SOCIOLOGY

Top timeline

Earliest horticultural and pastoral societies

Rise of agriculture and bureaucracy

European Middle Ages

Roman Empire

Modern *sapiens* e Earth

Cave art

First humans reach North America from Asia via Bering land bridge

First permanent settlements in Middle East mark "birth of civilization"

Domestication of dogs

Horticulture in Latin America

Invention of the wheel

Horticulture and pastoralism in Asia

Settlement in Nile region

Writing invented

Austrian "Iceman"

Settlement in Indus region

Great pyramids of Egypt

Domestication of horses

Muhammad

Confucius

Buddha

Moses

Plato

Jesus

European colonization begins

Galileo

EARLIEST CIVILIZATION

| 15,000 B.P. | 14,000 B.P. | 13,000 B.P. | 12,000 B.P. | 11,000 B.P. | 10,000 B.P. | 9,000 B.P. | 8,000 B.P. | 7,000 B.P. | 6,000 B.P. | 5,000 B.P. | 4,000 B.P. | 3,000 B.P. | 2,000 B.P. | 1,000 B.P. |

Lower timeline (upper band)

"Baby bust"

Women's movement intensifies

U.S. life expectancy 77 years

Civil Rights Movement

1969 Woodstock

1981 MTV debuts

1979 SugarHill Gang popularizes rap

1977 Disco peaks

1997 Backstreet Boys lead revival of pop

1999 Eminem merges musical styles

1964 British music invasion (The Beatles)

1974 Punk begins

1960 Rise of folk era and Motown

1991 Nirvana takes grunge mainstream

Rise of and Roll

1965 Foreign-born Japanese eligible for citizenship

1970 First Earth Day

1968 First interracial kiss on TV (*Star Trek*)

1980 Women earn majority of college degrees

1987 Rhode Island enacts statewide recycling law

2000 60% of U.S. women in labor force

1955 First McDonald's restaurant

1954 *Brown v. Board of Education*

son olor line"

1961 European colonization of Africa ends

1975 First women's shelter

1969 Stonewall riot begins gay rights movement

1981 First AIDS cases reported

1977 First gay TV character

1988 Last U.S. Playboy Club closes

Sept. 11, 2001 Terrorist attacks

2001 War on Terrorism

1973 *Roe v. Wade*

Revolutions in USSR and Eastern Europe 1989–1990

Persian Gulf War 1991

Iraq War 2003

950–1953

Vietnam War 1963–1975

PRESENT

1975

2000

Lower timeline (lower band)

1955 Cable TV invented

1960 Birth control pill invented

1965 Compact disc invented

1981 Space shuttle

1990 Human Genome Project

1977 First computerized arcade game

1957 Sputnik launched

1952 DNA discovered

1969 First human on moon

1975 Microsoft founded

1971 E-mail invented

1982 Modern Internet opens

1990s Expansion of the Internet

1968 First heart transplant

1993 First cloned cells

vented

Postindustrial era

cline in industrial jobs

Information Revolution

| 3 billion | 4 billion | 5 billion | 6 billion |

150.7 million

292.2 million

1959 Goffman debuts "dramaturgical analysis"

1981 Bernard nurtures gender studies

Piaget probes how we learn

THIS BOOK IS OFFERED TO TEACHERS OF SOCIOLOGY IN THE HOPE THAT IT WILL HELP OUR STUDENTS UNDERSTAND THEIR PLACE IN TODAY'S SOCIETY AND IN TOMORROW'S WORLD.

John J. Macionis

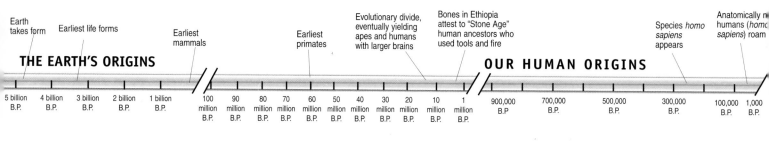

Age of dinosaurs

All humans are hunters and gatherers

Earth takes form

Earliest life forms

Earliest mammals

Earliest primates

Evolutionary divide, eventually yielding apes and humans with larger brains

Bones in Ethiopia attest to "Stone Age" human ancestors who used tools and fire

Species *homo sapiens* appears

Anatomically modern humans (*homo sapiens*) roam

THE EARTH'S ORIGINS

OUR HUMAN ORIGINS

| 5 billion B.P. | 4 billion B.P. | 3 billion B.P. | 2 billion B.P. | 1 billion B.P. | 100 million B.P. | 90 million B.P. | 80 million B.P. | 70 million B.P. | 60 million B.P. | 50 million B.P. | 40 million B.P. | 30 million B.P. | 20 million B.P. | 10 million B.P. | 1 million B.P. | 900,000 B.P | 700,000 B.P. | 500,000 B.P. | 300,000 B.P. | 100,000 B.P. | 1,000 B.P. |

Birth rates fall in Europe and U.S.

U.S. life expectancy 47 years

U.S. majority in cities

Immigration to U.S. restricted

Northward migration of African Americans

Great Depression

"Baby boom

1910 Jazz era begins

1938 Rise of bluegrass

1935 Swing era begins

T H E   M O D E R N   E R A

195
Ro

1921 First Miss America pageant

1932 First woman cabinet member

1942 Chemist Albert Hoffman takes first LSD "trip"

1948 Armed forces desegregate

1916 First sanitary landfill

1924 Native Americans eligible for citizenship

1938 Word "teenager" coined

900 20% of U.S. women in labor force

1917 Russian Revolution

1909 NAACP founded

1912 Sinking of Titanic

1920 Women win right to vote

1925 First College Board tests

1931 First woman governor

1947 Jackie Rob breaks baseball

1924 First woman senator

1933 First Major League baseball game under lights

World War I 1914–1918

World War II 1938–1945

Korean War

1925

1913 Ford assembly line

1927 Lindbergh flies across Atlantic

1940 First interstate road (PA Tpke)

1947 Aerosol spray can invented

1920 First commercial radio station

1914 First coast-to-coast telephone call

1926 Middle East starts pumping oil

1945 First atomic explosion

1948 Record debuts

1950

1914 First stop sign (Detroit)

1931 First electric guitar

1927 Television invented

1946 Computer invented

903 Airplane invented

1947 Transistor

De

---

2 billion

1902–1931 Cooley and Mead reflect on the self

1902 Simmel analyzes small groups

1931 W.I. Thomas discusses defining situations as real

1903 Du Bois describes racial consciousness

c.1915 Weber sees expanding bureaucracy

SOCIOLOGY

TENTH EDITION

JOHN J. MACIONIS

Kenyon College

PEARSON

Prentice
Hall

UPPER SADDLE RIVER, NEW JERSEY 07458

Library of Congress Cataloging-in-Publication Data

Macionis, John J.
    Sociology / John J. Macionis.—10th ed.
       p. cm.
    Includes bibliographical references and index.
    ISBN 0-13-184918-2 (alk. paper)
    1. Sociology.   I. Title
HM586.M33 2005
301—dc21   2001057794

Executive Editor: *Christopher DeJohn*
AVP, Publisher: *Nancy Roberts*
Editor in Chief of Development: *Rochelle Diogenes*
Development Editor: *Leslie Carr*
VP, Director of Production and Manufacturing:
    Barbara Kittle
Production Editor: *Barbara Reilly*
Copyeditors: *Margaret Riche, Amy Macionis*
Supplements Editor: *Erin Katchmar*
Proofreaders: *Alison Lorber, Beatrice Marcks*
Editorial Assistant: *Veronica D'Amico*
Prepress and Manufacturing Manager: *Nick Sklitsis*
Prepress and Manufacturing Buyer: *Mary Ann Gloriande*
Director of Marketing: *Beth Mejia*
Senior Marketing Manager: *Marissa Feliberty*
Marketing Assistant: *Adam Laitman*
Creative Design Director: *Leslie Osher*

Art Director: *Ximena Tamvakopoulos*
Interior and Cover Designer: *Ximena Tamvakopoulos*
Line Art Manager: *Guy Ruggiero*
Line Art Illustrations: *Lithokraft*
Maps: *Carto-Graphics*
Director, Image Resource Center: *Melinda Reo*
Manager, Rights and Permissions: *Zina Arabia*
Interior Image Specialist: *Beth Boyd-Brenzel*
Image Permissions Coordinator: *Debra Hewitson*
Photo Researcher: *Barbara Salz*
Cover Image Specialist: *Karen Sanatar*
Cover Art: Shoppng Mall on Grafton Street, © *Franklin
    McMahon/Corbis.*
Media Editor: *Kate Ramunda*
Media Project Manager: *Tina Rudowski*
Manager of Media Production: *Lynn Pearlman*

This book was set in 10/11 Janson by Lithokraft, and was printed and bound by RR Donnelley and Sons Company.
The cover was printed by The Lehigh Press, Inc.

For permission to use copyrighted material, grateful
acknowledgment is made to the copyright holders listed
on pages 680–81, which is considered an extension of this
copyright page.

Pearson Education LTD.
Pearson Education Singapore, Pte. Ltd
Pearson Education, Canada, Ltd
Pearson Education—Japan
Pearson Education Australia PTY, Limited

Pearson Education North Asia Ltd
Pearson Educación de Mexico, S.A. de C.V.
Pearson Education Malaysia, Pte. Ltd
Pearson Education, Upper Saddle River, New Jersey

10 9 8 7 6 5 4 3 2 1

ISBN 0-13-184918-2

Printed on Recycled Paper

BRIEF CONTENTS

CONTENTS

PART I

THE FOUNDATIONS OF SOCIOLOGY

In the Times   Military Mirrors Working Class America   25

 **Are Those Leaving Welfare Better Off Now? Yes and No   297**

PART IV
SOCIAL INSTITUTIONS

PART V
SOCIAL CHANGE

BOXES

APPLYING SOCIOLOGY

CRITICAL THINKING

GLOBAL SOCIOLOGY

DIVERSITY: RACE, CLASS, AND GENDER

MAPS

GLOBAL MAPS: WINDOW ON THE WORLD

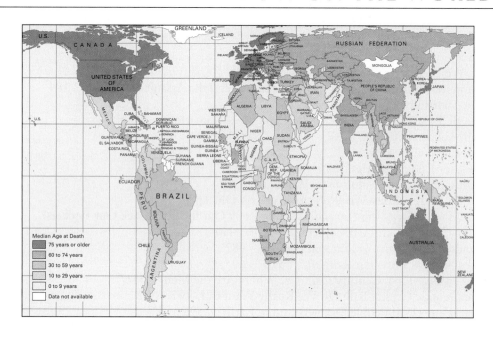

NATIONAL MAPS: SEEING OURSELVES

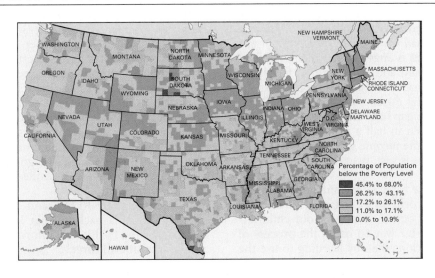

PREFACE

At the dawning of the modern age, the French philosopher François Voltaire expressed his certainty that humans were meant to live together in society and that the gift of society to each of us is the ability to develop a sense of justice. A young woman or man coming of age today has plenty of reasons to take a keen interest in human society and wonder about justice. The United States is engaged in military conflicts in Iraq and Afghanistan, and our nation is fighting a worldwide war against terrorism. Throughout the world, there are several dozen other ongoing military conflicts. At home, the gap between the rich and poor is greater than it has been in half a century, and it is increasing. Worldwide, the income gap between the richest and poorest nations is vast, twice as large as it was a century ago.

Facts such as these force us to confront vital questions: What kind of world do we live in? Is it the kind of world we want for ourselves and for our children? Surely there is no better way to begin the process of answering these questions than by learning to use the discipline of sociology.

There is another, happier reason to begin the study of society. Learning about the social world all around us is extremely rewarding and often great fun. The daily e-mail I receive from students throughout the United States and around the world is clear testimony both to the power of sociology to help people understand their world and to the pleasure they find in doing it. Ask the women and men who teach sociology in classrooms throughout North America and you will find that, in a large majority of cases, they enjoyed the first course they took so much that they continued, eventually deciding to make the study of society their life's work.

Sociology has the power to transform people, and many of these people go on to transform society. All instructors know the deep satisfaction that comes from making a difference in the lives of our students. There is no greater reward for our work and, in my case, no better reason for striving for ever-better revisions of *Sociology*, which, along with the briefer *Society: The Basics*, stand out—as they have for more than a decade—as the discipline's most widely used texts.

I hope you will find *Sociology* to be authoritative, comprehensive, stimulating, and—as so many students testify—plain fun to read. In addition to the book, every new copy of *Sociology, Tenth Edition*, comes with a CD-ROM that includes a number of learning tools, including short video selections that illustrate major concepts, theories, and research findings, and also a series of "author's tip" videos—one for each chapter—that focus on key chapter themes.

The third part of the learning package that is available free with each new book is access to two Web sites. The first is our full-featured Companion Website™ at http://www.prenhall.com/macionis From the main page, simply click on the cover of the text to access a comprehensive and interactive study guide. Select a chapter to find chapter summaries, learning objectives, suggested essay questions, and paper topics, as well as multiple-choice and true/false questions. The second, new to this edition, is a premium-content Web site called OneKey. It will serve as a one-stop shop for students and faculty, providing anytime, anywhere access to important course materials. OneKey will also offer a customized student study plan after the student takes a quick diagnostic quiz. Access to OneKey is free with a passcode that can be wrapped with *Sociology, Tenth Edition*.

Textbook, CD-ROM, and Web sites: A three-part, multimedia package that is the foundation for sound learning in this new information age. We invite you to examine all three!

ORGANIZATION OF THIS TEXT

Part I of the textbook and the CD-ROM introduces the foundations of sociology. Underlying the discipline is the *sociological perspective*—the focus of Chapter 1, which explains how this point of view brings the world to life in a new and instructive way. Chapter 2 spotlights *sociological investigation*, or the "doing of sociology." This chapter recognizes the methodological diversity of the discipline, explaining the scientific, interpretive, and critical orientations, and illustrating major research strategies with actual, well-known sociological work.

Part II surveys the foundations of social life. Chapter 3 focuses on the central concept of *culture*, emphasizing the cultural diversity that makes up our society and our world. The focus of Chapter 4 is the concept of *society*, presenting four time-honored models for understanding the structure and dynamics of social organization. This unique chapter provides introductory students with the background to understand the ideas of important thinkers—including Karl Marx, Max Weber, and Emile Durkheim, as well as Gerhard Lenski—that appear in subsequent chapters. Chapter 5 turns to *socialization*, exploring how we gain our humanity as we learn to participate in society. Chapter 6 provides a micro-level look at the patterns of *social interaction* that make up our everyday lives. Chapter 7 offers full-chapter coverage of *groups and organizations*, explaining the importance of group life and investigating how and why large organizations have come to dominate our way of life. Chapter 8 explains how the operation of society generates both *deviance and conformity* and also surveys the operation of the criminal justice system. Chapter 9 explains the social foundations of *human sexuality*. This chapter surveys sexual patterns in the United States and also explores variations in ideas and practices through history and around the world today.

Part III offers unparalleled discussion of social inequality, beginning with three chapters on *social stratification*. Chapter 10 introduces major concepts and presents theoretical explanations of *social inequality*. This chapter richly illustrates historical changes in stratification and how patterns of inequality vary in today's world. Chapter 11 surveys *social inequality in the United States*, confronting common perceptions of inequality and assessing how well they square with research findings. Chapter 12 extends the analysis with a look at *global stratification*, revealing the disparities in wealth and power that separate rich and poor nations. Both Chapters 11 and 12 pay special attention to how global developments affect stratification in the United States as they explore our nation's role in global inequality. Chapter 13, *gender stratification*, explains how gender is a central element in social stratification in the United States as it is worldwide. *Race and ethnicity*, additional important dimensions of social inequality that often intersect differences based on class and gender, are detailed in Chapter 14. *Aging and the elderly*, a topic of increasing concern to "graying" societies such as our own, is addressed in Chapter 15.

Part IV includes a full chapter on each social institution. Leading off is Chapter 16, *the economy and work*, because most sociologists recognize the economy as having the greatest impact on all other institutions. This chapter traces the rise and fall of industrial production in the United States and the emergence of a global economy, and explains what such transformations mean for the U.S. labor force. Chapter 17, *politics and government*, analyzes the distribution of power in U.S. society and surveys political systems around the world. In addition, this chapter includes discussion of the U.S. military, the threat of war, and terrorism as a new form of war. Chapter 18, *family*, explains the central importance of families to social organization and underscores the diversity of family life both here and in other societies. Chapter 19, *religion*, addresses the timeless human search for ultimate purpose and meaning, introduces major world religions, and explains how religious beliefs are linked to other dimensions of social life. Chapter 20, *education*, analyzes the expansion of schooling in industrial and postindustrial societies. Here again, schooling in the United States comes to life through contrasts with educational patterns in other countries. Chapter 21, *health and medicine*, reveals health to be a social issue just as much as it is a matter of biological processes. This chapter traces the historical emergence of scientific medicine, analyzes today's medical establishment as well as alternative approaches to health, and compares patterns of health in the United States to those in other countries.

Part V examines important dimensions of global social change. Chapter 22 highlights the powerful impact of *population growth* and *urbanization* in the United States and throughout the world with special attention to the *natural environment*. Chapter 23 explores forms of *collective behavior* and explains how people seek or resist social change by joining *social movements*. Chapter 24 concludes the text with an overview of *social change* that contrasts *traditional, modern, and postmodern societies*. This chapter rounds out the text by explaining how and why world societies change and critically analyzing the benefits and liabilities of traditional, modern, and postmodern ways of life.

CONTINUITY: ESTABLISHED FEATURES OF *SOCIOLOGY*

Everyone knows that introductory sociology texts have some things in common, but differences run deep. The extraordinary success of *Sociology* and *Society: The Basics*—far and away the texts most widely adopted by sociologists across North America—results from a combination of the following distinctive features.

The best writing style. Most important, this text offers a writing style widely praised by students and faculty alike as elegant and inviting. *Sociology* is the text that encourages students to read—even beyond their assignments. No one says it better than the students themselves, whose recent e-mail includes testimonials such as these:

> I want to thank you for providing us with such a comprehensive, easy-to-read, and engaging book for our use. . . . In fact, my professor thought it was so interesting and well done, she read the book from cover to cover. Your work has been a great service to us all. My sociology book is the only textbook I currently own that I actually enjoy reading. Thank you!

> My sociology class used your book, *Sociology*. It was by far the best textbook I have ever used. I actually liked to read it for pleasure as well as to study. I just want to say it was great.

Thanks for writing such a brilliant book. It has sparked my sociological imagination. This was the first textbook that I have ever read completely and enjoyed. From the moment that I picked the book up I started reading nonstop.

I have read four chapters ahead; it's like a good novel I can't put down! I just wanted to say thank you.

Your book is extremely well written and very interesting. I find myself reading it for pleasure, something I have never done with college texts. It is going to be the only collegiate textbook that I ever keep simply to read on my own. I am also thinking of picking up sociology as my minor due to the fact that I have enjoyed the class as well as the text so much. Your writing has my highest praise and utmost appreciation.

I am taking a Sociology 101 class using *Sociology*, a book that I have told my professor is the best textbook that I have ever seen, bar none. I've told her as well that I will be more than happy to take more sociology classes as long as there is a Macionis text to go with them.

I am fascinated by the contents of this textbook. In contrast to texts in my other classes, I actually enjoy reading *Sociology*. Thank you for such a thought-provoking, well-written textbook.

I have been in college for three years and I have not found a textbook more remarkable or thought provoking than your *Sociology*.

Dude, your book *rocks!*

A global perspective. *Sociology* has taken a leading role in expanding the horizons of our discipline beyond the United States. *Sociology* was the first text to mainstream global content, introduce global maps, and offer coverage of global issues such as stratification and the environment. Global content is not only mainstreamed in chapters but highlighted in global maps, Global Snapshot figures, and Global Sociology boxes. Such a global focus helps explain why this text has been adapted and translated into many other languages for use all over the world.

Race, class, gender, and age: A focus on national diversity. *Sociology* invites students from all social backgrounds to discover a fresh and exciting way to see the world and to understand themselves. Readers will find in this text the diversity of U.S. society—people of African, Asian, Middle Eastern, European, and Latino ancestry, as well as women and men of various class positions, in all parts of the country, and at all points in the life course. In addition to weaving race, class, and gender into all discussions, the text highlights these

factors through national maps, Diversity Snapshot figures, and Diversity: Race, Class, and Gender boxes. An independent survey of all introductory books gave this text top marks for mainstreaming race and ethnicity throughout the chapters (Stone, 1996).

A focus on diversity also means giving attention to rural issues. Although the media-based view of the United States highlights urban life, a large share of the U.S. population lives in rural areas, and a significant share of U.S. college students are from rural backgrounds.

Emphasis on critical thinking. Critical-thinking skills include the ability to challenge common assumptions by formulating questions, to identify and weigh appropriate evidence, and to reach reasoned conclusions. This text not only teaches but encourages students to think and to discover on their own. Many captions for the photography and fine art as well as for maps include questions that call out a response from readers. The Critical Thinking boxes include a series of three "What do you think?" questions. In addition, each chapter concludes with a list of Critical-Thinking Questions, a series of Applications and Exercises, and an invitation for readers to use the Research Navigator™ search engines to learn more on their own.

The broadest coverage so instructors can choose. No other text matches *Sociology's* twenty-four chapter coverage of the field. We offer such breadth—at no greater cost—expecting that few instructors will assign every chapter, but with the goal of supporting instructors as they choose exactly what they wish to teach.

Engaging and instructive chapter openings. One of the most popular features of *Sociology* is the engaging vignettes that begin each chapter. These openings—for instance, using the sociological perspective to show how society guides selection of marriage partners, using the tragic sinking of the *Titanic* to illustrate the life and death consequences of social inequality, and documenting the rising level of obesity in the United States to show how health is a social issue—spark the interest of readers as they introduce important themes. This revision retains eight of the best chapter-opening vignettes found in earlier editions and offers sixteen new ones as well.

Inclusive focus on women and men. Beyond devoting two full chapters to the important concepts of sex and gender, *Sociology* mainstreams gender into *every* chapter, showing how the topic at hand affects women and men differently and explaining how gender operates as a basic dimension of social organization.

Theoretically clear and balanced. *Sociology, Tenth Edition,* makes theory easy. Chapter 1 introduces the discipline's major theoretical approaches, which are used in all the chapters that follow. The text highlights not only the social-conflict, structural-functional, and symbolic-interaction paradigms, but incorporates feminist theory, intersection theory, social-exchange analysis, ethnomethodology, cultural ecology, and sociobiology.

Chapter 4—unique to this text—provides students with an easy-to-understand introduction to important social theorists *before* they encounter their work in later chapters. The ideas of Max Weber, Karl Marx, and Emile Durkheim, as well as Gerhard Lenski's historical overview of human societies, appear in distinct sections that instructors may assign together or refer to separately at different points in the course.

Recent research and the latest data. *Sociology, Tenth Edition,* blends classic sociological statements with the latest research, as reported in the leading publications in the field. The results of 300 new research publications inform this revision, and almost half of more than 2000 pieces of research cited throughout the book were published in the last five years. From chapter to chapter, the text's statistical data are the most recent available, typically for 2001, 2002, and 2003.

Learning aids. This text has many features to help students learn. In each chapter, **key concepts** are identified by boldfaced type, and following each appears *a precise, italicized definition.* A list of key concepts with their definitions appears at the end of each chapter, and a complete **Glossary** is found at the end of the book. Each chapter also contains a numbered **Summary** and four **Critical-Thinking Questions** that help students review material and assess their understanding. Following these are a number of **Applications and Exercises,** which provides students with activities to do on or near the campus. Each chapter also includes an annotated list of worthwhile **Sites to See** on the Internet.

Outstanding images: photography and fine art. This book offers the finest and most extensive program of photography and artwork available in any sociology textbook. The tenth edition of *Sociology* displays about 50 examples of fine art as well as more than 250 color photographs—more than in any other text. Each of these images is carefully selected by the author and appears with an insightful caption. Moreover, both photographs and artwork present people of various social backgrounds and historical periods. For example, alongside art by well-known Europeans such as Vincent Van

Gogh and U.S. artists including George Tooker, this edition has paintings by celebrated African American artists Henry Ossawa Tanner and Jonathan Green, outstanding Latino artists Wayne Healy, Carmen Lomas Garza, and Diego Rivera, Navajo painter Harrison Begay, and the engaging Australian painter and feminist Sally Swain.

Thought-provoking theme boxes. Although boxed material is common to introductory texts, *Sociology, Tenth Edition,* provides a wealth of uncommonly good boxes. Each chapter typically contains four boxes, which fall into five types that amplify central themes of the text. **Global Sociology** boxes provoke readers to think about their own way of life by examining the fascinating social diversity that characterizes our world. **Diversity: Race, Class, and Gender** boxes focus on multicultural issues and amplify the voices of women and people of color. **Critical Thinking** boxes teach students to ask sociological questions about their surroundings and help them evaluate important, controversial issues. **Applying Sociology** boxes show the value of the sociological perspective to understanding the world around us. **Controversy & Debate** boxes conclude each chapter by presenting several points of view on an issue of contemporary importance; these boxes are followed by a series of three "Continue the debate" questions that encourage student reaction and are sure to stimulate spirited class discussion.

Sociology, Tenth Edition, contains eighty-nine boxes in all. Nine are new to this edition, and many more are revised and updated. A complete listing of this text's boxes appears after the table of contents.

An unparalleled program of sixty global and national maps. This is the text that pioneered the use of global and national maps. Window on the World global maps—thirty in all, with many updated—are truly sociological maps offering a comparative look at the number of children typically born to women, income disparity, favored languages and religions, the extent of prostitution, permitted marriage forms, the practice of female genital mutilation, the degree of political freedom, the incidence of HIV infection, and a host of other issues. The global maps use the non-Eurocentric projection devised by cartographer Arno Peters that accurately portrays the relative size of all the continents. A complete listing of the Window on the World global maps follows the table of contents.

Seeing Ourselves national maps—thirty in all, with many updated for this edition—help to illuminate the social diversity of the United States. Most of these maps offer a close-up look at all 3,066 U.S.

counties, highlighting suicide rates, median per capita income, labor force participation, first-cousin marriage laws, religious diversity, average annual teacher salaries, and, as measures of popular culture, where people play golf or where households prefer to read newspapers or watch television. Each national map includes an explanatory caption that poses several questions to stimulate students' thinking about social forces. A complete listing of the Seeing Ourselves national maps follows the table of contents.

Linking technology to the text. At four or five points in each chapter, a Media logo directs students to visit carefully selected Web sites. These sites provide biographical material about sociologists, useful data, or information about an organization that deals with the topic at hand. In addition, an annotated list of even more Web sites is found at the end of each chapter.

INNOVATION: CHANGES IN THE TENTH EDITION

Each new edition of *Sociology* has broken new ground, one reason that the popularity of this text and its brief version keeps rising. Now, having reached the tenth edition, we renew the book once again with many fresh ideas and useful teaching tools. Two years in the making, this tenth edition is, quite simply, the best revision yet. Here is a brief overview of what's new in *Sociology*, *Tenth Edition*.

A greater focus on careers. Most students who enroll in a sociology course hope to find something useful for their future careers. They will. *Sociology*, *Tenth Edition*, reflects the discipline's *career relevance* more than ever before. Many chapters now apply sociological insights to careers—for example, read how today's marketers are learning to be more multicultural (Chapter 3, "Culture") and why physicians should understand the social dynamics of an office visit or a medical examination (Chapter 6, "Sociology of Everyday Life"). In addition, there is greatly expanded coverage of the entire criminal justice system (Chapter 8, "Deviance"), as well as a new discussion of nursing as part of the medical establishment (Chapter 21, "Health and Medicine").

Highlighting "sociology@work." For additional connections between sociology and careers, look for the "sociology@work" icon. These icons draw student attention to a discussion that has particular relevance to the world of work and identify not only career applications but include descriptions of people working as professional sociologists.

"In the *Times*" readings. What better way to bring sociology to life than to provide students with brief, well-written, highly interesting newspaper articles on the important chapter topics! Eleven of the chapters in this edition of *Sociology*—including *every* social institution chapter—are followed by a one- or two-page reading carefully edited from a recent article in *The New York Times*. The sociological articles were published in 2002 and 2003, and all present important and current issues that are sure to engage student readers. Here is a listing of the "In the *Times*" articles:

Chapter 1 ("The Sociological Perspective"): "Military Mirrors Working-Class America"

Chapter 3 ("Culture"): "Cultural Divide Over Parental Discipline"

Chapter 9 ("Sexuality"): "The Skin Wars Start Earlier and Earlier"

Chapter 11 ("Social Class in the United States"): "Are Those Leaving Welfare Better Off Now? Yes and No"

Chapter 16 ("Economy and Work"): "Immigrant Laborers Feel Stranded in Pacific Northwest as Day Jobs Dry Up"

Chapter 17 ("Politics and Government"): "After Sept. 11, a Legal Battle over Limits of Civil Liberty"

Chapter 18 ("Family"): "With the Blessing of Society, Europeans Opt Not to Marry"

Chapter 19 ("Religion"): "Putting the American in 'American Muslim'"

Chapter 20 ("Education"): "Students' Scores Rise in Math, Not in Reading"

Chapter 21 ("Health and Medicine"): "Good and Bad Marriage, Boon and Bane to Health"

Chapter 24 ("Social Change"): "No Wiggle Room in a Window War"

Student Snapshots. Among the popular features of *Sociology* are the Global Snapshot figures (comparing social patterns in the United States to those in other nations) and Diversity Snapshot figures (detailing differences by race, ethnicity, class, or gender). For this revision, we have added fourteen Student Snapshots, which document trends in the behavior and opinions of college students, based on the surveys conducted by the Higher Education Research Institute at the University of California at Los Angeles since 1968.

Learn more with Research Navigator™. Students using *Sociology*, *Tenth Edition*, can make use of two high-powered search engines found in the Research Navigator™ system. First, there is the search engine that scans a scholarly database compiled by EBSCO. Search using discipline screens to select only articles in the field of interest. Second, you can search the recent archives of *The New York Times* for news articles on any topic of your choosing. With Research Navigator™, more information is only a few keystrokes away.

Expanded and improved time line. An easy way to help students put their lives in historical perspective is the time line, an exclusive feature found inside the front cover of *Sociology, Tenth Edition*. For this revision, we have expanded the time line to three pages, adding more material about popular culture and social diversity, as well as a number of color images.

Keeping up with the field. An unfortunate fact is that some sociology textbooks do not reflect new work in the field, ignoring the latest ideas from sociology journals and new books in the field. By contrast, *Sociology, Tenth Edition*, is at the cutting edge, reflecting what's new in more than a dozen scholarly journals—including *American Journal of Sociology, American Sociological Review, Rural Sociology, Social Forces, Sociological Focus, Sociological Forum, Society, The Public Interest, Social Problems, Population Bulletin, Teaching Sociology, Contemporary Sociology*, and *Social Science Quarterly*—as well as popular publications that keep us abreast of current trends and events. If you don't have time to keep up with everything in the field (and most of us don't), be sure you have a text that does.

New chapter-opening vignettes. This revision keeps the best of the popular chapter-opening vignettes and adds sixteen new ones; overall, two-thirds of the openings are new to this edition.

Many new boxes. A total of eighty-nine boxes supports five themes of the text: Global Sociology; Diversity: Race, Class, and Gender; Critical Thinking; Applying Sociology; and, focusing on social policy, Controversy & Debate. Many boxes are revised and updated; nine boxes are completely new to this edition.

The latest statistical data. Instructors count on this text for including the very latest statistical data. The tenth edition comes through again, using both online and conventional sources to ensure that the very latest data from the U.S. Census Bureau, U.S. Department of Labor, the Centers for Disease Control, and numerous other agencies are found here. The author and Professor Carol A. Singer, government documents librarian at Bowling Green State University (Ohio), work together to ensure that, when you adopt *Sociology, Tenth Edition*, you can be sure your students will have the most recent data available at the time of publication. In addition, this revision incorporates 300 new research citations as well as many recent current events that spark the interest of students.

New topics. The tenth edition of *Sociology* is thoroughly updated with new and expanded discussions in every chapter. Here is a listing, by chapter, of just some of the new material:

- **Chapter 1 The Sociological Perspective**: A new opening vignette shows how love and marriage are guided by society; also find statistical updates on patterns of suicide in the United States; at the end of the chapter, students are invited to make use of the new Research Navigator™ search engines with instructions and keywords provided; finally, directly following this chapter, the first "In the *Times*" feature, which casts a sociological eye on the U.S. military, appears with discussion questions.

- **Chapter 2 Sociological Investigation**: The discussion of research ethics is expanded to include institutional review boards; there is a new discussion of the tension between uniformity and rapport in interviewing research.

- **Chapter 3 Culture**: A new chapter opening highlights the importance of multicultural marketing to today's corporations; a new box highlights emerging cyber-symbols in popular culture; there is new discussion of the number of cultures in today's world, noting a number of languages that are now in danger of disappearing; there is a critical update on the Sapir-Whorf thesis; directly after this chapter, an "In the *Times*" feature looks at cultural conflict involving childrearing practices of immigrant parents.

- **Chapter 4 Society**: This entire chapter has been carefully rewritten for even greater clarity; there is an expanded discussion about whether life in the United States is getting better or worse.

- **Chapter 5 Socialization**: This chapter features an increased number of examples and illustrations; there is expanded discussion of Kohlberg's theory of moral development; a research update highlights the difference class makes in the socialization process; there is expanded discussion of the effects of television programming on young people; a new Student Snapshot looks at patterns of trust; and the chapter includes a new discussion of the effects that events such as the September 11 terrorist attacks have on young people.

- **Chapter 6 Social Interaction in Everyday Life**: There is an updated ethnomethodology section; a major reorganization of the second half of the chapter includes a new section on the sociology of emotions; a new Critical Thinking box focuses on managing emotions in the experiences of women who have abortions; another new Critical Thinking box focuses on how people can detect lying, with applications to the war on terrorism.

- **Chapter 7 Groups and Organizations**: There is a new application of research on leadership styles focusing on President Bush's White House; there is an update on Stanley Milgram's "six degrees of separation" research; a new Student Snapshot describes the changing share of first-year college students engaged in volunteer work; a new example of bureaucratic ritualism notes that, after the September 11 terrorist attacks, the United States Postal Service insisted on delivering Osama bin Laden's mail; find a recent look at the nature of Japanese organizations in light of Japan's economic downturn; there is an expanded discussion of new, flatter organizations highlighting specific innovations by some of the most successful U.S. corporations.

- **Chapter 8 Deviance**: A new opening describes a recent corporate scandal, setting up the discussion of white-collar crime and corporate crime; there is an update on "weird laws" as well as gambling laws across the United States; a new Critical Thinking box asks whether the United States is becoming a society of cheaters; find new research in support of differential association theory; there are statistical updates on all crime rates, as well as the latest on the growing controversy surrounding the death penalty; a new Student Snapshot shows the trend in student opposition to the death penalty; there is greatly expanded coverage of the criminal justice system, with new sections on due process and community-based corrections, including probation and parole.

- **Chapter 9 Sexuality**: A new chapter opening sets up discussion of various social problems related to sex among young people; there is expanded discussion of variations in sexuality, which now includes coverage of intersexual people and gender reassignment; a new national map shows which states permit first-cousin marriages and which do not; a new figure helps students understand sexual orientation; a new Critical Thinking box takes a look at the campus culture of "hooking up"; and there is an update on the abortion controversy as the United States marks the 30th anniversary of *Roe v. Wade*; following this chapter, an "In the *Times*" feature describes the recent trend towards sexually provocative clothing for young teens and pre-teens.

- **Chapter 10 Social Stratification**: This chapter contains an update on social class in Japan; a major new section profiles the emerging class system in China; there are new examples of this country's highest-income people in a discussion of whether they are worth what they are paid; and a new table summarizes theories of stratification.

- **Chapter 11 Social Class in the United States**: A new chapter opening asks whether winning a $171-million lottery changes a grocer's social class; a new chapter Web link invites students to compare income inequality in the United States and Canada; new statistics provide the latest information on income and wealth inequality, mobility by income level, the working poor, and those below the poverty line; a new national map shows poverty rates for all U.S. counties; a new Critical Thinking box looks at charges of "runaway" CEO compensation during the last twenty years; there is an updated discussion of the effects of the 1996 welfare reforms; following this chapter, an "In the *Times*" feature looks at the current fate of families affected by welfare reform.

- **Chapter 12 Global Stratification**: A new chapter opening describes the sometimes deadly conditions of people working in garment sweatshops in poor countries such as Bangladesh; a new Diversity box describes *las colonias* in

southern Texas, often described as the "American Third World"; find statistical updates on important economic indicators for countries around the world; there is an expanded discussion of slavery in the modern world.

- **Chapter 13 Gender Stratification**: This chapter contains numerous research updates including new material on gender and the mass media, and also the link between having children and earning tenure in academia; find the latest statistics on working women and men—their jobs as well as their income and wealth—women's and men's schooling, gender and political power, and women's participation in the military; the latest survey data show changing attitudes toward gender equality, including a new Student Snapshot showing declining support among first-year students for conventional gender norms; there is also greater emphasis on intersection theory and the social standing of people with multiple disadvantages.

- **Chapter 14 Race and Ethnicity**: A new chapter opening points to the increasing racial and ethnic diversity of U.S. society; the chapter contains more comparative data that demonstrate the social construction of race; there are statistical updates on multiracial people in the United States, as well as the social standings of major categories of the U.S. population; a new discussion provides recently published data updating the classic Bogardus social distance research and adding discussion of hostility towards Muslims and Arabs after the September 11 attacks; coverage of affirmative action is brought up to date with discussion of the 2003 decision of the U.S. Supreme Court in the University of Michigan admissions policy case.

- **Chapter 15 Aging and the Elderly**: A new chapter opening shows how active—but aging—rock stars blur the line between youth and old age; a new Global Sociology box examines the surprising number of centenarians on the island of Sardinia; a new Applying Sociology box explains how the recent economic downturn has forced many older people to keep working; the discussion of the economics of retirement is expanded to include the idea of "staged retirement"; there is an expanded discussion of bereavement.

- **Chapter 16 The Economy and Work**: A new chapter opening describes the extent to which the rapidly expanding retailer Wal-Mart affects the entire U.S. economy; find updated statistics on labor force participation as well as unemployment for all categories of the population; the chapter now includes the latest on the increasing social diversity in the U.S. workplace; there is more coverage of workers—including white-collar employees—who have been forced to give up bonuses, salary, and benefits to keep their jobs in the weak economy; a new Student Snapshot shows the most often named "probable" careers of first-year college students; directly after this chapter, an "In the *Times*" feature looks at how immigrant laborers are faring in the weak economy after 2000.

- **Chapter 17 Politics and Government**: A new chapter opening highlights the War in Iraq, asking why nations often turn to violence to resolve disputes; a new Student Snapshot shows changing political leanings among college students; find updates on the extent of democracy in the world, the number of political action committees, as well as sociological analysis of the latest election results; there is more discussion of the effects of race, class, and gender on political attitudes; also find a new discussion of laws that bar convicted felons from voting—and estimates of the difference it would make if they could; a new short section discusses the role of the mass media in the War in Iraq; a new Controversy and Debate box asks whether Islam is compatible with political democracy and includes a new Global Snapshot figure; following the chapter, an "In the *Times*" feature examines the tradeoff between stronger security laws and weaker civil liberties.

- **Chapter 18 Family**: A new chapter opening tells the story of a successful single mother who has adopted two children from China, highlighting the diversity of today's families; find updates on all marriage and family statistics, including the cost of raising children, differences in average family income by race and ethnicity, the divorce rate, and reported family violence; a new section profiles family patterns among American Indian migrants to cities; a new figure shows the probabilities of children living with both biological parents until age eighteen for cohabiting and married parents; and a new Student Snapshot shows the historical trend in campus support for laws that prohibit homosexual relationships; following the chapter, a new "In the *Times*" feature describes the trend in Europe away from traditional marriage.

- **Chapter 19 Religion**: A new chapter opening points to the United States as the most religiously diverse nation on Earth; updates provide the latest on all the major religions of the world; the chapter includes the latest data on measures of religiosity in the United States as well as the size of various religious communities; find expanded coverage of the effects of religious belief on young people; a new Student Snapshot shows the rising share of first-year college students who claim no religious preference; there is expanded coverage of New Age spirituality; there is a new national map providing a recent look at the religious diversity of the United States; after the chapter, a new "In the *Times*" feature highlights the difficulties of U.S. Muslims after the September 11 attacks.

- **Chapter 20 Education**: A new chapter opening highlights the rising number of home-schooled children in the United States; there are updates on all education statistics; a new section on the expansion of higher education in the United States focuses on the growing importance of community colleges; a new Diversity box looks at racial differences in school discipline; find the latest events and trends in the school choice debate, including discussion of the

Bush administration's 2002 education bill; a new section and a new Student Snapshot highlight grade inflation in recent decades; there is a new discussion of the increase in home schooling; a new national map shows average teacher salaries for all fifty states; following this chapter, a new "In the *Times*" feature reports on recent trends in the performance of U.S. students.

- **Chapter 21 Health and Medicine**: A new chapter opening illustrates the link between society and health by documenting the rising level of obesity that now affects most people in the United States; a new national map shows the state of health in all 3,066 U.S. counties; a new Student Snapshot highlights self-assessment of health; new statistics update all measures of health in the United States, as well as global issues such as the AIDS epidemic; a new journal entry notes the Canadian policy of limiting doctors' income; a new section examines the extent and causes of the nursing shortage; following this chapter, a new "In the *Times*" feature explores the effects of marriage on health.

- **Chapter 22 Population, Urbanization, and Environment**: A new opening describes the declining population of Bisbee, North Dakota, one of hundreds of dying towns on the Great Plains; a new journal entry describes high fertility among the U.S. Amish; the chapter presents the latest statistical data on fertility, mortality, and population increase; a new discussion points out the decline of public life in the United States, with more urban activity taking place in private spaces, including malls and gated communities; there is an update on the increasing shortage of water around the world.

- **Chapter 23 Collective Behavior and Social Movements**: A new chapter opening shows how easily rumors—even when completely untrue—can spread; the chapter includes a number of recent examples of collective behavior, including the 2003 Rhode Island nightclub fire, the anti-war demonstrations that accompanied the War in Iraq, and public ignorance of the federal tax system; two Student Snapshots show a declining trend of student involvement in community action programs, and track political involvement; additional discussion focuses on the role of new information technology in creating "smart crowds"; there is a new section presenting the political-economy theory of social movements.

- **Chapter 24 Social Change: Traditional, Modern, and Postmodern Societies**: Find updates from the National Opinion Research Center on people's attitudes toward social change and modernity; a rewritten and expanded box tells the stories of both Brazil's Kaiapo Indians and the people of Hog Hammock, a Gullah community off the coast of Georgia, both of which are being drawn into modern ways of life with both good and bad consequences; following the chapter, a new "In the *Times*" feature describes the conflict between modern building codes and traditional Amish homes.

A WORD ABOUT LANGUAGE

This text's commitment to representing the social diversity of the United States and the world carries with it the responsibility to use language thoughtfully. In most cases, we prefer the terms *African American* and *person of color* to the word *black*. We use the terms *Hispanic* and *Latino* to refer to people of Spanish descent. Most tables and figures refer to "Hispanics" because this is the term the Census Bureau uses when collecting statistical data about our population.

Students should realize, however, that many individuals do not describe themselves using these terms. Although the term "Hispanic" is commonly used in the eastern part of the United States, and "Latino" and the feminine form "Latina" are widely heard in the West, throughout the United States people of Spanish descent identify with a particular ancestral nation, whether it be Argentina, Mexico, some other Latin American country, or Spain in Europe.

Likewise, the term "Asian Americans" is used by the government to collect data. Most people of Asian descent, however, think of themselves in terms of a specific country of origin (say, Japan, the Philippines, Taiwan, or Vietnam).

In this text, "Native American" refers to all the inhabitants of the Americas whose ancestors lived here prior to the arrival of Europeans. Here again, however, most people in this broad category identify with their historical society (say, Cherokee, Hopi, or Zuni). "American Indian" is the preferred name of Native Americans who live in the continental United States, not including Native peoples in Alaska or Hawaii.

Learning to think globally also leads us to use language carefully. This text avoids the word "American"—which literally designates two continents—to refer to just the United States. For example, referring to this country, the term "U.S. economy" is more correct than the "American economy." This convention may seem a small point, but it implies the significant recognition that we in this country represent only one society (albeit a very important one) in the Americas.

SUPPLEMENTS

Sociology, Tenth Edition, is the heart of an unprecedented multimedia learning package that includes a wide range of proven instructional aids as well as several new ones. As the author of the text, I maintain a keen interest in all the supplements to ensure their quality and integration with the text. The supplements for this revision have been thoroughly updated, improved, and expanded.

FOR THE INSTRUCTOR

Annotated Instructor's Edition (0-13-189124-3). The AIE is a complete student text annotated on every page by the author. Annotations—which have been thoroughly revised for this edition—have won praise from instructors for enriching class presentations. Margin notes include summaries of research findings, statistics from the United States or other nations, insightful quotations, information highlighting patterns of social diversity in the United States, and high-quality survey data from the National Opinion Research Center's (NORC) General Social Survey and the World Values Survey data from the Inter-university Consortium for Political and Social Research (CPSR).

Instructor's Manual (0-13-189125-1). Formerly called the *Data File*, this is the "instructor's manual" that is of interest even to those who have never used one before. It provides far more than detailed chapter outlines and discussion questions; it contains statistical profiles of the United States and other nations, summaries of important developments, and significant research and supplemental lecture material for every chapter of the text.

Test Item File (0-13-189128-6). Written by the text author, John Macionis, this key supplement is available in both printed and computerized forms. The file contains over 2500 items—at least 100 per chapter—in multiple-choice, true/false, and essay formats. Questions are identified as simple "recall" items or more complex inferential issues; the answers to all questions are page referenced to the text.

TestGEN-EQ (0-13-189126-X). This computerized software allows instructors to create their own personalized exams, to edit any or all of the existing test questions, and to add new questions. Other special features of this program include random generation of test questions, creation of alternate versions of the same test, scrambling question sequence, and test preview before printing.

Instructor Resource CD-ROM (0-13-189141-3). Pulling together all of the media assets available to instructors, this interactive CD allows instructors to insert media—video, PowerPoint, graphs, charts, maps—into their interactive classroom presentations.

Prentice Hall Film and Video Guide: Introductory Sociology, Sixth Edition (0-13-020659-8). Keyed to the chapters of this text, this guide describes more than 300 films and videos appropriate for classroom viewing. It also provides summaries, discussion questions, and rental sources for each film and video.

ABCNEWS *ABC News*/**Prentice Hall Video Library for Sociology.** Few will dispute that video is the most dynamic supplement you can use to enhance a class. However, the quality of the video material and how well it relates to your course still make all the difference. Prentice Hall and *ABC News* are working together to bring to you the best and most comprehensive video material available in the college market. Through its wide variety of award-winning programs—*Nightline, This Week, World News Tonight,* and *20/20*—ABC offers a resource for feature and documentary-style videos related to the chapters in *Sociology, Tenth Edition.* The programs have high production quality, present substantial content, and are hosted by well-known anchors. The author, working with editors at Prentice Hall, has carefully selected videos on topics that complement *Sociology, Tenth Edition,* and included notes on how to use them in the classroom. An excellent instructor's guide carefully integrates the videos into your lectures. The guide has a synopsis of each video showing its relation to the chapter and discussion questions to help students focus on how concepts and theories apply to real-life situations.

Volume I: Social Stratification (0-13-466228-8)
Volume II: Marriage/Families (0-13-209537-8)
Volume III: Race/Ethnic Relations (0-13-458506-2)
Volume IV: Criminology (0-13-375163-5)
Volume V: Social Problems (0-13-437823-7)
Volume VI: Intro to Sociology I (0-13-095066-1)
Volume VII: Intro to Sociology II (0-13-095060-2)
Volume VIII: Intro to Sociology III (0-13-095773-9)
Volume IX: Social Problems II (0-13-095774-7)
Volume X: Marriage/Families II (0-13-095775-5)
Volume XI: Race and Ethnic Relations II (0-13-021134-6)
Volume XII: Institutions (0-13-021133-8)
Volume XIII: Introductory Sociology IV (0-13-018507-8)
Volume XIV: Introductory Sociology V (0-13-018509-4)

Prentice Hall Introductory Sociology PowerPoint™ Transparencies. These PowerPoint™ slides combine graphics and text in a colorful format to help you convey sociological principles in a new and exciting way. Created in PowerPoint™, an easy-to-use software program, this set contains slides keyed to each chapter in the text. For easy download, they are available on the Instructor Resource CD-ROM or in the instructor resource area of the OneKey for Macionis, *Sociology, Tenth Edition.*

Prentice Hall Color Transparencies: Sociology Series VII. Full-color illustrations, charts, and other visual materials from the text as well as outside sources have been selected to make up this useful in-class tool. An Instructor's Guide, which offers suggestions for using each transparency in the classroom, is also available.

MEDIA SUPPLEMENTS

OneKey. A one-stop shop for both professors and students, this innovative, premium Web site will help professors more effectively prepare lectures and help students more efficiently review the course material. For professors, it will include PowerPoint™ presentations, all the instructor supplements, testing software, and videos. For students, it will include videos, flashcards, quizzes, and concept tips. Professor access to OneKey can be gained by contacting your Prentice Hall representative or by visiting http://www.prenhall. com/onekey for registration. Students can access OneKey when professors order a special package of *Sociology, Tenth Edition,* with a free OneKey access code wrapped with the text.

Interactive CD-ROM. Using video as a window to the world outside the classroom, this innovative CD-ROM offers students videos and animations—arranged by the themes of Seeing, Thinking, and Doing within each chapter—that reinforce the material covered in each chapter of the text. Students can watch relevant *ABC News* clips, view author video tips, and interact with the global and national maps, as well as review sociological concepts through additional video. The CD-ROM is available free with all new copies of *Sociology, Tenth Edition.*

Census2000 Interactive CD-ROM. Capturing the rich picture of our nation drawn by Census 2000, this CD-ROM brings related Census data into your classroom in a rich multimedia format. It uses files taken directly from the U.S. Census Bureau Web site—even recently released Census Briefs—organizes them around your course, and offers teaching aids to support student learning. This updated CD-ROM is free when packaged with *Sociology, Tenth Edition.*

Companion Website™. In tandem with the text, students and professors can now take full advantage of the Internet to enrich their study of sociology. The Macionis Companion Website™ continues to lead the way in providing students with avenues for delving deeper into the topics covered in the text. Features of the Web site include chapter objectives and study questions, as well as links to interesting material and information from other sites on the Web that will reinforce and enhance the content of each chapter. Access to the Macionis Companion Website™ is free to both students and instructors. Please visit the site at http://www.prenhall.com/macionis and click on the cover of *Sociology, Tenth Edition.*

Research Navigator™. Research Navigator™ can help students confidently and efficiently complete research assignments. Research Navigator™ does this by providing students and faculty with three exclusive databases of high-quality scholarly and popular articles and search engines. Gain access to Research Navigator™ through an access code found in the front of the *Prentice Hall Guide to Evaluating Online Resources: Sociology*. The *Evaluating Online Resources* guide can be wrapped with *Sociology, Tenth Edition*, at no additional cost.

- **EBSCO's ContentSelect™ Academic Journal Database**, organized by subject, contains 50–100 of the leading academic journals for each discipline. Instructors and students can search the online journals by keyword, topic, or multiple topics. Articles include abstract and citation information and can be cut, pasted, e-mailed, or saved for later use.

- *The New York Times* **Search-by-Subject Archive** provides articles specific to sociology and is searchable by keyword or multiple keywords. Instructors and students can view full-text articles from the world's leading journalists writing for *The New York Times*.

- **Link Library** offers editorially selected "Best of the Web" sites for Sociology. Link Libraries are continually scanned and kept up to date to provide the most relevant and accurate links for research assignments.

Prentice Hall Guide to Evaluating Online Resources: Sociology (with Research Navigator™). This guide focuses on developing the critical-thinking skills necessary to evaluate and use online sources. Encouraging students to become critical consumers of online sources, this guide walks students through the process of selecting and citing their online sources properly. It also includes a section on using Research Navigator™, Prentice Hall's own gateway to academically sound and current sources. This supplementary book along with the Research Navigator™ access code is free to students when packaged with *Sociology, Tenth Edition*. Please contact your Prentice Hall representative for more information.

Distance Learning Solutions. Prentice Hall is committed to providing our leading content to the growing number of courses being delivered over the Internet by developing relationships with the leading vendors—Blackboard™, Web CT™, and CourseCompass™, Prentice Hall's own easy-to-use course management system powered by Blackboard™. Please visit our technology solutions site at http://www.prenhall.com/demo

FOR THE STUDENT

Study Guide (0-13-189123-5). This complete guide helps students review and reflect on the material presented in *Sociology, Tenth Edition*. Each of the twenty-four chapters in the Study Guide provides an overview of the corresponding chapter in the student text, summarizes its major topics and concepts, offers applied exercises, and features end-of-chapter tests with solutions.

"10 Ways to Fight Hate" brochure (0-13-028146-8). Produced by the Southern Poverty Law Center, the leading hate-crime and crime-watch organization in the United States, this free supplement walks students through ten steps that they can take on their own campus or in their own neighborhood to fight hate every day.

IN APPRECIATION

The conventional practice of designating a single author obscures the efforts of dozens of women and men that have resulted in *Sociology, Tenth Edition*. I would like to express my thanks to the Prentice Hall editorial team, including Yolanda De Rooy, division president, Nancy Roberts, publisher, and Chris DeJohn, executive editor in sociology, for their steady enthusiasm and for pursuing both innovation and excellence. Day-to-day work on the book is shared by the author and the production team. Barbara Reilly, production editor at Prentice Hall, deserves much of the credit for the attractive page layout of the book; indeed, if anyone "sweats the details" more than the author, it is Barbara! Amy Marsh Macionis, the text's "in house" editor, checks virtually everything, untangling awkward phrases, eliminating errors, and correcting inconsistencies in statistical data from chapter to chapter. Amy is a most talented editor who is relentless in her pursuit of quality; my debt to her is great, indeed.

I also have a large debt of gratitude to the members of the Prentice Hall sales staff, the men and women who have given this text such remarkable support over the years. Thanks, especially, to Beth Mejia and Marissa Feliberty who direct our marketing campaign.

Thanks, too, to Ximena Tamuakopoulos for providing the interior and cover design of the book. Developmental and copy editing of the manuscript was provided by Margaret Riche and Amy Marsh Macionis. Barbara Salz researched our photographs and fine art.

It goes without saying that every colleague knows more about some topics covered in this book than the author does. For that reason, I am grateful to the hundreds of faculty and students who have written to me to offer comments and suggestions.

I also wish to thank the following colleagues for sharing their wisdom in ways that have improved this book by reviewing this or previous editions: Doug Adams (The Ohio State University), Kip Armstrong (Bloomsburg University), Rose Arnault (Fort Hays State University), Scott Beck (Eastern Tennessee State University), Lois Benjamin (Hampton University), Philip Berg (University of Wisconsin, La Crosse), Charlotte Brauchle (Southwest Texas Junior College), Bill Brindle (Monroe Community College), John R. Brouillette (Colorado State University), Cathryn Brubaker (DeKalb College), Brent Bruton (Iowa State University), Richard Bucher (Baltimore City Community College), Karen Campbell (Vanderbilt University), Harold Conway (Blinn College), Gerry Cox (Fort Hays State University), Lovberta Cross (Southwest Tennessee Community College), Robert Daniels (Mount Vernon Nazarene College), James A. Davis (Harvard University), Sumati Devadutt (Monroe Community College), Keith Doubt (Northeast Missouri State University), Denny Dubbs (Harrisburg Area Community College), Travis Eaton (Northeast Louisiana State University), Helen Rose Fuchs Ebaugh (University of Houston), John Ehle (Northern Virginia Community College), Roger Eich (Hawkeye Community College), Gerhard Falk (Buffalo State College), Heather Fitz Gibbon (The College of Wooster), Kevin Fitzpatrick (University of Alabama-Birmingham), Dona C. Fletcher (Sinclair Community College), Charles Frazier (University of Florida), Karen Lynch Frederick (St. Anselm College), Patricia Gagné (University of Kentucky, Louisville), Pam Gaiter (Collin County Community College), Jarvis Gamble (Owen's Technical College), Steven Goldberg (City College, City University of New York), Charlotte Gotwald (York College of Pennsylvania), Norma B. Gray (Bishop State Community College), Rhoda Greenstone (DeVry Institute), Jeffrey Hahn (Mount Union College), Harry Hale (Northeast Louisiana State University), Dean Haledjian (Northern Virginia Community College), Dick Haltin (Jefferson Community College), Marvin Hannah (Milwaukee Area Technical College), Charles Harper (Creighton University), Gary Hodge (Collin County Community College), Elizabeth A. Hoisington (Heartland Community College), Sara Horsfall (Stephen F. Austin State University), Peter Hruschka (Ohio Northern University), Glenna Huls (Camden County College), Jeanne Humble (Lexington Community College), Cynthia Imanaka (Seattle Central Community College), Patricia Johnson (Houston Community College), Ed Kain (Southwestern University), Paul Kamolnick (Eastern Tennessee State University), Irwin Kantor (Middlesex County College), Thomas Korllos (Kent State University), Rita Krasnow (Virginia Western Community College), Donald Kraybill (Elizabethtown College), Michael Lacy (Colorado State University), Michael Levine (Kenyon College), Stephen Light (State University of New York at Plattsburgh), George Lowe (Texas Tech University), Don Luidens (Hope College), Dale Lund (University of Utah), Larry Lyon (Baylor University), Li-Chen Ma (Lamar University), Karen E. B. McCue (University of New Mexico, Albuquerque), Meredith McGuire (Trinity College), Setma Maddox (Texas Wesleyan University), Errol Magidson (Richard J. Daley College), Mehrdad Mashayekhi (Georgetown University), Allan Mazur (Syracuse University), Jack Melhorn (Emporia State University), Ken Miller (Drake University), Richard Miller (Navarro College), Joe Morolla (Virginia Commonwealth University), Craig Nauman (Madison Area Technical College), Mark Packard (Southeast Community College), Toby Parcel (The Ohio State University), Anne Peterson (Columbus State Community College), Marvin Pippert (Roanoke College), Lauren Pivnik (Monroe Community College), Nevel Razak (Fort Hays State College), Jim Rebstock (Broward Community College), George Reim (Cheltenham High School), Virginia Reynolds (Indiana University of Pennsylvania), Laurel Richardson (The Ohio State University), Keith Roberts (Hanover College), Ellen Rosengarten (Sinclair Community College), Howard Schneiderman (Lafayette College), Ray Scupin (Linderwood College), Steve Severin (Kellogg Community College), Harry Sherer (Irvine Valley College), Walt Shirley (Sinclair Community College), Anson Shupe (Indiana University-Purdue University at Fort Wayne), Brenda Silverman (Onondaga Community College), Ree Simpkins (Missouri Southern State University), Glen Sims (Glendale Community College), Toni Sims (University of Louisiana, Lafayette), Nancy Sonleitner (University of Oklahoma), Larry Stern (Collin County Community College), Randy Ston (Oakland Community College), Verta Taylor (University of California-Santa Barbara), Vickie H. Taylor (Danville Community College), Mark J. Thomas (Madison Area Technical College), Kirby Throckmorton (University of Wisconsin, Stevens Point), Len Tompos (Lorain County Community College), Tim Tuinstra (Kalamazoo Valley Community College), Christopher Vanderpool (Michigan State University), Phyllis Watts (Tiffin University), Murray Webster (University of North Carolina, Charlotte), Debbie White (Collin County Community College), Marilyn Wilmeth (Iowa University), Stuart Wright (Lamar University), William Yoels (University of Alabama, Birmingham), Dan Yutze (Taylor University), Wayne Zapatek (Tarrant County Community College), and Frank Zulke (Harold Washington College).

Finally, this revision represents something of a milestone—the tenth edition of the text. For almost twenty years, hundreds of women and men at Prentice Hall—both in editorial positions and in sales—have labored with skill and enthusiasm to help make this book as good and as successful as it is. I am grateful to you all. Of everyone, Nancy Roberts, publisher, stands out as having worked with me since 1988, when she became sociology editor. I dedicate this edition of the book to the entire Prentice Hall family—and, especially, to Nancy Roberts, with my deepest admiration and thanks.

John J. Macionis

THE SOCIOLOGICAL PERSPECTIVE

BILL JACKLIN (ENGLISH)
Gridlock NYC

1998, oil on canvas, 152.4 × 152.4 cm. Private Collection/The Bridgeman Art Library.

IF YOU WERE TO ASK 100 people in the United States, "Why do couples marry?" it is a safe bet that at least 90 will reply, "People marry because they fall in love." Indeed, it is hard for us to imagine a marriage being happy without love; likewise, when people fall in love, we expect them to think about marriage.

But is the decision about whom to marry really so simple and so personal? There is plenty of evidence to show that, if love is the key to marriage, Cupid's arrow is carefully aimed by the society around us.

Consider the fact that society has many "rules" about whom one should and should not marry. For instance, right off the bat, U.S. society rules out half the population with laws that prohibit people from marrying someone of the same sex (even if a couple is deeply in love). But there are other rules as well. Sociologists have found that people (especially when they are young) are very likely to marry someone close in age, and people of all ages typically marry someone in the same racial category, of a similar social class background, with a similar level of education, and of an equal degree of physical attractiveness (Chapter 18 gives details). In truth, people do end up making choices about whom to marry, but society certainly narrows the field long before they do (Gardyn, 2002; Zipp, 2002).

When it comes to love and most other dimensions of our lives, the decisions people make do not simply result from the process philosophers call "free will." More correctly—and this is the essential wisdom we gain from the study of sociology—our social world guides our actions and life choices in much the same way that the seasons influence our clothing and activities.

THE SOCIOLOGICAL PERSPECTIVE

Sociology is *the systematic study of human society*. At the heart of sociology is a distinctive point of view called "the sociological perspective."

SEEING THE GENERAL IN THE PARTICULAR

Peter Berger (1963) described the sociological perspective as *seeing the general in the particular*. By this he meant that sociologists seek out general patterns in the behavior of particular people. Although every individual is unique, a society shapes the lives of its members. (People in the United States are much more likely to expect love to figure in marriage than, say, people living in a traditional village in rural Pakistan.) In addition, any society acts differently on various *categories* of people (say, women as opposed to men, the rich as opposed to the poor, and children as opposed to adults). In a classic study of women's hopes for their marriages, for example, Lillian Rubin (1976) discovered that a higher-income woman typically expected the man she married to be sensitive to others, to talk readily, and to share his feelings and experiences. Most of the lower-income women in her study, by contrast, were looking for a man who did not drink too much, was not violent, and held a steady job. Obviously, what women think they can expect in a marriage partner has a lot to do with social class position. More generally, people who come from more privileged social backgrounds tend to be more confident

We can easily grasp the power of society over the individual by imagining how different our lives would be had we been born in place of any of these children from, respectively, Bolivia, Ethiopia, Nepal, Botswana, the People's Republic of China, and El Salvador.

and optimistic about their lives. This is not surprising when we realize that they have more opportunities as well as the training and skills to take advantage of them. We begin to think sociologically by realizing how the society we live in—as well as the general categories into which we fall within that society—shapes our particular life experiences.

SEEING THE STRANGE IN THE FAMILIAR

At first, using the sociological perspective amounts to *seeing the strange in the familiar*. It would strike us all as strange indeed if one person were to say to another, "You fit all the right social categories; that means you would make a wonderful husband!" The point is that looking sociologically means challenging the familiar idea that we live our lives in terms of what we *decide*,

considering instead the initially strange notion that society shapes our experiences.

For individualistic North Americans, learning to see how society affects us may take a bit of practice. If someone asked you why you "chose" to enroll at your particular college, you might offer one of the following reasons:

"I wanted to stay close to home."
"I got a basketball scholarship."
"With a journalism degree from this university, I can get a good job."
"My girlfriend goes to school here."
"I didn't get into the school I *really* wanted to attend."

Such responses may well be true. But do they tell the whole story?

Thinking sociologically about going to college, we might first realize that, around the world, about 5 people in 100 receive a college degree. Even in the United States a century ago, going to college was not an option for most people. Today a look around the classroom shows that social forces still have much to do with college attendance. Typically, U.S. college students are young, generally between eighteen and twenty-four. Why? Because in our society, attending college is linked to this period of life. But more than age is involved, because fewer than half of all young men and women actually end up on campus.

Another factor is cost. Because higher education is so expensive, students tend to come from families with above-average incomes. As Chapter 20 ("Education") explains, if you are lucky enough to belong to a family earning more than $75,000 a year, you are three times more likely to go to college than someone whose family earns less than $20,000. Is it reasonable, in light of these data, to assume that attending college is simply a matter of personal choice?

SEEING INDIVIDUALITY IN SOCIAL CONTEXT

To see the power of society to shape individual choices, consider the number of children women have. In the United States, as shown in Global Map 1–1 on page 4, the average woman has slightly fewer than two children during her lifetime. In India, however, the average is about three; in South Africa, about four; in Cambodia, about five; in Saudi Arabia, about six; and in Niger, about seven.

Why these striking differences? As later chapters explain, women in poor countries have less schooling and fewer economic opportunities, are more likely to remain in the home, and are less likely to use contraception. Clearly, society has much to do with the decisions women and men make about childbearing.

Another illustration of the power of society to shape even our most private choices comes from the study of suicide. What could be a more personal choice than taking one's own life? But Emile Durkheim (1858–1917), one of sociology's pioneers, showed that social forces are at work even in the apparently isolated act of self-destruction.

Examining official records in his native France, Durkheim found that some categories of people were more likely than others to take their own lives. He found that men, Protestants, wealthy people, and the unmarried had significantly higher suicide rates than did women, Catholics and Jews, the poor, and married

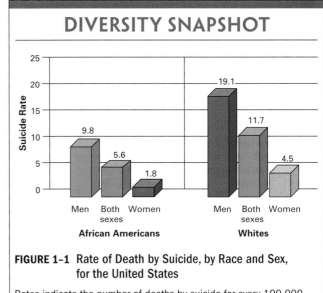

DIVERSITY SNAPSHOT

FIGURE 1-1 Rate of Death by Suicide, by Race and Sex, for the United States

Rates indicate the number of deaths by suicide for every 100,000 people in each category for 2000.

Source: U.S. National Center for Health Statistics (2002).

people. Durkheim explained the differences in terms of *social integration:* Categories of people with strong social ties had low suicide rates, whereas more individualistic categories of people had high suicide rates.

In the male-dominated society Durkheim studied, men certainly had more freedom than women. But despite its advantages, freedom weakens social ties and thus boosts the risk of suicide. Likewise, more individualistic Protestants were more prone to suicide than more tradition-bound Catholics and Jews, whose rituals foster stronger social ties. The wealthy have much more freedom than the poor, but, once again, at the cost of a higher suicide rate. Finally, can you see why single people are at greater risk of suicide than married people?

A century later, Durkheim's analysis still holds true (Thorlindsson & Bjarnason, 1998). Figure 1–1 shows suicide rates for four categories of the U.S. population. Keep in mind that suicide is very rare—a rate of 10 suicides for every 100,000 people is about the same as 4 inches in a mile. Even so, some interesting patterns are evident. In 2000, there were 11.7 recorded suicides for every 100,000 white people, about twice the rate for African Americans (5.6). For both races, suicide was more common among men than among women; white men (19.1) were more than

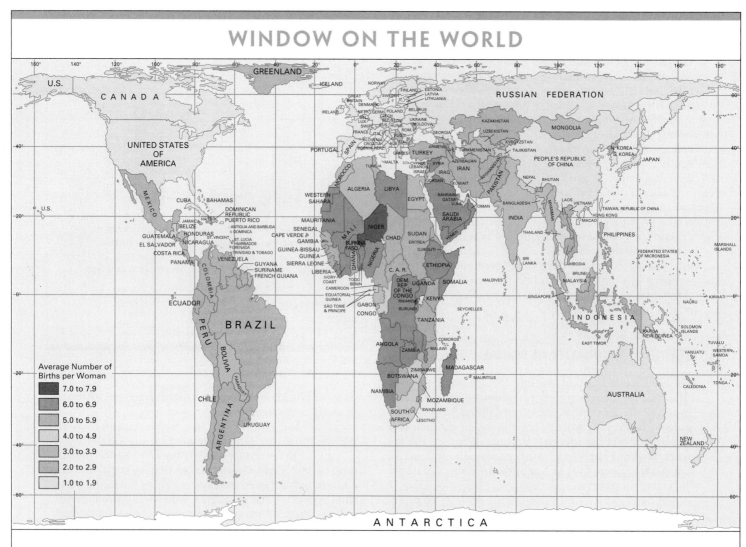

GLOBAL MAP 1–1 Women's Childbearing in Global Perspective

Is childbearing simply a matter of personal choice? A look around the world shows that it is not. In general, women living in poor countries have many more children than women in rich nations. Can you point to some of the reasons for this global disparity? In simple terms, such differences mean that if you had been born into another society (whether you are female or male), your life might have been quite different from what it is now.

Source: Data from Mackay (2000).

four times as likely as white women (4.5) to take their own lives. Among African Americans, the rate for men (9.8) was six times higher than for women (1.8). Following Durkheim's logic, the higher suicide rate among white people and men reflects their greater wealth and freedom; the lower rate among women and African Americans follows from their limited social choices. Just as in Durkheim's day, then, we can see general patterns in the personal actions of particular individuals.

GLOBAL SOCIOLOGY

The Global Village: A Social Snapshot of Our World

The Earth is home to 6.4 billion people who live in the cities and villages of 192 nations. To grasp the social shape of the world, imagine for a moment that the planet's population is reduced to a single settlement of 1,000 people. In this "global village," more than half (610) of the inhabitants are Asian, including 210 citizens of the People's Republic of China. Next, in terms of numbers, we would find 130 Africans, 120 Europeans, 85 people from Latin America and the Caribbean, 5 from Australia and the South Pacific, and just 50 North Americans, including 45 people from the United States.

A study of the settlement's ways of life would reveal some startling facts: The village is a rich place, with a seemingly endless array of goods and services for sale. Yet most of the inhabitants only dream about such treasures, because 80 percent of the village's total income is earned by just 200 people.

For the majority, the greatest problem is getting enough food. Every year, village workers produce more than enough to feed everyone; even so, half the village's people, including most of the children, do not get enough to eat, and many fall asleep hungry. The worst-off 200 residents (who, together, have less money than the richest person in the village) lack both clean drinking water and safe shelter. Weak and unable to work, some of them fall victim to life-threatening diseases every day.

Villagers boast of their community's many schools, including a fine university. About 50 inhabitants have completed a college degree, but almost half of the village's people can neither read nor write.

We in the United States, on average, would be among the richest people in this global village. Although we tend to credit ourselves for living well, the sociological perspective reminds us that our achievements are largely products of the privileged position our nation holds in the worldwide social system.

Sources: Calculations by the author based on data from Population Reference Bureau (2002) and United Nations Development Programme (2002).

THE IMPORTANCE OF GLOBAL PERSPECTIVE

December 10, Fez, Morocco. This medieval city—a web of narrow streets and alleyways—is alive with the laughter of playing children, the silence of veiled women, and the steady gaze of men leading donkeys laden with goods. Fez seems to have changed little over the centuries. Here, in northwest Africa, we are just a few hundred miles from the more familiar rhythms of Europe. Yet this place seems a thousand years away. Never have we had such an adventure! Never have we thought so much about home!

As new information technology draws even the farthest reaches of the Earth closer to each other, many academic disciplines are taking a **global perspective,** *the study of the larger world and our society's place in it.* What is the importance of a global perspective for sociology?

First, global awareness is a logical extension of the sociological perspective. Sociology shows us that our place in society profoundly affects our life experiences. It stands to reason, then, that the position of our society in the larger world system affects everyone in the United States. The box describes a "global village" to show the social shape of the world and the place of the United States within it.

Global Map 1–2 on page 6 provides a visual guide to the relative economic development of the world's countries. **High-income countries** are *nations with very productive economic systems in which most people have relatively high incomes.* The forty high-income countries include the United States and Canada, Argentina, the nations of Western Europe, South Africa, Israel, Saudi Arabia, Japan, and Australia. Taken together, these nations produce most of the world's goods and services and control most of the wealth. On average, individuals in these countries live well, not because they are smarter than anyone else, but because they had the good fortune to be born in an affluent region of the world.

The world's **middle-income countries** are *nations with moderately productive economic systems in*

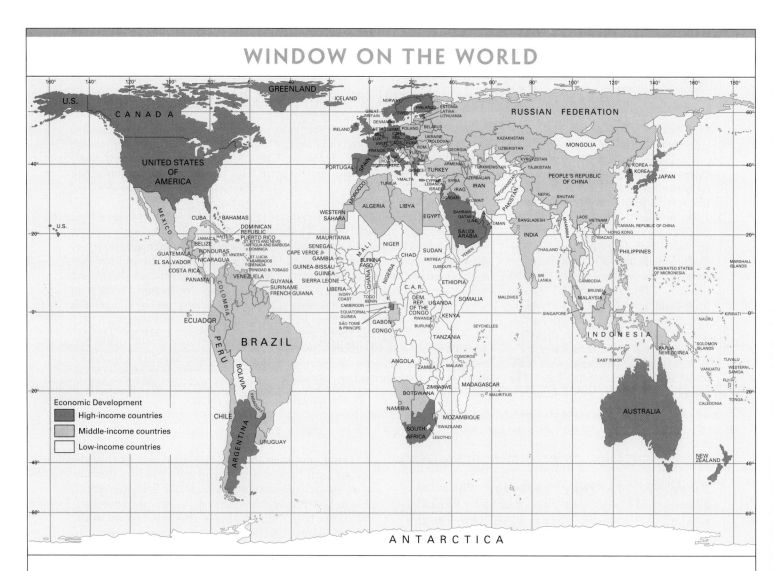

GLOBAL MAP 1–2 Economic Development in Global Perspective

In high-income countries—including the United States, Canada, Argentina, the nations of Western Europe, South Africa, Israel, Saudi Arabia, Australia, and Japan—a highly productive economy provides people, on average, with material plenty. Middle-income countries—including most of Latin America and the nations of Eastern Europe—are less economically productive, with a standard of living about average for the world as a whole but far below that of the United States. These nations also have a significant share of poor people who barely scrape by with meager housing and diet. In the low-income countries of the world, poverty is severe and extensive. Although small numbers of elites live very well in the poorest nations, most people struggle to survive on a small fraction of the income common in the United States.

Note: Data for this map are provided by the United Nations. High-income countries have a per capita gross domestic product (GDP) of at least $10,000. Many are far richer than this, however; the figure for the United States exceeds $34,000. Middle-income countries have a per capita GDP ranging from $2,500 to $10,000. Low-income countries have a per capita GDP below $2,500. Figures used here reflect the United Nations "purchasing power parities" system. Rather than directly converting income figures into U.S. dollars, this calculation estimates the local purchasing power of each domestic currency.

Source: Prepared by the author using data from United Nations Development Programme (2003). Map projection from *Peters Atlas of the World* (1990).

which people's incomes are about the global average. People who live in any of these roughly ninety nations—most of the countries of Eastern Europe, much of Asia, some of Africa, and almost all of Latin America—are as likely to live in rural villages as in cities; to walk or ride tractors, scooters, bicycles, or animals as to drive automobiles; and, on average, to receive just a few years of schooling. Most middle-income countries also have marked social inequality, so that some people are extremely rich (members of the business elite in nations across North Africa, for example), but many more lack safe housing and adequate nutrition.

Finally, about half of the world's people live in the sixty **low-income countries,** *nations with less productive economic systems in which most people are poor.* As Global Map 1–2 shows, most of the poorest countries in the world are in Africa. Here, again, a few people are very rich, but the majority struggle to get by with poor housing, unsafe water, too little food, limited sanitation, and, perhaps most seriously of all, little chance to improve their lives.

Chapter 12 ("Global Stratification") details the causes and consequences of global wealth and poverty. But every chapter of this text highlights life in the world beyond our own borders for four reasons:

1. **Where we live makes a great difference in shaping our lives.** As we saw in Global Map 1–1, women's lives are strikingly different in rich and poor countries. To understand ourselves and appreciate the lives of others, we must grasp the social landscape of the world—one good reason to pay attention to the thirty global maps found throughout this text.

2. **Societies throughout the world are increasingly interconnected.** Historically the United States took only passing note of the countries beyond its own borders. In recent decades, however, the United States and the rest of the world have become linked as never before. Electronic technology now transmits sounds, pictures, and written documents around the globe in seconds.

   One consequence of new technology, as later chapters explain, is that people all over the world now share many tastes in food, clothing, and music. With their economic clout, high-income countries such as the United States influence other nations, whose people eagerly gobble up our hamburgers, dance to pop music, and, more and more, speak the English language.

   As we spread our way of life around the world, the larger world also has an impact on us. About

One important reason to gain a global understanding is that, living in a high-income nation, we scarcely can appreciate the suffering that goes on in much of the world. This boy is growing up in the African nation of Ghana, where he carries water for cooking and drinking from a public faucet and sewerage flows freely over unpaved streets. In poor nations like this, children have only a fifty-fifty chance to grow to adulthood.

1 million documented immigrants enter the United States each year, bringing their fashions and foods to our shores, which greatly enhances the racial and cultural diversity of this country.

   Commerce across national boundaries has also created a global economy. Large corporations make and market goods worldwide, and global financial markets linked by satellite communication operate around the clock. Stock traders in New York follow the financial markets in Tokyo and Hong Kong even as wheat farmers in Iowa watch the price of grain in the former Soviet republic of Georgia. With eight out of ten new U.S. jobs involving international trade, global understanding has never been more important.

3. **Many problems that we face in the United States are far more serious elsewhere.** Poverty is a serious problem in the United States, but as Chapter 12 ("Global Stratification") explains, poverty in Latin America, Africa, and Asia is both more common and more serious. Similarly, although women have lower social standing than men in the United States, gender inequality is much greater in poor countries of the world.

4. **Thinking globally is a good way to learn more about ourselves.** We cannot walk the streets of a distant city without becoming keenly aware of what it means to live in the United States. Making global comparisons also leads to unexpected lessons. For instance, in Chapter 12 we visit a squatter settlement in Madras, India. There, despite a lack of basic material goods, people thrive in the love and support of family members. Why, then, is poverty in the United States associated with isolation and anger? Are material comforts—so crucial to our definition of a "rich" life—the best way to gauge human well-being?

In sum, in an increasingly interconnected world, we can understand ourselves only to the extent that we comprehend others (Macionis, 1993).

APPLYING THE SOCIOLOGICAL PERSPECTIVE

It is easy to apply the sociological perspective when we encounter people who differ from us—whether around the world or in our own hometowns—because they remind us that society shapes individual lives. But two other kinds of situations also help us to see the world with a sociological perspective: living on the margins of society and living through a social crisis.

SOCIOLOGY AND SOCIAL MARGINALITY

From time to time, everyone feels like an "outsider." For some categories of people, however, being an *outsider*—not part of the dominant group—is an everyday experience. The greater people's social marginality, the better able they are to use the sociological perspective.

For example, no African American grows up in the United States without understanding the importance of race. But white people, as the dominant majority, think less often about race and believe it affects only

people of color, not themselves. Women, gay people, people with disabilities, and the very old are also, to some degree, "outsiders." People at the margins of social life are aware of social patterns that others rarely think about. To become better at using the sociological perspective, therefore, we must step back from our familiar routines and look at our lives with new awareness and curiosity.

SOCIOLOGY AND SOCIAL CRISIS

Periods of change or crisis make everyone feel a little off balance and prompt us to use the sociological perspective. U.S. sociologist C. Wright Mills (1959) illustrated this idea using the Great Depression of the 1930s. As the unemployment rate soared to 25 percent, people out of work could not help but see general social forces at work in their particular lives. Rather than saying, "Something is wrong with me; I can't find a job," they took a sociological approach and realized, "The economy has collapsed; there are no jobs to be found!"

Just as social change fosters sociological thinking, sociological thinking can bring about social change. The more we learn how "the system" operates, the more we may want to change it in some way. Becoming aware of the power of gender, for example, many women and men have actively tried to reduce traditional gender role differences.

In short, an introduction to sociology is an invitation to learn a new way of looking at familiar patterns of social life. But is this invitation worth accepting? What are the benefits of applying the sociological perspective?

BENEFITS OF THE SOCIOLOGICAL PERSPECTIVE

Applying the sociological perspective to our daily lives benefits us in four ways:

1. **The sociological perspective helps us assess the truth of "common sense."** We all take many things for granted, but that does not make them true. One good example is the notion that we are free individuals who are personally responsible for our own lives. If we think people decide their own fate, we may be quick to praise particularly successful people as superior and consider others with more modest achievements personally deficient. A sociological approach, by contrast, encourages us to ask whether commonly held

APPLYING SOCIOLOGY

The Sociological Imagination: Turning Personal Problems into Public Issues

The power of the sociological perspective lies not just in changing individual lives but in transforming society. As C. Wright Mills saw it, society, not people's personal failings, is the cause of poverty and other social problems. The sociological imagination brings people together to create change by transforming personal *problems* into public *issues*.

In the following excerpt* Mills explains the need for a sociological imagination:

> When a society becomes industrialized, a peasant becomes a worker; a feudal lord is liquidated or becomes a businessman. When

_____

*In this excerpt, Mills uses "man" and male pronouns to apply to all people. Note that even an outspoken critic of society such as Mills reflected the conventional writing practices of his time as far as gender was concerned.

classes rise or fall, a man is employed or unemployed; when the rate of investment goes up or down, a man takes new heart or goes broke. When wars happen, an insurance salesman becomes a rocket launcher; a store clerk, a radar man; a wife lives alone; a child grows up without a father. Neither the life of an

 To find out more about C. Wright Mills, visit the Gallery of Sociologists at http://www.TheSociologyPage.com

individual nor the history of a society can be understood without understanding both.

> Yet men do not usually define the troubles they endure in terms of historical change. . . . The well-being they enjoy, they do not usually impute to the big ups and downs of the society in which they live. Seldom aware of the intricate

connection between the patterns of their own lives and the course of world history, ordinary men do not usually know what this connection means for the kind of men they are becoming and for the kinds of history-making in which they might take part. They do not possess the quality of mind essential to grasp the interplay of men and society, of biography and history, of self and world. . . .

> What they need . . . is a quality of mind that will help them to [see] what is going on in the world and . . . what may be happening within themselves. It is this quality . . . that . . . may be called the sociological imagination.

_____

Source: Mills (1959:3–5).

beliefs are actually true and, to the extent that they are not, why they are so widely held.

2. **The sociological perspective helps us see the opportunities and constraints in our lives.** Sociological thinking leads us to see that, in the game of life, we have a say in how to play our cards, but it is society that deals us the hand. The more we understand the game, the better players we will be. Sociology helps us "size up" our world so we can pursue our goals more effectively.

3. **The sociological perspective empowers us to be active participants in our society.** The more we understand about how society works, the more active citizens we become. For some, this may mean supporting society as it is; others may attempt nothing less

than changing the entire world in some way. Evaluating any aspect of social life—whatever your goal–requires identifying social forces and assessing their consequences. In the box, C. Wright Mills describes the power of using the sociological perspective.

4. **The sociological perspective helps us live in a diverse world.** North Americans represent just 5 percent of the world's people, and, as the remaining chapters of this book explain, many of the other 95 percent live very differently than we do. Still, like people everywhere, we tend to define our own way of life as "right," "natural," and "better." The sociological perspective encourages us to think critically about the relative strengths and weaknesses of all ways of life, including our own.

SOCIOLOGY, POLICY, AND CAREERS

The benefits of sociology go well beyond personal growth. Sociologists have helped shape public policy and law in countless ways, involving school desegregation, school busing, pornography regulation, and social welfare. For example, the work that Lenore Weitzman (1985) did on the financial hardships facing women after divorce "had a real impact on public policy and resulted in the passage of fourteen new laws in California" (Weitzman, 1996:538).

A background in sociology is also good preparation for the working world. The American Sociological

Association reports that sociologists are hired for hundreds of jobs in fields such as advertising, banking, criminal justice, education, government, health care, public relations, and research (Billson & Huber, 1993).

Most men and women who continue beyond a bachelor's degree to earn advanced training in sociology go on to careers in teaching and research. But an increasing number of professional sociologists work in all sorts of applied fields. Clinical sociologists, for example, work with troubled clients much as clinical psychologists do. A basic difference is that whereas psychologists focus on the individual, sociologists locate difficulties in a person's web of social relation-

In a short video, the author offers a personal response to the question, "Why would someone want to be a sociologist?" See the Video Gallery at http://www.TheSociologyPage.com

ships. Another type of applied sociology is evaluation research. In today's cost-conscious climate, administrators must evaluate the effectiveness of virtually every kind of program and policy. Sociologists, especially those with advanced research skills, are in high demand for this kind of work (Deutscher, 1999).

THE ORIGINS OF SOCIOLOGY

Like the "choices" made by individuals, major historical events rarely just "happen." The birth of sociology was itself the result of powerful social forces.

SOCIAL CHANGE AND SOCIOLOGY

Striking transformations during the eighteenth and nineteenth centuries greatly changed European society. Three changes were especially important in the development of sociology: the rise of a factory-based industrial economy, the explosive growth of cities, and new ideas about democracy and political rights.

A New Industrial Economy

During the Middle Ages in Europe, most people tilled fields near their homes or engaged in small-scale *manufacturing* (a word derived from Latin words meaning "to make by hand"). But by the end of the eighteenth century, inventors used new sources of energy—the power of moving water and then steam—to operate large machines in mills and factories. Instead of laboring at home or in tightly knit groups, workers became part of a large and anonymous labor force, toiling for strangers who owned the factories. This change in the system of production separated families and weakened the traditions that had governed community life for centuries.

The Growth of Cities

Across Europe, factories drew people in need of work. Along with this "pull" came the "push" of the *enclosure movement*. Landowners fenced off more and more ground, turning farms into grazing land for sheep, the source of wool for the thriving textile mills. Without land, countless tenant farmers left the countryside in search of work in the new factories.

As cities grew to unprecedented size, the new urban dwellers contended with mounting social problems, including pollution, crime, and homelessness. Living on streets crowded with strangers, they adapted to the new, impersonal social environment.

Political Change

During the Middle Ages, people viewed society as an expression of God's will: Royalty claimed to rule by "divine right," and each person up and down the social ladder played a part in the holy plan. This theological view of society is captured in lines from the old Anglican hymn "All Things Bright and Beautiful":

> The rich man in his castle,
> The poor man at his gate,
> God made them high and lowly
> And ordered their estate.

But economic development and the rapid growth of cities soon brought new political ideas. By about 1600, tradition was under spirited attack. In the writings of Thomas Hobbes (1588–1679), John Locke (1632–1704), and Adam Smith (1723–1790), we see a shift in focus

The birth of sociology was sparked by rapid social change. The discipline developed in those regions of Europe where the Industrial Revolution was most pronounced. Large cities grew as people left countless small villages in search of work in the new factories. As this image of a London soup kitchen suggests, tens of thousands of people struggled to survive in the new industrial cities, working for pennies a day and surrounded by strangers. These facts help to explain why early sociologists were, on the whole, critical of modern society.

from people's moral obligations to God and their rulers to the idea that people should pursue their own self-interest. In the new political climate, philosophers spoke of *individual liberty* and *individual rights*. Echoing Locke, our own Declaration of Independence asserts that every person has "certain unalienable rights," including "life, liberty, and the pursuit of happiness."

The French Revolution, which began in 1789, further exemplified this dramatic break with political and social tradition. The French social analyst Alexis de Tocqueville (1805–1859) declared that the changes in society brought about by the French Revolution amounted to "nothing short of the regeneration of the whole human race" (1955:13; orig. 1856).

A New Awareness of Society

Huge factories, exploding cities, a new spirit of individualism—these changes combined to make people aware of their surroundings. As the social ground trembled under people's feet, the new discipline of sociology was born in England, France, and Germany—precisely where the changes were greatest.

SCIENCE AND SOCIOLOGY

And so it was that the French social thinker Auguste Comte (1798–1857) coined the term *sociology* in 1838 to describe a new way of looking at society. Notice

that sociology is among the youngest academic disciplines—far newer than history, physics, or economics, for example.

Of course, Comte was not the first person to ponder the nature of society. The workings of the social world fascinated the brilliant thinkers of ancient civilizations, including the Chinese philosopher K'ung Fu-tzu, or Confucius (551–479 B.C.E.) and the Greek philosophers Plato (c. 427–347 B.C.E.) and Aristotle (384–322 B.C.E.).[1] Centuries later, the Roman emperor Marcus Aurelius (121–180), the medieval thinkers Saint Thomas Aquinas (c. 1225–1274) and Christine de Pisan (c. 1363–1431), and the English playwright William Shakespeare (1564–1616) took up the question.

Yet these thinkers were more interested in envisioning the ideal society than in analyzing society as it really was. Comte and other pioneers of sociology, by contrast, cared how society could be improved, but their major goal was to understand how society actually operates.

---

[1]Throughout this text, the abbreviation B.C.E. designates "before the common era." We use this terminology in place of the traditional B.C. ("before Christ") in recognition of the religious plurality of our society. Similarly, in place of the traditional A.D. (*anno Domini*, or "in the year of our Lord"), we use the abbreviation C.E. ("common era").

Here we see Galileo, one of the great pioneers of the scientific revolution, defending himself before church officials, who were greatly threatened by his claims that science could explain the operation of the universe. Just as Galileo challenged the common sense of his day, pioneering sociologists such as Auguste Comte later argued that society is neither rigidly fixed by God's will nor set by human nature. On the contrary, Comte claimed, society is a system we can study scientifically, and based on what we learn, we can act intentionally to improve our lives.

Comte (1975; orig. 1851–54) saw sociology as the product of a three-stage historical development. During the earliest, the *theological stage*, from the beginning of human history to the end of the European Middle Ages about 1350 C.E., people took a religious view of society, seeing it as an expression of God's will.

With the Renaissance, the theological approach gave way to what Comte called the *metaphysical stage* of history. During this period, people understood society as a natural rather than a supernatural phenomenon. Thomas Hobbes (1588–1679), for example, thought that society reflected not the perfection of God so much as the failings of a selfish human nature.

What Comte called the *scientific stage* of history began with the work of early scientists such as the Polish astronomer Copernicus (1473–1543), the Italian astronomer and physicist Galileo (1564–1642), and the English physicist and mathematician Isaac Newton (1642–1727). Comte's contribution came in applying the scientific approach, which was first used to study the physical world, to the study of society.[2]

---

[2]Illustrating Comte's stages, the ancient Greeks and Romans viewed the planets as gods; Renaissance metaphysical thinkers saw them as astral influences (giving rise to astrology); by the time of Galileo, scientists understood planets as natural objects behaving according to natural laws.

Comte thus favored **positivism,** defined as *a way of understanding based on science.* As a positivist, Comte believed that society conforms to invariable laws, much as the physical world operates according to gravity and other laws of nature.

At the beginning of the twentieth century, sociology emerged as an academic discipline in the United States, strongly influenced by Comte's ideas. Today, most sociologists still consider science a crucial part of sociology. But as Chapter 2 ("Sociological Investigation") explains, we now realize that human behavior is far more complex than the movement of planets or even the actions of other living things. Because humans are creatures of imagination and spontaneity, our behavior can never fully be explained by any rigid "laws of society." In addition, early sociologists such as Karl Marx (1818–1883), whose ideas are discussed in Chapter 4 ("Society"), were troubled by the striking inequality of the new industrial society. They wanted the new discipline of sociology not just to understand society but to bring about change toward social justice.

 For a biographical sketch of Comte, go to the Gallery of Sociologists at http://www. TheSociologyPage.com

GENDER AND RACE: MARGINAL VOICES

Auguste Comte and Karl Marx stand among the giants of sociology. In recent years, though, we have come to see the important contributions that others—pushed

We can use the sociological perspective to look at sociology itself. All of the most widely recognized pioneers of the discipline were men. This is because, in the nineteenth century, it was all but unheard of for women to be college professors, and few women took a central role in public life. But Harriet Martineau in England, Jane Addams in the United States, and others made contributions to sociology that we now recognize as important and lasting.

to the margins of society because of their gender or race—have made.

Harriet Martineau (1802–1876), born to a wealthy English family, first made her mark in 1853 by translating the writings of Auguste Comte from French into English. Subsequently, she became a noted scholar in her own right, exposing the evils of slavery and arguing for laws to protect factory workers and advance the standing of women.

In the United States, Jane Addams (1860–1935) was a sociological pioneer. Trained as a social worker, Addams spoke out on behalf of immigrants, who were entering the nation at the rate of 1 million per year. In 1889, Addams founded Hull House, a settlement house in Chicago that provided assistance to immigrant families. She also gathered sociologists and politicians to discuss the urban problems of the day. For her work on behalf of immigrants, Addams received the Nobel Peace Prize in 1931.

An important contribution to understanding race in the United States was made by yet another sociological pioneer, William Edward Burghardt Du Bois (1868–1963). Born to a poor Massachusetts family, Du Bois enrolled at Fisk University in Nashville, Tennessee, and then at Harvard University, where he earned the first doctorate awarded by that university to a person of color. Like Martineau and Addams, Du Bois believed that sociologists should try to solve social problems. He therefore studied the black community (1899), spoke out against racial inequality, and served as a founding member of the National Association for the Advancement of Colored People (NAACP).

Widespread belief in the inferiority of women and African Americans kept Martineau, Addams, and Du Bois at the margins of sociology. Looking back with a sociological eye, we can see how the forces of society were at work shaping even the history of sociology itself.

SOCIOLOGICAL THEORY

Weaving observations into understanding brings us to another aspect of sociology: theory. A **theory** is *a statement of how and why specific facts are related.* The job of sociological theory is to explain social behavior in the real world. Recall Emile Durkheim's theory that categories of people with low social integration (men, Protestants, the wealthy, and the unmarried) are especially prone to suicide. As Durkheim pondered the issue of suicide, he considered a number of possible theories. But which one was correct?

To evaluate a theory, as the next chapter explains, sociologists gather evidence using various methods of scientific research. Research allows sociologists to confirm some theories while rejecting or modifying others. Thus, Durkheim collected data that revealed patterns showing that certain categories of people are more likely to commit suicide. These patterns allowed Durkheim to settle on a theory that best squared with all available evidence. National Map 1–1 on page 14 displays the suicide rate for each of the fifty states and gives you a chance to do some theorizing of your own.

In building theory, sociologists face two basic questions: What issues should we study? How should we connect the facts? How sociologists answer these

SEEING OURSELVES

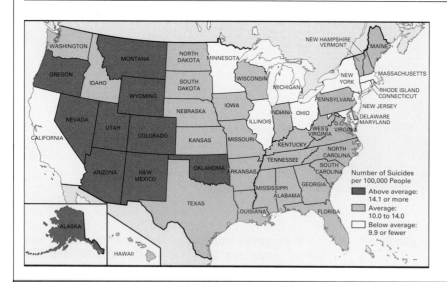

NATIONAL MAP 1–1
Suicide Rates across the United States

This map shows which states have high, average, and low suicide rates. Look for patterns. By and large, high suicide rates occur where people live far apart from one another. More densely populated states have low suicide rates. Do these data support or contradict Durkheim's theory of suicide? Why?

Source: U.S. National Center for Health Statistics (2002).

Number of Suicides per 100,000 People

- Above average: 14.1 or more
- Average: 10.0 to 14.0
- Below average: 9.9 or fewer

---

questions depends on their theoretical "road map" or paradigm (Kuhn, 1970). A **theoretical paradigm** is *a basic image of society that guides thinking and research.* Sociology has three major approaches: the structural-functional paradigm, the social-conflict paradigm, and the symbolic-interaction paradigm.

THE STRUCTURAL-FUNCTIONAL PARADIGM

The **structural-functional paradigm** is *a framework for building theory that sees society as a complex system whose parts work together to promote solidarity and stability.* As its name suggests, this paradigm points to **social structure,** meaning *any relatively stable pattern of social behavior.* Social structure gives our lives shape, whether it be in families, the workplace, or the classroom. Second, this paradigm looks for a structure's **social functions,** or *consequences for the operation of society as a whole.* All social structure—from a simple handshake to complex religious rituals—functions to keep society going, at least in its present form.

The structural-functional paradigm owes much to Auguste Comte, who pointed to the importance of social integration during a time of rapid change. Emile Durkheim, who helped establish sociology in French universities, also based his work on this approach. A third structural-functional pioneer was the

English sociologist Herbert Spencer (1820–1903). Spencer compared society to the human body. Just as the structural parts of the human body—the skeleton, muscles, and various internal organs—function interdependently to help the entire organism survive, social structures work together to preserve society. The structural-functional paradigm, then, organizes sociological observations by identifying various structures of society and investigating their functions.

The Gallery of Sociologists includes a biography of Herbert Spencer. Go to http://www.TheSociologyPage.com

As sociology developed in the United States, many of the ideas of Comte, Spencer, and Durkheim were carried forward by Talcott Parsons (1902–1979), the major U.S. proponent of the structural-functional paradigm. Parsons treated society as a system and sought to identify the basic tasks that any and all societies must perform to survive and the ways they accomplish these tasks.

Robert K. Merton (1910–2003) critically expanded our understanding of the concept of social function. Merton (1968) explains, first, that people rarely perceive all the functions of social structure. He describes as **manifest functions** *the recognized and intended consequences of any social pattern.* By contrast, **latent functions** are *consequences that are largely*

The approach of the structural-functional paradigm is conveyed by the painting St. Regis Indian Reservation *by Amy Jones (1937). Here we see society composed of major rounds of life, each serving a particular purpose that contributes to the operation of the entire system.*

Amy Jones, St. Regis Indian Reservation, 1937. Photo courtesy Janet Marqusee Fine Arts Ltd.

unrecognized and unintended. To illustrate, the obvious function of the U.S. system of higher education is to provide young people with the information and skills they need to perform jobs. Perhaps just as important, although less often acknowledged, is college's function as a "marriage broker," bringing together people of similar social backgrounds. Another latent function of higher education is keeping millions of young people out of the labor market, where, presumably, many of them would not find jobs.

Second, Merton explains, social patterns affect various members of a society differently. For example, conventional families may provide benefits to young children, but they also confer privileges on men while limiting the opportunities of women.

Third, some social patterns support a society's status quo while others disrupt it. Merton used the term **social dysfunction** to describe *any social pattern that may disrupt the operation of society.* Some disruptive patterns (such as crime) are widely viewed as harmful. But what is disruptive is not always bad, at least not from everyone's point of view. After all, crime is big business in the United States, providing jobs for millions of people who work within the criminal justice system.

Critical evaluation. The chief characteristic of the structural-functional paradigm is its vision of society as stable and orderly. The main goal of the sociologists who use this approach, then, is to figure out "what makes society tick."

In the mid-1900s, most sociologists favored the structural-functional paradigm. In recent decades, however, its influence has declined. By focusing on social stability and unity, critics point out, structural-functionalism tends to ignore inequalities of social class, race, and gender, which can generate considerable tension and conflict. In general, focusing on stability at the expense of conflict makes this paradigm somewhat conservative. As a critical response to this approach, sociologists developed another theoretical orientation: the social-conflict paradigm.

THE SOCIAL-CONFLICT PARADIGM

The **social-conflict paradigm** is *a framework for building theory that sees society as an arena of inequality that generates conflict and change.* Unlike the structural-functional emphasis on solidarity, this approach highlights inequality. Sociologists guided by this paradigm investigate how factors such as social class, race, ethnicity, gender, and age are linked to the unequal distribution of money, power, education, and social prestige. A conflict analysis rejects the idea that social structure promotes the operation of society as a whole, pointing out instead how social patterns benefit some people while depriving others. The box on page 16 highlights a key contribution regarding race made by W. E. B. Du Bois.

Sociologists using the social-conflict paradigm look at ongoing conflict between dominant and disadvantaged categories of people—the rich in relation to the poor, white people in relation to people of color, and men in relation to women. Typically, people on top strive to protect their privileges, while the disadvantaged try to gain more for themselves.

A conflict analysis of our educational system shows how schooling reproduces class inequality in

DIVERSITY: RACE, CLASS, AND GENDER

An Early Pioneer: Du Bois on Race

One of sociology's pioneers in the United States, William Edward Burghardt Du Bois, did not consider sociology a dry, academic discipline. On the contrary, he wanted to use sociology to solve the pressing problems of his time, especially racial inequality.

Du Bois spoke out against racial separation and served as a founding member of the National Association for the Advancement of Colored People (NAACP). He helped his colleagues in sociology—and people everywhere—to see the deep racial divisions in the United States. White people can simply be "Americans," Du Bois pointed out; African Americans, however, have a "double consciousness," reflecting their status as citizens who are never able to escape identification based on the color of their skin.

In his sociological classic *The Philadelphia Negro: A Social Study* (1899), Du Bois studied Philadelphia's African

American community, identifying both the strengths and the weaknesses of people wrestling with overwhelming social problems. He challenged the

widespread belief in black inferiority, attributing the problems of African Americans to white prejudice. His criticism extended also to successful people of color for being so eager to win white acceptance that they gave up all ties with the black community, which needed their help.

Du Bois described race as the major problem facing the United States in the twentieth century. Early in his career, he was optimistic about overcoming racial divisions. By the end of his life, however, he had grown bitter, believing that little had changed. At the age of ninety-three, Du Bois left the United States for Ghana, where he died two years later. Do you think, following Du Bois, that race is still a major problem in the twenty-first century?

Sources: Based, in part, on Baltzell (1967) and Du Bois (1967; orig. 1899).

---

every new generation. For example, secondary schools assign students to either college preparatory or vocational training programs. From a structural-functional point of view, such "tracking" benefits everyone by providing schooling that fits students' abilities. But conflict analysis counters that tracking often has less to do with talent than with social background, so that well-to-do students are placed in higher tracks while poor children end up in the lower tracks.

In this way, young people from privileged families receive the best schooling and later pursue high-income careers. The children of poor families, on the other hand, are not prepared for college and, like their parents before them, typically enter low-paying jobs. In both cases, the social standing of one generation is passed on to another, with schools justifying the

practice in terms of individual merit (Bowles & Gintis, 1976; Oakes, 1982, 1985).

Social conflict in the United States extends well beyond schools. Later chapters of this book explain how inequality based on class, gender, and race is rooted in the organization of society itself.

Many sociologists use the social-conflict paradigm not just to understand society but to bring about societal change that would reduce inequality. This was the goal of W. E. B. Du Bois and also of Karl Marx, whose writing was especially important in the development of the social-conflict paradigm. Marx had little patience with those who sought only to analyze society. In a well-known declaration (inscribed on his monument in London's Highgate Cemetery), Marx asserted, "The philosophers have only interpreted the world, in various ways; the point, however, is to change it."

The painting The New Nanny, by Paul Marcus, presents the essential wisdom of social-conflict theory: Society operates in a way that conveys wealth, power, and privilege to some at the expense of others. What categories of people does the artist suggest are advantaged and disadvantaged?

© Paul Marcus, The New Nanny, oil painting on wood, 48 × 72 in. Studio SPM, Inc.

Critical evaluation. The social-conflict paradigm has gained a large following in recent decades. Yet, like other approaches, it has come in for its share of criticism. Because the paradigm focuses on inequality, it largely ignores how shared values and mutual interdependence unify members of a society. In addition, say critics, to the extent that this paradigm pursues political goals, it loses any claim to scientific objectivity. As Chapter 2 ("Sociological Investigation") explains, however, conflict theorists counter that *all* theoretical approaches have political consequences, albeit different ones.

A final criticism of both the structural-functional and the social-conflict paradigms is that they paint society in broad strokes in terms of "family," "social class," "race," and so on. A third theoretical paradigm depicts society less in terms of broad social structures and more as everyday experiences.

THE SYMBOLIC-INTERACTION PARADIGM

The structural-functional and social-conflict paradigms share a **macro-level orientation,** meaning *a broad focus on social structures that shape society as a whole.* Macro-level sociology takes in the big picture, rather like observing a city from high above in a helicopter and seeing how highways help people move from place to place or how housing differs from rich to poor neighborhoods. Sociology also has a **micro-level**

orientation, *a close-up focus on social interaction in specific situations.* Exploring urban life in this way occurs at street level, where researchers might observe how children interact on a school playground, how pedestrians wait to board a bus, or how well-dressed people respond to a homeless person. The **symbolic-interaction paradigm,** then, is *a framework for building theory that sees society as the product of the everyday interactions of individuals.*

How does "society" result from the ongoing experiences of tens of millions of people? One answer, explained in Chapter 6 ("Social Interaction in Everyday Life"), is that society is nothing more than the shared reality that people construct as they interact with one another. That is, human beings are creatures who live in a world of symbols, attaching *meaning* to virtually everything. "Reality," therefore, is simply how we define our surroundings, our obligations toward others, even our own identities.

Of course, this process of definition is subjective and varies from person to person. For example, one person may define a homeless man as "just a bum looking for a handout" and ignore him, but another might see the man as a fellow human being in need and offer help. In the same way, one person may feel a sense of security passing by a police officer walking the beat, while another may be seized by nervous anxiety or outright rage. Sociologists who take a symbolic-interaction approach, therefore, view society as a complex, ever-changing mosaic of subjective meanings.

To understand how the symbolic-interaction paradigm views society, consider Sherry Karver's painting, Faces in the Crowd III. Just as the images seem to flow together in new and never quite predictable ways, society is never at rest; it is an ongoing process by which interacting people define and redefine reality.

Sherry Karver, Faces in the Crowd III, 2001, oil and photography on panel, 24 in. × 19 in. Courtesy of Lisa Harris Gallery, Seattle, Washington.

The symbolic-interaction paradigm has roots in the thinking of Max Weber (1864–1920), a German sociologist who emphasized the need to understand a setting from the point of view of the people in it. Weber's approach is discussed in Chapter 4 ("Society").

Since Weber's time, sociologists have taken micro-level sociology in a number of directions. Chapter 5 ("Socialization") discusses the ideas of George Herbert Mead (1863–1931), who explored how we build our personalities from social experience. Chapter 6 ("Social Interaction in Everyday Life") presents the work of Erving Goffman (1922–1982), whose *dramaturgical analysis* describes how we resemble actors on a stage as we play out our various roles. Other contemporary sociologists, including George Homans and Peter Blau,

have developed *social-exchange analysis*. In their view, social interaction is guided by what each person stands to gain and lose from others (Molm, 1997; Mulford et al., 1998). In the ritual of courtship, for example, people seek mates who offer at least as much—in terms of physical attractiveness, intelligence, and wealth—as they themselves have to offer.

Critical evaluation. The social-interaction paradigm corrects some of the bias found in macro-level approaches to society. Without denying the existence of macro-level social structures such as "the family" and "social class," the symbolic-interaction paradigm reminds us that society basically amounts to *people interacting*. That is, micro-level sociology tries to convey how individuals actually experience society. The other side of the coin is that, by focusing on day-to-day interactions, the symbolic-interaction paradigm ignores larger social structures, the effects of culture, and factors such as class, gender, and race.

Table 1–1 summarizes the main characteristics of the structural-functional paradigm, the social-conflict paradigm, and the symbolic-interaction paradigm. Each paradigm is helpful in answering particular kinds of questions. However, the fullest understanding of society comes from using the sociological perspective with all three, as we show with the following analysis of sports in the United States.

APPLYING THE PARADIGMS: THE SOCIOLOGY OF SPORT

People in the United States love sports. Not only do most young people engage in organized sports, but—for old and young alike—television is filled with sporting events, and the daily news media regularly report

 For more information on social aspects of sports, visit http://www.aafla.org

sports scores. In the United States, outstanding players such as Mark McGwire (baseball), Tiger Woods (golf), and Serena Williams (tennis) are among our most famous celebrities. Overall, sports in the United States are a multibillion-dollar industry. What sociological insights can the three theoretical paradigms give us into this familiar part of everyday life?

The Functions of Sports

A structural-functional approach directs attention to the ways in which sports help society operate. Their manifest functions include providing recreation,

TABLE 1-1 The Three Major Theoretical Paradigms: A Summary

Theoretical Paradigm	Orientation	Image of Society	Core Questions
Structural-functional	Macro-level	A system of interrelated parts that is relatively stable because of widespread agreement on what is morally desirable; each part has a particular function in society as a whole.	How is society integrated? What are the major parts of society? How are these parts interrelated? What are the consequences of each part for the overall operation of society?
Social-conflict	Macro-level	A system based on social inequality; each part of society benefits some categories of people more than others; social inequality leads to conflict, which, in turn, leads to social change.	How is society divided? What are the major patterns of social inequality? How do some categories of people try to protect their privileges? How do other categories of people challenge the status quo?
Symbolic-interaction	Micro-level	An ongoing process of social interaction in specific settings based on symbolic communication; individual perceptions of reality are variable and changing.	How is society experienced? How do human beings interact to create, maintain, and change social patterns? How do individuals try to shape the reality that others perceive? How does individual behavior change from one situation to another?

physical conditioning, and a relatively harmless way to "let off steam." Sports have important latent functions as well, from fostering social relationships to generating tens of thousands of jobs. Perhaps most important, sports encourage competition and the pursuit of success, both of which are central to our way of life.

Sports also have dysfunctional consequences. For example, colleges and universities intent on fielding winning teams sometimes recruit students for their athletic ability rather than their academic aptitude. Not only does this practice pull down the academic standards of a school, but it shortchanges athletes who devote little time to academic work (Upthegrove, Roscigno, & Charles, 1999).

Sports and Conflict

A social-conflict analysis begins by pointing out that sports are closely linked to social inequality. Some sports—including tennis, swimming, golf, sailing, and skiing—are expensive, so participation is largely limited to the well-to-do. Football, baseball, and basketball, however, are accessible to people of all income levels. In short, the games people play not only are a matter of choice but also reflect social standing.

Throughout history, sports have been oriented primarily toward males. For example, the first modern Olympic Games, held in 1896, barred women from competition; in the United States, even Little League teams in most parts of the country did not let girls play until recently. Such exclusion has been defended by incorrect notions that girls and women lack the strength and stamina to play sports or that they lose their femininity when they do. Thus, our society encourages men to be athletes while expecting women to be attentive observers and cheerleaders. Today, more women play professional sports than ever before, yet they continue to take a back seat to men, particularly in the sports with the most earnings and social prestige.

Although our society long excluded people of color from big league sports, the opportunity to earn high incomes in professional sports has expanded in recent decades. Major League Baseball first admitted African American players when Jackie Robinson broke the color line and joined the Brooklyn Dodgers in 1947. More than fifty years later, professional baseball retired the legendary Robinson's number 42 on *all* teams, and, in 2000, African Americans (12 percent of the U.S. population) accounted for 13 percent of Major League Baseball players,

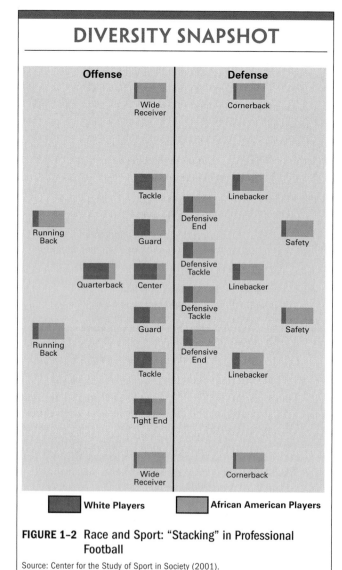

DIVERSITY SNAPSHOT

Offense   **Defense**

Wide Receiver — Cornerback

Tackle — Linebacker

Defensive End

Running Back — Guard — Safety

Defensive Tackle

Quarterback — Center — Linebacker

Defensive Tackle

Running Back — Guard — Safety

Defensive End

Tackle — Linebacker

Tight End

Wide Receiver — Cornerback

■ **White Players** ☐ **African American Players**

FIGURE 1–2 Race and Sport: "Stacking" in Professional Football

Source: Center for the Study of Sport in Society (2001).

is also true that some people of color make a particular effort to excel in athletics, where they perceive greater opportunity than in other careers (Steele, 1990; Hoberman, 1997, 1998; Edwards, 2000; Harrison, 2000). In recent years, in fact, African American athletes have earned higher salaries, on average, than white players.

But racial discrimination still taints professional sports in the United States. For one thing, race is linked to the *positions* athletes play on the field, in a pattern called "stacking." Figure 1–2 shows the result of a study of race in football. Notice that white players dominate in offense and also play the central positions on both sides of the line. More broadly, African Americans figure prominently in only five sports: baseball, basketball, football, boxing, and track. Across all of professional sports, the vast majority of managers, head coaches, and owners of sports teams are white (Gnida, 1995; Smith & Leonard, 1997; Center for the Study of Sport in Society, 2001).

 For more information on race and sports, go to http://www.sportinsociety.org

We might ask who benefits the most from professional sports. Although individual players get astronomical salaries, and millions of fans enjoy following their teams, sports are big business, generating profits for a small number of people (predominantly white men). In sum, sports in the United States are bound up with inequalities based on gender, race, and economic power.

Sports as Interaction

At a micro-level, a sporting event is a complex drama of face-to-face interaction. In part, play is guided by the players' assigned positions and the rules of the game. But players are also spontaneous and unpredictable. Informed by the symbolic-interaction paradigm, then, we see sports less as a system than as an ongoing process.

From this point of view, too, we expect each player to understand the game a little differently. Some thrive in a setting of stiff competition, whereas, for others, love of the game may be greater than the need to win.

Beyond different attitudes toward competition, team members also shape their particular realities according to the various prejudices, jealousies, and ambitions they bring to the game. Then, too, the behavior of any single player may change over time. A rookie in professional baseball, for example, may feel self-conscious during the first few games in the big

67 percent of National Football League (NFL) players, and 78 percent of National Basketball Association (NBA) players (Center for the Study of Sport in Society, 2001).

One reason for the increasing proportion of people of African descent in professional sports is that athletic performance—in terms of batting average or number of points scored per game—can be precisely measured and is not influenced by racial prejudice. It

CONTROVERSY & DEBATE

Is Sociology Nothing More than Stereotypes?

"Protestants are the ones who kill themselves!"

"People in the United States? They're rich, they love to marry, and they love to divorce!"

"Everybody knows that you have to be black to play professional basketball!"

Everyone, including the sociologist, loves to generalize. But beginning students of sociology may wonder how generalizations differ from stereotypes. For example, are the preceding statements sound generalizations or stereotypes?

These three statements are examples of a **stereotype,** *an exaggerated description applied to every person in some category.* First, rather than describing averages, each statement paints every individual in a category with the same brush; second, each ignores facts and distorts reality (even though many stereotypes do contain an element of truth); third, a stereotype sounds more like a "put-down" than a fair-minded assertion.

Good sociology, by contrast, involves making generalizations, but with three important conditions. First, *sociologists do not carelessly apply any generalization to all individuals.* Second, *sociologists make sure that a generalization squares with available facts.* Third, *sociologists offer generalizations fair-mindedly, with an interest in getting at the truth.*

Earlier in this chapter, we noted that the suicide rate among Protestants is higher than among Catholics or Jews. However, the statement "Protestants are the ones who kill themselves" is not a reasonable generalization because the vast majority of Protestants do no such thing. Moreover, it would be just as wrong to assume that a particular friend, because he is a Protestant male, is on the verge of self-destruction. (Imagine refusing to lend money to a roommate who happens to be a Baptist, explaining, "Well, given your risk of suicide, I might never get paid back!")

Second, sociologists shape their generalizations to available facts. A more factual version of the second statement at the beginning of this box is that, on average and by world standards, the U.S. population has a very high standard of living. It is also true that our marriage rate is one of the highest in the world. And, although few people take pleasure in divorcing, so is our divorce rate.

Third, sociologists strive to be fair-minded; that is, they are motivated by a passion for truth. The third statement, about African Americans and basketball, is not good sociology for two reasons. First, it is simply not true, and, second, it seems motivated by bias rather than truth-seeking.

Good sociology stands apart from harmful stereotyping. But a sociology course is an excellent setting for talking over common stereotypes. The classroom encourages discussion and offers the factual information you need to decide whether a particular assertion is accurate or just a stereotype.

Continue the debate . . .

1. *Do people in the United States have stereotypes of sociologists? What are they? Are they valid?*

2. *Do you think taking a sociology course dispels people's stereotypes? Why or why not?*

3. *Can you cite a stereotype of your own that sociology challenges?*

leagues. In time, however, most players fit in comfortably with the team. Coming to feel at home on the field was slow and painful for Jackie Robinson, who knew that many white players, and millions of white fans, resented his presence. In time, however, his outstanding ability and his confident and cooperative manner won him the respect of the entire nation.

The three theoretical approaches—the structural-functional paradigm, the social-conflict paradigm, and the symbolic-interaction paradigm—provide different insights, but none is more correct than the others. Applied to any issue, each paradigm generates its own interpretations; to appreciate fully the power of the sociological perspective, you should become familiar with all three. Together, they stimulate debates and controversies. In the final box, we review many of the ideas presented in this chapter by asking how sociological generalizations differ from common stereotypes.

SUMMARY

1. The sociological perspective shows "the general in the particular," or the power of society to shape our individual lives.

2. Because our culture emphasizes individual choice, seeing the power of society in our lives may seem, at first, like "seeing the strange in the familiar."

3. Differences in the number of children born to women around the world, as well as Emile Durkheim's research on suicide rates among some categories of people, show that society affects even our most personal choices and actions.

4. Global awareness is an important part of the sociological perspective because, first, people live very differently in various nations; second, societies of the world are becoming increasingly interconnected; third, many social problems are most serious beyond the borders of the United States; and, fourth, global awareness helps us better understand ourselves.

5. Socially marginal people are more likely than others to see the power of society. For everyone, periods of social crisis foster sociological thinking.

6. The benefits of using the sociological perspective include, first, helping us assess common beliefs; second, helping us appreciate the opportunities and limits in our lives; third, encouraging more active participation in society; and, fourth, increasing our awareness of social diversity in the world around us.

7. Sociology arose in response to vast changes in Europe during the eighteenth and nineteenth centuries. Three changes—the rise of an industrial economy, the explosive growth of cities, and the emergence of new political ideas—focused people's attention on how society operates.

8. Auguste Comte gave sociology its name in 1838. Earlier social thinkers focused on what society ought to be, but Comte's new discipline used scientific methods to understand society as it is.

9. A theory weaves observations into insight and understanding. Sociologists use various theoretical paradigms to construct theories.

10. The structural-functional paradigm focuses on how patterns of behavior contribute to the operation of society. This approach highlights stability and integration while minimizing inequality and conflict.

11. While emphasizing inequality, conflict, and change, the social-conflict paradigm downplays a society's integration and stability.

12. In contrast to these broad, macro-level approaches, the symbolic-interaction paradigm is a micro-level framework that focuses on face-to-face interaction in specific settings.

13. Because each paradigm highlights different dimensions of any social issue, the richest sociological understanding is derived from applying all three.

14. Sociological thinking involves generalizations. But unlike a stereotype, a sociological statement (a) is not applied carelessly to everyone in some category, (b) is supported by facts, and (c) is put forward in the fair-minded pursuit of truth.

KEY CONCEPTS

sociology (p. 1) the systematic study of human society

global perspective (p. 5) the study of the larger world and our society's place in it

high-income countries (p. 5) nations with very productive economic systems in which most people have relatively high incomes

middle-income countries (p. 5) nations with moderately productive economic systems in which people's incomes are about the global average

low-income countries (p. 7) nations with less productive economic systems in which most people are poor

positivism (p. 12) a way of understanding based on science

theory (p. 13) a statement of how and why specific facts are related

theoretical paradigm (p. 14) a basic image of society that guides thinking and research

structural-functional paradigm (p. 14) a framework for building theory that sees society as a complex system whose parts work together to promote solidarity and stability

social structure (p. 14) any relatively stable pattern of social behavior

social functions (p. 14) the consequences of any social pattern for the operation of society as a whole

manifest functions (p. 14) the recognized and intended consequences of any social pattern

latent functions (p. 14) the unrecognized and unintended consequences of any social pattern

social dysfunction (p. 15) any social pattern that may disrupt the operation of society

social-conflict paradigm (p. 15) a framework for building theory that sees society as an arena of inequality that generates conflict and change

macro-level orientation (p. 17) a broad focus on social structures that shape society as a whole

micro-level orientation (p. 17) a close-up focus on social interaction in specific situations

symbolic-interaction paradigm (p. 17) a framework for building theory that sees society as the product of the everyday interactions of individuals

stereotype (p. 21) an exaggerated description applied to every person in some category

CRITICAL-THINKING QUESTIONS

1. How would you contrast psychology and sociology in terms of perspective?

2. In what ways does using the sociological perspective make us seem less in control of our lives? In what ways does it give us greater power over our surroundings?

3. Consider the following argument: Sociology would not have arisen if human behavior were biologically programmed (like, say, the behavior of ants), nor could sociology exist if human behavior were random or chaotic. Sociology exists because humans live in a middle ground, being both spontaneous and guided by social structure.

4. What factors help explain why sociology developed where and when it did?

5. Guided by the discipline's three major theoretical paradigms, what kinds of questions might you ask about (a) television, (b) war, and (c) colleges and universities?

APPLICATIONS AND EXERCISES

1. Packaged in the back of this new textbook is an interactive CD-ROM that offers a variety of study and review materials intended to help you better understand the material covered in this chapter. For this chapter, the CD-ROM contains an author's tip video, interactive map animations, an interactive timeline, and flashcards with audio pronunciations of the more difficult words.

2. Spend several hours exploring your local area until you can draw a sociological map of the community. The map might indicate the categories of people and types of buildings found in various places (for example, "big single-family homes," "rundown business area," "new office buildings," "student apartments," and so on). What patterns do you see?

3. Look ahead to Figure 18–3 on page 477, which shows the U.S. divorce rate over the last century. Try to identify societal factors that pushed the divorce rate down after 1930, up again after 1940, down in the 1950s, up after 1960, and down again after 1980.

4. During a class, carefully observe the behavior of the instructor and the other students. What patterns do you see in who speaks? What about how people use space? What categories of people are taking the class in the first place?

5. Look at all the global maps found throughout the chapters of this book. (They are listed in the table of contents on page xviii). Make a list of the traits of high-income nations and the traits of low-income nations. Using these findings, write a sociological profile of both types of countries.

SITES TO SEE

http://www.prenhall.com/macionis

The author and publisher of this book invite you to visit the interactive Companion Website™ that accompanies this text. Begin by clicking on the cover of your book. You will find a chapter-by-chapter study guide, practice tests, suggested Web links, and links to other relevant material.

http://www.TheSociologyPage.com
(or **http://www.macionis.com**)

You can find dozens of additional links to Internet sites, as well as information—including short videos—about the discipline of sociology, at the author's home page. Bookmark this page as your doorway to the discipline.

http://plasma.nationalgeographic.com/mapmachine
http://www.nationalatlas.gov

These two sites provide a number of maps showing patterns and trends of interest to sociologists.

http://quickfacts.census.gov/qfd/
http://www.countrywatch.com

The first of these sites provides statistical data and other information about the United States, your own state, and your own county. The second offers a range of data about all 192 nations in the world.

INVESTIGATE WITH RESEARCH NAVIGATOR™

To access the full resources of Research Navigator™, please find the access code printed on the inside cover of *The Prentice Hall Guide to Evaluating Online Resources with Research Navigator™: Sociology, 2004*. You may have received this booklet if your instructor recommended this guide be packaged with new textbooks. (If your book did not come with this printed guide, you can purchase one through your college bookstore.) Visit our Research Navigator™ site at

http://www.researchnavigator.com Once at this site, click on "Register" under "New Users" and enter your access code to create a personal Login Name and Password. (When revisiting the site, use the same Login Name and Password to enter.) Browse the features of the Research Navigator™ Web site and search the databases of academic journals, newspapers, magazines, and Web links using keywords such as "sociology," "suicide," and "sports."

INTRODUCING... In the Times

The articles featured at the end of selected chapters throughout this text originally appeared in the pages of one of the world's leading newspapers: *The New York Times*.

Since its founding in 1851, *The New York Times* has become the publication that other media look to as a guide for responsible news coverage. *The New York Times* is the leader among news organizations in winning the Pulitzer Prize, journalism's top award.

We chose these particular articles because they look at current events through a sociological lens

and because they raise deeper issues related to topics covered in this text. Please keep in mind that these articles were originally published in a daily newspaper and, as such, each one is a snapshot of an issue at a particular point in time; however, great care was taken to ensure that the selections are of lasting interest.

These *New York Times* articles illustrate how sociology is a part of our everyday lives. Watching your favorite television show, reading the daily newspaper, or surfing the Internet can all be exercises in using your sociological imagination. Enjoy reading all eleven *In the Times* features and use the questions at the end of each article to analyze the issues with a sociological eye!

March 30, 2003

Military Mirrors Working-Class America

By DAVID M. HALBFINGER
and STEVEN A. HOLMES

They left small towns and inner cities, looking for a way out and up, or fled the anonymity of the suburbs, hoping to find themselves. They joined the all-volunteer military, gaining a free education or a marketable skill or just the discipline they knew they would need to get through life.

As the United States engages in its first major land war in a decade, the soldiers, sailors, pilots and others who are risking, and now giving, their lives in Iraq represent a slice of a broad swath of American society but by no means all of it.

Of the 28 servicemen killed who have been identified so far, 20 were white, 5 black, and 3 Hispanic—proportions that neatly mirror those of the military as a whole. But just one was from a well-to-do family, and with the exception of a Naval Academy alumnus, just one had graduated from an elite college.

A survey of the American military's . . . demographics paints a picture of a fighting force that is anything but a cross section of America. With minorities overrepresented and the wealthy and the underclass essentially absent, with political conservatism ascendant in the officer corps and Northeasterners fading from the ranks, America's 1.4 million-strong military seems to resemble the makeup of a two-year commuter or trade school outside Birmingham or Biloxi far more than that of a ghetto or barrio or four-year university in Boston.

Today's servicemen and women may not be Ivy Leaguers, but in fact they are better educated than the population at large: Reading scores are a full grade higher for enlisted personnel than for their civilian counterparts of the same age. While whites account for three of five soldiers, the military has become a powerful magnet for blacks, and black women in particular, who now outnumber white women in the Army. . . .

Sgt. Annette Acevedo, 22, a radio operator from Atlanta, could have gone to college but chose the Army because of all the benefits it offered: travel, health coverage, work experience and independence from her parents. The Army seemed a better opportunity to get started with her life and be a more independent person, she said. . . .

Though Hispanics are underrepresented in the military, their numbers are growing rapidly. Even as the total number of military personnel dropped 23 percent over the last decade, the number of Hispanics in uniform grew to 118,000 from 90,600, a jump of about 30 percent.

While blacks tend to be more heavily represented in administrative and support functions, a new study shows that Hispanics, like whites, are much more likely to serve in combat operations. But those Hispanics in combat jobs tend to be infantry grunts, particularly in the Marine Corps, rather than fighter or bomber pilots. . . .

Confronted by images of the hardships of overseas deployment and by the stark reality of casualties in Iraq, some have raised questions about the composition of the fighting force and about requiring what is, in essence, a working-class military to fight and die for an affluent America.

"It's just not fair that the people that we ask to fight our wars are people who join the military because of economic conditions, because they have fewer options," said Representative Charles B. Rangel, a Democrat from Manhattan and a Korean War veteran who is calling for restoring the draft.

Some scholars have noted that since the draft was abolished in 1973, the country has begun developing what could be called a warrior class or caste, often perpetuating itself from father or uncle to son or niece, whose political and cultural attitudes do not reflect the diversity found in civilian society, potentially foreshadowing a social schism between those who fight and those who ask them to.

It is an issue that today's soldiers grapple with increasingly as they watch their comrades, even their spouses, deploy to the combat zone. "As it stands right now, the country is riding on the soldiers who volunteer," said Sgt. Barry Perkins, 39, a career military policeman at Fort Benning, Ga. "Everybody else is taking a free ride."

What do you think?

1. What are some of the reasons people may give for joining the military? How are these reasons different from the reasons sociologists would give for why people join the military?
2. In the article, Charles Rangel states that it is not fair to have people fighting our wars who joined the military because they had fewer options than other people. Do you agree with his position? Why or why not?

CHAPTER

2

SOCIOLOGICAL INVESTIGATION

GUSTAVE CAILLEBOTTE (1848–1894, FRENCH)
Man on a Balcony

c. 1880, oil on canvas, 116 × 90 cm. Private Collection/The Bridgeman Art Library.

WHILE ON A VISIT to Atlanta during the winter holiday season, sociologist Lois Benjamin (1991) called on the mother of an old friend from college. Benjamin was anxious to learn about her friend, Sheba, a woman who had shared her own dream of earning a graduate degree, landing a teaching job, and writing books. Proudly, Benjamin had fulfilled her dream. But as she soon found out, Sheba had fallen disastrously short of her goal.

There had been early signs of trouble, Benjamin recalled. After college, Sheba began graduate work at a university in Canada. But in her letters to Benjamin, Sheba became more and more critical of the world and seemed to be cutting herself off from others. Some people thought that Sheba was suffering from a personality disorder. But as Sheba saw it, the problem was racism. As an African American woman, she felt she was the target of racial hostility. Before long, she flunked out of school, blaming her white professors for her failure. At this point, she left North America, finally earning a Ph.D. in England and then settling in Nigeria. Since then, Benjamin had not heard a word from her long-time friend.

Benjamin was happy to learn that Sheba had returned to Atlanta. But her delight dissolved into shock when she saw Sheba and realized that her friend, suffering a

mental breakdown, was barely responsive to anyone.

For months after, Sheba's emotional collapse troubled Benjamin. Obviously, Sheba was suffering from serious psychological problems. But Benjamin knew that many factors combine to cause such personal tragedy. Having experienced the sting of racism herself, Benjamin believed it had played a major role in Sheba's story. Partly as a tribute to her old friend, Benjamin set out to explore the effects of race in the lives of bright and well-educated African Americans in the United States.

Benjamin realized she was challenging the conventional wisdom that race poses less of a barrier today than in previous generations, especially to talented African Americans (W. J. Wilson, 1978). But her own experiences—and, she believed, Sheba's, too—seemed to contradict such thinking.

To test her ideas, Benjamin spent the next two years asking 100 successful African Americans across the country how race affected their lives. In the words of these "Talented One Hundred"[1] men and women, she found evidence that, even among privileged African Americans, racism remains a heavy burden.

[1]Benjamin derived her concept from the term "Talented Tenth" used by W. E. B. Du Bois (1967; orig. 1899) to describe African American leaders in his day.

Later in this chapter, we will take a closer look at Lois Benjamin's research. For the moment, notice how the sociological perspective helped her to spot broad social patterns in the lives of individuals. Just as important, Benjamin's work demonstrates the *doing* of sociology, the process of *sociological investigation.*

Many people think that scientists work only in laboratories, carefully taking measurements using complex equipment. But as this chapter explains, while some sociologists do conduct scientific research in laboratories, most work on neighborhood streets, in homes and workplaces, in schools and hospitals, in bars and prisons—in short, wherever people can be found.

This chapter examines the methods that sociologists use to conduct research. Along the way, we shall see that research involves not just procedures for gathering information but controversies about values: Should researchers strive to be objective? Or should they point to the need for change? Certainly, for example, Lois Benjamin did not undertake her study simply to show that racism exists; she wanted to bring racism out in the open as a way to challenge it. We shall tackle questions of values after addressing the basics of sociological investigation.

THE BASICS OF SOCIOLOGICAL INVESTIGATION

Sociological investigation starts with two simple requirements. The first was the focus of Chapter 1: *Use the sociological perspective.* This point of view reveals curious patterns of behavior all around us that call for further study. It was Lois Benjamin's sociological imagination that prompted her to wonder how race affects the lives of talented African Americans.

This brings us to the second requirement of sociological investigation: *Be curious and ask questions.* Benjamin sought to learn more about how race affects people with significant personal achievements. She asked questions: Who are the leaders of this nation's black community? What effect does being part of a racial minority have on their view of themselves? On the way white people perceive them and their work?

Seeing the world sociologically and asking questions are fundamental to sociological investigation. Yet they are only the beginning. They spark our curiosity, but then we face the task of finding answers to our questions. To understand the kind of insights sociology offers, we need to realize that there are various kinds of "truth."

SCIENCE AS ONE FORM OF TRUTH

When we say we "know" something, we can mean many things. Most people in the United States, for instance, claim to believe in the existence of God. Few would claim to have direct contact with God, but they say they believe all the same. We call this kind of knowing "belief" or "faith."

A second kind of truth rests on the pronouncement of some recognized expert. Parents with questions about raising their children, for example, may read books by an "expert" or consult a child psychologist.

A third type of truth is based on simple agreement among ordinary people. We come to "know" that, say, sexual intercourse among preteens is wrong because just about everyone says it is.

People's "truths" differ the world over, and we often encounter "facts" at odds with our own. Imagine being a Peace Corps volunteer who has just arrived in a small, traditional village in Latin America. Your job is to help local people increase their crop yield. On your first day in the fields, you observe a curious practice: After planting the seeds, the farmers lay a dead fish on top of the soil. In response to your question, they reply that the fish is a gift to the god of the harvest. A village elder adds sternly that the harvest was poor one year when no fish were offered.

From that society's point of view, using fish as gifts to the harvest god makes sense. The people believe in it, their experts endorse it, and everyone seems to agree that the system works. But with scientific training in agriculture, you have to shake your head and wonder. The scientific "truth" in this situation is something entirely different: The decomposing fish fertilize the ground, producing a better crop.

Science represents a fourth way of knowing. **Science** is *a logical system that bases knowledge on direct, systematic observation.* **Scientific sociology,** then, is *the study of society based on systematic observation of social behavior.* Standing apart from faith, the wisdom of "experts," and general agreement, scientific knowledge rests on **empirical evidence,** that is, *information we can verify with our senses.*

Our Peace Corps example does not mean, of course, that people in traditional villages ignore what their senses tell them, or that members of technologically advanced societies reject nonscientific ways of knowing. A medical researcher using science to develop a new drug for treating cancer, for example, may still practice her religion as a matter of faith; she may turn to experts when making financial decisions; and

Myths as well as scientific facts are an important dimension of human existence. In his painting, Creation of North Sacred Mountain, *Navajo artist Harrison Begay offers a mythic account of creation. A myth (from the Greek, meaning "story" or "word") may or may not be factual in the literal sense. Yet it conveys some basic truth about the meaning and purpose of life. Indeed, it is science, rather than art, that has no power to address such questions of meaning.*

she may derive political opinions from family and friends. In short, we all hold various kinds of truths at the same time.

COMMON SENSE VERSUS SCIENTIFIC EVIDENCE

Scientific evidence sometimes challenges our common sense. Here are six statements that many North Americans assume are true:

1. **Poor people are far more likely than rich people to break the law.** Watching a television show like *Cops*, one might well conclude that police arrest only people from "bad" neighborhoods. Chapter 8 ("Deviance") explains that poor people do stand out in the official arrest statistics. But research also shows that police and prosecutors are more likely to respond leniently to apparent wrong-doing by well-to-do people, as in the recent Winona Ryder shoplifting case. Further, some laws themselves are written in a way that criminalizes poor people more and affluent people less.

2. **The United States is a middle-class society in which most people are more-or-less equal.** Data presented in Chapter 11 ("Social Class in the United States") show that the richest 5 percent of U.S. families control more than half the nation's total wealth. If people are equal, then some are much "more equal" than others.

3. **Most poor people don't want to work.** Research described in Chapter 11 indicates that this statement is true of some but not most poor people. In fact, about half of poor individuals in the United States are children and elderly people whom no one would expect to work.

4. **Differences in the behavior of females and males reflect "human nature."** Much of what we call "human nature" is constructed by the society in which we are raised, as Chapter 3 ("Culture") explains. Further, as Chapter 13 ("Gender Stratification") argues, some societies define "feminine" and "masculine" very differently from the way we do.

5. **People change as they grow old, losing many interests as they focus on their health.** Chapter 15 ("Aging and the Elderly") reports that aging changes our personalities very little. Problems of health increase in old age but, by and large, elderly people keep their distinctive personalities.

6. **Most people marry because they are in love.** To members of our society, few statements are so self-evident. Surprisingly, however, in many societies marriage has little to do with love. Chapter 18 ("Family") explains why.

These examples confirm the old saying "It's not what we don't know that gets us into trouble as much as things we *do* know that just aren't so." We have all been brought up believing conventional truths, being

Common sense suggests that, in a world of possibilities, people fall in love with that "special someone." Sociological research reveals that the vast majority of people select partners who are very similar in social background to themselves.

bombarded by expert advice, and being pressured to accept the opinions of people around us. As adults, we need to evaluate critically what we see, read, and hear. Sociology can help us to do just that.

SCIENCE: BASIC ELEMENTS AND LIMITATIONS

In Chapter 1, we explained how early sociologists such as Auguste Comte and Emile Durkheim applied science to the study of society just as natural scientists investigate the physical world. The scientific approach to knowing, called *positivism*, assumes that an objective reality exists "out there." The job of the scientist is to discover this reality by gathering empirical evidence, facts we can verify with our senses.

In this chapter, we begin by introducing the major elements of scientific sociology. Then we shall discuss some limitations of scientific (or positivist) sociology and present alternative approaches.

CONCEPTS, VARIABLES, AND MEASUREMENT

A basic element of science is the **concept,** *a mental construct that represents some part of the world in a simplified form*. "Society" is a concept, as are the structural parts of societies, such as "the family" and "the economy."

Sociologists also use concepts to describe people, as when we speak of someone's "race" or "social class."

A **variable** is *a concept whose value changes from case to case*. The familiar variable "price," for example, changes from item to item in a supermarket. Similarly, we use the concept "social class" to identify people as "upper class," "middle class," "working class," or "lower class."

The use of variables depends on **measurement,** *a procedure for determining the value of a variable in a specific case*. Some variables are easy to measure, as when the checkout clerk adds up the cost of our groceries. But measuring sociological variables can be far more difficult. For example, how would you measure a person's "social class"? You might look at clothing, listen to patterns of speech, or note a home address. Or trying to be more precise, you might ask about income, occupation, and education.

Because almost any variable can be measured in more than one way, sociologists often have to make a judgment about which factors to consider. For example, having a very high income might qualify a person as "upper class." But what if the income comes from selling automobiles, an occupation most people think of as "middle class"? Would having only an eighth-grade education make the person "lower class"? In this case, sociologists sensibly (but arbitrarily) combine these three measures—income, occupation, and education—to assign social class, as described in Chapter 10 ("Social Stratification") and Chapter 11 ("Social Class in the United States").

Sociologists face another interesting problem in measuring variables: dealing with vast numbers of people. How, for instance, do you describe the income of millions of U.S. families? Reporting streams of numbers carries little meaning and tells us nothing about the people as a whole. Thus sociologists use *statistical measures* to describe people. The box explains how.

Defining Concepts

Measurement is always somewhat arbitrary because the value of any variable partly depends on how it is defined. In addition, deciding what abstract concepts such as "love," "family," or "intelligence" mean in real life can lead to lengthy debates before any attempt is made to measure them as variables.

Good research, therefore, requires that sociologists **operationalize a variable,** which means *specifying exactly what one is to measure before assigning a value to a variable*. Before measuring the concept of social class, for example, we would have to decide exactly what we

Three Useful (and Simple) Statistical Measures

We all talk about "averages," whether it is the average price of a gallon of gasoline or the average salary for new college graduates. Sociologists, too, are interested in averages, and they use three different statistical measures to describe what is typical.

Assume that we wish to describe the salaries paid to seven members of a sociology department at a local college:

$55,000 $42,000 $61,000 $180,000
$72,000 $55,000 $60,000

The simplest statistical measure is the *mode*, the value that occurs most often in a series of numbers. In this example, the mode is $55,000, since that value occurs two times, and each of the others occurs

only once. If all the values were to occur only once, there would be no mode; if two values occurred three times (or twice), there would be two modes. Although it is easy to identify, sociologists rarely use the mode because it is a very crude measure of the "average."

A more common statistical measure, the *mean*, refers to the arithmetic average of a series of numbers, calculated by adding all the values together and dividing by the number of cases. The sum of the seven incomes is $525,000. Dividing by seven yields a mean income of $75,000. But notice that the mean is not a very good "average" because it is higher than six of the seven incomes. Because the mean is "pulled" up or down by an especially high or low value

(in this case, the $180,000 paid to one sociologist, who also serves as academic dean and vice president of the university), it has the drawback of giving a distorted picture of any distribution with extreme scores.

The *median* is the middle case: the value that occurs midway in a series of numbers arranged from lowest to highest. Here the median income for the seven people is $60,000, because this number divides the series of numbers in half with three incomes higher and three lower. (With an even number of cases, the median is halfway between the two middle cases.) Because a median is unaffected by an extreme score, it gives a better picture of what is "average" than the mean does.

were going to measure: say, income level, years of schooling, occupational prestige. Sometimes sociologists measure several of these things; in such cases, they need to specify exactly how they plan to combine these variables into one overall score. When reading about research, always notice the way researchers operationalize each variable. How they define terms can greatly affect the results.

When deciding how to operationalize variables, sociologists may take into account the opinions of the people they study. Since 1977, for example, researchers at the U.S. Census Bureau have defined race and ethnicity as white, black, Hispanic, Asian or Pacific Islander, and American Indian or Alaskan Native. One problem with this system is that someone can be *both* Hispanic and white or black; similarly, people of Arab ancestry might not identify with *any* of these choices. Just as important, an increasing number of people in the United States are *multiracial* (Cose, 1997; O'Hare, 1998). As a result of such problems, the 2000 Census allowed people to describe their race and ethnicity by selecting more than one category.

Reliability and Validity

For a measurement to be useful, it must be reliable and valid. **Reliability** refers to *consistency in measurement*. A measurement is reliable if repeated measurements yield the same result time after time. But consistency does not guarantee **validity**, which means *actually measuring exactly what one intends to measure*.

Valid measurement is no easy matter, as an example will show. Say you want to study how religious people are. A reasonable strategy might be to ask how often respondents attend religious services. But is going to a church, temple, or mosque really the same thing as being religious? It may be that religious people do attend services more frequently, but people also join in religious rituals out of habit or because someone else wants them to. Moreover, some very spiritual people avoid organized religion altogether. Thus, even when a measurement yields consistent results (making it reliable), it may still not measure what we want it to (and lack validity). Later on, in Chapter 19 ("Religion"), we suggest that measuring religiosity should take account

Young people who live in the crowded inner city are more likely than those who live in the spacious suburbs to have trouble with the police. But does this mean that crowding causes delinquency? Researchers know that crowding and arrest rates do vary together, but they have demonstrated that the connection is spurious: Both factors rise in relation to a third factor—declining income.

of not only church attendance but also a person's beliefs and the degree to which a person lives by religious convictions. In sum, careful measurement is vital to sociological research, and often a challenge.

Relationships among Variables

Once measurements are made, investigators can pursue the real payoff: seeing how variables are related. The scientific ideal is **cause and effect,** *a relationship in which change in one variable causes change in another*. Cause-and-effect relationships occur around us every

day, as when studying for an exam results in a high grade. *The variable that causes the change* (in this case, studying) is called the **independent variable.** *The variable that changes* (the exam grade) is called the **dependent variable.** The value of one variable, in other words, depends on the value of another. Why is linking variables in terms of cause and effect important? Because this kind of relationship allows us to *predict* how one pattern of behavior will produce another.

But just because two variables change together does not mean that they are linked by a cause-and-effect relationship. Consider, for instance, that the marriage rate in the United States falls to its lowest point in January, exactly the same month that our national death rate peaks. This hardly means that people die because they fail to marry (or that the marriage rate falls because more people die). In fact, it is the dreary weather in much of the nation during January (and maybe also the post-holiday blahs) that causes both a low marriage rate and a high death rate. The flip side holds as well: The warmer and sunnier summer months have the highest marriage rates as well as the lowest death rates. Thus, researchers must look below the surface to untangle cause-and-effect relationships.

To take a second case, sociologists have long recognized that juvenile delinquency is more common among young people who live in crowded housing. Say we operationalize the variable "juvenile delinquency" as the number of times (if any) a person under the age of eighteen has been arrested, and we define "crowded housing" by a home's number of square feet of living space per person. We would find the variables related; that is, delinquency rates are, indeed, high in densely populated neighborhoods. But should we conclude that crowding in the home (in this case, the independent variable) is what causes delinquency (the dependent variable)?

Not necessarily. **Correlation** is *a relationship in which two (or more) variables change together*. We know that density and delinquency are correlated because they change together, as shown in part (a) of Figure 2–1. This relationship *may* mean that crowding causes misconduct, but it could also mean that some third factor is at work causing change in *both* of the variables under observation. To identify a third variable, think what kind of people live in crowded housing: people with less money and few choices—the poor. Poor children are also more likely to end up with police records. Thus, crowded housing and juvenile delinquency are found together because *both* are caused by a third factor—poverty—as shown in part (b) of

Figure 2–1. In short, the apparent connection between crowding and delinquency is "explained away" by a third variable—low income—that causes them both to change. So our original connection turns out to be a **spurious correlation,** *an apparent, although false, relationship between two (or more) variables caused by some other variable.*

Unmasking a correlation as spurious requires a bit of detective work, assisted by a technique called **control,** *holding constant all variables except one in order to see clearly the effect of that variable.* In the example above, we suspect that income level may be causing a spurious link between housing density and delinquency. To check, we control for income (that is, we hold income constant by looking at only young people of one income level) and see if a correlation between density and delinquency remains. If the correlation between density and delinquency is still there despite the control (that is, if young people living in more crowded housing show higher rates of delinquency than young people in less crowded housing, all with the same family income), we have more reason to think that crowding does, in fact, cause delinquency. But if the relationship disappears when we control for income, as shown in part (c) of the figure, we then know we have a spurious correlation. In fact, research shows that the correlation between crowding and delinquency just about disappears if income is controlled (Fischer, 1984). So we have now sorted out the relationship among the three variables, as illustrated in part (d) of the figure. Housing density and juvenile delinquency have a spurious correlation; evidence shows that both variables rise or fall according to people's income.

To sum up, correlation means only that two (or more) variables change together. Cause and effect rests on three conditions: (1) demonstrated correlation, (2) an independent (or causal) variable that precedes the dependent variable in time, and (3) no evidence that a third variable could be causing a spurious correlation between the two.

Natural scientists usually have an easier time than social scientists identifying cause-and-effect relationships because they can control many variables in a laboratory. Carrying out research in a workplace or on the streets, however, is a more difficult task, and sociologists must often be satisfied with demonstrating only correlation. Moreover, human behavior is highly complex, involving dozens of causal variables at any one time, so establishing all the cause-and-effect relationships in any situation is extremely difficult.

FIGURE 2-1 Correlation and Cause: An Example

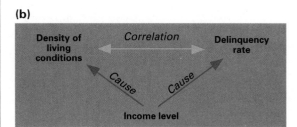

(a)

Density of living conditions ←— *Correlation* —→ Delinquency rate

If two variables vary together, they are said to be correlated. In this example, density of living conditions and juvenile delinquency increase and decrease together.

(b)

Density of living conditions ←— *Correlation* —→ Delinquency rate
Cause ↘ ↗ *Cause*
Income level

Here we consider the effect of a third variable: income level. Low income level may cause *both* high-density living conditions *and* a high delinquency rate. In other words, as income level decreases, both the density of living conditions and the delinquency rate increase.

(c)

Density of living conditions ····· *Correlation disappears* ····· Delinquency rate
Income level controlled

If we control income level—that is, examine only cases with the same income level—do those with higher-density living conditions still have a higher delinquency rate? The answer is "no." There is no longer a correlation between these two variables.

(d)

Density of living conditions ←— *Spurious correlation* —→ Delinquency rate
Cause ↘ ↗ *Cause*
Income level

This finding leads us to conclude that income level is a cause of both density of living conditions and delinquency rate. The original two variables (density of living conditions and delinquency rate) are thus correlated, but neither one causes the other. Their correlation is therefore *spurious.*

One principle of scientific research is that sociologists and other investigators should strive to be objective in their work, so that their personal values and beliefs do not distort their findings. But such an aloof attitude may discourage the relationship needed in order for people to open up and share information. Thus, as sociologists study human relationships, they have to be especially mindful of their own—when it comes to their subjects.

THE IDEAL OF OBJECTIVITY

Assume that ten people who work for a magazine in Fort Lauderdale, Florida, are collaborating on a story about that city's best restaurants. With the magazine picking up the tab, they head out on the town for a week of fine dining. Later, they get together to compare notes. Do you think one restaurant will be everyone's clear favorite? That hardly seems likely.

In scientific terms, each of the ten probably operationalizes the concept "best restaurant" differently. For one, it might be a place that serves delicious steaks at reasonable prices; for another, the choice might turn on a menu keyed to nutrition and health; for still

another, stunning decor and attentive service might be the deciding factors. Like so many other things in life, the best restaurant turns out to be mostly a matter of individual taste.

Personal values are fine when it comes to restaurants, but they pose a challenge to scientific research. Remember, science assumes reality is "out there." Scientists, then, need to study this reality without changing it in any way. Science, therefore, demands that researchers strive for **objectivity,** *personal neutrality in conducting research*. Objectivity means that researchers carefully hold to scientific procedures while reining in their own attitudes and beliefs in order not to bias the results.

Scientific objectivity is an ideal rather than a reality, of course, since no one can be completely neutral about anything. Even the subject a researcher chooses to study reflects a personal interest of one sort or another, as Lois Benjamin's research on race attests. But the scientific ideal is to keep a professional sense of detachment from how the results turn out. Holding to this ideal, we do our best to see that conscious or unconscious biases do not distort research. As an extra precaution, many researchers inform their readers about their personal leanings so that their conclusions are taken in the proper context.

Max Weber: Value-Free Research

The influential German sociologist Max Weber expected that people would select their research topics according to their personal beliefs and interests. Why else, after all, would one person study world hunger, another investigate the effects of racism, and still another examine how children fare in one-parent families? Knowing that people select topics that are *value-relevant*, Weber cautioned researchers to be *value-free* in their investigations. Only by being dispassionate (as we expect any professionals to be) can researchers study the world *as it is* rather than tell how they think *it should be*. This detachment, for Weber, is a crucial element of science that sets it apart from politics. Politicians, in other words, are committed to particular outcomes; scientists try to maintain an open-minded readiness to accept the results of their investigations, whatever they may be.

Weber's argument still carries much weight in sociology, although most sociologists concede that we can never be completely value-free or even aware of all our biases (Demerath, 1996). Moreover, sociologists are not "average" people: Most are white, highly educated, and more politically liberal than the population as a whole (L. Wilson, 1979). Sociologists need to

A basic lesson of social research is that being observed affects how people behave. Researchers can never be certain precisely how this will occur; while some people resent public attention, others become highly animated when they think they have an audience.

remember that they, too, are influenced by their own social backgrounds.

One way to limit distortion caused by personal values is **replication,** *repetition of research by other investigators.* If other researchers repeat a study using the same procedures and obtain the same results, we gain confidence that the results are accurate. The need for replication in scientific investigation probably explains why the search for knowledge is called *re*-search in the first place.

In any case, keep in mind that the logic of science does not guarantee objective, absolute truth. What science offers is an approach to knowledge that is *self-correcting* so that, in the long run, researchers stand the best chance of overcoming their biases. Objectivity and truth lie, then, not in any particular research, but in the scientific process itself.

SOME LIMITATIONS OF SCIENTIFIC SOCIOLOGY

Science is one important way of knowing. Yet, applied to social life, science has several important limitations:

1. **Human behavior is too complex for sociologists to predict precisely any individual's actions.** Astronomers calculate the movement of objects in the heavens with remarkable precision, but comets and planets are unthinking objects. Humans, by contrast, have minds of their own, so no two people react to any event in exactly the same way. Sociologists, therefore, must be satisfied with showing that *categories* of people typically act in one way or another. This is not a failing of sociology. It simply reflects the reality of what we do: study creative, spontaneous people.

2. **Because humans respond to their surroundings, the mere presence of a researcher may affect the behavior being studied.** An astronomer's gaze has no effect whatever on a distant comet. But most people react to being observed. Some become anxious, angry, or defensive; others try to "help" by doing what they think the researcher expects of them.

3. **Social patterns change; what is true in one time or place may not hold true in another.** The laws of physics apply tomorrow as well as today; they hold true all around the world. But human behavior is so variable that there are no unchanging sociological laws.

4. **Because sociologists are part of the social world they study, being value-free when conducting social research is difficult.** Barring a laboratory mishap, chemists are rarely personally affected by what goes on in test tubes. But sociologists live in their "test tube": the society they study. Therefore, social scientists face a greater challenge in controlling, or even recognizing, personal values that may distort their work.

A SECOND FRAMEWORK: INTERPRETIVE SOCIOLOGY

All sociologists agree that studying social behavior scientifically presents some real challenges. But some sociologists go further, suggesting that science as it is used to study the natural world misses a vital part of the social world: *meaning*.

Human beings do not simply act; we engage in *meaningful* action. Max Weber, who pioneered this framework, argued that the proper focus of sociology, therefore, must go beyond simply observing behavior to include *interpretation*—or learning what meaning people find in everyday life. **Interpretive sociology** is *the study of society that focuses on the meanings people attach to their social world*.

Interpretive sociology differs from scientific, or positivist, sociology in three ways. First, scientific sociology focuses on action, what people do; interpretive sociology, by contrast, focuses on the meaning people attach to behavior. Second, while scientific sociology sees an objective reality "out there," interpretive sociology sees reality constructed by people themselves in the course of their everyday lives. Third, while scientific sociology tends to favor *quantitative* data—that is, numerical measurements of social behavior—interpretive sociology favors *qualitative* data, researchers' accounts of how people understand their surroundings.

In sum, the scientific approach is well suited to research in a laboratory, where investigators stand back and take careful measurements. The interpretive approach is better suited to research in a natural setting, where investigators interact with people, learning how they make sense of their everyday lives.

Weber believed the key to interpretive sociology lay in *Verstehen*, the German word for "understanding." It is the interpretive sociologist's job not just to observe *what* people do but to understand *why* they act as they do. The thoughts and feelings of subjects—which scientists tend to dismiss because they are difficult to measure—now become the focus of the researcher's attention (Berger & Kellner, 1981; Neuman, 1997).

A THIRD FRAMEWORK: CRITICAL SOCIOLOGY

There is a third methodological approach in sociology. Like the interpretive approach, critical sociology developed in reaction to scientific research. This time, however, the issue was the scientific goal of objectivity.

Scientific sociology holds that reality is "out there" and the researcher's task is to study and document this reality. But Karl Marx, who founded the critical approach, rejected the idea that society exists as a "natural" system with a fixed order. To assume this, he claimed, amounts to saying that society cannot be changed. Scientific sociology, from this point of view, ends up supporting the status quo.

Critical sociology, by contrast, is *the study of society that focuses on the need for social change*. Rather than asking the scientific question "How does society work?" critical sociologists ask moral and political questions, especially "Should society exist in its present form?" Their answer, typically, is that it should not. One recent account of this approach, echoing Marx, claims that the point of sociology is "not just to research the social world but to change it in the direction of democracy and social justice" (Feagin & Vera, 2001:1). In making value judgments about how society should be improved, critical sociology rejects Weber's goal that researchers be value-free in favor of becoming social activists in pursuit of desirable change.

Sociologists using the critical approach seek to change not only society but the character of research itself. They consider their research subjects equals and encourage their participation in deciding what to study and how to do the work. Typically, researchers and subjects use their findings to provide a voice for less powerful people and to advance the political goal of a more equal society (Wolf, 1996; B. Hess, 1999; Feagin & Vera, 2001; Perrucci, 2001).

Scientific sociologists object to taking sides in this way, charging that critical sociology (whether feminist, Marxist, or some other critical approach), because of its political nature, lacks objectivity and is unable to correct for its own biases. Critical sociologists respond that *all* research is political or biased in that either it calls for change or it does not. Sociologists, they continue, have no choice about their work being political, but they can choose *which* positions to support.

Critical sociology is an activist approach tying knowledge to action—seeking not just to understand the world but also to improve it. Generally speaking, scientific sociology tends to appeal to researchers with more conservative political views; critical sociology appeals to those whose politics range from liberal to radical left.

What about the link between methodological approaches and theory? There is no precise connection; a sociologist who favors the critical approach, for example, may well use scientific methods to collect data. But each of the three methodological approaches does stand closer to one of the theoretical paradigms

TABLE 2-1 Three Methodological Approaches in Sociology

	Scientific	Interpretive	Critical
What is reality?	Society is an orderly system; reality is "out there."	Society is ongoing interaction; reality is socially constructed meanings.	Society is patterns of inequality; reality is that some dominate others.
How do we conduct research?	Gather empirical data, ideally, quantitative; researcher tries to be an objective observer.	Develop a qualitative account of the subjective sense people make of their world; researcher is a participant.	Research is a strategy to bring about desired change; researcher is an activist.
Corresponding theoretical paradigm	Structural-functional paradigm	Symbolic-interaction paradigm	Social-conflict paradigm

presented in Chapter 1 ("The Sociological Perspective"). The scientific approach corresponds to the structural-functional paradigm, the interpretive approach to the symbolic-interaction paradigm, and the critical approach to the social-conflict paradigm. Table 2–1 summarizes the differences among the three methodological approaches. Many sociologists favor one approach over another; however, it is important to become familiar with all three (Gamson, 1999).

GENDER AND RESEARCH

In recent years, sociologists have become aware that research is affected by **gender,** *the personal traits and social positions that members of a society attach to being female or male.* Margrit Eichler (1988) identifies five ways in which gender can shape research:

1. **Androcentricity.** Androcentricity (*andro-* in Greek means "male"; *centricity* means "being centered on") refers to approaching an issue from a male perspective. Sometimes researchers act as if only men's activities are important, ignoring what women do. For years researchers studying occupations focused on the paid work of men and overlooked the housework and child care traditionally performed by women. Clearly, research that seeks to understand human behavior cannot ignore half of humanity.

   Gynocentricity—seeing the world from a female perspective—is equally limiting to sociological investigation. However, in our male-dominated society, this problem arises less often.

2. **Overgeneralizing.** This problem occurs when researchers use data drawn from people of only one sex to support conclusions about "humanity" or "society." Gathering information about a community from a handful of male public officials and then drawing conclusions about the entire community illustrates the problem of overgeneralizing. In another case, studying child-rearing practices by collecting data only from women would allow researchers to draw conclusions about "motherhood" but not about the more general issue of "parenthood."

3. **Gender blindness.** Failing to consider the variable of gender at all is called "gender blindness." As is evident throughout this book, the lives of men and women differ in countless ways. A study of growing old in the United States would be flawed by gender blindness if it overlooked the fact that most elderly men live with their wives while elderly women typically live alone.

4. **Double standards.** Researchers must be careful not to distort what they study by judging men and women differently. For example, a family researcher who labels a couple as "man and wife" may define the man as the "head of household" and treat him accordingly, while assuming that the woman simply engages in family "support work."

5. **Interference.** Gender distorts a study if a subject reacts to the sex of the researcher, and it thereby interferes with the research operation. While studying a small community in Sicily, for instance, Maureen Giovannini (1992) found

many men responding to her as a woman rather than as a researcher. Gender dynamics precluded her from certain activities, such as private conversations with men, that were considered inappropriate for single women. Local residents also denied Giovannini access to places they considered off-limits to women.

There is nothing wrong with focusing research on one sex or the other. But all sociologists, as well as people who read their work, should be mindful of the importance of gender in any investigation.

RESEARCH ETHICS

Like all researchers, sociologists are aware that research can harm as well as help subjects or communities. For this reason, the American Sociological Association (ASA)—the major professional association of sociologists in North America—has established formal guidelines for conducting research (1997).

Sociologists must strive to be both technically competent and fair-minded in their work. Sociologists must disclose all research findings, without omitting significant data. They are ethically bound to make their results available to other sociologists, especially those who want to replicate a study.

 Read the professional Code of Ethics at the Web site of the American Sociological Association: http://www.asanet.org/members/ecointro.html

Sociologists must also ensure the safety of subjects taking part in a research project. Should research develop in a manner that threatens the well-being of participants, investigators must stop their work immediately. Researchers must also protect the privacy of anyone involved in a research project. This last promise can be difficult to keep, since researchers sometimes come under pressure (even from the police or courts) to disclose information. Therefore, researchers must think carefully about their responsibility to protect subjects, and they should discuss this issue with participants. In fact, ethical research requires the *informed consent* of participants, which means that subjects understand the responsibilities and risks that the research involves and agree—before the work begins—to take part.

Another important guideline concerns funding. Sociologists must include in their published results the sources of all financial support. They must also avoid conflicts of interest that may compromise the integrity of their work. For example, researchers must never accept funding from an organization that seeks to influence the research results for its own purposes.

The federal government, as well, plays a part in research ethics. Every college and university that seeks federal funding for research involving human subjects must have an *institutional review board* (IRB) that reviews grant applications and ensures that research will not violate ethical standards.

Finally, there are global dimensions to research ethics. Before beginning research in other countries, investigators must become familiar enough with that society to understand what people *there* are likely to perceive as a violation of privacy or a source of personal danger. In a multicultural society such as the United States, the same rule applies to studying people whose cultural background differs from one's own. The box offers some tips about how outsiders can effectively and sensitively study Hispanic communities.

THE METHODS OF SOCIOLOGICAL RESEARCH

A **research method** is *a systematic plan for conducting research*. The remainder of this chapter introduces four commonly used methods of sociological investigation. None is inherently better or worse than any other. Rather, in the same way that a carpenter selects a particular tool for a specific task, researchers choose a method—or mix several methods—according to whom they wish to study and what they wish to learn.

TESTING A HYPOTHESIS: THE EXPERIMENT

The logic of science is most clearly expressed in the **experiment,** *a research method for investigating cause and effect under highly controlled conditions*. Experimental research is *explanatory*; that is, it asks not just what happens but why. Typically, researchers devise an experiment to test a **hypothesis,** *an unverified statement of a relationship between variables*. A hypothesis typically takes the form of an *if-then* statement: *If* one thing were to happen, *then* something else would result.

The ideal experiment consists of four steps. First, the experimenter specifies the variable that is assumed to cause the change (the independent variable, or "the cause") as well as the variable that is changed (the dependent variable, or "the effect"). Second, the investigator determines the initial value of the dependent variable. Third, the investigator exposes the dependent variable to the independent variable (the "treatment"). Fourth, the researcher again measures the dependent variable to see what change took place. If

DIVERSITY: RACE, CLASS, AND GENDER

Studying the Lives of Hispanics

In a society as racially, ethnically, and religiously diverse as the United States, sociologists are always studying people who differ from themselves. Learning—in advance—some of the distinctive traits of any category of people can ease the research process and ensure that no hard feelings will be left when the work is finished.

Gerardo Marín and Barbara VanOss Marín have identified five areas of concern in conducting research with Hispanics:

1. **Terminology.** The Maríns point out that the term "Hispanic" is a label of convenience used by the Census Bureau. Few people of Spanish descent think of themselves as "Hispanic" or "Latino"; most identify with a particular country (generally, with a Latin American nation such as Mexico or Argentina, or with Spain).

2. **Cultural values.** By and large, the United States is a nation of individualistic, competitive people. Many Hispanics, by contrast, have a more collective orientation. An outsider, then, may judge the behavior of a Hispanic subject as conformist or overly trusting when, in fact, the

person is simply trying to be courteous. Researchers should also realize that Hispanic respondents might agree with a particular statement out of politeness rather than conviction.

3. **Family dynamics.** Generally speaking, Hispanic cultures have strong family loyalties. Asking subjects to reveal information about another family member may make them uncomfortable, or even angry. The Maríns add that, in the home, a researcher's request to speak privately with a Hispanic woman may provoke suspicion or outright disapproval from her husband or father.

4. **Time and efficiency.** Spanish cultures, the Maríns explain, tend to be

more concerned with the quality of relationships than with simply getting a job done. A non-Hispanic researcher who tries to hurry an interview with a Hispanic family, perhaps wishing not to delay the family's dinner, may be considered rude for not proceeding at a more sociable and relaxed pace.

5. **Personal space.** Finally, as the Maríns point out, people of Spanish descent typically maintain closer physical contact than many non-Hispanics. Consequently, researchers who seat themselves across the room from their subjects may appear "standoffish." Conversely, researchers may inaccurately label Hispanics "pushy" when they move closer than the non-Hispanic researcher finds comfortable.

Of course, Hispanics differ among themselves just like people in every other category, and these generalizations apply to some more than to others. But the challenge of being culturally aware is especially great in the United States, where hundreds of categories of people make up our multicultural society.

Source: Marín & Marín (1991).

the expected change did occur, the experiment supports the hypothesis; if not, the hypothesis must be modified.

But a change in the dependent variable could be due to something other than the supposed cause. To be certain that they identify the correct cause, researchers carefully control other factors that might intrude into the experiment and affect the outcome. Such control is most easily accomplished in a laboratory, a setting specially constructed to neutralize outside influences. Another strategy to gain control is dividing subjects into an *experimental group* and a *control group*. Early in the study, the researcher measures the dependent variable for subjects in both groups but later exposes only the experimental group to the independent variable or treatment. (The control group typically gets a

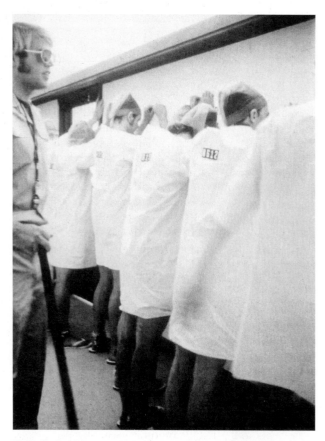

Philip Zimbardo's research helps to explain why violence is a common element in our society's prisons. At the same time, his work demonstrates the dangers that sociological investigation poses for subjects and the need for investigators to observe ethical standards that protect the welfare of people who participate in research.

"placebo," a treatment that the members of the group think is the same but really has no effect on the experiment.) Then the investigator measures the subjects in both groups again. Any factor occurring during the course of the research that influences people in the experimental group (say, a news event) would do the same to those in the control group, thus "washing out" the factor. By comparing the before and after measurements of the two groups, a researcher can assess how much of the change is due to the independent variable.

The Hawthorne Effect

Another concern of experimenters is that subjects' behavior may change simply because they are getting special attention, as one classic experiment revealed. In the late 1930s, the Western Electric Company hired researchers to investigate worker productivity in its Hawthorne factory near Chicago (Roethlisberger & Dickson, 1939). One experiment tested the hypothesis that increasing the available lighting would raise worker output. First, researchers measured worker productivity (the dependent variable). Then they increased the lighting (the independent variable) and measured output a second time. The resulting increased productivity supported the hypothesis. But when the research team later turned the lighting back down, productivity increased again. What was going on? In time, the researchers realized that the employees were working harder (even if they could not see as well) simply because people were paying attention to them. From this research, social scientists coined the term **Hawthorne effect** to refer to *a change in a subject's behavior caused simply by the awareness of being studied.*

An Illustration of an Experiment: The Stanford County Prison

Prisons can be violent settings, but is this due simply to the "bad" people who end up there? Or, as Philip Zimbardo suspected, does the prison itself somehow generate violent behavior? This question led Zimbardo to devise a fascinating experiment, which he called the "Stanford County Prison" (Zimbardo, 1972; Haney, Banks, & Zimbardo, 1973).

Zimbardo contended that, once inside a prison, even emotionally healthy people are prone to violence. Thus, Zimbardo treated the *prison setting* as the independent variable capable of causing *violence*, the dependent variable.

To test this hypothesis, Zimbardo's research team first constructed a realistic-looking "prison" in the basement of the psychology building on the campus of Stanford University. Then they placed an ad in a Palo Alto newspaper, offering to pay young men to help with a two-week research project. To each of the seventy who responded they administered a series of physical and psychological tests and then selected the healthiest twenty-four.

The next step was to assign randomly half the men to be "prisoners" and half to be "guards." The plan called for the guards and prisoners to spend the next two weeks in the mock prison. The prisoners began their part of the experiment soon afterward when the Palo Alto police "arrested" them at their homes. After searching and handcuffing the men, the police drove them to the local police station, where they were fingerprinted. Then police transported their captives to the Stanford prison, where the guards locked them up. Zimbardo started his video camera rolling and watched to see what would happen next.

The experiment turned into more than anyone had bargained for. Both guards and prisoners soon became embittered and hostile toward one another. Guards humiliated the prisoners by assigning them tasks such as cleaning out toilets with their bare hands. The prisoners, for their part, resisted and insulted the guards. Within four days, the researchers removed five prisoners who displayed "extreme emotional depression, crying, rage and acute anxiety" (Haney, Banks, & Zimbardo, 1973:81). Before the end of the first week, the situation had become so bad that the researchers had to cancel the experiment. Zimbardo explains:

> The ugliest, most base, pathological side of human nature surfaced. We were horrified because we saw some boys (guards) treat others as if they were despicable animals, taking pleasure in cruelty, while other boys (prisoners) became servile, dehumanized robots who thought only of escape, of their own individual survival and of their mounting hatred for the guards. (Zimbardo, 1972:4)

The events that unfolded at the "Stanford County Prison" supported Zimbardo's hypothesis that prison violence is rooted in the social character of jails themselves, not in the personalities of guards and prisoners. This finding raises questions about our society's prisons, suggesting the need for basic reform. But also note how this experiment reveals the potential of research to threaten the physical and mental well-being of subjects. Such dangers are not always as obvious as they were in this case. Therefore, researchers must consider carefully the potential harm to subjects at all stages of their work and end any study, as Zimbardo did, if subjects may suffer harm of any kind.

ASKING QUESTIONS: SURVEY RESEARCH

A **survey** is *a research method in which subjects respond to a series of statements or questions in a questionnaire or an interview*. The most widely used of all research methods, surveys are particularly well suited to studying attitudes—such as beliefs about politics, religion, or race—since there is no way to observe directly what people think. Sometimes surveys provide clues about cause and effect, but typically they yield *descriptive* findings, painting a picture of people's views on some issue.

Population and Sample

A survey targets some **population,** *the people who are the focus of research*. Lois Benjamin, in her study of racism described at the beginning of this chapter, studied a select population—100 talented African Americans. A survey population can also be very large: Political pollsters predict election returns using surveys that treat every adult in the country as the population.

Obviously, however, contacting millions of people would overwhelm even the most well-funded and patient researcher. Fortunately, there is an easier way that yields accurate results: Researchers collect data from a **sample,** *a part of a population that represents the whole*. Everyone uses the logic of sampling all the time. If you look at students sitting near you in a lecture hall and notice five or six heads nodding off, you might conclude that the class finds the day's lecture dull. In reaching this conclusion, you are making a judgment about *all* the people (the "population") from observing *some* of the people (the "sample").

But how can we know if a sample actually represents the entire population? One answer is *random sampling*, in which researchers draw a sample from the population randomly so that every element in the population has an equal chance to be selected. The mathematical laws of probability dictate that a random sample is quite likely to represent the population.

Beginning researchers sometimes make the mistake of assuming that "randomly" walking up to people on a street produces a sample that is representative of the entire city. Unfortunately, such a strategy does

 For a discussion of the use of polls in political campaigns, go to http://faculty.vassar.edu/lowry/polls.html

not give every person an equal chance to be included in the sample. For one thing, any street, whether in a rich neighborhood or a college town, contains more of some kinds of people than others. For another, any researcher is apt to find some people more approachable than others, yet another bias.

Although good sampling is no simple task, it offers a considerable savings in time and expense. We are spared the tedious work of contacting everyone in a population, yet we can obtain essentially the same results.

Using Questionnaires

Selecting subjects is only the first step in carrying out a survey. Also needed is a plan for asking questions and recording answers. Most surveys use a questionnaire for this purpose.

A focus group is a small group of people who assemble to discuss some issue or product in detail. Typically, a group leader directs the discussion, encouraging the participants to speak freely and honestly about the topic at hand. Here we see corporate executives monitoring a focus group discussion of one of their products. In this case, the executives sit behind a one-way mirror so that their presence does not influence the focus group members.

A **questionnaire** is *a series of written questions a researcher presents to subjects.* One type of questionnaire provides not only the questions but a series of fixed responses (similar to a multiple-choice examination). This *closed-ended format* makes it relatively easy to analyze the results, but by narrowing the range of responses, it can also distort the findings. For example, Frederick Lorenz and Brent Bruton (1996) found that how many hours per week students say they study for a college course depends on the options offered to them. When the researchers presented students with options ranging from one hour or less to nine hours or more, 75 percent said that they studied four hours or less per week. But when subjects in a comparable group were given choices ranging from four hours or less to twelve hours or longer (a higher figure that suggests students should study more), they suddenly became more studious, only 34 percent reporting that they studied four hours or less each week.

A second type of questionnaire, using an *open-ended format,* allows subjects to respond freely, expressing various shades of opinion. The drawback of this approach is that the researcher has to make sense out of what can be a bewildering array of answers.

The researcher must also decide how to present questions to subjects. Most often, researchers use a *self-administered survey,* mailing or e-mailing questionnaires to respondents and asking them to complete the form and send it back. Since no researcher is present when subjects read the questionnaire, it must be both inviting and clearly written. *Pretesting* a self-administered questionnaire with a small number of people before sending it to the entire sample can prevent the costly problem of finding out—too late—that instructions or questions were confusing.

Using the mail or e-mail allows a researcher to contact a large number of people over a wide geographic area at minimal expense. But many people treat such questionnaires as junk mail, so that typically no more than half are completed and returned (in 2000, the public returned just two-thirds of U.S. Census Bureau forms as requested). Researchers must send follow-up mailings (or, as the Census Bureau does, visit people's homes) to coax reluctant subjects to respond.

Finally, keep in mind that many people are not capable of completing a questionnaire on their own. Young children obviously cannot, nor can many hospital patients, or a surprising number of adults who simply lack the required reading and writing skills.

Conducting Interviews

An **interview** is *a series of questions a researcher administers in person to respondents.* In a closed-format design, researchers read a question or statement and then ask the subject to select a response from several alternatives. Generally, interviews are open-ended so that subjects can respond as they choose and researchers can probe with follow-up questions. However, the researcher must guard against influencing a subject, which is as easy as raising an eyebrow when a person begins to answer.

Although subjects are more likely to complete a survey if contacted personally by the researcher, interviews have some disadvantages: Tracking people down

CRITICAL THINKING

Survey Questions: A Word or Two Makes All the Difference

Do people approve of their president? Pollsters find that approval ratings rise or fall depending on a few small words. During the Clinton years, surveys showed that a majority of adults held a favorable opinion of Mr. Clinton as president. But if researchers asked people what they thought of Mr. Clinton *as a person*, his approval ratings typically tumbled 20 percent.

This difference shows that how researchers word questions affects people's responses. In 1998, *Newsweek* magazine hired a team of researchers to measure public attitudes toward abortion. The results of this national survey showed once again just how important a few

words can be in shaping public response. One question put it this way: "Do you personally believe that abortion is wrong?" In this case, 57 percent of respondents said "yes," while 36 percent said "no" (the rest either were not sure or did not answer). Looking at these results, one might well conclude that a majority of people are anti-abortion. Yet, another question was worded this way: "Whatever your own personal view of abortion, do you favor or oppose a woman in this country having the choice to have an abortion with the advice of her doctor?" Now 69 percent favored available abortion, and just 24 percent opposed it—clear support for the abortion rights side of the debate.

Are people of two minds on the abortion question? Probably most people listen carefully to the wording of the questions. While a slight majority *personally* consider abortion wrong, a larger majority believe that women—with medical advice—should be able to have an abortion if they decide to.

One final example. Look at the wording in these questions: The first is "Do you think that the police force is doing a good job?" The second, "Do you agree that the police force is doing a good job?" Which one is more likely to elicit stronger support for the police? Why?

Source: Data taken from Witt (1999).

is costly and time-consuming, especially if subjects do not live in the same area. Telephone interviews allow far greater "reach," but the impersonality of cold calls by telephone (and reaching answering machines) can lower the response rate.

In both questionnaires and interviews, how a question is worded greatly affects how people answer. For example, when asked if they object to homosexuals serving in the military, most adults in the United States say "yes." Yet, ask them if the government should exempt homosexuals from military service, and most say "no" (NORC, 1991). Emotionally loaded language can also sway subjects. For instance, using the term "welfare mothers" rather than "women who receive public assistance" adds an emotional element to a question that encourages people to answer negatively. The box takes a closer look at the importance of wording in conducting public opinion polls.

Moreover, researchers may confuse respondents by asking a double question, like "Do you think that the government should reduce the deficit by cutting spending and raising taxes?" The problem here is that a subject could very well agree with one part of the question but reject the other, so that forcing a subject

to say "yes" or "no" distorts the opinion the researcher is trying to measure.

All these examples suggest that conducting a good interview means standardizing the technique—treating all subjects in the same way. But this, too, can lead to problems. Drawing people out requires establishing rapport, which, in turn, depends on responding naturally to the particular person being interviewed—as one would in a normal conversation. In the end, researchers have to decide where to strike the balance between uniformity on the one hand and rapport on the other (Lavin & Maynard, 2001).

An Illustration: Studying the African American Elite

We opened this chapter by recounting how Lois Benjamin came to investigate the effects of racism on talented African American men and women. Benjamin suspected that personal achievement did not prevent hostility based on color. She based this view on her own experiences after becoming the first black professor in the history of the University of Tampa. But was she the exception or the rule? To answer this question,

TABLE 2-2 The Talented 100: Lois Benjamin's African American Elite

Sex	Age	Childhood Racial Setting	Childhood Region	Highest Educational Degree	Occupational Sector	Income	Political Orientation
Male 63%	35 or younger 6%	Mostly black 71%	West 6%	Doctorate 32%	College or university 35%	More than $50,000 64%	Radical left 13%
Female 37%	36 to 54 68%	Mostly white 15%	North or Central 32%	Medical or law 17%	Private, profit 17%	$35,000 to $50,000 18%	Liberal 38%
	55 or older 26%	Racially mixed 14%	South 38%	Master's 27%	Private, nonprofit 9%	$20,000 to $34,999 12%	Moderate 28%
			Northeast 12%	Bachelor's 13%	Government 22%	Less than $20,000 6%	Conservative 5%
			Other 12%	Less 11%	Self-employed 14%		Depends on issue 14%
					Retired 3%		Unknown 2%
100%	100%	100%	100%	100%	100%	100%	100%

Source: Adapted from Lois Benjamin, *The Black Elite: Facing the Color Line in the Twilight of the Twentieth Century* (Chicago: Nelson-Hall, 1991), p. 276.

Benjamin set out to discover whether—and how—racism plagued members of the African American elite.

Opting to conduct a survey, Benjamin chose to interview subjects rather than distribute a questionnaire because, first, she wanted to enter into a conversation with her subjects, to ask follow-up questions, and to pursue topics that she could not anticipate. A second reason Benjamin favored interviews over questionnaires is that racism is a sensitive topic. A supportive investigator can make it easier for subjects to respond to painful questions (Bergen, 1993).

Choosing to conduct interviews made it necessary to limit the number of people in the study. Benjamin settled for 100 men and women. Even this small number kept Benjamin busy for more than two years scheduling, traveling, and meeting with respondents. She spent two more years transcribing the tapes of her interviews, sorting out what the hours of talk told her about racism, and writing up her results.

In selecting a sample, Benjamin first considered using all the people listed in *Who's Who in Black America*. But she rejected this idea in favor of starting out with people she knew and asking them to suggest others. This strategy is called *snowball sampling* because the number of individuals included grows rapidly over time.

Snowball sampling is appealing because it is an easy way to do research—we begin with familiar people who provide introductions to their friends and colleagues. The drawback, however, is that snowball sampling rarely produces a sample that is representative of the larger population. Benjamin's sample probably contained many like-minded individuals, and it was certainly biased toward people willing to talk openly about race. She understood these problems and did try to make her sample as varied as she could in terms of sex, age, and region of the country. Table 2–2 presents a statistical profile of Benjamin's respondents; the box provides some tips on how to read tables.

Benjamin based all her interviews on a series of questions, with an open-ended format so that her subjects could say whatever they wished. As usually happens, the interviews took place in a wide range of settings. She met subjects in offices (hers or theirs), in hotel rooms, and in cars. In each case, Benjamin tape-recorded the conversation, which lasted from two-and-one-half to three hours, so she would not be distracted by taking notes.

As research ethics demand, Benjamin offered full anonymity to participants. Even so, many—including notables such as Vernon E. Jordan, Jr. (former president of the National Urban League) and Yvonne Walker-Taylor (first woman president of Wilberforce University)—were accustomed to being in the public eye and permitted Benjamin to use their names.

Reading Tables: An Important Skill

A table provides a lot of information in a small amount of space, so learning to read tables can increase your reading efficiency. When you spot a table, look first at the title to see what information it contains. The title tells you that Table 2–2 presents a profile of the 100 subjects participating in Lois Benjamin's research. Across the top of the table, you will see eight variables that define these men and women. Reading down each column, note the categories within each variable; the percentages in each column add up to 100.

Starting at the top left, we see that Benjamin's sample was mostly men (63 percent versus 37 percent women). In terms of age, most of the respondents (68 percent) were in the middle stage of life, and most had grown up in a predominantly black community in the South or the North or Central regions of the United States.

These individuals are, indeed, a professional elite. Notice that half have earned either a doctorate (32 percent) or a medical or law degree (17 percent). Given their extensive education (and Benjamin's own position as a professor), we should not be surprised that the largest share (35 percent) work in academic institutions. In terms of income, these are affluent individuals, with most (64 percent) earning more than $50,000 annually during the 1980s (a salary that only 25 percent of all U.S. workers make even today).

Finally, we see that these 100 individuals are generally left-of-center in their political views. In part, this reflects their extensive schooling (which encourages progressive thinking) and the tendency of academics to fall on the liberal side of the political spectrum.

What surprised Benjamin most about her research was how eagerly many informants responded to her request for an interview. These normally busy men and women appeared to go out of their way to contribute to her project. Furthermore, once the interviews were underway, many became very emotional. Benjamin reports that, at some point in the conversation, about 40 of her 100 subjects cried. For them, apparently, the research provided an opportunity to release feelings and share experiences never revealed before. How did Benjamin respond to such sentiments? She reports that she laughed and cried along with her respondents.

Benjamin's research is less scientific and more interpretive sociology (she wanted to find out what race meant to her subjects) and critical sociology (she undertook the study partly to document that racial prejudice still exists). Indeed, many subjects reported fearing that race might someday undermine their success, and others spoke of a race-based "glass ceiling" preventing them from reaching the highest positions in our society. Summarizing her findings, Benjamin concluded that, despite the improving social standing of African Americans, black people in the United States still feel the sting of racial hostility.

IN THE FIELD: PARTICIPANT OBSERVATION

Lois Benjamin's research demonstrates that sociological investigation takes place not only in laboratories but "in the field," that is, where people carry on their everyday lives. The most widely used strategy for field study is **participant observation**, *a research method in which investigators systematically observe people while joining them in their routine activities.*

Participant observation allows researchers an inside look at social life in settings ranging from nightclubs to religious seminaries. Cultural anthropologists commonly employ participant observation (which they call *fieldwork*) to study communities in other societies. They term their descriptions of unfamiliar cultures *ethnographies*. Sociologists prefer to call their accounts of people in particular settings *case studies*.

At the beginning of a field study, most investigators do not have a specific hypothesis in mind. In fact, they may not yet realize what the important questions will turn out to be. Thus, most field research is *exploratory* and *descriptive*.

As its name suggests, participant observation has two sides. On the one hand, getting an "insider's" look depends on becoming a participant in the setting— "hanging out" with others, trying to act, think, and

Anthropologists and photographers Angela Fisher and Carol Beckwith have documented fascinating rituals around the world. As part of their fieldwork, they lived for months with the Himba in Namibia, in order to gain their acceptance and trust. During this time, a village man was killed by a lion. Later, his wives fell under the control of a lion spirit, apparently sent by the husband to bring these women to him in the afterlife. In the ritual shown above, photographed by Fisher and Beckwith, the women seek to rid themselves of the curse.

even feel the way they do. Compared to experiments and survey research, then, participant observation has fewer hard-and-fast rules. But it is precisely this flexibility that allows investigators to explore the unfamiliar and adapt to the unexpected.

Unlike other research methods, participant observation requires that the researcher become immersed in the setting not for a week or two, but for months or even years. At the same time, however, the researcher must maintain some distance as an "observer," mentally stepping back to record field notes and, eventually, to interpret them. Because the investigator must both "play the participant" to win acceptance and gain access to people's lives and "play the observer" to maintain the distance needed for thoughtful analysis, there is an inherent tension in this method. Carrying out the twin roles of insider participant and outsider observer often comes down to a series of careful compromises.

Most sociologists carry out participant observation alone, so they—and readers, too—must remember that the results depend on the work of a single person. Participant observation usually falls within interpretive sociology, yielding mostly qualitative data—the researcher's accounts of people's lives and what they think of themselves and the world around them—

although researchers sometimes collect some quantitative (numerical) data. From a scientific point of view, participant observation is a "soft" method that relies heavily on personal judgment and lacks scientific rigor. Yet, its personal approach is also a strength: Whereas a highly visible team of sociologists attempting to administer, say, formal surveys would disrupt many social settings, a sensitive participant-observer can often gain considerable insight into people's natural behavior.

An Illustration: *Street Corner Society*

In the late 1930s, a young graduate student at Harvard University named William Foote Whyte (1914–2000) was fascinated by the lively street life of a nearby, rather rundown section of Boston. His curiosity ultimately led him to carry out four years of participant observation in this neighborhood, which he called "Cornerville," and in the process to produce a sociological classic.

At the time, Cornerville was home to first- and second-generation Italian immigrants. Many were poor, and popular wisdom in the rest of Boston considered Cornerville a place to avoid: a poor, chaotic slum inhabited by racketeers. Unwilling to accept easy stereotypes, Whyte set out to discover for himself exactly what kind of life went on inside this community. His celebrated book, *Street Corner Society* (1981; orig. 1943), describes Cornerville as a highly organized community with a distinctive code of values, complex social patterns, and particular social conflicts.

In beginning his investigation, Whyte considered a range of research methods. He could have taken questionnaires to one of Cornerville's community centers and asked local people to fill them out. Or he could have invited members of the community to come to his Harvard office for interviews. But it is easy to see that such formal strategies would have prompted little cooperation from the local people and would have yielded few insights. Whyte decided, therefore, to ease into Cornerville life and patiently build an understanding of this rather mysterious place.

Soon enough, Whyte discovered the challenges of even getting started in field research. After all, an upper-middle-class WASPy graduate student from Harvard did not exactly fit into Cornerville life. He soon found out, for example, that even an outsider's friendly overture could seem pushy and rude. Early on, Whyte dropped in at a local bar, hoping to buy a woman a drink and encourage her to talk about Cornerville. But looking around the room, he could find no woman alone. Presently, he thought he might have an opportunity when a fellow sat down with two women. He gamely asked, "Pardon me. Would you mind if I joined you?" Instantly, he realized his mistake:

> There was a moment of silence while the man stared at me. Then he offered to throw me down the stairs. I assured him that this would not be necessary, and demonstrated as much by walking right out of there without any assistance. (1981:289)

As this incident suggests, gaining entry to a community is the crucial (and sometimes hazardous) first step in field research. "Breaking in" requires patience, ingenuity, and a little luck. Whyte's big break came in the form of a young man named "Doc," whom he met in a local social service agency. Listening to Whyte's account of his bungled efforts to make friends in Cornerville, Doc was sympathetic and decided to take Whyte under his wing and introduce him to others in the community. With Doc's help, Whyte soon became a neighborhood regular.

Whyte's friendship with Doc illustrates the importance of a *key informant* in field research. Such people not only introduce a researcher to a community but often remain a source of information and help. But using a key informant also has its risks. Because any person has a particular circle of friends, a key informant's guidance is certain to "spin" the study in one way or another. Moreover, in the eyes of others, the reputation of the key informant—for better or worse—usually rubs off on the investigator. In sum, a key informant is helpful at the outset, but a participant-observer soon must seek a broad range of contacts.

Having entered the Cornerville world, Whyte began his work in earnest. But he soon realized that a field researcher needs to know when to speak up and when simply to look, listen, and learn. One evening, he joined a group discussing neighborhood gambling. Wanting to get the facts straight, Whyte asked innocently, "I suppose the cops were all paid off?" In a heartbeat,

> the gambler's jaw dropped. He glared at me. Then he denied vehemently that any policeman had been paid off and immediately switched the conversation to another subject. For the rest of that evening I felt very uncomfortable.

The next day, Doc offered some sound advice:

> "Go easy on that 'who,' 'what,' 'why,' 'when,' 'where' stuff, Bill. You ask those questions and people will clam up on you. If people accept you, you can just hang around, and you'll learn the answers in the long run without even having to ask the questions." (1981:303)

In the months and years that followed, Whyte became familiar with life in Cornerville and married a local woman with whom he would spend the rest of his life. In the process, he learned that this neighborhood was hardly the stereotypical slum. On the contrary, most immigrants worked hard, many were quite successful, and some even boasted of sending children to college. In short, Whyte's book is fascinating reading about the deeds, dreams, and disappointments of people living in one ethnic community, and it contains a richness of detail that can come only from long-term participant observation.

Whyte's work shows that participant observation is a method rife with tensions and contrasts. Its flexibility allows a researcher to respond to the unexpected but makes replication difficult. Participation means getting close to people, but observation depends on keeping some distance. Because no elaborate equipment or laboratory is needed, little expense is involved. But this method is costly in terms of time—most studies take a year or more, which probably explains why participant observation is used less

The U.S. Census Bureau collects a vast amount of information about the population of this country. Data are available in Census Bureau publications found in your local library or on the Internet at www.census.gov

often than the other methods described in this chapter. Yet the depth of understanding gained through interpretive research of this kind greatly enriches our knowledge of many types of human communities.

USING AVAILABLE DATA: SECONDARY AND HISTORICAL ANALYSIS

Not all research requires investigators to collect their own data. Sometimes, sociologists conduct **secondary analysis,** *a research method in which a researcher uses data collected by others.*

The most widely used statistics in social science are gathered by government agencies. The U.S. Census Bureau continuously updates information on the U.S. population. Comparable data on Canada are available from Statistics Canada, a branch of that nation's government. For international data, there are various publications of the United Nations and the World Bank. In short, a wide range of data about the whole world is as close as your library or the Internet.

For easy access to many data links, visit http://www. TheSociologyPage.com

Using available data—whether government statistics or the findings of individual researchers—saves time and money. This approach, therefore, has special

appeal to sociologists with low budgets. Even more important, government data are generally better than what most researchers could obtain on their own.

Still, secondary analysis has inherent problems. For one thing, available data may not exist in precisely the form needed. Further, there are always questions about the meaning and accuracy of work done by others. For example, in his classic study of suicide, Emile Durkheim soon discovered that there was no way to know whether a death classified as a suicide was really an accident, and vice versa. In addition, various agencies use different procedures and categories in collecting data, so comparisons are difficult. In the end, then, using secondhand data is a little like shopping for a used car: Bargains are plentiful, but you have to shop carefully to avoid ending up with a "lemon."

To illustrate, let's assume that reading about Lois Benjamin's account of African American elites sparks your interest in this country's well-off minorities. How many such people are there? Where do they live? National Map 2–1 graphically displays Census Bureau data that address these questions. These statistics are the best available, and at no cost. Yet to use them means accepting the Census Bureau's racial and ethnic categories (until 2000, for example, people could check only one racial category). It also means accepting as accurate people's self-reported income. Further, if you were to use this map for your own purposes, you would also have to accept the given definitions of "well-off" and "above average" even though they may not exactly fit your purpose.

An Illustration: A Tale of Two Cities

To people trapped in the present, secondary analysis offers a key to unlocking secrets of the past. The award-winning study *Puritan Boston and Quaker Philadelphia,* by E. Digby Baltzell (1979b), exemplifies a researcher's power to analyze the past using historical sources.

A chance visit to Bowdoin College in Maine prompted Baltzell to begin his investigation. Entering the college library, he gazed upon portraits of the celebrated author Nathaniel Hawthorne, the eminent poet Henry Wadsworth Longfellow, and Franklin Pierce, the fourteenth U.S. president. He was startled to learn that all three of these great men had been members of a single class at Bowdoin, graduating in 1825. How could it be, Baltzell mused, that this small college had graduated more famous people in a single year than his own, much bigger University of Pennsylvania had

SEEING OURSELVES

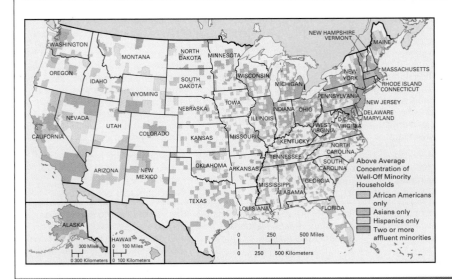

NATIONAL MAP 2–1

Well-Off Minorities across the United States

Based on 1990 Census data, this map identifies the counties with an above-average share of well-off minority households—earning at least $50,000 a year. (For the entire country in 2000, about one-third of African American and Hispanic families and more than half of Asian families fell into this category.) Where do well-off members of each minority live? Do members of one category tend to live where members of another category predominate? Can you explain this pattern?

Source: Adapted from *American Demographics* magazine, December, 1992, pp. 34–35. Reprinted with permission. © 1992, *American Demographics* magazine, Ithaca, New York. Data taken from the 1990 Census.

---

graduated in its entire history? To answer this question, Baltzell was soon poring over historical documents to see if New England had indeed produced more famous people than his native Pennsylvania.

For data, Baltzell turned to the *Dictionary of American Biography*, twenty volumes profiling more than 13,000 outstanding men and women in fields such as politics, law, and the arts. The *Dictionary* told Baltzell *who* was great; but he also wanted some way to measure *how* great people were. He decided to base his ranking on the *Dictionary*'s statement that, the more impressive the person's achievements, the longer the biography. So counting the number of lines in a biography yielded a reasonable measure of "greatness."

By the time Baltzell had identified the seventy-five individuals with the longest biographies, he saw a striking pattern. Massachusetts had the most by far, with twenty-one of the seventy-five top achievers. The New England states, combined, claimed thirty-one of the entries. By contrast, Pennsylvania could boast of only two, and all the states in the Middle Atlantic region had just twelve. Looking more closely, Baltzell discovered that most of New England's great achievers had grown up in and around the city of Boston. Again, in stark contrast, almost no one of comparable standing came from his own Philadelphia, a city with many more people than Boston.

What could explain this remarkable pattern? Baltzell drew inspiration from the German sociologist Max Weber (1958; orig. 1904–05), who argued that a region's record of achievement was largely a result of its predominant religious beliefs (see Chapter 4, "Society"). In the religious differences that set Boston apart from Philadelphia, Baltzell found the answer to his puzzle. Boston was a Puritan settlement, founded by people who were determined in their pursuit of excellence and public achievement. Philadelphia, by contrast, was settled by Quakers, who were equally determined to shun public notice.

Both the Puritans and the Quakers were fleeing religious persecution in England, but the two religious beliefs produced quite different cultural patterns. Convinced of humanity's innate sinfulness, Boston Puritans built a rigid society in which family, church, and school regulated people's behavior. They celebrated hard work as a means of glorifying God and viewed public success as a reassuring sign of God's blessing. In other words, Puritanism fostered a disciplined life in which people both sought and respected achievement.

Philadelphia's Quakers, on the other hand, built their way of life on the belief that all human beings are basically good. They saw little need for strong social institutions to "save" people from sinfulness. They believed in equality, so that even those who became rich

TABLE 2-3 Four Research Methods: A Summary

Method	Application	Advantages	Limitations
Experiment	For explanatory research that specifies relationships between variables; generates quantitative data.	Provides the greatest opportunity to specify cause-and-effect relationships; replication of research is relatively easy.	Laboratory settings have an artificial quality; unless the research environment is carefully controlled, results may be biased.
Survey	For gathering information about issues that cannot be directly observed, such as attitudes and values useful for descriptive and explanatory research; generates quantitative or qualitative data.	Sampling, using questionnaires, allows surveys of large populations; interviews provide in-depth responses.	Questionnaires must be carefully prepared and may yield a low return rate; interviews are expensive and time-consuming.
Participant observation	For exploratory and descriptive study of people in a "natural" setting; generates qualitative data.	Allows study of "natural" behavior; usually inexpensive.	Time-consuming; replication of research is difficult; researcher must balance roles of participant and observer.
Secondary analysis	For exploratory, descriptive, or explanatory research whenever suitable data are available.	Saves time and expense of data collection; makes historical research possible.	Researcher has no control over possible biases in data; data may only partially fit current research needs.

considered themselves no better than anyone else. Thus, rich and poor alike lived modestly and discouraged one other from standing out by seeking fame or even public office.

In Baltzell's sociological imagination, Boston and Philadelphia took the form of two social "test tubes": Puritanism was poured into one, Quakerism into the other. Centuries later, we can see that different "chemical reactions" occurred in each case. The two belief systems apparently led to different attitudes toward personal achievement, which, in turn, shaped the history of each region. Moreover, we can see the results of these cultural differences even today. Boston's Kennedys (despite being Catholic) are only one of that city's families that exemplify the Puritan pursuit of recognition and leadership, but there has *never* been a family with such public stature in the entire history of Philadelphia.

Baltzell's study uses scientific logic, but it also illustrates the interpretive approach by showing how people understood their world. His research reminds us that sociological investigation often involves mixing methodological approaches and a lively sociological imagination.

Table 2–3 summarizes the four major methods of sociological investigation. We now turn to our final consideration: the link between research results and sociological theory.

THE INTERPLAY OF THEORY AND METHOD

No matter how they gather data, sociologists have to turn facts into meaning by building theory. They do this in two ways: inductive logical thought and deductive logical thought.

Inductive logical thought is *reasoning that transforms specific observations into general theory*. In this mode, a researcher's thinking runs from the specific to the general and goes something like this: "I have some interesting data here; I wonder what they mean?" E. Digby Baltzell's research illustrates the inductive logical model. His data showed that one region of the country (the Boston area) had produced many more high achievers than another (the Philadelphia region). He worked "upward" from ground-level observations to the high-flying theory that religious values were a key factor in shaping people's attitude toward achievement.

A second type of logical thought moves "downward," in the opposite direction: **Deductive logical thought** is *reasoning that transforms general theory into specific hypotheses suitable for testing*. The researcher's thinking runs from the general to the specific: "I have this hunch about human behavior; let's collect some data and put it to the test." Working deductively, the researcher first states the theory in the form of a hypothesis and then selects a method by which to test it. To the extent that the data support the hypothesis, we conclude that the theory is correct; data that refute the hypothesis tell us that the theory should be revised or perhaps rejected entirely.

Philip Zimbardo's Stanford County Prison experiment illustrates deductive logic. Zimbardo began with the general idea that prisons change human behavior. He then developed a specific, testable hypothesis: Placed in a prison setting, even emotionally well-balanced young men will behave violently. The violence that erupted soon after his experiment began supported Zimbardo's hypothesis. Had his experiment produced friendly behavior between prisoners and guards, his original theory would have needed reformulation.

Just as researchers often employ several methods over the course of one study, they typically use *both* kinds of logical thought. Figure 2–2 illustrates both types of reasoning: inductively building theory from observations and deductively making observations to test a theory.

Finally, turning facts into meaning usually involves organizing and presenting statistical data. Precisely how sociologists arrange their numbers affects the conclusions they reach. In short, preparing one's results amounts to spinning reality in one way or another.

Often, we conclude that an argument must be true simply because there are statistics to back it up. However, we must look at statistics with a cautious eye. After all, researchers choose what data to present, they interpret their statistics, and they may use tables and graphs to steer readers toward particular conclusions. The final box, on pages 52–53, takes a closer look at this important issue.

PUTTING IT ALL TOGETHER: TEN STEPS IN SOCIOLOGICAL INVESTIGATION

We can draw the material in this chapter together by outlining ten steps in the process of carrying out sociological investigation. Each step is represented by an important question:

1. **What is your topic?** Being curious and using the sociological perspective can generate ideas for social research at any time and in any place. The issue you choose for study is likely to have some personal significance.

2. **What have others already learned?** You are probably not the first person with an interest in some issue. Visit the library to see what theories and methods other researchers have applied to your

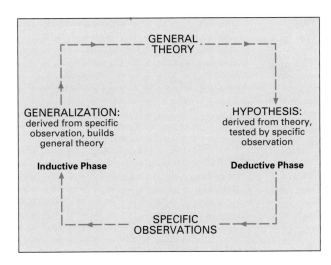

FIGURE 2-2 Deductive and Inductive Logical Thought

topic. In reviewing the existing research, note problems that have come up.

3. **What, exactly, are your questions?** Are you seeking to explore an unfamiliar social setting? To describe some category of people? To investigate cause and effect among variables? If your study is exploratory or descriptive, identify *whom* you wish to study, *where* the research will take place, and *what* kinds of issues you want to explore. If it is explanatory, you also must formulate the hypothesis to be tested and operationalize each variable.

4. **What will you need to carry out research?** How much time and money are available to you? Is special equipment or skills necessary? Can you do the work yourself? You should answer all these questions as you plan the research project.

5. **Are there ethical concerns?** Not all research raises serious ethical questions, but you must be sensitive to the possibility. Can the research cause harm or threaten anyone's privacy? How might you design the study to minimize the chances for injury? Will you promise anonymity to the subjects? If so, how will you ensure that anonymity is maintained?

6. **What method will you use?** Consider all major research strategies, as well as combinations of approaches. Keep in mind that the appropriate method depends on the kind of questions you are asking as well as the resources available to you.

CONTROVERSY & DEBATE

Can People Lie with Statistics?

Is research—especially research involving numbers—always as "factual" as we think? Not according to the great English politician Benjamin Disraeli, who remarked, "There are three kinds of lies: lies, damned lies, and statistics!" In a world that bombards us with numbers—often described as "scientific facts" or "official figures"—it is worth pausing to consider that "statistical evidence" is not necessarily the same as truth. For one thing, any researcher can make mistakes. For another, because data do not speak for themselves, someone has to interpret what they mean. Sometimes, people (even sociologists) "dress up" their data almost the way politicians deliver campaign speeches—with an eye more to winning you over than to getting at the truth.

The best way not to fall prey to statistical manipulation is to understand how people can mislead with statistics:

1. **People select their data.** Many times, the data presented are not

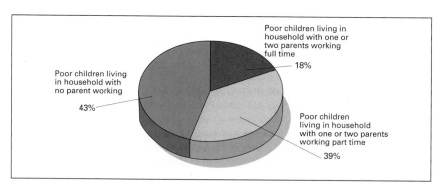

Poor children living in household with one or two parents working full time — 18%

Poor children living in household with no parent working — 43%

Poor children living in household with one or two parents working part time — 39%

wrong, but they are not the whole story. Let's say someone who thinks that television is ruining our way of life presents statistics indicating that we watch more TV today than a generation ago. Moreover, during the same period, College Board scores have fallen. Both sets of data may be correct, but the suggestion that television is lowering test scores remains unproven. Moreover, a person more favorable to television might counter with the additional "fact" that the U.S.

population spends much more money buying books today than it did a generation ago, suggesting that television creates new intellectual interests. In sum, people can find statistics that seem to support just about any argument.

2. **People interpret their data.** Another way people manipulate statistics is to "package" them with a ready-made interpretation, as if numbers can mean only one thing. One publication, for example, presented the results of a study of U.S. children

7. **How will you record the data?** Your research method is the system for data collection. Record all information accurately and in a way that will make sense later (it may be some time before you actually write up the results of your work). Be alert for any bias that may creep into the research.

8. **What do the data tell you?** Study the data in terms of your initial questions and decide how to interpret the data you have collected. If your study involves a specific hypothesis, you must decide whether to confirm, reject, or modify the hypothesis. Keep in mind that there may be several ways to look at your data, depending on which theoretical paradigm you apply, and you should consider all interpretations.

9. **What are your conclusions?** Prepare a final report stating your conclusions. How does your work advance sociological theory? Improve research methods? Does your study have policy implications? What would the general public find interesting in your work? Finally, evaluate your own work, noting problems that arose and questions left unanswered.

10. **How can you share what you've learned?** Consider sending your research paper to a campus newspaper or magazine or making a presentation to a class, a campus gathering, or perhaps a meeting of professional sociologists. The point is to share what you have learned with others and to let them respond to your work.

living in poverty (National Center for Children in Poverty, cited in *Population Today*, 1995). As the figure shows, the researchers reported that 43 percent of these children lived in a household with no working parent, 39 percent lived in a household with one or two parents employed part time, and 18 percent lived in a household with one or two parents working full time. The researchers labeled this figure "Majority of Children in Poverty Live with Parents Who Work." Do you think this interpretation is accurate or misleading?

3. People use graphs to spin the truth. Especially in newspapers and other popular media, we find statistics in the form of charts and graphs.

Graphs help explain data, showing, for example, an upward or downward trend. But using graphs also gives people the opportunity to "spin" data in various ways. What trend we think we see depends, in part, on the time frame used in a graph. During the last ten years, for instance, the U.S. crime rate has fallen. But if we were to look at the last fifty years, we would see an opposite trend: The crime rate pushed sharply upward.

The scale used to draw a graph is also important because it lets a researcher "inflate" or "deflate" a trend. Both graphs below present identical data for College Board SAT verbal scores between 1967 and 2003. But the left-hand graph stretches the scale to show

a downward trend; the right-hand graph compresses the scale, showing a steady trend. So, understanding what statistics do—or don't—mean depends on being a careful reader!

Continue the debate . . .

1. Why do you think people are so quick to accept "statistics" as true?

2. From a scientific point of view, is spinning the truth acceptable? What about from the view of a critical approach trying to advance social change?

3. Can you find a news story on some social issue that you think presents biased data or conclusions? What are the biases?

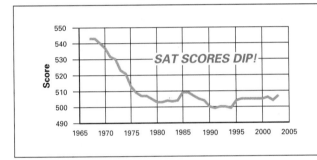

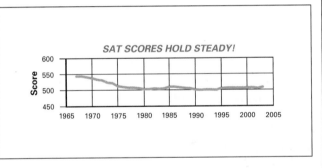

SUMMARY

1. Two basic requirements for sociological investigation are (a) using the sociological perspective and (b) being curious and asking questions about the world around us.

2. Scientific sociology studies society by systematically observing social behavior. This methodological approach requires carefully operationalizing concepts and ensuring that measurement is both reliable (consistent) and valid (precise).

3. A goal of science is to discover how variables are related. Correlation means that two or more variables change value together. A cause-and-effect relationship means that change in one variable actually causes change in another variable. When a cause-and-effect

relationship exists, a researcher who knows the value of an independent variable can predict the value of some dependent variable.

4. Although investigators select topics according to their personal interests, the scientific ideal of objectivity demands that they try to suspend personal values and biases as they conduct research.

5. Interpretive sociology is a methodological approach that focuses on the meaning that people attach to their behavior. Reality is not "out there" but is constructed by people in their everyday interaction.

6. Critical sociology is a methodological approach that uses research as a means of social change. Critical sociology

rejects the scientific principle of objectivity, claiming that all research has a political character.

7. The logic of science is most clearly expressed in the experiment, which is performed under controlled conditions and tries to specify causal relationships between two (or more) variables.

8. Surveys measure people's attitudes or behavior using questionnaires or interviews.

9. Participant observation is a method in which a researcher directly observes a social setting while participating in it for an extended period of time.

10. Secondary analysis is making use of existing data. This method is easier and often more efficient than collecting data firsthand, and it allows the study of historical issues.

11. Theory and research are linked in two ways. Deductive logical thought starts with general theories and generates specific hypotheses suitable for testing. Inductive logical thought starts with specific observations and builds general theories.

KEY CONCEPTS

science (p. 28) a logical system that bases knowledge on direct, systematic observation

scientific sociology (p. 28) the study of society based on systematic observation of social behavior

empirical evidence (p. 28) information we can verify with our senses

concept (p. 30) a mental construct that represents some part of the world in a simplified form

variable (p. 30) a concept whose value changes from case to case

measurement (p. 30) a procedure for determining the value of a variable in a specific case

operationalize a variable (p. 30) specifying exactly what one is to measure before assigning a value to a variable

reliability (p. 31) consistency in measurement

validity (p. 31) actually measuring exactly what one intends to measure

cause and effect (p. 32) a relationship in which change in one variable (the independent variable) causes change in another (the dependent variable)

independent variable (p. 32) a variable that causes change in another (dependent) variable

dependent variable (p. 32) a variable that is changed by another (independent) variable

correlation (p. 32) a relationship in which two (or more) variables change together

spurious correlation (p. 33) an apparent, although false, relationship between two (or more) variables caused by some other variable

control (p. 33) holding constant all variables except one in order to see clearly the effect of that variable

objectivity (p. 34) personal neutrality in conducting research

replication (p. 35) repetition of research by other investigators

interpretive sociology (p. 36) the study of society that focuses on the meanings people attach to their social world

critical sociology (p. 36) the study of society that focuses on the need for social change

gender (p. 37) the personal traits and social positions that members of a society attach to being female or male

research method (p. 38) a systematic plan for conducting research

experiment (p. 38) a research method for investigating cause and effect under highly controlled conditions

hypothesis (p. 38) an unverified statement of a relationship between variables

Hawthorne effect (p. 40) a change in a subject's behavior caused simply by the awareness of being studied

survey (p. 41) a research method in which subjects respond to a series of statements or questions in a questionnaire or an interview

population (p. 41) the people who are the focus of research

sample (p. 41) a part of a population that represents the whole

questionnaire (p. 42) a series of written questions a researcher presents to subjects

interview (p. 42) a series of questions a researcher administers in person to respondents

participant observation (p. 45) a research method in which investigators systematically observe people while joining them in their routine activities

secondary analysis (p. 48) a research method in which a researcher uses data collected by others

inductive logical thought (p. 50) reasoning that transforms specific observations into general theory

deductive logical thought (p. 50) reasoning that transforms general theory into specific hypotheses suitable for testing

CRITICAL-THINKING QUESTIONS

1. What does it mean to say that there are various kinds of truth? What are the advantages and limitations of science as a way of knowing?

2. How does interpretive sociology differ from scientific sociology? What about critical sociology? Which approach best describes the work of these founders of sociology: Emile Durkheim, Max Weber, and Karl Marx?

3. Why do some sociologists argue, and others disagree, that objectivity is essential to sound research? Why do other sociologists disagree?

4. What are some differences between "hard" research (such as scientific experiments) and "soft" research (such as participant observation)?

APPLICATIONS AND EXERCISES

1. Imagine that you are observing your instructor in an effort to assess his or her skills as a teacher. Operationalize the concept "good teaching." What specific traits might you identify as relevant evidence? Do you think students are always good judges of strong teaching?

2. Drop by to see at least three sociology instructors (or other social science instructors) during their office hours. Ask each the extent to which sociology is an objective science. Do they agree about the character of their discipline? Why or why not?

3. You can do sociological research while watching television. In recent years, some critics have claimed that African Americans are not very visible on primetime television. Select a sample of primetime shows and systematically keep track of the race of major characters. Notice that you will have to decide what "primetime" means, what a "major" character is, how to gauge someone's "race," and other issues before you begin. Sketch out a research plan.

4. Packaged in the back of this new textbook is an interactive CD-ROM that offers a variety of video and interactive review materials intended to help you better understand the material covered in this chapter. For this chapter, the CD-ROM contains a relevant clip from *ABC News*, an author's tip video, interactive map animations, an interactive time line, and flashcards with audio pronunciations of the more difficult words.

SITES TO SEE

http://www.prenhall.com/macionis

Visit the interactive Companion Website™ that accompanies this text. Begin by clicking on the cover of your book. You will find a chapter-by-chapter study guide, practice tests, suggested Web links, and links to other relevant material.

http://www.ameristat.org

The Population Reference Bureau offers statistical data for the United States at this Web site.

http://quickfacts.census.gov/qfd/

Data for any county in the United States are available from this Census Bureau Web site. Visit this site and prepare a sociological profile of your local area.

http://www.TheSociologyPage.com
(or **http://www.macionis.com**)

You can find more than fifty Web links to sociological journals and other sources of data and information by visiting the "Links Library" at the author's personal Web site.

INVESTIGATE WITH RESEARCH NAVIGATOR™

Follow the instructions on page 24 of this text to access the features of **Research Navigator™**. Once at the Web site, enter your Login Name and Password. Then, to use the **Content Select™** database, enter keywords such as "science," "questionnaire," and "participant observation," and the search engine will supply relevant and recent scholarly and popular press publications. Use the *New York Times* **Search-by-Subject Archive** to find recent news articles related to sociology and the **Link Library** feature to find relevant Web links organized by the key terms associated with this chapter.

CHAPTER 3

CULTURE

UTAGAWA KUNISADA (1786–1864, JAPANESE)
Painting and Calligraphy Party at the Manpachiro Teahouse

1827, color woodblock print, 18.7 × 25.4 cm. Fitzwilliam Museum, University of Cambridge, UK/The Bridgeman Art Library.

BACK IN 1990, EXECUTIVES of Charles Schwab & Co. assembled at the investment brokerage's headquarters. During their meeting, officials discussed strategies to expand the company's business. One conclusion that came from this meeting was that the company would profit by taking greater account of the increasing racial and ethnic diversity of the United States.

In particular, officials noted, Census Bureau data showed the number of Asian Americans was rising very rapidly, not only in San Francisco but across the country. The data also showed a trend that is still true today: that Asian Americans are, on average, affluent, with more than one-third earning more than $75,000 a year (in today's dollars).

Schwab therefore launched a diversity initiative, assigning three executives to work exclusively on building awareness of the company among Asian Americans. In the years since then, the scope of the initiative has grown: Today, Schwab employs more than 300 people who are fluent in Chinese, Japanese, Korean, Vietnamese, or another Asian language. This is important because research shows that most Asian Americans who come to the United States prefer to communicate in their first language. In addition, the company has launched Web sites using Chinese and other Asian languages. Finally, the company has opened branch offices in many Asian American neighborhoods in cities on the East and West Coasts.

What has been the result of this diversity initiative? Schwab claims a substantial increase in its share of business with Asian Americans. Because estimates place the annual buying power of Asian Americans at more

than $250 billion, any company would do well to follow Schwab's lead. Indeed, businesses gain an advantage by learning to attract the interest of not only Asian Americans but African Americans, Hispanics, and all segments of the U.S. population (Fattah, 2002).

The truth is that the United States is the most *multicultural* of all the world's nations, a fact that reflects this nation's long history of receiving immigrants from elsewhere. Indeed, the cultural diversity of the world as a whole is truly astounding, involving not only differences in musical tastes and preferred foods, but also differences in family patterns and beliefs about right and wrong. Some of the world's people have many children, while others have few; some honor the elderly while others are obsessed with youth. Some societies are peaceful while others are warlike; and segments of humanity embrace a thousand different religious beliefs as well as particular ideas about what is polite and rude, beautiful and ugly, pleasant and repulsive. This amazing human capacity for so many different ways of life is a matter of human culture.

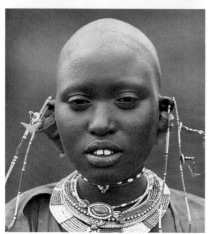  

Human beings around the globe create diverse ways of life. Such differences begin with outward appearance: Contrast the women shown here from Brazil, Kenya, New Guinea, and South Yemen, and the men from Taiwan (Republic of China), India, Canada, and New Guinea. Less obvious, but of even greater importance, are internal differences, since culture also shapes our goals in life, our sense of justice, and even our innermost personal feelings.

WHAT IS CULTURE?

Culture is *the values, beliefs, behavior, and material objects that together form a people's way of life.* Culture includes what we think, how we act, and what we own. Culture is both a bridge to our past and a guide to the future (Soyinka, 1991).

To understand all that culture entails, we must distinguish between thoughts and things. **Nonmaterial culture** is *the intangible world of ideas created by members of a society,* ideas that range from altruism to zen. **Material culture,** on the other hand, is *the tangible things created by members of a society,* everything from armaments to zippers.

Not only does culture shape what we do, but it also helps form our personalities—what we commonly, but wrongly, describe as "human nature." The warlike Yąnomamö of the Brazilian rain forest think aggression is natural, whereas, halfway around the world, the Semai of Malaysia live in peace and cooperation. The cultures of the United States and Japan both stress achievement and hard work, but members of our society value individualism more than the Japanese, who value collective harmony.

Given the extent of cultural differences in the world and people's tendency to view their own way of life as "better" or "natural," it is no wonder that travelers often find themselves feeling uneasy as they enter an unfamiliar culture. This uneasiness is **culture shock,** *personal disorientation when experiencing an unfamiliar way of life.* People can experience culture shock right here in the United States, when, say, African Americans explore an Iranian neighborhood in Los Angeles, college students venture into the Amish countryside in Ohio, or New Yorkers travel through small towns in the Deep South. But culture shock is most intense when we travel abroad: The box on page 60 tells the story of a U.S. researcher making his first visit to the home of the Yąnomamö people living in the Amazon region of South America.

 The author offers a short video discussing the challenges and benefits of travel at http://www.TheSociologyPage.com

December 1, Istanbul, Turkey. Harbors everywhere, it seems, have two things in common: ships and cats. Istanbul, the tenth port on our voyage, is awash with felines, prowling about in search of an easy meal. People certainly change from place to place—but not cats.

Behavior that people in one society consider routine can be chilling to members of another culture. In the Russian city of St. Petersburg, this young mother and her six-week-old son brave the 17°F temperatures for a dip in a nearby lake. To Russians, this is something of a national pastime. To some members of our society, however, this practice may seem cruel or even dangerous.

No way of life is "natural" to humanity, even though most people around the world view their own behavior that way. What comes naturally to members of our species is creating culture. Every other form of life—from ants to zebras—behaves in uniform, species-specific ways. To a traveler, the enormous diversity of human life stands out in contrast to the behavior of, say, cats, which is the same everywhere. This uniformity follows from the fact that most living creatures are guided by *instincts,* biological programming over which animals have no control. A few animals—notably chimpanzees and related primates—have the capacity for limited culture, as researchers have noted by observing them use tools and teach simple skills to their offspring. But the creative power of humans far exceeds that of any other form of life. In short, *only humans rely on culture rather than instinct to ensure the survival of their kind* (M. Harris, 1987). To understand how human culture came to be, we need to look back at the history of our species.

GLOBAL SOCIOLOGY

Confronting the Yąnomamö: The Experience of Culture Shock

A small aluminum motorboat chugged steadily along the muddy Orinoco River, deep within South America's vast tropical rain forest. Anthropologist Napoleon Chagnon was nearing the end of a three-day journey to the home territory of the Yąnomamö, one of the most technologically simple societies on Earth.

Some 12,000 Yąnomamö live in villages scattered along the border of Venezuela and Brazil. Their way of life could hardly be more different from our own. The Yąnomamö wear little clothing and live without electricity, automobiles, or other familiar conveniences. Their traditional weapon, used for hunting and warfare, is the bow and arrow. Most of the Yąnomamö had had little contact with the outside world, so Chagnon would be as strange to them as they would be to him.

By 2:00 in the afternoon, Chagnon had almost reached his destination. The heat and humidity were almost unbearable. He was soaked with perspiration, and his face and hands swelled from the bites of gnats swarming around him. But he scarcely noticed, so excited was he that in just a few moments he would

be face to face with people unlike any he had ever known.

Chagnon's heart pounded as the boat slid onto the riverbank. Chagnon and his guide climbed from the boat and headed toward the sounds of a nearby village, pushing their way through the dense undergrowth. Chagnon describes what happened next:

I looked up and gasped when I saw a dozen burly, naked, sweaty, hideous men staring at us down the shafts of their drawn arrows! Immense wads of green tobacco were stuck between their lower teeth and lips making them look even more hideous, and

strands of dark green slime dripped or hung from their nostrils—strands so long that they clung to their [chests] or drizzled down their chins.

My next discovery was that there were a dozen or so vicious, underfed dogs snapping at my legs, circling me as if I were to be their next meal. I just stood there holding my notebook, helpless and pathetic. Then the stench of the decaying vegetation and filth hit me and I almost got sick. I was horrified. What kind of welcome was this for the person who came here to live with you and learn your way of life, to become friends with you? (1992:11–12)

Fortunately for Chagnon, the Yąnomamö villagers recognized his guide and lowered their weapons. Though reassured that he would survive the afternoon, Chagnon was still shaken by his inability to make any sense of the people surrounding him. And this was to be his home for a year and a half! He wondered why he had forsaken physics to study human culture in the first place.

Source: Chagnon (1992).

CULTURE AND HUMAN INTELLIGENCE

Scientists tell us that our planet is 4.5 billion years old (see the time line inside the front cover of this text). Life appeared about 1 billion years later. Fast-forward another 2 to 3 billion years and we find dinosaurs ruling the Earth. It was when these giant creatures disappeared—some 65 million years ago—that our history took a crucial turn with the appearance of the creatures we call primates.

The importance of primates is that they have the largest brains relative to body size of all living creatures. About 12 million years ago, primates began to evolve along two different lines, setting humans apart from the great apes, our closest relatives. Then, some 3 million years ago, our distant human ancestors climbed down from the trees of central Africa to move about in the tall grasses. There, walking upright, they learned the advantages of hunting in groups and made use of fire, tools, and weapons, built simple shelters, and fashioned basic clothing. These Stone Age achievements may seem modest, but they mark the point at which our ancestors set off on a distinct evolutionary course, making culture their primary strategy for survival. By about 250,000 years ago, our own species—*Homo sapiens* (derived from the Latin meaning "thinking person")—finally emerged. Humans continued to evolve so that, by about 40,000 years ago, people who looked more or less like ourselves roamed the Earth. With larger brains, these "modern" *Homo sapiens* developed culture rapidly, as the wide range of tools and cave art from this period suggests.

By about 12,000 years ago, the founding of permanent settlements and the creation of specialized occupations in the Middle East (in what today is Iraq and Egypt) marked the "birth of civilization." At this point, the biological forces we call instincts were long gone in favor of a more efficient survival scheme: *fashioning the environment for ourselves.* Ever since, humans have made and remade their worlds in countless ways, resulting in today's fascinating cultural diversity.

CULTURE, NATION, AND SOCIETY

The term "culture" calls to mind other similar terms, such as "nation" and "society," although each has a slightly different meaning. *Culture* refers to a shared way of life. A *nation* is a political entity, that is, a territory with designated borders, such as the United States, Canada, Peru, or Zimbabwe. *Society*, the topic of the next chapter, is the organized interaction of people in a nation or within some other boundary.

The United States, then, is both a nation and a society. But many nations, including the United States, are *multicultural*; that is, their people follow various ways of life that blend (and sometimes clash).

HOW MANY CULTURES?

In the United States, how many cultures are there? One clue is that the Census Bureau lists more than 200 languages spoken in this country, most of which were brought by immigrants from nations around the world.

Globally, experts document almost 7,000 languages, suggesting the existence of as many distinct cultures. Yet the number of languages spoken around the world is declining, and roughly half now are spoken by fewer than 10,000 people. Experts expect that the coming decades may see the disappearance of dozens of these languages, from Gullah, Pennsylvania German, and Pawnee (all spoken in the United States), to Han (spoken in northwest Canada), to Oro in the Amazon region (Brazil), to Sardinian (spoken on the European island of Sardinia), to Aramaic (the

People throughout the world communicate not just with spoken words but also with bodily gestures. Because gestures vary from culture to culture, they can occasionally be the cause for misunderstandings. For instance, the commonplace "thumbs up" gesture we use to express "Good job!" can get a person from the United States into trouble in Australia, where people take it to mean "Up yours!"

language of Jesus of Nazareth in the Middle East), to Nushu (spoken in southern China and the only language known to be used only by women), to Wakka Wakka and several other Aboriginal tongues spoken in Australia. Why the decline? Likely reasons for the trend include high-technology communication, increasing international migration, and an expanding global economy (UNESCO, 2001; Barovick, 2002).

THE COMPONENTS OF CULTURE

Although cultures vary greatly, they all have five common components: symbols, language, values and beliefs, norms, and material culture, including technology. We begin with the one that underlies all the others: symbols.

SYMBOLS

Like all creatures, humans use their senses to experience the surrounding world, but unlike others, we also try to give the world *meaning*. Humans transform elements of the world into **symbols,** *anything that carries*

Around the world, McDonald's is a symbol of U.S. culture. This is why anti-war activists in Buenos Aires, Argentina, chose this site in 2003 to protest the U.S.-led war in Iraq.

a particular meaning recognized by people who share a culture. A word, a whistle, a wall of graffiti, a flashing red light, a raised fist—all serve as symbols. We can see the human capacity to create and manipulate symbols reflected in the very different meanings associated with the simple act of winking the eye, which can convey interest, understanding, or insult.

We are so dependent on our culture's symbols that we take them for granted. Sometimes, however, we become keenly aware of a symbol when someone uses it in an unconventional way, as when a person burns a U.S. flag during a political demonstration. Entering an unfamiliar culture also reminds us of the power of symbols; culture shock is really the inability to "read" meaning in new surroundings. Not understanding the symbols of a culture leaves a person feeling lost and isolated, unsure of how to act, and sometimes frightened.

Because people attach different meanings to the world, culture shock is a two-way process. On the one hand, travelers *experience* culture shock when encountering people whose way of life is different. For example, North Americans who consider dogs beloved household pets might be put off by the Masai of eastern Africa, who ignore and never feed them. The same travelers might be horrified to find that, in parts of Indonesia and the northern regions of the People's Republic of China, people roast dogs for dinner.

On the other hand, a traveler *inflicts* culture shock on local people by acting in ways that offend them. A North American who asks for a cheeseburger in an Indian restaurant offends Hindus, who consider cows sacred and never to be eaten.

Global travel provides almost endless opportunities for misunderstanding. In unfamiliar settings, we need to remember that even behavior that seems innocent and normal to us can offend others.

Symbolic meanings also vary within a single society. A fur coat may represent a prized symbol of success or the inhumane treatment of animals. In debates about whether several southern states should continue to display the Confederate flag, some people see this flag as a symbol of regional heritage and pride; others, however, see the flag as a symbol of racial oppression (Broughton, 2001).

Finally, societies create new symbols all the time. The box offers a case in point, describing some of the new cyber-symbols that have developed along with our increasing use of computers for communication.

LANGUAGE

In infancy, an illness left Helen Keller (1880–1968) blind and deaf. Without these two senses, she was cut off from the symbolic world, and her social development was greatly limited. Only when her teacher, Anne Mansfield Sullivan, broke through Keller's isolation using sign language did Helen Keller begin to

APPLYING SOCIOLOGY

The New Cyber-Symbols

It all started with the "smiley" figure that shows one is happy or telling a joke. Now a new language of gestures is emerging as creative people use computer keystrokes to create emoticons, symbols that convey thoughts and emotions. Here is a sampling of the new cyber-language. (Rotate this page 90° to the right to appreciate the emoticon faces.)

:-)   I'm smiling at you.

:`-)   I'm so happy (laughing so hard) that I'm starting to cry.

:-O   Wow!

:-x   My lips are sealed!

:-l l I'm angry with you!

:-P   I'm sticking my tongue out at you!

:-(I feel sad.

:-   Things look grim.

%-}   I think I've had too much to drink.

-:(Somebody cut my hair into a mohawk!

+O:-) I've just been elected pope!

@}———>——— Here's a rose for you!

Computers are as popular in Japan as they are in the United States. The Japanese have their own emoticons:

(^_^)   I'm smiling at you.

(\`^o^\`) This is exciting!

(^o^)   I am happy.

\(^o^)/ Banzai! This is wonderful!

How far will this new keyboard language go? If you're creative enough, anything is possible. Here's a routine that has been making the rounds on the Internet. It's called "Mr. Asciihead learns the Macarena"! To see Mr. Asciihead in action, go to the link at http://www.TheSociologyPage.com

```
 o        o        o        o
.l.      \l.      \l/      //
/\       >\       /<       >\

 o       <o      <o>      o>       o
 X        \       |       <l      <l>
/<       >\      /<       >\      /<
```

Sources: Pollack (1996) and Krantz (1997).
"Mr. Asciihead" is the creation of Leow Yee Ling.

---

realize her human potential. This remarkable woman, who later became a renowned educator herself, recalls the moment she grasped the concept of language:

> We walked down the path to the well-house, attracted by the smell of honeysuckle with which it was covered. Someone was drawing water, and my teacher placed my hand under the spout. As the cool stream gushed over one hand, she spelled into the other the word *water*, first slowly, then rapidly. I stood still, my whole attention fixed upon the motions of her fingers. Suddenly I felt a misty consciousness as of something forgotten—a thrill of returning thought; and somehow the mystery of language was revealed to me. I knew then that "w-a-t-e-r" meant the wonderful cool something that was flowing over my hand. That living word awakened my soul; gave it light, hope, joy, set it free! (1903:21–24)

To learn more about the life of Helen Keller, go to http://www.helen-keller.freeservers.com

Language, the key to the world of culture, is *a system of symbols that allows people to communicate with one another.* Humans have devised hundreds of alphabets, and even conventions for writing differ. Most people in Western societies write from left to right, but people in northern Africa and western Asia write right to left, and people in eastern Asia write from top to bottom. Global Map 3–1 on page 64 shows where one finds the three most widely spoken languages.

Language not only allows communication but also ensures the continuity of culture. Language is a cultural heritage and the key to **cultural transmission,** *the process by which one generation passes culture to the next.* Just as our bodies contain the genes of our ancestors, so our culture contains countless symbols of those who came before us. Language is the key that unlocks centuries of accumulated wisdom.

Every society transmits culture through speech, a process sociologists call the "oral cultural tradition." Some 5,000 years ago, however, humans invented writing, although, at that time, only a privileged few learned to read and write. Not until the twentieth

WINDOW ON THE WORLD

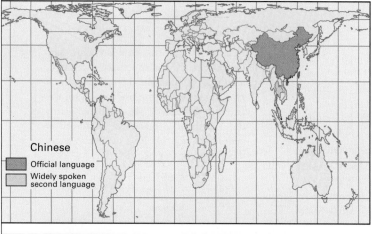

Chinese
■ Official language
□ Widely spoken second language

GLOBAL MAP 3–1
Language in Global Perspective

Chinese (including Mandarin, Cantonese, and dozens of other dialects) is the native tongue of one-fifth of the world's people, almost all of whom live in Asia. Although all Chinese people read and write with the same characters, they use several dozen dialects. The "official" dialect, taught in schools throughout the People's Republic of China and the Republic of Taiwan, is Mandarin (the dialect of Beijing, China's historic capital city). Cantonese, the language of Canton, is the second most common Chinese dialect; it differs in sound from Mandarin roughly the way French differs from Spanish.

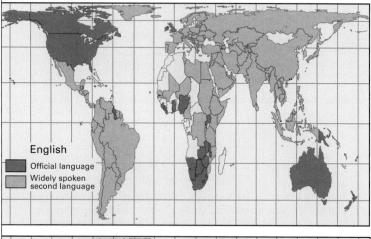

English
■ Official language
□ Widely spoken second language

English is the native tongue or official language in several world regions (spoken by one-tenth of humanity) and has become the preferred second language in most of the world.

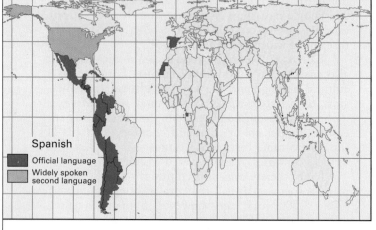

Spanish
■ Official language
□ Widely spoken second language

The largest concentration of Spanish speakers is in Latin America and, of course, Spain. Spanish is also the second most widely spoken language in the United States.

Source: *Peters Atlas of the World* (1990); updated by the author.

century did high-income nations boast of nearly universal literacy. Still, at least 10 percent of U.S. adults (some 20 million people) are functionally illiterate, unable to read and write in a society that increasingly demands symbolic skills. In low-income countries of the world, about one-third of men and one-half of women are illiterate (The World Bank, 2003).

Language may link us with the past, but it also sets free the human imagination. Connecting symbols in new ways, we can conceive of an almost limitless range of ideas and possibilities. Among all life forms, language sets humans apart as the only creatures who are self-conscious, aware of our limitations and ultimate mortality, yet able to dream and to hope for a future better than the present.

Language: Only for Humans?

Creatures great and small direct sounds, smells, and gestures toward one another. In most cases, these signals are instinctive. But some animals have at least some ability to use symbols to communicate with one another and with humans.

Consider the remarkable achievement of a twenty-three-year-old pygmy chimp named Kanzi. Chimpanzees lack the physical ability to mimic human speech. But researcher E. Sue Savage-Rumbaugh discovered that Kanzi could learn language by listening to and observing people. Under Savage-Rumbaugh's supervision, Kanzi has developed a vocabulary of several hundred words, and he has learned to "speak" by pointing to pictures on a special keyboard. He can respond to requests like "Will you get a diaper for your sister?" or "Put the melon in the potty." Kanzi's abilities go beyond mere rote learning because he can respond to requests he has not heard before. In short, Kanzi has the language ability of a human child of two-and-one-half years (Linden, 1993).

Still, the language skills of chimps, dolphins, and a few other animals are limited. Even specially trained animals cannot, on their own, pass on language skills to others of their kind. But the achievements of Kanzi and others caution us against assuming that humans alone can lay any claim to culture.

Does Language Shape Reality?

Does someone who speaks Cherokee, an American Indian language, experience the world differently from other North Americans who think in, say, English or Spanish? Edward Sapir and Benjamin Whorf claimed the answer is "yes," since each language has its own distinctive symbols that serve as the building blocks of reality (Sapir, 1929, 1949; Whorf, 1956; orig. 1941). Further, they noted that each language has words or expressions not found in any other symbolic system. Finally, all languages fuse symbols with distinctive emotions so that, as multilingual people can attest, a single idea may "feel" different when spoken in Spanish rather than in English or Chinese (Falk, 1987).

Formally, then, the **Sapir-Whorf thesis** states that *people perceive the world through the cultural lens of language.* In the decades since Sapir and Whorf published their work, however, scholars have taken issue with this thesis. Current thinking is that, while we do fashion reality out of our symbols, evidence does not support the notion that language *determines* reality the way Sapir and Whorf claimed. For example, we know that children understand the idea of "family" long before they learn that word; similarly, adults can imagine new ideas or things before devising a name for them (Kay & Kempton, 1984; Pinker, 1994).

VALUES AND BELIEFS

What accounts for the popularity of Hollywood film characters such as James Bond, Dirty Harry, Rambo, and Erin Brockovich? Each is ruggedly individualistic, going it alone and relying on personal skill and savvy to challenge "the system." In applauding such characters, we are endorsing certain **values,** *culturally defined standards by which people assess desirability, goodness, and beauty and that serve as broad guidelines for social living.* Values are statements, from the standpoint of a culture, of what ought to be.

Values are broad principles that underlie **beliefs,** *specific statements that people hold to be true.* In other words, values are abstract standards of goodness, and beliefs are particular matters that individuals consider true or false. For example, because most U.S. adults share the value of providing equal opportunities for all, they believe a qualified woman could serve as president of the United States (NORC, 2003).

Cultural values and beliefs not only affect how we perceive our surroundings but also help form our personalities. We learn from families, friends, schools, and religious organizations to think and act according to particular principles, to believe worthy "truths," and to pursue worthy goals. Even so, in a nation as large and diverse as the United States, few cultural values and beliefs are shared by everyone. Our long

Australian feminist artist Sally Swain alters a famous artist's painting to make fun of our culture's tendency to ignore the everyday lives of women. This spoof is entitled Mrs. Warhol Is of Two Minds about What to Cook for Dinner.

history of immigration has made the United States a cultural mosaic. In this regard, this country differs from many nations—such as China and Japan—that are more culturally homogeneous.

Key Values of U.S. Culture

Although U.S. culture is not uniform, sociologist Robin Williams (1970) has identified ten values that are widespread and viewed by many as central to our way of life:

1. **Equal opportunity.** People in the United States endorse not *equality of condition* but *equality of opportunity*. This means that society should provide everyone with the chance to get ahead according to individual talents and efforts.

2. **Achievement and success.** Our way of life encourages competition so that each person's rewards should reflect personal merit. Moreover, greater success confers worthiness on a person—the mantle of being a "winner."

3. **Material comfort.** Success in the United States generally means making money and enjoying what it will buy. Although people sometimes say that "money won't buy happiness," most pursue wealth all the same.

4. **Activity and work.** Popular U.S. heroes, from film's famed archaeologist Indiana Jones to golf champion Tiger Woods, are "doers" who get the job done. Our culture values *action* over *reflection* and controlling events over passively accepting one's fate.

5. **Practicality and efficiency.** People in the United States value the practical over the theoretical, "doing" over "dreaming." Activity has value to the extent that it earns money. "Major in something that will help you get a job!" parents say to their college-age children.

6. **Progress.** We are an optimistic people who, despite waves of nostalgia, believe that the present is better than the past. We celebrate progress, equating the "very latest" with the "very best."

7. **Science.** We expect scientists to solve problems and improve the quality of our lives. We believe we are rational people, which probably explains our cultural tendency (especially among men) to devalue emotion and intuition as sources of knowledge.

8. **Democracy and free enterprise.** Members of our society recognize individual rights that should not be overridden by government. We believe a just political system is based on free elections in which adults select their leaders and on an economy that responds to the choices of individual consumers.

9. **Freedom.** Our cultural value of freedom means that we favor individual initiative over collective conformity. While we acknowledge that everyone has responsibilities to others, we believe that people should be free to pursue their personal goals with minimal interference from anyone else.

In the United States, many people measure the quality of their lives in terms of the material things they have been able to accumulate. Here, a family living in American Canyon, California, proudly shows off their possessions. Do you think material things are a good measure of quality of life? Why or why not?

10. **Racism and group superiority.** Despite strong notions about individualism and freedom, there remains a tendency for most people in the United States to evaluate individuals according to gender, race, ethnicity, and social class. In general, U.S. culture values males above females, whites above people of color, people with northwest European backgrounds above those whose ancestors came from other lands, and rich above poor. Although we like to describe ourselves as a nation of equals, there is little doubt that some of us rank as "more equal" than others.

Values: Sometimes in Conflict

Looking over Williams's list, we see that some values are inconsistent and even opposed to one another (Lynd, 1967; Bellah et al., 1985; Ray, 1997). For example, people in the United States believe in equality of opportunity, yet they may also degrade others because of their sex or race.

Conflict between values reflects the cultural diversity of U.S. society and also cultural change by which new trends develop alongside older traditions. Recently, for example, what some observers call a "culture of victimization" has arisen to challenge our society's long-time belief in individual responsibility (J. Best, 1997; Furedi, 1998). The box on pages 68–69 takes a closer look.

Value conflict causes strain and often leads to awkward balancing acts in our beliefs. Sometimes we decide one value is more important than another by, for example, supporting equal opportunity while opposing the acceptance of homosexual people in the U.S. military. In such cases, we simply learn to live with the contradictions.

NORMS

Most people in the United States are eager to gossip about "who's hot" and "who's not." Members of American Indian societies, however, typically condemn such behavior as rude and divisive. Both patterns illustrate the operation of **norms,** *rules and expectations by which a society guides the behavior of its members.* Some norms are *proscriptive,* stating what we should *not* do, as when health officials warn us to avoid casual sex. *Prescriptive* norms, on the other hand, state what we *should* do, as when U.S. schools teach "safe-sex" practices.

Most important norms in a culture apply everywhere and at all times. For example, parents expect obedience from young children regardless of the setting. Other norms depend on the situation. In the United States, we expect the audience to applaud after a musical performance; we may applaud (although it is not expected) at the end of a classroom lecture; we do not applaud at the end of a religious sermon.

CRITICAL THINKING

Don't Blame Me! The "Culture of Victimization"

A University of North Carolina law student walked down the street, took aim with an M-1 rifle, and killed two men he had never met. Later, from a psychiatric hospital, he sued his therapist for not doing enough to prevent his actions. A jury awarded him $500,000. A New York man leaped in front of a subway train; lucky enough to survive, he sued the city, claiming that the train had failed to stop in time to prevent his serious injuries. His award: $650,000. In Washington, D.C., after realizing that he had been videotaped smoking crack cocaine in a hotel room, the city's mayor blamed his woman companion for "setting him up" and suggested that the police had been racially motivated in arresting him. After more than a dozen women accused an Oregon senator of sexual harassment, he claimed his

behavior had been caused by his problem with alcohol. In the most celebrated case of its kind, a former city politician gunned down the mayor of San Francisco and a city council member, blaming his violence on insanity caused by eating too much junk food (the so-called "Twinkie defense").

In each of these cases, someone denied personal responsibility for an action, claiming instead to be a victim. More and more, members of our society are pointing the finger elsewhere, which prompted Irving Horowitz (1993) to declare that our way of life is becoming a "culture of victimization" in which "everyone is a victim" and "no one accepts responsibility for anything."

One indication of this victimization trend is the proliferation of "addictions," a term once associated only with uncontrollable drug use. We now hear

about gambling addicts, compulsive overeaters, sex addicts, and even people who excuse runaway credit-card debt as a shopping addiction. Bookstores overflow with manuals to help people deal with numerous new medical or psychological conditions ranging from the "Cinderella complex" to the "Casanova complex" and even "soap opera syndrome." And U.S. courts are clogged by lawsuits blaming someone for misfortunes that we used to accept as part of life.

What's going on here? Is U.S. culture changing? Historically, our cultural ideal was "rugged individualism," the idea that people are responsible for whatever triumph or tragedy befalls them. But this value has eroded in a number of ways. First, everyone is more aware (partly through the work of sociologists) of how society shapes our

Mores and Folkways

William Graham Sumner (1959; orig. 1906), an early U.S. sociologist, recognized that some norms are more important to our lives than others. Sumner coined the term **mores** (pronounced *more-ays*) to refer to *norms that are widely observed and have great moral significance*. Mores, or *taboos*, include our society's prohibition against adults engaging in sexual relations with children.

People pay less attention to **folkways**, *norms for routine or casual interaction*. Examples include ideas about appropriate greetings and proper dress. In short, mores distinguish between right and wrong, whereas folkways draw a line between right and *rude*. A man who does not wear a tie to a formal dinner party may raise eyebrows for violating folkways. If, however, he were to arrive at the party wearing *only* a tie, he would violate cultural mores and invite more serious sanctions.

Social Control

Mores and folkways are the basic rules of everyday life. Although we sometimes resist pressure to conform, we all can see that norms make our dealings with others more orderly and predictable. Observing or breaking the rules of social life prompts a response from others, in the form of reward or punishment. Sanctions— whether an approving smile or a raised eyebrow—operate as a system of **social control,** *attempts by society to regulate people's thought and behavior.*

As we learn cultural norms, we acquire the capacity to evaluate our own behavior. Doing wrong (say, downloading a term paper from the Internet) can cause both *shame* (the painful sense that others disapprove of our actions) and *guilt* (a negative judgment we make of ourselves). Only cultural creatures can experience shame and guilt. This is probably what Mark Twain had in mind when he remarked that people "are the only animals that blush—or need to."

lives. Thus, categories of people well beyond those who have suffered real historical disadvantages (such as Native Americans, African Americans, and women) now say they are victims. The latest victims include white males who claim that "everybody gets special treatment but us."

Second, especially since they began advertising their services in 1977, many lawyers encourage a sense of injustice among clients they hope to represent in court. The number of million-dollar lawsuit awards has risen more than twenty-five-fold in the last twenty-five years.

Finally, a proliferation of "rights groups" promotes what Amitai Etzioni calls "rights inflation." Beyond the traditional constitutional liberties are many newly claimed rights: those of hunters (as well as animals), the rights of smokers (and non-smokers), the right of women to control their bodies (and the rights of the unborn), the right to own a gun (and the right to be safe from violence). Expanding claims for unmet rights create victims (and victimizers) on all sides.

Does this shift toward victimization signal a fundamental realignment in our individualistic culture? Perhaps, but the new popularity of being a victim also springs from some established cultural forces. For example, the claim to victim-

ization depends on a longstanding belief that everyone has the right to life, liberty, and the pursuit of happiness. What is new, however, is that the explosion of "rights" now does more than alert us to clear cases of injustice: It lessens our responsibility for our own lives.

What do you think?

1. *Do you think our cultural emphasis on individualism is less strong today than in the past? Why?*

2. *Do you think the United States has experienced "rights inflation"? Why or why not?*

3. *Does using the sociological perspective encourage us to view people as victims? Why or why not?*

Sources: Based on Etzioni (1991), Taylor (1991), Hollander (1995), and Roche (1999).

"IDEAL" AND "REAL" CULTURE

Values and norms do not describe actual behavior so much as they suggest how we *should* behave. We must remember that *ideal* culture always differs from *real* culture—what actually occurs in everyday life. To illustrate, most women and men agree on the importance of sexual fidelity in marriage. Even so, in one study, about 25 percent of married men and 10 percent of married women reported having been sexually unfaithful to their spouses at some point in their marriage (Laumann et al., 1994). But a culture's moral prodding is important all the same, calling to mind the old saying "Do as I say, not as I do."

MATERIAL CULTURE AND TECHNOLOGY

In addition to intangible elements such as values and norms, every culture includes a wide range of tangible (from the Latin meaning "touchable") human creations, which sociologists call *artifacts*. The Chinese eat with chopsticks rather than knives and forks, the Japanese put mats rather than rugs on the floor, many men and women in India prefer flowing robes to the close-fitting clothing common in the United States. The material culture of a people may seem as strange to outsiders as their language, values, and norms.

A society's artifacts partly reflect underlying cultural values. The warlike Yanomamö carefully craft their weapons and prize the poison tips on their arrows. By contrast, our society's emphasis on individualism and independence goes a long way toward explaining our high regard for the automobile: We own 217 million motor vehicles—more than one for every licensed driver—and, in recent years, half of all cars sold in the United States are large sports utility vehicles.

In addition to reflecting values, material culture also reflects a society's **technology,** *knowledge that people use to make a way of life in their surroundings.* The more complex a society's technology, the more its

Standards of beauty—including the color and design of everyday surroundings—vary significantly from one culture to another. These two Nankani women put the finishing touches on their lavishly decorated homes. Members of North American and European societies, by contrast, make far less use of bright colors and intricate detail so that their housing appears much more subdued.

many Yąnomamö are eager to acquire modern technology (such as steel tools and shotguns), they are generally well fed by world standards, and most are very satisfied with their lives (Chagnon, 1992). Remember, too, that while our powerful and complex technology has produced work-reducing devices and seemingly miraculous medical treatments, it has also contributed to unhealthy levels of stress and created weapons capable of destroying in a blinding flash everything that humankind has achieved.

Finally, technology is not equally distributed within our population. Although many of us cannot imagine life without personal computers, televisions, and CD players, many members of U.S. society cannot afford these luxuries. Others reject them on principle. The Amish, who live in small farming communities across Pennsylvania, Ohio, and Indiana, shun most modern conveniences on religious grounds. With their traditional black garb and horse-drawn buggies, the Amish may seem like a curious relic of the past. Yet their communities flourish, grounded in strong families that give everyone a sense of identity and purpose. Some researchers have studied the Amish only to conclude that these communities are "islands of sanity in a culture gripped by commercialism and technology run wild" (Hostetler, 1980:4; Kraybill, 1994:28).

NEW INFORMATION TECHNOLOGY AND CULTURE

Many rich nations, including the United States, have entered a postindustrial phase based on computers and new information technology. While industrial production is centered on factories and machinery generating material goods, postindustrial production is based on computers and other electronic devices that create, process, store, and apply information.

In an information economy, workers need symbolic skills in place of the mechanical skills of the industrial age. Symbolic skills include the ability to speak, write, compute, design, and create images in art, advertising, and entertainment. New information technology also enables us to *generate culture* on an unprecedented scale. The box takes a closer look.

CULTURAL DIVERSITY: MANY WAYS OF LIFE IN ONE WORLD

In the United States, we are aware of our cultural diversity when we hear the distinctive accents of people from New England, the Midwest, or the Deep South. Ours is also a nation of religious pluralism, a land of class

members are able (for better or worse) to shape the world for themselves. Advanced technology has allowed us to crisscross the country with superhighways and to fill them with automobiles. At the same time, reliance on internal-combustion engines releases carbon dioxide into the atmosphere, which contributes to global warming.

Because we attach great importance to science and praise sophisticated technology, people in our society tend to judge cultures with simpler technology as less advanced. Some facts support such an assessment. For example, life expectancy for children born in the United States now exceeds seventy-seven years; the lifespan of the Yąnomamö is only about forty years.

However, we must be careful not to make self-serving judgments about other cultures. Although

Virtual Culture: Is It Good for Us?

January 16, Orlando, Florida. Disney World is a delight to the kids but a little disturbing to the sociologist. It is ready-made culture: Streets, stores, and events artificially recreate a nineteenth-century small town populated with Disney characters. Here, life is carefully controlled to ensure a good time, with the ultimate purpose of relieving us of whatever cash we have.

The Information Revolution is generating symbols—words, sounds, and images—faster than ever before and spreading these symbols across the nation and around the world. What does this new information technology mean for our way of life?

In centuries past, culture was a way of life transmitted from generation to generation. It was a heritage—a society's collective memory—that was authentically our own because it had belonged to our ancestors (B. Schwartz, 1996). But in the emerging cyber-society, more and more cultural symbols are new, intentionally *created* by a small cultural elite of composers, writers, filmmakers, and others who work in the expanding information economy.

To illustrate, consider the changing character of cultural heroes, people who serve as role models and represent cultural ideals. A century ago, our heroes were real men and women who had made a difference in the life of this nation—George Washington, Abigail Adams, Betsy Ross, Davy Crockett, Daniel Boone, Abraham Lincoln, and Harriet Tubman. Of course, when a society makes a hero of someone (almost always well after the person has died), it "cleans up" the person's biography, highlighting the successes and overlooking the shortcomings. Even so, these people were authentic parts of our history and shaped the hopes and

dreams of children growing up a century ago.

Today's youngsters, by contrast, are fed a steady diet of *virtual culture*, images that spring from the minds of contemporary culture makers and that reach them via a screen: on television, in the movies, or through computer cyberspace. Today's "heroes" are Powerpuff Girls, Rug Rats, Spongebob, Batman, Barbie, and Barney, a continuous flow of Disney characters, and the ever-smiling Ronald McDonald. Some of these cultural icons embody values that shape our way of life. But they have no historical reality, and almost all have been created for a single purpose: to make money.

What do you think?

1. *Over the course of the twenty-first century, do you think virtual culture will become increasingly important? Why or why not?*

2. *Does virtual culture erode or enhance our cultural traditions? Is that good or bad?*

3. *What image of this country do U.S. movies and television shows give to people abroad?*

Source: Thanks to Roland Johnson (1996) for the basic idea for this box.

---

differences, and a home to individualists who try to be like no one else. Over the centuries, heavy immigration In two brief videos, the author considers issues of cultural relativism at http://www. TheSociologyPage.com has made the United States the most *multicultural* of all high-income countries. By contrast, historic isolation has made Japan the most *monocultural* of all high-income nations.

Between 1820 (when the government began keeping track of immigration) and 2001, more than 67 million people have come to these shores. Moreover, our cultural mix continues to increase as each year almost 1 million more people arrive. A century ago, as shown in Figure 3–1 on page 72, almost all immigrants hailed from Europe; today, most newcomers are from Latin America and Asia. To understand the reality of life in

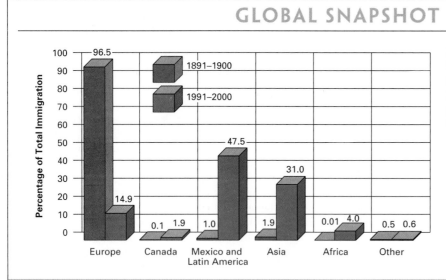

FIGURE 3-1
**Recorded Immigration
to the United States, by Region of Birth,
1891-1900 and 1991-2000**

Source: U.S. Department of Commerce (1930) and U.S. Immigration and Naturalization Service (2002).

the United States, we must move beyond broad cultural patterns and shared values to consider cultural diversity.

HIGH CULTURE AND POPULAR CULTURE

Cultural diversity can involve social class. In fact, in everyday talk, we usually use the term "culture" to mean art forms such as classical literature, music, dance, and painting. We describe people who regularly go to the opera or the theater as "cultured," because we think they appreciate the "finer things in life."

We speak less generously of ordinary people, assuming that everyday culture is somehow less worthy. We are tempted to judge the music of Beethoven as "more cultured" than the blues, couscous as better than cornbread, and polo as more polished than Ping-Pong.

Such judgments imply that many cultural patterns are readily accessible to only some members of a society (Hall & Neitz, 1993). Sociologists use the term **high culture**[1] to refer to *cultural patterns that distinguish a*

society's elite; **popular culture** designates *cultural patterns that are widespread among a society's population.*

Common sense may suggest that high culture is superior to popular culture, but sociologists are uneasy with such judgments, for two reasons. First, neither elites nor ordinary people share all the same tastes and interests; people in both categories differ in numerous ways. Second, do we praise high culture because it is inherently better than popular culture, or simply because its supporters have more money, power, and prestige? For example, there is no difference between a violin and a fiddle; however, we name the instrument one way when it is used to produce music typically enjoyed by a person of higher position and the other way when the musician plays works appreciated by individuals with lower social standing.

How are high culture and popular culture spread across the United States? National Map 3–1 gives some idea, showing preferred alcoholic beverages from coast to coast.

SUBCULTURE

The term **subculture** refers to *cultural patterns that set apart some segment of a society's population.* Surfers, Polish Americans, motorcyclists, jazz musicians, computer "nerds," campus poets, and wilderness campers—all display subcultural patterns.

---

[1]The term "high culture" is derived from the term "highbrow." A century ago, people influenced by phrenology—the bogus nineteenth-century theory that personality was affected by the shape of the human skull—praised the tastes of those they termed "highbrows" while dismissing the appetites of "lowbrows."

SEEING OURSELVES

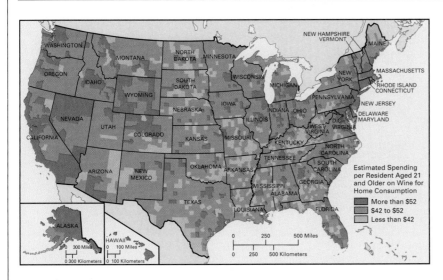

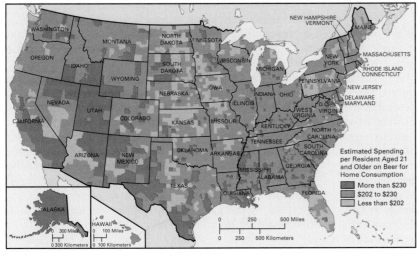

NATIONAL MAP 3–1
What'll Ya Have? Popular Beverages across the United States

What people consume is one mark of their status as a "highbrow" or "lowbrow." Drinking wine at home is an indicator of highbrow standing. Well-to-do people not only enjoy a glass of wine with dinner but drink water from bottles rather than the tap, prefer Grey Poupon to Gulden's mustard, and favor Häagen-Dazs over the local Tastee-Freeze. Drinking beer, on the other hand, marks a person as a "lowbrow." Such a person has a low to moderate income, consumes a good deal of snack food, and frequents fast-food restaurants. On the maps, where have the "highbrows" and the "lowbrows" created centers of "high culture" and "popular culture"?

Source: *American Demographics* magazine, March 1998, p. 19. Reprinted with permission. © 1998, *American Demographics* magazine, Ithaca, New York.

It is easy, but often inaccurate, to place people in some subcultural category, because almost everyone participates in many subcultures without necessarily having much commitment to any of them. In some cases, however, ethnicity and religion do set people apart from one another, sometimes with tragic results. Consider, for example, the former nation of Yugoslavia in southeastern Europe. The recent Balkan war is only the latest chapter in a long history of hatred based on cultural differences. Before its breakup, this *one* small country used *two* alphabets, professed *three* religions, spoke *four* languages, was home to *five* major nationalities, was divided into *six* political republics, and absorbed the cultural influences of *seven* surrounding countries. Clearly, subcultures are a source not only of pleasing variety but also of tension

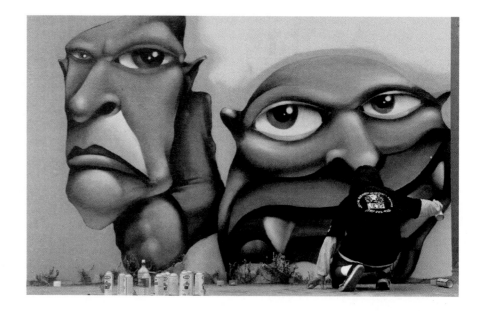

Whether visual expression in lines and color is revered as "art" or dismissed as "graffiti" or even condemned as "vandalism" depends on the social standing of the creator. How would you characterize images such as this one, common in cities across North America? Is this art? Why or why not?

and outright violence (cf. Sekulic, Massey, & Hodson, 1994).

Many people view the United States as a "melting pot" where many nationalities blend into a single new culture; indeed, about eight in ten U.S. adults describe their way of life as "American" (Gardyn, 2001). But given so much cultural diversity, how accurate is the "melting pot" image? For one thing, subcultures involve not just *difference* but *hierarchy*. Too often, what we view as "dominant" or "mainstream" culture are patterns favored by powerful segments of the population, while we view the lives of disadvantaged people as "subculture." For example, are the cultural patterns of rich skiers in Aspen, Colorado, any less a "subculture" than the cultural patterns of street gangs in Los Angeles, California? Some sociologists, therefore, prefer to level the playing field of society by emphasizing multiculturalism.

MULTICULTURALISM

Multiculturalism is *an educational program recognizing the cultural diversity of the United States and promoting the equality of all cultural traditions.* Multiculturalism is a sharp turn away from the past, when our society downplayed cultural diversity and defined itself primarily in terms of its European (and especially English) immigrants. Today, a spirited debate asks whether we should continue to stress these historical traditions or highlight our cultural diversity (Orwin, 1996; Rabkin, 1996).

E pluribus unum, the familiar Latin phrase that appears on all U.S. coins, means "out of many, one." This motto symbolizes not only our national political union but also the idea that immigrants from around the world have come together to form a new way of life.

But from the outset, the many cultures did not melt together as much as harden into a hierarchy. At the top were the English, who formed a majority early in U.S. history and established English as the nation's dominant language. Further down, people of other backgrounds were advised to model themselves after "their betters." In practice, then, "melting" was really a process of Anglicization—adoption of English ways. As multiculturalists see it, early in our history, this society set up the English way of life as an ideal to which all should aspire and by which all should be judged.

Ever since, historians have reported events from the point of view of the English and other people of European ancestry, paying little attention to the perspectives and accomplishments of Native Americans and people of African and Asian descent. Multiculturalists call this view **Eurocentrism,** *the dominance of European (especially English) cultural patterns.* Molefi Kete Asante, an advocate of multiculturalism, argues that, "like the fifteenth-century Europeans who could not cease believing that the Earth was the center of the universe, many today find it difficult to cease viewing European culture as the center of the social universe" (1988:7).

One contested issue involves language. Some people believe English should be the official language of

SEEING OURSELVES

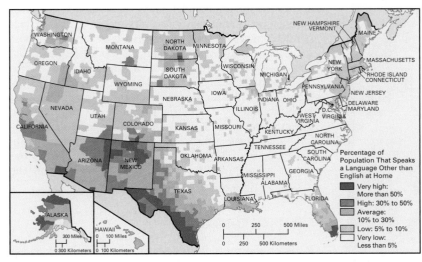

NATIONAL MAP 3–2
Language Diversity
across the United States

Of more than 262 million people over the age of five in the United States, the 2000 Census reports that 47 million (18 percent) typically speak a language other than English at home. Of these people, 60 percent speak Spanish, 15 percent use an Asian language, and the remaining 25 percent communicate with some other tongue (the Census Bureau lists 25 languages, each of which is favored by more than 100,000 people in the United States). The map shows that non-English-speakers are concentrated in certain regions of the country. Which ones? What do you think accounts for this pattern?

Percentage of Population That Speaks a Language Other than English at Home

- Very high: More than 50%
- High: 30% to 50%
- Average: 10% to 30%
- Low: 5% to 10%
- Very low: Less than 5%

0 250 500 Miles
0 250 500 Kilometers

ALASKA
0 300 Miles
0 300 Kilometers

HAWAII
0 100 Miles
0 100 Kilometers

Source: *Time,* January 30, 1995. Copyright © 1995 *Time,* Inc. Reprinted by permission.

the United States. By 2003, legislatures in twenty-seven states had enacted laws making it the official language. But some 47 million men and women—nearly one in six—speak a language other than English at home. Spanish is the second most commonly spoken language, and several hundred other tongues are also heard across the country, including Italian, German, French, Filipino, Japanese, Korean, and Vietnamese, as well as a host of Native American languages. National Map 3–2 shows where in the United States large numbers of people speak a language other than English at home.

Proponents also paint multiculturalism as a way of coming to terms with our country's increasing social diversity. With the Asian and Hispanic populations of this country increasing rapidly, some analysts predict that today's children will live to see people of African, Asian, and Hispanic ancestry become a *majority* of this country's population.

Moreover, they claim, multiculturalism is a good way to strengthen the academic achievement of African American children. To offset Eurocentrism, some multicultural educators are calling for **Afrocentrism,** *the dominance of African cultural patterns,* which they see as a corrective for centuries of minimizing or altogether ignoring the cultural achievements of African societies and African Americans.

Although multiculturalism has found favor in recent years, it has provoked its share of criticism as well. Opponents say it encourages divisiveness rather than unity, urging people to identify with their own category rather than with the nation as a whole. Instead of recognizing any common standards of truth, say critics, multiculturalism maintains that we should evaluate ideas according to the race (and sex) of those who present them. Our common humanity thus dissolves into an "African experience," an "Asian experience," and so on.

But the bottom line, say critics, is that multiculturalism actually harms minorities themselves. Multicultural policies (from African American studies to all-black dorms) seem to endorse the same racial segregation that our nation has struggled so long to end. Furthermore, in the early grades, an Afrocentric curriculum may deny children a wide range of important knowledge and skills by forcing them to study only certain topics from a single point of view. The historian Arthur Schlesinger, Jr. (1991:21), puts the matter bluntly: "If a Kleagle of the Ku Klux Klan wanted to use the schools to handicap black Americans, he could

Any society is actually made up of countless different cultural patterns, some of which may seem strange, indeed, to most people. What cultural values are evident in the pierced noses and tattoos of these two men? Are these values completely at odds with our individualistic way of life?

During the 1960s, for example, a youth-oriented counterculture rejected mainstream culture as overly competitive, self-centered, and materialistic. Instead, hippies and other counterculturalists favored a cooperative lifestyle in which "being" took precedence over "doing" and the capacity for personal growth—or "expanded consciousness"—was prized over material possessions like homes and cars. Such differences led some people to "drop out" of the larger society.

Countercultures are still flourishing. At the extreme, small bands of religious militants exist in the United States, engaging in violence intended to threaten our way of life. Evidence suggests that members of al-Qaeda, one such group under the leadership of Osama bin Laden, lived for years in this country before carrying out the September 11 attacks on the World Trade Center and the Pentagon.

CULTURAL CHANGE

Perhaps the most basic human truth of this world is "All things shall pass." Even the dinosaurs, which thrived on this planet for 160 million years (see the time line), remain today only as fossils. Will humanity survive for millions of years to come? All we can say with certainty is that, given our reliance on culture, for as long as we survive, the human record will show continuous change.

Figure 3–2 shows changes in attitudes among first-year college students between 1969 (the height of the 1960s counterculture) and 2001. Some attitudes have changed only slightly: Today, as a generation ago, most men and women look forward to raising a family. But today's students are less concerned with developing a philosophy of life and much more interested in making money.

Change in one dimension of a culture usually sparks changes in others. For example, today's college women are much more interested in making money because women are now far more likely to be in the labor force than they were several generations ago. Working for income may not change their interest in raising a family, but it does push back the age at first marriage as well as push up the divorce rate. Such connections illustrate the principle of **cultural integration,** *the close relationships among various elements of a cultural system.*

Cultural Lag

Some elements of culture change faster than others. William Ogburn (1964) observed that technology

hardly come up with anything more effective than the 'Afrocentric' curriculum."

Is there any common ground in this debate? Almost everyone agrees that we need greater appreciation of our cultural diversity. But precisely where the balance is to be struck—between the *pluribus* and the *unum*—is likely to remain an issue for some time to come.

COUNTERCULTURE

Cultural diversity also includes outright rejection of conventional ideas or behavior. **Counterculture** refers to *cultural patterns that strongly oppose those widely accepted within a society.*

moves quickly, generating new elements of material culture (like test-tube babies) faster than nonmaterial culture (such as ideas about parenthood) can keep up with them. Ogburn called this inconsistency **cultural lag**, *the fact that some cultural elements change more quickly than others, disrupting a cultural system.* For example, how are we to apply traditional notions about motherhood and fatherhood when one woman can give birth to a child by using another woman's egg, which has been fertilized in a laboratory with the sperm of a total stranger?

Causes of Cultural Change

Cultural changes are set in motion in three ways. The first is *invention*, the process of creating new cultural elements. Invention has given us the telephone (1876), the airplane (1903), and the computer (1947), each of which has had a tremendous impact on our way of life. The process of invention goes on constantly, as indicated by the thousands of applications submitted annually to the U.S. Patent Office. The time line shows other inventions that have helped change our way of life.

Discovery, a second cause of cultural change, involves recognizing and better understanding something already in existence—from a distant star, to the foods of another culture, to women's athletic prowess. Many discoveries result from painstaking scientific research, and others from a stroke of luck, as in 1898, when Marie Curie left a rock on a piece of photographic paper, noticed that emissions from the rock had exposed the paper, and thus discovered radium.

The third cause of cultural change is *diffusion*, the spread of cultural traits from one society to another. Because new information technology sends information around the globe in seconds, cultural diffusion has never been greater than it is today.

Certainly our own society has contributed many significant cultural elements to the world, ranging from computers to jazz music. Of course, diffusion works the other way, too, so that much of what we assume to be "American" actually comes from elsewhere. Most clothing, furniture, clocks, newspapers, money, and even the English language are derived from other cultures (Linton, 1937a).

ETHNOCENTRISM AND CULTURAL RELATIVISM

December 10, a small village in rural Morocco. Watching many of our fellow travelers browsing through a tiny ceramics

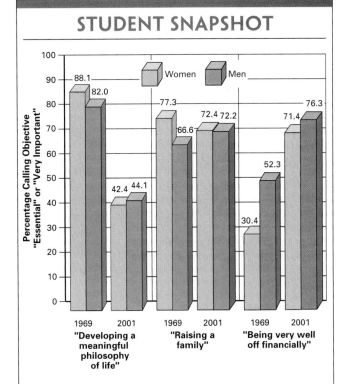

FIGURE 3-2 Life Objectives of First-Year College Students, 1969–2001

Source: Astin et al. (2002).

factory, we have little doubt that North Americans are among the world's greatest shoppers. We delight in surveying hand-woven carpets in China or India, inspecting finely crafted metals in Turkey, or collecting the beautifully colored porcelain tiles we find here in Morocco. Of course, all these items are wonderful bargains. But one major reason for the low prices is unsettling: Many products from the world's low- and middle-income countries are produced by children—some as young as five or six—who work long days for pennies per hour.

In the world's low-income countries, most children must work to provide their families with needed income. This young child in Dhaka, Bangladesh, is sorting discarded materials in a factory that makes recycled lead batteries. Is it ethnocentric for people living in high-income nations to condemn the practice of child labor because we think youngsters belong in school? Why or why not?

We think of childhood as a time of innocence and freedom from adult burdens like regular work. In poor countries throughout the world, however, families depend on income earned by children. So what people in one society think of as right and natural, people elsewhere find puzzling and even immoral. Perhaps the Chinese philosopher Confucius had it right when he noted that "All people are the same; it's only their habits that are different."

Just about every imaginable idea or behavior is commonplace somewhere in the world, and this cultural variation causes travelers equal measures of excitement and distress. The Australians flip light switches down to turn them on, while North Americans flip them up; the Japanese name intersections, while North Americans name streets; Egyptians move very close to others in conversation, while North Americans are used to maintaining several feet of "personal space." Bathrooms lack toilet paper in much of rural Morocco, causing considerable consternation among North Americans, who recoil at the thought of using the left hand for bathroom hygiene.

Given that a particular culture is the basis for everyone's reality, it is no wonder that people everywhere exhibit **ethnocentrism,** *the practice of judging another culture by the standards of one's own culture.* Some degree of ethnocentrism is necessary for people to be emotionally attached to their way of life. But ethnocentrism also generates misunderstanding and sometimes conflict.

Even our language is culturally biased. Centuries ago, people in Europe and North America referred to China as the "Far East." But this term, unknown to the Chinese, is an ethnocentric expression for a region that is "far east" *of us.* The Chinese name for their country translates as "Central Kingdom," suggesting that they, like us, see their own society as the center of the world. The map shows ethnocentrism at work in a "down under" view of the Western Hemisphere.

The logical alternative to ethnocentrism is **cultural relativism,** *the practice of evaluating a culture by its own standards.* Cultural relativism can be difficult for travelers to adopt: It requires not only openness to unfamiliar values and norms, but also the suspension of cultural standards we have known all our lives. Even so, as people of the world come into increasing contact with one another, the importance of understanding other cultures becomes ever greater.

As the opening to this chapter explained, businesses in the United States are learning the value of  marketing to a culturally diverse population. Similarly, businesses are learning that success in the global economy depends on awareness of cultural patterns around the world. IBM, for example, now provides technical support for its products using Web sites in twenty-two languages (Fonda, 2001).

This trend is a change from the past, when many corporations used marketing strategies that lacked

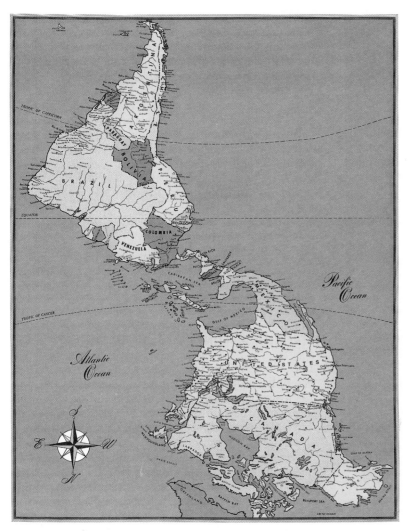

The View from "Down Under"

North America should be "up" and South America "down," or so we think. But because we live on a globe, such notions are conventions rather than absolutes. The reason this map of the Western Hemisphere looks wrong to us is not that it is geographically inaccurate; it simply violates our ethnocentric assumption that the United States should be "above" the rest of the Americas.

sensitivity to cultural diversity. Coors's phrase "Turn It Loose" startled Spanish-speaking customers by proclaiming that the beer would cause diarrhea. Braniff airlines turned "Fly in Leather" into clumsy Spanish reading "Fly Naked." Eastern Airlines transformed its slogan "We Earn Our Wings Daily" into "We Fly Every Day to Heaven." Even Frank Purdue fell victim to poor marketing when his pitch "It Takes a Tough Man to Make a Tender Chicken" ended up in Spanish words reading "A Sexually Excited Man Will Make a Chicken Affectionate" (Helin, 1992).

But cultural relativity introduces problems of its own. If almost any kind of behavior is normative *somewhere* in the world, does that mean everything is equally right? Does the fact that some Indian and Moroccan families benefit from having their children work long hours justify child labor?

Since we all are members of a single species, surely there must be some universal standards of proper conduct. But what are they? And in trying to develop them, how can we avoid imposing our own standards of fair play on others? There are no simple answers. But when confronting an unfamiliar cultural practice, resist making judgments before grasping what "they" think of the issue. Remember, also, to think about your own way of life as others might see it. After all, what we gain most from studying others is better insight into ourselves.

A GLOBAL CULTURE?

Today, more than ever before, we can observe many of the same cultural practices the world over. Walking the streets of Seoul (South Korea), Kuala Lumpur (Malaysia), Madras (India), Cairo (Egypt), and Casablanca (Morocco), we find people wearing jeans, hear familiar pop music, and see advertising for many of the same products we use in this country. Recall, too, from Global Map 3–1, that English is rapidly emerging as the preferred second language around the world. Are we witnessing the birth of a single global culture?

Societies now have more contact with one another than ever before, involving the flow of goods, information, and people:

1. **The global economy: the flow of goods.** There has never been more international trade. The global economy has spread many of the same consumer goods (from cars and TV shows to music and fashions) throughout the world.

2. **Global communications: the flow of information.** Satellite-based communications enable people to experience the sights and sounds of events taking place thousands of miles away—often as they happen.

3. **Global migration: the flow of people.** Knowing about the rest of the world motivates people to move where they imagine life will be better. Moreover, today's transportation technology, especially air travel, makes relocating easier than ever before. As a result, in most countries, significant numbers of people were born elsewhere (including some 33 million people in the United States, 12 percent of the population).

These global links make the cultures of the world more similar. But there are three important limitations to the global culture thesis. First, the global flow of goods, information, and people is uneven. Generally speaking, urban areas (centers of commerce, communication, and people) have stronger ties to one another, while many rural villages remain isolated. Then, too, the greater economic and military power of North America and Western Europe means that these regions influence the rest of the world more than happens the other way around.

Second, the global culture thesis assumes that people everywhere are able to *afford* various new goods and services. As Chapter 12 ("Global Stratification") explains, desperate poverty in much of the world deprives people of even the basic necessities of a safe and secure life.

Third, although many cultural practices are now found throughout the world, people everywhere do not attach the same meanings to them. Do children in Tokyo draw the same lessons from reading *Harry Potter* as their counterparts in New York or London? Similarly, we enjoy foods from around the world while knowing little about the lives of the people who created them. In short, people everywhere still see the world through their own cultural lenses (Featherstone, 1990; Hall & Neitz, 1993).

THEORETICAL ANALYSIS OF CULTURE

Culture helps us make sense of ourselves and the surrounding world. And sociologists have the special task of comprehending culture. They use several theoretical approaches.

STRUCTURAL-FUNCTIONAL ANALYSIS

The structural-functional paradigm depicts culture as a complex strategy for meeting human needs. Borrowing from the philosophical doctrine of *idealism*, this approach considers values the core of a culture (Parsons, 1966; R. Williams, 1970). Cultural values, in other words, give meaning to life and bind people together. Countless other aspects of culture function in various ways to support a way of life.

Thinking functionally helps us understand an unfamiliar way of life. Take, for example, the Amish farmer plowing hundreds of acres of an Ohio farm with a team of horses. His farming methods may violate our cultural value of efficiency, but from the Amish point of view, hard work functions to develop the discipline necessary to sustain a traditional way of life. Long days of working together not only make the Amish self-sufficient but also unify families and communities.

Of course, Amish practices have dysfunctions as well. The hard work and strict religious discipline are too demanding for some, who end up leaving the community. Then, too, religious devotion sometimes prevents compromise, resulting in lasting divisions within Amish communities (Kraybill, 1989; Kraybill & Olshan, 1994).

If cultures are strategies for meeting human needs, we would expect to find many common patterns around the world. The term **cultural universals** refers to *traits that are part of every known culture.*

Comparing hundreds of cultures, George Murdock (1945) identified dozens of cultural universals. One common element is the family, which functions everywhere to control sexual reproduction and to oversee the care of children. Funeral rites, too, are found everywhere, because all human communities cope with the reality of death. Jokes are another cultural universal, serving as a safe means of releasing social tensions.

Critical evaluation. The strength of the structural-functional paradigm is showing how culture operates to meet human needs. Yet, by emphasizing a society's dominant cultural patterns, this approach largely ignores cultural diversity. Moreover, because this approach emphasizes cultural stability, it downplays the importance of change. In short, cultural systems are not as stable or a matter of as much agreement as structural functionalism leads us to believe.

SOCIAL-CONFLICT ANALYSIS

The social-conflict paradigm stresses the link between culture and inequality. Any cultural trait, from this point of view, benefits some members of society at the expense of others.

We might well begin a conflict analysis by asking why certain values dominate a society in the first place. Many conflict theorists, especially Marxists, argue that culture is shaped by a society's system of economic production. "It is not the consciousness of men that determines their being," Marx proclaimed, "it is their social being that determines their consciousness" (Marx & Engels, 1978:4; orig. 1859). Social-conflict theory, then, is rooted in the philosophical doctrine of *materialism*, which holds that a society's system of material production (such as our own capitalist economy) has a powerful effect on the rest of a culture. This materialist approach contrasts with the idealist leanings of structural functionalism.

Social-conflict analysis ties our competitive values to our society's capitalist economy, which serves the interests of the nation's wealthy elite. The culture of capitalism further teaches us to think that rich and powerful people work harder or longer than others and therefore deserve their wealth and privileges. Viewing capitalism as somehow "natural" also discourages efforts to reduce economic disparity.

Eventually, however, the strains of inequality erupt into movements for social change. Two recent examples in the United States are the civil rights movement and the women's movement. Both seek

This Christmas Eve dinner at the Los Angeles Mission brings together affluent volunteers and poor, homeless people. What questions does structural-functional analysis lead us to ask about this setting? What about social-conflict analysis?

greater equality, and both, too, encounter opposition from defenders of the status quo.

Critical evaluation. The social-conflict paradigm suggests that cultural systems do not address human needs equally, allowing some people to dominate others. This inequity, in turn, generates pressure toward change.

Yet, by stressing the divisiveness of culture, this paradigm understates the ways that cultural patterns integrate members of society. Thus, we should consider both social-conflict and structural-functional insights for a fuller understanding of culture.

SOCIOBIOLOGY

We know culture is a human creation, but does human biology influence how this process unfolds? A third theoretical paradigm, standing with one leg in biology and one in sociology, is **sociobiology,** *a theoretical*

Using an evolutionary perspective, sociobiologists point to a double standard by which men treat women as sexual objects more than women treat men that way. While this may be so, many sociologists counter that behavior—such as that shown in Ruth Orkin's photograph, American Girl in Italy—is more correctly understood as resulting from a culture of male domination.

Copyright 1952, 1980 Ruth Orkin/Getty Images, Inc.

paradigm that explores ways in which human biology affects how we create culture.

Sociobiology rests on the theory of evolution proposed by Charles Darwin in his book *On the Origin of Species* (1859). Darwin asserted that living organisms change over long periods of time as a result of *natural selection*, a matter of four simple principles. First, all living things live to reproduce themselves. Second, the blueprint for reproduction is in the genes, the basic units of life that carry traits of one generation into the next. Third, some random variation in genes allows a species to "try out" new life patterns in a particular environment. This variation allows some organisms to survive better than others and pass on their advantageous genes to their offspring. Finally, over thousands of generations, the genetic patterns that promote reproduction survive and become dominant. In this way, as biologists say, a species *adapts* to its environment, and dominant traits emerge as the "nature" of the organism.

Sociobiologists claim that the large number of cultural universals reflects the fact that all humans are members of a single biological species. It is our common biology that underlies, for example, the apparently universal "double standard" of sexual behavior. As sex researcher Alfred Kinsey put it, "Among all people everywhere in the world, the male is more likely than the female to desire sex with a variety of partners" (quoted in Barash, 1981:49). But why?

We all know that children result from joining a woman's egg with a man's sperm. But the biological importance of a single sperm and of a single egg are quite different. For healthy men, sperm represent a "renewable resource" produced by the testes throughout most of the life course. A man releases hundreds of millions of sperm in a single ejaculation—technically, enough to fertilize every woman in North America (Barash, 1981:47). A newborn female's ovaries, however, contain her entire lifetime allotment of follicles, or immature eggs. A woman generally releases a single egg cell from her ovaries each month. So, whereas a man is biologically capable of fathering thousands of offspring, a woman is able to bear only a relatively small number of children.

Given this biological difference, men reproduce their genes most efficiently by being promiscuous—readily engaging in sex. This scheme, however, opposes the reproductive interests of women. Each of a woman's relatively few pregnancies demands that she carry the child for nine months, give birth, and provide care for some time afterward. Thus, efficient reproduction on the part of the woman depends on carefully selecting a mate whose qualities (beginning with the likelihood that he will simply stay around) will contribute to their child's survival and, later, successful reproduction (Remoff, 1984).

The "double standard" certainly involves more than biology and is tangled up with the historical

GLOBAL SOCIOLOGY

The United States and Canada: Are They Culturally Different?

The United States and Canada are two of the largest high-income countries in the world, and they share a common border of about 4,000 miles. But do the United States and Canada share the same culture?

One important point to make right away is that both nations are *multicultural*. Just as immigration has brought people to the United States from all over the world, it has done the same to Canada. In both countries, most early immigrants came from Europe, but in recent decades most immigrants have come from nations in Asia and Latin America. The Canadian city of Vancouver, for example, has a large Chinese community on the same order as the Latino community in Los Angeles, California.

Canada and the United States differ in one important respect—historically, Canada has had *two* dominant cultures: French (about 25 percent of the population) and British (roughly 40 percent). People of French ancestry are a large majority of the province of Quebec

(where French is the official language) and a large minority of New Brunswick (which is officially bilingual).

Are the dominant values of Canada much the same as those we have described for the United States? Seymour Martin Lipset (1985) finds that they differ to some degree. The United States declared its independence from Great Britain in 1776, whereas Canada did not formally separate from Great Britain until 1982. Thus, Lipset continues, the dominant culture of Canada lies somewhere between the culture of the United States and that of Great Britain.

For example, the culture of the United States is more individualistic, whereas Canada's is more collective. In the United States, individualism is seen in the historical importance of the cowboy, a self-sufficient type of person, and even outlaws such as Jesse James and Billy the Kid are looked on as heroes because they challenged authority. In Canada, by contrast, it is the Mountie—Canada's well-known police

officer—who is looked on with great respect.

Politically, people in the United States tend to think individuals ought to do things for themselves. In Canada, however, much as in Great Britain, there is a strong sense that government should look after the interests of everyone. This is one reason, for example, that Canada has a much broader social welfare system (including universal health care) than the United States (the only high-income nation without such a program). It also helps explain the fact that about half of all households own one or more guns in the United States, where the idea that individuals are entitled to own a gun is strong—albeit, controversial. In Canada, on the other hand, few households have a gun, and the government greatly restricts gun ownership, as in Great Britain.

Sources: Lipset (1985) and Macionis & Gerber (2001).

---

domination of women by men (Barry, 1983). But sociobiology suggests that this cultural pattern, like many others, has an underlying bio-logic. Simply put, the double standard exists around the world because biological differences lead women and men everywhere to favor distinctive reproductive strategies.

Critical evaluation. Sociobiology has generated intriguing theories about the biological roots of some cultural patterns. But the approach remains controversial for several reasons.

First, some critics fear that sociobiology may revive biological arguments, from a century ago, that touted the superiority of one race or sex. But defenders counter that sociobiology rejects the past pseudoscience of racial

superiority. In fact, sociobiology unites all of humanity because all people share a single evolutionary history. Sociobiology does assert that men and women differ biologically in some ways that culture cannot overcome. But far from claiming that males are somehow more important than females, sociobiology emphasizes that both sexes are vital to human reproduction.

Second, say the critics, sociobiologists have little evidence to support their theories. Research to date suggests that biological forces do not determine human behavior in any rigid sense. Rather, humans *learn* behavior within a cultural system. The contribution of sociobiology, then, lies in explaining why some cultural patterns are learned more easily than others (Barash, 1981).

CULTURE AND HUMAN FREEDOM

Underlying the discussion in this chapter is an important question: To what extent are cultural creatures free? Does culture bind us to each other and to the past? Or does culture enhance our capacity for individual thought and independent choices?

CULTURE AS CONSTRAINT

As symbolic creatures, humans cannot live without culture. But the capacity for culture does have some drawbacks. We may be the only animals who name ourselves, but living in a symbolic world means that we are also the only creatures who experience alienation. Moreover, culture is largely a matter of habit, limiting our choices as generations pass along troubling patterns, such as racial prejudice, to the young.

Moreover, our society's emphasis on competitive achievement urges us toward excellence, yet this same pattern also isolates us from one another. Material things comfort us in some ways but divert us from the security and satisfaction that come from close relationships and spiritual strength.

CULTURE AS FREEDOM

For better or worse, human beings are cultural creatures, just as ants and bees are prisoners of their biology. But there is a crucial difference. Biological instincts create a ready-made world; culture, by contrast, forces us to choose as we make and remake a world for ourselves. No better evidence of this freedom exists than the cultural diversity of our own society and the even greater human diversity around the world.

Learning more about this cultural diversity is one goal shared by sociologists. The final box offers some contrasts between the cultures of the United States and Canada. But wherever we may live, the better we understand the workings of the surrounding culture, the better prepared we are to use the freedom it offers us.

SUMMARY

1. Culture is a way of life shared by members of a society. Several species display a limited capacity for culture, but only human beings rely on culture for survival.

2. As the human brain evolved, the first elements of culture appeared some 3 million years ago; culture replaced biological instincts as our species' primary strategy for survival.

3. Culture relies on symbols. Language is the symbolic system by which one generation transmits culture to the next.

4. Values are culturally defined standards of what ought to be; beliefs are statements that people who share a culture hold to be true.

5. Cultural norms, which guide human behavior, are of two kinds: Mores have great moral significance, whereas folkways are everyday matters of politeness.

6. "High culture" refers to patterns that distinguish a society's elite; "popular culture" refers to widespread social patterns.

7. The United States stands among the most culturally diverse societies in the world. "Subculture" refers to distinctive cultural patterns supported by some part of a population, and "counterculture" to patterns strongly at odds with a conventional way of life. Multiculturalism is an educational effort to enhance an awareness and appreciation of cultural diversity.

8. Invention, discovery, and diffusion all generate cultural change. Cultural lag results as some parts of a cultural system change faster than others.

9. Ethnocentrism involves judging others by the standards of one's own culture. By contrast, "cultural relativism" means evaluating another culture according to its own standards.

10. Global cultural patterns result from the worldwide flow of goods, information, and people.

11. Structural-functional analysis views culture as a relatively stable system built on core values. Cultural patterns function to maintain the overall system.

12. The social-conflict paradigm envisions culture as a dynamic arena of inequality and conflict. Cultural patterns benefit some categories of people more than others.

13. Sociobiology studies how humanity's evolutionary past shapes cultural patterns.

14. Culture can constrain social possibilities; yet, as cultural creatures, we have the capacity to shape and reshape our world to meet our needs and pursue our dreams.

KEY CONCEPTS

culture (p. 59) the values, beliefs, behavior, and material objects that together form a people's way of life

nonmaterial culture (p. 59) the intangible world of ideas created by members of a society

material culture (p. 59) the tangible things created by members of a society

culture shock (p. 59) personal disorientation when experiencing an unfamiliar way of life

symbols (p. 61) anything that carries a particular meaning recognized by people who share a culture

language (p. 63) a system of symbols that allows people to communicate with one another

cultural transmission (p. 63) the process by which one generation passes culture to the next

Sapir-Whorf thesis (p. 65) the thesis that people perceive the world through the cultural lens of language

values (p. 65) culturally defined standards by which people assess desirability, goodness, and beauty and that serve as broad guidelines for social living

beliefs (p. 65) specific statements that people hold to be true

norms (p. 67) rules and expectations by which a society guides the behavior of its members

mores (p. 68) norms that are widely observed and have great moral significance

folkways (p. 68) norms for routine or casual interaction

social control (p. 68) attempts by society to regulate people's thought and behavior

technology (p. 69) knowledge that people use to make a way of life in their surroundings

high culture (p. 72) cultural patterns that distinguish a society's elite

popular culture (p. 72) cultural patterns that are widespread among a society's population

subculture (p. 72) cultural patterns that set apart some segment of a society's population

multiculturalism (p. 74) an educational program recognizing the cultural diversity of the United States and promoting the equality of all cultural traditions

Eurocentrism (p. 74) the dominance of European (especially English) cultural patterns

Afrocentrism (p. 75) the dominance of African cultural patterns

counterculture (p. 76) cultural patterns that strongly oppose those widely accepted within a society

cultural integration (p. 76) the close relationships among various elements of a cultural system

cultural lag (p. 77) the fact that some cultural elements change more quickly than others, disrupting a cultural system

ethnocentrism (p. 78) the practice of judging another culture by the standards of one's own culture

cultural relativism (p. 78) the practice of evaluating a culture by its own standards

cultural universals (p. 80) traits that are part of every known culture

sociobiology (p. 81) a theoretical paradigm that explores ways in which human biology affects how we create culture

CRITICAL-THINKING QUESTIONS

1. In the United States, hot dogs, hamburgers, French fries, and ice cream have long been considered national favorites. What cultural patterns help explain the love of these kinds of foods?

2. What cultural lessons do games like King of the Mountain, Tag, or Keep Away teach our children? What about a schoolroom spelling bee? What cultural values are expressed by children's stories such as *The Little Engine that Could* and popular board games such as Chutes and Ladders, Monopoly, and Risk?

3. To what extent, in your opinion, is a global culture emerging? Do you regard the prospect of a global culture as positive or negative? Why?

4. Have you ever identified with one or more subcultures? If so, which? How are they distinctive?

APPLICATIONS AND EXERCISES

1. Try to find someone on campus who has lived in another country. Ask for a chance to discuss how the culture of that society differs from the way of life here. Look for ways in which the other person sees U.S. culture differently from most people.

2. Make a list of words with the prefix "self" ("self-service," "self-image," "self-esteem," "self-destructive," and so on); there are hundreds of them. What does this high number suggest about our way of life?

3. Watch a Disney film like *The Little Mermaid, Aladdin, Pocahontas,* or *Mulan.* All of these films share cultural themes, which is one reason for their popularity. According to these films, how should young people behave toward their parents? What makes these films especially "American"?

4. Make a list of ten things you can do in sixty seconds. Did you find this task easy? Would people in a more traditional society make this kind of list? Why or why not?

5. Packaged in the back of this new textbook is an interactive CD-ROM that offers a variety of video and interactive review materials intended to help you better understand the material covered in this chapter. For this chapter, the CD-ROM contains a relevant clip from *ABC News,* an author's tip video, interactive map animations, an interactive time line, and flashcards with audio pronunciations of the more difficult words.

SITES TO SEE

http://www.prenhall.com/macionis

Visit the interactive Companion Website™ that accompanies this text. Begin by clicking on the cover of your book. You will find a chapter-by-chapter study guide, practice tests, suggested Web links, and links to other relevant material.

http://www.TheSociologyPage.com
(or **http://www.macionis.com**)

Visit the author's Web page to view short videos on the lessons and challenges of traveling in an unfamiliar setting.

http://www.nationalgeographic.com

The National Geographic Society offers information on world cultures, including search engines and a library of maps.

http://www.gorilla.org

What does a 450-pound gorilla say? Anything she wants! The Gorilla Foundation offers a look at the sign language used by a 450-pound gorilla named Koko.

http://www.aaanet.org

Anthropologists study cultures all over the world. This is the Web site for the American Anthropological Association, where you can find out more about this discipline, which is closely related to sociology.

 ## INVESTIGATE WITH RESEARCH NAVIGATOR™

Follow the instructions on page 24 of this text to access the features of **Research Navigator™**. Once at the Web site, enter your Login Name and Password. Then, to use the **Content Select™** database, enter keywords such as "ethnocentrism," "multiculturalism," and "immigration," and the search engine will supply relevant and recent scholarly and popular press publications. Use the *New York Times* **Search-by-Subject Archive** to find recent news articles related to sociology and the **Link Library** feature to find relevant Web links organized by the key terms associated with this chapter.

May 29, 2002

Cultural Divide Over Parental Discipline

By YILU ZHAO

When a Chinese immigrant mother beat her 8-year-old son with a broomstick last month because he had not been doing his homework, she thought she was acting within the bounds of traditional Chinese disciplinary practices. . . .

The next day, when the boy's reddish welts were seen by his teachers, his school in Rego Park, Queens, reported the incident to the Administration for Children's Services, the city agency that protects children. That evening, the police went to the home in Rego Park, and her three children, 6 to 8, were put in foster care. The parents were investigated for child abuse.

. . . The handling of the case touched a nerve in immigrant communities, where many parents have disciplinary ideas that differ from mainstream American views.

"It's something cultural," said David Chen, the executive director of the Chinese-American Planning Council, a nonprofit organization, referring to corporal punishment among Chinese immigrants. "The Chinese believe I hit you because I love you. The harder I hit you, the more I love you."

As more such incidents involving immigrant families occur and are reported in New York's ethnic media, from Korean newspapers to Spanish TV, advocacy groups are joining with public schools to educate immigrants about America's child welfare laws. . . .

When the Coalition for Asian American Children and Families, an advocacy group, printed a brochure to advise parents on child abuse issues, it addressed fundamental cultural beliefs.

"In the Chinese culture, the family is most important," it said. "A Chinese family might expect their child to support the family by doing well in school and obeying his parents.

"In America, the individual is the most important. American society might consider the family's discipline to be too strong, especially if the child is hurt physically or emotionally."

The clash about how to discipline a child is not new in New York City, where half of the population are immigrants and their children. Many immigrant parents have said for years that American parents are too permissive, and that children are disrespectful to elders. . . .

Well-meaning advice can put parents in a predicament, said social workers, since many parents know no other way to discipline children.

Mrs. Liu, a Chinatown resident who would give only her last name, said she had been at a loss after she learned about local laws. "I don't even dare to touch him," said Mrs. Liu, referring to her mischievous 11-year-old son. "Every time I want to hit him, he threatens to call 911 and have me arrested."

Joe Semidei, a director of the Committee for Hispanic Children and Families, said his organization teaches parents other ways to discipline children.

Mr. Semidei said: "Here are some examples: You are not going to the baseball game this weekend if you do this. But you are going to have a new toy if you do that. You negotiate with the kids and lay the boundaries. Here in America, you reinforce good discipline by rewards."

But many immigrant parents see this as bribery. . . . They grow more antagonistic toward the child welfare system when their children encounter negligent foster parents or guardians.

"Some Chinese kids have become addicted to drugs in foster care, and a few teenage girls got pregnant," said Xuejun Chi, who was a university professor in China and is now a social worker at the Y.M.C.A. in Chinatown. "When their parents eventually get them back, they are so messed up. The parents ask, 'How has the system cared for them any better than I did?'"

Children's Services is willing to become more sensitive to cultural differences. "Our goal is to keep families together, not to break them up," said Kathleen Walsh, a spokeswoman. "But our ultimate goal is to keep the children safe." The agency has formed an immigrant issues group, which meets once every three months, when officials are briefed by immigrant community leaders about their groups' cultural practices.

What do you think?

1. Do you think it is ethnocentric to expect the Chinese families described in this article to discipline their children according to cultural norms common in the United States? Or would you support a culturally relativist approach to letting these parents do what seems right to them?
2. Can you cite other cultural patterns brought by immigrants that have come into conflict with established cultural norms? What about such patterns changing U.S. culture?

SOCIETY

ALEXANDER CALDER (1898–1976)

St. Regis Restaurant

1925. Oil on canvas. 64.1 × 76.2 cm. © 2004 ARS, N.Y. © Art Resource, N.Y. Location: Private Collection.

SIDIDI AG INAKA HAS NEVER logged onto the Internet using a computer, sent a fax, or even spoken on a cell phone. In today's high-technology world, these facts may seem strange enough. But how about this: Neither Inaka nor anyone in his family has ever seen a television or even read a newspaper.

Are these people visitors from another planet? Prisoners on some remote island? Not at all. They are Tuareg nomads who wander the vastness of the Sahara in western Africa, north of the city of Timbuktu in the nation we know as Mali. Known as the "blue men of the desert" for the flowing blue robes worn by both men and women, the Tuareg herd camels, goats, and sheep and live in camps where the sand blows and the daytime temperature often reaches 120 degrees. Life is hard, but most try to hold onto traditional ways. With a look of determination, Inaka says, "My father was a nomad, his father was a nomad, I am a nomad, my children will be nomads."

The Tuareg are among the poorest people of the world, living a simple and difficult existence. When the rains fail to come, they and their animals are at risk of their lives. Inaka and his people are a society set apart, isolated from the rest of humanity and virtually untouched by modern ideas and advanced technology. To many, no doubt, they seem a curious throwback to the past. But Inaka does not complain: "This is the life of my ancestors. This is the life that we know" (Buckley, 1996; Matloff, 1997; Lovgren, 1998).

Many kinds of human societies have existed in the past, and we still find remarkable diversity today. But what is a society? How and why have societies changed over the course of human history?

Society refers to *people who interact in a defined territory and share a culture.* In this chapter, we shall examine this deceptively simple term from four different angles. We begin with the approach of **Gerhard Lenski,** describing the changing character of human societies over the last 10,000 years. Lenski highlights the importance of *technology* in defining the character of any society. Then we turn to three of sociology's founders. **Karl Marx,** like Lenski, understood human history as a long and complex process. For Marx, however, the story of society spins around *social conflict* that arises from how people produce material goods. **Max Weber** took another approach, showing that the power of *ideas* also shapes society. Weber contrasted the traditional thinking of simple societies with the rational thought that dominates our modern way of life. Finally, **Emile Durkheim** helped us to see the different ways that traditional and modern societies hang together.

All four visions of society answer important questions: What makes simple people, such as the Tuareg of the Sahara, so different from the society familiar to us? How and why do all societies change? What forces divide a society? What forces hold it together? Finally, after looking at the trends over time, we conclude this chapter by asking whether societies are getting better or worse.

In technologically simple societies, successful hunting wins men great praise. However, the gathering of vegetation by women is a more dependable and easily available source of nutrition.

GERHARD LENSKI: SOCIETY AND TECHNOLOGY

Members of our society, who take telephones and television as well as schools and hospitals for granted, must wonder at the nomads of the Sahara, who live the same simple life their ancestors did centuries ago. The work of Gerhard Lenski (Lenski, Nolan, & Lenski, 1995; Nolan & Lenski, 1999) helps us understand the great differences among societies that have flourished and declined throughout human history.

Lenski uses the term **sociocultural evolution** to refer to *the changes that occur as a society acquires new technology.* Societies with simple technology, such as the Tuareg, have little control over nature, so they can support only a small number of people. Technologically complex societies, while not necessarily "better," support hundreds of millions of people who live highly specialized lives.

New technology sends ripples of change through a society's entire way of life. When our ancestors first discovered how to harness the power of the wind using a sail, they set the stage for building sailing ships, which took them to new lands, stimulated trade, and increased their military might. Moreover, the more

technology a society has, the faster it changes. Technologically simple societies change very slowly; Sididi Ag Inaka says he "lives the life of his ancestors." Modern, high-technology societies, on the other hand, change so quickly that dramatic transformations can occur during a single lifetime. Imagine asking someone who lived just a few generations ago for an opinion about beepers, phone sex, artificial hearts, test-tube babies, genetic engineering, e-mail, smart bombs, space shuttles, the threat of nuclear holocaust, transsexualism, computer hackers, and "tell all" talk shows.

Drawing on Lenski's work, we will describe five types of societies according to their technology: hunting and gathering societies, horticultural and pastoral societies, agrarian societies, industrial societies, and postindustrial societies.

HUNTING AND GATHERING SOCIETIES

The simplest of all kinds of societies live by **hunting and gathering,** *the use of simple tools to hunt animals and gather vegetation.* From the emergence of our species 3 million years ago until just 12,000 years before the present, *all* humans were hunters and gatherers. Even in 1800, there were many hunting and gathering societies in the world. Today, however, just a few remain, including the Aka and Pygmies of central Africa, the Bushmen of southwestern Africa, the Aborigines of Australia, the Kaska Indians of northwest Canada, and the Batek and Semai of Malaysia (Endicott, 1992; Hewlett, 1992).

With little control over their environment, hunters and gatherers spend most of their time searching for game and collecting plants to eat. Only in lush areas where food is plentiful do hunters and gatherers have leisure time. Moreover, it takes a lot of land to support even a few people, so hunting and gathering societies are small bands with a few dozen members. They must also be nomadic, moving on as they deplete vegetation in one area or follow migratory animals. Although periodically returning to favored sites, they rarely form permanent settlements.

Hunting and gathering societies are built on kinship. The family obtains and distributes food, protects its members, and teaches the children. Everyone's life is much the same and is focused on getting the next meal. There is some specialization related to age and gender. The very young and the very old contribute what they can, while healthy adults secure most of the food. Women gather vegetation—the more reliable food source—while men take on the less certain task

Pastoralism historically has flourished in regions of the world where arid soil does not support crops. Pastoral people still thrive in northern Africa, living today much as they did a thousand years ago.

of hunting. Although men and women perform different tasks, most hunters and gatherers probably see the sexes as having about the same social importance (Leacock, 1978).

Hunting and gathering societies have few formal leaders. Most recognize a *shaman*, or spiritual leader, who enjoys high prestige but receives no greater material rewards and must work to find food like everyone else. In short, hunting and gathering societies are egalitarian.

Hunters and gatherers employ simple weapons—the spear, bow and arrow, and stone knife—but rarely to wage war. Their real enemy is the forces of nature: Storms and droughts can destroy their food supply, and there is little they can do in the event of accident or illness. Such vulnerability encourages cooperation and sharing, raising everyone's odds of survival. Nonetheless, many die in childhood, and no more than half reach the age of twenty (Lenski, Nolan, & Lenski, 1995:104).

During the twentieth century, technologically complex societies slowly closed in on the few remaining hunters and gatherers, reducing their food supply. Lenski claims that now hunting and gathering societies are disappearing from the Earth. Fortunately, study of this way of life has produced valuable information about human history and our fundamental ties to the natural world.

HORTICULTURAL AND PASTORAL SOCIETIES

Ten to twelve thousand years ago, a new technology began to change the lives of human beings (see the time line inside the front cover). People discovered **horticulture,** *the use of hand tools to raise crops.* Using a hoe to work the soil and a digging stick to punch holes in the ground to plant seeds may seem simple and obvious, but horticulture was an invention that allowed people to give up gathering in favor of "growing their own." Humans first planted gardens in the fertile regions of the Middle East and then in Latin America and Asia. Within some 5,000 years, cultural diffusion spread knowledge of horticulture throughout most of the world.

Not all societies abandoned hunting and gathering in favor of horticulture. Hunters and gatherers living amid plentiful vegetation and game probably took little note of the new technology (Fisher, 1979). Then, too, people inhabiting arid regions (such as the Sahara in western Africa or the Middle East) or mountainous areas found horticulture of little value. Such people (including the Tuareg) turned to **pastoralism,** *the domestication of animals.* Today, societies that mix horticulture and pastoralism thrive in South America, Africa, and Asia.

Domesticating plants and animals greatly increased food production, so societies could support not dozens but hundreds of people. Pastoralists remained nomadic, leading their herds to fresh grazing

Of Egypt's 130 pyramids, the Great Pyramids at Giza are the largest. Each of the three major structures stands more than forty stories high and is composed of 3 million massive stone blocks. Some 4,500 years ago, tens of thousands of people labored to construct these pyramids so that one man, the pharaoh, might have a godlike monument for his tomb. Clearly social inequality in this agrarian society was striking.

lands. Horticulturalists, by contrast, formed settlements, moving only when they depleted the soil. Joined by trade, these settlements formed societies with populations climbing into the thousands.

Once a society is capable of producing a *material surplus*—more resources than are needed to support day-to-day living—not everyone has to secure food. Some make crafts, engage in trade, cut hair, apply tattoos, or serve as priests. Compared to hunting and gathering societies, then, horticultural and pastoral societies are more specialized and complex. Domestication of plants and animals makes simpler societies

more productive. But advancing technology is never entirely beneficial. Lenski points out that, compared to hunters and gatherers, horticulturalists and pastoralists have more social inequality and, in many cases, engage in slavery, protracted warfare, and even cannibalism.

As some families produce more food than others, they assume positions of relative power and privilege. Forging alliances—including marriage—with other elite families allows social advantages to endure over generations. Along with social hierarchy, simple government, backed by military force, emerges in pastoral and horticultural societies to shore up the dominance of elites. However, without the ability to communicate or to travel over large distances, a ruler can control only a small number of people, so there is little empire building.

Hunters and gatherers believe many spirits inhabit the world. Horticulturalists, however, practice ancestor worship and conceive of God as Creator. Pastoral societies carry this belief further, seeing God as directly involved in the well-being of the entire world. This view of God ("The Lord is my shepherd, . . ." Psalm 23) is widespread among members of our own society because Christianity, Islam, and Judaism all began as Middle Eastern pastoral religions.

AGRARIAN SOCIETIES

About 5,000 years ago, another technological revolution was underway in the Middle East and would eventually transform most of the world. This was the discovery of **agriculture**, *large-scale cultivation using plows harnessed to animals or more powerful energy sources.* So great was the social significance of the animal-drawn plow and other technological innovations of the period—including irrigation, the wheel, writing, numbers, and the use of various metals—that this era qualifies as "the dawn of civilization" (Lenski, Nolan, & Lenski, 1995:177).

Using animal-drawn plows, farmers could cultivate fields vastly larger than the garden-sized plots worked by horticulturalists. Plows have the additional advantage of turning and aerating the soil to increase fertility. As a result, farmers work the same land for generations, which, in turn, encourages permanent settlements. Now able to produce a surplus of food and to transport goods by using animal-powered wagons, agrarian societies greatly expand their land area and population. About 100 C.E., for example, the agrarian Roman Empire boasted a population of

DIVERSITY: RACE, CLASS, AND GENDER

Technology and the Changing Status of Women

In the earliest human societies, women produced more food than men did. Hunters and gatherers valued meat highly, but men's hunting was not a dependable source of nourishment. Thus, vegetation gathered by women was the primary means of ensuring survival. Similarly, it was women who took charge of the tools and seeds used in horticulture. For their part, men engaged in trade and tended herds of animals. Only at harvest time did men and women work side by side.

Then, about 5,000 years ago, humans discovered how to mold metals. This technology spread by cultural diffusion, primarily along male-dominated trade networks. Thus, it was men who developed the metal plow and, because they already managed animals, thought to hitch the implement to a cow.

The metal plow marked the beginning of agriculture, and for the first time, men took over the dominant role in food production. Elise Boulding explains how this technological breakthrough undermined the social standing of women:

The shift of the status of the woman farmer may have happened quite rapidly, once there were two male specializations relating to agriculture: plowing and the care of cattle. This situation left women with all the subsidiary tasks, including weeding and carrying water to the fields. The new fields were larger, so women had to work just as many hours as they did before, but now they worked at more secondary tasks. . . . This would contribute further to the erosion of the status of women.

Sources: Based on Boulding (1976) and Fisher (1979).

---

70 million spread over some 2 million square miles (Stavrianos, 1983; Nolan & Lenski, 1999).

As always, increasing production meant more specialization. Tasks once performed by everyone, such as clearing land and securing food, became distinct occupations. Specialization also made the early barter system obsolete, and money became the standard of exchange. Because money made trade easier, cities grew and their populations soared into the millions.

Agrarian societies exhibit dramatic social inequality. In many cases, including the United States early in its history, peasants or slaves represent a significant share of the population. Freed from manual work, elites can then engage in the study of philosophy, art, and literature. This explains the historical link between "high culture" and social privilege noted in Chapter 3.

Among hunters and gatherers and also among horticulturists, women are the primary providers of food. Agriculture, however, propels men into a position of social dominance (Boulding, 1976; Fisher, 1979). The box looks more closely at the declining position of women at this point in the course of sociocultural evolution.

In many societies, religion reinforces the power of agricultural elites by defining work as a moral obligation. Many of the "Wonders of the Ancient World," such as the Great Wall of China and the

To see several wonders of the ancient world—all made primarily with muscle power—click on http://unmuseum.mus.pa.us/wonders.htm

Great Pyramids of Egypt, were possible only because emperors and pharaohs wielded absolute power, subjecting their people to a lifetime of labor without wages.

In agrarian societies, then, elites acquire unparalleled power. To maintain control of large empires, leaders require the services of a wide range of administrators. Thus, along with the growing economy, the political system emerges as a distinct sphere of life.

Of the societies described so far, agrarian societies have the greatest specialization and the most social inequality. Agrarian technology also gives people a greater range of life choices, the reason that agrarian societies differ more from one another than horticultural and pastoral societies do.

INDUSTRIAL SOCIETIES

Industrialism, as found in the United States, Canada, and other rich nations of the world, is *the production of goods using advanced sources of energy to drive large machinery.* Until the industrial era, the major source of energy was the muscles of humans and other animals.

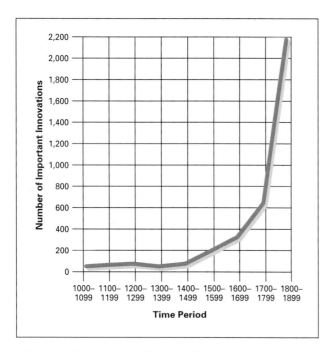

FIGURE 4–1 The Increasing Number of Technological Innovations

This figure illustrates the dramatic change in the number of technological innovations in Western Europe after the beginning of the Industrial Revolution in the mid-eighteenth century. Technological innovation occurred at an accelerating rate because each innovation combined with existing cultural elements to produce many additional innovations.

Source: Lenski, Nolan, & Lenski (1995).

But about 1750, mills and factories began to use water and then steam boilers to power ever-larger machinery.

With industrial technology, societies began to change faster, as shown in Figure 4–1. Industrial societies transformed themselves more in one century than they had during the past thousand years. As explained in Chapter 1 ("The Sociological Perspective"), this stunning change prompted the birth of sociology itself. During the nineteenth century, railroads and steamships revolutionized transportation, and steel-framed skyscrapers dwarfed the cathedrals that symbolized an earlier age.

In the twentieth century, automobiles further changed Western societies, and electricity powered modern conveniences such as lighting, refrigerators, elevators, and washing machines. Electronic communication, including the telephone, radio, television, and computers, soon followed, making the world seem smaller and smaller.

Work, too, has changed. In agrarian societies, most men and women work in the home or in the nearby fields. Industrialization, however, draws people away from home to factories situated near energy sources (such as coal fields) and filled with large machinery. Industrial workers are far more productive, of course, but lost in the process are close working relationships, strong kinship ties, and many of the traditional values, beliefs, and customs that guide agrarian life.

Occupational specialization has become more pronounced than ever. In fact, industrial people often size up one another in terms of their jobs rather than according to their kinship ties (as nonindustrial people do). Rapid change and movement from place to place also generate anonymity, cultural diversity, and numerous subcultures and countercultures, as described in Chapter 3 ("Culture").

Industrial technology recasts the family, too, lessening its traditional significance as the center of social life. No longer does the family serve as the primary setting for economic production, learning, and religious worship. And as Chapter 18 ("Family") explains, technological change also underlies the trend away from traditional families to greater numbers of single people, divorced people, single-parent families, and stepfamilies.

Lenski explains that, early in the industrialization process, only a small segment of the population enjoys the benefits of advancing technology. In time, however, wealth spreads and more people live longer and more comfortably. Though poverty remains a serious problem in industrial societies today, the standard of living has risen about fivefold over the last century, and social inequality has declined. One reason for this social leveling, described in Chapter 10 ("Social Stratification"), is that industrial societies require an educated and skilled labor force. While most people in nonindustrial societies are illiterate, industrial societies provide state-funded schooling and confer numerous political rights on almost everyone. Industrialization, in fact, intensifies demands for a political voice, as seen most recently in South Korea, Taiwan, the People's Republic of China, the nations of Eastern Europe, and the former Soviet Union.

POSTINDUSTRIAL SOCIETIES

Many industrial societies, including the United States, have now entered yet another phase of technological development, and we can extend Lenski's analysis to take account of recent trends. A generation ago, sociologist

Does advancing technology make society better? In some ways, perhaps. However, many films—including Frankenstein *(1931) and* Jurassic Park III *(2001)—have expressed the concern that new technology not only solves old problems but creates new ones. All the sociological theorists discussed in this chapter shared this ambivalent view of the modern world.*

Daniel Bell (1973) coined the term **postindustrialism** to refer to *technology that supports an information-based economy*. Whereas production in industrial societies centers on factories and machinery generating material goods, postindustrial production is based on computers and other electronic devices that create, process, store, and apply information. Thus, members of industrial societies learn and apply mechanical skills, and people in postindustrial societies develop information-based skills for working with computers and other forms of high-technology communication.

With this shift in key skills and the emergence of postindustrialism, a society's occupational structure changes dramatically. Chapter 16 ("The Economy and Work") explains that a postindustrial society uses less and less of its labor force for industrial production. At the same time, the ranks of clerical workers, managers, and other people who process information (in fields ranging from academia and advertising to marketing and public relations) swell.

The Information Revolution is most pronounced in rich nations, yet the new technology affects the entire world. As discussed in Chapter 3 ("Culture"), a new, worldwide flow of goods, people, and information ties societies together and creates a global culture.

And just as industrial technology joined local communities to create a national economy, so postindustrial technology joins nations to build a global economy.

Table 4–1 on pages 96–97 summarizes how technology shapes societies at different stages of sociocultural evolution.

THE LIMITS OF TECHNOLOGY

Technology remedies many human problems by raising productivity, reducing infectious disease, and sometimes simply relieving boredom. But it provides no quick fix for social problems. Poverty, for example, remains the plight of millions of women and men in the United States (detailed in Chapter 11, "Social Class in the United States") and 1 billion people worldwide (see Chapter 12, "Global Stratification"). Moreover, technology creates new problems that our ancestors (and people like the chapter-opening story's Sididi Ag Inaka today) hardly could imagine. Industrial societies provide more personal freedom, but often at the cost of the sense of community that characterized preindustrial life. Further, although the most powerful nations in the world today rarely engage

TABLE 4-1 Sociological Evolution: A Summary

Type of Society	Historical Period	Productive Technology	Population Size
Hunting and Gathering Societies	Only type of society until about 12,000 years ago; still common several centuries ago; the few examples remaining today are threatened with extinction	Primitive weapons	25–40 people
Horticultural and Pastoral Societies	From about 12,000 years ago, with decreasing numbers after about 3000 B.C.E.	Horticultural societies use hand tools for cultivating plants; pastoral societies are based on the domestication of animals	Settlements of several hundred people, connected through trading ties to form societies of several thousand people
Agrarian Societies	From about 5,000 years ago, with large but decreasing numbers today	Animal-drawn plow	Millions of people
Industrial Societies	From about 1750 to the present	Advanced sources of energy; mechanized production	Millions of people
Postindustrial Societies	Emerging in recent decades	Computers that support an information-based economy	Millions of people

in all-out warfare, they have stockpiles of nuclear weapons that could return us to a technologically primitive state—if we survived at all.

Advancing technology has also contributed to a major social problem involving the environment. Each stage in sociocultural evolution has introduced more powerful sources of energy and increased our appetite for the Earth's resources. An issue of vital concern, discussed in Chapter 22 ("Population, Urbanization, and Environment"), is whether we can continue to pursue material prosperity without permanently damaging our planet.

In some respects, then, technological advances have improved life and brought the world's people closer, into a "global village." But establishing peace, ensuring justice, and sustaining a safe environment are problems that technology alone cannot solve.

KARL MARX: SOCIETY AND CONFLICT

The first of our classic visions of society comes from Karl Marx (1818–1883), an early giant in the field of sociology. A keen observer of the industrial transformation of Europe, Marx spent most of his adult life in London, then the capital of the vast British Empire. He was awed by the productive power of the new factories. Great Britain and other industrial nations were producing more goods than ever before, with resources from around the world funneling into its factories at a dizzying rate.

 For biographical information on Karl Marx, go to http://www.TheSociologyPage.com and click on Marx in the Gallery of Sociologists.

What astounded and disturbed Marx was that industry's riches were concentrated in the hands of a few.

Type of Society	Settlement Pattern	Social Organization	Examples
Hunting and Gathering Societies	Nomadic	Family-centered; specialization limited to age and sex; little social inequality	Pygmies of central Africa Bushmen of southwestern Africa Aborigines of Australia Semai of Malaysia Kaska Indians of Canada
Horticultural and Pastoral Societies	Horticulturalists form small permanent settlements; pastoralists are nomadic	Family-centered; religious system begins to develop; moderate specialization; increased social inequality	Middle Eastern societies about 5000 B.C.E. Various societies today in New Guinea and other Pacific islands Yąnomamö today in South America
Agrarian Societies	Cities become common, but they generally contain only a small proportion of the population	Family loses significance as distinct religious, political, and economic systems emerge; extensive specialization; increased social inequality	Egypt during construction of the Great Pyramids Medieval Europe Numerous predominantly agrarian societies of the world today
Industrial Societies	Cities contain most of the population	Distinct religious, political, economic, educational, and family systems; highly specialized; marked social inequality persists, diminishing somewhat over time	Most societies today in Europe and North America, Australia, and Japan, which generate most of the world's industrial production
Postindustrial Societies	Population remains concentrated in cities	Similar to industrial societies, with information processing and other service work gradually replacing industrial production	Industrial societies noted above are now entering the postindustrial stage

A walk around London revealed striking contrasts of splendid affluence and wretched squalor. A handful of aristocrats and industrialists lived in fabulous mansions staffed by servants, where they enjoyed luxury and privilege. Most people, though, labored long hours for low wages and lived in slums or even slept in the streets, where many eventually died from disease brought on by poor nutrition.

Marx wrestled with a basic contradiction: In a society so rich, how could so many be so poor? Just as important, Marx asked, how can this situation be changed? Many people think Karl Marx set out to tear societies apart. But he was motivated by compassion and sought to help a badly divided society forge a new and just social order.

The key to Marx's thinking is the idea of **social conflict**, *the struggle between segments of society over valued resources.* Social conflict can, of course, take many forms: Individuals may quarrel, some colleges have longstanding sports rivalries, and nations sometimes go to war. For Marx, however, the most significant form of social conflict was class conflict arising from the way a society produces material goods.

SOCIETY AND PRODUCTION

Living in the nineteenth century, Marx observed the early stage of industrial capitalism in Europe. This economic system, Marx noted, turned a small part of the population into **capitalists**, *people who own and operate factories and other businesses in pursuit of profits.* A capitalist seeks profit by selling a product for more than it costs to produce. Capitalism transforms most

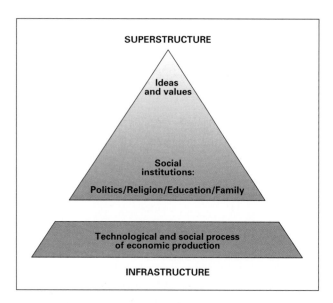

SUPERSTRUCTURE

Ideas
and values

Social
institutions:
Politics/Religion/Education/Family

Technological and social process
of economic production

INFRASTRUCTURE

FIGURE 4–2 Karl Marx's Model of Society

This diagram illustrates Marx's materialist view that economic production underlies and shapes the entire society. Economic production involves both technology (industry, in the case of capitalism) and social relationships (for capitalism, the relationship between the capitalists, who control economic production, and the workers, who are the source of labor). On this infrastructure, or foundation, rests society's superstructure, which includes its major social institutions as well as core cultural values and ideas. Marx maintained that every part of a society supports the economic system.

economy. Just as Lenski argues that technology molds a society, Marx argued that the economy is a society's "real foundation" (1959:43; orig. 1859).

Marx viewed the economic system as society's *infrastructure* (*infra* is Latin, meaning "below"). Other social institutions, including the family, the political system, and religion, are built on this foundation, forming society's *superstructure*. These institutions apply economic principles to other areas of life, as illustrated in Figure 4–2. For example, social institutions maintain capitalists' dominant position by protecting their wealth and lawfully transmitting property from one generation to the next through the family.

Generally speaking, members of industrial-capitalist societies do not view their legal or family systems as hotbeds of social conflict. On the contrary, individuals come to see their right to private property as "natural." People in the United States find it easy to think that affluent people have earned their wealth and that those who are poor or out of work lack skills or motivation. Marx rejected this reasoning, arguing that grand wealth clashing with grinding poverty is merely one set of human possibilities—the one generated by capitalism (Cuff & Payne, 1979).

Marx rejected capitalist common sense, therefore, as **false consciousness,** *explanations of social problems as the shortcomings of individuals rather than as the flaws of society.* Marx was saying, in effect, that industrial capitalism itself is responsible for many social problems. False consciousness, he continued, harms people by hiding the real cause of their problems.

CONFLICT AND HISTORY

Marx believed that most societies evolve gradually over time. But sometimes, they erupt in rapid, revolutionary change. Marx observed (as did Lenski) that change is caused partly by technological advance. But most change, he maintained, results from social conflict.

To put Lenski's analysis in Marxist terms, early hunters and gatherers formed primitive communist societies. *Communism* is a system by which people share more-or-less equally in the production of food and other material goods. Although resources were meager in hunting and gathering societies, they were shared by all rather than privately owned. In addition, everyone did much the same work, so there was little chance of social conflict.

Horticulture introduced social inequality, Marx noted. Among horticultural, pastoral, and early agrarian

of the population into industrial workers, whom Marx called the **proletarians,** *people who sell their productive labor for wages.* To Marx, conflict between capitalists and workers is inevitable in a system of capitalist production. To keep profits high, capitalists keep wages low. Workers, naturally, want higher wages. Since profits and wages come from the same pool of funds, conflict is the result. As Marx saw it, this conflict could end only with the end of capitalism itself.

All societies are composed of **social institutions,** defined as *the major spheres of social life, or societal subsystems, organized to meet human needs.* In his analysis of society, Marx argued that one institution—the economy—dominates all the others and defines the character of a society. Drawing on the philosophical doctrine of *materialism*, which says that how humans produce material goods shapes their experiences, Marx believed that the political system, family, religion, and education generally operate to support a society's

Jan Jules Geoffrey's painting The Starving reveals the fate of many migrants drawn to cities across Europe as the Industrial Revolution was getting underway. Karl Marx saw in such suffering a fundamental contradiction of modern society: Industrial technology promises material plenty for all, but capitalism concentrates wealth in the hands of a few.

Jan Jules Geoffroy, The Starving, 1886. Museo Civico Revoltella, Trieste, Italy/The Art Archive/Picture Desk.

societies—which Marx lumped together as the "ancient world"—warfare was frequent and the victors made their captives slaves. A small elite (the "masters") and their slaves were locked into an irreconcilable pattern of social conflict (Zeitlin, 1981).

Agriculture brought still more wealth to members of the elite, fueling further social conflict. Agrarian serfs, occupying the lowest reaches of European feudalism from about the twelfth to the eighteenth centuries, were only slightly better off than slaves. In Marx's view, both the church and the state defended the feudal system as God's will. Thus, to Marx, feudalism amounted to little more than "exploitation, veiled by religious and political illusions" (Marx & Engels, 1972:337; orig. 1848).

Gradually, new productive forces eroded the feudal order. As trade steadily increased, the merchants and skilled craftsworkers in cities formed a class, the *bourgeoisie* (a French word meaning "of the town"). Expanding trade made the bourgeoisie richer and richer. After about 1800, the bourgeoisie also controlled factories, becoming true capitalists with power that soon rivaled that of the ancient, land-owning nobility. For their part, the nobility looked down their noses at this upstart "commercial" class; but in time, it was the capitalists who gained control of European societies. To Marx's way of thinking, then, new technology was only part of the Industrial Revolution. It was

also a class revolution by which capitalists overthrew the old, agrarian elite.

Industrialization also led to the growth of the proletariat. English landowners converted fields once tilled by serfs into grazing land for sheep to produce wool for the textile mills. Forced from the land, millions of people migrated to cities to work in factories. Marx envisioned these workers one day joining together to form a unified class and thus, setting the stage for an historic confrontation. This time, the class revolution would lift the exploited workers over the oppressing capitalists.

CAPITALISM AND CLASS CONFLICT

"The history of all hitherto existing society is the history of class struggles." With these words, Marx and his collaborator Friedrich Engels began their best-known statement, the *Manifesto of the Communist Party* (1972:335; orig. 1848). Industrial capitalism, like earlier types of society, contains two major social classes—the ruling class and the oppressed—reflecting the two basic positions in the productive system. Like masters and slaves in the ancient world, and like nobles and serfs in feudal systems, capitalists and proletarians are engaged in class conflict now. Today, as in the past, one

Karl Marx, shown here at work on the Manifesto of the Communist Party *with his friend, benefactor, and collaborator Friedrich Engels, was surely the pioneering sociologist who had the greatest influence on the world as a whole. Through the second half of the last century, 1 billion people—nearly one-fifth of humanity—lived in societies organized on Marxist principles.*

class controls the other as productive property. Marx used the term **class conflict** (and sometimes *class struggle*) to refer to *conflict between entire classes over the distribution of a society's wealth and power.*

Class conflict is nothing new. What distinguishes the conflict in capitalist society, Marx pointed out, is how out in the open it is. Agrarian nobles and serfs, for all their differences, were bound together by long-standing traditions and mutual obligations. Industrial capitalism dissolved those ties so that loyalty and honor were replaced by "naked self-interest." With no personal ties to their oppressors, Marx saw no reason for the proletarians to put up with their situation.

Though industrial capitalism brought class conflict out in the open, Marx realized that revolution would not easily follow. First, workers must *become aware* of their oppression and see capitalism as its true cause. Second, they must *organize and act* to address their problems. This means workers must replace false consciousness with **class consciousness,** *workers' recognition of themselves as a class unified in opposition to capitalists and, ultimately, to capitalism itself.* Because the inhumanity of early capitalism was plain for him to see, Marx concluded that industrial workers would soon rise up to destroy capitalism.

And what of the capitalists? The capitalists' vast wealth makes them strong, indeed. But Marx saw a weakness in the capitalist armor. Motivated by a desire for personal gain, capitalists fear competition with other capitalists. Marx thought, therefore, that capitalists would be slow to band together, even though they, too, share common interests. Furthermore, he reasoned, because capitalists keep employees' wages low in order to maximize profits, the workers' resolve would grow ever stronger. In the long run, Marx believed, capitalists would contribute to their own undoing.

CAPITALISM AND ALIENATION

Marx also condemned capitalist society for producing **alienation,** *the experience of isolation and misery resulting from powerlessness.* Dominated by capitalists, workers are nothing more than a commodity—a source of labor—hired and fired at will. Dehumanized by their jobs (especially monotonous, repetitive factory work), workers find little satisfaction and feel unable to improve their situation. Here we see another contradiction of capitalist society: As people develop technology to gain power over the world, the capitalist economy gains more control over people.

Marx cited four ways in which capitalism alienates workers:

1. **Alienation from the act of working.** Ideally, people work to meet immediate needs and to develop their personal potential. Capitalism, however, denies workers a say in what they make or how they make it. Further, much work is tedious, a constant repetition of routine tasks. The fact that today we replace workers with machines whenever possible would not have surprised Marx. As far as he was concerned, capitalism had turned human beings into machines long ago.

2. **Alienation from the products of work.** The product of work belongs not to workers but to capitalists,

APPLYING SOCIOLOGY

Alienation and Industrial Capitalism

These excerpts from the book *Working* by Studs Terkel illustrate how dull, repetitive jobs can alienate men and women.

Phil Stallings is a twenty-seven-year-old auto worker in a Ford assembly plant in Chicago:

I start the automobile, the first welds. From there it goes to another line, where the floor's put on, the roof, the trunk, the hood, the doors. Then it's put on a frame. There is hundreds of lines. . . . I stand in one spot, about two-or three-feet area, all night. The only time a person stops is when the line stops. We do about thirty-two jobs per car, per unit. Forty-eight units an hour, eight hours a day. Thirty-two times forty-eight times eight. Figure it out. That's how many times I push that button.

The noise, oh it's tremendous. You open your mouth and you're liable to get a mouthful of sparks.

[Shows his arms.] That's a burn, these are burns. You don't compete against the noise. You go to yell and at the same time you're straining to maneuver the gun to where you have to weld.

You got some guys that are uptight, and they're not sociable. It's too rough. You pretty much stay to yourself. You get involved with yourself. You dream, you think of things you've done. I drift back continuously to when I was a kid and what me and my brothers did. The things you love most are what you drift back into.

It don't stop. It just goes and goes and goes. I bet there's men who have lived and died out there, never seen the end of the line. And they never will—because it's endless. It's like a serpent. It's just all body, no tail. It can do things to you. (1974:221–22)

Twenty-four-year-old Sharon Atkins is a college graduate working as a telephone receptionist for a large midwestern business:

I don't have much contact with people. You can't see them. You don't know if they're laughing, if they're being satirical or being kind. So your conversations become very abrupt. I notice that in talking to people. My conversation would be very short and clipped, in short sentences, the way I talk to people all day on the telephone. . . .

You try to fill up your time with trying to think about other things: what you're going to do on the weekend or about your family. You have to use your imagination. If you don't have a very good one and you bore easily, you're in trouble. Just to fill in time, I write real bad poetry or letters to myself and to other people and never mail them. The letters are fantasies, sort of rambling, how I feel, how depressed I am.

. . . I never answer the phone at home. (1974:58)

---

who sell it for profit. Thus, Marx reasoned, the more of themselves workers invest in their work, the more they lose.

3. **Alienation from other workers.** Through work, Marx claimed, people build bonds of community. Industrial capitalism, however, makes work competitive rather than cooperative. As the box illustrates, factory work provides little chance for human companionship.

4. **Alienation from human potential.** Industrial capitalism alienates workers from their human potential. Marx argued that a worker "does not fulfill himself in his work but denies himself, has a feeling of misery rather than well-being, does not freely develop his physical and mental energies, but is physically exhausted and mentally debased. The worker, therefore, feels himself to be at home only during his leisure time, whereas at work he feels homeless" (1964a:124–25; orig. 1844). In short, industrial capitalism distorts an activity that should express the best qualities in human beings into a dull and dehumanizing experience.

Marx viewed alienation, in its various forms, as a barrier to social change. But he hoped that industrial workers would overcome their alienation by uniting into a true social class, aware of the cause of their problems and ready to transform society.

The rise to power of Ayatollah Rohullah Khomeini in Iran in 1979 shows the power of religion to drive people toward change. In part, this revolution targeted an unpopular dictator; but it was also an expression of fundamentalist Islam, which has become more pronounced in the world in the decades since Khomeini's death in 1989.

REVOLUTION

The only way out of the trap of capitalism, argued Marx, is to remake society. He envisioned a more humane production system, one that would provide for the social needs of all. He called this system *socialism*. Although Marx knew well the obstacles to a socialist revolution, he was nevertheless disappointed that he had not lived to see workers in England rise up. Still, convinced of the immorality of capitalism, he was sure that, in time, the working majority would realize they held the key to a better future. This change would certainly be revolutionary, and perhaps even violent. In the end, Marx believed, a socialist society would bring class conflict to an end.

Chapter 10 ("Social Stratification") explains more about changes in industrial-capitalist societies since Marx's time and why the revolution he wanted never

took place. In addition, as Chapter 17 ("Politics and Government") explains, Marx failed to foresee that the revolution he imagined could take the form of repressive regimes—such as Stalin's government in the Soviet Union—that would end up killing tens of millions of people (Hamilton, 2001). But in his own time, Marx looked toward the future with hope (Marx & Engels, 1972:362; orig. 1848): "The proletarians have nothing to lose but their chains. They have a world to win."

MAX WEBER: THE RATIONALIZATION OF SOCIETY

With knowledge of law, economics, religion, and history, Max Weber (1864–1920) produced what many regard as the greatest individual contribution to sociology. This scholar, born to a prosperous family in Germany, generated ideas so wide-ranging that, in this discussion, we can touch on only his vision of how modern society differs from earlier types of social organization.

 For biographical information about Max Weber, visit http://www.TheSociologyPage.com and click on his name in the Gallery of Sociologists.

In line with the philosophical approach called *idealism*, Weber emphasized how human ideas shape society. He understood the power of technology, and he shared many of Marx's ideas about social conflict. But he countered Marx's materialist analysis by arguing that societies differ mainly in terms of how their members think about the world. For Weber, then, ideas—especially beliefs and values—were the key to understanding society. Weber saw modern society as the product, not just of new technology and capitalism, but of a new way of thinking. This emphasis on ideas, in contrast with Marx's focus on production, has led scholars to describe Weber's work as "a debate with the ghost of Karl Marx" (Cuff & Payne, 1979:73–74).

Weber compared social patterns in different times and places. To make the comparisons, he relied on the **ideal type,** *an abstract statement of the essential characteristics of any social phenomenon.* For example, he explored religion by contrasting the ideal "Protestant" with the ideal "Jew," "Hindu," and "Buddhist," knowing that these models precisely described no actual individuals. Note that Weber's use of the word "ideal" does not mean that something is "good" or "the best." We can analyze criminals as well as ministers in ideal terms. We have already used ideal types in comparing "hunting and gathering societies" with "industrial societies" and "capitalism" with "socialism."

TWO WORLDVIEWS: TRADITION AND RATIONALITY

Rather than categorizing societies by their technology or productive systems, Max Weber focused on ways people view the world. In simple terms, Weber said, members of preindustrial societies are *traditional,* whereas people in industrial-capitalist societies are *rational.*

By **tradition,** Weber meant *sentiments and beliefs passed from generation to generation.* In other words, traditional people are guided by the past. They consider particular actions right and proper solely because they have been accepted for so long.

But, argued Weber, people in modern societies favor **rationality,** *a way of thinking that emphasizes deliberate, matter-of-fact calculation of the most efficient means to accomplish a particular task.* Sentiment has no place in a rational worldview, which treats tradition simply as one kind of information. Typically, modern people choose to think and act on the basis of present and future consequences—evaluating jobs, schooling, and even relationships in terms of what they put into them and what they expect to receive in return.

Weber viewed both the Industrial Revolution and capitalism as evidence of a surge of rationality. He used the phrase **rationalization of society** to mean *the historical change from tradition to rationality as the dominant mode of human thought.* He went on to say that modern society has been "disenchanted," as scientific thinking and technology have swept away sentimental ties to the past.

The willingness to adopt the latest technology, then, is one strong indicator of how rationalized a society is. To illustrate the global pattern of rationalization, Global Map 4–1 on page 104 shows where in the world personal computers are found. In general, the high-income countries of North America and Europe use personal computers the most, whereas in low-income nations, they are rare.

Using Weber's comparative perspective—and the data found in the map—we can say that various societies value technological advance differently. What one society might consider a breakthrough, another might deem unimportant, and a third might strongly oppose as a threat to tradition. The Tuareg nomads, described at the beginning of this chapter, shrug off the notion of using telephones: Why would anyone want such a thing on the desert? In the United States, the Amish refuse to have telephones in their homes for religious reasons.

In Weber's view, then, the extent of technological innovation in a society depends on how people understand their world. Many people throughout history have had the opportunity to adopt new technology,

A common fear among thinkers in the early industrial era was that people—now slaves to the new machines—would be stripped of their humanity. No one better captured this idea than the comic actor Charlie Chaplin, who starred in the 1936 film Modern Times.
The Museum of Modern Art/Film Stills Archive.

but only in the rational cultural climate of Western Europe did people exploit scientific discoveries to spark the Industrial Revolution (1958; orig. 1904–5).

IS CAPITALISM RATIONAL?

Is industrial capitalism a rational economic system? Here, again, Weber and Marx came down on opposite sides. Weber considered industrial capitalism the essence of rationality, since capitalists pursue profit in whatever ways they can. Marx, however, believed capitalism irrational because it failes to meet the basic needs of most of the people (Gerth & Mills, 1946:49).

WEBER'S GREAT THESIS: PROTESTANTISM AND CAPITALISM

To look more closely at Weber's analysis we must consider how industrial capitalism emerged in the first place. Weber contended that industrial capitalism is the legacy of Calvinism—a Christian religious movement

WINDOW ON THE WORLD

GLOBAL MAP 4–1 High Technology in Global Perspective

Countries with traditional cultures either cannot afford, ignore, or sometimes even resist technological innovation; nations with highly rationalized ways of life quickly embrace such changes. Personal computers, central to today's high technology, are numerous in high-income countries such as the United States. In low-income nations, by contrast, they are unknown to most people.

Source: International Telecommunication Union (2002).

Personal Computers per 1,000 People

- 150.0 or more
- 50.0 to 149.9
- 20.0 to 49.9
- 5.0 to 19.9
- Fewer than 5.0
- No data

---

that arose from the Protestant Reformation. Calvinists, Weber explained, approached life in a highly disciplined and rational way. Moreover, central to the religious doctrine of John Calvin (1509–1564) was *predestination*, the idea that an all-knowing and all-powerful God has predestined some people for salvation and others for damnation. With everyone's fate set before birth, Calvinists believed that people could do nothing to change their destiny. Worse, they did not even know what their destiny was. Thus, Calvinists swung between hopeful visions of spiritual salvation and anxious fears of eternal damnation.

Not knowing one's fate was intolerable, and Calvinists gradually came to a resolution of sorts. Why shouldn't those chosen for glory in the next world, they reasoned, see signs of divine favor in *this* world? Such a conclusion prompted Calvinists to interpret worldly prosperity as a sign of God's grace. Eager to acquire this reassurance, Calvinists threw themselves into a quest for success, applying rationality, discipline, and hard work to their tasks. Their pursuit of wealth was not for its own sake, since self-indulgent spending was clearly sinful. Neither were Calvinists moved to share their wealth with the poor, since poverty was a sign of rejection by God. Their duty was to carry forward what they held to be a personal *calling* from God: reinvesting their profits for still greater success. In such deliberate activity, Calvinists built the foundation of capitalism, using wealth to create more wealth, saving their money, and eagerly adopting new technology.

The rational pursuit of wealth distinguished Calvinism from other world religions. For example, Catholicism, the traditional religion in most of Europe, gave rise to a passive, "otherworldly" view: Good deeds performed humbly on Earth would bring rewards in heaven. For Catholics, material wealth had none of the spiritual significance that motivated Calvinists. And so it was, Weber concluded, that industrial capitalism developed primarily in areas of Europe where Calvinism was strong.

Weber's study of Calvinism provides striking evidence of the power of ideas to shape society (versus Marx's contention that ideas merely reflect the process of economic production). But Weber was not one to accept simple explanations; he knew that industrial capitalism has many causes. In fact, one purpose of Weber's research was to counter Marx's narrow, strictly economic explanation of modern society.

Although later generations of Calvinists were less religious, their success seeking and personal discipline remained, and a *religious* ethic became simply a *work* ethic. In other words, industrial capitalism can be seen as "disenchanted" religion, with wealth now valued for its own sake. It is revealing that the practice of "accounting," which to early Calvinists meant keeping a daily record of moral deeds, before long was simply a matter of keeping track of money.

RATIONAL SOCIAL ORGANIZATION

According to Weber, then, rationality gave rise to the Industrial Revolution and capitalism and thereby defined modern society. Weber went on to identify seven characteristics of rational social organization:

1. **Distinctive social institutions.** Among hunters and gatherers, the family is the center of all activity. Gradually, however, other social institutions, including religious, political, and economic systems, become separate from family life. In modern societies, new institutions—education and health care—also appear. The separation of social institutions is a rational way to meet human needs efficiently.

2. **Large-scale organizations.** Modern rationality is clearly evident in the spread of large-scale organizations. As early as the horticultural era, political officials oversaw religious observances, public works, and warfare. In medieval Europe, the Catholic church grew into a huge organization with thousands of officials. In our modern, rational society, the federal government employs millions, and most people work for one large organization or another.

3. **Specialized tasks.** Unlike members of traditional societies, individuals in modern societies perform a wide range of specialized jobs. The classified pages of any city's telephone directory show just how many different occupations there are today.

4. **Personal discipline.** Modern society puts a premium on self-discipline. For early Calvinists, discipline was rooted in religious belief. Although now distanced from its religious origins, discipline is still encouraged by cultural values such as achievement, success, and efficiency.

5. **Awareness of time.** In traditional societies, people measure time according to the rhythm of sun and seasons. Modern people, by contrast, schedule events precisely by the hour and even the minute. Interestingly, clocks began appearing in European cities some 500 years ago, about the time commerce began to expand. Soon, people began to think (to borrow Benjamin Franklin's phrase) "time is money."

6. **Technical competence.** Members of traditional societies size up one another on the basis of *who* they are—how they are joined to others in the web of kinship. Modern rationality prompts us to judge people according to *what* they are, that is, with an eye toward their skills and abilities.

7. **Impersonality.** Finally, in a rational society technical competence takes priority over close relationships, so the world becomes impersonal. People interact

Max Weber agreed with Karl Marx that modern society is alienating to the individual, but they identified different causes of this estrangement. For Marx, economic inequality is the culprit; for Weber, the issue is pervasive and dehumanizing bureaucracy. George Tooker's painting Landscape with Figures echoes Weber's sentiments.

George Tooker, Landscape with Figures, 1963, egg tempera on gesso panel, 26 × 30 in. Private collection. Reproduction courtesy D.C. Moore Gallery, N.Y.C.

as specialists concerned with particular tasks, rather than as individuals broadly concerned with one another. Because feelings are difficult to control, modern people tend to devalue emotion.

All these characteristics can be found in one important expression of modern rationality: bureaucracy.

Rationality and Bureaucracy

Although the medieval church grew large, Weber explained, it remained basically traditional and resisted change. Truly rational organizations that are both efficient and open to change appeared only in the last few centuries. The kind of organization Weber termed *bureaucracy* arose along with capitalism as an expression of the rationality that shapes modern society. Indeed, Weber explained, bureaucracy and capitalism have much in common:

> Today, it is primarily the capitalist market economy which demands that the official business of public administration be discharged precisely, unambiguously, continuously, and with as much speed as possible. Normally, the very large capitalist enterprises are themselves unequaled models of strict bureaucratic organization. (1978:974; orig. 1921)

As Chapter 7 ("Groups and Organizations") explains, we find aspects of bureaucracy in today's businesses, government agencies, labor unions, and universities. Weber considered bureaucracy highly rational because its elements—offices, duties, and policies—help achieve specific goals as efficiently as possible. Thus, Weber concluded, the defining elements of modern society—capitalism, bureaucracy, and science—are all expressions of the same underlying factor: rationality.

Rationality and Alienation

Max Weber joined with Karl Marx in recognizing the efficiency of industrial capitalism. Weber also agreed that modern society generates widespread alienation, although he offered different reasons. Whereas Marx thought alienation was caused by economic inequality, Weber blamed the stifling effect of bureaucracy's countless rules and regulations. Bureaucracies, Weber warned, treat people as a series of cases rather than as unique individuals. In addition, working for large organizations demands highly specialized and often tedious routines. In the end, Weber envisioned modern society as a vast and growing system of rules seeking to regulate everything and thereby to crush the human spirit.

Like Marx, Weber found it ironic that modern society—meant to serve humanity—turns on its creators and enslaves them. Just as Marx described the human toll of industrial capitalism, Weber portrayed the modern individual as "only a small cog in a ceaselessly moving mechanism that prescribes to him an endlessly fixed routine of march" (1978:988; orig. 1921). Although Weber could see the advantages of modern society, he was deeply pessimistic about the future. He feared that, in the end, the rationalization of society would reduce human beings to robots.

EMILE DURKHEIM: SOCIETY AND FUNCTION

"To love society is to love something beyond us and something in ourselves." These are the words (1974:55; orig. 1924) of Emile Durkheim (1858–1917), another of sociology's founders. In them we find one more influential vision of human society.

Durkheim's observation that people with weak social bonds are prone to self-destructive behavior stands as stark evidence of the power of society to shape individual lives. When rock-and-roll singers become famous, they are wrenched out of familiar life patterns and existing relationships, sometimes with deadly results. The history of rock and roll contains many tragic stories of this kind, including (from left) Janis Joplin's and Jimi Hendrix's deaths by drug overdose (both 1970) and Jim Morrison's (1971) and Kurt Cobain's (1994) suicides.

STRUCTURE: SOCIETY BEYOND OURSELVES

Emile Durkheim's great insight was recognizing that society exists beyond ourselves. Society is more than the individuals who compose it; society has a life of its own that stretches beyond our personal experiences. Society was here long before we are born, it shapes us while we live, and it will remain long after we are gone. Patterns of human behavior—cultural norms, values, and beliefs—exist as established structures and thus are *social facts* that have an objective reality beyond the lives of individuals.

 Durkheim is included in the Gallery of Sociologists at http://www.TheSociologyPage.com

Because society looms larger than any one of us, it has the power to guide our thoughts and actions. This is why studying individuals alone (as psychologists or biologists do) can never capture the essence of the human experience. Society is more than the sum of its parts; it exists as a complex organism rooted in our collective life. A classroom of third-graders taking a math test, a family gathered around a table sharing a meal, people quietly waiting their turn in a doctor's office—all are examples of the countless situations that have a familiar organization apart from any particular individual who has ever participated in them.

Once created by people, then, society takes on a life of its own and demands a measure of obedience from its creators. We experience the reality of society in the order of our lives or as we face temptation and feel the tug of morality.

FUNCTION: SOCIETY AS SYSTEM

Having established that society has structure, Durkheim turned to the concept of *function*. The significance of any social fact, he explained, is more than what individuals see in our immediate lives; social facts help society as a whole to operate.

As an illustration, consider crime. Of course, individuals experience pain and loss as a result of crime. But taking a broader view, Durkheim saw that crime is vital to the ongoing life of society itself. As Chapter 8 ("Deviance") explains, only by defining acts as criminal do people construct and defend morality, which gives purpose and meaning to our collective life. For this reason, Durkheim rejected the common view of crime as "pathological." On the contrary, he concluded, crime is "normal" for the most basic of reasons: A society could not exist without it (1964a, orig. 1893; 1964b, orig. 1895).

PERSONALITY: SOCIETY IN OURSELVES

Durkheim contended that society is not only "beyond ourselves" but also "in ourselves," helping to form our personalities. How we act, think, and feel is drawn from the society that nurtures us. Society shapes us in another way as well—serving as the moral discipline that regulates our behavior and reins in our desires. Durkheim held that human beings need the restraint of society because, with insatiable appetites, we are in

Historically, members of human societies engaged in many of the same activities: searching out food and securing shelter. Modern societies, explained Durkheim, display a rapidly expanding division of labor. Increasing specialization is evident in the streets of countries in the process of industrialization: On a Bombay street, a man earns a small fee for cleaning ears.

constant danger of being overpowered by our own desires. As he put it, "The more one has, the more one wants, since satisfactions received only stimulate instead of filling needs" (1966:248; orig. 1897). Society gives us life, then, but it must also rein us in.

Nowhere is the need for societal regulation better illustrated than in Durkheim's study of suicide (1966; orig. 1897), described in Chapter 1 ("The Sociological Perspective"). Why is it that rock stars—from Janis Joplin to Jim Morrison, from Jimi Hendrix to Kurt Cobain—seem so prone to self-destruction? Durkheim had the answer long before anyone made electric music: Now as back then, the *highest* suicide rates are found among categories of people with the *lowest* level of societal regulation. In short, the enormous freedom of the young, rich, and famous exacts a high price in terms of the risk of suicide.

MODERNITY AND ANOMIE

Compared to traditional societies, modern societies impose fewer restrictions on everyone. Durkheim acknowledged the advantages of modern-day freedom, but he warned of increased **anomie**, *a condition in which society provides little moral guidance to individuals.*

The pattern by which many celebrities are "destroyed by fame" well illustrates the destructive effects of anomie. Sudden fame tears people from their families and familiar routines; it disrupts established values and norms; and it breaks down society's support and regulation of an individual—sometimes with fatal results. Thus, Durkheim explained, an individual's desires must be balanced by the claims and guidance of society—a balance that is sometimes difficult in the modern world.

EVOLVING SOCIETIES: THE DIVISION OF LABOR

Like Marx and Weber, Durkheim saw firsthand the rapid social transformation of Europe during the nineteenth century. But Durkheim made his own sense of this change.

In preindustrial societies, explained Durkheim, tradition operates as the social cement that binds people together. In fact, what he termed the *collective conscience* is so strong that the community moves quickly to punish anyone who dares to challenge conventional ways of life. Durkheim used the term **mechanical solidarity** to refer to *social bonds, based on common sentiments and shared moral values, that are strong among members of preindustrial societies.* In practice, mechanical solidarity springs from *likeness.* Durkheim called these bonds "mechanical" because people are linked together in a lockstep, with a more-or-less automatic sense of belonging together.

With industrialization, Durkheim continued, mechanical solidarity becomes weaker and weaker, and people cease to be bound by tradition. But this does not mean that society dissolves. Modern life generates a new type of solidarity. Durkheim called this new social integration **organic solidarity,** defined as *social bonds, based on specialization and interdependence, that are strong among members of industrial societies.* Where solidarity was once rooted in likeness, it is now based on *differences* among people who find that their specialized work—as plumbers, consultants, midwives, or sociology instructors—make them rely on one another for many of their daily needs.

For Durkheim, then, the key to change in a society is an expanding **division of labor,** or *specialized economic activity.* Max Weber said that modern societies specialize in order to become more efficient, and Durkheim filled out the picture by showing that members of modern societies count on tens of thousands of others—most of them strangers—for the goods and services needed every day. That is, as members of

APPLYING SOCIOLOGY

The Information Revolution:
What Would Durkheim (and Others) Have Thought?

New technology is rapidly reshaping our society. Were they alive today, the founding sociologists discussed in this chapter would be eager observers of the current scene. Let's imagine for a moment the kinds of questions Emile Durkheim, Max Weber, and Karl Marx might ask about the effects of computer technology on society.

Emile Durkheim, who emphasized the increasing division of labor in modern society, probably would wonder if new information technology is pushing specialization even further. There is good reason to think that it is. Because electronic communication (say, a Web site) gives anyone a vast market (already, about 600 million people access the Internet), people can specialize far more than if they were confined to a limited geographic area. For example, while most small-town lawyers have a general practice, an information age attorney (living anywhere) can provide specialized guidance on, say, prenuptial agreements or electronic copyright law. Indeed, as we move into the electronic age, the number of highly specialized

microbusinesses in all fields—some of which end up becoming very large—is increasing rapidly.

Durkheim might also point out that the Internet threatens to increase anomie. In part, the reason is that computer use has a tendency to isolate people from personal relationships with others. Then, too, while the Internet offers a flood of information, it provides little in the way of moral guidance about what is true or worth knowing.

Max Weber believed that modern societies are distinctive because their members share a rational worldview, and, of course, nothing illustrates this worldview better than bureaucracy. But will bureaucracy continue to dominate the social scene in the twenty-first century? Here is one reason to think it may not: While it may make sense for organizations to regulate workers performing the kinds of routine tasks that were common in the industrial era, much work in the postindustrial era involves imagination. Consider such "new age" work as designing homes, composing music, and writing software. The creativity involved cannot be regulated in

the same way as, say, assembling automobiles on an assembly line. Perhaps this is the reason many high-technology companies have done away with dress codes and time clocks.

Finally, what might Karl Marx make of the Information Revolution? Since Marx considered the earlier Industrial Revolution a *class* revolution that allowed the owners of industry to dominate society, he would probably wonder whether a new symbolic elite is gaining power over us. Some analysts point out, for example, that film and television writers, producers, and performers now enjoy vast wealth, international prestige, and enormous power (Lichter, Rothman, & Lichter, 1990). Similarly, just as people without industrial skills stayed at the bottom of the class system in past decades, so people without symbolic skills are likely to become the "underclass" of the twenty-first century.

Durkheim, Weber, and Marx greatly improved our understanding of industrial societies. As we continue into the postindustrial age, there is plenty of room for new generations of sociologists to carry on.

modern societies, we depend more and more on people we trust less and less. Why do we look to people we hardly know and whose beliefs may well differ from our own? Durkheim's answer was "Because we can't live without them."

So modernity rests far less on *moral consensus* and far more on *functional interdependence*. Herein lies what we might call "Durkheim's dilemma": The technological power and greater personal freedom of modern society come at the cost of declining morality and the rising risk of anomie.

Like Marx and Weber, Durkheim worried about the direction society was taking. But of the three, Durkheim was the most optimistic. He praised our greater freedom and privacy while hoping we would be able to create laws and other norms to regulate our behavior.

Finally, can we apply Durkheim's views to the Information Revolution? The box suggests that he and the other theorists we have considered in this chapter would have had much to say about today's new computer technology.

CONTROVERSY & DEBATE

Is Society Getting Better or Worse?

Optimism has been a defining trait of U.S. culture; as time goes on, we tend to think, life gets better. There are some good reasons to think this way. To begin, over the last century, the average U.S. income has gone up fourfold, even when inflation is taken into account. Opportunities for higher education have also expanded greatly: Since 1900, we have seen a tenfold increase in the share of U.S. adults who are college graduates.

That's not all. Back in 1900, it was the rare home that had a telephone, and outside of large cities, none had electricity. No one had even heard of television, and the only "horsepower" available was the kind with four legs. Today, almost every home has at least one telephone, a host of electric appliances, television sets, videocassette recorders, and DVD players; most U.S. homes are air-conditioned, are linked to the Internet, and have a garage that keep's one or more automobiles protected. Indeed, not only is life better, but there is also more of it: People born in 1900 lived an average of just forty-seven years; children born today can look forward to reaching age eighty.

But in recent years, our historic optimism may be on the decline. One recent national survey found 67 percent of U.S. adults agreeing that, for the average person, life is getting worse, not better (30 percent disagreed, and 3 percent offered no opinion; NORC, 2003:208). Surely, rough economic times have played a major part in this rising pessimism. The news has been full of stories of corporate CEOs looting companies and forcing them into bankruptcy, throwing people out of work, and often dissolving their pensions as well. Even more people are losing confidence that hard work pays off. Consider this: Even though more households than ever have two or more people in the labor force, average family earnings have risen only slightly. Other trends are also troubling. After 1960, the divorce rate soared upward, and the crime rate went up as well. Researchers tell us that people are not as happy as they used to be. Statistics show the suicide rate is up (Myers, 2000).

Modern society may give us more things, but we are working harder than ever to hold onto them and are less sure that they are our ticket to happiness. Even as we now move farther and faster than ever before, we seem to lack a sense of community. As the economic scandals of the last few years suggest, our cultural individualism seems to have dissolved into pure selfishness. Therefore, it is little surprise that pessimism is on the rise and a majority of U.S. adults claim to believe that "you can't be too careful in dealing with people" (NORC, 2003:181).

The evidence, then, is mixed: In some ways life is getting better and in others it is getting worse. How do we make sense of this complex issue?

The theorists whose ideas we have examined in this chapter can help us. It is easy to equate "high tech" with "progress" and to expect technological discoveries to keep making life better. But as Lenski explains, history shows us that advancing technology may offer real advantages, but it is no guarantee of a better life. Marx, Weber, and Durkheim also noted that, as modern society becomes more and more productive, there is a dangerous tendency toward individualism. For Marx, capitalism is the culprit, elevating money to a godlike status and fostering a culture of selfishness. In Weber's analysis the modern spirit of rationality erodes traditional ties of kinship and neighborhood while expanding bureaucracy, which, he warned, manipulates and isolates people. For Durkheim, members of modern societies may need one another, but they are more and more strangers to each other and share few moral norms by which to judge right and wrong.

This chapter has shown us that technological advances certainly change society. But invention of this kind is no solution to many of the problems that plague us. On the contrary, evidence suggests that new technology makes some problems worse, forcing us to work even harder at the task of building a satisfying and just society.

CRITICAL EVALUATION: FOUR VISIONS OF SOCIETY

This chapter opened with several important questions about society. We will conclude by summarizing how each of the four visions of society answers these questions.

What Holds Societies Together?

How is something as complex as society possible? Lenski claims that members of a society are united by a shared culture, although cultural patterns vary according to a society's level of technological development. He also points out that, as technology becomes more complex, inequality divides a society more and more, although industrialization reduces inequality somewhat.

Marx saw not unity but social division based on class position. From his point of view, elites may force an uneasy peace, but true social unity will occur only if production becomes a cooperative endeavor. To Weber, the members of a society share a worldview. Just as tradition joined people together in the past, so modern societies have created rational, large-scale organizations that connect people's lives. Finally, Durkheim made solidarity the focus of his work. He contrasted the mechanical solidarity of preindustrial societies, which is based on shared morality, with modern society's organic solidarity, which is based on specialization.

How Have Societies Changed?

According to the Lenski model of sociocultural evolution, societies differ primarily in terms of changing technology. Modern society stands out in this regard with its enormous productive power. Marx also stressed historical differences in productive systems yet pointed to the persistence of social conflict (except perhaps among simple hunters and gatherers). For Marx, modern society is distinctive only because it brings that conflict out in the open. Weber considered the question of change from the perspective of how people look at the world.

Members of preindustrial societies have a traditional outlook, whereas modern people take a rational worldview. Finally, for Durkheim, traditional societies are characterized by mechanical solidarity based on moral likeness. In industrial societies, mechanical solidarity gives way to organic solidarity based on productive specialization.

Why Do Societies Change?

As Lenski sees it, social change is first and foremost a matter of technological innovation that, over time, transforms an entire society. Marx's materialist approach highlights the struggle between classes as the "engine of history," pushing societies toward revolution and reorganization. Weber, on the other hand, pointed out how ideas contribute to social change. He demonstrated how a particular worldview—Calvinism—advanced the Industrial Revolution, which, in turn, reshaped just about all of society. Finally, Durkheim pointed to an expanding division of labor as the key dimension of social change.

The fact that these four approaches are so different does not mean that any one of them is right or wrong in an absolute sense. Society is exceedingly complex, and our understanding of society benefits from applying all four visions, as shown in the final box.

SUMMARY

Gerhard Lenski

1. Sociocultural evolution explores the effects of technological advances on societies.

2. The earliest hunting, and gathering societies were composed of a small number of family-centered nomads. Such societies have all but vanished from today's world.

3. Horticulture began some 12,000 years ago as people created hand tools for cultivation. Pastoral societies domesticate animals and create networks of trade.

4. Agriculture, about 5,000 years old, is large-scale cultivation using animal-drawn plows. This technology allows societies to expand into vast empires, with greater productivity, more specialization, and increasing inequality.

5. Industrialization began 250 years ago in Europe as people used new energy sources to operate large machinery.

6. In postindustrial societies, production shifts from heavy machinery making material things to computers and related technology processing information.

Karl Marx

7. Marx's materialist analysis points up conflict between social classes.

8. Conflict in "ancient" societies involved masters and slaves; in agrarian societies, nobles oppose serfs; in industrial-capitalist societies, capitalists oppose the proletariat.

9. Industrial capitalism alienates workers in four ways: from the act of working, from the products of work, from other workers, and from their own potential.

10. Marx believed that once workers overcame their false consciousness, they would overthrow the industrial-capitalist system.

Max Weber

11. Weber's idealist approach argues that ideas have a powerful effect on society.

12. Weber contrasted the tradition of preindustrial societies with the rationality of modern, industrial societies.

13. Weber traced the origins of capitalism to Calvinist religious beliefs. In his analysis, capitalism is "disenchanted" religion.

14. Weber feared that rationality, especially in efficient bureaucratic organizations, would stifle human creativity.

Emile Durkheim

15. Durkheim explained that society has an objective existence apart from individuals.

16. Durkheim related social elements to the larger society through their functions.

17. Societies require solidarity. Traditional societies have mechanical solidarity, which is based on moral likeness; modern societies depend on organic solidarity, which is based on specialization (the division of labor).

KEY CONCEPTS

society (p. 89) people who interact in a defined territory and share a culture

sociocultural evolution (p. 90) Lenski's term for the changes that occur as a society acquires new technology

hunting and gathering (p. 90) the use of simple tools to hunt animals and gather vegetation

horticulture (p. 91) the use of hand tools to raise crops

pastoralism (p. 91) the domestication of animals

agriculture (p. 92) large-scale cultivation using plows harnessed to animals or more powerful energy sources

industrialism (p. 93) the production of goods using advanced sources of energy to drive large machinery

postindustrialism (p. 95) technology that supports an information-based economy

social conflict (p. 97) the struggle between segments of society over valued resources

capitalists (p. 97) people who own and operate factories and other businesses in pursuit of profits

proletarians (p. 98) people who sell their productive labor for wages

social institutions (p. 98) the major spheres of social life, or societal subsystems, organized to meet human needs

false consciousness (p. 98) Marx's term for explanations of social problems as the shortcomings of individuals rather than as the flaws of society

class conflict (p. 100) conflict between entire classes over the distribution of a society's wealth and power

class consciousness (p. 100) Marx's term for workers' recognition of themselves as a class unified in opposition to capitalists and, ultimately, to capitalism itself

alienation (p. 100) the experience of isolation and misery resulting from powerlessness

ideal type (p. 102) an abstract statement of the essential characteristics of any social phenomenon

tradition (p. 103) sentiments and beliefs passed from generation to generation

rationality (p. 103) a way of thinking that emphasizes deliberate, matter-of-fact calculation of the most efficient means to accomplish a particular task

rationalization of society (p. 103) Weber's term for the historical change from tradition to rationality as the dominant mode of human thought

anomie (p. 108) Durkheim's designation of a condition in which society provides little moral guidance to individuals

mechanical solidarity (p. 108) Durkheim's term for social bonds, based on common sentiments and shared moral values, that are strong among members of preindustrial societies

organic solidarity (p. 108) Durkheim's term for social bonds, based on specialization and interdependence, that are strong among members of industrial societies

division of labor (p. 108) specialized economic activity

CRITICAL-THINKING QUESTIONS

1. Would you say that development of new technology is the same as "progress"? Why or why not?

2. Explain how Marx's materialist view of society differs from the idealist view held by Weber.

3. Both Marx and Weber were concerned that modern society alienated people. How are their approaches different? How do their concepts of alienation compare to Durkheim's concept of anomie?

4. Marx, Weber, and Durkheim each argued that people create society, but that, once created, society takes on a life of its own and shapes people's behavior. Can you explain each social thinker's reasoning?

APPLICATIONS AND EXERCISES

1. Hunting and gathering people mused over the stars, and we still know the constellations in terms they used—mostly the names of animals and hunters. As a way of revealing what's important to *our* way of life, write a short paper imagining the meanings we would give clusters of stars if we were starting from scratch.

2. Spend an hour in your home trying to identify every device that has a computer chip in it. How many did you find? Were you surprised by the number?

3. Watch an old Tarzan movie or another film about technologically simple people. How are they portrayed in the film?

4. Packaged in the back of this new textbook is an interactive CD-ROM that offers a variety of video and interactive review materials intended to help you better understand the material covered in this chapter. For this chapter, the CD-ROM contains a relevant clip from *ABC News*, an author's tip video, interactive map animations, an interactive time line, and flashcards with audio pronunciations of the more difficult words.

 ## SITES TO SEE

http://www.prenhall.com/macionis

Visit the interactive Companion Website™ that accompanies this text. Begin by clicking on the cover of your book. You will find a chapter-by-chapter study guide, practice tests, suggested Web links, and links to other relevant material.

http://www.hewett.norfolk.sch.uk/curric/soc/durkheim/durk.htm
http://csf.colorado.edu:80/psn/marx/index.html

These two sites provide a close-up look at the work of two great sociologists.

http://www.TheSociologyPage.com
(or http://www.macionis.com)

Biographical sketches of Marx, Weber, and Durkheim, as well as other social thinkers, are found at the author's Web site.

http://www2.pfeiffer.edu/~lridener/DSS/DEADSOC.HTML

Visit the Dead Sociologists' Society to learn more about Marx, Weber, and other sociologists.

http://www.gwu.edu/~ccps/

Visit the Web site for the Communitarian Network, an organization concerned with balancing modern individuality with traditional social responsibility.

 ## INVESTIGATE WITH RESEARCH NAVIGATOR™

Follow the instructions on page 24 of this text to access the features of **Research Navigator™**. Once at the Web site, enter your Login Name and Password. Then, to use the **Content Select™** database, enter keywords such as "Karl Marx," "technology," and "Emile Durkheim," and the search engine will supply relevant and recent scholarly and popular press publications. Use the *New York Times* **Search-by-Subject Archive** to find recent news articles related to sociology and the **Link Library** feature to find relevant Web links organized by the key terms associated with this chapter.

SOCIALIZATION

WAYNE HEALY
Bolero Familiar Serigraph
2002. 36 in. × 50 in. Monoprint.

O N A COLD winter day in 1938, a social worker walked quickly to the door of a rural Pennsylvania farmhouse. Investigating a case of possible child abuse, the social worker entered the home and soon discovered a five-year-old girl hidden in a second-floor storage room. The child, whose name was Anna, was wedged into an old chair with her arms tied above her head so that she couldn't move. She was wearing filthy clothes, and her arms and legs were as thin as matchsticks (Davis, 1940).

Anna's situation can only be described as tragic. She had been born in 1932 to an unmarried and mentally impaired woman of twenty-six who lived with her strict father. Enraged by his daughter's "illegitimate" motherhood, the grandfather did not even want the child in his house.

For her first six months, therefore, Anna was shuttled among various welfare agencies. When her mother was no longer able to pay for her care, Anna returned to the hostile home of her grandfather.

To lessen the grandfather's anger, Anna's mother moved Anna to the storage room and gave her just enough milk to keep her alive. There she stayed—day after day, month after month, with almost no human contact—for five long years.

Learning of the discovery of Anna, sociologist Kingsley Davis (1940) immediately went to see her. He found her with local authorities at a county home. Davis was appalled by the emaciated child, who could not laugh, speak, or even smile. Anna was completely unresponsive, as if alone in an empty world.

SOCIAL EXPERIENCE: THE KEY TO OUR HUMANITY

Socialization is so basic to human development that we may overlook its importance. But here, in a terrible case of an isolated child, we can see what humans would be like without social contact. Although physically alive, Anna hardly seems to have been human. Her plight reveals that, without social experience, a child is incapable of thought, emotion, or meaningful action—more an *object* than a *person*.

Sociologists use the term **socialization** to refer to *the lifelong social experience by which individuals develop their human potential and learn culture.* Unlike other living species, whose behavior is biologically set, humans need social experience to learn their culture and to survive. Social experience is also the foundation of **personality,** *a person's fairly consistent patterns of acting, thinking, and feeling.* We build a personality by internalizing—or taking in—our surroundings. But without social experience, as Anna's case shows, personality hardly develops at all.

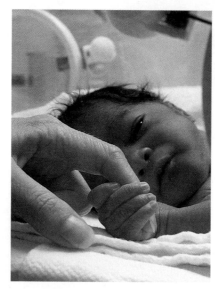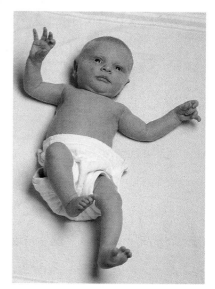

Human infants display various reflexes—biologically based behavior patterns that enhance survival. The sucking reflex, which actually begins before birth, enables the infant to obtain nourishment. The grasping reflex, triggered by placing a finger on the infant's palm causing the hand to close, helps the infant to maintain contact with a parent and, later on, to grasp objects. The Moro reflex, activated by startling the infant, has the infant swinging both arms outward and then bringing them together across the chest. This action, which disappears after several months of life, probably developed among our evolutionary ancestors so that a falling infant could grasp the body hair of a parent.

HUMAN DEVELOPMENT: NATURE AND NURTURE

Helpless at birth, the human infant depends on others to provide nourishment and care. Anna's case makes these facts clear. But a century ago, most people mistakenly believed that human behavior was the product of our biology.

The Biological Sciences: The Role of Nature

Charles Darwin's groundbreaking study of evolution, described in Chapter 3 ("Culture"), explained that each species evolves over thousands of generations as genetic variations improve its ability to survive and reproduce. Traits that enhance survival emerge as a species' "nature." For this reason people once assumed that humans, like other life forms, had an instinctive "human nature." Given our tendency to see our own way of life as "natural," people argued that our economic system reflects "instinctive human competitiveness," that some people are "born criminals," or that women are "naturally" emotional while men are "innately" rational (Witkin-Lanoil, 1984).

People trying to understand cultural diversity also misunderstood Darwin's thinking. From centuries of world exploration, Western Europeans knew that people around the world behaved quite differently from each other. But Europeans linked these differences to biology rather than culture. It was an easy, although very damaging, next step to claim that members of technologically simple societies were biologically less evolved and therefore, less human. This ethnocentric view helped justify colonialism: Why not exploit others if they seem not to be human in the same sense that you are?

The Social Sciences: The Role of Nurture

In the twentieth century, biological explanations of human behavior came under fire. Psychologist John B. Watson (1878–1958) developed a theory called *behaviorism*, which holds that behavior is not instinctive but learned. Thus, people everywhere are equally human, differing only in their learned cultural patterns. Watson, in short, rooted human behavior not in nature but in *nurture*.

Today, social scientists are cautious about describing *any* human behavior as instinctive. This does not mean that biology plays *no* part in human behavior. Human life, after all, depends on the functioning of the body. We also know that children often share biological traits (like height and hair color) with their parents and that heredity plays a part in intelligence, musical and artistic aptitude, and personality (such as how one reacts to frustration). In fact, unless children use their brains early in life, the brain itself does not fully develop. At the same time, whether a person *realizes* any inherited potential depends on an environmental factor—having an opportunity to develop it (Plomin & Foch, 1980; Goldsmith, 1983; Begley, 1995).

Without denying the importance of nature, then, nurture matters more in shaping human behavior. More precisely, *nurture is our nature.*

SOCIAL ISOLATION

Studying socialization is difficult. Of course, researchers must never experiment on human beings by placing them in total isolation. But forty years ago, researchers did carry out a revealing study of the effects of social isolation, in which they used nonhuman primates. The study highlighted the importance of socialization, just as the case of Anna does.

Studies of Nonhuman Primates

Psychologists Harry Harlow and Margaret Harlow (1962) placed rhesus monkeys—whose behavior is in some ways surprisingly similar to human behavior—in various conditions of social isolation. They found that complete isolation (with adequate nutrition) for even six months seriously disturbed the monkeys' development. When returned to their group, these monkeys were passive, anxious, and fearful.

The Harlows then placed infant rhesus monkeys in cages with an artificial "mother" made of wire mesh with a wooden head and the nipple of a feeding tube where the breast would be. These monkeys, too, were later unable to interact with others.

But when the researchers covered the artificial "mother" with soft terry cloth, the infant monkeys would cling to it. Because these monkeys showed less developmental damage than earlier groups, the Harlows concluded that the monkeys benefited from this closeness. The experiment confirmed how important it is that adults cradle infants affectionately.

Early in the twentieth century, most people in the United States thought biology shaped human behavior. The discipline of anthropology helped demonstrate the primary importance of environment in human development. The best known of all anthropologists was Margaret Mead (1901–1978), who spent her life comparing the behavior of people living in different cultural settings.

Finally, the Harlows discovered that infant monkeys could recover from about three months of isolation. But by about six months, isolation caused irreversible emotional and behavioral damage.

Studies of Isolated Children

Tragic cases of children isolated by abusive family members show the damage caused by depriving human beings of social experience. We will review three such cases.

Anna: The rest of the story. The rest of Anna's story squares with the Harlows' findings. After her discovery, Anna received extensive attention and soon showed improvement. When Kingsley Davis visited her after ten days, he found her more alert and even smiling with obvious pleasure. Over the next year, Anna made steady progress, showing more interest in other people and gradually learning to walk. After a year and a half, she could feed herself and play with toys.

As the Harlows might have predicted, however, Anna's five years of social isolation had caused permanent damage. At age eight, her mental development was less than a two-year-old's. Not until she was almost ten did she begin to use words. Since Anna's mother was mentally retarded, perhaps Anna was similarly challenged. The riddle was never solved, because Anna died at age ten from a blood disorder, possibly related to years of abuse (Davis, 1940, 1947).

Another case: Isabelle. A second case involves another girl, found at about the same time as Anna and under much the same circumstances. After more than six years of virtual isolation, this girl—known as Isabelle—displayed the same lack of responsiveness as Anna. Unlike Anna, though, Isabelle benefited from a special learning program directed by psychologists. Within a week, Isabelle was attempting to speak, and a year and a half later, she knew some 2,000 words. The psychologists concluded that intensive effort had propelled Isabelle through six years of normal development in only two years. By the time she was fourteen, Isabelle was attending sixth-grade classes, damaged by her early ordeal but on her way to a somewhat normal life (Davis, 1947).

A third case: Genie. A more recent case of childhood isolation involves a California girl abused by her parents (Curtiss, 1977; Pines, 1981; Rymer, 1994). From age two, Genie was tied to a potty chair in a dark garage. In 1970, when she was found at age thirteen, Genie weighed only fifty-nine pounds and had the mental development of a one-year-old. With

 Read a transcript of the PBS *Nova* television program about the life of Genie at http://www.pbs.org/wgbh/nova/transcripts/2112gchild.html

intensive treatment, she became physically healthy, but her language ability remains that of a young child. Genie lives today in a home for developmentally disabled adults.

Conclusion. All the evidence points to the crucial role of social experience in personality development. Human beings can recover from abuse and short-term isolation. But there is a point—precisely when is unclear from the small number of cases studied—at which isolation in infancy causes permanent developmental damage.

UNDERSTANDING SOCIALIZATION

Socialization is a complex, lifelong process. The following sections highlight the work of six researchers who have made lasting contributions to our understanding of human development.

SIGMUND FREUD: THE ELEMENTS OF PERSONALITY

Sigmund Freud (1856–1939) lived in Vienna at a time when most Europeans considered human behavior

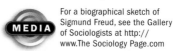 For a biographical sketch of Sigmund Freud, see the Gallery of Sociologists at http://www.The Sociology Page.com

biologically fixed. Trained as a physician, Freud gradually turned to the study of personality and mental disorder and eventually developed the celebrated theory of psychoanalysis.

Basic Human Needs

Freud believed that biology plays a major part in human development, although not in terms of specific instincts, as is the case in other species. Rather, he theorized that humans have two basic needs that are there at birth. First is a need for bonding, which Freud called the "life instinct," or *eros* (from the Greek god of love). Second, we have an aggressive drive he called the "death instinct," or *thanatos* (from the Greek, meaning "death"). These opposing forces operate at an unconscious level and generate deep inner tension.

Freud's Model of Personality

Freud joined basic needs with the influence of society to form a model of personality with three parts: id, ego, and superego. The **id** (the Latin word for "it") represents *the human being's basic drives*, which are unconscious and demand immediate satisfaction. Rooted in biology, the id is present at birth, making a newborn a bundle of demands for attention, touching, and food. But society opposes the self-centered id, which is why one of the first words a child learns is "no."

To avoid frustration, a child must learn to approach the world realistically. This is done through the **ego** (Latin for "I"), which is *a person's conscious efforts to balance innate pleasure-seeking drives with the demands of society*. The ego develops as we become aware of ourselves and at the same time realize that we cannot have everything we want.

The personalities we develop depend largely on the environment in which we live. As William Kurelek shows in this painting, Prairie Childhood, based on his childhood in the Alberta, Canada, prairies, a young person's life on a farm is often characterized by periods of social isolation and backbreaking work. How would such a boy's personality be likely to differ from that of his wealthy cousin raised in a large city, such as Montreal?

William Kurelek, Prairie Childhood. The Estate of William Kurelek and the Isaacs Gallery, Toronto.

Finally, the human personality develops the **superego** (Latin meaning "above" or "beyond" the ego), which is *the cultural values and norms internalized by an individual*. The superego operates as our conscience, telling us *why* we cannot have everything we want. The superego begins to form as a child becomes aware of parental control, and it matures as the child comes to understand that everyone's behavior must take cultural norms into account.

Personality Development

To the id-centered child, the world is a bewildering array of physical sensations that bring either pleasure or pain. As the superego develops, however, the child learns the moral concepts of right and wrong. Initially, in other words, children can feel good only in a physical way (such as by being held and cuddled), but after three or four years, they feel good or bad according to how they judge their behavior against cultural norms (doing "the right thing").

The id and superego remain in conflict, but in a well-adjusted person, the ego manages these two opposing forces. When conflicts are not resolved during childhood, they may surface as personality disorders later on.

Culture, in the form of the superego, serves to *repress* selfish demands, forcing people to look beyond themselves. Often, the competing demands of self and society result in a compromise that Freud called *sublimation*. Sublimation redirects selfish drives into socially acceptable behavior. Sexual urges, for example, may lead to marriage, just as aggression gives rise to competitive sports.

Critical evaluation. Freud's work was controversial in his own time. More recently, critics have charged that Freud's work presents humans in male terms and devalues women (Donovan & Littenberg, 1982). His theories are also difficult to test scientifically. But Freud influenced everyone who later studied the human personality. Of special importance to sociology is his notion that we internalize social norms and that childhood experiences have a lasting impact on our personalities.

JEAN PIAGET: COGNITIVE DEVELOPMENT

Swiss psychologist Jean Piaget (1896–1980) studied human *cognition*, that is, how people think. As Piaget watched his

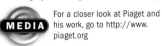
For a closer look at Piaget and his work, go to http://www.piaget.org

In a well-known experiment, Jean Piaget demonstrated that children over the age of seven had entered the concrete operational stage of development because they could recognize that the quantity of liquid remained the same when poured from a wide beaker into a tall one.

own three children, he wondered not just *what* they knew but *how* they made sense of the world. Piaget went on to identify four stages of cognitive development.

The Sensorimotor Stage

Stage one is the **sensorimotor stage,** *the level of human development at which individuals experience the world only through their senses.* For about the first two years of life, the infant knows the world only through the five senses: touching, tasting, smelling, looking, and listening. "Knowing" to young children amounts to direct, sensory experience.

The Preoperational Stage

About age two, children enter the **preoperational stage,** *the level of human development at which individuals first use language and other symbols.* Now children begin to think about the world mentally and with imagination. But "pre-op" children between about two and six still attach meaning only to specific experiences and objects. They can identify a favorite toy but cannot explain what *kinds* of toys they like.

Lacking abstract concepts, a child also cannot judge size, weight, or volume. In one of his best-known experiments, Piaget placed two identical glasses containing equal amounts of water on a table. He asked several children ages five and six if the

amount in each glass was the same. They nodded that it was. The children then watched Piaget take one of the glasses and pour its contents into a taller, narrower glass, so the level of the water in the glass was higher. He asked again if each glass held the same amount. The typical five- and six-year-old now insisted that the taller glass held more water. By about age seven, children are able to think abstractly and realize that the amount of water stays the same.

The Concrete Operational Stage

Next comes the **concrete operational stage,** *the level of human development at which individuals first perceive causal connections in their surroundings.* Between ages seven and eleven, children focus on how and why things happen. In addition, children now attach more than one symbol to a particular event or object. If, for example, you say to a child of five, "Today is Wednesday," she might respond, "No, it's my birthday!" indicating that she can use just one symbol at a time. But a ten-year-old at the concrete operational stage would be able to respond, "Yes, and this Wednesday is my birthday!"

The Formal Operational Stage

The last stage in Piaget's model is the **formal operational stage,** *the level of human development at which individuals think abstractly and critically.* At about age twelve, young people begin to reason abstractly rather than thinking only of concrete situations. If, for example, you were to ask a child of seven, "What would you like to be when you grow up?" you might receive a concrete response such as "a teacher." But most teenagers can think more abstractly and might reply, "I would like a job that helps others." This capacity for abstract thought also lets young people understand metaphors. Hearing the phrase "A penny for your thoughts" might lead a child to ask for a coin, but the adolescent will recognize a gentle invitation to intimacy.

Critical evaluation. While Freud saw human beings torn by opposing forces of biology and culture, Piaget saw the mind as active and creative. He saw an ability to engage the world unfolding in stages as the result of both biological maturation and social experience.

One criticism of Piaget's theory is that the cognitive development of some children, depending on their innate abilities and their environment, is faster or slower than that of others. Therefore, children may reach the various stages of development sooner or later than the age guidelines noted above.

Finally, do people everywhere pass through all four of Piaget's stages? Living in a traditional society that changes slowly limits the capacity for abstract and critical thought. Even in our own society, perhaps 30 percent of people never reach the formal operational stage (Kohlberg & Gilligan, 1971).

LAWRENCE KOHLBERG: MORAL DEVELOPMENT

Lawrence Kohlberg (1981) built on Piaget's work in studying *moral reasoning*, how individuals judge situations as right or wrong. Here, again, development occurs in stages.

Young children who experience the world in terms of pain and pleasure (Piaget's sensorimotor stage) are at the *preconventional* level of moral development. At this early stage, in other words, "rightness" amounts to "what feels good to me." For example, a young child may simply reach for something on a table that looks interesting, which is the reason parents of young children typically try to "childproof" their homes.

The *conventional* level, Kohlberg's second stage, appears by the teen years (corresponding to Piaget's final, formal operational stage). At this point, young people lose some of their selfishness as they learn to define right and wrong in terms of what pleases parents and what is consistent with broader cultural norms. Individuals at this stage also try to assess intention in reaching moral judgments instead of simply observing what others do. For example, they understand that stealing food in order to feed a hungry family is more defensible morally than stealing a book just to save money.

In Kohlberg's final stage of moral development, the *postconventional* level, individuals move beyond their society's norms to consider abstract ethical principles. Now they think about liberty, freedom, or justice, perhaps arguing that what is legal still may not be right. When African American activist Rosa Parks refused to give up her seat on a Birmingham, Alabama, bus in 1955, she violated that city's segregation laws in pursuit of racial justice.

Critical evaluation. Like the work of Piaget, Kohlberg's model presents moral development in distinct stages. But here again, the precise time frame will vary from person to person. Moreover, many people in the United States apparently never reach the postconventional level of moral reasoning, although exactly why is still an open question. In addition, this model may not apply in the same way to people in all societies.

Another problem with Kohlberg's research is that his subjects were all boys. Kohlberg commits the research error, described in Chapter 2 ("Sociological Investigation"), of generalizing the results of male subjects to all people. This problem led a colleague, Carol Gilligan, to investigate how gender affects moral reasoning.

CAROL GILLIGAN: THE GENDER FACTOR

Carol Gilligan, whose approach is highlighted in the box on page 122, compared the moral development of girls and boys and concluded that the two sexes use different standards of rightness.

Gilligan (1982, 1990) claims that males have a *justice perspective*, relying on formal rules to define right and wrong. Girls, on the other hand, have a *care and responsibility perspective*, judging a situation with an eye toward personal relationships. For example, as boys see it, stealing is wrong because it breaks the law. Girls are more likely to wonder why someone would steal and to be sympathetic toward a person who steals, say, to feed a hungry child.

Kohlberg considers rule-based male reasoning superior to the person-based female approach. But Gilligan notes that impersonal rules dominate men's lives in the workplace, whereas personal relationships are more relevant to women's lives as mothers and caregivers. Why, then, Gilligan asks, should we set up male standards as the norms by which to judge everyone?

Critical evaluation. Gilligan's work sharpens our understanding of human development and gender issues in research. Yet what accounts for the differences she documents between females and males? Is it nature or nurture? Are girls naturally more caring or are they socialized that way? In Gilligan's view, cultural conditioning is at work. Thus, as more women organize their lives around the workplace, the moral reasoning of women and men will become more similar.

GEORGE HERBERT MEAD: THE SOCIAL SELF

George Herbert Mead (1863–1931) developed a theory of *social behaviorism* to explain how social experience creates individual personality (1962; orig. 1934). His approach calls to mind the behaviorism of psychologist John B. Watson, described earlier. Both saw the power of environment to shape behavior. But

 MEDIA A short biography of George Herbert Mead is included in the Gallery of Sociologists at http://www.TheSociologyPage.com

CRITICAL THINKING

The Importance of Gender in Research

Carol Gilligan, an educational psychologist at Harvard University, has shown how gender guides social behavior. Her early work exposed the gender bias in studies by Kohlberg and others who had used only male subjects. But as her research progressed,  Gilligan made a major discovery: Boys and girls actually use different strategies in making moral decisions. Therefore, by ignoring gender, we end up with an incomplete view of human behavior.

Gilligan has also looked at the effect of gender on self-esteem. Her research team interviewed more than 2,000 girls, ages six to eighteen, over a five-year period. She found a clear pattern: Young girls start out eager and confident, but their self-esteem slips away as they pass through adolescence.

Why? Gilligan claims that the answer lies in our society's socialization of females. In our society, the ideal woman is calm, controlled, and eager to please. Then, too, as girls move from the elementary grades to secondary school, they encounter fewer women teachers and find that most authority figures are men. As a result, by their late teens, girls must struggle to regain the personal strength they had a decade before.

Ironically, when Gilligan and her colleagues returned to a private school—one site of their research—to present their findings, they found further evidence of their theory. Most younger girls who had been interviewed were eager to have their names appear in the forthcoming book, but the older girls were hesitant: Many were fearful that they would be talked about.

What do you think?

1. *How does Gilligan's research show the importance of gender in understanding society?*

2. *How does her work show that socialization may not be a direct and linear progression?*

3. *Do you think boys are subject to some of the same pressures and difficulties as girls? How?*

Sources: Gilligan (1990) and Winkler (1990).

---

whereas Watson focused on outward behavior, Mead studied inward *thinking*, humanity's defining trait.

The Self

Mead's central concept is the **self,** *that part of an individual's personality composed of self-awareness and self-image.* Mead's genius was in seeing the self as the product of social experience.

First, said Mead, *the self develops only with social experience.* The self is not part of the body, and it does not exist at birth. Mead rejected the position that personality is guided by biological drives (as Freud asserted) or biological maturation (as Piaget claimed). For Mead, self develops only as the individual interacts with others. In the absence of interaction, as we see from cases of isolated children, the body grows, but no self emerges.

Second, Mead explained, *social experience is the exchange of symbols.* Only people use words, a wave of the hand, or a smile to create meaning. We can train a dog using reward and punishment, but the dog attaches no meaning to its actions. Human beings, by contrast, find meaning in action by imagining people's underlying intentions. In short, a dog responds to *what you do*; a human responds to *what you have in mind* as you do it. Thus, you can train a dog to go to the hallway and bring back an umbrella. But because it doesn't understand intention, if the dog cannot find the umbrella it is incapable of the *human* response: to look for a raincoat instead.

Third, Mead continued, *understanding intention requires imagining the situation from the other's point of view.* Using symbols, we imagine ourselves "in another person's shoes" and see ourselves as that person does. We can therefore anticipate how others will respond to us even before we act. A simple toss of a ball requires stepping outside ourselves to imagine how another will catch our throw. Social interaction, then, involves seeing ourselves as others see us—a process that Mead termed *taking the role of the other*.

The Looking-Glass Self

In effect, others represent a mirror (which people used to call a "looking glass") in which we can see ourselves.

What we think of ourselves, then, depends on what we think others think of us. For example, if we think others see us as clever, we will think of ourselves in the same way. But if we feel they think of us as clumsy, then that is how we will see ourselves. Charles Horton Cooley (1864–1929) used the phrase **looking-glass self** to mean *a self-image based on how we think others see us* (1964; orig. 1902).

The I and the Me

Mead's fourth point is that *by taking the role of the other, we become self-aware.* The self, then, has two parts. As subject, the self is active and spontaneous. Mead called the active side of the self the "I" (the subjective form of the personal pronoun). But the self is also an object, as we imagine ourselves as others see us. Mead called the objective side of the self the "me" (the objective form of the personal pronoun). All social experience has both components: We initiate an action (the I-phase of self) and then we continue the action based on how others respond to us (the me-phase of self).

Development of the Self

According to Mead, then, the key to developing the self is learning to take the role of the other. With limited social experience, infants can do this only through *imitation*. That is, they mimic behavior without understanding underlying intentions and so have no self.

As children learn to use language and other symbols, the self emerges through *play*, which involves taking the roles of *significant others*, especially parents. Playing "mommy and daddy" (often putting themselves, literally, "in the shoes" of a parent) helps young children imagine the world from a parent's point of view.

Gradually, children learn to take the roles of several others at once. Now they can move from simple play (say, playing catch) involving one other to complex *games* (like baseball) involving many others. By about age seven, most children have the social experience needed to engage in team sports.

Figure 5–1 on page 124 charts the progression from imitation to play to games. But a final stage in the development of self remains. A game involves taking the role of others in just one situation, but social life demands that we see ourselves in terms of cultural norms as *anyone* else might. Mead used the term **generalized other** to refer to *widespread cultural norms and values we use as a reference in evaluating ourselves.*

George Herbert Mead wrote: "No hard-and-fast line can be drawn between our own selves and the selves of others." The painting Manyness by Rimma Gerlovina and Valeriy Gerlovin conveys this important truth. Although we tend to think of ourselves as unique individuals, each person's characteristics develop in an ongoing process of interaction with others.

Rimma Gerlovina and Valeriy Gerlovin, Manyness, 1990. © the artists, New City, N.Y.

As life goes on, the self continues to change along with our social experiences. But no matter how much events and circumstances affect us, we always remain creative beings, able to act back on the world. Thus, Mead concluded, we play a key role in our own socialization.

Critical evaluation. Mead's work explores the character of social experience itself. In symbolic interaction, he believed he had found the root of both self and society.

Some criticize Mead's view as completely social, allowing no biological element at all. In this, Mead stands apart from Freud (who identified general drives within the organism) and Piaget (whose stages of development are tied to biological maturity).

Be careful not to confuse Mead's concepts of the I and the me with Freud's id and superego. For Freud, the id originates in our biology, while Mead rejected any biological element of self (although he never

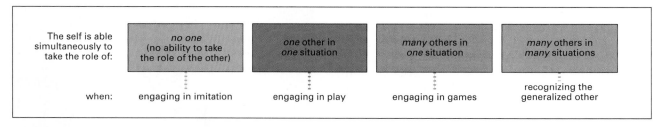

The self is able simultaneously to take the role of:	*no one* (no ability to take the role of the other)	*one* other in *one* situation	*many* others in *one* situation	*many* others in *many* situations
when:	engaging in imitation	engaging in play	engaging in games	recognizing the generalized other

FIGURE 5-1 Building on Social Experience

George Herbert Mead described the development of the self as a process of gaining social experience. That is, the self develops as we expand our capacity to take the role of the other.

specified the origin of the I). Moreover, while the id and the superego are locked in continual combat, the I and the me work cooperatively together (Meltzer, 1978).

ERIK H. ERIKSON: EIGHT STAGES OF DEVELOPMENT

Although some analysts (including Freud) point to childhood as the crucial time when personality takes shape, Erik H. Erikson (1902–1994) took a broader view of socialization. He explained that we face challenges throughout the life course. Erikson outlined eight stages of human development, each linked to a major life challenge (1963; orig. 1950).

> **Stage 1—Infancy: the challenge of trust (versus mistrust).** Between birth and about eighteen months, infants face the first of life's challenges: to establish a sense of trust that their world is a safe place. Family members play a key role in how the child meets this challenge.
>
> **Stage 2—Toddlerhood: the challenge of autonomy (versus doubt and shame).** The next challenge, up to age three, is to learn skills for coping with the world confidently. Failing to gain self-control leads children to doubt their abilities.
>
> **Stage 3—Preschool: the challenge of initiative (versus guilt).** Four- and five-year-olds must learn to engage their surroundings—including people outside the family—or experience guilt at failing to meet the expectations of parents and others.
>
> **Stage 4—Preadolescence: the challenge of industriousness (versus inferiority).** Between ages six and thirteen, children enter

school, make friends, and strike out on their own more and more. They either feel proud of their accomplishments or fear that they do not measure up.

> **Stage 5—Adolescence: the challenge of gaining identity (versus confusion).** During the teen years, young people struggle to establish their own identity. In part, teenagers identify with others, but they also want to be unique. Almost all teens experience some confusion as they struggle to establish an identity.
>
> **Stage 6—Young adulthood: the challenge of intimacy (versus isolation).** The challenge for young adults is to form and maintain intimate relationships with others. Falling in love (as well as making close friends) involves balancing the need to bond with the need to have a separate identity.
>
> **Stage 7—Middle adulthood: the challenge of making a difference (versus self-absorption).** The challenge of middle age is contributing to the lives of others in the family, at work, and in the larger world. Failing at this, people become stagnant, caught up in their own limited concerns (think of Scrooge in Dickens's classic *A Christmas Carol*).
>
> **Stage 8—Old age: the challenge of integrity (versus despair).** Near the end of our lives, Erikson explains, people hope to look back on what they have accomplished with a sense of integrity and satisfaction. For those who have been self-absorbed, old age brings only a sense of despair over missed opportunities.

Critical evaluation. Erikson's theory views personality formation as a lifelong process. Further, success at one stage (say, as an infant gaining trust) prepares us for meeting the next challenge.

One problem with this model is that not everyone confronts these challenges in the exact order presented by Erikson or at exactly the ages specified. Nor is it clear that failure to meet the challenge of one stage of life means that a person is doomed to fail later on. A broader question, raised earlier in our discussion of Piaget's ideas, is whether people in other cultures and in other times in history would define a successful life in the same terms as Erikson.

In sum, Erikson's model helps us make sense of socialization and points out how the family, the school, and other settings shape us. We now take a close look at these agents of socialization.

AGENTS OF SOCIALIZATION

Every social experience we have affects us in at least a small way. However, several familiar settings have special importance in the socialization process.

THE FAMILY

The family has the greatest impact on socialization. Infants are totally dependent on others, and the responsibility typically falls on parents and other family members. At least until children begin school, the family also has the job of teaching children skills, values, and beliefs. Overall, research suggests, nothing is more likely to produce a happy, well-adjusted child than being in a loving family (Gibbs, 2001).

Not all family learning results from intentional teaching by parents. Children also learn from the kind of environment adults create. Whether children learn to see themselves as strong or weak, smart or stupid, loved or simply tolerated, and, as Erik Erikson suggests, whether they see the world as trustworthy or dangerous, largely depends on their surroundings.

The family also gives children a social position in terms of race, religion, ethnicity, and class. In time, all these elements become part of a child's self-concept.

Research shows that the class position of parents affects how they raise their children (Ellison, Bartkowski, & Segal, 1996). Class position shapes not just how much money parents have to spend, but what they expect of their children. Surveys show that, when asked to pick from a list of traits that are most desirable in a child, lower-class people in the United States favor obedience and conformity. Well-to-do people,

Sociological research indicates that affluent parents tend to encourage creativity in their children while poor parents tend to foster conformity. While this general difference may be valid, parents at all class levels can and do provide loving support and guidance by simply involving themselves in their children's lives. Henry Ossawa Tanner's painting The Banjo Lesson stands as a lasting testament to this process.

Henry Ossawa Tanner, The Banjo Lesson, 1893. Oil on canvas. Hampton University Museum, Hampton, Virginia.

by contrast, choose good judgment and creativity (NORC, 2003).

Why the difference? Melvin Kohn (1977) explains that people of lower social standing usually have limited education and perform routine jobs under close supervision. Expecting that their children will hold similar positions, they encourage obedience and may even use physical punishment like spanking to get it. Well-off parents, with more schooling, usually have jobs that demand imagination and creativity. These

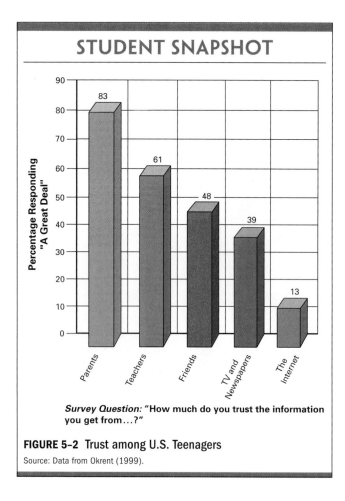

STUDENT SNAPSHOT

Percentage Responding "A Great Deal"

- Parents: 83
- Teachers: 61
- Friends: 48
- TV and Newspapers: 39
- The Internet: 13

Survey Question: "How much do you trust the information you get from…?"

FIGURE 5-2 Trust among U.S. Teenagers

Source: Data from Okrent (1999).

the process, they learn the importance that society attaches to race and gender. Studies confirm that children tend to cluster in play groups made up of one race and gender (Lever, 1978; Finkelstein & Haskins, 1983).

Schools teach children a wide range of knowledge and skills. But schools informally convey other lessons, which might be called the *hidden curriculum.* Activities such as spelling bees and sports foster the value of competition and showcase success. Children also receive countless informal lessons that their society's way of life is morally good.

School is also most children's first experience with bureaucracy. The school day runs on impersonal rules and a strict time schedule. Not surprisingly, these are the hallmarks of the many organizations that will employ them later in life.

Finally, schools socialize children into gender roles. Researchers report that, at school, boys engage in more physical activities and spend more time outdoors, while girls often volunteer to help teachers with various housekeeping chores. Similarly, boys engage in more aggressive behavior in the classroom, while girls are typically quieter and more well behaved (Best, 1983; Jordan & Cowan, 1995). Gender differences continue in college, as women tend toward majoring in the arts or humanities and men lean toward economics, the physical sciences, and computing.

PEER GROUPS

By the time they enter school, children have discovered the **peer group,** *a social group whose members have interests, social position, and age in common.* Unlike the family and school, the peer group lets children escape the direct supervision of adults. Among their peers, children learn how to form relationships on their own. Peer groups also offer the chance to discuss interests that adults may not share with their children (such as clothing and popular music) or tolerate in them (such as drugs and sex).

Not surprisingly, then, parents express concern about who their children's friends are. In a rapidly changing society, peer groups have great influence, and the attitudes of young and old may differ because of a "generation gap." The importance of peer groups typically peaks during adolescence, when young people begin to break away from their families and think of themselves as adults.

Even during adolescence, however, parental influence on children remains strong. Peers may affect short-term interests such as music or films, but parents

parents, therefore, try to inspire the same qualities in their children. All parents, then, act in ways that encourage their children to follow in their footsteps.

Furthermore, middle-class parents typically provide their children with an extensive program of leisure activities, including sports, travel, and music lessons. These enrichment activities—far less available to children growing up in low-income families—represent important *cultural capital* that advances learning and fosters a sense of confidence that these children will succeed later in life (Lareau, 2002).

THE SCHOOL

Schooling enlarges children's social worlds to include people with backgrounds different from their own. In

retain greater sway over long-term goals, such as going to college (Davies & Kandel, 1981). Figure 5–2 shows the results of a recent survey of teenagers confirming that teens still place their greatest trust in their parents.

Finally, any neighborhood or school is a social mosaic of many peer groups. As Chapter 7 ("Groups and Organizations") explains, individuals tend to view their own group in positive terms and to discredit others. Moreover, people are influenced by peer groups they would like to join, a process sociologists call **anticipatory socialization,** *learning that helps a person achieve a desired position.* In school, for example, young people may mimic the styles and slang of the group they hope to join. Or at a later point in life, a young lawyer who hopes to become a partner in her law firm may conform to the attitudes and behavior of the firm's partners in order to be accepted.

THE MASS MEDIA

September 29, the Pacific Ocean, nearing Japan. We have been out of sight of land for two weeks now, which makes this ship our entire social world. But more than land, many of the students miss television! Tapes of Dawson's Creek are a hot item.

The **mass media** are *impersonal communications aimed at a vast audience.* The term "media" comes from Latin meaning "middle," suggesting that media serve to connect people. *Mass* media arise as communications technology (first newspapers and then radio, television, films, and the Internet) spreads information on a mass scale.

In the United States today, the mass media have an enormous effect on our attitudes and behavior, shaping people's opinions about issues as well as what they buy. Television, introduced in 1939, soon became the dominant medium, and 98 percent of U.S. households have a TV (just 94 percent have telephones) and 88 percent have more than one. Two out of three households also have cable television. As Figure 5–3 shows, the United States has one of the highest rates of television ownership in the world. Some categories of people—including those with lower incomes—spend the most time watching TV. National Map 5–1 on page 128 shows where in the United States people are more likely to be television

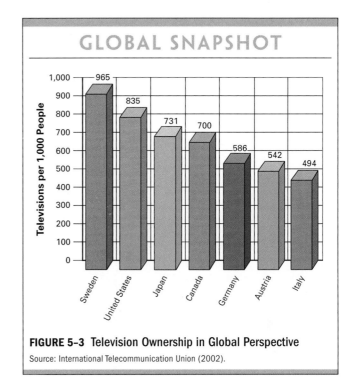

FIGURE 5–3 Television Ownership in Global Perspective

Source: International Telecommunication Union (2002).

watchers and where they are more likely to spend their leisure time reading newspapers.

The Extent of Television Viewing

Just how "glued to the tube" are we? Survey data show that the average household has at least one set turned on for seven hours each day, and that people spend almost half their free time watching television (Nielsen, 1997; Seplow & Storm, 1997; Cornell, 2000). A study by the Kaiser Family Foundation found that youngsters between age two and age eighteen average five-and-one-half hours per day "consuming media," including almost three hours a day watching television and the rest divided between watching videotapes and playing video games (McPherson, 1999).

 Read the report from the Kaiser Family Foundation on young people and the mass media: http://www.kff.org/content/1999/1535/KidsReport%20FINAL.pdf

Years before children learn to read, television watching is a regular routine. In fact, children grow up spending as many hours in front of a television as they

SEEING OURSELVES

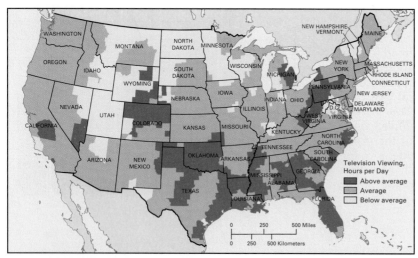

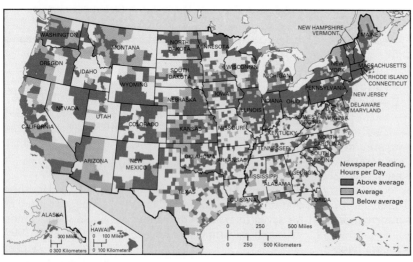

NATIONAL MAP 5–1
Television Viewing
and Newspaper Reading
across the United States

The map on the left identifies U.S. counties where television watching is above average, average, and below average. The map below provides comparable information for time devoted to reading newspapers. What do you think accounts for the high level of television viewing across much of the South and in rural West Virginia? Does your theory also account for patterns of newspaper reading?

Source: *American Demographics* magazine, August 1993, p. 64; *American Demographics* magazine, November 1998, p. 46. Reprinted with permission. ©1993, 1998 *American Demographics* magazine, Ithaca, New York.

do in school or interacting with their parents. This is so despite research that suggests television makes children more passive and less likely to use their imagination (APA, 1993; Fellman, 1995).

Television and Political Bias

Comedian Fred Allen once quipped that we call television a "medium" because it is rarely well done. For a variety of reasons, television (as well as other mass media) provokes plenty of criticism. Some liberal critics argue that television shows mirror our society's patterns of inequality and rarely challenge the status quo. Although women now have many more starring roles than in the past, most programs depict men in positions of power over women. Moreover, for most of television's history, racial and ethnic minorities have not been visible at all or have been included only in stereotypical roles (such as African Americans playing butlers, Asian Americans playing gardeners, or Hispanics playing new immigrants). In recent years, however, minorities have become more visible on television. One example: The fall 2002 television lineup featured three times as many Hispanic actors as were used ten years before, and these men and women played a far larger range of characters (Brown, 1990; Lichter & Amundson, 1997; Fetto, 2003a).

On the other side of the fence, conservative critics charge that the television and film industries are led by a liberal "cultural elite." In recent years, they claim, "politically correct" media have advanced liberal causes—including feminism and gay rights—while excluding a conservative perspective (Woodward, 1992b; Prindle, 1993; Prindle & Endersby, 1993; Rothman, Powers, & Rothman, 1993; Goldberg, 2002). On the other hand, the increasing popularity of the Fox Network—which includes Sean Hannity, Bill O'Reilly, and other more conservative commentators—suggests that people can now find programming consistent with political "spin" from both sides of the political spectrum.

Television and Violence

A large share of U.S. adults is concerned about the extent of mass media violence. In 1996, the American Medical Association (AMA) issued the startling statement that violence in television and films had reached levels that were a health hazard to this country's people. More recently, a study found a strong link between the amount of time elementary schoolchildren spend watching television and using video games and aggressive behavior (Robinson et al., 2001). Moreover, three-fourths of U.S. adults report walking out of a movie or turning off a television show due to high levels of violence. An analysis of programming shows that almost two-thirds of television programs contain violence and that, in most violent scenes, violent characters show no remorse and are not punished (B. Wilson, 1998).

In 1997, the television industry adopted a rating system for shows. But larger questions remain: Does watching sexual or violent programming harm people as much as critics say it does? More important, why do the mass media contain so much sex and violence in the first place?

In sum, television and the other mass media enrich our lives with entertaining and educational programming. The media also increase our exposure to diverse cultures and provoke discussion of current issues. At the same time, the power of the media, especially television, to shape how we think remains highly controversial.

Finally, other spheres of life beyond those just described also play a part in social learning. For most people in the United States, these include religious organizations, the workplace, the military, social clubs, and, for small-town residents, the local post office, where people stop to chat every day. In the end, socialization proves to be not a simple matter of learning but a complex balancing act. In the process of taking in and evaluating all sorts of conflicting information, we form our own distinctive personalities and worldviews.

SOCIALIZATION AND THE LIFE COURSE

Although childhood has special importance in the socialization process, learning continues throughout our lives. An overview of the life course reveals that our society organizes human experience according to age—childhood, adolescence, adulthood, and, finally, old age.

CHILDHOOD

A few years ago, the Nike corporation, maker of popular athletic shoes, came under fire. Their shoes are made in Taiwan and Indonesia, in many cases by young children who work in factories rather than go to school. Some 250 million of the world's children work, half of them full time, earning about fifty cents an hour (Human Rights Watch, 2003). Global Map 5–1 on page 131 shows that child labor is most common in the nations of Africa and Asia.

Criticism of Nike springs from the fact that most North Americans think of *childhood*—roughly the first twelve years of life—as a carefree time for learning and play. In fact, explains historian Philippe Ariès (1965), the whole idea of "childhood" is fairly new. During the Middle Ages, children of four or five were treated like adults and expected to fend for themselves. Even a century ago, children in North America and Europe had much the same life as children in poor countries today: Most worked long hours, in mines and textile mills, under dangerous conditions, for little pay.

We defend our idea of childhood because children are biologically immature. But a look back in time and around the world shows that the concept of "child-

 A Web site that reports on the state of children working as soldiers around the world is http://www.hrw.org/campaigns/crp/index.htm

hood" is based in culture (LaRossa & Reitzes, 2001). In rich countries, not

Historian Philippe Ariès looked at the art of a period for evidence of how the society viewed childhood. This 1732 painting by Antonio David shows Scottish Prince Charles Edward Stuart ("Bonnie Prince Charlie"). Are you surprised to learn that the prince is only twelve years of age?

Antonio David (1702–66, Italian), Portrait of Prince Charles Edward Stuart (1720–88), alias "Bonnie Prince Charlie," c. 1732, oil on copper, 10.2 × 7.9 cm. Philip Mould, Historical Portraits Ltd., London, UK/The Bridgeman Art Library.

everyone has to work, so childhood can be extended to allow time for young people to learn the skills they will need in a high-technology workplace.

Given this extended childhood, it is no surprise that many people worry about children growing up too fast. In part, this "hurried child" syndrome results from changes in the family—including high divorce rates and both parents in the labor force—that leave children with less supervision. Then, too, "adult" programming on television (not to mention in films and on the Internet) carries grown-up concerns such as sex, drugs, and violence into young people's lives. Today's ten- to twelve-year-olds, says one executive of a children's television channel, have about the same interests and experiences typical of twelve- to fourteen-year-olds

a generation ago (Hymowitz, 1998). Perhaps it should be no surprise that, compared to kids fifty years ago, today's children have higher levels of stress and anxiety (Gorman, 2000).

ADOLESCENCE

Just as industrialization helped create childhood as a distinct stage of life, adolescence emerged as a buffer between childhood and adulthood. We generally link adolescence, or the teenage years, to emotional and social turmoil as parents spar with young people who are trying to develop their own identities. Here, again, we are tempted to attribute teenage turbulence to the biological changes of puberty. But this turmoil more correctly reflects cultural inconsistency. For example, the mass media glorify sex, and schools hand out condoms, while, at the same time, parents urge restraint. Consider, too, that an eighteen-year-old may face the adult duty of going to war but lacks the adult right to drink alcohol. In short, adolescence is a time of social contradictions when people are no longer children but not yet adults.

As is true of all stages of life, adolescence varies according to social background. Most young people from working-class families move directly from high school into the adult world of work and parenting. Wealthier teens, however, have the resources to attend college and perhaps graduate school, thereby stretching adolescence into the late twenties and even past thirty.

ADULTHOOD

Adulthood, which begins between the late teens and the early thirties, depending on social background, is a time of accomplishment. Having completed their schooling, people embark on careers and raise families of their own. Personalities are now largely formed, although a marked change in a person's environment—such as unemployment, divorce, or serious illness—may cause significant change in the self.

Early Adulthood

During early adulthood—until about age forty—young adults learn to manage day-to-day affairs for themselves, often juggling conflicting priorities: parents, partner, children, schooling, and work (Levinson et al., 1978). Women, especially, often try to "do it all," since our culture gives them the major responsibility for child rearing and housework, even if they have demanding jobs outside the home (Hochschild & Machung, 1989).

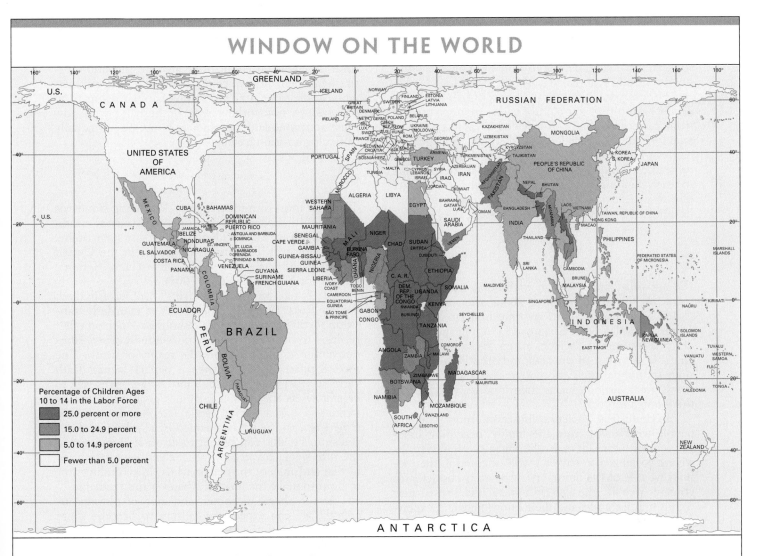

GLOBAL MAP 5–1 Child Labor in Global Perspective

Industrialization prolongs childhood and discourages children from work and other activities deemed suitable only for adults. Thus, child labor is uncommon in the United States and other high-income countries. In less economically developed nations of the world, however, children are a vital economic asset, and they typically begin working as soon as they are able.

Source: The World Bank (2003) and author estimates; map projection from *Peters Atlas of the World* (1990).

Middle Adulthood

In middle adulthood—roughly ages forty to sixty—people sense that their life circumstances are pretty well set. They also become more aware of the fragility of health, whereas the young typically take good health for granted. Women who have spent many years raising a family find middle adulthood especially trying. Children grow up and require less attention, and husbands become absorbed in their careers, leaving some women with spaces in their lives that are difficult to fill. Many women who divorce also face serious financial problems (Weitzman, 1985, 1996). For all these reasons, an increasing number of women in middle adulthood return to school and seek new careers.

For everyone, growing older means facing physical decline, a prospect our culture makes more painful for women. Because good looks are defined as more important for women, wrinkles, added weight, and graying hair can be traumatic. Men, of course, have their own difficulties. Some must admit that they are never going to reach their career goals. Others realize that the price of career success has been neglect of family or personal health (Farrell & Rosenberg, 1981; Wolf, 1990).

OLD AGE

Old age—the later years of adulthood and the final stage of life itself—begins about the mid-sixties. Again, societies attach different meanings to this stage of life. As explained in Chapter 15 ("Aging and the Elderly"), traditional societies often give older people control over most of the land and other wealth. Also, since traditional societies change slowly, older people amass great wisdom during their lifetime, which earns them much respect.

In industrial societies, however, most younger people work apart from the family, becoming independent of their elders. In the midst of rapid change, we are socialized to have a youth orientation that defines what is old as unimportant or even obsolete. To younger people, the elderly appear unaware of new trends and fashions, and their knowledge and experience may seem of little value.

It is likely that U.S. society's anti-elderly bias will diminish as the share of older people steadily increases. The percentage of the U.S. population over age sixty-five has more than tripled since the beginning of the twentieth century, so that today there are more seniors than there are teenagers. Moreover, life expectancy is still increasing, so that most men and women in their mid-sixties (the "young elderly") can look forward to decades more of life. In the twenty-first century, the Census Bureau (1999) predicts, the fastest-growing segment of our population will be those over eighty-five ("the oldest old"), whose numbers will soar nearly fivefold.

Old age differs in an important way from earlier stages in the life course. Growing up typically means entering new roles and assuming new responsibilities; growing old, by contrast, is the opposite experience—

leaving roles that provided both satisfaction and social identity. Retirement can be a period of restful activity, or it can mean the loss of valued routines and sometimes outright boredom. Like any life transition, retirement demands learning new, different patterns while at the same time *un*learning familiar habits from the past. A nonworking wife or husband who now must accommodate a partner at home has an equally difficult transition to make.

DYING

Through most of human history, low living standards and simple medical technology meant that death, caused by disease or accident, came at any stage of life. Today, however, 85 percent of people in the United States die after the age of fifty-five (U.S. National Center for Health Statistics, 2003).

After observing many dying people, Elisabeth Kübler-Ross (1969) described death as an orderly transition involving five distinct responses. A person's first reaction to the prospect of dying is usually *denial*, since our culture tends to ignore the reality of death. The second phase is *anger*, when a person facing death views it as a gross injustice. Third, anger gives way to *negotiation* as the person imagines avoiding death by striking a bargain with God. The fourth response, *resignation*, is often accompanied by psychological depression. Finally, adjustment to death is completed in the fifth stage, *acceptance*. Rather than being paralyzed by fear and anxiety, the person whose life is ending now sets out to make the most of whatever time remains.

As the share of women and men of old age increases, we can expect our culture to become more comfortable with the idea of death. In recent years, for example, people in the United States and elsewhere have come to discuss death more openly, and the trend is to view dying as preferable to painful or prolonged suffering. Moreover, more married couples now prepare for death with legal and financial planning. This openness may ease somewhat the pain of the surviving spouse, a consideration for women, who, more often than not, outlive their husbands.

THE LIFE COURSE: AN OVERVIEW

This survey of the life course leads us to two major conclusions. First, although each stage of life is linked to the biological process of aging, the life course is largely a social construction. For this reason, people in other societies may experience a stage of life quite

DIVERSITY: RACE, CLASS, AND GENDER

The Development of Self among High School Students

Adolescence is a time when people are concerned about identity, that is, answering questions such as "Who am I?" and "What should I strive to become?" Depending on their race and ethnicity, however, young people develop very different answers to these questions.

Grace Kao (2000) investigated the identity and aspirations of students enrolled in Johnstown High School, a large (3,000-student) school in a Chicago suburb. Johnstown High is considered a good school, with above-average test scores. It is also racially and ethnically diverse: 47 percent of the students are white, 43 percent are African American, 7 percent are Hispanic, and 3 percent are of Asian descent.

Kao interviewed sixty-three Johnstown students—female and male—both individually and in small groups with others of their race and ethnicity. From these interviews, she documented the importance of racial and ethnic stereotypes in the development of a student's

sense of self. Moreover, Kao found, not only is there wide agreement about these stereotypes, but students in various racial and ethnic categories also apply these stereotypes to themselves.

What are these stereotypes? White students are seen as hard-working and studious, motivated by a desire for high grades. African American students, by contrast, are viewed as less studious. As some see it, the reason is that they are less intelligent; as others see it, they simply don't try as hard. In any case, students see African Americans as at high risk of failure in school. Hispanics are seen as destined for manual occupations—as gardeners or manual laborers—so that doing well in school is less important to them. Finally, Asian American students are seen as hard-working high achievers. Again, some attribute this achievement to "being smart," while others see it as a focus on academics rather than, say, sports.

From her interviews, Kao concludes that most students take these stereotypes

very personally. That is, they assume that these beliefs are true and expect to perform in school more or less as the stereotype predicts. One reason, Kao explains, is that young people—whether white, black, Hispanic, or Asian—tend to socialize both in and out of school—with others like themselves, so existing beliefs are reinforced.

Another reason is that, while students of all racial and ethnic categories say they *want* to do well in school, they measure success *only in relation to their own category*. To African American students, in other words, "success" means doing as well as other black students, and not flunking out. To Hispanics, "success" means avoiding manual labor and ending up with any job in an office. Whites and Asians, by contrast, define "success" as earning high grades and living up to the high achievement embodied in the stereotype. For all these young people, then, "self" develops through the lens of how U.S. society defines race and ethnicity.

differently, or for that matter, they may not recognize it at all. Second, in any society, the stages of the life course present characteristic problems and transitions that involve learning something new and, in many cases, unlearning familiar routines.

Societies organize the life course according to age; other forces, such as class, race, ethnicity, and gender, also shape people's lives. Thus, the general patterns we have described apply somewhat differently to various categories of people (cf. Duncan et al., 1998). The box provides an example of how race and ethnicity can shape the academic performance of high school students in the United States.

People's life experiences also vary according to when, in the history of the society, they are born. A

cohort is *a category of people with a common characteristic, usually their age*. Age-cohorts are likely to be influenced by the same economic and cultural trends, so that members have similar attitudes and values (Riley, Foner, & Waring, 1988). Women and men born in the 1940s and 1950s, for example, grew up during a time of economic expansion that gave them a sense of optimism. Today's college students, who have grown up in an age of economic uncertainty, are less confident of the future.

Finally, specific events often shape the lives of an entire population. The terrorist attacks of September 11, 2001, "changed the world" for many people in the United States and elsewhere. A typical reaction was that of Adrienne Ulmer, a seventeen-year-old who had

To facilitate the filing of first-hand reports from the battle front during the recent War in Iraq, members of the press were "embedded" in highly regimented military units. During this time, they experienced life in a total institution. What do you think were some of the adjustments these reporters had to make?

graduated from a South Carolina high school several months before. "Since the attack on September 11, I believe anything can happen anywhere, even in our back yard," she explained. "It made me appreciate my family, my religion, the places where I grew up, everybody who has loved me." Ulmer was interviewed as part of a survey of the effect of September 11 on young people, three-fourths of whom characterized the attacks as "the most important event in my life." At the same time, evidence suggests that the effects of such events may subside over time: Six months later, there was evidence that the greater attention to family and religion was beginning to wane (Horatio Alger Association, 2001).

RESOCIALIZATION: TOTAL INSTITUTIONS

A final type of socialization, currently experienced by 2 million people in the United States, involves being confined—usually against their will—in prisons or mental hospitals. This is the world of the **total institution,** *a setting in which people are isolated from the rest of society and manipulated by an administrative staff.*

According to Erving Goffman (1961), total institutions have three distinctive characteristics. First, staff members supervise all spheres of daily life, including where residents (often called "inmates") eat, sleep, and work. Second, the environment of a total institution is highly standardized, with institutional food, uniforms, and one set of activities for everyone. Third, formal rules and daily schedules dictate when, where, and how inmates perform their daily routines.

Total institutions impose such regimentation for one reason: **resocialization,** *radically changing an inmate's personality by carefully controlling the environment.* Prisons and mental hospitals physically isolate inmates behind fences, barred windows, and locked doors and control their access to the telephone, mail, and visitors. When inmates are cut off in this way, the institution becomes their entire world, so it is easier for the staff to produce long-term change—or at least short-term compliance.

Resocialization is a two-part process. First, the staff breaks down the new inmate's existing identity, using what Goffman describes as "abasements, degradations, humiliations, and profanations of self" (1961:14). For example, an inmate must give up personal possessions, including clothing and grooming articles used to maintain a distinctive appearance. Instead, the staff provides standard-issue clothes so everyone looks alike. The staff subjects new inmates to "mortifications of self," including searches, head shaving, medical examinations, and fingerprinting, and then assigns each a serial number. Once inside the walls, individuals also give up their privacy, as guards routinely monitor their living quarters.

In the second part of the resocialization process, the staff tries to build a new self in the inmate through a system of rewards and punishments. Having a book to read, watching television, or making a telephone call may seem trivial to outsiders, but in the rigid environment of the total institution, these simple privileges can be powerful motivations to conform. In the end, the length of confinement typically depends on how well the inmate cooperates with the staff.

Resocialization can bring about considerable change in an inmate, but total institutions affect different people in different ways. While some inmates are considered "rehabilitated" or "recovered," others may change little, and still others may become hostile and bitter. Furthermore, over a long period of time, the rigidly controlled environment can leave some *institutionalized,* without the capacity for independent living.

But what about the rest of us? Does socialization crush our individuality or empower us? The final box takes a closer look at this important question.

CONTROVERSY & DEBATE

Are We Free within Society?

Throughout this chapter, we have stressed one key theme: Society shapes how we think, feel, and act. If this is so, then in what sense are we free? To answer this important question, consider the Muppets, puppet stars of television and film. Watching the antics of Kermit the Frog, Miss Piggy, and the rest of the troupe, we almost believe they are real rather than objects animated from backstage. Similarly, as the sociological perspective points out, human beings are like puppets in that we, too, respond to backstage forces. Society, after all, gives us a culture and shapes our lives according to class, race, and gender. In the face of such social forces, can we really claim to be free?

Sociologists speak with many voices when addressing this question. One response, with politically liberal overtones, is that individuals are *not* free of society—in fact, as social creatures, we never could be. But if we are constrained to life within society, it is important to make our home as just as possible. That is, we should work to lessen class differences and other barriers to opportunity for minorities, including women.

Another approach, this time with conservative overtones, is that we *are* free because society can never dictate our dreams. Our history as a nation, right from the revolutionary act that led to its founding, is one story after another of individuals pursuing personal goals in spite of great odds.

We find both attitudes in George Herbert Mead's analysis of socialization. Mead recognized that society makes demands on us and sometimes limits us. But he also saw that human beings are spontaneous and creative, capable of continually acting back—individually and collectively—on society. Thus, Mead noted the power of society while still affirming the human capacity to evaluate, to criticize, and, ultimately, to choose and change.

In the end, then, we may resemble puppets, but only on the surface. A crucial difference—one that gives us a large measure of freedom—is that we can stop, look up at the "strings" that animate much of our action, and even yank on them defiantly (Berger, 1963:176). If our pull is persistent enough, we can do more than we might think. As Margaret Mead once mused, "Do not make the mistake of thinking that concerned people cannot change the world; it's the only thing that ever has."

Continue the debate . . .

1. *Do you think our society affords more freedom to males than to females? Why or why not?*

2. *What about modern, high-income countries compared to traditional, low-income nations? Are some of the world's people more free than others?*

3. *Does an understanding of sociology increase your freedom? Why?*

SUMMARY

1. Socialization is the lifelong process by which individuals develop their humanity and particular personalities.

2. A century ago, people thought most human behavior was guided by biological instinct. Today, we recognize that human behavior is mostly a result of nurture rather than nature.

3. The permanently damaging effects of social isolation reveal that social experience is essential to human development.

4. Sigmund Freud's model of the human personality has three parts: The id represents innate human drives (the life and death instincts); the superego is internalized cultural values and norms; and the ego resolves competition between the demands of the id and the restraints of the superego.

5. Jean Piaget believed that human development reflects both biological maturation and increasing social experience. He identified four stages of cognitive development: sensorimotor, preoperational, concrete operational, and formal operational.

6. Lawrence Kohlberg applied Piaget's approach to moral development. We first judge rightness in preconventional terms, according to our individual needs. Next, conventional moral reasoning takes account of parental attitudes and cultural norms. Finally, postconventional reasoning allows us to criticize society itself.

7. In response to Kohlberg's use of only male subjects, Carol Gilligan discovered that while males rely on abstract standards of rightness, females look at the effect of decisions on relationships.

8. To George Herbert Mead, social experience generates the self, which he described as partly autonomous (the I) and partly guided by society (the me). Although infants engage in imitation, the self develops through play and games and eventually includes the generalized other.

9. Charles Horton Cooley used the term *looking-glass self* to explain that we see ourselves as we imagine others see us.

10. Erik H. Erikson identified challenges that individuals face at each stage of life from infancy to old age.

11. Usually the first setting of socialization, the family has the greatest influence on a child's attitudes and behavior.

12. Schools expose children to greater social diversity and introduce them to impersonal performance evaluations.

13. Peer groups free children from adult supervision and take on great significance during adolescence.

14. The mass media, especially television, have a considerable impact on the socialization process. The average U.S. child spends as much time watching television as attending school or interacting with parents. Research has linked television and video games to aggressive behavior in young children.

15. Each stage of the life course—childhood, adolescence, adulthood, and old age—is socially constructed in ways that vary from society to society.

16. People in high-income countries typically fend off death until old age. Accepting death is part of socialization for the elderly.

17. Total institutions, such as prisons and mental hospitals, try to resocialize inmates, that is, to radically change their personalities.

18. Socialization shows the power of society to shape our thoughts, feelings, and actions. Yet, as humans, we have the ability to act back, shaping both ourselves and our social world.

KEY CONCEPTS

socialization (p. 115) the lifelong social experience by which individuals develop their human potential and learn culture

personality (p. 115) a person's fairly consistent patterns of acting, thinking, and feeling

id (p. 118) Freud's term for the human being's basic drives

ego (p. 118) Freud's term for a person's conscious efforts to balance innate pleasure-seeking drives with the demands of society

superego (p. 119) Freud's term for the cultural values and norms internalized by an individual

sensorimotor stage (p. 120) Piaget's term for the level of human development at which individuals experience the world only through their senses

preoperational stage (p. 120) Piaget's term for the level of human development at which individuals first use language and other symbols

concrete operational stage (p. 120) Piaget's term for the level of human development at which individuals first perceive causal connections in their surroundings

formal operational stage (p. 120) Piaget's term for the level of human development at which individuals think abstractly and critically

self (p. 122) George Herbert Mead's term for that part of an individual's personality composed of self-awareness and self-image

looking-glass self (p. 123) Cooley's term for a self-image based on how we think others see us

generalized other (p. 123) George Herbert Mead's term for widespread cultural norms and values we use as a reference in evaluating ourselves

peer group (p. 126) a social group whose members have interests, social position, and age in common

anticipatory socialization (p. 127) learning that helps a person achieve a desired position

mass media (p. 127) impersonal communications aimed at a vast audience

cohort (p. 133) a category of people with a common characteristic, usually their age

total institution (p. 134) a setting in which people are isolated from the rest of society and manipulated by an administrative staff

resocialization (p. 134) radically changing an inmate's personality by carefully controlling the environment

CRITICAL-THINKING QUESTIONS

1. What do cases of social isolation teach us about the importance of social experience to human beings?

2. State the two sides of the nature-nurture debate. Why does the assertion "Nurture is human nature" point to the fact that nature and nurture are not in opposition?

3. We have all seen young children place their hands in front of their faces and exclaim, "You can't see me!" They assume that if they cannot see you, then you cannot see them. What does this behavior suggest about a young child's ability to "take the role of the other"?

Should a parent expect a young child to "see things from *my* point of view"?

4. What are the common themes in the ideas of Freud, Piaget, Kohlberg, Gilligan, Mead, and Erikson? In what ways do their theories differ?

APPLICATIONS AND EXERCISES

1. Discuss the following question in your sociology class: In what ways does gender affect socialization? (Remember to consider the entire life cycle.) What about ways in which social class affects socialization?

2. Find a copy of the book (or video) *Lord of the Flies*, a tale based on a Freudian model of personality. Jack (and his hunters) represent the power of the id; Piggy consistently opposes them as the superego; Ralph stands between the two as the ego, the voice of reason. William Golding wrote the book after taking part in the bloody D-Day landing in France during World War II. Do you agree with his belief that violence is part of human nature?

3. Watch several hours of prime-time programming on network or cable television. Keep track of every time

any element of violence is shown. For fun, assign each program a "YIP rating," for the number of Years In Prison a person would serve for committing all the violent acts you witness (Fobes, 1996). On the basis of observing this small (and unrepresentative) sample of programs, what are your conclusions?

4. Packaged in the back of this new textbook is an interactive CD-ROM that offers a variety of video and interactive review materials intended to help you better understand the material covered in this chapter. For this chapter, the CD-ROM contains a relevant clip from *ABC News*, an author's tip video, interactive map animations, an interactive time line, and flashcards with audio pronunciations of the more difficult words.

SITES TO SEE

http://www.prenhall.com/macionis

Visit the interactive Companion Website™ that accompanies this text. Begin by clicking on the cover of your book. You will find a chapter-by-chapter study guide, practice tests, suggested Web links, and links to other relevant material.

http://www.prenticehall.ca/macionis/massmedia.html

An online chapter on the mass media is available at the Web site for Macionis Canadian texts.

http://www.nd.edu/~rbarger/kohlberg.html

This Web site is dedicated to the ideas and research of Lawrence Kohlberg.

http://www.TheSociologyPage.com
(or http://www.macionis.com)

At the author's Web site, you can find brief biographies of George Herbert Mead and Charles Horton Cooley, as well as of other sociologists discussed in this chapter.

http://freud.t0.or.at

Visit the Sigmund Freud Museum of Vienna, Austria, at this site.

http://www.unicef.org/sowc02/
http://www.savethechildren.org

Here are two sites that provide information on the state of the world's children.

INVESTIGATE WITH RESEARCH NAVIGATOR

Follow the instructions found on page 24 of this text to access the features of **Research Navigator**™. Once at the Web site, enter your Login Name and Password. Then, to use the **Content Select**™database, enter keywords such as "Sigmund Freud," "childhood," and "television violence," and the search

engine will supply relevant and recent scholarly and popular press publications. Use the *New York Times* **Search-by-Subject Archive** to find recent news articles related to sociology and the **Link Library** feature to find relevant Web links organized by the key terms associated with this chapter.

SOCIAL INTERACTION
IN EVERYDAY LIFE

ANDREW MACARA (ENGLISH)
Playground, Sri Lanka

1998, oil on canvas, 71.1 × 91.4 cm. Private Collection/The Bridgeman Art Library.

HAROLD AND Sybil are on their way to another couple's home in an unfamiliar area near Rochester, New York. They are now late because for the last twenty minutes they have traveled in

circles searching in vain for Brindle Road. Harold, gripping the wheel ever more tightly, is doing a slow burn. Sybil, sitting next to him, looks straight ahead, afraid to utter a word. Both realize that the day is off to a bad start (Tannen, 1990:62).

Harold and Sybil are lost in more ways than one: They are unable to understand why they are growing enraged at their situation and at each other. Consider their plight from Harold's point of view: Like most men, Harold cannot tolerate getting lost, and the longer he drives around, the more incompetent he feels. Sybil, on the other hand, cannot understand why Harold does not pull over and ask someone where Brindle Road is. If she were driving, she

thinks to herself, they would already have arrived and would now be comfortably settled in with friends.

Why don't men like to ask for directions? Because men value their independence, they are uncomfortable asking for help (and also reluctant to accept it). To ask someone for assistance is the same as saying, "You know something I don't." If it takes Harold a few more minutes to find Brindle Road on his own—and keep his self-respect in the process—he thinks it's a good bargain.

If men pursue self-sufficiency and are aware of hierarchy, women are more attuned to others and strive for connectedness. From Sybil's point of view, asking for help is right because sharing information reinforces social bonds. Asking for directions seems as natural to her as searching on his own is to Harold. Obviously, getting lost is sure to generate conflict as long as neither one understands the other's point of view.

Such everyday experiences are the focus of this chapter. We begin by presenting several important sociological concepts that describe the building blocks of common experience and then go on to explore the almost magical way that face-to-face interaction generates reality. The central concept is **social interaction,** *the process by which people act and react in relation to others.* Through social interaction, we create the reality in which we live. This chapter explains how.

SOCIAL STRUCTURE: A GUIDE TO EVERYDAY LIVING

<u>October 21, Ho Chi Minh City, Vietnam.</u> This morning we leave the ship and make our way along the docks toward the center of Ho Chi Minh City, known to an earlier generation as Saigon. The

In any rigidly ranked setting, no interaction can proceed until people assess each other's social standing. Thus, military personnel wear clear insignia to designate their level of authority. Don't we size up one another in much the same way in routine interactions, noting a person's rough age, quality of clothing, and manner for clues about social position?

government security officers wave us through the heavy metal gates. Pressed against the fence surrounding the port are dozens of men who operate cyclos (bicycles with a small carriage attached to the front), the Vietnamese equivalent of taxicabs. We wave them off but spend the next twenty minutes shaking our heads at several drivers who pedal alongside pleading for our business. The pressure is uncomfortable. We decide to cross the street but realize suddenly that there are no stop signs or signal lights—and the street is an unbroken stream of bicycles, cyclos, motorbikes, and small trucks. What to do? The locals don't bat an eye; they just

For a short video ("Sociology and Cultural Relativism") on the difficulty of traveling to unfamiliar places, see http://www.TheSociologyPage.com

walk at a steady pace across the street, parting waves of vehicles that close in again immediately behind them. Walk right into traffic? With our small children on our backs? Yup, we did it; that's the way it works in Vietnam.

Members of every society rely on social structure to make sense out of everyday situations. As one family's introduction to the streets of Vietnam suggests, the world can be disorienting—even frightening—when cultural norms are not what we expect. So what, then, are the building blocks of our daily lives?

STATUS

One building block of social structure is **status,** *a social position that a person occupies.* Sociologists do not use the term "status" in its everyday meaning of "prestige," as when a college president has more "status" than a newly hired assistant professor. Rather, both "president" and "professor" are statuses within the collegiate organization.

Every status is part of our social identity and helps define our relationship to others. As Georg Simmel (1950:307; orig. 1902), one of the founders of sociology, put it, "The first condition of having to deal with somebody . . . is knowing with *whom* one has to deal."

STATUS SET

Everyone occupies many statuses at once. The term **status set** refers to *all the statuses a person holds at a given time.* A teenage girl is a *daughter* to her parents, a *sister* to her brother, a *friend* to members of her social circle, a *student* at her college, and a *goalie* on her soccer team. Just as status sets branch out in many directions, they also change over the life course. A child grows into a parent, a student becomes a lawyer, and people marry to become husbands and wives, sometimes becoming single again as a result of death or divorce. Joining an organization or finding a job enlarges our status set; withdrawing from activities makes it smaller. Over a lifetime, people gain and lose dozens of statuses.

ASCRIBED AND ACHIEVED STATUS

Sociologists classify statuses in terms of how people obtain them. An **ascribed status** is *a social position a person receives at birth or assumes involuntarily later in life.*

Role models teach us that any one person can truly make a difference for our world. In December, 1955, the driver of a city bus in Montgomery, Alabama, asked passenger Rosa Parks to give up her seat, as required by law, so a white man could sit down. She refused and was arrested, fingerprinted, and later fined $14 for the offense. This courageous act prompted Birmingham's African American population to boycott city buses, leading to the repeal of the bus-segregation law.

Examples of ascribed statuses include being a daughter, a Cuban, a teenager, or a widower. Ascribed statuses are matters about which people have little or no choice.

By contrast, an **achieved status** refers to *a social position a person assumes voluntarily that reflects personal ability and effort.* Among achieved statuses in the United States are being an honors student, an Olympic athlete, a spouse, a computer programmer, or a thief.

In reality, most statuses involve some combination of ascription and achievement. That is, people's ascribed statuses influence the statuses they achieve. People who achieve the status of lawyer, for example, are likely to share the ascribed benefit of being born into relatively well-off families. By the same token, many less desirable statuses, such as criminal or being unemployed, are more easily achieved by people born into poverty.

MASTER STATUS

Some statuses matter more than others. A **master status** is *a status that a society defines as having special importance for social identity, often shaping a person's entire life.* For most people, one's occupation is a master status because it conveys a great deal about social background, education, and income. In a few cases, one's name is a master status; being a "Bush" or a "Kennedy" is enough by itself to push an individual into the limelight.

In a negative sense, serious illness also operates as a master status. Sometimes even lifelong friends avoid cancer patients or people with acquired immuno-deficiency syndrome (AIDS), simply because of their illness. Most societies of the world also limit the opportunities of women, whatever their abilities, making gender a master status (cf. Webster & Hysom, 1998).

Sometimes a physical disability serves as a master status to the point where we dehumanize people by perceiving them only in terms of their disability. In the box on page 142, two people with disabilities describe the problem.

ROLE

A second component of social interaction is **role**, *behavior expected of someone who holds a particular status.* People *hold* a status and *perform* a role (Linton, 1937b). Holding the status of student, for example, means one will attend classes, complete assignments, and, more broadly, devote a lot of time to personal enrichment through academic study.

Both statuses and roles vary by culture. In the United States, the status "uncle" refers to a sibling of either mother or father. In Vietnam, however, the word for "uncle" is different on the mother's and father's sides of the family, and the two men have different responsibilities. Of course, in every society, actual

Physical Disability as Master Status

Physical disability operates in much the same ways as class, gender, or race in defining individuals in the eyes of others. In the following interviews, two women explain how a physical disability can become a master status—an all-important trait that overshadows everything else about them. The first voice is of twenty-nine-year-old Donna Finch, who lives with her husband and son in Muskogee, Oklahoma, and holds a master's degree in social work. She is also blind.

Most people don't expect handicapped people to grow up, they are always supposed to be children. . . . You aren't supposed to date, you aren't supposed to have a job, somehow you're just supposed to disappear. I'm not saying this is true of anyone else, but in my own case I think I was more intellectually mature than most children, and more

emotionally immature. I'd say that not until the last four or five years have I felt really whole.

Rose Helman is an elderly woman who has retired and lives near New York City. She suffers from spinal meningitis and is also blind.

You ask me if people are really different today than in the '20s and '30s. Not too much. They are still fearful of the handicapped. I don't know if fearful is the right word, but uncomfortable at least. But I can understand it somewhat; it happened to me. I once asked a man to tell me which staircase to use to get from the subway out to the street. He started giving me directions that were confusing, and I said, "Do you mind taking me?" He said, "Not at all." He grabbed me on the side with my dog on it, so I asked him to take my other arm. And he said, "I'm sorry, I have no other arm." And I said, "That's all right, I'll hold onto the jacket." It felt funny hanging onto the sleeve without the arm in it.

Source: Orlansky & Heward (1981).

role performance varies according to an individual's unique personality, although some societies permit more individual expression of a role than others.

ROLE SET

Because we occupy many statuses at once—a status set—everyday life is a mix of multiple roles. Robert Merton (1968) introduced the term **role set** to identify *a number of roles attached to a single status.*

Figure 6–1 shows four statuses of one individual, each status linked to a different role set. First, as a

professor, this person interacts with students (the teacher role) and with other academics (the colleague role). Second, in her work as a researcher, she gathers and analyzes data (the laboratory role) that she uses in her publications (the author role). Third, the woman occupies the status of "wife," with a conjugal role (such as confidante and sexual partner) toward her husband, with whom she shares a domestic role toward the household. Fourth, she holds the status of "mother," with routine responsibilities for her children (the maternal role), as well as toward their school and other organizations in her community (the civic role).

ROLE CONFLICT AND ROLE STRAIN

Most people in high-income nations such as the United States juggle a host of responsibilities demanded by their various statuses and roles. As many mothers can testify, parenting as well as working outside the home can be both physically and emotionally draining. The trend of more women's entering the labor force is also increasing role conflict for men, many of whom have greater responsibilities for both jobs and children (Kanazawa, 2001). Sociologists thus recognize **role conflict** as *conflict among the roles corresponding to two or more statuses.*

We experience role conflict when we find ourselves pulled in various directions while trying to respond to the many statuses we hold. One response to role conflict is deciding that "something has to go." More than one politician, for example, has decided not to run for office because the demands of a campaign would interfere with family life. In other cases, people wait to have children in order to stay on the "fast track" for career success.

Even roles linked to a single status may make competing demands on us. **Role strain** refers to *tension among the roles connected to a single status.* A plant supervisor may enjoy being friendly with other workers. At the same time, however, the supervisor has production goals and must maintain the personal distance needed to evaluate employees. In short, although not all cases of role strain present serious problems, performing the various roles attached to even one status can be something of a balancing act (Gigliotti & Huff, 1995).

One strategy for minimizing role conflict is to "compartmentalize" our lives so that we perform roles linked to one status at one time and place and carry out roles corresponding to another status in a completely different setting. A familiar example of this scheme is deciding to "leave the job at work" before heading home to one's family.

ROLE EXIT

After she herself left the life of a Catholic nun to become a university sociologist, Helen Rose Fuchs Ebaugh (1988) began to study *role exit,* the process by which people disengage from important social roles. Studying a range of "exes," including ex-nuns, ex-doctors, ex-husbands, and ex-alcoholics, Ebaugh identified elements common to the process of becoming an "ex."

According to Ebaugh, the process begins as people come to doubt their ability to continue in a certain

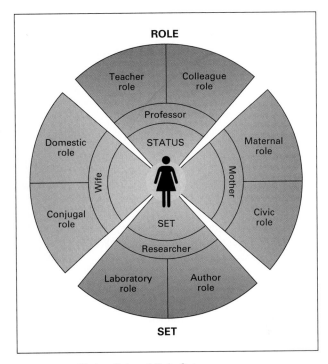

FIGURE 6-1 Status Set and Role Set

role. As they imagine alternative roles, they ultimately reach a tipping point when they decide to pursue a new life. Even at this point, however, a past role can continue to influence their lives. "Exes" carry away a self-image shaped by an earlier role, which can interfere with building a new sense of self. An ex-nun, for example, may hesitate to wear makeup and stylish clothing.

"Exes" must also rebuild relationships with people who knew them in their "earlier life." Learning new social skills is another challenge. For example, Ebaugh reports, nuns who begin dating after decades in the church are often startled to learn that sexual norms are very different from those they knew as teenagers.

THE SOCIAL CONSTRUCTION OF REALITY

More than eighty years ago, the Nobel Prize–winning Italian playwright Luigi Pirandello wrote the play *The Pleasure of Honesty.* The main character is Angelo Baldovino—a brilliant man with a checkered past. Baldovino enters the fashionable home of the Renni family and introduces himself in a most peculiar way:

Flirting is an everyday experience in reality construction. Each person offers information to the other, and hints at romantic interest. Yet the interaction proceeds with a tentative and often humorous air so that either individual can withdraw at any time without further obligation.

Inevitably we construct ourselves. Let me explain. I enter this house and immediately I become what I have to become, what I can become: I construct myself. That is, I present myself to you in a form suitable to the relationship I wish to achieve with you. And, of course, you do the same with me. (1962:157–58; orig. 1917)

Baldovino's introduction suggests that, while behavior is guided by status and role, we also have the ability to shape who we are and to guide what happens in any given situation from moment to moment. "Reality," in other words, is not as fixed as we may think.

The phrase **social construction of reality** describes *the process by which people creatively shape reality through social interaction.* This idea is the familiar foundation of the symbolic-interaction paradigm, described in earlier chapters (Berger & Luckmann, 1966; Maines, 2000). As Angelo Baldovino's remark suggests, especially when we enter an unfamiliar situation quite a bit of "reality" remains unclear in everyone's mind. So we "present ourselves" in terms that suit the setting and our purposes, we try to guide what happens next, and, as others do the same, reality emerges.

Social interaction, then, amounts to a complex negotiation. Most everyday situations involve at least some agreement about what's going on, in part, because people recognize the various statuses of the people involved. Even so, individuals have to act in expected ways in order to make the status believable to others; that is, a professor who expects to be "taken seriously" must act in a professorial manner (Ridgeway & Erickson, 2000).

Of course, participants are likely to hold different perceptions of events to the extent that they have different interests and intentions. In any interaction, in other words, each participant has at least slightly different ideas about what "reality" should be. Our very choice of words is one way we put a "spin" on events. The box applies this idea to the language used by the military to create (or conceal?) reality.

"STREET SMARTS"

What people commonly call "street smarts" really amounts to constructing reality. In his biography *Down These Mean Streets,* Piri Thomas recalls moving to an apartment in Spanish Harlem. Returning home one evening, young Piri found himself cut off by Waneko, the leader of the local street gang, who was flanked by a dozen others.

"Whatta ya say, Mr. Johnny Gringo," drawled Waneko.

Think man, I told myself, *think your way out of a stomping. Make it good.* "I hear you 104th Street coolies are supposed to have heart," I said. "I don't know this for sure. You know there's a lot of streets where a whole 'click' is made out of punks who can't fight one guy unless they all jump him for the stomp." I hoped this would push Waneko into giving me a fair one. His expression didn't change.

"Maybe we don't look at it that way."

APPLYING SOCIOLOGY

The "Spin" Game: Choosing Our Words Carefully

Military organizations choose their words carefully in order to "sanitize" the horror of war and make military action seem necessary and good. William Lutz, an English professor at Rutgers University, collected examples of language used by U.S. military officers in the Persian Gulf War. Read the following military terminology and the straight-talk translations. Do these military terms convey a reality or do they try to alter it? What do you think would happen if a general gave a news conference using everyday language rather than military jargon?

Military language	Everyday meaning
Incontinent ordnance	Bombs or shells that miss their targets and hit civilians
Area denial weapons	Cluster bombs that kill or destroy everything within a particular area
Coercive potential	The capacity of bombs and shells to kill or injure the enemy
Suppressing assets	Reducing the enemy's ability to fight, by killing people and destroying equipment
Ballistically induced aperture	Bullet hole
Scenario-dependent postcrisis environment	Whether we win or lose

Crazy, man, I cheer inwardly, *the* cabron *is falling into my setup.* . . . "I wasn't talking to you," I said. "Where I come from, the pres is president 'cause he got heart when it comes to dealing."

Waneko was starting to look uneasy. He had bit on my worm and felt like a sucker fish. His boys were now light on me. They were no longer so much interested in stomping me as seeing the outcome between Waneko and me. "Yeah," was his reply. . . .

I knew I'd won. Sure, I'd have to fight; but one guy, not ten or fifteen. If I lost, I might still get stomped, and if I won I might get stomped. I took care of this with my next sentence. "I don't know you or your boys," I said, "but they look cool to me. They don't feature as punks."

I had left him out purposely when I said "they." Now his boys were in a separate class. I had cut him off. He would have to fight me on his own, to prove his heart to himself, to his boys, and most important, to his turf. He got away from the stoop and asked, "Fair one, Gringo?" (1967:56–57)

This situation reveals the drama—sometimes subtle, sometimes savage—by which human beings creatively build reality. But of course, not everyone enters a situation with equal standing. Should a police officer have come upon the fight between Piri and Waneko, both young men might well have ended up in jail.

THE THOMAS THEOREM

By displaying his wits and fighting with Waneko until they both tired, Piri Thomas won acceptance and became one of the gang. What took place that evening in Spanish Harlem is an example of the **Thomas theorem,** named after W. I. Thomas (1966:301; orig. 1931): *Situations that are defined as real are real in their consequences.*

Applied to social interaction, the Thomas theorem means that although reality is initially "soft" as it is fashioned, it can become "hard" in its effects. In the case we have described, local gang members saw Piri Thomas act in a worthy way, so in their eyes he *became* worthy.

ETHNOMETHODOLOGY

How can we become more aware of the social reality in which we play a part? Harold Garfinkel (1967) helped answer this question when he devised

SEEING OURSELVES

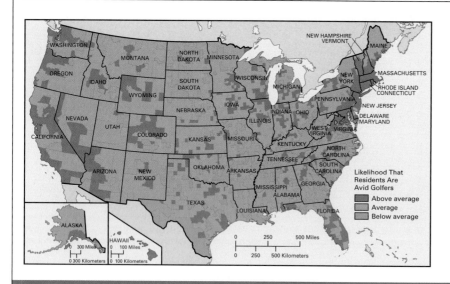

NATIONAL MAP 6–1
Teeing Off across the United States

The map shows the popularity of the game of golf in all 3,141 counties in the United States in 2000. More than 25 million people across the country enjoy golf, but they are not typical in a number of respects. Looking at the map, what patterns can you see? As a hint, serious golfers tend to be white men who are somewhat older than the national average and who have incomes much higher than average.

Source: *American Demographics* magazine, August 2000, p. 50. Reprinted with permission from *American Demographics*. © 2000 by Intertec Publishing, a Primedia Company.

---

ethnomethodology, *the study of the way people make sense of their everyday surroundings.* This approach begins by pointing out that everyday behavior rests on a number of assumptions, usually taken for granted. When we ask someone the simple question, "How are you?" we might wonder how the person is physically, mentally, spiritually, or financially. Of course, the common assumption is that we are really not interested in details regarding any of these things; rather, we are "just being polite."

Ethnomethodology also suggests that one good way to discover the assumptions we make about reality is to purposely break the rules. To test the assertion we just made, for example, wait for the next time someone says, "Hey, how ya doin'?" Then, to see what the person assumes the question means, offer details from your last physical exam, or explain all the good and bad things that have happened since you woke up that morning. Furthermore, to test assumptions about how people should space themselves while talking, slowly move closer to the other person as the interaction unfolds.

The results are predictable, because we all have some idea of what the "rules" of everyday interaction are. People become confused and irritated by such antics—a reaction which helps us to see not only what the rules are but also how important our everyday reality is to us.

REALITY BUILDING: CLASS AND CULTURE

People do not build everyday experience out of thin air. In part, how we act or what we see in our surroundings depends on our interests. Scanning the night sky, for example, lovers discover romance, while scientists view the same stars as hydrogen atoms fusing into helium. Social background, too, directs our perceptions, so that residents of, say, Spanish Harlem experience a different world than do those people living on Manhattan's high-income Upper East Side.

In truth, there is a lot of diversity in the reality construction that goes on across the United States. Take the kinds of sports people play, games that also

All the maps found in this text become interactional at the Companion Website™: http://www.prenhall.com/macionis

play a part in the way we think of ourselves and the impressions others have of us. Golf—like any other sport—is far more popular among some segments of the U.S. population than among others. National Map 6–1 gives a geographical look, showing where people are—and are not—likely to tee off.

In global perspective, reality construction varies even more. Consider these everyday situations: People waiting for a bus in London typically "queue up" in a straight line; people in New York rarely are so orderly.

People build reality from their surrounding culture. Yet, because cultural systems are marked by diversity and even outright conflict, reality construction always involves tensions and choices. Turkey is a nation with a mostly Muslim population, but it is also a country that has embraced Western culture. Here, women confront starkly different definitions of what is "feminine."
Staton R. Winter, The New York Times.

The law forbids women in Saudi Arabia to drive cars, a ban unheard of in the United States. Finally, global events also shape reality: Consider the heightened level of fear and anxiety (as well as a heightened sense of patriotism) that followed the September 11 terrorist attacks in 2001.

The general conclusion is that people build reality from the surrounding culture. Chapter 3 ("Culture") explains how people the world over find different meanings in specific gestures, so that sometimes travelers find themselves building a most unexpected reality. Similarly, in a study of popular culture, JoEllen Shively (1992) showed western films to men of European descent and to Native American men. Both categories claimed to enjoy the films but for different reasons. White men interpreted the films as praising rugged people striking out for the West to impose their will on nature. Native American men, by contrast, saw in the same films a celebration of land and nature apart from any human ambitions.

DRAMATURGICAL ANALYSIS: "THE PRESENTATION OF SELF"

Erving Goffman (1922–1982) spent much of his life explaining how people in their everyday behavior are very much like actors performing on a stage. If we imagine ourselves as directors observing what goes on in some situational "theater," we can understand Goffman's **dramaturgical analysis**—*the study of social interaction in terms of theatrical performance.*

Dramaturgical analysis offers a fresh look at the concepts of status and role. A status is like a part in a play, and a role serves as a script, supplying dialogue and action for the characters. Goffman described each individual's "performance" as the **presentation of self,** *a person's efforts to create specific impressions in the minds of others.* This process, sometimes called *impression management,* has several distinctive elements (Goffman, 1959, 1967).

PERFORMANCES

As we present ourselves in everyday situations, we convey information—consciously and unconsciously—to others. An individual's performance includes dress (costume), objects carried along (props), and tone of voice and particular gestures (manner). In addition, people craft their performance according to the setting (stage). We may joke loudly in a restaurant, for example, but lower our voices when entering a church. Individuals design settings, such as homes or offices, to bring about desired reactions in others.

I didn't ask you to undress so I could examine you. I asked you to undress because it's essential to the doctor-patient relationship that I be fully clothed and you be sitting there in your underwear.

SIPRESS

An Application: The Doctor's Office

Consider how a physician uses an office to convey particular information to the audience of patients. Physicians enjoy high prestige and power in the United States, a fact evident upon entering a doctor's office. First, the physician is nowhere to be seen. Instead, in what Goffman describes as the "front region" of the setting, the patient encounters a receptionist who serves as a gatekeeper, deciding if and when the patient can meet the doctor. Who waits to see whom is, of course, a power game: In any setting, the less powerful person is the one who waits. And a simple survey of the doctor's waiting room, with patients (often impatiently) waiting to gain entry to the inner sanctum, leaves little doubt that the physician is the one who controls events.

The physician's private office and examination room are the "back region" of the setting. Here, the patient confronts a wide range of props, such as medical books and framed degrees, that reinforce the impression that the physician has the specialized knowledge necessary to call the shots. In the office, the physician usually remains seated behind a desk—the larger and grander the desk, the greater the

statement of power—while the patient is provided with only a chair.

The physician's appearance and manner convey still more information. The usual costume of white lab coat may have the practical function of keeping clothes from becoming soiled, but its social function is to let others know at a glance the physician's status. A stethoscope around the neck or a medical chart in hand has the same purpose. A doctor's highly technical language, frequently mystifying, is also a statement of power. Finally, patients use the title "doctor," but they, in turn, are frequently addressed by their first names, a practice that further underscores the physician's dominant position. The overall message of a doctor's performance is clear: "I will help you, but you must allow me to take charge."

SOCIOLOGY @ WORK

NONVERBAL COMMUNICATION

Novelist William Sansom describes a fictional Mr. Preedy, an English vacationer on a beach in Spain:

He took care to avoid catching anyone's eye. First, he had to make it clear to those potential companions of his holiday that they were of no concern to him whatsoever. He stared through them, round them, over them—eyes lost in space. The beach might have been empty. If by chance a ball was thrown his way, he looked surprised; then let a smile of amusement light his face (Kindly Preedy), looked around dazed to see that there were people on the beach, tossed it back with a smile to himself and not a smile *at* the people. . . .

[He] then gathered together his beach-wrap and bag into a neat sand-resistant pile (Methodical and Sensible Preedy), rose slowly to stretch his huge frame (Big-Cat Preedy), and tossed aside his sandals (Carefree Preedy, after all). (1956; quoted in Goffman, 1959:4–5)

Without uttering a single word, Mr. Preedy offers a great deal of information about himself to anyone observing him. This illustrates the process of **nonverbal communication,** *communication using body movements, gestures, and facial expressions rather than speech.*

People use many parts of the body to generate *body language,* that is, to convey information to others. Facial expressions are the most significant form of body language. Smiling, for instance, conveys pleasure, although we distinguish among the deliberate

 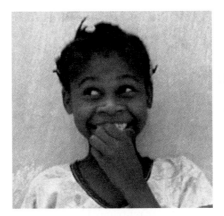 

Hand gestures vary widely from one culture to another. Yet people everywhere define a chuckle, grin, or smirk in response to someone's performance as an indication that one does not take another person seriously. Therefore, the world over, people who cannot restrain their mirth tactfully cover their faces.

smile of Kindly Preedy on the beach, a spontaneous smile of joy at seeing a friend, a pained smile of embarrassment, and the full, unrestrained smile of self-satisfaction we often associate with "the cat who ate the canary."

Eye contact is another crucial element of nonverbal communication. Generally, we use eye contact to invite social interaction. Someone across the room "catches our eye," sparking a conversation. Avoiding another's eyes, by contrast, discourages communication. Hands, too, speak for us. Common hand gestures in our society convey, among other things, an insult, a request for a ride, an invitation for someone to join us, or a demand that others stop in their tracks. Gestures also supplement spoken words. Pointing in a menacing way at someone gives greater emphasis to a word of warning, just as shrugging the shoulders adds an air of indifference to the phrase "I don't know" and rapidly waving the arms lends urgency to the single word "Hurry!"

Body Language and Deception

As any actor knows, it is very difficult to pull off a perfect performance. In everyday performances, unintended body language can contradict our planned meaning. A teenage boy offers an explanation for getting home late, for example, but his mother doubts his words because he avoids looking her in the eye. The movie star on a television talk show claims that her recent flop at the box office is "no big deal," but the nervous swing of her leg suggests otherwise. In practical terms, careful observation of nonverbal communication

(most of which is not easily controlled) provides clues to deception, in much the same way that a lie detector records telltale changes in breathing, pulse rate, perspiration, and blood pressure.

Look at the two facial photographs in the box on page 150. Can you tell which one is an honest smile and which one is a deception? Detecting phony performances is difficult, because no bodily gesture directly indicates that one is lying. Even so, because any performance involves so many expressions, few people can lie without making a slip and raising the suspicions of a careful observer. Therefore, the key to detecting deceit is to scan the whole performance with an eye for inconsistencies.

 For more information about facial expression and honesty, visit the following Web site: http://www.bbc.co.uk/science/humanbody/humanface/expertarticle_ekman.shtml

GENDER AND PERSONAL PERFORMANCES

Because women are socialized to be less assertive than men, they tend to be more sensitive to nonverbal communication. Moreover, gender plays an important part in personal performances. Based on the work of Nancy Henley, Mykol Hamilton, and Barrie Thorne (1992), we can extend our discussion of personal performances to spotlight the importance of gender.

Demeanor

Demeanor—general conduct or deportment—is a clue to personal power. Simply put, powerful people enjoy more freedom in how they act; subordinates act more

APPLYING SOCIOLOGY

Spotting Lies in an Age of Terrorism

It is no secret that we live in dangerous times; checking the terror alert status has become a regular part of U.S. citizens' lives as this country engages in a worldwide war against terrorism. One of the biggest problems in efforts to combat terror is trying to figure out who the enemy is. There is no simple way to identify someone bent on causing harm. But research by social scientists plays a part here by pointing out clues that anyone can use to tell when someone else is lying.

According to Paul Ekman, a specialist in analyzing social interaction, an observer can find clues to deception by paying attention to four elements of a performance: words, voice, body language, and facial expressions.

1. **Words.** People who are good liars mentally rehearse their lines, but they cannot always avoid inconsistencies that suggest deception. In addition, a simple slip of the tongue—something the person did not mean to say in quite that way—often occurs in even a carefully prepared performance. Any such "leak" might indicate a person is concealing information. Of course, doing so is no certain indication of being a criminal, much less a terrorist.

2. **Voice.** Tone and patterns of speech contain clues to deception because they are hard to control. Especially when trying to hide a powerful emotion, a person cannot easily prevent the voice from trembling or breaking. Similarly, the individual may speak more quickly (suggesting anger) or slowly (indicating sadness). Terrorists are most vulnerable here since, according to Ekman, they typically are trying to manage a strong hatred and disdain for police or other officials who are asking them questions.

3. **Body language.** A "leak" from body language may tip off an observer to deception as well. Subtle body movements, for example, give the impression of nervousness, as does sudden swallowing or rapid breathing. These are especially good clues

to deception because few people can control them. Powerful emotions that flash through a performance— what Ekman calls a "hot spot"—are good clues to deception.

4. **Facial expressions.** Ekman explains that there are forty-three distinct muscles in the face that humans use to create expressions. Therefore, facial expressions are even more difficult to control than other body language. Look at the two faces in the photos. Can you tell which is a lying face? It's the one on the left. While a real smile usually has a relaxed expression and lots of "laugh lines" around the eyes, a phony smile seems forced and unnatural, with fewer wrinkles around the mouth and eyes.

We all try to fake emotions—some more successfully than others—at some time in our lives. Obviously, the ability to hide powerful emotions to the degree that terrorists do is a practiced art. For this reason, Paul Ekman's recent work includes training people to be able to tell when someone is (and is not) telling a lie.

Sources: Based on Ekman (1985), Golden (1999b), and M. Kaufman (2002).

formally and self-consciously. Off-color remarks, swearing, or putting one's feet on the desk may be acceptable for the boss, but not for a secretary. Similarly, powerful people can interrupt others whenever they wish, whereas subordinates are expected to display deference through silence (Smith-Lovin & Brody, 1989; Henley, Hamilton, & Thorne, 1992; Johnson, 1994).

Since women generally occupy positions of lesser power, demeanor is a gender issue as well. As Chapter

13 ("Gender Stratification") explains, about 40 percent of all working women in the United States hold clerical or service jobs that place them under the control of supervisors, who are usually men. Women, then, craft their personal performances more carefully than men and defer more often in everyday interaction.

Use of Space

How much space does a personal performance require? Power plays a key role because using more space is a sign of personal importance. Thus, men typically command more space than women, whether pacing back and forth before an audience or casually lounging on a beach. Why? Our culture traditionally has measured femininity by how *little* space women occupy (the standard of "daintiness") and masculinity by how *much* territory a man controls (the standard of "turf").

For both sexes, the concept of **personal space** refers to *the surrounding area over which a person makes some claim to privacy*. In the United States, people typically position themselves several feet apart when speaking; throughout the Middle East, by contrast, people stand much closer. But just about everywhere, men often intrude into women's personal space. A woman's encroachment on a man's personal space, however, is often seen as a sexual overture. Here, again, women have less power in everyday interaction than men.

Staring, Smiling, and Touching

Eye contact encourages interaction. Women more than men work to sustain eye contact. But men have their own distinctive brand of eye contact: *staring*. As Henley, Hamilton, and Thorne see it, men staring at women are claiming dominance and defining women as sexual objects.

Although frequently conveying pleasure, *smiling* can also be a sign of appeasement or submission. In a male-dominated world, therefore, women smile more than men.

Finally, mutual *touching* conveys intimacy and caring. Apart from close relationships, however, touching is generally something men do to women (and rarely, in our culture, to other men). A male physician touches the shoulder of his female nurse as they examine a report, a young man touches the back of his woman friend as he guides her across the street, or a male skiing instructor touches young women as he teaches them to ski. In such examples, the touching may evoke little response, but it amounts to a subtle ritual by which men claim dominance over women.

IDEALIZATION

Complex motives underlie human behavior. Even so, Goffman suggests, we construct performances to *idealize* our intentions. That is, we try to convince others (and perhaps ourselves) that what we do reflects ideal cultural standards rather than selfish motives.

Idealization is easily illustrated in the world of physicians and patients. In a hospital, physicians engage in a performance commonly described as "making rounds." Entering the room of a patient, the physician often stops at the foot of the bed and silently examines the patient's chart. Afterward, physician and patient converse briefly. In ideal terms, this routine involves a physician making a personal visit to inquire about a patient's condition.

In reality, the picture is not so perfect. A physician may see several dozen patients a day and remember little about many of them, so that reading the chart is a chance to recall the patient's name and medical problems. Revealing the impersonality of much medical care would undermine the cultural ideal of the physician as one who is deeply concerned about the welfare of others.

Physicians, college professors, and other professionals typically idealize their motives for entering their chosen careers. They describe their work as "making a contribution to science," "helping others," "serving the community," and even "answering a calling from God." Rarely do they admit the less honorable, although common, motives of seeking the income, power, prestige, and leisure these occupations provide.

More generally, idealization is part of civility. Smiling and speaking politely to people we do not like are little lies that ease our way through social interactions. Even when we suspect that others are putting on an act, we are unlikely to challenge their performances, for reasons we explained next.

EMBARRASSMENT AND TACT

The visiting speaker mispronounces the college's name; the senator rises from the table to speak, unaware of the napkin that still hangs from her neck; the president becomes ill at a state dinner. As carefully as individuals may craft their performances, slipups of all kinds occur. The result is *embarrassment*, or discomfort following a spoiled performance. Goffman describes embarrassment simply as "losing face."

Embarrassment is an ever-present danger because, first, all performances typically contain some deception. And second, most performances involve

To most people in the United States, these expressions convey anger, fear, disgust, happiness, surprise, and sadness. But do people elsewhere in the world define them in the same way? Research suggests that all human beings experience the same basic emotions and display them to others in the same basic ways. But culture plays a part by specifying the situations that trigger one emotion or another.

many elements that, in a thoughtless moment, can shatter the intended impression.

A curious fact is that an audience usually overlooks flaws in a performance, allowing an actor to avoid embarrassment. If we do point out a misstep ("Excuse me, but did you know your fly is open?"), we do it quietly and only to help someone avoid even greater loss of face. In Hans Christian Andersen's classic fable "The Emperor's New Clothes," the child who blurts out that the emperor is parading about naked tells the truth but is scolded for being rude.

Often, too, members of an audience actually help the performer recover a flawed performance. *Tact*, then, amounts to helping someone "save face." After hearing a supposed expert make an embarrassingly inaccurate remark, for example, people may tactfully ignore the comment. Or mild laughter may indicate that they wish to treat what was said as a joke. Or a listener may simply respond, "I'm sure you didn't mean that," noting the statement but not allowing it to destroy the actor's performance. With this in mind, we can understand Abraham Lincoln's comment "Tact is the ability to describe others the way they see themselves."

Why is tact so common? Because embarrassment provokes discomfort not simply in the actor but in *everyone*. Just as a theater audience feels uneasy when

an actor forgets a line, people who observe awkward behavior are reminded of how fragile their own performances are. Socially constructed reality thus works like a dam holding back a sea of chaos. Should one person's performance spring a leak, others tactfully help make repairs. Everyone, after all, lends a hand in building reality, and no one wants it suddenly swept away.

In sum, Goffman's research shows that, although behavior is spontaneous in some respects, it is more patterned than we like to think. Almost 400 years ago, Shakespeare captured this idea in memorable lines that still ring true:

> All the world's a stage,
> And all the men and women merely players:
> They have their exits and their entrances;
> And one man in his time plays many parts.
> *As You Like It*, II

INTERACTION IN EVERYDAY LIFE: THREE APPLICATIONS

We have now examined the major elements of social interaction. The final sections of this chapter illustrate these lessons by focusing on three important dimensions of everyday life: emotions, language, and humor.

EMOTIONS: THE SOCIAL CONSTRUCTION OF FEELING

Emotions—more commonly called *feelings*—are a vital element of human social life. Indeed, emotions evolved as a survival strategy to form cooperative social groups (Turner, 2000; Massey, 2002). In the present, the importance of emotions in everyday life is evident in the fact that what we *do* often matters less than how we *feel* about it.

Emotions seem very personal because they are "inside." Even so, as we now explain, just as society guides our behavior, so it guides our emotional life.

The Biological Side of Emotions

Studying people all over the world, Paul Ekman (1980a, 1980b) reports that people everywhere express six basic emotions: happiness, sadness, anger, fear, disgust, and surprise (see also Lutz & White, 1986; Lutz, 1988). Moreover, Ekman found, people everywhere use much the same facial expressions to display these emotions. Indeed, Ekman argues, some emotional responses seem to be "wired" into human beings, that is, biologically programmed in our facial features, muscles, and central nervous system.

Why? Over the evolution of the human species, emotions may have had a biological root, but they serve a social purpose: supporting group life. That is, emotions are powerful forces that allow us to overcome our individualism and forge connections with others. Thus, the capacity for emotion arose in our ancestors along with the capacity for culture (Turner, 2000). This fact helps explain Ekman's finding that a surprising degree of the emotional life of human beings is universal rather than culturally variable.

The Cultural Side of Emotions

But culture does play an important role in guiding human emotions. First, Ekman explains, culture defines *what triggers* an emotion. Whether people define, say, the departure of an old friend as joyous (calling out happiness), insulting (causing anger), a loss (causing sadness), or a mystical event (provoking surprise and awe) has a lot to do with the culture. Second, culture provides rules for the *display* of emotions. For example, most people in the United States express emotions more freely with family members than with workplace colleagues. Similarly, we expect children to express emotions to parents, although parents tend to guard their emotions in front of their children. Third, culture guides how we

Many of us think emotions are simply part of our biological makeup. While there is a biological foundation to human emotion, sociologists have demonstrated that what triggers an emotion—as well as when, where, and to whom the emotion is displayed—is shaped by culture. For example, many jobs not only regulate a worker's behavior, but also expect workers to display a particular emotion, as in the case of the always-smiling airline flight attendant. Can you think of other jobs that regulate emotions in this way?

value emotions. Some societies encourage the expression of emotion, whereas others belittle emotion and expect members to suppress their feelings and maintain a "stiff upper lip." Gender also plays a part here because, traditionally at least, many cultures expect women to show emotions yet they condemn emotional expression by men as a sign of weakness. In some cultures, of course, this pattern is less pronounced or even reversed.

Emotions on the Job

In the United States most people are freer to express their feelings at home than on the job. The reason is that, as Arlie Russell Hochschild (1979, 1983) explains, the typical company tries to regulate not only the behavior but also the emotions of its employees. Take

the case of an airline flight attendant who offers passengers a beverage and a smile. Although this smile might convey real pleasure at serving the customer, Hochschild's study of flight attendants points to a different conclusion: The smile is an emotional script demanded by the airline

CRITICAL THINKING

Managing Feelings: The Case of Women's Abortion Experiences

Few issues today generate as much emotion as abortion. In a study of women's abortion experiences, sociologist Jennifer Keys (2002) discovered emotional scripts or "feeling rules" that guide how women feel about ending a pregnancy.

Keys begins by explaining that emotional scripts arise from the political controversy surrounding abortion. The antiabortion movement defines abortion as a personal tragedy: the "killing of an unborn child." Given this definition, women who terminate a pregnancy through abortion are doing something very wrong and can expect to feel grief, guilt, and regret. Indeed, so intense are these feelings, according to advocates of this position, that such women often suffer from "postabortion syndrome."

Those who take the pro-choice position have an opposing view of abortion. From this point of view, the woman's problem is the *unwanted pregnancy;* abortion is a medical solution. Therefore, the emotion common to women who terminate a pregnancy should be not guilt but relief.

In her research, Keys conducted in-depth interviews with forty women who had recently had abortions and found that all of them activated scripts as they "framed" their situation in an anti-abortion or pro-choice manner. In part, this construction of reality reflected the women's own attitudes about abortion. In addition, however, the women's

partners and friends typically encouraged specific feelings about the event. Ivy, one young woman in the study, had a close friend who was also pregnant. "Congratulations!" she exclaimed, when she learned of Ivy's condition. "We're going to be having babies together!" Such a statement established one "feeling rule"—having a baby is *good*—which sent the message to Ivy that her planned abortion should trigger guilt. Working in the other direction, Jo's partner was horrified by the news that she was pregnant. Doubting his own ability to be a father, he blurted out, "I would rather put a gun to my head than have this baby!" His panic not only defined having the child as a mistake but alarmed Jo as well. Clearly, her partner's reaction helped frame Jo's decision to terminate the pregnancy as a matter of relief from a terrible problem.

Medical personnel also play a part in this process of reality construction by using specific terms. Nurses and doctors who talk about "the baby" encourage the antiabortion framing of abortion and provoke grief and guilt. On the contrary, those who use language such as "pregnancy tissue," "fetus," or "the contents of the uterus" encourage the pro-choice framing of abortion as a simple medical procedure leading to relief. Olivia began using the phrase "products of conception," which she picked up from her doctor. Denise spoke of her procedure as "taking the extra cells out of my body. Yeah, I did feel some guilt

when I thought that this was the beginning of life, but my body is full of life—you have lots of cells in you."

After the procedure, most women reported actively trying to manage their feelings. Explained Ivy, "I never used the word 'baby.' I kept saying to myself that it was not formed yet. There was nothing there yet. I kept that in my mind." On the other hand, Keys found that all of the women in her study who leaned toward the antiabortion position did use the term "baby." When interviewed, Gina explained, "I do think of it as a baby. The truth is that I ended my baby's life and I should not have done that. Thinking that makes me feel guilty. But—considering what I did—maybe I *should* feel guilty." Believing that what she had done was wrong, in other words, Gina actively called out the feeling of guilt—in part, Keys concluded, to punish herself.

What do you think?

1. *In your own words, what are "emotional scripts" or "feeling rules"?*

2. *Can you provide examples of "feeling rules" in your own life?*

3. *In light of this discussion, to what extent is it correct to say that our feelings are not as personal as we might have thought?*

Sources: McCaffrey & Keys (2000) and Keys (2002).

as the right way to do the job. Therefore, we see that Goffman's "presentation of self" involves not just surface acting but also the "deep acting" of emotions.

With these patterns in mind, it is easy to see that we socially construct our emotions as part of our

everyday reality, a process sociologists call *emotion management.* The box relates how women who decide to have an abortion display very different emotions about the experience depending on their initial view of terminating a pregnancy.

LANGUAGE: THE SOCIAL CONSTRUCTION OF GENDER

As Chapter 3 ("Culture") explains, language is the thread that joins members of a society into the symbolic web we call culture. Language conveys not only a surface meaning but also deeper levels of meaning. One such level involves gender. Language defines men and women differently in at least three ways, involving power, value, and attention.[1]

Language and Power

A young man proudly rides his new motorcycle up his friend's driveway and boasts, "Isn't she a beauty?" On the surface, the question has little to do with gender. Yet, why does he use the pronoun "she" rather than "he" or "it" to refer to his prized possession? The answer is that men often use language to establish control over their surroundings. That is, a man attaches a female pronoun to a motorcycle (or car, boat, or other object) because it reflects the power of *ownership*.

Another control function of language relates to people's names. Traditionally in the United States and in many other parts of the world, a woman takes the family name of the man she marries. While few people in this country consider this an explicit statement of a man's ownership of a woman, many think it reflects male dominance. For this reason, an increasing share of married women (almost 15 percent) have kept their own name or merged the two family names.

Language and Value

The English language usually treats as masculine whatever has greater value, force, or significance. For instance, the adjective "virtuous," meaning "morally worthy" or "excellent," is derived from the Latin word *vir*, meaning "man." By contrast, the disparaging adjective "hysterical" is derived from the Greek word *hystera*, meaning "uterus."

In many familiar ways, language also confers different value on the two sexes. Traditional masculine terms such as "king" and "lord" have retained their positive meaning, while comparable terms, such as "queen," "madam," and "dame," have acquired negative connotations in contemporary usage. Language thus both mirrors social attitudes and helps to perpetuate them.

Why do we associate ownership with men and characterize what is owned as feminine? How easily can you imagine renaming this boat with the gender reversed?

Similarly, use of the suffixes "ette" and "ess" to denote femininity usually devalues the words to which they are added. For example, a "major" has higher standing than a "majorette," as does a "host" in relation to a "hostess." And, certainly, men's groups with names such as the Los Angeles Rams carry more stature than women's groups with names like the Radio City Music Hall Rockettes.

Language and Attention

Language also shapes reality by directing greater attention to masculine activity. In the English language, the plural pronoun "they" is gender-neutral. But the corresponding singular pronouns "he" and "she" specify gender. According to traditional grammatical practice, we use "he," along with the possessive "his" and the objective "him," to refer to *all* people. Thus, we assume that the bit of wisdom "He who hesitates is lost" refers to women as well as to men. But this practice also reflects the cultural pattern of overlooking the existence of women.

The English language has no gender-neutral third-person singular personal pronoun. In recent years, however, the plural pronouns "they" and "them" increasingly have gained currency as a singular pronoun

---

[1]The following sections draw primarily on Henley, Hamilton, & Thorne (1992). Additional material comes from Thorne, Kramarae, & Henley (1983) and Romaine (1999).

DIVERSITY: RACE, CLASS, AND GENDER

Gender and Language: "You Just Don't Understand!"

In the story that opened this chapter, a couple faces a situation that rings all too true to many people: When lost, men grumble to themselves and perhaps blame their partners but avoid asking others for directions. For their part, women can't seem to understand such behavior.

Deborah Tannen, who has conducted extensive research on the linguistic differences that separate the sexes, explains. Men, she claims, see most daily encounters as competitive situations; so getting lost is bad enough without asking for help and thereby letting someone else get "one up" on them. By contrast, because women in the United States hold a generally subordinate position, they are socialized to ask for help. Sometimes, Tannen points out, women will ask for assistance even when they don't need it.

A similar gender-linked problem common to couples involves what men call "nagging." Consider the following exchange (adapted from Adler, 1990:74):

Sybil: What's wrong, honey?

Harold: Nothing . . .

Sybil: Something is bothering you; I can tell.

Harold: I told you nothing is bothering me. Leave me alone.

Sybil: But I can see that there is a problem . . .

Harold: OK. Just why do you think there is a problem?

Sybil: Well, for one thing, you're bleeding all over your shirt.

Harold [now irritated]: It doesn't bother me.

Sybil [losing her temper]: WELL, IT SURE IS BOTHERING ME!

Harold: I'll go change my shirt.

The problem couples face in communicating is that what one partner *intends* by a comment is not always what the other *hears* in the words. To Sybil,

the opening question is an attempt at cooperative problem solving. She can see that something is wrong with Harold (who has cut himself while doing yard work), and she wants to help him. But Harold interprets her pointing out his problem as belittling and tries to close off the discussion. Sybil, confident that Harold needs just to understand that she only wants to be helpful, repeats herself. This reaction sets in motion a vicious circle in which Harold, thinking his wife is nagging because she thinks he cannot take care of himself, responds by digging in his heels. His response, in turn, makes Sybil all the more sure that she needs to do something. And round it goes until somebody gets angry.

In the end, Harold gives in only to the extent that he agrees to change his shirt. But notice he still refuses to discuss the original problem. Misunderstanding his wife's motives, Harold just wants Sybil to leave him alone. Likewise, Sybil fails to understand her husband's view of the situation and walks away thinking that he is a stubborn grouch.

Sources: Adler (1990) and Tannen (1990).

("A person should do as they please"). This violates grammatical rules, yet there is no doubt that English is changing to accept such gender-neutral constructions.

Grammar aside, the mix of gender and language is likely to remain a source of miscommunication between women and men. In the box, Harold and Sybil, whose misadventures in trying to find a friend's home opened this chapter, return to illustrate how the two sexes often seem to be speaking different languages.

REALITY PLAY: THE SOCIAL CONSTRUCTION OF HUMOR

Humor is an important part of everyday life. But while everyone laughs at a joke, few people think about what makes something funny or why humor is a part of every culture in the world. We can apply many of the ideas developed in this chapter as we explore the character of humor.[2]

The Foundation of Humor

Humor is a form of reality play, that is, a product of reality construction. Specifically, humor stems from the contrast between two different realities. Generally, one reality is *conventional*, that is, what people expect in a specific situation. The other reality is *unconventional*, an unexpected violation of cultural patterns. Humor, therefore, arises from contradiction, ambiguity, and double meanings found in differing definitions of the same situation. Note how this principle works in the newspaper headlines in the box on page 158.

There are countless ways to mix realities and thereby generate humor. Contrasting realities emerge from statements that contradict themselves, like "Nostalgia is not what it used to be." Switching words can create humor, as in Oscar Wilde's line "Work is the curse of the drinking class." Even reordering syllables does the trick, as in the case of the (probably fictitious) country song that goes "I'd rather have a bottle in front of me than a frontal lobotomy."

Of course, a joke can be built the other way around, so that the comic leads the audience to expect an unconventional answer then delivers a very ordinary one. When a reporter asked the famous desperado Willy Sutton why he robbed banks, for example, he replied dryly, "Because that's where the money is." However a joke is constructed, the greater the opposition or incongruity between the two definitions of reality, the greater the humor.

When telling jokes, the comedian uses various strategies to strengthen this opposition and make the joke funnier. One common technique is for the comic to present the first, or conventional, remark in conversation with another actor, then to turn toward the audience to deliver the second, unexpected line. In a Marx Brothers film, Groucho waxes philosophical when he says, "Outside of a dog, a book is a man's best friend." Then, raising his voice and turning to the camera, he adds, "And *inside* of a dog, it's too dark to read!" Such "changing of channels" underscores the incongruity of the two parts. Following the same logic, stand-up comics may "reset" the audience to conventional expectations by interjecting, "But, seriously, folks . . ." after one joke and before the next one.

To construct the strongest contrast in meaning, comedians pay careful attention to their performances—the precise words they use and the timing of their delivery. A joke is "well told" if the comic creates the sharpest possible opposition between the realities, just as humor falls flat in a careless performance. Since the key to humor lies in the opposition of realities, we can see why the climax of a joke is called the "*punch* line."

The Dynamics of Humor: "Getting It"

Someone who does not understand both the conventional and the unconventional realities in a joke may complain, "I don't get it." To "get" humor, the audience must understand the two realities involved well enough to appreciate their difference. But comics may make getting the joke harder still by leaving out some important piece of information. The audience, therefore, must pay attention to the stated elements of the joke and then fill in the missing pieces on their own.

As a simple case, consider the reflection of movie producer Hal Roach upon reaching his one hundredth birthday: "If I had known I would live to be one hundred, I would have taken better care of myself!" Here, "getting" the joke depends on realizing that Roach must have taken pretty good care of himself since he lived to be one hundred in the first place. Or take one of W. C. Fields's lines: "Some weasel took the cork out of my lunch." "Some lunch!" we think to ourselves to "finish" the joke.

Here is an even more complex joke: What do you get if you cross an insomniac, a dyslexic, and an agnostic? Answer: A person who stays up all night wondering if there is a dog. To get this one, you must know, first, that insomnia is an inability to sleep, that dyslexia causes a person to reverse the letters in words; and that an agnostic doubts the existence of God.

Why would an audience be required to make this sort of effort in order to understand a joke? Simply because our enjoyment of a joke is heightened by the pleasure of having completed the puzzle necessary to "get it." In addition, getting the joke also confers a favored insider status. We can also understand the frustration of *not* getting a joke: fear of being judged stupid coupled with being excluded from a pleasure shared by others. Not surprisingly, outsiders in such a situation sometimes fake getting the joke, or someone may tactfully explain the joke so the other person doesn't feel left out.

But as the old saying goes, if you have to explain a joke, it won't be very funny. Besides taking the edge off the language and timing on which the *punch* depends, an explanation removes the mental involvement and greatly reduces the listener's pleasure.

---

[2]The ideas discussed here are those of the author (1987), except as otherwise noted. The general approach draws on work discussed in this chapter, especially on the ideas of Erving Goffman.

CRITICAL THINKING

Double Take: Real Headlines That Make People Laugh

Humor is generated by the mixing of two distinct and opposing realities. Here are several real headlines from recent newspapers. Read each one and identify the conventional meaning intended by the writer as well as the unconventional interpretation that generates humor.

"Include Your Children When Baking Cookies"

"Drunk Gets Nine Months in Violin Case"

"Survivor of Siamese Twins Joins Parents"

"Iraqi Head Seeks Arms"

"Stud Tires Out"

"Prostitutes Appeal to Pope"

"Panda Mating Fails: Veterinarian Takes Over"

"Soviet Virgin Lands Short of Goal Again"

"Typhoon Rips through Cemetery: Hundreds Dead"

"Squad Helps Dog Bite Victim"

"Miners Refuse to Work after Death"

"Killer Sentenced to Die for Second Time in Ten Years"

"Something Went Wrong in Jet Crash"

"British Left Waffles on Falkland Islands"

"Stolen Painting Found by Tree"

What do you think?

1. *For each headline, do you see the expected and unexpected meanings?*

2. *Which headlines are funniest? Why?*

3. *Can you think of other everyday examples of humor?*

Source: Thanks to Kay Fletcher.

The Topics of Humor

The fact that people the world over smile and laugh makes humor a universal human trait. But people differ in what they find funny, so humor rarely travels well.

October 1, Kobe, Japan. Can you share a joke with people who live halfway around the world? At dinner, I ask two Japanese college women to tell me a joke. "You know 'crayon'?" Asako asks. I nod. "How do you ask for a crayon in Japanese?" I respond that I have no idea. She laughs out loud as she says what sounds like "crayon crayon." Her companion Mayumi laughs, too. My wife and I sit awkwardly, straight-faced. Asako relieves some of our embarrassment by explaining that the Japanese word for "give me" is kureyo, which sounds like "crayon." I force a smile.

What is humorous to the Japanese, then, may be lost on the Chinese, Iraqis, or people in the United States. To some degree, too, the social diversity of our own country means that different types of people will find humor in different situations. New Englanders, southerners, and westerners have their own brands of humor, as do Latinos and Anglos, fifteen- and forty-year-olds, Wall Street bankers and southwestern rodeo riders.

But for everyone, humor deals with topics that lend themselves to double meanings or *controversy*. For example, the first jokes many of us learned as children were about culturally taboo bodily functions. The mere mention of "unmentionable acts" or even certain parts of the body can dissolve young faces in laughter.

Are there jokes that do break through the culture barrier? Yes, but they must touch upon universal human experiences such as, say, turning on a friend:

I think of a number of jokes, but none seems likely to work. Understanding jokes about the United States is difficult for people who have never been there. Is there something more universal? Inspiration: "Two fellows are walking in the woods and come upon a huge bear. One guy leans over and tightens up the laces on his running shoes. 'Jake,' says the other, 'what are you doing? You can't outrun this bear!' 'I don't have to outrun the bear,' responds Jake, 'I just have to outrun you!' Smiles all around.

Humor and health have always been related. During the Middle Ages, people used the word "humors" (derived from the Latin *humidus*, meaning "moist") to mean a balance of bodily fluids that regulates a person's well-being. Researchers today document the power of humor to reduce stress and improve health, confirming the old saying "Laughter is the best medicine" (Robinson, 1983; Haig, 1988). But at the extreme, people who always take conventional reality lightly risk being defined as deviant or even mentally ill (a common stereotype depicts insane people as laughing uncontrollably, and we have long dubbed mental hospitals "funny farms").

Then, too, every social group considers certain topics too sensitive for humorous treatment. Of course, one can joke about such things, but doing so courts criticism for telling a "sick" joke (and, therefore, *being* sick). People's religious beliefs, tragic accidents, or appalling crimes are the stuff of "sick" jokes or no jokes at all. After the September 11 terrorist attacks, late-night comedy shows were off the air for a week (Kleiner, 2002).

The Functions of Humor

Humor is found everywhere because it works as a safety valve that vents potentially disruptive sentiments with little harm. That is, humor provides a way to express an opinion on a sensitive topic without being serious. Having said something controversial, a person can also use humor to diffuse the situation by simply stating, "I didn't mean anything by what I said; it was just a joke!"

Similarly, people use humor to relieve tension in uncomfortable situations. One study of medical examinations found most patients begin to joke with doctors to ease their own nervousness (Baker et al., 1997).

Humor and Conflict

If humor holds the potential to comfort those who laugh, it can also be used to harm others. Men who tell jokes about women, for example, typically are voicing some measure of hostility toward them (Powell & Paton, 1988; Benokraitis & Feagin, 1995). Similarly, jokes at the expense of gay people reveal the tensions surrounding sexual orientation in the United States. Humor is often a sign of real conflict in situations where one or both parties choose nt to bring the conflict out into the open (Primeggia & Varacalli, 1990).

"Put-down" jokes function to make one category of people feel good at the expense of another. After collecting and analyzing jokes from many societies, Christie Davies (1990) concluded that conflict among ethnic groups is one driving force behind humor

Because humor involves challenging established conventions, most U.S. comedians—including George Lopez—have been social "outsiders," members of racial and ethnic minorities.

almost everywhere. The typical ethnic joke makes fun of some disadvantaged category of people, thereby making the jokester and the audience superior. Given the Anglo-Saxon traditions of U.S. society, Poles and other ethnic and racial minorities have long been the butt of jokes, as have Newfoundlanders ("Newfies") in eastern Canada, the Irish in Scotland, Sikhs in India, Turks in Germany, Hausas in Nigeria, Tasmanians in Australia, and Kurds in Iraq.

Disadvantaged people, of course, also make fun of the powerful, although usually with some care. Women in the United States joke about men, just as African Americans find humor in white people's ways, and poor people poke fun at the rich. Throughout the world, people target their leaders with humor, and officials in some countries take such jokes seriously enough to suppress them (Speier, 1998).

In sum, the significance of humor is much greater than we may think. Humor is a means of mental escape from a conventional world that is never entirely to our liking (Flaherty, 1984, 1990; Yoels & Clair, 1995). Indeed, this fact helps explain why so many of our nation's comedians come from among the ranks of historically oppressed peoples, including Jews and African Americans. As long as we maintain a sense of humor, we assert our freedom and are not prisoners of reality. By putting a smile on our faces, we change ourselves and the world just a little.

SUMMARY

1. Social structure provides guidelines for behavior, making everyday life understandable and predictable.

2. A major component of social structure is status. Within an entire status set, a master status has special significance for a person's identity.

3. Ascribed statuses are involuntary, whereas achieved statuses are earned. In practice, most statuses are both ascribed and achieved.

4. Role is the dynamic expression of a status. Incompatible roles linked to two or more statuses generate role conflict; likewise, incompatible roles linked to a single status cause role strain.

5. The "social construction of reality" refers to the idea that we build the social world through our interactions with others.

6. The Thomas theorem states, "Situations defined as real become real in their consequences."

7. Ethnomethodology reveals people's assumptions about and understandings of their social world.

8. Dramaturgical analysis views everyday life as theatrical performance, noting that people try to create particular impressions in the minds of others.

9. Social power affects performances, one reason that men's behavior typically differs from women's.

10. Everyday behavior carries the ever-present danger of embarrassment, or "loss of face." People use tact to prevent others' performances from breaking down.

11. Although the same basic emotions are found everywhere, culture dictates what triggers emotions, how we display emotions, and what value we attach to emotion. In everyday life, presentations of self involve managing emotions as well as overt behavior.

12. Language is vital to the process of socially constructing reality. In various ways, language defines women and men differently, generally to the advantage of men.

13. Humor stems from the difference between conventional and unconventional definitions of a situation. Because humor is an element of culture, people throughout the world find different situations funny.

KEY CONCEPTS

social interaction (p. 139) the process by which people act and react in relation to others

status (p. 140) a social position that a person occupies

status set (p. 140) all the statuses a person holds at a given time

ascribed status (p. 140) a social position a person receives at birth or assumes involuntarily later in life

achieved status (p. 141) a social position a person assumes voluntarily that reflects personal ability and effort

master status (p. 141) a status that a society defines as having special importance for social identity, often shaping a person's entire life

role (p. 141) behavior expected of someone who holds a particular status

role set (p. 142) a number of roles attached to a single status

role conflict (p. 143) conflict among the roles corresponding to two or more statuses

role strain (p. 143) tension among the roles connected to a single status

social construction of reality (p. 144) the process by which people creatively shape reality through social interaction

Thomas theorem (p. 145) W. I. Thomas's assertion that situations that are defined as real are real in their consequences

ethnomethodology (p. 146) Harold Garfinkel's term for the study of the way people make sense of their everyday surroundings

dramaturgical analysis (p. 147) Erving Goffman's term for the study of social interaction in terms of theatrical performance

presentation of self (p. 147) Erving Goffman's term for a person's efforts to create specific impressions in the minds of others

nonverbal communication (p. 148) communication using body movements, gestures, and facial expressions rather than speech

personal space (p. 151) the surrounding area over which a person makes some claim to privacy

CRITICAL-THINKING QUESTIONS

1. Consider ways in which a physical disability can serve as a master status. What assumptions do people commonly make about the mental ability or the sexuality of someone with a physical disability such as cerebral palsy?

2. The word "conversation" has the same root as the religious term "convert," suggesting that we engage one another with the expectation of change on the part of everyone involved. In what sense, then, does good-faith conversation require open-mindedness on everyone's part?

3. George Jean Nathan once quipped, "I only drink to make other people interesting." What does this statement mean in terms of reality construction? Can you identify the elements of humor in it?

4. Here is a joke about sociologists: "Question—How many sociologists does it take to change a light bulb? Answer—None, because there is nothing wrong with the light bulb; it's the *system* that needs to be changed!" What makes this joke funny? What sorts of people are likely to get it? What kinds of people probably won't? Why?

APPLICATIONS AND EXERCISES

1. Write down as many of your own statuses as you can. Do you consider any a master status? To what extent are each of your statuses ascribed and achieved?

2. During the next twenty-four hours, every time somebody asks, "How are you?" stop and actually give a truthful answer. What happens when you respond to a "polite" question in an unexpected way? (Listen to what people say and also note their body language.) What does this experiment suggest about everyday interactions?

3. This chapter illustrated Erving Goffman's ideas with a description of a physician's office. Investigate the offices of several professors in the same way. What furniture is there, and how is it arranged? What "props" do professors use? How are the offices of physicians and professors different? Which are tidier? Why?

4. Spend an hour or two walking around the businesses of your town (or shops at a local mall). Observe the presence of women and men at each location. From your observations, would you conclude that physical space is "gendered"?

5. Packaged in the back of this new textbook is an interactive CD-ROM that offers a variety of video and interactive review materials intended to help you better understand the material covered in this chapter. For this chapter, the CD-ROM contains a relevant clip from *ABC News*, an author's tip video, interactive map animations, an interactive time line, and flashcards with audio pronunciations of the more difficult words.

 SITES TO SEE

http://www.prenhall.com/macionis

Visit the interactive Companion Website™ that accompanies this text. Begin by clicking on the cover of your book. You will find a chapter-by-chapter study guide, practice tests, suggested Web links, and links to other relevant material.

http://www.census.gov/genealogy/www/namesearch.html

Many interesting patterns of everyday life involve names. This Census Bureau Web site has a search engine for names. Study the frequency of different last names (or investigate first names) in the U.S. population. What patterns can you find? How many others share your own name?

http://www.ai.mit.edu/projects/humanoid-robotics-group/

Is it possible to build a machine capable of human interaction? That is the goal of robotics engineers at the Massachusetts Institute of Technology. Their Web site provides details and photographs. Look over their work and think about issues raised in this chapter. In what ways are machines able, and unable, to mimic human behavior?

 INVESTIGATE WITH RESEARCH NAVIGATOR™

Follow the instructions on page 24 of this text to access the features of **Research Navigator™**. Once at the Web site, enter your Login Name and Password. Then, to use the **Content Select™** database, enter keywords such as "non-verbal communication," "emotions," and "humor," and the search engine will supply relevant and recent scholarly and popular press publications. Use the *New York Times* **Search-by-Subject Archive** to find recent news articles related to sociology and the **Link Library** feature to find relevant Web links organized by the key terms associated with this chapter.

GROUPS AND ORGANIZATIONS

BILL JACKLIN (ENGLISH)
Saluting Policemen

1998, oil on canvas, 40.6 × 40.6 cm. Private Collection / The Bridgeman Art Library.

BACK IN 1948, PEOPLE IN Pasadena, California, paid little attention to the opening of a new restaurant. Yet one small business—owned by brothers Maurice and Richard McDonald—would transform not only the entire restaurant industry but introduce a new organizational model copied by countless businesses of all kinds.

The McDonald brothers' basic concept—which we now call "fast food"—was to serve meals quickly and cheaply to large numbers of people. The brothers trained employees to perform highly specialized jobs, so that one person grilled hamburgers while others "dressed" them, made French fries, whipped up milkshakes, and presented the food to the customers in assembly-line fashion.

As the years went by, the McDonald brothers prospered, and they decided to move their single restaurant from Pasadena to San Bernardino. It was there, in 1954, that Ray Kroc, a traveling blender and mixer merchant, paid them a visit.

Kroc was fascinated by the efficiency of the brothers' system and saw the potential for a whole chain of fast-food restaurants. The three launched the plan as partners. Soon, however, Kroc bought out the McDonalds and went on to become one of the greatest success stories of all time. Today, more than 30,000 McDonald's restaurants serve 46 million people every day throughout the United States and in 118 other nations around the world.

The success of McDonald's is evidence of more than just the popularity of hamburgers. Its larger importance, as we shall see presently, lies in the extent to which the principles that guide this company are coming to dominate social life in the United States and elsewhere (Ritzer, 1993, 1998, 2000; Stross, 2002).

We begin with an examination of *social groups*, the clusters of people with whom we interact in much of our daily lives. As this chapter explains, the scope of group life in the United States expanded greatly over the course of the twentieth century. Having evolved from a close-knit world of families, local neighborhoods, and small businesses, our society now turns on the operation of huge businesses and other bureaucracies that sociologists describe as *formal organizations*. Understanding how this expanding scale of life came to be, and what it means for us as individuals, are this chapter's main objectives.

SOCIAL GROUPS

Almost everyone seeks a sense of belonging, which is the experience of group life. A **social group** is *two or more people who identify and interact with one another.* Human beings come together in couples, families, circles of friends, churches, clubs, businesses, neighborhoods, and large organizations. Whatever its form, a group is made up of people with shared experiences, loyalties, and interests. In short, while keeping their individuality, members of social groups also think of themselves as a special "we."

Not every collection of individuals can be called a group. People with a status in common, such as women, homeowners, gay men, soldiers, millionaires, and Roman Catholics, are not a group, but a *category*. Though they know others who hold the same status, the vast majority are strangers to one another.

As human beings, we live our lives as members of groups. Such groups may be large or small, temporary or long-lasting, and can be based on kinship, cultural heritage, or some shared interest.

What about students sitting together in a campus lecture hall or bathers enjoying a hot day at the beach? Some people in such settings may interact, but only with a few others. These temporary, loosely formed collections of people are better termed a *crowd*. In general, crowds are too anonymous and transitory to qualify as groups.

The right circumstances, however, can turn a crowd into a group. Disasters, tragedies, and common enemies can make people see strangers in a new way. After the September 11 terrorist attacks, for example, many New Yorkers (and people across the United States) have a renewed appreciation for neighbors and friends.

PRIMARY AND SECONDARY GROUPS

Acquaintances commonly greet one another with a smile and a "Hi! How are you?" The response is usually "Just fine, thanks. How about you?" This answer, of course, is often more scripted than truthful. In most cases, providing a detailed account of how you are *really* doing would make most people feel so awkward they would beat a hasty retreat.

Sociologists designate two types of social groups, depending on the degree of genuine personal concern that members show for one another. According to

Charles Horton Cooley (1864–1929), a **primary group** is *a small social group whose members share personal and enduring relationships.* Bound by *primary relationships*, people typically spend a great deal of time together, engage in a wide range of activities, and feel that they know one another well. Although not without conflict, from time to time, members of primary groups display real concern for each other's welfare. The family (the focus of Chapter 18) is every society's most important primary group.

For a biographical sketch of Charles Horton Cooley, see the Gallery of Sociologists at http://www.TheSociologyPage.com

Cooley called these personal and tightly integrated groups "primary" because they are among the first groups we experience in life. In addition, the family and early play groups hold primary importance in the socialization process, shaping attitudes, behavior, and social identity.

Primary relationships give people a comforting sense of security, evident in the heightened sense of family many people experienced in the wake of the September 11 attacks (Hart, 2001). In normal times, people enjoy the familiar social circle of family or friends, where they can "be themselves" without worrying about the impression they are making.

Members of primary groups help one another in many ways, but they generally think of their ties as ends in themselves rather than as a means to other ends. In other words, we prefer to think that kinship and friendship link people who "belong together." Moreover, members of a primary group tend to view each other as unique and irreplaceable. Especially in the family, we are bound to others by emotion and loyalty. Brothers and sisters may not always get along, but they always remain siblings.

In contrast to the primary group, the **secondary group** is *a large and impersonal social group whose members pursue a specific goal or activity.* In most respects, secondary groups have precisely the opposite characteristics of primary groups. *Secondary relationships* involve weak emotional ties and little personal knowledge of one another. Most secondary groups are short-term, beginning and ending without particular significance. An example of a secondary group is students in a college sociology course, who may interact with others in the class but who probably will not see many of the students again after the semester ends.

Secondary groups include many more people than primary groups. For example, dozens or even hundreds of people may work together in the same office, yet most of them pay only passing attention to one another. In some cases, time may transform a group from secondary to primary, as with co-workers who share an office for many years. But generally, members of a secondary group do not think of themselves as "we."

Whereas members of primary groups display a *personal orientation*, people in secondary groups have a *goal orientation*. Secondary ties need not be hostile or cold, of course. Interaction among students, co-workers, and business associates is often pleasant even if it is impersonal. But while primary-group members define themselves according to *who* they are in terms of kinship or personal qualities, people in secondary groups look to one another for *what* they are or what they can do for each other. Put simply, people in secondary groups tend to "keep score," mindful of what they give others and what they receive in return. This goal orientation means that secondary-group members usually remain formal and polite. In a secondary relationship, therefore, we ask the question "How are you?" without expecting a truthful answer.

Table 7–1 summarizes the characteristics that distinguish primary and secondary groups. Keep in mind that these traits define two types of groups in ideal terms; many real groups contain elements of both. But putting these concepts at opposite ends of a continuum helps us describe and analyze group life.

Many people think that small towns and rural areas have mostly primary relationships and that large cities are characterized by more secondary ties. This generalization holds much truth, but some urban neighborhoods—especially those populated by people of a single ethnic or religious category—are very tightly knit.

GROUP LEADERSHIP

How do groups operate? One important element of group dynamics is leadership. Though many small friendship groups have no leader at all, most large secondary groups have a formal chain of command.

Two Leadership Roles

Groups typically benefit from two kinds of leadership. **Instrumental leadership** refers to *group leadership that emphasizes the completion of tasks*. Members look to instrumental leaders to make plans, give orders, and "get things done." **Expressive leadership,** on the other hand, *focuses on collective well-being*. Expressive leaders take less of an interest in achieving goals than in promoting the well-being of members, raising group morale, and minimizing tension and conflict among members.

TABLE 7–1	Primary Groups and Secondary Groups: A Summary	
	Primary Group ←—————→	Secondary Group
Quality of Relationships	Personal orientation	Goal orientation
Duration of Relationships	Usually long-term	Variable; often short-term
Breadth of Relationships	Broad; usually involving many activities	Narrow; usually involving few activities
Subjective Perception of Relationships	As ends in themselves	As means to an end
Examples	Families, circles of friends	Co-workers, political organizations

Because they concentrate on performance, instrumental leaders usually have formal, secondary relations with other group members. Instrumental leaders give orders and reward or punish members according to their contribution to the group's efforts. Expressive leaders, however, build more personal, primary ties. They offer sympathy to a member going through a tough time, keep the group united, and lighten a tense moment with humor. Whereas successful instrumental leaders enjoy more *respect* from members, expressive leaders generally receive more personal *affection*.

Historically, in U.S. families, the two types of leadership have been linked to gender. Cultural norms bestowed instrumental leadership on men, who, as fathers and husbands, assumed primary responsibility for earning income and making major family decisions. Expressive leadership traditionally belonged to women: Mothers and wives encouraged supportive and peaceful relationships among family members. One result of this division of labor was that many children had greater respect for their fathers but closer personal ties with their mothers (Parsons & Bales, 1955; Macionis, 1978a).

Greater equality between the sexes has blurred this gender-based distinction between instrumental and expressive leadership. In most group settings, women and men now assume both leadership roles.

Three Leadership Styles

Sociologists also characterize leadership in terms of decision-making style. *Authoritarian leadership* focuses

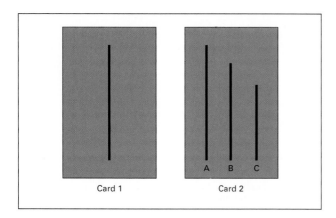

FIGURE 7-1 Cards Used in Asch's Experiment in Group Conformity

Source: Asch (1952).

on instrumental concerns, takes personal charge of decision making, and demands strict compliance from subordinates. Although this leadership style may win little affection from the group, a fast-acting authoritarian leader is appreciated in a crisis.

Democratic leadership is more expressive and makes a point of including everyone in the decision-making process. Although less successful when crises leave little time for discussion, democratic leaders generally draw on the ideas of all members to develop creative solutions to problems.

Laissez-faire leadership (a French phrase roughly meaning "to leave alone") allows the group to function more-or-less on its own. This style typically is the least effective in promoting group goals (White & Lippitt, 1953; Ridgeway, 1983).

A leader may adopt each of the three styles in different situations. Vice President Richard Cheney recently commented that President Bush had a more authoritarian style in his role as commander in chief of the armed forces and a more democratic style working with Congress on economic issues.

GROUP CONFORMITY

One way groups influence the behavior of members is by promoting conformity. "Fitting in" provides a secure feeling of belonging, but at the extreme, group pressure can be unpleasant and, at times, dangerous. Group pressure can influence us to conform or obey, as experiments by Solomon Asch and Stanley Milgram showed.

Asch's Research

Solomon Asch (1952) conducted a classic experiment that showed the power of groups to generate conformity. Asch recruited students allegedly for a study of visual perception. Before the experiment began, he explained to all but one member in a small group that their real purpose was to put pressure on the remaining person. Arranging six to eight students around a table, Asch showed them a "standard" line, as drawn on Card 1 in Figure 7–1, and asked them to match it to one of three lines on Card 2.

Anyone with normal vision could easily see that the line marked "A" on Card 2 is the correct choice. Initially, as planned, everyone made the matches correctly. But then Asch's secret accomplices began answering incorrectly, leaving the naive subject (seated at the table so as to answer next to last) bewildered and uncomfortable.

What happened? Asch found that one-third of all subjects conformed to the others by answering incorrectly. Apparently, many of us are willing to compromise our own judgment to avoid being different, even from people we do not know.

Milgram's Research

Stanley Milgram, a former student of Solomon Asch, conducted conformity experiments of his own. In Milgram's controversial study (1963, 1965; Miller, 1986), a researcher explained to male recruits that they would be taking part in a study of how punishment affects learning. One by one, he assigned the subjects to the role of "teacher" and placed another individual—actually an accomplice of Milgram's—in a connecting room to pose as a "learner."

The teacher watched as the learner was seated in what looked like an electric chair. The researcher applied electrode paste to one of the learner's wrists, explaining that this would "prevent blisters and burns." The researcher then attached an electrode to the wrist

For more on Milgram's research, go to http://www.smallworld.sociology.columbia.edu/

and secured the leather straps, explaining that these would "prevent excessive movement while the learner was being shocked." The researcher assured the teacher that although the shocks would be painful, they would cause "no permanent tissue damage."

The researcher then led the teacher back to the next room, explaining that the "electric chair" was connected to a "shock generator," a realistic-looking piece of equipment with a label that read "Shock Generator, Type ZLB, Dyson Instrument Company, Waltham, Mass." On the front was a dial that appeared to regulate electric current from 15 volts (labeled "Slight Shock") to 300 volts (marked "Intense Shock") to 450 volts (marked "Danger: Severe Shock").

Seated in front of the "shock generator," the teacher was told to read aloud pairs of words. Then the teacher was to repeat the first word of each pair and wait for the learner to recall the second word. Whenever the learner failed to answer correctly, the teacher was told to apply an electric shock.

The researcher directed the teacher to begin at the lowest level (15 volts) and to increase the shock by 15 volts every time the learner made a mistake. And so the teacher did. At 75, 90, and 105 volts, the teacher heard moans from the learner; at 120 volts, shouts of pain; at 270 volts, screams; at 315 volts, pounding on the wall; after that, deadly silence. None of forty subjects assigned to the role of teacher during the initial research even questioned the procedure before reaching 300 volts, and twenty-six of the subjects—almost two-thirds—went all the way to 450 volts.

Although Milgram was aware that the electric shock generator was phony and that the person in the other room was in on the study, he was "shocked" to see how readily people obeyed authority figures, even if it meant hurting others. Perhaps, Milgram imagined, this experiment helps to explain how, during wartime, ordinary people hurt or kill others as they simply "follow orders."

Milgram (1964) then modified his research to see if Solomon Asch had documented such a high degree of group conformity only because the task he used to measure group conformity—matching lines—was trivial. Could groups of ordinary people—not authority figures—also pressure people to administer electrical shocks?

This time, Milgram formed a group of three teachers, two of whom were his accomplices. Each of the three teachers was to suggest a shock level when the learner made an error; the group would then administer the *lowest* of the three suggestions. This arrangement gave the naive subject the power to deliver a lesser shock regardless of what the others proposed.

The accomplices suggested increasing the shock level with each error, putting pressure on the third member to do the same. And in fact, they succeeded. Although the rate of compliance was lower than when a single "authority figure" gave the orders, on average subjects in this study applied voltages three to four times higher than subjects who acted alone in control

conditions. Thus, Milgram's research suggests that people are likely to follow directions from not only "legitimate authority figures" but from groups of ordinary individuals, even when it means inflicting harm on another person.

Janis's "Groupthink"

Experts, too, cave in to group pressure, says Irving L. Janis (1972, 1989). Janis contends that a number of U.S. foreign policy errors, including the ill-fated Vietnam War and the failure to foresee Japan's attack on Pearl Harbor during World War II, resulted from group conformity among our highest-ranking political leaders.

Common sense tells us that group discussion improves decision making. Janis counters that group members often seek consensus that closes off other points of view. Janis called this process **groupthink,** *the tendency of group members to conform, resulting in a narrow view of some issue.*

A classic example of groupthink led to the disastrous 1961 invasion of the Bay of Pigs in Cuba. Looking back, Arthur Schlesinger, Jr., an adviser to President John F. Kennedy, confessed to feeling guilty for "having kept so quiet during those crucial discussions in the Cabinet Room," adding that the group discouraged anyone from challenging what, in hindsight, Schlesinger considered "nonsense" (quoted in Janis, 1972:30, 40).

REFERENCE GROUPS

How do we assess our own attitudes and behavior? Frequently, we use a **reference group,** *a social group that serves as a point of reference in making evaluations and decisions.*

A young man who imagines his family's response to a woman he is dating is using his family as a reference group. Similarly, a young woman assessing her salary is likely to use co-workers of about the same age and experience as a standard of reference. As these examples suggest, reference groups can be primary or secondary. In either case, our membership in groups affects the judgments we make.

We also use groups that we do *not* belong to for reference. Being well prepared for a job interview means showing up dressed the way people in that company dress for work. Conforming to groups we do not belong to as a strategy to win acceptance illustrates the process of *anticipatory socialization,* described in Chapter 5 ("Socialization").

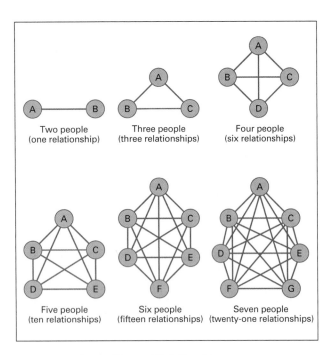

Two people
(one relationship)

Three people
(three relationships)

Four people
(six relationships)

Five people
(ten relationships)

Six people
(fifteen relationships)

Seven people
(twenty-one relationships)

FIGURE 7–2 Group Size and Relationships

Stouffer's Research

Samuel A. Stouffer (1949) conducted a classic study of reference group dynamics during World War II. Researchers asked soldiers to rate their own or any competent soldier's chances of promotion in their army unit. One might guess that soldiers serving in outfits with a high promotion rate would be optimistic about their own advancement. Yet Stouffer's research pointed to the opposite conclusion: Soldiers in army units with low promotion rates were actually more positive about their chances of moving ahead.

The key to understanding Stouffer's results lies in the groups against which soldiers measured themselves. Those having assignments with lower promotion rates looked around them and saw people making no more headway than they were. That is, although they had not been promoted, neither had many others, so they did not feel deprived. Soldiers in units with a higher promotion rate, however, could easily think of people who had been promoted sooner or more often than they. With such people in mind, even soldiers who had been promoted were likely to feel shortchanged.

The lesson is that we do not make judgments about ourselves in isolation, nor do we compare ourselves with just anyone. Regardless of our situation in *absolute* terms, we form a subjective sense of our well-being by looking at ourselves in relation to specific reference groups (Merton, 1968; Mirowsky, 1987).

IN-GROUPS AND OUT-GROUPS

Everyone favors some groups over others, whether because of political outlook, social prestige, or just manner of dress. On the college campus, for example, left-leaning student activists may look down on fraternity members, whom they consider conservative; the Greeks, in turn, may snub the computer "nerds" and "grinds," who work too hard. Virtually every social landscape has a comparable mix of positive and negative evaluations.

Such judgments illustrate another important element of group dynamics: the opposition of in-groups and out-groups. An **in-group** is *a social group commanding a member's esteem and loyalty.* An in-group exists in relation to an **out-group,** *a social group toward which one feels competition or opposition.* In-groups and out-groups are based on the idea that "we" have valued traits that "they" lack.

Tensions among groups sharpen their boundaries and give people a clearer social identity. At the same time, the group dynamics foster stereotypes and distort reality. Specifically, members of in-groups generally hold overly positive views of themselves and unfairly negative views of various out-groups.

Power also plays a part in intergroup relations. A powerful in-group can define others as a lower-status out-group. Historically, for example, many white people have viewed people of color as an out-group and have subordinated them socially, politically, and economically. Minorities who have internalized these attitudes struggle to overcome negative self-images. In short, in-groups and out-groups foster loyalty and also generate conflict (Tajfel, 1982; Bobo & Hutchings, 1996).

GROUP SIZE

If you are the first person to arrive at a party, you are in a position to watch some fascinating group dynamics. Until about six people enter the room, those present usually share a single conversation. But as more people arrive, the group soon divides into two or more clusters. Size plays an important role in how group members interact.

To understand the effects of group size, consider the mathematical number of relationships among two to seven people. As Figure 7–2 shows, two people form a single relationship; adding a third person results in three relationships; adding a fourth person yields six. Increasing the number of people one at a time, then, expands the number of relationships much more rapidly since every new individual can interact with everyone already there. Thus, by the time seven people join one conversation, twenty-one "channels" connect them. With so many open channels at this point, the group usually divides.

The Dyad

German sociologist Georg Simmel (1858–1918) studied the social dynamics in the smallest groups. Simmel (1950; orig. 1902) used the term **dyad** to designate *a social group with two members.*

Simmel explained that social interaction in a dyad is typically more intense than in larger groups because neither member shares the other's attention with anyone else. In the United States, love affairs, marriages, and the closest friendships are dyadic.

But like a stool with only two legs, dyads are unstable. Both members of a dyad must work to keep the relationship going; if either withdraws, the group collapses. Because the stability of marriages is important to society, the marital dyad is supported by legal, economic, and often religious ties.

The Triad

Simmel also studied the **triad,** *a social group with three members.* A triad contains three relationships, each joining two of the three people. A triad is more stable than a dyad because one member can act as a mediator should the relationship between the other two become strained. Such group dynamics help explain why members of a dyad (say, a married couple) often seek out a third person (often a counselor) to air tension between them.

On the other hand, two of the three can pair up to press their views on the third, or two may intensify their relationship, leaving the other feeling left out. For example, when two of the three develop a romantic interest in each other, they will understand the old saying, "Two's company, three's a crowd."

 For more about Georg Simmel, see his biography in the Gallery of Sociologists at http://www.TheSociologyPage.com

As groups grow beyond three people, they become more stable and capable of withstanding the loss of even several members. At the same time, increases in group size reduce the intense personal interaction possible only in the smallest groups. Larger groups are thus based less on personal attachment and more on formal rules and regulations. Such formality helps a group

The triad, illustrated by Jonathan Green's painting Friends, *includes three people. A triad is more stable than a dyad because conflict between any two persons can be mediated by the third member. Even so, should the relationship between any two become more intense in a positive sense, those two are likely to exclude the third.*

Jonathan Green, Friends, 1992. Oil on masonite, 14 in. × 11 in. © Jonathan Green, Naples, Florida. Collection of Patric McCoy.

persist over time, though the group is not immune to change. After all, their numerous members give large groups more contact with the outside world, opening the door to new attitudes and behavior (Carley, 1991).

SOCIAL DIVERSITY: RACE, CLASS, AND GENDER

Race, ethnicity, class, and gender play a part in group dynamics. Peter Blau (1977; Blau, Blum, & Schwartrz 1982; South & Messner, 1986) points out four ways in which social diversity influences intergroup contact:

1. **Large groups turn inward.** Blau explains that the larger a group is, the more likely its members are to have relationships just among themselves. Say a

Today's college campuses value social diversity. One of the challenges of this movement is ensuring that all categories of students are fully integrated into campus life. This is not always easy. Following Blau's theory of group dynamics, as the number of minority students increases, these men and women are able to form a group unto themselves, perhaps interacting less with others.

college is trying to enhance social diversity by increasing the number of international students. These students may add a dimension of difference, but as their numbers rise, they become more likely to form their own social group. Thus, efforts to promote social diversity may have the unintended effect of promoting separatism.

2. **Heterogeneous groups turn outward.** The more internally diverse a group is, the more likely its members are to interact with outsiders. Members of campus groups that recruit people of both sexes and various social backgrounds typically have more intergroup contact than those with members of one social type.

3. **Social equality promotes contact.** To the extent that all groups have the same social standing, members of all the groups will interact. Thus,

whether groups keep to themselves or not depends on how much the groups form a social hierarchy. For example, if sororities all recruit women of a particular social class, members of these elite groups may have little contact with members of lower-status groups.

4. **Physical boundaries create social boundaries.** To the extent that a social group is physically segregated from others (by having its own dorm or dining area, for example), its members are less likely to associate with other people.

NETWORKS

A **network** is *a web of weak social ties.* Think of a network as a "fuzzy" group containing people who come into occasional contact but who lack a sense of boundaries and belonging. If we think of a group as a "circle of friends," then we might describe a network as a "social web" expanding outward, often reaching great distances and including large numbers of people.

Some networks are close to being groups, as is the case with college friends who stay in touch after graduation by e-mail and telephone. More commonly, however, a network includes people we *know of*—or who *know of us*—but with whom we interact rarely, if at all. As one woman with a widespread reputation as a community organizer explains, "I get calls at home, someone says, 'Are you Roseann Navarro? Somebody told me to call you. I have this problem' " (quoted in Kaminer, 1984:94).

Network ties often give us the sense that we live in a "small world." In a widely known classic experiment, Stanley Milgram (1967; Watts, 1999) gave letters to subjects in Kansas and Nebraska intended for a few specific people in Boston who were unknown to the original subjects. No addresses were supplied, and the subjects in the study were instructed to send the letters to others they knew personally who might know the target people. Milgram found that the target people received the letters with, on average, six subjects helping out. This result lead Milgram to conclude that just about everyone is connected to everyone else by "six degrees of separation." Later research, however, has cast doubt on Milgram's conclusions. Examining Milgram's original data, Judith Kleinfeld (2002) points out that most of Milgram's letters (240 out of 300) never arrived at all. Those that did typically were given to subjects who were affluent, a circumstance leading Kleinfeld to conclude that richer people are far better connected across the country than ordinary women and men.

GLOBAL SOCIOLOGY

The Internet: A Global Network

Its origins seem right out of the 1960s cold war film *Dr. Strangelove*. Three decades ago, U.S. government officials and scientists were trying to figure out how to run the country after an atomic attack, which, they assumed, would knock out telephones and television. The brilliant solution was to devise a communication system with no central headquarters, no one in charge, and no main power switch—in short, an electronic web that would link the country in one vast network.

By 1985, a web of high-speed data lines was in place and the Internet was about to be born. Today, the Internet connects thousands of colleges and universities, as well as tens of thousands of government offices, all of which share in the cost of its operation. Businesses and individuals at home also connect to this "information superhighway" using a telephone-line modem and a subscription to a commercial Internet "gateway."

How many people use the Internet? A rough estimate is that, in 2003, about 600 million people in 180 (of 192) countries around the world are connected by the largest network in history.

What does the network offer to individuals? Popular "search engines" such as Google (http://www.google.com) provide information and additional site listings for just about any topic you can imagine. Another popular activity is electronic mail, with which you can start a cyber romance with a pen pal, write to your textbook author (macionis@kenyon.edu), or even send a message to the president of the United States (president@whitehouse.gov). Through the Internet, you can also join discussion groups, visit museums and college campuses for "virtual tours," locate data from government agencies (a good starting point is http://www.census.gov), explore Web pages of sociological interest (try the author's Web site, at http://www.TheSociologyPage.com), or

review for exams in this course (http://www.prenhall.com/macionis). With no formal rules for its use, the Internet's potential is limited only by our imagination.

Ironically, perhaps, it is precisely this freedom that disturbs some people. Critics claim that "electronic democracy" threatens our political system, parents fear that their children will access sexually explicit "adult sites," and purists bristle as the Internet becomes ever more flooded with advertising.

In its "anything goes" character, of course, the Internet is like the real world. Not surprisingly, therefore, a recent trend is that more and more users now employ passwords, fees, and other "gates" to create restricted subnetworks limited to people like themselves. From one vast network, then, is emerging a host of social groups.

Sources: Based, in part, on Elmer-DeWitt (1993, 1994b), Hafner (1994), and O'Connor (1997).

Network ties may be weak, but they can be a powerful resource. For immigrants seeking to become established in a new community, businesspeople seeking to expand their operations, or anyone looking for a job, *whom you know* is often just as important as *what you know* (cf. Luo, 1997; Hagan, 1998; Petersen, Saporta, & Seidel, 2000).

Networks are based on people's colleges, clubs, neighborhoods, political parties, and personal interests. Obviously, some networks contain people with considerably more wealth, power, and prestige than others, which is what the expression "well connected" means. The networks of more privileged categories of people—including whites in comparison to African Americans and Hispanics—are a valuable form of "social capital," which is more likely to yield higher-paying jobs (Kasinitz & Rosenberg, 1996; Green, Tigges, & Diaz, 1999; Lin, Cook, & Burt, 2001).

Some people also have denser networks than others; that is, they are connected to more people. Typically, the most extensive social networks include people who are young, well educated, and living in large cities (Markovsky et al., 1993; Kadushin, 1995; O'Brien, Hassinger, & Dershem, 1996; Fernandez & Weinberg, 1997; Podolny & Baron, 1997).

Gender, too, shapes networks. Although the networks of men and women are typically the same size, women include more relatives (and other women) in their networks, whereas those of men include more co-workers (and mostly men). Research suggests that women's ties do not carry quite the same clout as typical "old boy" networks. Even so, research suggests that as gender equality increases in the United States, the networks of women and men are becoming more alike (Wright, 1995; Mencken & Winfield, 1999; Reskin & McBrier, 2000; Torres & Huffman, 2002).

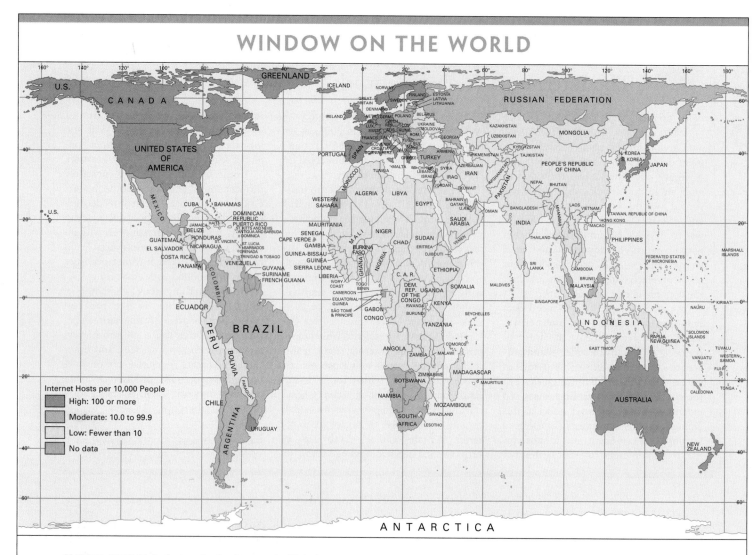

GLOBAL MAP 7–1 Access to the Internet in Global Perspective

This map shows access to the Internet around the world in terms of the number of Internet hosts for every 10,000 people. Most high-income countries and many middle-income nations are rated as having high Internet access. By contrast, about half the world's nations (mostly those with low average incomes) offer little access. What effect does this have on people's access to information? What are the likely consequences of this disparity for the future in terms of global inequality?

Source: The World Bank (2001).

Finally, new information technology has generated a global network of unprecedented size in the form of the Internet. The box on page 171 takes a closer look at this twenty-first-century form of communication, and Global Map 7–1 shows access to the Internet around the world.

FORMAL ORGANIZATIONS

A century ago, most people lived in small groups of family, friends, and neighbors. Today, our lives revolve more and more around **formal organizations,** *large secondary groups organized to achieve their goals efficiently.*

Formal organizations, such as business corporations and government agencies, differ from families and neighborhoods in an important way: Their greater size makes social relations less personal and fosters a formal, planned atmosphere. In other words, formal organizations operate in a deliberate way, not to meet personal needs but to accomplish complex jobs.

When you think about it, organizing almost 290 million members of society is remarkable, involving countless jobs, from collecting taxes to delivering the mail. To carry out most of these tasks, we rely upon large formal organizations. The U.S. government, the nation's largest formal organization, employs more than 5 million people in hundreds of agencies and the armed forces. Large formal organizations develop lives and cultures of their own so that, as members come and go, their operation can stay the same over many years.

TYPES OF FORMAL ORGANIZATIONS

Amitai Etzioni (1975) identified three types of formal organizations, distinguished by the reasons people participate: utilitarian organizations, normative organizations, and coercive organizations.

Utilitarian Organizations

Just about everyone who works for income belongs to a *utilitarian organization*, one that pays people for their efforts. Large businesses, for example, generate profits for their owners and income for their employees. Joining utilitarian organizations is usually a matter of individual choice, although, obviously, most people must join one or another utilitarian organization to make a living.

Normative Organizations

People join *normative organizations* not for income but to pursue some goal they think is morally worthwhile. Sometimes called *voluntary associations*, these include community service groups (such as the PTA, the Lions Club, the League of Women Voters, and the Red Cross), as well as political parties and religious organizations. In global perspective, people living in high-income nations with relatively democratic political systems are likely to join voluntary associations; the United States stands out as a nation of "joiners" (Curtis, Grabb, & Baer, 1992; Curtis, Baer, & Grabb, 2001; Schofer & Fourcade-Gourinchas, 2001). Figure 7–3 shows that a majority of first-year college students claim to have participated in volunteer work during the past year, and since 1990, the trend has been for more of them to do so.

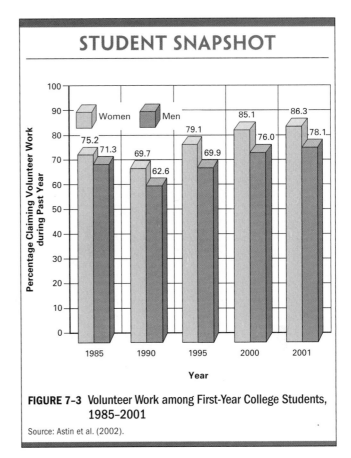

STUDENT SNAPSHOT

FIGURE 7–3 Volunteer Work among First-Year College Students, 1985–2001

Source: Astin et al. (2002).

Coercive Organizations

Coercive organizations have an involuntary membership. That is, people are forced to join these organizations as a form of punishment (prisons) or treatment (some psychiatric hospitals). Coercive organizations have special physical features, such as locked doors and barred windows, and are supervised by security personnel. They isolate people as "inmates" or "patients" for a period of time, seeking to radically change attitudes and behavior. Recall from Chapter 5 ("Socialization") the power of a total institution to transform a human being's overall sense of self.

From differing vantage points, any particular organization may fall into all of these categories. A psychiatric hospital, for example, serves as a coercive organization for a patient, a utilitarian organization for a psychiatrist, and a normative organization for a part-time hospital volunteer.

Although formal organization is vital to modern, high-income nations, it is far from new. Twenty-five centuries ago, the Chinese philosopher and teacher K'ung Fu-Tzu (known to Westerners as Confucius) endorsed the idea that government offices should be filled by the most talented young men. This led to what was probably the world's first system of civil service examinations. Here, would-be bureaucrats compose essays to demonstrate their knowledge of Confucian texts.

ORIGINS OF BUREAUCRACY

Formal organizations date back thousands of years. Elites who controlled early empires relied on officials to collect taxes, undertake military campaigns, and construct monumental structures, from the Great Wall of China to the pyramids of Egypt.

These early organizations had two limitations, however. First, they lacked the technology to communicate quickly, to travel over large distances, and to collect and store information. Second, tradition is strong in preindustrial societies, so the organizational goals were to preserve cultural systems, not to change them. But during the last few centuries, what Max Weber called a "rational worldview" emerged in parts of the

world, a process described in Chapter 4 ("Society"). In Europe and North America, the Industrial Revolution ushered in a new organizational structure concerned with efficiency, what Weber called "bureaucracy."

CHARACTERISTICS OF BUREAUCRACY

Bureaucracy is *an organizational model rationally designed to perform tasks efficiently.* Bureaucratic officials deliberately enact and revise policy to increase efficiency. To appreciate the power and scope of bureaucratic organization, consider this: Any one of nearly 300 million phones in the United States can connect you, within seconds, to any other phone—in homes, businesses, automobiles, or even a hiker's backpack on a remote mountain trail in the Adirondacks. Such instant communication was beyond the imagination of people who lived in the ancient world.

Of course, the telephone system depends on technology such as electricity, fiber optics, and computers. But neither could the system exist without the organizational ability to keep track of every telephone call—noting which phone calls which other phone, when, and for how long—and then to present this information in the form of more than 100 million monthly telephone bills.

What specific traits promote organizational efficiency? Max Weber (1978; orig. 1921) identified six key elements of the ideal bureaucratic organization:

1. **Specialization.** Our ancestors spent most of their time looking for food and shelter. Bureaucracy, by contrast, assigns individuals highly specialized duties.

2. **Hierarchy of offices.** Bureaucracies arrange personnel in a vertical ranking of offices. Each person is supervised by "higher-ups" in the organization while, in turn, supervising others in lower positions. Usually, with few people at the top and many at the bottom, bureaucratic organizations take the form of a pyramid.

3. **Rules and regulations.** Cultural tradition counts for little in a bureaucracy. Instead, rationally enacted rules and regulations guide a bureaucracy's operation. Ideally, a bureaucracy operates in a completely predictable way.

4. **Technical competence.** Bureaucratic officials and staff have the technical competence to carry out their duties. Bureaucracies typically recruit new members according to set criteria and regularly monitor their performance. Such impersonal

evaluation contrasts sharply with the ancient custom of favoring relatives, whatever their talents, over strangers.

5. **Impersonality.** Bureaucracy puts rules ahead of personal whim so that clients as well as workers are all treated uniformly. From this detached approach stems the notion of the "faceless bureaucrat."

6. **Formal, written communications.** According to an old saying, the heart of bureaucracy is not people but paperwork. Rather than casual, face-to-face talk, bureaucracy relies on formal, written memos and reports, which accumulate in vast files and guide the operation of the organization.

Bureaucratic organization promotes efficiency by carefully recruiting personnel and limiting the unpredictable effects of personal taste and opinion. Table 7–2 summarizes the differences between small social groups and large formal organizations.

ORGANIZATIONAL ENVIRONMENT

No organization operates in a vacuum. How any organization performs depends not only on its own goals and policies but also on the **organizational environment,** *factors outside the organization that affect its operation.* These factors include technology, economic and political trends, current events, the available workforce, and other organizations.

Modern organizations are shaped by the *technology* of computers, telephone systems, and copiers. Computers give employees access to more information and people than ever before. At the same time, computer technology allows managers to monitor closely the activities of workers (Markoff, 1991).

Economic and political trends affect organizations. All organizations are helped or hindered by periodic economic growth or recession. Most industries also face competition from abroad as well as changes in law—such as new environmental standards—at home.

Current events can have significant effects on organizations that are far removed from the location of the events themselves. The September 11 terrorist attacks, for example, were followed by an economic slowdown throughout the United States.

Population patterns, such as the size and composition of the surrounding populace, also affect organizations. The average age, typical education, and social diversity of a local community determine the available workforce and, sometimes, the market for an organization's products or services.

TABLE 7-2 Small Groups and Formal Organizations: A Comparison

	Small Groups	Formal Organizations
Activities	Members typically engage in many of the same activities.	Members typically engage in distinct, highly specialized activities.
Hierarchy	Often Informal or nonexistent	Clearly defined, corresponding to offices
Norms	Informal application of general norms	Clearly defined rules and regulations
Membership Criteria	Variable; often based on personal affection or kinship	Technical competence to carry out assigned tasks
Relationships	Variable; typically primary	Typically secondary, with selective primary ties
Communications	Typically casual and face to face	Typically formal and in writing
Focus	Person-oriented	Task-oriented

Other organizations also contribute to the organizational environment. To be competitive, a hospital must be responsive to the insurance industry and to organizations representing doctors, nurses, and other workers. It must also keep abreast of the equipment and procedures available at nearby facilities, as well as their prices.

THE INFORMAL SIDE OF BUREAUCRACY

Weber's ideal bureaucracy deliberately regulates every activity. In actual organizations, however, human beings are creative (and stubborn) enough to resist bureaucratic blueprints. Informality may amount to simply cutting corners in one's job, but it can also provide needed flexibility (Scott, 1981).

Informality comes partly from the personalities of organizational leaders. Studies of U.S. corporations document that the qualities and quirks of individuals—including personal charisma and interpersonal skills—can have a great effect on organizational outcomes (Halberstam, 1986; Baron, Hannan, & Burton, 1999).

George Tooker's painting Government Bureau *is a powerful statement about the human costs of bureaucracy. The artist depicts members of the public in monotonous similitude—reduced from human beings to mere "cases" to be disposed of as quickly as possible. Set apart from others by their positions, officials are "faceless bureaucrats" concerned more with numbers than with providing genuine assistance (notice that the artist places the fingers of the officials on calculators).*

George Tooker, Government Bureau, 1956. Egg tempera on gesso panel, 19⅝ × 29⅝ inches. The Metropolitan Museum of Art, George A. Hearn Fund, 1956 (56.78). Photograph © 1984 The Metropolitan Museum of Art.

Authoritarian, democratic, and laissez-faire types of leadership (described earlier in this chapter) reflect individual personality as much as any organizational plan. Then, too, in the real world of organizations, leaders and their cronies sometimes seek to benefit personally by abusing organizational power. High-profile examples include some of the corporate scandals (the collapse of Enron and other companies) of recent years. More commonly, leaders take credit for the efforts of their subordinates. Many secretaries, for example, have far more authority and responsibility than their official job titles and salaries suggest.

Communication offers another example of informality within large organizations. Memos and other written communications are the formal way to spread information through the organization. Typically, however, individuals also create informal networks, or "grapevines," that spread information quickly, if not always accurately. Grapevines, using both word-of-mouth and e-mail, are particularly important to subordinates because higher-ups may try to keep important information from them.

The spread of e-mail has "flattened" organizations somewhat, allowing even the lowest-ranking employee to bypass immediate superiors and communicate directly with the organization's leader or with all fellow employees at once. Some organizations object to "open-channel" communication and limit the use of e-mail. Microsoft Corporation (whose founder, Bill Gates, has an unlisted address yet still receives hundreds of e-mail messages a day) has developed "screens" that allow messages from only approved people to reach a particular computer terminal (Gwynne & Dickerson, 1997).

Using new information technology as well as age-old human ingenuity, members of organizations often try to break free of rigid rules in order to personalize procedures and surroundings. Such efforts suggest that we now take a closer look at some of the problems of bureaucracy.

PROBLEMS OF BUREAUCRACY

We rely on bureaucracy to manage countless dimensions of everyday life efficiently, but many people are, at best, uneasy about large organizations. Bureaucracy can dehumanize and manipulate us, and some say it poses a threat to political democracy.

Bureaucratic Alienation

Max Weber touted bureaucracy as a model of productivity. Nonetheless, Weber was keenly aware of bureaucracy's ability to *dehumanize* the people it is supposed to serve. The same impersonality that fosters efficiency also keeps officials and clients from responding to each other's unique, personal needs. On the contrary, officials we encounter at large governmental or corporate agencies must treat each client impersonally—as a standard "case."

Formal organizations create *alienation*, according to Weber, by reducing the human being to "a small cog in a ceaselessly moving mechanism" (1978:988; orig. 1921). Although formal organizations are intended to benefit humanity, Weber feared that people could well end up serving formal organizations.

Bureaucratic Inefficiency and Ritualism

Inefficiency, the failure of an organization to carry out the work that it exists to perform, is a familiar problem. According to one report, the General Services Administration, the government agency that buys equipment for federal workers, takes up to three years to process a request for a new computer. This delay ensures that by the time the computer arrives, it is already out of date (Gwynne & Dickerson, 1997).

The problem of inefficiency is captured in the concept of "red tape" (a phrase derived from the red tape used by eighteenth-century English administrators to wrap official parcels and records; Shipley, 1985). "Red tape" refers to a tedious preoccupation with organizational routine and procedures. Robert Merton (1968) points out that red tape amounts to a new twist to the already-familiar concept of group conformity. He coined the term **bureaucratic ritualism** to designate *a preoccupation with rules and regulations to the point of thwarting an organization's goals.* After the September 11 attacks, for example, the U.S. Postal Service continued to deliver mail addressed to Osama bin Laden to a post office in Afghanistan, despite the policy of the U.S. government to disrupt his terror network and objections of the FBI. It took an act of Congress to change postal policy (Bedard, 2002).

Ritualism stifles individual creativity and strangles organizational performance. In part, ritualism arises from the fact that organizations, which pay modest, fixed salaries, give officials little financial stake in performing efficiently. Then, too, bureaucratic ritualism stands as another form of the alienation that Weber feared would arise from bureaucratic rigidity (Whyte, 1957; Merton, 1968; Coleman, 1990; Kiser & Schneider, 1994).

Bureaucratic Inertia

Although bureaucrats sometimes have little motivation to be efficient, they have every reason to protect their jobs. Officials may even strive to keep an organization going when its original purpose has been realized. As Weber put it, "Once fully established, bureaucracy is among the social structures which are hardest to destroy" (1978:987; orig. 1921).

Bureaucratic inertia refers to *the tendency of bureaucratic organizations to perpetuate themselves.* Formal organizations tend to take on a life of their own beyond their formal objectives. For example, the U.S.

According to Max Weber, bureaucracy is an organizational strategy that promotes efficiency. Impersonality, however, also fosters alienation among employees, who may become indifferent to the formal goals of the organization. The behavior of this municipal employee in Bombay, India, is understandable to members of formal organizations almost anywhere in the world.

Department of Agriculture has offices in almost all U.S. counties, even though, these days, only one county in seven has any working farm (Littman, 1992).

Usually, an organization stays in business by redefining its goals. The Agriculture Department, for example, now performs a number of tasks not directly related to farming, including nutritional and environmental research.

OLIGARCHY

Early in this century, Robert Michels (1876–1936) pointed out the link between bureaucracy and political **oligarchy,** *the rule of the many by the few* (1949; orig. 1911). According to what Michels called "the iron law of oligarchy," the pyramid shape of bureaucracy places a few leaders in charge of organizational resources.

Max Weber credited a strict hierarchy of responsibility with high organizational efficiency. But Michels countered that this hierarchical structure also concentrates power and thus endangers democracy because

The ideas of scientific management were most successfully applied by Henry Ford, who pioneered the automobile assembly line. As shown in this 1928 photograph of the Dearborn, Michigan, plant, Ford divided up the job of building cars into hundreds of different tasks, each performed by a worker as the cars moved along an assembly line. The result was that new cars could be produced so cheaply that most of these autoworkers could afford to buy one.

officials can—and often do—use their access to information, resources, and the media to promote their personal interests. Again, think of the corporate fraud and outright looting by some executives in the recent corporate scandals.

Furthermore, bureaucracy also insulates officials from the public, as in the case of the corporate president or public official who is "unavailable for comment" to the local press, or the U.S. president who withholds documents from Congress claiming "executive privilege." Oligarchy, then, thrives in the hierarchical structure of bureaucracy and reduces the accountability of leaders to the people (Tolson, 1995).

Political competition, term limits, and a system of checks and balances prevent the U.S. government from becoming an out-and-out oligarchy. Even so, incumbents enjoy a significant advantage in U.S. politics. In the 2000 congressional elections, only 15 of 437 congressional officeholders running for reelection were defeated by their challengers (Giroux, 2000; Pierce, 2000).

THE EVOLUTION OF FORMAL ORGANIZATIONS

The problems of bureaucracy—especially the alienation it produces and its tendency toward oligarchy—stem from two organizational traits: hierarchy and rigidity. To Weber, bureaucracy was a top-down system: Rules and regulations made at the top guide every facet of people's lives down the chain of command. A century ago in the United States, Weber's ideas took hold in an organizational model called *scientific management*. We begin with a look at this model and then describe three challenges over the course of the twentieth century that gradually led to a new model: the *flexible organization*.

SCIENTIFIC MANAGEMENT

Frederick Winslow Taylor (1911) had a simple message: Most businesses in the United States were sadly inefficient. Managers had little idea of how to increase their business's output, and workers relied on the same tired skills of earlier generations.

To increase efficiency, Taylor explained, business should apply the principles of science. **Scientific management,** then, is *the application of scientific principles to the operation of a business or other large organization.*

Scientific management involves three steps. First, managers carefully observe the task performed by each worker, identifying all the operations involved and measuring the time needed for each. Second, managers analyze their data, trying to discover ways for workers to perform each task more efficiently. For example, managers might decide to provide workers with different tools, or to reposition various work operations within the factory. Third, management provides guidance and incentives for workers to do their jobs more quickly. If a factory worker moves twenty tons of pig iron in one day, for example, management shows the worker how to move forty tons a day and then provides higher wages for higher productivity. Applying scientific principles in this way, Taylor concluded, companies become more profitable, workers earn higher wages, and, in the end, consumers pay lower prices. As auto pioneer Henry Ford put it, "Save ten steps a day for each of 12,000 employees, and you will have saved fifty miles of wasted motion and misspent energy" (Allen & Hyman, 1999:209).

In the early 1900s, the Ford Motor Company and many businesses followed Taylor's lead and improved their efficiency. As time went on, however, formal organizations faced three new challenges, involving race and gender, rising competition from abroad, and the changing nature of work. We look briefly at each in turn.

THE FIRST CHALLENGE: RACE AND GENDER

During the 1960s, critics pointed out that big businesses and other organizations were inefficient—and also unfair—in their hiring practices. Rather than hiring on the basis of competence, as Weber had proposed, they excluded women and other minorities. As a result, most managers were white men.

Patterns of Privilege and Exclusion

Even by the end of the twentieth century, as Figure 7–4 shows, non-Hispanic white men in the United States—35 percent of the working-age population—still held 57 percent of management jobs. Non-Hispanic white women also made up 35 percent of the population but held just 28 percent of managerial positions (U.S. Equal Employment Opportunity Commission, 2003). The members of other minorities lagged further behind.

According to Rosabeth Moss Kanter (1977; Kanter & Stein, 1979), excluding women and minorities from the workplace ignores the talents of more than half the population. Furthermore, underrepresented people in an organization often feel like socially isolated out-groups—uncomfortably visible, taken less seriously, and given fewer chances for promotion.

"Opening up" an organization, Kanter claims, improves everyone's on-the-job performance by motivating employees to become "fast-trackers" who work harder and are more committed to the company. By contrast, an organization with many "dead end" jobs makes workers less productive because they have nowhere to go in their careers. An open organization also encourages leaders to seek out the input of everyone, which benefits the organization. It is officials in rigid organizations—those who have little reason themselves to be creative—who jealously guard their privileges and ride herd on their employees.

The "Female Advantage"

Some organizational researchers argue that including more women brings special management skills that strengthen an organization. Deborah Tannen (1994) claims, for example, that women have a greater "information focus," and more readily ask questions in

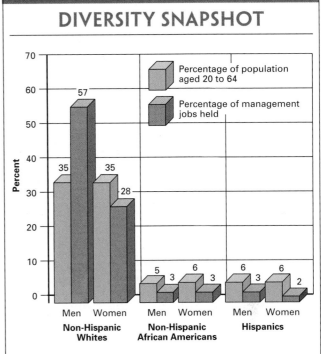

FIGURE 7–4 U.S. Managers in Private Industry by Race, Sex, and Ethnicity, 2001

Sources: U.S. Census Bureau (2002) and U.S. Equal Employment Opportunity Commission (2003).

order to understand an issue. Men, on the other hand, have an "image focus" that makes them wonder how asking questions in a particular situation will affect their reputation.

In another study of women executives, Sally Helgesen (1990) found three other gender-linked patterns. First, women place greater value on communication skills than men and share information more than men do. Second, women are more flexible leaders who typically give their employees greater autonomy. Third, compared to men, women tend to emphasize the interconnectedness of all organizational operations. Thus, women bring a "female advantage" to companies striving to be more flexible and democratic.

In sum, one challenge to conventional bureaucracy is to become more open and flexible in order to take advantage of everyone's experience, ideas, and creativity. The result goes right to the bottom line: greater profits.

THE SECOND CHALLENGE: THE JAPANESE WORK ORGANIZATION

In 1980, the corporate world in the United States was shaken to discover that the most popular automobile model sold in this country was not a Chevrolet, Ford, or Plymouth but the Honda Accord, made in Japan. To people old enough to remember the 1950s, the words "made in Japan" generally meant a cheap, poorly made product. But times had changed. The success of the Japanese auto industry (and shortly afterward, companies making electronics, cameras, and other products) soon had analysts buzzing about the "Japanese organization." How else could so small a country challenge the world's economic powerhouse?

Japanese organizations were never entirely different from their counterparts in the United States. But building on that nation's more collective spirit, Japanese organizations have always had a greater emphasis on cooperation. William Ouchi (1981) highlights five differences between formal organizations in Japan and those in the United States:

1. **Hiring and advancement.** U.S. organizations typically hold out promotions and raises in salary as prizes that employees win through individual competition. Many Japanese companies, however, have hired new school graduates together, giving all employees similar salary and responsibilities. Only after several years is anyone likely to be singled out for special advancement.

2. **Lifetime security.** Employees in the United States expect to move from one company to another to advance their careers. U.S. companies are also quick to lay off employees during an economic setback. For years, however, many Japanese firms hired workers "for life," which fostered strong, mutual loyalties. If jobs became obsolete, these companies would avoid layoffs by retraining workers for new positions.

3. **Holistic involvement.** While we tend to see the home and the workplace as distinct spheres, Japanese companies play a much larger role in workers' lives. Many provide home mortgages, sponsor recreational activities, and schedule social events. Such interaction beyond the workplace was believed to strengthen collective identity and offer the respectful Japanese employees a chance to voice suggestions and criticisms informally.

4. **Broad-based training.** U.S. workers are highly specialized, and many spend an entire career doing one thing. But a Japanese organization is more likely to train workers in all phases of its operation, again with the idea that employees will remain with the company for life.

5. **Collective decision making.** In the United States, key executives make the important decisions. Although Japanese leaders also take responsibility for their organization's performance, they are more likely to involve workers in "quality circles," where they can discuss decisions that affect them. A closer working relationship is also encouraged by Japan's lower salary difference between executives and workers—about 10 percent of the difference typical in the United States.

These characteristics have given the Japanese a very strong sense of organizational loyalty. Because they identify personal interests with company interests, workers have been likely to realize their ambitions through the organization. Even so, by the end of the 1980s, the Japanese economy entered hard times that have continued to the present. As a result of this economic downturn, fewer organizations are willing to offer workers lifetime security and the other advantages Ouchi notes above. Today, while Japanese organizations remain relatively more collectivist in their orientation, differences between Japanese and U.S. companies are smaller than they used to be.

THE THIRD CHALLENGE: THE CHANGING NATURE OF WORK

Perhaps the greatest pressure to modify conventional organizations is coming from changes in the nature of work itself. Chapter 4 ("Society") described the shift from industrial to postindustrial production. Rather than working in factories using heavy machinery to make *things*, more and more people are using computers and other electronic technology to create or process *information*. The postindustrial society, then, is characterized by information-based organizations.

Frederick Taylor developed his concept of scientific management at a time when jobs involved tasks that, while often backbreaking, were routine. Workers shoveled coal, poured liquid iron into molds, welded body panels to automobiles on an assembly line, or shot hot rivets into steel girders to build skyscrapers. In addition, a large part of the U.S. labor force in Taylor's day was immigrants, most of whom had little

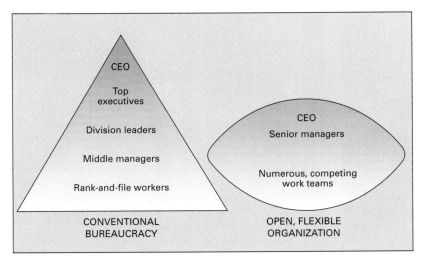

FIGURE 7–5 Two Organizational Models

The conventional model of bureaucratic organizations has a pyramid shape, with a clear chain of command. Directives flow from the top down, and reports of performance flow from the bottom up. Such organizations have extensive rules and regulations, and their workers have highly specialized jobs. More open and flexible organizations have a flatter shape, more like a football. With fewer levels in the hierarchy, responsibility for generating ideas and making decisions is shared throughout the organization. Many workers do their jobs in teams and have a broad knowledge of the entire organization's operation.

Source: Created by the author.

schooling and many of whom knew little English. The routine nature of industrial jobs, coupled with the limited skills of the labor force, led Taylor to treat work as a series of fixed tasks, set down by management and followed by employees.

Many of today's information age jobs are very different: The work of designers, artists, writers, composers, programmers, business owners, and others now demands creativity and imagination. What does this mean for formal organizations? Here are several ways in which today's organizations differ from those of a century ago:

1. **Creative autonomy.** As one Hewlett Packard executive put it, "From their first day of work here, people are given important responsibilities and are encouraged to grow" (cited in Brooks, 2000:128). Today's organizations now treat employees with information age skills as a vital resource. While executives do set production goals, they cannot dictate how a worker is to accomplish tasks that require imagination and discovery. Thus, highly skilled workers have *creative autonomy*, which means less day-to-day supervision as long as they generate good ideas in the long run.

2. **Competitive work teams.** Organizations typically give several groups of employees the freedom to work on a problem, offering the greatest rewards to those who come up with the best solution. Competitive work teams, a strategy first used by Japanese organizations, draw out the creative contributions of everyone and, at the same time,

reduce the alienation often found in conventional organizations (Yeatts, 1991, 1994; Maddox, 1994).

3. **A flatter organization.** By spreading responsibility for creative problem solving throughout the workforce, organizations take on a flatter shape. That is, the pyramid shape of conventional bureaucracy is replaced by an organizational form with fewer levels in the chain of command, as shown in Figure 7–5.

4. **Greater flexibility.** The typical industrial age organization was a rigid structure guided from the top. Such organizations may accomplish a good deal of work, but they are not especially creative or able to respond quickly to changes in their larger environment. The ideal model in the information age is a *flexible* organization, one that both generates new ideas and, in a rapidly changing global marketplace, adapts quickly.

As David Brooks puts it, "The machine is no longer held up as the standard that healthy organizations should emulate. Now it's the ecosystem" (2000:128). Thus, "smart" companies seek out intelligent, creative people (America Online's main building is called "Creative Center One") and nurture the growth of their talents.

Keep in mind, however, that this trend toward creativity does not extend to all organizations. On the contrary, many of today's jobs involve little or no creative work at all. Why? The postindustrial economy has created two very different types of work: high-skill creative work and low-skill service work.

The best of today's "information-age jobs"—including working at the popular search-engine Web site Google—allow people lots of personal autonomy as long as they produce good ideas. At the same time, many other jobs—such as working the counter at McDonald's—involve the same routines and strict supervision found in factories a century ago.

Work in the fast-food industry, for example, is routine and highly supervised, and thus has much more in common with the factory work of a century ago than with the work of teams in information organizations. Therefore, at the same time that some organizations have taken on a flexible, flatter form, others continue to use the rigid chain of command, as we now explain.

THE "MCDONALDIZATION" OF SOCIETY[1]

As noted in the opening to this chapter, McDonald's has enjoyed enormous success, now operating more than 30,000 restaurants in the United States and around the world. Japan now has more than 2,400 Golden Arches, and the world's largest McDonald's is found in China's capital city of Beijing.

October 9, Macao. Here we are, halfway around the world, in the Portuguese colony of Macao off the coast of China. Few people here speak English, and life on the streets seems a world apart from the urban rhythms of New York,

Chicago, or Los Angeles. Then I turn the corner and stand face to face with (who else?) Ronald McDonald! After eating who-knows-what for so long, forgive me for giving in to the lure of the Big Mac. But the most amazing thing is that the food—the burger, the fries, and the drink—looks, smells, and tastes exactly the same as it does back home 10,000 miles away!

McDonald's may be found almost everywhere these days, but in the United States, it is more than a restaurant—it is a symbol of our way of life. Not only do people around the world associate McDonald's with the United States, but here at home, one poll found that 98 percent of schoolchildren could identify Ronald McDonald, making him as well known as Santa Claus.

Even more important, the organizational principles that underlie McDonald's are coming to dominate our entire society. Our culture is becoming "McDonaldized," an awkward way of saying that we model many aspects of life on this restaurant chain: Parents buy toys at worldwide chain stores like Toys 'Я' Us; we drive to Jiffy Lube for a ten-minute oil change; face-to-face communication is sliding more and more toward voice mail, e-mail, and junk mail;

---

[1]Much of the material in this section is based on Ritzer (1993, 1998, 2000).

more vacations take the form of resort and tour packages; television presents news in the form of ten-second sound bites; college admissions officers size up students they have never met by their GPA and SAT scores; and professors assign ghost-written textbooks[2] and evaluate students with tests mass-produced for them by publishing companies. The list goes on and on.

McDonaldization: Four Principles

What do all such developments have in common? According to George Ritzer (1993), the McDonaldization of society involves four basic organizational principles:

1. **Efficiency.** Ray Kroc, the marketing genius behind the expansion of McDonald's, set out to serve a hamburger, French fries, and a milkshake to a customer in fifty seconds. Today, one of the company's most popular items is the Egg McMuffin, an entire breakfast in a single sandwich. In the restaurant, customers bus their own trays or, better still, drive away from the pickup window taking with them the packaging and whatever mess they make.

   Efficiency is now central to our way of life. We tend to think that anything done quickly is, for that reason alone, good.

2. **Calculability.** The first McDonald's operating manual set the weight of a regular raw hamburger at 1.6 ounces, its size at 3.875 inches across, and its fat content at 19 percent. A slice of cheese weighs exactly half an ounce. Fries are cut precisely 9/32 of an inch thick.

   Think about how many objects around your home, the workplace, and the campus are designed and mass-produced according to a uniform plan. Not just our environment but our life experiences—from traveling the nation's interstates to sitting at home viewing television—are more standardized than ever before.

3. **Uniformity and predictability.** An individual can walk into a McDonald's restaurant almost anywhere and receive the same sandwiches, drinks, and desserts prepared in precisely the same way.[3] Predictability, of course, is the result of a highly rational system that specifies every course of action and leaves nothing to chance.

4. **Control through automation.** The most unreliable element in the McDonald's system is human beings. People, after all, have good and bad days, sometimes let their minds wander, or simply decide to try something a different way. To minimize the unpredictable human element, McDonald's has automated its equipment to cook food at fixed temperatures for set lengths of time. Even the cash register at a McDonald's is little more than pictures of the items, so that ringing up a customer's order is as simple as possible.

Similarly, automatic teller machines are replacing banks, highly automated bakeries now produce bread with scarcely any human intervention, and chickens and eggs (or is it eggs and chickens?) emerge from automated hatcheries. In supermarkets, laser scanners are phasing out checking groceries by hand. We do most of our shopping in malls, where everything—from temperature and humidity to the kinds of stores and products—is carefully controlled and supervised (Ide & Cordell, 1994).

Can Rationality Be Irrational?

There can be no argument about the popularity or efficiency of McDonald's. But there is another side to the story.

Max Weber observed the expansion of formal organizations with alarm, fearing that they would cage the imagination and crush the human spirit. As Weber saw it, rational systems were efficient but dehumanizing, and McDonaldization bears him out. Each of the four principles just discussed limits human creativity, choice, and freedom. Echoing Weber, Ritzer states that "the ultimate irrationality of McDonaldization is that people could lose control over the system and it would come to control us" (1993:145). Not surprisingly, perhaps, McDonald's itself now owns a large stake in more upscale restaurants (such as Chipotle's

---

[2]Half a dozen popular sociology texts were not authored by the person or persons whose names appear on the cover. This book is not one of them.

[3]As McDonald's has "gone global," a few products have been added or modified according to local tastes. For example, in Uruguay, customers enjoy the McHuevo (hamburger with poached egg on top); Norwegians can buy McLaks (grilled salmon sandwiches); the Dutch favor Groenteburger (vegetable burger); in Thailand, McDonald's serves Samurai pork burgers (pork burgers with teriyaki sauce); the Japanese can purchase Chicken Tatsuta Sandwich (chicken seasoned with soy and ginger); Filipinos eat McSpaghetti (spaghetti with tomato sauce and bits of hot dogs); and in India, where Hindus eat no beef, McDonald's sells a vegetarian Maharaja Mac (Sullivan, 1995).

CONTROVERSY & DEBATE

Computer Technology, Large Organizations, and the Assault on Privacy

Late for a meeting with a new client, Sarah drives her car through a yellow light as it turns red at a main intersection. A computer notes the infraction and photographs the rear of the car, showing the license plate number. At the same moment, another camera photographs the driver's seat, showing Sarah behind the wheel. In seven days, she receives a summons to appear in court.

Joe finishes dressing and calls an 800 number to check the pollen count. As he listens to a recorded message, a Caller ID computer identifies Joe, records the call, and pulls up Joe's profile from a public records database. The computer adds to the profile the fact that Joe suffers from allergies. Several weeks later, tens of thousands of profiles are sold to a drug company, which sends Joe and others a free sample of its new allergy medication.

At a local department store, Nina uses her American Express card to buy an expensive new watch and some sleepwear. The store's computer adds Nina's name to its database of "buyers of expensive jewelry" and "buyers of sexy lingerie." The store trades its database with other companies, and within a month Nina receives four jewelry catalogues and an adult video brochure (Bernstein, 1997; Hamilton, 2001).

Are these cases of protecting the public and providing consumers with interesting products, or are they violating people's privacy? The answer is both: The same systems that help organizations operate efficiently also let them invade our lives and manipulate us. So, as large organizations have expanded in the United States, privacy has declined.

Small-town life in the past, of course, gave people little privacy. But at least if

people knew something about you, you were just as likely to know something about them. Today, unknown people "out there" are accumulating more information about each of us all the time.

In part, the loss of privacy is a result of more and more complex computer technology. Are you aware that every e-mail you send and every Web site you visit leaves a record in one or more computers? Most of these records can be retrieved by people you don't know, as well as by employers and other people you do know.

Another part of today's loss of privacy reflects the number and size of formal organizations. As we have explained in this chapter, large organizations tend to treat people impersonally, and they have a huge appetite for information. Mix large organizations with ever more complex computer technology, and it is no wonder that most people in the United States are concerned about who knows what about them—

and Pret A Manger) that offer food that is more sophisticated, fresh, and healthful (Philadelphia, 2002).

THE FUTURE OF ORGANIZATIONS: OPPOSING TRENDS

Early in the twentieth century, ever-larger organizations arose in the United States, most taking on the bureaucratic form described by Max Weber. In many respects, these organizations resembled armies led by powerful generals who issued orders to their captains and lieutenants. Foot soldiers, working in the factories, did what they were told.

With the emergence of a postindustrial economy after mid-century, as well as rising competition from abroad, many organizations have evolved toward a flatter, more flexible model that prizes communication and creativity. Such "intelligent organizations" (Pinchot & Pinchot, 1993; Brooks, 2000) have become more productive than ever. Just as important, for highly skilled people whose information age work demands "creative autonomy," these organizations create less of the alienation that so worried Max Weber.

But this is only half the story. Though the postindustrial economy has created many highly skilled jobs, it has created even more routine service jobs, as exemplified by McDonald's, where one in

and what people are doing with this information.

For decades, the level of personal privacy in the United States has been declining. Early in the twentieth century, when state agencies began issuing driver's licenses, for example, they generated files for every licensed driver. Today, officials can dispatch this information at the touch of a button to other organizations, including police departments. Similarly, the Internal Revenue Service and the Social Security Administration, as well as government agencies that benefit veterans, students, the unemployed, and the poor, all collect extensive information.

Business organizations now do much the same thing, and few people are aware that their choices and activities have ended up in a company's database. Most people find credit cards indispensable—the U.S. population now holds more than 1 billion of them, averaging more than five per adult—but one price we pay for the convenience of credit-card purchases is that each time we make one we automatically generate records that can end up almost anywhere.

Then there are the small cameras that are found not only at traffic intersections, but also in stores, public buildings, and parking garages and across college campuses. The number of surveillance cameras that monitor our movements is rapidly increasing with each passing year. So-called security cameras may increase public safety in some ways—say, by discouraging a mugger or even a terrorist—but only at the cost of some of the privacy we have left.

In the wake of the September 11, 2001, terrorist attacks, the federal government took steps (including the USA Patriot Act) to enhance national security. Today, government officials more closely monitor not just who enters the country but pay closer attention to everyone's behavior. In other words, national security and privacy do not go together very well. Thus, concern about the erosion of privacy in the United States is now greater than ever.

Of course, some legal protections remain. All the states have laws that give citizens rights to examine some records about themselves kept by employers, banks, credit bureaus, and even the government. The U.S. Privacy Act of 1974 also limits the exchange of personal information among government agencies and permits citizens to examine and correct most government files. But the fact is that so many private as well as public organizations now have information about us—experts estimate that 90 percent of U.S. households are profiled in databases somewhere—that current laws do not effectively address the privacy problem, and many believe recent security laws have made it much worse.

Continue the debate . . .

1. *Do you believe that the concern about national security is eroding privacy? How?*

2. *Internet search engines such as YAHOO! (http://www.yahoo.com) have "people search" programs that let you locate almost anyone. Do you think such programs pose a threat to personal privacy?*

3. *In your opinion, will the degree of personal privacy continue to decline in the years to come? Why or why not? Is there anything ordinary people can do?*

Sources: Wright (1998), *Business Week* (2000), Rosen (2000), Hamilton (2001), and Heymann (2002).

eight adults in the United States has worked at some time (Ritzer, 1998). Work of this kind, which Ritzer terms "McJobs," offers few of the benefits that today's highly skilled workers enjoy. On the contrary, the automated routines that define work in the fast-food industry, telemarketing, and similar fields are very much the same as Frederick Taylor described a century ago.

Moreover, the organizational "flexibility" that gives better-off workers more autonomy carries, for rank-and-file employees, the ever-present threat of "downsizing" (Sennett, 1998). That is, organizations facing global competition are eager to have creative employees, but they are also eager to cut costs by eliminating as many routine jobs as possible. The net result is that some people are better off than ever while others worry about holding their jobs and struggle to make ends meet—a trend that Chapter 11 ("Social Class in the United States") explores in detail.

In spite of the recent corporate scandals that have tarnished the reputation of U.S. corporations, there is little doubt that U.S. organizations as a whole operate with remarkable efficiency. Indeed, there are few places on Earth where the mail arrives as quickly and dependably as it does in the United States (J. Wilson, 1991). But we should remember that the future is far brighter for some than for others. In addition, as the final box explains, organizations pose an increasing threat to our privacy—something to keep in mind as we envision our organizational future.

SUMMARY

1. Social groups are the building blocks of society that join members as well as perform various tasks.
2. Primary groups tend to be small and person-oriented; secondary groups are typically large and goal-oriented.
3. Instrumental leadership is concerned with realizing a group's goals; expressive leadership focuses on members' morale and well-being.
4. Because group members often seek consensus, groups may pressure members toward conformity.
5. Individuals use reference groups—both in-groups and out-groups—to form attitudes and make evaluations.
6. Georg Simmel characterized the dyad relationship as intense but unstable; a triad, he added, can easily dissolve into a dyad by excluding one member.
7. Peter Blau explored how group size, homogeneity, and social standing and the physical segregation of groups all affect members' behavior.
8. Social networks are relational webs that link people with little common identity and limited interaction. The Internet is a vast electronic network linking millions of people worldwide.
9. Formal organizations are large secondary groups that seek to perform complex tasks efficiently. They are classified as utilitarian, normative, or coercive, depending on their members' reasons for joining.
10. Bureaucratic organization expands in modern societies to perform tasks efficiently. Bureaucracy is based on specialization, hierarchy, rules and regulations, technical competence, impersonal interaction, and formal, written communications.
11. Technology, political and economic trends, population patterns, and other organizations all combine to form the environment in which a particular business or agency must operate.
12. Ideally, bureaucracy promotes efficiency, but it can also lead to alienation and oligarchy and contribute to the erosion of personal privacy.
13. Frederick Taylor's scientific management shaped U.S. organizations a century ago. Since then, organizations have evolved toward a more open and flexible form as they have (a) included a larger share of women and other minorities; (b) responded to global competition, especially from Japan; and (c) shifted their focus from industrial production to postindustrial information processing.
14. Reflecting the collective spirit of Japanese culture, formal organizations in Japan are based more on personal ties than their counterparts in the United States.
15. The "McDonaldization" of society involves increasing automation and impersonality.
16. The future of organizations is likely to involve opposing trends: toward more creative autonomy for highly skilled information workers and toward supervision and discipline for less-skilled service workers.

KEY CONCEPTS

social group (p. 163) two or more people who identify and interact with one another

primary group (p. 164) a small social group whose members share personal and enduring relationships

secondary group (p. 164) a large and impersonal social group whose members pursue a specific goal or activity

instrumental leadership (p. 165) group leadership that emphasizes the completion of tasks

expressive leadership (p. 165) group leadership that focuses on collective well-being

groupthink (p. 167) the tendency of group members to conform, resulting in a narrow view of some issue

reference group (p. 167) a social group that serves as a point of reference in making evaluations and decisions

in-group (p. 168) a social group commanding a member's esteem and loyalty

out-group (p. 168) a social group toward which one feels competition or opposition

dyad (p. 169) a social group with two members

triad (p. 169) a social group with three members

network (p. 170) a web of weak social ties

formal organization (p. 172) a large secondary group organized to achieve its goals efficiently

bureaucracy (p. 174) an organizational model rationally designed to perform tasks efficiently

organizational environment (p. 175) factors outside an organization that affect its operation

bureaucratic ritualism (p. 177) a preoccupation with rules and regulations to the point of thwarting an organization's goals

bureaucratic inertia (p. 177) the tendency of bureaucratic organizations to perpetuate themselves

oligarchy (p. 177) the rule of the many by the few

scientific management (p. 178) Frederick Taylor's term for the application of scientific principles to the operation of a business or other large organization

CRITICAL-THINKING QUESTIONS

1. How do primary groups differ from secondary groups? Identify examples of each in your own life.

2. According to Max Weber, what are the six characteristic traits of bureaucracy? In what ways do new, more flexible organizations differ?

3. George Ritzer (1996:1), a critic of McDonaldization, suggests that fast-food restaurants carry the following label: "Sociologists warn us that habitual use of McDonald's systems are destructive to our physical and psychological well-being as well as to society as a whole." Do you agree? Why or why not?

4. The twentieth century was the first one with the widespread use of initials, such as IRS, IRA, IMF, IBM, CIA, WPA, PLO, NATO, CNN, WB, WWF, CDC, and so on. What does this usage suggest about social trends?

APPLICATIONS AND EXERCISES

1. Spend several hours observing customers at a fast-food restaurant. Think about ways in which not just employees but also *customers* are trained to behave in certain ways. For example, customers' norms include lining up to order and finding their own table. What other norms are at work?

2. Visit a large public building with an elevator. Observe groups of people as they approach the elevator, and enter the elevator with them. Watch their behavior: What happens to conversations as the elevator doors close? Where do people fix their eyes? Can you account for these patterns?

3. Make a list of in-groups and out-groups on your campus. What traits account for groups' falling into each category? Ask several people to comment on your list to see if they agree with your classification.

4. Using available publications (and some assistance from an instructor), try to draw an organizational pyramid for your college or university showing the key offices and how they supervise and report to each other.

5. Packaged in the back of this new textbook is an interactive CD-ROM that offers a variety of video and interactive review materials intended to help you better understand the material covered in this chapter. For this chapter, the CD-ROM contains a relevant clip from *ABC News*, an author's tip video, interactive map animations, an interactive time line, and flashcards with audio pronunciations of the more difficult words.

 ## SITES TO SEE

http://www.prenhall.com/macionis

Visit the interactive Companion Website™ that accompanies this text. Begin by clicking on the cover of your book. You will find a chapter-by-chapter study guide, practice tests, suggested Web links, and links to other relevant material.

http://www.saturn.com

Visit the Saturn car company Web site to read about Saturn's "flatter" organizational structure.

http://www.riotmanhattan.com/old_riot_site/webcam.html

This Web site uses a camera placed at New York City's Fifth Avenue at Forty-fifth Street. Do you think Internet technology of this kind threatens people's privacy? Why or why not?

http://groups.yahoo.com/

A number of Web sites, including this one, let people build their own social groups for chat or posting photos and other information. Take a look, and see what you think about "virtual groups."

 ## INVESTIGATE WITH RESEARCH NAVIGATOR™

Follow the instructions on page 24 of this text to access the features of **Research Navigator™**. Once at the Web site, enter your Login Name and Password. Then, to use the **Content Select™** database, enter keywords such as "social network," "bureaucracy," and "Max Weber," and the search engine will supply relevant and recent scholarly and popular press publications. Use the *New York Times* **Search-by-Subject Archive** to find recent news articles related to sociology and the **Link Library** feature to find relevant Web links organized by the key terms associated with this chapter.

CHAPTER

8

DEVIANCE

ADAM HERNANDEZ
Drive-by Asesino

Diptych. 1992. Oil on canvas. 55" × 60¼"

DENNIS KOZLOWSKI WAS on a roll. As the chief executive officer of Tyco International, a large Bermuda-based manufacturing corporation, Kozlowski was buying new companies so fast he had earned the nickname "Deal-a-Month Dennis." His reputation was that of a frugal and level-headed business leader. "We don't believe in perks," he boasted in a business magazine interview.

On the face of it, Tyco was a highly successful and responsibly run business. But all that was to change. In 2002, the company suddenly collapsed as it became clear that Tyco had misreported its profits. As the person in charge, Kozlowski stood accused of grand larceny, enterprise corruption, falsifying business records—in short, of looting the company of more than $600 million for his own benefit. The victims, of course, were the people who worked for Tyco as well as those who had invested in the company by buying its stock.

The details of the alleged crime are staggering. Prosecutors claim Kozlowski used company money for one extravagant purchase after another, including a $30-million New York apartment (among the lavish furnishings was a $6,000 shower curtain), paintings by the likes of Monet and Renoir, and a 130-foot yacht. In 2001, he even charged more than $1 million to the company to cover half the cost of a fortieth birthday party for his second wife, Angie (some seventy-five guests were whisked by jet to the Mediterranean island of Sardinia, where Jimmy Buffet joined them to sing "Margaritaville" to the guest of honor). In short, Kozlowski lived very well—on other people's money.

Kozlowski has been indicted by a criminal court. But it is far from clear that he will spend much time in jail. Some early indications: After the indictment, he was still spending more than $350,000 per month, and his wife was able to put up $10 million bail so he would not have to await trial in jail. The couple promptly left to spend the winter holidays on the ski slopes in Colorado (Sloan, 2002; Lavelle, 2003; Smart, 2003).

Kozlowski is only one of a number of executives who have been involved in corporate scandals in the past several years. Enron, Global Crossing, World-Com, Adelphia Communications, and other large businesses have floundered or collapsed under charges that their leaders, led by personal greed, engaged in massive violations of the law. This chapter explores the issue of crime and criminal offenders, showing that those accused of wrongdoing do not always fit the common stereotype of the "street" criminal.

More broadly, we tackle the question of why societies develop standards of right and wrong in the first place. As we shall see, law is simply one part of a complex system of social control: Society teaches us all to conform, at least most of the time, to countless rules. We begin our investigation by defining several basic concepts.

WHAT IS DEVIANCE?

Deviance is *the recognized violation of cultural norms.* Norms guide almost all human activities, so the concept of deviance is quite broad. One category of deviance is **crime,** *the violation of a society's formally enacted criminal law.* Even criminal deviance spans a wide range of behavior, from minor traffic violations to sexual assault to murder.

Most familiar examples of nonconformity are negative instances of rule breaking, such as stealing from a convenience store, abusing a child, or driving while intoxicated. But we also define especially righteous people—students who speak up too much in class or people who are overly enthusiastic about new computer technology—as deviant, even if we accord them a measure of respect (Huls, 1987). What deviant actions or attitudes—whether negative or positive—have in common is some element of *difference* that causes us to regard another person as an "outsider" (Becker, 1966).

Not all deviance involves action or even choice. The very *existence* of some categories of individuals can be troublesome to others. To the young, elderly people may seem hopelessly "out of it"; and to some whites, the mere presence of people of color may cause discomfort. Able-bodied people often view people with disabilities as an out-group, just as affluent people may shun the poor for falling short of their standards.

SOCIAL CONTROL

All of us are subject to **social control,** *attempts by society to regulate people's thought and behavior.* Often, this process is informal, as when parents praise or scold their children or friends make fun of someone's clothing or musical taste. Serious deviance, however, may involve the **criminal justice system,** *a formal response by police, courts, and prison officials to alleged violations of the law.*

In sum, deviance is much more than a matter of individual choice or personal failing. *How* a society defines deviance, *who* is branded as deviant, and *what*

 Visit the Juvenile Justice and Delinquency Prevention Web site to see the available research reports: http://ojjdp.ncjrs.org/pubs/alpha.html

people decide to do about deviance all have to do with the way society is organized. Only gradually, however, have people recognized this fact, as we shall now explain.

THE BIOLOGICAL CONTEXT

Early interest in understanding crime focused on biological factors. In 1876, Caesare Lombroso (1835–1909), an Italian physician who worked in prisons, theorized that criminals could be identified by physical traits—having low foreheads, prominent jaws and cheekbones, big ears, lots of body hair, and unusually long arms. All in all, Lombroso claimed that criminals resembled our apelike ancestors.

But the physical features that Lombroso pointed to can be found throughout the entire population. We now know that no physical attributes, of the kind described by Lombroso, set off criminals from noncriminals (Goring, 1972; orig. 1913).

At mid-century, William Sheldon (Sheldon, Hartl, & McDermott, 1949) took a different tack, suggesting that body structure might predict criminality. He cross-checked hundreds of young men for body type and criminal history, and concluded that criminality was most likely among boys with muscular, athletic builds. Sheldon Glueck and Eleanor Glueck (1950) confirmed Sheldon's conclusion but cautioned that a powerful build does not necessarily cause criminality. Parents, they suggested, tend to be somewhat distant from powerfully built sons, who, in turn, grow up to display less sensitivity toward others. Moreover, in a self-fulfilling prophecy, people who expect muscular boys to act like bullies may provoke the aggressive behavior they expect.

Today, genetics research seeks possible links between biology and crime. Though no conclusive evidence connects criminality to any specific genetic trait, people's overall genetic makeup, in combination with social influences, probably accounts for some tendency toward criminality. In other words, biological factors may have a real, but modest, effect on whether or not an individual becomes a criminal (Wilson & Herrnstein, 1985; Jencks, 1987; Pallone & Hennessy, 1998).

Critical evaluation. At best, biological theories offer a limited explanation of crime. Recent sociobiological research—noting, for example, that violent crime is overwhelmingly male and that parents are more likely to abuse foster children than natural children—is promising, but we know too little about the links between genes and human behavior to draw firm conclusions (Daly & Wilson, 1988).

Furthermore, because a biological approach looks at the individual, it offers no insight into how some kinds of behaviors come to be defined as deviant in the first place. Therefore, although there is much to be learned about how human biology may affect behavior, research currently puts far greater emphasis on social influences (Gibbons & Krohn, 1986; Liska, 1999).

PERSONALITY FACTORS

Like biological theories, psychological explanations of deviance focus on individual abnormality. Some personality traits are hereditary, but most psychologists think that personality is shaped primarily by social experience. Deviance, then, is viewed as the product of "unsuccessful" socialization.

Classic research by Walter Reckless and Simon Dinitz (1967) illustrates the psychological approach. Reckless and Dinitz began by asking a number of teachers to categorize twelve-year-old male students as either likely or unlikely to get into trouble with the law. They then interviewed both the boys and their mothers to assess each boy's self-concept and how he related to others. Analyzing their results, Reckless and Dinitz found that the "good boys" displayed a strong conscience (what Freud called superego), could handle frustration, and identified with cultural norms and values. The "bad boys," by contrast, had a weaker conscience, displayed little tolerance of frustration, and felt out of step with conventional culture.

As we might expect, the "good boys" had fewer run-ins with the police than the "bad boys." Since all the boys lived in an area where delinquency was widespread, the investigators attributed staying out of trouble to a personality that reined in deviant impulses. Based on this idea, Reckless and Dinitz call their analysis *containment theory*.

Critical evaluation. Psychologists have shown that personality patterns have some connection to deviance. Recent research shows that some serious criminals qualify as psychopaths, that is, they do not feel guilt or shame, they have no fear of punishment, and they have little sympathy for the people they harm (Herpertz, 2001). Even so, the fact is that most serious crimes are committed by people who do not have personality disorders, in other words, by individuals whose psychological profiles are *normal*.

The kind of deviance people create reflects the moral values they embrace. The Berkeley campus of the University of California has long celebrated its open-minded tolerance of sexual diversity. Thus, in 1992, when Andrew Martinez decided to attend classes wearing virtually nothing, people were reluctant to accuse "The Naked Guy" of immoral conduct. However, in Berkeley's politically correct atmosphere, it was not long before school officials banned Martinez from campus—charging that his nudity constituted a form of sexual harassment.

Overall, both biological and psychological research view deviance as an individual trait, without exploring how conceptions of right and wrong initially arise, why people define some rule breakers but not others as deviant, or what role power plays in shaping a society's system of social control. To explore these issues, we now turn to a sociological analysis of deviance.

THE SOCIAL FOUNDATIONS OF DEVIANCE

Although we tend to view deviance in terms of the free choice or personal failings of individuals, all behavior—deviance as well as conformity—is shaped by society. Three social foundations of deviance, identified here, will be detailed later in this chapter:

1. **Deviance varies according to cultural norms.** No thought or action is inherently deviant; it becomes deviant only in relation to particular norms. Because norms vary from place to place, deviance also varies. State law permits prostitution in rural areas of Nevada, although the practice is outlawed in the rest of the United States. Eleven states have gambling casinos; twenty-nine have casinos on Indian reservations. In all other states, casino gambling is illegal, although forty states operate their own lotteries.

   Further, most cities and towns have at least one unique statute. For example, Mobile, Alabama, outlaws the wearing of stiletto high-heeled shoes; Amityville, New York, bans building a private home with more than one front door; South Padre Island, Texas, bans wearing ties; Mount Prospect, Illinois, has a law against keeping pigeons or bees; Los Angeles bans gas-powered leaf blowers; Hoover, South Dakota, does not allow fishing with a kerosene lantern; and Beverly Hills regulates the number of tennis balls allowed on the court at one time (Sanders & Horn, 1998; Steele, 2000).

   Around the world, what is considered deviant is even more diverse. Albania outlaws any public display of religious faith, such as "crossing" oneself; Cuba and Vietnam can prosecute their citizens for meeting with foreigners; Singapore prohibits the sale of chewing gum; police in Iran can arrest a woman simply for wearing makeup; and U.S. citizens risk arrest for traveling to Libya or Iraq.

2. **People become deviant as others define them that way.** Everyone occasionally violates cultural norms, even to the extent of breaking the law. For example, most of us at some time or other have "borrowed" a pen or other supplies from our workplace. Many of us also have walked around talking to ourselves. Whether such behavior is sufficient to define us as criminal or mentally ill depends on how others perceive, define, and respond to it.

3. **Both norms and the way people define rule-breaking involve social power.** The law, declared Karl Marx, is the means by which powerful people protect their interests. A homeless person who stands on a street corner denouncing the government risks arrest for disturbing the peace; a mayoral candidate during an election campaign does exactly the same thing and gets police protection. In short, norms and how we apply them reflect social inequality.

THE FUNCTIONS OF DEVIANCE: STRUCTURAL-FUNCTIONAL ANALYSIS

The key insight of the structural-functional paradigm is that deviance is a necessary part of social organization. This point was made a century ago by Emile Durkheim.

EMILE DURKHEIM: THE FUNCTIONS OF DEVIANCE

In his pioneering study of deviance, Emile Durkheim (1964a, orig. 1893; 1964b, orig. 1895) made the surprising statement that there is nothing abnormal about deviance. In fact, it performs four essential functions:

1. **Deviance affirms cultural values and norms.** As moral creatures, people must prefer some attitudes and behaviors to others. But any conception of virtue rests on an opposing idea of vice: There can be no good without evil and no justice without crime. Deviance, then, is needed to define and sustain morality.

2. **Responding to deviance clarifies moral boundaries.** By defining some people as deviant, people draw a boundary between right and wrong. For example, a college marks the line between academic honesty and cheating by punishing students who plagiarize.

3. **Responding to deviance promotes social unity.** People typically react to serious deviance with collective outrage. In this way, Durkheim explained, they reaffirm the moral ties that bind them. For example, after the September 11, 2001, terrorist attacks, people across the United States were joined by a common desire to protect the country and bring those responsible to justice.

4. **Deviance encourages social change.** Deviant people push a society's moral boundaries, suggesting alternatives to the status quo and encouraging change. Today's deviance, declared Durkheim, can become tomorrow's morality (1964b:71). For example, rock 'n' roll, condemned as morally degenerate in the 1950s, became a multibillion-dollar industry just a few years later.

An Illustration: The Puritans of Massachusetts Bay

Kai Erikson's (1966) classic study of the Puritans of Massachusetts Bay brings Durkheim's theory to life. Erikson shows that even the Puritans, a disciplined and highly religious group, created deviance to clarify their moral boundaries. In fact, Durkheim might well have had the Puritans in mind when he wrote:

> Imagine a society of saints, a perfect cloister of exemplary individuals. Crimes, properly so called, will there be unknown; but faults which appear [insignificant] to the layman will create there the same scandal that the ordinary offense does in ordinary consciousness. . . . For the same reason, the perfect and upright man judges his smallest failings with a severity that the majority reserve for acts more truly in the nature of an offense. (1964b:68–69)

In short, deviance is not a matter of a few "bad apples"; it is a necessary condition of "good" social living.

Deviance may be universal, but the *kind* of deviance people generate depends on the moral issues they seek to clarify. The Puritans, for example, experienced a number of "crime waves," including the well-known outbreak of witchcraft in 1692. With each response, the Puritans sharpened their views on crucial moral issues. They answered questions about the range of proper beliefs by celebrating some of their members and condemning others as deviant.

Perhaps most fascinating of all, Erikson discovered that even though the offenses changed, the proportion of people the Puritans defined as deviant remained steady over time. This stability, concludes Erikson, confirms Durkheim's contention that deviants serve to mark a society's changing moral boundaries. In other words, by constantly defining a small number of people as deviant, the Puritans maintained the moral shape of their society.

MERTON'S STRAIN THEORY

Some deviance may be necessary for a society to function, but Robert Merton (1938, 1968) argued that excessive deviance results from particular social arrangements. Specifically, the extent and kind of deviance depend on whether a society provides the *means* (such as schooling and job opportunities) to achieve cultural *goals* (such as financial success).

Artists have always pushed the boundaries of the cultural system, often becoming controversial in the process. For years, critics have sought to silence artists whose work offended them; for their part, artists have demanded freedom of speech, often using their art as a political weapon. Here, artists fly a banner at a political demonstration in front of the U.S. Capitol building.

Conformity, says Merton, lies in pursuing conventional goals through approved means. Thus, the U.S. "success story" is someone who acquires wealth and prestige through talent, schooling, and hard work. But not everyone who seeks conventional success has the opportunity to attain it. For example, people raised in poverty may have little hope of becoming successful if they play by the rules. According to Merton, the strain between our culture's emphasis on wealth and the lack of opportunities to get rich gives rise, especially among the poor, to theft, the sale of illegal drugs, and other forms of street crime. Merton called this type of deviance *innovation*—using unconventional means (street crime) to achieve a culturally approved goal (wealth). Figure 8–1 shows that innovation involves accepting a cultural goal (financial success) but rejecting the conventional means (hard work at a "straight" job).

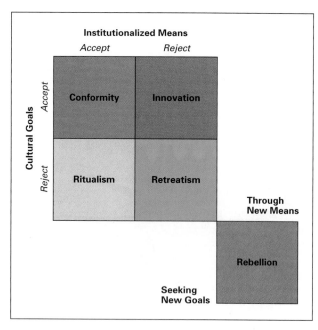

FIGURE 8–1 Merton's Strain Theory of Deviance
Source: Merton (1968).

The inability to succeed by normative means may also lead to another type of deviance that Merton calls *ritualism* (see Figure 8–1). For example, low-level bureaucrats, knowing they will achieve only limited financial success, stick closely to the rules in order to at least feel respectable.

A third response to the inability to succeed is *retreatism*—the rejection of both cultural goals and means, so that one, in effect, "drops out." Some alcoholics, drug addicts, and street people are retreatists. The deviance of retreatists lies in their unconventional lifestyle and, perhaps more seriously, in their apparent willingness to live this way.

The fourth response to failure is *rebellion*. Like retreatists, rebels reject both the cultural definition of success and the normative means of achieving it. Rebels—such as radical "survivalists"—go one step further by forming a counterculture and advocating alternatives to the existing social order.

DEVIANT SUBCULTURES

Richard Cloward and Lloyd Ohlin (1966) extended Merton's theory, proposing that crime results not just from limited legitimate (legal) opportunity but also from readily accessible illegitimate (illegal) opportunity. In short, deviance or conformity arises from the *relative opportunity structure* that frames a person's life.

The life of Al Capone, a notorious gangster, illustrates Cloward and Ohlin's theory. As the son of poor immigrants, Capone faced barriers of poverty and ethnic prejudice, which lowered his odds of achieving success in conventional terms. Yet, as a young man during Prohibition (the banning of alcoholic beverages in the United States from 1920 to 1933), Capone found in his neighborhood people who could teach him how to be a bootlegger—a source of illegitimate opportunity. Where the structure of opportunity favors criminal activity, Cloward and Ohlin predict the development of *criminal subcultures.* The existence of criminal gangs across the United States is evidence of just such opportunity that encourages criminal activity (Sheley et al., 1995).

But what happens when people cannot identify *any* kind of opportunity, legal or illegal? Then, deviance may take the form of "*conflict subcultures*" (armed street gangs), where violence is ignited by frustration and a desire for respect. Alternatively, those who fail to succeed, even through criminal means, may fall into "*retreatist subcultures*," dropping out and abusing alcohol or other drugs.

Albert Cohen (1971; orig. 1955) suggests that delinquency is most pronounced among lower-class youths because they have the least opportunity to achieve conventional success. Defined as outsiders by society as a whole, they seek self-respect by creating a delinquent subculture that "defines as meritorious the characteristics they *do* possess, the kinds of conduct of which they *are* capable" (1971:66). Being feared on the street, for example, may win few points with the larger society, but it may satisfy a youth's desire to "be somebody" in the local neighborhood.

Walter Miller (1970; orig. 1958) adds that delinquent subcultures are characterized by (1) *trouble,* arising from frequent conflict with teachers and police; (2) *toughness,* the value placed on physical size and strength, especially among males; (3) *smartness,* the ability to succeed on the streets, to outsmart or "con" others, and to avoid being similarly taken advantage of; (4) *a need for excitement,* the search for thrills, risk, or danger; (5) *a belief in fate,* a sense that people lack control over their own lives; and (6) *a desire for freedom,* often expressed as hostility toward authority figures.

Finally, Elijah Anderson (1994, 2002) explains that in poor urban neighborhoods, most people manage to conform to conventional ("decent") values. Yet,

Young people cut off from legitimate opportunity often form deviant subcultures as a strategy to gain the prestige denied them by the larger society. Once exclusively a male phenomenon, girl gangs are increasingly evident in many large cities.

faced with neighborhood crime and violence, indifference or even hostility from police, and sometimes even neglect by their own parents, some young men adopt a "street code," a protective strategy based on earning respect, establishing a reputation, and retaliating against anyone who threatens harm. At the extreme, explains Anderson, even a violent death is better than being "dissed" (disrespected) by others. Some are able to escape the dangers, but the risk of ending up in jail—or worse—is very high for these young men pushed to the margins of our society.

Critical evaluation. Durkheim made an important contribution by pointing out the functions of deviance. However, evidence shows that a community does not always come together in reaction to crime; sometimes fear of crime drives people to withdraw from public life (Liska & Warner, 1991; Warr & Ellison, 2000).

Merton's strain theory has been criticized for explaining some kinds of deviance (theft, for example) far better than others (such as crimes of passion). Moreover, not everyone seeks success in the conventional terms of wealth, as strain theory implies.

The general argument of Cloward and Ohlin, Cohen, Miller, and Anderson—that deviance reflects the opportunity structure of society—has been confirmed by subsequent research (cf. Allan & Steffensmeier, 1989; Uggen, 1999). However, these theories, too, fall short in assuming that everyone shares the same cultural standards for judging right and wrong.

Moreover, we must be careful not to define deviance in ways that unfairly focus attention on poor people. If we define crime as including the kind of corporate fraud described in the opening to this chapter as well as street theft, then more affluent people will be counted among criminals. Indeed, there is some evidence that many people in the United States are becoming more casual about breaking the rules; the box on page 196 takes a closer look.

A final criticism is that all structural-functional theories imply that everyone who breaks the rules is labeled deviant. Becoming deviant, however, is actually a highly complex process, as the next section explains.

LABELING DEVIANCE: SYMBOLIC-INTERACTION ANALYSIS

The symbolic-interaction paradigm explains how people define deviance in everyday situations. From this point of view, definitions of deviance and conformity are surprisingly flexible.

LABELING THEORY

The central contribution of symbolic-interaction analysis is **labeling theory,** *the assertion that deviance and conformity result not so much from what people do as from how others respond to those actions.* Labeling

CRITICAL THINKING

Deviant (Sub)Culture: Has It Become Okay to Cheat?

It's been a bad couple of years for the idea of playing by the rules. First, we learn that the executives of—not one but several—major U.S. corporations are guilty of fraud and outright stealing on a scale most of us cannot even imagine. Then it turns out that some of the accounting companies, whose task it is to check the books and keep corporations honest, are in cahoots with the bad corporations. Perhaps worst of all, the Catholic church, which should be a model of correct behavior for all of us, has been embroiled in a scandal of its own. In this case, the allegations are that hundreds of priests have sexually abused parishioners (most of them children) while church officials busied themselves covering up the crimes. By the beginning of 2003, more than 300 priests in the United States had to be removed from their duties.

Plenty of people are offering explanations for this widespread pattern of wrongdoing. With regard to the highly competitive corporate world, some suggest that the pressure to win by whatever means necessary can be overwhelming. As one analyst put it, "You can get away with your embezzlements and your lies—but you can never get away with *failing.*"

Such thinking might be part of the explanation for wrongdoing in the corporate world, but it offers little insight into the problem of abusive priests. Moreover, in some ways at least, cheating seems to have become a way of life for just about everybody. For example, the Internal Revenue Service reports that many U.S. taxpayers cheat on their taxes, failing to pay an estimated $200 billion each year (averaged out, that amounts to about $1,600 for each U.S. taxpayer). The music industry claims that it has lost a vast amount of money because of illegal piracy of recordings, a common practice especially among young people. Perhaps most disturbing of all, surveys of high school students reveal that three-fourths claim to have cheated on a test at least once during the past year.

Emile Durkheim considered society a moral enterprise, built on a set of rules about what people should and should not do. Years earlier, another French thinker named Blaise Pascal made the contrasting claim that "cheating is the foundation of society." The question today is which of the two statements is closer to the truth.

What do you think?

1. *In your opinion, how widespread is cheating today at your college?*

2. *Do you think people who cheat consider what they are doing wrong or not? Why?*

3. *What do you think are the reasons for this apparent increase in dishonesty?*

Source: Based on "Our Cheating Hearts" (2002).

theory stresses the relativity of deviance, the idea that people may define the same behavior in any number of ways. Howard S. Becker claims that deviance is nothing more than behavior people define as deviant (1966:9).

Consider these situations: A college student takes an article of clothing from a roommate's drawer, a married woman at a convention in a distant city has sex with an old boyfriend, a mayor gives a big city contract to a major campaign contributor. We might define the first situation as carelessness, borrowing, or theft. The consequences of the second case depend largely on whether the woman's behavior becomes known back home. In the third situation, is the official choosing the best contractor or paying off a political debt? The social construction of reality is a highly variable process of detection, definition, and response.

Primary and Secondary Deviance

Edwin Lemert (1951, 1972) observed that some episodes of norm violation—say, skipping school or underage drinking—provoke slight reaction from others and have little effect on a person's self-concept. Lemert calls such passing episodes *primary deviance.*

But what happens if other people notice someone's deviance and make something of it? For example, if people begin to describe a young man as an "alcohol abuser" and evict him from their social circle, he may become embittered, drink even more, and seek the company of others who approve of his behavior. In this way, the response to initial deviance sets in motion *secondary deviance*, by which a person repeatedly violates a norm and begins to take on a deviant identity. The development of secondary deviance is one application of the Thomas theorem (discussed in Chapter 6, "Social Interaction in Everyday Life"), which states that situations defined as real become real in their consequences.

Stigma

Secondary deviance marks the start of what Erving Goffman (1963) calls a "deviant career." As individuals develop a stronger commitment to deviant behavior, they typically acquire a **stigma,** *a powerfully negative label that greatly changes a person's self-concept and social identity.*

A stigma operates as a master status (see Chapter 6), overpowering other aspects of social identity so that a person is discredited in the minds of others, becoming socially isolated. Sometimes an entire community formally stigmatizes an individual through what Harold Garfinkel (1956) calls a *degradation ceremony.* A criminal prosecution is one example, operating much the way a high school graduation does but in reverse: A person stands before the community to be labeled in a negative rather than a positive way.

Retrospective and Projective Labeling

Once people stigmatize an individual, they may engage in *retrospective labeling,* interpreting someone's past in light of some present deviance (Scheff, 1984). For example, after discovering that a priest has sexually molested a child, others rethink his past, perhaps musing, "He always did want to be around young children." Retrospective labeling can distort a person's biography by being highly selective and serving to deepen a deviant identity.

Similarly, people may engage in *projective labeling* of a stigmatized person. That is, they use a deviant identity to predict future action. People might say of the priest, for example, "He's just going to keep at it until he gets caught." The more others think such things, of course, the greater is the chance that they will come true.

Labeling Difference as Deviance

Attaching labels to behavior can be used as a strategy to control other people's behavior. Take as an example a homeless man who, on a cold night, resists efforts by police to take him to a city shelter. The man's presence may be irritating to those who live nearby, but if he is

The world is full of people who are unusual in one way or another. This Indian man grew the fingernails on one hand for more than thirty years just to do something that no one else had ever done. Should we define such behavior as harmless eccentricity or as evidence of mental illness?

breaking no law, there may be little the police can do. However, if the police label the man mentally ill and claim that he is unable to know what is best for himself, forcing him to the shelter becomes far easier.

The psychiatrist Thomas Szasz warns that people often apply labels such as "insane" or "mentally ill" to people who are merely "different." The only way to avoid this kind of abuse, Szasz continues, is to abandon the concept of mental illness entirely (1961; 1970, orig. 1961; 1994; 1995). The world is full of people whose "differences" in thought or action may irritate us, but such differences are no grounds for defining someone as mentally ill. Such labeling, Szasz claims, simply enforces conformity to the standards of people powerful enough to impose their will on others.

The vast majority of health care professionals reject Szasz's claim that mental illness is nothing more

John Allen Muhammad and a young companion were charged with the random shooting of thirteen people in the Washington, D.C., area in 2002. In 2003, he was convicted of murder and sentenced to death. In all, ten people died in these shootings, and millions lived in fear for weeks until the shootings stopped. In cases in which people commit deadly violence, do you think the perpetrators are more correctly understood to be "bad" (and deserving of punishment) or "sick" (and deserving of treatment)? Why?

than a fiction. They say that it is, on the contrary, a form of illness—one closely bound up with physical illness. But most agree that it is important to think critically about how we define "difference." First, people who are mentally ill are no more to blame for their condition than people who suffer from cancer or some other physical ailment. In short, having a mental or physical illness is no grounds for being blamed as "deviant." Second, ordinary people without the medical knowledge to diagnose mental illness should avoid using powerful terms such as "psychotic" or "crazy" to describe others. Using such labels to describe someone who may just be different amounts to imposing one's own standards of behavior on everyone else.

THE MEDICALIZATION OF DEVIANCE

Labeling theory, particularly the ideas of Szasz and Goffman, helps explain an important shift in the way our society understands deviance. Over the last fifty years, the growing influence of psychiatry and medicine in the United States has led to the **medicalization of deviance,** *the transformation of moral and legal deviance into a medical condition.*

Medicalization amounts to swapping one set of labels for another. In moral terms, we evaluate people or their behavior as "bad" or "good." However, the scientific objectivity of modern medicine passes no moral judgment, instead using clinical diagnoses such as "sick" or "well."

To illustrate, until the mid-twentieth century, people generally viewed alcoholics as morally weak people easily tempted by the pleasure of drink. Gradually, however, medical specialists redefined alcoholism so that most people now consider alcoholism a disease, rendering people "sick" rather than "bad." Similarly, obesity, drug addiction, child abuse, sexual promiscuity, and other behaviors that used to be strictly moral matters are widely defined today as illnesses for which people need help rather than punishment.

The Difference Labels Make

Whether we define deviance as a moral or a medical issue has three consequences. First, it affects *who responds* to deviance. An offense against common morality usually brings about a reaction from members of the community or the police. A medical label, however, places the situation under the control of clinical specialists, including counselors, psychiatrists, and physicians.

A second difference is *how people respond* to deviance. A moral approach defines deviants as "offenders" subject to punishment. Medically, however, they are patients who need treatment (for their own good, of course). Whereas punishment is designed to fit the crime, treatment programs are tailored to the patient and may involve virtually any therapy that a specialist thinks will prevent future illness (von Hirsh, 1986). As a result, while punishment is regulated by law, treatment provides less assurance of "due process" and can, in theory, involve almost anything.

Third, and most important, the two labels differ on *the personal competence of the deviant person.* Morally speaking, whether we are right or wrong, at least we take responsibility for our own behavior. Once defined as sick, however, we are seen as lacking the capacity to control (or, if "mentally ill," even understand) our actions. People who are labeled incompetent are, in turn, subject to treatment, often against their will. For this reason alone, attempts to define deviance in medical terms should be made only with extreme caution.

SUTHERLAND'S DIFFERENTIAL ASSOCIATION THEORY

Learning any behavioral pattern—whether conforming or deviant—is a social process that takes place in groups. Therefore, according to Edwin Sutherland (1940), a person's tendency toward conformity or deviance depends on the amount of contact with others who encourage—or reject—conventional behavior. This is Sutherland's theory of *differential association*.

A number of studies confirm the idea that young people are more likely to engage in delinquency if they believe members of their peer groups encourage such activity (Akers et al., 1979; Miller & Mathews, 2001). One recent investigation focused on why some eighth-grade students engaged in consensual sex. A strong predictor of such behavior for young girls was having a boyfriend who, presumably, encouraged the onset of sexual relations. Moreover, the girls who became sexually active were those who believed their girlfriends would approve of such activity. Similarly, boys were encouraged to become sexually active by friends who rewarded them with high status in the peer group (Little & Rankin, 2001).

HIRSCHI'S CONTROL THEORY

The sociologist Travis Hirschi (1969; Gottfredson & Hirschi, 1995) developed *control theory*, which states that social control depends on imagining the consequences of one's behavior. Hirschi assumes that everyone finds at least some deviance tempting. But the prospect of a ruined career is sufficient to deter most people; for some, just imagining the reactions of family and friends is enough. On the other hand, individuals who feel they have little to lose by deviance are likely to become rule-breakers.

Specifically, Hirschi links conformity to four different types of social control:

1. **Attachment.** Strong social attachments encourage conformity; weak relationships, especially in the family and in school, leave people freer to engage in deviance.

2. **Opportunity.** The greater a person's access to legitimate opportunity, the greater the advantages of conformity. By contrast, someone with little confidence in future success is more likely to drift toward deviance.

3. **Involvement.** Extensive involvement in legitimate activities—such as holding a job, going to school,

In some gangs, young people learn attitudes and skills that promote violence. Gangs offer their members a sense of belonging and social importance, but the price of membership is often high. This graffiti memorial to a fallen gang member is found in Bridgeport, Connecticut.

and playing sports—inhibits deviance (Langbein & Bess, 2002). People without these activities—those who simply "hang out" waiting for something to happen—have time and energy for deviant activity.

4. **Belief.** Strong belief in conventional morality and respect for authority figures restrain tendencies toward deviance. People who have a weak conscience (and who are left unsupervised) are more vulnerable to temptation (Osgood et al., 1996).

Hirschi's analysis draws together a number of earlier ideas about the causes of deviant behavior. Note that a person's relative social privilege and strength of moral character give that individual a stake in conforming to conventional norms (Sampson & Laub, 1990; Free, 1992).

Critical evaluation. The various symbolic-interaction theories see deviance as process. Labeling theory links deviance not to *action* but to the *reaction* of others. Thus, some people come to be defined as deviant while others who think or behave in the same way are not. The concepts of secondary deviance, deviant careers, and stigma demonstrate how being labeled deviant can become a lasting self-concept.

Yet labeling theory has several limitations. First, this theory's highly relative view of deviance ignores the fact that some kinds of behavior, such as murder, are condemned just about everywhere (Wellford, 1980). Labeling theory thus works best in the case of less serious deviance, such as drug abuse or sexual promiscuity. Second, research on the consequences of deviant labeling is inconclusive (Smith & Gartin, 1989; Sherman & Smith, 1992). Does deviant labeling produce further deviance or discourage it? Third, not everyone resists being labeled deviant; some people actually seek it out (Vold & Bernard, 1986). For example, people take part in civil disobedience and willingly subject themselves to arrest in order to call attention to social injustice.

Both Sutherland's differential association theory and Hirschi's control theory have had considerable influence in sociology. But they provide little insight into why a society's norms and laws define certain kinds of activities as deviant in the first place. This important question is addressed by social-conflict analysis, the focus of the next section.

DEVIANCE AND INEQUALITY: SOCIAL-CONFLICT ANALYSIS

The social-conflict paradigm demonstrates how deviance reflects social inequality. That is, *who* or *what* is labeled "deviant" depends on which categories of people hold power in a society.

DEVIANCE AND POWER

Alexander Liazos (1972) points out that the people we tend to define as deviants—those we dismiss as "nuts" and "sluts"—are typically those who share the trait of powerlessness. That is, bag ladies (not corporate polluters) and unemployed men on street corners (not arms dealers) carry the stigma of deviance.

Social-conflict theory explains this pattern in three ways: First, the norms—and especially laws—of any society generally reflect the interests of the rich and powerful. People who threaten the wealthy, either by taking their property or by advocating a more egalitarian society, are defined as "common thieves" or "political radicals." As noted in Chapter 4 ("Society"), Karl Marx argued that the law and all other social institutions support the interests of the rich. Or as Richard Quinney puts it, "Capitalist justice is by the capitalist class, for the capitalist class, and against the working class" (1977:3).

Second, even if their behavior is called into question, the powerful have the resources to resist deviant labels. Some—but not many—of the corporate executives involved in recent scandals have faced arrest on criminal charges. Those who end up going to court, of course, have the means to employ the best lawyers available.

Third, the widespread belief that norms and laws are natural and good masks their political character. For this reason, although we may condemn the *unequal application* of the law, we give little thought to whether the *laws themselves* are inherently unfair (Quinney, 1977).

DEVIANCE AND CAPITALISM

In the Marxist tradition, Steven Spitzer (1980) argues that deviant labels are applied to people who interfere with the operation of capitalism. First, because capitalism is based on private control of wealth, people who threaten the property of others—especially the poor who steal from the rich—are prime candidates for being labeled deviant. Conversely, the rich who exploit the poor are less likely to be labeled deviant. For example, landlords who charge poor tenants high rents and evict anyone who cannot pay are not considered criminals; they are simply "doing business."

Second, because capitalism depends on productive labor, people who cannot or will not work risk being labeled deviant. Many members of our society think people who are out of work—even through no fault of their own—are somehow deviant.

Third, capitalism depends on respect for authority figures, so people who resist authority are labeled deviant. Examples are children who skip school or talk back to parents and teachers, and adults who do not cooperate with employers or police.

Fourth, anyone who directly challenges the capitalist status quo is likely to be defined as deviant. In this category are labor organizers, radical environmentalists, and antiwar activists.

On the other side of the coin, society positively labels whatever enhances the operation of capitalism. For example, winning athletes enjoy celebrity status because they express the values of individual achievement and competition that are vital to capitalism. Moreover, Spitzer notes, we condemn using drugs of escape (marijuana, psychedelics, heroin, and crack) as deviant but endorse drugs (such as alcohol and caffeine) that promote adjustment to the status quo.

The capitalist system also strives to control people who don't fit into the system. The elderly, people with mental or physical disabilities, and Robert Merton's retreatists (people addicted to alcohol or other drugs) are a "costly yet relatively harmless burden" on society. Such people, claims Spitzer, are subject to control by social welfare agencies. But people who openly challenge the capitalist system, including the inner-city underclass and revolutionaries—Merton's innovators and rebels—are controlled by the criminal justice system and, in times of crisis, military forces such as the National Guard.

Notice that both the social welfare and criminal justice systems blame individuals, not the system, for social problems. Welfare recipients are deemed unworthy freeloaders; poor people who vent their rage at their plight are labeled rioters; anyone who challenges the government is branded a radical or a Communist; and those who attempt to acquire illegally what they cannot obtain otherwise are rounded up as common criminals.

WHITE-COLLAR CRIME

In a sign of things to come, a Wall Street stockbroker named Michael Milken made headlines back in 1987 when he was jailed for business fraud. Milken attracted attention because not since the days of Al Capone had anyone made so much money in one year. In Milken's case, earnings reached $550 million—*about $1.5 million a day* (Swartz, 1989).

Milken committed a **white-collar crime,** defined by Edwin Sutherland (1940) as *crime committed by people of high social position in the course of their occupations* (Sutherland & Cressey, 1978). As the Milken case indicates, white-collar crimes do not involve violence and rarely bring police with drawn guns to the scene. Rather, white-collar criminals use their powerful occupational positions to enrich themselves and others, often causing significant public harm in the process (Hagan & Parker, 1985; Vold & Bernard, 1986). For this reason, sociologists sometimes call white-collar offenses that occur in government offices and corporate board rooms *crime in the suites* as opposed to *crime in the streets.*

The most common white-collar crimes are bank embezzlement, business fraud, bribery, and antitrust violations. Sutherland (1940) explains that such white-collar offenses typically end up in a civil hearing rather than a criminal courtroom. *Civil law* regulates business dealings between private parties, while *criminal law*

In the wake of the recent collapse of many large corporations due to fraud and other illegal activities, some corporate executives are facing criminal charges. Here, Andrew S. Fastow, chief financial officer of the Enron Corporation, is escorted to a court appearance by FBI agents. In your opinion, what share of the executives involved in corporate crime will ever serve jail time?

defines the individual's moral responsibilities to society. In practice, then, someone who loses a civil case pays for damage or injury but is not labeled a criminal. Furthermore, corporate officials are protected by the fact that most charges of white-collar crime target the organization rather than individuals.

In the rare cases in which white-collar criminals are charged and convicted, the odds are about fifty-fifty that they will not go to jail. One accounting shows that just 55 percent of the embezzlers convicted in the U.S. federal courts in 2001 served prison sentences; the rest were put on probation and/or paid a fine (U.S. Bureau of Justice Statistics, 2002).

CORPORATE CRIME

Sometimes whole companies, rather than individuals acting on their own, break the law. **Corporate crime** is *the illegal actions of a corporation or people acting on its behalf.*

Corporate crime ranges from knowingly selling faulty or dangerous products to deliberately polluting the environment to corporate leadership's engaging in

TABLE 8-1	Sociological Explanations of Deviance: A Summary
Theoretical Paradigm	**Major Contributions**
Structural-functional analysis	What is deviant may vary, but deviance is found in all societies; deviance and the social response it provokes sustain the moral foundation of society; deviance may also guide social change.
Symbolic-interaction analysis	Nothing is inherently deviant but may become defined as such through the response of others; the reactions of others are highly variable; labeling someone deviant may lead to the development of secondary deviance and deviant careers.
Social-conflict analysis	Laws and other norms reflect the interests of powerful members of society; those who threaten the status quo generally are defined as deviant; social injury caused by powerful people is less likely to be considered criminal than is social injury caused by people who have little social power.

massive fraud (Benson & Cullen, 1998). The collapse of the Enron corporation in 2001 following extensive violations of legal business and accounting practices was the first of a number of very serious corporate scandals. Estimates of the loss to stockholders and employees as a result of corporate wrongdoing exceed $50 billion, which is four times the annual loss in the entire United States resulting from common theft (Lavella, 2002).

As is the case with white-collar crime, most cases go unpunished, and many never even become a matter of public record. (In one of the harsher sentences of 2002, Alfred Taubman, former Sotheby's CEO convicted of fixing art auction prices, was fined $7.5 million and sentenced to one year and a day in a minimum security federal prison camp that critics describe as "Club Fed"; Clark, 2002a). Furthermore, the cost of corporate crime goes beyond dollars to human lives. The collapse of Enron, Global Crossing, Tyco International, and other corporations in recent years has cost tens of thousands of people their jobs and their pensions. Even more seriously, for decades coal-mining companies have knowingly put miners at risk from inhaling coal dust, so that hundreds of people die annually of "black lung" disease. The death toll from all job-related hazards that are known to companies

probably exceeds 100,000 annually (Reiman, 1998; Carroll, 1999; Jones, 1999b).

ORGANIZED CRIME

Organized crime is *a business supplying illegal goods or services.* Sometimes criminal organizations force people to do business with them, as when a gang extorts money from shopkeepers for "protection." In most cases, however, organized crime involves selling illegal goods and services—including sex, drugs, and gambling—to a willing public.

For more than a century, organized crime has flourished in the United States. The scope of its operations expanded among some immigrants who found that this society was not willing to share all its opportunities with them. Thus, some ambitious minorities (such as Al Capone, described earlier) made their own success, especially during Prohibition (1920–1933), when the U.S. government banned the production and sale of alcoholic beverages coast to coast.

The Italian Mafia is a well-known example of organized crime. But other criminal organizations involve African Americans, Chinese, Colombians, Cubans, Haitians, and Russians, as well as others of almost every racial and ethnic category. Moreover, today's organized crime involves a wide range of activities, from selling illegal drugs to prostitution to credit-card fraud to marketing false identification papers to illegal immigrants (Valdez, 1997).

Critical evaluation. According to social-conflict theory, a capitalist society's inequality in wealth and power guides the creation and application of laws and other norms. The criminal justice and social welfare systems thus act as political agents, controlling categories of people who threaten the capitalist system.

Like other approaches to deviance, however, social-conflict theory has its critics. First, this approach implies that laws and other cultural norms are created directly by the rich and powerful. At the very least, this is an oversimplification, as laws also protect workers, consumers, and the environment, sometimes opposing the interests of corporations and the rich.

Second, social-conflict analysis implies that criminality springs up only to the extent that a society treats its members unequally. However, as Durkheim noted, deviance exists in all societies, whatever the economic system.

The sociological explanations for crime and other types of deviance that we have discussed are summarized in Table 8–1.

CRITICAL THINKING

Hate-Crime Laws: Do They Punish Actions or Attitudes?

On a cool October evening, nineteen-year-old Todd Mitchell, an African American, was standing with some friends in front of their apartment complex in Kenosha, Wisconsin. They had just seen the film *Mississippi Burning* and were fuming over a scene that showed a white man beating a young black boy who is kneeling in prayer.

"Do you feel hyped up to move on some white people?" asked Mitchell. Minutes later, they saw a young white boy walking toward them on the other side of the street. Mitchell commanded, "There goes a white boy; go get him!" The group swarmed around the youngster, beating him bloody and leaving him on the ground in a coma. The attackers took the fourteen-year-old's tennis shoes as a trophy.

Police soon arrested the teenagers and charged them with the beating. Todd Mitchell went to trial as the ringleader, and the jury found him guilty of aggravated battery *motivated by racial hatred.* Instead of the usual two-year sentence, Mitchell went to jail for four years.

As this case illustrates, hate-crime laws punish a crime more severely if the offender is motivated by bias against some category of people. Supporters make three arguments in favor of hate-crime legislation. First, the offender's intentions are always important in the weighing of criminal responsibility, so considering hatred an intention is nothing new. Second, crimes motivated by racial or other bias inflame the public mood more than crimes carried out, say, for monetary gain. Third, victims of hate crimes typically suffer greater injury than victims of crimes with other motives.

Critics counter that while some hate-crime cases involve hard-core racism, most are impulsive acts by young people. Even more important, critics maintain, hate-crime laws are a threat to First Amendment guarantees of free speech. Hate-crime laws allow courts to sentence offenders not just for their actions but for their attitudes. As Harvard law professor Alan Dershowitz cautions, "As much as I hate bigotry, I fear much more the Court attempting to control the minds of its citizens." In short, according to critics, hate-crime statutes open the door to punishing beliefs rather than behavior.

In 1993, the U.S. Supreme Court upheld the sentence handed down to Todd Mitchell. In a unanimous decision, the justices stated that the government should not punish an individual's beliefs. But, they reasoned, a belief is no longer protected when it becomes the motive for a crime.

What do you think?

1. *Do you think crimes motivated by hate are more harmful than those motivated by, say, greed? Why or why not?*

2. *On balance, do you favor or oppose hate-crime laws? Why?*

3. *Do you think minorities such as African Americans should be subject to hate-crime laws just as white people are? Why or why not?*

Mourners carry the casket of Won Jon Loon, who was gunned down on his way to church by members of a white supremacist group.

Sources: Greenhouse (1993), Jacobs (1993), Terry (1993), and Sullivan (2002).

DEVIANCE AND SOCIAL DIVERSITY

What is defined as deviant has much to do with the relative power and privilege of different categories of people. The following sections offer two examples: how racial and ethnic hostility motivate hate crimes, and how gender is linked to deviance.

HATE CRIMES

The term **hate crime** refers to *a criminal act against a person or a person's property by an offender motivated by racial or other bias.* A hate crime may express hostility toward someone's race, religion, ancestry, sexual orientation, or physical disability. The federal

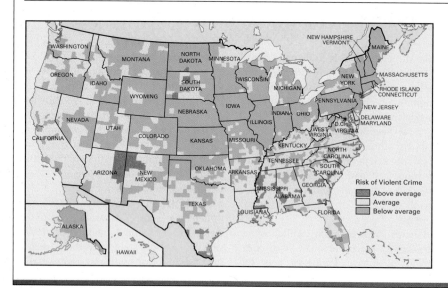

NATIONAL MAP 8–1
The Risk of Violent Crime across the United States

This map shows the risk of becoming a victim of violent crime. In general, the risk is highest in low-income, rural counties that have a large population of men between the ages of fifteen and twenty-four. After reading through this section of the text, see whether you can explain this pattern.

Source: *American Demographics* magazine, December 2000. Reprinted with permission of *American Demographics*, © 2000 by Intertec Publishing, a Primedia Company.

Risk of Violent Crime
Above average
Average
Below average

government records about 10,000 incidents of hate crimes each year.

Most people were stunned by the brutal killing in 1998 of Matthew Shepard, a gay student at the University of Wyoming, by two men filled with hate toward homosexuals. The National Gay and Lesbian Task Force reports that one in five lesbians and gay men is physically assaulted and that more than 90 percent are verbally abused because of sexual orientation (cited in Berrill, 1992:19–20). Victims of hate-motivated violence are especially likely to be people who contend with multiple stigmas, such as gay men of color. Yet hate crimes can victimize anyone: A recent study found that about 25 percent of the hate crimes based on race targeted white people (Jenness & Grattet, 2001).

By 2002, forty-five states and the federal government had enacted legislation that increased penalties for crimes motivated by hatred. Supporters are gratified, but opponents charge that such laws punish "politically incorrect" thoughts. The box on page 203 takes a closer look at the issue of hate-crime laws.

DEVIANCE AND GENDER

Virtually every society in the world applies more stringent normative controls to women than to men.

Historically, our society has centered the lives of women on the home. Even today, in the United States, women's opportunities in the workplace, in politics, in athletics, and in the military are limited. Elsewhere in the world, women face even greater barriers. In Saudi Arabia, women cannot vote or legally operate motor vehicles; in Iran, women who dare to expose their hair in public can be whipped; in 2002, a Nigerian court convicted a divorced woman of bearing a child out of wedlock and sentenced her to death by stoning (Eboh, 2002).

Gender also figures in the theories of deviance noted earlier. Robert Merton's strain theory, for example, seems masculine in that it defines cultural goals in terms of financial success. Traditionally, at least, accumulating wealth has more to do with the lives of men, while women are socialized to define success in terms of relationships, particularly marriage and motherhood (Leonard, 1982). A more woman-focused theory might recognize the strain that results from the cultural ideal of equality clashing with the reality of gender-based inequality.

In labeling theory, too, gender influences how we define deviance because people commonly use different standards to judge the behavior of females and males. Further, because society puts men in positions of power over women, men often escape direct responsibility for actions that victimize women. In the past, at least, men who sexually harassed or assaulted women were labeled only mildly deviant, if they were punished at all.

By contrast, women who are victimized may have to convince an unsympathetic audience that they were not to blame for their own sexual harassment. Research confirms an important truth: Whether people define a situation as deviance—and, if so, whose deviance it is—depends on the sex of both the audience and the actors (King & Clayson, 1988).

Finally, despite its focus on social inequality, much social-conflict analysis does not address the issue of gender. If economic disadvantage is a primary cause of crime, as conflict theory suggests, why do women (whose economic position is much worse than men's) commit far *fewer* crimes than men do?

CRIME

Crime is the violation of criminal laws enacted by a locality, a state, or the federal government. Technically, all crimes are composed of two elements: the *act* itself (or, in some cases, the failure to do what the law requires) and *criminal intent* (in legal terminology, *mens rea*, or "guilty mind"). Intent is a matter of degree, ranging from willful conduct to negligence. Someone who is negligent does not deliberately set out to hurt anyone but acts (or fails to act) in a way that results in harm. Prosecutors weigh the degree of intent in deciding whether, for example, to charge someone with first-degree murder, second-degree murder, or negligent manslaughter. Alternatively, they may consider a killing justifiable, as in self-defense.

TYPES OF CRIME

In the United States, the Federal Bureau of Investigation gathers information on criminal offenses and regularly reports the results in a publication called *Crime in the United States.* Two major types of crime make up the FBI "crime index."

Crimes against the person are *crimes that direct violence or the threat of violence against others.* Such violent crimes include murder and manslaughter (legally defined as "the willful killing of one human being by another"), aggravated assault ("an unlawful attack by one person

Read a report by the Department of Housing and Urban Development on gun violence in public housing projects: http://www.huduser.org/periodicals/rrr/rrr_3_2000/0300_1.html

upon another for the purpose of inflicting severe or aggravated bodily injury"), forcible rape ("the carnal knowledge of a female forcibly and against her will"), and robbery ("taking or attempting to take anything of value from the care, custody, or control of a person or persons by force or threat of force or violence and/or putting the victim in fear"). National Map 8–1 shows the risk of violent crime for all the counties across the United States.

Crimes against property encompass *crimes that involve theft of property belonging to others.* Property crimes include burglary ("the unlawful entry of a structure to commit a [serious crime] or a theft"), larceny-theft ("the unlawful taking, carrying, leading, or riding away of property from the possession of another"), auto theft ("the theft or attempted theft of a motor vehicle"), and arson ("any willful or malicious burning or attempt to burn the personal property of another").

A third category of offenses, not included in major crime indexes, is **victimless crimes,** *violations of law in which there are no readily apparent victims.* Also called "crimes without complaint," they include illegal drug use, prostitution, and gambling. The term "victimless crime" is misleading, however. How victimless is a crime when young people have to steal to support a drug habit? What about a young pregnant woman who smokes crack and permanently harms her baby? Perhaps it is more correct to say that people who commit such crimes are both offenders and victims.

Because public views of victimless crimes vary so much, laws differ from place to place. In the United States, although gambling and prostitution are legal in very limited areas, both activities are common across the country. Homosexual (and some heterosexual) behavior among consenting adults is legally restricted in about half the states. Where such laws exist, enforcement is light and selective.

CRIMINAL STATISTICS

Statistics gathered by the Federal Bureau of Investigation show crime rates rising from 1960 to 1990, declining through 2000, and rising slightly in 2001. Even so, police tally nearly 12 million serious crimes each year. Figure 8–2 on page 206 shows the trends for various serious crimes.

One should always read crime statistics with caution, however, because they include only crimes known to the police. Almost all homicides are reported, but assaults—especially among people who know each

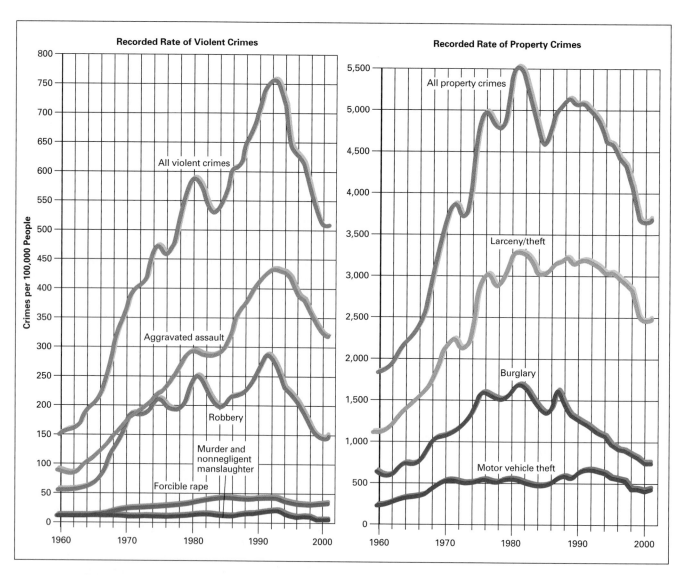

FIGURE 8–2 Crime Rates in the United States, 1960–2001

The graphs represent crime rates for various violent crimes and property crimes during recent decades.

Source: U.S. Federal Bureau of Investigation (2002).

other—often are not. Police records include an even smaller share of property crimes, especially when the losses are small.

Researchers check official crime statistics using *victimization surveys,* in which they ask a representative sample of people about their experience with crime. According to these surveys, the crime rate is about three times higher than official reports indicate (Russell, 1995b).

THE "STREET" CRIMINAL: A PROFILE

Using government crime reports, we can draw a general description of the categories of people most likely to be arrested for violent and property crimes.

Age

Official crime rates rise sharply during adolescence and peak in the late teens, falling thereafter. People between the ages of fifteen and twenty-four represent just 14 percent of the U.S. population, but in 2001 they accounted for 39.1 percent of all arrests for violent crimes and 46.9 percent of arrests for property crimes.

A disturbing trend is that young people are responsible for a larger share of some serious crimes. In the 1990s, according to the most recent government statistics, juveniles accounted for a rising share of arrests for robbery, rape, and arson (U.S. Federal Bureau of Investigation, 2001).

Gender

Although each sex makes up roughly half the population, police collared males in 69.6 percent of all property crime arrests in 2001. In other words, men are arrested more than twice as often as women for property crimes. In the case of violent crimes, the disparity is even greater: 82.7 percent of those arrested were males and just 17.3 percent were females (a five-to-one ratio).

It may be that law enforcement officers are reluctant to define women as criminals. In global perspective, in fact, the greatest gender difference in crime rates occurs in societies that most severely limit the opportunities of women. In the United States, however, the difference in arrest rates for women and men is narrowing, which probably reflects increasing sexual equality in our society. Between 1992 and 2001, a 17.8 percent *increase* in arrests of women contrasted to a *drop* of 3.6 percent in arrests of men (U.S. Federal Bureau of Investigation, 2002).

Social Class

The FBI does not assess the social class of arrested persons, so no statistical data of the kind given for age and gender are available. But plenty of research confirms that street crime is more widespread among people of lower social position (Wolfgang, Figlio, & Sellin, 1972; Clinard & Abbott, 1973; Braithwaite, 1981; Thornberry & Farnsworth, 1982; Wolfgang, Thornberry, & Figlio, 1987).

Yet the link between class and crime is more complicated than it appears on the surface. For one thing, many people look on the poor as less worthy than the rich, whose wealth and power confer "respectability" (Tittle & Villemez, 1977; Tittle, Villemez, & Smith, 1978; Elias, 1986). Moreover, while crime—especially violent crime—is a serious problem in the poorest inner-city communities, most of these crimes are committed by a few hard-core offenders. The majority of the people who live in poor communities have no

Criminal statistics can be used to construct a portrait of offenders in the United States. But these data have some limitations. For one thing, they are based not on convictions in a court of law but on arrests made and reported to the FBI by police. Two patterns are clear: Those arrested for serious crimes are likely to be young and they are likely to be male.

criminal records at all (Wolfgang, Figlio, & Sellin, 1972; Elliott & Ageton, 1980; Harries, 1990).

Moreover, the connection between social standing and criminality depends on what kind of crime one is talking about (Braithwaite, 1981). If we expand our definition of crime beyond street offenses to include white-collar crime and corporate crime, the "common criminal" suddenly looks much more affluent and, like some of the executives involved in the kind of corporate scandals described in the opening to this chapter, may live in a $100-million home.

Race and Ethnicity

Both race and ethnicity are strongly correlated to crime rates, although the reasons are many and complex. Official statistics show that 64.4 percent of arrests for index crimes in 2001 involved white people. However, arrests of African Americans were higher than of whites in proportion to their representation in the general population. African Americans represent 12.3 percent of the population but 31.4 percent of

"You look like this sketch of someone who's thinking about committing a crime."

arrests for property crimes (versus 66.0 percent for whites) and 37.6 percent of arrests for violent crimes (60.2 percent for whites) (U.S. Federal Bureau of Investigation, 2002).

What accounts for the disproportionate number of arrests among African Americans? Several factors come into play. First, prejudice related to color or class often means that police arrest black people or citizens report African Americans to police as potential offenders more often than they do white people. Specifically, research shows that there is a strong stereotype linking being black (and especially black and male) to criminality (Covington, 1995; Chiricos, McEntire, & Gertz, 2001; Quillian & Pager, 2001).

 Here is a government report on racial differences in violent crime victimization: http://www.ojp.usdoj.gov/bjs/abstract/vvr98.htm

Second, race in the United States closely relates to social standing, which, as we have already explained, affects the likelihood of engaging in street crimes. Many poor people living in the midst of affluence come to perceive society as unjust and therefore are more likely to turn to crime to get their share (Blau & Blau, 1982; Anderson, 1994; Martinez, 1996).

Third, black and white family patterns differ: Two-thirds of non-Hispanic black children (compared to one-fifth of non-Hispanic white children) are born to single mothers. In general, single-parenting means that children grow up with less supervision and greater risk of getting into trouble. Further, single-parent families are at high risk for being poor. The fact that one-third of African American children grow up in poverty (compared to one-eighth of white children) surely contributes to the proportionately higher crime rates for African Americans (Courtwright, 1996; Jacobs & Helms, 1996; Piquero, MacDonald, & Parker, 2002; U.S. Census Bureau, 2002).

Fourth, remember that the official crime index excludes arrests for offenses ranging from drunk driving to white-collar violations. This omission contributes to the view of the typical criminal as a person of color. If we broaden our definition of crime to include driving while intoxicated, business fraud, embezzlement, stock swindles, and cheating on income tax returns, the proportion of white criminals rises dramatically.

Keep in mind, too, that categories of people with high arrest rates are also at higher risk for being victims of crime. In the United States, for example, African Americans are almost six times as likely to die as a result of homicide as white people (Murphy, 2000; Rogers et al., 2001).

Finally, some categories of the population have unusually low rates of arrest. People of Asian descent, who account for about 4 percent of the population, figure in only 1.1 percent of all arrests. As Chapter 14 ("Race and Ethnicity") documents, Asian Americans enjoy higher-than-average educational achievement and income. Moreover, Asian American culture emphasizes family solidarity and discipline, both of which keep criminality down.

CRIME IN GLOBAL PERSPECTIVE

By world standards, the crime rate in the United States is high. Although recent crime trends are downward, there were 15,980 murders in the United States in 2001, about one every half hour around the clock. In large cities such as New York, rarely does a day pass with no murder; in fact, more people in New York are hit with stray bullets than are deliberately gunned down in most large cities elsewhere in the world.

Overall, the rates of serious violent and property crimes in the United States are several times higher than in Europe. The contrast is even greater between our society and the nations of Asia, including India and Japan, where rates of violent and property crime are among the lowest in the world.

Elliott Currie (1985) suggests that crime stems from our culture's emphasis on individual economic success, frequently at the expense of strong families and neighborhoods. The United States also has extraordinary cultural diversity, a result of centuries of immigration, which can weaken community ties. Moreover, economic inequality is higher in this country than in most other high-income nations. Thus, our society's relatively weak social fabric, combined with considerable frustration among the have-nots, generates widespread criminal behavior.

Another factor contributing to violence in the United States is extensive private ownership of guns. About two-thirds of murder victims in the United States die from shootings. Since the early 1990s, in Texas and several other southern states shooting deaths have exceeded automobile-related fatalities. The rate of handgun deaths (that is, controlling for population size) is about six times higher than in Canada, a country that strictly regulates and limits handgun ownership.

Surveys suggest that almost half of U.S. households own at least one gun (J. Wright, 1995; NORC, 2003). Put differently, there are more guns than adults in this country, and one-third of these weapons are handguns that figure in violent crime. In large part, gun ownership reflects people's fear of crime: Gun ownership is especially high among people who have been victims of serious crime (Ross, 2001). Yet, the relationship also works in reverse, because the easy availability of guns in this country also makes crime more deadly.

But as critics of gun control point out, waiting periods and background checks at retail gun stores (mandated by the 1993 "Brady bill") do not keep guns out of the hands of criminals, who almost always obtain guns illegally (J. Wright, 1995). Moreover, we should be cautious about assuming that gun control would be a magic bullet in the war on crime. Elliott Currie (1985) notes, for example, that the number of Californians killed each year by knives alone exceeds the number of Canadians killed by weapons of all kinds. However, most experts do think that stricter gun control would lower the level of deadly violence.

Crime rates are soaring in some of the largest cities of the world, including Manila in the Philippines, and São Paulo, Brazil, which have rapid population growth and millions of desperately poor people. In rural areas, however, strong kinship and community ties typically help control crime informally.

Some kinds of crime have always been multinational, such as terrorism, espionage, and illegal trade in weapons (Martin & Romano, 1992). But today, the "globalization" we are experiencing on many fronts also extends to crime. A recent case in point is the illegal drug trade. In part, the problem of illegal drugs in the United States is a "demand" issue. That is, there is a high demand for cocaine and other drugs in this country, and legions of young people risk arrest or even violent death to enter the lucrative drug trade. But the "supply" side of the issue is just as important. In the South American nation of Colombia, at least 20 percent of the people depend on cocaine production for their livelihood. Furthermore, not only is cocaine Colombia's most profitable export, but it outsells all other exports—including coffee—combined. Clearly, then, understanding global crime such as drug dealing means understanding social and economic conditions in this country and elsewhere.

Countries have different strategies for dealing with crime. The use of the death penalty provides a case in point. According to Amnesty International (2003), three nations account for 81 percent of the world's government-sanctioned executions: China, Iran, and the United States. Global Map 8–1 on page 210 identifies countries that employ capital punishment in response to crime and those that do not. The global trend is toward abolition of the death penalty: Amnesty International (2003) reports that since 1985 more than fifty nations have ended it.

THE CRIMINAL JUSTICE SYSTEM

December 10, Casablanca, Morocco. Casablanca! An exciting mix of African, European, and Middle Eastern cultures. Returning from a stroll through the

WINDOW ON THE WORLD

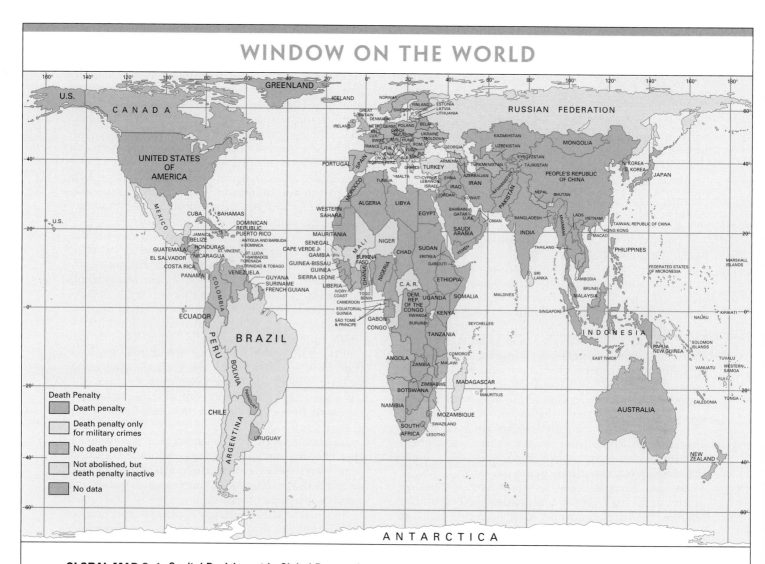

GLOBAL MAP 8–1 Capital Punishment in Global Perspective

The map identifies eighty-three countries and territories in which the law provides for the death penalty for ordinary crimes; in fifteen more, the death penalty is reserved for exceptional crimes under military law or during times of war. The death penalty does not exist in seventy-six countries and territories; in twenty-one more, although the death penalty remains in law, no execution has taken place in more than a decade. Compare rich and poor nations: What general pattern do you see? In what way do the United States and Japan stand out?

Source: Amnesty International Website against the Death Penalty. Available August 27, 2003, at http://web.amnesty.org/pages/deathpenalty-countries-eng

medina, the medieval section of this coastal North African city, we confront lines of police along a boulevard, standing between us and our ship in the harbor. The police are providing security for many important leaders attending an Islamic conference in a nearby hotel. Are the streets closed? No one asks; people seem to observe an invisible line some fifty feet from the police officers. I play the brash urbanite and start across the street to inquire (in broken French) if we can pass by; but I stop cold as several officers draw a bead on me with their eyes. Their fingers nervously tap at the grips on their automatic weapons. This is no time to strike up a conversation.

The criminal justice system is a society's formal system of social control. In some of the world's countries, military police keep a tight rein on people's behavior; in others, including the United States, police have more limited powers  and respond only to specific violations of criminal law. We shall briefly introduce the major components of the U.S. criminal justice system: police, the courts, and the system of punishment and corrections. First, however, we introduce an important principal that underlies the entire system, the principle of due process.

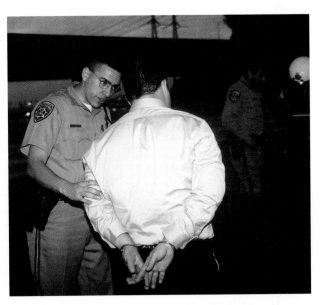

Police must be allowed discretion if they are to handle effectively the many different situations they face every day. At the same time, it is important to treat people fairly. Here, we see a police officer deciding whether or not to charge a motorist for driving while intoxicated. What factors do you think enter into this decision?

DUE PROCESS

Due process is a simple but very important idea meaning that the criminal justice system must operate within the bounds of law. This principal is grounded in the first ten amendments to the U.S. Constitution—known as the Bill of Rights—adopted by Congress in 1791. The Constitution offers various protections to any person charged with a crime, including the right to counsel, the right to refuse to testify against oneself, the right to confront one's accusers, freedom from being tried twice for the same crime, and freedom from being "deprived of life, liberty, or property without due process of law." Furthermore, the Constitution gives all people the right to a speedy and public trial, with a jury if desired, and freedom from excessive bail as well as cruel and unusual punishment.

 To read the Bill of Rights, go to http://www.archives.gov/ national_archives_experience/ bill_of_rights.html

In general terms, the concept of due process means that anyone charged with a crime must receive (1) fair notice of the proceedings, (2) a hearing on the charges conducted according to law and with the ability to present a defense, and (3) a judge or jury that weighs evidence impartially (Inciardi, 2000).

The idea of due process limits the power of government with an eye toward this nation's cultural support of individual rights and freedoms. Of course, deciding exactly how far government can go is an ongoing process that makes up much of the work of the judicial system, especially the U.S. Supreme Court.

POLICE

The police serve as the primary point of contact between the criminal justice system and a society's population. Police must follow due process, meaning they, like all citizens, are bound by law. Moreover, in the United States (unlike many other countries) police are expected to be both responsive and accountable to the public (Bayley, 1998).

Of course, there is only so much the 659,104 full-time police officers in the United States (in 2001) can do to monitor the activities of 285 million people. As a result, the police exercise considerable discretion about which situations warrant their attention and how to handle them.

How, then, do police carry out their duties? In a study of police behavior in five cities, Douglas Smith

In the United States, the death penalty itself is now on trial. In the last thirty years, 100 people have been released from death row after new evidence showed their innocence. In their effort to bring an end to capital punishment in this country, people opposed to the execution of offenders stage a protest at virtually every execution that takes place. Do you support the use of the death penalty? Why or why not?

and Christy Visher (1981; Smith, 1987) concluded that, because they must act swiftly, police officers quickly size up a situation in terms of six factors. First, the more serious they think the situation is, the more likely they are to make an arrest. Second, officers take account of the victim's wishes in deciding whether or not to make an arrest. Third, the odds of arrest go up the more uncooperative a suspect is. Fourth, officers are more likely to take into custody someone they have arrested before, presumably because previous arrests suggest likelihood of guilt. Fifth, the presence of observers prompts police to take stronger control of a situation, if only to move the encounter from the street (the suspect's turf) to the police department (where law officers have the edge). Sixth, all else being equal, police officers are more likely to arrest people of color than whites, perceiving suspects of African or Hispanic descent as either more dangerous or more likely to be guilty.

COURTS

After arrest, a court determines a suspect's guilt or innocence. In principle, our courts rely on an adversarial process involving attorneys—one representing the defendant and another the state—in the presence of a judge, who is responsible for ensuring due process.

In practice, however, about 90 percent of criminal cases are resolved prior to court appearance through **plea bargaining,** *a legal negotiation in which a prosecutor* *reduces a charge in exchange for a defendant's guilty plea.* For example, the state may offer a defendant charged with burglary a lesser charge of possessing burglary tools in exchange for a guilty plea.

Plea bargaining is widespread because it spares the state the time and expense of trials. A trial is usually unnecessary if there is little disagreement on the facts of the case. Moreover, since the number of cases entering the system annually has doubled over the last decade, prosecutors could not possibly bring every case to trial. By quickly resolving most of their work, then, the courts channel their resources into the most important cases.

But plea bargaining pressures defendants (who are always presumed innocent) to plead guilty. A person can exercise the right to a trial, but only at the risk of receiving a more severe sentence if found guilty. Furthermore, low-income defendants enter the process with the guidance of a public defender—an attorney provided by the court who is often overworked and usually underpaid and who may devote little time even to a serious case (Novak, 1999). Overall, plea bargaining may be efficient, but at the cost of undercutting the adversarial process as well as the rights of defendants.

PUNISHMENT

Punishing wrongdoers is as old as society itself. But the ideas about *why* society should punish have changed over the course of history. Scholars point to four basic reasons to punish: retribution, deterrence, rehabilitation, and societal protection. They are summarized in Table 8–2.

Retribution

The oldest justification for punishment is to satisfy people's need for **retribution,** *an act of moral vengeance by which society inflicts on the offender suffering comparable to that caused by the offense.* Retribution rests on a view of society as a moral balance. When criminality upsets this balance, punishment exacted in comparable measure restores the moral order, as suggested in the biblical dictum "An eye for an eye."

During the Middle Ages, most people viewed crime as sin—an offense against God as well as society—that warranted a harsh response. Today, although critics point out that retribution does little to reform the offender, many people consider vengeance reason enough for punishment.

Deterrence

A second justification for punishment is **deterrence,** *the attempt to discourage criminality through punishment.* Deterrence is based on the eighteenth-century Enlightenment idea that humans are calculating and rational creatures who will not break the law if they think that the pains of punishment will outweigh the pleasures of crime.

Deterrence emerged as a reform measure in response to the harsh punishments based on retribution. Why put someone to death for stealing, reformists reasoned, if theft can be discouraged with a prison sentence? As the concept of deterrence gained widespread acceptance, the execution and physical mutilation of criminals in most high-income societies were replaced by milder forms of punishment, such as imprisonment.

Punishment can deter in two ways. *Specific deterrence* convinces an individual offender that crime does not pay. Through *general deterrence*, the punishment of one person serves as an example to others.

Rehabilitation

The third justification for punishment is **rehabilitation,** *a program for reforming the offender to prevent subsequent offenses.* Rehabilitation arose along with the social sciences in the nineteenth century. Since then, sociologists have claimed that crime and other deviance spring from a social environment marked by

TABLE 8–2 Four Justifications for Punishment: A Summary	
Retribution	The oldest justification for punishment. Punishment is atonement for a moral wrong; in principle, punishment should be comparable in severity to the deviance itself.
Deterrence	An early modern approach. Deviance is considered social disruption, which society acts to control. People are viewed as rational and self-interested; deterrence works because the pains of punishment outweigh the pleasures of deviance.
Rehabilitation	A modern strategy linked to the development of social sciences. Deviance is viewed as the product of social problems (such as poverty) or personal problems (such as mental illness). Social conditions are improved; treatment is tailored to the offender's condition.
Societal Protection	A modern approach easier to implement than rehabilitation. If society is unable or unwilling to rehabilitate offenders or reform social conditions, people are protected by the incarceration or execution of the offender.

poverty or a lack of parental supervision. Logically, then, if offenders learn to be deviant, they can also learn to obey the rules; the key is controlling the environment. *Reformatories* or *houses of correction* provided controlled settings where people could learn proper behavior (recall the description of total institutions in Chapter 5, "Socialization").

Like deterrence, rehabilitation motivates the offender to conform. But rehabilitation emphasizes constructive improvement, whereas deterrence and retribution simply make the offender suffer. In addition, where retribution demands that the punishment fit the crime, rehabilitation tailors treatment to each offender. Thus, identical crimes would prompt similar acts of retribution but different rehabilitation programs.

Societal Protection

A final justification for punishment is **societal protection,** *a means by which society renders an offender incapable of further offenses temporarily through incarceration*

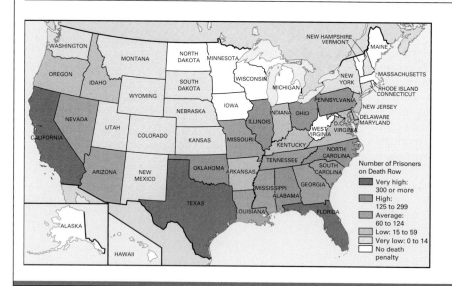

NATIONAL MAP 8–2
Capital Punishment
across the United States

The United States and Japan are the only high-income nations in which the government imposes the death penalty. Yet within the United States, the fifty states have broadly divergent capital punishment laws: Half of the 3,581 prisoners on death row are in five states. What regional pattern do you see in the map? Can you account for this pattern?

Source: U.S. Bureau of Justice Statistics (2002).

Number of Prisoners on Death Row

- Very high: 300 or more
- High: 125 to 299
- Average: 60 to 124
- Low: 15 to 59
- Very low: 0 to 14
- No death penalty

or permanently by execution. Like deterrence, societal protection is a rational approach to punishment and seeks to protect society from crime.

Currently, 2 million people are incarcerated in the United States. In response to tougher public attitudes and an increasing number of drug-related arrests, the U.S. prison population has tripled since 1980. The size of inmate populations is going up in most high-income countries, yet the United States incarcerates a larger share of its population than any other country in the world (Sutton, 2000; The Sentencing Project, 2002).

Critical evaluation. Assessing the actual consequences of punishment is no simple task.

The value of retribution lies in Durkheim's contention that punishing the deviant person increases people's moral awareness. Appropriately, then, punishment was traditionally a public event. Although the last public execution in the United States took place in Kentucky in 1937, today's mass media ensure public awareness of executions carried out inside prison walls (Kittrie, 1971).

Does punishment deter crime? Our society has a high rate of **criminal recidivism,** *subsequent offenses by people previously convicted of crimes,* despite its high rate of punishment. About three-fourths of prisoners in state

penitentiaries have been jailed before, and about half will be back in prison within a few years after release. In light of such patterns, it is far from clear that punishment really deters crime (McNulty, 1994; Petersilia, 1997; DeFina & Arvanites, 2002). Then, too, only about one-third of all crimes are known to police, and of these, only about one in five results in an arrest. The adage "Crime doesn't pay" rings hollow when we recognize that only a small share of offenses are ever punished.

General deterrence is even more difficult to investigate scientifically, since we have no way of knowing how people might act if they were unaware of the punishments meted out to others. In the debate over capital punishment, opponents point to research suggesting that the death penalty has limited value as a general deterrent. Moreover, the United States is the only Western high-income nation that routinely executes serious offenders. A troubling fact is that some death sentences have been pronounced against innocent people. Between 1973 and 2003, almost 100 people have been released from death row after new evidence established their innocence, which means the death penalty itself is now on trial. Before leaving office in January, 2003, Illinois Governor George Ryan—who has characterized his state's judicial system as seriously flawed—commuted sentences for all 157 of the state's death row inmates to life in prison (Tanber, 1998; Alter, 2000; Yunker, 2001; Babwin, 2003; Levine, 2003). National Map 8–2 identifies the thirty-eight states that have the death penalty and shows that half the prisoners on death row are in just five of these states.

Despite growing controversy over the death penalty, a majority of U.S. adults (63 percent) say they support capital punishment for people convicted of murder (NORC, 2003:121). Figure 8–3 shows that opposition to the death penalty among students was high in 1970 but fell until 1995, with opposition rising since then.

Prisons provide short-term societal protection by keeping offenders off the streets, but they do little to reshape attitudes or behavior in the long term (Carlson, 1976; Wright, 1994). Perhaps rehabilitation is an

 Human Rights Watch has issued a report on rape in prison: http://www.hrw.org/ reports/2001/prison/

unrealistic expectation, because according to Sutherland's theory of differential association, locking up criminals together for years probably strengthens criminal attitudes and skills. Incarceration also severs whatever social ties inmates may have in the outside world and thus, following Hirschi's control theory, leaves individuals prone to commit more crimes upon their release.

Finally, the stigma of being an ex-convict can be a powerful barrier to building a new life. One study of young offenders in Philadelphia found that boys who were sentenced to long prison terms—and thus most likely to acquire a criminal stigma—went on to commit both more crimes and more serious ones (Wolfgang, Figlio, & Sellin, 1972).

COMMUNITY-BASED CORRECTIONS

Prisons keep convicted criminals off the streets. But the evidence suggests that they do little to rehabilitate most offenders. Furthermore, prisons are expensive, costing approximately $25,000 per year to support each inmate in addition to the costs of building the facilities. Is there an alternative to incarceration?

One alternative is **community-based corrections,** *correctional programs located within society at large rather than behind prison walls.* Community-based corrections have a number of advantages, including (1) reducing prison overcrowding, (2) reducing costs, and (3) allowing for supervision of convicts while eliminating the hardships of prison life as well as the stigma that accompanies being incarcerated. In general, the idea of community-based corrections is not

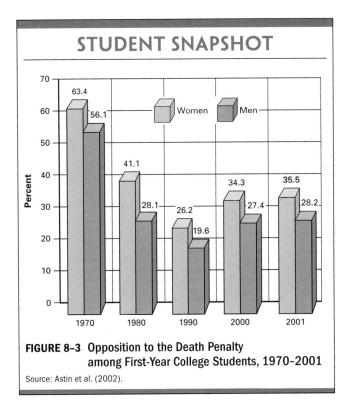

STUDENT SNAPSHOT

FIGURE 8-3 Opposition to the Death Penalty among First-Year College Students, 1970–2001

Source: Astin et al. (2002).

so much to punish as to reform; individuals assigned to such programs, therefore, are usually those who have committed less serious offenses and appear to be good prospects for avoiding future criminal violations (Inciardi, 2000).

Probation

One form of community-based corrections is *probation,* a policy of permitting a convicted offender to remain in the community under conditions imposed by a court and subject to regular supervision. Courts may require that a probationer receive counseling, attend a drug treatment program, hold a job, avoid "consorting with known criminals," or anything else they deem appropriate. Typically, a probationer must check in with an officer of the court (the "probation officer") on a regular schedule. Should the probationer fail to comply with conditions set by the court or commit a subsequent offense, the court may revoke probation in favor of incarceration.

APPLYING SOCIOLOGY
Violent Crime Is Down—But Why?

During the 1980s, crime rates shot upward. Just about everyone lived in fear of violent crime, and in many larger cities, the numbers killed and wounded made whole neighborhoods seem like war zones. There seemed to be no solution to the problem.

Then, in the 1990s, something good and unexpected happened: Serious crime rates began to fall until, by 2001, they had dropped by one-third to levels not seen in more than a generation. Why? Applying the perspectives and theories presented in this chapter, we can identify several reasons:

1. **A reduction in the youth population.** We have already noted that young people (particularly males) are responsible for much violent crime. Between 1990 and 2000, the population aged fifteen to twenty-four dropped by 5 percent (in part because of the legalization of abortion in 1973).

2. **Changes in policing.** Much of the drop in crime (and the earlier rise in crime) has taken place in large cities. New York City, where the number of murders fell from 2,245 in 1990 to just 649 in 2001, has adopted a policy of *community policing*, which means that police are concerned not just about making arrests but about preventing crime before it happens. Officers get to know the areas they patrol and stop young men for jaywalking or other minor infractions in order to check them for concealed weapons (the word has

gotten around that you risk arrest for carrying a gun). Moreover, there are *more* police at work in large cities. Los Angeles, for example, added more than 2,000 police in the 1990s, and it, too, saw its violent crime rate fall during that period.

3. **More prisons.** From 1985 until 2001, the number of inmates in U.S. jails and prisons soared from 750,000 to 2 million. The main reason for this increase is tough laws that demand prison time for many crimes, especially drug offenses. As one analyst put it, "When you lock up an extra million people, it's got to have some effect on the crime rate" (Zimring, cited in Witkin, 1998:31).

4. **A better economy.** The U.S. economy boomed during the 1990s. With unemployment down, more people were working, and the likelihood that some would turn to crime out of economic desperation was reduced. The logic here is simple: More jobs, fewer crimes. By the

One reason that crime has gone down is that there are 2 million people incarcerated in this country. This has caused severe overcrowding of facilities such as this Maricopa County, Arizona, prison.

same token, of course, the recent economic downturn may well push crime rates up somewhat.

5. **The declining drug trade.** Many analysts agree that the most important factor in reducing rates of violent crime was the decline of crack cocaine. Crack came on the scene about 1985, and violence spread as young people—especially in the inner cities and increasingly armed with guns—became part of a booming drug trade. With legitimate job opportunities low and a rising opportunity to make money illegally, a generation of young people became part of a wave of violence. Widespread crack cocaine use also explains the trend, noted earlier, of the younger age of violent criminals.

By the early 1990s, however, the popularity of crack began to fall as people saw the damage it was causing to entire communities. This realization, coupled with steady economic improvement and stiffer sentences for drug offenses, brought the turnaround in violent crime.

Keep in mind that the current picture looks better relative to what it was a decade ago. The crime problem, says one researcher, "looks better, but only because the early 1990s were so bad. So let's not fool ourselves into thinking everything is resolved. It's not."

Sources: Based on Boggess & Bound (1997), Blumstein & Rosenfeld (1998), Fagan, Zimring, & Kim (1998), Witkin (1998), Winship & Berrien (1999), Donahue & Leavitt (2000), and Rosenfeld (2002).

Shock Probation

A related strategy is *shock probation*, a policy by which a judge orders a convicted offender to prison for a length of time, but then stipulates that only a portion of the sentence will be served in actual incarceration, with the remainder suspended in favor of probation. Shock probation is, then, a mix of prison and probation that is used to impress on the offender the seriousness of the situation, while still withholding full-scale incarceration. In some cases, shock probation takes place in a special "boot camp" facility where offenders might spend one to three months in a military-style setting intended to teach discipline and respect for authority (Cole & Smith, 2002).

Parole

Parole is a policy of releasing inmates from prison to serve the remainder of their sentences supervised within the local community. Although some sentences specifically deny the possibility of parole, most inmates become eligible for parole after serving a specified share of a sentence. At this time, a parole board evaluates the risks and benefits of an early release from prison and, if parole is granted, monitors the offender's conduct until the sentence is completed.

Should the offender not comply with the conditions of parole or be arrested for another crime, the board can revoke parole and return the person to prison to complete the sentence there.

Critical evaluation. Evaluations of probation and parole are mixed. There is little question that these programs are much less expensive than incarceration and that, by monitoring selected offenders in the community, they free up room in prisons for those who commit more serious crimes. Yet research suggests although probation and shock probation do seem to work for some people, they do not significantly reduce recidivism. Similarly, parole is useful to prison officials as a means to encourage good behavior among inmates who hope for early release. Yet, levels of crime among those released on parole are high. Indeed, recidivism among parolees is so high that a number of states have ended parole programs entirely (Inciardi, 2000).

Evaluations of all aspects of the criminal justice system point to a sobering truth: We should never imagine that the criminal justice system can eliminate crime. As the box explains, while police, courts, and prisons play a part affecting crime rates, more is involved. As this chapter has described, crime and other forms of deviance are not just the acts of "bad people" but reflect the operation of society itself.

SUMMARY

1. Deviance refers to norm violations ranging from mild breaches of etiquette to serious violence.

2. Biological research, from Caesare Lombroso's nineteenth-century observations of convicts to recent research in human genetics, has yet to offer much insight into the causes of deviance.

3. Psychological study links deviance to abnormal personality resulting from either biological or environmental causes. Psychological theories help explain some kinds of deviance.

4. Deviance has societal rather than individual roots because it varies according to cultural norms, because people are socially defined as deviant, and because deviance reflects patterns of social power.

5. Using the structural-functional paradigm, Durkheim explained that deviance serves to affirm norms and values, clarifies moral boundaries, promotes social unity, and encourages social change.

6. The symbolic-interaction paradigm is the basis of labeling theory, which holds that deviance lies in people's reaction to a person's behavior, not in the behavior itself. Acquiring a stigma of deviance can lead to secondary deviance and a deviant career.

7. Based on Karl Marx's ideas, social-conflict theory holds that laws and other norms reflect the interests of powerful members of society. Although white-collar and corporate crime cause extensive social harm, offenders are rarely branded as criminals.

8. Official statistics show that arrest rates peak in late adolescence, then drop steadily with advancing age. About 70 percent of those arrested for property crimes and 83 percent of those arrested for violent crimes are male.

9. People of lower social position commit more street crime than people with greater social privilege. When white-collar and corporate crimes are included among criminal offenses, however, the disparity in overall criminal activity goes down.

10. More whites than African Americans are arrested for street crimes. However, African Americans are arrested more often than whites in proportion to their respective

populations. Asian Americans have lower-than-average rates of arrest.

11. The concept of due process, which is based in the U.S. Constitution (Bill of Rights), guides the operation of the criminal justice system.

12. Police exercise considerable discretion in their work. Arrest is more likely if the offense is serious, bystanders are present, or the accused is African American or Hispanic.

13. Most prosecutions of criminal cases never go to trial but are resolved through plea bargaining. While efficient, this method puts less powerful people at a disadvantage.

14. Justifications of punishment include retribution, deterrence, rehabilitation, and societal protection. Because its consequences are difficult to evaluate scientifically, punishment—like deviance itself—sparks controversy among sociologists and the public as a whole.

15. Community-based corrections include probation and parole. Such policies reduce the cost of supervising people convicted of crimes as well as prison overcrowding but have not been shown to greatly reduce recidivism.

KEY CONCEPTS

deviance (p. 190) the recognized violation of cultural norms

crime (p. 190) the violation of a society's formally enacted criminal law

social control (p. 190) attempts by society to regulate people's thought and behavior

criminal justice system (p. 190) a formal response by police, courts, and prison officials to alleged violations of the law

labeling theory (p. 195) the assertion that deviance and conformity result not so much from what people do as from how others respond to those actions

stigma (p. 197) a powerfully negative label that greatly changes a person's self-concept and social identity

medicalization of deviance (p. 198) the transformation of moral and legal deviance into a medical condition

white-collar crime (p. 201) crime committed by people of high social position in the course of their occupations

corporate crime (p. 201) the illegal actions of a corporation or people acting on its behalf

organized crime (p. 202) a business supplying illegal goods or service

hate crime (p. 203) a criminal act against a person or a person's property by an offender motivated by racial or other bias

crimes against the person (p. 205) (violent crimes) crimes that direct violence or the threat of violence against others

crimes against property (p. 205) (property crimes) crimes that involve theft of property belonging to others

victimless crimes (p. 205) violations of law in which there are no readily apparent victims

plea bargaining (p. 212) a legal negotiation in which a prosecutor reduces a charge in exchange for a defendant's guilty plea

retribution (p. 213) an act of moral vengeance by which society inflicts on the offender suffering comparable to that caused by the offense

deterrence (p. 213) the attempt to discourage criminality through punishment

rehabilitation (p. 213) a program for reforming the offender to prevent subsequent offenses

societal protection (p. 213) a means by which society renders an offender incapable of further offenses temporarily through incarceration or permanently by execution

criminal recidivism (p. 214) subsequent offenses by people previously convicted of crimes

community-based corrections (p. 215) correctional programs located within society at large rather than behind prison walls

CRITICAL-THINKING QUESTIONS

1. How does a sociological view of deviance differ from the commonsense notion that bad people do bad things?

2. List Durkheim's functions of deviance. From his point of view, can society ever be free of deviance? Why or why not?

3. An old saying is "Sticks and stones can break my bones, but names can never hurt me." Explain how labeling theory challenges this statement.

4. A recent study found that one in three black men between the ages of twenty and twenty-nine is in jail, on probation, or on parole (Mauer, 2000). What factors, noted in this chapter, help explain this pattern?

APPLICATIONS AND EXERCISES

1. Research computer crime. What new kinds of crime are emerging in the information age? Is computer technology also generating new ways of tracking lawbreakers?

2. Rent a wheelchair (check with a local pharmacy or medical supply store), and use it as much as possible for a day or two. Not only will you gain a firsthand understanding of the physical barriers to getting around, but you will also discover that people respond to you in many new ways.

3. Watch an episode of the real-action police show *Cops*. Based on this program, how would you profile the people who commit crimes?

4. Packaged in the back of this new textbook is an interactive CD-ROM that offers a variety of video and interactive review materials intended to help you better understand the material covered in this chapter. For this chapter, the CD-ROM contains a relevant clip from *ABC News*, an author's tip video, interactive map animations, an interactive time line, and flashcards with audio pronunciations of the more difficult words.

 SITES TO SEE

http://www.prenhall.com/macionis

Visit the interactive Companion Website™ that accompanies this text. Begin by clicking on the cover of your book. You will find a chapter-by-chapter study guide, practice tests, suggested Web links, and links to other relevant material.

http://www.civilrights.org/

The Leadership Conference on Civil Rights maintains this site dealing with hate crimes and other issues of civil rights.

http://www.spr.org/

The organization Stop Prisoner Rape hosts this site dealing with the problem of rape in U.S. prisons.

http://www.mcso.org

This site provides a look at the operations of the well-known Maricopa County, Arizona, sheriff's office.

http://www.ncadp.org
http://www.uaa.alaska.edu/just/death/intl.html

These sites provide information on the death penalty. The first presents the views of the National Coalition to Abolish the Death Penalty. The second provides data on the death penalty in global perspective.

http://www.cybercrime.gov

This site, operated by the U.S. Department of Justice, provides a great deal of information on computer crime and issues surrounding intellectual property.

 INVESTIGATE WITH RESEARCH NAVIGATOR™

Follow the instructions on page 24 of this text to access the features of **Research Navigator™**. Once at the Web site, enter your Login Name and Password. Then, to use the **Content Select™** database, enter keywords such as "crime," "rape," and "prison," and the search engine will supply relevant and recent scholarly and popular press publications. Use the *New York Times* **Search-by-Subject Archive** to find recent news articles related to sociology and the **Link Library** feature to find relevant Web links organized by the key terms associated with this chapter.

SEXUALITY

KATE, EMILY, AND Tara stream through the door of the pizza shop a few blocks from their Princeton, New Jersey, high school, where they have just started their sophomore year.

They survey the room to see who is there while pushing their book bags beneath their favorite table and then walk to the counter to place their order (three plain slices, three diet colas). Minutes later, food in hand, the girls slide into their seats to talk about their favorite topic: sex.

Tara begins, "Now that we've had sex, Tom says I'm being a tease if we hook up and I say I just want to kiss."

"Me, too," Kate interrupts, scarcely waiting for her friend to finish. "It's like once you do it, you have to do it all the time! I don't know how it's supposed to be—he has a temper and sometimes—if I don't feel like anything—he gets really mad."

Emily, who has been eating her pizza in silence, has not yet had sex. But, listening to her friends, she is glad, although she would never say so (based on Mulrine, 2002).

There is nothing new about young people being interested in sex. But more of today's teens are doing more than talk—they are having sex, and at a younger age. According to the government's Centers for Disease Control (2001), about 10 percent of young people in the United States report losing their virginity by age thirteen, and half do so by age sixteen. Among high-school sophomores such as the girls in our opening, one in six has already had at least four sexual partners.

Why does more and earlier sexual activity concern many people? There are a number of reasons. As this chapter explains, the United States has a high rate of pregnancy among teenagers. In addition, a significant number of young women become victims of sexual violence. Then, too, all sexually active people (especially those with multiple partners) run the risk of infection with a sexually transmitted disease. It is also true that many young people—and a number of their parents—understand too little about sexuality.

This chapter, written from a sociological point of view, presents some of what researchers have learned about human sexuality. Our main concern is to investigate patterns of sexual behavior, including the various ways societies define sex and the diverse ways in which people express themselves sexually.

UNDERSTANDING SEXUALITY

How much of the day goes by without your giving any thought at all to sexuality? If you are like most people, the answer is "not very much." That is because sexuality is not just about "having sex." Sexuality is a theme found throughout society, apparent on campus, in the workplace, and especially in the mass media. The sex industry—including pornography and prostitution— is a multibillion-dollar business in its own right. In addition, sexuality is an important part of how we think about ourselves, just as it affects how others evaluate us. In truth, there are few areas of life in which sexuality does *not* play some part.

But in spite of its significance in life, many people understand little about sexuality. Moreover, through much of our history, sex has been a cultural taboo so that, at least in polite conversation, people did not even talk about it. As a result, while sex can produce much pleasure, it also causes confusion and sometimes outright fear. Even scientists long considered sex off limits as a topic of research. It was not until the middle of the twentieth century that researchers turned their attention to this vital dimension of social life. Since then, as this chapter reports, we have learned a great deal about human sexuality.

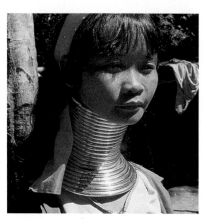

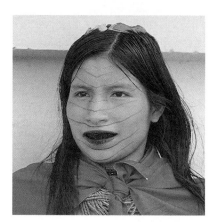

We claim that beauty is in the eye of the beholder, which suggests the importance of culture in setting standards of attractiveness. All of the people pictured here—from Morocco, South Africa, Nigeria, Myanmar (Burma), Japan, and Ecuador—are beautiful to members of their own society. At the same time, sociobiologists point out that, in every society on Earth, people are attracted to youthfulness. The reason is that, as sociobiologists see it, attractiveness underlies our choices about reproduction, which is most readily accomplished in early adulthood.

SEX: A BIOLOGICAL ISSUE

Sex refers to *the biological distinction between females and males.* From a biological point of view, sex is the means by which humans reproduce. A female ovum and a male sperm, each containing twenty-three chromosomes (biological codes that guide physical development), combine to form a fertilized embryo. One pair of chromosomes determines the child's sex. To this pair the mother contributes an X chromosome and the father contributes either an X or a Y. A second X from the father produces a female (XX) embryo; a Y from the father produces a male (XY) embryo. Thus, a child's sex is determined biologically at the moment of conception.

Within weeks, the sex of an embryo starts to guide its development. If the embryo is male, testicular tissue starts to produce large amounts of testosterone, a hormone that triggers the development of male genitals. If little testosterone is present (the adrenal gland in both females and males also produces testosterone), the embryo develops female genitals. In the United States, about 105 boys are born for every 100 girls, but a higher death rate among males makes females a slight majority by the time people reach their mid-thirties (U.S. National Center for Health Statistics, 2002).

SEX AND THE BODY

What sets females and males apart are differences in the body. Right from birth, the two sexes have different **primary sex characteristics,** namely, *the genitals, organs used for reproduction.* At puberty, as individuals reach sexual maturity, additional sex differentiation takes place. At this point in their development, individuals begin to exhibit **secondary sex characteristics,** *bodily development, apart from the genitals, that distinguishes biologically mature females and males.* To allow for pregnancy, giving birth, and nurturing infants, mature females have wider hips, breasts, and soft fatty tissue that provides a reserve supply of nutrition for pregnancy and breast-feeding. Mature males, on the other hand, typically develop more muscle in the upper body, more extensive body hair, and deeper voices. Of course, these are general differences, since some males are smaller and have less body hair and higher voices than some females.

Keep in mind that *sex* refers to biological traits that distinguish females and males. *Gender,* on the other hand, is a dimension of culture that refers to the personal traits and patterns of behavior (including social opportunities and privileges) that a culture attaches to being female or male. Chapter 13 ("Gender Stratification") describes the importance of gender in social life.

Intersexual People

Sex is not always as clear-cut as we have just described. The term **intersexual people** refers to *people whose anatomy (including genitals) includes both female and male characteristics.* Another term for intersexual people is hermaphrodites, a word derived from Hermaphroditus (the offspring of the mythological Greek gods Hermes and Aphrodite), who embodied both sexes. A true hermaphrodite is a person with both a female ovary and a male testis.

Our culture is uneasy about sexual ambiguity, a fact evident in the requirement that parents record the sex of their new child at birth as either female or male. It is also true that, in the United States, some people respond to hermaphrodites with confusion or even disgust. But other cultures lead people to respond quite differently: The Pokot of eastern Africa, for example, pay little attention to what they consider a simple biological error, and the Navajo look on intersexual people with awe, seeing in them the full potential of both the female and the male (Geertz, 1975).

Transsexuals

Transsexuals are *people who feel they are one sex even though biologically they are the other.* Tens of thousands of people in the United States have the experience of feeling "trapped" in a body of the wrong sex and a desire to be the other sex. Most become *transgendered;* that is, they begin to disregard conventional ideas about how females and males should look and behave. One option is to *cross-dress,* that is, to wear clothing conventionally associated with people of the other sex. Many go one step further and undergo *gender reassignment,* surgical alteration of their genitals. While this medical procedure is complex and takes months or even years, it provides many people with a joyful sense of finally becoming who they really are (Tewksbury & Gagné, 1996; Gagné, Tewksbury, & McGaughey, 1997).

SEX: A CULTURAL ISSUE

Sexuality has a biological foundation. But like all dimensions of human behavior, sexuality is also very much a cultural issue. Biology is sufficient to explain the strange mating rituals of the animal world, but humans have no similar biological program. That is, humans have a biological "sex drive" in the sense that people find sex pleasurable and may want to engage in sexual activity, but our biology does not dictate any specific ways of being sexual any more than our desire to eat dictates any particular foods or table manners.

Cultural Variation

Almost any sexual practice shows considerable variation from one society to another. In his pioneering study of sexuality in the United States, Alfred Kinsey (1948) found that most heterosexual couples reported having intercourse in a single position—face to face, with the woman on the bottom and the man on top. Halfway around the world, in the South Seas, most couples *never* have sex in this way. In fact, when the people of the South Seas learned of this practice from Western missionaries, they poked fun at it as the strange "missionary position."

Even the simple practice of showing affection has extensive cultural variation. Whereas most people in the United States readily kiss in public, the Chinese kiss only in private. The French kiss publicly, often twice (once on each cheek), while Belgians go them one better, kissing three times (starting on either cheek). The Maoris of New Zealand rub noses, and most people in Nigeria don't kiss at all.

SEEING OURSELVES

NATIONAL MAP 9–1
First-Cousin Marriage Laws across the United States

There is no single view on first-cousin marriages in the United States: Twenty-four states forbid such unions, nineteen allow them, and seven allow them with restrictions.* In general, states that permit first-cousin marriages are found in New England, the Southeast, and the Southwest.

*Of the seven states that allow first-cousin marriages with restrictions, six states permit them only when couples are past childbearing age.

Source: www.CousinCouples.com (2003).

First-Cousin Marriages
- Allowed
- Allowed with Restrictions
- Not Allowed

Modesty, too, is culturally variable. If a woman entering a bath is disturbed, what body parts does she cover? Helen Colton (1983) reports that an Islamic woman covers her face, a Laotian woman covers her breasts, a Samoan woman covers her navel, a Sumatran woman covers her knees, and a European woman covers her breasts with one hand and her genital area with the other.

Around the world, some societies tend to restrict sexuality, while others are more permissive. In China, for example, norms closely regulate sexuality so that few people have sexual intercourse before they marry. In the United States, however—at least in recent decades—intercourse prior to marriage has become the norm (about 70 percent claim to be sexually active by the end of high school), and many people may choose to have sex even when there is no strong commitment between them.

THE INCEST TABOO

Are any cultural views of sex the same everywhere? The answer is yes. One cultural universal—an element found in every society the world over—is the **incest taboo,** *a norm forbidding sexual relations or marriage between certain relatives.* In the United States, the law as well as cultural mores prohibits close relatives (including brothers and sisters, parents and children) from having sex or marrying. But exactly which family members are included in a society's incest taboo varies from one place to another. National Map 9–1 shows that twenty-four U.S. states outlaw marriage between first cousins; twenty-six states do not.

Moreover, some societies (such as the North American Navajo) apply incest taboos only to the mother and others on her side of the family. There are also societies (including ancient Peru and ancient Egypt) on record that have approved brother-sister marriages among the nobility (Murdock, 1965; orig. 1949).

Why does the incest taboo exist everywhere? Biology is part of the reason: Reproduction between close relatives of any species risks offspring with mental or physical problems. But this fact does not explain why, of all living species, only humans observe an incest taboo. In other words, controlling sexuality among close relatives seems a necessary element of social organization. For one thing, the incest taboo limits sexual competition in families by restricting sex to spouses (ruling out, for example, sex between parent and child). Second, since family ties define people's rights and obligations toward each other, reproduction among close relatives would hopelessly confuse kinship; if a mother and son had a daughter, for example, what would the child's relation be to the other two? Third, by requiring people to marry

Over the course of the last century, sexual attitudes in the United States have become more accepting of human sexuality. In 1925, women in Chicago were charged with indecent exposure and trucked off to the police station for wearing these "revealing" bathing suits.

outside their immediate families, the incest taboo integrates the larger society as people look widely for partners to form new families.

The incest taboo has been an enduring sexual norm in the United States and elsewhere. But in this country, many sexual norms have changed over time. During the twentieth century, as we now explain, our society experienced both a sexual revolution and, later, a sexual counterrevolution.

SEXUAL ATTITUDES IN THE UNITED STATES

What do people in the United States think about sex? Our cultural orientation toward sexuality has always been inconsistent. On the one hand, most European immigrants arrived with rigid notions about "correct" sexuality, which, ideally, meant that sex was permitted only within marriage and only for the purpose of reproduction. As explained in Chapter 8 ("Deviance"), the Puritan settlers of New England demanded conformity in all attitudes and behavior, and they imposed severe penalties for any misconduct—even if the sexual "misconduct" took place in the privacy of one's home. Efforts to regulate sexuality continued long after: As late as the 1960s, for example, some states legally banned the sale of condoms in stores. Until 2003, thirteen states still had laws on the books

banning sex between same-sex partners; even today, eleven states have "fornication" laws that can be used to punish heterosexual intercourse among unmarried couples.

But this is just one side of the story of sexuality in the United States. As Chapter 3 ("Culture") explains, our culture is also individualistic, and many believe in giving people freedom to do pretty much as they wish as long as they cause no direct harm to others. Such thinking—that what people do in the privacy of their own home is *their* business—makes sex a matter of individual freedom and personal choice.

So which is it? Is the United States a restrictive or a permissive society when it comes to sexuality? The answer is that it is both. On the one hand, many people in the United States still view sexual conduct as an important indicator of personal morality. On the other, sex is exploited and glorified everywhere in U.S. culture—and strongly promoted by the mass media—as if to say that "anything goes." Within this general framework, we turn now to changes in sexual attitudes and behavior over the course of the twentieth century.

THE SEXUAL REVOLUTION

During the last century, people witnessed profound changes in sexual attitudes and practices. The first

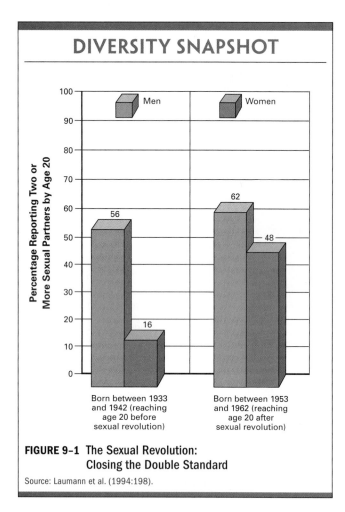

FIGURE 9–1 The Sexual Revolution: Closing the Double Standard

Source: Laumann et al. (1994:198).

scientists were studying *sex* that set off a national conversation. At that time, after all, many people were uneasy talking about sex even privately at home.

Kinsey's two books (1948, 1953) became best-sellers partly because they revealed that people in the United States, on average, were far less conventional in sexual matters than most had thought. Thus, these books fostered a new openness toward sexuality, which helped advance the sexual revolution.

In the late 1960s, the sexual revolution truly came of age. Youth culture dominated public life, and expressions like "if it feels good, do it" and "sex, drugs, and rock and roll" summed up a new freedom about sexuality. Some people were turned off by the idea of "turning on," of course, but the baby boom generation born between 1945 and 1960 became the first cohort in U.S. history to grow up with the idea that sex was part of people's lives, married or not.

Technology, too, played a part in the sexual revolution. "The pill," introduced in 1960, not only prevented pregnancy but also made sex more convenient. Unlike a condom or diaphragm, which has to be used at the time of intercourse, the pill could be taken anytime during the day. Now women as well as men could engage in sex without any special preparation.

The sexual revolution had special significance for women because, historically, women were subject to greater sexual regulation than men. According to the so-called "double standard," society allows (and even encourages) men to be sexually active, while expecting women to remain chaste before marriage and faithful to their husbands afterward. The survey data shown in Figure 9–1 support this conclusion. Among people born in the United States between 1933 and 1942 (that is, people who are in their sixties and seventies today), 56 percent of men but just 16 percent of women report having had two or more sexual partners by the time they were age twenty. Compare this wide gap to the pattern among the baby boomers born between 1953 and 1962 (people now in their forties and fifties), who came of age after the sexual revolution. In this category, 62 percent of men and 48 percent of women say they had two or more sexual partners by age twenty (Laumann et al., 1994:198). Thus, while the sexual revolution increased sexual activity overall, it changed behavior among women more than among men.

A general trend, then, is that greater openness about sexuality develops as societies develop economically and as the opportunities for women increase. With these facts in mind, we can understand the global pattern of birth control use shown in Global Map 9–1.

indications of this change occurred in the 1920s, as millions of women and men migrated from farms and small towns to rapidly growing cities. There, living apart from their families and meeting in the workplace, young people enjoyed considerable sexual freedom. Indeed, this is one reason the decade became known as the "Roaring Twenties."

In the 1930s and 1940s, the Great Depression and World War II slowed the rate of change. But in the postwar period, after 1945, Alfred Kinsey set the stage for what later came to be known as the *sexual revolution*. Kinsey and his colleagues published their first study of sexuality in the United States in 1948, and it raised eyebrows everywhere. It was not so much what Kinsey said about sexual behavior—although he did present some startling results—as simply the fact that

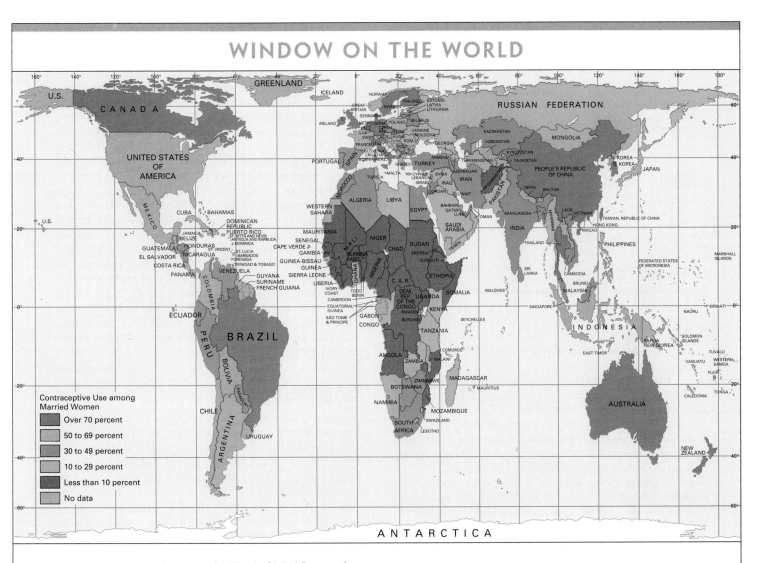

GLOBAL MAP 9–1 Contraceptive Use in Global Perspective

The map shows the percentage of married women using modern contraception methods (such as barrier methods, contraceptive pill, implants, injectables, intrauterine contraceptive devices [IUDs], or sterilization). In general, how do high-income nations differ from low-income nations? Can you explain this difference?

Source: Data from Mackay (2000).

Contraceptive Use among Married Women
- Over 70 percent
- 50 to 69 percent
- 30 to 49 percent
- 10 to 29 percent
- Less than 10 percent
- No data

THE SEXUAL COUNTERREVOLUTION

The sexual revolution made sex a topic of everyday discussion and sexual activity more a matter of individual choice. But given that U.S. society has always been of two minds about sex, the sexual revolution was also controversial. By 1980, the climate of sexual freedom that had marked the late 1960s and 1970s was criticized by some as evidence of our country's moral decline. Add to this fact the increasing fears about sexually transmitted diseases (STDs)—especially the beginning of the AIDS epidemic—and

TABLE 9–1 How We View Premarital and Extramarital Sex

Survey Question: "There's been a lot of discussion about the way morals and attitudes about sex are changing in this country. If a man and a woman have sexual relations before marriage, do you think it is always wrong, almost always wrong, wrong only sometimes, or not wrong at all? What about a married person having sexual relations with someone other than the marriage partner?"

	Premarital Sex	Extramarital Sex
"Always wrong"	26.7%	78.5%
"Almost always wrong"	8.0	13.4
"Wrong only sometimes"	19.4	4.2
"Not wrong at all"	43.4	2.1
"Don't know"/No answer	2.5	1.8

Source: *General Social Surveys, 1972–2002: Cumulative Codebook* (Chicago: National Opinion Research Center, 2003), pp. 233–34.

the stage was set for the beginning of the *sexual counterrevolution.*

Politically speaking, the sexual counterrevolution was a conservative call for a return to "family values," replacing sexual freedom with sexual responsibility. In practice, this turnaround meant moving sex back within marriage. Critics objected not just to the idea of "free love" but to trends such as cohabitation (living together) and having children out of wedlock.

Looking back, we can see that the sexual counterrevolution did not greatly change the idea that individuals should decide for themselves when and with whom to have a sexual relationship. But whether for moral reasons or concerns about STDs, more people began choosing to limit their number of sexual partners or to abstain from sex entirely.

PREMARITAL SEX

In light of the sexual revolution and the sexual counterrevolution, how much has sexual behavior in the United States really changed? One interesting trend involves premarital sex, that is, the likelihood that young people will have sexual intercourse before marriage.

Consider, first, what U.S. adults *say* about premarital intercourse. Table 9–1 shows that about 35 percent characterize sexual relations before marriage as "always wrong" or "almost always wrong."

Another 19 percent consider premarital sex "wrong only sometimes," and 43 percent say premarital sex is "not wrong at all." Public opinion is much more accepting of premarital sex today than a generation ago, but even so, our society remains divided on this issue.

Now consider what young people *do* regarding premarital intercourse. For women, there has been a marked change over time. The Kinsey studies (1948, 1953; see also Laumann et al., 1994) reported that among people born in the early 1900s, about 50 percent of men but just 6 percent of women had had premarital sexual intercourse before age nineteen. Studies of baby boomers, born after World War II, show a slight increase in premarital intercourse among men and a large increase—to about one-third—among women. The most recent studies, targeting men and women born in the 1970s, show that 76 percent of men and 66 percent of women had had premarital sexual intercourse by their senior year in high school (Laumann et al., 1994:323–24). Thus, although general public attitudes remain divided on premarital sex, this behavior is broadly accepted among young people today.

SEX BETWEEN ADULTS

To hear the mass media tell it, people in the United States are very active sexually. But do popular images reflect reality? The Laumann study (1994) found that frequency of sexual activity varied widely in the U.S. population. The patterns breaks down this way: One-third of adults report having sex with a partner a few times a year or not at all; another one-third have sex once or several times a month; the remaining one-third have sex with a partner two or more times a week. In short, no single stereotype accurately describes sexual activity in the United States.

Moreover, despite the widespread image of "swinging singles," it is married people who have sex with partners the most. In addition, married people report the highest level of satisfaction—both emotional and physical—with their partners (Laumann et al., 1994).

EXTRAMARITAL SEX

What about married people having sex with someone other than their marriage partner? What people commonly call "adultery" (sociologists prefer a less emotionally loaded term like "extramarital sex") is widely condemned. Table 9–1 shows that more than 90 percent of U.S. adults consider a married person having sex with someone other than the marital partner "always wrong" or "almost always wrong." The norm of sexual fidelity within marriage has been and remains a strong element of U.S. culture.

But in terms of behavior, the cultural ideal often differs from real life. It probably comes as no surprise that extramarital sexual activity is more common than people say it should be. At the same time, extramarital sex is not as frequent as many believe. The Laumann study reports that about 25 percent of married men and 10 percent of married women have had at least one extramarital sexual experience. Or the other way around: 75 percent of men and 90 percent of women remain sexually faithful to their partners throughout their married lives (Laumann et al., 1994:214; NORC, 2003:1227).

SEXUAL ORIENTATION

Over recent decades, public opinion about sexual orientation has shown a remarkable change. **Sexual orientation** is *a person's romantic and emotional attraction to another person.* The norm in all human societies is **heterosexuality** (*hetero* is a Greek word meaning "the other of two"), meaning *sexual attraction to someone of the other sex.* Yet, in every society, a significant share of people favor **homosexuality** (*homo* is the Greek word for "the same"), *sexual attraction to someone of the same sex.* When thinking about these categories, keep in mind that homosexuality and heterosexuality are not mutually exclusive. That is, people do not necessarily fall into one category or the other, but may have both sexual orientations to varying degrees.

The fact that sexual orientation is not clear-cut points to the importance of a third category: **bisexuality,** that is, *sexual attraction to people of both sexes.* Some bisexual people are equally attracted to males and females; many others, however, are more attracted to one sex than the other. Finally, one additional sexual orientation is **asexuality,** meaning *no sexual attraction to people of either sex.* Figure 9–2 describes each of these sexual orientations in relation to the others.

It is also important to note that sexual *attraction* is not the same thing as sexual *behavior.* Many people, no doubt, have experienced attraction to someone of the same sex, but fewer ever experience same-sex behavior, in large part because of cultural constraints on our actions.

Cultural systems do not accept all sexual orientations equally. In the United States and around the world, heterosexuality is the norm because, biologically

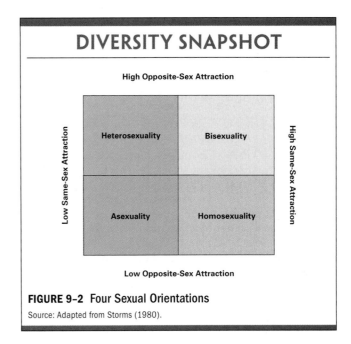

FIGURE 9–2 Four Sexual Orientations
Source: Adapted from Storms (1980).

speaking, heterosexual relations permit human reproduction. Even so, most societies tolerate homosexuality. In fact, among the ancient Greeks, upper-class men considered homosexuality the highest form of relationship, partly because they looked down on women as intellectually inferior. As men saw it, heterosexuality was necessary only so they could have children, and "real" men preferred homosexual relations (Kluckhohn, 1948; Ford & Beach, 1951; Greenberg, 1988).

WHAT GIVES US A SEXUAL ORIENTATION?

The question of *how* people come to have a sexual orientation in the first place is vigorously debated. But the arguments cluster into two general positions: first, that sexual orientation is a product of society, and second, that sexual orientation is a product of biology.

Sexual Orientation: A Product of Society

This approach argues that people in any society construct a set of meanings that lets them make sense of sexuality. Understandings of sexuality, therefore, differ from place to place and over time. For example, Michel Foucault (1990; orig. 1978) points out that there was no distinct category of people called "homosexuals" until the late nineteenth century, when scientists and, eventually, the public as a whole began labeling people that way. Through most of history, in other words, some people no doubt had what we would call "homosexual experiences." But neither they nor others saw in this behavior the basis for any special identity.

Anthropologists provide further evidence that sexual orientation is socially constructed. Studies show that various kinds of homosexuality exist in different societies. In Siberia, for example, the Chukchee Eskimo have a ritual practice in which one man dresses like a female and does a woman's work. In Tahitian culture, a "mahu" is a woman who takes on a transgendered role in which she displays both feminine and masculine sexual behavior. The Sambia, who dwell in the Eastern Highlands of New Guinea, have a ritual in which young boys perform oral sex on older men in the belief that ingesting semen will enhance their masculinity. The existence of such diverse patterns around the world points to the fact that sexual orientation and sexual expression have much to do with society itself (Herdt, 1993; Murray & Roscoe, 1998; Blackwood & Wieringa, 1999).

Finally, some studies conducted by sociologists support the position that sexual orientation is rooted in socialization. One recent study of opposite-sex twins (one girl and one boy), for example, linked a higher rate of homosexual orientation to being raised in a gender-neutral environment as opposed to a conventional pattern of raising boys to be masculine and girls to be feminine. Another clue to the importance of socialization was the fact that same-sex twins who had an older sibling—one who served as a gender role model for the twins—had a much lower rate of homosexual orientation (Bearman & Bruckner, 2002).

Sexual Orientation: A Product of Biology

A growing body of evidence suggests that sexual orientation is innate, that is, rooted in human biology in much the same way that people are born right-handed or left-handed. Arguing this position, Simon LeVay (1993) links sexual orientation to the structure of the human brain. LeVay studied the brains of both homosexual and heterosexual men and found a small but important difference in the size of the hypothalamus, a part of the brain that regulates hormones. Such an anatomical difference, some claim, plays a part in shaping sexual orientation.

Genetics, too, may influence sexual orientation. One study of forty-four pairs of brothers—all homosexual—found that thirty-three pairs had a distinctive genetic pattern involving the X chromosome. Moreover, the gay brothers had an unusually high number of gay male relatives—but only on their mother's side, the source of the X chromosome. Such evidence leads some researchers to think there may be a "gay gene" (Hamer & Copeland, 1994).

Critical evaluation. Mounting evidence supports the conclusion that sexual orientation is rooted in biology, although it is likely that society as well as biology plays a part in guiding sexual orientation (Gladue, Green, & Hellman, 1984; Weinrich, 1987; Troiden, 1988; Isay, 1989; Puterbaugh, 1990; Angier, 1992; Gelman, 1992). Further, we must bear in mind that sexual orientation is not a matter of neat categories. That is, most people who think of themselves as homosexual have had some heterosexual experiences, just as many people who think of themselves as heterosexual have had some homosexual experiences. Thus, the task of explaining sexual orientation is extremely complex.

There is also a political issue here with great importance for gay men and lesbians. To the extent that sexual orientation is based in biology, homosexuality is not a matter of choice any more than, say, skin color. If this is so, shouldn't gay men and lesbians expect the same legal protection from discrimination as African Americans? (Herek, 1991)

HOW MANY GAY PEOPLE?

What share of the U.S. population is gay? This is a difficult question to answer because, as we have explained, sexual orientation not a matter of neat categories. Moreover, people are not always willing to reveal their sexuality to strangers or even to family members. Pioneering sex researcher Alfred Kinsey (1948, 1953) estimated that about 4 percent of males and 2 percent of females have an exclusively same-sex orientation, although he estimated that at least one-third of men and one-eighth of women have had at least one homosexual experience leading to orgasm.

The American Psychological Association posts answers to commonly asked questions regarding sexual orientation at http://www.apa.org/pubinfo/answers.html

In light of the Kinsey studies, many social scientists put the gay share of the population at 10 percent. But a more recent national survey of sexuality in the United States indicates that how one operationalizes "homosexuality" makes a big difference in the results (Laumann et al., 1994; Tarmann, 2002). As part (a) of Figure 9–3 shows, about 9 percent of U.S. men and about 4 percent of U.S. women aged between eighteen and fifty-nine reported homosexual activity *at some time* in their lives. The second set of numbers shows that, in most cases, these experiences occur before puberty only. Finally, the figures for those claiming a homosexual identity—2.8 percent for men and 1.4 percent for women—are similar.

Finally, Kinsey treated sexual orientation as an "either/or" trait: To be more homosexual was, by definition, to be less heterosexual. But same-sex and other-sex attractions can operate independently (as shown back in Figure 9–2). Bisexual people feel a strong attraction to people of both sexes; by contrast, asexual people experience little sexual attraction to people of either sex.

In the national survey noted above, less than 1 percent of adults described themselves as bisexual. But bisexual experiences appear to be fairly common (at least for a time) among younger people, especially on college campuses (Laumann et al., 1994; Leland, 1995). Many bisexuals, then, do not think of themselves as either gay or straight, and their behavior reflects elements of both gay and straight living.

THE GAY RIGHTS MOVEMENT

In recent decades, the public attitude toward homosexuality has been moving toward greater acceptance (Loftus, 2001). In 1973, as shown in part (b) of Figure 9–3, about three-fourths of U.S. adults claimed homosexual relations were "always wrong" or "almost always wrong." Although that percentage changed little during the 1970s and 1980s, by 2002 it dropped to less than 60 percent (NORC, 2003:234).

In large measure, this change came about through the gay rights movement that arose in the middle of the twentieth century (Chauncey, 1994). At that time, most people did not discuss homosexuality, and it was common for companies (including the federal government and the armed forces) to fire anyone suspected of being gay. Mental health professionals, too, took a hard line, describing homosexuals as having a sexual disorder, sometimes placing them in mental hospitals, where, presumably, they might be cured.

In this climate of intolerance, most lesbians and gay men remained "in the closet"—closely guarding the secret of their sexual orientation. But the gay rights movement gained strength during the 1960s.

FIGURE 9-3 Sexual Orientation in the United States: Survey Data

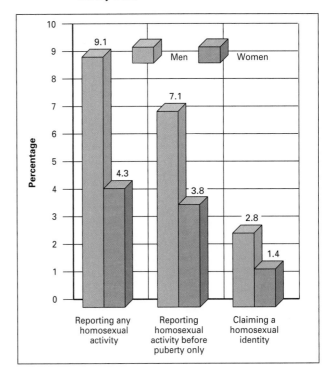

(a) How Many Gay People?

Source: Adapted from Laumann et al. (1994).

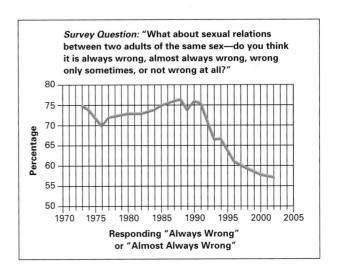

(b) Attitudes toward Homosexual Relations, 1973–2002

Source: NORC (2003).

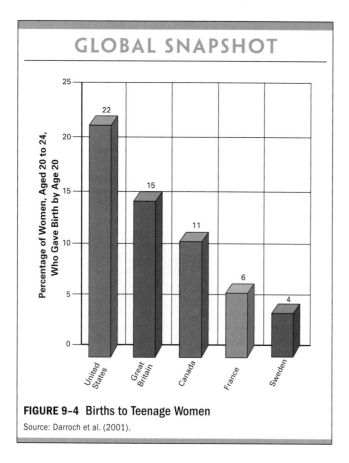

GLOBAL SNAPSHOT

FIGURE 9–4 Births to Teenage Women

Source: Darroch et al. (2001).

TEEN PREGNANCY

Surveys indicate that more than 1 million U.S. teens become pregnant each year, and most of them did not intend to. Being sexually active—especially having intercourse—demands a high level of responsibility, since pregnancy can result. Teenagers may be biologically mature, but many are not emotionally mature and may not appreciate all the consequences of their actions. As Figure 9–4 shows, this country's teen birth rate is well above that of other high-income countries.

For young women of all racial and ethnic categories, both weak families and low income sharply raise the risk of becoming sexually active and having an unplanned child. The opposite is also true: Having an unplanned child raises the risk that a young woman (and sometimes the young father-to-be) will face numerous disadvantages, including not finishing school and becoming poor (Alan Guttmacher Institute, 2002).

Did the sexual revolution raise the level of teenage pregnancy? Surprisingly, perhaps, the answer is no. The rate in 1950 was actually much higher than the rate today, but the reason is that people married younger at that time and many married as teens. In fact, many pregnancies led to quick marriages. As a result, there was a high number of pregnant teenagers, but almost 90 percent were married. Today, by contrast, the number of pregnant teens has fallen, but

 Read a new report from the Alan Guttmacher Institute on trends in teenage sex and pregnancy: http://www. agi-usa.org/pubs/ib_1-02.pdf

about 80 percent of today's cases are women who are not married. In a slight majority (57 percent) of today's teen pregnancies, these women keep their babies; in the remainder, they have abortions (29 percent) or miscarriages (14 percent) (Henshaw, 2001; Alan Guttmacher Institute, 2003). National Map 9–2 shows pregnancy rates for women between the ages of fifteen and nineteen in the United States.

Concern about the high rate of teenage pregnancy has led to sex education programs in schools. But such programs are controversial, as the box on page 234 explains.

PORNOGRAPHY

In general terms, **pornography** is *sexually explicit material that causes sexual arousal*. But what, exactly, is or is not pornographic has long been a matter of debate. Recognizing that people have different attitudes about

One early milestone occurred in 1973, when the American Psychiatric Association declared that homosexuality was not an illness but simply "a form of sexual behavior."

Gay rights activists also began using the term **homophobia** to describe *the dread of close personal interaction with people thought to be gay, lesbian, or bisexual* (Weinberg, 1973). The concept of homophobia (literally, "fear of sameness") turns the tables on society: Instead of asking "What's wrong with gay people?" the question becomes "What's wrong with people who can't accept those with a different sexual orientation?"

SEXUAL ISSUES AND CONTROVERSIES

Sexuality lies at the heart of a number of controversies in the United States. Here we take a look at four public issues: teen pregnancy, pornography, prostitution, and sexual violence.

SEEING OURSELVES

NATIONAL MAP 9–2
Teenage Pregnancy Rates across the United States

The map shows pregnancy rates for 1997 for women aged fifteen to nineteen. In what regions of the country are rates high? Where are they low? What explanation can you offer for these patterns?

Source: U.S. Centers for Disease Control and Prevention (2000).

Pregnancies per 1,000 Women Aged 15 to 19

Above average
Average
Below average

the portrayal of sexuality, the U.S. Supreme Court gives local communities the power to decide for themselves what violates "community standards" of decency and lacks any redeeming social value.

Definitions aside, pornography is surely popular in the United States: X-rated videos, telephone "sex lines," and a host of sexually explicit movies and magazines together constitute roughly a $10-billion-a-year industry. That figure is rising rapidly as people find more pornography at more and more Web sites—now estimated to be in the hundreds of thousands—on the Internet.

Traditionally, people have criticized pornography on *moral* grounds. As national surveys confirm, 60 percent of U.S. adults are concerned that "sexual materials lead to a breakdown of morals" (NORC, 2003:235). Today, however, pornography is also seen as a *power* issue because it so often depicts women as the sexual playthings of men.

Some critics also see pornography as a cause of violence against women. While it is difficult to document a scientific cause-and-effect relationship between what people view and how they act, research does support the idea that pornography makes men think of women as objects rather than as people. The public shares a concern about pornography and violence, with almost half of adults holding the opinion

that pornography encourages people to commit rape (NORC, 2003:235).

People everywhere object to sexual material they find offensive, but many also value free speech and want to protect artistic expression. Nevertheless, pressure to restrict pornography is building from an unlikely coalition of conservatives (who oppose pornography on moral grounds) and progressives (who condemn it for political reasons).

PROSTITUTION

Prostitution is *the selling of sexual services*. Often called "the world's oldest profession," prostitution has always been widespread, and about one in five adult men in the United States reports having paid for sex at some time (NORC, 2003:1226). Even so, to the extent that people think of sex as an expression of interpersonal intimacy, they find the idea of sex for money disturbing. As a result, prostitution is against the law everywhere in the United States except for parts of Nevada.

Around the world, prostitution is greatest in poor countries, where patriarchy is strong and traditional cultural norms limit women's ability to earn a living. Global Map 9–2 on page 235 shows where in the world prostitution is most widespread.

CRITICAL THINKING

Sex Education: Solution or Problem?

Most schools today have sex education programs that teach the basics of sexuality. Instructors explain to young people how their bodies grow and change, how reproduction occurs, and how to avoid pregnancy by using birth control or abstaining from sex.

Half of U.S. teenage boys report having sex by the time they reach sixteen, and half of girls report doing so by seventeen. These numbers are much the same in most high-income nations; what accounts for the higher U.S. teen pregnancy rate is less use of contraceptives. "Sex ed" programs, then, seem to make sense. But critics point out that as the number of sex education programs has expanded, the level of teenage sexual activity has actually gone *up*. This trend seems to suggest that sex education may not be discouraging sex

among youngsters and, maybe, that learning more about sex encourages young people to become sexually active sooner. Critics also say that it is parents who should be instructing their children about sex, since, unlike teachers, parents can also teach their beliefs about what is right and wrong.

But supporters of sex education counter that research does not support the conclusion that sex education makes young people more sexually active. More generally, they argue that it is the larger culture—one that celebrates sexuality—that encourages children to become sexually active. If this is the case, the sensible strategy is to ensure that they understand what they are doing and take reasonable precautions to protect themselves from unwanted pregnancy and sexually transmitted diseases.

What do you think?

1. *Schools can teach the facts about sexuality. But do you think they can address the emotional issues that often accompany sex? What about the moral issues? Why or why not?*

2. *What about parents? Are they doing their job in instructing children about sex? Ask members of your class how many received instruction in sexual matters from their parents.*

3. *Overall, do you think young people know too little about sexuality? Do you think they know too much? What specific changes would you suggest to address the problem of unwanted pregnancy among teens?*

Sources: Stodghill (1998), the Alan Guttmacher Institute (2001), and Voss & Kogan (2001).

Types of Prostitution

While most prostitutes (many prefer the morally neutral term "sex workers") are women, they fall into different categories. *Call girls* are elite prostitutes, typically women who are young, attractive, and well educated and who arrange their own "dates" with clients by telephone. The classified pages of any large city newspaper contain numerous ads for "escort services," by which women (and a much smaller number of men) offer both companionship and sex for a fee.

Sex workers in a middle category are employed in "massage parlors" or brothels under the control of managers. These people have less choice about their clients, receive less money for their services, and get to keep no more than half of what they make.

At the bottom of the sex-worker hierarchy are *street walkers*, women and men who "work the streets" of large cities. Female street walkers are often under the control of male pimps who take most of their earnings.

Street walkers are at the highest risk of violence from pimps and clients. In addition, many of the people selling sex on the street are children, about one-third of whom have experienced sexual abuse at home (Davidson, 1998; Estes, 2001).

Most, but not all, prostitutes offer heterosexual services. Gay prostitutes also trade sex for money. Researchers report that many gay prostitutes have suffered rejection by family and friends because of their sexual orientation (Weisberg, 1985; Boyer, 1989; Kruks, 1991).

A Victimless Crime?

Prostitution is against the law almost everywhere in the United States, but many people consider it a victimless crime (see Chapter 8, "Deviance"). Thus, instead of enforcing prostitution laws all the time, police stage occasional crackdowns. Our society seems to want to control prostitution while assuming that nothing will completely eliminate it.

WINDOW ON THE WORLD

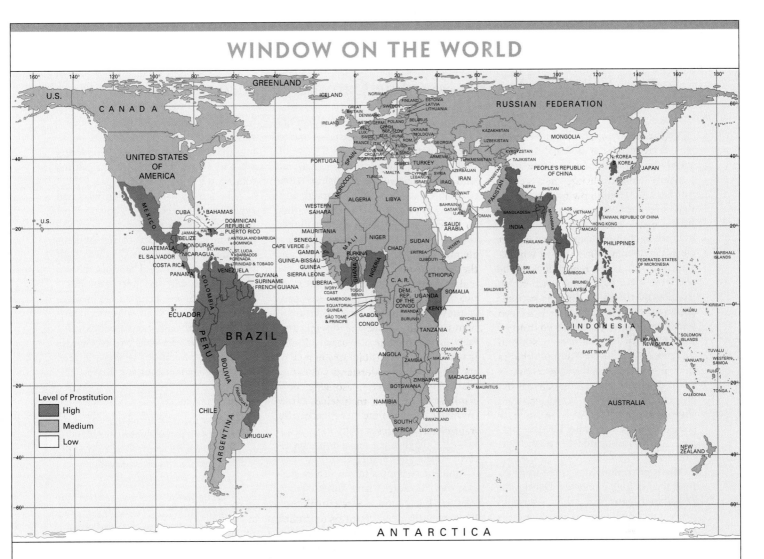

GLOBAL MAP 9–2 Prostitution in Global Perspective

Generally speaking, prostitution is widespread in societies where women have low standing. Officially, at least, the People's Republic of China boasts of gender equality, including the elimination of "vice" such as prostitution, which oppresses women. By contrast, in much of Latin America, where patriarchy is strong, prostitution is common. In many Islamic societies patriarchy is also strong, but religion is a counterbalance, so prostitution is limited. Western, high-income nations have a moderate amount of prostitution.

Sources: *Peters Atlas of the World* (1990) and Mackay (2000).

Is selling sex a victimless crime that hurts no one? Certainly, many people who take a "live-and-let-live" attitude about prostitution would say it is. But this view overlooks the fact that prostitution subjects many women to abuse and outright violence and plays a part in spreading sexually transmitted diseases, including AIDS. In addition, many poor women become trapped in a life of selling sex, generally to the benefit of others, while they put their own lives at risk.

CRITICAL THINKING

When Sex Is Only Sex: The Campus Culture of "Hooking Up"

Have you ever been in a sexual situation and not been sure of the right thing to do? What are the social norms on campus for sexual relationships? Most colleges and universities have initiated awareness programs that highlight two important rules. First, sexual activity must take place only when both participants have given clear statements of consent. The consent principle is what separates having sex from date rape. Second, no one should knowingly expose another person to a sexually transmitted disease, especially when the partner is unaware of the danger.

These rules are very important; yet they say little about the larger issue of what sex *means*. For example, when is it appropriate to have a sexual relationship? Does agreeing to have sex with someone mean you really like that person? Are you obligated to see the person again?

Two generations ago, there were informal rules for campus sex. Dating was considered part of the courtship process in which women and men evaluated each other as possible marriage partners, while they sharpened their own sense of what they wanted in a mate. Because, on average, marriage took place at a younger age, a number of college students became engaged and married while they were still in school. Having "honorable intentions" meant

that one's engaging in sex was a sign of a serious—potentially marital—interest in the other person.

Of course, not all sexual activity fell under the umbrella of courtship. A fair share of men (and some women, too) have always looked for sex where they could find it. But in an era that linked sex and courtship, it was easy to understand how casual sex could lead to one partner feeling "used."

Today, the sexual culture of the campus is very different. Partly because people now marry much later, the culture of courtship has largely disappeared. About three-fourths of women in a recent national survey point to a new campus pattern—the culture of "hooking up." What exactly is "hooking up"? Most describe it in words like these: "When a girl and a guy get together for a physical encounter—anything from kissing to having sex—and don't necessarily expect anything further."

Student responses to the survey suggest that "hookups" have three characteristics. First, most couples who hook up know little about each other. Second, a typical hookup involves people who have been drinking alcohol, usually at a campus party. Third, most women are critical of the culture of hooking up and express little satisfaction with these encounters. Certainly, some people who hook up simply walk away, happy to have enjoyed a sexual experience free of

further obligation. But given the powerful emotions that sex can unleash, hooking up often leaves someone wondering what to expect next: "Will you call me tomorrow?" "Will I see you again?"

The survey asked women who had experienced a recent hookup to report how they felt—a day later—about the experience. A majority of respondents said they felt "awkward," about half felt "disappointed" and "confused," and one in four said she felt "exploited." Clearly, for many people, sex involves something more than a physical encounter. Further, because today's campus climate is very sensitive to charges of sexual exploitation, is there a need for clearer standards of fair play?

What do you think?

1. *To what extent is the pattern of hooking up found on your campus? Are you aware of differences between heterosexual and homosexual encounters in this regard?*

2. *What do you see as the advantages of sex without commitment? What are the disadvantages of this kind of relationship?*

3. *Do you think college students need more guidance about sexual issues? If so, who should provide this guidance?*

Source: Based, in part, on Marquardt & Glenn (2001).

SEXUAL VIOLENCE AND ABUSE

Ideally, sexual activity occurs within a loving relationship; in reality, however, sex can be twisted by hate and violence. Sexual violence, which ranges from verbal abuse to rape and physical assault, is widespread in the United States.

Rape

Although some people think rape is a form of sex, it is actually an expression of power—a violent act that uses sex to hurt, humiliate, or control another person. The U.S. Federal Bureau of Investigation reports that about 90,000 women are raped each year. This number reflects only the reported cases, and the actual number of rapes is almost certainly several times higher than that (U.S. Federal Bureau of Investigation, 2002).

The official definition of rape, according to the federal government, is "the carnal knowledge of a female forcibly and against her will." Thus, official rape statistics include only victims who are women. But men, too, are raped—in perhaps 10 percent of all cases. A small number of cases are reported each year involving men who are raped by women, but most men are raped by other men. The offenders typically are not homosexual: They are heterosexuals who are motivated by a desire not for sex but to dominate another person (Groth & Birnbaum, 1979; Gibbs, 1991a).

Date Rape

A common myth is that rape involves strangers. In reality, however, only about 5 percent of rapes fit this pattern. On the contrary, almost 95 percent of rapes involve people who know one another—more often than not, pretty well—and these crimes usually take place in familiar surroundings, especially the home. For this reason, the term "date rape" or "acquaintance rape" refers to forcible sexual violence against women by men they know (Laumann et al., 1994).

A second misconception linked to date rape is the notion that a woman who has been raped must have done something to encourage the man and make him think she wanted to have sex. Perhaps the victim agreed to go out with the offender. Maybe she even invited him into her room. But of course, acting in this way no more justifies rape than it would any other kind of physical assault.

Although rape is a physical assault, it often leaves emotional and psychological scars. Beyond the brutality of being physically violated, rape by an acquaintance also undermines a victim's sense of trust. Psychological scars are especially serious among the half of rape victims who are under eighteen; one-third of these young victims are attacked by their own fathers or stepfathers (Greenfield, 1996).

How common is date rape? In a recent study of high school girls in the United States, 20 percent of those surveyed reported being the victim of sexual or physical violence inflicted by a boy she was dating (Dickinson, 2001).

Nowhere has the issue of date rape been more widely discussed than on college campuses, where the problem is even greater. The collegiate environment

A lot of campus rapes start here.

Whenever there's drinking or drugs, things can get out of hand. So it's no surprise that many campus rapes involve alcohol. But you should know that under any circumstances, sex without the other person's consent is considered rape. A felony, punishable by prison. And drinking is no excuse.

That's why, when you party, it's good to know what your limits are. You see, a little sobering thought now can save you from a big problem later.

© 1990 Rape Treatment Center, Santa Monica Hospital

Experts agree that one factor that contributes to the problem of sexual violence on the college campus is the widespread use of alcoholic beverages. What policies are in force on your campus to discourage the kind of drinking that leads to one person imposing sex on another?

promotes easy friendships and encourages trust among young people who have much to learn about relationships and about themselves. Yet, as the box explains, while college life encourages communication, it also provides few social norms that help guide the young people's sexual experiences. Not surprisingly, then, the campus also invites sexual violence.

 A government report on the sexual victimization of college women is available at http://www.ojp.usdoj.gov/bjs/abstract/svcw.htm

To counter the problem, many schools now actively address the issue of rape. In addition, greater attention is now focused on the use of alcohol, which increases the likelihood of sexual violence.

THEORETICAL ANALYSIS OF SEXUALITY

We can better understand how society influences human sexuality by using sociology's various theoretical paradigms. In the following sections, we apply the three major paradigms in turn.

STRUCTURAL-FUNCTIONAL ANALYSIS

The structural-functional approach highlights the contribution of any social pattern to the overall operation of society. Because sexuality is an important dimension of social life, society regulates sexual behavior.

The Need to Regulate Sexuality

From a biological point of view, sex allows our species to reproduce. But culture and social institutions regulate *with whom* and *when* people reproduce. For example, most societies condemn married people for having sex with someone other than their spouse. To do otherwise—to give the forces of sexual passion free rein—would threaten family life and, especially, the raising of children.

Another example, discussed earlier in this chapter, is the incest taboo. The fact that this norm exists everywhere clearly shows that no society permits completely free choice in sexual partners. Reproduction by family members other than married partners would break down the system of kinship and muddle relationships among people.

Historically, the social control of sexuality was strong, mostly because sex commonly led to childbirth. Moreover, offspring, as well as parents, were subject to these controls. We see this in the traditional distinction between "legitimate" reproduction (within marriage) and "illegitimate" reproduction (outside marriage). But once a society devises the means to effectively control births, its norms become more permissive. This occurred in the United States, where, over the course of the twentieth century, sex moved beyond its basic reproductive function and became accepted as a form of intimacy and even recreation (Giddens, 1992).

Latent Functions: The Case of Prostitution

It is easy to see that prostitution is harmful because it spreads disease and exploits women. But are there latent functions that help explain why prostitution is so widespread? Definitely, explains Kingsley Davis (1971): Prostitution performs several useful functions.

Prostitution is one way to meet the sexual needs of a large number of people who do not have ready access to sex, including soldiers, travelers, and people who are not physically attractive, or who have trouble establishing relationships. Moreover, adds Davis, the availability of this kind of sex on demand may even help to stabilize some strong but loveless marriages that might otherwise collapse. Then, too, some people favor prostitution because they want sex without the "trouble" of a relationship. As one analyst put it, "Men don't pay for sex, they pay to leave" (Miracle, Miracle, & Baumeister, 2003:421).

Critical evaluation. The structural-functional paradigm helps us to appreciate the important part sexuality plays in how society is organized. The incest taboo and other cultural norms also suggest that society has always paid attention to who has sex with whom and, especially, who reproduces with whom.

At the same time, this approach overlooks the great diversity of sexual ideas and practices found within every society. Moreover, sexual patterns change over time, just as they differ in remarkable ways around the world. To appreciate the varied and changeable character of sexuality, we turn to the symbolic-interaction paradigm.

SYMBOLIC-INTERACTION ANALYSIS

The symbolic-interaction paradigm highlights how, as people interact, they construct everyday reality. As Chapter 6 ("Social Interaction in Everyday Life") explains, the process of reality construction is highly variable, so that one group's or society's views of sexuality may well differ from another's. In the same way, how people understand sexuality can and does change over time.

The Social Construction of Sexuality

Almost all social patterns involving sexuality saw considerable change over the course of the twentieth century. One good illustration is the changing importance of virginity. A century ago, our society's norm—for women, at least—was virginity before marriage. This norm was strong because, in a society yet to devise effective birth control, virginity was the only assurance a man had that his bride-to-be was not carrying another man's child.

Today, however, we have gone a long way toward separating sex from reproduction, and as a result, the virginity norm has weakened. In the United States, among those born between 1963 and 1974, just 16.3 percent of men and 20.1 percent of women reported being virgins at first marriage (Laumann et al., 1994:503).

Another example of our society's construction of sexuality involves young people. A century ago, childhood was a time of innocence in sexual matters. In recent decades, however, our thinking has changed. Though we expect children will not be sexually active, most people believe children should be educated about sex by the time they are teenagers so that they can make intelligent choices about their sexual behavior.

Global Comparisons

The broader our view, the more variation we see in the meanings people attach to sexuality. One classic study showed that some cultures are far more accepting of childhood sexuality than others. Anthropologist Ruth Benedict (1938), who spent years learning the ways of life of the Melanesian people of southeast New Guinea, reported that adults paid little attention when young children engaged in sexual experimentation with one another. Parents in Melanesia shrugged off such activity because, before puberty, sex cannot lead to reproduction. Is it likely that most parents in the United States would respond the same way?

Sexual practices, too, vary as a part of culture. Male circumcision of infant boys (the practice of removing all or part of the foreskin of the penis) is common in the United States but rare in most other parts of the world. Similarly, female circumcision (the practice of removing the clitoris) is rare in the United States and much of the world but common in parts of Africa and the Middle East (Crosette, 1995; Huffman, 2000). (For more about female circumcision, see the box on page 341.)

Critical evaluation. The strength of the symbolic-interaction paradigm lies in revealing the constructed character of familiar social patterns. Understanding that people "construct" sexuality, we can better appreciate the variety of sexual practices found over the course of history and around the world.

One limitation of this approach, however, is that not everything is so variable. Throughout our own history—and around the world—men are more likely to see women in sexual terms than the other way around. If this pattern is widespread, some broader social structure must be at work, as we shall see in the next section.

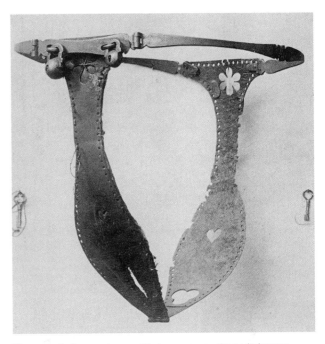

The control of women's sexuality is a common theme in human history. During the Middle Ages, Europeans devised the "chastity belt"—a metal device locked about a woman's groin that prevented sexual intercourse (and probably interfered with other bodily functions as well). While such devices are all but unknown today, the social control of sexuality continues. Can you point to examples?

SOCIAL-CONFLICT ANALYSIS

The social-conflict paradigm highlights dimensions of inequality. This approach, therefore, shows how sexuality both reflects patterns of social inequality and also helps create them.

Sexuality: Reflecting Social Inequality

Recall our discussion of prostitution, a practice outlawed almost everywhere in the United States. Even so, enforcement of these laws is uneven at best, especially when it comes to who is and is not likely to be arrested. Although two parties are involved, the record shows that police are far more likely to arrest (less powerful) female prostitutes than (more powerful) male clients. Similarly, of all women engaged in prostitution, it is street walkers—women with the least income and those most likely to be minorities—who face the highest risk of arrest (COYOTE, 2000). Then, too, we might wonder whether so many women

The Abortion Controversy

A black van pulls up in front of the storefront in a busy section of the city. Two women get out of the front seat and cautiously scan the sidewalk. After a moment, one nods to the other and they open the rear door to let a third woman out of the van. Standing to the right and left of their charge, the two quickly whisk her inside the building.

Is this a description of two federal marshals escorting a convict to a police station? It might be. But it is actually an account of two clinic workers escorting a woman who has decided to have an abortion. Why are they so cautious? Anyone who has read the papers in recent years knows about the heated confrontations at abortion clinics across North America. In fact, some opponents have even targeted and killed several doctors who perform abortions. Overall, the 862,000 abortions performed each year make this probably the most hotly contested issue in the United States today.

Abortion has not always been so controversial. During the colonial era, midwives and other healers performed abortions with little community opposition and with full approval of the law. But controversy arose about 1850, when early medical doctors sought to eliminate the competition they faced from midwives and other traditional health providers, whose income was derived largely from terminating pregnancies. By 1900, medical doctors had succeeded in getting every state to pass a law banning abortion.

Such laws did not end abortions, but the number of abortions fell dramatically. In addition, these laws drove abortion "underground," so that many women—especially those who were poor—had little choice but to seek help from unlicensed "back-alley" abortionists, sometimes with tragic results.

By the 1960s, opposition to abortion laws was rising. In 1973, the U.S. Supreme Court rendered a landmark decision (in the cases of *Roe* v. *Wade* and *Doe* v. *Bolton*), striking down all state laws banning abortion. In effect, this action established a woman's legal access to abortion.

In the wake of the Court's decision, the abortion controversy has grown.

On one side of the issue are people who describe themselves as "pro-choice," supporting a woman's right to choose abortion. On the other side are those who call themselves "pro-life," opposing abortion as morally wrong; these people would like to see the Supreme Court reverse its 1973 decision.

How strong is the support for each side of the abortion controversy? A recent national survey asked a sample of adults the question "Should it be possible for a pregnant woman to obtain a legal abortion if the woman wants it for any reason?" In response, 41.9 percent said "yes" (placing them in the pro-choice camp) and 55.5 percent said "no" (the pro-life position); the remaining 2.6 percent offered no opinion (NORC, 2003:227).

A closer look, however, shows that particular circumstances make a big difference in how people see this issue. The figure shows that a large majority of U.S. adults favor legal abortion if a pregnancy seriously threatens a woman's health, if she became pregnant as a result of rape, or if a fetus is likely to have a serious defect. The bottom line, then,

would be involved in prostitution at all if they had economic opportunities equal to those of men.

Sexuality: Creating Social Inequality

Social-conflict theorists, especially feminists, point to sexuality as being at the root of inequality between women and men. How can this be? Defining women in sexual terms amounts to devaluing them from full human beings into objects of men's interest and attention. Is it any wonder that the word "pornography" comes from the Greek word *porne*, meaning "a man's sexual slave"?

If men define women in sexual terms, it is easy to see why many people consider pornography—almost all of which is consumed by males—a power issue. Since pornography typically depicts women seeking to please men, it supports the idea that men have power over women.

Some more radical critics doubt that this element of power can ever be removed from heterosexual relations (Dworkin, 1987). While most social-conflict theorists do not reject heterosexuality entirely, they do agree that sexuality can and does degrade women. Further, critics point out that our culture often depicts sexuality in terms of sport (men "scoring" with

looks like this: About 42 percent support access to abortion under *any* circumstances, but nearly 90 percent support access to abortion under *some* circumstances.

Many pro-life people feel strongly that abortion is nothing more than killing unborn children—some 40 million in the thirty years since 1973. To them, people never have the right to end innocent life in this way. But pro-choice people are no less committed to their position. As they see it, the abortion debate is really about the standing of women in society. Why? For the simple reason that women must have control over their own sexuality. If pregnancy dictates the course of women's lives, women will never be able to compete with men on equal terms, whether it is on campus or in the workplace. Thus, the pro-choice position concludes, women must have access to legal, safe abortion as a necessary condition to women's full participation in society—a position that almost everyone supports.

Continue the debate . . .

1. *The more conservative, pro-life people see abortion as a moral issue, while more liberal, pro-choice people see abortion as a power issue. Can you see a parallel to how conservatives and liberals view the issue of pornography?*

2. *Surveys show that men and women have almost the same opinions about abortion. Does this surprise you? Why?*

3. *Why do you think the abortion controversy is often so bitter? Why has our nation been unable to find a middle ground on which all can agree?*

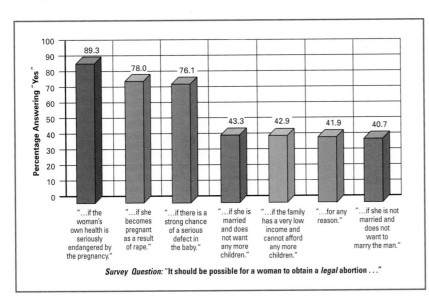

When Should the Law Allow a Woman to Choose Abortion?

Source: NORC (2003).

Sources: Based on Tannahill (1992), NORC (2003), Simon (2003), and various news reports.

women) and also violence ("slamming," "banging," and "hitting on," for example, are verbs used for both fighting and sex).

Queer Theory

Finally, social-conflict theory has taken aim not only at the domination of women by men but also at the domination of homosexuals by heterosexuals. In recent years, just as many lesbians and gay men have come out in search of public acceptance, so have some sociologists tried to add a gay voice to their discipline. The term **queer theory** refers to *a growing body of research findings that challenges the heterosexual bias in U.S. society.*

Queer theory begins with the assertion that our society is characterized by **heterosexism,** *a view stigmatizing anyone who is not heterosexual as "queer."* Our heterosexual culture victimizes a wide range of people, including gay men, lesbians, bisexuals, intersexuals, transsexuals, and even asexual people. Further, although most people agree that bias against women (sexism) and people of color (racism) is wrong, heterosexism is widely tolerated and sometimes well within the law. This country's military forces, for example, would never discharge a soldier simply for being a woman—even a sexually active woman—because that would be a clear case of gender discrimination. But the military forces can discharge her for homosexuality if she is a sexually active lesbian.

Heterosexism also exists at a more subtle level in our everyday understanding of the world. When we describe something as "sexy," for example, don't we really mean attractive to *heterosexuals*?

Critical evaluation. Applying the social-conflict paradigm shows how sexuality is both a cause and an effect of inequality. In particular, this paradigm helps us understand men's power over women and heterosexual people's domination of homosexual people.

At the same time, this approach overlooks the fact that many people do not see sexuality as a power issue. On the contrary, many couples enjoy a vital sexual relationship that deepens their commitment to one another. In addition, the social-conflict paradigm pays little attention to strides U.S. society has made toward eliminating longstanding inequality. Men, in public at least, are less likely to describe women as sex objects than a few decades ago; moreover, rising public concern about sexual harassment (see Chapter 13, "Gender Stratification) has had some effect in reducing expressions of sexuality in the workplace. Likewise, there is ample evidence that the gay rights movement has secured greater opportunities and social acceptance for gay people.

We bring this chapter to a close with a look at what is perhaps the most divisive sexuality issue of all: **abortion,** *the deliberate termination of a pregnancy.* The issue cuts to the heart of almost everyone's sense of justice, as described in the box on pages 240–41.

SUMMARY

1. U.S. culture long defined sex as a taboo topic. The Kinsey studies (1948, 1953) were among the first publications by social scientists on human sexuality.

2. Sex refers to the biological distinction between females and males, which is determined at conception as a male sperm joins a female ovum. Gender is a cultural concept referring to the personal traits and social positions that members of a society attach to being female or male.

3. Males and females are distinguished not only by their genitals (primary sex characteristics) but also by bodily development as they mature (secondary sex characteristics). Intersexual people (also called "hermaphrodites") have some combination of both male and female genitalia. Transsexuals are people who feel they are one sex, although, biologically, they are the other.

4. For most species, sex is rigidly directed by biology; for human beings, sex is a matter of cultural definition as well as personal choice. The variations in patterns of kissing, as well as standards of beauty, around the world reveal the cultural foundation of sexual practices.

5. Historically, U.S. society has held rigid attitudes toward sexuality, although these attitudes have become more permissive over time. Thus, we see that sex is a social, as well as a biological, issue.

6. The sexual revolution, which has roots back in the 1920s but came of age in the 1960s and 1970s, brought a far greater openness in matters of sexuality. Research shows that changes in sexuality were greater for women than for men. By 1980, a sexual counterrevolution was taking form, condemning permissiveness in favor of a return to more conservative "family values" and marked by increasing fear of sexually transmitted diseases.

7. The share of people in the United States who have premarital sexual intercourse increased during the twentieth century. Research shows that about three-fourths of young men and two-thirds of young women have had intercourse by their senior year in high school.

8. The level of sexual activity varies within the population of U.S. adults: One-third report having sex with a partner a few times a year or not at all; another one-third have sex once or several times a month; the remaining one-third have sex with a partner two or more times a week.

9. Although extramarital sex is widely condemned, about 25 percent of married men and 10 percent of married women report being sexually unfaithful to their spouses at some time.

10. Sexual orientation refers to a person's romantic and emotional attraction to another person. Four major orientations are heterosexuality, homosexuality, bisexuality, and asexuality. Sexual orientation reflects both biological and cultural factors.

11. The share of the population that is homosexual depends on how researchers define "homosexuality." About 9 percent of adult men and 4 percent of adult women report having some homosexual experience, compared with 2.8 percent of men and 1.4 percent of women who say they have a homosexual identity.

12. The gay rights movement has worked to gain greater acceptance for gay people. Largely because to this movement, the share of the U.S. population condemning homosexuality as morally wrong has steadily decreased and stands now at about half.

13. Some 1 million teenagers become pregnant each year in the United States. Although the rate of teenage pregnancy has dropped since 1950, more of today's pregnant teens are unmarried and, especially when they drop out of school, are at high risk of poverty.

14. With no universal definition of pornography, the law allows local communities to set standards of decency. Many conservatives condemn pornography as immoral; by contrast, many liberals condemn it as demeaning to women.

15. Prostitution, the selling of sexual services, is illegal almost everywhere in the United States. Although many people think of prostitution as a victimless crime,

others point out that it victimizes women and spreads sexually transmitted diseases.

16. Some 90,000 rapes are reported each year in the United States, but the actual number is several times greater. Although many people think of rape as a sexual act, rape is really a violent expression of power. Most rapes involve people who know one another.

17. Structural-functional theory highlights society's need to regulate sexual activity. A universal norm in this regard is the incest taboo, which keeps kinship relations clear.

18. The symbolic-interaction paradigm points up how people attach various meanings to sexuality. Thus, societies differ from one another in terms of sexual attitudes and practices; similarly, sexual patterns change within any one society over time.

19. Social-conflict theory links sexuality to inequality. From this point of view, men dominate women, in part, by devaluing them as only sexual objects.

KEY CONCEPTS

sex (p. 222) the biological distinction between females and males

primary sex characteristics (p. 223) the genitals, organs used for reproduction

secondary sex characteristics (p. 223) bodily development, apart from the genitals, that distinguishes biologically mature females and males

intersexual people (hermaphrodites) (p. 223) people whose anatomy (including genitals) includes both female and male characteristics

transsexuals (p. 223) people who feel they are one sex even though biologically they are the other

incest taboo (p. 224) a norm forbidding sexual relations or marriage between certain relatives

sexual orientation (p. 229) a person's romantic and emotional attraction to another person

heterosexuality (p. 229) sexual attraction to someone of the other sex

homosexuality (p. 229) sexual attraction to someone of the same sex

bisexuality (p. 229) sexual attraction to people of both sexes

asexuality (p. 229) no sexual attraction to people of either sex

homophobia (p. 232) the dread of close personal interaction with people thought to be gay, lesbian, or bisexual

pornography (p. 232) sexually explicit material that causes sexual arousal

prostitution (p. 233) the selling of sexual services

queer theory (p. 241) a growing body of research findings that challenges the heterosexual bias in U.S. society

heterosexism (p. 241) a view stigmatizing anyone who is not heterosexual as "queer"

abortion (p. 242) the deliberate termination of a pregnancy

CRITICAL-THINKING QUESTIONS

1. What do sociologists mean by the term *sexual revolution*? What did the sexual revolution change? Can you suggest some of the reasons that these changes occurred?

2. What is sexual orientation? Why is this characteristic difficult for researchers to measure?

3. What evidence can you point to supporting the view of U.S. society as permissive about sexuality? In what ways does U.S. society try to control sexuality?

4. What do you think is the most important sexuality related issue facing U.S. society today? Give reasons for your choice.

APPLICATIONS AND EXERCISES

1. The most complete study of sexual patterns in the United States to date is *The Social Organization of Sexuality: Sexual Practices in the United States* by Edward Laumann and others. You can find this book in your campus or community library. Get a copy and browse through some of the chapters most interesting to you. Afterward, think about the value of doing sociological research on sexuality.

2. Contact your school's student services office and ask for information about the extent of sexual violence on your campus. Do school officials think most sexual violence is reported or not? What policies and procedures does your school have to respond to sexual violence?

3. Sex is not always a simple matter of female or male. Do you think that health care policies should cover gender-reassignment surgery for people who want it? Why or why not?

4. Packaged in the back of this new textbook is an interactive CD-ROM that offers a variety of video and interactive review materials intended to help you better understand the material covered in this chapter. For this chapter, the CD-ROM contains a relevant clip from *ABC News*, an author's tip video, interactive map animations, an interactive time line, and flashcards with audio pronunciations of the more difficult words.

 SITES TO SEE

http://www.prenhall.com/macionis

Visit the interactive Companion Website™ that accompanies this text. Begin by clicking on the cover of your book. You will find a chapter-by-chapter study guide, practice tests, suggested Web links, and links to other relevant material.

http://www.teenpregnancy.org

Visit the Web site of the National Campaign to Prevent Teen Pregnancy, an organization formed to guide teens toward responsible sexual behavior. You can find data for your state at this site. What are the key parts of this organization's program? How effective would you imagine it is? Why?

http://www.qrd.org

This Web site, the Queer Resource Directory, looks at a wide range of issues—including family, religion, education, and health—from a queer theory perspective. Visit this site to see in what ways various social institutions can be considered "heterosexist." Do you agree? Why?

http://www.gay.com

This is a search engine for all sorts of information on issues involving homosexuality.

 **INVESTIGATE WITH RESEARCH NAVIGATOR™**

Follow the instructions on page 24 of this text to access the features of **Research Navigator™**. Once at the Web site, enter your Login Name and Password. Then, to use the **Content Select™** database, enter keywords such as "sexuality," "incest," "intersexuality," and "abortion," and the search engine will supply relevant and recent scholarly and popular press publications. Use the *New York Times* **Search-by-Subject Archive** to find recent news articles related to sociology and the **Link Library** feature to find relevant Web links organized by the key terms associated with this chapter.

September 2, 2003

The Skin Wars Start Earlier and Earlier

By GUY TREBAY

The front lines are drawn in the cool nonspace of every suburban mall. Here, at the Abercrombie & Fitch store in Westchester . . . pictures of half-nude models hang coyly above registers, and shoppers skirmish amiably over cropped miniskirts and skimpy tank tops against an aural backdrop of the White Stripes.

The combatants, if they can be called that, are parents and their daughters, and the fraught territory they are contesting is adolescent sexuality. When *The Washington Post* reported last summer that fashions for girls in the "tween" years were "long on skin, short on modesty," it was noting a reality that many parents of teenagers know only too well. . . .

"The 'whore wars' are a big issue," said Donna Cristen, who was shopping for back-to-school clothing on Thursday with her daughter, Tess, 13. Ms. Cristen's reference was to a term that arose on the Internet, where commentators like Betsy Hart of CNN complained that stores as mainstream as J. C. Penney, Target, and The Limited Too were increasingly carrying clothing that could seem designed to suit the needs of women who work the Lincoln Tunnel on-ramp. . . .

"Everything in stores now is so provocative, you have to keep a close watch," Ms. Cristen said, referring to the plethora of spaghetti strap blouses, midriff-baring tank tops, platform shoes, thongs, T-shirts emblazoned with double-entendre slogans and camisoles with built-in bras, all pitched by retailers at girls who have barely crossed the threshold of puberty. . . .

Randi Cardia, who lives in Manhattan and has two teenage daughters, described a majority of the clothes offered for them as "hooker wear." "There are a lot of us out there that are just appalled that someone hasn't taken a stand," Ms. Cardia said. . . .

"It's normal now to see these 12-year-old or younger girls trying to be Britney and Christina, with their pierced bellybuttons, their tiny little tube tops, their strappy shoes and their shorts showing the tops of their buttocks," said Ms. Cardia, who, discouraged by the current run of back-to-school offerings, shops with her daughters at stores that cater to boys. . . .

Many schools have been forced to modify dress codes to address concerns that are as much practical as moral. "If you can't sit on the floor in a discussion group about a piece of literature without calling attention to yourself," said John Fierro, the principal of Dorchester Elementary School in Woodcliff Lake, N.J., referring to the micro-miniskirts now popular among middle-school girls, "you're not appropriately dressed." . . .

"In marketing circles, they talk about K.G.O.Y.," an abbreviation for Kids Getting Older Younger, said Alissa Quart, the author of *Branded: The Buying and Selling of Teenagers* (Perseus Books, 2003). "You want to get them younger, so they're full of aspiration not only to look older but to spend older."

That this strategy works seemed clear at Delia's, an apparel store in the Westchester mall, which was packed on Thursday with young shoppers pawing through racks of $22 T-shirts imprinted with phrases like "Parental Guidance Suggested." It is by no means obvious how well such guidance is heard. . . . "You'll never hear a mother say, 'You can't wear that to school,'" she said. . . .

"You don't want to sound censorious or reactionary," Ms. Quart said. "But kids watch HBO. They see late-night TV. They see the 200 channels teeming with quasi-pornographic imagery." . . .

"Parents have to think about a life of commerce these kids are caught up in and teach them some media literacy," Ms. Quart suggested. Kimora Lee Simmons, designer of the hugely popular Baby Phat line, said they also "have to sit their kids down and take some major responsibility when they start wearing clothes that make them look like hootchie mamas, stuff that was never designed with children in mind."

What do you think?

1. Why are today's clothing manufacturers encouraging adult patterns of sexuality among young girls? What about teen stars such as Britney Spears and Christina Aguilera—how important is sexuality to their performances?
2. Does the pattern described in this article apply only to girls or does it also apply to boys? Explain your answer.

SOCIAL STRATIFICATION

Structure of Society in Mayan Civilisation

National Anthropological Museum, Mexico/The Art Archive/Picture Desk.

ON APRIL 10, 1912, the ocean liner *Titanic* slipped away from the docks of Southampton, England, on its maiden voyage across the North Atlantic to New York. A proud symbol of the new industrial age, the towering ship carried 2,300 men, women, and children, some enjoying more luxury than most travelers today could imagine. Poor people, however, crowded the lower decks, journeying to what they hoped would be a better life in the United States.

Two days out, the crew received radio warnings of icebergs in the area but paid little notice. Then, near midnight, as the ship steamed swiftly westward, a lookout was stunned to see a massive shape rising out of the calm ocean directly ahead. Moments later, the *Titanic* collided with a huge iceberg, as tall as the ship itself, which split open its side as if the grand vessel were just a giant tin can.

Seawater flooded the lower levels, pulling the ship down by the bow. Within twenty-five minutes of impact, people were rushing for the lifeboats. By 2:00 A.M., the bow was completely submerged and the stern high above the water. Within minutes, all lights went out. Clinging to the deck, quietly observed by those in lifeboats, hundreds of helpless passengers and crew solemnly passed their final minutes before the ship disappeared into the frigid Atlantic (Lord, 1976).

The tragic loss of more than 1,600 lives when the *Titanic* sank made news around the world. Looking back dispassionately at this terrible accident with a sociological eye, however, we note that some categories of passengers had much better odds of survival than others. In an age of conventional gallantry, women and children boarded the lifeboats first, so that 80 percent of the casualties were men. Class, too, was at work. More than 60 percent of people holding first-class tickets were saved because they were on the upper decks, where warnings were sounded first and lifeboats were accessible. Only 36 percent of the second-class passengers survived, and of the third-class passengers on the lower decks, only 24 percent escaped drowning. On board the *Titanic*, class turned out to mean much more than the quality of one's cabin. Class was a matter of life or death.

The fate of those aboard the *Titanic* dramatically illustrates how social inequality affects the way people live—and sometimes whether they live at all. This chapter explores the important concept of social stratification. Chapter 11 continues the story by examining social inequality in the United States, and Chapter 12 examines how our country fits into a global system of wealth and poverty.

WHAT IS SOCIAL STRATIFICATION?

For tens of thousands of years, humans the world over lived in small hunting and gathering societies.

The personal experience of poverty is captured in Sebastiao Salgado's photograph, which stands as a universal portrait of human suffering. The essential sociological insight is that, however strongly individuals feel its effects, our social standing is largely a consequence of the way in which a society (or a world of societies) structures opportunity and reward. To the core of our being, then, we are all the products of social stratification.

Although members of these bands might single out one person as swifter, stronger, or particularly skillful in collecting food, everyone had roughly the same social standing. As societies became more complex—a process detailed in Chapter 4 ("Society")—a major change came about. Societies began to elevate some categories of people above others, giving segments of the population more money, power, and prestige than others.

Social stratification is *a system by which a society ranks categories of people in a hierarchy.* Social stratification is a matter of four basic principles:

1. **Social stratification is a trait of society, not simply a reflection of individual differences.** Many of us think of social standing in terms of personal talent and effort, and as a result, we often exaggerate the extent to which we control our own fate. Did a higher percentage of the first-class passengers on the *Titanic* survive because they were smarter or better swimmers than second- and third-class passengers? Hardly. They fared better because of the system of privilege at work on the ship. Similarly, children born into wealthy families are more likely than children born into poverty to enjoy good health, earn a college degree, find a good job, and live a long life. Neither the rich nor the poor are responsible for creating social stratification, yet this system shapes the lives of us all.

2. **Social stratification persists over generations.** To see that stratification is a trait of societies rather than individuals, we need only look at how inequality persists across generations. In all societies, parents pass their social position on to their children.

    Some individuals, especially in high-income societies, experience **social mobility,** *a change in one's position in the social hierarchy.* Social mobility may be upward or downward. We celebrate the achievements of Shania Twain or Michael Jordan, both of whom rose from modest beginnings to fame and fortune. But people also move downward because of business setbacks, unemployment, or illness. More often, people move *horizontally;* that is, they switch one job for another at about the same social level. For most people, social standing remains much the same over a lifetime.

3. **Social stratification is universal but variable.** Social stratification is found everywhere. Yet, *what* is unequal and *how* unequal it is varies from one society to another. In some societies, inequality is mostly a matter of prestige; in others, wealth or power is the key dimension of difference. Moreover, some societies display more inequality than others.

4. **Social stratification involves not just inequality but beliefs.** Any system of inequality not only gives some people more than others but also defines these arrangements as fair. Just as *what* is unequal differs from society to society, so does the explanation of *why* people should be unequal.

CASTE AND CLASS SYSTEMS

Sociologists distinguish between "closed" systems, which allow for little change in social position, and "open" systems, which permit considerable social mobility (Tumin, 1985).

THE CASTE SYSTEM

A **caste system** is *social stratification based on ascription, or birth*. A pure caste system is closed because birth alone determines one's destiny, and there is little or no opportunity for social mobility based on individual effort. Caste systems, then, rank people in rigid categories, where they live out their lives.

Two Illustrations: India and South Africa

Many of the world's societies, most of them agrarian, approximate caste systems. One example is India, or at least India's traditional villages, where most of the people still live. The Indian system of castes (or *varna*, a Sanskrit word that means "color") is composed of four categories: Brahmin, Kshatriya, Vaishya, and Shudra. On the local level, however, each of these is composed of hundreds of subcaste (or *jati*) groups.

Caste has also played an important role in the history of South Africa. Until recently, this nation's policy of apartheid gave the 5 million South Africans of European ancestry a commanding share of wealth and power, dominating some 35 million black South Africans. In a middle position were another 3 million mixed-race people, known as "coloreds," and about 1 million Asians. The box on page 250 describes the current state of South Africa's racial caste system.

In a caste system, birth shapes people's lives in four ways. First, traditional caste groups have specific occupations, so that generations of a family perform the same type of work. In rural India, although some occupations (such as farming) are open to all, castes are identified with the work their members do (as priests, barbers, leather workers, sweepers, and so on). In South Africa, whites still hold most of the desirable jobs, and most blacks perform manual labor and other low-level service work.

Second, maintaining a rigid social hierarchy depends on people marrying within their own categories; "mixed" marriages would blur the ranking of children. Caste systems therefore demand that people marry others like themselves. Sociologists call this pattern *endogamous* marriage (*endo* stems from the Greek, meaning "within"). Traditionally, Indian parents select their children's marriage partners, often before the children reach their teens. Until 1985, South Africa outlawed marriage (and even sex) between the races; today, interracial couples are legal, but because most blacks and whites still live in separate areas, they are rare.

Third, caste norms guide people to stay in the company of "their own kind." Hindus in India support

In India, the traditional caste system still guides people's choice of work, especially in rural areas. Below the four basic castes are the Harijans, people defined as "outcasts" or "untouchables." These people perform jobs, such as cleaning the streets, defined as unclean for others of higher social position.

this segregation, believing that a ritually "pure" person of a higher caste will be "polluted" by contact with someone of lower standing. Apartheid in South Africa operated in much the same way.

Fourth, and finally, caste systems rest on powerful cultural beliefs. Indian culture is built on Hindu moral belief in accepting one's life work, whatever it may be. In South Africa, although apartheid is no longer law, most people still distinguish "white jobs" from "black jobs."

Caste and Agrarian Life

Caste systems exist in agrarian societies because the life-long routines of agriculture depend on a rigid sense of duty and discipline. Thus, caste persists in rural India, more than sixty years after being formally outlawed and even as its grip has relaxed in big cities, where people

GLOBAL SOCIOLOGY

Race as Caste: A Report from South Africa

At the southern tip of the African continent lies South Africa, a country about the size of Alaska, with a population of about 44 million in 2003. Long inhabited by black people, the region attracted white Dutch traders and farmers in the mid-seventeenth century. Early in the nineteenth century, a second wave of colonization saw British immigrants push the Dutch inland. By the early 1900s, the British had taken over the country, proclaiming it the Union of South Africa. In 1961, the United Kingdom gave up control and recognized the independence of the Republic of South Africa.

But freedom was a reality only for the white minority. Years before, to ensure their political control over the black majority, whites had instituted a policy of apartheid, or racial separation. Apartheid was made law in 1948, denying blacks national citizenship, ownership of land, and any formal voice in the government. In effect, black South Africans became a lower caste, receiving little schooling and performing menial, low-paying jobs. Under this system, even "middle-class" white households had at least one black household servant.

The prosperous white minority defended apartheid, claiming that blacks threatened their cultural traditions or, more simply, were inferior beings. But resistance to apartheid rose steadily,

prompting whites to resort to brutal military repression to maintain their power.

Steady resistance—especially from younger blacks, impatient for a political voice and economic opportunity—gradually forced change. Adding to the pressure was criticism from most other industrial nations, including the United States. By the mid-1980s, the tide began to turn as the South African government granted limited political rights to people of mixed race and Asian ancestry. Next came the right of all people to form labor unions, to enter occupations once restricted to whites, and to own property. Officials also began to dismantle the system of laws that separated the races in public places.

The rate of change increased in 1990, with Nelson Mandela's release from prison. In 1994, the first national election open to all people of all races elected

Mandela president—an event that ended centuries of white minority rule.

Despite this dramatic political change, however, social stratification in South Africa is still based on race. Even with the right to own property, one-third of black South Africans have no jobs, and the majority remain dirt poor. The worst off are some 7 million *ukuhleleleka*, which means "marginal people" in the Xhosa language. Soweto-by-the-Sea may sound like a summer getaway, but it is home to thousands of *ukuhleleleka*, who live crammed into shacks made of packing cases, corrugated metal, cardboard, and other discarded materials. There is no electricity for lights or refrigeration. Without plumbing, people use buckets to haul sewage; women line up to take a turn at a single water tap that serves more than 1,000 people. Any job is hard to come by; and those who do find work are lucky to earn $200 a month.

South Africa's current president, Thabo Mbeki, elected in 1999, leads a nation still twisted by centuries of racial caste. Economic development, based partly on tourism, holds out hope of a bright future. But the country can shed its past only by providing all its people with real opportunity.

Sources: Fredrickson (1981), Wren (1991), Hawthorne (1999), and Mabry & Masland (1999).

exercise greater choice in their work and marriage partners. Similarly, the rapid industrialization of South Africa made personal choice and individual rights more important, so that the abolition of apartheid was only a matter of time. In mature industrial nations such as the United States, some caste elements survive, but treating people categorically on the basis of race or sex now invites charges of racism and sexism.

Note that the erosion of caste does not signal an end to social stratification. On the contrary, it simply marks a change in its character, as the next sections explain.

THE CLASS SYSTEM

Farming demands the lifelong discipline created by caste systems. But industrial production depends on developing people's specific talents, giving rise to a **class system,** *social stratification based on both birth and individual achievement.*

A class system is more open, so that individuals who acquire schooling and skills may be socially mobile in relation to their parents and siblings. Such mobility, in turn, blurs class distinctions, so that even blood relatives may have different social standings. Social boundaries also break down as people immigrate from abroad or move from the countryside to the city, lured by greater opportunity for education and work (Lipset & Bendix, 1967; Cutright, 1968; Treiman, 1970). Typically, newcomers take low-paying jobs and, in the process, push others up the social ladder (Tyree, Semyonov, & Hodge, 1979).

Categorizing people according to their color, sex, or social background has come to be seen as wrong in industrial societies, and all people acquire political rights and roughly equal standing before the law. Moreover, in industrial societies, work is not fixed at birth but involves some personal choice. Greater individualism also translates into more freedom in selecting a marriage partner.

Meritocracy

Compared to agrarian societies where caste is the rule, industrial societies move toward **meritocracy,** *social stratification based on personal merit.* Because industrial societies need to develop a broad range of capabilities (beyond farming), stratification is based not solely on the accident of birth but also on "merit," by which we mean the job one does and how well one does it. To advance meritocracy, industrial societies expand equality of opportunity, although people expect inequality of outcomes.

In a pure meritocracy, social position would depend entirely on a person's ability and effort. Such a system would have ongoing social mobility, blurring social categories as individuals continuously move up or down in the system, depending on their latest performance. In caste societies, "merit" (from the Latin, meaning

"worthy of praise") means persisting in low-skill jobs such as farming. Caste systems honor those who do their work dutifully and remain "in their place."

Caste systems waste human potential, of course, but they are very orderly. And herein lies the answer to an important question: Why do industrial societies keep castelike qualities (such as letting wealth pass from generation to generation) rather than become complete meritocracies? The reason is that a pure meritocracy diminishes the importance of families and other social groupings. Economic performance is not everything, after all. Would we want to evaluate our family members solely on their jobs? Probably not. Therefore, class systems in industrial societies move toward meritocracy to promote productivity and efficiency but retain caste elements to maintain order and social cohesion.

Status Consistency

Status consistency is *the degree of consistency in a person's social standing across various dimensions of social inequality.* A caste system has limited social mobility and high status consistency, so that the typical person has the same relative ranking with regard to wealth, power, and prestige. The greater mobility of class systems, however, produces less status consistency. In the United States, then, a college professor with an advanced degree might enjoy high social prestige but earn less than someone who runs a popular pizzeria. Low status consistency means that *classes* are less well defined than *castes.*

ASCRIPTION AND ACHIEVEMENT: THE UNITED KINGDOM

The mix of caste and meritocracy in class systems is well illustrated by the United Kingdom (Great Britain—composed of England, Wales, and Scotland—and Northern Ireland), an industrial nation with a long agrarian history.

The Estate System

In the Middle Ages, England had a castelike system of three *estates.* The *first estate* was a hereditary nobility composed of barely 5 percent of the population; they controlled most of the land—the chief form of wealth (Laslett, 1984). Most nobles had no occupation, since they deemed engaging in a trade or any other work for income beneath them. Well tended by servants, nobles used their leisure time to develop skills in riding and

In 2002, Queen Elizabeth II celebrated her silver jubilee, marking fifty years on the throne as England's monarch. Perhaps it is a sign of more egalitarian times that the event was not a performance of the London Philharmonic but a rock and roll concert—a popular culture ritual—intended to appeal to ordinary people both in England and around the world.

warfare as well as to cultivate refined tastes in art, music, and literature.

To prevent vast landholdings from being divided by heirs, the law of *primogeniture* (from the Latin meaning "firstborn") demanded that all landholdings pass to the oldest son or other male relation. Younger sons had to find other means of support. Some entered the clergy—often termed the *second estate*—where their spiritual power was upheld by the church's extensive landholdings. Other young men of high birth became military officers, or lawyers, or took up other professions considered honorable for gentlemen. In an age when no woman could inherit her father's property and few women had the opportunity to earn a living on their own, a noble daughter depended for her security on marrying well.

Below the nobility and the clergy, the vast majority of men and women formed the *third estate*, or commoners. Most commoners were serfs working land owned by nobles. With little education, most were illiterate.

As the Industrial Revolution expanded England's economy, some commoners living in cities made enough money to challenge the nobility. Greater emphasis on meritocracy, the growing importance of money, and expanded schooling and legal rights to more people eventually blurred social rankings and gave rise to a class system.

Perhaps it is a sign of the times that, these days, traditional titles are put up for sale by nobles who simply need the money. In 1996, for example, the title "Lord of Wimbledon" was put on the block by Earl Spencer—Princess Diana's brother—to raise the $300,000 he needed to redo the plumbing in one of his large homes (McKee, 1996).

The United Kingdom Today

Today, the United Kingdom has a class system, though it retains the mark of a long feudal past. A small cluster of British families owns inherited estates, attends expensive schools, and exercises considerable political influence. A traditional monarch, Queen Elizabeth II, stands as the United Kingdom's head of state, and Parliament's House of Lords is composed of peers, about half of noble birth. Control of the government, however, has passed to the House of Commons, where the prime minister and other commoners typically reach their position by achievement—winning an election—rather than by birth.

Further down in the class hierarchy, roughly one-fourth of the British people form the "middle class." Many earn comfortable incomes from professions and business and are likely to have investments in the form of stocks and bonds.

Below the middle class, about half of all Britons think of themselves as "working class," earning modest incomes through manual work. In recent decades, the decline of British industries such as coal mining and steel production has led to high unemployment among working-class families. Some have slipped into poverty, joining the remaining one-fourth of Britons, who are socially and economically deprived. Lower-class people—or, more simply, the poor—are heavily concentrated in northern and western regions of the United Kingdom, which are plagued by economic decay.

Today's British class system mixes caste elements and meritocracy, producing a highly stratified society in which people are quite unequal, although some move both upward and downward. One legacy of the historical estate system, however, is that social mobility occurs less frequently in the United Kingdom than it does in the United States (Kerckhoff, Campbell, & Winfield-Laird, 1985). This more rigid system of inequality in the United Kingdom is reflected in the importance attached to accent. Distinctive patterns of speech develop in any society when people are separated from one another over many generations. Whereas people in the United States treat accent as a clue to where one lives (there is little mistaking a midwestern "twang" or a southern "drawl"), Britons use accent as a mark of social class, for example, distinguishing elites who speak "the king's English" from working people with the "cockney" accent common in London's East End. So different are these two accents that the British seem to be, as the saying goes, a single people divided by a common language.

London's *Sunday Times* recently presented a list of the richest people not only in Great Britain but also in various other nations. Find "The Rich List" at http://www.sunday-times. co.uk/richlist/

ANOTHER EXAMPLE: JAPAN

Social stratification in Japan also mixes caste and meritocracy. Japan is at once the world's oldest continuously operating monarchy and a modern society where wealth follows individual achievement.

Feudal Japan

By the fifth century C.E., Japan was an agrarian society with a rigid caste system composed of nobles and commoners and ruled by an imperial family. The emperor ruled by divine right, and his military leader (or *shogun*) oversaw a number of regional warlords.

Below the nobility were the *samurai*, a warrior caste whose name means "to serve." This second rank of Japanese society was made up of soldiers who learned martial skills and who lived by a code of honor based on absolute loyalty to their leaders.

As in Great Britain, most people in Japan at this time in history were commoners who labored to scrape out a bare subsistence. Unlike their European counterparts, however, Japanese commoners were not

lowest in rank. At the bottom were the *burakumin*, or "outcasts," shunned by lord and commoner alike. Much as the lowest caste groups in India, these outcasts lived apart from others, performed the most distasteful work, and, like everyone else, could not change their standing.

Modern Japan

By the 1860s (the time of the Civil War in the United States), the nobles realized that Japan could not enter the modern industrial era with its traditional caste system. Besides, as in Britain, some nobles were happy to have their children marry wealthy commoners who had more money than they did. As Japan opened up to the larger world, the traditional caste system weakened. In 1871, the Japanese legally banned the social category of "outcast," although even today people look down on descendants of this rank. After Japan's defeat in World War II, the nobility, too, lost legal standing, and the emperor remains only as a symbol of Japan's traditions, with little real power.

Social stratification in Japan is a far cry from the rigid caste system of centuries ago. Today, Japanese society consists of "upper," "upper-middle," "lower-middle," and "lower" classes. No firm boundaries exist, and many people do move between classes over time. But because Japanese culture tends to respect tradition, family background is never far from the surface in the sizing up of someone's social standing. Officially, everyone has equal standing before the law, although, in practice, many people still look at one another through the centuries-old lens of caste (Hiroshi, 1974; Norbeck, 1983).

Finally, traditional ideas about gender continue to shape Japanese society. Legally, the two sexes are equal, but men dominate women in many ways. Japanese parents are more likely to send sons than daughters to college, so a significant gender gap exists in education. Following the recent economic downturn in Japan, many more women have entered the labor force. But most working women fill lower-level support positions in the corporate world, only rarely assuming leadership roles. Thus, individual achievement in Japan's modern class system operates in the shadow of centuries of traditional male privileges (Brinton, 1988; French, 2002).

THE FORMER SOVIET UNION

The former Union of Soviet Socialist Republics (U.S.S.R.), which rivaled the United States as a

After the collapse of the Soviet Union in 1991, that nation began a transition toward a market economy. Since then, some people have become quite rich, but others have lost their jobs as old, inefficient factories closed. As a result, the problem of poverty has become widespread, affecting perhaps one-third of the Russian people. Scenes like this one—a Moscow woman begging for money—have become all too common.

military superpower during much of the twentieth century, was born out of revolution in 1917. The Russian Revolution put an end to the feudal estate system ruled by a hereditary nobility and transferred farms, factories, and other productive property from private ownership to state control.

A Classless Society?

The Russian Revolution was guided by the ideas of Karl Marx, who wrote that private ownership of productive property is the basis of social classes (see Chapter 4, "Society"). When the state took control of the economy, Soviet officials boasted that they had created the first modern, classless society.

Outside the Soviet Union, however, analysts were skeptical of this claim (Lane, 1984). They pointed out that the jobs people held actually fell into four unequal categories. At the top were high government officials, or *apparatchiks*. Next came the Soviet intelligentsia, including lower government officials, college professors, scientists, physicians, and engineers. Below them were manual workers and, at the lowest level, the rural peasantry.

These categories enjoyed very different living standards, so the former Soviet Union was not really classless at all. But putting factories, farms, colleges, and hospitals under state control did limit economic inequality (although sharp differences of power emerged) compared to capitalist societies such as the United States.

The Second Russian Revolution

After decades of organizing Soviet society according to the ideas of Karl Marx (and revolutionary leader Vladimir Lenin), the Soviet Union shook with change after Mikhail Gorbachev became president in 1985. Gorbachev introduced a program popularly known as *perestroika*, meaning "restructuring." He saw that, while the Soviet system had reduced economic inequality, nearly everyone was poor, and living standards lagged far behind those of higher-income nations in the West. Gorbachev sought to generate economic expansion by reducing the inefficient centralized control of the economy.

Gorbachev's economic reforms turned into one of the most dramatic social movements in history. Throughout Eastern Europe, socialist governments toppled, and in 1991 the Soviet Union itself collapsed. People blamed their poverty and their lack of basic freedoms on a repressive ruling class of Communist party officials. In the Soviet Union, for example, just 6 percent of the population formed the Communist party, which ran the whole country.

The Soviet story shows that social inequality involves more than economic resources. Soviet society may not have had the extremes of wealth and poverty found in the United Kingdom, Japan, and the United States. But an elite class existed all the same, one based on power rather than wealth. Thus, even though both Mikhail Gorbachev and his successor Boris Yeltsin earned far less than a U.S. president, they wielded awesome power.

What about social mobility in the Soviet Union? During the twentieth century there was as much upward social mobility in the Soviet Union as in the United Kingdom, Japan, and even the United States. Rapidly expanding industry and government drew many poor rural peasants into factories and offices (Dobson, 1977; Lane, 1984; Shipler, 1984). This trend illustrates what sociologists call **structural social mobility,** *a shift in the social position of large numbers of people due more to changes in society itself than to individual efforts.*

November 24, Odessa, Ukraine. The first snow of our voyage flies over the decks as our ship puts in at Odessa, the former Soviet Union's southernmost port on the Black Sea. A short distance from the dock, we gaze up the Potemkin Steps—the steep stairway leading to the city proper where the first shots of the Russian Revolution rang out. It has been several years since our last visit and much has changed; indeed, the Soviet Union itself has collapsed. Has life improved? For some people, certainly: There are now chic boutiques where well-dressed shoppers buy fine wines, designer clothes, and imported perfumes. But for most, life seems much worse. Flea markets line the curbs as families sell home furnishings. Many are desperate in a town where meat sells for $4 a pound and the average person earns about $30 a month. Even the city has to save money by shutting off street lights at eight o'clock. The spirits of most people seem as dim as Odessa's streets.

During the 1990s, the forces of structural mobility in the new Russian Federation were mostly downward. One important indicator is that the average life span for Russian men dropped by eight years, and for women, two years. Many factors are involved in this decline, including Russia's poor health care system, but the Russian people clearly have suffered in the turbulent period of economic change that began in 1991.

In the long run, closing inefficient state industries may improve the nation's economic performance. In the short run, some workers have made gains by

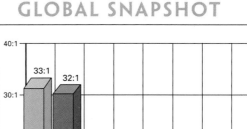

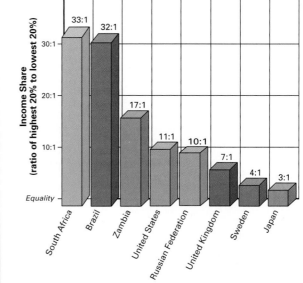

FIGURE 10-1 Economic Inequality in Selected Countries

These data are the most recent available, representing income share for various years between 1993 and 2001.

Sources: U.S. Census Bureau (2002) and The World Bank (2003).

joining growing private companies. Yet many citizens (including those locked in low-wage state-run companies) face hard times as living standards fall. Therefore, as the Russian economy moves unevenly toward private ownership of business, the gulf between rich and poor has grown greater than in the United States, as shown in Figure 10–1. Thus, while some praise the recent changes, others hang on, hoping for a higher living standard (Specter, 1997b; Bohlen, 1998; Gerber & Hout, 1998; Gerber, 2002; The World Bank, 2003).

CHINA: EMERGING SOCIAL CLASSES

Sweeping political and economic change has affected not just the Russian Federation but also the People's Republic of China. After the Communist revolution in 1949, the state took control of all farms, factories, and other productive property. Communist party leader Mao Zedong

Medieval Europeans accepted rigid social hierarchy as part of a divine plan for the world. This fifteenth-century painting by the Limbourg brothers shows nobles and high church officials well served by soldiers and servants.

Limbourg Brothers, Les Tres Riches Heures–January–Purged, 1400–D. 1416, Flemish. By courtesy of The Board of Trustees of The Victoria & Albert Museum, London/Bridgeman Art Library, London/SuperStock.

declared all types of work to be equally important, so that, officially, social classes no longer existed.

The new program greatly reduced economic inequality. But as in the case of the Soviet Union, social differences remained. The country was ruled by a political elite with enormous power and considerable privilege; below them were managers of large factories as well as skilled professionals; next came industrial workers; and faring least well were rural peasants, who were not even permitted to leave their villages and migrate to cities.

Further economic change came in 1978, when Mao died and Deng Xiaoping became China's leader. Gradually, the state loosened its hold on the economy, so that a new class of business owners emerged. Party leaders remain in control of the country, and some have prospered as they have joined the ranks of the small but wealthy elite who control new privately run industries. Much of this new economic growth has been concentrated in coastal areas, where living standards have soared above those in China's rural interior.

Today, a new class system is emerging with a mix of the old political hierarchy and a new business hierarchy. At this early stage, scholars point to the new system's complexity and debate its likely future. But one lesson of China is clear: With new patterns of inequality emerging over time, social stratification is highly dynamic (Bian, 2002).

IDEOLOGY: THE POWER BEHIND STRATIFICATION

Noting the extent of social inequality around the world, we might wonder how societies persist without sharing resources more equally. Castelike systems in Great Britain and Japan lasted for centuries, placing land and power in the hands of several hundred families. For 2,000 years, people in India have accepted the idea that they should be privileged or poor because of the accident of birth.

A major reason that social hierarchies endure, then, is **ideology,** *cultural beliefs that justify particular social arrangements, including patterns of inequality.* A belief—for example, the idea that the rich are smart and the poor are lazy—is ideological to the extent that it defines the wealthy as worthy and suggests that poor people deserve their plight.

Plato and Marx on Ideology

The ancient Greek philosopher Plato (427–347 B.C.E.) defined *justice* as agreement about who should have what. Every culture, Plato explained, considers some type of inequality "fair." Karl Marx, too, understood this fact, although he was far more critical of inequality than Plato. Marx took capitalist societies to task for channeling wealth and power to a few and defending the process as "a law of the marketplace." Capitalist law, Marx continued, defines the right to own property, and inheritance ensures that money stays within the same families from one generation to the next. In short, Marx concluded, culture and institutions combine to shore up a society's elite, which is why established hierarchies last a long time.

CRITICAL THINKING

Is Getting Rich "The Survival of the Fittest"?

"The survival of the fittest"—we have all heard these words used to describe society as a competitive jungle. The phrase was coined by one of sociology's pioneers, Herbert Spencer (1820–1903), whose ideas about social inequality are still widespread today.

Spencer, who lived in England, eagerly followed the work of the natural scientist Charles Darwin (1809–1882). Darwin's theory of biological evolution holds that a species changes physically over thousands of generations as it adapts to the natural environment. Spencer, thinking to apply Darwin's theory to the operation of society, proposed that society is a "jungle" with the "fittest" people rising to the top and the weak gradually sinking into miserable poverty.

In the United States, Spencer's distortion of Darwin's theory was popular among the powerful industrialists of the time. John D. Rockefeller (1839–1937), who made a vast fortune building the oil industry, recited Spencer's "social gospel" to young children in Sunday school. As Rockefeller saw it, the growth of giant corporations—and the astounding wealth of their owners—was merely a basic fact of nature. Neither Spencer nor Rockefeller had much sympathy for the poor, seeing poverty as evidence of not measuring up in a competitive world. Spencer opposed social welfare programs, charging that they penalized society's "best" members (through taxes) and rewarded society's "worst" members (through welfare benefits).

Today's sociologists are quick to point out that social standing is not a simple matter of personal effort, as Spencer contended. Nor is it the case that our society's "fattest"—the companies or people who earn lots of money—necessarily benefit society as a whole. Yet Spencer's view that people get more or less what they deserve in life remains part of our individualistic culture.

What do you think?

1. *What did Herbert Spencer mean when he said society encourages "the survival of the fittest"?*

2. *Why do you think that Spencer's ideas are still popular in the United States today?*

3. *In what sense do highly paid people benefit society? In what ways do they not?*

Historical Patterns of Ideology

Ideology changes as a society's economy and technology change. Because agrarian societies depend on the routine labor of their people, they develop caste systems that view performing the duties of one's "station" as a moral responsibility within a natural order. With the rise of industrial capitalism, personal initiative gains value, and an ideology of meritocracy develops. Wealth and power become prizes won by those who perform the best. Under industrial capitalism, the poor, the object of charity under feudalism, are scorned as personally undeserving. This harsh view is expressed in the work of Herbert Spencer, as explained in the box.

History shows how difficult it is to change social stratification. However, challenges to the status quo always arise. Traditional notions of a "woman's place," for example, have given way to economic opportunity for women. The continuing progress toward racial equality in South Africa also exemplifies widespread rejection of the ideology of apartheid.

THE FUNCTIONS OF SOCIAL STRATIFICATION

Why are societies stratified at all? One answer, consistent with the structural-functional paradigm, is that social inequality plays a vital part in the operation of society. This argument was set forth some fifty years ago by Kingsley Davis and Wilbert Moore (1945).

THE DAVIS-MOORE THESIS

The **Davis-Moore thesis** states that *social stratification has beneficial consequences for the operation of a society.* How else, ask Davis and Moore, can we explain the fact that some form of social stratification has been found in every known society?

Davis and Moore note that modern societies have hundreds of occupational positions of varying importance. Certain jobs—say, washing windows, cutting grass, or answering a telephone—are fairly easy and can be performed by almost anyone. Other jobs—such as designing new generations of computers or transplanting human organs—are difficult and demand the scarce talents of people with extensive (and expensive) training.

Therefore, Davis and Moore explain, the greater the functional importance of a position, the more rewards a society attaches to it. This strategy promotes productivity and efficiency, since rewarding important work with income, prestige, power, and leisure encourages people to do these jobs and to work better, longer, and harder. Unequal rewards benefit some individuals, then, and a system of unequal rewards (which is what social stratification is) benefits society as a whole.

Davis and Moore concede that any society can be egalitarian, but only to the extent that people are willing to let *anyone* perform *any* job. Equality also demands that someone who carries out a job poorly be rewarded the same as someone who performs it well. Such a system clearly offers little incentive for people to try their best and thereby reduces a society's productive efficiency.

The Davis-Moore thesis suggests why some form of stratification exists everywhere; it does not state precisely what rewards a society should give to any occupational position or just how unequal rewards should be. The point, however, is simply that positions a society considers more important must carry enough reward to draw talent away from less important work.

Critical evaluation. Although the Davis-Moore thesis is an important contribution to sociological analysis, it has provoked criticism. Melvin Tumin (1953) wondered, first, how we assess how important any occupation really is. Obviously, we cannot say that important jobs are simply those with high rewards because that amounts to circular reasoning (that is, we assume important jobs have high rewards, but then we define a job's importance by its level of reward so that our thesis is correct by definition). Perhaps the high rewards our society gives to, say, physicians, partly results from deliberate efforts by the medical profession to limit the supply of physicians and thereby increase the demand for their services.

Moreover, living in a society that places so much importance on money, we tend to overestimate the significance of high-paying work; beyond making money, how do stockbrokers or people who trade international currencies really contribute to society? For the same reason, it is difficult for us to see the importance of work that is not oriented toward making money, such as parenting, creative writing, playing music in a symphony, or just being a good friend to someone in need (Packard, 2002).

In short, how well does the income paid to people reflect their contribution to society? With an income approaching $100 million per year, television personality Oprah Winfrey earns more in two days than George W. Bush makes all year as president of the United States. Would anyone argue that hosting a talk show is more important than leading the country? The box takes a closer look at the link between pay and societal importance.

Second, Tumin claims that the Davis-Moore thesis ignores ways in which social stratification can *prevent* the development of individual talent. Born to privilege, rich children may develop their abilities, something many gifted poor children may never do.

Third, by suggesting that social stratification benefits all of society, the Davis-Moore thesis ignores how social inequality promotes conflict and even outright revolution. This criticism leads us to the social-conflict paradigm, which provides a very different explanation for social hierarchy.

 Do corporate CEOs deserve their high salaries? The AFL-CIO offers a critical view at its Web site, where it tracks CEO salaries: http://www.aflcio.org/corporateamerica/paywatch/

STRATIFICATION AND CONFLICT

Social-conflict analysis argues that, rather than benefiting society as a whole, social stratification provides some people with advantages over others. This analysis draws heavily on the ideas of Karl Marx, with contributions from Max Weber.

KARL MARX: CLASS AND CONFLICT

Karl Marx, whose ideas are discussed fully in Chapter 4 ("Society"), explained that most people have one of two basic relationships to the means of production: They either (1) own productive property or (2) labor for others. This productive role is the basis of social class. In medieval Europe, the nobility and church officials owned the productive land; peasants toiled as farmers. Similarly, in industrial class systems, the capitalists (or the bourgeoisie) control factories, which use the labor of workers (the proletariat).

Marx saw great inequality in wealth and power arising from capitalism, which, he argued, made class conflict inevitable. In time, he believed, oppression and misery would drive the working majority to organize and ultimately overthrow capitalism.

CRITICAL THINKING

Big Bucks: Are the Rich Worth What They Earn?

For an hour of work, a Los Angeles priest earns about $5, a hotel maid in New Orleans about $7, a bus driver in San Francisco about $15, a Phoenix bartender about $20, and a Detroit auto worker roughly $25. These wages shrink in comparison to the $40,000 that Barry Bonds earns per hour playing baseball for the San Francisco Giants. And what about the $100,000 that actor Jim Carrey makes for every hour he spends making a movie? Or the $600,000 Michael Jordan used to make for every hour he played basketball for the Chicago Bulls?

The Davis-Moore thesis suggests that rewards reflect an occupation's value to society. But are the talents of Michael Jordan, who earned more than $30 million each year playing basketball, worth more than the efforts of all 100 U.S. senators or of 1,000 police officers? In short, do earnings really reflect people's social importance?

In industrial-capitalist societies such as the United States, salaries should reflect the market forces of supply and demand. In simple terms, the more you create value in a market system, the more you are worth in financial rewards. According to this view, movie and television stars, top athletes, writers of popular songs, doctors and other professionals, and many business executives have rare talents that are much in demand; thus, they earn many times

more than the typical worker in the United States. Even Elvis Presley's estate—more than twenty-five years after the popular singer's death—still pulls in tens of millions of dollars in royalties each year.

But critics of the Davis-Moore thesis question whether the market is really a good evaluator of occupational importance. First, they say, the U.S. economy is dominated by a small pro-

Julia Roberts is among the highest-paid women in the film industry, making millions for starring in each picture. Why does she earn so much more than many lower-paid actors?

portion of people who manipulate the system for their own benefit. Corporate executives, for example, benefit from "suite deals," paying themselves multi-million-dollar salaries and bonuses whether their companies do well or not. As the Oracle software company spiraled downward, for example, CEO Larry Ellison earned more than $700 million from company stock options—an amount it would take a college teacher 10,000 years to earn (Benjamin, 2002; Broder, 2002).

Equating income with social worth, then, is risky business. Those who defend the market as a measure of occupational worth ask what would be better. But as critics see it, our economic system amounts to a closed game in which only a handful of people have the money to play.

What do you think?

1. *Do you think that highly paid entertainers and athletes deserve a thousand times more than an average worker? Why or why not?*

2. *We would all agree that parents perform a vital task as they raise children. Why is parenting unpaid work?*

3. *What about the argument that higher pay would improve the quality and performance of teachers? Do you agree? Why or why not?*

Marx lived at a time when a few great industrialists were amassing their fortunes. Andrew Carnegie, J. P. Morgan, John D. Rockefeller, and John Jacob Astor (one of the few very rich passengers to perish on the *Titanic*) lived in fabulous mansions adorned with priceless art and staffed by dozens of servants. Their wealth was staggering: Andrew Carnegie, founder of U.S. Steel, reportedly earned some $20 million a year at the beginning of the twentieth century (more than $100 million in today's dollars), at a time when the average worker earned roughly $500 a year (Baltzell, 1964; Pessen, 1990).

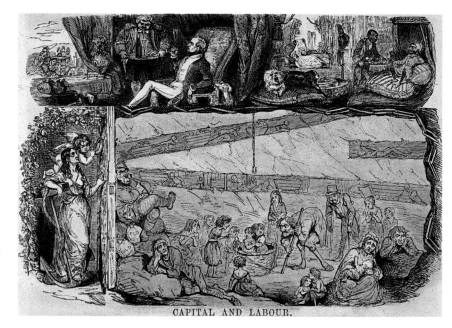

This cartoon, titled "Capital and Labour," appeared in the English press in 1843, when the ideas of Karl Marx were first gaining attention. It links the plight of that country's coal miners to the privileges enjoyed by those who owned coal-fired factories.

CAPITAL AND LABOUR.

But, according to Marx, the capitalist elite draws strength not just from the operation of the economy. Through the family, opportunity and wealth are passed down from generation to generation. Moreover, the legal system defends private property and inheritance. Finally, elite children mix at exclusive schools, forging social ties that will benefit them throughout their lives. In short, from Marx's point of view, capitalist society *reproduces the class structure in each new generation.*

Critical evaluation. Marx's analysis of how capitalism creates conflict between classes has greatly influenced sociological thinking. But because it is revolutionary, calling for the overthrow of capitalist society, Marxism is also highly controversial.

One of the strongest criticisms of Marxism is that it denies a central tenet of the Davis-Moore thesis: Motivating people to perform various social roles requires some system of unequal rewards. Marx separated reward from performance, endorsing a more-or-less equal system based on the principle of "from each according to his ability; to each according to his needs" (Marx & Engels, 1972:388; orig. 1848). Perhaps this severing of rewards from performance is exactly what caused low productivity in the former Soviet Union and other socialist economies around the world.

Defenders of Marx counter that considerable evidence supports Marx's view of humanity as inherently social rather than selfish (Clark, 1991; Fiske, 1991). We should not assume, therefore, that individual rewards (much less, money alone) are the only way to motivate people to perform social roles.

A second problem is that the revolutionary developments Marx considered inevitable within capitalist societies have, by and large, failed to happen. The next section explores why the socialist revolution Marx predicted and promoted has not occurred, at least in advanced capitalist societies.

WHY NO MARXIST REVOLUTION?

Despite Marx's prediction, capitalism is still thriving. Why have workers in the United States and other industrial societies not overthrown capitalism? Ralf Dahrendorf (1959) suggests four reasons:

1. **The fragmentation of the capitalist class.** Today, millions of stockholders, rather than single families, own most large companies. Moreover, the day-to-day operation of large corporations is now in the hands of a managerial class, whose members may or may not be major stockholders. With stock widely held—even with the recent downturn, about 40 percent of U.S. adults are in the market—more and more people have a direct stake in preserving the capitalist system.

2. **A higher standard of living.** As Chapter 16 ("The Economy and Work") explains, a century ago most workers were in factories or on farms performing **blue-collar occupations,** *lower-prestige work that involves mostly manual labor.* Today, most workers hold **white-collar occupations,** *higher-prestige work that involves mostly mental activity.* These jobs are in sales, management, and other service fields. Most of today's white-collar workers do not think of themselves as an "industrial proletariat." Just as important, the average U.S. worker's income rose almost tenfold over the course of the twentieth century, even allowing for inflation, and the number of hours worked per week has dropped. As a result, most workers today are far better off than workers were a century ago, a case of structural mobility helping people accept the status quo.

3. **More worker organizations.** Workers have organizational clout that they lacked a century ago. With the right to organize into labor unions, workers make demands of management backed up by threats of work slowdowns and strikes. In other words, worker-management disputes are settled without a threat to the capitalist system.

4. **More extensive legal protections.** During the twentieth century, the government passed laws to make the workplace safer and developed programs, such as unemployment insurance, disability protection, and Social Security, to provide workers with greater financial security.

A Counterpoint

These developments suggest that U.S. society has smoothed many of capitalism's rough edges. Yet, many claim that Marx's analysis of capitalism is still largely valid (Domhoff, 1983; Stephens, 1986; Boswell & Dixon, 1993; Hout, Brooks & Manza, 1993). First, wealth remains highly concentrated, with 40 percent of all privately owned property in the hands of just 1 percent of the U.S. population (Keister, 2000). Second, many of today's white-collar jobs offer no more income, security, or satisfaction than factory work did a century ago. Third, many benefits enjoyed by today's workers came about through the class conflict Marx described, and workers still struggle to hold onto what they have. Fourth, while workers have gained legal protections, the law still protects the private property of the rich. Therefore, social-conflict theorists conclude, the absence of a socialist revolution in the United States does not negate Marx's analysis of capitalism.

TABLE 10–1 Two Explanations of Social Stratification: A Summary	
Structural-Functional Paradigm	**Social-Conflict Paradigm**
Social stratification benefits society as a whole.	Social stratification benefits some at the expense of others.
Linking greater rewards to more important work raises societal productivity.	The organization of society allows some people to command great wealth and power.
There is widespread agreement that some people deserve more rewards than others.	There is widespread opposition to existing social inequality.
Social stratification is typically stable, enduring over time.	Social stratification is unstable, changing over time.

Table 10–1 summarizes the contributions of the two contrasting sociological approaches to an understanding of social stratification.

MAX WEBER: CLASS, STATUS, AND POWER

Max Weber, whose approach to social analysis is described in Chapter 4 ("Society"), agreed with Karl Marx that social stratification is a form of social conflict, but he considered Marx's two-class model simplistic. Instead, he thought social stratification involves three distinct dimensions of inequality.

The first dimension is economic inequality—the issue so vital to Marx—which Weber termed *class* position. Weber thought of "classes" not as crude categories but as a continuum ranging from high to low. Weber's second dimension of social stratification is *status,* or social prestige, and the third is *power.*

The Socioeconomic Status Hierarchy

Marx viewed social prestige and power as simple reflections of economic position and did not treat them as distinct dimensions of inequality. But Weber noted that status consistency in modern societies is often quite low: A local government official, say, might wield considerable power yet enjoy moderate social status and have little wealth.

Weber's contribution, then, is portraying social stratification in industrial societies as a multidimensional ranking rather than a hierarchy of clearly defined classes. In line with Weber's thinking, sociologists use

The extent of social inequality in agrarian systems is greater than that found in industrial societies. One indication of the unchallenged power of rulers is the monumental structures built over years with the unpaid labor of common people. Although the Taj Mahal in India is among the world's most beautiful buildings, it is merely a tomb for a single individual.

the term **socioeconomic status (SES)** to refer to *a composite ranking based on various dimensions of social inequality.*

Because people vary on the three dimensions of class, status, and power, Weber saw society not in terms of distinct classes, as Marx did, but as a broad range of self-interested social categories, say, government officials, small business owners, or factory workers. Social conflict, for Weber, was therefore both variable and complex.

Inequality in History

Weber noted that each of his three dimensions of social inequality stands out at different points in the evolution of human societies. Agrarian societies emphasize status or social prestige, typically in the form of honor. Members of these societies (whether they be, say, nobles or servants) gain status by conforming to cultural norms that correspond to their rank.

Industrialization and the development of capitalism level traditional rankings based on birth but generate striking financial inequality. Thus, Weber argued, the crucial difference among people in industrial societies is the economic dimension of class.

Over time, industrial societies witness the growth of a bureaucratic state. Bigger government and the spread of all kinds of other organizations make power more important in the stratification system. Especially in socialist societies, because government regulates many aspects of life, high-ranking officials become the new elite.

Historical analysis points to a final difference between Weber and Marx. Marx thought societies could eliminate social stratification by abolishing private ownership of productive property. Weber doubted that overthrowing capitalism would significantly diminish social stratification. It might lessen economic disparity, he reasoned, but socialism would simultaneously increase inequality by expanding government and concentrating power in the hands of a political elite. Popular uprisings against entrenched bureaucracies in Eastern Europe and the former Soviet Union support Weber's position.

Critical evaluation. Weber's multidimensional view of social stratification has enormously influenced sociologists. But critics (particularly those who favor Marx's ideas) argue that, although social class boundaries may have blurred, today's high-income societies still show striking patterns of social inequality.

Moreover, as we shall see in Chapter 11 ("Social Class in the United States"), income inequality has increased in recent years. In light of the rising wealth of the super-rich, some think that Marx's view of the rich versus the poor is closer to the mark than Weber's multidimensional hierarchy.

STRATIFICATION AND TECHNOLOGY: A GLOBAL PERSPECTIVE

We can weave together a number of observations made in this chapter by considering the relationship between a society's technology and its type of social stratification. This analysis draws on Gerhard Lenski's model of sociocultural evolution, detailed in Chapter 4 ("Society").

HUNTING AND GATHERING SOCIETIES

With simple technology, hunters and gatherers produce only what is necessary for day-to-day living. Some people may produce more than others, but the group's survival depends on all sharing what they have. Thus, no categories of people emerge as better off than others.

HORTICULTURAL, PASTORAL, AND AGRARIAN SOCIETIES

As technological advances create a surplus, social inequality increases. In horticultural and pastoral societies, a small elite controls most of the surplus. Large-scale agriculture is more productive still, and marked inequality—as great as at any time in human history—means that various categories of people lead strikingly different lives. Agrarian nobility typically exercise godlike power over the masses.

INDUSTRIAL SOCIETIES

Industrialization turns the tide, lessening inequality. Prompted by the need to develop individual talents for the more specialized economy, meritocracy takes hold and erodes the power of the traditional elites. Industrial productivity also raises the standard of living of the historically poor majority. Furthermore, specialized work demands schooling for all, sharply reducing illiteracy. A literate population, in turn, presses for a greater voice in political decision making, further diminishing social inequality and reducing men's domination of women.

Over time, even wealth becomes somewhat less concentrated (a countering of the trend predicted by Marx). In the 1920s, the richest 1 percent of the U.S. population owned about 40 percent of all wealth, a figure that fell to 30 percent by the 1980s (Williamson & Lindert, 1980; Beeghley, 1989; *1991 Green Book*). Such trends help explain why Marxist revolutions occurred in *agrarian* societies—such as the former Soviet Union (1917), Cuba (1959), and Nicaragua (1979)— where social inequality is most pronounced, rather than in industrial societies as Marx had predicted. However, wealth inequality increased after 1990 and is once again what it was in the 1920s (Keister, 2000).

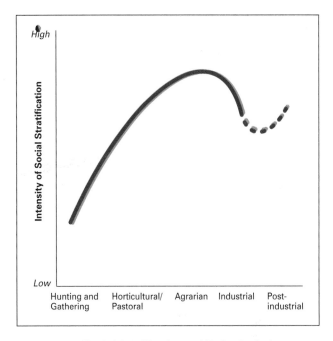

FIGURE 10-2 Social Stratification and Technological Development: The Kuznets Curve

The Kuznets curve shows that greater technological sophistication generally is accompanied by more pronounced social stratification. The trend reverses itself as industrial societies relax rigid, castelike distinctions in favor of greater opportunity and equality under the law. Political rights are more widely extended, and there is even some leveling of economic differences. (Kuznets's curve may also be usefully applied to the relative social standing of the two sexes.) However, the emergence of postindustrial society has brought an upturn in economic inequality, as indicated by the broken line added by the author.

Source: Created by the author, based on Kuznets (1955) and Lenski (1966).

THE KUZNETS CURVE

In human history, then, technological progress first increases and then moderates the extent of social stratification. Greater inequality is functional for agrarian societies, but industrial societies benefit from a more egalitarian climate. This historical trend, recognized by the Nobel Prize–winning economist Simon Kuznets (1955, 1966), is illustrated by the Kuznets curve, shown in Figure 10–2.

Patterns of social inequality around the world today generally square with the Kuznets curve. Global Map 10–1 on page 264 shows that high-income nations that have passed through the industrial era (including

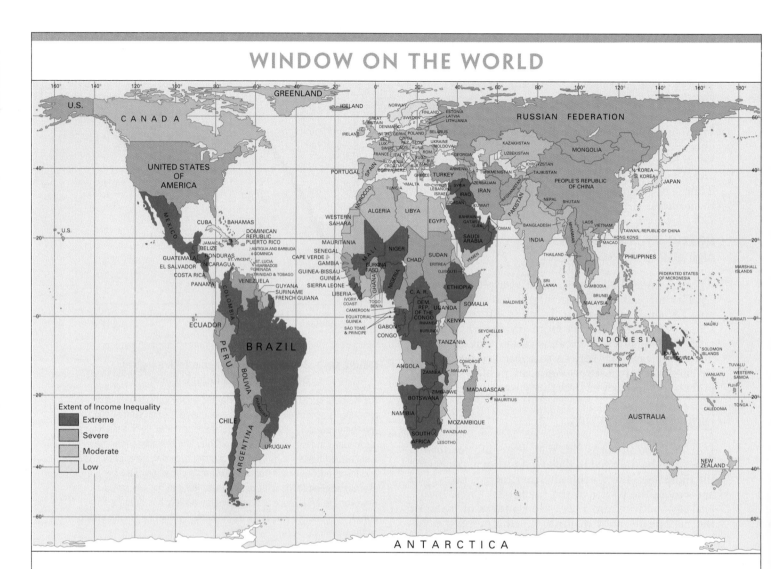

GLOBAL MAP 10–1 Income Disparity in Global Perspective

Societies throughout the world differ in the rigidity and extent of their social stratification and in overall standard of living. This map highlights income inequality. Generally speaking, the United States stands out among high-income nations, such as Great Britain, Sweden, Japan, and Australia, as having greater income inequality. The less economically developed countries of Latin America and Africa, including Colombia, Brazil, and the Central African Republic, as well as much of the Arab world, exhibit the most pronounced inequality of income. Is this pattern consistent with the Kuznets curve?

Source: Based on Gini coefficients obtained from The World Bank (2003).

Recent decades have seen increasing inequality of income and wealth in the United States. Learning the facts about social inequality is important; however, you also must consider the importance of values. Do you think it is fair that some have so much more than others? Why or why not?

the United States, Canada, and the nations of Western Europe) have somewhat less income inequality than nations in which agriculture remains a major part of the economy (as is common in Latin America and Africa). Of course, income disparity reflects not just technological development but also political and economic priorities. Of all high-income nations, the United States has the most income inequality.

And what of the future? A glance back at Figure 10–2 shows that we have extended the trend described by Kuznets to the postindustrial era (the broken line) to show increased social inequality. That is, as the Information Revolution moves ahead, U.S. society is experiencing greater economic inequality (discussed in the next chapter), suggesting that the long-term trend may differ from what Kuznets observed half a century ago (Nielsen & Alderson, 1997).

SOCIAL STRATIFICATION: FACTS AND VALUES

The year was 2081 and everybody was finally equal. They weren't only equal before God and the law. They were equal every which way. Nobody was smarter than anybody else. Nobody was better looking than anybody else. Nobody was stronger or quicker than anybody else. All this equality was due to the 211th, 212th, and 213th Amendments to the Constitution and the

unceasing vigilance of agents of the Handicapper General.

With these words, novelist Kurt Vonnegut, Jr. (1961), begins the story of "Harrison Bergeron," an imaginary account of a future United States in which all social inequality has been abolished. Vonnegut warns that, although perhaps appealing in principle, equality can be a dangerous concept in practice. His story describes a nightmare of social engineering in which every individual talent that makes one person different from another is systematically neutralized by the government.

To eradicate differences that make one person "better" than another, Vonnegut's state requires that physically attractive people wear masks that make them average looking, that intelligent people wear earphones that generate distracting noise, and that the best athletes and dancers be fitted with weights to make them as clumsy as everyone else. In short, although we may imagine that social equality would liberate people to make the most of their talents, Vonnegut concludes that an egalitarian society could exist only if everyone is reduced to the lowest common denominator.

Like Vonnegut's story, all of this chapter's explanations of social stratification involve value judgments. The Davis-Moore thesis states not only that social stratification is universal but that it is actually necessary to efficient social organization. Class differences in

CONTROVERSY & DEBATE

The Bell Curve Debate: Are Rich People Really Smarter?

It is rare when a social science book captures the attention of people across the country. But *The Bell Curve: Intelligence and Class Structure in American Life* (1994) by Richard J. Herrnstein and Charles Murray did that and more. The book ignited a firestorm of controversy over why social stratification divides our society and, just as important, what should be done about it.

The Bell Curve is a long (800 pages) book that addresses many complex issues, but at bottom it puts forth eight propositions:

1. There exists something we can describe as "general intelligence"; people with more of it tend to be more successful in their careers than those with less.

2. At least half the variation in human intelligence is transmitted genetically from one generation to another; the remaining variability is due to environmental factors that affect socialization.

3. Over the course of the twentieth century—and especially since the Information Revolution began several decades ago—intelligence has become more necessary in our society's most important jobs.

4. At the same time, the best U.S. colleges and universities have shifted their admissions policies away from favoring children of inherited wealth to admitting young people with high grades and the highest scores on standardized tests such as the Scholastic Assessment Test (SAT), American College Testing Program (ACT), and Graduate Record Examination (GRE).

5. As a result of these changes in the workplace and higher education, our society is coming to be dominated by a "cognitive elite," who are, on average, not only better trained than most people but actually more intelligent.

6. Intelligent people tend to interact with others like themselves—both on the campus and in the workplace—which raises the odds that they will pair up, marry, and have intelligent children, thus extending the "cognitive elite" into another generation.

7. The same process is at work at the other end of the social ladder: Poor people who, on average, have lower intelligence, are also socially segregated, tend to marry others with similar social background, and thus pass along their more modest abilities to their children.

Thus, Herrnstein and Murray conclude:

8. Because membership in the affluent elite or the impoverished underclass

U.S. society, then, reflect both variation in human abilities and the relative importance of different jobs. From this point of view, equality is undesirable because it could be achieved only in an inefficient society that cared little for developing individual talent and rewarding excellence.

Social-conflict analysis, advocated by Karl Marx, takes a much more positive view of equality. Marx considered inequality dysfunctional to societies, for the simple reason that it causes both human suffering and conflict between haves and have-nots. As he saw it, social stratification springs from injustice and greed. Thus, Marx advocated sharing resources equally, believing that equality would enhance human well-being.

The box addresses the connection between intelligence and social class. This issue—also a mix of fact and value—is among the most troublesome in social science, partly because of the difficulty in defining and measuring "intelligence," but also because the very idea that elites are somehow "better" than others challenges our democratic culture.

The next chapter ("Social Class in the United States") examines inequality in our own nation, highlighting recent economic polarization. Then, in Chapter 12 ("Global Stratification"), we survey the entire world, explaining why some nations have so much more wealth than others. At all levels, as we shall see, the study of social stratification involves a mix of facts and values about the shape of a just society.

is at least partly rooted in intelligence received mostly by genetic inheritance, we should not be surprised that the poor contend with high levels of social problems, such as crime and drug abuse. Further, we should expect that programs to help the poor (including, say, Head Start and affirmative action) will achieve limited practical results.

Evaluating the claims made in *The Bell Curve* must begin with a hard look at the concept of intelligence. Critics of the book argue that most of what we call "intelligence" is the result not of genetic inheritance but of socialization. Intelligence tests, in other words, do not measure cognitive *ability* as much as they measure cognitive *performance*. One way we know this is so is that average IQ scores have been rising as the U.S. population becomes more educated. If schooling is so important to intelligence, then, we might well expect rich children to perform better on such tests because of their educational advantages.

Most researchers who study intelligence agree that genetics plays a part in children's intelligence, but most conclude that perhaps 25 to 40 percent is inherited—less than Herrnstein and Murray claim. Therefore, *The Bell Curve* misleads readers when it states that social stratification is both natural and inevitable. In fact, say critics, this book amounts to a new version of the social Darwinism popular a century ago, which justified the great wealth of industrial tycoons as "the survival of the fittest."

Perhaps the more today's competitive society seems like a jungle, the more people think of stratification as a matter of blood rather than upbringing. But despite any flaws, *The Bell Curve* raises issues we cannot easily ignore. If some people are, indeed, smarter than others, shouldn't we expect that most of the smarter ones will end up in higher social positions? Is that fair or not? Wouldn't we expect the top people in various fields to be at least a little smarter than the rest of us? Are there also dangers in having a smart elite? Don't most of our society's

elites live apart from the problems—including crime, homelessness, and poor schools—that plague most of the population? Finally, what can our society do to ensure that all people will have the opportunity to develop their abilities as fully as possible?

Continue the debate. . .

1. *Do you think there is such a thing as "general intelligence"? Why or why not?*

2. *Do you think that well-off people, on average, are more intelligent than people of low social position? If so, how do we know which factor is causing the other?*

3. *Do you think social scientists should study issues such as differences in human intelligence if their results could justify social inequality? Why or why not?*

Sources: Herrnstein & Murray (1994), Jacoby & Glauberman (1995), Kohn (1996), and Arrow, Bowles, & Durlauf (2000).

SUMMARY

1. Social stratification is the ranking of people in a hierarchy. Stratification (a) is a trait of society, not just a result of individual differences; (b) endures over many generations; (c) is universal yet variable in form; and (d) is supported by cultural beliefs.

2. Caste systems, common in agrarian societies, are based on ascription (birth), permit little social mobility, and shape a person's entire life, including occupation and marriage.

3. Class systems, with an element of meritocracy, are found in industrial societies and allow social mobility based on individual achievement.

4. With public ownership of productive property, socialist societies claim to be classless. Although such societies usually exhibit less economic inequality than their

capitalist counterparts, they are characterized by much greater inequality in power.

5. Social stratification is difficult to change because it is supported by various social institutions and because cultural values and beliefs—ideology—define certain kinds of inequality as just.

6. The Davis-Moore thesis states that social stratification is universal because it promotes economic productivity in a society. In class systems, unequal rewards attract the most able people to the most important jobs.

7. Critics of the Davis-Moore thesis note that (a) it is difficult to assess objectively the functional importance of any job; (b) stratification prevents many people from developing their abilities; and (c) social stratification benefits some at the expense of others, causing social conflict.

8. For Karl Marx, main architect of social-conflict analysis, conflict in industrial societies places the capitalists (bourgeoisie), who own the means of production and seek profits, in opposition to the proletariat, who provide labor in exchange for wages.

9. The socialist revolution that Marx predicted has not occurred in industrial societies such as the United States. Some sociologists consider this to be evidence that Marx's analysis was flawed; others, however, point out that our society is marked by pronounced social inequality and class conflict.

10. Max Weber identified three dimensions of social inequality: economic class, social status or prestige, and power. Because people's standing on the three dimensions may differ, stratification takes the form of a multidimensional hierarchy rather than distinct classes.

11. Historically, says Gerhard Lenski, technological advances have made societies more unequal. Some reversal of this trend occurs in industrial societies, as shown by the Kuznets curve. However, the new postindustrial economy in the United States shows some increase in economic inequality.

12. The study of social inequality rests not only on facts but also on politics and values concerning how a society should be organized.

KEY CONCEPTS

social stratification (p. 248) a system by which a society ranks categories of people in a hierarchy

social mobility (p. 248) a change in one's position in the social hierarchy

caste system (p. 249) social stratification based on ascription, or birth

class system (p. 251) social stratification based on both birth and individual achievement

meritocracy (p. 251) social stratification based on personal merit

status consistency (p. 251) the degree of consistency in a person's social standing across various dimensions of social inequality

structural social mobility (p. 255) a shift in the social position of large numbers of people due more to changes in society itself than to individual efforts

ideology (p. 256) cultural beliefs that justify particular social arrangements, including patterns of inequality

Davis-Moore thesis (p. 257) the assertion that social stratification is a universal pattern because it has beneficial consequences for the operation of a society

blue-collar occupations (p. 261) lower-prestige work that involves mostly manual labor

white-collar occupations (p. 261) higher-prestige work that involves mostly mental activity

socioeconomic status (SES) (p. 262) a composite ranking based on various dimensions of social inequality

CRITICAL-THINKING QUESTIONS

1. How is social stratification a creation of society rather than simply a reflection of individual differences?

2. How do caste and class systems differ? What do they have in common? Why does industrialization introduce a measure of meritocracy into social stratification?

3. According to the Davis-Moore thesis, why should a college president earn more than a professor or a secretary? What would happen if all employees were paid the same?

4. In what respects do you think Karl Marx's predictions about capitalism have failed? In what respects are they correct?

APPLICATIONS AND EXERCISES

1. What evidence is there of social stratification on your college campus? In what ways are students unequal? Does family background or individual talent seem to be more important in shaping students' lives?

2. Sit down with parents, grandparents, or other relatives and assess how your family's lifestyle has changed over the last three generations. Has social mobility taken place? If so, describe the change. Was it caused by the efforts of individuals or changes in society itself?

3. What are the "seven deadly sins," the human failings recognized by the Catholic church during the Middle

Ages? Why are these traits dangerous to an agrarian caste system? Are they a threat to a modern, capitalist class system? Why?

4. Packaged in the back of this new textbook is an interactive CD-ROM that offers a variety of video and interactive review materials intended to help you better understand the material covered in this chapter. For this chapter, the CD-ROM contains a relevant clip from *ABC News*, an author's tip video, interactive map animations, an interactive time line, and flashcards with audio pronunciations of the more difficult words.

 SITES TO SEE

http://www.prenhall.com/macionis

Visit the interactive Companion Website™ that accompanies this text. Begin by clicking on the cover of your book. You will find a chapter-by-chapter study guide, practice tests, suggested Web links, and links to other relevant material.

http://www.TheSociologyPage.com

You can find additional links that deal with social stratification at the author's home page.

http://www.bea.doc.gov

This Web site is run by the government's Bureau of Economic Analysis. Here you will find income data by county and many other statistics about social inequality. See what you can learn about stratification in your part of the country.

http://www.cbpp.org

This site, developed by the Center on Budget and Policy Priorities, has data and analysis of issues involving social inequality.

 INVESTIGATE WITH RESARCH NAVIGATOR™

Follow the instructions on page 24 of this text to access the features of **Research Navigator**™. Once at the Web site, enter your Login Name and Password. Then, to use the **Content Select**™ database, enter keywords such as "social class," "apartheid," and "Karl Marx," and the search engine

will supply relevant and recent scholarly and popular press publications. Use the *New York Times* **Search-by-Subject Archive** to find recent news articles related to sociology and the **Link Library** feature to find relevant Web links organized by the key terms associated with this chapter.

SOCIAL CLASS
IN THE UNITED STATES

PAUL MARCUS
Upstairs-Downstairs
Studio SPM Inc. © Paul Marcus.

THE MONDAY MORNING SUN streamed through the small kitchen window as Alcario Castellano sipped his coffee and reached for the morning paper that his wife, Carmen, had left on her chair. After scanning the headlines, the sixty-six-year-old retired grocery clerk flipped open the second section looking for the winning numbers for California's weekly

lottery. Castellano had stopped by a local liquor store on Saturday night to purchase a ticket, lured by the lottery's $141-million grand prize—the largest in U.S. history.

Finding the winning numbers, Castellano carried the paper to the refrigerator and plucked his ticket from the magnet that held it to the door. He sat down again and hunched over the table, carefully checking the numbers, one by one. "Wait a minute," he said to himself, leaning back in the chair, his voice rising with excitement. "What's going on here? Is this real? C-A-R-M-E-N!!!"

His wife rushed in, and the two checked the numbers again and again. They all matched up. Castellano was an instant multimillionaire. It *was* real.

The following Thursday, the Castellanos arrived at the lottery's district office in San Jose to claim their prize. After verifying that this was, indeed, the only winning ticket, an official asked the couple how they wanted their winnings. They smiled nervously at each other and replied that they had chosen to take the money in a single lump sum rather than in annual payments over twenty years. The official explained that, in that case, the total would be $70,794,365. Then there was the matter of taxes, which would cut that number almost in half. Still, the Castellanos would receive over $42,000,000. The couple hardly seemed to hear what was being said. It was all a dream come true.

After signing the required forms, the Castellanos turned to several reporters standing nearby. The couple explained that, two weeks ago, they had decided to sell their house and move south, where the cost of living was more affordable. "Now," Carmen turned, smiling at her husband, "now we can stay" (based on Davis, 2001).

The amazing good fortune of Alcario and Carmen Castellano made headlines across the United States. Indeed, there is something "American" about the story: A retired grocer—who never seemed to be able to make ends meet—suddenly becomes one of the richest people in town. But this story also raises some important questions about social inequality in the United States. Just how common is it that people "make it" by getting rich? Does a windfall like the one in this case make someone a member of the upper

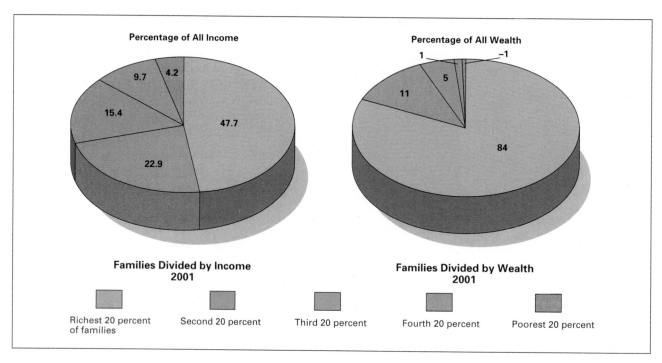

Percentage of All Income

4.2
9.7
15.4
22.9
47.7

Percentage of All Wealth

1
−1
5
11
84

**Families Divided by Income
2001**

**Families Divided by Wealth
2001**

Richest 20 percent of families

Second 20 percent

Third 20 percent

Fourth 20 percent

Poorest 20 percent

FIGURE 11–1 Distribution of Income and Wealth in the United States

Sources: Income data from U.S. Census Bureau (2002); wealth data are author estimates based on Keister (2000) and Russell & Mogelonsky (2000).

class? How socially unequal are people in this country in the first place? This chapter answers all these questions, explaining what separates us, how different we are, and why the differences are getting greater.

DIMENSIONS OF SOCIAL INEQUALITY

Many people think of the United States as a more-or-less equal society. Unlike countries in Europe, this nation never had a nobility. With the significant exception of our racial history, we have never known a caste system that rigidly ranked categories of people.

Even so, U.S. society is highly stratified. Not only do the rich have most of the money, but they also receive more schooling, enjoy better health, and consume the lion's share of goods and services. Such privileges contrast sharply with the poverty of millions of women and men in this same country who worry about paying next month's rent or a doctor's bill when a child becomes ill.

So why do many people think of the United States as a middle-class society? We underestimate the extent of social inequality for many reasons. For one thing, our legal system declares that everyone stands equal before the law. Second, our culture celebrates individual effort and downplays the importance of birth. Third, although we may read about high-paid celebrities or the occasional winner of a big lottery prize, most of us do not personally know anyone who is either "super-rich" or extremely poor. In short, we interact mostly with people like ourselves (Kelley & Evans, 1995). Finally, because the United States is such a rich country, it seems that everyone is at least pretty well off.

When people do face up to social inequality, they often speak of a "ladder of social class," as if inequality were a matter of a single factor such as money. On the contrary, social class in the United States has several dimensions. Socioeconomic status (SES), as discussed in Chapter 10 ("Social Stratification"), reflects not just money (income and wealth and the power they provide) but also occupational prestige and schooling.

INCOME

One important dimension of inequality is **income,** *wages or salary from work and earnings from investments.* The Census Bureau reports that the median U.S. family income in 2001 was $51,407. The first part of

Figure 11–1 illustrates the distribution of income among all U.S. families.[1] The richest 20 percent of families (earning at least $94,151 annually, with a mean of $159,644) received 47.7 percent of all income, while the bottom 20 percent (earning less than $24,000, with a mean of $14,021) received only 4.2 percent.

Table 11–1 provides a closer look at income distribution. In 2001, the highest-paid 5 percent of U.S. families earned at least $164,104 (averaging $280,312), or 21.0 percent of all income, more than the total earnings of the lowest-paid 40 percent. At the very top of the income pyramid, the richest half of 1 percent earned at least $1.5 million. In short, while a small number of people earn very high incomes, the majority make do with far less.

Chapter 10 ("Social Stratification") explained that social inequality declines along with industrialization (illustrated by the Kuznets curve, Figure 10–2). Thus, the United States has less income inequality than, say, Venezuela (in South America), Kenya (Africa), or Sri Lanka (Asia). However, as Figure 11–2 indicates, the United States has more income inequality than most other high-income nations.

---

[1]The Census Bureau reports both mean and median income for families ("two or more persons related by blood, marriage or adoption") and households ("two or more persons sharing a living unit"). In 2001, mean family income was $66,863, higher than the median because high-income families pull up the mean but not the median. For households, the figures are somewhat lower—a mean of $58,208 and a median of $42,228—mostly because families average 3.2 persons, and households average 2.6.

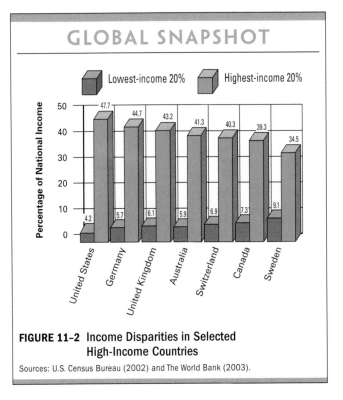

GLOBAL SNAPSHOT

FIGURE 11-2 Income Disparities in Selected High-Income Countries

Sources: U.S. Census Bureau (2002) and The World Bank (2003).

TABLE 11-1 U.S. Family Income, 2001

Highest paid . . .	Annually earns at least . . .
0.5%	$1,500,000
1	335,000
5	164,000
10	112,000
20	94,000
30	74,000
40	63,000
50	53,000
60	41,000
70	31,000
80	24,000
90	10,000

Sources: Kennickell, Starr-McCluer, & Surette (2000), U.S. Census Bureau (2002), and author calculations.

WEALTH

Income is only a part of a person's or family's **wealth,** *the total value of money and other assets, minus outstanding debts.* Wealth—including stocks, bonds, and real estate—is distributed even less equally than income.

The second part of Figure 11–1 shows the distribution of wealth. The richest 20 percent of U.S. families own roughly 84 percent of the country's entire wealth. High up in this privileged category are the wealthiest

Find a government report on U.S. wealth inequality at http://www.census.gov/hhes/www/wealth/1998_2000/wealth98_00.html

5 percent of families—the "very rich," who own 60 percent of all private property. Richer still, with wealth into the tens of millions, are the 1 percent of families that qualify as "super-rich" and possess about 40 percent of this nation's privately held resources (Keister, 2000; Keister & Moller, 2000). Capping the wealth pyramid (and allowing for recent stock market declines), the ten richest U.S. families have a combined net worth exceeding $220 billion (*Forbes,* 2002). This amount equals the total property of 3.1 million average families, including enough people to fill the cities of Chula Vista, California; Chicago, Illinois; Chattanooga, Tennessee; and Clearwater, Florida.

TABLE 11-2 The Relative Social Prestige of Selected Occupations in the United States

White-Collar Occupations	Prestige Score	Blue-Collar Occupations	White-Collar Occupations	Prestige Score	Blue-Collar Occupations
Physician	86		Funeral director	49	
Lawyer	75		Realtor	49	
College/university professor	74		Bookkeeper	47	
Architect	73			47	Machinist
Chemist	73			47	Mail carrier
Physicist/astronomer	73		Musician/composer	47	
Aerospace engineer	72			46	Secretary
Dentist	72		Photographer	45	
Member of the clergy	69		Bank teller	43	
Psychologist	69			42	Tailor
Pharmacist	68			42	Welder
Optometrist	67			40	Farmer
Registered nurse	66			40	Telephone operator
Secondary-school teacher	66			39	Carpenter
Accountant	65			36	Brick/stone mason
Athlete	65			36	Child-care worker
Electrical engineer	64		File clerk	36	
Elementary-school teacher	64			36	Hairdresser
Economist	63			35	Baker
Veterinarian	62			34	Bulldozer operator
Airplane pilot	61			31	Auto body repairperson
Computer programmer	61		Retail apparel salesperson	30	
Sociologist	61			30	Truck driver
Editor/reporter	60		Cashier	29	
	60	Police officer		28	Elevator operator
Actor	58			28	Garbage collector
Radio/TV announcer	55			28	Taxi driver
Librarian	54			28	Waiter/waitress
	53	Aircraft mechanic		27	Bellhop
	53	Firefighter		25	Bartender
Dental hygienist	52			23	Farm laborer
Painter/sculptor	52			23	Household laborer
Social worker	52			22	Door-to-door salesperson
	51	Electrician		22	Janitor
Computer operator	50			09	Shoe shiner

Source: Adapted from *General Social Surveys 1972–2002: Cumulative Codebook* (Chicago: National Opinion Research Center, 2003), pp. 1488–1506.

The wealth of the average U.S. household, currently about $71,600, rose through the 1990s and fell somewhat with the economic downturn beginning in 2000. Household wealth reflects the value of homes, cars, investments, insurance policies, retirement pensions, furniture, clothing, and all other personal property, minus a home mortgage

Compare economic inequality in the United States to that found in Canada by visiting http://www.ccsd.ca/facts.html

and other debts. The wealth of average people is not only less than that of the rich, however, but also different in kind. While most people's wealth centers on a home and a car—that is, property that generates no income—the wealth of the rich is mostly in the form of stocks and other income-producing investments.

When financial assets are balanced against debits, the lowest-ranking 40 percent of U.S. families have virtually no wealth at all. The negative percentage shown in Figure 11–1 for the poorest 20 percent of the population means that these families actually live in debt.

POWER

In the United States, wealth is an important source of power. Therefore, the small share of families that controls most of the nation's wealth also shapes the agenda of an entire society. Thomas Jefferson (1953; orig. 1785), the third U.S. president and a wealthy man himself, cautioned that a true democracy could not exist if property remained in the hands of a small number of families.

Chapter 17 ("Politics and Government") presents the debate surrounding wealth and power. Some analysts argue that, while the rich have certain advantages, they do not dominate the political process. Others counter that the political system mostly serves the interests of the "super-rich."

OCCUPATIONAL PRESTIGE

Beyond generating income, work is also an important source of social prestige. We commonly evaluate each other according to the kind of work we do, respecting those who do what we consider important work and looking down on those with less prestigious jobs.

Sociologists monitor the relative prestige of various occupations (NORC, 2003). Table 11–2 shows that people accord high prestige to occupations—such as physician, lawyer, and engineer—that require extensive training and generate high income. On the other hand, less prestigious work—waiting tables, for  example—not only pays less but usually requires less ability and schooling. Occupational prestige rankings are much the same in all high-income nations (Ma, 1987; Lin & Xie, 1988).

In any society, high-prestige occupations go to privileged categories of people. In Table 11–2, for example, the highest-ranking occupations are dominated by men. One has to go thirteen jobs down the list until we find an occupation—"registered nurse"—in which most workers are women. Similarly, many of the lowest-prestige jobs are commonly performed by people of color.

SCHOOLING

Industrial societies expand opportunities for schooling, but some people receive much more than others. Table 11–3 shows schooling for U.S. women and men

TABLE 11-3 Schooling of U.S. Adults, 2002 (aged 25 and over)		
	Women	**Men**
Not a high school graduate	**15.6%**	**16.2%**
8 years or less	6.7	7.1
9–11 years	8.9	9.1
High school graduate	**84.4**	**83.8**
High school only	33.1	31.0
1–3 years college	26.2	24.3
College graduate or more	25.1	28.5

Source: U.S. Census Bureau (2003).

aged twenty-five and older. In 2002, although 84 percent completed high school, only about 26 percent were college graduates.

Schooling affects both occupation and income, since most (but not all) of the better-paying white-collar jobs shown in Table 11–2 require a college degree or other advanced study. Most blue-collar jobs, which bring lower income and social prestige, require less schooling.

SOCIAL STRATIFICATION AND BIRTH

As we discussed in Chapter 10, the class system in the United States is partly a meritocracy; that is, social position reflects individual talent and effort. But birth also plays a big part in shaping what we become later in life.

ANCESTRY

Nothing affects social standing in the United States as much as being born into a particular family. Family is our point of entry into the social system and has a strong bearing on schooling, occupation, and income. Research suggests that at least half our country's richest individuals—those with hundreds of millions of dollars in wealth—acquired their fortunes mostly from inheritance (Thurow, 1987; Queenan, 1989). By the same token, inherited poverty just as surely shapes the future of others.

GENDER

Of course, both men and women are found in families at every class level. Yet, on average, women have less income, wealth, and occupational prestige than men. Therefore, in the United States, there are about six times more poor families headed by women (3.5 million) than there are poor families headed by men (583,000). From another angle, families headed by women are more than twice as likely to be poor (26.4 percent) than families headed by men (13.1 percent) (U.S. Census Bureau, 2002). Chapter 13 ("Gender Stratification") examines the connection between gender and social stratification.

RACE AND ETHNICITY

Race is closely linked to social position in the United States. White people receive more schooling and have higher overall occupational standing than African Americans. Thus, the median African American family's income was $33,598 in 2001, just 59 percent of the $57,328 earned by non-Hispanic white families. This disparity makes a real difference in people's lives. For example, non-Hispanic white families are more likely to own their homes (74 percent do) than black families (48 percent) (U.S. Census Bureau, 2002).

Much—but not all—of the disparity in income is due to the larger share of single-parent families among African Americans. If only families headed by married couples are compared, African Americans earned 81 percent as much as non-Hispanic white families.

Over time, the income differential builds into a huge "wealth gap" (Altonji et al., 2000). A recent survey of U.S. households by the Federal Reserve found that median wealth for minority families (about $17,100) is just 14 percent of the median ($120,900) for non-Hispanic whites (Aizcorbe, Kennickell, & Moore, 2003). Race is significant even among affluent families, as the box explains.

Social ranking involves ethnicity, as well. Historically, people of English ancestry have enjoyed the most wealth and wielded the greatest power in the United States. The Latino population—now the largest U.S. racial or ethnic minority—has long been disadvantaged. In 2001, the median income among Hispanic families was $34,490, or 60 percent of the comparable figure for all non-Hispanic white families. A detailed examination of how race and ethnicity affect social standing is presented in Chapter 14 ("Race and Ethnicity").

RELIGION

Religion, too, has a bearing on social standing in the United States. Among Protestant denominations, with which almost two-thirds of individuals identify, Episcopalians and Presbyterians have significantly higher social standing, on average, than Lutherans and Baptists. Jews, on average, also have high social standing, while Roman Catholics hold a more modest position (Davidson, Pyle, & Reyes, 1995).

Back in 1960, John Fitzgerald Kennedy, a member of one of this country's wealthiest and most powerful families, had to overcome religious opposition to become our first (and, so far, only) Catholic president. Understandably, then, throughout our history, upward mobility has sometimes meant converting to a higher-ranking religion (Baltzell, 1979b).

SOCIAL CLASSES IN THE UNITED STATES

As Chapter 10 ("Social Stratification") explained, rankings in a caste system are rigid and obvious to all. Defining social categories in a more fluid class system, however, is not so easy.

Consider the joke about a couple who orders a pizza, asking that it be cut into six slices because they aren't hungry enough to eat eight. All sociologists agree that social inequality exists in the United States; they just can't agree on how to divide up the population. Some, following Karl Marx, see two major classes: capitalists and proletariat. Others find as many as six classes (Warner & Lunt, 1941) or even seven (Coleman & Rainwater, 1978). Still others side with Max Weber, favoring not clear-cut classes but a multi-dimensional status hierarchy.

Defining classes in U.S. society is difficult because of our relatively low level of status consistency. Especially near the middle of the hierarchy, standing in one dimension often contradicts standing in another. A government official, for example, may have the power to administer a multimillion-dollar budget yet may earn only a modest personal income. Similarly, members of the clergy enjoy great prestige but moderate power and low pay. Or consider a lucky day trader on the stock market who wins no special respect but makes a lot of money.

Finally, the social mobility typical of class systems means that social position may change during a person's lifetime. This mobility, which is must common mean the middle of the hierarchy, further blurs class boundaries. With these reservations in mind, we can describe four general social classes in the United States: the upper class, the middle class, the working class, and the lower class.

THE UPPER CLASS

Families in the upper class—5 percent of the U.S. population—earn at least $164,000 annually and may earn ten times that much or more. As a general rule, the more

DIVERSITY: RACE, CLASS, AND GENDER

The Color of Money: Being Rich in Black and White

African American families earn 59 cents for every dollar a non-Hispanic white family earns, which helps explain why black families are three times as likely to be poor. But there is another side to black America—an affluent side—that has expanded dramatically in recent decades.

The number of affluent families—those with incomes over $80,000 a year—is increasing faster among African Americans than among whites. In 2001, 1.2 million African American families (14 percent) were financially privileged, 50 percent more than the number in 1990 when inflation is taken into account, and ten times the number in 1970. About 13 percent of Latino families also ranked as well-off, along with 32 percent of non-Hispanic white families.

The color of money is the same for everyone, but black and white affluence differs in several ways. First, well-off people of African descent are not *as rich* as their white counterparts. Sixty-five percent of affluent non-Hispanic white families

(21 percent of all such families) earn more than $100,000 a year, compared to 53 percent of affluent African American families (7 percent of all black families).

Second, African Americans are more likely than white people to achieve affluence through multiple incomes. From another angle, 11.3 percent of non-Hispanic white men and 3.0 percent of non-Hispanic white women earn more than $80,000, compared to just 2.9 percent of black men and 1.2 percent of black women. Rich black families, then, are more likely to contain two, and perhaps more, working people.

Third, affluent African Americans are more likely to receive their income from salaries than from investments. Among wealthy white families, more than 80 percent of families have investment income, compared to two-thirds of affluent African American families.

Beyond differences in income, affluent people of color must deal with social barriers that do not limit whites. Even African Americans with the money to purchase a home, for example, may find they are unwelcome as neighbors. This is one reason that a smaller share of well-off African American families (54 percent) live in the suburbs (the richest areas of the country) than affluent white families (68 percent).

Affluent Americans come in all colors. But having money does not override as the importance society attaches to race.

Sources: Weicher (1995), Lach (1999), and U.S. Census Bureau (2002).

a family's income comes from inherited wealth in the form of stocks and bonds, real estate, and other investments, the stronger a family's claim to being upper class.

In 2002, *Forbes* magazine profiled the richest 400 people in the United States and noted that they had a *minimum* net worth of $550 million (down in the last few years) and included 225 billionaires. This economic upper class is Karl Marx's "capitalists"—those who own the means of production and thus most of the nation's private wealth. Many members of the upper class work as top corporate executives or senior government officials; many others work mostly at managing their own money.

Upper-Uppers

The *upper-upper class*, sometimes called "blue bloods" or simply "society," includes less than 1 percent of the U.S. population (Coleman & Neugarten, 1971; Baltzell, 1995). Membership is almost always the result of birth, as suggested by the quip that the easiest way to become an upper-upper is to be born one. Most of these families possess enormous wealth, primarily inherited. For this reason, members of the upper-upper class are said to have *old money*.

Set apart by their wealth, upper-uppers live in old, exclusive neighborhoods, such as Beacon Hill in

People often distinguish between the "new rich" and those with "old money." Men and women who suddenly begin to earn high incomes tend to spend their money on "status symbols" because they enjoy the new thrill of high-roller living and they want others to know of their success. Those who grow up surrounded by wealth, on the other hand, are used to a privileged way of life and are more quiet about it. Thus, the "conspicuous consumption" of the lower-upper class (left) can differ dramatically from the more private pursuits and understatement of the upper-upper class (right).

Boston, Rittenhouse Square or the Main Line in Philadelphia, the Gold Coast of Chicago, and Nob Hill in San Francisco. Their children typically attend private schools with others of similar background and complete their education at high-prestige colleges and universities. In the tradition of European aristocrats, they study liberal arts rather than vocational skills.

Women of the upper-upper class often maintain a full schedule of volunteer work for charitable organizations. While helping the larger community, such charitable activities also build networks that broaden this elite's power (Ostrander, 1980, 1984).

Lower-Uppers

Most upper-class people actually fall into the *lower-upper class*. The queen of England is in the upper-upper class. J. K. Rowling, author of the Harry Potter books, is in the lower-upper class. The major difference, in other words, is that lower-uppers are the "working rich," for whom earnings rather than inherited wealth are the primary source of income. In fact, some lower-uppers are actually richer than many upper-uppers: In 2002, Rowling earned $77 million from her books, while the queen's income (mostly from her wealth) provided her with only about $12 million for the year (Orecklin, 2003).

In the United States, what we often call the American Dream has been to earn enough to join the ranks of the lower-upper class. The athlete who signs a

million-dollar contract, the actress who lands a starring role in a Hollywood film, the computer whiz who becomes an Internet entrepreneur, and even the retired grocery clerk who wins a huge lottery jackpot—these are the talented achievers and lucky people who reach the lower-upper class. Although "new rich" families have the money to live in expensive communities, most do not have the background or connections to gain entry to the exclusive clubs and associations of "old money" families.

THE MIDDLE CLASS

Made up of 40 to 45 percent of the U.S. population, the large middle class has a tremendous influence on our culture. Television programs and movies usually depict middle-class people, and most commercial advertising is directed toward these "average" consumers. The middle class contains far more racial and ethnic diversity than the upper class.

Upper-Middles

The top half of this category is termed the *upper-middle class*, based on above-average income in the range of $80,000 to $160,000 a year. Such income allows upper-middle-class families to accumulate considerable property—a comfortable house in a fairly expensive area, several automobiles, and investments.

Two-thirds of upper-middle-class children receive a college education, and postgraduate degrees are common. Many go on to high-prestige careers as physicians, engineers, lawyers, accountants, and business executives. Lacking the power of the richest people to influence national or international events, upper-middles often play an important role in local political affairs.

Average-Middles

The rest of the middle class falls near the center of the U.S. class structure. *Average-middles* typically work at less prestigious white-collar jobs (as middle managers, high school teachers, and sales clerks) or in highly skilled blue-collar jobs (say, as building contractors). Household income is between $40,000 and $80,000 a year, which is roughly the national average.

Middle-class people accumulate a small amount of wealth over the course of their working lives, mostly in the form of a house and a retirement account. Middle-class men and women are likely to be high school graduates, but the odds are just fifty-fifty that they will complete a college degree, typically at a less-expensive, state-supported school.

THE WORKING CLASS

About one-third of the population falls within the working class (sometimes called the *lower-middle class*). In Marxist terms, the working class forms the core of the industrial proletariat. Their blue-collar jobs usually yield a family income of between $25,000 and $40,000 a year, somewhat below the national average, and they have little or no wealth. Working-class families are thus vulnerable to financial problems caused by unemployment or illness.

Many working-class jobs provide little personal satisfaction—requiring discipline but rarely imagination—and subject workers to continual supervision. These jobs also offer fewer benefits, such as medical insurance and pension plans. About half of working-class families own their own homes, usually in lower-cost neighborhoods. College is a goal that only about one-third of working-class children realize.

THE LOWER CLASS

The remaining 20 percent of our population constitute the lower class. Low income makes their lives unstable and insecure. In 2001, the federal government

For decades, farm families who worked hard could expect to fall within the U.S. middle class. But the trend toward large-scale agribusiness has put the future of the small family farm in doubt. While many young people in rural areas are turning away from farming toward other careers, some carry on, incorporating high technology into their farm management in their determined efforts to succeed.

classified 32.9 million people (11.7 percent of the population) as poor. Millions more—called the "working poor"—are just barely better off, holding low-prestige jobs that provide not only little satisfaction but salaries that are close to minimum wage. Barely half manage to complete high school, and only one in four reaches college.

Society segregates the lower class, especially when the poor are racial or ethnic minorities. About 60 percent of lower-class families do not own their own homes, typically renting in the least desirable neighborhoods. Although poor neighborhoods are usually found in our inner cities, lower-class families also live in rural communities, especially across the South.

Most communities contain people of various class levels. In the country as a whole, however, some areas are more wealthy than others. National Map 11–1 on page 280 shows one measure of social class—per capita income—for all the counties in the United States.

THE DIFFERENCE CLASS MAKES

September 2, Mount Vernon, Ohio. My bike leans right, leaving the trail

SEEING OURSELVES

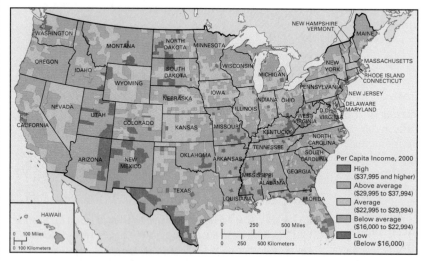

NATIONAL MAP 11-1
Per Capita Income
across the United States, 2000

This map shows the median per person income (that is, how much money, on average, a person has to spend) in the more than 3,000 counties that make up the United States, for the year 2000. The richest counties, shown in dark green, are not spread randomly across the country. Nor are the poorest U.S. counties, which are shown in dark red. Looking at the map, what patterns do you see in the distribution of wealth and poverty across the United States? What can you say about wealth and poverty in urban and rural areas?

Per Capita Income, 2000

High ($37,995 and higher)
Above average ($29,995 to $37,994)
Average ($22,995 to $29,994)
Below average ($16,000 to $22,994)
Low (Below $16,000)

Source: *American Demographics*, April 2000, pp. 42–43. ©2000 *American Demographics* magazine. Courtesy of Intertec Publishing/A Primedia Company. All rights reserved.

for the rest station that offers a stretch and a drink of water. Here I encounter Linda, a thirty-something woman who seems to be having trouble with her new roller blades. Eye contact and a perplexed look are a call for help, so I walk over to see what I might do. Several of her boot buckles require adjustment. Close up, she doesn't look well. "Are you OK?" I gently ask. "Very tired," Linda responds and goes on to explain why. Now divorced, she cannot pay off her debts with one low-income job. So she works an 11 A.M. to 7 P.M. shift as a computer clerk at a bank in town, catches four hours of sleep, and then drives an hour to Columbus, where she sits at another computer, processing catalog orders from 2 A.M. until 10 A.M. That leaves just enough time to drive back to Mount Vernon to start all over again at the bank.

Social stratification affects nearly every dimension of our lives. We will briefly examine some of the ways social standing is linked to our health, values, politics, and family life.

HEALTH

Health is closely related to social standing. Children born into poor families are three times more likely than children born to privileged families to die from disease, neglect, accidents, or violence during their first years of life. Among adults, people with above-average incomes are twice as likely as low-income people to describe their health as excellent. Moreover, richer people live, on average, seven years longer because they eat more nutritious food, live in safer and less stressful environments, and receive better medical care (U.S. National Center for Health Statistics, 2003).

VALUES

Cultural values, too, vary from class to class. The "old rich" have an unusually strong sense of family history since their social position is based on wealth passed down from generation to generation. Secure in their birthright privileges, upper-uppers also favor understated manners and tastes, while many "new rich" practice *conspicuous consumption*, buying things they know others will notice. They use clothes, homes, cars, boats, and even airplanes to make a statement about their social position.

Affluent people with greater education and financial security are also more tolerant of controversial behavior such as homosexuality. Working-class people, who grow up in an atmosphere of greater supervision and discipline and are less likely to attend college, tend to be less tolerant (Baltzell, 1979b; Lareau, 2002; NORC, 2003).

POLITICS

Do political attitudes follow class lines? The answer is yes, but the pattern is complex. A desire to protect their wealth prompts well-off people to be more conservative on *economic* issues, favoring, for example, lower taxes. But on *social* issues, such as abortion and other feminist concerns, highly educated, affluent people are more liberal. People of lower social standing, on the other hand, tend to be economic liberals, favoring expanded government social programs, but support a more conservative social agenda (NORC, 2003).

A more clear pattern emerges when it comes to political involvement. Higher-income people, who are better served by the system, are more likely to vote and to join political organizations than people with low incomes. In 2000, about half of adults with family incomes of $35,000 voted compared to three-fourths of those with family incomes of $75,000 (Samuelson, 2003).

FAMILY AND GENDER

Social class also shapes family life. Most lower-class families are somewhat larger than middle-class families because of earlier marriage and less use of birth control. In addition, working-class parents encourage children to conform to conventional norms and to respect authority figures. Parents of higher social standing, however, transmit a different "cultural capital" to their children, teaching them to express their individuality and imagination more freely. In both cases, parents are looking to the future: The odds are that less privileged children will take jobs that require they closely follow rules, whereas more advantaged children will enter fields that require more creativity (Kohn, 1977; McLeod, 1995; Lareau, 2002).

Compared to high-income people, low-income people are half as likely to report good health and, on average, live about seven fewer years. The toll of low income—played out in inadequate nutrition, little medical care, and high stress—is easy to see on the faces of the poor, who look old before their time.

Of course, the more money a family has, the better parents can develop their children's talents and abilities. An affluent family earning $100,100 a year will spend $254,400 raising a child born in 2002 to the age of eighteen. Middle-class people, with an annual income of $52,900, will spend $173,880, and a lower-income family, earning less than $39,700, will spend $127,080 (Lino, 2003). Privilege, then, begets privilege as family life reproduces the class structure in each generation.

Class also shapes our world of relationships. In a classic study of married life, Elizabeth Bott (1971; orig. 1957) found that most working-class couples divide their responsibilities according to gender; middle-class couples, by contrast, are more egalitarian, sharing more activities and expressing greater intimacy. More recently, Karen Walker (1995) discovered that working-class friendships typically provide material assistance; middle-class friendships, however, are likely to involve shared interests and leisure pursuits.

"So long, Bill. This is my club. You can't come in."

SOCIAL MOBILITY

Ours is a dynamic society marked by significant social movement. Earning a college degree, landing a higher-paying job, or marrying someone who earns a high income contributes to *upward social mobility;* dropping out of school, losing a job, or divorcing (especially for women) may signal *downward social mobility.*

Over the long term, though, social mobility is not so much a matter of individual changes as of changes in society itself. During the first half of the twentieth century, for example, industrialization expanded the U.S. economy, pushing up living standards. Even without being very good swimmers, so to speak, people rode a rising tide of prosperity. More recently, *structural social mobility* in a downward direction has dealt many people economic setbacks.

Sociologists distinguish between shorter- and longer-term changes in social position. **Intragenerational social mobility** is *a change in social position occurring during a person's lifetime.* **Intergenerational**

social mobility, *upward or downward social mobility of children in relation to their parents,* is important because it usually reveals long-term changes in society that affect almost everyone.

MYTH VERSUS REALITY

In few societies do people think about "getting ahead" as much as in the United States. Moving up, after all, is the American Dream. But is there as much social mobility as we like to think?

Studies of intergenerational mobility (almost all of which, unfortunately, have focused only on men) show that almost 40 percent of the sons of blue-collar workers attain white-collar jobs and almost 30 percent of sons born into white-collar families end up doing blue-collar work. *Horizontal mobility*—a change of occupation at one class level—is even more common, so that about 80 percent of sons show at least some type of social mobility in relation to their fathers (Blau & Duncan, 1967; Featherman & Hauser, 1978; Hout, 1998).

Research points to four general conclusions about social mobility in the United States:

1. **Social mobility over the course of the last century has been fairly high.** The widespread belief that the United States allows considerable social mobility is true. Mobility is what we would expect in an industrial class system.

2. **The long-term trend in social mobility has been upward.** Industrialization, which greatly expanded the U.S. economy, and the growth of white-collar work over the course of the twentieth century have boosted living standards.

3. **Within a single generation, social mobility is usually small.** Most young families increase their income over time as they gain education and skills. For example, a typical family headed by someone aged thirty earned about $46,000 in 2001; a typical family headed by someone aged fifty earned $68,000 (Duncan et al., 1998; U.S. Census Bureau, 2002). Yet only a very few people move "from rags to riches." While a sharp rise in wealth (the lottery winner in our chapter opening) or a steep drop in wealth (Martha Stewart claimed her stock trading scandal cost her $400 million) may attract media attention, most social mobility involves limited movement *within* one class level rather than striking moves *between* classes.

4. **Social mobility since the 1970s has been uneven.** Real income (adjusted for inflation) rose steadily during

the twentieth century until the 1970s, when it hit a plateau. During the 1980s, real income changed little for many people, rising slowly until the recent economic downturn began in 2000.

MOBILITY BY INCOME LEVEL

General trends often mask the experiences of different categories of people. Figure 11–3 shows how U.S. families at different income levels fared between 1980 and 2001. Well-to-do families (the highest 20 percent, but, like all the quintiles, not all the same families over the entire period) saw their incomes jump 59 percent, from an average $100,206 in 1980 to $159,644 in 2001. People in the middle of the population also had gains, albeit more modest ones. The lowest-income 20 percent saw only a 7.5 percent increase in earnings.

For families at the top of the income scale (the highest 5 percent), the last twenty-one years have been a windfall. These families, with an average income of almost $150,000 in 1980, were averaging almost $300,000 in 2001, about twice as much (U.S. Census Bureau, 2002).

MOBILITY: RACE, ETHNICITY, AND GENDER

White people, in a more privileged position to begin with, have been more upwardly mobile in recent decades than people of African or Hispanic ancestry. Through the economic expansion of the 1980s and 1990s, many more African Americans entered the ranks of the wealthy. But overall, the real income of African Americans has changed little in two decades. African American families earned nearly the same percentage of white family income in 2001 (62 percent) as in 1970 (61 percent). Compared to white families, Latino families lost ground between 1975 (when their average income was 67 percent of white family income) and 2001 (when it had slipped to 64 percent) (Featherman & Hauser, 1978; Pomer, 1986; U.S. Census Bureau, 2002).

Historically, women have had less opportunity for upward mobility than men, because so many working women hold clerical jobs (such as secretary) and service positions (such as waitress) that offer few promotions. In addition, when marriages end in divorce (as almost half do), women commonly experience downward social mobility; they lose not only income but a host of benefits, including health care and insurance coverage (Weitzman, 1996).

Over time, however, the earnings gap between women and men has been narrowing. Women working

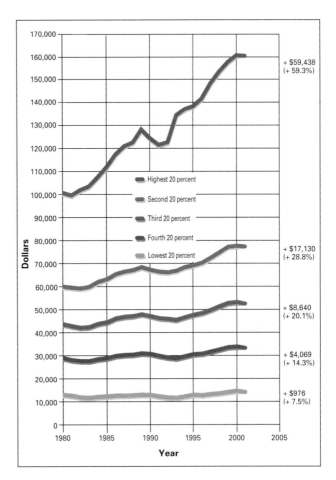

FIGURE 11-3 Mean Income, U.S. Families, 1980–2001 (in 2001 dollars, adjusted for inflation)

Source: U.S. Census Bureau (2002).

full time in 1980 earned 60 percent as much as men working full time; by 2001, women were earning 76 percent as much. Unfortunately, most of this change was due to a *drop* in men's earnings through the 1980s, while women's income stayed about the same (U.S. Census Bureau, 2002).

THE AMERICAN DREAM: STILL A REALITY?

The expectation of upward social mobility is deeply rooted in our culture. Through most of our history, economic expansion fulfilled this promise by raising living standards. Research shows that, for some people, this American Dream is still alive and well. One indication is that more people have become rich. In

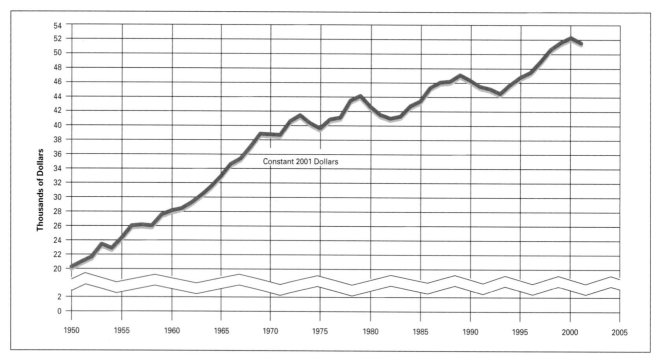

FIGURE 11-4 Median Income, U.S. Families, 1950–2001

Source: U.S. Census Bureau (2002).

1967, for example, just 3 percent of U.S. households earned $100,000 or more (in 2001 dollars, controlled for inflation); by 2001, this share had more than tripled to 14 percent. Moreover, even with the recent economic downturn, there are now at least 5 million millionaires in the United States, four times the number a decade ago (D'Souza, 1999; Rank & Hirschl, 2001; U.S. Census Bureau, 2002).

Yet not all indicators are positive. Note these disturbing trends:

1. **For many workers, earnings have stalled.** The annual income of a fifty-year-old man working full time climbed 49 percent between 1958 and 1974 (from $25,671 to $38,190 in constant 2001 dollars). Between 1974 and 2001, however, this worker's income rose only slightly, even as the number of hours worked increased and the cost of necessities like housing and medical care went up (Russell, 1995a; U.S. Census Bureau, 2002). For the nation as a whole, Figure 11–4 shows a 100 percent rise in median family income between 1950 and 1973 but only a 25 percent rise since then.

2. **Multiple job-holding is up.** According to the Bureau of Labor Statistics, 4.7 percent of the U.S. labor

force worked at two or more jobs in 1975; by 2001, the share had risen to 5.4 percent.

3. **More jobs offer little income.** In 1979, the Census Bureau classified 12 percent of full-time workers as "low-income earners" because they made less than $6,905; by 1998, this segment had increased to 15.4 percent, earning less than the comparable figure of $15,208.

4. **Young people are remaining at home.** Half of young people aged eighteen to twenty-four are now living with their parents. Since 1975, the average age at marriage has moved upward four years (to 25.3 years for women and 26.9 years for men).

In sum, for many lower-income people, the last several decades have brought hard times. The rising share of low-paying jobs has brought downward mobility for millions of families, creating widespread fear that the chance for a middle-class life is slipping away (Newman, 1993).

Over the last generation, the rich, by contrast, have become richer. At the very top of the pile, as the box explains, the highest-paid corporate executives have enjoyed a runaway rise in their earnings.

CRITICAL THINKING

As CEOs Get Richer: The Great Mansions Return

I grew up in Elkins Park, Pennsylvania, an older suburban community just to the north of Philadelphia. Elkins Park was at that time and still is a mostly middle-class community, although, like most of suburbia, some neighborhoods boast bigger houses and others have homes that are far more modest.

What was special about the Elkins Park of my childhood was that scattered over the area were a handful of great mansions, built a century ago by early Philadelphia industrialists. The great "estates" that surrounded these mansions back in the early 1900s had been fields and rolling meadows. By about 1940, however, most of the land was split off into lots for the newer middle-class suburbanites. The great mansions suddenly seemed out of place, with heirs disagreeing over who should live there and how to pay the rising taxes. As a result, many of the great mansions were sold, the buildings were taken down, and the remaining land was subdivided. The few mansions that still stood became the headquarters of religious or civic organizations that did not have to pay high taxes.

In the 1960s, when I was a teenager, a short ride on my bicycle could take me past what was left of the Breyer estate (built by the founder of the ice cream company, and now the township police building), the Curtis estate (built by a magazine publisher; it became a community park), the Wanamaker estate (built by the founder of a large Philadelphia department store), and the Wiedner estate (probably the grandest of them all, built by transportation magnate Peter A. B. Wiedner and modeled on a French chateau, complete with door knobs and window pulls covered in gold).

In their day, these structures were not just home to a family and its many servants; they were also monuments to a time when the rich were, well, *really* rich. By contrast, the community that emerged on the grounds once owned by these wealthy families is middle class, with homes built on quarter-acre lots. Some of the larger houses have a back stairway (originally intended for use by a maid or housekeeper), but thinking back to the 1960s, I can recall only one of my friends whose house had a maid (and the maid was his mother).

Is the so-called "Gilded Age" of great wealth gone? Hardly. By the 1980s, a new wave of great mansions was being built in the United States. Take architect Thierry Despont, who mostly designs huge houses for super-rich people. One of Despont's "smaller" homes might be 20,000 square feet (about ten times the size of the average U.S. house), and the larger ones go all the way up to 60,000 square feet (as big as any from a century ago and almost the size of the White House). These megahomes have kitchens as large as a college classroom, exercise rooms, indoor swimming pools, and even indoor tennis courts.

Megahouses are being built by newly rich chief executive officers (CEOs) of large corporations. While CEOs have always made more money than most people, recent years have witnessed executive pay soaring out of sight. Between 1970 and 2001, the average U.S. family saw only a modest increase in income (about 10 percent after inflation is taken into account). Yet, according to *Fortune* magazine, during that period the average compensation for the 100 highest-paid CEOs skyrocketed from $1.3 million (about 40 times the earnings of

an average worker of that time) to $37.5 million (roughly a 2,500 percent increase and equal to 1,000 times as much as the earnings of today's average worker). Some CEOs, of course, earn far more: In the year before Enron collapsed, for example, Kenneth Lay earned about $150 million. Assuming Lay worked forty-eight hours per week and fifty weeks that year, that sum amounts to more than $60,000 *per day.*

Analysts put forward numerous theories to account for this sharp increase in CEO pay. Some contend that, in today's competitive global economy, many CEOs are true "superstars," who build company profits and deserve every penny they earn. Some take a less generous view, suggesting that CEOs have stacked their corporate boards of directors with friends, whose "payback" includes approving enormous paychecks and bonuses. In any case, executive pay has become a national scandal. In light of the harm that this pay scandal (not to mention cases of outright executive wrongdoing) has done to the corporate world, it may be most accurate simply to say that we have been living in an era of unbridled greed. The question is whether or not this era is coming to an end.

What do you think?

1. *Do you consider increasing economic inequality a problem? Why or why not?*

2. *How many times more than an average worker should a CEO earn? Why?*

3. *Do you think very high CEO pay hurts stockholders? The general public? Why or why not?*

Source: Written by the author, based on Krugman (2002) and with material from Myers (2000).

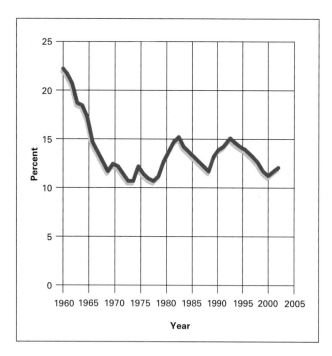

FIGURE 11–5 The Poverty Rate in the United States, 1960–2001

Source: U.S. Census Bureau (2002).

THE GLOBAL ECONOMY AND U.S. CLASS STRUCTURE

Underlying the recent shifts in U.S. class structure is global economic change. Much of the industrial production that gave U.S. workers high-paying jobs a generation ago has moved overseas. With less industry at home, the United States now serves as a vast market for industrial goods such as cars and popular items like stereos, cameras, and computers made in Japan, Korea, and elsewhere.

High-paying jobs in manufacturing, held by 26 percent of the U.S. labor force in 1960, support only 14 percent of workers today. In their place, the economy now offers "service work," which often pays far less. A traditionally high-paying corporation like USX (formerly United States Steel) now employs fewer people than the expanding McDonald's chain, and fast-food clerks make only a fraction of what steel workers earn.

The global reorganization of work is not bad news for everyone. On the contrary, the global economy creates upward social mobility for educated people who specialize in law, finance, marketing, and computer technology. Moreover, global economic expansion has helped push up the stock market (even with the recent declines) almost eightfold between 1980 and 2002, reaping profits for families with money to invest.

But the same trend has hurt many "average" workers, who have seen their factory jobs relocate overseas. Moreover, many companies have "downsized"—cutting the ranks of their work force—to become competitive in world markets. As a result, although half of all households contain two or more workers—double the share in 1950—many people are working harder simply to hold on to what they have (Reich, 1991; Nelson, 1998; Schlesinger, 1998; Sennett, 1998).

POVERTY IN THE UNITED STATES

Social stratification creates both "haves" and "have-nots." All systems of social inequality create poverty—or at least **relative poverty,** *the deprivation of some people in relation to those who have more.* A more serious but preventable problem is **absolute poverty,** *a deprivation of resources that is life-threatening.*

As Chapter 12 ("Global Stratification") explains, upward of 1 billion human beings—one in six—live at or near absolute poverty. Even in the affluent United States, families go hungry, live in inadequate housing, and suffer poor health because of wrenching poverty.

THE EXTENT OF U.S. POVERTY

In 2001, the government tallied 32.9 million men, women, and children—11.7 percent of the population—as poor. This count of relative poverty refers to families with incomes below an official poverty line, which for a family of four was set at $18,104. The poverty line is about three times what the government estimates people must spend for food. But the income of the average poor family was just 60 percent of this amount. Thus, the typical poor family had to get by on about $10,873 in 2001 (U.S. Census Bureau, 2002). Figure 11–5 shows that the official poverty rate fell during the 1960s and has stayed about the same since then.

Poor people know very well the consequences of living on the edge—not being able to afford the jackets or expensive sneakers their children want so badly and, worse, worrying about what will happen if one of the family becomes injured or ill. In short, poverty means a life of daily stress, insecurity, and—for several million adults and children in the United States—hunger.

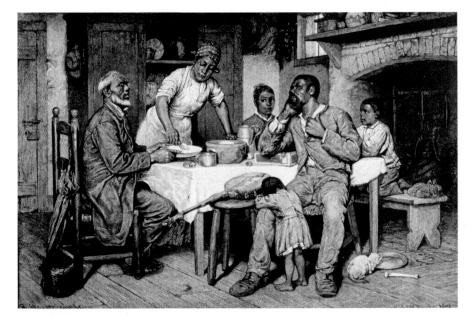

This woodcut from the 1880s depicting a family sharing a meal with a visiting pastor captures the humanity and humility of impoverished people. This message—that the poor are human beings, most doing the best they can to get by—is important to remember in a society that tends to define poor people as morally unworthy and deserving of their bitter plight.

WHO ARE THE POOR?

Although there is no simple profile of the poor, poverty is pronounced among certain categories of our population. Where these categories overlap, the problem is especially serious.

Age

A generation ago, it was the elderly who were at greatest risk for poverty, but no longer. Thanks to better retirement programs offered today by private employers and the government, the poverty rate for people over age sixty-five fell from 30 percent in 1967 to 10.1 percent—well below the national average—in 2001. Even so, with the number of older people increasing, about 10 percent (3.4 million) of the poor are elderly people.

Today, the burden of poverty falls most heavily on children. In 2001, 16.3 percent of people under age eighteen (11.7 million children) were poor. Tallied another way, four in ten of the U.S. poor are children.

Race and Ethnicity

Two-thirds of all poor people are white; 25 percent are African Americans. But in relation to their overall numbers, African Americans are about three times as likely as non-Hispanic whites to be poor. In 2001, 22.7 percent of African Americans (8.1 million people)

lived in poverty, compared to 21.4 percent of Latinos (8.0 million), 10.2 percent of Asians and Pacific Islanders (1.3 million), and 7.8 percent of non-Hispanic whites (15.3 million). The poverty gap between whites and minorities has changed little since 1975.

As we might expect, child poverty is especially high among minorities. Whereas 10 percent of non-Hispanic white children are poor, 28 percent of Latino children and 30 percent of African American youngsters are poor (U.S. Census Bureau, 2002).

Gender and Family Patterns

Of all poor people over age eighteen, 60 percent are women and 40 percent are men. This disparity reflects the fact that women who head households bear the brunt of poverty. Of all poor families, 51 percent are headed by women with no husband present, while just 9 percent of poor families are headed by single men.

The term **feminization of poverty** describes *the trend by which women represent an increasing proportion of the poor.* In 1960, 25 percent of all poor households were headed by women; the majority of poor families had both wives and husbands in the home. By 2001, however, the share of poor households headed by a single woman had more than doubled to 51 percent.

The feminization of poverty is thus part of a larger change: the rapidly increasing number of households

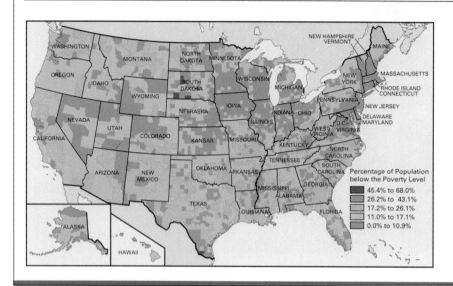

NATIONAL MAP 11–2
Poverty across the United States

This map shows that the poorest counties in the United States—where the poverty rate is more than twice the national average—are in Appalachia, spread across the Deep South, along the border with Mexico, near the "four corners" region of the southwest, and in the Dakotas. Can you provide some reasons for this pattern?

Source: U.S. Census Bureau (2001).

Percentage of Population below the Poverty Level
- 45.4% to 68.0%
- 26.2% to 43.1%
- 17.2% to 26.1%
- 11.0% to 17.1%
- 0.0% to 10.9%

at all class levels headed by single women. This trend, coupled with the fact that households headed by women are at high risk of poverty, is why women and their children make up an increasing share of the U.S. poor.

Urban and Rural Poverty

The greatest concentration of poverty is found in central cities, where the 2001 poverty rate stood at 16.5 percent. Suburbs, too, have destitute people, but their poverty rate is just 8.2 percent. Thus, the poverty rate for urban areas as a whole is 11.1 percent—lower than the 14.2 percent found in rural areas. National Map 11–2 shows that most of the counties with the highest poverty rate in the United States are rural.

EXPLAINING POVERTY

For the richest nation on Earth to have tens of millions of poor people raises serious questions. It is true, as some analysts remind us, that many of the people counted among the officially poor in the United States are far better off than the poor in other countries: 41 percent of U.S. poor families own a home, 70 percent own a car, 97 percent have a color television, and only

a few percent report often going without food (Rector, 1998; Gallagher, 1999). Nevertheless, poverty harms the overall well-being of millions of people in this country.

Figure 11–6 shows that the public is divided over what to do about poverty. More than one-fourth of respondents to this national survey look to the government to help poor people; slightly fewer think people must take responsibility for themselves. More than 46 percent, however, straddle the fence, thinking both government and individuals share this responsibility.

We now focus on two opposing explanations for poverty. Together, they lead to a lively and important political debate.

One View: Blame the Poor

One approach holds that *the poor are mostly responsible for their own poverty.* Throughout our history, people in the United States have valued self-reliance and have believed that social standing is mostly a matter of individual talent and effort. This view sees society offering plenty of opportunity to anyone able and willing to take advantage of it. Thus, anyone who is poor cannot or will not work, women and men with few skills, little schooling, and little motivation. This argument represents the right side of the continuum in Figure 11–6.

In his study of Latin American cities, anthropologist Oscar Lewis (1961) concluded that the poor become trapped in a *culture of poverty*, a lower-class subculture that can destroy people's ambition. Socialized in poor families, children become resigned to their plight, producing a self-perpetuating cycle of poverty.

In 1996, hoping to break the cycle of poverty in the United States, Congress changed the welfare system that had provided federal funds to assist poor people since 1935. Now the federal government sends money to the states to give to needy people, but benefits carry strict time limits: in most cases, no more than two years at a stretch and a total of five years if an individual moves in and out of the welfare system. The stated purpose of this reform was to move people from dependency on government and force them to be self-supporting.

 A report on food scarcity in the United States is found at this Internet address: http://www.ers.usda.gov/publications/fanrr35/

Counterpoint: Blame Society

The opposing position, argued by William Julius Wilson (1996a, 1996b; Mouw, 2000), holds that *society is primarily responsible for poverty*. Wilson points to the loss of jobs in the inner cities as the primary cause of poverty, claiming that there is simply not enough work to support families. Thus, Wilson sees any lack of trying on the part of poor people as a *result of little opportunity* rather than a *cause of poverty*. From this point of view, then, Oscar Lewis's analysis amounts to "blaming the victims" for their own suffering (Ryan, 1976; Billings & Blee, 2000). The view that looks to government to overcome poverty is at the left side of the continuum in Figure 11–6. The box on page 290 provides a closer look at Wilson's argument and how it would shape public policy.

Weighing the Evidence

What evidence supports one side or the other of the poverty controversy? Government statistics show that 44 percent of the heads of poor households did not work at all during 2001, and an additional 35 percent worked only part time (U.S. Census Bureau, 2002). Such facts seem to support the "blame the poor" side, since one major cause of poverty is *not holding a job*.

But the *reasons* that people do not work seem more consistent with the "blame society" position.

Survey Question: "Some people think that the government in Washington should do everything possible to improve the living standards of all poor Americans [they are at point 1 below]. Other people think it is not the government's responsibility, and that each person should take care of himself [they are at point 5 below]. Where would you place yourself on this scale, or haven't you made up your mind on this?

1	2	3	4	5	Don't know/ no answer 2.6%
16.9%	10.4%	46.1%	12.6%	11.4%	

"I strongly agree the government should improve living standards"   "I agree with both answers"   "I strongly agree that people should take care of themselves"

FIGURE 11-6 Government or Individuals: Who Is Responsible for Poverty?

Source: NORC (2003:293).

Middle-class women may be able to combine working and child rearing, but this juggling is much harder for poor women, who cannot afford child care—and few employers provide child-care programs for their employees. Moreover, as William Julius Wilson explains, many people are idle not because they are avoiding work but because there are not enough jobs to go around. In short, most poor people in the United States find few options and alternatives (Popkin, 1990; Schiller, 1994; Edin & Lein, 1996; Wilson, 1996a; Pease & Martin, 1997; Duncan, 1999).

The Working Poor

But not all poor people are jobless, and the *working poor* command the sympathy and support of people on both sides of the poverty debate (Schwarz & Volgy, 1992). In 2001, 21 percent of heads of poor families (1.3 million women and men) worked at least fifty weeks of the year and yet could not escape poverty. Another 35 percent of these heads of families (2.2 million people) remained poor despite part-time employment. Put differently, about 3 percent of full-time workers earn so little that they remain poor (U.S. Census Bureau, 2002). In short, the working poor suffer from low income due to, first, working too few hours and, second, earning wages that are too low. Keep in mind that a full-time worker earning $6 per hour (more than the minimum wage of $5.15 per

CRITICAL THINKING

When Work Disappears: The Result Is Poverty

The U.S. economy has created tens of millions of new jobs in recent decades. Yet African Americans who live in inner cities have faced a catastrophic loss of work. William Julius Wilson points out that, while people continue to talk about welfare reform, neither major political party (Democrats or Republicans) has said anything about the lack of work in central cities.

With the loss of inner-city jobs, Wilson continues, for the first time in U.S. history a large majority of the adults in our inner cities are not working. Studying the Washington Park area of Chicago, Wilson found a troubling trend. Back in 1950, most adults in this African American community had jobs, but by the mid-1990s, two-thirds did not. As one elderly woman who moved to the neighborhood in 1953 explained:

> When I moved in, the neighborhood was intact. It was intact with homes, beautiful homes, mini-mansions, with stores, laundromats, with Chinese cleaners. We had drugstores. We had hotels. We had doctors over on 39th street. We had doctor's offices in the neighborhood. We had the middle class and the upper-middle class. It has gone from affluent to where it is today. (Wilson, 1996b:28)

But *why* has this neighborhood declined? Wilson's eight years of research point to one answer: There are barely any jobs. It is the loss of work that has pushed people into desperate poverty, weakened families, and made people turn to welfare. In nearby Woodlawn, Wilson identified more than 800 businesses that had operated in 1950; today,

just 100 remain. Moreover, a number of major employers in the past—including Western Electric and International Harvester—closed their plant doors in the late 1960s. The inner cities have fallen victim to economic change, including downsizing and industrial jobs moving overseas.

Wilson paints a grim picture. But he also believes the answer lies in creating new jobs. Wilson proposes attacking the problem in stages. First, the government could hire people to do all kinds of work, from clearing slums to putting up new housing. Such a program, modeled on the Works Progress Administration (WPA) enacted in 1935 during the Great Depression, would move people from welfare to work and, in the process, create much-needed hope. In addition, federal and state governments must improve schools by enacting performance standards and providing more funding. Of special importance is teaching children language skills and computer skills to prepare

them for the jobs being created by the Information Revolution. Improved regional public transportation would connect cities (where people need work) and suburbs (where most jobs now are). In addition, more child-care programs would help single mothers and fathers balance the responsibilities of employment and parenting.

Wilson claims that his proposals are well grounded in research. But he knows politics revolves around other considerations as well. For one thing, to the extent that the public *thinks* there are plenty of jobs, they will conclude that the poor are simply avoiding work, and change will be even less likely. Moreover, he concedes that his proposals, at least in the short term, are more expensive than continuing to funnel welfare assistance to jobless communities.

But for the long term, he asks, what are the costs of allowing our cities to decay while suburbs prosper? Of allowing a new generation of preschoolers to join the ranks of the restless and often angry people for whom there is no work? What would be the benefits of affording everyone the hope and satisfaction that are supposed to define our way of life?

What do you think?

1. *According to Wilson, why are many of this country's inner-city neighborhoods so poor?*

2. *What does he think we can do to address this problem?*

3. *Do you agree with his analysis of poverty? Why or why not?*

Source: Based on Wilson (1996b).

Some 1.3 million people in the United States work full time and yet do not earn enough to escape poverty. This hotel worker washes windows to earn $7 an hour or about $14,500 per year. Would you favor higher wages for such workers? Why or why not?

hour) cannot lift an urban family of four above the poverty line.

The working poor also include another 5 million families that are only slightly better off, with income above the poverty line but less than 150 percent of the poverty line (an urban family of four with an income between about $18,000 and $27,000). Among families in this category, 83 percent have at least one full-time worker. Therefore, with only low-wage jobs available, many people who work hard can boost incomes above the poverty line, but not by much (O'Hare, 2002).

 For a profile of the working poor, visit http://www.bls.gov/cps/cpswp2000.htm

To sum up, individual ability and personal initiative do play a part in shaping everyone's social position. However, the weight of sociological evidence points to society—not individual character traits—as the primary cause of poverty. Society must be at fault because a rising share of jobs available offer only low wages. In addition, the poor are *categories* of people—women heads of families, people of color, people isolated from the larger society in inner-city areas—who face special barriers and limited opportunities.

HOMELESSNESS

There is no precise count of homeless people. Fanning out across the cities of the United States on the night of March 27, 2000, Census Bureau officials tallied 170,706 people at emergency and homeless shelters. But the actual number is surely higher, especially in light of the recent economic downturn, which has many urban homeless shelters filled to the point of overcrowding. A rough estimate is that a full count of the homeless might reach 500,000 *on any given night*, with as many as three times that number—1.5 million people—homeless *at some time during the course of a year* (U.S. Census Bureau, 2000; Wickham, 2000; Marks, 2001).

The familiar stereotypes of homeless people—men sleeping in doorways and women carrying everything they own in a shopping bag—have been replaced by the "new homeless": people thrown out of work because of plant closings, those forced out of apartments by rent increases or condominium conversions, and others unable to meet mortgage or rent payments because of low wages or no work at all. Today, no stereotype paints a complete picture of the homeless.

Most homeless people report that they do not work, but 44 percent say they work at least part time (HUD, 1999). But working or not, virtually all homeless people have one thing in common: *poverty*. For that reason, the explanations of poverty already offered also apply to homelessness. Some blame the *personal traits* of the homeless themselves. One-third of homeless people are substance abusers, and one-fourth are mentally ill. More broadly, a fraction of 1 percent of our population, for one reason or another, seems

CONTROVERSY & DEBATE

The Welfare Dilemma

In 1996, Congress ended the federal public assistance that guaranteed some income to all poor people. The new state-run programs require people who receive aid to enroll in a job-training program or find work—or have their benefits cut off.

Almost no one likes "welfare." Liberals criticize welfare for doing too little to help the poor; conservatives charge that it hurts the people it is supposed to help; and the poor themselves find welfare a complex and often degrading program.

So what, exactly, *is* welfare? The term "welfare" refers to a host of policies and programs designed to improve the well-being of the U.S. population. Until the welfare reform of 1996, most people used the term to refer to one part of the overall system—Aid for Dependent Children (AFDC), a program of monthly financial support for parents (mostly single women) to care for themselves and their children. In 1996, some 5 million households received AFDC for some part of the year.

Did AFDC help or hurt the poor? There are two sides to the debate. Conservative critics argue that, rather than reducing child poverty, AFDC actually made the problem worse for two reasons. First, this form of welfare weakened families, they say, because for years

after the program began, public assistance regulations provided benefits to poor mothers only if no husband lived in the home. As conservatives see it, AFDC operated as an economic incentive to women to have children outside marriage, and they blamed it for the rapid rise of out-of-wedlock births among poor people. To conservatives, the connection between being poor and not being married is clear: Fewer than one in ten married-couple families were poor; more than nine in ten AFDC families were headed by an unmarried woman.

Second, conservatives also believe that welfare encouraged poor people to become dependent on government handouts. This, they say, is the main reason that eight of ten poor heads of households did not have full-time jobs. Furthermore, more than half of nonpoor single mothers worked full time, compared with only 5 percent of single mothers receiving AFDC. Conservatives thus claim that welfare strayed from its original purpose of short-term help to nonworking women with children (typically, after divorce or death of a husband) and became a way of life. Once trapped in dependency, poor women were likely to raise children who would, themselves, be poor as adults.

Liberals charge that their opponents use a double standard in evaluating

government programs. Why, they ask, do people object to government money going to poor mothers and children when most "welfare" actually goes to richer people? The AFDC budget was $25 billion annually—no small sum, to be sure—but just half of the $50 billion in home mortgage deductions that homeowners pocket each year. And it pales in comparison to the $300 billion in annual Social Security benefits Uncle Sam provides to senior citizens, most of whom are well-off. And what about "corporate welfare" to big companies? Their tax write-offs and other benefits run into hundreds of billions of dollars per year. As liberals see it, "wealthfare" is far greater than "welfare."

Second, liberals claim that conservatives paint a distorted picture of public assistance. The popular image of do-nothing "welfare queens" masks the fact that most poor families that turned to public assistance were truly needy. Moreover, the typical household receiving AFDC received barely $400 per month, hardly enough to attract people to a "life of welfare dependency." And in constant dollars, AFDC payments actually declined over time. In fact, liberals fault public assistance as a "Band-Aid™ approach" to the serious social problems of too few jobs and too much income inequality in the United States.

unable to cope with our complex and highly competitive society (Bassuk, 1984; Whitman, 1989).

Others, however, see homelessness as resulting from *societal factors*, including low wages and a lack of low-income housing (Kozol, 1988; Schutt, 1989; Bohannan, 1991). Supporters of this position point out that one-third of all homeless people are entire families, and children are the fastest-growing category

of the homeless. A minister in a Pennsylvania town that has lost hundreds of industrial jobs because of plant closings describes the real-life effects of economic recession:

> Yes, there are new jobs. There's a new McDonald's and a Burger King. You can take home [enough to] barely pay the rent. What do you do if someone

As for the charge that public assistance weakens families, liberals concede that the proportion of single-parent families has risen, but they doubt AFDC was to blame. Rather, single parenting is a broad cultural trend found at all class levels in many countries.

Thus, liberals conclude, AFDC was attacked not because it failed but, rather, because it benefited a part of the population that many consider undeserving. Our cultural tradition of equating wealth with virtue and poverty with vice allows rich people to display privilege as a badge of ability, while poverty is a sign of personal failure. According to Richard Sennett and Jonathan Cobb (1973), the negative stigma of poverty is the "hidden injury of class."

The figure shows that people in the United States, more than people in other industrial societies, tend to see poverty as a mark of laziness and personal failure. It should not be surprising, then, that Congress replaced the federal AFDC program with state-run programs called Temporary Assistance for Needy Families (TANF). The federal government provides funding, and states set their own qualifications and benefits, but they must limit assistance

to two consecutive years (with a lifetime limit of five years).

By 2002, TANF had moved about half of single parents on welfare into jobs or job training, and the rate of out-of-wedlock births started to fall after 1996. Therefore, President George W. Bush and other supporters of welfare reform declared the new program to be

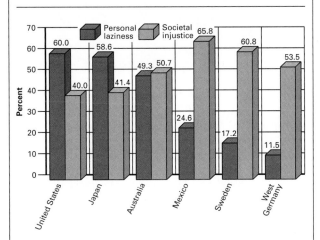

GLOBAL SNAPSHOT

Assessing the Causes of Poverty

Survey Question: "Why are there people in this country who live in need?" Percentages reflect respondents' identification of either "personal laziness" or "societal injustice" as the primary cause of poverty.

*Percentages for each country may not add up to 100 because less frequently identified causes of poverty were omitted from this figure.

Source: Inglehart et al. (2000).

a success. However, critics point out that most of the "success stories"—that is, people who are now working—earn so little that they are hardly better off than before (and half of these jobs provide no health insurance). In other words, welfare reform has slashed the number of people receiving welfare, but it has done far less to reduce poverty. In addition, say the critics, many of these working women now spend less time with their children. In sum, the welfare debate goes on.

Continue the debate . . .

1. *How does our cultural emphasis on self-reliance help explain the controversy surrounding public assistance? Why, then, do people not criticize benefits (like home mortgage deductions) for more well-off people?*

2. *Do you approve of the benefit time limits built into the new TANF program? Why or why not?*

3. *Why do you think the welfare reforms have done little to reduce poverty?*

Sources: Corcoran et al. (2000), U.S. Department of Health and Human Services (2000), Iceland & Kim (2001), Rogers-Dillon (2001), Hofferth (2002), Lichter & Crowley (2002), and Lichter & Jayakody (2002).

gets sick? What do you do for food and clothes? These may be good jobs for a teenager. Can you ask a thirty-year-old man who's worked for GM since he was eighteen to keep his wife and kids alive on jobs like that? There are jobs cleaning rooms in the hotel. . . . Can you expect a single mother with three kids to hold her life together with that kind of work? (Kozol, 1988:6)

No one disputes that a large proportion of homeless people are personally impaired to some degree, but how much is cause and how much is effect is difficult to untangle. Structural changes in the U.S. economy, coupled with reduced aid to low-income people and a real estate market that puts housing out of the reach of the poorest members of U.S. society—contribute to homelessness (Ratnesar, 1999).

Homelessness is found throughout the United States as well as other high-income nations. Here, homeless people gather under a bridge in Hamburg, Germany. Why do you think that the public tends not to view homelessness (and, more generally, poverty) as a serious social problem?

Most homeless people live in urban areas. A Housing and Urban Development (HUD) study of more than 4,000 poor people across the United States—most of them homeless at the time they were interviewed—reports that 92 percent are urban: 71 percent reside in central cities and 21 percent live in suburbs. Just 8 percent live in rural areas (HUD, 1999). Rural homelessness not only involves lower numbers but is often less visible. As one volunteer in a rural Ohio county explains, "Here, you don't see people sleeping in a park or under a bridge" (Splain, 2000:1a). Yet social service agencies in this small county (of 15,000 people) serve some 400 people a year. Some are transients, moving from place to place, some are living with friends or relatives, some are sleeping in a car. This varied pattern explains why people who live in rural areas may not be aware that they, too, have homeless in their communities.

 Find the HUD report on homelessness at http://www.huduser.org/publications/homeless/homelessness/contents.html

We close this chapter with a look at welfare, a topic that focuses our thinking about how to respond to issues such as poverty and homelessness.

 A report by the U.S. Conference of Mayors on homelessness in this country is found at http://www.usmayors.org/uscm/news/press_releases/documents/hunger_121802.asp

Finally, social stratification extends far beyond the borders of the United States. In fact, the most striking social inequality is found not within any one nation but in the different living standards among nations around the world. In Chapter 12 ("Global Stratification"), we broaden our investigation by looking at global inequality.

SUMMARY

1. Social stratification in the United States involves inequality of many kinds, including income, wealth, and power.

2. White-collar jobs generally offer greater income and prestige than blue-collar work. Many of the jobs typically held by women offer low social prestige or income.

3. Schooling is also a resource that is distributed unequally. More than 80 percent of people over age twenty-five complete high school, but only one-fourth are college graduates.

4. Family ancestry, race and ethnicity, gender, and religion all affect a person's social position.

5. The upper class (5 percent of the population) includes the richest and most powerful families. Most members of the upper-upper class, or the "old rich," inherit their wealth; the lower-upper class, or the "new rich," amass wealth from high incomes.

6. The middle class (40 to 45 percent) enjoys financial security, but only some of these people (the upper-middle class) have substantial wealth.

7. With below-average incomes, most members of the working class or lower-middle class (33 percent) have blue-collar jobs, and only one-third of their children reach college.

8. About one-fifth of the U.S. population belongs to the lower class; more than half of these people live below the government's poverty line. People of African and Hispanic descent, as well as women, are disproportionately represented in the lower class.

9. Social class shapes our lives, including health, attitudes, and patterns of family living.

10. Some social mobility is common in the United States as it is in other high-income countries; typically, however, only small changes occur from one generation to the next.

11. The growing global economy has increased the wealth of rich families in the United States but stalled or even lowered the standard of living of low-income families.

12. The government classifies 32.9 million people as poor. About 40 percent of the poor are children under age eighteen. Two-thirds of the poor are white, but African Americans and Hispanics are disproportionately represented among people with low income. The *feminization of poverty* means more poor families are headed by women.

13. The *culture of poverty* thesis suggests that poverty is caused by shortcomings in the poor themselves. Others believe that poverty is caused by society's unequal distribution of jobs and wealth.

14. Our cultural emphasis on individual responsibility helps explain why public assistance for the poor has long been controversial.

KEY CONCEPTS

income (p. 272) wages or salary from work and earnings from investments

wealth (p. 273) the total value of money and other assets, minus outstanding debts

intragenerational social mobility (p. 282) a change in social position occurring during a person's lifetime

intergenerational social mobility (p. 282) upward or downward social mobility of children in relation to their parents

relative poverty (p. 286) the deprivation of some people in relation to those who have more

absolute poverty (p. 286) a deprivation of resources that is life-threatening

feminization of poverty (p. 287) the trend by which women represent an increasing proportion of the poor

CRITICAL-THINKING QUESTIONS

1. If you were trying to assess a person's social class and could ask the individual only *one* question, what would it be? Why?

2. When you think back to Alcario Castellano, the retired grocer in our chapter opening, what is your estimate of his social class position before and after his claiming a $42.3-million lottery prize? Specify the reasons for your answer.

3. Would you be in favor of class-based affirmative action? That is, should our society give people born to lower-class families an edge in college admission and company hiring? Why or why not?

4. Our society is always ready to assist the "worthy" poor, including elderly people, whom we do not expect to fend for themselves. At the same time, we are less generous toward the "unworthy poor," able-bodied people who, we assume, could take care of themselves but do not. If this is so, why do you think we have not done more to reduce poverty among children, who surely fall into the "worthy" category?

APPLICATIONS AND EXERCISES

1. Develop several simple questions that assess various dimensions of social standing (you might consider income, wealth, education, job prestige, and power, among others). Ask the questions of half a dozen people who are finished with school. According to your data, what is the extent of status consistency for these subjects?

2. During an evening of television viewing, assess the social class level of the characters you see on various shows. In each case, explain why you assign someone a particular social position. What patterns do you find?

3. Visit the social services office that oversees financial assistance to people with low incomes in your community. See what you can learn about the effect of the 1996 welfare reforms.

4. Packaged in the back of this new textbook is an interactive CD-ROM that offers a variety of video and interactive review materials intended to help you better understand the material covered in this chapter. For this chapter, the CD-ROM contains a relevant clip from *ABC News*, an author's tip video, interactive map animations, an interactive time line, and flashcards with audio pronunciations of the more difficult words.

 ## SITES TO SEE

http://www.prenhall.com/macionis

Visit the interactive Companion Website™ that accompanies this text. Begin by clicking on the cover of your book. You will find a chapter-by-chapter study guide, practice tests, suggested Web links, and links to other relevant material.

http://quickfacts.census.gov/qfd/index.html
http://www.bea.doc.gov

These two sites, the first run by the Census Bureau and the second by the government's Bureau of Economic Analysis, provide state-by-state and county-by-county income data. Visit these sites and see what you can learn about social standing in your part of the country.

http://www.secondharvest.org/whoshungry/
   hunger_study_intro.html
http://www.jcpr.org
http://www.nber.org

Here are three Web sites that are worth a visit to learn more about poverty in the United States. The first is operated by

America's Second Harvest, a hunger-fighting organization; the second by the Joint Center for Poverty Research; and the third by the National Bureau of Economic Research.

http://www.researchforum.org
http://www.childrensdefense.org/states/data.html

In the United States, children are at high risk of poverty. The two sites noted above introduce you to the Research Forum on Children, Families, and the New Federalism and the Children's Defense Fund, both of which are concerned about child poverty.

http://www.iwpr.org

The Institute for Women's Policy Research investigates the interplay of gender and poverty.

http://www.journalofpoverty.org

This Web site describes a journal that focuses on poverty issues.

 ## INVESTIGATE WITH RESEARCH NAVIGATOR™

Follow the instructions on page 24 of this text to access the features of **Research Navigator™**. Once at the Web site, enter your Login Name and Password. Then, to use the **Content Select™** database, enter keywords such as "homelessness," "welfare reform," and "poverty," and the search engine will

supply relevant and recent scholarly and popular press publications. Use the *New York Times* **Search-by-Subject Archive** to find recent news articles related to sociology and the **Link Library** feature to find relevant Web links organized by the key terms associated with this chapter.

The New York Times

In the Times

October 20, 2003

Are Those Leaving Welfare Better Off Now? Yes and No

By **LESLIE KAUFMAN**

By many measures, the overhaul of welfare has been a success. Seven years after Congress rewrote the rules in an effort to end long-term dependency on benefits, hundreds of thousands of Americans have moved from welfare to work, many of them substantially raising their incomes. . . .

But several recent studies by state governments and urban-policy researchers point to a result that has been less obvious and slower to emerge: a significant number of those who have left the welfare rolls have no jobs, and are sinking deeper into poverty. . . .

There are 2.4 million fewer American families on the federal welfare rolls than in 1996, when there were 4.4 million.

More than half have left welfare for work, although many who left for jobs did not keep them. Others have gone off welfare voluntarily, possibly because they chafed under the new rules or turned to other sources of support. And roughly a third have been forced out because they failed to comply with stricter state requirements or reached the five-year lifetime limit on federal benefits. . . .

Many urban-policy researchers and advocates for the poor . . . argue that the deepening poverty among former welfare recipients reflects flaws in the legislation that were entirely predictable and need to be corrected.

They say the people who are losing ground face all sorts of obstacles that keep them from work . . . like learning disabilities, depression, minor illnesses or a lack of transportation. Families with more obvious handicaps are frequently exempted from the work rules under the 1996 law. . . .

Census Bureau figures for 2002 showed the number of people living in severe poverty with incomes less than half of the poverty rate had grown by 600,000 over the previous year . . . Researchers say they suspect many of the new severely poor are people who left welfare, because benefits automatically lift families out of this lowest category.

Tracy Lawrence, 34, a single mother in Hartford, was cut off from benefits two years ago after she reached her lifetime limit. Ms. Lawrence insists her chronic stomach problems make her too sick to work, but has not been able to provide adequate proof to state authorities to be exempted from the work rules. Welfare was not her only income. She also received and still receives food stamps, gifts from her mother and small child-support payments from the father of her 6-year-old daughter. Perhaps most important, she pays only $77 a month for rent in state housing.

Still, she says life is much harder without the federal check. "I can't buy shampoo or personal care items because they are not covered by food stamps," she said. Clothing is not covered, either, and she said she had been unable to find her daughter a winter coat or snow boots at local charities. She has received a notice of eviction because she is months behind on her rent, and fears her phone will be cut off as well. . . .

Cynthia Brown of New Haven is also feeling the pinch. Ms. Brown, 31, who says she is healthy, has spent most of her life on welfare. . . . In 2001, Connecticut denied her benefits, saying she had already hit her lifetime limit. Ms. Brown and her three children did not cope well. They lived with an aunt in public housing until she made them leave, fearing the overcrowding would cause her to lose her lease. They lived in a park for a week and then in a homeless shelter for three months, until Ms. Brown obtained subsidized housing and a year's extension on welfare. . . .

Two months before the extension will expire, Ms. Brown says she is earnestly looking for work but has not found any. She was briefly employed at Yale as a cook, but says she lost the job after her cutting skills were found wanting. Now, she says, her only chance is that something in her life will go so wrong that she will be exempted from the state's rules.

"I am hoping for a disaster," she said.

What do you think?

1. Do you think people on welfare should be required to look for work? What role should the government play in helping them find work?
2. Do you consider the 1996 welfare reform to be a success or not? Explain.

Adapted from the original article by Leslie Kaufman published in *The New York Times* on October 20, 2003. Copyright © 2003 by The New York Times Company. Reprinted with permission.

GLOBAL STRATIFICATION

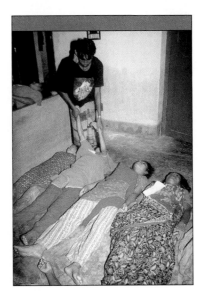

ORE THAN 1,000 workers were busily sewing together polo shirts on the fourth floor of the garment factory in Narsingdi, a small town about thirty miles northeast of Dhaka, Bangladesh's capital city. The thumping of hundreds of sewing machines combined to produce a steady roar that never stopped throughout the long working day.

But in an instant everything changed when a spark jumped from an electric gun a worker was using to shoot spot remover on a stained piece of fabric. The can of flammable liquid burst into flames. Nearby workers rushed to smother the fire with shirts, but it was too late. In a room filled with combustible materials, the flames spread quickly.

More than 1,000 people scrambled toward the narrow staircase that led to the street. A human wave poured down the steep steps but was blocked at the bottom by a folding metal gate that factory bosses kept locked to prevent workers from leaving during work hours. Panicked, the people turned, only to collide with the hundreds behind them. In a single minute of screaming voices, thrusting legs, and pounding hearts, dozens were crushed and trampled. By the time the gates were opened and the fire put out, fifty-two garment workers lay dead.

Garment factories like this one are big business in Bangladesh, where clothing makes up 75 percent of the country's total economic exports. Moreover, half of the garments shipped from Bangladesh end up in clothing stores in the United States. The reason so much of the clothing we buy is made in poor countries like Bangladesh is simple economics; Bangladeshi garment workers labor for close to twelve hours a day, typically seven days a week, and yet earn only between $400 and $500 a year.

Tanveer Chowdhury manages the garment factory owned by his family. Speaking to reporters, he complained bitterly about the tragedy. "This fire has cost me $586,373, and that does not include $70,000 for machinery and $20,000 for furniture. I made commitments to meet deadlines, and I still have the deadlines. I am now paying for air freight at $10 a dozen when I should be shipping by sea at 87 cents a dozen."

There was one other cost Mr. Chowdhury had not considered. To compensate families for the loss of their loved ones in the fire, he eventually agreed to pay $1,952 per person. In Bangladesh, life—like labor—is cheap (based on Bearak, 2001).

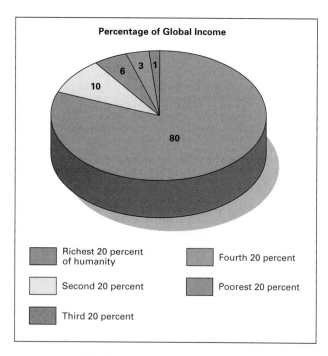

Percentage of Global Income

6   3   1

10

80

Richest 20 percent of humanity

Second 20 percent

Third 20 percent

Fourth 20 percent

Poorest 20 percent

FIGURE 12–1 Distribution of World Income

Sources: Calculated by the author based on United Nations Development Programme (2000) and The World Bank (2001).

These garment workers in Bangladesh are part of the roughly 1 billion of the world's people who work hard every day and yet remain poor. As this chapter explains, although poverty is a reality in the United States and other nations, the greatest social inequality is not *within* nations but *between* them (Goesling, 2001). Therefore, we can understand the full dimensions of poverty only by using a global perspective.

GLOBAL STRATIFICATION: AN OVERVIEW

Chapter 11 ("Social Class in the United States") described social inequality in the United States. In global perspective, however, social stratification is far more pronounced. Figure 12–1 divides the world's total income by fifths of the population. Recall that the richest 20 percent of the U.S. population earn about 48 percent of the national income (see Figure 11–1). The richest 20 percent of global population, however, receive about 80 percent of world income. At the other extreme, the poorest 20 percent of the U.S. population earn 4 percent of our national income, but the poorest fifth of the world's people struggles to survive on just 1 percent of global income.

Because global income is so concentrated, even people in the United States with income below the government's poverty line live far better than the majority of the Earth's people. The average person living in a rich nation such as the United States is quite well-off by world standards. At the very top of the pyramid, the wealth of the world's three richest *individuals* roughly equals the annual economic output of the world's forty-eight poorest *countries* (Annan, 1998).

A WORD ABOUT TERMINOLOGY

A familiar model for describing global stratification, developed after World War II, labeled rich, industrial countries the "First World," less industrialized, socialist countries the "Second World," and nonindustrialized, poor countries the "Third World." But the "Three Worlds" model is now less useful. For one thing, it was a product of cold war politics by which the capitalist West (the First World) faced off against the socialist East (the Second World), while other nations (the Third World) remained more or less on the sidelines. But the sweeping changes in Eastern Europe and the collapse of the former Soviet Union mean that a distinctive Second World no longer exists.

A second problem is that the "Three Worlds" model lumped together more than 100 countries as the Third World. In reality, some relatively better-off nations of the Third World (such as Chile in South America) have fifteen times the per person productivity of the poorest countries of the world (including Ethiopia in East Africa).

These facts call for a modestly revised system of classification. Here, we define *high-income countries* as the richest forty nations with the highest overall standard of living. Next, the world's ninety *middle-income countries* are somewhat poorer, with economic development more-or-less typical of the world as a whole. Finally, the remaining sixty *low-income countries* have the lowest productivity and the most severe and extensive poverty.

This new model has two advantages over the older "Three Worlds" system, First, it focuses on economic development rather than whether societies are capitalist or socialist. Second, it gives a better picture of the relative economic development of various countries because it does not lump together all lower-income nations into a single "Third World."

Still, classifying the 192 nations on Earth into any three categories ignores many striking differences. These nations have rich and varied histories, speak different languages, and take pride in their distinctive cultures.

When natural disasters strike high-income countries, property loss is great but loss of life is low. In low-income countries, the converse is true: Poor people have less property to lose, but many die.

Keep in mind, too, that even in poor countries, some people are very rich. In Bangladesh, for example, members of the Chowdhury family, who own the garment factory noted in the chapter opening, earn as much as $1 million per year, which is several thousand times more than their workers earn. Of course, the full extent of global inequality is even greater, because the most well-off people in rich countries such as the United States earn hundreds of millions per year and live worlds apart from the poorest people in low-income nations such as Bangladesh, Haiti, or Sudan.

HIGH-INCOME COUNTRIES

In nations where the Industrial Revolution first took place more than two centuries ago, productivity increased more than one-hundredfold. To understand the power of industrial and computer technology, consider that the small European nation of Holland is more productive than the vast continent of Africa south of the Sahara; likewise, tiny South Korea outproduces all of India.

A look back at Global Map 1–2 on page 6 identifies the forty high-income countries of the world. They include the United States and Canada, Argentina, the nations of Western Europe, Israel, Saudi Arabia, South Africa, Singapore, Hong Kong (now part of the People's Republic of China), Japan, South Korea, Australia, and New Zealand.

Taken together, countries with the most developed economies cover roughly 25 percent of the Earth's land area, including parts of five continents, and lie mostly in the Northern Hemisphere. In 2003, the population of these nations was about 1 billion, or about 18 percent of the Earth's people. About three-fourths of the people in high-income countries live in or near cities.

Significant cultural differences exist among high-income countries; for example, the nations of Europe recognize more than thirty official languages. But these societies share a productive capacity that generates, on average, a rich material life for their people. Per capita income ranges from about $11,000 annually (in Slovakia and Argentina) to more than $29,000 annually (in the United States and Norway).[1] In fact, people in high-income countries enjoy more than three-fourths of the world's total income.

---

[1]High-income countries have a per capita annual income of at least $10,000. For middle- and low-income countries, the comparable figures are $2,500 to $10,000 and $2,500 or less. All data reflect the United Nations concept of purchasing power parities, which avoids distortion caused by conversion of all currencies to U.S. dollars. Instead, the data represent the local purchasing power of each nation's currency.

Japan represents the world's high-income countries, in which industrial technology and economic expansion have produced material prosperity. The presence of market forces is evident in this view of downtown Tokyo (above, left). The Russian Federation represents the middle-income countries of the world. Industrial development and economic performance were sluggish under socialism; as a result, Moscow residents had to wait in long lines for their daily needs (above, right). The hope is that the introduction of a market system will raise living standards, although in the short run, Russian citizens must adjust to increasing economic disparity. Bangladesh (left) represents the world's low-income countries. As the photograph suggests, these nations have limited economic development and rapidly increasing populations. The result is widespread poverty.

Production in rich nations is capital-intensive; that is, it is based on factories, big machinery, and advanced technology. High-income countries also stand at the forefront of the Information Revolution, with most of the largest corporations that design and market computers, as well as most computer users. In addition, high-income countries control the world's financial markets, so that daily events in the financial exchanges of New York, London, and Tokyo affect people throughout the world.

MIDDLE-INCOME COUNTRIES

Middle-income countries have a per capita income ranging between $2,500 and $10,000, roughly the median for the world's nations. Two-thirds of the people in middle-income countries live in cities, and industrial jobs are common. The remaining one-third of people

live in rural areas, where most are poor and lack access to schools, medical care, adequate housing, and even safe drinking water.

Looking back at Global Map 1–2 (page 6), we see that about ninety of the world's nations fall into the middle-income category. At the high end are Chile (Latin America), Mauritius (Africa), and Malaysia (Asia), where annual income is about $9,000. At the low end are Ecuador (Latin America), Albania (Europe), Morocco (Africa), and Indonesia (Asia), with roughly $3,000 annually in per capita income.

One cluster of middle-income countries includes the former Soviet Union and the nations of Eastern Europe (in the past, known as the Second World). These countries had mostly socialist economies until popular revolts between 1989 and 1991 swept aside their governments. Since then, these nations have begun to introduce market systems, but so far, the results have been uneven. Some (including Poland) have

DIVERSITY: RACE, CLASS, AND GENDER

Las Colonias: "America's Third World"

"We wanted to have something for ourselves," explains Olga Ruiz, who has lived in the border community of College Park, Texas, for eleven years. There is no college in College Park, nor does this dusty stretch of rural land even have water or sewer lines. Yet this town is one of some 1,800 settlements that have sprouted up in southern Texas along the 1,200-mile border from El Paso down to Brownsville. Together, they are home to between 500,000 and 700,000 people, numbers expected to pass 1 million within five years.

Many people speak of *las colonias* (Spanish for "the colonies") as "America's Third World" because these desperately poor communities look much like their counterparts in Mexico or many other middle- or low-income nations. But this is the United States, and almost all of the people living in the *colonias* are Hispanic Americans, 85 percent of them legal residents, and more than half U.S. citizens.

Anastacia Ledsema, now seventy-two years old, moved to a *colonia* called Sparks more than forty years ago. Born in Mexico, Ledsema married a Texas man and, together, they paid $200 for a one-quarter-acre lot in a new border community. For months, they camped out on their land. Step by step, they invested their labor and their money to build a modest house. Not until seven years ago did their small community get running water—a service that had been promised by developers years before. When the water line finally did arrive, however, things changed more than they expected. "When we got water," recalls Ledsema, "that's when so many people came in." The population of Sparks quickly doubled to about 3,000, overwhelming the water supply.

The residents of all the *colonias* know that they are poor. Indeed, the Census Bureau recently declared one border community to be the most impoverished county in the entire United States. Concerned over the lack of basic services in so many of these communities, Texas officials have banned any new settlements. But most of the people who move here—even those who start off sleeping in their car or truck—see these communities as the first step on the path to the "American Dream." Oscar Solis, a neighborhood leader in Panorama Village, with a population of about 150, is proud to show visitors around the small but growing town. "All of this work we have done ourselves," he says with a smile, "to make our dream come true."

Source: Based on Schaffer (2002).

improving economies, while living standards in others (including Russia) have fallen.

The remaining middle-income nations include Chile and Brazil in South America, as well as Namibia and Botswana in Africa. Taken together, middle-income countries span roughly 47 percent of the Earth's land area and include about 3.3 billion people, or more than one-half of humanity. Some countries (such as Russia) are far less crowded than others (such as El Salvador), but compared to high-income countries, these societies are densely populated.

LOW-INCOME COUNTRIES

Low-income countries, where most people are very poor, are mostly agrarian societies with some industry. Many of these sixty nations, identified in Global Map 1–2 on page 6, are found in Central and East Africa as well as Asia. Low-income countries cover 28 percent of the planet's land area and are home to 28 percent of its people. Population density is, therefore, generally high, although greater in Asian countries (such as Bangladesh and Vietnam) than in Central African nations (like Chad and the Democratic Republic of the Congo).

In poor countries, 31 percent of the people live in cities; most inhabit villages and farms as their ancestors did. In fact, half the world's people are peasants, people with a strong sense of cultural tradition. With limited industrial technology, peasants are not very productive, one reason that many endure severe poverty. Hunger, disease, and unsafe housing frame the lives of the world's poorest people.

People living in affluent nations such as the United States find it hard to grasp the scope of human want in much of the world. From time to time, televised

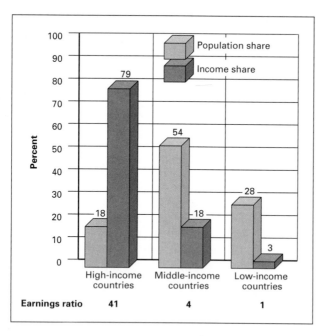

FIGURE 12-2 The Relative Share of Income and Population by Level of Economic Development

Sources: Calculated by the author based on United Nations Development Programme (2000) and The World Bank (2001).

pictures of famine in very poor countries such as Ethiopia and Bangladesh give us a shocking glimpse of the poverty that makes every day a life-and-death struggle. Behind these images lie cultural, historical, and economic forces that we shall explore in the remainder of this chapter.

GLOBAL WEALTH AND POVERTY

October 14, Manila, the Philippines. What caught my eye was how clean she was—a girl no more than seven or eight years old. She was wearing a freshly laundered dress, and her hair was carefully combed. She followed us with her eyes: Camera-toting Americans stand out in this neighborhood, one of the poorest in the entire world.

Fed by methane from decomposing garbage, the fires never go out on Smokey Mountain, the vast garbage dump on the north side of Manila. Smoke envelops the hills of refuse like a thick fog. But Smokey Mountain is more than a dump; it is a neighborhood that is home to thousands of people. It is hard to imagine a setting more hostile to human life. Amid the smoke and the squalor, men and women do what they can to survive. They pick plastic bags from the garbage and wash them in the river and collect cardboard boxes or anything else they can sell. What chance do their children have, in families that earn scarcely a few hundred dollars a year? With barely any opportunity for schooling? Year after year, breathing this air? Against this backdrop of human tragedy, one lovely little girl has put on a fresh dress and gone out to play.

Now our taxi driver threads his way through heavy traffic as we head for the other side of Manila. The change is amazing: The smoke and smell of the dump give way to neighborhoods that could be in Miami or Los Angeles. On the bay in the distance floats a cluster of yachts. No more rutted streets; now we glide quietly along wide boulevards lined with trees and filled with expensive Japanese cars. We pass shopping plazas, upscale hotels, and highrise office buildings. Every block or so we see the gated entrance to an exclusive residential enclave with security guards standing watch. Here, in large, air-conditioned homes, the rich of Manila live and many of the poor work.

Low-income nations are home to some rich and many poor people. The fact that most people live with incomes of barely several hundred dollars a year means that the burden of poverty is far greater than among the poor of the United States. This is not to suggest that poverty here is a minor problem. In so rich a country, too little food, substandard housing, and no medical care for tens of millions of people—almost half of them children—amount to a national tragedy. The box on page 303 profiles the striking poverty that exists along the southwestern border of the United States. Yet poverty in low-income countries is both *more severe* and *more extensive* than in the United States.

THE SEVERITY OF POVERTY

Poverty in poor countries is more severe than it is in rich countries. A key reason that the quality of life differs so much around the world is that economic productivity is lowest in precisely the regions where population growth is highest. Figure 12–2 shows the proportion of world population and global income for countries at each level of economic development. High-income countries are by far the most advantaged, with 79 percent of global income supporting just 18 percent of humanity. In middle-income nations, 54 percent of the world's people earn 18 percent of global income. This leaves 28 percent of the planet's population with just 3 percent of global income. In short, for every dollar received by individuals in a low-income country, someone in a high-income country takes home forty-one dollars.

The data in Table 12–1 further illustrate these disparities. The first column of figures gives gross domestic product (GDP) for selected high-, middle-, and low-income countries.[2] The United States, a large and highly productive nation, had a 2001 GDP of $10 trillion; Japan's GDP was more than $4 trillion. A comparison of GDP figures shows that the world's richest nations are thousands of times more productive than the poorest countries.

The second column of figures in Table 12–1 indicates per capita GDP in terms of what the United Nations (1995) calls "purchasing power parities," what people can buy using their income in the local economy. The per capita GDP for rich countries like the United States, Sweden, and Canada is very high—exceeding $24,000. For middle-income countries, such as Botswana and Latvia, the figures are much lower, in

---

[2]Gross domestic product (GDP) includes all the goods and services on record as produced by a country's economy in a given year, excluding income earned outside the country by individuals or corporations. Gross national product (GNP) adds in the foreign earnings. For countries that invest heavily abroad (Kuwait, for example), GDP is much smaller than GNP; for countries in which other nations invest heavily (Hong Kong), GDP is much greater than GNP. For countries that both invest heavily abroad and have high foreign investment at home (including the United States), the two measures are about the same.

TABLE 12-1 Wealth and Well-Being in Global Perspective, 2001

Country	Gross Domestic Product (US$ billions)	GDP per Capita (PPP US$)*	Quality of Life Index
High Income			
Norway	166	29,620	.944
Sweden	210	24,180	.941
Australia	369	25,370	.939
United States	10,065	34,320	.937
Canada	695	27,130	.937
Japan	4,141	25,130	.932
United Kingdom	1,424	24,160	.930
France	1,310	23,990	.925
South Korea	422	15,090	.879
Middle Income			
Eastern Europe			
Poland	176	9,450	.841
Lithuania	12	8,470	.824
Russian Federation	310	7,100	.779
Ukraine	38	4,350	.766
Latin America			
Mexico	618	8,430	.800
Brazil	503	7,360	.777
Venezuela	125	5,670	.775
Asia			
Malaysia	88	8,750	.790
Thailand	115	6,400	.768
China, P. R.	1,159	4,020	.721
Middle East			
Iran	114	6,000	.719
Syria	20	3,280	.685
Africa			
Algeria	55	6,090	.704
Botswana	5	7,820	.614
Low Income			
Latin America			
Bolivia	8	2,300	.672
Haiti	4	1,860	.467
Asia			
Bangladesh	47	1,610	.502
Pakistan	59	1,890	.499
Africa			
Guinea	3	1,960	.425
Democratic Republic of the Congo	5	680	.363
Ethiopia	6	810	.359
Sierra Leone	1	470	.275

*These data are the United Nations purchasing power parity (PPP) calculations, which avoid currency rate distortion by showing the local purchasing power of each domestic currency.

Source: United Nations Development Programme, *Human Development Report 2003* (New York: Oxford University Press, 2003).

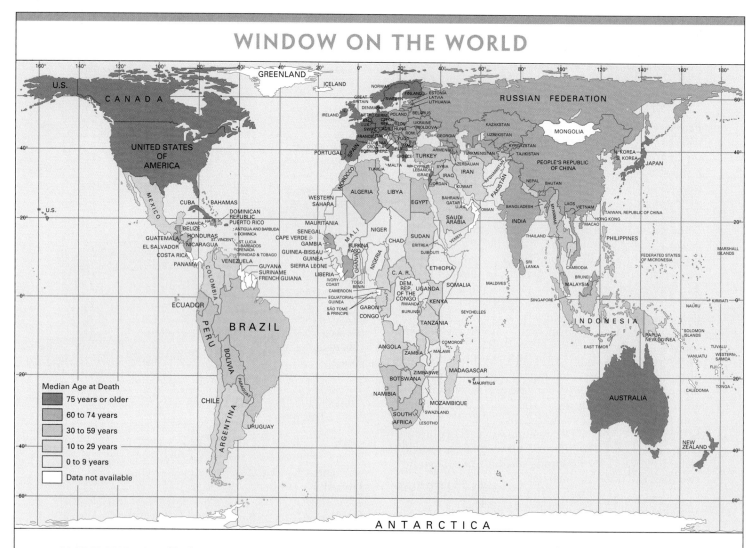

GLOBAL MAP 12–1 Median Age at Death in Global Perspective

This map identifies the age below which half of all deaths occur in any year. In the high-income countries of the world, including the United States, it is mostly the elderly who face death, that is, people age seventy-five or older. In middle-income countries, including most of Latin America, most people die years or even decades earlier. In low-income countries, especially in Africa and parts of Asia, it is children who die, half of them never reaching their tenth birthday.

Sources: The World Bank (1993) with updates by the author; map projection from *Peters Atlas of the World* (1990).

Median Age at Death
- 75 years or older
- 60 to 74 years
- 30 to 59 years
- 10 to 29 years
- 0 to 9 years
- Data not available

the $7,800 range. In the world's low-income countries, per capita annual income is just a few hundred dollars. In the Democratic Republic of the Congo or in Ethiopia, for example, a typical person labors all year to make what the average worker in the United States earns in several days.

The last column of Table 12–1 measures quality of life in the various nations. This index, calculated by the United Nations, is based on income, education (extent of adult literacy and average years of schooling), and longevity (how long people typically live). Index values are decimals that fall between hypothetical extremes of one (highest) and zero (lowest). By this calculation, Norwegians enjoy the highest quality of life (.944), with residents of the United States close behind (.937). At the other extreme, people in the African nation of Sierra Leone have the lowest quality of life (.275).

Relative versus Absolute Poverty

The distinction between relative and absolute poverty, made in Chapter 11 ("Social Class in the United States"), has an important application to global inequality. People living in rich countries generally focus on *relative poverty*, meaning that some people lack resources that are taken for granted by others. Relative poverty, by definition, cuts across every society, whether rich or poor.

More important in global perspective, however, is *absolute poverty*, a lack of resources that is life-threatening. Human beings in absolute poverty lack the nutrition necessary for health and long-term survival. To be sure, some absolute poverty exists in the United States. But such immediately life-threatening poverty strikes only a small proportion of the U.S. population; in low-income countries, by contrast, one-third or more of the people are in desperate need.

Find a UN report on world hunger at http://www.fao.org/NEWS/1999/img/SOFI99-E.PDF

Because absolute poverty is deadly, one global indicator of this problem is median age at death. Global Map 12–1 identifies the age by which half of all people born in a nation die. In rich societies, most people die after the age of seventy-five; in poor countries, half of all deaths occur among children under the age of ten.

THE EXTENT OF POVERTY

Poverty in poor countries is more extensive than it is in rich nations such as the United States. Chapter 11 ("Social Class in the United States") indicated that the U.S. government officially classifies about 12 percent of the population as poor. In low-income countries, however, most people live no better than the poor in the United States, and many are far worse off. As Global Map 12–1 shows, the high death rates among children in Africa indicate that absolute poverty is greatest there, where half the population is malnourished. In the world as a whole, at any given time, 15 percent of the people—about 1 billion—suffer from chronic undernutrition, which leaves them less able to work and puts

Tens of millions of children fend for themselves on the streets of Latin America, where many fall victim to disease, drug abuse, and outright violence. What do you think must be done to put an end to scenes like this one in San Salvador, the capital city of El Salvador?

them at high risk of disease (Kates, 1996; United Nations Development Programme, 2001).

The typical adult in a rich nation, such as the United States, consumes about 3,500 calories a day, an excess that contributes to widespread obesity and related health problems. The typical adult in a low-income country not only does more physical labor but consumes just 2,000 calories a day. The result is undernourishment: too little food, or not enough of the right kinds of food.

In the ten minutes it takes to read this section of the chapter, about 300 people in the world who are sick and weakened from hunger will die. This number amounts to about 40,000 people a day, or 15 million people each year. Clearly, easing world hunger is one of the most serious responsibilities facing humanity today.

POVERTY AND CHILDREN

Death comes early in poor societies, where families lack adequate food, safe water, secure housing, and access to medical care. Organizations combating child poverty estimate that at least 100 million children living in cities

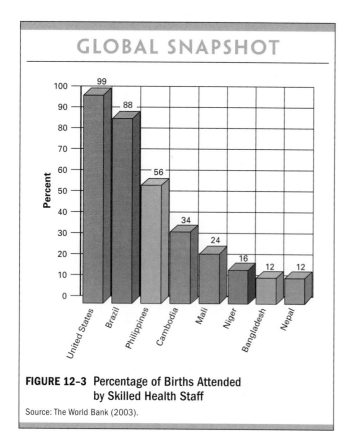

GLOBAL SNAPSHOT

FIGURE 12-3 Percentage of Births Attended
by Skilled Health Staff

Source: The World Bank (2003).

under bridges, or in alleyways (Ross, 1996; United Nations Development Programme, 2000; Collymore, 2002).

POVERTY AND WOMEN

In rich societies, much of the work women do is undervalued, underpaid, or overlooked entirely. In poor societies, women face even greater disadvantages. Most of the people who work in the kind of sweatshops described in the opening to this chapter, for example, are women.

Women in low-income societies may be underpaid, but their families depend on this income. Even so, tradition bars women from many jobs; in Bangladesh, for example, women work in garment factories because that society's conservative Muslim religious norms bar them from most other paid work and limit their opportunity for advanced schooling (Bearak, 2001). At the same time, traditional norms in poor societies give women primary responsibility for child rearing and maintaining the household. The United Nations estimates that, in poor countries around the world, men own 90 percent of the land, a far greater gender disparity in wealth than is found in high-income nations. It is no surprise, then, that about 70 percent of the world's 1 billion people living near absolute poverty are women (Hymowitz, 1995).

Read about a woman who spent six years working in a sweatshop in Saipan producing clothing for sale by GAP in the United States: http://www.globalexchange.org/education/speakers/CarmencitaChieAbad.html

Finally, women in poor countries have limited access to reproductive health care. Less access to birth control has the effect of keeping the birth rate high, as well as keeping women in the home with their children. In addition, the world's poorest women typically give birth without help from trained health care personnel. Figure 12–3 draws a stark contrast between low- and high-income countries in this regard.

SLAVERY

Poor societies are vulnerable to many obvious problems, such as hunger and illiteracy. But many also contend with the age-old problem of slavery. Many nations ended slavery about the time that they developed industrial economies: The British Empire banned slavery in 1833 and the United States did the same in 1865. Yet, in poor countries today, according

in poor countries beg, steal, sell sex, or work for drug gangs to provide income for their families. Such a life almost always means dropping out of school and puts children at high risk of disease and violence. Many girls, with little or no access to medical assistance, become pregnant, a case of children who cannot support themselves being forced to have still more children.

Analysts estimate that another 100 million of the world's children leave their families altogether, sleeping and living on the streets as best they can or

Read more about the plight of street children at http://www.hrw.org/children/street.htm

perhaps trying to migrate to the United States. Roughly half of these street children are found in Latin America, where perhaps half of all children grow up in poverty, living in Mexico City, Rio de Janeiro, or some other large city. Such cities may be known to many in the United States as exotic travel destinations, but they are also home to thousands of street children living in makeshift huts,

GLOBAL SOCIOLOGY

"God Made Me to Be a Slave"

Fatma Mint Mamadou is a young woman living in North Africa's Islamic Republic of Mauritania. Asked her age, she pauses, smiles, and shakes her head. She has no idea when she was born. Nor can she read or write. What she knows is tending camels, herding sheep, hauling bags of water, sweeping, and serving tea to her owners. This young woman is one of perhaps 90,000 slaves in Mauritania.

In the central region of this nation, having dark brown skin almost always means being a slave to an Arab owner. Fatma accepts her situation; she has known nothing else. She explains in a matter-of-fact voice that she is a slave as was her mother before her and her grandmother before that. "Just as God created a camel to be a camel," she shrugs, "he created me to be a slave."

Fatma, her mother, and her brothers and sisters live in a squatter settlement on the edge of Nauakchott, Mauritania's capital city. Their home is a nine-by-twelve-foot hut that they built from wood scraps and other materials taken from construction sites. The roof is nothing more than a piece of cloth; there is no plumbing or furniture. The nearest water comes from a well a mile down the road.

Human slavery continues to exist in the twenty-first century.

In this region, slavery began 500 years ago, about the time Columbus sailed west toward the New World. Then, as Arab and Berber tribes raided local villages, they made slaves of the people. So it has been for dozens of generations ever since. In 1905, the French colonial rulers of Mauritania banned slavery. After the nation gained independence in 1961, the new government reaffirmed the ban. But such proclamations have done little to change strong traditions. Indeed, people like Fatma have no idea what freedom to choose means.

The next question is more personal: "Are you and other girls ever raped?" Again, Fatma hesitates. With no hint of emotion, she responds, "Of course, in the night the men come to breed us. Is that what you mean by rape?"

Source: Based on Burkett (1997).

---

to Anti-Slavery International (ASI), as many as 400 million men, women, and children (almost 7 percent of humanity) live in conditions that amount to slavery (Janus, 1996).

ASI distinguishes four types of slavery. In *chattel slavery*, one person owns another. The number of chattel slaves is difficult to estimate because this practice is against the law almost everywhere. Nevertheless, the buying and selling of slaves still takes place in many countries in Asia, the Middle East, and, especially, in Africa. The box describes the reality of one slave's life in the African nation of Mauritania.

A second, more common form of bondage is *child slavery*, in which desperately poor families let their children take to the streets, where they are readily victimized by others. Perhaps 100 million children—

many in poor countries of Latin America—fall into this category.

Third, *debt bondage* is the practice by which employers hold workers by paying them too little to meet their debts. In this case, workers receive wages, but not enough to cover the food and housing provided by an employer; to all practical purposes, they are enslaved. Many workers in sweatshops in poor countries fall into this category.

Fourth, *servile forms of marriage* may also amount to slavery. In India, Thailand, and some African nations, families marry off women against their will. Many end up as slaves working for their husband's family; some are forced into prostitution.

Finally, one additional form of slavery is *human trafficking*, the moving of men, women, and children from one place to another and then placing them in conditions of forced labor. Women or men brought to a new country on the promise of a job and then forced to become prostitutes or agricultural laborers and "parents" who adopt children from another country and who then force them to work in sweatshops are examples of trafficking in human beings. Such activity is big business: Next to trading in guns and drugs, trading in people brings the greatest profit to organized crime around the world (Orhant, 2002).

In 1948, the United Nations issued its Universal Declaration of Human Rights, which states, "No one shall be held in slavery or servitude; slavery and the slave trade shall be prohibited in all their forms." Unfortunately, more than fifty years later, this social evil persists.

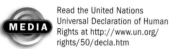 Read the United Nations Universal Declaration of Human Rights at http://www.un.org/rights/50/decla.htm

CORRELATES OF GLOBAL POVERTY

What accounts for the severe and extensive poverty throughout much of the world? The rest of this chapter weaves together explanations from the following facts about poor societies:

1. **Technology.** About one-quarter of people in low-income countries farm the land using human muscle or beasts of burden. Because of these limited energy sources, agricultural production is modest.

2. **Population growth.** As Chapter 22 ("Population, Urbanization, and Environment") explains, the poorest countries have the world's highest birth rates. Despite the death toll from poverty, the populations of many poor countries in Africa, for example, double every twenty-five years. In these countries, half the people are teenagers or younger. With so many people entering their childbearing years, a wave of population growth will roll into the future. In recent years, for example, the population of Chad swelled by 3.3 percent annually, so that even with economic development, living standards have fallen.

3. **Cultural patterns.** Poor societies are usually traditional. Adhering to long-established ways of life, people resist innovations—even those that promise a richer material life. The box explains why traditional people in India respond to their poverty differently than poor people in the United States.

4. **Social stratification.** Low-income societies distribute their wealth very unequally. Chapter 10 ("Social Stratification") explained that social inequality is more pronounced in agrarian societies than in industrial societies. In Brazil, for example, half of all farmland is owned by just 1 percent of the people (Bergamo & Camarotti, 1996).

5. **Gender inequality.** Extreme gender inequality in poor societies means that economic and educational opportunities are not available to women, and as a result, women typically have many children. An expanding population, in turn, slows economic development. Many analysts therefore conclude that raising living standards in much of the world depends on improving the social standing of women.

6. **Global power relationships.** A final cause of global poverty lies in the relationships among the nations of the world. Historically, wealth flowed from poor societies to rich nations through **colonialism,** *the process by which some nations enrich themselves through political and economic control of other nations.* The countries of Western Europe colonized much of Latin America beginning roughly 500 years ago. Such global exploitation allowed some nations to develop economically at the expense of other nations.

   Although 130 former colonies gained their independence during the twentieth century, exploitation continues through **neocolonialism** (*neo* is the Greek for "new"), *a new form of global power relationships that involves not direct political control but economic exploitation by multinational corporations.* **Multinational corporations** are *large businesses that operate in many countries* and wield tremendous economic power. Corporate leaders can impose their will on countries where they do business to create favorable economic conditions, just as colonizers did in the past (Bonanno, Constance, & Lorenz, 2000).

GLOBAL STRATIFICATION: THEORETICAL ANALYSIS

There are two major explanations for the unequal distribution of the world's wealth and power: *modernization theory* and *dependency theory.* Each theory suggests a different path toward relieving the suffering of hungry people in much of the world.

A Different Kind of Poverty: A Report from India

Most North Americans know that India is one of the poorest nations on Earth. A vast country with a per capita gross domestic product (GDP) of only $2,840 a year, India is home to one-third of the world's hungry people.

But most North Americans do not readily understand the reality of poverty in India. Most of the country's 1 billion people live in conditions far worse than those the U.S. government labels "poor." A traveler's first experience of Indian life can be shocking. Madras, for example, one of India's largest cities with 7 million inhabitants, seems chaotic to an outsider—streets choked with motorbikes, trucks, carts pulled by oxen, and waves of people. Along the roadway, vendors sit on burlap cloth and hawk fruits, vegetables, and cooked food while people nearby work, talk, bathe, and sleep.

Madras is dotted with thousands of shanty settlements, home to half a million people from rural villages who have come in search of a better life. Shantytowns are clusters of huts built with branches, leaves, and pieces of discarded cardboard and tin. These dwellings offer little privacy and lack refrigeration, running water, and bathrooms. A visitor from the United States may feel uneasy in such an area, knowing that the poorest sections of our own inner cities seethe with frustration and sometimes explode with violence.

But India's people understand poverty differently than we do. No restless young men hang out on corners, no drug dealers work the streets, and there is little danger of violence. In the United States, poverty often means anger and isolation; in India,

even shantytowns are organized around strong families—children, parents, and often grandparents—who offer a smile and a welcome to a stranger.

For traditional people in India, life is shaped by *dharma*, the Hindu concept of duty and destiny that teaches people to accept their fate, whatever it may be. Mother Teresa, who worked among the poorest of India's people, went to the heart of the cultural differences: "Americans have angry poverty," she explained. "In India, there is worse poverty, but it is a happy poverty."

Perhaps we should not describe anyone who clings to the edge of survival as happy. But poverty in India is eased by the strength and support of families and communities, a sense that existence has a purpose, and a worldview that encourages each person to accept whatever life offers. As a result, a visitor may well come away from a first encounter with Indian poverty in confusion: "How can people be so poor, and yet apparently content, active, and *joyful*?"

Source: Based on the author's research in Madras, India, November 1988.

MODERNIZATION THEORY

Modernization theory is *a model of economic and social development that explains global inequality in terms of technological and cultural differences between nations.* In simple terms, modernization theory claims that some societies are rich because "they earned it."

Modernization theory emerged in the 1950s, a time when U.S. society was fascinated by new developments in technology. To showcase the power of productive technology, and also to counter the growing influence of the Soviet Union, U.S. policy makers drafted a market-based foreign policy that has been with us ever since.[3]

[3]The following discussion of modernization theory draws primarily on Rostow (1960, 1978), Bauer (1981), and Berger (1986); see also Firebaugh (1996) and Firebaugh & Sandu (1998).

Historical Perspective

Modernization theorists point out that, as recently as several centuries ago, the entire world was poor. Because poverty is the norm throughout human history, it is *affluence* that demands an explanation.

Affluence came within reach of a growing share of people in Western Europe during the late Middle Ages as the scope of world exploration and trade expanded. Soon, the Industrial Revolution was underway, transforming first Western Europe and then North America. Industrial technology coupled with the spirit of capitalism created new wealth on an unprecedented scale. At the outset, this new wealth benefited only a few. But industrial technology was so productive that gradually the living standard of even the poorest people began to rise. Absolute poverty, which had plagued humanity throughout history, was finally in decline.

During the twentieth century, the standard of living in high-income countries, where the Industrial Revolution began, jumped at least fourfold. Many middle-income nations in Asia and Latin America have industrialized, and they, too, have become richer. But with limited industrial technology, low-income countries have changed much less.

The Importance of Culture

Why didn't the Industrial Revolution sweep away poverty the world over? Modernization theory points out that not every society has been eager to adopt new technology. Doing so requires a cultural environment that emphasizes the benefits of innovation and material prosperity.

Modernization theory identifies *tradition* as the greatest barrier to economic development. In some societies, strong family systems and a reverence for the past discourage people from adopting new technologies that would raise their living standards. Even today, many people—from the North American Amish to Islamic people in rural regions of the Middle East and Asia to the Semai of Malaysia—oppose technological advances as a threat to their family relationships, customs, and religious beliefs.

Max Weber (1958; orig. 1904–5) found that at the end of the Middle Ages, Western Europe was quite another story: a cultural environment that favored change. As discussed in Chapter 4 ("Society"), the Protestant Reformation had reshaped traditional Catholicism to generate a progress-oriented way of life. Wealth—regarded with suspicion by the Catholic church—became a sign of personal virtue, and the growing importance of individualism steadily replaced the traditional emphasis on kinship and community. Taken together, these new cultural patterns nurtured the Industrial Revolution, which propelled a large segment of the population from poverty to prosperity.

Rostow's Stages of Modernization

Modernization theory holds that the door to affluence is open to all. Indeed, as technological advances diffuse around the world, all societies should gradually industrialize and prosper. According to W. W. Rostow (1960, 1978), modernization occurs in four stages:

1. **Traditional stage.** Socialized to venerate the past, people in traditional societies cannot easily imagine how life could be different from what they know. Therefore, with lives built around families and local communities, they follow well-worn paths that allow for little individual freedom or change. Life is often spiritually rich but lacking in material abundance.

   A century ago, much of the world was in this initial stage of economic development. Nations such as Bangladesh, Niger, and Somalia are still at the traditional stage and remain impoverished.

2. **Take-off stage.** As a society shakes off the grip of tradition, people start to use their talents and imagination, sparking economic growth. A market emerges as people produce goods not just for their own consumption but to trade with others for profit. Greater individualism, a willingness to take risks, and a desire for material goods also take hold, often at the expense of family ties and time-honored norms and values.

   Great Britain reached take-off by about 1800, the United States by 1820. Thailand, a middle-income country in eastern Asia, is now at this stage. Such development typically is speeded by help from rich nations, including foreign aid, the availability of advanced technology and investment capital, and opportunities for schooling abroad.

3. **Drive to technological maturity.** During this stage, "growth" is a widely accepted concept that fuels a society's pursuit of higher living standards. A diversified economy drives a population eager to enjoy the benefits of industrial technology. At the same time, however, people begin to realize (and sometimes lament) that industrialization is

In rich nations such as the United States, most parents expect their children to enjoy years of childhood, largely free from the responsibilities of adult life. This is not the case in poor nations across Latin America, Africa, and Asia. Poor families depend on whatever income their children can earn, and many children as young as six or seven work full days weaving or performing other kinds of manual labor. Child labor lies behind the low prices of many products imported for sale in this country.

eroding traditional family and local community life. Great Britain reached this point by about 1840, the United States by 1860. Today, Mexico, the U.S. territory of Puerto Rico, and South Korea are among the nations driving to technological maturity.

Societies in stage three have greatly reduced absolute poverty. Cities swell with people who leave rural villages in search of economic opportunity; occupational specialization makes relationships less personal, and heightened individualism generates social movements demanding greater political rights. Societies approaching technological maturity also provide basic schooling for all their people and advanced training for some. The newly educated consider tradition "backward" and push for further change. The social position of women steadily becomes more equal to that of men.

4. **High mass consumption.** Economic development steadily raises living standards, as mass production stimulates industrial consumption. Simply put, people soon learn to "need" the expanding array of goods that their society produces.

The United States, Japan, and other rich nations moved into this stage by 1900. Now entering this level of economic development are two former British colonies that are prosperous small societies of eastern Asia: Hong Kong (part of the People's Republic of China) and Singapore (independent since 1965).

The Role of Rich Nations

Modernization theory claims that high-income countries play four important roles in global economic development:

1. **Helping control population.** Since population growth is greatest in the poorest societies, rising population can overtake economic advances. Rich nations can help limit population growth by exporting birth control technology and promoting its use. Once economic development is underway, birth rates should decline, as they have in industrialized nations, because children are no longer an economic asset.

2. **Increasing food production.** Rich nations can export "high tech" farming methods to poor nations and thus raise agricultural yields. Such techniques—collectively referred to as the "Green Revolution"—include new hybrid seeds, modern irrigation methods, and chemicals that fertilize the land and control insects.

3. **Introducing industrial technology.** Rich nations can accelerate economic growth in poor societies by introducing machinery and information technology, which raise productivity. Industrialization

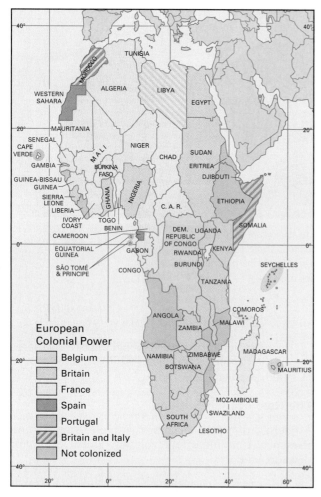

European
Colonial Power

	Belgium
	Britain
	France
	Spain
	Portugal
	Britain and Italy
	Not colonized

FIGURE 12–4 Africa's Colonial History

also shifts the labor force from farming to skilled industrial and service jobs.

4. **Providing foreign aid.** Investment capital from rich nations can boost the prospects of poor societies striving to reach Rostow's "take-off" stage. Foreign aid can purchase fertilizer and fund irrigation projects, which increase agricultural productivity. Financial and technical assistance can also build power plants and factories to improve industrial output.

Critical evaluation. Modernization theory has many influential supporters among social scientists (Parsons, 1966; W. Moore, 1977, 1979; Bauer, 1981; Berger,

1986; Firebaugh & Beck, 1994; Firebaugh, 1996, 1999; Firebaugh & Sandu, 1998). Moreover, for decades it has shaped the foreign policy of the United States and other rich nations. Proponents point to rapid economic development in Asia—including South Korea, Taiwan, Singapore, and Hong Kong—as proof that the affluence that accompanied industrialization in Western Europe and North America is within reach of all countries.

But modernization theory comes under fire from analysts who favor a more egalitarian socialist society as a thinly veiled defense of capitalism. Its most serious flaw, according to critics, is that modernization simply has not occurred in many poor countries. The United Nations reported in 1996 that living standards in a number of nations, including Haiti and Nicaragua in Latin America, and Sudan, Ghana, and Rwanda in Africa, were actually lower than in 1960 (United Nations Development Programme, 1996).

A second criticism of modernization theory is that it fails to recognize how rich nations, which benefit from the status quo, often block paths to development for poor countries. Centuries ago, critics charge, rich countries industrialized from a position of global *strength.* Can we expect poor countries today to do so from a position of global *weakness?*

Third, critics continue, modernization theory treats rich and poor societies as separate worlds, ignoring how international relations affect all nations. To begin with, it was colonization that boosted the fortunes of Europe. This economic windfall has left countries in Latin America and Asia reeling to this day.

Fourth, critics contend that modernization theory holds up the world's most developed countries as the standard for judging the rest of humanity, thus revealing an ethnocentric bias. We should remember that our Western conception of "progress" has led us to degrade the physical environment throughout the world and to rush headlong into a competitive, materialistic way of life.

Fifth, and finally, modernization theory draws criticism for suggesting that the causes of global poverty lie almost entirely in the poor societies themselves. Critics see this analysis as little more than "blaming the victims" for their own plight. Instead, these critics argue, an analysis of global inequality should focus as much on the behavior of *rich* nations as on that of poor nations (Wiarda, 1987).

Such concerns reflect a second major approach to understanding global inequality. We now turn to dependency theory.

DEPENDENCY THEORY

Dependency theory is *a model of economic and social development that explains global inequality in terms of the historical exploitation of poor nations by rich ones*. This analysis puts the primary responsibility for global poverty on rich nations. It holds that some countries became rich only by looting the resources of poor countries and, in the process, making poor nations *dependent* on them. This destructive process, which began centuries ago, persists today.

Historical Perspective

Everyone agrees that before the Industrial Revolution there was little affluence in the world. Dependency theory asserts, however, that people living in poor countries were actually better off economically in the past than their descendants are now. André Gunder Frank (1975), a noted proponent of this theory, argues that the colonial process that helped develop rich nations also *underdeveloped* poor societies.

Dependency theory is based on the idea that the economic positions of rich and poor nations of the world are linked together by the global economy. Poor nations are not simply lagging behind rich ones on the "path of progress"; rather, the prosperity of the most developed countries came largely at the expense of the least developed ones. In short, then, global commerce made some nations rich only by making other nations poor. Both are products of the global commerce beginning five centuries ago.

The Importance of Colonialism

Late in the fifteenth century, Europeans began surveying the Americas to the west, Africa to the south, and Asia to the east looking to establish colonies. They were so successful that, by 1900, the small nation of Great Britain controlled about one-fourth of the world's land, boasting that "the sun never sets on the British Empire." The United States, itself originally thirteen small British colonies on the eastern seaboard of North America, soon pushed across the continent, purchased Alaska, and gained control of Haiti, Puerto Rico, Guam, the Philippines, the Hawaiian Islands, and part of Cuba.

Meanwhile, Europeans and Africans engaged in a brutal form of human exploitation—the slave trade—from about 1500 until 1850. But then, even as industrializing nations were rejecting slavery, Europeans took control of Africa itself. As Figure 12–4 shows,

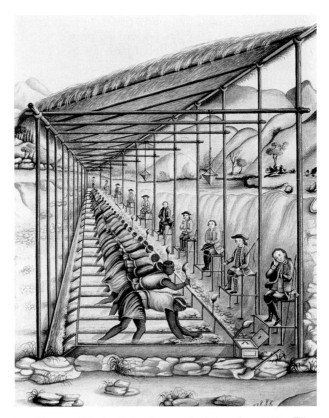

Brazil is among the leading nations producing precious stones. This trade developed when Brazil was colonized by the Portuguese. In this early watercolor from around 1775, the artist, Carlos Juliao, shows slaves washing precious stones under the watchful eyes of European overseers with whips. Dependency theory highlights how colonization both robbed nations of their natural resources and brutally oppressed their people.

European powers dominated most of the African continent until the early 1960s.

Formal colonialism has almost disappeared from the world. However, according to dependency theory, political liberation has not translated into economic autonomy. Far from it: The economic relationship between poor and rich nations perpetuates the colonial pattern of domination. This neocolonialism is the essence of the capitalist world economy.

Wallerstein's Capitalist World Economy

Immanuel Wallerstein (1974, 1979, 1983, 1984) explains global stratification using a model of the "capitalist world economy." Wallerstein's term *world economy* suggests that the prosperity or poverty of any country is the product of a global economic system. He traces the roots of the global economy to the onset of colonization 500 years ago, when Europeans began gathering wealth from the rest of the world. Because the world economy is based in the high-income countries, it is capitalist in character.[4]

Wallerstein calls the rich nations the *core* of the world economy. Colonialism enriched this core by funneling raw materials from around the world to Western Europe, where they fueled the Industrial Revolution. Today, multinational corporations operate profitably worldwide, channeling wealth to North America, Western Europe, Australia, and Japan.

Low-income countries, on the other hand, represent the *periphery* of the world economy. Drawn into the world economy by colonial exploitation, poor nations continue to support rich ones by providing inexpensive labor and a vast market for industrial products. The remaining countries are considered the *semiperiphery* of the world economy. They include middle-income countries like Mexico and South Africa that have closer ties to the global economic core.

According to Wallerstein, the world economy benefits rich societies (by generating profits) and harms the rest of the world (by perpetuating poverty). The world economy thus makes poor nations dependent on rich ones. This dependency involves three factors:

1. **Narrow, export-oriented economies.** Poor nations produce only a few crops for export to rich countries. Examples include coffee and fruit from Latin American nations, oil from Nigeria, hardwoods from the Philippines, and palm oil from Malaysia.

   Today's multinational corporations purchase raw materials cheaply in poor societies and transport them to core nations where factories process them for profitable sale. Thus, poor nations develop few industries of their own.

2. **Lack of industrial capacity.** Without an industrial base, poor societies face a double bind: They count on rich nations to buy their inexpensive raw materials, and they try to buy from them whatever expensive manufactured goods they can

afford. In a classic example of this dependency, British colonialists encouraged the people of India to raise cotton but prevented them from weaving their own cloth. Instead, the British shipped Indian cotton to their own textile mills in Birmingham and Manchester, manufactured the cloth, and shipped finished goods back to India for profitable sale.

Dependency theorists claim the Green Revolution—widely praised by modernization theorists—works the same way. Poor countries sell cheap raw materials to rich nations and then try to buy expensive fertilizers, pesticides, and tractors in return. Rich countries profit from this exchange much more than poor nations.

3. **Foreign debt.** Unequal trade patterns have plunged poor countries into debt to the core nations. Collectively, the poor nations of the world owe rich countries some $2.3 trillion, including hundreds of billions of dollars owed to the United States. Such staggering debt paralyzes a country with high unemployment and rampant inflation (Walton & Ragin, 1990; The World Bank, 2003).

The Role of Rich Nations

Nowhere is the difference between modernization theory and dependency theory drawn more sharply than in the role each assigns to rich nations. Modernization theory maintains that rich societies *produce wealth* through capital investment and technological innovation. Accordingly, as poor nations adopt progrowth policies and more productive technology, they, too, will prosper. By contrast, dependency theory views global inequality in terms of how countries *distribute wealth*, arguing that rich nations have *over*developed themselves as they have *under*developed the rest of the world.

Dependency theorists dismiss the idea that programs developed by rich countries to control population and boost agricultural and industrial output raise living standards in poor countries. Instead, they contend, such programs actually benefit rich nations and the ruling elites, not the poor majority, in low-income countries (Lappé, Collins, & Kinley, 1981; Kentor, 2001).

Hunger activists Frances Moore Lappé and Joseph Collins (1986; Lappé, Collins, & Rosset, 2001) maintain that the capitalist culture of the United States encourages people to think of poverty as somehow inevitable. In this line of reasoning, poverty

---

[4]While based on Wallerstein's ideas, this section also reflects the work of Frank (1980, 1981), Delacroix & Ragin (1981), Bergesen (1983), Dixon & Boswell (1996), and Kentor (1998).

Although the world continues to grow richer, billions of people are being left behind. The shantytown of Cité Soleil ("City of the Sun") near Port-au-Prince, the capital of Haiti, is built around an open sewer. What would you estimate life expectancy to be in such a place?

results from "natural" processes, including having too many children, and natural disasters such as droughts. But global poverty is far from inevitable; it results from deliberate policies. Lappé and Collins point out that the world already produces enough food to allow every person on the planet to become fat. Moreover, India and most of Africa actually *export* food, even though many of their own people go hungry.

According to Lappé and Collins, the contradiction of poverty amid plenty stems from the rich-nation policy of producing food for profits, not for people. That is, corporations in rich nations cooperate with elites in poor countries to grow and export profitable crops such as coffee, which means using land that could otherwise produce staples such as beans and corn for local families. Governments of poor countries support the practice of "growing for export" because they need food profits to repay foreign debt. At the core of this vicious circle, according to Lappé and Collins, is the capitalist corporate structure of the global economy.

Critical evaluation. The main idea of dependency theory is that no nation develops (or fails to develop) in isolation, because the global economy shapes the destiny of all nations. Citing Latin America and other poor regions of the world, dependency theorists claim that development simply cannot proceed under the constraints now imposed by rich countries. Rather,

they call for radical reform of the entire world economy so that it operates in the interests of the majority of people.

Critics, however, charge that dependency theory wrongly treats wealth as a zero-sum commodity, as if no one gets richer without someone else getting poorer. Not so, critics continue, since corporations, small business owners, and farmers can and do create new wealth through their drive and imaginative use of new technology. After all, they point out, the entire world's wealth has swelled sixfold since 1950.

Second, critics continue, dependency theory is wrong in blaming rich nations for global poverty because many of the world's poorest countries (like Ethiopia) have had little contact with rich nations. On the contrary, a long history of trade with rich countries has dramatically improved the economies of nations, including Sri Lanka, Singapore, and Hong Kong (all former British colonies), as well as South Korea and Japan. In short, say the critics, most evidence shows that foreign investment by rich nations fosters economic growth, as modernization theory claims, not economic decline, as dependency theorists claim (Vogel, 1991; Firebaugh, 1992).

Third, critics contend that dependency theory is simplistic in pointing the finger at a single factor—world capitalism—as the cause of global inequality (Worsley, 1990). Dependency theory thereby casts poor societies as passive victims and ignores factors

TABLE 12-2 Modernization Theory and Dependency Theory: A Summary		
	Modernization Theory	**Dependency Theory**
Historical Pattern	The entire world was poor several centuries ago; the Industrial Revolution brought affluence to high-income countries; as industrialization gradually transforms poor societies, all nations are likely to become more equal and alike.	Global parity was disrupted by colonialism, which made some countries rich while making others poor; barring radical change in the world capitalist system, rich nations will grow richer and poor nations will become poorer.
Primary Causes of Global Poverty	Characteristics of poor societies cause their poverty, including lack of industrial technology, traditional cultural patterns that discourage innovation, and rapid population growth.	Global economic relations—historical colonialism and now multinational corporations—have enriched high-income countries while making low-income nations economically dependent.
Role of Rich Nations	Rich countries can and do assist poor nations through population control programs, technology transfers that increase food production and stimulate industrial development, and capital investment in the form of foreign aid.	Rich countries have concentrated global resources, conferring advantages on themselves while generating massive foreign debt in low-income countries; rich nations impede the economic development of poor nations.

inside these countries that contribute to their economic plight. Sociologists have long recognized the vital role of culture in shaping people's willingness to embrace or resist change. Under the rule of the conservative Muslim Taliban, for example, Afghanistan became economically isolated, and its living standards were among the lowest in the world. Is it reasonable to blame capitalist nations for this country's stagnation? With close economic ties to the larger world, Saudi Arabia, by contrast, is included among the high-income nations.

Nor should rich societies be saddled with responsibility for the reckless behavior of foreign leaders whose corruption and militaristic campaigns impoverish their countries (examples include the regimes of Ferdinand Marcos in the Philippines, François Duvalier in Haiti, Manuel Noriega in Panama, Mobutu Sese Seko in Zaire, and Saddam Hussein in Iraq). Governments may even use food supplies as a weapon in internal political struggles, leaving the masses starving in the African nations of Ethiopia, Sudan, and Somalia. Likewise, many countries throughout the world have done little to improve the status of women or control population growth.

Fourth, critics chide dependency theorists for downplaying the economic dependency fostered by the former Soviet Union. The Soviet army seized control of most of Eastern Europe during World War II and then politically and economically dominated those countries. Many see the uprisings between 1989 and 1991 as a wholesale rejection of the Soviet Union's socialist colonial system.

Fifth, critics claim this approach is more protest than policy since it offers only vague solutions to global poverty. Most dependency theorists urge poor nations to end all contact with rich countries, and some call for nationalizing foreign-owned industries. In other words, dependency theory amounts to a thinly disguised call for some sort of world socialism. In light of the difficulties socialist societies have had in meeting the needs of their own people, critics ask, should we really expect such a system to rescue the entire world from poverty?

Table 12–2 summarizes the main arguments of modernization theory and dependency theory.

GLOBAL STRATIFICATION: LOOKING AHEAD

Among the most important trends in recent decades is the development of a global economy. In the United States, rising production and sales abroad bring profits to many corporations and their stockholders, especially those who already have substantial wealth. At the same time, the global economy has moved manufacturing jobs abroad, closing factories in this country and hurting many average workers. The net result: economic polarization in the United States.

As this chapter has noted, however, the greatest economic inequality exists between the world's countries. The concentration of wealth among high-income countries, coupled with the grinding poverty of low-income nations, may well be the biggest problem facing humanity in the twenty-first century.

Finding answers to questions about global poverty, therefore, takes on great urgency. Both modernization theory and dependency theory have their merits and their limitations. In searching for truth, we must consider empirical evidence. Over the course of the twentieth century, living standards rose around the world. Even so, as shown in Figure 12–5, the poorest of the world's people are being left behind. It is true that the economic output of the poorest quarter of the world's people almost tripled over the course of the twentieth century; however, the economic output of the other quartiles of the world's people increased about sixfold. By this measure, although all people are better off in *absolute* terms, there was almost twice as much *relative* economic inequality in the world in 2000 as there was in 1900.

What are the trends in recent decades? There is evidence that income inequality between nations stabilized and now shows a slight decline (Schultz, 1998; Firebaugh, 1999, 2000; Goesling, 2001). In a closer look, the United Nations (1996) reported that people in about one-third of the world's countries were living far better in 1996 than they were in 1980. These nations, identified in Global Map 12–2 on page 320, include most of the high-income countries, but they also include dozens of poorer countries, especially in Asia. These prospering nations are evidence that the market forces endorsed by modernization theory can raise living standards.

In another one-third of the world's countries, however, living standards were actually lower in 1996 than they were in 1980. A rising wave of poverty, especially in the nations of sub-Saharan Africa, supports the dependency theory assertion that current economic arrangements are leaving hundreds of millions of people behind.

This mixed report calls into question both modernization and dependency theories, and both camps are revising their views of proper "paths to development." On the one hand, few societies seeking economic growth favor a market economy completely free of government control, a position that challenges orthodox modernization theory and its free-market approach to development. On the other hand, recent upheavals in the former Soviet Union and Eastern Europe demonstrate that a global reevaluation of socialism is underway. Since these uprisings follow decades of poor economic performance and political repression, many poor societies are reluctant to consider a government-controlled path to development. Because

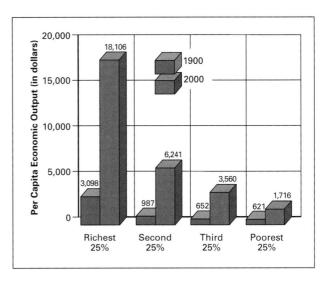

FIGURE 12-5 The World's Increasing Economic Inequality

Source: International Monetary Fund (2000).

dependency theory historically has supported socialist economic systems, changes in world socialism will generate new thinking here as well.

Perhaps the basic problem caused by poverty is hunger. As the final box on page 321 explains, while there is little doubt that we have the necessary food, many analysts wonder if we have the determination to provide for everyone on the planet.

Although the world's future is uncertain, we have learned a great deal about global stratification. One insight, offered by modernization theory, is that poverty is partly a *problem of technology*. A higher standard of living for a surging world population depends on poor nations' raising their agricultural and industrial productivity. A second insight, derived from dependency theory, is that global inequality is also a *political issue*. Even with higher productivity, the human community must address crucial questions concerning how resources are distributed, both within societies and around the globe.

Note, too, that while economic development increases living standards, it also places greater strains on the natural environment. Imagine, for example, if the 1 billion people in India were suddenly to become middle class, with automobiles guzzling gasoline and spewing hydrocarbons into the atmosphere.

Finally, the vast and increasing gulf that separates the world's richest and poorest people puts everyone at greater risk of conflict, as the most impoverished

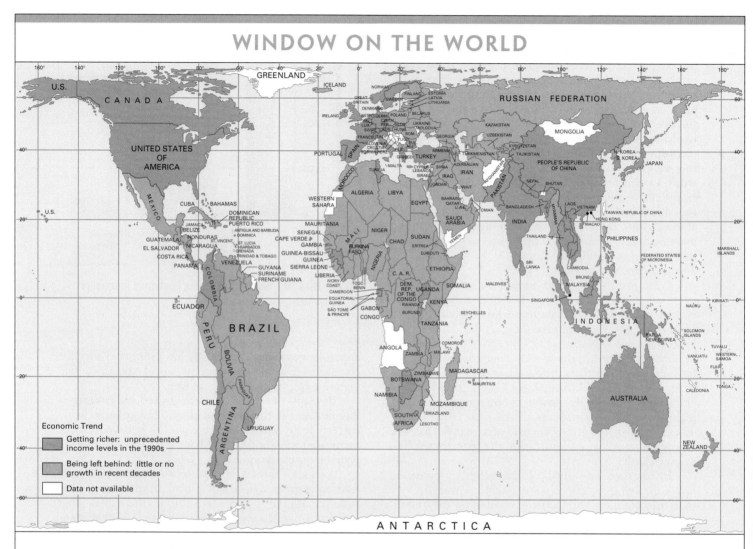

GLOBAL MAP 12–2 Prosperity and Stagnation in Global Perspective

In about sixty nations of the world, people are enjoying a higher standard of living than ever before. These prospering countries include some rich nations (such as the United States and the countries of Western Europe) and some poor nations (especially in Asia). For most countries, however, living standards have remained steady or even slipped in recent decades. Especially in Eastern Europe and the Middle East, some nations have experienced economic setbacks since the 1980s. And in sub-Saharan Africa, some nations are no better off than they were in 1960. The overall pattern is economic polarization, with an increasing gap between rich and poor nations.

Source: United Nations Development Programme (1996); updates by the author.

people feel resentment toward the United States and other rich nations. Indeed, few doubt that global poverty is one underlying cause of terrorism and thus is a threat to the national security of the United States (Lindauer & Weerapana, 2002). In the long run, we can achieve peace on this planet only by ensuring that all people enjoy a significant measure of dignity and security.

CONTROVERSY & DEBATE

Will the World Starve?

The animals' feet leave their prints
on the desert's face.
Hunger is so real, so very real,
that it can make you walk around
a barren tree looking for
nourishment.
Not once,
Not twice,
Not thrice . . .

These lines, by Indian poet Amit Jayaram, describe the appalling hunger found in Rajasthan, in northwest India. As this chapter has explained, however, hunger casts its menacing shadow not only over Asia but also over much of Africa, as well as parts of Latin America, and even North America. Throughout the world, hundreds of millions of adults do not eat enough food to enable them to work. Most tragically, some 10 million children die each year as a result of hunger. As we begin the twenty-first century, what are the prospects for ending the wretched misery of daily hunger?

Pessimists point out that the population of poor countries is increasing by 73 million people annually—equivalent to adding another Egypt to the world every year. Poor countries can scarcely feed the people they have now; how will they ever feed *twice* as many people a generation in the future?

In addition, hunger forces poor people to exploit the Earth's resources by using short-term strategies for food

production, which leads to long-term disaster. For example, farmers are cutting rain forests in order to increase their farmland; but without the protective canopy of trees, it is only a matter of time before much of this land turns to desert. Taken together, rising populations and shortsighted policies raise the specter of unprecedented hunger, human misery, and political calamity.

But there are also some grounds for optimism. Thanks to the Green Revolution, food production the world over has increased sharply during the last fifty years, well outpacing the growth in population. The world's economic productivity has risen steadily, so that the average person on the planet now has more income to purchase food and other necessities than ever before. This growth has also increased daily calorie intake, life expectancy, access to safe water, and adult literacy, and around the world infant mortality is half of what it was in 1960.

So what are the prospects for eradicating world hunger? Overall, we see less hunger in both rich and poor countries, and a smaller *share* of the world's people are hungry now than in 1960. But as global population increases, with 96 percent of children born in middle- and low-income countries, the *number* of lives at risk is as great today as ever before. Thus, many low-income countries have made solid gains, but more are stagnating or even losing ground.

The best-case region of the world is eastern Asia, where incomes, controlled for inflation, have tripled over the last generation. It is to Asia that optimists in the global hunger debate point for evidence that poor countries can and do raise living standards and reduce hunger. The worst-case region of the world is sub-Saharan Africa, where living standards have fallen over the last decade. It is here that high technology is least evident and birth rates are highest. Pessimists typically look to Africa when they argue that poor countries are losing ground in the struggle to feed their people.

Television brings home the tragedy of hunger when news cameras focus on starving people in places like Ethiopia and Somalia. But hunger—and early death from illness—is the plight of millions all year round. The world has the food to feed everyone; the question is whether we have the moral determination.

Continue the debate . . .

1. *In your opinion, what are the primary causes of global hunger?*

2. *Do you place more responsibility for solving this problem on poor countries or rich ones? Why?*

3. *Do you consider yourself an optimist or a pessimist about the problem of global hunger? Why?*

Sources: United Nations Development Programme (1996, 1997, 1998, 1999, 2000, 2001, 2002, 2003).

SUMMARY

1. Around the world, social stratification is more pronounced than in the United States. About 18 percent of the world's people live in industrialized, high-income

countries such as the United States and receive 79 percent of all income. Another 54 percent of humanity live in middle-income countries with significant industrialization, receiving about 18 percent of all in-come. And 28 percent of the world's population live in low-income countries with limited industrialization and earn only 3 percent of global income.

2. Although relative poverty is found everywhere, poor societies grapple with widespread, absolute poverty. Worldwide, the lives of some 1 billion people are at risk because of poor nutrition. About 15 million people, most of them children, die annually from various causes because they lack adequate nourishment.

3. Nearly everywhere in the world, women are more likely than men to be poor. Gender bias against women is greatest in poor, agrarian societies.

4. The poverty found in much of the world is a complex problem reflecting limited industrial technology, rapid population growth, traditional cultural patterns, internal social stratification, male domination, and global power relationships.

5. Modernization theory maintains that successful development hinges on breaking out of traditional cultural patterns to acquire advanced technology.

6. Modernization theorist W. W. Rostow identifies four stages of development: traditional, take-off, the drive to technological maturity, and high mass consumption.

7. Arguing that rich societies hold the keys to creating wealth, modernization theory claims rich nations can assist poor nations by providing population control programs, agricultural technology such as hybrid seeds and fertilizers that increase food production, industrial technology that includes machinery and information technology, and foreign aid to help build power plants and factories.

8. Critics of modernization theory say that rich nations do not spread economic development around the world. Further, they claim, poor nations cannot follow the same path to development taken by rich nations centuries ago.

9. Dependency theory claims global wealth and poverty are the historical products of the capitalist world economy because of colonialism and, more recently, the operation of multinational corporations.

10. Immanuel Wallerstein views the high-income countries as the advantaged "core" of the capitalist world economy; middle-income nations are the "semiperiphery," and poor societies form the global "periphery."

11. Three key factors—export-oriented economies, a lack of industrial capacity, and foreign debt—perpetuate poor countries' dependency on rich nations.

12. Critics of dependency theory argue that this approach overlooks the sixfold increase in the world's wealth over the course of the twentieth century. Furthermore, the world's poorest societies are not those with the strongest ties to rich countries.

13. Both modernization theory and dependency theory offer useful insights into global inequality. Some evidence supports each view. But as global inequality continues to increase, there is an urgent need to address the various problems caused by worldwide poverty.

KEY CONCEPTS

colonialism (p. 310) the process by which some nations enrich themselves through political and economic control of other nations

neocolonialism (p. 310) a new form of global power relationships that involves not direct political control but economic exploitation by multinational corporations

multinational corporation (p. 310) a large business that operates in many countries

modernization theory (p. 311) a model of economic and social development that explains global inequality in terms of technological and cultural differences between nations

dependency theory (p. 315) a model of economic and social development that explains global inequality in terms of the historical exploitation of poor nations by rich ones

CRITICAL-THINKING QUESTIONS

1. Based on what you have read here and elsewhere, what is your prediction about the extent of global hunger fifty years from now? Will the problem be more or less serious? Why?

2. What is the difference between relative and absolute poverty? Use these two concepts to describe social stratification in the United States and around the world.

3. Why do many analysts argue that economic development in low-income countries depends on raising the social standing of women?

4. State the basic tenets of modernization theory and dependency theory. What are several criticisms of each approach?

APPLICATIONS AND EXERCISES

1. Keep a log book of mass media advertising mentioning low-income countries (selling, say, coffee from Colombia or exotic vacations to India). What image of life in low-income countries does the advertising present? In light of this chapter, how accurate is this image?

2. Millions of students from abroad study on U.S. campuses. See if you can identify a woman and a man on your campus who were raised in a poor country. Approach them, explain that you have been studying global stratification, and ask if they are willing to share what life is like back home. You may be able to learn quite a bit from them.

3. Use the global maps in this text (or the animated maps on the CD-ROM) to identify social traits associated with the world's richest and poorest nations. Try to use both modernization theory and dependency theory to build explanations of the patterns you find.

4. Packaged in the back of this new textbook is an interactive CD-ROM that offers a variety of video and interactive review materials intended to help you better understand the material covered in this chapter. For this chapter, the CD-ROM contains a relevant clip from *ABC News*, an author's tip video, interactive map animations, an interactive time line, and flashcards with audio pronunciations of the more difficult words.

 ## SITES TO SEE

http://www.prenhall.com/macionis

Visit the interactive Companion Website™ that accompanies this text. Begin by clicking on the cover of your book. You will find a chapter-by-chapter study guide, practice tests, suggested Web links, and links to other relevant material.

http://members.aol.com/casmasalc/

This is the Web site for the Coalition against Slavery in Mauritania and Sudan. This site provides information about the problem of slavery as well as links to similar organizations.

http://www.census.gov/ipc/www/idbnew.html
http://www.prb.org/

These two sites, operated by the U.S. Census Bureau and the Population Reference Bureau, offer a statistical profile of world nations.

http://www1.worldbank.org/publications/pdfs/14978frontmat.pdf

Here is a recent report by The World Bank on strategies to reduce global poverty.

http://www.fh.org
http://www.worldconcern.org
http://www.worldvision.org
http://www.care.org

Here are a number of additional Web sites that address global inequality. The first is operated by Food for the Hungry, the second takes you to the home page for World Concern, the third organization is World Vision, the fourth is CARE. Visit them all and watch for differences in the focus and strategies of the various organizations.

http://www.unicef.org/sowc02/

This UN site explores the state of the world's children.

 ## INVESTIGATE WITH RESEARCH NAVIGATOR™

Follow the instructions on page 24 of this text to access the features of **Research Navigator™**. Once at the Web site, enter your Login Name and Password. Then, to use the **Content Select™** database, enter keywords such as "world poverty," "world hunger," and "slavery," and the search engine will supply relevant and recent scholarly and popular press publications. Use the *New York Times* **Search-by-Subject Archive** to find recent news articles related to sociology and the **Link Library** feature to find relevant Web links organized by the key terms associated with this chapter.

GENDER STRATIFICATION

FERNANDO BOLERO (B. 1932, COLOMBIAN)
El Patron

1968, oil on canvas, 186.7 × 114.3 cm. Private Collection/The Bridgeman Art Library.

At first we traveled quite alone . . . but before we had gone many miles, we came on other wagon-loads of women, bound in the same direction. As we reached different cross-roads, we saw wagons coming from every part of the country and, long before we reached Seneca Falls, we were a procession.

S O WROTE CHARLOTTE Woodward in her journal as she made her way along the rutted dirt roads of upstate New York to the town of Seneca Falls. The year was 1848, a time when slavery was legal in much of the United States, and the social standing of all women was subordinate in every way to that of men. Back then, in much of the United States, women—regardless of color—could not own property or keep their wages if they were married; women could not draft a will; women were barred from filing lawsuits in court, including suits seeking custody of their children; women could not attend college; and husbands were widely viewed as having unquestioned authority over their wives and children.

Some 300 women gathered at Wesleyan Chapel in Seneca Falls to challenge this second-class citizenship. They listened as their leader, Elizabeth Cady Stanton, called for expanding women's rights and opportunities, including the right to vote. To many, such a proposal seemed absurd and outrageous; even many attending the conference were shocked by the idea. Stanton's husband, Henry, rode out of town in protest (Gurnett, 1998).

Much has changed in the century and a half since the Seneca Falls convention, and many of Stanton's proposals are now accepted as matters of basic fairness. But as this chapter explains, women and men still lead different lives, in the United States and elsewhere in the world; in most respects, men still dominate. This chapter explores the importance of gender and explains how, like class position, gender is a major dimension of social stratification.

GENDER AND INEQUALITY

Chapter 9 ("Sexuality") discussed the biological differences that divide the human population into categories of female and male. **Gender** refers to *the personal traits and social positions that members of a society attach to being female or male.* Gender, then, is a dimension of social organization, shaping how we interact with others and how we think about ourselves. More important, gender also involves *hierarchy*, ranking men and women differently in terms of power, wealth, and other resources. This is why sociologists speak of **gender stratification**, *the unequal distribution of wealth, power, and privilege between men and women.* Gender, in short, affects the opportunities and constraints each of us faces throughout life (Ferree & Hall, 1996; Riley, 1997).

MALE-FEMALE DIFFERENCES

Many people think there is something "natural" about gender distinctions because, after all, there are biological differences between the sexes. But we must be careful not to think of social differences in biological terms. In 1848, for example, women were denied the

Sex is a biological distinction that develops prior to birth. Gender is the meaning that a society attaches to being female or male. Gender differences are a matter of power, as what is masculine typically has social priority over what is feminine. The importance of gender is not evident among infants, of course, but the ways in which we think of boys and girls set in motion patterns that will continue for a lifetime.

vote because many people assumed that they "naturally" lacked sufficient intelligence and political interest. But such attitudes had nothing to do with biology. Rather, they reflected the *cultural conventions* of that time and place.

Figure 13–1 presents another example of women's "natural" inferiority—athletics. In 1925, most people would have doubted that the best women runners could ever finish a marathon in anywhere near the time that men could. Yet today, as the figure shows, the best women routinely post better times than the fastest men of decades past, and the performance gap between the sexes has narrowed greatly. Here again, most of the differences between men and women turn out to be socially created.

There are some differences in physical ability between the sexes. On average, males are 10 percent taller, 20 percent heavier, and 30 percent stronger, especially in their upper bodies (Ehrenreich, 1999). On the other hand, women outperform men in the ultimate game of life itself: Whereas life expectancy for men in the United States is 74.4 years, women can expect to live 79.8 years (U.S. National Center for Health Statistics, 2003).

In adolescence, males show greater mathematical ability, whereas adolescent females excel in verbal skills, a difference that reflects both biology and socialization (Maccoby & Jacklin, 1974; Baker et al., 1980; Lengermann & Wallace, 1985; Tavris & Wade, 2001). However, research points to no overall differences in intelligence between males and females.

Biologically, then, men and women differ in limited ways, neither one being naturally superior. But culture can define the two sexes very differently, as the global study of gender shows.

GENDER IN GLOBAL PERSPECTIVE

The best way to see the cultural foundation of gender is by making global comparisons. Here, we review three studies that highlight how different the ideas of "masculine" and "feminine" can be.

The Israeli Kibbutzim

In Israel, collective Jewish settlements are called *kibbutzim*. The kibbutz (singular form) is especially important for gender research because gender equality is one of its goals, with men and women sharing in domestic work and leadership roles.

Members of kibbutzim consider gender irrelevant to most of everyday life. Both men and women take care of children, cook and clean, repair buildings, and make day-to-day decisions concerning life in the kibbutz. Girls and boys are raised in the same way, and from the first weeks of life, children live together in dormitories. Women and men in kibbutzim have achieved remarkable (although not complete) social equality. Thus, kibbutzim are evidence of the wide latitude cultures have in defining what is feminine and what is masculine.

Margaret Mead's Research

Anthropologist Margaret Mead carried out ground-breaking research on gender. To the extent that gender reflects biological facts of sex, she reasoned, people everywhere should define "feminine" and "masculine" in the same way; if gender is cultural, these conceptions should vary.

Mead studied three societies in New Guinea (1963; orig. 1935). In the mountainous home of the Arapesh, Mead observed men and women with remarkably similar attitudes and behavior. Both sexes, she reported, were cooperative and sensitive to others—in short, what our culture would label "feminine."

Moving south, Mead then studied the Mundugumor, headhunters and cannibals who stood in striking contrast to the gentle Arapesh. In this culture, both sexes were typically selfish and aggressive, traits we define as "masculine."

Finally, traveling west to the Tchambuli, Mead discovered a culture that, like our own, defined females and males differently. But, Mead reported, the Tchambuli *reversed* many of our notions of gender: Females were dominant and rational, and males were submissive, emotional, and nurturing toward children. From her observations, Mead concluded that gender rests on culture: What one culture defines as masculine, another may see as feminine.

Some critics view Mead's findings as "too neat," as if she saw in these three societies just the patterns she was looking for. Deborah Gewertz (1981) challenged Mead's "reversal hypothesis," claiming that Tchambuli males are really more aggressive and Tchambuli females more submissive. Gewertz explains that Mead visited the Tchambuli (who actually call themselves the Chambri) during the 1930s, after they had lost much of their property in tribal wars. Working in the home, she claims, was a temporary role for Chambri men.

George Murdock's Research

In a broader study of more than 200 preindustrial societies, George Murdock (1937) found some global agreement about which tasks are feminine and which masculine. Hunting and warfare generally fall to men, while home-centered tasks such as cooking and child care tend to be women's work. With their simple technology, preindustrial societies apparently assign roles reflecting men's and women's physical attributes. With greater size and strength, men hunt game and protect the group; because women bear children, they assume domestic duties.

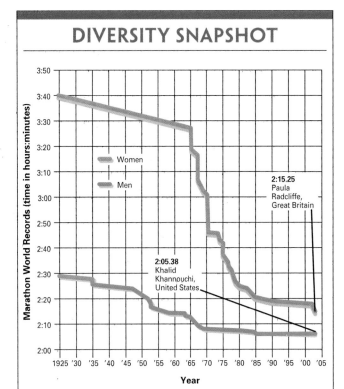

FIGURE 13-1 Men's and Women's Athletic Performance

Do men naturally outperform women in athletic competition? The answer is not obvious. Early in the twentieth century, men outdistanced women by many miles in marathon races. But as opportunities for women in athletics have increased, women have been closing the performance gap. Only ten minutes separate the current world marathon records for women (set in 2003) and for men (set in 2002).

But beyond this general pattern, Murdock found significant variation. Consider agriculture: Women did the farming in about the same number of societies as men, but in most, the two sexes divided this work. When it came to many other tasks—from building shelters to tattooing the body—Murdock found that societies of the world were as likely to turn to one sex as the other.

In Sum: Gender and Culture

Global comparisons show us that, by and large, societies do not consistently define most tasks as either

In every society, people assume certain jobs, patterns of behavior, and ways of dressing are "naturally" feminine while others are just as obviously masculine. But in global perspective, we see remarkable variety in such social definitions. These men, Wodaabe pastoral nomads who live in the African nation of Niger, are proud to engage in a display of beauty most people in our society would consider feminine.

feminine or masculine. With industrialization, moreover, the importance of muscle power declines, so people have even more options and gender differences are further reduced (Nolan & Lenski, 1999). Thus, gender is simply too variable across cultures to be considered a simple expression of biology. Instead, as with many other elements of culture, what it means to be female and male is mostly a creation of society.

PATRIARCHY AND SEXISM

Although conceptions of gender vary, everywhere in the world we find some degree of **patriarchy** (literally, "rule by fathers"), *a form of social organization in which males dominate females.* Of course, some men are far more advantaged than others; but in general, males have more social resources than females (Arrighi, 2001).

Matriarchy, on the other hand, is *a form of social organization in which females dominate males.* Although there is no clear case of matriarchy, women's power can rival that of men. During the 1700s and 1800s among the Seneca of North America, for example, women did the farming and controlled the food supply. Therefore, men had to obtain women's support for their objectives (such as a military campaign) or women could simply withhold the necessary food (Freedman, 2002).

Even today, as Global Map 13–1 shows, there is significant variation in the relative power and privilege of females and males around the world. According to a

United Nations report, three Nordic countries—Norway, Sweden, and Finland—afford women the highest social standing relative to men; by contrast, women in the Central African nations of Niger and Chad as well as the Asian nation of Afghanistan and the East African nation of Djibouti have the lowest social standing compared to men. Of the world's nations, the United States ranked eighth in terms of gender equality (United Nations Development Programme, 1995).

Sexism, *the belief that one sex is innately superior to the other,* is the ideological basis of patriarchy. Sexism is not just a matter of individual attitudes; it is built into the institutions of society. *Institutional sexism* pervades the U.S. economy, for example, with women highly concentrated in low-paying jobs. Similarly, the legal system in this country has long excused violence against women, especially on the part of boyfriends, husbands, and fathers (Landers, 1990).

The Costs of Sexism

Sexism stunts the talents and limits the ambitions of the half of the human population who are women. Although men benefit in some respects from sexism, their privilege comes at a high price. Masculinity in our culture calls for men to engage in many high-risk behaviors, including using tobacco and alcohol, participating in physically dangerous sports, and driving recklessly (motor vehicle accidents are the leading cause of death among young males). Moreover, as Marilyn French

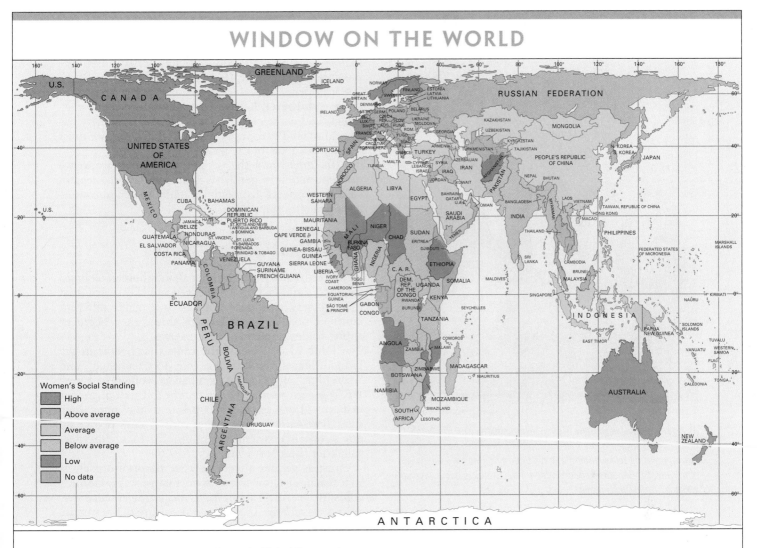

GLOBAL MAP 13–1 Women's Power in Global Perspective

Women's social standing in relation to men's varies around the world. In general, women fare better in rich countries than in poor countries. Even so, some nations stand out: In the Nordic nations of Norway, Sweden, and Finland, women come closest to social equality with men.

Source: Data taken from Seager (1997).

(1985) argues, patriarchy compels men to seek control not only of women but also of themselves and their world. Thus, masculinity is closely linked not only to accidents but to suicide, violence, and stress-related diseases. The Type A personality—marked by chronic impatience, driving ambition, competitiveness, and free-floating hostility—is a recipe for heart disease and almost perfectly matches the behavior that our culture considers masculine (Ehrenreich, 1983).

Finally, insofar as men seek control over others, they lose opportunities for intimacy and trust. As one analyst put it, competition is supposed to separate "the

As a general rule, patriarchy is strongest in nations with traditional cultures and limited economic development. Here we see a man in Eritrea traveling to a wedding with his three wives walking alongside him. While gender stratification in the United States is not always so obvious, it remains a reality in this country as well.

men from the boys." In practice, however, it separates men from men and everyone else (Raphael, 1988).

Is Patriarchy Inevitable?

In preindustrial societies, women have little say over pregnancy and childbirth, so the scope of their lives is limited. At the same time, men's greater height and physical strength are highly valued resources. But industrialization—including birth control technology—gives people choices about how to live. In today's postindustrial societies, biological differences offer little justification for patriarchy.

But legitimate or not, male dominance remains in the United States and elsewhere. Does this mean that patriarchy is inevitable? Some researchers claim that biological factors such as differences in hormones and slight differences in brain structure confer on the two sexes a tendency toward somewhat different motivations and behaviors—especially aggressiveness in males—making patriarchy difficult, perhaps even impossible, to eliminate (Goldberg, 1974, 1987; Rossi, 1985; Popenoe, 1993b; Udry, 2000, 2001). Most sociologists, however, believe that gender is a social construct that *can* be changed. Just because no society has yet eliminated patriarchy does not mean that we must remain prisoners of the past.

To understand the persistence of patriarchy, we now examine how gender is rooted and reproduced in society, a process that begins in childhood and continues throughout our lives.

GENDER AND SOCIALIZATION

From birth until death, gender shapes human feelings, thoughts, and actions. Children quickly learn that their society considers females and males different kinds of people; by about age three, they begin to apply gender standards to themselves.

Table 13–1 presents the traits that people in the United States traditionally link to "feminine" and "masculine" behavior. As similar as women and men are, it is curious that we are taught to think of gender in terms of one sex being opposite to the other, even though research suggests that most young people do not develop consistently feminine or masculine personalities (Bernard, 1980; Bem, 1993).

Just as gender affects how we think of ourselves, so it teaches us how to act in normative ways. **Gender roles** (or sex roles) are *attitudes and activities that a society links to each sex.* Insofar as our culture defines males as ambitious and competitive, we expect them to play team sports and aspire to positions of leadership. To the extent that we define females as deferential and emotional, we expect them to be supportive helpers and quick to show their feelings.

GENDER AND THE FAMILY

The first question people usually ask about a newborn—"Is it a boy or a girl?"—looms large because the answer involves not just sex but the likely direction of the child's entire life.

In fact, gender is at work even before the birth of a child because, especially in lower-income nations, parents hope their firstborn will be a boy rather than a girl. Soon after birth, family members usher infants into the "pink world" of girls or the "blue world" of boys

(Bernard, 1981). Parents even send gender messages in the way they handle daughters and sons. One researcher at an English university presented an infant dressed as either a boy or a girl to a number of women; her subjects handled the "female" child tenderly, with frequent hugs and caresses, and treated the "male" child more aggressively, often lifting him up high in the air or bouncing him on the knee (Bonner, 1984; Tavris & Wade, 2001). The lesson is clear: The female world revolves around passivity and emotion, while the male world puts a premium on independence and action.

GENDER AND THE PEER GROUP

About the time they enter school, children move outside the family and make friends with others of the same age. Considerable research points to the fact that young children tend to form single-sex play groups (Martin & Fabes, 2001).

Peer groups teach additional lessons about gender. After spending a year watching children at play, Janet Lever (1978) concluded that boys favor team sports with complex rules and clear objectives such as scoring a run or making a touchdown. Because such games nearly always have winners and losers, they reinforce masculine traits of aggression and control.

Girls, too, play team sports. But, Lever explains, girls also play hopscotch, jump rope, or simply talk, sing, or dance. These activities have few rules, and rarely is "victory" the ultimate goal. Instead of teaching girls to be competitive, Lever explains, female peer groups promote the interpersonal skills of communication and cooperation, presumably the basis for girls' future roles as wives and mothers.

Lever's observations recall Carol Gilligan's (1982) gender-based theory of moral reasoning, discussed in Chapter 5 ("Socialization"). Boys, Gilligan contends, reason according to abstract principles. For them, "rightness" amounts to "playing by the rules." Girls, on the other hand, consider morality a matter of responsibility to others. Thus, the games we play offer important lessons for our later lives.

GENDER AND SCHOOLING

Gender shapes our interests and beliefs about our own abilities, guiding areas of study and, eventually, career choices (Correll, 2001). In high school, more girls than boys learn secretarial skills and take vocational classes such as cosmetology and food services. Classes in woodworking and auto mechanics attract mostly young men.

TABLE 13-1 Traditional Notions of Gender Identity

Feminine Traits	Masculine Traits
Submissive	Dominant
Dependent	Independent
Unintelligent and incapable	Intelligent and competent
Emotional	Rational
Receptive	Assertive
Intuitive	Analytical
Weak	Strong
Timid	Brave
Content	Ambitious
Passive	Active
Cooperative	Competitive
Sensitive	Insensitive
Sex object	Sexually aggressive
Attractive because of physical appearance	Attractive because of achievement

In college, the pattern continues, with men disproportionately represented in mathematics and the sciences, including physics, chemistry, and biology. Women cluster in the humanities (such as English), the fine arts (painting, music, dance, and drama), and the social sciences (including anthropology and sociology). New areas of study are also likely to be gender-typed. Computer science, for example, enrolls mostly men, whereas courses in gender studies enroll more women.

GENDER AND THE MASS MEDIA

Since television first captured the public imagination in the 1950s, white males have held center stage, and until the early 1970s, racial and ethnic minorities were all but absent from prominent television roles. Today, while we expect to see both sexes on camera, men are still more likely to play the brilliant detectives, fearless explorers, and skilled surgeons. Women, by contrast, play the less capable characters, often important only for the sexual interest they add to the story.

Historically, advertisements have shown women in the home, happily using cleaning products or appliances, serving food, and modeling clothes. Men, on the other hand, predominate in ads for cars, travel, banking services, and alcoholic beverages. The authoritative "voice-over"—the faceless voice that describes a product on television and radio—is almost always male (Courtney & Whipple, 1983; Davis, 1993).

Further, a careful study of gender in advertising reveals that men usually appear taller than women,

DIVERSITY: RACE, CLASS, AND GENDER

Pretty Is as Pretty Does: The Beauty Myth

The Duchess of Windsor once quipped, "A woman cannot be too rich or too thin." The first half of her observation might apply to men as well, but what about the second? The answer lies in the fact that the vast majority of ads placed by the $20-billion-a-year cosmetics industry and the $40-billion diet industry target women.

According to Naomi Wolf (1990), our culture promotes a "beauty myth" that is damaging to women. The beauty myth arises, first, because society teaches women to measure themselves in terms of physical appearance (Backman & Adams, 1991). Yet the standards of beauty (such as the *Playboy* centerfold or the 100-pound New York fashion model) are unattainable for most women.

The beauty myth also teaches women to prize relationships with men and to use beauty to attract men. Striving for beauty drives women to be ex-

tremely disciplined but also forces them to be highly attuned and responsive to men. Beauty-minded women, in short, try to please men and avoid challenging male power.

The beauty myth affects males, as well: Men should want to possess beautiful women. Thus, our ideas about beauty reduce women to objects and motivate men to possess women as if they were dolls rather than human beings.

In sum, there can be little doubt that the idea of beauty is important in everyday life. The question, according to Wolf, is whether beauty is about how we look or how we act.

Source: Based on Wolf (1990).

implying male superiority. Women, by contrast, are more frequently presented lying down (on sofas and beds) or, like children, seated on the floor. Men's facial expressions and behavior exude competence and imply dominance, whereas women often appear childlike, submissive, and sexual. While men focus on the products being advertised, women often focus on the men (Goffman, 1979; Cortese, 1999).

Advertising also actively perpetuates what Naomi Wolf calls the "beauty myth." The box takes a closer look.

GENDER AND SOCIAL STRATIFICATION

Gender implies more than how people think and act. It is also about social hierarchy. The reality of gender stratification can be seen, first, in the world of work.

WORKING WOMEN AND MEN

Back in 1900, just 20 percent of U.S. women were in the labor force. In 2002, 60 percent of women aged

sixteen and over worked for income, and three-fourths of working women worked full time. The traditional view that earning an income is exclusively a "man's role" no longer holds true, as Figure 13–2 shows.

Factors that have changed the U.S. labor force include the decline of farming as an occupation, the

growth of cities, a shrinking family size, and a rising divorce rate. Thus, the United States, along with most other nations of the world, considers women working for income the rule rather than the exception. In fact, 59 percent of U.S. married couples depend on two incomes. As Global Map 13–2 on page 334 shows, women represent almost half the U.S. work force; however, this is not the case in many of the poorer nations of the world.

In the past, many women in the U.S. labor force were childless. But today, 63 percent of married women with children under age six work for income, as do 77 percent of married women with children between six and seventeen years of age. For widowed, divorced, or separated women with children, the comparable figures are 76 percent of women with younger children and 87 percent of women with older children (U.S. Census Bureau, 2002).

Gender and Occupations

Although the shares of men and women in the labor force have been converging in all high-income nations, the work they do remains different (van der Lippe & van Dijk, 2002). The U.S. Department of Labor (2003) reports a high concentration of women in two job types. Administrative support work draws 22 percent of working women, most of whom are secretaries, typists, or stenographers. Often, these are called "pink-collar" jobs because 78 percent are filled by women. Another 18 percent of employed women do service work. Most of these jobs are in food service industries, child care, and health care.

Table 13–2 shows the ten occupations with the highest concentrations of women. Overall, although more women now work for pay, they are segregated in the labor force in jobs at the low end of the pay scale, with limited opportunities for advancement and usually supervised by men (Bianchi & Spain, 1996; Bellas & Coventry, 2001; U.S. Department of Labor, 2003).

Men dominate most other job categories, including the building trades, where 99 percent of brick and

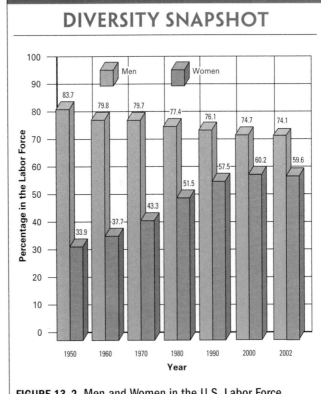

DIVERSITY SNAPSHOT

FIGURE 13-2 Men and Women in the U.S. Labor Force

Source: U.S. Department of Labor (2003).

TABLE 13-2 Jobs with the Highest Concentrations of Women, 2002		
Occupation	Number of Women Employed	Percentage in Occupation Who Are Women
1. Family child-care provider	457,000	99.4
2. Secretary	2,302,000	98.6
3. Dental hygienist	133,000	98.1
4. Dental assistant	224,000	98.0
5. Prekindergarten and kindergarten teacher	647,000	97.7
6. Private household child-care worker	229,000	97.6
7. Receptionist	1,068,000	97.1
8. Stenographer	146,000	95.2
9. Licensed practical nurse	382,000	94.9
10. Speech therapist	117,000	94.3

Source: U.S. Department of Labor, Bureau of Labor Statistics, tables from *Employment and Earnings*. [Online] Available June 20, 2003, at http://www.bls.gov/cps/#annual

stone masons and heavy equipment mechanics are men. Likewise, men are 89 percent of engineers; 84 percent of police officers and detectives; 71 percent of judges and lawyers; 69 percent of physicians; and 66 percent of corporate managers. According to a recent survey, the top earners in Fortune 500 corporations include 2,162 men (96 percent of the total) and 93 women (4 percent). Just eleven of the 1,000 largest U.S. corporations have a woman as their chief executive officer (Catalyst, 2003; U.S. Department of Labor, 2003).

 Read a summary of a study about the small number of women in top corporate jobs at http://www.catalystwomen.org/ press_room/press_releases/ 20030603.htm#top

Gender stratification in the workplace is easy to see: Female nurses assist male physicians, female secretaries serve male executives, and female flight attendants are under the command of male airplane pilots. Moreover, in any field, the greater the income and

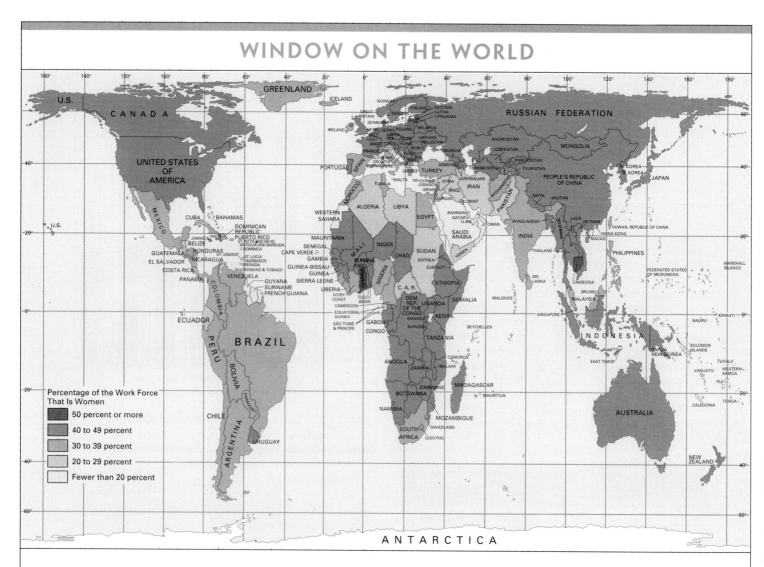

GLOBAL MAP 13–2 Women's Paid Employment in Global Perspective

This map shows the percentage of the labor force made up of women. A country's level of technological development plays an important part here. In 2002, women were 47 percent of the labor force in the United States, up almost 10 percent over the last generation. In high-income nations, overall, nearly one-half of the labor force is made up of women. In poor societies, however, women work even harder than in this country, but they are less likely to be paid for their efforts. In Latin America, for example, women represent about one-third of the paid labor force; in Islamic societies of northern Africa and the Middle East, the figure is significantly lower. One exception to this rule is central and southern Africa, where, traditionally, women make up a large share of farmers.

Sources: *Peters Atlas of the World* (1990); updated by the author from The World Bank (2003).

prestige associated with a job, the more likely it is to be held by a man. For example, women represent 98 percent of kindergarten teachers, 83 percent of elementary school teachers, 58 percent of secondary school teachers, 43 percent of college and university professors, and 19 percent of college and university presidents (*Chronicle of Higher Education*, 2002; U.S. Department of Labor, 2003).

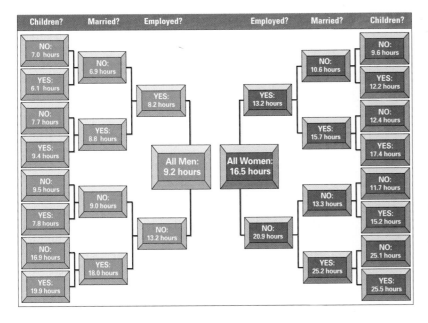

| Children? | Married? | Employed? | | Employed? | Married? | Children? |

FIGURE 13-3 Housework: Who Does How Much?

Overall, women average 16.5 hours of housework per week, compared with 9.2 hours for men. This pattern holds whether people are employed or not, married or not, and parenting or not.

Source: Adapted from Stapinski (1998).

How are women kept out of certain jobs? By defining some kinds of work as "masculine," companies define women as unsuitable workers. In a study of coal mining in southern West Virginia, Suzanne E. Tallichet (2000) found that most men considered it "unnatural" for women to join them working in the mines. Women who did, therefore, risked being defined, themselves, as "unnatural" and subject to labeling as "sexually loose" or as lesbians. Such labeling made these women outcasts, presented a challenge to holding the job, and made advancement all but impossible.

But one challenge to male domination in the workplace comes from women who are entrepreneurs. Women now own more than 9 million small businesses in the United States, double the number just a decade ago and more than one-third of the total. Although a large majority of these businesses are one-person operations, women-owned businesses employ one-fourth of the entire labor force. Through starting their own businesses, women have shown that they can make opportunities for themselves outside larger, male-dominated companies (Mergenhagen, 1996; Winters, 1999; U.S. Small Business Administration, 2001).

HOUSEWORK: WOMEN'S "SECOND SHIFT"

In the United States, housework has always been something of a cultural contradiction: We claim that it is essential to family life, but housework carries little prestige or other reward (Bernard, 1981). With women's entry into the labor force, the amount of housework performed by women has declined, but the *share* women do has stayed about the same. Figure 13–3 shows that, overall, women average 16.5 hours a week of housework, compared to 9.2 hours for men. Among all categories of people, the figure shows, women do significantly more housework than men (Stapinski, 1998).

In sum, men support the idea of women entering the labor force, and most count on the money women earn. But many men resist taking on a more equal share of household duties (Lennon & Rosenfeld, 1994; Heath & Bourne, 1995; Harpster & Monk-Turner, 1998; Stratton, 2001).

GENDER, INCOME, AND WEALTH

In 2001, the median earnings of women working full time were $29,215, whereas men working full time earned $38,275. Thus, for every dollar earned by men, women earned 76 cents. These earning differences are greatest among older workers—older working women typically have less education and seniority than older working men—and smaller among younger workers.

Among all full-time workers of all ages, 39 percent of women earned less than $25,000 in 2001, compared with 24 percent of comparable men. At the upper end of the income scale, men were three times more likely

Although only about 12 percent of the richest people in the United States are women, a number of women have reached the very top of the economic pyramid. Oprah Winfrey, who became both very wealthy and hugely influential as a result of her television show, is one example. As part of a business empire, she recently launched O, The Oprah Magazine.

than women (15.8 percent versus 5.5 percent) to earn more than $75,000 (U.S. Census Bureau, 2002).

The main reason women earn less is the *kind* of work they do: largely clerical and service jobs. In effect, jobs and gender interact. People still perceive jobs with less clout as "women's work," just as people devalue certain work simply because it is performed by women (Blum, 1991; England, 1992; Bellas, 1994; Huffman, Velasco, & Bielby, 1996; England, Hermsen, & Cotter, 2000).

In recent decades, proponents of gender equality have proposed a policy of "comparable worth." That is, people should be paid not according to the historical double standard, but according to the level of skill and responsibility involved in the work. Several nations, including Great Britain and Australia, have adopted comparable worth policies, but these policies

have found limited acceptance in the United States. As a result, working women in this country lose as much as $1 billion annually.

A second cause of gender-based income disparity has to do with the family. Both men and women have children, of course, but our culture defines parenting as more a woman's duty than a man's. Pregnancy and raising small children keep many young women out of the labor force at a time when their male peers are making significant career advancements. When women workers return to the labor force, they have less job seniority than their male counterparts (Stier, 1996; Waldfogel, 1997).

Moreover, women who choose to have children may be reluctant or unable to maintain fast-paced jobs that tie up their evenings and weekends. To avoid role strain, they may take jobs that offer a shorter commuting distance, more flexible hours, or employer child-care services. Women pursuing both a career and a family are often torn between their dual responsibilities in ways that men are not. Consider this: At age forty, 90 percent of men but only 35 percent of women in executive positions have at least one child (F. Schwartz, 1989). In academia, the same pattern holds: Young women with one or more children were 22 percent less likely to earn tenure than comparable men in the same field (Shea, 2002).

This *Monthly Labor Review* article traces women's earnings in recent decades: http://www.bls.gov/opub/mlr/1999/12/art2full.pdf

The two factors noted so far—type of work and family responsibilities—account for about two-thirds of the earnings disparity between women and men. A third factor—discrimination against women—accounts for most of the remainder (Pear, 1987; Fuller & Schoenberger, 1991). Because discrimination is illegal, it is practiced in subtle ways. Corporate women often encounter a *glass ceiling*, a barrier that is invisible because it is denied by company officials even though it effectively prevents women from rising above middle management (Benokraitis & Feagin, 1995; Yamagata et al., 1997).

For all these reasons, then, women earn less than men in all major occupational categories. Even so, many people think that women own most of this country's wealth, perhaps because women typically outlive men.

Government statistics, however, tell a different story: Sixty-one percent of individuals with $1 million or more in assets are men, although widows are highly represented in this elite club (U.S. Internal Revenue Service, 2003). Just 12 percent of the individuals identified in 2001 by *Forbes* magazine as the richest people in the United States were women.

GENDER AND EDUCATION

In the past, women received little schooling because their lives revolved around the home. But times have changed. By 1980, women earned a majority of all associate's and bachelor's degrees; in 2001, that proportion stood at 58 percent (U.S. National Center for Education Statistics, 2003).

College doors have opened to women, and differences in men's and women's majors are becoming smaller. In 1970, for example, women earned just 17 percent of bachelor's degrees in the natural sciences, computer science, and engineering; by 2001, that proportion had doubled to 35 percent.

In 1993, for the first time, women also earned a majority of postgraduate degrees, often a springboard to high-prestige jobs. In all areas of study in 2001, women earned 59 percent of master's degrees and 45 percent of doctorates (including 58 percent of all Ph.D.s in sociology). Women have also broken into many graduate fields that used to be almost all

 A report from the U.S. National Center for Education Statistics on gender and education can be found at http://nces.ed. gov/pubs2000/2000030.pdf

male. For example, in 1970 only a few hundred women received a master's of business administration (M.B.A.) degree, compared to more than 47,000 in 2001 (41 percent of all such degrees) (U.S. National Center for Education Statistics, 2003).

Men continue to dominate some professional fields, however. In 2001, men received 53 percent of law degrees (LL.B. and J.D.), 57 percent of medical degrees (M.D.), and 61 percent of dental degrees (D.D.S. and D.M.D.) (U.S. National Center for Education Statistics, 2003). Our society still defines high-paying professions (and the drive and competitiveness needed to succeed in them) as masculine. Nevertheless, the proportion of women in all these professions is rising steadily. For example, the American Bar Association reports that the law school class of 2004 across the United States is about evenly split between women and men (Gest, 2001).

GENDER AND POLITICS

A century ago, almost no women held elected office in the United States. In fact, women were legally barred from voting in national elections until ratification of the Nineteenth Amendment to the Constitution in 1920. A few women, however, were candidates for political office even before they could vote. The Equal Rights party supported Victoria Woodhull for the

TABLE 13-3 Significant "Firsts" for Women in U.S. Politics

Year	Event
1869	Law allows women to vote in Wyoming territory; Utah follows suit in 1870.
1872	First woman to run for the presidency (Victoria Woodhull) represents the Equal Rights party.
1917	First woman elected to the House of Representatives (Jeannette Rankin of Montana).
1924	First women elected state governors (Nellie Taylor Ross of Wyoming and Miriam ["Ma"] Ferguson of Texas); both followed their husbands into office. First woman to have her name placed in nomination for vice-presidency at the convention of a major political party (Lena Jones Springs).
1931	First woman to serve in the Senate (Hattie Caraway of Arkansas); completed the term of her husband upon his death and won reelection in 1932.
1932	First woman appointed to the presidential cabinet (Frances Perkins, secretary of labor in the cabinet of President Franklin D. Roosevelt).
1964	First woman to have her name placed in nomination for the presidency at the convention of a major political party (Margaret Chase Smith, a Republican).
1972	First African American woman to have her name placed in nomination for the presidency at the convention of a major political party (Shirley Chisholm, a Democrat).
1981	First woman appointed to the U.S. Supreme Court (Sandra Day O'Connor).
1984	First woman to be successfully nominated for the vice-presidency (Geraldine Ferraro, a Democrat).
1988	First woman chief executive to be elected to a consecutive third term (Madeleine Kunin, governor of Vermont).
1992	Political "Year of the Woman" yields record number of women in the Senate (six) and the House (forty-eight), as well as (1) first African American woman to win election to U.S. Senate (Carol Moseley-Braun of Illinois), (2) first state (California) to be served by two women senators (Barbara Boxer and Dianne Feinstein), and (3) first woman of Puerto Rican descent elected to the House (Nydia Velazquez of New York).
1996	First woman appointed secretary of state (Madeleine Albright).
2000	Record number of women in the Senate (thirteen) and the House (sixty).
2000	First First Lady to win elected political office (Hillary Rodham Clinton, senator from New York).

Sources: Based on data compiled from Sandra Salmans, "Women Ran for Office before They Could Vote," *New York Times*, July 13, 1984, p. A11; and news reports.

U.S. presidency in 1872; perhaps it was a sign of the times that she spent election day in a New York City jail. Table 13–3 identifies later milestones in women's gradual movement into political life.

SEEING OURSELVES

NATIONAL MAP 13–1
Women in State Government across the United States

Although women make up half of U.S. adults, just 22 percent of the seats in state legislatures are held by women. Look at the state-by-state variation in the map. In which regions of the country have women gained the greatest political power? What factors do you think account for this pattern?

Source: Center for American Women and Politics, Eagleton Institute of Politics, Rutgers University, "Women in State Legislatures 2003." [Online] Available June 20, 2003, at http://www.cawp.rutgers.edu/pdf/stleg.pdf

Share of State Legislative Seats Held by Women

- High: 30.0% and over
- Above average: 25.0% to 29.9%
- Average: 20.0% to 24.9%
- Below average: 15.0% to 19.9%
- Low: 14.9% and under

U.S. average: 22.3%

Today, thousands of women serve as mayors of cities and towns across the United States, and tens of thousands hold responsible administrative posts in the federal government. At the state level, 22 percent of legislators in 2003 were women (up from just 6 percent in 1970). National Map 13–1 shows where in the United States women have made the greatest political gains.

Less change has occurred at the highest levels of politics, although a majority of U.S. adults claim they would support a qualified woman for any office, including the presidency. After the 2002 national elections, 6 of the 50 state governors were women (12 percent), and, in Congress, women held 59 of 435 seats in the House of Representatives (14 percent), and 14 of 100 seats (14 percent) in the Senate (Center for American Women and Politics, 2003).

For the latest on women in national politics, visit http://www.cawp.rutgers.edu

In global perspective, although women are half the Earth's population, they hold just 15.2 percent of seats in the world's 181 parliaments. Although this percentage represents a rise from 3 percent fifty years ago, only in the Nordic nations of Sweden, Denmark, Finland, and Norway (ranging from 45.3 percent to 36.4 percent) does the share of parliamentary seats held by women even approach their share of the population (Inter-Parliamentary Union, 2003).

GENDER AND THE MILITARY

Since colonial times, women have served in the armed forces. Yet, in 1940, at the outset of World War II, just 2 percent of armed forces personnel were women. By the 2003 War in Iraq, women represented about 7 percent of all deployed U.S. troops. By mid-December, 2003, eight of the 460 War in Iraq casualties were women. In 2003, women represented 15 percent of all people in the armed forces.

Although women make up a rising share of the U.S. military, only the Coast Guard makes all assignments available to women. At the other extreme, the Marine Corps denies women access to two-thirds of its jobs. Those who defend limited roles for women in the military claim that women lack the physical strength of men. Critics counter that military women are better educated and score higher on intelligence tests than their male counterparts. But the heart of the issue is our society's deeply held view of women as *nurturers*—people who give life and help others—which clashes with the image of women trained to kill.

Although integrating women into military culture has been difficult, women in all branches of the armed forces are taking on more and more military assignments. One reason is that high technology blurs the distinction between combat and noncombat personnel.

A combat pilot can fire missiles by radar at a target miles away, while nonfighting medical evacuation teams go right to the battle site (McNeil, 1991; May, 1991; Segal & Hansen, 1992; Wilcox, 1992; Kaminer, 1997).

ARE WOMEN A MINORITY?

A **minority**[1] is *any category of people distinguished by physical or cultural difference that a society sets apart and subordinates.* Given the clear economic disadvantage of being a woman in our society, it seems reasonable to say that U.S. women are a minority even though they outnumber men.

Even so, most white women do not think of themselves this way (Lengermann & Wallace, 1985). The reason is partly that, unlike racial minorities (including African Americans) and ethnic minorities (say, Hispanics), white women are well represented at all levels of the class structure, including the very top.

Bear in mind that at every class level, women typically have less income, wealth, education, and power than men. In fact, patriarchy makes women dependent for much of their social standing on men—first their fathers and later their husbands (Bernard, 1981).

MINORITY WOMEN: INTERSECTION THEORY

If women are defined as a minority, what about minority women? Are they doubly handicapped? This question lies at the heart of **intersection theory,** *the investigation of the interplay of race, class, and gender, often resulting in multiple dimensions of disadvantage.* Research shows that disadvantages linked to gender and race may combine so that some categories of people face greater challenges (Arrighi, 2001; McCall, 2001a; Ovadia, 2001).

Income data illustrate the validity of this theory. If we look first at race and ethnicity, the median income in 2001 for African American women working full time was $27,297, which is 86 percent as much as the $31,794 earned by non-Hispanic white women; Hispanic women earned $21,973—just 69 percent as much as their white counterparts. If we look at gender, African American women earned 86 percent as much as African American men, while Hispanic women earned 87 percent as much as Hispanic men.

With these disadvantages combined, African American women earned 63 percent as much as

The basic insight of intersection theory is that various dimensions of social stratification—including race and gender—can add up to great disadvantages for some categories of people. Just as African Americans earn less than whites, women earn less than men. Thus, African American women confront a "double disadvantage," earning just 63 cents for every dollar earned by non-Hispanic white men. How would you explain the fact that some categories of people are much more likely to end up in low-paying jobs like this one?

non-Hispanic white men, and Hispanic women earned 51 percent as much (U.S. Census Bureau, 2002). These disparities reflect minority women's lower positions in the occupational and educational hierarchies compared to white women (Bonilla-Santiago, 1990). These data confirm that, while gender has a powerful effect on our lives, it never operates alone. Class position, race and ethnicity, and gender intersect to form a multilayered system of disadvantage for some and privilege for others (Ginsburg & Tsing, 1990; St. Jean & Feagin, 1998).

VIOLENCE AGAINST WOMEN

As noted in the opening to this chapter, about 150 years ago, men claimed the right to rule their households, even to the point of using physical discipline against their wives. Even today, a great deal of "manly" violence is directed at women. A government report estimates 402,000 aggravated assaults against women annually. To this number can be added 217,000 rapes or sexual assaults and perhaps 2 million

---

[1]We use the term "minority" instead of "minority group" because, as explained in Chapter 7 ("Groups and Organizations"), a minority is a category, not a group.

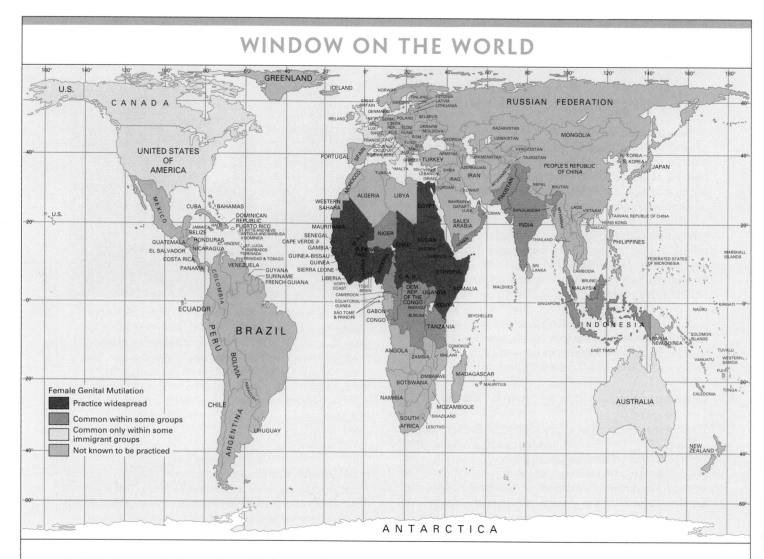

GLOBAL MAP 13–3 Female Genital Mutilation in Global Perspective

Female genital mutilation, also called female circumcision, is known to be performed in more than forty countries around the world. Across Africa, the practice is common and affects a majority of girls in the eastern African nations of Sudan, Ethiopia, and Somalia. In several Asian nations, including India, the practice is limited to a few ethnic minorities. In the United States, Canada, several European nations, and Australia, there are reports of the practice among some immigrants.

Source: Data taken from Seager (1997).

simple assaults (Goetting, 1999; U.S. Bureau of Justice Statistics, 2003).

Gender violence is also an issue on college and university campuses. A report from the Department of Justice (2001) states that, in 2000, 1.7 percent of female college students were victims of rape, and another 1.1 percent were victims of attempted rape. In 90 percent of all cases the victims knew the offenders, and most of the assaults took place in the woman's living quarters.

GLOBAL SOCIOLOGY

Female Genital Mutilation: Violence in the Name of Morality

Meserak Ramsey, a woman born in Ethiopia and now working as a nurse in California, paid a visit to a friend's nearby home. Soon after arriving, she noticed her friend's eighteen-month-old daughter huddled in the corner of a room in obvious distress. "What's wrong?" she asked.

Ramsey was shocked when the woman said her daughter had recently had a clitoridectomy, or female circumcision, whereby the clitoris is surgically removed. This procedure—performed by a midwife, a tribal practitioner, or a doctor, and typically without anesthesia—is common in two dozen African nations, including Nigeria, Togo, Somalia, and Egypt, and is known to exist among certain cultural groups in other nations around the world.

Among members of highly patriarchal societies, husbands demand that their wives be virgins at marriage and remain sexually faithful thereafter. The point of female circumcision is to eliminate sexual sensation, which, people assume, makes the girl less likely to

violate sexual norms and thus be more desirable to men. In about one-fifth of all cases, an even more severe procedure, called infibulation, is performed, in which the entire external genital area is removed and the surfaces are stitched together, leaving only a small hole for urination. Before marriage, a husband retains the right to open the wound and ensure himself of his bride's virginity.

How many women have undergone genital mutilation? Worldwide, estimates place the number at more than 100 million. In the United States, hundreds and probably thousands of such procedures are performed every year. In most cases, immigrant mothers and grandmothers who have themselves been mutilated insist that young girls in their family follow their example. Indeed, many immigrant women demand the procedure *because* their daughters now live in the United States, where sexual mores are more lax. "I don't have to worry about her now," the girl's mother explained to Meserak Ramsey. "She'll be a good girl."

The medical consequences of genital mutilation can be serious. Pain is intense and can persist for years. There is also danger of infection, infertility, and even death. And, of course, female circumcision results in the loss of sexual pleasure. Meserak Ramsey knows this all too well. She herself underwent genital mutilation as a young girl; she is one of the lucky ones who has had few medical problems since. But the extent of her suffering is suggested by this story: She had invited a young U.S. couple to stay at her home. Late at night, she heard the woman cry out and burst into their room to investigate, only to learn that the couple was making love and the woman had just had an orgasm. "I didn't understand," Ramsey recalls. "I thought that there must be something wrong with American girls. But now I know that there is something wrong with me." Or with a system that inflicts such injury in the name of traditional morality.

Sources: Based on Crossette (1995) and Boyle, Songora, & Foss (2001).

Off the campus as well, most gender-linked violence occurs where men and women interact most: in the home. It may be true, as Richard Gelles (cited in Roesch, 1984) once noted, that with the exception of the police and the military, the family is the most violent organization in the United States. Both sexes suffer from family violence, although, by and large, women sustain more serious injuries than men (Shupe, Stacey, & Hazlewood, 1987; Gelles & Cornell, 1990; Smolowe, 1994).

Violence against women also occurs in casual relationships. As noted in Chapter 8 ("Deviance"), most rapes involve not strangers but men known, and often trusted, by the victim. Dianne Herman (2001) claims that abuse of women is built into our way of life. All

forms of violence against women—from the wolf whistles that intimidate women on city streets to a pinch in a crowded subway to physical assaults that occur at home—express what she calls a "rape culture" of men trying to dominate women. Sexual violence, she explains, is fundamentally about *power*, not sex, and therefore should be understood as a dimension of gender stratification.

In global perspective, violence against women is built into culture in other ways. One case in point is the practice of female genital mutilation, a painful surgical procedure performed in more than forty countries and known to occur in the United States, as shown in Global Map 13–3. The box presents a case of genital mutilation that took place in California.

Many private companies and public organizations have adopted policies to discourage forms of behavior that might create a "hostile or intimidating environment." In practice, such policies seek to remove sexuality from the workplace so that employees can do their jobs while steering clear of traditional notions about female and male relationships. The hope is that sexual harassment policies will develop a comfortable informal atmosphere in which people can interact freely and easily.

Sexual Harassment

Sexual harassment refers to *comments, gestures, or physical contact of a sexual nature that are deliberate, repeated, and unwelcome.* During the 1990s, sexual harassment became an issue of national importance that rewrote the rules for workplace interaction.

Most (but not all) victims of sexual harassment are women. The reason is that, first, our culture encourages men to be sexually assertive and to perceive women in sexual terms. As a result, social interaction in the workplace, on campus, and elsewhere can readily take on sexual overtones. Second, most individuals in positions of power—including business executives, physicians, assembly line supervisors, professors, and military officers—are men who oversee the work of women. In surveys carried out in widely different work settings, half of the women respondents report receiving unwanted sexual attention (Paul, 1991; NORC, 2003).

Sexual harassment is sometimes blatant and direct: A supervisor solicits sexual favors from a subordinate

by threatening reprisal if the advances are refused. Courts have declared such quid pro quo sexual harassment (the Latin phrase means "one thing in return for another") to be a violation of civil rights.

More often, however, sexual harassment involves subtle behavior—sexual teasing, off-color jokes, pinups displayed in the workplace—that may or may not be *intended* to harass anyone. But, by the *effect* standard favored by many feminists, such actions amount to creating a *hostile environment* (Cohen, 1991; Paul, 1991). Incidents of this kind are far more complex because they involve different perceptions of the same behavior. For example, a man may think that repeatedly complimenting a co-worker on her appearance is simply being friendly. The co-worker may believe that men who tend to think of women in sexual terms do not take them seriously as colleagues, an attitude that can easily harm women's prospects for advancement.

Pornography

Chapter 9 ("Sexuality") defined *pornography* as sexually explicit material that causes sexual arousal. Keep in mind, however, that people take different views of what is and what is not pornographic. Likewise, the law gives local municipalities the power to draw the lines that define what sexually explicit materials violate "community standards" of decency and lack any redeeming social value.

People may disagree about what pornography is, but there is little doubt that, in the United States, pornography is big business. Taken together, sexually explicit videos, movies, magazines, telephone chat, and Internet sites represent more than $10 billion in sales each year.

Traditionally, U.S. society has viewed pornography as a *moral* issue. National survey data show that 57 percent of U.S. adults express concern that "sexual materials lead to a breakdown of morals" (NORC, 2003:235). But pornography also plays a part in gender stratification. From this point of view, pornography is really a *power* issue because most pornography dehumanizes women as the playthings of men. Worth noting, in this context, is that the term *pornography* comes from the Greek word *porne*, meaning a harlot who acts as a man's sexual slave.

In addition, there is widespread concern that pornography promotes violence against women. Depicting women as merely the sexual playthings of men amounts to defining women as weak and undeserving of respect. Men may show contempt for women defined this way by striking out against them. Surveys show that about half of U.S. adults think that pornography encourages men to commit rape (NORC, 2003:235).

Like sexual harassment, pornography raises complex and conflicting issues. While most people object to offensive material, many also think we must protect free speech and artistic expression. Nevertheless, public support to restrict pornography is building, reflecting both the longstanding concern that pornography undermines morality and more recent concerns that it is demeaning and threatening to women.

THEORETICAL ANALYSIS OF GENDER

Each of sociology's major theoretical paradigms addresses the significance of gender in social organization.

STRUCTURAL-FUNCTIONAL ANALYSIS

The structural-functional paradigm views society as a complex system of many separate but integrated parts. From this point of view, gender serves as a means to organize social life.

As Chapter 4 ("Society") explained, members of hunting and gathering societies had little power over the forces of biology. Lacking effective birth control, women were frequently pregnant, and the responsibilities of child care kept them close to home. At the same time, men's greater strength made them more suited for warfare and hunting game. Over the centuries, this sexual division of labor became institutionalized and largely taken for granted (Lengermann & Wallace, 1985; Freedman, 2002).

Industrial technology, however, opens up vastly greater cultural possibilities. Because human muscles are no longer the main energy source, the physical strength of men becomes less significant. In addition, the ability to control reproduction gives women greater choice in shaping their lives. Modern societies relax traditional gender roles as they come to see the enormous amount of human talent they waste; yet change comes slowly, because gender is deeply embedded in culture.

Talcott Parsons: Gender and Complementarity

As Talcott Parsons (1942, 1951, 1954) observed, gender helps to integrate society, at least in its traditional form. Gender forms a *complementary* set of roles that links men and women into family units for carrying out various important tasks. Women take primary responsibility for managing the household and raising

In the 1950s, Talcott Parsons proposed that sociologists interpret gender as a matter of differences. As he saw it, masculine men and feminine women formed strong families and made for an orderly society. In recent decades, however, social-conflict theory has reinterpreted gender as a matter of inequality. From this point of view, U.S. society places men in a position of dominance over women.

children. Men connect the family to the larger world as they participate in the labor force.

Parsons further argued that socialization teaches the two sexes the appropriate gender identity and skills needed for adult life. Thus, society teaches boys—presumably destined for the labor force—to be rational, competitive, and self-assured. This complex of traits Parsons termed *instrumental*. To prepare girls for child rearing, their socialization stresses *expressive* qualities, such as emotional responsiveness and sensitivity to others.

Society, explained Parsons, encourages gender conformity by instilling in men and women a fear that straying too far from accepted standards of masculinity or femininity courts rejection by the other sex. In simple terms, women are taught to view nonmasculine men as sexually unattractive, while men learn to shun unfeminine women.

Critical evaluation. Structural functionalism puts forward a theory of complementarity by which gender integrates society both structurally (in terms of what people do) and morally (in terms of what they believe). Influential a half century ago, this approach has lost much of its standing today.

First, functionalism assumes a singular vision of society that is not shared by everyone. For example, many women have always worked outside the home because of economic necessity, a fact not reflected in Parsons's conventional, middle-class view of family life. Second, Parsons's analysis ignores the personal strains and social costs of rigid, traditional gender roles (Giele, 1988). Third, for those who seek sexual equality, what Parsons describes as gender "complementarity" amounts to little more than women submitting to male domination.

SOCIAL-CONFLICT ANALYSIS

From a social-conflict point of view, gender involves differences not just in behavior but in power. Consider the striking parallel between the way ideas about gender have benefited men and the way oppression of racial and ethnic minorities has benefited whites (Hacker, 1951, 1974; Collins, 1971; Lengermann & Wallace, 1985). That is, conventional ideas about gender promote not cohesion but division and tension, with men seeking to protect their privileges as women challenge the status quo.

As earlier chapters explain, the social-conflict paradigm draws heavily on the approach of Karl Marx. Yet Marx was a product of his time insofar as his writings focused almost exclusively on men. However, his friend and collaborator Friedrich Engels did develop a theory of gender stratification (1902; orig. 1884).

Friedrich Engels: Gender and Class

Looking back through history, Engels saw that in hunting and gathering societies, the activities of women and men, while different, had the same importance. A successful hunt brought men great prestige, but the vegetation gathered by women provided most of a group's food supply. As technological advances led to the production of a surplus, however, social equality and communal sharing gave way to private property and, ultimately, a class hierarchy. With the rise of agriculture, then, men gained significant power over women. With surplus wealth to pass on to heirs, men (at least those in the higher classes) wanted to be sure of paternity; in order to do that, they had to be able to regulate the sexuality of women. The desire to control property, then, led to the creation of monogamous marriage and the family. Women were taught to remain virgins until marriage, to stay faithful to their husbands thereafter, and to build their lives around bearing and raising one man's children.

Capitalism, Engels continued, intensifies male domination. For one thing, capitalism creates more wealth, which confers greater power on men as owners of property and primary wage earners. Second, an expanding capitalist economy depends on turning people, especially women, into consumers who seek personal fulfillment through buying and using products. Third, to free themselves to work in factories, men can demand that women maintain the home. The double exploitation of capitalism, as Engels saw it, lies in paying men low wages for their labor and paying women no wages at all (Barry, 1983; Jagger, 1983; Vogel, 1983; Freedman, 2002).

Critical evaluation. Social-conflict analysis highlights how society places the two sexes in positions of unequal wealth, power, and privilege. It is decidedly critical of conventional ideas about gender, claiming that society would be better off if it minimized or even eliminated this dimension of social structure.

But social-conflict analysis also has its critics. One problem is that this approach sees conventional families—defended by traditionalists as morally positive—as harmful to society. Second, from a more practical point of view, social-conflict analysis minimizes the extent to which women and men live together cooperatively, and often happily, in families. A third problem lies in the assertion that capitalism is the basis of gender stratification. In fact, agrarian countries are typically more patriarchal than industrial-capitalist societies. Moreover, socialist nations—including the People's Republic of China and the former Soviet Union—did move women into the work force but, by and large, provided women with very low pay in sex-segregated jobs (Moore, 1992; Rosendahl, 1997; Haney, 2002).

FEMINISM

Feminism is *the advocacy of social equality for men and women, in opposition to patriarchy and sexism.* The first wave of the feminist movement in the United States began in the 1840s as women opposed to slavery, including Elizabeth Cady Stanton and Lucretia Mott, drew parallels between the oppression of African Americans and the oppression of women. The Seneca Falls convention, described in the chapter opening, began the social movement by which women finally won the right to vote in 1920. But other disadvantages persisted, and a second wave of feminism arose in the 1960s and continues today.

BASIC FEMINIST IDEAS

Feminism views the personal experiences of women and men through the lens of gender. How we think of ourselves (gender identity), how we act (gender roles), and our sex's social standing (gender stratification) are all rooted in the operation of society.

Although people who consider themselves feminists disagree about many issues, most support five general principles:

1. **Working to increase equality.** Feminist thinking is decidedly political, linking ideas to action. Feminism is critical of the status quo and advocates change toward social equality for women and men in the United States and around the world.

2. **Expanding human choice.** Feminists maintain that cultural conceptions of gender divide the full range of human qualities into two opposing and limited spheres: the female world of emotions and cooperation and the male world of rationality and competition. As an alternative, feminists propose a "reintegration of humanity" by which all individuals can develop all human traits (French, 1985).

3. **Eliminating gender stratification.** Feminism opposes laws and cultural norms that limit the education, income, and job opportunities of women. For this reason, feminists have long supported passage of the Equal Rights Amendment (ERA) to the U.S. Constitution, which states, "Equality of rights under the law shall not be denied or abridged by the United States or any State on account of sex." The ERA was first proposed in Congress in 1923. Although surveys show widespread public support, it has yet to become law.

4. **Ending sexual violence.** Today's women's movement seeks to eliminate sexual violence. Feminists argue that patriarchy distorts the relationships between women and men, encouraging violence against women in the form of rape, domestic abuse, sexual harassment, and pornography (Dworkin, 1987; Freedman, 2002).

5. **Promoting sexual freedom.** Finally, feminism supports women's control over their sexuality and reproduction. Feminists support the free availability of birth control information. As Figure 13–4 shows, contraceptives are much less

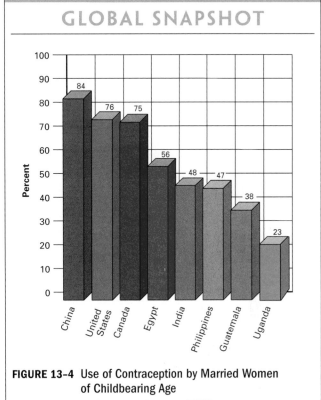

GLOBAL SNAPSHOT

FIGURE 13-4 Use of Contraception by Married Women of Childbearing Age

Source: United Nations Development Programme (2003).

available in most of the world than they are in the United States. Most feminists also support a woman's right to choose whether to bear children or terminate a pregnancy, rather than allowing men—as husbands, physicians, and legislators—to control their reproduction. Over time, the feminist social movement has voiced increasing support for gay people's efforts to overcome the many barriers they face in a predominantly heterosexual culture (Jagger, 1983; Ferree & Hess, 1995; Armstrong, 2002).

TYPES OF FEMINISM

Although feminists agree on the importance of gender equality, they disagree on how to achieve it—through liberal feminism, socialist feminism, or radical feminism (Barry, 1983; Jagger, 1983; Stacey, 1983; Vogel, 1983; Ferree & Hess, 1995; Armstrong, 2002; Freedman, 2002).

These three women made enormous contributions to the women's movement during the twentieth century. Margaret Higgins Sanger (1883–1966) was a pioneer activist in the crusade for women's reproductive rights. Margaret Mead (1901–1978), probably the best known anthropologist of all time, showed how definitions of femininity and masculinity are rooted in culture rather than biology. In 1949, Simone De Beauvoir (1908–1986) published The Second Sex, *one of the first books to explore systematically the importance of gender to social life.*

Liberal Feminism

Liberal feminism is rooted in the classic liberal thinking that individuals should be free to develop their own talents and pursue their own interests. Liberal feminists accept the basic organization of our society but seek to expand the rights and opportunities of women, in part by passage of the Equal Rights Amendment.

Liberal feminists also endorse reproductive freedom for all women. They respect the family as a social institution but seek changes, including more widely available maternity leave and child care for parents who work.

Given their belief in the rights of individuals, liberal feminists do not think that all women need to work together collectively. Both women and men, through their individual achievement, are capable of improving their lives—as long as society removes legal and cultural barriers.

Socialist Feminism

Socialist feminism evolved from the ideas of Karl Marx and Friedrich Engels, in part as a critical response to Marx's inattention to gender (Philipson & Hansen, 1992). From this point of view, capitalism increases patriarchy by concentrating wealth and power in the hands of a small number of men.

Socialist feminists do not think the reforms sought by liberal feminism go far enough because they do not recognize that the structural foundation of patriarchy is capitalism. The bourgeois family that limits women's opportunities rests on capitalism and must be changed if we are to replace "domestic slavery" with some collective means of carrying out housework and child care. Moreover, replacing the traditional family can come about only through a socialist revolution that creates a state-centered economy to meet the needs of all. Such a basic transformation of society requires that women and men pursue their personal liberation not individually, as liberal feminists propose, but collectively.

Radical Feminism

Radical feminism also finds liberal feminism inadequate. Moreover, radical feminists do not believe that even a socialist revolution would end patriarchy. Instead, to attain equality, society must eliminate gender itself.

One way to achieve this goal is to use new reproductive technology (see Chapter 18, "Family") to separate women's bodies from the process of childbearing. With an end to motherhood, radical feminists reason, society could leave behind the entire family system, liberating women, men, and children from the tyranny of family, gender, and sex itself (Dworkin, 1987). Thus, radical feminism envisions an egalitarian and gender-free society, a revolution more sweeping than that sought by Marx.

OPPOSITION TO FEMINISM

Today, just one-fifth of U.S. adults express attitudes in opposition to feminism, a share that has declined over time (NORC, 2003). Figure 13–5 shows a downward trend in opposition to feminism among college students after 1970; note, however, little change in recent years and a continuing gender gap by which a larger share of men than women express antifeminist attitudes.

Feminism provokes criticism and resistance from both men and women who hold conventional ideas about gender. Some men oppose sexual equality for the same reasons that many white people have historically opposed social equality for people of color: They do not want to give up their privileges. Other men and women, including those who are neither rich nor powerful, distrust a social movement (especially its radical expressions) that attacks the traditional family and rejects centuries-old patterns of male-female relations.

Furthermore, some men find that feminism threatens the basis of their status and self-respect: their masculinity. Men who have been socialized to value strength and dominance feel uneasy about feminist ideas of men as gentle and warm (Doyle, 1983). Similarly, some women whose lives center on their husbands and children may think feminism disparages the social roles that give meaning to their lives. In general, resistance to feminism is strongest among women who have the least education and those who do not work (Marshall, 1985; Ferree & Hess, 1995).

Race and ethnicity play some part in shaping people's attitudes toward feminism. In general, African Americans (especially African American women) express the greatest support of feminist goals, followed by whites, with Hispanic Americans holding somewhat more traditional attitudes when it comes to gender (Kane, 2000).

Resistance to feminism is also found within academic circles. Some sociologists charge that feminism ignores a growing body of evidence that men and women do think and act in somewhat different ways, which may make absolute gender equality impossible. Furthermore, say critics, with its drive to enhance women's presence in the workplace, feminism belittles the crucial and unique contribution women make to the development of children, especially in the first years of life (Baydar & Brooks-Gunn, 1991; Popenoe, 1993b; Gibbs, 2001a).

Finally, there is the question of *how* women should go about improving their social standing. A large majority of U.S. adults believe women should have equal rights, but 70 percent also say that women should advance individually, according to their abilities; only

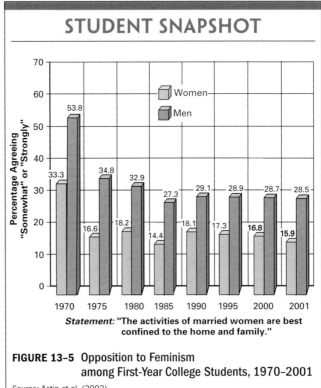

STUDENT SNAPSHOT

Percentage Agreeing "Somewhat" or "Strongly"

1970: Women 33.3, Men 53.8
1975: Women 16.6, Men 34.8
1980: Women 18.2, Men 32.9
1985: Women 14.4, Men 27.3
1990: Women 18.1, Men 29.1
1995: Women 17.3, Men 28.9
2000: Women 16.8, Men 28.7
2001: Women 15.9, Men 28.5

Statement: "The activities of married women are best confined to the home and family."

FIGURE 13-5 Opposition to Feminism among First-Year College Students, 1970–2001

Source: Astin et al. (2002).

10 percent favor women's rights groups or collective action (NORC, 2003:345).

In sum, most opposition to feminism is directed toward its socialist and radical forms, while support for liberal feminism is widespread. Moreover, we are seeing an unmistakable trend toward greater gender equality. In 1977, 65 percent of all adults endorsed the statement "It is much better for everyone involved if the man is the achiever outside the home and the woman takes care of the home and family." By 2002, however, the share supporting this statement had dropped sharply, to 38 percent (NORC, 2003:253).

LOOKING AHEAD: GENDER IN THE TWENTY-FIRST CENTURY

At best, predictions about the future are informed speculation. So, just as economists disagree about what the inflation rate will be a year from now, sociologists can offer only general observations about the likely future of gender and society.

CONTROVERSY & DEBATE

A Closer Look: Are Men *Really* So Privileged?

When Hanover High School, in Massachusetts, held its graduation in June, it was the ninth year in a row that a female student sat onstage as class valedictorian. Almost all of the school's academic prizes—even the science prize—went to young women.

It is no surprise to college students that women outnumber men on the campus. But is this evidence that men are not quite as privileged as we sometimes think? It is men, this chapter argues, who dominate society. Men enjoy higher earnings, control more wealth, exercise more power, get more respect, and do less housework than women. But a closer look reveals some facts that suggest that the male world is, indeed, less privileged in a number of ways.

If men are so privileged in our society, why do they turn to crime more often than women? Moreover, the criminal justice system does not give men any special privileges. Probably most people would not be surprised to learn that police are reluctant to arrest a woman, especially if she has children. This fact helps explain why 78 percent of arrests for serious crime put the handcuffs on a man. Neither do men get a break from the courts: Males make up 92 percent of the U.S. prison population. And even though women kill, all but 3 of the roughly 400 offenders executed during the last several decades have been men.

Culture is not always generous to men either. "Real men" work and play hard; they typically drink and smoke, speed on the highways, and place undo stress on themselves. Given this view of maleness, is it any wonder that men are twice as likely as women to suffer serious assault, three times more likely to fall victim to homicide, and four times more likely to commit suicide? In light of such statistics, how do we explain our national preoccupation with violence against *women*? Perhaps, critics suggest, we are in the grip of a cultural double standard: We accept harm that comes to males while showing sympathy for the far fewer cases in which violence victimizes women. It is this same double standard, the argument continues, that moves women and children out of harm's way and expects men to "go down with the ship" or to die defending their country on the battlefield.

Across the United States, it is boys more than girls who flunk out, drop out, or are kicked out of school. Girls are the majority in high school advanced placement classes, while boys are more likely to be diagnosed with a learning disability. Boys are less likely than girls to go to college, and those

To begin, change so far has been remarkable. A century and a half ago, women occupied a position of striking subordination. Husbands controlled property in marriage, and laws barred women from most jobs, from holding political office, and from voting. Although women remain socially disadvantaged, the movement toward equality has surged ahead. Two-thirds of people entering the work force during the 1990s were women, and in 2000, for the first time, a majority of U.S. families had both husband and wife in the paid labor force. Clearly, today's economy depends a great deal on the earnings of women.

Many factors have contributed to this transformation. Perhaps most important, industrialization has both broadened the range of human activity and shifted the nature of work from physically demanding tasks that favor male strength to jobs that require thought and imagination. This change puts women and men on an even footing. Additionally, since we can control reproduction, women's lives are less constrained by unwanted pregnancies.

Many women and men have also deliberately pursued social equality. For example, complaints about sexual harassment in the workplace are now taken much more seriously. And as more women assume positions of power in the corporate and political worlds, social changes in the twenty-first century may be as great as those we have already witnessed.

Gender is an important part of personal identity and family life, and it is deeply woven into our ways of life. Therefore, efforts to change social patterns involving gender will continue to provoke opposition, as the final box illustrates. On balance, however, while changes may be incremental, we are seeing movement toward a society in which women and men enjoy equal rights and opportunities.

who do earn lower grades while women claim most of the academic awards. The pattern holds for just about all segments of society and for new immigrants as well as for children born in the United States.

Child custody is another sore point for many men. Despite decades of consciousness-raising in pursuit of gender fairness and clear evidence that men earn more than women, courts across the United States routinely award the primary care of children to mothers. To make matters worse, men separated from their children by the courts are often stigmatized as "runaway fathers" or "deadbeat dads," even though government studies show that women are more likely to refuse to pay court-ordered child support (in 35 percent of cases) than men (25 percent).

Finally, male advocates point out that affirmative action laws now cover three-fourths of the population but notably exclude white males. Therefore, in today's affirmative action climate, women have the inside track to college

(where they now outnumber men) as well as in the work force (where businesses know they will be called to account for their hiring practices).

Even nature seems to plot against men, as, on average, women live five years longer. The controversial question is this: When society plays favorites, who is favored?

Continue the debate . . .

1. *Do you think the criminal justice system favors women over men? Or do men simply get what they deserve? Why, in your opinion, are so many more men than women in prison?*

2. *On your campus, do men's organizations (such as fraternities and athletic teams) enjoy special privileges? What about women's organizations?*

3. *On balance, do you agree or disagree that men are advantaged over women? Provide specific evidence to support your answer.*

Sources: Based on Scanlon (1992), Rosenfeld (1998), Kleinfeld (1999), Campo-Flores (2002), and CBS (2002).

SUMMARY

1. Gender refers to the meaning a culture attaches to being female or male. Because society gives men more power and other resources than it gives women, gender is an important dimension of social stratification.

2. Although some degree of patriarchy exists everywhere, gender varies historically and across cultures.

3. Through the socialization process, people incorporate gender into their personalities (gender identity) and their actions (gender roles). The major agents of socialization—family, peer groups, schools, and the mass media—reinforce cultural definitions of what is feminine and masculine.

4. Gender stratification shapes the workplace. Although a majority of women are now in the paid labor force,

most hold clerical or service jobs. Unpaid housework remains a task performed mostly by women, whether or not they hold jobs outside the home.

5. In comparisons of all female and male workers, women earn 76 percent as much as men. This disparity stems from differences in jobs and family responsibilities, as well as from discrimination.

6. Women now earn a slight majority of all bachelor's and master's degrees. Men still receive a slight majority of all doctorates and professional degrees.

7. The number of women in politics has increased sharply in recent decades. Still, the vast majority of elected officials, especially at the national level, are men and women make up only 15 percent of U.S. military personnel.

8. Intersection theory investigates the intersection of race, class, and gender, which often causes multiple disadvantages.

9. Because women have a distinctive social identity and are disadvantaged, they are a minority, although most white women do not think of themselves that way. Minority women encounter greater social disadvantages than white women and earn much less than white men.

10. Violence against women is a widespread problem in the United States. Our society is also grappling with the issue of sexual harassment and debating the issue of pornography.

11. Structural-functional analysis suggests that, in preindustrial societies, distinctive roles for males and females reflect biological differences between the sexes. In industrial societies, marked gender inequality becomes dysfunctional and gradually decreases. Talcott Parsons claimed that complementary gender roles promote the social integration of families and society as a whole.

12. Social-conflict analysis views gender as a dimension of social inequality and conflict. Friedrich Engels tied gender stratification to the development of private property.

13. Feminism endorses the social equality of the sexes and opposes patriarchy and sexism. Feminism also seeks to eliminate violence against women and to give women control over their reproduction.

14. There are three variants of feminist thinking: Liberal feminism seeks equal opportunity for both sexes within the existing society; socialist feminism advocates abolishing private property as the means to social equality; radical feminism seeks to create a gender-free society.

15. Although two-thirds of adults in the United States support the Equal Rights Amendment, this legislation, first proposed in Congress in 1923, has yet to become part of the U.S. Constitution.

KEY CONCEPTS

gender (p. 325) the personal traits and social positions that members of a society attach to being female or male

gender stratification (p. 325) the unequal distribution of wealth, power, and privilege between men and women

patriarchy (p. 328) a form of social organization in which males dominate females

matriarchy (p. 328) a form of social organization in which females dominate males

sexism (p. 328) the belief that one sex is innately superior to the other

gender roles (sex roles) (p. 330) attitudes and activities that a society links to each sex

minority (p. 339) any category of people distinguished by physical or cultural difference that a society sets apart and subordinates

intersection theory (p. 339) the investigation of the interplay of race, class, and gender, often resulting in multiple dimensions of disadvantage

sexual harassment (p. 342) comments, gestures, or physical contact of a sexual nature that are deliberate, repeated, and unwelcome

feminism (p. 344) the advocacy of social equality for men and women, in opposition to patriarchy and sexism

CRITICAL-THINKING QUESTIONS

1. In what ways are sex and gender related? In what respects are they distinct?

2. What techniques do the mass media employ in order to "sell" conventional ideas about gender to women and men?

3. Why is gender a dimension of social stratification? How does gender intersect other dimensions of inequality based on class, race, and ethnicity?

4. Consider the following two statements: "He fathered the child" and "She mothered the child." Describe the differences in meaning. How do you account for these differences?

5. A number of European nations, including Great Britain, Norway, Denmark, and Finland, require that at least 25 percent of candidates for national offices be women. Because women members are just 14 percent of the U.S. Congress, should the United States do likewise?

APPLICATIONS AND EXERCISES

1. Take a walk through a business area of your local community. Which businesses are frequented almost entirely by women? By men? By both men and women? Try to explain the patterns you find.

2. Watch several hours of children's television programming on a Saturday morning. Notice the advertising, which mostly sells toys and breakfast cereal. Keep track of what share of toys are "gendered," that is, aimed at one sex or the other. What traits do you associate with toys intended for boys and those intended for girls?

3. Do some research on the history of women's issues in your state. When was the first woman sent to Congress? What laws once existed that restricted the work women could do? Do any such laws exist today? Did your state support the passage of the Equal Rights Amendment or not? What share of political officials today is women?

4. Packaged in the back of this new textbook is an interactive CD-ROM that offers a variety of video and interactive review materials intended to help you better understand the material covered in this chapter. For this chapter, the CD-ROM contains a relevant clip from *ABC News*, an author's tip video, interactive map animations, an interactive time line, and flashcards with audio pronunciations of the more difficult words.

 SITES TO SEE

http://www.prenhall.com/macionis

Visit the interactive Companion Website™ that accompanies this text. Begin by clicking on the cover of your book. You will find a chapter-by-chapter study guide, practice tests, suggested Web links, and links to other relevant material.

http://www.now.org

Visit the Web site for the National Organization for Women to discover the goals and strategies of this organization.

http://www.iwpr.org

Another informative site is run by the Institute for Women's Policy Research. Identify the issues this organization finds most important. Would you characterize this site as feminist? Why or why not?

http://www.wwwomen.com/

This site provides a search engine for locating all sorts of information concerning women.

http://www.educationindex.com/women/

This site provides numerous and widely varied links to sites concerned with women's issues.

http://www.feminist.org

The Feminist Majority Foundation Online offers information about feminist issues and the feminist movement.

http://www.ncjrs.org/pdffiles1/nij/182369.pdf

A report from the U.S. Department of Justice about sexual violence on the college campus can be found at this Web site.

 INVESTIGATE WITH RESEARCH NAVIGATOR™

Follow the instructions on page 24 of this text to access the features of **Research Navigator**™. Once at the Web site, enter your Login Name and Password. Then, to use the **Content Select**™ database, enter keywords such as "gender," "feminism," and "sexual harassment," and the search engine will supply relevant and recent scholarly and popular press publications. Use the *New York Times* **Search-by-Subject Archive** to find recent news articles related to sociology and the **Link Library** feature to find relevant Web links organized by the key terms associated with this chapter.

RACE AND ETHNICITY

RON WADDAMS

Ordered

1998. Acrylic on board. 92 × 92 cm. Private collection, Bridgeman Art Library.

I F YOU TRIED TO IMAGINE A "typical American neighborhood," something very much like Sequoia Way might come to mind, a very average-looking street on the south side of Sacramento, California. The winding road is lined with one-story frame houses, and most of the people living in them consider themselves middle class.

But how do you envision the people who live in that "typical American neighborhood"? The real-life residents of Sequoia Way include Tom and Debra Burruss, who moved in three years ago; Tom is African American, Debra is white. Next door live Ken Wong and Binh Lam, a Vietnamese couple. Across the street live the Cardonas, who are Mexican American. Next to them are the Farrys: He is white and she is Japanese. The local elementary school enrolls 347 students, 189 of whom speak a language other than English at home. You get the idea. This "all-American neighborhood" comes in more flavors than you find at Baskin-Robbins (adapted from Stodghill & Bower, 2002).

Not surprisingly, perhaps, Sacramento is sometimes called the most integrated city in the United States. There, non-Hispanic whites make up only 41 percent of the population. This city captures a trend for the United States as a whole, because everywhere, racial and ethnic diversity is increasing rapidly.

This chapter examines the meaning of race and ethnicity, explains how these social constructs have shaped our history, and suggests why they will play an ever greater part in social life as we move through the twenty-first century.

THE SOCIAL MEANING OF RACE AND ETHNICITY

People frequently confuse "race" and "ethnicity." For this reason, we begin by defining these terms.

RACE

A **race** is *a socially constructed category composed of people who share biologically transmitted traits that members of a society consider important.* People may classify each other racially based on physical characteristics such as skin color, facial features, hair texture, and body shape.

Physical diversity appeared among our human ancestors as the result of their living in different geographic regions of the world. In regions of intense heat, for example, humans developed darker skin (from the natural pigment melanin) as protection from the sun; in regions with moderate climates, people have lighter skin. Such differences are, literally, only skin deep because *every* human being on Earth is a member of a single biological species.

Migration has mixed genetic traits the world over. Especially pronounced is the physical mix found in the Middle East (that is, western Asia), historically a crossroads of human migration. Greater physical uniformity characterizes more isolated people, such as the island-dwelling Japanese. But every population has some genetic mixture, and increasing contact among

The range of biological variation in human beings is far greater than any system of racial classification allows. This fact is made obvious by trying to place all of the people pictured here into simple racial categories.

the world's people ensures even more racial blending in the future.

Although we think of race in terms of biological elements, race is a socially constructed concept. At one level, research shows that white people rate black subjects as darker in skin tone than black people rate the same subjects (Hill, 2002). Furthermore, a number of people (especially biracial and multiracial people) are defined by others—and define themselves—differently from setting to setting (Harris & Sim, 2002). More broadly, entire societies define physical traits differently. Typically, people in the United States "see" fewer racial categories (commonly, black, white, and Asian) than people in Brazil, who distinguish between "branca" (white), "parda" (brown), "morena" (brunette), "mulata" (mulatto), "preta" (black), and "amarela" (yellow) (Inciardi, Surratt, & Telles, 2000). In some countries (the United States, for one), people consider these differences more important; in others (such as Brazil), people consider them less important.

Moreover, in any society, definitions and meanings concerning race change over time. For example, in 1900, many white people in the United States

viewed those of Irish and Italian ancestry as "racially different," a practice that was far less common by 1950 (Loveman, 1999). Today, the Census Bureau allows people to describe themselves using more than one racial category (a total of sixty-three racial options), thus recognizing a wide range of multiracial people (Porter, 2001).

Racial Types

Scientists invented the concept of race more than a century ago as they tried to organize the world's physical diversity, constructing three racial types. They called people with relatively light skin and fine hair *Caucasoid*; they called people with darker skin and coarse hair *Negroid*; and they labeled people with yellow or brown skin and distinctive folds on the eyelids *Mongoloid*.

Sociologists consider such terms misleading, at best, and harmful, at worst. For one thing, nowhere do we find biologically "pure" people. The skin color of people we might call "Caucasoid" (or "Indo-European," "Caucasian," or, more commonly, "white") ranges from very light (typical in Scandinavia) to very dark (in southern India). The same variation exists among so-called "Negroids" (Africans or, more commonly, "black" people) and "Mongoloids" (that is, "Asians"). In fact, many "white" people (say, in southern India) actually have darker skin than many "black" people (the Negroid Aborigines of Australia). Overall, the three racial categories differ in only 6 percent of their genes, less than the genetic variation *within* each category (Boza, 2002; Harris & Sim, 2002).

Why, then, do people make so much of race? The underlying reason is that racial categories rank people in a hierarchy, allowing some people to feel that they are inherently "better" than others (Zuberi, 2001). Because racial ranking shapes access to wealth and prestige, societies may construct racial categories in extreme ways. Throughout much of the twentieth century, for example, many southern U.S. states labeled as "colored" anyone with as little as one thirty-second African ancestry (that is, one African American great-great-great-grandparent). Today, the law allows parents to declare the race of a child as they wish. Even so, most members of U.S. society are still very sensitive to people's racial background.

A Trend toward Mixture

Over many generations and throughout the Americas, the genetic traits from around the world have intermingled. Many "black" people, therefore, have a significant Caucasoid ancestry, just as "white" people have some Negroid genes. In short, whatever people may think, race is no black-and-white issue.

As the chapter-opening description of a California neighborhood suggests, people are now more willing to define themselves as multiracial. When completing their 2000 census forms, almost 7 million people described themselves by checking two or more racial categories. Further, the official number of interracial births tripled over the last twenty years to 172,000 annually, about 5 percent of all births.

ETHNICITY

Ethnicity is *a shared cultural heritage.* People define themselves—or others—as members of an *ethnic category* based on having common ancestors, language, or religion that confers a distinctive social identity. The United States is a multiethnic society that favors the English language; even so, more than 47 million people (18 percent) speak Spanish, Italian, German, French, Chinese dialects, or some other tongue in

Fifty years ago, in some states, marrying someone of another race violated the law. Since then, the number of multiracial couples has risen steadily, and the number of recorded interracial births has tripled since the mid-1980s. The result is that more and more people consider themselves to be multiracial. What effect will this trend have on the use of traditional racial categories?

their homes. In California, more than one-third of the population speaks a language other than English at home. Similarly, the United States is a predominantly Protestant nation, but most people of Spanish, Italian, and Polish descent are Roman Catholic, while many of Greek, Ukrainian, and Russian descent belong to the Eastern Orthodox church. More than 6 million Jewish Americans with ancestral ties to various nations share a religious history. Similarly, more than 7 million men and women are Muslim; there are more Muslims than Episcopalians in the United States (Blank, 1998).

Like race, ethnicity is socially constructed. On an individual level, people play up or play down cultural traits so that they fit in or stand apart from the surrounding society. More broadly, societies define some ethnic differences as important and other as not. A century ago, for example, Catholics were widely considered "different" in the predominantly Protestant United States. This is far less the case today. Similarly, U.S. society defines people of Spanish descent as "Latin," but not people of Italian descent, even though Italy probably has a more "Latin" culture than Spain. Instead, Italians generally are defined as "Europeans" and thus less different (Camara, 2000; Brodkin, 2001).

TABLE 14-1 Racial and Ethnic Categories in the United States, 2000		
Racial or Ethnic Classification*	**Approximate U.S. Population**	**Percentage of Total Population**
Hispanic descent	**35,305,818**	**12.5%**
Mexican	20,640,711	7.3
Puerto Rican	3,406,178	1.2
Cuban	1,241,685	0.4
Other Hispanic	10,017,244	3.6
African descent	**34,658,190**	**12.3**
Nigerian	165,481	0.1
Ethiopian	86,918	<
Cape Verdean	77,103	<
Ghanaian	49,944	<
South African	45,569	<
Native American descent	**2,475,956**	**0.9**
American Indian	1,815,653	0.6
Eskimo	45,919	<
Other Native American	614,384	0.2
Asian or Pacific Island descent	**10,641,833**	**3.8**
Chinese	2,432,585	0.9
Filipino	1,850,314	0.7
Asian Indian	1,678,765	0.6
Vietnamese	1,122,528	0.4
Korean	1,076,872	0.4
Japanese	796,700	0.3
Cambodian	171,937	<
Hmong	169,428	<
Laotian	168,707	<
Other Asian or Pacific Islander	1,173,997	0.4
West Indian descent	**1,869,504**	**0.7**
Arab descent	**1,202,871**	**0.4**
Non-Hispanic European descent	**194,552,774**	**70.9**
German	42,885,162	15.2
Irish	30,528,492	10.8
English	24,515,138	8.7
Italian	15,723,555	5.6
Polish	8,977,444	3.2
French	8,309,908	3.0
Scottish	4,890,581	1.7
Dutch	4,542,494	1.6
Norwegian	4,477,725	1.6
Two or more races	**6,826,228**	**2.4**

*People of Hispanic descent may be of any race. Many people also identify with more than one ethnic category. Therefore, figures total more than 100 percent.

< Indicates less than 1/10 of 1 percent.

Sources: U.S. Census Bureau (2001, 2002, 2003).

Race and ethnicity, then, are both socially defined, one involving biological traits, the other cultural traits. Of course, the two may go hand in hand. Japanese Americans, for example, have distinctive physical traits and—for those who maintain a traditional way of life—a distinctive culture as well. Table 14–1 presents the broad sweep of racial and ethnic diversity in the United States, as recorded by the 2000 census.

People can modify their ethnicity by discarding cultural traditions or, like many people of Native American descent in recent years, reviving their heritage (Nagel, 1994; Spencer, 1994). For most people, ethnicity is even more complex than race, because most people identify with several ethnic backgrounds. Golf star Tiger Woods, for example, describes himself as one-eighth American Indian, one-fourth Thai, and one-fourth Chinese, as well as one-eighth white and one-fourth black (Whyte, 1997).

MINORITIES

March 3, Dallas, Texas. Sitting in the lobby of just about any hotel in a major U.S. city presents a lesson in contrasts: The majority of the guests checking in and out are white; the majority of hotel employees who carry luggage, serve the food, and clean the rooms are people of color.

As Chapter 13 ("Gender Stratification") described, a **minority** is *any category of people distinguished by physical or cultural difference that a society sets apart and subordinates.* Both race and ethnicity are the basis for minority standing. As shown in Table 14–1, non-Hispanic white people (70 percent of the total) are still a majority in the United States. But the share of minorities is increasing. Today, minorities are a majority in three states and half the nation's 100 largest cities (U.S. Census Bureau, 2002). Within a century, minorities are likely to form a majority of the entire U.S. population. National Map 14–1 shows where a minority-majority already exists.

Minorities have two major characteristics. First, they share a *distinctive identity*, which may be based on physical or cultural traits. Second, minorities experience *subordination*. As the remainder of this chapter shows, U.S. minorities typically have lower income, lower occupational prestige, and limited schooling. These facts mean that class, race, and ethnicity, as well as gender, are overlapping and reinforcing dimensions of social stratification. The box on page 358 profiles the struggles of recent Latin American immigrants.

Of course, not all members of any minority category are disadvantaged. For example, some Latinos are quite wealthy, certain Chinese Americans are celebrated business leaders, and African Americans are included

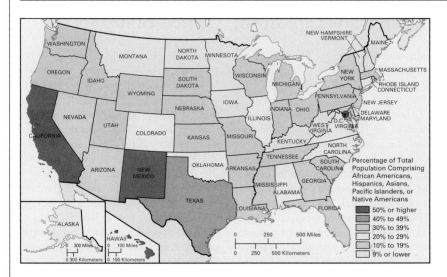

NATIONAL MAP 14–1
Where the Minority-Majority Already Exists

By 2000, minorities had become a majority in three states—Hawaii, California, and New Mexico—and the District of Columbia. With a 45 percent minority population, Texas is approaching a minority-majority. At the other extreme, Vermont and Maine have the lowest share of racial and ethnic minorities (about 2 percent). Why are states with high minority populations in the South and Southwest?

Source: "America 2000: A Map of the Mix," *Newsweek*, September 18, 2000, p. 48. Copyright © 2000 Newsweek, Inc. All rights reserved. Reprinted by permission.

among our nation's leading scholars. But even job success rarely allows individuals to escape their minority standing (Benjamin, 1991). That is, race or ethnicity often serves as a *master status* (described in Chapter 6, "Social Interaction in Everyday Life") that overshadows personal accomplishments.

Finally, minorities are usually—but not always—a small proportion of a society's population. For example, black South Africans are disadvantaged even though they are a numerical majority in their country. In the United States, women represent slightly more than half the population but are still struggling to gain the opportunities and privileges enjoyed by men.

PREJUDICE

November 19, Jerusalem, Israel. We are driving along the outskirts of this historic city—a holy place to Jews, Christians, and Muslims—when Razi, our taxi driver, spots a small group of fellasha—Ethiopian Jews—on a street corner. "Those people," he points to the group, "may be Jews like me, but they are different. They don't drive cars. They don't want to improve themselves. Even

when our country offers them schooling, they don't take it." He shakes his head and pronounces the Ethiopians "socially incorrigible."

Prejudice is *a rigid and unfair generalization about an entire category of people.* Prejudice is unfair insofar as people rigidly describe all people in some category as the same based on little or no direct evidence. Prejudice may target people of a particular social class, sex, sexual orientation, age, political affiliation, physical disability, race, or ethnicity.

Prejudices are *prejudgments*, and they may be positive or negative. Our positive prejudices tend to exaggerate the virtues of people like ourselves, while our negative prejudices condemn those who differ from us. Negative prejudice runs along a continuum from mild avoidance to outright hostility. Because attitudes are rooted in culture, everyone has at least some measure of prejudice.

Take a test for prejudice at http://www.tolerance.org/hidden_bias/index.html

STEREOTYPES

Prejudice often takes the form of a **stereotype** (*stereo* is derived from Greek meaning "hard" or "solid"), *an*

DIVERSITY: RACE, CLASS, AND GENDER

Hard Work: The Immigrant Life in the United States

Early in the morning, it is already hot in Houston as a line of pickup trucks snakes slowly into a dusty yard, where 200 laborers have been gathering since dawn, hoping for a day's work. The driver of the first truck opens his window and tells the foreman that he is looking for a crew to spread boiling tar on a roof. Abdonel Cespedes, the foreman, turns to the crowd, and after a few minutes, three workers step forward and climb into the back of the truck. The next driver is looking for two experienced house painters. The scene is repeated over and over, as men and a few women leave to dig ditches, spread cement, hang drywall, open clogged septic tanks, or crawl under houses to poison rats.

As each driver pulls into the yard, the foreman asks, "How much?" Most offer five dollars an hour. Cespedes automatically responds, "Six-fifty; the going rate is $6.50 for an hour's hard work." Sometimes he convinces them to pay that much, but usually not. The workers, who come from Mexico, El Salvador, and Guatemala, know that many of them will end up with no work at

all this day. Most accept five dollars an hour because they know, when the long day is over, they will have earned fifty dollars.

Labor markets like this one are common in large cities, especially across the southwestern United States. The surge in immigration in recent years has brought millions of people in search of work, and most have little schooling and speak little English.

Manuel Barrera has taken a day's work moving the contents of a store that has closed to a storage site. He arrives at the boarded-up store and gazes at the mountains of heavy furniture that he must carry out to a moving van,

drive across town, and then carry again. He sighs, knowing that it is even hotter in the building than it is outside. He will have no break for lunch. No one says anything about toilets. Barrera shakes his head: "I will do this kind of work because it puts food on the table. But I did not foresee it would turn out like this."

The hard truth is that immigrants to the United States do the jobs that no one else wants. At the bottom level of the national economy, immigrants work in restaurants and hotels, on construction crews, and in private homes cooking, cleaning, and caring for children. Across the United States, about half of all housekeepers, household cooks, tailors, and restaurant waiters are men or women born abroad. Few immigrants make much more than minimum wage ($5.15 per hour), and rarely do immigrant workers receive health or pension benefits. Many well-off families take the labor of immigrants as much for granted as their sport utility vehicles and cell phones.

Source: Based on Booth (1998).

exaggerated description applied to every person in some category. Many white people hold stereotypical views of minorities. Stereotyping is especially harmful to minorities in the workplace. If company officials see workers through the lens of a stereotype, they will make assumptions about their abilities, steering minorities toward certain jobs and limiting their access to better opportunities (Kaufman, 2002).

But minorities, too, apply stereotypes to whites and also to other minorities (Smith, 1996; Cummings & Lambert, 1997). Surveys show, for example, that

more African Americans than whites express the belief that Asians engage in unfair business practices; similarly, more Asians than whites criticize Hispanics for having too many children (Perlmutter, 2002).

MEASURING PREJUDICE: THE SOCIAL DISTANCE SCALE

One measure of prejudice is *social distance*, that is, how closely people are willing to interact with members of

STUDENT SNAPSHOT

(a) I would accept a[n] [member of this category] as a . . .

1	2	3	4	5	6	7
family member by marriage	close friend	neighbor	co-worker	speaking acquaintance	visitor to my country	I would bar from my country

(b) Mean Scores for All Categories

		Spread of Averages
1925	2.14	2.85
1946	2.14	2.57
1956	2.08	1.75
1966	1.92	1.55
1977	1.93	1.38
2001	1.44	0.87

(c) Mean Social Distance Score by Category in 2001

Top One-Third		Middle One-Third		Bottom One-Third	
Americans	1.07	Jews	1.38	Dominicans	1.51
Italians	1.15	American Indians	1.40	Japanese	1.52
Canadians	1.20	Africans	1.43	Cubans	1.53
British	1.23	Polish	1.44	Koreans	1.54
Irish	1.24	Other Hispanics	1.45	Mexicans	1.55
French	1.28	Filipinos	1.46	Indians (India)	1.60
Greeks	1.32	Chinese	1.47	Haitians	1.63
Germans	1.33	Puerto Ricans	1.48	Vietnamese	1.69
African Americans	1.34	Jamaicans	1.49	Muslims	1.88
Dutch	1.35	Russians	1.50	Arabs	1.94

FIGURE 14–1 Bogardus Social Distance Research

Source: Parrillo (2003a).

some category. Almost eighty years ago, Emory Bogardus (1925) developed the seven-point *social distance scale* shown in Figure 14–1. Bogardus asked students at U.S. colleges and universities to look at this scale and indicate how closely they were willing to interact with people in thirty racial and ethnic categories. At one extreme, (point 7) students could express the greatest social distance (most negative prejudice) by declaring that a particular category of people should be barred from the country entirely. At the other extreme (point 1), students could express the least social distance (most social acceptance) by saying they would accept members of a particular category into their family through marriage.

Bogardus's (1925, 1967; Owen, Elsner, & McFaul, 1977) major finding was that people felt much more social distance from some categories than from others. In general, students in his survey expressed the most social distance from Hispanics, African Americans, Asians, and Turks, saying that they would be willing to tolerate such people as co-workers but not as neighbors, friends, or family members. They expressed the least social distance from those from northern and western Europe—English and Scottish people—and also Canadians, whom they were willing to have marry into their families.

What patterns of social distance do we find among college students today? A recent study using the same social distance scale reported three major findings (Parrillo, 2003a)[1]:

1. A trend toward greater social acceptance has continued. Today's students express less social distance from all minorities than students did decades ago.

---

[1]Parrillo dropped seven of the categories used by Bogardus (Armenians, Czechs, Finns, Norwegians, Scots, Swedes, and Turks), claiming they were no longer visible minorities. He added nine new categories (Africans, Arabs, Cubans, Dominicans, Haitians, Jamaicans, Muslims, Puerto Ricans, and Vietnamese), claiming these are visible minorities today. This change probably encouraged higher social distance scores, making the downward trend all the more significant.

Part (b) of Figure 14–1 shows that the average (mean) score on the social distance scale declined from 2.14 in 1925 to 1.93 in 1977 to 1.44 in 2001. Respondents (81 percent of whom were white) showed notably greater acceptance of African Americans, a category that moved up from near the bottom in 1925 to the top one-third in 2001.

2. **People see less difference between various minorities.** The earliest studies found the range (spread of averages) of social distance for different minorities equal to almost three points on the scale. As part (b) of the figure shows, the most recent research produced a range of less than one point.

3. **The September 11, 2001, terrorist attacks may have contributed to low social acceptance of Arabs and Muslims.** The recent study was conducted several weeks after September 11, 2001. Perhaps the fact that the nineteen men who attacked the World Trade Center and the Pentagon were Arabs and Muslims is part of the reason that students ranked these categories last on the social distance scale. It should be noted, however, that not a single student declared that Arabs or Muslims should be barred from the country. On the contrary, the 2001 scores (1.94 for Arabs and 1.88 for Muslims) show higher social acceptance than students in 1977 expressed toward eighteen of the thirty categories of people.

RACISM

A powerful and destructive form of prejudice, **racism** is *the belief that one racial category is innately superior or inferior to another.* Racism has pervaded world history. The ancient Greeks, the peoples of India, and the Chinese—despite their many notable achievements—were all quick to consider people unlike themselves inferior.

Racism has also been widespread in the United States, where notions about racial inferiority supported slavery. Today, overt racism in this country has declined because our more egalitarian culture urges us to evaluate people, in Dr. Martin Luther King, Jr.'s words, "not by the color of their skin but the content of their character."

 Racism can give rise to hate crimes. For more information, go to http://www.civilrights.org/issues/hate/

Even so, racism remains a serious problem everywhere, and people still contend that some racial and ethnic categories are "better" than others. As the box explains, however, racial differences in mental abilities result from environment rather than biology.

THEORIES OF PREJUDICE

Where does prejudice come from? Social scientists have offered many answers to this question, focusing their attention on frustration, personality, culture, and social conflict.

Scapegoat Theory

Scapegoat theory holds that prejudice springs from frustration among people who are themselves disadvantaged (Dollard et al., 1939). Take the case of a white woman frustrated by her low-paying job in a textile factory. Directing hostility at the powerful factory owners carries obvious risk; therefore, she may blame her low pay on the presence of minority co-workers. Her prejudice may not improve her situation, but it is a relatively safe way to vent anger, and it may give her the comforting feeling that at least she is superior to someone.

A **scapegoat,** then, is *a person or category of people, typically with little power, whom people unfairly blame for their own troubles.* Because they are usually "safe targets," minorities are often used as scapegoats.

Authoritarian Personality Theory

T. W. Adorno and others (1950) considered extreme prejudice a personality trait of some individuals. These *authoritarian personalities* rigidly conform to conventional cultural values and see moral issues as clear-cut matters of right and wrong. People with authoritarian personalities also look upon society as naturally competitive and hierarchical, with "better" people (like themselves) inevitably dominating those who are weaker (including all minorities).

Adorno also found that people tolerant toward one minority are likely to be accepting of all. They tend to be more flexible in their moral judgments and treat all people as equals.

Adorno thought that people with little schooling, especially those raised by cold and demanding parents, develop authoritarian personalities. Filled with anger and anxiety as children, they grow into hostile, aggressive adults, seeking scapegoats whom they consider inferior.

Culture Theory

A third theory contends that although extreme prejudice may be found in some people, some prejudice is found in everyone. Why? Because prejudice is embedded in culture, as the Bogardus social distance

CRITICAL THINKING

Does Race Affect Intelligence?

Are Asian Americans smarter than white people? Are whites more intelligent than African Americans? Throughout the history of the United States, many people have painted one category of people as intellectually more gifted than another. Moreover, people have used such thinking to justify privileges for the allegedly superior category and to bar supposedly inferior people from entering this country.

Scientists tell us that the distribution of human intelligence forms a "bell curve," as shown in the figure. They define average intelligence as an *intelligence quotient* (IQ) score of 100 (technically, an IQ score is mental age, as measured by a test, divided by age in years, the result being multiplied by 100; thus, an eight-year-old who performs like a ten-year-old has an IQ of $10/8 = 1.25 \times 100 = 125$).

In a controversial study of intelligence and social inequality, Richard Herrnstein and Charles Murray (1994) reported that much research links race and intelligence. Specifically, they explained, the average IQ of people with European ancestry is 100, that of people with East Asian ancestry is 103, and that of people of African descent is 90.

Such assertions fly in the face of our democratic and egalitarian sentiments, which say no racial type is inherently "better" than another. Critics charge that more well-off people do better on IQ tests simply because they have more schooling and other cultural advantages.

Most social scientists acknowledge that IQ tests do measure something important that we think of as "intelligence," and they agree that *individuals* vary in intellectual aptitude. But they reject the idea that any *category* of people, on average, is "smarter" than any other. So how do we explain the overall differences in IQ scores by race?

Thomas Sowell (1994, 1995) explains that most of this difference results not from biology but from environment. Tracing IQ scores for various racial and ethnic categories through the early twentieth century, Sowell found that immigrants from European nations such as Poland, Lithuania, Italy, and Greece, as well as from Asian countries including China and Japan, scored 10 to 15 points below the U.S. average. But by the end of the twentieth century, people in these same categories had IQ scores that were average or above average. Among Italian Americans, for example, average IQ jumped almost 10 points; among Polish and Chinese Americans, the increase was almost 20 points.

Because genetic changes occur over thousands of years, biology cannot explain this rapid rise in IQ scores. The only plausible explanation is changing cultural patterns. The children of early immigrants improved their intellectual performance as their standard of living rose and their opportunity for schooling increased.

Sowell found that a similar pattern applies to African Americans. Historically, the average IQ score of African Americans living in the North has been about 10 points higher than the average score of those living in the South. Furthermore, among the descendants of African Americans who migrated from the South to the North after 1940, IQ scores went up just as they did with descendants of earlier immigrants. Thus, if environmental factors are the same for various categories of people, racial IQ differences largely disappear.

What changes in IQ test scores tell us, concludes Sowell, is that *cultural patterns matter*. Asians score higher on tests not because they are smarter but because they have been raised to value learning and pursue excellence. For their part, African Americans are no less intelligent than anyone else, but they carry a legacy of disadvantage that can undermine self-confidence and discourage achievement.

What do you think?

1. *If IQ scores reflect people's environment, are they valid measures of intelligence? Might they be harmful?*

2. *According to Thomas Sowell, why do some racial and ethnic categories show dramatic, short-term gains in average IQ scores?*

3. *Do you think parents and schools influence a child's IQ score? If so, how?*

Sources: Herrnstein & Murray (1994) and Sowell (1994, 1995).

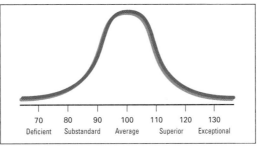

70	80	90	100	110	120	130
Deficient	Substandard		Average		Superior	Exceptional

IQ: The Distribution of Intelligence

Racial and ethnic stereotypes are deeply embedded in our culture and language. Many people speak of someone "gypping" another without realizing that this word insults European Gypsies, a category of people long pushed to the margins of European societies. What about terms such as "Dutch treat," "French kiss," or "Indian giver"?

studies, noted earlier, illustrate. Bogardus found that students across the country had mostly the same attitudes toward specific categories of the population, feeling closer to some and further from others. Moreover, social distance research shows that, by and large, attitudes stay the same over decades. Finally, we know prejudice is cultural because minorities express the same attitudes as white people toward categories other than their own. Such patterns suggest that individuals hold prejudices because they live in a "culture of prejudice," which teaches us to view certain categories of people as "better" or "worse" than others.

Conflict Theory

A fourth explanation proposes that prejudice helps powerful people oppress others. To the extent that people look down on illegal Latino immigrants in the Southwest, for example, employers can pay the immigrants low wages for hard work. Similarly, elites benefit from prejudice that divides workers along racial and ethnic lines, preventing them from working together to advance their common interests (Geschwender, 1978; Olzak, 1989).

Another conflict-based argument, advanced by Shelby Steele (1990), is that minorities themselves cultivate a climate of *race consciousness* in order to win greater power and privileges. Minorities promote race consciousness, Steele explains, by claiming they are victims who are entitled to special consideration. While this strategy may yield short-term gains, Steele points out that such thinking can spark a backlash from white people or others who oppose "special treatment" for anyone on the basis of race or ethnicity.

DISCRIMINATION

Closely related to prejudice is **discrimination**, *treating various categories of people unequally*. Whereas *prejudice* refers to attitudes, discrimination is a matter of action. Like prejudice, discrimination can be either positive (providing special advantages) or negative (subjecting people to obstacles). Discrimination also ranges from subtle to blatant.

INSTITUTIONAL PREJUDICE AND DISCRIMINATION

We typically think of prejudice and discrimination as the hateful ideas or actions of specific people. But decades ago, Stokely Carmichael and Charles Hamilton (1967) pointed out that far greater harm results from **institutional prejudice and discrimination**, *bias inherent in the operation of society's institutions*, including schools, the police, and the workplace. For example, research shows that banks provide less favorable terms for home mortgages to minorities than to whites, even when the applicants have the same income and live in similar neighborhoods (Gotham, 1998).

According to Carmichael and Hamilton, the white majority is slow to recognize institutional prejudice and discrimination because it often involves respected public officials and long-established practices. A case in point is the U.S. Supreme Court's *Brown v. Board of Education of Topeka*, the 1954 decision that ended legally segregated schools. The principle of "separate but equal" had been the law of the land, supporting racial inequality by allowing school segregation. Today, fifty years later, the law has changed, but most U.S. students still attend schools that are overwhelmingly one race or the other. One key reason is that much of the U.S. population still lives in racially segregated urban areas, with most African Americans living in central cities and most white people (and Asian Americans) living beyond the city limits in suburbs.

PREJUDICE AND DISCRIMINATION: THE VICIOUS CIRCLE

Prejudice and discrimination reinforce each other. The Thomas theorem, discussed in Chapter 6 ("Social Interaction in Everyday Life"), offers a simple explanation of this fact: *Situations defined as real become real in their consequences* (Thomas, 1966:301; orig. 1931).

As W. I. Thomas recognized, stereotypes become real to those who believe them, sometimes even to those who are victimized by them. Prejudice on the part of white people toward people of color, for example, does not produce *innate* inferiority, but it can produce *social* inferiority, pushing minorities into low-paying jobs, inferior schools, and racially segregated housing. Then, to the extent that white people see social disadvantage as evidence that minorities do not measure up, there emerges a new round of prejudice and discrimination, giving rise to a vicious circle, as shown in Figure 14–2.

MAJORITY AND MINORITY: PATTERNS OF INTERACTION

Social scientists describe patterns of interaction among racial and ethnic categories in a society in terms of four models: pluralism, assimilation, segregation, and genocide.

PLURALISM

Pluralism is *a state in which people of all races and ethnicities are distinct but have social parity.* In other words, people may differ in appearance or social heritage but share resources roughly equally.

The United States is pluralistic to the extent that our society promises equal standing under the law. Moreover, large cities contain countless "ethnic villages," where people proudly display the traditions of their immigrant ancestors. These include New York's Spanish Harlem, Little Italy, and Chinatown; Philadelphia's Italian South Philly; Chicago's Little Saigon; and Latino East Los Angeles. New York City alone has 189 different ethnic newspapers (Paul, 2001; Logan, Alba, & Zhang, 2002).

But the United States is not really pluralistic for three reasons. First, while most people value their cultural heritage, few want to live just with others exactly like themselves (NORC, 2003). Second, our tolerance of social diversity goes only so far. One reaction to the rising number of U.S. minorities is a social movement

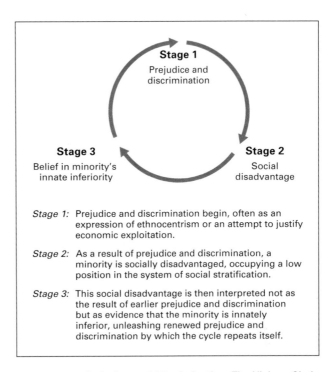

Stage 1
Prejudice and discrimination

Stage 2
Social disadvantage

Stage 3
Belief in minority's innate inferiority

Stage 1: Prejudice and discrimination begin, often as an expression of ethnocentrism or an attempt to justify economic exploitation.

Stage 2: As a result of prejudice and discrimination, a minority is socially disadvantaged, occupying a low position in the system of social stratification.

Stage 3: This social disadvantage is then interpreted not as the result of earlier prejudice and discrimination but as evidence that the minority is innately inferior, unleashing renewed prejudice and discrimination by which the cycle repeats itself.

FIGURE 14–2 Prejudice and Discrimination: The Vicious Circle

Prejudice and discrimination can form a vicious circle, perpetuating themselves.

to make English this nation's official language. Third, as we shall see later in this chapter, it is simply a fact that people of various colors and cultures do not have equal social standing.

ASSIMILATION

Many people think of the United States as a "melting pot" where different nationalities blend together. But rather than everyone's "melting" into some new cultural pattern, most minorities adopt the dominant culture established by earlier settlers with higher status. Why? Because doing so is both the avenue to upward social mobility and a way to escape the prejudice and discrimination directed at more visible foreigners (Newman, 1973). Sociologists use the term **assimilation** to describe *the process by which minorities gradually adopt patterns of the dominant culture.* Assimilation involves changing modes of dress, values, religion, language, and friends.

The amount of assimilation varies by category. For example, Canadians have "melted" more than Cubans, the Dutch more than Dominicans, Germans

In an effort to force assimilation, the U.S. Bureau of Indian Affairs took American Indian children from their families and placed them in boarding schools like this one—Oklahoma's Riverside Indian School. There, they were taught the English language by non-Indian teachers with the goal of making them into "Americans." As this photo from about 1890 suggests, discipline in these schools was strict.

more than the Japanese. However, critics of the strategy of assimilation suggest that it paints minorities as "the problem" and defines them rather than majority people as the ones who need to do all the changing.

Note, too, that assimilation involves changes in ethnicity but not in race. For example, many descendants of Japanese immigrants discard their traditions but retain their racial identity. For racial traits to diminish over generations requires **miscegenation,** *biological reproduction by partners of different racial categories.* Although interracial marriage is becoming more common, it still amounts to only 3 percent of all marriages (U.S. Census Bureau, 2003).

SEGREGATION

Segregation refers to *the physical and social separation of categories of people.* Some minorities, especially religious orders like the Amish, voluntarily segregate themselves. Usually, however, majorities segregate minorities by excluding them. Residential neighborhoods, schools, occupations, hospitals, and even cemeteries may be segregated. While pluralism fosters distinctiveness without disadvantage, segregation enforces separation that harms a minority.

Racial segregation has a long history in the United States, beginning with slavery and evolving into racially separated housing, schools, buses, and trains. Decisions such as in the 1954 *Brown* case have reduced de jure (Latin, meaning "by law") discrimination in this country. However, de facto ("in fact") segregation continues to this day in the form of countless neighborhoods that are home to people of a single race.

Despite some recent decline, segregation persists in the United States. For example, Lavonia, Michigan, is 96 percent white, while neighboring Detroit is 83 percent African American. Kurt Metzger (2001:2) explains, "Livonia was pretty much created by white flight [from Detroit] and has stayed pretty much that." Further, research shows that, across the country, whites (especially those with young children) avoid neighborhoods where African Americans live (Emerson, Yancey, & Chai, 2001; Krysan, 2002). At the extreme, Douglas Massey and Nancy Denton (1989) document the *hypersegregation* of poor African Americans in some inner cities. Hypersegregation means having little contact of any kind with other people beyond a local communitiy. Hypersegregation disadvantages only a few percent of poor white people but about 20 percent of all poor African Americans (Jagarowsky & Bane, 1990; Krivo et al., 1998).

GENOCIDE

Genocide is *the systematic killing of one category of people by another.* This deadly form of racism and ethnocentrism, which violates every moral standard, has occurred time and time again in human history.

Genocide figured prominently in contact between Europeans and the original inhabitants of the Americas. From the sixteenth century on, the Spanish, Portuguese, English, French, and Dutch forcibly colonized vast empires. Although most native people died after contracting diseases brought by Europeans, for which they had no natural defenses, many others were killed deliberately (Matthiessen, 1984; Sale, 1990).

During the twentieth century, unimaginable horror befell European Jews during Adolf Hitler's reign of terror known as the Holocaust. From about 1935 to 1945, the Nazis murdered more than 6 million Jewish men, women, and children. The Soviet dictator Josef Stalin murdered on an even greater scale, killing perhaps 30 million real and imagined enemies during decades of violent rule. Between 1975 and 1980, Pol Pot's communist regime in Cambodia butchered all "capitalists," including anyone able to speak a Western language; in all, some 2 million people (one-fourth of the population) perished in the Cambodian "killing fields" (Shawcross, 1979).

Tragically, genocide continues. Recent examples include Hutus killing Tutsis in the African nation of Rwanda and Serbs killing Bosnians in the Balkans of Eastern Europe.

These four patterns of minority-majority interaction have all been played out in the United States. While many people proudly point to patterns of pluralism and assimilation, it is also important to recognize the degree to which U.S. society has been built on segregation (of African Americans) and genocide (of Native Americans). The remainder of this chapter examines how these four patterns have shaped the history and present social standing of major racial and ethnic categories in the United States.

RACE AND ETHNICITY IN THE UNITED STATES

Give me your tired, your poor,
Your huddled masses yearning to breathe free,
The wretched refuse of your teeming shore,
Send these, the homeless, tempest-tossed to me:
I lift my lamp beside the golden door.

These words by Emma Lazarus, inscribed on the Statue of Liberty, express cultural ideals of human dignity, personal freedom, and opportunity. Indeed, the United States has provided more of the "good life" to more immigrants than any other nation. But as the history of this nation's racial and ethnic minorities reveals, our country's golden door has opened more widely for some than for others.

NATIVE AMERICANS

The term "Native Americans" refers to the societies— including Aleuts, Eskimos, Cherokee, Zuni, Sioux, Mohawk, Aztec, and Inca—that first settled the Western Hemisphere. Some 30,000 years before Christopher Columbus stumbled on the Americas, migrating peoples crossed a land bridge from Asia to North America where the Bering Strait (off the coast of Alaska) lies today. Gradually, they made their way throughout North and South America.

When the first Europeans arrived late in the fifteenth century, Native Americans numbered in the millions. But by 1900, after centuries of conflict

During World War II, the U.S. Army turned to members of the Navajo who devised a code for communication based on their native language. Throughout the war in the Pacific, the opposing Japanese forces intercepted messages but were never able to make sense of them. Thus, the Navajo "code talkers" played a vital role in the eventual U.S. victory.

and acts of genocide, the "vanishing Americans" numbered just 250,000 (Dobyns, 1966; Tyler, 1973). As shown in National Map 14–2 on page 366, the lands they controlled had also shrunk dramatically.

Columbus first referred to Native Americans as "Indians" because he wrongly thought he had reached India. Actually, he landed in the Bahama Islands in the Caribbean. Columbus found the island people passive and peaceful, in stark contrast to materialistic and competitive Europeans (Matthiessen, 1984; Sale, 1990). Yet, early Europeans justified seizing land by calling their victims thieves and murderers (Unruh, 1979; Josephy, 1982).

After the Revolutionary War, the new U.S. government took a pluralist approach to Native American societies while it sought to gain more land through treaties. The payments it offered for the land were far from fair, however, and when Native Americans refused to surrender their homelands, the U.S. government

SEEING OURSELVES

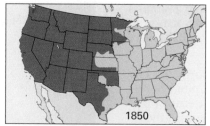
1790

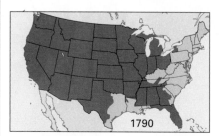
1850

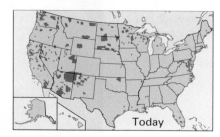
1880

1850

Today

NATIONAL MAP 14–2
Land Controlled by Native Americans, 1790–1998

Two hundred years ago, Native Americans controlled three-fourths of the land that eventually became today's United States. Today, Native Americans control 314 reservations, scattered across the United States, that account for just 2 percent of the country's land area. How would you characterize these locations?

Source: Copyright © 1998 by The New York Times Co. Reprinted by permission. All rights reserved.

used superior military power to evict them. By the early 1800s, few Native Americans remained east of the Mississippi River.

In 1871, the United States declared Native Americans wards of the government and tried to force assimilation. Native Americans continued to lose their land and were well on their way to losing their culture as well. Reservation life fostered dependency, replacing ancestral languages with English and traditional religion with Christianity. Officials of the Bureau of Indian Affairs took children from their parents and put them in boarding schools, where they were resocialized as "Americans." Authorities gave local control of reservation life to the few Native Americans who supported government policies, and they distributed reservation land, traditionally held collectively, as private property to individual families (Tyler, 1973).

Not until 1924 were Native Americans entitled to U.S. citizenship. After that, many migrated from reservations, adopting mainstream cultural patterns and marrying non–Native Americans. Today, four out of ten Native Americans consider themselves biracial or multiracial (Raymond, 2001; Wellner, 2001), and many large cities now have sizable Native American populations. As Table 14–2 shows, however, Native American income is far below the U.S. average, and relatively few Native Americans earn a college degree.[2]

From in-depth interviews with Native Americans in a western city, Joan Albon (1971) linked low Native American social standing to a range of cultural factors, including a noncompetitive view of life and a reluctance to pursue higher education. In addition, she noted, many Native Americans have dark skin, which makes them targets of prejudice and discrimination.

Like other racial and ethnic minorities in the United States, Native Americans have recently reasserted pride in their cultural heritage. Native American organizations report a surge in membership, and many children can speak native languages better than

MEDIA For more information on Native Americans, visit this site: http://www.nativeweb.org

their parents (Fost, 1991; Johnson, 1991; Nagel, 1996). Native Americans now operate a wide range of successful businesses (Raymond, 2001). Moreover, the legal autonomy of reservations has turned out to be an ace-in-the-hole for some tribes,

---

[2]In making comparisons of education and, especially, income, keep in mind that various categories of the U.S. population have different median ages. In 2000, the median age for all U.S. people was 35.3 years. Non-Hispanic white people have a median age of 38.6 years; for Native Americans, the figure is 28.0 years. Because people's schooling and income increase over time, such an age difference accounts for some of the disparities shown in Table 14–2.

which have built lucrative gaming casinos. But such financial windfalls have enriched relatively few Native peoples, and most casino profits go to non-Indian investors (Bartlett & Steele, 2002). While some prosper, most Native Americans remain severely disadvantaged and share a profound sense of the injustice they have suffered at the hands of white people.

WHITE ANGLO-SAXON PROTESTANTS

White Anglo-Saxon Protestants (WASPs) were not the first people to inhabit the United States, but they soon dominated this nation after European settlement began. Most WASPs are of English ancestry, but the category also includes Scots and Welsh. With some 32 million people of English ancestry, one in nine members of our society claims some WASP background, and WASPs are found at all class levels. National Map 14–3 on page 368 shows the highest concentrations of WASPs across the United States.

Historically, WASP immigrants were highly skilled and motivated to achieve by what we now call the Protestant work ethic. Because of their high social standing, WASPs were not subject to the prejudice and discrimination experienced by other categories of immigrants. In fact, the historical dominance of WASPs has led others to want to become more like them (Jones, 2001).

WASPs were never one single social group; especially in colonial times, considerable hostility separated English Anglicans and Scots-Irish Presbyterians (Parrillo, 1994). But, later on, most WASPs joined together to oppose the arrival of "undesirables" such as Germans in the 1840s and Italians in the 1880s. Meanwhile, richer people who were already here moved out to exclusive suburban neighborhoods and joined restrictive clubs. Thus, the 1880s—the decade that saw the Statue of Liberty first welcome immigrants to the United States—also saw the founding of the first country club with only WASP members (Baltzell, 1964).

By about 1950, however, the social elite were no longer mostly WASPs, as indicated by the 1960 election of John Fitzgerald Kennedy as the first Irish Catholic president. Yet the WASP cultural legacy remains. English is this country's dominant language, and Protestantism the majority religion. Our legal system also reflects its English origins. But the historical dominance of WASPs is most evident in the widespread use of the terms "race" and "ethnicity" to describe everyone but them.

TABLE 14-2 The Social Standing of Native Americans, 2000		
	Native Americans	Entire United States
Median family income	$31,064	$50,891
Percentage in poverty	27.1%	11.3%
Completion of four or more years of college (age 25 and over)	$9.3%*	25.6%

*Author estimate based on latest available data.
Source: U.S. Census Bureau (2001).

AFRICAN AMERICANS

Although Africans accompanied European explorers to the New World in the fifteenth century, most accounts mark the beginning of black history in the United States as 1619, when a Dutch trading ship brought twenty Africans to Jamestown, Virginia. Whether these people arrived as slaves or indentured servants who paid their passage by agreeing to work for a period of time, being of African descent on these shores soon became virtually synonymous with being a slave. In 1661, Virginia enacted the first law recognizing slavery (Sowell, 1981).

Slavery was the foundation of the southern colonies' plantation system. White people ran plantations with slave labor, and until 1808, some were also slave traders. Traders—including Europeans, Africans, and North Americans—forcibly transported some 10 million Africans to various countries in the Americas, including 400,000 to the United States. On board small sailing ships, hundreds of slaves were chained together for the several weeks it took to cross the Atlantic Ocean. Filth and disease killed many and drove others to suicide. If supplies ran low, slave traders simply threw slaves overboard. Overall, perhaps half died en route (Tannenbaum, 1946; Franklin, 1967; Sowell, 1981).

Surviving the journey was a mixed blessing, bringing a life of servitude. Although some slaves worked in cities at various trades, most labored in the fields,

 Read first-person accounts of slavery in the United States at this Library of Congress site: http://lcweb2.loc.gov/ammem/snhtml

often from daybreak until sunset, and even longer during the harvest. The law allowed owners to impose whatever disciplinary measures they deemed necessary to ensure that slaves would work hard and obey. Even killing a slave rarely prompted legal action. Owners also divided slave families at public auctions

SEEING OURSELVES

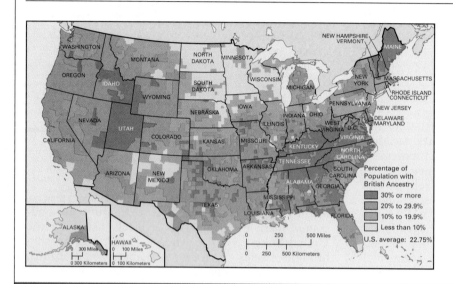

NATIONAL MAP 14–3
The Concentration of People of WASP Ancestry across the United States

Many people associate white Anglo-Saxon Protestants with elite communities along the eastern and western seaboards of the United States. But the highest concentrations of WASPs are in Utah (because of migrations of Mormons with English ancestry), Appalachia, and northern New England (because of historic immigration). Overall, however, WASPs form a large share of the U.S. population almost everywhere except Alaska, South Texas, and the upper Great Plains. Do you know why?

Source: From Rodger Doyle, *Atlas of Contemporary America.* Copyright © 1994 by Facts on File, Inc. Reprinted with permission of Facts on File, Inc.

---

where human beings were bought and sold as pieces of property. Unschooled and dependent on their owners for all their basic needs, slaves had little control over their lives (Franklin, 1967; Sowell, 1981).

Some free persons of color lived in both the North and the South, laboring as small-scale farmers, skilled workers, and small-business owners. But the lives of most African Americans stood in glaring contradiction to the principles of equality and freedom on which the United States was founded. The Declaration of Independence states:

> We hold these Truths to be self-evident, that all Men are created equal, that they are endowed by their Creator with certain unalienable Rights, that among these are Life, Liberty, and the Pursuit of Happiness.

However, most white people did not apply these ideals to black people. In the 1857 case of *Dred Scott v. Sanford* case, the U.S. Supreme Court addressed the question "Are blacks citizens?" by writing, "We think they are not, and that they are not included, and were not intended to be included, under the word 'citizens' in the Constitution, and can therefore claim none of the rights and privileges which that instrument provides for and secures for citizens of the United

States" (quoted in Blaustein & Zangrando, 1968:160). Thus arose what Swedish sociologist Gunnar Myrdal (1944) termed the "American dilemma": a democratic society's denial of basic rights and freedoms to an entire category of people. People would speak of equality, in other words, but do little to make all categories of people equal. On the contrary, many white people resolved this dilemma by defining black people as innately inferior and undeserving of equality (Leach, 2002).

In 1865, the Thirteenth Amendment to the Constitution outlawed slavery. Three years later, the Fourteenth Amendment reversed the *Dred Scott* ruling, giving citizenship to all people born in the United States. The Fifteenth Amendment, ratified in 1870, stated that neither race nor previous condition of servitude could deprive anyone of the right to vote. However, so-called Jim Crow laws—classic cases of institutional discrimination—segregated U.S. society into two racial castes. Especially in the South, white people beat and lynched black people (and some white people) who challenged the racial hierarchy.

The twentieth century brought dramatic changes for African Americans. After World War I, tens of thousands of men, women, and children fled the South as part of the "Great Migration," seeking jobs

The efforts of these four women greatly advanced the social standing of African Americans in the United States. Pictured above, from left to right: Sojourner Truth (1797–1883), born a slave, became an influential preacher and outspoken abolitionist who was honored by President Lincoln at the White House. Harriet Tubman (1820–1913), after escaping from slavery herself, masterminded the flight from bondage of hundreds of African American men and women via the "Underground Railroad." Ida Wells-Barnett (1862–1931), born to slave parents, became a partner in a Memphis newspaper and served as a tireless crusader against the terror of lynching. Marian Anderson (1902–1993), an exceptional singer whose early career was restrained by racial prejudice, broke symbolic "color lines" by singing in the White House (1936) and on the steps of the Lincoln Memorial to a crowd of almost 100,000 people (1939).

in northern factories. Most found more economic opportunity but also discovered that others considered them socially below white immigrants arriving from Europe (Tolnay, 2001).

In the 1950s and 1960s, a national civil rights movement led to landmark judicial decisions outlawing segregated schools as well as overt discrimination in employment and public accommodations. In addition, the "black power" movement gave African Americans a renewed sense of pride and purpose.

Gains notwithstanding, people of African descent continue to occupy a subordinate position in the United States, as shown in Table 14–3 on page 370. The median income of African American families in 2001 ($33,598) was only 59 percent of non-Hispanic white family income ($57,328), a ratio that has changed little in thirty years.[3] Black families remain three times as likely as white families to be poor.

_____

[3]Here again, a median age difference (non-Hispanic white people, 38.6; black people, 30.2) accounts for some of the income and educational disparities. More important is a higher proportion of one-parent families among blacks than whites. If we compare only married-couple families, African Americans (median income $51,514 in 2001) earned 81 percent as much as whites ($63,862).

The number of African Americans securely in the middle class rose by more than half between 1980 and 2001; 48 percent earn more than $35,000 a year, and 33 percent earn $50,000 or more. Taken together, African Americans now have more than half a trillion dollars in annual purchasing power. But African Americans remain largely working class, and many have seen earnings slip during the last fifteen years as urban factory jobs have been lost to other countries where labor costs are lower. Thus, black unemployment is at least twice as high as white unemployment; among African American teenagers in many cities, the figure exceeds 40 percent (Horton et al., 2000; DeJong & Madamba, 2001b; McCall, 2001b; Raymond, 2001; Smith, 2002; U.S. Department of Labor, 2003).

Since 1980, African Americans have made remarkable educational progress. The share of adults completing high school rose from half to more than three-fourths, nearly closing the gap between whites and blacks. Between 1980 and 2001, the share of African American adults with at least a college degree rose from 8 to 17 percent. But as Table 14–3 shows, African Americans are still at just over half the national standard when it comes to completing four years of college.

TABLE 14-3 The Social Standing of African Americans, 2001		
	African Americans	Entire United States
Median family income	$33,598*	$51,407
Percentage in poverty	22.7%*	11.7%
Completion of four or more years of college (age 25 and over)	17.0%*	26.7%

*For purposes of comparison with other tables in this chapter, 2000 data are as follows: median family income, $34,204; percentage in poverty, 22.1%; completion of four or more years of college, 16.6%.

Sources: U.S. Census Bureau (2001, 2002).

The political clout of African Americans has also increased. As a result of black migration to the cities and white flight to the suburbs, half of this country's ten largest cities have elected African American mayors. Yet, in 2003, African Americans accounted for just 37 members of the House of Representatives (8.5 percent of 435), none (out of 100) in the Senate, and no state governors (*CQ Weekly*, 2003).

Do banks refuse loans unfairly to African Americans? Go to http://www.hud.gov/library/bookshelf18/pressrel/subprime.html

In sum, for more than 350 years, African Americans have struggled for social equality. As a nation, the United States has come far in this pursuit. Overt discrimination is now illegal, and research documents a long-term decline in prejudice against them (Firebaugh & Davis, 1988; Wilson, 1992; NORC, 2003).

In 1913, fifty years after the abolition of slavery, W. E. B. Du Bois pointed to the extent of black achievement. But Du Bois also cautioned that racial caste remained strong in the United States. Almost a century later, this racial hierarchy persists.

ASIAN AMERICANS

Although Asian Americans share some racial traits, enormous cultural diversity characterizes this category of people with ancestors from dozens of nations. In 2000, the total number of Asian Americans exceeded 10 million, approaching 4 percent of the U.S. population. The largest category of Asian Americans is people of Chinese ancestry (2.4 million), followed by those of Filipino (1.8 million), Asian Indian (1.7 million), Vietnamese (1.1 million), Korean (1 million), and Japanese (800,000) descent. More than one-third of Asian Americans live in California.

Young Asian Americans command attention and respect as high achievers and are disproportionately found at our country's best colleges and universities. Many of their elders, too, have made economic and social gains so that most Asian Americans now live in middle-class suburbs (O'Hare, Frey, & Fost, 1994). Yet, despite (and sometimes because of) this achievement, Asian Americans often find that others are aloof or outright hostile to them (Chua-Eoan, 2000).

At the same time, the "model minority" image of Asian Americans hides the fact that many Asian Americans remain poor. We now focus on the history and current standing of Chinese Americans and Japanese Americans—the longest-established Asian American minorities—and conclude with a brief look at the most recent arrivals (Takaki, 1998).

Chinese Americans

Chinese immigration to the United States began in 1849 with the economic boom of California's gold rush. New towns and businesses sprang up overnight, and the demand for cheap labor attracted some 100,000 Chinese immigrants. Most Chinese workers were young men willing to take tough, low-status jobs shunned by whites. But the economy soured in the 1870s, and desperate whites began to compete with the Chinese for whatever work could be found. Suddenly the hard-working Chinese posed a threat. In short, economic hard times led to prejudice and discrimination (Ling, 1971; Boswell, 1986).

Soon, the law barred Chinese people from many occupations, and public opinion turned hostile against "the Yellow Peril." Everyone seemed to line up against the Chinese, as expressed in the popular phrase of the time that someone up against great odds did not have "a Chinaman's chance" (Sung, 1967; Sowell, 1981).

In 1882, the U.S. government passed the first of several laws curbing Chinese immigration. Because Chinese men in this country outnumbered Chinese women by twenty to one, and no more women were arriving, the Chinese population in the United States tumbled to about 60,000 by 1920 (Hsu, 1971; Lai, 1980). Chinese women already here were in high demand, so they soon became less submissive to men (Sowell, 1981).

Responding to racial hostility, some Chinese moved eastward; many more sought the safety of urban Chinatowns. There, Chinese traditions flourished, and kinship networks, called clans, provided financial help to individuals and represented the interests of all. At the same time, however, Chinatowns discouraged

TABLE 14-4 The Social Standing of Asian Americans, 2001

	All Asian Americans	Chinese Americans	Japanese Americans	Korean Americans	Filipino Americans	Entire United States
Median family income	$60,158	$57,174*	$71,336*	$46,924*	$64,621*	$51,407
Percentage in poverty	10.2%	10.2%*	5.1%*	9.9%*	4.6%*	11.7%
Completion of four or more years of college (age 25 and over)	47.2%	51.0%*	43.2%*	43.2%*	49.0%*	26.7%

*Author estimates based on latest available data.
Source: U.S. Census Bureau (2002, 2003).

residents from learning the English language, so their job opportunities were limited (Wong, 1971).

A growing need for labor during World War II prompted President Franklin Roosevelt to end the ban on Chinese immigration in 1943 and to extend the rights of citizenship to Chinese Americans born abroad. Many responded by moving out of China-towns and pursuing cultural assimilation. In Honolulu back in 1900, for example, 70 percent of Chinese people lived in Chinatown; today, the figure is below 20 percent.

For information of interest to Chinese Americans, go to http://www.ocanatl.org/

By 1950, many Chinese Americans had experienced upward social mobility. Today, people of Chinese ancestry are no longer restricted to self-employment in laundries and restaurants; many hold high-prestige positions, especially in fields related to science and new information technology.

As shown in Table 14–4, the median family income of Chinese Americans in 2001 ($57,174) stood above the national average ($51,407). The higher income of all Asian Americans reflects, on average, a larger number of family members in the labor force.[4] Chinese Americans also have a record of educational achievement, with twice the national average of college graduates.

Despite their success, many Chinese Americans still grapple with subtle (and sometimes blatant) prejudice and discrimination. Such hostility is one reason

that poverty among Chinese Americans remains above the national average. Poverty is higher yet among those who remain in the restrictive circle of China-towns, working in restaurants or other low-paying jobs, raising the question of whether racial and ethnic enclaves help their residents or exploit them (Portes & Jensen, 1989; Zhou & Logan, 1989; Kinkead, 1992; Gilbertson & Gurak, 1993).

Japanese Americans

Japanese immigration began slowly in the 1860s, reaching only 2,000 by 1890. Most came to the Hawaiian Islands (annexed by the United States in 1898 and made a state in 1959) as a source of cheap labor. After 1900, however, as the number of Japanese immigrants to California rose (reaching 140,000 by 1915), white hostility increased (Takaki, 1998). In 1907, the United States signed an agreement with Japan curbing the entry of men—the chief economic threat—while allowing women to enter this country to ease the Japanese sex ratio imbalance. In the 1920s, state laws in California and elsewhere segregated the Japanese and banned interracial marriage. Not until 1952 was citizenship extended to foreign-born Japanese.

Overall, Japanese immigrants probably faced less prejudice and discrimination than their Chinese counterparts for three reasons. First, there were fewer of them. Second, the Japanese knew more about the United States than the Chinese did, which helped them assimilate (Sowell, 1981). Third, Japanese immigrants preferred rural farming to clustering in cities. Even so, in 1913, California barred further land purchases by Japanese immigrants. Many foreign-born Japanese (called *Issei*) responded by placing farmland in the names of their U.S.-born children (*Nisei*), who were constitutionally entitled to citizenship.

---

[4]Median age for all Asian Americans in 2000 was 32.7 years, somewhat below the national median of 35.3 and the non-Hispanic white median of 38.6. But specific categories vary widely in median age: Japanese, 36.1; Chinese, 32.1; Filipino, 31.1; Korean, 29.1; Asian Indian, 28.9; Cambodian, 19.4; Hmong, 12.5 (U.S. Census Bureau, 2000, 2001).

Between 1942 and 1944, more than 100,000 men, women, and children of Japanese ancestry were forcibly removed from their homes and businesses and taken to detention camps. Here, a mother fights back tears as the army prepares to move her and her three small children (note the identification tags) from Bainbridge Island (off the coast of Washington state) to the mainland.

Japanese Americans faced their greatest challenge after December 7, 1941, when Japan bombed the U.S. naval fleet at Hawaii's Pearl Harbor. Rage toward the Japanese living in the United States was made worse by fear that Japanese Americans might spy for Japan or commit acts of sabotage. Within a year, President Franklin Roosevelt signed Executive Order 9066, requiring 110,000 people of Japanese descent to be relocated to inland military camps (Sun, 1998).

The Japanese internment was sharply criticized. First, it targeted an entire category of people, not one of whom was known to have committed any disloyal act. Second, roughly two-thirds of those imprisoned were *Nisei*, U.S. citizens by birth. Third, the United States was also at war with Germany and Italy, but no comparable action was taken against people of German or Italian ancestry.

Relocation meant selling homes, furnishings, and businesses for pennies on the dollar, making the Japanese American population suddenly poor. In military prisons—surrounded by barbed wire and guarded by armed soldiers—families crowded into single rooms, often in buildings that had previously sheltered livestock (Fujimoto, 1971; Bloom, 1980). The internment ended in 1944, when the Supreme Court declared it unconstitutional. In 1988, Congress awarded $20,000 as token compensation to each victim.

After World War II, Japanese Americans staged a dramatic recovery. They entered many new occupations, and because their culture highly values education and hard work, Japanese Americans have enjoyed remarkable success. In 2001, the median income of Japanese American households was almost 50 percent above the national average. The rate of poverty among Japanese Americans was less than half the national figure.

To learn about Japanese culture and society, go to http://www.jinjapan.org

Upward social mobility has encouraged cultural assimilation and interracial marriage. The third and fourth generations of Japanese Americans (the *Sansei* and *Yonsei*) rarely live in residential enclaves, as many Chinese Americans do, and most marry non-Japanese partners. In the process, some have abandoned their traditions, including the Japanese language. A good proportion of Japanese Americans, however, belong to associations as a way of maintaining their ethnic identity (Fugita & O'Brien, 1985). Unfortunately, some appear to be caught between two worlds: no longer culturally Japanese, yet, because of racial differences, not completely accepted in the larger society.

Recent Asian Immigrants

More recent immigrants from Asia include Filipinos, Indians, Koreans, Vietnamese, Samoans, and Guamanians. Overall, the Asian American population increased by 48 percent between 1990 and 2000 and currently accounts for one-third of all immigration (U.S. Citizenship and Immigration Services, 2003). A brief look at Koreans and Filipinos—both from countries that have had special ties to the United States—shows the social diversity of newly arriving people from Asia.

Koreans. Korean immigration to the United States followed the U.S. involvement in the Korean War

(1950–53). U.S. troops in South Korea experienced Korean culture firsthand, and some soldiers found Korean spouses. For South Koreans, contact with the troops raised interest in the United States.

The entrepreneurial spirit is strong among all Asian immigrants. Asians are slightly more likely than Latinos, three times more likely than African Americans, and eight times more likely than Native Americans to own and operate small businesses (U.S. Small Business Administration, 2001). Among all Asian Americans, moreover, Koreans are the most likely to own small businesses. For example, residents of New York City know that most small grocery stores there are Korean-owned; those who live in Los Angeles know that Koreans operate a large share of liquor stores.

Although many Koreans work long hours, Korean American family income is slightly below the national average, as shown in Table 14–4. Moreover, Korean Americans face limited social acceptance, even among other categories of Asian Americans.

Filipinos. The large number of immigrants from the Philippines is explained partly by the fact that the United States controlled the Philippine Islands between 1898 (when Spain ceded it as partial settlement of the Spanish-American War) and 1946 (when the Philippines became an independent republic).

The data in Table 14–4 suggest that Filipinos generally have fared well. But a closer look reveals a mixed pattern, with some Filipinos highly successful in the professions (especially in medicine) and others struggling to get by in low-skill jobs (Parrillo, 1994, 2003b).

For many Filipino families, the key to high income is working women. Almost three-fourths of Filipino American women are in the labor force, compared to just half of Korean American women. Moreover, many of these women are professionals, reflecting the fact that 42 percent of Filipino American women have a four-year college degree, compared to just 26 percent of Korean American women.

In sum, a survey of Asian Americans presents a complex picture. The Japanese come closest to gaining social acceptance, but surveys reveal greater prejudice against Asian Americans than against African Americans (Parrillo, 2003a). Median income data suggest that, while many Asian Americans remain poor, many others have prospered. Yet high average income reflects the fact that Asian Americans are heavily concentrated in regions—Hawaii, California, and New York—where incomes are high but so are costs of living (Takaki, 1998). Then, too, many Asian Americans remain poor. Finally,

Of all ethnic minorities, people of Asian Indian descent are the most well off, with a large share working in medicine or holding other professional positions. How do you explain the pattern by which some ethnic categories, on average, have higher or lower social standing than others?

with an exceptionally high immigration rate, people of Asian ancestry are sure to play a central role in U.S. society in the decades to come (Lee, 1994; Whelan, 2001).

HISPANIC AMERICANS

In 2000, the number of Hispanics in the United States topped 35 million (12.5 percent of the population), surpassing the number of African Americans and making Hispanics the largest racial or ethnic minority (U.S. Census Bureau, 2003). Keep in mind, though, that few people who fall into this category describe themselves as "Hispanic" or "Latino." Like Asian Americans, Hispanics are really a cluster of distinct populations, each identifying with a particular ancestral nation (Marín &

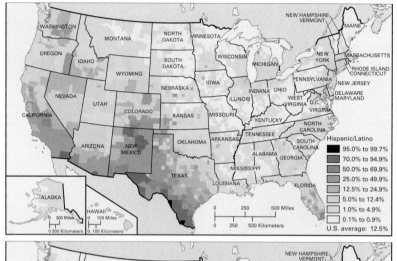

NATIONAL MAP 14–4
The Concentration of Hispanics/Latinos, African Americans, and Asian Americans, by County, 2000

In 2000, people of Hispanic or Latino descent represented 12.5 percent of the U.S. population, compared with 12.3 percent African Americans and 3.6 percent Asian Americans. These three maps show the geographic distribution of these categories of people in 2000. Comparing them, we see that the southern half of the United States is home to far more minorities than the northern half. But do the three concentrate in the same areas? What patterns do the maps reveal?

Source: U.S. Census Bureau (2001).

TABLE 14-5 The Social Standing of Hispanic Americans, 2001

	All Hispanics	Mexican Americans	Puerto Ricans	Cuban Americans	Entire United States
Median family income	$34,490*	$33,533	$30,095	$35,217	$51,407
Percentage in poverty	21.4%*	22.8%	26.1%	16.5%	11.7%
Completion of four or more years of college (age 25 and over)	11.1%*	7.5%	14.0%	18.6%	26.7%

*For purposes of comparison with other tables in this chapter, 2000 data for all Hispanics are as follows: median family income, $35,050; percentage in poverty, 21.2%; completion of four or more years of college, 10.6%.

Source: U.S. Census Bureau (2003).

Marín, 1991). About two out of three Hispanics (some 24 million) are Mexican Americans, or "Chicanos." Puerto Ricans are next in population size (3 million), followed by Cuban Americans (1.2 million). Many other nations of Latin America are represented by smaller numbers.

Although the Hispanic population is increasing all over the country, most still live in the Southwest (Wellner, 2002a). One out of four Californians is a Latino (in greater Los Angeles, almost half the people are Latino). National Map 14–4 locates the Hispanic, African American, and Asian American populations across the United States.

For information about Hispanic/Latino culture, go to http://www.lanic.utexas.edu/la/region/hispanic

Median family income for all Hispanics—$34,490 in 2001—is well below the national average.[5] As the following sections explain, however, some categories of Hispanics fare better than others.

Mexican Americans

Some Mexican Americans (also known as "Chicanos") are descendants of people who lived in a part of Mexico annexed by the United States after the Mexican American War (1846–48). Most, however, are more recent immigrants. Indeed, more immigrants now come to the United States from Mexico than from any other nation.

Like many other immigrants, many Mexican Americans have worked as low-wage laborers on farms and in factories. Table 14–5 shows that the 2001 median family income for Mexican Americans was $33,533, about two-thirds the national standard. Almost one-fourth of Chicano families are poor, twice

the national average. Mexican Americans also have a high dropout rate. Even more troubling, research suggests that many Mexican immigrant families make few economic gains even over several generations (Livingston & Kahn, 2002).

Puerto Ricans

Puerto Rico (like the Philippines) became a possession of the United States when the Spanish-American War ended in 1898. In 1917, Puerto Ricans (but not Filipinos) became U.S. citizens.

New York City is home to about 1 million Puerto Ricans. However, about one-third of this community is severely disadvantaged. Adjusting to cultural patterns on the mainland—including, for many, learning English—is a major challenge; also, Puerto Ricans with dark skin encounter prejudice and discrimination. As a result, more people return to Puerto Rico each year than arrive on the mainland: During the 1990s, the Puerto Rican population of New York actually fell by 100,000 (Navarro, 2000).

This "revolving door" pattern limits assimilation. Three-fourths of Puerto Rican families in the United States speak Spanish at home, compared to about half of Mexican American families (Sowell, 1981; Stevens & Swicegood, 1987). Speaking Spanish keeps ethnic identity strong but also limits economic opportunity. Puerto Ricans also have a higher incidence of women-headed households than other Hispanics, a pattern that puts families at greater risk of poverty.

Table 14–5 shows that the 2001 median family income for Puerto Ricans was $30,095, more than half the national average. Although long-term mainland residents have made economic gains, more recent immigrants from Puerto Rico continue to struggle to find work. When the differences are averaged out, Puerto Ricans remain the most socially disadvantaged Hispanic minority (Rivera-Batiz & Santiago, 1994; Holmes, 1996b).

[5]The 2000 median age of the U.S. Hispanic population was 25.8 years, well below the national median of 35.3 years. This differential accounts for some of the disparity in income and education.

The strength of family bonds and neighborhood ties in Latino communities is evident in Carmen Lomas Garza's painting Cakewalk.

Carmen Lomas Garza, Cakewalk, acrylic painting, 36 × 48 inches. © 1987 Carmen Lomas Garza. Photo credit: M. Lee Fatherree. Collection of Paula Maciel-Benecke and Norbert Benecke, Aptos, CA.

Cuban Americans

Within a decade after the 1959 Marxist revolution led by Fidel Castro, 400,000 Cubans had fled to the United States. Most settled in Miami. Those who came were, for the most part, highly educated business and professional people who wasted little time becoming as successful in the United States as in their homeland (Fallows, 1983; Krafft, 1993).

Table 14–5 shows that the 2001 median household income for the 1.2 million Cuban Americans was $35,217, surpassing that of other Hispanics, yet still below the national average. Of all Hispanics, Cubans are the most likely to speak Spanish in their homes: Eight out of ten families do. However, their cultural distinctiveness and highly visible communities, like Miami's Little Havana, provoke hostility from some people.

WHITE ETHNIC AMERIANS

The term "white ethnics" recognizes the ethnic heritage—and social disadvantages—of many white people. White ethnics are non-WASPs whose ancestors lived in Ireland, Poland, Germany, Italy, or other European countries. More than half the U.S. population falls into one or another white ethnic category (Alba, 1990).

Unprecedented emigration from Europe during the nineteenth century first brought Germans and Irish and then Italians and Jews to our shores. Despite cultural differences, all shared the hope that the United States would offer greater political freedom and economic opportunity than their homelands. Most did live better in this country, but the belief that "the streets of America were paved with gold" turned out to be a far cry from reality. Many immigrants found only hard labor for low wages.

White ethnics also endured their share of prejudice and discrimination. Many employers shut their doors to immigrants, posting signs that warned "None need apply but Americans" (Handlin, 1941:67). By 1921, the federal government passed a quota system greatly limiting immigration, especially by southern and eastern Europeans, who were likely to have darker skin and different cultural backgrounds from the dominant WASPs. This system continued until 1968 (Fallows, 1983).

In response to this hostility, many white ethnics formed supportive residential enclaves. Some also established footholds in certain businesses and trades: Italian Americans entered the construction industry; the Irish worked in construction and in civil service jobs; Jews predominated in the garment industry; many Greeks (like the Chinese) worked in the retail food business (Newman, 1973).

Many working-class people still live in traditional neighborhoods, although those who prospered gradually assimilated. Most descendants of immigrants

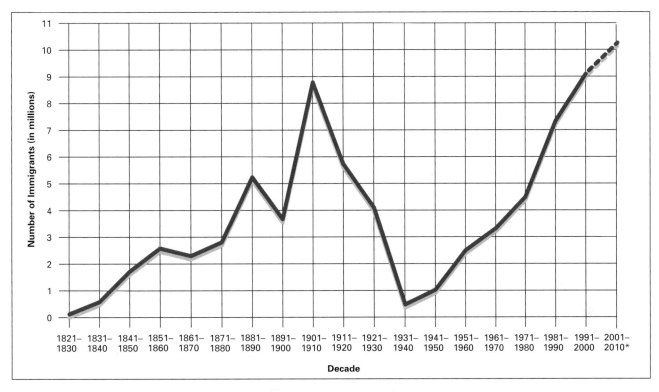

FIGURE 14–3 Immigration to the United States, by Decade

*Projection based on 2001–2002 data.

Source: U.S. Citizenship and Immigration Services (2003).

who labored in sweatshops and lived in overcrowded tenements now lead more comfortable lives. As a result, their ethnic heritage has become a source of pride.

RACE AND ETHNICITY: LOOKING AHEAD

The United States has been, and will long remain, a land of immigrants. Immigration has brought striking cultural diversity and tales of hope, struggle, and success told in hundreds of tongues.

Most immigrants arrived in a great wave that peaked about 1910. The next two generations saw gradual economic gains and some assimilation. The government also extended citizenship to Native Americans (1924), foreign-born Filipinos (1942), Chinese Americans (1943), and Japanese Americans (1952).

As Figure 14–3 indicates, another wave of immigration began after World War II and swelled as the government relaxed immigration laws in the 1960s.

During the 1990s, nearly 1 million people came to the United States each year, more than twice the number that arrived during the "Great Immigration" a century ago (although newcomers now enter a country that has five times as many people). Today's immigrants come not from Europe but from Latin America and Asia, with Mexicans, Filipinos, and South Koreans arriving in the largest numbers.

New arrivals face the same kind of prejudice and discrimination experienced by those who came before them. Indeed, recent years have witnessed rising hostility toward foreigners (sometimes termed *xenophobia*, with Greek roots meaning "fear of what is strange"). In 1994, California voters passed Proposition 187, which cut off social services (including schooling) to illegal immigrants. More recently, voters there mandated that all children learn English in school. In 2000, some landowners along the southwest border of the United States took up arms to discourage the large number of illegal immigrants crossing the border from Mexico, and some political candidates have

CONTROVERSY & DEBATE

Affirmative Action: Solution or Problem?

Barbara Gruttner, who is white, claimed that she was the victim of racial discrimination. She maintained that the University of Michigan Law School unfairly denied her application for admission, while admitting many less qualified African American applicants. The basis of her claim was the fact that Michigan, a state university, admitted just 9 percent of white students with her grade point average and law school aptitude test scores, while admitting 100 percent of comparable African American applicants.

In 2003, the Supreme Court heard Gruttner's complaint in a review of the admissions policies of both the law school and the undergraduate program at the University of Michigan. In a 6 to 3 decision, the Court ruled against Gruttner, claiming that the University of Michigan Law School could take account of the race of applicants in the interest of creating a socially diverse student body. At the same time, however, the Court struck down the university's undergraduate admissions policy, which was a point system that took account of grades and college board scores but also gave underrepresented minorities a numerical bonus. A point system of this kind, the Court ruled, is too close to the rigid quota systems rejected by the Court in the past.

Overall, although the Supreme Court continued to oppose any quota-like systems, it reaffirmed the importance of racial diversity on the campus. Thus, colleges and universities can take account of race in order to increase the number of traditionally underrepresented students, as long as race is treated as one variable in a process that evaluates each applicant as an individual (Stout, 2003).

This important court decision is merely the latest in a long debate over

the policy of affirmative action. But how did this controversial policy begin? The answer takes us back to the end of World War II, when the U.S. government funded higher education for veterans of all races. The G.I. Bill held special promise for African Americans, most of whom needed financial assistance to enroll in college. The program was so successful that, by 1960, some 350,000 black men and women were on college campuses with government funding.

But a problem remained: These individuals were not finding the kinds of jobs for which they were qualified. In short, educational opportunity was not producing economic opportunity.

Thus, in 1965, the Johnson administration introduced a program called "affirmative action" to provide a broader "net of opportunity" for qualified minorities in the job market. Employers were instructed to monitor hiring, promotion, and admissions policies to eliminate discrimination—even if unintended—against minorities.

Defenders of affirmative action see it, first, as a sensible response to our nation's racial and ethnic history, especially for African Americans, who suffered through two centuries of slavery and a century of segregation under Jim Crow laws. Throughout our history, they claim, being white gave people a big

called for drastic action to cut off further immigration. For many people, fear of terrorism has led to demands to limit immigration, especially from Middle Eastern nations (Ragavan, 2002). More broadly, as the final box explains, the debate over affirmative action rages as hotly as ever.

Some newcomers try to blend into U.S. society; others try to maintain some of their traditional culture. Still others become part of visible ethnic communities, so that the Little Havanas and Koreatowns of today stand alongside the Little Italys and Germantowns of the past. What all newcomers share with those already here, however, is the hope that their racial and ethnic identity can be a source of pride and strength rather than a badge of inferiority.

advantage. Thus, minority preference today is a step toward fair compensation for unfair majority preference in the past.

Second, given our racial history, the promise of a color-blind society strikes many analysts as hollow. They claim that, because prejudice and discrimination are rooted deep in the fabric of U.S. society, simply saying we are now color-blind does not mean everyone competes fairly.

Third, proponents maintain that affirmative action has worked. Where would minorities be if the government had not enacted this policy almost four decades ago? Major employers, such as fire and police departments in large cities, began hiring minorities and women for the first time only because of affirmative action. This program has played an important part in expanding the African American middle class. Furthermore, affirmative action has increased interracial interaction on the campus—a benefit to all students—and has advanced the careers of a generation of black students.

About 80 percent of African Americans claim that affirmative action is needed to ensure them equal opportunity. But affirmative action draws criticism from others. Indeed, a 2003 poll shows that 73 percent of white people and 56 percent of Hispanics oppose preferences for African Americans. One consequence of this concern is that, by the mid-1990s, courts began to trim back such policies. Critics argue, first, that affirmative action started out as a temporary remedy to ensure fair competition but became a system of "group preferences" and quotas. In other words, the policy did not remain true to the goal of promoting color blindness as set out in the 1964 Civil Rights Act. By the 1970s, it had become "reverse discrimination," favoring people not because of their performance but because of their race, ethnicity, or sex.

Second, critics contend that affirmative action polarizes society. If treating people according to race was wrong in the past, it is wrong now. Moreover, why should whites today, many of whom are far from privileged, be penalized for past discrimination that was in no way their fault? Our society has undone most of the institutional prejudice and discrimination of earlier times, opponents continue, so that minorities can and do enjoy success according to their personal merit. Giving entire categories of people special treatment inevitably compromises standards of excellence, calls into question the real accomplishments of minorities, and offends public opinion.

A third argument against affirmative action is that it benefits those who need it least. Favoring minority-owned corporations or allocating places in law school helps already-privileged people. Affirmative action has done little for the African American underclass that most needs a leg up.

In sum, there are good reasons to argue for and against affirmative action. Indeed, people who believe in a society where no racial or ethnic category dominates fall on both sides of the debate. The disagreement, then, is not whether people of all colors should have equal opportunity, but whether a particular policy—affirmative action—is part of the solution or part of the problem.

Continue the debate. . .

1. *In view of the fact that, historically, society has favored males over females and whites over people of color, would you agree that white males have received more "affirmative action" than anyone? Why or why not?*

2. *Should affirmative action include only disadvantaged categories of minorities (say, African Americans and Native Americans) and exclude more affluent categories (such as Japanese Americans)? Why or why not?*

3. *What do you think about the assertion that state universities ought to admit applicants with an eye toward advancing minorities and thereby lessening racial inequality? Isn't that goal as important as the goal of admitting the most qualified individuals?*

Sources: Bowen & Bok (1999), Fetto (2002), Fineman & Lipper (2003), Kantrowitz & Wingert (2003), and NORC (2003).

SUMMARY

1. Races are socially constructed categories by which societies set apart people with various physical traits. Although scientists identified three broad categories—Caucasoids, Mongoloids, and Negroids—there are no pure races.

2. Ethnicity is based not on biology but on people's shared cultural heritage. Just as people may or may not choose to emphasize their cultural distinctiveness, societies may or may not set categories of people apart because of their cultural heritage.

3. Minorities, including people of various races and ethnicities, are categories of people society sets apart, making them both distinct and disadvantaged.

4. Prejudice is a rigid and unfair generalization about a category of people. The social distance scale is one measure of prejudice. Racism, a destructive type of prejudice, asserts that one race is innately superior or inferior to another.

5. Discrimination is a pattern of action by which a person treats various categories of people unequally.

6. Pluralism means that racial and ethnic categories, although distinct, have equal social standing. Assimilation is a process by which minorities gradually adopt the patterns of the dominant culture. Segregation is the physical and social separation of categories of people. Genocide is the extermination of a category of people.

7. Native Americans, the earliest human inhabitants of the Americas, have endured genocide, segregation, and forced assimilation. Today, the social standing of Native Americans is well below the national average.

8. WASPs predominated among the original European settlers of the United States, and many continue to enjoy high social position today.

9. African Americans experienced two centuries of slavery. Emancipation in 1865 gave way to segregation by law.

Today, despite legal equality, African Americans are still disadvantaged.

10. Chinese and Japanese Americans have suffered both racial and ethnic hostility. Although some prejudice and discrimination continue, both categories now have above-average income and schooling. Asian immigrants, especially Koreans and Filipinos, now account for one-third of all immigration to the United States.

11. Hispanics, the largest U.S. minority, include many ethnicities sharing a Spanish heritage. Mexican Americans, the largest Hispanic minority, are concentrated in the Southwest. Cubans, concentrated in Miami, are the most affluent Hispanic category; Puerto Ricans, one-third of whom live in New York, are the poorest.

12. White ethnics are non-WASPs of European ancestry. Although they made gains during the twentieth century, many white ethnics still struggle for economic security.

13. Immigration has increased in recent years. No longer primarily from Europe, most immigrants now arrive from Latin America and Asia.

KEY CONCEPTS

race (p. 353) a socially constructed category composed of people who share biologically transmitted traits that members of a society consider important

ethnicity (p. 355) a shared cultural heritage

minority (p. 356) any category of people distinguished by physical or cultural difference that a society sets apart and subordinates

prejudice (p. 357) a rigid and unfair generalization about an entire category of people

stereotype (p. 357) an exaggerated description applied to every person in some category

racism (p. 360) the belief that one racial category is innately superior or inferior to another

scapegoat (p. 360) a person or category of people, typically with little power, whom people unfairly blame for their own troubles

discrimination (p. 362) treating various categories of people unequally

institutional prejudice and discrimination (p. 362) bias inherent in the operation of society's institutions

pluralism (p. 363) a state in which people of all races and ethnicities are distinct but have social parity

assimilation (p. 363) the process by which minorities gradually adopt patterns of the dominant culture

miscegenation (p. 364) biological reproduction by partners of different racial categories

segregation (p. 364) the physical and social separation of categories of people

genocide (p. 364) the systematic killing of one category of people by another

CRITICAL-THINKING QUESTIONS

1. What is the difference between race and ethnicity? What does it mean to say that race (and also ethnicity) is socially constructed?

2. Do you think all people of color, even if they are rich, should be considered minorities? Why or why not?

3. Many historians claim that the history of the United States is the history of immigrants. Do you agree with this statement? Is the statement as true today as it was in the past?

4. Many people wrongly assume that only white people display prejudice and discrimination. To what extent do minorities exhibit prejudice and discrimination against whites? Against other minorities?

APPLICATIONS AND EXERCISES

1. Does your college or university take account of race and ethnicity in its admissions policies? Ask to speak with an admissions officer to see what you can learn about your school's policies and the reasons for them. Ask whether there is a "legacy" policy that favors applicants with a parent who attended the school.

2. Give several of your friends or family members a quick quiz, asking them what share of the U.S. population is white, Hispanic, African American, and Asian American (see Table 14–1). If they are like most people, they will exaggerate the share of all minorities and understate the white proportion (Labovitz, 1996). What do you make of the results?

3. There are probably immigrants on your campus or in your local community. Have you ever thought about asking them to tell you about their homeland and their experiences since arriving in the United States? Most people would be pleased to be asked, and you can learn a great deal.

4. Packaged in the back of this new textbook is an interactive CD-ROM that offers a variety of video and interactive review materials intended to help you better understand the material covered in this chapter. For this chapter, the CD-ROM contains a relevant clip from *ABC News*, an author's tip video, interactive map animations, an interactive time line, and flashcards with audio pronunciations of the more difficult words.

 ## SITES TO SEE

http://www.prenhall.com/macionis

Visit the interactive Companion Website™ that accompanies this text. Begin by clicking on the cover of your book. You will find a chapter-by-chapter study guide, practice tests, suggested Web links, and links to other relevant material.

http:www.naacp.org
http://www.adl.org/adl.asp

These two organizations—the National Association for the Advancement of Colored People and the Anti-Defamation League—are concerned with combating prejudice and discrimination and advancing the social standing of minorities

in the United States. Determine each organization's strategies and goals.

http://w3.access.gpo.gov/eop/ca/index.html

This worthwhile data site, operated by the Council of Economic Advisors, provides an assessment of the social and economic well-being of various racial and ethnic categories of this country's population.

http://www.collegeboard.com/repository/minorityhig_3948.pdf

Read the report of the College Board's National Task Force on Minority High Achievement, which analyzes racial and ethnic differences in higher education.

 ## INVESTIGATE WITH RESEARCH NAVIGATOR™

Follow the instructions on page 24 of this text to access the features of **Research Navigator**™. Once at the Web site, enter your Login Name and Password. Then, to use the **Content Select**™ database, enter keywords such as "race," "ethnicity," and "racial profiling," and the search engine will

supply relevant and recent scholarly and popular press publications. Use the *New York Times* **Search-by-Subject Archive** to find recent news articles related to sociology and the **Link Library** feature to find relevant Web links organized by the key terms associated with this chapter.

AGING AND THE ELDERLY

P. J. CROOK (B. 1945, ENGLISH)

Sunday (Reading in Bed)

Twentieth Century, acrylic on canvas and wood, 132.1 × 101.6 cm.
© Courtesy of Theo Waddington Fine Art/Private Collectiion/The Bridgeman Art Library.

THE SIGNATURE CHIME OF Keith Richards's guitar beginning the song "Street Fighting Man" brought the crowd to life. The screaming grew louder as Mick Jagger—his cocky strut and edgy sneer as energetic as ever—took center stage. Amid flashing lights and deafening screams, "The World's Greatest Rock and Roll Band" began to tear into a two-hour set, opening with a song that Jagger and Richards had written before many of the people attending the concert were born.

Does it seem strange that two men now in their sixties are still banging out rock and roll? Certainly, the 2002–2003 tour's huge audiences don't think so. In fact, most of the most popular concert tours in recent years—including those of Paul McCartney, Tina Turner, Brian Wilson, Elton John, and Crosby, Stills, Nash, and Young—feature superstars who are old enough to qualify for senior citizen discounts (Campbell, 2002; Margolis, 2002).

From a sociological perspective, the extended careers of aging rock stars reveal that the line between "young" and "old" is today less clear than ever. Indeed, the United States is experiencing a revolution in aging as people live longer and the "baby boomers"—that large segment of U.S. women and men born between 1945 and 1960—move closer to what has traditionally been called "old age." This chapter explores this aging revolution, the changing meaning that people attach to "growing old," and the various challenges and transitions linked to aging.

THE GRAYING OF THE UNITED STATES

A quiet but powerful revolution is reshaping the United States. In 1900, the United States was a young nation with half the population under age twenty-three; just 4 percent had reached sixty-five. But the elderly population—that is, women and men aged sixty-five or older—increased tenfold during the last century. By 2000, the number of seniors exceeded 35 million. Seniors already outnumbered

teenagers, and as shown in Figure 15–1 on page 384, they accounted for 12.4 percent of the entire population. By 2030, the number of seniors will double to some 70 million, and almost half the country's people will be over forty (Himes, 2001; U.S. Census Bureau, 2001).

Global Map 15–1 on page 385 shows that it is in the rich nations, such as the United States, that the share of elderly people is increasing most rapidly. Typically, two factors combine to drive up the share of the population that is elderly: low birth rates (meaning that there are fewer children) and increasing longevity (meaning that people typically live longer).

In the United States, the ranks of the elderly will swell even more rapidly as the first of the baby boomers—now some 75 million strong—reach age sixty-five in 2010. There are serious questions about the ability of the current Social Security system to meet the needs of so many older people (Gendell, 2002).

 Find information on aging and older people at the National Institute on Aging Web site: http://www.nia.nih.gov/

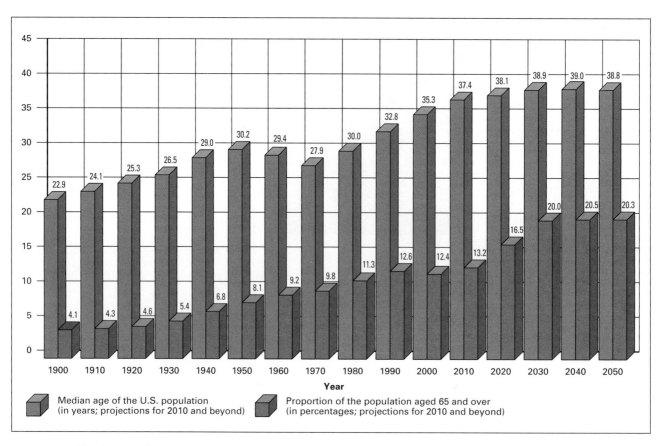

FIGURE 15–1 The Graying of U.S. Society

Source: U.S. Census Bureau (2000, 2001).

THE BIRTH RATE: GOING DOWN

The first factor contributing to the graying of our society is a declining birth rate. The birth rate in the United States has been falling for more than a century. One reason is that, as societies industrialize, children are more likely to survive into adulthood, so couples bear fewer children. Another reason is that, although children are an economic asset to farming families, they are an economic liability to families in industrial societies. In other words, children no longer contribute to their family's financial well-being but instead are a major expense.

Also, as more and more women work outside the home for income, they want to have fewer children. Advances in birth control technology during the last century have provided the means to avoid unwanted births.

LIFE EXPECTANCY: GOING UP

The second factor contributing to the graying of U.S. society is an increase in life expectancy. It surprises many people to learn that, in 1900, a typical female born in the United States lived just forty-eight years, and a male, forty-six years. By contrast, females born in 2002 can look forward to living 79.8 years, while males can expect to live 74.4 years (U.S. National Center for Health Statistics, 2003).

A longer life span is one consequence of the Industrial Revolution. Greater material wealth and advances in medicine raise living standards; people benefit from better housing and nutrition and live longer. At the same time, medical advances have virtually eliminated infectious diseases—such as smallpox, diphtheria, and measles—that killed many infants and children a century ago. More recent medical strides

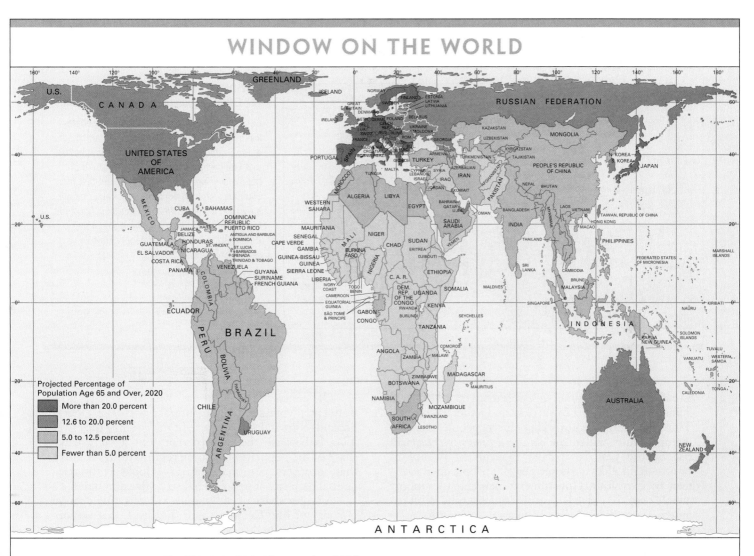

GLOBAL MAP 15–1 The Elderly in Global Perspective, 2020

Here we see projections of the share of population aged sixty-five and older in the year 2020, one generation from now. What relationship do you see between a country's income level and the size of its elderly population?

Source: U.S. Census Bureau (2000).

help us fend off cancer and heart disease, which claim most of the U.S. population, but now later in life.

As life becomes longer, the oldest segment of the U.S. population—people over eighty-five—is increasing rapidly and is already thirty-five times greater than in 1900. These men and women now number 4.2 million (about 1.5 percent of the total population). Projections put their number at 19 million (about 5 percent of the total) by the year 2050 (Kaufman, 1990; Harbert & Ginsberg, 1991; U.S. Census Bureau, 2001).

We can only begin to imagine how this major increase in the elderly population will change our society. As the number of older people retiring from the labor force goes up, the proportion of nonworking adults—

SEEING OURSELVES

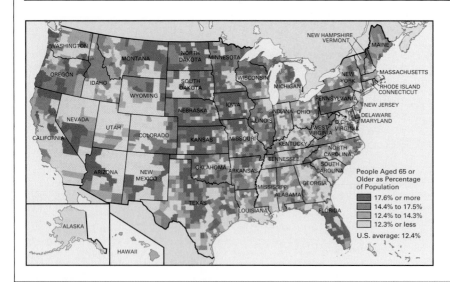

NATIONAL MAP 15–1
The Elderly Population of the United States

Common sense suggests that elderly people live in the Sunbelt, savoring the warmer climate of the South and Southwest. Although it is true that Florida has a disproportionate share of people over age sixty-five, it turns out that most counties with high percentages of older people are in the Midwest. What do you think accounts for this pattern? Hint: Which regions of the United States do *younger* people leave in search of jobs?

Source: U.S. Census Bureau (2001).

People Aged 65 or
Older as Percentage
of Population
- 17.6% or more
- 14.4% to 17.5%
- 12.4% to 14.3%
- 12.3% or less

U.S. average: 12.4%

already about ten times greater than in 1900—will demand ever more health care and other resources. Thus, the ratio of nonworking elderly people to working-age adults, called the *old-age dependency ratio*, will rise by the year 2050 from the current twenty to twenty-eight elderly people per 100 people aged eighteen to sixty-four. Government spending to support people over sixty-five is already rising sharply. With tomorrow's swelling elderly population looking for support from a smaller share of younger workers, what security can today's young people expect in their old age? (Treas, 1995; Edmondson, 1996; Riche, 2000).

AN AGING SOCIETY: CULTURAL CHANGE

As the number of people and the share of the population over sixty-five push upward, cultural patterns, too, are changing. Through much of the twentieth century, the young rarely mingled with the old, so that most people know little about old age. But as this country's elderly population steadily increases, age segregation will decline. Younger people will see more seniors at shopping malls, in movie theaters, at sporting events, and on the highways. Moreover, the design of buildings—from homes to stores to colleges—is likely to change to ease access for older people.

Of course, tomorrow as well as today, how frequently younger people interact with the elderly depends a great deal on where in the country they live. This is because the elderly represent a far greater share of the population in some regions of the country than in others. National Map 15–1 looks at the residential patterns of people aged sixty-five and older.

A larger share of old people will certainly change our way of life. Keep in mind, however, that seniors are quite socially diverse. Being "elderly" is a category open to everyone, if we are lucky enough to live that long. Elders in the United States represent not just men and women but all cultures, classes, races, and ethnic backgrounds.

THE "YOUNG OLD" AND THE "OLD OLD"

Analysts sometimes distinguish two cohorts of the elderly, which have roughly equal size (Himes, 2001). The younger elderly are between sixty-five and seventy-five and typically live independently with good health and financial security; they are likely to be living as couples. The older elderly are past age seventy-five, and are more likely to have health and money problems and to be dependent on others. Because of their greater longevity, women outnumber men in the elderly population, an imbalance that grows greater with advancing age. Among the "oldest old," those over age eighty-five, about 60 percent are women.

GROWING OLD: BIOLOGY AND CULTURE

Studying the graying of the United States is the focus of **gerontology** (derived from the Greek word *geron*, meaning "an old person"), *the study of aging and the elderly.* Gerontologists—who work within many disciplines, including medicine, psychology, and sociology—investigate not only how people change as they grow old, but also the different ways societies around the world define old age.

BIOLOGICAL CHANGES

Aging consists of gradual, ongoing changes in the body. But how individuals experience life's transitions—whether we welcome our maturity or complain about physical decline—depends largely on how a cultural system defines the various stages of life. In general, U.S. culture takes a positive view of biological changes that occur early in life. Through childhood and adolescence, people look forward to expanding opportunities and responsibilities.

But our youth-oriented culture takes a dimmer view of the biological changes that develop later in life. Few people receive congratulations for getting old, at least not until they reach eighty-five or ninety. Rather, we commiserate with friends as they turn forty, fifty, and sixty and make jokes to avoid facing up to the fact that advancing age puts people, sooner or later, on a slippery slope of physical and mental decline. We assume, in short, that by age fifty or sixty, people stop growing *up* and begin growing *down.*

Growing old brings on predictable changes: gray hair, wrinkles, loss of height and weight, and an overall decline in strength and vitality. After age fifty, bones become more brittle, so that injuries take longer to heal, and the odds of contracting chronic illnesses (such as arthritis and diabetes) and life-threatening conditions (like heart disease and cancer) rise steadily. The sensory abilities—taste, sight, touch, smell, and especially hearing—become less keen with age (Treas, 1995; Metz & Miner, 1998).

Though health becomes more fragile with advancing age, the vast majority of older people are not disabled by their physical condition. Only about one in ten seniors reports trouble walking, and fewer than one in twenty needs intensive care in a hospital or nursing home. No more than 1 percent of the elderly are bedridden. Overall, only 17 percent of people over age sixty-five characterize their health as "fair" or "poor"; 73 percent consider their overall condition "good" or "excellent." In fact, the share of seniors reporting good or excellent health is going up (*Population Today*, 1997; U.S. National Center for Health Statistics, 2003).

However, patterns of well-being vary greatly within the elderly population. More health problems beset those over age seventy-five. Moreover, because women typically live longer than men, they suffer more from chronic disabilities like arthritis. In addition, well-to-do people live and work in safer and more healthful environments and can afford better medical care. About 78 percent of elderly people with incomes exceeding $35,000 assess their own health as "excellent" or "good"; that figure drops below 55 percent among people with incomes under $20,000. Lower income and stress linked to prejudice and discrimination also explain why 60 percent of older African Americans assess their health in positive terms, compared to 75 percent of elderly white people (Feagin, 1997; U.S. National Center for Health Statistics, 2003).

PSYCHOLOGICAL CHANGES

Just as we tend to overstate the physical problems of old age, it is easy to exaggerate the psychological changes that accompany growing old. The conventional wisdom about intelligence over the life course can be summed up as "What goes up, must come down" (Baltes & Schaie, 1974).

If we operationalize intelligence to refer to skills like sensorimotor coordination—the ability to arrange objects to match a drawing—we do find a steady decline after midlife. The ability to learn new material and think quickly also declines, although not until around age seventy. But the ability to apply familiar ideas holds steady with advancing age, and the ability to engage in thoughtful reflection and spiritual growth actually increases (Baltes & Schaie, 1974; Schaie, 1980; Metz & Miner, 1998).

We all wonder if we will think or feel differently as we get older. Gerontologists report that, for better or worse, the answer is usually "no." The most common personality changes with advancing age are becoming less materialistic, more mellow in attitudes, and more thoughtful. Generally, therefore, two elderly people who were childhood friends would recognize in

The reality of growing old is as much a matter of culture as it is of biology. In the United States, being elderly often means being inactive; yet, in rural regions of Iraq and other more traditional societies, old people commonly continue many familiar and productive routines.

each other the same personality traits that brought them together as youngsters (Neugarten, 1971, 1972, 1977; Wolfe, 1994).

AGING AND CULTURE

November 1, approaching Kandy, Sri Lanka. Our little van struggles up the steep mountain incline. Breaks in the lush vegetation offer spectacular views that interrupt our conversation about growing old. "Then there are no old age homes in your country?" I ask. "In Colombo and other cities, I am sure," our driver responds, "but not many. We are not like you Americans." "And how is that?" I counter, stiffening a bit. His eyes remain fixed on the road: "We would not leave our fathers and mothers to live alone."

When do people grow old? How do younger people regard society's oldest members? How do elderly people view themselves? The answers to these questions vary from place to place, showing that, while aging is a biological process, it is also a matter of culture.

At one level, how long and well people live depend on a society's technology and standard of living. Through most of human history, as the English philosopher Thomas Hobbes (1588–1679) put it, people's lives were "nasty, brutish, and short" (although Hobbes himself made it to the ripe old age of ninety-one). In his day, most people married and had children

 For data and graphics on aging in global perspective, visit this MEDIA UN site: http://www.un.org/ esa/population/publications/ aging99/fa99.htm

while in their teens, became middle-aged in their twenties, and began to succumb to various illnesses in their thirties and forties. Thus, many greats of the past never reached what we would call old age at all: The English poet Keats died at age twenty-six; Mozart, the Austrian composer, died at thirty-five. Among famous writers, none of the three Brontë sisters lived to the end of their thirties; Edgar Allan Poe died at forty, Henry David Thoreau at forty-five, Oscar Wilde at forty-six, and Shakespeare at fifty-two.

About a century ago, rising living standards and advancing medical technology in the United States and Western Europe extended longevity to about age fifty. (As Global Map 15–2 shows, this is still the figure in many lower-income nations today.) Since then, increasing affluence in rich countries has added almost thirty more years to the average life span.

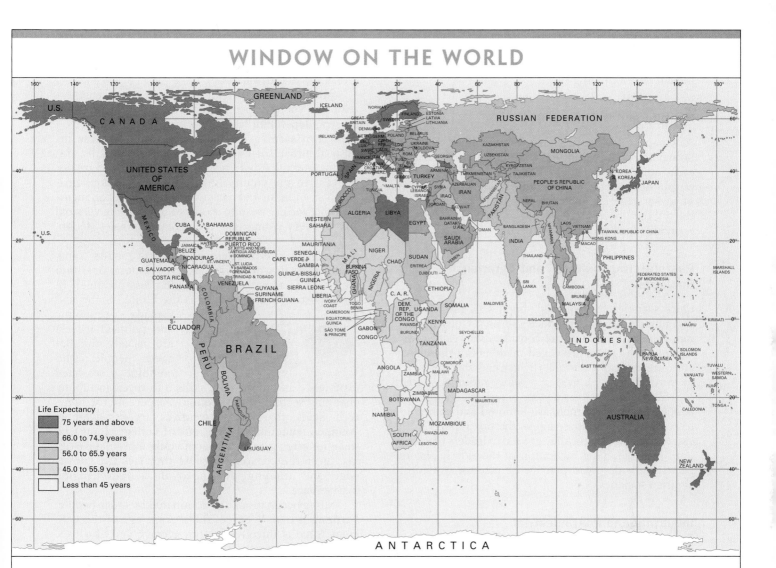

GLOBAL MAP 15–2 Life Expectancy in Global Perspective

Life expectancy shot upward over the course of the twentieth century in high-income countries, including Canada, the United States, Western Europe, Japan, and Australia. A newborn in the United States can now expect to live about seventy-seven years, and our life expectancy would be greater still were it not for the high risk of death among infants born into poverty. Because poverty is the rule in much of the world, lives are correspondingly shorter, especially in parts of Africa, where life expectancy may be less than forty years.

Source: Population Reference Bureau (2003).

Just as important as longevity is the value societies attach to their senior members. As Chapter 10 ("Social Stratification") explains, all societies distribute basic resources unequally. We now turn to the importance of age in this process.

AGE STRATIFICATION: A GLOBAL SURVEY

Like race, ethnicity, and gender, age is a basis for social ranking. **Age stratification,** then, is *the unequal distribution of wealth, power, and privilege among* *people at different stages of the life course.* As is true of the other dimensions of social hierarchy, age stratification varies according to a society's level of technological development.

Hunting and Gathering Societies

As Chapter 4 ("Society") explains, without the technology to produce a surplus of food, hunters and gatherers must be nomadic. Therefore, survival depends on physical strength and stamina. Thus, as members of these societies grow old (in this case, about age thirty), they become less active and are considered an economic burden (Sheehan, 1976).

Pastoral, Horticultural, and Agrarian Societies

Once societies control food supplies by raising crops and animals, they can produce a surplus. Consequently, individuals can accumulate considerable wealth over a lifetime. The most privileged members of these societies are typically the elderly, a trend that gives rise to **gerontocracy,** *a form of social organization in which the elderly have the most wealth, power, and prestige.* Old people, particularly men, are honored and sometimes feared by their families, and as the box reports in the case of the Sardinians, they are active leaders of society until they die. This veneration of the elderly also explains the widespread practice of ancestor worship in agrarian societies.

Industrial and Postindustrial Societies

We have noted that industrialization pushes living standards upward and advances medical technology and thus increases human life expectancy. But although industrialization adds to the *quantity* of life, it can harm the *quality* of life for old people. Contrary to the practice in traditional societies, industrial societies give little power and prestige to the elderly. The reason is that, with industrialization, the prime source of wealth shifts from land (typically controlled by the oldest members of society) to businesses and other goods (often owned and managed by younger people). Consider that, in low-income nations, the share of people over age sixty-five in the labor force is 76 percent of men and 44 percent of women. In high-income countries these percentages drop dramatically to 23 percent of men and 16 percent of women. These

figures help explain why the peak earning years among U.S. workers, on average, occur around age fifty; after that, earnings decline (UN Population Division, 1999; U.S. Census Bureau, 2000).

Modern living also physically separates the generations as younger people move away to pursue their careers, depending less on their parents and more on their own earning power. Furthermore, because industrial, urban societies change rapidly, the skills, traditions, and life experiences that served the old are not relevant to the young. Finally, the tremendous productivity of industrial nations means that not all members of a society need to work, so most of the very old and the very young play nonproductive roles (Cohn, 1982).

The long-term effect of all these factors transforms *elders* (a word with positive connotations) into *the elderly* (a term commanding far less prestige). In postindustrial societies such as the United States and

 A U.S. Department of Agriculture report on the effects of aging in rural communities is found at http://www.ers.usda.gov/publications/rdrr90/rdrr90.pdf

Canada, economic and political leaders are usually middle-aged people who combine seasoned experience and up-to-date skills. However, in rapidly changing sectors of the economy, especially the high-tech fields, many key executives are considerably younger, sometimes barely out of college. Industrial societies often give older people only marginal participation in the economy because they lack the knowledge and training demanded in a fast-changing marketplace.

Some occupations are dominated by older people. Farming is one: Whereas the average age of the U.S. labor force is thirty-eight, the average age of a U.S. farmer is fifty-seven, and 35 percent of farmers are over the age of sixty-five. Certainly some older men and women remain at the helm of corporations and other businesses; more commonly, however, older people predominate only in traditional occupations (working as farmers, barbers, tailors, and shop clerks) and in jobs that involve minimal activity (as night security guards, for instance) (Kaufman & Spilerman, 1982; Yudelman & Kealy, 2000).

Japan: An Exceptional Case

Throughout the last century, Japan stood out as an exception to the rule. Japan has about the same share of seniors as the United States, but its more traditional culture values older people. Most aged people in Japan live with an adult daughter or son, and they

Growing (Very) Old: A Report from Sardinia

Giovanni Frau sits quietly, shaded from the afternoon sun, in the piazza (village square) of Orroli, a small town on the Mediterranean island of Sardinia, lying to the east of Italy. Frau attracts little attention from the people passing by, but he is something of a celebrity: At the age of 111, he may well be the oldest person alive.

Frau is not the only one growing very old on Sardinia. His friend Vincenza Orgiana, who lives down the road, just turned 106, and during the past year, five others in the town have celebrated their 100th birthdays. All this in a town of only 2,748 people. In fact, records indicate that 220 Sardinians are at least 100 years old, twice the number found in nearby countries with much larger populations.

Several places in the world have an unusual number of people who have lived remarkably long lives. Sardinia is one, the Caucasus region to the north is another, as is the Japanese island of Okinawa to the east.

How do we explain such longevity? The answer certainly is not advanced medical technology, so important to people in the United States; many residents of Orroli have never seen a physician or entered a hospital. One theory is biological: All these regions are isolated, with a limited genetic mix that may play a part in long life. But the most important factor is probably cultural, including diet and patterns of physical activity. Rural Sardinians eat none of the fatty and highly processed foods that are so popular in the United States. They eat great amounts of local fruits and homegrown vegetables, consume almost no

sugar, and enjoy a small daily ration of local wine. (Sardinians often raise their glasses and say, "May you live to be 100.") Without television or other mass media, and little money for fancy appliances or power equipment, villagers of all ages lead active lives based on regular physical work.

Perhaps most important, a strong sense of tradition and community gives everyone a clear sense of purpose and a strong sense of belonging. The elderly—the word "elders" is more accurate—are at the center of social life, in marked contrast to our own society's practice of pushing old people to the margins. Elders are indispensable guardians of a way of life and preside at all ceremonial occasions, where they transmit their knowledge to the young. Elders feel needed because, in their own minds and everyone else's, they are.

Sources: Based on Israely (2002) and also Benet (1971) and Specter (1998).

play a significant role in family life. Elderly men in Japan are also more likely than their U.S. counterparts to stay in the labor force, and in many Japanese corporations, the oldest employees enjoy the greatest respect. But even Japan has steadily become more like other industrial nations, where growing old means giving up some measure of social importance. Further, the prolonged economic downturn has left Japanese families less able to care for their older members, a circumstance that may further erode the traditional importance of elders (Palmore, 1982; Yates, 1986; Ogawa & Retherford, 1997).

TRANSITIONS AND CHALLENGES OF AGING

We confront change at each stage of life. Old age has its rewards; but of all stages of the life course, it presents the greatest challenges.

Physical decline in old age is less serious than most younger people think. But even so, older people endure more pain, become resigned to limiting their activities, adjust to greater dependence on others, lose dear friends and relatives, and face up to their own mortality. Moreover, because our culture places such a high value on youthfulness, aging in the United States often means

TABLE 15-1 Living Arrangements of the Elderly, 2000*		
	Men	**Women**
Living alone	17.0%	39.6%
Living with spouse	72.6	41.3
Living with other relatives or nonrelatives	10.4	19.1

*In 2000, the percentage of elderly people living in a nursing home was 4.5 percent. These elders represented men and women who fell within each of the above categories.

Source: U.S. Census Bureau (2000, 2001).

added fear and self-doubt (Hamel, 1990). As one retired psychologist commented about old age, "Don't let the current hype about the joys of retirement fool you. They are not the best of times. It's just that the alternative is even worse" (Rubenstein, 1991:13).

FINDING MEANING

Recall from Chapter 5 ("Socialization") Erik Erikson's (1963, 1980) theory that elderly people must resolve a tension of "integrity versus despair." No matter how much they still may be learning and achieving, older people recognize that their lives are nearing an end. Thus, the elderly spend more time reflecting on their past, including disappointments as well as accomplishments. Integrity, to Erikson, means assessing one's life realistically. Without such honesty, this stage of life may turn into a time of despair—a dead end with little positive meaning.

In a classic study of people in their seventies, Bernice Neugarten (1971) found that some people cope with growing older better than others. Worst off are those who fail to come to terms with aging; they develop *disintegrated and disorganized personalities* marked by despair. Many of these people end up as passive residents of hospitals or nursing homes.

Slightly better off are those people with *passive-dependent personalities*. They have little confidence in their abilities to cope with daily events, sometimes seeking help even if they do not actually need it. Always in danger of social withdrawal, their level of life satisfaction is relatively low.

A third category have *defended personalities*, living independently but fearful of aging. They try to shield themselves from the reality of old age by fighting to stay youthful and physically fit. While it is good to be

concerned about health, setting unrealistic standards breeds stress and disappointment.

Most of Neugarten's subjects, however, displayed what she termed *integrated personalities:* These are the people who cope well with the challenges of growing old. As Neugarten sees it, the key to successful aging lies in maintaining one's dignity and self-confidence and accepting the inevitability of advancing age.

SOCIAL ISOLATION

Being alone can cause anxiety at any age, but isolation is most common among elderly people. Retirement closes off one source of social interaction, physical problems may limit mobility, and negative stereotypes of the elderly as "over the hill" may discourage younger people from close social contact with them.

The greatest cause of social isolation, however, is the death of significant others. Few experiences affect people as profoundly as the death of a spouse. One study found that almost three-fourths of widows and widowers cited loneliness as their most serious problem (Lund, 1989). In such cases, people must rebuild their lives in the glaring absence of others with whom, in many cases, they spent most of their adult lives.

The problem of social isolation falls more heavily on women because they typically outlive their husbands. Table 15–1 shows that three-fourths of men aged sixty-five and over live with spouses, whereas only four in ten elderly women do. Moreover, 40 percent of older women (especially the "older elderly") live alone, compared to 17 percent of older men (U.S. Census Bureau, 2001).

For most older people, family members are the major source of social support. The majority of older people have at least one adult child living no more than ten miles away. About half of these nearby children visit their parents at least once a week, although much research confirms that daughters are more likely than sons to visit regularly (Stone, Cafferata, & Sangl, 1987; Lin & Rogerson, 1994; Rimer, 1998).

RETIREMENT

Work not only provides us with earnings but is also an important part of our personal identity. Thus, retirement means not only a reduction in income but also reduced social prestige and perhaps some loss of purpose in life.

Some organizations help ease this transition. Colleges and universities, for example, confer the title "professor emeritus" (from the Latin, meaning "fully earned") on retired faculty members, many of whom are permitted to keep library privileges, a parking space, and an e-mail account. Indeed, these highly experienced faculty can be a valuable resource not only to students but to younger professors as well (Parini, 2001).

Because seniors are socially diverse, there is no single formula for successful retirement. Part-time work keeps many people entering old age, busy as well as providing some extra cash. Grandparenting is another source of pleasure for older people. Volunteer work is another path to rewarding activity, especially for those who have saved enough so that they do not have to work—one reason that volunteerism is increasing more among seniors than in any other age category (Mergenhagen, 1996b; Gardyn, 2000; Savishinsky, 2000; Shapiro, 2001).

Although retirement is a familiar idea, the concept emerged only within the last century in high-income countries. High-income societies are so productive that not everyone needs to work; in addition, advanced technology places a premium on up-to-date skills. Therefore, retirement emerges as a strategy to permit younger workers—presumably, those with the most current knowledge and training—to predominate in the labor force. Fifty years ago, most companies in the United States even had a mandatory retirement age, typically between sixty-five and seventy (although Congress enacted laws phasing out such policies in the 1970s until, by 1987, almost none existed). Then, too, the introduction of private and public pension programs in high-income countries makes it financially possible for older people to retire, whereas in poor societies, most people work until they can work no more.

At the same time, retirement patterns reflect the health of the national economy. Generally speaking, when economic times are good, people save more and think about retiring early. Such has been the case in the United States: As the economy expanded during the 1980s and 1990s, more people retired earlier, causing the median retirement age to fall from sixty-eight in 1950 to sixty-three by 2000. The economic downturn that began in 2000 has had the opposite effect: Today we hear talk about "staged retirement," in which people continue working well past the age of sixty-five, reducing their hours as they build financial security (Gendall, 2001; Kadlec, 2002). And some retired people, faced with declining value of their investments, are realizing that to make ends meet, they have to go back to work. The box on page 394 takes a closer look.

Women and men experience stages of the life course in different ways. Most men, for example, pass through old age with the support of a partner. Women, who typically outlive men, endure much of their old age alone.

AGING AND POVERTY

By the time they reach sixty-five, most people have paid off their home mortgages and their children's college expenses. But now medical care, household help, and home utility bills typically go up. At the same time, retirement often means a significant decline in income. Even with recent economic setbacks, today's seniors are more affluent than ever before, with a median net worth of about $160,000 in 2000. Most of this amount is in the form of home equity, however, and many lack enough savings or pension benefits to be self-supporting (Himes, 2001). Social Security is the major source of income for most people over sixty-five. Not

APPLYING SOCIOLOGY

Back to Work! When Will We Get to Retire?

Old age was looking like the "golden years" for sixty-year-old Martha Perry. She had worked hard for decades, and it had paid off. The sale of her small business, added to years of regular savings, netted her a total of about $1 million. With additional income from Social Security, Perry figured she was set for the rest of her life. She looked forward to playing golf, enjoying an active social life, and traveling around the world.

That was before the stock market tumble that began in 2000. Two years later, her accountant gave her some bad news: Her nest egg had lost almost half its value. With barely half the income she expected—only about $16,000 a year—Perry's travel plans have been put on hold. "I'm going to have to look for part-time work," she says, shaking her head. "But something tells me it's going to end up being full-time work."

The recent recession has hit everyone hard, but older people who rely on investment income have suffered more than most. Many have seen their retirement vanish as quickly as the money in their 401(k) investment portfolios. Like millions of others, Martha Perry is reading the want ads.

This trend helps explain why the share of older people in the labor force has changed direction and is now going up. Certainly, some seniors are happy to continue their careers, and others enjoy working part time. But in the past, many did so out of choice, enjoying their jobs but knowing they could retire whenever they wanted to. Now people fear they no longer have a choice. Worse, they wonder whether they will ever be able to step out of the labor force. For those who do not like the jobs they have, of course, the future will be far less happy.

All economic downturns come to an end. But analysts caution that it is unlikely investment gains will return to the double-digit levels of the 1990s anytime soon. The bottom line: less talk about "early retirement" and more older people in the work force.

Source: Kadlec (2002).

surprisingly, then, the risk of poverty rises after midlife, as shown in Figure 15–2.

The rate of poverty among the elderly fell sharply from about 35 percent in 1960 to 10.1 percent in 2001—below the 11.7 percent rate for the entire population. Moreover, since about 1980, seniors have posted a 32 percent increase in average income (in constant dollars), whereas the income of people under thirty-five has increased by only 15 percent (U.S. Census Bureau, 2002).

Several factors have boosted the financial strength of seniors. Better health now allows people who want to work to stay in the labor force, employer pension programs are more generous, and more of today's couples earn double incomes. Government policy, too, has played a part, with programs benefiting the elderly (including Social Security) amounting to almost half of all government spending, even as spending on children has remained flat.

But disadvantages associated with race and ethnicity persist in old age. In 2001, the poverty rate among elderly Hispanics (21.8 percent) and African Americans (21.9 percent) was two to three times higher than the rate for elderly, non-Hispanic whites (8.1 percent) (U.S. Census Bureau, 2002).

Gender also shapes the lives of people as they age. Among full-time workers, women over sixty-five had median earnings of $34,159 in 2001, compared to $47,985 for men over sixty-five. A quick calculation shows that these older full-time working women earned just 71 percent as much as comparable men; thus, the income gap linked to gender is greater among older than among younger people (recall that *all* working women earn 76 percent as much as *all* working men). This is because older women typically have much less schooling than men their age, so they hold lower-paying jobs.

But because most elderly people have retired from the labor force, a more realistic financial assessment must take account of all seniors, both those who are working and those who are not. From this point of view, median individual income is far lower: $11,313 for women, which is 57 percent of the $19,688 earned by men (U.S. Census Bureau, 2002). In light of these low averages, it is easy to understand why seniors are concerned about the costs of health care and prescription drugs, which are rising fast and may double by 2010 (Fetto, 2003).

In the United States, then, although the elderly are faring better than ever, growing old (especially for women and other minorities) still raises the risk of poverty. One study found that poor elderly households typically spend three-fourths of their income on basic necessities, which means that these people are just getting by (Koelln, Rubin, & Picard, 1995).

Note, too, that poverty among the elderly is often hidden from view. Because of personal pride and a desire to stay independent, many elderly people conceal financial problems even from their own families. People who have supported their children for years find it difficult to admit that they can no longer provide for themselves.

CAREGIVING[1]

In an aging society, the need for caregiving is bound to increase. **Caregiving** refers to *informal and unpaid care provided to a dependent person by family members, other relatives, or friends.* Although parents provide caregiving to children, the term is more often applied to the needs of elderly men and women. Indeed, today's middle-aged adults are called the "sandwich generation" because many will spend as much time caring for their aging parents as for their own children.

Who Are the Caregivers?

Surveys show that 80 percent of caregiving to elders is provided by family members, most from one person. Most caregivers are nearby, typically living only minutes away from the older person. In addition, 75 percent of all caregiving is provided by women, most often daughters and, next, wives. The gender norm is so strong that daughters-in-law are more likely than sons to care for an aging parent (Himes, 2001).

About two-thirds of caregivers are married, and one-third are also responsible for young children. When we add the fact that half of all caregivers also have a part- or full-time job, it is clear that caregiving is a responsibility over and above what most people already consider a full day's work. Half of all primary caregivers spend more than twenty hours per week providing elder care.

[1]This section is based on Lund (1993), as well as helpful personal communication.

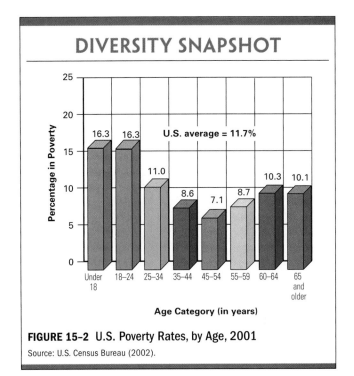

DIVERSITY SNAPSHOT

FIGURE 15–2 U.S. Poverty Rates, by Age, 2001
Source: U.S. Census Bureau (2002).

Elder Abuse

Abuse of older people takes many forms, from passive neglect to active torment; it includes verbal, emotional, financial, and physical harm. Research suggests that 1 million elderly people (3 percent) suffer serious maltreatment each year, and three times as many (about 10 percent) suffer abuse at some point. Like other forms of family violence, abuse of the elderly often goes unreported because the victims are reluctant to talk about their plight (Clark, 1986; Pillemer, 1988; Holmstrom, 1994; Thompson, 1997, 1998).

Many caregivers contend with fatigue, emotional distress, and guilt over not being able to do more. Abuse is most likely to occur if the caregiver not only finds the work difficult but also (1) works full time, (2) cares for young children, (3) is poor, (4) feels little affection for the older person, (5) finds the elderly person very difficult, and (6) gets no support or help from others.

But the relatively small share of cases involving abuse should not overshadow the positive side of caregiving. Helping another person is a selfless act of human kindness that affirms the best in us and provides a source of personal enrichment and satisfaction (Lund, 1993).

AGEISM

In earlier chapters, we explained how ideology—including racism and sexism—serves to justify the social disadvantages of minorities. Sociologists use the parallel term **ageism** for *prejudice and discrimination against older people.* Elderly people are the primary targets of ageism, although middle-aged people can suffer as well, most seriously in the workplace where they find many employers prefer to hire younger workers (Kelley-Moore, 2002).

Like racism and sexism, ageism can be blatant (as when a college decides not to hire a sixty-year-old professor because of her age) or subtle (as when a nurse speaks to elderly patients in a condescending tone, as if they were children). Also like racism and sexism, ageism builds physical traits into stereotypes. In the case of the elderly, people consider gray hair, wrinkled skin, and stooped posture signs of personal incompetence. Negative stereotypes portray the aged as helpless, confused, resistant to change, and generally unhappy. Even sentimental views of sweet little old ladies and eccentric old gentlemen are stereotypes that gloss over individuality and ignore years of experience and accomplishment (Butler, 1975; Cohen, 2001).

Sometimes, ageism contains a kernel of truth. Statistically speaking, old people are more likely than young people to be mentally and physically impaired. But we slip into ageism when we make unwarranted generalizations about an entire category of people, most of whom do not conform to the stereotypes.

Betty Friedan (1993), a pioneer of today's feminist movement, believes ageism is deeply rooted in our culture. Friedan points out that few elderly people appear in the mass media; only a small percentage of television shows, for example, include main characters over sixty. More generally, when most of us think about older people, it is often in negative terms: This older man *lacks* a job, that older woman has *lost* her vitality, and seniors *look back* to their youth. In short, says Friedan, we often treat being old as if it were a disease—marked by decline and deterioration—for which there is no cure.

Nevertheless, Friedan believes that older women and men in the United States are discovering that in fact they have more to contribute than others give them credit for. Advising small business owners, designing housing for the poor, teaching children to read—there are countless ways in which older people can enhance their own lives and at the same time help others.

THE ELDERLY: A MINORITY?

There is little doubt that elderly people in the United States face social disadvantages. Does that mean that the elderly are a minority in the same way as, say, African Americans or women?

The elderly appear to meet the definition of a minority because they have a clear social identity based on their age, and they are subject to prejudice and discrimination. But Gordon Streib (1968) counters that we should not think of elderly people as a minority for several reasons. First, minority status is usually both permanent and exclusive. That is, a person is an African American or a woman *for life* and cannot become part of the dominant category of whites or men. But being elderly is an *open* status because people are elderly for only part of their lives, and everyone who has the good fortune to live long enough grows old.

 Find data on the well-being of the U.S. elderly population at http://www.agingstats.gov

Moreover, whereas elderly people are disadvantaged economically, it is also true that the seniors at risk of being poor fall into categories of people—women, African Americans, Hispanics—who are at higher risk of being poor throughout the life course. As Streib sees it, it is not so much that "the old grow poor" as that "the poor grow old."

Perhaps, then, old people are not a minority in the same sense as other categories. Instead, perhaps we should describe the elderly as a distinctive segment of our population that faces characteristic challenges. As we have explained, some challenges are brought on by physical decline. But others—including social isolation, adjustment to retirement, and risk of poverty, abuse, and ageism—are products of society.

We turn now to theoretical perspectives that offer insights into how society shapes the lives of the elderly.

THEORETICAL ANALYSIS OF AGING

Sociology's major theoretical paradigms shed light on the process of aging in the United States. We examine each in turn.

STRUCTURAL-FUNCTIONAL ANALYSIS: AGING AND DISENGAGEMENT

Drawing on the ideas of Talcott Parsons—an architect of the structural-functional paradigm—Elaine Cumming and William Henry (1961) lay the groundwork for this approach, explaining that aging threatens to disrupt society as physical decline and death take their toll. In response, society *disengages* the elderly—gradually transferring statuses and roles from the old to the young so that tasks are performed with minimal interruption.

Disengagement is thus a strategy that ensures the orderly operation of society by removing aging people from productive roles while they are still able to perform them. Disengagement has an added benefit in a rapidly changing society, since young workers typically bring the most up-to-date skills and training to their work. Formally, then, **disengagement theory** is *the idea that society enhances its orderly operation by disengaging people from positions of responsibility as they reach old age.*

Disengagement provides benefits to aging people as well. Although most sixty-year-olds in the United States wish to keep working, most begin to think about retirement and perhaps cut back a bit on their careers. Exactly when people begin to disengage from their careers, of course, depends on a number of factors, including health, enjoyment of the job, and the person's financial assets. Retiring is not the same as being inactive; some people begin a different kind of job, while others develop hobbies or engage in volunteer work. In general, though, people in their sixties start to think less about what they *have* been doing and begin to think more about what they *want* to do with the rest of their lives (Palmore, 1979b; Carstensen, 1995; Schultz & Heckhausen, 1996; Voltz, 2000).

Critical evaluation. Disengagement theory explains why rapidly changing high-income societies typically define their oldest members as socially marginal. But there are several limitations to this approach.

First, especially in recent years, many workers have found they cannot disengage from paid work because they do not have the financial resources to fall back on. Second, some elderly people—regardless of their financial circumstances—simply do not want to disengage from their earlier productive roles. Disengagement, after all, comes at a high personal price, including loss of friends and social prestige. Third, it is far from clear that the societal benefits of disengagement outweigh its social costs, which include the loss of human resources and the need to care for people who might otherwise be able to care for themselves. Indeed, as the numbers of elderly people swell, finding ways to help seniors remain independent is a high priority. Fourth, any rigid system of disengagement does not take account of the widely differing abilities of the elderly.

In the United States, it is common for businesses to offer a "senior discount" to people over sixty-five (or sometimes even fifty-five). What is the reason for this practice? Would you prefer a policy of offering discounts to single parents with children, a category of people at much higher risk of poverty?

SYMBOLIC-INTERACTION ANALYSIS: AGING AND ACTIVITY

A second approach draws heavily on the symbolic-interaction paradigm. **Activity theory** is *the idea that a high level of activity enhances personal satisfaction in old age.* Because we build social identity through various activities, disengagement is bound to reduce satisfaction and meaning in the lives of older people. What seniors need, in short, is not to be pushed out of roles but to have a wide range of productive or recreational possibilities. The importance of such options increases when we realize that a sixty-five-year-old today can look forward to about twenty more years of life (Robinson, Werner, & Godbey, 1997; Smart, 2001; Walsh, 2001).

Activity theory does not reject the notion of job disengagement; it simply says that people need to find new roles to replace those they leave behind. Research confirms that elderly people who maintain a high activity level derive the most satisfaction from their lives.

Activity theory also recognizes that the elderly are diverse, with highly variable interests, needs, and physical abilities. Therefore, the activities that people pursue and the pace at which they pursue them are always an individual matter (Neugarten, 1977; Palmore, 1979a; Moen, Dempster-McClain, & Williams, 1992).

Critical evaluation. Activity theory shifts the focus of analysis from the needs of society (as stated in disengagement theory) to the needs of the elderly themselves. It emphasizes the social diversity among elderly people, an important consideration in the formulation of any government policy.

A limitation of this approach, from a structural-functionalist point of view, is the tendency to exaggerate the well-being and competence of the elderly. Do we really want to depend on elderly people to perform crucial roles? From another perspective, activity theory falls short by ignoring the fact that many problems that older people face—such as poverty—have more to do with society than with themselves. We turn now to that point of view: social-conflict theory.

SOCIAL-CONFLICT ANALYSIS: AGING AND INEQUALITY

A social-conflict analysis is based on the idea that different age categories have different opportunities and different access to social resources that create a system of age stratification. By and large, middle-aged people in the United States enjoy the greatest power and the most opportunities and privileges, while the elderly and children have less power and prestige and a higher risk of poverty. Employers often replace more senior workers with younger men and women as a way of keeping down wages. As a result, older people become second-class citizens (Atchley, 1982; Phillipson, 1982).

To conflict theorists, an age-based hierarchy is inherent in an industrial-capitalist society. In line with Marxist thought, Steven Spitzer (1980) points out that a profit-oriented society devalues any category of people that is economically less productive. To the extent that older people do not work, our society labels them as mildly deviant.

Social-conflict analysis also draws attention to social diversity in the elderly population. Differences of class, race, ethnicity, and gender divide older people as they do everyone else. Thus, some seniors have far greater economic security, greater access to top-flight medical care, and more options for personal satisfaction

in old age than others. Likewise, elderly white people typically enjoy advantages denied to older minorities. And women—an increasing majority as people age—suffer the social and economic disadvantages of both sexism and ageism.

Critical evaluation. Social-conflict theory adds to our understanding of the aging process by underscoring age-based inequality and explaining how capitalism devalues elderly people who are less productive. But it is not capitalism that creates the lower social standing, according to critics; the real culprit is *industrialization*. Thus, the elderly are not better off under a socialist system, as a Marxist analysis implies. Furthermore, the notion that either industrialization or capitalism dooms the elderly to economic distress is challenged by the long-term rise in income and well-being among the U.S. elderly.

DEATH AND DYING

> To every thing there is a season,
> And a time for every matter under heaven:
> A time to be born and a time to die . . .

These well-known lines from the Bible's Book of Ecclesiastes state two basic truths about human existence: the fact of birth and the inevitability of death. Just as life varies throughout history and around the world, so does death have many faces. We conclude this chapter with a brief look at the changing character of death, the final stage in the process of growing old.

HISTORICAL PATTERNS OF DEATH

In the past, confronting death was commonplace. No one assumed that a newborn child would live for long, a fact that led many parents to delay naming children until they were one or two years old. For those fortunate enough to survive infancy, illness, accident, and natural catastrophe made life uncertain at best.

Sometimes, in fact, food shortages forced societies to protect the majority by sacrificing the least productive members. *Infanticide* is the killing of newborn infants, and *geronticide* is the killing of the elderly.

If death was routine, it was also readily accepted. Medieval Christianity assured believers, for example, that death fit into the divine plan for human existence. Here is how the historian Philippe Ariès describes Sir Lancelot, one of King Arthur's Knights of the Round Table, preparing for death when he thinks he is mortally wounded:

His gestures were fixed by old customs, ritual gestures which must be carried out when one is about to die. He removed his weapons and lay quietly upon the ground. . . . He spread his arms out, his body forming a cross . . . in such a way that his head faced east toward Jerusalem. (1974:7–8)

As societies gradually learned more about health and medicine, death became less of an everyday experience. Fewer children died at birth, and accidents and disease took a smaller toll among adults. People today view dying as extraordinary, except when it occurs among the very old or is associated with war or catastrophe. Consider that in 1900, about one-third of all deaths in the United States occurred before the age of five, and fully two-thirds before the age of fifty-five. Today, by contrast, 85 percent of our population die *after* the age of fifty-five. Death and old age are closely linked in our culture.

THE MODERN SEPARATION OF LIFE AND DEATH

Now removed from everyday experience, death somehow seems unnatural. If social conditions prepared our ancestors to accept death, modern society, with its youth culture and aggressive medical technology, fosters a desire for eternal youth and immortality. Death has become separated from life.

Death is also *physically* removed from everyday activities. The clearest evidence of this is that many of us have never seen a person die. While our ancestors typically died at home in the presence of family and friends, most deaths today occur in impersonal settings such as hospitals and nursing homes. Even in hospitals, dying patients occupy a special part of the building, and hospital morgues are located well out of sight of patients and visitors alike (Sudnow, 1967; Ariès, 1974; Lee, 2002).

ETHICAL ISSUES: CONFRONTING DEATH

Moral questions are more pressing than ever, now that technological advances give humans the power to prolong life and thereby draw a line separating life from death. We now grapple with how to use these new powers—or whether to use them at all.

When Does Death Occur?

Perhaps the most basic question is the most difficult: Exactly how do we define death? Common sense suggests that life ceases when breathing and heartbeat

In many traditional societies, people express great respect not only for elders but also for their ancestors. Dani villagers in New Guinea mummified the body of this elder in a sitting position so that they could continue to honor him and feel his presence in their daily lives.

stop. But the ability of medical personnel to resuscitate someone after a heart attack and artificially sustain breathing makes such definitions of death obsolete. Medical and legal experts in the United States continue to debate the meaning of death, but many now consider death an *irreversible* state involving no response to stimulation, no movement or breathing, no reflexes, and no indication of brain activity (Ladd, 1979; Wall, 1980; Jones, 1998).

The Right-to-Die Debate

Today, many aging people are less afraid of death than of the prospect of being kept alive at all costs. In other words, medical technology now threatens personal autonomy by letting doctors rather than the dying person decide when life is to end. In response, people who support a right-to-die movement now seek control over their deaths just as they seek control over their lives (Ogden, 2001).

GLOBAL SOCIOLOGY

Death on Demand: A Report from the Netherlands

Marcus Erich picked up the telephone and dialed his brother Arjen's number. In a quiet voice, thirty-two-year-old Marcus announced, "It's Friday at five o'clock." When the time came, Arjen was there, having driven to his brother's farmhouse an hour south of Amsterdam. They said their final good-byes. Soon afterward, Marcus's physician arrived. Marcus and the doctor spoke for a few moments, and then the doctor prepared a "cocktail" of barbiturates and other drugs. As Marcus drank the mixture, he made a face, joking, "Can't you make this sweeter?"

As the minutes passed, Marcus lay back and his eyes closed. But after half an hour, he was still breathing. At that point, according to their earlier agreement, the physician administered a lethal injection. Minutes later, Marcus's life came to an end.

Events like this take us to the heart of the belief that people have a "right to die." Marcus Erich was dying from the virus that causes AIDS. For five years, his body had been wasting away, and he was suffering greatly with no hope of recovery. He wanted his doctor to end his life.

The Netherlands, a small nation in northwestern Europe, has gone further than any other in the world in allowing mercy killing, or euthanasia. A 1981 Dutch law allows a physician to assist in a suicide if the following five conditions are met:

1. The patient must make a voluntary, well-considered, and repeated request to a doctor for help in dying.

2. The patient's suffering must be unbearable and without prospect of improvement.

3. The doctor and the patient must discuss alternatives.

4. The doctor must consult with at least one colleague who has access to the patient and the patient's medical records.

5. The assisted suicide must be performed in accordance with sound medical practice.

Official records indicate that doctors end 3,000 to 4,000 lives per year in the Netherlands. But because many cases are never reported, the actual number may well be twice that.

Sources: Based on della Cava (1997) and Mauro (1997).

After deliberation, patients, families, and physicians may decide to forgo "heroic measures" to keep a person alive. Physicians and family members may decide to issue a "do not resuscitate" order, which will allow a patient to die. *Living wills*—documents stating which medical procedures an individual wants and does not want under specific conditions—are now widely used.

A more difficult issue involves mercy killing, or **euthanasia**—*assisting in the death of a person suffering from an incurable disease.* Euthanasia (from the Greek, meaning "a good death") poses an ethical dilemma because it involves not just refusing treatment but actively taking steps to end life. In euthanasia, some see an act of kindness, while others see a form of killing.

Is there a right to die? People with incurable diseases can forgo treatment that might prolong their lives. But whether a doctor should be allowed to help bring about death is a matter of debate. In only one state—Oregon—have voters passed a right-to-die initiative ("The Death with Dignity Act," 1997). Although this law has been challenged repeatedly ever

since, Oregon physicians can legally assist in ending the lives of patients; in 2002, Oregon physicians legally assisted in thirty-eight suicides (Cain, 2001; Ogden, 2001; McCall, 2003). In 1997, the U.S. Supreme Court (*Vacco v. Quill*) weighed in, declaring that the U.S. Constitution recognizes no "right to die."

Those who support the right-to-die movement hold up the Netherlands as a model nation in this regard. There we find the most permissive euthanasia law in the world. How does the Dutch system operate? The box takes a closer look.

Should the United States hold the line on euthanasia or follow the lead of the Dutch? Right-to-die advocates maintain that a person facing extreme suffering should be able to choose to live or die. And if death is the choice, medical assistance can help people toward a "good death." Surveys show that a majority of U.S. adults support the option of dying with a doctor's help (Rosenbaum, 1997; NORC, 2003).

On the other side of the debate, opponents fear that laws allowing physician-assisted suicide will

Whereas a hospital tries to save and extend life, a hospice tries to give dying people greater comfort. The setting is, as much as possible, personal, and the dying person can have the companionship and support of family members.

invite abuse. Pointing to the Netherlands, critics cite surveys indicating that, in most cases, the five conditions for physician-assisted suicide are not met. In particular, most physicians do not consult with another doctor or even report the euthanasia to authorities. Of greater concern, however, is the fact that in about one-fifth of all physician-assisted suicides, the patient never explicitly asks to die. This is so even though half of these patients are conscious and capable of making decisions for themselves (Gillon, 1999). Opponents, therefore, fear that legalizing physician-assisted suicide puts a nation on a slippery slope toward more and more euthanasia. Can anyone deny, they ask, that ill people may be pushed into accepting death by doctors who consider suicide the right choice for the terminally ill or by family members who are weary of caring for them or want to avoid the expenses of medical care?

However the right-to-die debate turns out, our society has now entered a new era when it comes to dying. More often, individuals, family members, and medical personnel must face death not as a medical fact but as a negotiated outcome (Flynn, 1991; Humphrey, 1991; Markson, 1992; Wolfson, 1998).

BEREAVEMENT

Elisabeth Kübler-Ross (1969) found that most people usually confront their own death in stages (see Chapter 5, "Socialization"). Initially, individuals react with *denial*, followed by *anger*; then they try to *negotiate* a divine intervention. Gradually, they fall into *resignation* and finally reach *acceptance*.

According to some researchers, bereavement follows the same pattern of stages. Those close to a dying person, for instance, may initially deny the reality of impending death and then, with time, gradually reach a point of acceptance. Other investigators, however, question any linear "stage theory," arguing that bereavement is an unpredictable process (Lund, Caserta, & Dimond, 1986; Lund, 1989; Cutcliffe, 1998). Experts do agree, however, that how family and friends view an impending death affects the person who is dying. By accepting an approaching death, others help the dying person do the same; denying death isolates the dying person, who is unable to share feelings and experiences with others.

Many dying people find support in the *hospice movement*. Unlike a hospital, which is designed to cure disease, a hospice helps people have a good death. These care centers for dying people try to minimize pain and suffering—either there or at home—and encourage family members to stay close by. Most hospices also provide social support for family members experiencing bereavement (Stoddard, 1978; Foliart & Clausen, 2001).

Even under the most favorable circumstances, though, bereavement may involve profound grief. Research documents that bereavement is less intense for someone who accepts the death of a loved one and has brought satisfactory closure to the relationship. Such closure also allows family and friends to better comfort one another after death occurs.

Looking ahead in the twenty-first century, the elderly will represent an increasing share of the U.S. population. How do you think this trend will affect the experiences and attitudes of the young?

Of course, reaching closure is not possible when a death is unexpected. Especially in such cases, social disorientation may be profound and may last for years. One study of middle-aged women who had recently experienced the death of their husbands found that many felt they had lost not only a spouse but also their reason for living. Therefore, dealing successfully with bereavement requires the time and social support necessary to form a new sense of self and recognize new life options (Atchley, 1983; Danforth & Glass, 2001).

LOOKING AHEAD: AGING IN THE TWENTY-FIRST CENTURY

This chapter has explored the graying of the United States and other high-income nations. We can be sure that the ranks of the elderly will swell dramatically in this century: By 2050, the elderly population will exceed the population of the entire country in 1900. Moreover, one in four of these seniors will be over eighty-five. Within the next fifty years, then, society's oldest members will gain a far greater voice in everyday life. Careers relating to gerontology—the study of the elderly—are sure to gain in importance.

The reshaping of our society's age structure raises many serious concerns. With more people in their old age (and living longer once they enter old age), will we have the support services to sustain them? Remember that, as the elderly make demands, a smaller share of younger people will be there to respond. What about the spiraling medical care costs of an aging society? As the baby boomers enter old age, some analysts paint a

doomsday picture of the United States as a "twenty-first century Calcutta," with desperate and dying elderly people everywhere (Longino, 1994:13).

But not all the signs are ominous. For one thing, the health of tomorrow's elderly people (that is, today's middle-aged adults) is better than ever: Smoking is way down, and people are eating more healthfully. Such trends suggest that the elderly may well become more vigorous and independent. Moreover, tomorrow's seniors will enjoy the benefits of steadily advancing medical technology, although, as the final box explains, the claim of the old on our nation's resources is already hotly debated.

Another positive sign is the growing financial strength of the elderly. Although recent years have been stressful, it is likely that tomorrow's elderly will draw on greater affluence than ever before. Note, too, that the baby boomers will be the first generation of U.S. seniors with women who have been in the labor force most of their lives, a fact reflected in their substantial savings and pensions.

At the same time, younger adults will face a mounting responsibility to care for aging parents. Indeed, a falling birth rate coupled with a growing elderly population means that an increasing share of caregiving will be required by the very old.

Most of us need to learn more about caring for aging parents, which includes far more than meeting physical needs. More important lessons involve learning about communication, expressing love, and facing up to eventual death. In caring for parents, of course, we will also teach important lessons to our children, including the skills they will need, one day, to care for us.

CONTROVERSY & DEBATE

Setting Limits: Must We "Pull the Plug" on Old Age?

As the elderly population soars in the United States, as new technology gives us more power to prolong life, and as life-extending care gets increasingly expensive, many now wonder just how much old age we can afford. Currently, about half the average person's lifetime spending for medical care occurs during the final years of life, and the share is rising. Against the spiraling costs of prolonging life, then, we well may ask if what is technically possible is necessarily desirable. In the decades to come, warns gerontologist Daniel Callahan (1987), an elderly population ready and eager to extend their lives will eventually force us either to "pull the plug" on old age or short-change everyone else.

To even raise this issue, Callahan concedes, seems cold and heartless. But consider that the bill for the elderly's health topped $200 billion in 2000—more than twice what it cost in 1980. This dramatic increase reflects our current policy of directing more and more medical resources to studying and treating the diseases and disabilities of old age.

So Callahan makes the case for limits. First, the more we spend on behalf of the elderly, the less we have to provide for others. With poverty a growing problem among children, can we afford to spend more and more on the oldest members of our society?

Second, Callahan reminds us, a *longer* life does not necessarily mean a *better* life. Cost aside, does heart surgery that prolongs the life of an eighty-four-year-old woman a year or two truly improve the quality of her life? Cost considered, would those resources yield more "quality of life" if used, say, to give a ten-year-old child a kidney transplant? Or to provide basic care and comfort to hundreds of low-income seniors?

Third, Callahan urges us to reconsider our view of death as an enemy to be conquered at all costs. Rather, he suggests, a more realistic stance for an aging society is to treat death as a natural end to the life course. If we cannot make peace with death for our own well-being, then in light of society's limited resources we must do it for the benefit of others.

But not everyone agrees. Shouldn't people who have worked all their lives and made our society what it is enjoy our generosity in their final years? Would it be right to deny medical care to aging people able and willing to pay for it?

What is clear is that, in the twenty-first century, we face questions that few would have imagined even fifty years ago: Is peak longevity good for everyone? Is it even *possible* for everyone?

Continue the debate . . .

1. *Should doctors and hospitals use a double standard, offering more complete care to the youngest people and more limited care to society's oldest members? Why or why not?*

2. *Do you think that a goal of the medical establishment should be to extend life at all costs?*

3. *How should society balance the needs of high-income seniors with the needs of those with little or no money to pay for medical care as they age?*

Sources: Callahan (1987), Kapp (2001), and U.S. Census Bureau (2002).

SUMMARY

1. The proportion of elderly people in the U.S. population has risen from 4 percent in 1900 to 12 percent today; by 2030, 20 percent of our people will be elderly.

2. Gerontology, the study of aging and the elderly, focuses on how people change in old age, and on how various cultures define aging.

3. Most younger people exaggerate the extent of disability among the elderly. Growing old is accompanied by a rising rate of disease and disability, but most seniors are healthy.

4. Psychological research confirms that growing old does not result in overall loss of intelligence or radical changes in personality.

5. The age at which people are defined as old varies historically: Until several centuries ago, old age began as early as thirty. In poor societies today, where life expectancy is substantially lower than in North America, people become old at fifty or even forty.

6. Worldwide, industrialization fosters a decline in the social standing of the elderly relative to younger people.

7. As people age, they face social isolation brought on by retirement, physical disability, and the death of friends or spouse. Even so, most elderly people enjoy the support of family members.

8. Since 1960, poverty among the elderly has dropped sharply. The aged poor include categories of people—such as single women and people of color—who are at high risk of poverty at any age.

9. Most caregiving for the elderly population is performed by family members, typically women, who are likely to be caring for children as well.

10. Ageism—prejudice and discrimination against old people—is used to justify age stratification.

11. Although income falls among seniors, the fact that this category includes men and women of all races, ethnicities, and social classes suggests that older people are not a minority.

12. Disengagement theory, based on structural-functional analysis, suggests that society helps the elderly disengage from positions of social responsibility before the onset of disability or death. This process provides for the orderly transfer of statuses and roles from the older to the younger generation.

13. Activity theory, based on symbolic-interaction analysis, claims that a high level of activity affords people personal satisfaction in old age.

14. Age stratification is one focus of social-conflict analysis. A capitalist society's emphasis on economic efficiency leads to devaluing those who are less productive, including the elderly.

15. Modern society has set death apart from everyday life, prompting a cultural denial of human mortality. In part, this attitude is related to the fact that most people now die in old age. Recent trends suggest that people are confronting death more directly and seeking control over the process of dying.

KEY CONCEPTS

gerontology (p. 387) the study of aging and the elderly

age stratification (p. 389) the unequal distribution of wealth, power, and privilege among people at different stages of the life course

gerontocracy (p. 390) a form of social organization in which the elderly have the most wealth, power, and prestige

caregiving (p. 395) informal and unpaid care provided to a dependent person by family members, other relatives, or friends

ageism (p. 396) prejudice and discrimination against older people

disengagement theory (p. 397) the idea that society enhances its orderly operation by disengaging people from positions of responsibility as they reach old age

activity theory (p. 397) the idea that a high level of activity enhances personal satisfaction in old age

euthanasia (mercy killing) (p. 400) assisting in the death of a person suffering from an incurable disease

CRITICAL-THINKING QUESTIONS

1. What factors are causing the populations of high-income nations to become, on average, older? What are some of the likely consequences of the graying of the United States?

2. In general, are the most popular faculty on the campus young instructors or old instructors? Does age play into the ways students evaluate a professor?

3. In what ways does the United States have a "youth culture"? Provide specific examples.

4. Political analyst Irving Kristol (1996) praised the elderly as "our most exemplary citizens" because, compared to younger people, they do not kill, steal, use illegal drugs, or fall deep into debt. Moreover, they are twice as likely as young people to vote. Overall, do you think the elderly receive the respect and social support they deserve? Why or why not?

APPLICATIONS AND EXERCISES

1. What practices and policies does your college or university have for helping older faculty make the transition to retirement? Ask several faculty nearing retirement—and several already retired—for their views. In what ways does retiring from an academic career seem harder or easier than retiring from other kinds of work?

2. Look through an issue of any popular magazine—say, *Time, Newsweek,* or *People*—and note the images of men and women featured in the stories and pictured in the advertising. How well are elderly people represented in such publications?

3. Obtain a copy of a living will and try to respond to all the questions it asks. Does filling out such a form help clarify your own thinking about confronting death?

4. The *Journal of Medical Ethics* (vol. 25, no. 1, February 1999) has several research articles investigating the alleged abuse of euthanasia laws in the Netherlands. Read the articles and decide if you think, on balance, doctor-assisted suicide is a good or a bad idea.

5. Packaged in the back of this new textbook is an interactive CD-ROM that offers a variety of video and interactive review materials intended to help you better understand the material covered in this chapter. For this chapter, the CD-ROM contains a relevant clip from *ABC News,* an author's tip video, interactive map animations, an interactive time line, and flashcards with audio pronunciations of the more difficult words.

 ## SITES TO SEE

http://www.prenhall.com/macionis

Visit the interactive Companion Website™ that accompanies this text. Begin by clicking on the cover of your book. You will find a chapter-by-chapter study guide, practice tests, suggested Web links, and links to other relevant material.

http://www.census.gov/prod/2001pubs/p95-01-1.pdf

This report, by the U.S. Census Bureau and the National Institute on Aging, provides data on aging with a global perspective.

http://www.nhpco.org

Learn about hospices by visiting the Web site for the National Hospice and Palliative Care Organization. Then check your local telephone book to contact people who operate a hospice in your community.

http://www.seniornet.org/php/

This is the site for SeniorNet, a nonprofit organization that is bringing seniors into the age of the Internet. Run by volunteers, SeniorNet offers low-cost computer and Internet instruction to the elderly at several hundred training sites across the United States.

http://www.aoa.gov

This site, operated by the Department of Health and Human Services, provides a look at likely trends involving the elderly over the course of the twenty-first century.

 ## INVESTIGATE WITH RESEARCH NAVIGATOR™

Follow the instructions on page 24 of this text to access the features of **Research Navigator™**. Once at the Web site, enter your Login Name and Password. Then, to use the **Content Select™** database, enter keywords such as "retirement," "ageism," and "death," and the search engine will supply relevant and recent scholarly and popular press publications. Use the *New York Times* **Search-by-Subject Archive** to find recent news articles related to sociology and the **Link Library** feature to find relevant Web links organized by the key terms associated with this chapter.

THE ECONOMY AND WORK

DIEGO RIVERA (1886–1957)

Peasants

ERE'S A QUICK quiz about the U.S. economy (Hint: All five questions have the same right answer):

- Which business do 100 million people in the United States visit each week?

- Which U.S. company, on average, opens a new store every day?

- Which U.S. company is the largest U.S. employer after the federal government?

- Which U.S. company will create nearly 800,000 new jobs over the next five years?

- Which single company accounted for 25 percent of all the growth in U.S. economic output during the second half of the 1990s?

You have probably guessed that the correct answer is Wal-Mart, the global discount store chain founded by Sam Walton, who opened his first store in Arkansas back in 1962. By 2003, Wal-Mart had some $240 billion in annual sales from 3,500 stores in the United States and 1,200 stores in other countries, from Brazil to China (Saporito, 2003).

But not everyone is happy about the expansion of Wal-Mart. Across the United States, people have formed a social movement to keep Wal-Mart out of their local communities, fearing the loss of local businesses and, in some cases, local culture. Then, too, critics claim that the merchandising giant pays low wages, keeps out unions, and sells many products made in sweatshops abroad (Rousseau, 2002).

This chapter examines the economy, widely considered the most influential of all social institutions. (The other major social institutions are examined in subsequent chapters: Chapter 17, "Politics and Government"; Chapter 18, "Family"; Chapter 19, "Religion"; Chapter 20, "Education"; and Chapter 21, "Health and Medicine.") As the story of Wal-Mart's expansion suggests, the economy of the United States and the entire world is dominated by a number of giant corporations. Who benefits from these megabusinesses? Who loses? These are questions of interest to sociologists who debate how the economy ought to work, whose interests it ought to serve, and what companies and workers owe each other.

THE ECONOMY: HISTORICAL OVERVIEW

The **economy** is *the social institution that organizes a society's production, distribution, and consumption of goods and services.* As an institution, the economy operates in a generally predictable manner. *Goods* are commodities ranging from necessities (food, clothing, shelter) to luxury items (cars, swimming pools, yachts). *Services* are activities that benefit others (for example, the work of priests, physicians, teachers, and software specialists).

We value goods and services because they ensure survival or because they make life easier or more interesting. Also, what people produce as workers and what they buy as consumers constitute important parts of

As societies industrialize, a smaller and smaller share of the labor force works in agriculture. In the United States, much of what agricultural work remains is performed by immigrants from lower-income nations. This grape worker in southern California is a recent immigrant from Mexico.

social identity, as when we say, "He's a steel worker," or "She drives a Mercedes." How goods and services are distributed, too, shapes the lives of everyone by giving more resources to some and fewer to others.

The economies of modern high-income nations are the result of centuries of social change. We turn now to three technological revolutions that reorganized production and, in the process, transformed social life.

THE AGRICULTURAL REVOLUTION

Members of the earliest human societies were hunters and gatherers living off the land. In these technologically simple societies, there was no distinct economy. Rather, producing and consuming were all part of family life.

As Chapter 4 ("Society") explained, when people harnessed animals to plows, beginning some 5,000 years ago, a new agricultural economy was created that was fifty times more productive than hunting and gathering. The resulting surplus meant that not everyone had to produce food, so many took on specialized work: making tools, raising animals, or building dwellings. Soon towns sprang up, linked by networks of traders dealing in food, animals, and other goods. These four factors—agricultural technology, job specialization, permanent settlements, and trade—made the economy a distinct social institution.

THE INDUSTRIAL REVOLUTION

By the mid-eighteenth century, a second technological revolution was underway, first in England and then in North America. The development of industry was to bring even more change to the economy than agriculture had. Industrialization changed the economy in five fundamental ways:

1. **New sources of energy.** Throughout history, "energy" had meant the muscle power of people or animals. But in 1765, the English inventor James Watt introduced the steam engine. One hundred times stronger than muscle power, early steam engines soon drove heavy machinery.

2. **Centralization of work in factories.** Steam-powered machines soon moved work from homes to factories, the centralized and impersonal workplaces housing the machines.

3. **Manufacturing and mass production.** Before the Industrial Revolution, most people grew or gathered raw materials (such as grain, wood, or wool). In an industrial economy, the focus shifted so that most people's workday was spent turning raw materials into a wide range of finished products (such as furniture and clothing).

4. **Specialization.** Centuries ago, artisans working at home made products from start to finish. In the

DIVERSITY: RACE, CLASS, AND GENDER
Women in the Mills of Lowell, Massachusetts

Few people paid much attention as Francis Cabot Lowell, ancestor of two prominent Boston families, the Cabots and the Lowells, stepped off a ship returning from England in 1810. But Lowell carried with him documents that would change the course of the U.S. economy: plans, based on machinery operating in England, for this country's first power loom textile factory.

Lowell built his factory beside a waterfall on the Merrimack River in Massachusetts, so he could use waterpower to turn large looms to weave cloth. Soon, the productive factory transformed a small farming village into a thriving industrial town that, at his death, was renamed in his honor.

From the outset, 90 percent of the mill workers were women. Factory owners preferred women because they could be paid $2 to $3 a week, half the wages men received. Many immigrant men were willing to work for low wages, but prejudice disqualified "foreigners" from any job at all.

Recruiters, driving wagons through the small towns of New England, urged parents to send their daughters to the mills, where, they promised, the young women would be properly supervised as they learned skills and discipline. The offer appealed to many parents who could barely provide for their children, and the prospect of getting out on their own surely excited many young women. Back then, after all, there were few occupations open to women, and those that were—

including teaching and household service—paid even less than factory work.

At the Lowell factory, young women lived in dormitories, paying one-third of their wages for room and board. They were subject to a curfew and, as a condition of employment, regularly attended church. Any morally questionable conduct (such as bringing men to their rooms) brought firm disciplinary action.

Besides fulfilling their promise to parents, factory owners had another motive for their strict rules: They knew that closely supervised women could not organize among themselves. Working twelve or thirteen hours a day, six days a week, the Lowell employees had good reason to seek improvements in their working conditions. Yet any public criticism of the factory, or even possessing "radical" literature, could cost a worker her job.

Sources: Based on Eisler (1977) and Wertheimer (1982).

factory, a laborer repeated a single task over and over, making only a small contribution to the finished product. Such specialization raised productivity but lowered the skill level of the average worker.

5. **Wage labor.** Instead of working for themselves in a household (in what is called a cottage industry), factory workers became wage laborers working for strangers, who often cared less for them than for the machines they operated.

The Industrial Revolution gradually raised the standard of living as countless new products and services filled an expanding marketplace. Yet the benefits of industrial technology were shared very unequally, especially at the beginning. Some factory owners made vast fortunes, while the majority of industrial workers lived close to poverty. Children, too, worked in factories or in coal mines for pennies a day. Women factory workers, among the lowest paid, endured special problems, as the box explains.

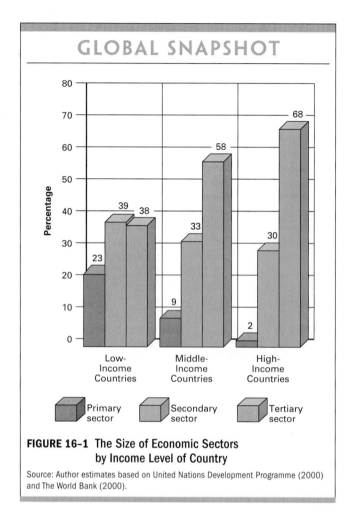

GLOBAL SNAPSHOT

FIGURE 16–1 The Size of Economic Sectors by Income Level of Country

Source: Author estimates based on United Nations Development Programme (2000) and The World Bank (2000).

THE INFORMATION REVOLUTION AND THE POSTINDUSTRIAL SOCIETY

By about 1950, the nature of production was changing once again. The United States was creating a **postindustrial economy,** *a productive system based on service work and high technology.* Automated machinery (and, more recently, robotics) reduced the role of human labor in production so that fewer people work in industrial jobs and most now work in service positions, including sales, public relations, health care, advertising, and banking. The postindustrial era, then, is distinguished by a shift from industrial work to service work.

Driving this change is a third technological breakthrough: the computer. Just as the Industrial Revolution did two-and-a-half centuries ago, the Information Revolution has introduced new kinds of products and

new forms of communication and has altered the character of work. In general, we see three changes:

1. **From tangible products to ideas.** The industrial era was defined by the production of goods; in the postindustrial era, work involves manipulating symbols. Computer programmers, writers, financial analysts, advertising executives, architects, editors, and all sorts of consultants make up the labor force of the information age.

2. **From mechanical skills to literacy skills.** The Industrial Revolution required mechanical skills, but the Information Revolution requires literacy skills: effective speaking, clear writing, and of course, knowing how to use a computer. People able to communicate effectively enjoy new opportunities; people with limited skills face declining prospects.

3. **From factories to almost anywhere.** Industrial technology drew workers into factories located near power sources, but computer technology allows workers to be almost anywhere. Laptop computers, cell phones, and portable facsimile (fax) machines now turn the home, a car, or even an airplane into a "virtual office." New information technology, in short, blurs the line between work and home life.

SECTORS OF THE ECONOMY

The three revolutions we have just described reflect a shifting balance among the three sectors of a society's economy. The **primary sector** is *the part of the economy that draws raw materials from the natural environment.* The primary sector—agriculture, raising animals, fishing, forestry, and mining—is largest in low-income nations. Figure 16–1 shows that 23 percent of the economic output of low-income countries is from the primary sector, compared to 9 percent of economic activity in middle-income nations and just 2 percent in high-income countries such as the United States.

The **secondary sector** is *the part of the economy that transforms raw materials into manufactured goods.* This sector grows quickly as societies industrialize. It includes operations such as refining petroleum into gasoline and turning metals into tools and automobiles. The globalization of industry means that just about all the world's countries have a significant share of their workers in the secondary sector. Indeed, as Figure 16–1 shows, the secondary sector accounts for a greater share of economic output in low-income countries than it does in high-income nations.

The **tertiary sector** is *the part of the economy that involves services rather than goods.* Accounting for 38 percent of the labor force in low-income countries, the tertiary sector grows with industrialization and dominates the economies of middle-income countries (58 percent of economic output) and high-income, postindustrial nations (68 percent). Today, about 74 percent of the U.S. labor force is in service work, including secretarial and clerical work and positions in food service, sales, law, health care, law enforcement, advertising, and teaching.

THE GLOBAL ECONOMY

New information technology is drawing people around the world closer together and creating a **global economy,** *expanding economic activity with little regard for national borders.* The development of a global economy has four major consequences. First, we see a global division of labor so that different regions of the world specialize in one sector of economic activity. As Global Map 16–1 on page 412 shows, agriculture represents more than half the total economic output of the world's poorest countries. Global Map 16–2 indicates that most of the economic output of high-income countries, including the United States, is in the service sector. The poorest nations, then, specialize in producing raw materials, while the richest nations, including the United States, specialize in the production of various services.

Second, an increasing number of products pass through more than one nation. Look no further than your morning coffee, which may well have been grown in Colombia and transported to New Orleans on a freighter, registered in Liberia, which was made in Japan with steel from Korea, and which was fueled by oil from Venezuela.

A third consequence of the global economy is that national governments no longer control the economic activity that takes place within their borders. In fact, governments cannot even regulate the value of their national currencies because dollars, euros, pounds sterling, yen, and other currencies are traded around the clock in the financial markets of Tokyo, London, and New York. Global markets are the result of satellite communications that link the world's cities.

A fourth consequence of the global economy is that a small number of businesses, operating internationally, now control a vast share of the world's economic activity. A rough estimate is that the 600

The rise of a global economy means that more and more products originally produced in one country are now made and consumed around the world. *What do you see as some of the good consequences of globalization? What about harmful consequences?*

largest multinational companies account for half the entire world's economic output (Kidron & Segal, 1991; Gergen, 2002).

The world is still divided into 192 politically distinct nations. But increasing international economic activity makes "nationhood" less significant than it was even a decade ago.

ECONOMIC SYSTEMS: PATHS TO JUSTICE

October 20, Saigon, Vietnam. Sailing up the narrow Saigon River is an unsettling experience for anyone who came of age during the 1960s. We need to remember that Vietnam is a country, not a war, and that thirty years have passed since the last U.S. helicopter lifted off the rooftop of the U.S. embassy, ending our country's presence there.

Saigon is on the brink of becoming a boomtown. Neon signs bathe the city's waterfront in color; hotels, bankrolled by Western corporations, push skyward from a dozen construction sites; taxi

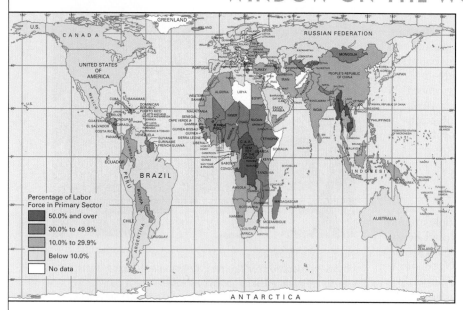

GLOBAL MAP 16–1
Agricultural Employment in Global Perspective

The primary sector of the economy is largest in the nations that are least developed. Thus, in the poor countries of Africa and Asia, up to half of all workers are farmers. This picture is altogether different in the world's most economically developed countries—including the United States, Canada, Great Britain, and Australia—which have 2 percent of their work force in agriculture.

Percentage of Labor Force in Primary Sector
- 50.0% and over
- 30.0% to 49.9%
- 10.0% to 29.9%
- Below 10.0%
- No data

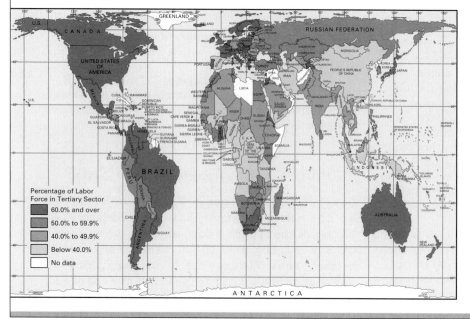

GLOBAL MAP 16–2
Service-Sector Employment in Global Perspective

The tertiary sector of the economy becomes ever larger as a nation's income level rises. In the United States, Canada, the countries of Western Europe, Australia, and Japan, about two-thirds of the labor force perform service work.

Percentage of Labor Force in Tertiary Sector
- 60.0% and over
- 50.0% to 59.9%
- 40.0% to 49.9%
- Below 40.0%
- No data

Sources: The author, using data from United Nations Development Programme (2000) and The World Bank (2000, 2001); map projection from *Peters Atlas of the World* (1990).

meters record fares in U.S. dollars, not Vietnamese dong; Visa and American Express stickers decorate the doors of fashionable shops that cater to tourists from Japan, France, and the United States.

There is a heavy irony here: After decades of fighting, the loss of millions of human lives, and the victory of communist forces, the Vietnamese are doing an about-face and turning toward capitalism. What we see today is what might well have happened had the U.S. forces won the war.

Every society's economic system makes a statement about *distributive justice* by determining who is entitled to what. Two general economic models are capitalism and socialism. No nation anywhere in the world has an economy that is completely one or the other; capitalism and socialism represent two ends of a spectrum along which all actual economies can be located. We will look at each of these two models in turn.

CAPITALISM

Capitalism is *an economic system in which natural resources and the means of producing goods and services are privately owned.* An ideal capitalist economy has three distinctive features:

1. **Private ownership of property.** In a capitalist economy, individuals can own almost anything. The more capitalist an economy is, the more private ownership there is of wealth-producing property, such as factories, real estate, and natural resources.

2. **Pursuit of personal profit.** A capitalist society encourages the accumulation of private property and considers the profit motive natural, simply a matter of doing business. Further, claimed the Scottish philosopher Adam Smith (1723–1790), the individual pursuit of self-interest helps the entire society prosper (1937:508; orig. 1776).

3. **Competition and consumer sovereignty.** A purely capitalist economy is a free-market system with no government interference (sometimes called a *laissez-faire economy*, from the French words meaning "to leave alone"). Adam Smith stated that a freely competitive economy regulates itself by the "invisible hand" of the laws of supply and demand.

   Consumers regulate a free-market economy, Smith explained, by selecting the goods and services offering the greatest value. As producers compete for the customer's business, they provide the highest-quality goods at the lowest possible prices. In Smith's time-honored phrase, from narrow self-interest comes the "greatest good for the greatest number of people." Government

Although the United States has a mostly capitalist economy, the role of government increased over the course of the twentieth century and is now a familiar part of everyday life. By contrast, back in the 1800s in small towns across the country, the only evidence of government was a single building—a post office. Shown here is the original post office for Duluth, Minnesota.

control of an economy, on the other hand, distorts market forces by reducing the quantity and quality of goods and shortchanging consumers.

"Justice," in a capitalist context, amounts to freedom of the marketplace, where one can produce, invest, and buy according to individual self-interest. The worth of products and labor is determined by the dynamic process of supply and demand. The increasing popularity of Wal-Mart, described in the opening to this chapter, reflects the fact that the company provides a high level of value to customers who choose to shop there.

The United States is a capitalist nation in that the vast majority of businesses are privately owned. Even so, government plays an extensive role in economic affairs. The government itself owns and operates a number of businesses, including almost all of this country's schools, roads, parks and museums, the U.S. Postal Service, the Amtrak railroad system, and the entire U.S. military. The U.S. government also had a major hand in building the Internet. In addition, governments use taxation and other forms of regulation to influence what companies produce, to control the

Global comparisons indicate that socialist economies generate greater economic equality although living standards remain relatively low. Capitalist economies, by contrast, generate more economic inequality although living standards are relatively high. As the Russian Federation has moved from socialism toward capitalism, there is widespread evidence of increasing economic inequality, including the building of large mansions by those who have become rich. This complex is being built by a business tycoon in the suburbs of the Russian capital, an area coming to be known as "the Beverly Hills of Moscow."

quality and cost of merchandise, and to motivate consumers to conserve natural resources.

Furthermore, government sets minimum wage levels, enforces workplace safety standards, regulates corporate mergers, provides farm price supports, and supplements income in the form of Social Security, public assistance, student loans, and veterans' benefits to a majority of the people in the United States. In fact, local, state, and federal governments together are the country's biggest employer, with 16 percent of the nonfarm labor force on their payrolls (U.S. Census Bureau, 2001).

SOCIALISM

Socialism is *an economic system in which natural resources and the means of producing goods and services are collectively owned.* In its ideal form, a socialist economy is the exact opposite of capitalism.

1. **Collective ownership of property.** A socialist economy limits rights to private property, especially property used to generate income. Government controls such property and makes housing and other goods available to all, not just to the people with the most money.

2. **Pursuit of collective goals.** The individualistic pursuit of profit is also at odds with the collective orientation of socialism. What capitalism celebrates as the "entrepreneurial spirit," socialism condemns as greed; individuals are urged to work for the common good of all.

3. **Government control of the economy.** Socialism rejects capitalism's laissez-faire approach in favor of a *centrally controlled* or *command economy* operated by the government. (Commercial advertising thus plays little role in socialist economies.)

In a socialist context, "justice" is not freedom to compete and accumulate wealth but meeting everyone's basic needs in a roughly equal manner. From a socialist point of view, cutting back on workers' wages and benefits to boost company earnings is putting profits before people and is thus an injustice.

The People's Republic of China and some two dozen other nations in Asia, Africa, and Latin America model their economies on socialism, placing almost all wealth-generating property under state control (McColm et al., 1991; Freedom House, 2003). The extent of world socialism has declined in recent years as the countries in Eastern Europe and the former Soviet Union have geared their economies toward a market system.

Socialism and Communism

Many people think of *socialism* and *communism* as much the same. More precisely, **communism** is *a hypothetical economic and political system in which all members of a society are socially equal.* Karl Marx viewed socialism as one important step on the path toward the ideal of a communist society that abolishes all class divisions. In many socialist societies today, the dominant political party describes itself as communist, but nowhere has the communist goal been achieved.

Capitalism still thrives in Hong Kong (left), evident in streets choked with advertising and shoppers. Socialism is more the rule in China's capital of Beijing (right), a city dominated by government buildings rather than a downtown business district.

Why? For one thing, social stratification involves differences of power as well as wealth. In general, socialist societies have reduced economic differences by regulating people's range of choices. In the process, government did not "wither away" as Karl Marx imagined. On the contrary, government has grown, and socialist political elites have enormous power and privilege.

Probably Marx would have agreed that a communist society is a *utopia* (from Greek words meaning "not a place"). Yet Marx considered communism a worthy goal and might well have objected to so-called "Marxist" societies such as North Korea, the People's Republic of China, Cuba, and the former Soviet Union for falling short of the promise of communism.

WELFARE CAPITALISM AND STATE CAPITALISM

Some nations of Western Europe, including Sweden and Italy, have combined a market-based economy with broad social welfare programs. Analysts call this "third way" **welfare capitalism,** *an economic and political system that combines a mostly market-based economy with extensive social welfare programs.*

Under welfare capitalism, the government owns some of the largest industries and services, such as transportation, the mass media, and health care.

In Sweden and Italy, about 12 percent of economic production is "nationalized," or state-controlled. Most industry is left in private hands, although subject to extensive government regulation. High taxation (aimed especially at the rich) funds a wide range of social welfare programs, including universal health care and child care (Olsen, 1996).

Yet another blend of capitalism and socialism is **state capitalism,** *an economic and political system in which companies are privately owned but cooperate closely with the government.* State capitalism is the rule among the nations along the Pacific Rim. Japan, South Korea, and Singapore, for example, are all capitalist countries, but their governments work in partnership with large companies, supplying financial assistance and controlling foreign imports to help their businesses compete in world markets (Gerlach, 1992).

RELATIVE ADVANTAGES OF CAPITALISM AND SOCIALISM

In practice, which economic system works best? Comparing economic models is difficult because all countries mix capitalism and socialism to varying degrees. Moreover, nations differ in cultural attitudes toward work, the available natural resources, the levels of

TABLE 16-1 Employed Persons in the Labor Force by Sex, Race, and Ethnicity, 2002		
	Employed Persons	
Category of the Population	Number (in millions)	Percentage
Men (aged 16 and over)	72.9	69.7%
White	61.8	70.8
African American	7.0	61.1
Hispanic	9.8	74.5
Women (aged 16 and over)	63.6	56.3
White	52.2	56.4
African American	7.9	55.8
Hispanic	6.7	52.9

Source: U.S. Department of Labor, Bureau of Labor Statistics, tables 3 and 4 from *Employment and Earnings*. [Online] Available November 11, 2003, at http://www.bls.gov/cps

technological development, and the patterns of trade (Gregory & Stuart, 1985). Despite these complicating factors, some crude comparisons are revealing.

Economic Productivity

One key dimension of economic performance is productivity. A commonly used measure of economic output is gross domestic product (GDP), the total value of all goods and services produced annually. Per capita (per person) GDP allows us to compare the economic performance of nations of different population sizes.

Averaging the economic output of mostly capitalist countries—the United States, Canada, and the nations of Western Europe—at the end of the 1980s yielded a per capita GDP of about $13,500. The comparable figure for the mostly socialist former Soviet Union and nations of Eastern Europe was about $5,000. This means that the capitalist countries outproduced the socialist nations by a ratio of 2.7 to 1 (United Nations Development Programme, 1990).[1]

Economic Equality

How resources are distributed within a society is another important measure of how well an economic system works. One comparative study of Europe, when that region was split between mostly capitalist and mostly socialist countries, compared the earnings of the richest and poorest 5 percent of the populations

---

[1]A recent comparison of socialist North Korea (per capita GDP of $1,000) and capitalist South Korea ($18,000) provides an even sharper contrast (Omestad, 2003).

(Wiles, 1977). The result was that, in societies with mostly capitalist economies, the rich earned ten times more than the poor; the ratio for socialist countries was about five to one. The study concluded that, while capitalist economies support a higher overall standard of living, they also show greater income inequality. Or put otherwise, socialist economies create more economic equality but with a lower overall living standard.

Personal Freedom

One additional consideration in evaluations of capitalism and socialism is the personal freedom each affords its people. Capitalism emphasizes *freedom to* pursue one's self-interest. Capitalism, after all, depends on the freedom of producers and consumers to interact, with little interference by the state. On the other hand, socialism emphasizes *freedom from* basic want. Equality is the goal, which requires state intervention in the economy, which in turn limits the personal choices of citizens.

No system has yet been able to offer both political freedom and economic equality. In the capitalist United States, the political system guarantees many personal freedoms, but are these freedoms worth as much to a poor person as to a rich one? On the other side of the coin, China or Cuba has more economic equality but restricts the rights of its people to express themselves freely and to move freely inside and outside the country.

CHANGES IN SOCIALIST COUNTRIES

In 1989 and 1990, the nations of Eastern Europe, which had been seized by the Soviet Union at the end of World War II, shook off their socialist regimes. These nations—including the German Democratic Republic, Czechoslovakia, Hungary, Romania, and Bulgaria—are moving toward market systems after decades of state-controlled economies. In 1992, the Soviet Union itself formally dissolved, and the economy moved toward a market system. Ten years later, three-fourths of state enterprises were partly or entirely under private ownership (Montaigne, 2001).

There were many reasons for these sweeping changes. First, the mostly socialist economies underproduced in comparison with their capitalist counterparts. They were successful in achieving remarkable economic equality, but living standards were low compared to those of Western Europe. Second, Soviet socialism was heavy-handed, rigidly controlling the media and restricting individual freedoms. In short, socialism did away with *economic* elites, as Karl Marx

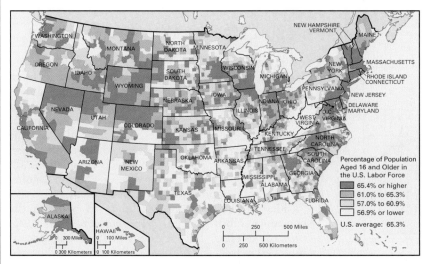

NATIONAL MAP 16–1
Labor Force Participation
across the United States

Counties with high levels of labor force participation have steady sources of employment, including military bases, recreation areas, and large cities. By contrast, counties with low employment rates generally include a high proportion of elderly people (as well as students). Gender is another important consideration: What do you think is the typical level of employment in regions of the country (stretching from the South up into the coal-mining districts of Kentucky and West Virginia) where traditional cultural norms encourage women to remain at home?

Percentage of Population
Aged 16 and Older in
the U.S. Labor Force

- 65.4% or higher
- 61.0% to 65.3%
- 57.0% to 60.9%
- 56.9% or lower

U.S. average: 65.3%

Sources: *American Demographics Desk Reference Series #4*. Reprinted with permission. ©1992 *American Demographics* magazine, Ithaca, New York. Data from the 1990 decennial census.

predicted. But as Max Weber foresaw, socialism increased the power of *political* elites.

So far, the market reforms in Eastern Europe are proceeding unevenly. Some nations (the Czech Republic, Slovakia, Poland, and the Baltic states of Latvia, Estonia, and Lithuania) are faring pretty well, but others (Romania, Bulgaria, and the Russian Federation) have been buffeted by price increases and falling living standards. Officials hope that expanding production will eventually bring a turnaround. However, there is already evidence that any improvement in living standards will be accompanied by increasing economic disparity (Pohl, 1996; Buraway, 1997; Specter, 1997a).

WORK IN THE POSTINDUSTRIAL ECONOMY

Economic change is not restricted to the socialist world. In 2002, 136 million people in the United States—representing almost two-thirds of those aged sixteen and over—were working for income. As shown in Table 16–1, a larger share of men (69.7 percent) than of women (56.3 percent)

Find a government report on youth in the U.S. labor force at http://www.bls.gov/opub/rylf/rylfhome.htm

had jobs, although this gap is closing. Among men, 61.1 percent of African Americans were employed, compared to 70.8 percent of white men and 74.5 percent of Hispanics. Among women, 55.8 percent of African Americans were employed, compared to 56.4 percent of white women and 52.9 percent of Hispanics.

National Map 16–1 shows labor force participation across the United States. Because working is the major source of income for most people, regions with greater labor force participation are more affluent.

THE DECLINE OF AGRICULTURAL WORK

In 1900, about 40 percent of the U.S. labor force engaged in farming. In 2002, just 2 percent were in agriculture. Figure 16–2 on page 418 shows the shrinking role of the primary sector in the U.S. economy.

Although farming involves far fewer people today, it is more productive than ever. A century ago, a typical farmer grew food for five people; today, one farmer feeds seventy-five. This dramatic rise in productivity reflects new varieties of crops, chemicals that raise yields, and more efficient farm machinery and farming techniques. The average U.S. farm has also doubled in size since 1950, to about 500 acres.

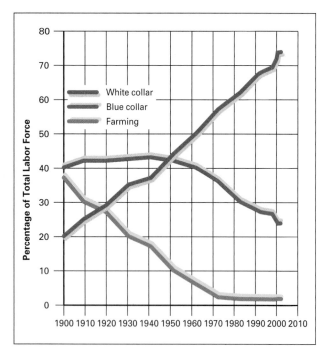

FIGURE 16–2 The Changing Pattern of Work
in the United States, 1900–2002

Sources: Author estimates based on U.S. Department of Labor (2003).

little of the income and prestige of the white-collar professions and, often, fewer rewards than factory work. In sum, many jobs in this postindustrial era provide only a modest standard of living.

THE DUAL LABOR MARKET

Sociologists see the jobs in today's economy falling into two categories. The **primary labor market** includes *jobs that provide extensive benefits to workers*. This segment of the labor market includes the traditional white-collar professions such as medicine and law, as well as upper-management positions. These are jobs that people think of as *careers*, interesting work that provides high income and more job security. Such occupations require a broad education rather than on-the-job training and offer solid opportunity for advancement.

Few of these advantages apply to work in the **secondary labor market,** *jobs that provide minimal benefits to workers*. This segment of the labor force is employed in low-skilled, blue-collar assembly-line operations and low-level service-sector jobs, including clerical positions. Workers in the secondary labor market receive lower income, have less job security and fewer benefits, and find less satisfaction in their work. Women and other minorities are overly represented in the secondary labor market work force (Hunnicutt, 1990; Greenwald, 1994; Nelson, 1994; Kalleberg, Reskin, & Hudson, 2000).

LABOR UNIONS

The changing U.S. economy has seen a decline in **labor unions,** *organizations of workers that seek to improve wages and working conditions through various strategies, including negotiations and strikes.* During the Great Depression of the 1930s, union membership increased rapidly until it reached more than one-third of nonfarm workers by 1950. By 1970, union rolls had peaked at almost 25 million. Since then, membership has declined to about 13 percent of nonfarm workers, or 16.3 million men and women. If we look more closely, 37 percent of government workers are members of unions compared to just 9 percent of private sector (nongovernmental) workers (Clawson & Clawson, 1999; Goldfield, 2000).

The pattern of union decline holds in most high-income countries. Yet unions claim a far smaller share of workers in the United States than elsewhere. In Canada and Japan, about 33 percent of workers belong to unions; across Europe, about 40 percent; in the

The family farms of yesterday have been replaced by *corporate agribusinesses.* Agriculture may be more productive, but the transformation has required painful adjustments in farming communities across the country as a way of life is lost (Dudley, 2000).

FROM FACTORY WORK TO SERVICE WORK

In the early 1900s, industrialization swelled the ranks of blue-collar workers. By 1950, however, a white-collar revolution had moved a majority of workers into service occupations. By 2002, 74 percent of the labor force worked in the service sector, and 92 percent of new jobs were being created in this sector (U.S. Department of Labor, 2003).

As Chapter 11 ("Social Class in the United States") explained, the expansion of service work is one reason many people call the United States a middle-class society. But much service work—including sales and clerical positions and jobs in hospitals and restaurants—carries

Scandinavian countries, the share is 80 percent (Western, 1993, 1995).

The widespread decline in union memberships follows the shrinking industrial sector of the economy. Newer service jobs—such as sales jobs at the retailer Wal-Mart described in the chapter opening—are less likely to be unionized. Citing low wages and numerous worker complaints, however, unions are trying to organize Wal-Mart employees, so far without success. Indeed, lower job security in recent years has given unions a short-term boost. Long-term gains, however, probably depend on the ability of unions to adapt to the new global economy. Union members in the United States, used to seeing foreign workers as "the enemy," will have to build new international alliances (Church, 1994; Greenhouse, 2000; Rousseau, 2002).

PROFESSIONS

All kinds of jobs today are called *professional*—we hear of professional tennis players, professional house cleaners, and even professional exterminators. As distinct from *amateur* (from the Latin for "lover," meaning someone who acts out of love for the activity itself), a professional does some task for a living. But what exactly is a *profession*?

A **profession** is *a prestigious white-collar occupation that requires extensive formal education*. Those performing this kind of work make a profession, or public declaration, to abide by certain principles. Professions include the ministry, medicine, law, academia, and, more recently, architecture, accountancy, and social work. Occupations are professions to the extent that they demonstrate the following four characteristics (W. Goode, 1960; Ritzer & Walczak, 1990):

1. **Theoretical knowledge.** Professionals have a theoretical understanding of their field rather than mere technical training. Anyone can master first-aid skills, for example, but physicians have a theoretical understanding of human health.

2. **Self-regulating practice.** The typical professional is self-employed, "in practice" rather than working for a company. Professionals oversee their own work and observe a code of ethics.

3. **Authority over clients.** Because of their expertise, professionals are sought out by clients, who value their advice and follow their directions.

4. **Community orientation rather than self-interest.** The traditional professing of duty states an intention to serve others rather than merely to seek income.

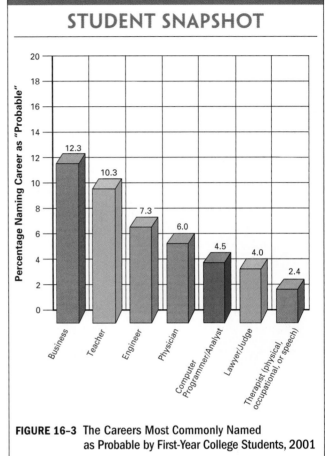

STUDENT SNAPSHOT

FIGURE 16–3 The Careers Most Commonly Named as Probable by First-Year College Students, 2001

Source: Astin et al. (2002).

In almost all cases, professional work requires a college degree and also a graduate degree. Not surprisingly, therefore, professions are well represented among the occupations beginning college students name as their probable careers, as shown in Figure 16–3.

Many occupations that do not qualify as true professions nonetheless seek to *professionalize* their services. Claiming professional standing often begins by renaming the work to imply special, theoretical knowledge, thereby distancing the field from its previously less distinguished reputation. Stockroom workers become "inventory supply managers," and exterminators are reborn as "insect control specialists."

Interested parties may also form a professional association to formally attest to their skills. This organization then licenses people who perform the work and

This Depression-era photo is a powerful statement of the personal collapse and private despair that afflict men and women who are out of work. How does a sociological perspective help us to understand being out of work as more than a personal problem?

writes a code of ethics that emphasizes the occupation's role in the community. In its effort to win public acceptance, a professional association may also establish schools or other training facilities and perhaps start a professional journal (Abbott, 1988). Not all occupations try to claim professional status. Some *paraprofessionals*, including paralegals and medical technicians, possess specialized skills but lack the extensive theoretical education required of full professionals.

SELF-EMPLOYMENT

Self-employment—earning a living without working for an organization—was once common in the United States. About 80 percent of the labor force was self-employed in 1800, compared to just 7.1 percent of workers today (8.3 percent of men and 5.8 percent of women) (U.S. Department of Labor, 2003).

Lawyers, physicians, and other professionals are well represented among the ranks of the self-employed. But most self-employed workers are small business owners, plumbers, carpenters, freelance writers, editors, artists, and long-distance truck drivers. Overall, the self-employed are more likely to have blue-collar than white-collar jobs.

Finally, a notable trend in the U.S. economy is that women now own nearly 40 percent of this country's small businesses, and their share is rising. More-

 Visit the Web site of the Small Business Administration: http://www.sba.gov

over, the 9.1 million firms owned by U.S. women now employ almost 30 million people and generate close to $4 trillion in annual sales (U.S. Small Business Administration, 2001).

UNEMPLOYMENT AND UNDEREMPLOYMENT

Every society has some unemployment. Few young people entering the labor force find a job right away; workers may leave their jobs to seek new work or stay at home raising children; some may be on strike; others suffer from long-term illnesses; and still others are illiterate or without the skills to perform useful work.

But unemployment is also caused by the economy itself. Jobs disappear as occupations become obsolete, businesses close in the face of foreign competition or economic recession, and companies downsize to become more profitable. Since 1980, the 500 largest U.S. businesses have eliminated some 5 million jobs—one-fourth of the total. The economic slowdown that began in 2000 led to millions of people losing their jobs, especially people with white-collar jobs who had typically weathered downturns in the past (Cullen, 2002).

In 2002, 8.4 million people over the age of sixteen were unemployed, about 5.8 percent of the civilian labor force. As a glance back at National Map 16–1 shows, some regions of the country, including parts of West Virginia and New Mexico, have high unemploy-

Read a report on employment patterns of African American men at http://www.brookings.edu/es/urban/publications/offnerexsum.htm

ment, in some cases twice the national average. Today, research shows that rural residents are at especially high risk of unemployment (Stofferahn, 2000).

Figure 16–4 shows that unemployment among African Americans (10.2 percent) is twice the rate among white people (5.1 percent). For both races, men have slightly higher levels of unemployment than women.

DIVERSITY SNAPSHOT

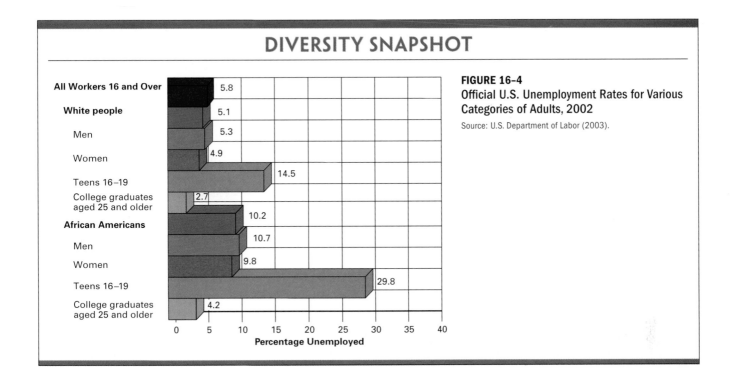

All Workers 16 and Over 5.8

White people 5.1

Men 5.3

Women 4.9

Teens 16–19 14.5

College graduates aged 25 and older 2.7

African Americans 10.2

Men 10.7

Women 9.8

Teens 16–19 29.8

College graduates aged 25 and older 4.2

0 5 10 15 20 25 30 35 40
Percentage Unemployed

FIGURE 16–4
Official U.S. Unemployment Rates for Various Categories of Adults, 2002

Source: U.S. Department of Labor (2003).

Underemployment, too, is a problem for millions of workers. The government reports that more than 31 million people work part time, that is, no more than thirty-four hours weekly. While 80 percent are satisfied with this arrangement, 20 percent (6 million workers) say they want more work but cannot find it (U.S. Department of Labor, 2003).

The economic downturn in recent years has created a new kind of underemployment. The bankruptcy of large corporations, including Enron and Worldcom, has left thousands of workers—the ones lucky enough to have kept their jobs—unable to collect their travel costs and other expenses. Similarly, after filing for bankruptcy USAirways forced flight attendants to take an 8.4 percent salary reduction. Across the United States, as many as 1 million workers have kept their jobs only by agreeing to cutbacks in pay or to the loss of bonuses or other benefits (Eisenberg, 2001; Clark, 2002b).

THE UNDERGROUND ECONOMY

The U.S. government requires individuals and businesses to report their economic activity, especially earnings. Unreported income makes a transaction part of the **underground economy,** *economic activity involving income unreported to the government as required by law.*

On a small scale, most people participate in the underground economy from time to time: A family makes extra money by holding a garage sale, or teenagers baby-sit for neighbors without reporting the income. Of course, far more of the underground economy is attributable to criminal activity, such as prostitution, bribery, theft, illegal gambling, loan-sharking, and the sale of illegal drugs.

But the single largest segment of contributors to the underground economy is people who fail to report some or all of their legally obtained income when it comes time to file income tax returns. Self-employed persons such as carpenters, physicians, and small business owners may understate their income on tax forms; food servers and other service workers may not report their earnings from tips. Individually, the omissions and misrepresentations may be small, but millions of individuals' hedging on income tax returns adds up to perhaps $170 billion annually in lost tax revenues (Speer, 1995).

DIVERSITY: RACE, CLASS, AND GENDER

Twenty-First-Century Diversity: Changes in the Workplace

An upward trend in the U.S. minority population is changing the workplace. As the figure shows, the number of non-Hispanic white men in the U.S. labor force will rise by a modest 4 percent between 2000 and 2010, the number of African American men will increase by 15 percent, the number of Hispanic men will increase by 31 percent, and the number of Asian American and Native American men will increase by the even greater 42 percent.

Among non-Hispanic white women, the projected rise is 8 percent; among African American women, 26 percent; and among Hispanic women, 43 percent. Asian American and Native American women will show the greatest gains, estimated at 47 percent.

The overall result is that, within a decade, non-Hispanic white men will represent just 37 percent of all workers, a figure that will continue to drop. Therefore, companies that welcome social diversity will tap the largest talent pool and enjoy a competitive advantage.

Welcoming social diversity means, first, recruiting talented workers of both sexes as well as all colors and cultural backgrounds. But developing the potential of all employees requires meeting the needs of women and other minorities, which may not be the same as those of white men. For example, corporations are being pressed to provide child care at the workplace.

Second, businesses must develop effective ways to defuse tensions that arise from social differences. They will have to work harder at treating workers equally and respectfully; also, no corporate culture can tolerate racial or sexual harassment.

Third, companies will have to rethink current promotion practices. At present, only 4 percent of Fortune 500 top executives are women, and just 1 percent are other minorities. In a broad survey of U.S. companies, the U.S. Equal Employment Opportunity Commission confirmed that non-Hispanic white men (35 percent of adults aged twenty to sixty-four) hold 57 percent of management jobs; the comparable figures for non-Hispanic white women are 35 and 28 percent; for African Americans, 12 and 6 percent; and for Hispanics, 13 and 5 percent.

In sum, "glass ceilings" that prevent skilled workers from advancing not only discourage effort but deprive companies of their largest source of talent: women and other minorities.

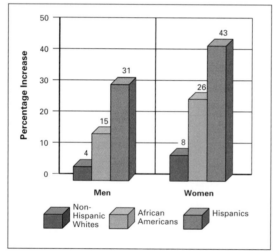

Projected Increase in the Numbers of People in the U.S. Labor Force, 2000–2010

Source: Fullerton & Toossi (2001).

Sources: Fullerton & Toossi (2001), Catalyst (2003), and U.S. Equal Employment Opportunity Commission (2003).

WORKPLACE DIVERSITY: RACE AND GENDER

Traditionally, white men have been the mainstay of the U.S. labor force. However, our nation's proportion of minorities is rising rapidly. Between 1990 and 2000, the African American population increased by 16 percent, more than five times the 3 percent rate for non-Hispanic white people. The jump in the Hispanic population was even greater, at 58 percent, and the increase among Asian Americans was 48 percent. The box takes a closer look at how the increasing social diversity of our society will affect the workplace.

NEW INFORMATION TECHNOLOGY AND WORK

July 2, Ticonderoga, New York. The manager of the local hardware store scans the barcodes of a bagful of items. "The computer not only totals the costs," she

Although the Information Revolution is centered in high-income countries such as the United States, the effects of high technology are becoming evident even in low-income nations. Do you think the expansion of information technology will change the lives of rural people such as these peasants in Vietnam? If so, how?

explains, "but it also keeps track of inventory, placing orders from the warehouse and deciding which products to continue to sell and which to discontinue." "Sounds like what you used to do, Maureen," I respond with a smile. "Yep," she nods, with no smile at all.

Another workplace issue is the increasing role of computers and other new information technology. The Information Revolution is changing what people do in some basic ways (Zuboff, 1982; Rule & Brantley, 1992; Vallas & Beck, 1996):

1. **Computers are deskilling labor.** Just as industrial machinery replaced the master craftsworkers of an earlier era, so computers now threaten the skills of managers. More business operations are based not on executive decisions but on computer modeling. In other words, a machine decides whether to place an order, resupply a client, or approve a loan application.

2. **Computers are making work more abstract.** Most industrial workers have a "hands-on" relationship with their product. Postindustrial workers manipulate symbols in pursuit of abstract goals such as making a company more profitable or software more user-friendly.

3. **Computers limit workplace interaction.** As workers spend more time at computer terminals, they become isolated from other workers.

4. **Computers enhance employers' control of workers.** Computers allow supervisors to monitor employees' output continuously, whether they work at computer terminals or on assembly lines.

Such changes remind us that technology is not socially neutral. Rather, it shapes the way we work and alters the balance of power between employers and employees. Understandably, then, people welcome some aspects of the Information Revolution and oppose others.

CORPORATIONS

At the core of today's capitalist economy lies the **corporation,** *an organization with a legal existence, including rights and liabilities, apart from that of its members.* Incorporating makes an organization a legal entity unto itself, able to enter into contracts and own property. Of the more than 24 million businesses in the United States, 5 million are incorporated (U.S. Census Bureau, 2002). Incorporating also protects the wealth of owners from lawsuits arising from business debts or as a result of harm to consumers; often, it also means a lower tax rate on the company's profits.

ECONOMIC CONCENTRATION

Forty percent of U.S. corporations are small, with assets under $100,000. The largest corporations, however, dominate our country's economy. In 2001, 576

Them That's Got, Gets: The Case of Corporate Welfare

Would you like the government to slash your income taxes and end sales tax on your purchases? What about offering you money to buy a new house at a below-market interest rate? Would you like the government to hook up all your utilities for free and pay your water and electric bills?

For an ordinary person, such deals sound too good to be true. But our tax money is doing exactly this—not for families, but for big corporations. All a large company has to do is declare a willingness to relocate and then wait for the offers from state and local governments to come pouring in.

Supporters call government aid to corporations "public-private partnerships." They point to the jobs corporations create, sometimes in areas hard hit by earlier business closings. For a city or county with a high unemployment rate, the promise of a new factory is simply too good to pass up. If incentives in the form of tax relief or free utilities are needed to seal the deal, the money is considered well spent.

Critics, however, call such arrangements "corporate welfare." They agree that companies create

new jobs, but they point out that the corporations get much more than they give. In 1991, for example, the state of Indiana offered $451 million in incentives to lure United Airlines to build an aircraft maintenance facility there. United Airlines built the facility and hired 6,300 people. But some simple math shows that the cost to Indiana came out to be a whopping $72,000 *per job*. Much the same happened in 1993, when Alabama offered $253 million in incentives to Mercedes-Benz to build an automobile assembly plant in Tuscaloosa. The plant opened and 1,500 people were hired—at an average cost to Alabama of $169,000 for each worker. In 1997, Pennsylvania gave $307 million in incentives to a Norwegian

company to reopen part of Philadelphia's naval shipyard. Once the deal was signed, 950 people were hired, at a cost of $323,000 per job. In 2002, Georgia spent $67,000 per job to clinch the deal for a new Daimler-Benz auto plant. Across the country, the pattern is much the same. Overall, government support to corporations exceeds $15 billion each year, more than the welfare given to poor people.

Nationwide, while new plants do create some jobs, most jobs are simply moved from one place to another. But not all jobs pay well. Nor is there any guarantee that, once settled, a corporation will stay, since businesses are free to make a better deal to move once again to another location. In 1993, state and local governments in Kentucky granted General Electric $19 million in tax breaks to build a washing-machine factory near Louisville. In 1999, GE pulled up stakes, putting 1,500 local people out of work, so that the company could move to new factories in Georgia and Mexico, where wages were lower.

Sources: Adapted from Bartlett & Steele (1998) and various news reports.

corporations had assets exceeding $1 billion, representing three-fourths of all corporate assets and profits (U.S. Census Bureau, 2002).

The largest U.S. corporation in terms of sales is Wal-Mart, with $94.7 billion in total assets. Wal-Mart employs more people than the state governments of California, Texas, Washington, New York, Ohio, Michigan, and Florida combined. Its sales ($245 billion in 2003) equal the tax revenues of nearly half the states.

CONGLOMERATES AND CORPORATE LINKAGES

Economic concentration creates **conglomerates,** *giant corporations composed of many smaller corporations.* Conglomerates form as corporations enter new markets, spin off new companies, or merge with other companies. For example, RJR-Nabisco is a conglomerate that sells not only cigarettes but dozens of family household products.

Many conglomerates are linked because they own each other's stock, the result being worldwide corporate alliances of staggering size. General Motors, for example, owns Opel (Germany), Vauxhall (Great Britain), and half of Saab (Sweden) and has partnerships with Suzuki, Isuzu, and Toyota (Japan). Similarly, Ford owns Jaguar and Aston Martin (Great Britain) and a share of Mazda (Japan), Kia (Korea), and Volvo (Sweden).

Corporations are also linked through *interlocking directorates,* networks of people who serve as directors of many corporations (Scott & Griff, 1985; Weidenbaum, 1995; Kono et al., 1998). On the board of directors of any large corporation, one is likely to find people who also have seats on the boards of dozens or even hundreds of other companies. These boardroom connections provide access to valuable information about each other's products and marketing strategies. While perfectly legal, such linkages sometimes encourage illegal activity, such as price fixing, as the companies share information about their pricing structures.

CORPORATIONS: ARE THEY COMPETITIVE?

According to the capitalist model, businesses operate independently in a competitive market. But with extensive linkages, large corporations do not operate independently. Moreover, a small number of large corporations dominates many markets; large corporations, therefore, are not truly competitive.

U.S. law forbids the practice of **monopoly,** *the domination of a market by a single producer,* because, with no competition, a company could simply dictate prices. But **oligopoly,** *the domination of a market by a few producers,* is both legal and common. Oligopoly arises because the vast investment needed to enter a major market, such as the auto industry, is beyond the reach of all but the biggest companies. Moreover, true competition means risk, which big business tries to avoid.

The federal government seeks to regulate corporations in order to protect the public interest. Yet, as recent corporate scandals have shown us (Chapter 8, "Deviance," has a discussion of corporate crime), when corporations misbehave, millions of people are harmed, and regulation is typically too little, too late. Furthermore, the U.S. government is the corporate world's single biggest customer. The federal government also steps in to support struggling corporations, sometimes with billion-dollar bailout programs. In addition, as the box explains, state governments' aid to corporations has drawn fire as "corporate welfare."

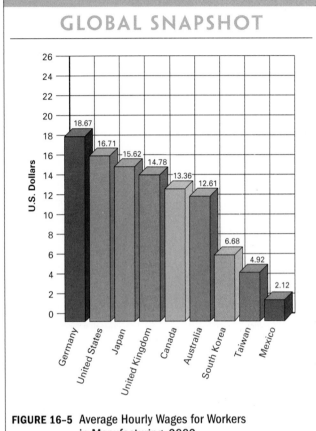

GLOBAL SNAPSHOT

FIGURE 16-5 Average Hourly Wages for Workers in Manufacturing, 2002

Source: U.S. Department of Labor (2003).

CORPORATIONS AND THE GLOBAL ECONOMY

Corporations have grown so large that they account for most of the world's economic output. The biggest corporations are based in the United States, Japan, and Western Europe, but they consider the entire world one huge marketplace. In fact, many large U.S. companies such as McDonald's generate most of their sales outside the United States.

Global corporations are well aware that poor nations contain most of the world's people and resources. In addition, as shown in Figure 16–5, labor costs are attractively low: A manufacturing worker in Mexico labors for almost two weeks to earn what a German worker earns in a single day.

The impact of multinationals on poor countries is controversial, as Chapter 12 ("Global Stratification")

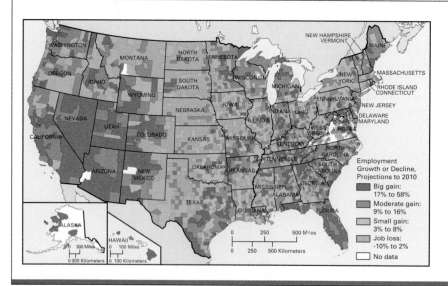

NATIONAL MAP 16–2
Where the Jobs Will Be:
Projections to 2010

The economic prospects of counties across the United States are not the same. Much of the midsection of the country is projected to lose jobs. By contrast, the coastal regions and most of the West are rapidly gaining jobs. What factors might account for this pattern?

Source: Used with permission of Woods & Poole Economics, Washington, D.C.

Employment Growth or Decline, Projections to 2010
- Big gain: 17% to 58%
- Moderate gain: 9% to 16%
- Small gain: 3% to 8%
- Job loss: -10% to 2%
- No data

---

explained. On one side of the argument, modernization theorists claim that multinationals, unleashing the great productive power of capitalism, raise living standards in poor nations. Specifically, corporations offer poor societies capital investment, tax revenues, new jobs, and advanced technology that, together, accelerate economic growth (Rostow, 1978; Madsen, 1980; Berger, 1986; Firebaugh & Beck, 1994; Firebaugh & Sandu, 1998; Firebaugh, 1999).

Dependency theorists counter that multinationals make global inequality worse. Multinationals, they say, create few jobs because they block the development of local industries and push poor countries to make goods for export rather than food and other products for local people. From this standpoint, multinationals make poor nations poorer (Wallerstein, 1979; Delacroix & Ragin, 1981; Bergesen, 1983; Walton & Ragin, 1990; Dixon & Boswell, 1996; Kentor, 1998).

While modernization theory hails the market as the key to progress and affluence for all the world's people, dependency theory calls for replacing market systems with government-based economic policies. The final box takes a closer look at the issue of market versus government economies.

 MEDIA Statistics and analysis for any number of economic issues can be found at the Web site of the U.S. Department of Labor: http://www.dol.gov

LOOKING AHEAD: THE ECONOMY OF THE TWENTY-FIRST CENTURY

Social institutions are a society's way of meeting people's needs. But as we have seen, the U.S. economy only partly succeeds in this respect. Although highly productive, our economy provides for some much better than for others. Moreover, the Information Revolution continues to change our economy. First, the share of the U.S. labor force in manufacturing is half what it was in 1960; service work, especially computer-related jobs, makes up the difference. For industrial workers, then, the postindustrial economy has brought rising unemployment and declining wages. Our society must face up to the challenge of providing millions of men and women with the language and computer skills they need to succeed in the new economy. Of course, as the recent economic collapse of many "dot.coms" shows, even this new type of work is not immune to a downturn. In addition, there are regional differences in the economic outlook: National Map 16–2 shows which regions are projected to gain jobs and which are expected to lose them by the end of the decade.

A second transformation that will mark this new century is the expansion of the global economy. Two centuries ago, the ups and downs of a local economy

CONTROVERSY & DEBATE

The Market: Does the "Invisible Hand" Look Out for Us or Pick Our Pockets?

"The market" or "government planning"? Governments rely on one or the other to determine what products and services companies will produce and what people will consume. So important is this question that the answer largely determines how nations define themselves, choose their allies, and identify their enemies.

Historically, U.S. society has relied on the "invisible hand" of the market to make economic decisions. Market dynamics move prices up or down according to the supply of products and buyer demand. The market thus coordinates the efforts of countless people, each of whom—to restate Adam Smith's insight—is motivated only by self-interest. Defenders of the market system—most notably economists Milton Friedman and Rose Friedman (1980)—remind us that a more-or-less freely operating market system is the key to this country's high standard of living.

But others point to the contributions government makes to the U.S. economy. First, government must step in to carry out tasks that no private company could do as well. For example, Adam Smith looked to government to defend the country against external enemies. Government (in partnership with private companies) also plays a key role in constructing and maintaining public projects such as roads, utilities, schools, libraries, and museums.

But the Friedmans counter that, whatever the task, government usually ends up being very inefficient. The least satisfying goods and services available today—public schools, the postal service, and passenger railroad service—are government-operated. The products we

most enjoy—household appliances, computers and other new electronics, fashionable clothes—are products of the market. Thus, while some government presence in the economy is necessary, the Friedmans and other supporters of free markets believe that minimal state regulation best serves the public interest.

But supporters of government intervention in the economy have additional arguments in their arsenal. For one thing, they claim, the market has little incentive to produce anything that is not profitable. Therefore, few private companies set out to meet the needs of poor people, since, by definition, poor people have little money to spend.

Second, the market has certain self-destructive tendencies that only the government can curb. In 1890, for example, the government passed the Sherman Antitrust Act to break up the monopolies that controlled the nation's oil and steel production. Since then—and especially since President Franklin Roosevelt's New Deal of the 1930s—government has taken a strong regulatory role to control inflation (by setting interest rates), enhance the well-being of workers (by imposing workplace safety standards), and benefit consumers (by setting standards for product quality). Despite such interventions, advocates of a stronger government role point out that corporations in U.S. society are so powerful that the government still cannot effectively challenge the capitalist elite.

Third, because the market magnifies social inequality, the government must step in on the side of social justice. Since capitalist economies concentrate income and wealth in the hands of a

few, a government system of taxation that applies higher rates to the rich counters this tendency.

Does the market's "invisible hand" look out for us or pick our pockets? While most people in the United States favor a free market, they also support government intervention that benefits the public. Indeed, in recent years, public confidence in corporations has fallen, while confidence in the federal government has gone up. Government's job is not only to ensure national security but also to maintain economic stability. Therefore, government helps businesses by providing investment capital, maintaining roads and other public services, and shielding companies from foreign competition. It is no surprise, then, that people in the United States and around the world continue to debate the optimal balance of market forces and government decision making.

Continue the debate . . .

1. *Why do free-market defenders assert that "a government is best that governs least"? What do you think?*

2. *What difference does it make in people's everyday lives if a society's economy is more a market system or more government-centered?*

3. *What is your impression of the successes and failures of socialist economic systems? What about "welfare capitalism" as found in Sweden?*

Sources: Friedman & Friedman (1980), Erber (1990), Paul (2002), and NORC (2003).

reflected events and trends in a single town. One century ago, communities were economically linked so that one town's prosperity depended on producing goods demanded by people elsewhere in the country. Today, it makes little sense to speak of a national economy, because what people in a Kansas farm town produce and consume may be affected as much by what happens in the wheat-growing region of Russia as by events in their own state capital. In short, U.S. workers and business owners are generating products and services in response to factors and forces that are distant and unseen.

Finally, analysts around the world are rethinking conventional economic models. The global economy shows that socialism is less productive than capitalism, one important reason for the collapse of the socialist regimes in Eastern Europe and the former Soviet Union. But capitalism, too, is changing and now operates with significant government regulation, partly to address the economic inequality generated by market systems.

What will be the long-term effects of these changes? Two conclusions seem inescapable. First, the economic future of the United States and other nations will be played out in a global arena. The emergence of the postindustrial economy in the United States is inseparable from the increasing industrial production of other nations. Second, we must address the related issues of global inequality and population increase (Firebaugh, 1999, 2000). Whether the world economy ultimately reduces or deepens the disparity between rich and poor societies may well be what will steer our planet toward peace or war.

SUMMARY

1. The economy is the major social institution by which a society produces, distributes, and consumes goods and services.

2. In technologically simple societies, the economy is simply part of family life. Agrarian societies show some productive specialization. Industrialization rapidly expands the economy through greater specialization and new energy sources that power machines in large factories.

3. The postindustrial economy is characterized by a shift from producing goods to producing services. Just as the Industrial Revolution propelled the industrial economy of the past, the Information Revolution is now advancing the postindustrial economy.

4. The primary sector of the economy, which generates raw materials, dominates in preindustrial societies. The secondary, manufacturing sector prevails in industrial societies. The tertiary, service sector dominates in postindustrial societies.

5. The expanding global economy now produces and consumes products and services with little regard for national boundaries. Today, the 600 largest corporations, operating internationally, account for most of the world's economic output.

6. Capitalism is based on the private ownership of productive property and the pursuit of profit in a competitive marketplace. Socialism is grounded in the collective ownership of productive property through government control of the economy.

7. Although the U.S. economy is predominantly capitalist, government is broadly involved in economic life. Government plays a greater role in the "welfare capitalist" economies of some Western European nations, such as Sweden, and the "state capitalism" of many Asian nations, including Japan.

8. Capitalism is very productive, providing a high average standard of living. A capitalist system allows the freedom to act according to one's self-interest. Socialism is less productive but generates greater economic equality. A socialist system offers freedom from basic want.

9. In the United States, agricultural work has declined to just 2 percent of the labor force. Blue-collar jobs have also dwindled, accounting for 24 percent of the labor force. The share of white-collar service occupations, however, has risen to more than 70 percent of the labor force.

10. While work in the primary labor market provides greater rewards, many new jobs in the United States are service positions in the secondary labor market.

11. A profession is a special category of white-collar work based on theoretical knowledge, occupational autonomy, authority over clients, and a claim to serving the community.

12. Today, 7.1 percent of U.S. workers are self-employed. Although many professionals fall into this category, most self-employed workers have blue-collar occupations.

13. Unemployment has many causes, including the operation of the economy itself; in 2002, 5.8 percent of the U.S. labor force was without work.

14. The underground economy, which includes criminal as well as legal activity, generates income unreported to the government.

15. Corporations form the core of the U.S. economy. The largest corporations, which are conglomerates, account for most corporate assets and profits. Many large corporations operate as multinationals, producing and distributing products in nations around the world.

KEY CONCEPTS

economy (p. 407) the social institution that organizes a society's production, distribution, and consumption of goods and services

postindustrial economy (p. 410) a productive system based on service work and high technology

primary sector (p. 410) the part of the economy that draws raw materials from the natural environment

secondary sector (p. 410) the part of the economy that transforms raw materials into manufactured goods

tertiary sector (p. 411) the part of the economy that involves services rather than goods

global economy (p. 411) expanding economic activity with little regard for national borders

capitalism (p. 413) an economic system in which natural resources and the means of producing goods and services are privately owned

socialism (p. 414) an economic system in which natural resources and the means of producing goods and services are collectively owned

communism (p. 414) a hypothetical economic and political system in which all members of a society are socially equal

welfare capitalism (p. 415) an economic and political system that combines a mostly market-based economy with extensive social welfare programs

state capitalism (p. 415) an economic and political system in which companies are privately owned but cooperate closely with the government

primary labor market (p. 418) jobs that provide extensive benefits to workers

secondary labor market (p. 418) jobs that provide minimal benefits to workers

labor unions (p. 418) organizations of workers that seek to improve wages and working conditions through various strategies, including negotiations and strikes

profession (p. 419) a prestigious white-collar occupation that requires extensive formal education

underground economy (p. 421) economic activity involving income unreported to the government as required by law

corporation (p. 423) an organization with a legal existence, including rights and liabilities, apart from that of its members

conglomerate (p. 424) a giant corporation composed of many smaller corporations

monopoly (p. 425) the domination of a market by a single producer

oligopoly (p. 425) the domination of a market by a few producers

CRITICAL-THINKING QUESTIONS

1. As a social institution, what is the economy supposed to do? How well do you think the U.S. economy does its job?

2. In what specific ways did the Industrial Revolution change the U.S. economy? How is the Information Revolution changing the economy once again?

3. What key characteristics distinguish capitalism from socialism? Compare these two systems in terms of productivity, economic inequality, and personal freedoms.

4. What does it mean to say that we now have a global economy? How does the operation of the global economy affect your life?

APPLICATIONS AND EXERCISES

1. The profile of the overall U.S. economy—74 percent of output is in the service sector, 24 percent in the industrial sector, and 2 percent in the primary sector—obscures great variety within this country. Visit the library and locate data that profile your own city, county, or state.

2. Visit a discount store such as Wal-Mart or K-Mart and select an area of the store of interest to you. Do a little "fieldwork," inspecting products to see where they are made. Does your research support the existence of a global economy?

3. What share of the faculty on your campus have temporary teaching contracts? Talk with several tenured faculty, as well as several visiting professors: What differences can you discover in their working conditions and their attitude toward their job?

4. Packaged in the back of this new textbook is an interactive CD-ROM that offers a variety of video and interactive review materials intended to help you better understand the material covered in this chapter. For this chapter, the CD-ROM contains a relevant clip from *ABC News*, an author's tip video, interactive map animations, an interactive time line, and flashcards with audio pronunciations of the more difficult words.

 ## SITES TO SEE

http://www.prenhall.com/macionis

Visit the interactive Companion Website™ that accompanies this text. Begin by clicking on the cover of your book. You will find a chapter-by-chapter study guide, practice tests, suggested Web links, and links to other relevant material.

http://www.bls.gov/

Visit this Web site operated by the Bureau of Labor Statistics, where you will find a wide range of interesting data and reports.

http://www.nber.org

Another worthwhile site is run by the National Bureau of Economic Research, which explains the operation of the economy.

http://www2.kenyon.edu/Projects/Famfarm/

Students at Kenyon College, in central Ohio, prepared this Web site as part of their study of family farms in the local, rural county.

http://www.fao.org

The Food and Agriculture Organization is a part of the United Nations concerned with how well the global economy meets the needs of the world's people. From its main page, look for its annual report, titled "State of Food Insecurity in the World."

 ## INVESTIGATE WITH RESEARCH NAVIGATOR™

Follow the instructions on page 24 of this text to access the features of **Research Navigator™**. Once at the Web site, enter your Login Name and Password. Then, to use the **Content Select™** database, enter keywords such as "unemployment," "corporations," and "capitalism," and the search engine will supply relevant and recent scholarly and popular press publications. Use the *New York Times* **Search-by-Subject Archive** to find recent news articles related to sociology and the **Link Library** feature to find relevant Web links organized by the key terms associated with this chapter.

January 27, 2002

Immigrant Laborers Feel Stranded in Pacific Northwest as Day Jobs Dry Up

By SAM HOWE VERHOVEK

TACOMA, Wash.—Finding work was not a problem for José Padilla for most of the last two and a half years. Landscaping in Phoenix, laying carpet in Denver and, most recently, packing apples near Wenatchee in central Washington.

"Everywhere I went there were jobs to do," said Mr. Padilla, 26, from a village in Jalisco Province in Mexico.

But as he stood in the wind and rain the other morning outside a day laborers' center here, part of a line of more than 60 men, he found himself confronting a new reality. There was no work that day, just as there had been none in three of the last four days he had shown up at the site. . . .

With the economy in particular decline in the Pacific Northwest, where Oregon and Washington have the two highest unemployment rates in the nation, hundreds of immigrant laborers have left agricultural areas on the eastern side of the Cascade Mountains in recent months, looking for work in the urban areas on the western side.

But with the market for such unskilled work drying up, many are finding little or no work at all, and some describe themselves as virtually stranded in the cities. . . .

The problem is most visible in Seattle, at places like the Casa Latina Day Workers Center, a gathering place that has for four years matched Mexican and Central American immigrants with contractors and homeowners.

For much of that time, with the Puget Sound economy roaring, the workers seemed to have the upper hand. Almost anyone who showed up at Casa Latina could find a job for the day, even if the worker was in the United States illegally.

Today many more men show up each day, competing for fewer jobs, said David Ayala, lead organizer at the center. . . .

Several men waiting for work the other day said they were homeless. . . . Most said they could no longer send money to their families in Mexico or Central America, their reason for traveling to the United States in the first place. Others said they felt stuck here, with no way out.

"I came here because I heard there were jobs, jobs, jobs in Seattle, $10 an hour or more," said Raúl, also 26, from San Pedro Sula, Honduras, who declined to give his full name because he is not a legal immigrant. "Now I would do anything to just be able to go home," Raúl said about the city where his wife and his son and daughter, both 6, live. But with a bus or plane ticket costing $600 or more, Raúl wondered whether he could ever afford to go.

Those who had worked on the farms of central Washington said they had traveled to Seattle temporarily, looking for work in the fallow winter months . . .

In past years, they said, they had . . . gone home to see their families for the winter or, perhaps, traveled to Florida or Texas, where farm work could be found. But many said they were remaining in Seattle because they could not afford to go elsewhere or because they were worried about security crackdowns along the border and in the United States. . . .

"I think it's harder just to travel around the country," said a 32-year-old at Casa Latina who gave his first name as Pedro. He has found work over the last three years even though he is here illegally and has no photo identification. Last year, he took a bus to Missouri to work in a poultry-processing plant.

"I've heard that Greyhound wants to see a driver's license or a passport or something," Pedro said. . . .

Mr. Ayala said he was seeing a growing number of workers who have grown destitute and demoralized. "The street changes you," he said, describing several regulars at Casa Latina who recently became homeless and who have found only sporadic work despite showing up at the job center every day.

"You wind up feeling like a mouse, just trying to figure out where to go at night," Mr. Ayala said. "You forget your whole goal in coming here to begin with. Now you're just trying to survive."

What do you think?

1. Do the people in this article conform to the common stereotype of the poor as not trying very hard? Explain.
2. What, if anything, do you think society owes people who want to work but who cannot find jobs?

CHAPTER

17

POLITICS AND GOVERNMENT

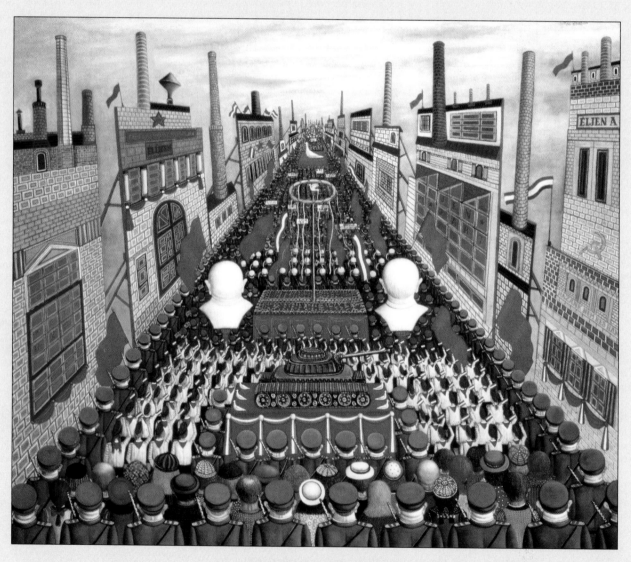

TAMAS GALAMBOS
Bright Winds Are Blowing Our Banner

1980. 150 × 170 cm. Private Collection. Bridgeman Art Library.

ON THE EVENING of March 17, 2003, the president of the United States stood before television cameras in the White House and spoke in a serious tone: "My fellow citizens, events in Iraq have now reached the final days of decision." President Bush then recounted how the Gulf War of 1991 had ended only on the condition that Iraq "reveal and destroy all its weapons of mass destruction." During the last twelve years, the president continued, Iraq had failed to do so, despite diplomatic pressure by the United Nations and the United States. Characterizing the Iraqi government as a "regime with a history of reckless aggression," President Bush maintained that the Iraqi government still held weapons of mass destruction, which threatened the security of many nations, including the United States. Therefore, the president laid down an ultimatum: Unless Saddam Hussein and his sons left the country within forty-eight hours, opening the door to peaceful disarmament, the United States and other nations would disarm Iraq by using military force.

Saddam Hussein defied the ultimatum, and two days later, the United States unleashed a barrage of high technology weapons. With such technological superiority, the ability of the United States to defeat Iraq militarily could not be in doubt, and within three weeks, the coalition forces were entering the capital city of Baghdad. But as many critics have pointed out, winning a military engagement is no sure road to peace. Indeed, the emergence of the United States as a global superpower has provoked both praise and condemnation around the world.

Power relationships define our world. What is power? How do governments gain popular support? Why do nations sometimes turn to war as a means of resolving differences? This chapter addresses these questions by investigating *politics*, the dynamics of power within societies and among nations. Formally, **politics**—or "the polity"—is *the social institution that distributes power, sets a society's agenda, and makes decisions*. The fact that the U.S. population was divided over the military campaign to disarm Iraq, however, suggests that politics is often a matter of controversy.

POWER AND AUTHORITY

We begin with a basic observation by sociologist Max Weber (1978; orig. 1921). Every society, Weber claimed, is based on **power,** which he defined as *the ability to achieve desired ends despite resistance from others*. To a large degree, the exercise of power is the business of **government,** *a formal organization that directs the political life of a society*. Governments demand compliance on the part of a population; yet, as Weber explained, most governments do not openly threaten their people. Most of the time, people respect (or, at least, accept) their political system.

Brute force is the most basic form of power. The rule of Saddam Hussein was criticized as brutal toward anyone who did not comply with the will of the leader. Yet, Weber explained, no government is likely to stay in power if compliance comes *only* from the threat of sheer force, since there could never be enough police to watch everyone (and who would watch the police?). Therefore, a government tries to build support from the people for its goals and its means of pursuing them.

Every government, then, tries to establish its power as legitimate in the eyes of the people. This brings us to Weber's concept of **authority,** *power that people perceive as legitimate rather than coercive.* How can governments transform raw power into more stable authority? Weber pointed to three ways, which societies employ according to their level of economic development: traditional authority, rational-legal authority and charismatic authority.

TRADITIONAL AUTHORITY

Preindustrial societies, Weber explained, rely on **traditional authority,** *power legitimized through respect for long-established cultural patterns.* Woven into a society's collective memory, traditional authority may seem almost sacred. Chinese emperors in antiquity were legitimized by tradition, as were nobles in medieval Europe. The power of tradition can be so strong that—for better or worse—people typically viewed hereditary rulers as almost godlike.

But traditional authority declines as societies industrialize. Hannah Arendt (1963) pointed out that traditional authority is compelling only so long as everyone shares the same heritage and worldview. Modern scientific thinking, the specialization demanded by industrial production, and the social change and cultural diversity brought on by immigration all weaken tradition. Thus, a U.S. president would never claim to rule by the grace of God. Even so, some upper-class families with names like Bush, Kennedy, Roosevelt, and Rockefeller are so well established in this country's political life that their members can enter the political arena with some measure of traditional authority (Baltzell, 1964).

If traditional authority plays only a small part in U.S. national politics, it persists in other aspects of everyday life. *Patriarchy,* the domination of women by men, is a traditional form of power that is widespread, although increasingly challenged. Less controversial is the traditional authority parents exert over their children. The fact that traditional authority is linked to a person's status as parent is obvious every time a parent answers a doubting child's "Why?" with "Because I said so!" The parent's decision is not open for debate because it would defeat the parent's traditional authority over the child by putting the two on an equal footing.

RATIONAL-LEGAL AUTHORITY

Weber defined **rational-legal authority** (sometimes called *bureaucratic authority*) as *power legitimized by legally enacted rules and regulations.* Rational-legal authority, then, is power legitimized in the operation of lawful government.

As Chapter 7 ("Groups and Organizations") explains, Weber viewed bureaucracy as the organizational backbone of rational-thinking, modern societies. Moreover, just as a rational worldview promotes bureaucracy, so it erodes traditional customs and practices. Instead of venerating the past, members of today's high-income societies seek justice through formally enacted rules of law.

Rationally enacted rules also underlie many power relationships in everyday life. The authority of deans and classroom teachers, for example, rests on the offices they hold in bureaucratic colleges and universities (one reason we call people in authority "officers"). The police, too, are officers within the bureaucracy of local government. In contrast to traditional authority, rational-legal authority flows not from family background but from a position in the formal organization of government. Thus, whereas a traditional monarch rules for life, a modern president accepts and gives up power according to law, which shows that presidential authority lies in the office, not in the person.

CHARISMATIC AUTHORITY

Finally, Weber claimed that power can be transformed into authority through charisma. **Charismatic authority** is *power legitimized through extraordinary personal abilities that inspire devotion and obedience.* Unlike its traditional and rational-legal counterparts, then, charismatic authority depends less on a person's ancestry or office and more on individual personality.

Charismatic leaders have surfaced throughout history and have used their personal skills to turn an audience into followers. In the process, often enough, they make their own rules and challenge the status

In 2003, just 28 of the world's 192 nations were political monarchies where single families pass power from generation to generation. The African nation of Swaziland recently celebrated the coronation of a young king.

quo. Examples of charismatic leaders include Jesus of Nazareth, Nazi Germany's Adolf Hitler, liberator of India Mahatma Gandhi, and civil rights leader Dr. Martin Luther King, Jr. The fact that all charismatics share a goal of radically transforming society makes them highly controversial (and explains why few charismatics die of old age).

For more about the life of Dr. King, go to http://www.lib.lsu.edu/hum/mlk

Because charismatic authority flows from a single individual, the leader's death creates a crisis. The survival of a charismatic movement, Max Weber explained, requires the **routinization of charisma,** *the transformation of charismatic authority into some combination of traditional and bureaucratic authority.* After the death of Jesus, his followers institutionalized his teachings in a church built on tradition and bureaucracy. Routinized in this way, the Roman Catholic church has lasted for some 2,000 years.

POLITICS IN GLOBAL PERSPECTIVE

Political systems have changed over the course of history. Technologically simple hunting and gathering societies, once found all over the planet, operated like one large family without formal government. Leadership generally fell to a man with unusual strength, hunting skill, or personal charisma. But with few resources, such leaders could barely control their own people, much less rule a large area (Nolan & Lenski, 1999).

Agrarian societies are larger, are characterized by specialized activity, and produce a material surplus. In these societies, a small elite gains control of most of the wealth and power, moving politics from the family to become a social institution in its own right. Some leaders may claim a divine right to rule, gaining some measure of Weber's traditional authority. Leaders may also benefit from rational-legal authority to the extent that their rule is supported by law.

As societies grow even bigger, politics takes the form of a national government, or *political state.* But the effectiveness of a political state depends on the available technology. Centuries ago, armies moved slowly, and communication over even short distances was uncertain. For this reason, the early political empires—such as Mesopotamia in the Middle East about 5,000 years ago—took the form of many small *city-states.*

More complex technology brings about the larger-scale system of *nation-states.* Currently, the world has 192 independent nation-states, each with a somewhat distinctive political system. Generally speaking, however, the world's political systems can be analyzed in terms of four categories: monarchy, democracy, authoritarianism, and totalitarianism.

MONARCHY

Monarchy (with Latin and Greek roots meaning "one ruler") is *a type of political system in which a single family rules from generation to generation.* Monarchy was typical in the ancient agrarian societies; the Bible, for example, tells of great kings such as David and Solomon. In the world today, twenty-eight nations have royal families;[1] some trace their ancestry back for centuries. In Weber's terms, then, monarchy is legitimized by tradition.

During the Middle Ages, *absolute monarchs* in much of the world claimed to rule by divine right. Today, although claims of divine right are rare, monarchs in a number of nations—including Kuwait, Saudi Arabia, and Brunei—still have almost absolute control over their people.

With industrialization, however, monarchs gradually pass from the scene in favor of elected officials. All the European nations where monarchs remain are *constitutional monarchies* in that these traditional leaders are little more than symbolic heads of state; actual governing is the responsibility of elected officials, led by a prime minister and guided by a constitution. In these nations, nobility formally reigns, but elected officials actually rule.

DEMOCRACY

The historical trend in the modern world is toward **democracy,** *a type of political system that gives power to the people as a whole.* More accurately, a system of *representative democracy* puts authority in the hands of elected leaders who, from time to time, compete for office in elections.

Most rich countries of the world claim to be democratic (including those that still have royal families). Industrialization and democratic government go together because both require a literate populace. Moreover, the traditional legitimization of power in an agrarian monarchy gives way, with industrialization, to rational-legal authority. Thus, democracy and rational-legal authority are linked just as monarchy and traditional authority are.

But high-income countries such as the United States are not truly democratic, for two reasons. First, there is the problem of bureaucracy. The U.S. federal government has close to 3 million regular

employees, 6 million contract workers, 1.4 million uniformed military personnel, and 2.4 million employees paid by various grants and special funding—about 13 million workers in all. In addition, another 18 million people work in some 80,000 local governments across the country. Most people who operate the government are not directly accountable to the people (Edwards, 1985; Etzioni-Halevy, 1985; Light, 1999).

The second problem involves economic inequality, since rich people have far more political clout than poor people. One reason George W. Bush got off to such a fast start in the 2000 presidential campaign was that, as a rich man with many rich friends, he was able to raise more than $50 million very quickly. Media magnate Michael Bloomberg spent almost $70 million of his own money (about $90 per vote cast for him) in his successful bid to be elected mayor of New York City in 2001. In short, in the game of politics, few doubt that "money talks." Given the even greater resources of billion-dollar corporations and labor unions, how well does our "democratic" system hear the voices of average people? (Burns, Francia, & Herrnson, 2000; Williams, 2001)

Still, democratic nations provide many rights and freedoms. Global Map 17–1 shows one assessment of the extent of political freedom around the world. According to Freedom House, an organization that tracks political trends, by 2003, 89 of the world's 192 nations (with 44 percent of the global population) were "free," respecting many civil liberties. This number represents a strong gain for democracy: Just 76 nations were free a decade earlier (Freedom House, 2003).

Democracy and Freedom: Capitalist and Socialist Approaches

Despite the problems we have just described, rich capitalist nations such as the United States claim to operate as democracies. Of course, socialist countries like Cuba and the People's Republic of China make the same claim. This curious fact suggests that we need to look more closely at *political economy,* that is, the interplay of politics and economics.

The political life of the United States, Canada, and the nations of Europe is largely shaped by the economic principles of capitalism, described in Chapter 16. The pursuit of profit within a market system requires that "freedom" be defined in terms of people's rights to act in their own self-interest. Thus, the capitalist approach to political freedom translates into

---

[1]In Europe, these include Sweden, Norway, Denmark, Great Britain, the Netherlands, Liechtenstein, Luxembourg, Belgium, Spain, and Monaco; in the Middle East, Jordan, Saudi Arabia, Oman, Qatar, Bahrain, and Kuwait; in Africa, Lesotho, Swaziland, and Morocco; in Asia, Brunei, Samoa, Tonga, Thailand, Malaysia, Cambodia, Nepal, Bhutan, and Japan.

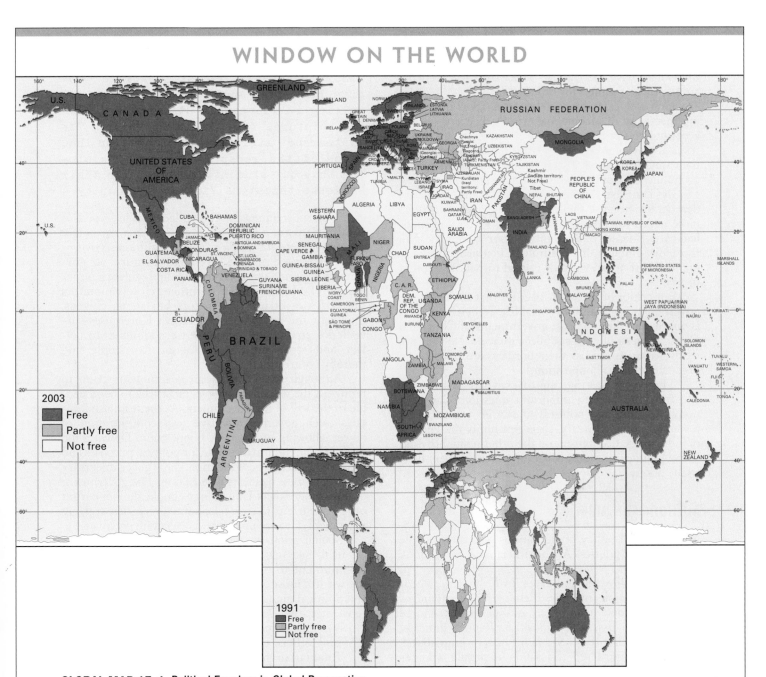

GLOBAL MAP 17–1 Political Freedom in Global Perspective

In 2003, 89 of the world's nations, containing 44 percent of all people, were politically "free"; that is, they offered their citizens extensive political rights and civil liberties. Another 55 countries, which included 21 percent of the world's people, were "partly free," with more limited rights and liberties. The remaining 48 nations, home to 35 percent of humanity, fall into the category of "not free." In these countries, government sharply restricts individual initiative. Between 1980 and 2003, democracy made significant gains, largely in Latin America and Eastern Europe. In Asia, India (containing 1 billion people) returned to the "free" category in 1999. In 2000, Mexico joined the ranks of nations considered "free" for the first time.

Source: Freedom House (2003).

personal liberty, the freedom to act in whatever ways maximize personal profit or other advantage. From this point of view, moreover, "democracy" means that individuals have the right to select their leaders from among those running for office.

However, capitalist societies are marked by a striking inequality of income and wealth. If everyone acts according to self-interest, in other words, the inevitable result is that some people have much more power to get their way than others. It is this elite that dominates the economic and political life of the society.

By contrast, socialist systems claim they are democratic because their economies meet everyone's basic needs for housing, schooling, work, and medical care. Despite being a much poorer country than the United States, for example, Cuba provides basic medical care to all without regard to people's ability to pay.

But critics of socialism counter that the extensive government regulation of social life in these countries is oppressive. The socialist governments of China and Cuba, for example, do not allow their people to move freely within or across their borders and tolerate no organized political opposition.

These contrasting approaches to democracy and freedom raise an important question: Can economic equality and political liberty go together? To foster economic equality, socialism limits the choices of individuals. Capitalism, on the other hand, provides broad political liberties, which, in practice, mean little to the poor.

AUTHORITARIANISM

As a matter of policy, some nations give their people little voice in politics. **Authoritarianism** is *a political system that denies popular participation in government.* An authoritarian government cares little about the needs of ordinary people, provides them with no legal means to remove leaders from office, and makes use of force in response to dissent or opposition. Reports indicate, for example, that Iraq's Saddam Hussein imprisoned, tortured, or murdered thousands of people who resisted his rule.

Several of Iraq's neighbors, including the absolute monarchies in Saudi Arabia and Bahrain, are also authoritarian, as are the military juntas in the African nations of Congo and Ethiopia. But heavy-handed government does not always breed popular opposition. The box looks at the "soft authoritarianism" that thrives in the small Asian nation of Singapore.

TOTALITARIANISM

October 22, near Saigon, Vietnam. Six U.S. students in our study-abroad program have been arrested, allegedly for talking to Vietnamese students and taking pictures at the university. The Vietnamese Minister of Education has canceled the reception tonight, claiming that our students meeting with their students threatens Vietnam's security.

The most intensely controlled political form is **totalitarianism,** *a highly centralized political system that extensively regulates people's lives.* Totalitarian governments emerged in the twentieth century as governments gained the ability to rigidly regulate a population. The Vietnamese government closely monitors the activities of not just visitors but all its citizens. Similarly, the government of North Korea uses surveillance equipment and powerful computers to collect and store information about its people and thereby control them.

Although some totalitarian governments claim to represent the will of the people, most seek to bend people to the will of the government. As the term itself implies, such governments have *total* concentration of power, allowing no organized opposition. Denying the populace the right to assemble for political purposes and controlling access to information, these governments try to make citizens feel fearful and alone. The government of the former Soviet Union, for example, did not permit ordinary citizens to own telephone directories, copying equipment, fax machines, or even accurate city maps.

Socialization in totalitarian societies is intensely political, seeking not just compliance but personal commitment to the system. In North Korea, one of the world's most totalitarian states, pictures of leaders and political messages are everywhere, reminding citizens that they owe total allegiance to the state. Government-controlled schools and mass media present only official versions of events.

Totalitarian governments span the political spectrum from fascist (including Nazi Germany) to communist (including North Korea). In some totalitarian states, businesses are privately owned (as was the case in Nazi Germany and in Chile under Augusto Pinochet); in others, businesses are government-owned (as in North Korea, Cuba, and the former Soviet Union). In all cases, however, one party claims total control of the society and permits no opposition.

GLOBAL SOCIOLOGY

"Soft Authoritarianism" or Planned Prosperity? A Report from Singapore

To many, Singapore, a tiny nation on the tip of the Malay Peninsula with a population of 4 million, seems an Asian paradise. Surrounded by poor societies grappling with rapidly growing populations, rising crime rates, and squalid, sprawling cities, Singapore—with its affluence, cleanliness, and safety—makes North American visitors think more of a theme park than a country.

In fact, since gaining its independence from Malaysia in 1965, Singapore has startled the world with its economic development; its per capita income rivals that of France. In contrast to the United States, Singapore has scarcely any social problems such as crime, slums, unemployment, or children living in poverty. In fact, people in Singapore don't even contend with traffic jams, graffiti on subway cars, or litter in the streets.

The key to Singapore's orderly environment is the ever-present hand of government, which actively promotes traditional morality and regulates just about everything. The state owns and manages most of the country's housing and has a hand in many businesses. It provides tax incentives for family planning and completing additional years of schooling. To keep traffic under control, the government slaps hefty surcharges on cars, pushing the price of a basic sedan up to around $40,000.

Singapore has tough anti-crime laws that mandate death by hanging for drug dealing and permit police to detain a person suspected of a crime without charge or trial. The government has outlawed some religious groups (including Jehovah's Witnesses) and bans pornography outright. To keep the city clean, the state forbids smoking in public, bans eating on a subway, imposes stiff fines for littering, and has even outlawed the sale of chewing gum.

In economic terms, Singapore defies familiar categories. Government control of scores of businesses, including television stations, telephone service, airlines, and taxis, seems socialist. Yet, unlike most socialist enterprises, these businesses are operated efficiently and very profitably. Moreover, Singapore's capitalist culture applauds economic growth (although the government cautions people against the evils of excessive materialism), and hundreds of multinational corporations are based here.

Singapore's political climate is as unusual as its economy. Freedom House characterizes Singapore as "partly free." The law provides for elections of political leaders, but one party—the People's Action party—dominates the political process and currently controls eighty-one of the eighty-three seats in the country's Parliament. In fact, the People's Action party has ruled Singapore without opposition since the country's independence thirty years ago. Just as important, members of this society feel the presence of government far more than their counterparts in the United States.

Clearly, Singapore is not a democratic country in the conventional sense. But most people in this prospering nation wholeheartedly endorse their way of life. What Singapore's political system offers is a simple bargain: Government demands unflinching loyalty from the populace; in return, it provides security and prosperity. Critics charge that this system amounts to a "soft authoritarianism" that stifles dissent and controls people's lives. Most of the people of Singapore, however, know the struggles of living elsewhere and, for now at least, consider the trade-off a good one.

Sources: Adapted from Branegan (1993) and Freedom House (1999).

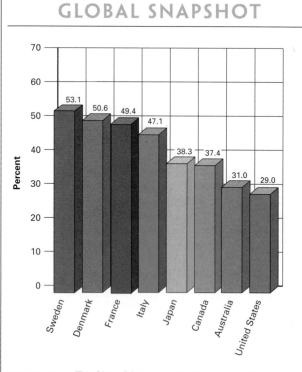

GLOBAL SNAPSHOT

FIGURE 17-1 The Size of Government: Government Expenditures as a Percentage of Gross Domestic Product, 2001

Source: U.S. Census Bureau (2002).

because they have enormous power to shape events throughout the world. In other words, politics is dissolving into business as corporations grow larger than governments.

Then, too, the Information Revolution has made national politics accessible to people around the world. Electronic mail over the Internet, cellular phones, satellite transmission systems, and fax machines mean that countries can no longer conduct their political affairs in complete privacy.

Finally, several thousand *nongovernmental organizations* (NGOs) are now in operation, most with global membership and focus. Typically, these organizations seek to advance universal principles, such as human rights (Amnesty International) or an ecologically sustainable world (Greenpeace). In this century, NGOs will almost certainly play a key part in forming a global political culture (Boli & Thomas, 1997).

In sum, just as individual nations are losing control of their own economies, governments cannot fully manage the political events occurring within their borders.

POLITICS IN THE UNITED STATES

After fighting a revolutionary war against Great Britain to gain political independence, the United States replaced the British monarchy with a democratic political system. Since then, our nation's political development has reflected its distinctive history, cultural heritage, and capitalist economy.

A GLOBAL POLITICAL SYSTEM?

Chapter 16 ("The Economy and Work") described the emergence of a global economy, in which large corporations operate with little regard to national boundaries. Is there a parallel development of a global political system?

On one level, the answer is no. Although most of the world's economic activity now involves more than one nation, the planet remains divided into nation-states, just as it has been for centuries. The United Nations (founded in 1945) was a step toward global government. But as the debate leading up to the war in Iraq makes clear, this body is often divided, and member nations still operate largely according to their own interests.

On another level, however, politics has become a global process. In the minds of some analysts, multinational corporations represent a new political order

U.S. CULTURE AND THE RISE OF THE WELFARE STATE

The political culture of the United States can be summed up in a word: individualism. This emphasis derives from the Bill of Rights, which guarantees freedom from undue government interference. It was this individualism that the nineteenth-century poet and essayist Ralph Waldo Emerson had in mind when he said, "The government that governs best is the government that governs least."

But most people today stop short of Emerson's position, recognizing that government is necessary to ensure national defense, maintain law and order, and support schools, highways, and other infrastructure. Moreover, the U.S. government has grown into a vast and complex **welfare state**—*a range of government agencies and programs that provides benefits to the population.* Government benefits begin even before birth

TABLE 17-1 The Political Spectrum: A National Survey, 2002

Survey Question: "We hear a lot of talk these days about liberals and conservatives. I'm going to show you a seven-point scale on which the political views people might hold are arranged from extremely liberal—point 1—to extremely conservative—point 7. Where would you place yourself on this scale?"

1	2	3	4	5	6	7
Extremely liberal	Liberal	Slightly liberal	Middle of the road	Slightly conservative	Conservative	Extremely conservative
3.4%	10.4%	11.6%	38.0%	15.2%	15.3%	3.0%

[*Don't know/no answer* 3.0%]

Source: *General Social Surveys, 1972–2002: Cumulative Codebook* (Chicago: National Opinion Research Center, 2003), p. 98.

(through prenatal nutrition programs) and continue into old age (through Social Security and Medicare). Some programs are especially important to the poor, who are not well served by our capitalist economic system; but students, farmers, homeowners, small business operators, veterans, performing artists, and even executives of giant corporations also get various subsidies and supports. In fact, a majority of U.S. adults now look to government for at least part of their income (Caplow et al., 1982; Devine, 1985; Bartlett & Steele, 1998).

Today's welfare state is the result of a gradual increase in the size and scope of government. In 1789, when the presence of the federal government amounted to little more than a flag in most communities, the entire federal budget was a mere $4.5 million ($1.50 for every person in the nation). Since then, it has steadily risen, reaching $2 trillion in 2002 (a per capita figure of $7,100).

Similarly, when our nation was founded, one government employee served every 1,800 citizens. Today, there is one official for every fourteen citizens—a total of 20 million government employees, more than are engaged in U.S. manufacturing (U.S. Census Bureau, 2002).

As much as government has expanded in this country, the U.S. welfare state is still smaller than that in many other high-income nations. Figure 17–1 shows that government is larger in most of Europe, and especially in the Scandinavian countries.

THE POLITICAL SPECTRUM

Who supports a bigger welfare state? Who wants to cut it back? Such questions tap attitudes that form the *political spectrum*, which ranges from extremely liberal on the left to extremely conservative on the right.

Table 17–1 shows how adults in the United States describe their political orientation. One-fourth of the respondents fall on the liberal, or "left," side, and one-third describe themselves as conservative to some degree, placing themselves on the political "right." The remaining 38 percent claim to be moderates, in the political "middle" (NORC, 2003:98).

One reason so many people identify themselves as "moderates" is that most of us are more conservative on some issues and more liberal on others (Barone & Ujifusa, 1981; McBroom & Reed, 1990). One cluster of attitudes concerns *economic issues*, which focus on economic inequality and the opportunities available for various categories of people. Others concern *social issues*, which involve moral questions about how people ought to live.

Economic Issues

Economic issues came to the fore during the Great Depression of the 1930s as President Franklin Delano Roosevelt developed a number of programs together known as "the New Deal." These programs, which included Social Security, greatly expanded government efforts to promote the economic well-being of the U.S. population. Then as now, economic liberals supported enlarging the welfare state, while economic conservatives did not.

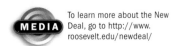 To learn more about the New Deal, go to http://www.roosevelt.edu/newdeal/

Today, both the more liberal Democratic party and the more conservative Republican party support popular government programs such as Social Security. Democrats, however, support greater government regulation of the overall economy. Republicans, by contrast, seek to trim the size and scope of government involvement in the economy.

Lower-income people have more pressing financial needs and so they tend to focus on economic issues, such as the level of the minimum wage. Higher-income people, by contrast, provide support for many social issues, such as animal rights.

Economic liberals (mostly Democrats) believe that the power of the government is needed to maintain a healthy economy and ensure an adequate supply of jobs. Economic conservatives (likely to be Republicans) counter that government intervention tends to block market forces and reduces economic productivity.

Social Issues

Social issues are moral questions, ranging from abortion to the death penalty to gay rights and the treatment of minorities. Social liberals endorse equal rights and opportunities for all categories of people, view abortion as a matter of individual choice, and oppose the death penalty because, in their view, it does little to discourage crime and has been unfairly applied to minorities.

The "family values" agenda of social conservatives supports traditional gender roles and opposes gay marriage, affirmative action, and other "special programs" that take account of people's group membership rather than their individual abilities and efforts. Social conservatives condemn abortion as morally wrong and support the death penalty as a just response to heinous crime (Macionis, 2005).

Of the two major political parties, Republicans are more conservative on both economic and social issues, while Democrats are more liberal. In practice, then, Republicans endorse traditional values and celebrate individual initiative, while Democrats support government action to enhance people's well-being and to reduce inequality. Yet each party has conservative and liberal wings so that there may be little difference between a liberal Republican and a conservative Democrat. Furthermore, both Republicans and Democrats favor big government—as long as it advances their particular aims. Conservative Republicans (like Presidents Ronald Reagan and George W. Bush) have sought to increase military strength, for example, while more liberal Democrats (like President Bill Clinton) tried to expand the government's "social safety net" by extending government-regulated health care coverage to all citizens.

Class, Race, and Gender

Well-to-do people tend to be conservative on economic issues (because they have wealth to protect) but liberal on social issues (due, in large part, to higher levels of education). Low-income people display the opposite pattern, being economically liberal yet socially conservative (Erikson, Luttbeg, & Tedin, 1980; McBroom & Reed, 1990).

African Americans, both rich and poor, tend to be more liberal than whites (especially on economic issues) and, for half a century, have voted Democratic (more than 90 percent supported Democrat Al Gore in 2000). Historically, Latinos, Asian Americans, and Jews have also supported the Democratic party.

Overall, women tend to be somewhat more liberal than men. Among U.S. adults, women lean toward the Democratic party, while men are somewhat more likely to vote for Republican candidates. Figure 17–2 shows the same pattern among college students. Although there have been changes in student attitudes—being more liberal in the 1970s, more conservative in the 1980s, and shifting a bit toward the liberal side in the 1990s—women in college have remained consistently more liberal than their male counterparts (Astin et al., 2002; NORC, 2003).

Party Identification

Because many people hold mixed political attitudes—espousing liberal views on some issues and taking conservative stands on others—party identification in the United States is weak. In a recent national survey of party identification among U.S. adults, 43.1 percent claimed to favor the Democratic Party and 34.8 percent favored the Republican Party; yet just 14.8 percent of adults claimed to be "strong Democrats," and just 11.4 percent claimed to be "strong Republicans." Another 19.1 percent described themselves as "independent" (NORC, 2003). This lack of strong party identification is one reason each of the two major parties gains or loses power from election to election. Republicans scored a landslide victory in the 1994 congressional elections, for example, while the Democrats held the White House in 1996 and gained ground in Congress in 1996, 1998, and 2000. In 2002, the tide turned again as Republicans made gains in Congress.

Finally, there is an urban-rural divide in U.S. politics: People in urban areas typically vote Democratic and those in rural areas Republican. The box on page 444 takes a closer look at the national political scene, and National Map 17–1 on page 445 shows the county-by-county results for the 2000 election.

SPECIAL-INTEREST GROUPS

For years, a debate has raged across the United States about the extent to which government should regulate the private ownership of firearms. Organizations such as Handgun Control, Inc., support stricter gun laws, while

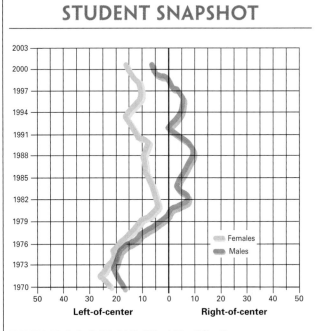

STUDENT SNAPSHOT

FIGURE 17–2 Left/Right Political Identification of College Students, 1970–2001

Source: Astin et al. (2002).

the National Rifle Association opposes them. Each of these organizations is an example of a **special-interest group,** *a political alliance of people interested in some economic or social issue.* Special-interest groups, which To learn more about how researchers conduct political polls, go to http://faculty.vassar.edu/lowry/polls.html include associations of elderly people, women, farmers, tour bus operators, fireworks producers, environmentalists, and countless others, flourish in nations such as the United States, where political parties are relatively weak. Special-interest groups employ *lobbyists* (Washington, D.C., is home to more than 15,000 of them) to work on their behalf.

Political action committees (PACs) are *organizations formed by special-interest groups, independent of political parties, to raise and spend money in support of political aims.* Political action committees channel most of their funds directly to candidates likely to support their interests. Although legal reforms have limited direct contributions to candidates, since the 1970s the number of PACs has grown to 3,945 (U.S. Federal Election Commission, 2003).

DIVERSITY: RACE, CLASS, AND GENDER

The Rural-Urban Divide: Election 2000

An important—and often over-looked—dimension of diversity in the United States involves where people live: in rural versus urban places. Sociologists have long debated how the two settings differ (see Chapter 22, "Population, Urbanization, and Environment"). But one thing is certain: Rural and urban politics are quite different.

Take a look at National Map 17–1, which shows the county-by-county results from the 2000 presidential election. The first thing that is striking about the map is that Republican George W. Bush won in almost 80 percent of U.S. counties—2,477 out of a total of 3,153 (which appear in various shades of red). Democrat Al Gore, by contrast, won in just 676 counties (which appear in a shade of blue). Gore actually won the popular vote across the country, although Bush was victorious in the election by winning the majority of votes in the electoral college.

The reason Bush won more counties while Gore received more votes is that Republican counties tend to be rural, with relatively small populations. Democrats, by contrast, do better in the fewer counties containing large cities. In Nevada, for example, the map shows just the Las Vegas area in "Gore blue," while the remainder of the state is painted "Bush red." In Oregon, Gore won enough votes in Portland to carry the entire state, even though almost all the remaining counties went for Bush.

Political analyst Stuart Rothenberg (cited in Simon, 2000) sums it up: "There is a cultural gap between liberal, urban, Democratic America and rural, small-town, Republican America." With this difference in mind, we can understand why there was stronger support for the recent Gulf War in rural counties, while demonstrations opposing the war were centered in large cities.

Source: Based on Bai (2001).

With the costs of campaigns rising rapidly, most candidates eagerly accept support from political action committees. In the 2002 congressional elections, 40 percent of all funding came from PACs; twenty-five percent of all donations to senatorial election campaigns were PAC contributions. Supporters claim that PACs represent the interests of a vast array of businesses, unions, and church groups and are a legitimate part of the political process. Critics counter that organizations supplying cash to politicians expect to be treated favorably in return, so that, in effect, PACs buy political influence (Allen & Broyles, 1991; Cook, 1993; Center for Responsive Politics, 2003).

In 2000, the candidates for the U.S. presidency spent some $3 billion on their campaigns, and another $3 billion was spent by those running for all other political offices. Does having the most money matter? The answer is yes: Race for race, 90 percent of the time the candidate with the most money won the election. Concerns about the power of money have prompted considerable discussion across the country. In 2002, Congress passed a modest reform that is likely to reduce—only slightly—the political power of money (Lindlaw, 2002).

VOTER APATHY

A disturbing fact of U.S. political life is that many people are indifferent about voting. The long-term trend has been toward wider *eligibility* to vote—the Fifteenth Amendment, ratified in 1870, enfranchised African American men; the Nineteenth Amendment extended voting rights to women in 1920; in 1971, the Twenty-sixth Amendment lowered the voting age to eighteen years. Compared to a century ago, however, a smaller percentage of today's eligible citizens actually *do* vote. In the 2000 presidential election, which turned on a few hundred votes, less than 60 percent of eligible voters actually went to the polls, a lower share than in most other high-income nations.

Who is and is not likely to vote? Women and men are equally likely to cast a ballot. People over sixty-five, however, are twice as likely to vote as college-age adults (half of whom never even registered before the 2000 election). Non-Hispanic white people are more likely to vote (62 percent voted in 2000) than African Americans (57 percent), and Hispanics (45 percent) are the least likely of all to vote. Generally speaking, people with a bigger stake in U.S. society—homeowners,

SEEING OURSELVES

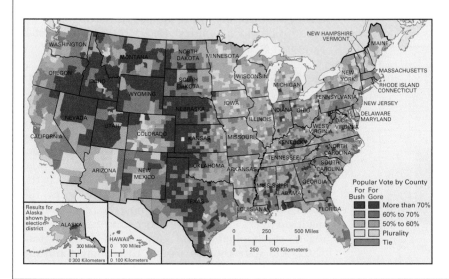

NATIONAL MAP 17–1
The Presidential Election, 2000: Popular Vote by County

The 2000 presidential election was the closest in more than a century. Almost 80 percent of the nation's counties went for George W. Bush, but densely populated areas, especially along both coasts, provided strong support for Al Gore. What social differences do you think distinguish the areas that voted Republican and Democratic? Why are rural areas mostly Republican whereas cities tend to be Democratic?

Popular Vote by County
For Bush / For Gore
More than 70%
60% to 70%
50% to 60%
Plurality
Tie

Results for Alaska shown by election district

parents with young children, people with more schooling and good jobs—are more likely to vote. Income matters, too: People earning more than $75,000 are twice as likely to vote (75 percent voted in 2000) as people earning between $5,000 and $10,000 (41 percent voted) (Lewis, McCracken, & Hunt, 1994; DeLuca, 1998; Fetto, 1999; U.S. Census Bureau, 2002).

Of course, we should expect some nonvoting because, at any given time, millions of people are sick or away from home or have recently moved to a new neighborhood and have yet to reregister. Registering and voting also depend on the ability to read and write, so the tens of millions of U.S. adults who have limited literacy skills are discouraged from voting. Finally, people with physical disabilities that limit mobility have a lower turnout than the general population (Schur & Kruse, 2000; Brians & Grofman, 2003).

Conservatives suggest that apathy amounts to *indifference* to politics because most people are, by and large, content with their lives. Liberals and especially political radicals counter that apathy reflects *alienation* from politics: People are so deeply dissatisfied with society that they doubt elections make any real difference. Figure 17–3 on

Learn more about voting, public opinion, and political participation at this Web site: http://www.umich.edu/~nes/

page 446 confirms that most high-income people *do* vote and most low-income people *don't.* The fact that it is the disadvantaged and powerless people who are least likely to vote suggests that the liberal explanation for apathy is probably closer to the truth.

NONVOTING BY CONVICTED CRIMINALS

Although the right to vote is one foundation of U.S. democracy, forty-eight of the fifty states (all except Vermont and Maine) have laws that bar felons—people convicted of serious crimes—from voting. Typically, therefore, people in jail, on probation, or on parole have no political voice. Ten states go further and bar many or all ex-felons from ever voting again.

Do such laws make a difference in U.S. elections? The answer is yes: The number of people prevented from voting by these laws approaches 10 million. Noting that convicted felons show better than a two-to-one preference for Democratic over Republican candidates, and even allowing for expected voter apathy, one recent study concluded that, were these laws not in force, Democrats would have won more congressional races and Al Gore would have defeated George W. Bush for the presidency in 2000 (Uggen & Manza, 2002).

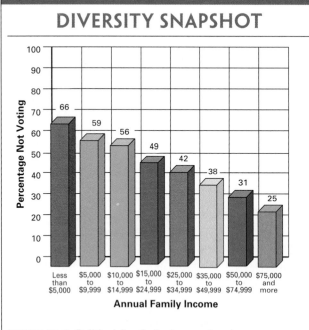

FIGURE 17-3 Political Apathy by Income Level

Percentage of adults who reported not voting in the 2000 presidential election, by annual family income.

Source: U.S. Census Bureau (2002).

THEORETICAL ANALYSIS OF POWER IN SOCIETY

Sociologists have long debated the distribution of power in the United States. Power is a very difficult topic to study because decision making is complex and takes place behind closed doors. Moreover, it is difficult to separate a theory of power from the theorists' political leanings. Nevertheless, three competing models of power in the United States have emerged.

THE PLURALIST MODEL: THE PEOPLE RULE

The **pluralist model,** closely linked to structural-functional theory, is *an analysis of politics that sees power as dispersed among many competing interest groups.* Pluralists claim, first, that politics is an arena of negotiation. With limited resources, no organization can expect to realize all its goals. Organizations therefore operate as *veto groups,* realizing some success but mostly keeping opponents from achieving all their

ends. The political process, then, relies heavily on negotiating alliances and compromises among numerous interest groups so that policies gain wide support. In short, pluralists see power as widely dispersed throughout society, with all people having at least some voice in the political system (Dahl, 1961, 1982; Rothman & Black, 1998).

THE POWER-ELITE MODEL: A FEW PEOPLE RULE

The **power-elite model,** based on social-conflict theory, is *an analysis of politics that sees power as concentrated among the rich.* The term *power elite* was coined by C. Wright Mills (1956), who argued that a small upper class holds most of society's wealth, prestige, and power.

Mills claimed that the power elite head up the three major sectors of U.S. society: the economy, the government, and the military. Thus, the power elite is made up of the "super-rich" (corporate executives and major stockholders); top officials in Washington, D.C., and state capitals around the country; and the highest-ranking officers in the U.S. military.

Further, Mills explained, these elites move from one sector to another, building power as they go. Vice President Dick Cheney, for example, has moved back and forth between powerful positions in the corporate world and the federal government. Colin Powell moved from a top position in the U.S. military to become secretary of state. More broadly, when President George W. Bush took office, he assembled a cabinet in which all but one member were already millionaires.

Power-elite theorists challenge the claim that the United States is a political democracy. They maintain that the concentration of wealth and power is simply too great for the average person's voice to be heard. They reject the pluralist idea that various centers of power serve as checks and balances on one another. Instead, the power-elite model holds that people at the top encounter no real opposition (Bartlett & Steele, 2000; Moore et al., 2002).

THE MARXIST MODEL: BIAS IN THE SYSTEM ITSELF

A third approach to understanding U.S. politics is the **Marxist political-economy model,** *an analysis that explains politics in terms of the operation of a society's economic system.* Like the power-elite model, the Marxist model rejects the idea that the United States operates as a political democracy. But whereas the power-elite model focuses on the disproportionate wealth and power of certain individuals, the Marxist model highlights bias rooted within this nation's institutions, especially its

TABLE 17-2 Three Models of U.S. Politics: A Summary

	Pluralist Model	Power-Elite Model	Marxist Model
How is power distributed in U.S. society?	Highly dispersed.	Concentrated.	Concentrated.
Is the United States basically democratic?	Yes, because voting offers everyone a voice, and no one group or organization dominates society.	No, because a small share of the people dominates the economy, government, and military.	No, because the bias of the capitalist system is to concentrate wealth and power.
How should we understand voter apathy?	Apathy is indifference; after all, even poor people can organize for a greater voice if they want it.	Apathy is understandable, given how difficult it is for ordinary people to oppose the rich and powerful.	Apathy is alienation generated by a system that will always leave most people powerless.

economy. As noted in Chapter 4 ("Society"), Karl Marx claimed that a society's economic system (capitalist or socialist) shapes its political system. Therefore, the power elites do not simply appear on the scene; they are creations of capitalism itself.

From this point of view, reform of the political system—say, by limiting the amount of money that rich people can contribute to political candidates—is unlikely to bring about true democracy. The problem does not lie in the *people* who exercise great power or the *people* who don't vote; the problem is rooted in the *system* itself, what Marxists term the "political-economy of capitalism." In other words, until the United States establishes an economic democracy, in which companies are operated by all workers collectively, there can be no real political democracy.

Critical evaluation. Table 17–2 summarizes the three models of the U.S. political system. Which of these three models is correct? Over the years, research has shown that a case can be made for all three. In the end, how one views this country's political system, and how one thinks it ought to operate, turns out to be as much a matter of political values as of scientific fact.

Classic research by Nelson Polsby (1959) supports the pluralist model. Polsby studied the political scene in New Haven, Connecticut, and concluded that key decisions on various issues—including education, urban renewal, the electoral nominating process—were made by different groups. He found, too, that few of the upper-class families listed in New Haven's *Social Register* were also economic leaders. Thus, Polsby concluded, no one segment of society rules all the others.

Robert Dahl also investigated New Haven's history, finding that, over time, power had become more and more dispersed. Thus, Dahl's research also supports the pluralist model. As he put it, "No one, and certainly no group of more than a few individuals, is entirely lacking in [power]" (1961:228).

Supporting the power-elite position is classic research by Robert Lynd and Helen Lynd (1937) in Muncie, Indiana (which they called "Middletown," to suggest that it was a typical city). They documented the fortune amassed by a single family—the Balls—from their business manufacturing glass canning jars. The Lynds showed how the Ball family dominated the city's life. If anyone doubted the Balls' prominence, one had only to note that the local bank, a university, a hospital, and a department store all bore the family name. In Muncie, according to the Lynds, the power elite boiled down more-or-less to a single family.

From the Marxist perspective, the point is not to look at which individuals make decisions. Rather, as Alexander Liazos (1982:13) explains, "The basic tenets of capitalist society shape everyone's life: the inequalities of social classes and the importance of profits over people." As long as the basic institutions of society are organized to meet the needs of the few rather than the many, Liazos concludes, a democratic society is impossible.

Clearly, the U.S. political system gives almost everyone the right to participate in the political process through elections. But the power-elite and Marxist models point out that, at the very least, the U.S. political system is far less democratic than most people think. Most citizens may have the right to vote, but the major political parties and their candidates typically support only those positions acceptable to the most powerful segments of society and consistent with the operation of our capitalist economy (Bachrach & Baratz, 1970).

Increasing security in a time of danger generally means reducing freedom. As part of the ongoing "war on terror," security teams are far more evident in public places. In what ways does increased police surveillance threaten our freedoms?

Whatever the reasons, many people in the United States appear to be losing confidence in their leaders. More than 80 percent of U.S. adults report having, at best, only "some confidence" that members of Congress and other government officials will do what is best for the country (NORC, 2003:977, 1132).

POWER BEYOND THE RULES

Politics is always a matter of disagreement over a society's goals and the means to achieve them. Political systems, therefore, try to resolve controversy within a system of rules. But political activity sometimes breaks the rules or tries to do away with the entire system.

REVOLUTION

Political revolution is *the overthrow of one political system in order to establish another.* Reform involves change *within* a system, through modification of the law or, in the extreme case, a coup d'état (in French, literally, "stroke of the state"), in which one leader topples another. Revolution, however, involves not just change at the top but a change of the system itself.

No type of political system is immune to revolution; nor does revolution invariably produce any one kind of government. Our country's Revolutionary War transformed colonial rule by the British monarchy into a democratic government. French revolutionaries in

1789 also overthrew a monarch, only to set the stage for the return of monarchy in the person of Napoleon. In 1917, the Russian Revolution replaced monarchy with a socialist government built on the ideas of Karl Marx. In 1991, the Soviet Union dissolved, and shortly thereafter, the new Russian Federation moved toward a market system and a greater political voice for its people.

Despite their striking variety, revolutions share a number of traits (Tocqueville, 1955, orig. 1856; Davies, 1962; Brinton, 1965; Skocpol, 1979; Lewis, 1984; Tilly, 1986):

1. **Rising expectations.** Common sense suggests that revolution would be more likely when people are grossly deprived, but history shows that most revolutions occur when people's lives are improving. Rising expectations, rather than bitter resignation, fuel revolutionary fervor.

2. **Unresponsive government.** Revolutionary zeal gains strength when a government is unwilling to reform, and especially when the demands for reform are made by powerful segments of society.

3. **Radical leadership by intellectuals.** The English philosopher Thomas Hobbes (1588–1679) observed that intellectuals provide the justification for revolution, and universities often are the center of political change. Students played a critical role in China's prodemocracy movement and the uprisings in Eastern Europe.

4. **Establishing a new legitimacy.** Overthrowing a political system is not easy, but more difficult still is ensuring a revolution's long-term success. Some revolutionary movements are unified mostly by hatred of the past regime and fall apart once new leaders are installed. Revolutionaries must also guard against counterrevolutionary drives led by the deposed leaders; this explains the speed and ruthlessness with which victorious revolutionaries typically dispose of former rulers.

Scientific analysis cannot declare that a revolution is good or bad. The full consequences of such an upheaval depend on one's values and, in any case, become evident only after many years. More than a decade after the 1991 revolution, for example, the future of the former Soviet Union remains unsettled.

TERRORISM

On September 11, 2001, terrorists hijacked four commercial airliners; one crashed in a wooded area, and the other three were flown into public buildings full of people. The attack, which killed some 3,025 innocent individuals (representing sixty-eight nations), completely destroyed the World Trade Center in New York and seriously damaged the Pentagon in Washington, D.C. Not since the attack on Pearl Harbor at the outbreak of World War II had the United States suffered such a blow. Indeed, this event was the most serious terrorist act ever recorded.

Terrorism refers to *acts of violence or the threat of such violence used as a political strategy by an individual or a group.* Like revolution, terrorism is a political act beyond the rules of established political systems. According to Paul Johnson (1981), terrorism has four distinguishing characteristics.

First, terrorists try to paint violence as a legitimate political tactic, even though such acts are condemned by virtually every nation. Terrorists also bypass (or are excluded from) established channels of political negotiation. Terror is, therefore, a weak organization's strategy to harm a stronger foe. Indeed, terrorism has become almost commonplace in international politics. In 2002, there were 199 acts of terrorism worldwide, which claimed 725 lives and injured 2,013 people. Of these, 77 (39 percent) were directed against the United States (U.S. State Department, 2003).

Read the U.S. State Department's annual report on global terrorism at http://www.usis.usemb.se/terror/rpt2002/index.html

Not all terrorism is the work of individuals or groups. Since 1950, China has sought to maintain control of Tibet by force. This Tibetan refugee displays instruments of torture used against him by officials of the Chinese government.

These numbers represent a significant drop from 2001, in which 355 recorded attacks, including those committed on September 11, killed 3,295 people and injured 2,283. In that year, 62 percent of the attacks were aimed against the United States.

Second, terrorism is employed not just by groups but also by governments against their own people. *State terrorism* is the use of violence, generally without support of law, by government officials. State terrorism is lawful in some authoritarian and totalitarian states, which survive by inciting fear and intimidation. Saddam Hussein, for example, relied on secret police and state terror to shore up his power in Iraq.

Third, democratic societies reject terrorism in principle, but they are especially vulnerable to terrorists because they afford extensive civil liberties to their people and have less extensive police networks. In contrast, totalitarian regimes make widespread use of state terrorism, although, at the same time, their extensive police power minimizes opportunities for individual acts of terror against the government.

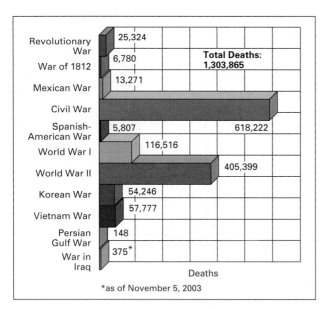

War	Deaths
Revolutionary War	25,324
War of 1812	6,780
Mexican War	13,271
Civil War	618,222
Spanish-American War	5,807
World War I	116,516
World War II	405,399
Korean War	54,246
Vietnam War	57,777
Persian Gulf War	148
War in Iraq	375*

Total Deaths: 1,303,865

Deaths

*as of November 5, 2003

FIGURE 17–4 Deaths of Americans in Eleven U.S. Wars

Sources: Compiled from various sources by Maris A. Vinovskis (1989) and the author.

Hostage taking and outright killing provoke popular anger, and there is little doubt that the September 11 attacks united the United States. But taking action against terrorists is problematic. The first step is identifying those responsible. Because most terrorist groups are shadowy organizations with no formal connection to any established state, it is difficult to point a finger of responsibility and a reprisal may be all but impossible. Yet, as terrorism expert Brian Jenkins warns, the failure to respond "encourages other terrorist groups, who begin to realize that this can be a pretty cheap way to wage war" (quoted in Whitaker, 1985:29). At the same time, a forcible military reaction to terrorism may risk confrontation with other governments.

Fourth, and finally, terrorism is always a matter of definition. Governments claim the right to maintain order, even by force, and may brand opposition groups that use violence as "terrorists." Similarly, political differences may explain why one person's "terrorist" is another's "freedom fighter." Ironically, in Afghanistan, some of the "terrorists" that the United States and other nations targeted in the wake of the September 11, 2001, attacks were the same people whom the world had widely praised as "freedom fighters" in the 1980s when they fought the invading Soviet army.

WAR AND PEACE

Perhaps the most critical political issue is **war,** *organized, armed conflict among the people of various nations, directed by their governments.* War is as old as humanity, of course, but understanding it now takes on greater urgency because modern military technology gives humanity the capacity to destroy itself.

For almost all of the twentieth century, nations somewhere on Earth were in violent conflict. In our nation's short history, we have participated in eleven large-scale wars—from the Revolutionary War to the War in Iraq in 2003—resulting in the deaths of more than 1.3 million U.S. men and women and injury to many times that number, as shown in Figure 17–4. Thousands more died in "undeclared wars" and "limited military actions" in the Dominican Republic, Nicaragua, Lebanon, Grenada, Panama, Haiti, Bosnia, and elsewhere, as well as the ongoing "war on terrorism" (Barone, 2002).

THE CAUSES OF WAR

Wars occur so often that we might think that there is something natural about armed confrontation. But although many animals are naturally aggressive, there is no evidence that human beings inevitably wage war under any particular circumstances. Indeed, as Ashley Montagu (1976) points out, governments around the world have to use considerable coercion in order to mobilize their people for war.

Like all forms of social behavior, warfare is a product of *society* that varies in purpose and intensity from place to place. The Semai of Malaysia, among the most peace-loving of the world's peoples, rarely resort to violence. In contrast, the Yąnomamö, described in Chapter 3 ("Culture"), are quick to wage war.

If society holds the key to war or peace, under what circumstances *do* humans go to battle? Quincy Wright (1987) identifies five factors that promote war:

1. **Perceived threats.** Societies mobilize in response to a perceived threat to their people, territory, or culture. Leaders justified the recent U.S.–led military campaign to disarm Iraq, for example, as necessary in order to eliminate the threat posed by Saddam Hussein and his weapons of mass destruction.

2. **Social problems.** When internal problems generate widespread frustration at home, a society's leaders may divert public attention by attacking

an external "enemy" as a form of scapegoating. While U.S. leaders claimed the War in Iraq was a matter of national security, there is little doubt that the onset of the war diverted attention from the struggling national economy and led to sharply higher public support for President Bush.

3. **Political objectives.** Poor nations, such as Vietnam, have used wars to end foreign domination. On the other hand, powerful countries, such as the United States, may benefit from a periodic show of force (recall the recent deployments of troops in Somalia, Haiti, Bosnia, Afghanistan, and Iraq) that enhances global political stature.

4. **Moral objectives.** Nations rarely claim to fight just to gain wealth and power or to satisfy the egos of national leaders. Leaders infuse military campaigns with moral urgency. By calling the 2003 War in Iraq "Operation Iraqi Freedom," U.S. leaders portrayed the mission as a morally justified war against an evil tyrant.

5. **The absence of alternatives.** A fifth factor promoting war is the absence of alternatives. Although the goal of the United Nations is to maintain international peace, the UN has had limited success in resolving tensions among nations and thus preventing war.

TERRORISM: A NEW KIND OF WAR?

In the wake of the terrorist attacks on September 11, 2001, U.S. government officials spoke of terrorism as a new kind of war. As we have explained, war has historically followed certain patterns: It is played out according to some basic rules; the warring parties are known to each other; and the objectives of the warring parties—which often involve control of territory—are clearly stated.

Terrorism, however, breaks from these patterns. The identity of terrorist individuals and organizations may not be known, terrorists may deny their responsibility, and their goals may be unclear. Indeed, the 2001 terrorist attacks against the United States were not attempts to defeat the nation militarily or to secure territory. They were carried out by people representing not a country but a cause, one not well understood in the United States. In short, they were expressions of anger and hate, an effort to destabilize the country, an effort to incite widespread anger and fear.

Conventional warfare is symmetrical, with two nations sending their armies into battle. By contrast, terrorism is an unconventional form of warfare, an asymmetrical conflict in which a small number of attackers use terror and their own willingness to die in order to level the playing field against a much more powerful enemy. Further, while the terrorists may be ruthless, the nation under attack must exercise restraint in its response to terror because little may be known about the identity and location of those responsible. It is for this reason that the U.S. response to the 2001 attack continues to unfold years later.

In the War in Iraq, the line between conventional war and terrorism sometimes blurred. Members of the Iraqi army made use of civilians as human shields in combat as well as sending soldiers into the field in civilian uniforms. As one U.S. officer stated, "The enemy has gone asymmetric on us. There's treachery. There's ambushes. It's not conventional" (Ratnesar, 2003:35). The reason for such tactics, of course, was to give a less powerful army an edge against a more technologically advanced foe.

THE COSTS AND CAUSES OF MILITARISM

The cost of armed conflict extends far beyond battlefield casualties. Together, the world's nations spend more than $1 trillion annually ($150 for every person on the planet) for military purposes. Such expenditures divert resources from the desperate struggle for survival by hundreds of millions of poor people.

For years, defense has been the U.S. government's largest single expenditure, accounting for 17 percent of all federal spending, or $348 billion in 2002. The war on terrorism (as well as the War in Iraq) has only pushed this number higher. The United States now stands as the world's single superpower, with more military might than the next nine countries combined (Gergen, 2002).

For decades, military spending went up as a result of the *arms race* between the United States and the former Soviet Union, which dropped out of the race after its collapse in 1991. But some analysts (who support power-elite theory) claim high spending has yet another cause: the domination of U.S. society by a **military-industrial complex,** *the close association of the federal government, the military, and defense industries.* The roots of militarism, then, lie not just in external threats to our security but also in the institutional structures here at home (Marullo, 1987; Barnes, 2002).

A final reason for continuing militarism is regional conflict. During the 1990s, for example, localized wars broke out in Bosnia, Chechnya, and Zambia, and tensions today run high in the Middle East as well

In recent years, the world has become aware of the death and mutilation caused by millions of land mines placed in the ground during wartime and left there afterward. Civilians—many of them children—maimed by land mines receive treatment in this Kabul, Afghanistan, clinic.

as between India and Pakistan. Even limited wars have the potential to escalate and draw in other countries, including the United States. India and Pakistan—both nuclear powers—moved to the brink of war in 2002, raising fears of atomic war. In 2003, the announcement by North Korea that it, too, had joined the nuclear club ensures that tensions will remain high in Asia as well.

NUCLEAR WEAPONS

The world still contains 20,000 nuclear warheads, representing a destructive force equivalent to the weight of every human being on the planet in TNT. If even a small fraction of this stockpile is used in war, life as we know it could end on much of the Earth. Albert Einstein, whose genius contributed to the development of nuclear weapons, reflected, "The unleashed power of the atom has changed everything *save our modes of thinking*, and we thus drift toward unparalleled catastrophe." In short, nuclear weapons make unrestrained war unthinkable in a world not yet capable of peace.

Great Britain, France, and the People's Republic of China all have substantial nuclear capability, but the vast majority of nuclear weapons are based in the United States and the Russian Federation. Although these two nations have reduced their stockpile of nuclear warheads, the danger of catastrophic war increases with **nuclear proliferation,** *the acquisition of nuclear weapons technology by more and more nations.* Israel, India, Pakistan, and North Korea also possess some nuclear weapons, and other nations (including Iran and Libya) are in the process of developing them. Although a few nations stopped the development of nuclear weapons—Argentina and Brazil halted work in 1990, South Africa dismantled its arsenal in 1991, and Belarus, Ukraine, and Kazakhstan are reported to have dismantled their weapons after the collapse of the Soviet Union—by 2010 as many as fifty nations could have the ability to fight a nuclear war. Such a trend makes any regional conflict infinitely more dangerous (McGeary, 1998; Thomas, Barry, & Liu, 1998; Ratnesar, 2003).

MASS MEDIA AND WAR

The War in Iraq was the first war in which television crews traveled with U.S. troops, reporting as the campaign unfolded. The mass media provided ongoing and detailed reports of events; cable television made available live coverage of the war twenty-four hours a day, seven days a week.

Those media outlets critical of the war—especially the Arab news channel Al Jezeera—tended to report the slow pace of the conflict, the casualties to the U.S. and allied forces, and the deaths and injuries suffered by Iraqi civilians, information that would increase pressure to end the war. Media outlets supportive of the war—including most news organizations in the United States—tended to report the rapid pace of the war and the casualties to Iraqi forces, and to downplay harm to Iraqi civilians as minimal and unintended. In sum, the power of the mass media to provide selective information to a worldwide audience means that television and other media are almost as important to the outcome of a conflict as the military that fight in the field.

PURSUING PEACE

How can the world reduce the dangers of war? Here are the most recent approaches to peace:

1. **Deterrence.** The logic of the arms race linked security to a "balance of terror" between rival

CRITICAL THINKING

Information Warfare: Let Your Fingers Do the Fighting

For decades, scientists and military officials have studied how to use computers to defend against missiles and planes. More recently, however, the military has recognized that new information technology can fundamentally transform warfare itself, replacing rumbling tanks and screaming aircraft with electronic weapons that would silently penetrate an enemy country's computer system and render it unable to transmit information.

In such "virtual wars," soldiers seated at workstation monitors would dispatch computer viruses to shut down the enemy's communication links, causing telephones to fall silent, air traffic control and railroad switching systems to fail, computer systems to feed phony orders to field officers, and television stations to broadcast "morphed" news bulletins urging people to turn against their leaders.

Like the venom of a poisonous snake, the weapons of "information warfare" might quickly paralyze an enemy before a conventional attack. Perhaps, too, the use of new information technology weaponry might not just precede conventional fighting but might prevent it entirely. If the victims of computer warfare could be limited to a nation's communications links rather than its citizens and cities, wouldn't we all be more secure?

Yet so-called "info-war" also poses new dangers to the world's most powerful nations, since, presumably, it would take only a few highly skilled operators with sophisticated electronic equipment to wreak communications havoc on them. The United States may be militarily without equal in the world, but given our increasing reliance on high technology, we are also more vulnerable to cyber-attack than any other nation. As a result, in 1996, the Central Intelligence Agency began work on a defensive "cyber-war center" to help prevent what one official termed an "electronic Pearl Harbor." Congress has already appropriated more than $2 billion to ensure the security of the U.S. computer infrastructure, including several hundred scholarships to train computer specialists who agree to work for the government after they graduate.

What do you think?

1. *Do you think it is realistic to expect virtual warfare to replace conventional battlefield fighting? Why or why not?*

2. *Can you see ways in which new information technology might increase the chances to resolve disputes peacefully?*

3. *Do you think computer technology might increase the dangers of war? If so, how?*

Sources: Waller (1995), Weiner (1996), and Page (2000).

---

nations. Based on the principle of *mutual assured destruction (MAD)*—meaning that the side launching a first-strike nuclear attack against the other would suffer massive retaliation—deterrence kept the peace during more than fifty years of "cold war" between the United States and the Soviet Union. But this strategy fueled an enormously expensive arms race and had little effect on nuclear proliferation. Deterrence also does little to prevent war initiated by a powerful nation (such as the United States) against a weaker foe (such as the Taliban regime in Afghanistan or Saddam Hussein's Iraq).

2. **High technology defense.** If technology created the weapons, perhaps it can also protect us from the threat of war. This is the idea behind the *strategic defense initiative (SDI)* proposed by the Reagan administration in 1981 and supported today by President Bush. Under SDI, satellites and ground installations would destroy enemy missiles soon after they were launched. Partly in response to the recent terrorist attacks, two-thirds of U.S. adults now support SDI (Thompson & Waller, 2001; *Society*, 2002). However, critics claim that the "Star Wars" system as it is called would be, at best, a leaky umbrella. Others worry that deploying such a system will spark another massive arms race.

Worth noting, too, is that sophisticated technology raises not only new possibilities for defense, but also new strategies for waging war. The box takes a closer look at the possibilities for "information warfare."

CONTROVERSY & DEBATE

Islam and Freedom: A "Democracy Gap"?

As the United States and its allies launched the war on Iraq, President Bush spoke of his hopes of liberating the Iraqi people and afterward, by holding up the example of a democratic Iraq, of bringing change to much of the Islamic world. As a recent study by Freedom House shows, however, the president is up against some long odds.

Freedom House reports that 47 of the world's 192 nations have an Islamic majority population. As the figure shows, just 11 (23.4 percent) of these 47 countries have democratic governments, and Freedom House rates only one—Mali—as "free." Of the 145 nations without a majority Islamic population, 110 (75.9 percent) have democratic governments, and 84 are rated as "free." In other words, countries without Islamic majorities are

three times more likely to have democratic governments as countries with Islamic majorities. Therefore, Freedom House concludes, countries with Islamic majority populations display a disturbing "democracy gap."

This relative lack of democracy holds for all world regions that have Islamic-majority nations—Africa, Central Europe, the Middle East, and Asia. The pattern is especially strong among the sixteen Islamic-majority states in the Middle East and North Africa that are ethnically Arabic—none is an electoral democracy.

What explains this "democracy gap"? Freedom House points to four factors. First, countries with Islamic-majority populations typically are less economically developed, with limited

schooling for their people and widespread poverty. Second, these countries have cultural traditions that rigidly control the lives of women, providing them with few economic, educational, or political opportunities. Third, while most other countries limit the power of religious elites in government, and some, including the United States, even mandate a "separation of church and state," Islamic-majority nations endorse involving Islamic leaders in government. In just two recent cases—Iran and Afghanistan under the Taliban—have Islamic leaders actually taken formal control of government; commonly, however, they exert considerable influence on political outcomes.

Fourth, and finally, the enormous wealth that comes from Middle Eastern

---

3. **Diplomacy and disarmament.** Some analysts believe that the best path to peace is diplomacy rather than technology (Dedrick & Yinger, 1990). Diplomacy can enhance security if nations commit to resolving differences at the negotiating table, and especially if they then agree to reduce weapons stockpiles.

   But disarmament has limitations. Successful diplomacy depends on everyone involved making efforts to resolve a common problem (Fisher & Ury, 1988). Furthermore, while the United States and the former Soviet Union have succeeded in negotiating arms reduction agreements, the threat from other nations such as North Korea is increasing.

4. **Resolving underlying conflict.** In the end, reducing the dangers of war may depend on resolving underlying conflicts by promoting justice around the world. Such a goal is easier stated than accomplished, of course. Even as the United States claims to fight in order to liberate the

people of Iraq from the tyranny of Saddam Hussein, many Islamic people see the United States as systematically oppressing the Muslim world. Perhaps the world needs to consider the wisdom of spending thousands of times as much money on militarism as we do on efforts to find peaceful solutions (Sivard, 1988; Kaplan & Schaffer, 2001).

LOOKING AHEAD: POLITICS IN THE TWENTY-FIRST CENTURY

Political systems are subject to ongoing change. As the twenty-first century unfolds, several problems and trends are likely to command widespread attention.

One vexing problem in the United States is the inconsistency between our democratic ideals and our low turnout at the polls. Perhaps, as conservative pluralist theorists contend, many people do not bother to vote because they are content with their lives. But perhaps liberal power-elite theorists are right to say that oil also plays a part in preventing democratic government. In Iraq, Saudi Arabia, Kuwait, Qatar, and other nations, this resource has provided astounding riches to a small number of families, money that they can use to shore up their political control. In addition, oil wealth permits elites to build airports and other modern facilities without encouraging broader economic development that would raise the living standards of the majority.

For all these reasons, Freedom House concludes that the road to democracy for Islamic-majority nations is likely to be long. Yet, there are also reasons to think that today's patterns do not predict those of tomorrow. Looking back to 1950, a survey of the world would have noted that very few Catholic-majority countries (mostly in Europe and Latin America) had democratic governments. Today, however, most of these nations are

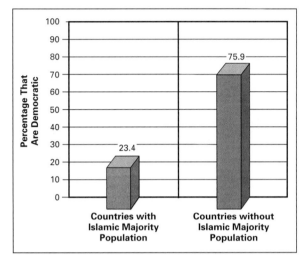

Democracy in Countries with and without Islamic-Majority Populations

Source: Karatnycky (2002).

democratic. Note, too, that a majority of the world's Muslim people—who live in Nigeria, Turkey, Bangladesh, India, Indonesia, and the United States—already live under democratic governments.

Continue the debate . . .

1. *Do you think the United States is right or wrong in seeking to bring about a democratic political system in Iraq? Why?*

2. *Do you expect to see greater democracy in Islamic-majority countries fifty years from now? Why or why not?*

3. *Can you point to several reasons that Muslim people might object to the kind of political system we call "democracy"? Explain.*

Source: Based on Karatnycky (2002).

people withdraw from a system that concentrates wealth and power in the hands of a few. Or as radical Marxist critics claim, perhaps people find that our political system gives little real choice, limiting options and policies to what is consistent with our capitalist economic system. In any case, widespread apathy and low confidence in government appear to demand significant political reforms.

A second trend discussed in this chapter is the expansion of a global political process. Just as the Information Revolution is changing the economy, so it is changing politics (although perhaps more slowly). Communications technology now allows news and political analysis to flow instantly from one point in the world to another: In 2003, one could sit at home and watch the War in Iraq unfold on live television. But will such an avalanche of information spreading around the globe advance the cause of democracy? Or will new information technology provide governments with new tools to control their citizens?

A third issue is the global rethinking of political models. The cold war between the United States and

the former Soviet Union encouraged people to think of politics in terms of the two opposing models, capitalism and socialism. Today, however, a wider discussion includes a broader range of political systems, linking government to economic production in various ways. The "welfare capitalism" found in Sweden and the "state capitalism" found in Japan and South Korea (see Chapter 16, "The Economy and Work") are just two possibilities. The final box takes a look at the emerging debate over the chances for democratic governments emerging in the world's Islamic countries.

Fourth, many countries have large stockpiles of nuclear weapons, and this deadly technology is spreading around the world. On almost every continent, regional conflicts threatening the peace raise the risk of eventual nuclear war somewhere in the world.

Fifth, and finally, the emergence of terrorism on a large scale endangers many countries. No nation has been the target of terrorists more than the United States, and since 2001, countering terrorism has kept the U.S. military engaged in Afghanistan, Iraq, and elsewhere.

SUMMARY

1. Politics is the major social institution by which a society distributes power and organizes decision making. Max Weber explained that raw power is transformed into authority by tradition, rationally enacted rules and regulations, or the personal charisma of a leader.

2. Monarchy, based on traditional authority, is common in preindustrial societies. Although constitutional monarchies persist in some industrial nations, industrialization favors democracy based on rational-legal authority and extensive bureaucracy.

3. Authoritarian political regimes deny popular participation in government. Totalitarian political systems go even further, tightly regulating people's everyday lives.

4. The world is divided into 192 politically independent nation-states. A political trend, however, is the growing wealth and power of multinational corporations that operate around the world. In an age of computers and other new information technology, governments can no longer control the flow of information across their boundaries.

5. Government has expanded in the United States during the past two centuries and now offers extensive public benefits and, to some extent, regulates the economy. The welfare state in the United States is less extensive than in most other high-income nations.

6. The political spectrum—from the liberal left to the conservative right—involves attitudes on economic issues (such as government regulation of the economy) and social issues (including the rights and opportunities of various segments of the population).

7. Special-interest groups advance the political aims of specific segments of the population. These groups employ lobbyists and political action committees (PACs) to influence the political process.

8. Affiliation with political parties is relatively weak in the United States, and many people switch their party support from election to election.

9. Political apathy runs high in the United States: About half of eligible voters go to the polls in presidential elections. Millions of people convicted of serious crimes lose their right to vote.

10. The pluralist model holds that political power is widely dispersed in the United States; the power-elite model takes an opposing view, arguing that power is concentrated in a small, wealthy segment of the population. The Marxist political-economy view claims that our political agenda is determined by a capitalist economy, so that true democracy is impossible.

11. Revolution radically transforms a political system. Terrorism, another unconventional political tactic, employs violence in the pursuit of political goals and is widely used by groups against a much more powerful enemy. Terrorism is emerging as a new form of asymmetrical warfare.

12. War is armed conflict directed by governments. The development and spread of nuclear weapons have increased the threat of global catastrophe. World peace ultimately depends on resolving the tensions and conflicts that fuel militarism.

KEY CONCEPTS

politics (p. 433) the social institution that distributes power, sets a society's agenda, and makes decisions

power (p. 433) the ability to achieve desired ends despite resistance from others

government (p. 433) a formal organization that directs the political life of a society

authority (p. 434) power that people perceive as legitimate rather than coercive

traditional authority (p. 434) power legitimized through respect for long-established cultural patterns

rational-legal authority (also **bureaucratic authority**) (p. 434) power legitimized by legally enacted rules and regulations

charismatic authority (p. 434) power legitimized through extraordinary personal abilities that inspire devotion and obedience

routinization of charisma (p. 435) the transformation of charismatic authority into some combination of traditional and bureaucratic authority

monarchy (p. 435) a type of political system in which a single family rules from generation to generation

democracy (p. 436) a type of political system that gives power to the people as a whole

authoritarianism (p. 438) a political system that denies popular participation in government

totalitarianism (p. 438) a highly centralized political system that extensively regulates people's lives

welfare state (p. 440) a range of government agencies and programs that provides benefits to the population

special-interest group (p. 443) a political alliance of people interested in some economic or social issue

political action committee (PAC) (p. 443) an organization formed by a special-interest group, independent of political parties, to raise and spend money in support of political aims

pluralist model (p. 446) an analysis of politics that sees power as dispersed among many competing interest groups

power-elite model (p. 446) an analysis of politics that sees power as concentrated among the rich

Marxist political-economy model (p. 446) an analysis that explains politics in terms of the operation of a society's economic system

political revolution (p. 448) the overthrow of one political system in order to establish another

terrorism (p. 449) acts of violence or the threat of such violence used as a political strategy by an individual or a group

war (p. 450) organized, armed conflict among the people of various nations, directed by their governments

military-industrial complex (p. 451) the close association of the federal government, the military, and defense industries

nuclear proliferation (p. 452) the acquisition of nuclear weapons technology by more and more nations

CRITICAL-THINKING QUESTIONS

1. What is the difference between authority and power? How does the basis of authority differ in preindustrial and industrial societies? Why does democracy gradually replace monarchy as societies industrialize?

2. Identify various positions along the political spectrum. How do economic issues differ from social issues? How is social standing linked to being liberal or conservative on each kind of issue?

3. Contrast the pluralist, power-elite, and Marxist models of societal power. Which do you find most convincing? Why?

4. How is terrorism a new form of asymmetrical warfare? What are some challenges in trying to win the war on terrorism?

APPLICATIONS AND EXERCISES

1. The day after every presidential election (held the first Tuesday in November), national newspapers such as *The New York Times* publish an analysis of who voted and for whom. Visit the library and locate one of these issues to obtain a "scorecard" for the most recent election. To what extent did men and women vote for different presidential candidates? What about people of various racial categories? Ages? Religions? Income levels? Which variables affected political attitudes the most?

2. Along with several other people, make a list of leaders who have demonstrated personal charisma. Discuss why someone is on a list. Do you think personal charisma today is something more than "being good on television"? If so, precisely what is it?

3. Do a little research to trace the increase in the size of the federal government over the last fifty years (a Web site to start at is http://www.census.gov). Then do further searching to see what you can learn about how organizations at different points along the political spectrum (from socialist organizations on the left through the Democratic and Republican parties to right-wing militia groups) view the size of the current welfare state.

4. Members of the all-volunteer army are drawn heavily from the working class in the United States. In order to share the burden and danger of defending this country, should the United States reintroduce a lottery draft system? Why or why not?

5. Freedom House, an organization that studies civil rights and political liberty around the world, publishes an annual report, *Freedom in the World*. Find a copy in the library, or examine the trends or political profiles of countries of interest to you on the Web at http://www.freedomhouse.org

6. Packaged in the back of this new textbook is an interactive CD-ROM that offers a variety of video and interactive review materials intended to help you better understand the material covered in this chapter. For this chapter, the CD-ROM contains a relevant clip from *ABC News*, an author's tip video, interactive map animations, an interactive time line, and flashcards with audio pronunciations of the more difficult words.

 ## SITES TO SEE

http://www.prenhall.com/macionis

Visit the interactive Companion Website™ that accompanies this text. Begin by clicking on the cover of your book. You will find a chapter-by-chapter study guide, practice tests, suggested Web links, and links to other relevant material.

http://www.state.gov/g/drl/rls/hrrpt/2001/

Access the recent report on human rights worldwide.

http://www.cawp.rutgers.edu/

The Center for American Women and Politics is a resource providing information on and analysis of women in politics and government.

http://www.amnesty.org

Amnesty International operates a Web site that offers information about human rights around the world.

http://www.usis.usemb.se/terror/index.html

This Web site provides information on global terrorism.

http://www.coara.or.jp/~ryoji/abomb/e-index.html

Few of us have firsthand experience of the horrors of war. This Web site provides a personal account of the dropping of the first atomic bomb on the Japanese city of Hiroshima.

http://thomas.loc.gov

Review legislation currently before Congress by visiting this Web site.

 ## INVESTIGATE WITH RESEARCH NAVIGATOR™

Follow the instructions on page 24 of this text to access the features of **Research Navigator™**. Once at the Web site, enter your Login Name and Password. Then, to use the **Content Select™** database, enter keywords such as "democracy," "political economy," and "terrorism," and the search engine will supply relevant and recent scholarly and popular press publications. Use the *New York Times* **Search-by-Subject Archive** to find recent news articles related to sociology and the **Link Library** feature to find relevant Web links organized by the key terms associated with this chapter.

August 4, 2002

After Sept. 11, a Legal Battle Over Limits of Civil Liberty

This article was reported and written by Adam Liptak, Neil A. Lewis, and Benjamin Weiser.

In the fearful aftermath of Sept. 11, Attorney General John Ashcroft vowed to use the full might of the federal government and "every available statute" to hunt down and punish "the terrorists among us."

The roundup that followed the attacks, conducted with wartime urgency and uncommon secrecy, led to the detentions of more than 1,200 people suspected of violating immigration laws, being material witnesses to terrorism or fighting for the enemy.

The government's effort . . . has provoked a sprawling legal battle, now being waged in federal courthouses around the country, that experts say has begun to redefine the delicate balance between individual liberties and national security.

The main combatants are the attorney general and federal prosecutors on one side and a network of public defenders, immigration and criminal defense lawyers, civil libertarians and some constitutional scholars on the other, with federal judges in between.

. . . As [the government] has pushed civil liberties protections to their limits, the courts, particularly at the trial level, have pushed back. . . . Federal judges have, however, allowed the government to hold two American citizens without charges in military brigs, indefinitely, incommunicado and without a road map for how they might even challenge their detentions. . . .

Late on Sept. 12, federal agents pulled two nervous Indian men, Mohammed Jaweed Azmath and Syed Gul Mohammed Shah, off an Amtrak train near Fort Worth. They were carrying box cutters, black hair dye and about $5,000 in cash and had also shaved their body hair.

The agents' suspicions were obvious. The hijackers had used box cutters and knives to take control of the aircraft and had received letters instructing them to "shave excess hair from the body." An F.B.I. affidavit dated Sept. 15 said there was probable cause to believe that both of the Indian men were involved in, or "were associated" with, those responsible for the Sept. 11 attacks.

But even though government officials told reporters that the men had been detained as material witnesses, their lawyers now say that they were held last fall only on immigration violations.

The distinction is important because a material witness warrant brings the automatic appointment of a government-paid lawyer, while the government does not have to supply a visa violator with counsel.

As a result, the authorities were able to question each of the men repeatedly about terrorism without a lawyer present, their current lawyers say. . . .

The Indian men were held in isolation in jails in New York for extended periods. It was 91 days before Mr. Azmath received a lawyer and 57 days before Mr. Shah did, their lawyers say.

"It's wrong to keep a man in jail for 57 days and never bring him before a magistrate to advise him of his rights," Mr. Shah's lawyer, Lawrence K. Feitell, said in an interview. "It's wrong not to provide him with an attorney at the threshold. It's wrong to depict this as an I.N.S. investigation, when in truth and in fact, it's the main inquiry into the World Trade Center debacle."

Anthony L. Ricco, the lawyer for Mr. Azmath, said his client was interrogated "oftentimes for several hours a day, with multiple interviewers, getting rapid-fire questions from three or four different people."

. . . The detention issues also carry an emotional punch. Many of the Arabs and Muslims caught in the government dragnet were cabdrivers, construction workers or other types of laborers, and some spent up to seven months in jail before being cleared of terrorism ties and deported or released. . . . Law enforcement officials have acknowledged that only a few of these detainees had any significant information about possible terrorists.

What do you think?

1. Do you think national security and individual freedoms are now in conflict in the United States? If so, which do you think people consider more important? Why?

2. Is it proper for the government to target certain categories of people as a means to ensure national security? Why or why not?

CHAPTER 18

FAMILY

WILLIAM CUMMING
Family (Lake Chelan)

2002. Tempera on board. 56" × 56". Courtesy of William Cumming and Woodside Braseth Gallery, Seattle.

DIANE CARP HAD THE career of her dreams: She worked as a nurse in a pediatric intensive care unit, finding great satisfaction in helping sick children. Despite long hours at the hospital, she saved time to teach nursing classes at the nearby university and work on several research projects. She is widely known and well respected in her community.

With so many responsibilities at work, it may be no surprise to learn that Diane Carp never quite got around to marrying. She recalls, "I had always thought I had such a rewarding career. . . . Part of me kept saying that I did not need the other stuff, the husband and the kids. Then, suddenly I was forty, and I realized that if I were going to do something, I had better do it now."

Carp decided she wanted a child and set out to adopt an infant girl from China, one of the few countries that permits adoption by foreigners who are single and over forty. She filled out volumes of paperwork and sent off her application. Fifteen months later, she was in China for the joyful first meeting with her daughter, Kai Li. So wonderful has this experience been for them that today, five years later, Carp is going through the process once again so that Kai Li will have a little sister.

"I have friends who say, 'Hey, I have someone I'd really like you to meet.' I reply, 'Well, thanks, but I really don't have time for another relationship.' I would rather devote the extra time to helping another child" (Padawer, 2001).

Diane Carp's story illustrates an important trend—families in the United States conform to no one model and are more diverse than ever. Families differ because people's desires and situations differ. At the same time, however, family diversity sparks a good deal of debate. One in three U.S. children is born to an unmarried woman; add the effect of a high divorce rate, and the result is that half of U.S. children live with just one parent for some time before reaching eighteen. Diane Carp recently commented, "If I had my druthers, I would rather my daughter have a father. But that was not an option."

So while some people claim the family is falling apart, others counter that families are merely changing. For better or worse, in fact, the family is changing faster than any other social institution (Bianchi & Spain, 1996). When Diane Carp was born, the typical family included a working husband, a homemaker wife, and their young children. Today, just one in four U.S. households fits that description.

This chapter explores the changes in family life, especially considering their effects on children. We begin with some basic concepts.

THE FAMILY: BASIC CONCEPTS

The **family** is *a social institution found in all societies that unites people in cooperative groups to oversee the bearing and raising of children.* Family ties are also called **kinship,** *a social bond based on blood, marriage, or adoption.* All societies contain families, but exactly whom people call their kin has varied through history and varies today from one culture to another. In the

Families vary from culture to culture and also over time. But everywhere, people celebrate the ritual of marriage that extends kinship into a new generation. This idea is expressed clearly in David Botello's painting, Wedding Photos at Hollenbeck Park.

David Botello, Wedding Photos at Hollenbeck Park, 1990.

United States, most people regard a **family unit** as *a social group of two or more people, related by blood, marriage, or adoption, who usually live together.* Initially, individuals are born into a family composed of parents and siblings; this is sometimes called the *family of orientation* because of its importance to socialization. In adulthood, people form a *family of procreation* in order to have or adopt children of their own.

Throughout the world, families form around **marriage,** *a legally sanctioned relationship, usually involving economic cooperation as well as sexual activity and childbearing, that people expect to be enduring.* Our cultural belief that marriage is the right setting for having children explains the historical description of children born out of wedlock as *illegitimate.* Moreover, *matrimony*, in Latin, means "the condition of motherhood." The link between having children and being married has weakened, however, as the share of children born to single women (one in three) has increased.

Today, some people object to defining only married couples and children as "families" because this definition endorses a single standard of moral conduct. Also, because some businesses and government programs still use this conventional definition, some unmarried but committed partners—whether heterosexual or homosexual—may be excluded from health care and other benefits. More and more, however, organizations are coming to recognize *families of affinity*, that is, people with or without legal or blood ties who feel they belong together and wish to define themselves as a family.

The Census Bureau uses the conventional definition of family.[1] Thus, sociologists who use Census Bureau data describing "families" must accept this definition. But the national trend is toward a more inclusive definition of family.

THE FAMILY: GLOBAL VARIATIONS

In preindustrial societies, people take a wide view of family ties, recognizing the **extended family** as *a family unit that includes parents and children as well as other kin.* This group is also called the *consanguine family* because it includes everyone with "shared blood." With industrialization, however, increasing social mobility and geographic migration give rise to the **nuclear family,** *a family unit composed of one or two parents and their children.* The nuclear family is also called the *conjugal family*, meaning "based on marriage." Although many members of our society live in extended families, the nuclear family is most common.

Family change has been greatest in nations that have the most expansive welfare state (see Chapter 17, "Politics and Government"). In the box, sociologist

[1]According to the U.S. Census Bureau, there were 109.3 million U.S. households in 2001. Of these, 74.3 million (68 percent) were family households. The remaining living units contained single people or unrelated individuals living together. In 1960, 85 percent of all households were families.

GLOBAL SOCIOLOGY

The Weakest Families on Earth? A Report from Sweden

The Swedes have managed to avoid many of the social problems——the violent crime, drug abuse, and savage poverty—that blight whole cities in the United States. Instead, this Scandinavian nation seems to fulfill the promise of the modern welfare state, with an extensive and professional government bureaucracy that sees to virtually all human needs.

But one drawback of an expanding welfare state, according to David Popenoe, is that Sweden has the weakest families on Earth. Because people look to the government, not spouses, for economic assistance, Swedes are less likely to marry than members of any other high-income society. For the same reason, Sweden also has a high share of adults living alone (more than 20 percent, about the same as in the United States). Moreover, a large proportion of couples live together outside marriage (25 percent versus 9 in the United States), and half of all Swedish children (compared to one in three in the United States) are born to unmarried parents. Average household size in Sweden is also the smallest in the world (2.2 persons versus 2.6 in the United States). Finally, Swedish couples (whether married or not) are more likely to break up than partners in any other country. According to Popenoe, the family "has probably become weaker in Sweden than anywhere else—certainly among advanced Western nations. Individual family members are the most autonomous and least bound by the group" (1991:69).

Popenoe contends that a growing culture of individualism and self-fulfillment, along with the declining influence of religion, began eroding Swedish families in the

1960s. The movement of women into the labor force also played a part. Today, Sweden has the lowest proportion of women who are homemakers (10 percent versus 22 percent in the United States) and the highest percentage of women in the labor force (77 percent versus 60 percent in the United States).

But most important, according to Popenoe, is the expansion of the welfare state. The Swedish government offers its citizens a lifetime of services. Swedes can count on the government to deliver and school their children, provide comprehensive health care, support them when they are out of work, and, when the time comes, pay for their funeral.

Many Swedes supported the growth of welfare, thinking it would *strengthen* families. But Popenoe claims that by expanding benefits, government actually has been *replacing* families. Take the case of child care: The Swedish government operates child-care centers, staffed by professionals and available regardless of

parents' income. However, the government offers no subsidy for parents who desire to care for children in their own home. In effect, then, government benefits operate as incentives for people to let the state do what family members used to do for themselves.

But if Sweden's system has solved so many social problems, why should anyone care about the erosion of family life? For two reasons, says Popenoe. First, it is very expensive for government to provide many "family" services; this is the main reason that Sweden has one of the highest rates of taxation in the world. Second, can government employees in large child-care centers provide children with the level of love and emotional security available from two parents living as a family? Unlikely, says Popenoe, noting that small, intimate groups can accomplish some human tasks much better than large organizations.

Popenoe concludes that the Swedes have gone too far in delegating family responsibilities to government. But, he wonders, have we in the United States gone far enough? With the birth of a child, a Swedish parent may apply for up to eighteen months' leave at 90 percent of regular salary. The 1993 Family and Medical Leave Act guarantees U.S. workers only ninety days—without pay—to care for newborns or sick family members. Should our society follow Sweden's lead? If we look to government to help working parents care for children, will such a program strengthen or weaken families?

In Sweden, unmarried women bear half of all children, 50 percent higher than the percentage of births by single women in the United States.

Sources: Herrstrom (1990), Popenoe (1991, 1994), and U.S. Census Bureau (2002).

David Popenoe takes a look at Sweden, which, he claims, has the weakest families in the world.

MARRIAGE PATTERNS

Cultural norms, and often laws, identify people as suitable or unsuitable marriage partners. Some marital norms promote **endogamy,** *marriage between people of the same social category.* Endogamy limits marriage prospects to others of the same age, race, religion, or social class. By contrast, **exogamy** mandates *marriage between people of different social categories.* In rural areas of Pakistan and India, for example, people are expected to marry someone of the same caste (endogamy) but from a different village (exogamy). The logic of endogamy is that people of similar position pass along their standing to their offspring, thereby maintaining the traditional social hierarchy. Exogamy, on the other hand, builds alliances and encourages cultural diffusion.

In high-income nations, laws prescribe **monogamy** (from the Greek, meaning "one union"), *marriage that unites two partners.* The high level of divorce and remarriage in the United States, however, suggests that *serial monogamy* might be a more accurate description of this nation's marital practice. Global Map 18–1 shows that, whereas monogamy is the rule throughout the Americas and in Europe, many lower-income countries—especially in Africa and southern Asia—permit **polygamy** (from the Greek, meaning "many unions"), *marriage that unites three or more people.* Polygamy takes two forms. By far the more common form is **polygyny** (from the Greek, meaning "many women"), *marriage that unites one man and two or more women.* For example, Islamic nations in the Middle East and Africa permit men up to four wives. Even so, most Islamic families are monogamous because few men can afford to support several wives and even more children.

Polyandry (from the Greek, meaning "many men" or "many husbands") is *marriage that unites one woman and two or more men.* One case of this rare pattern is seen in Tibet, a mountainous land where agriculture is difficult. There, polyandry discourages the division of land into parcels too small to support a family and divides the work of farming among many men.

Most world societies, at some time, have permitted more than one marital pattern. Even so, as noted, most actual marriages have been monogamous (Murdock, 1965; orig. 1949). This cultural preference for monogamy reflects two facts of life: Supporting multiple spouses is a heavy financial burden, and the number of men and women in most societies is roughly the same.

RESIDENTIAL PATTERNS

Just as societies regulate mate selection, so they designate where a couple resides. In preindustrial societies, most newlyweds live with one set of parents who offer them protection, support, and assistance. Most common is the norm of **patrilocality** (Greek for "place of the father"), *a residential pattern in which a married couple lives with or near the husband's family.* But some societies (such as the North American Iroquois) favor **matrilocality** (meaning "place of the mother"), *a residential pattern in which a married couple lives with or near the wife's family.* Societies that engage in frequent local warfare tend toward patrilocality, so sons are close to home to offer protection. On the other hand, societies that engage only in distant warfare may be either patrilocal or matrilocal, depending on whether it is sons or daughters who have greater economic value (Ember & Ember, 1971, 1991).

Industrial societies show yet another pattern. Finances permitting, they favor **neolocality** (Greek meaning "new place"), *a residential pattern in which a married couple lives apart from both sets of parents.*

PATTERNS OF DESCENT

Descent refers to *the system by which members of a society trace kinship over generations.* Most preindustrial societies trace kinship through just the father's or the mother's side of the family. **Patrilineal descent,** the more common, is *a system tracing kinship through men.* Children are related to others only through their fathers, so that fathers typically pass property on to their sons. Patrilineal descent characterizes most pastoral and agrarian societies, in which men produce the most valued resources. Less common is **matrilineal descent,** *a system tracing kinship through women.* Matrilineal descent, through which mothers pass property to their daughters, is found more frequently in horticultural societies, where women are the primary food producers.

Industrial societies with greater gender equality recognize **bilateral descent** ("two-sided descent"), *a system tracing kinship through both men and women.* In this pattern, children recognize people on both the father's side and the mother's side as relatives.

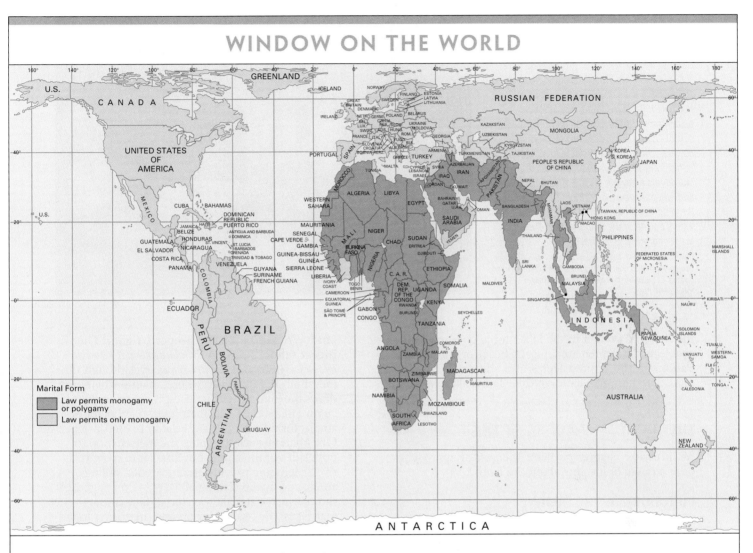

GLOBAL MAP 18–1 Marital Form in Global Perspective

Monogamy is the legally prescribed form of marriage throughout the Western Hemisphere and in much of the rest of the world. In most African nations and in southern Asia, however, polygamy is permitted by law. In many cases, this practice reflects the historic influence of Islam, a religion that allows a man to have up to four wives. Even so, most marriages in these countries are monogamous, primarily for financial reasons.

Source: *Peters Atlas of the World* (1990).

PATTERNS OF AUTHORITY

The predominance of polygyny, patrilocality, and patrilineal descent in the world reflects the universal presence of patriarchy. Wives and mothers exercise considerable power in every society, but as Chapter 13 ("Gender Stratification") explains, no truly matriarchal society has ever existed.

In industrial societies like the United States, more egalitarian family patterns are evolving, especially as

The family is a basic building block of society because it performs important functions, such as conferring social position and regulating sexual activity. To most family members, however, the family (at least in ideal terms) is a "haven in a heartless world" in which individuals enjoy the feeling of belonging and find emotional support. Marc Chagall conveyed the promise of marriage in his painting, To My Wife. *Looking at the painting, how does the artist characterize marriage?*

Marc Chagall (1887–1985), painting, To My Wife, 1933–44. Georges Pompidou Centre, Paris. The Bridgeman Art Library, London. © 2003 Artists Rights Society (ARS), New York/ADAGP, Paris.

the share of women in the labor force goes up. However, even here, men are typically heads of households. Parents in the United States also still prefer boys to girls, and most give children their father's last name.

THEORETICAL ANALYSIS OF THE FAMILY

As in earlier chapters, several theoretical approaches offer a range of insights about the family.

FUNCTIONS OF THE FAMILY: STRUCTURAL-FUNCTIONAL ANALYSIS

According to the structural-functional paradigm, the family performs several vital tasks. In fact, the family operates as the backbone of society.

1. **Socialization.** As explained in Chapter 5 ("Socialization"), the family is the first and most important setting for child rearing. Ideally, parents help children become well-integrated, contributing members of society (Parsons & Bales, 1955). Of course, family socialization continues throughout the life cycle. Adults change within marriage, and as any parent knows, mothers and fathers learn as much from their children as their children learn from them.

2. **Regulation of sexual activity.** Every culture regulates sexual activity in the interest of maintaining

kinship organization and property rights. The **incest taboo** is *a norm forbidding sexual relations or marriage between certain relatives.* Although the incest taboo exists everywhere, exactly where one draws the line in defining incest varies from one culture to another. The matrilineal Navajo, for example, forbid marrying any relative of one's mother. Our bilateral society applies the incest taboo to both sides of the family but limits it to close relatives, including parents, grandparents, siblings, aunts, and uncles (National Map 9–1 on page 224 shows which states allow or forbid first-cousin marriages). But even brother-sister marriages found approval among the ancient Egyptian, Incan, and Hawaiian nobility (Murdock, 1965; orig. 1949).

Reproduction between close relatives of any species can mentally and physically harm offspring. Yet only human beings observe an incest taboo, a fact suggesting that the main reason to control incest is social. Why? First, the incest taboo limits sexual competition in families by restricting sexuality to spouses. Second, because kinship defines people's rights and obligations toward each other, reproduction among close relatives would hopelessly confuse kinship ties and threaten social order. Third, forcing people to marry outside their immediate families integrates the larger society.

3. **Social placement.** Families are hardly necessary for people to reproduce, but they help maintain

social organization. Parents confer their own social identity—in terms of race, ethnicity, religion, and social class—on their children at birth.

4. **Material, emotional, and financial security.** Many people view the family as a "haven in a heartless world," looking to kin for physical protection, emotional support, and financial assistance. Thus, people living in families tend to be happier and healthier than people who live alone. Evidence also shows that, compared to single people, people living in families are better off financially (Waite & Gallagher, 2000; U.S. Census Bureau, 2002).

Critical evaluation. Structural-functional analysis explains why society, at least as we know it, depends on families. But this approach glosses over the great diversity of U.S. family life and also ignores how other social institutions (say, government) could meet some of the same human needs. Finally, structural-functionalism overlooks negative aspects of family life, including patriarchy and family violence.

INEQUALITY AND THE FAMILY: SOCIAL-CONFLICT ANALYSIS

The social-conflict paradigm also considers the family as being central to our way of life. But rather than focusing on ways that kinship benefits society, conflict theorists point out how the family perpetuates social inequality:

1. **Property and inheritance.** Friedrich Engels (1902; orig. 1884) traced the origin of the family to the need of men (especially in the upper classes) to identify heirs so they could transmit property to their sons. Families thus support the concentration of wealth and reproduce the class structure in each succeeding generation (Mare, 1991). More recent research points out both that marriage raises family income and that higher-income people are more likely to marry—in both ways, marriage supports class differences (Goldstein & Kenney, 2001).

2. **Patriarchy.** To know their heirs, men must control the sexuality of women. Families thus transform women into the sexual and economic property of men. A century ago in the United States, most wives' earnings belonged to their husbands. Today, men still have more power than women in most marriages, while women still bear most of

Women have long been taught to see marriage as the key to a happy life. Social-conflict theory, however, points to the fact that marriage often means a lifetime sentence to unpaid domestic labor. Susan Pyzow's painting, Bridal Bouquet, *makes the point.*

© Susan Pyzow, Bridal Bouquet, *watercolor on paper, 10 × 13.5 in. Studio SPM Inc.*

the responsibility for child rearing and housework (Presser, 1993; Keith & Schafer, 1994; Benokraitis & Feagin, 1995; Stapinski, 1998; England, 2001).

3. **Racial and ethnic inequality.** Racial and ethnic categories persist over generations only to the degree that people marry others like themselves. Thus, endogamous marriage shores up racial and ethnic hierarchies.

Critical evaluation. Social-conflict analysis shows another side of family life: its role in social stratification.

The decision for a young woman or man to marry generally involves not only the partners themselves but their parents and other family members. In George Smith's painting, The Expected Lover—Will They Give Their Consent?, a young woman waits anxiously for her prospective partner to arrive so that they may ask her parents to bless their marriage. Do you think such parental approval is as important today as it was a century ago? Why or why not?

George Smith (1829–1901, English) The Expected Lover— Will They Give Their Consent? Nineteenth century, oil on panel, 61 × 73.5 cm. Private collection/Bonhams, London, UK/The Bridgeman Art Library.

Engels criticized the family as part and parcel of capitalism. Yet noncapitalist societies have families (and family problems) all the same. The family may be linked to social inequality, as Engels argued, but the family carries out societal functions not easily accomplished by other means.

CONSTRUCTING FAMILY LIFE: MICRO-LEVEL ANALYSIS

Both structural-functional and social-conflict analyses view the family as a structural system. Micro-level approaches, by contrast, explore how individuals shape and experience family life.

Symbolic-Interaction Analysis

Ideally, family living offers an opportunity for intimacy, a word with Latin roots meaning "sharing fear." That is, as family members share activities, they build emotional bonds. Of course, the fact that parents act as authority figures often limits their closeness with younger children. Only as people reach adulthood do kinship ties open up to include confiding in and turning to one another for help with daily tasks and responsibilities (Macionis, 1978a).

Social-Exchange Analysis

Social-exchange analysis, another micro-level approach, depicts courtship and marriage as forms of negotiation (Blau, 1964). Dating allows each person to assess the advantages and disadvantages of taking the other as a spouse, always keeping in mind the value of what one has to offer in return. In essence, exchange analysts suggest, people "shop around" to make the best "deal" they can in a partner.

Physical attractiveness is one important dimension of exchange. In patriarchal societies, men bring wealth and power to the marriage marketplace, and women bring beauty. The importance of beauty explains women's traditional concern with their appearance and their sensitivity about revealing their age. But as women have joined the labor force, they are less dependent on men to support them, so that the terms of exchange are converging for men and women.

Critical evaluation. Micro-level analysis balances structural-functional and social-conflict visions of the family as an institutional system. Both the interaction and exchange viewpoints show how individuals shape the experience of family life for themselves. This approach, however, misses the bigger picture, namely,

GLOBAL SOCIOLOGY

Early to Wed: A Report from Rural India

Sumitra Jogi cries as her wedding is about to begin. Are they tears of joy? Not exactly. This "bride" is an eleven-month-old squirming in the arms of her mother. The groom? A boy of six.

In a remote, rural village in India's western state of Rajasthan, two families gather at midnight to celebrate a traditional wedding ritual. It is May 2, in Hindu tradition an especially good day to marry. Sumitra's father smiles as the ceremony begins; her mother cradles the infant, who has fallen asleep. The groom, dressed in a special costume with a red and gold turban on his head, gently reaches up and grasps the baby's hand. Then, as the ceremony reaches

its conclusion, the young boy leads the child and mother around the wedding fire three-and-one-half times, as the audience beams at the couple's first steps together as husband and wife.

Child weddings are illegal in India, but in the rural regions, traditions are strong and marriage laws are hard to enforce. Thus, experts estimate, thousands of children marry each year. "In rural Rajasthan," explains one social welfare worker, "all the girls are married by age fourteen. These are poor, illiterate families, and they don't want to keep girls past their first menstrual cycle."

For the immediate future, Sumitra Jogi will remain with her parents. But in eight or ten years, a second ceremony

will send her to live with her husband's family, and her married life will begin.

If the responsibilities of marriage lie years in the future, why do families push their children to marry at such an early age? Parents of girls know that the younger the bride, the smaller the dowry offered to the groom's family. Then, too, when girls marry this young, there is no question about their virginity, which raises their value on the marriage market. Arranged marriages are an alliance between families. No one thinks about love or the fact that the children are too young to understand what is taking place.

Source: Based on Anderson (1995).

that family life is similar for people in the same social and economic categories. U.S. families vary in predictable ways, according to social class and ethnicity, and as the next section explains, they typically evolve through distinct stages linked to the life course.

STAGES OF FAMILY LIFE

The family is a dynamic institution, with marked changes across the life course. New families begin with courtship and evolve as the new partners settle into the realities of married life. Next, for most couples at least, come the years spent raising children, leading to the later years of marriage after the children have left home to form families of their own. We will look briefly at each of these four stages.

COURTSHIP

November 2, Kandy, Sri Lanka. Winding through the rain forest of this beautiful island, our van driver, Harry, recounts how he met his wife. Actually,

it was more of an arrangement: The two families were both Buddhist and of the same caste. "We got along well, right from the start," recalls Harry. "We had the same background. I suppose she or I could have said 'no.' But love marriages happen in the city, not in the village where I grew up."

In rural Sri Lanka, and in rural areas of low- and middle-income countries throughout the world, most people consider courtship too important to be left to the young (Stone, 1977). An *arranged marriage* is an alliance between two extended families of similar social standing and usually involves not just an exchange of children but also of wealth and favors. Romantic love has little to do with marriage, and parents may make such arrangements when their children are very young. A century ago in Sri Lanka and India, for example, half of all girls married before reaching age fifteen (Mayo, 1927; Mace & Mace, 1960). As the box explains, in some parts of the world, child marriage persists today.

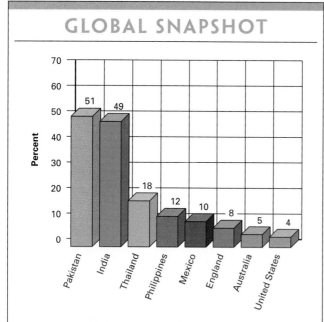

GLOBAL SNAPSHOT

FIGURE 18-1 Percentage of College Students Who Express a Willingness to Marry without Romantic Love

Source: Levine (1993).

Because traditional societies are culturally homogeneous, almost any member of the opposite sex has been suitably socialized to be a good spouse. Thus, parents can arrange marriages with little thought about whether or not the two individuals involved are *personally* compatible; they can be confident that the partners will be *culturally* compatible.

Industrialization erodes the importance of extended families as it weakens tradition. Young people choose their own mates and delay marriage until they have financial security and the experience needed to select a suitable partner. Dating sharpens courtship skills and allows sexual experimentation.

Take a look at "virtual courtship" using the Internet to find a partner at http://www.loveme.com

Romantic Love

Our culture celebrates *romantic love*—affection and sexual passion for another person—as the basis for marriage. We find it hard to imagine marriage without love, and popular culture—from fairy tales

like "Cinderella" to today's romance novels—portrays love as the key to a successful marriage. However, as Figure 18–1 shows, in many countries romantic love plays a much smaller role in marriage.

Our society's emphasis on romance motivates young people to "leave the nest" to form new families of their own, and physical passion can help a new couple through the difficult adjustments of living together (Goode, 1959). On the other hand, because feelings wax and wane, romantic love is a less stable foundation for marriage than social and economic considerations—one reason that the divorce rate is much higher in the United States than in nations where culture limits its choices in partners.

But even here, sociologists point out, society aims Cupid's arrow more than we like to think. Most people fall in love with others of the same race, of comparable age, and of similar social class. Our society "arranges" marriages by encouraging **homogamy** (literally, "like marrying like")—*marriage between people with the same social characteristics.*

SETTLING IN: IDEAL AND REAL MARRIAGE

Our culture gives the young an idealized, "happily ever after" picture of marriage. Such optimism can lead to disappointment, especially for women, who are taught to view marriage as the key to happiness. Also, romantic love involves a good deal of fantasy. We fall in love with others not necessarily as they are but as we want them to be (Berscheid & Hatfield, 1983).

Sexuality, too, can be a source of disappointment. In the romantic haze of falling in love, people may unrealistically expect marriage to be an endless sexual honeymoon, only to face the sobering realization that sex becomes a less-than-all-consuming passion. Although the frequency of marital sex does decline over time, about two in three married people report that they are satisfied with the sexual dimension of their relationship. In general, couples with the best sexual relationships experience the most satisfaction in their marriages. Sex may not be the key to marital bliss, but, more often than not, good sex and good relationships go together (Blumstein & Schwartz, 1983; Laumann et al., 1994).

Infidelity—*sexual activity outside marriage*—is another area where the reality of marriage does not coincide with our cultural ideal. In a recent survey, 92 percent of U.S. adults said sex outside of marriage is "always wrong" or "almost always wrong." Even so, 21 percent of men and 13 percent of women indicated on a private, written questionnaire that they had, at least once, been sexually unfaithful to their partners (NORC, 2003:234, 1227).

CHILD REARING

Despite the demands children make on us, adults in this country overwhelmingly identify raising children as one of life's greatest joys (NORC, 2003: 1071). Today, however, few people want more than three children, as Table 18–1 on page 472 documents. This is a change from two centuries ago, when *eight* children was the U.S. average.

Big families pay off in preindustrial societies because children supply needed labor. Thus, people regard having children as a wife's duty, and without effective birth control, childbearing is a regular event. Of course, a high death rate in preindustrial societies means many children never reach adulthood; as late as 1900, one-third of children born in the United States died by age ten (Wall, 1980).

Industrialization transforms children, economically speaking, from an asset to a liability. It now costs more than $200,000 to raise one child, including college tuition (Lino, 2003). No wonder the average size of the U.S. family steadily dropped during the twentieth century to one child per family.[2]

The trend toward smaller families is most pronounced in high-income nations. But the picture differs in low-income countries in Latin America, Asia, and, especially, Africa, where many women have few alternatives to bearing children. In such societies, as a glance back to Global Map 1–1 on page 4 shows, four to six children is still the norm.

Parenting is not only expensive, it is also a lifetime commitment. As our society has given people greater choice about family life, more U.S. adults have opted  to delay childbirth or to remain childless. In 1960, almost 90 percent of women between twenty-five and twenty-nine who had ever married had at least one child; today, this proportion is just 69 percent (U.S. Census Bureau, 2003).

Here is a report about the quality of care children receive from relatives: http://www.urban.org/url.cfm?ID=310270

"Son, you're all grown up now. You owe me two hundred and fourteen thousand dollars."

About two-thirds of parents in the United States say they would like to devote more of their time to child rearing (Snell, 1990; Clark 2002). But unless we accept a lower standard of living, economic realities demand that most parents pursue careers outside the home, even if that means giving less attention to their families.

Children of working parents spend most of the day at school. But after school, about 3 million children (roughly 10 percent of  the total) are *latchkey kids* who fend for themselves (Sonenstein, 2002). Traditionalists in the "family values" debate charge that many mothers work at the expense of their children, who receive less parenting. Progressives counter that such criticism targets women for wanting the same opportunities men have long enjoyed.

Congress took a step toward easing the conflict between family and job responsibilities by passing the

---

[2]According to the U.S. Census Bureau, the median number of children per family was 0.90 in 2002. Among families with children, the medians were .91 for whites, 1.27 for African Americans, and 1.47 for Hispanics.

TABLE 18–1 The Ideal Number of Children for U.S. Adults, 2002	
Number of Children	**Proportion of Respondents**
0	1.4%
1	3.2
2	49.2
3	24.6
4	8.9
5	1.8
6 or more	0.7
"As many as you want"	8.7
No response	1.5

Source: *General Social Surveys, 1972–2002: Cumulative Codebook* (Chicago: National Opinion Research Center, 2003), p. 230.

Family and Medical Leave Act in 1993. This law allows up to ninety days of unpaid leave from work because of a new child or a serious family emergency. Still, most adults in this country have to juggle parental and occupational responsibilities. When parents work, who cares for the kids? The box provides the answer.

THE FAMILY IN LATER LIFE

Increasing life expectancy in the United States means that, barring divorce, couples are likely to remain married for a long time. By about age sixty, almost all have finished the task of raising children. The remaining years of marriage bring a return to living with only one's spouse.

Like the birth of children, their departure—the "empty nest"—requires adjustments, although a marriage often becomes closer and more satisfying in midlife. Years of living together may diminish a couple's sexual passion for each other, but mutual understanding and companionship often increase.

Personal contact with children usually continues, since most older adults live a short distance from at least one of their children. Moreover, one-third of all U.S. adults (60 million) are grandparents. Most grandparents help with child care and other responsibilities; 2.4 million grandparents have primary responsibility for raising their grandchildren. Among African Americans (who have a high rate of single parenting), grandmothers have a central position in family life (Crispell, 1993; Jarrett, 1994; Rutherford, 1999; Clemetson, 2000; U.S. Census Bureau, 2003).

The other side of the coin is that more adults in midlife now care for aging parents. The "empty nest" may not be filled by a parent coming to live in the home, but many adults find that caring for parents, who now live to eighty and beyond, can be as taxing as raising young children. The oldest of the "baby boomers"—currently in their fifties—are called the "sandwich generation" because they (especially the women) will spend as many years caring for their aging parents as they did caring for their children (Lund, 1993).

The final, and surely the most difficult, transition in married life comes with the death of a spouse. Wives typically outlive their husbands because of women's longer life expectancy and the fact that women usually marry men several years older. Wives can thus expect to spend some years as widows. The challenge of living alone following the death of a spouse is especially great for men, who usually have fewer friends than widows and may lack housekeeping skills.

U.S. FAMILIES: CLASS, RACE, AND GENDER

Dimensions of inequality—social class, ethnicity and race, and gender—are powerful forces that shape marriage and family life. This discussion addresses each factor in turn, but bear in mind that they overlap in our lives.

SOCIAL CLASS

Social class frames a family's financial security and range of opportunities. Interviewing working-class women, Lillian Rubin (1976) found that wives thought a good husband was one who held a steady job, did not drink too much, and was not violent. Rubin's middle-class informants, by contrast, never mentioned such things; these women simply *assumed* a husband would provide a safe and secure home. Their ideal husband was someone they could talk to easily, sharing feelings and experiences.

Clearly, what women (and men) think they can hope for in marriage—and what they end up with—is linked to their social class. Much the same holds for children; boys and girls lucky enough to be born into more affluent families enjoy better mental and physical health, develop more self-confidence, and go on to greater achievement than children born to poor parents (Rubin, 1976; Fitzpatrick, 1988; McLeod & Shanahan, 1993; Duncan et al., 1998).

APPLYING SOCIOLOGY

Who's Minding the Kids?

Traditionally, the task of providing daily care for young children fell to mothers. But with a majority of mothers and fathers now in the labor force, finding quality, affordable child care is a high priority for parents.

A recent study reported on various child-care arrangements used by mothers who work. As the figure shows, 54 percent of children under age five receive care at home from a parent (27 percent) or a relative (27 percent). The remaining 46 percent are cared for by a nonrelative: 28 percent attend preschool or a day-care program, 14 percent go to the home of a nonrelative, and only 4 percent of children are cared

for in their own home by a nanny or babysitter.

The use of day-care programs has doubled over the last decade because

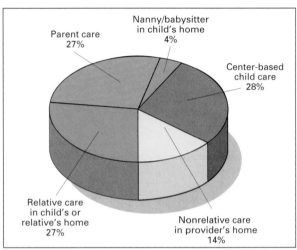

Parent care
27%

Nanny/babysitter
in child's home
4%

Center-based
child care
28%

Relative care
in child's or
relative's home
27%

Nonrelative care
in provider's home
14%

many parents cannot find in-home care for their children. Some day-care centers are so big that they amount to "tot lots" where parents "park" their children for the day. The impersonality of such settings and the rapid turnover in staff prevent the warm and consistent nurturing that young children need in order to develop a sense of trust. Other child-care centers offer a secure and healthful environment. Research suggests that *good* care centers are good for children; *bad* facilities are not.

Sources: Capizzano, Adams, & Sonenstein (2001), Sonenstein et al. (2002), and U.S. Census Bureau (2002).

ETHNICITY AND RACE

As Chapter 14 ("Race and Ethnicity") discusses, ethnicity and race are powerful social forces, and the effects of both ripple through family life. Keep in mind, however, that like white families, American Indian, Hispanic, African American, and other categories of families are diverse and conform to no single stereotype (Allen, 1995).

American Indian Families

American Indians display a wide variety of family types. Some patterns emerge, however, among people who migrate from tribal reservations to cities. Women and men who arrive in cities often seek out others—especially kin and members of the same tribe—for assistance in getting settled. One recent study, for example, tells the story of two women migrants to the San Francisco area who met at a meeting of an Indian organization and realized they were of the same tribe.

The women and their children decided to share an apartment, and soon after, the children began to refer to one another as brothers, sisters, and cousins. As the months passed, the two mothers came to think of themselves as sisters.

Migration also creates many "fluid households" with changing membership. In another case from this research, a large apartment in San Francisco was rented by a woman, her aunt, and their children. Over the course of the next month, however, they welcomed into their home more than 30 other urban migrants, who stayed for a short time while they found housing of their own. Such patterns of mutual assistance, often involving real and fictional kinship, are common among low-income people (Lobo, 2002).

Hispanic Families

Many Latinos enjoy the loyalty and support of extended families. Traditionally, too, Hispanic parents exercise greater control over children's courtship,

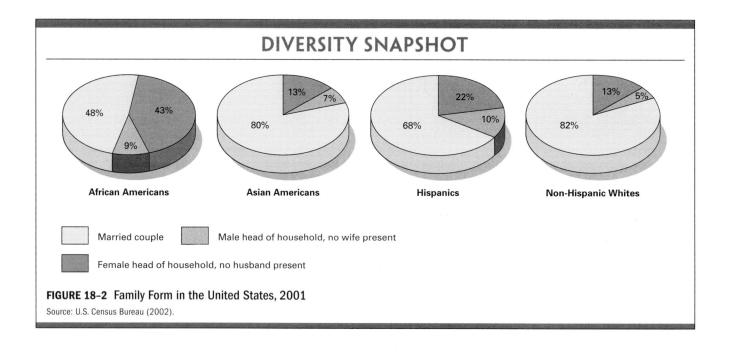

DIVERSITY SNAPSHOT

African Americans
- 48% Married couple
- 9%
- 43%

Asian Americans
- 80%
- 13%
- 7%

Hispanics
- 68%
- 22%
- 10%

Non-Hispanic Whites
- 82%
- 13%
- 5%

■ Married couple   ■ Male head of household, no wife present

■ Female head of household, no husband present

FIGURE 18–2 Family Form in the United States, 2001

Source: U.S. Census Bureau (2002).

considering marriage an alliance of families, not just a union based on romantic love. Some Hispanic families also adhere to conventional gender roles, encouraging machismo—strength, daring, and sexual prowess—among men, while women are both honored and closely supervised.

Assimilation into the larger society, however, is changing these traditional patterns. Many Puerto Ricans who migrate to New York, for example, do not maintain the strong extended families they knew in Puerto Rico. Traditional male authority over women has also diminished, especially among affluent Hispanic families—whose number has tripled in the last twenty years (Nielsen, 1990; O'Hare, 1990; Lach, 1999).

While some Hispanics have prospered, the overall social standing of this segment of the U.S. population remains below average. The U.S. Census Bureau (2003) reports that the typical Hispanic family had an income of $34,490 in 2001, or 67 percent of the national standard. As a result, many Hispanic families suffer the stress of unemployment and other poverty-related problems.

African American Families

African American families face economic disadvantages: As explained in earlier chapters, the typical African American family earned $33,598 in 2001, or

65 percent of the national standard. People of African ancestry are three times as likely as whites to be poor, and poverty means that families experience unemployment, underemployment, and, in some cases, a physical environment of crime and drug abuse.

Under these circumstances, maintaining stable family ties is difficult. For example, 25 percent of African American women in their forties have never married, compared to about 10 percent of white women of the same age. This means that African American women—often with children—are more likely to be single heads of households. As Figure 18–2 shows, women headed 43 percent of all African American families in 2001, compared to 22 percent of Hispanic families, 13 percent of Asian or Pacific Islander families, and 13 percent of non-Hispanic white families (U.S. Census Bureau, 2002).

Regardless of race, single-mother families are always at high risk of poverty. Nineteen percent of single families headed by non-Hispanic white women are poor. Higher yet is the poverty rate among families headed by African American women (35 percent) and Hispanic women (37 percent)—good evidence of how the intersection of class, race, and gender can put women at a disadvantage. African American families with both wife and husband in the home, which represent half the total, are much stronger economically, earning 81 percent as much as comparable non-Hispanic white families. But

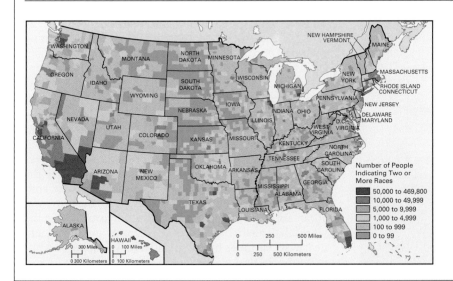

NATIONAL MAP 18–1
Racially Mixed People
across the United States

Where are racially mixed marriages most common? No precise data of this kind are currently available, but the Census Bureau does publish the distribution of racially mixed people—those, presumably, who have parents of two different racial categories. This map shows the distribution of people who described themselves as racially mixed in the 2000 Census. What can you say about where such people reside and, thus, where racially mixed marriages are most common?

Source: U.S. Census Bureau (2001).

Number of People Indicating Two or More Races
- 50,000 to 469,800
- 10,000 to 49,999
- 5,000 to 9,999
- 1,000 to 4,999
- 100 to 999
- 0 to 99

69 percent of African American children are born to single women, and 30 percent of African American boys and girls are growing up poor, so that such families carry much of the burden of child poverty in the United States (U.S. Census Bureau, 2002; U.S. National Center for Health Statistics, 2002).

Racially Mixed Marriages

Most spouses have similar social backgrounds with regard to class, race, and ethnicity. But over the course of the twentieth century, ethnicity mattered less and less. Thus, a woman of German and French ancestry might readily marry a man of Irish and English background without inviting disapproval from their families or from society in general.

Race remains a more formidable consideration, however. Before a 1967 Supreme Court decision (*Loving v. Virginia*), interracial marriage was illegal in sixteen states. Today, African, Asian, and Native Americans represent 17 percent of the U.S. population, so we would expect about the same share of marriages to be mixed if people ignored race in choosing spouses. The actual proportion of mixed marriages is 2.9 percent, showing that race still matters in social relations. But the number of racially mixed marriages is steadily rising, and most U.S. teens now claim they have dated someone of another race.

Black-white marriages are most numerous, as the large African American population (12 percent of the U.S. total) would lead us to expect. Proportionately, though, most whites involved in racially mixed marriages are likely to have partners of Asian ancestry (U.S. Census Bureau, 2001). National Map 18–1 shows where people who described themselves in Census 2000 as being multiracial live, which is a good indicator of the prevalence of racially mixed marriages.

GENDER

Regardless of race, Jessie Bernard (1982) said that every marriage is actually *two* different relationships: a woman's marriage and a man's marriage. The reason is that few marriages are composed of two equal partners. While patriarchy has weakened, most people still expect men to be older and taller than their wives and to have more prominent careers.

Bernard wondered, therefore, why many people think that marriage benefits women more than men? The positive stereotype of the carefree bachelor contrasts sharply with the negative image of the lonely spinster, suggesting that women are fulfilled only through being wives and mothers.

But, Bernard continued, married women in fact have poorer mental health, less happiness, and more

Divorce may be a solution for a couple in an unhappy marriage, but it can be a problem for children who experience the withdrawal of a parent from their social world. In what ways can divorce be harmful to children? Is there a positive side to divorce? How might separating parents better prepare their children for the transition of parental divorce?

passive attitudes toward life than single women. Married men, on the other hand, generally live longer, are mentally better off, and report being happier overall than single men. These differences suggest why, after divorce, men are more eager than women to find a new partner.

Bernard concluded that there is no better guarantor of long life, health, and happiness for a man than a woman well socialized to devote her life to taking care of him and providing the security of a well-ordered home. She was quick to add that marriage *could* be healthful for women if husbands did not dominate wives and expect them to perform virtually all the housework. Indeed, research confirms that the wives with the best mental health have husbands who share responsibilities for earning income, raising children, and keeping the home (Ross, Mirowsky, & Huber, 1983; Mirowsky & Ross, 1984).

TRANSITIONS AND PROBLEMS IN FAMILY LIFE

The newspaper columnist Ann Landers once remarked that one marriage in twenty is wonderful, five in twenty are good, ten in twenty are tolerable, and the remaining four are "pure hell." Families can be a source of joy, but for some, the reality falls far short of the ideal.

DIVORCE

U.S. society strongly supports marriage, and about nine out of ten people at some point "tie the knot." But many of today's marriages unravel. Figure 18–3 shows the tenfold increase in the U.S. divorce rate over the last century. By 2001, four in ten marriages were ending in divorce (for African Americans, the rate was about six in ten). Ours is the highest divorce rate in the world, half again higher than in Canada and Japan, and nearly seven times higher than in Italy (Japanese Ministry of Health, Labour, and Welfare, 2002).

The high U.S. divorce rate has many causes (Weitzman, 1985; Gerstel, 1987; Furstenberg & Cherlin, 1991; Etzioni, 1993; Popenoe, 1999; Greenspan, 2001):

1. **Individualism is on the rise.** Today's family members spend less time together. We have become more individualistic and more concerned about personal happiness and earning income than about the well-being of families and children.

2. **Romantic love often subsides.** Because our culture bases marriage on romantic love, relationships may fail when sexual passion fades. Many people end a marriage in favor of a new relationship that renews excitement and romance.

3. **Women are now less dependent on men.** Increasing participation in the labor force has reduced wives' financial dependency on husbands. Therefore, women find it easier to leave unhappy marriages.

4. **Many of today's marriages are stressful.** With both partners working outside the home in most cases, jobs leave less time and energy for family life. Thus, raising children becomes that much harder. Children do stabilize some marriages, but divorce is most common during the early years of marriage, when many couples have young children.

5. **Divorce is socially acceptable.** Divorce no longer carries the powerful stigma it did a century ago. Family and friends are now less likely to discourage couples in conflict from divorcing.

6. **Legally, a divorce is easier to get.** In the past, courts required divorcing couples to show that one or both were guilty of behavior such as adultery or physical abuse. Today, all states allow divorce if a couple simply thinks their marriage has failed. Concern about easy divorces, shared by more than half of U.S. adults, has led some states to consider rewriting their marriage laws (Nock, Wright, & Sanchez, 1999; Phillips, 2001; NORC, 2003:232).

Who Divorces?

At greatest risk of divorce are young spouses—especially those who marry after a brief courtship—with little money, who have yet to mature emotionally. The chance of divorce also rises if the couple marries after an unexpected pregnancy or if one or both partners have substance-abuse problems. People whose parents divorced also have a higher divorce rate themselves. Researchers suggest that a role-modeling effect is at work: Children who see parents go through divorce are more likely to consider divorce themselves (Amato, 2001). Finally, people who are not religious divorce more readily than those who are.

Divorce also is more common when both partners have successful careers, perhaps because of the strains of a two-career marriage but also because financially secure people do not feel compelled to stay in an unhappy home. Finally, men and women who divorce once are more likely to divorce again, probably because high-risk factors follow them from one marriage to another (Glenn & Shelton, 1985).

Because mothers usually secure custody of children but fathers typically earn more income, the well-being of children often depends on fathers' making court-ordered child-support payments. As Figure 18–4 on page 478 indicates, courts award child support in 59 percent of all divorces involving children. Yet, in any given year, half the children legally entitled to support receive only partial payments or no payments at all. Because some 3.3 million "deadbeat dads" fail to support their youngsters, federal legislation now mandates that employers withhold money from the earnings of parents who fail to pay up; and in 1998, refusing to make child-support payments or moving to another state to avoid making them became a felony (U.S. Census Bureau, 2002).

Divorce may be hardest on children. Divorce can tear young people from familiar surroundings, entangle them in bitter feuding, and distance them from a parent they love. Most serious of all, many children

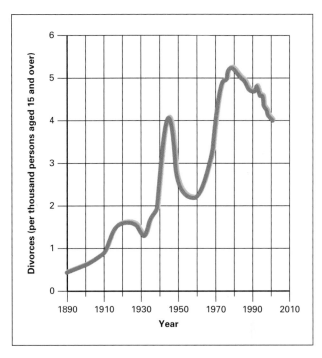

FIGURE 18-3 The Divorce Rate for the United States, 1890-2001

Sources: U.S. Census Bureau (2001) and U.S. National Center for Health Statistics (2002).

blame themselves for their parents' breakup. Divorce changes the course of many children's entire lives, causing emotional and behavioral problems and raising the risk of dropping out of school and getting into trouble with the law. Many experts counter that divorce is better for children than their staying in a family torn by tension and violence. In any case, parents should remember that, when couples think about divorce, more than their own well-being is at stake (Wallerstein & Blakeslee, 1989; Adelson, 1996; Popenoe, 1996; Cherlin, Chase-Landale, & McRae, 1998; Amato & Sobolewski, 2001).

REMARRIAGE

Four out of five people who divorce remarry, most within five years. Nationwide, almost half of all marriages are now remarriages for at least one partner. Men, who derive greater benefits from wedlock, are more likely than women to remarry.

Remarriage often creates *blended families*, composed of children and some combination of biological

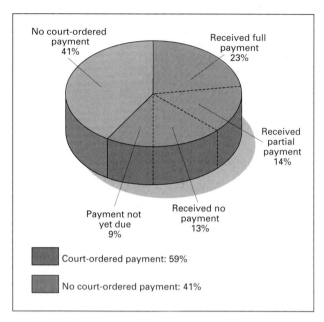

No court-ordered
payment
41%

Received full
payment
23%

Received
partial
payment
14%

Received no
payment
13%

Payment not
yet due
9%

Court-ordered payment: 59%

No court-ordered payment: 41%

FIGURE 18–4 Payment of Child Support after Divorce
Source: U.S. Census Bureau (2002).

parents and stepparents. With brothers, sisters, half sisters, a stepdad—not to mention a biological parent who lives elsewhere and may now be married to someone else with other children—young people in blended families face the challenge of defining many new relationships and deciding just who is part of the nuclear family. Parents often have trouble defining responsibility for household work among people unsure of their relations to each other. Then, too, when the custody of children is an issue, ex-spouses can be a source of interference for people in a new marriage. In all these cases, adjustments are necessary, and family dynamics typically change over time. At the same time, blended families offer both young and old the chance to relax rigid family roles (Furstenberg & Cherlin, 1991, 2001; McLanahan, 2002).

 Find a new report on remarriage and other family issues by the Centers for Disease Control at http://www.cdc.gov/nchs/data/series/sr_23/sr23_022.pdf

FAMILY VIOLENCE

The ideal family is a source of pleasure and support. However, the disturbing reality of many homes is **family violence,** *emotional, physical, or sexual abuse of*

one family member by another. Sociologist Richard J. Gelles calls the family "the most violent group in society with the exception of the police and the military" (quoted in Roesch, 1984:75).

Violence against Women

Family brutality often goes unreported to police. Even so, the U.S. Bureau of Justice Statistics (2003) estimates that about 700,000 people are victims of domestic violence each year. Of this total, 85 percent of cases involve violence against women, and the remaining 15 percent involve violence against men. Of women who are victims of homicide, 33 percent (but just 4 percent of men) are killed by spouses or, more often, ex-spouses. Nationwide, the death toll from family violence is about 1,250 women each year. Overall, women are more likely to be injured by a family member than to be mugged or raped by a stranger or hurt in an automobile accident (Straus & Gelles, 1986; Schwartz, 1987; Shupe, Stacey, & Hazlewood, 1987; Blankenhorn, 1995).

Historically, the law defined wives as the property of their husbands, so that no man could be charged with raping his wife. Today, however, all states have enacted *marital rape laws* that allow wives to charge husbands with rape. The law no longer regards domestic violence as a private family matter; it gives victims more options. Now, even without a formal separation or divorce, a woman can obtain court protection from an abusive spouse. Half the states have enacted "stalking laws" that prohibit an ex-partner from following or otherwise threatening someone. Finally, communities across the United States have established shelters to provide counseling and temporary housing for women and children driven from their homes by domestic violence.

Violence against Children

Family violence also victimizes children. Each year, there are roughly 3 million reports of alleged child abuse and neglect, about 1,300 of them involving a child's death. Child abuse entails more than physical injury; abusive adults misuse power and trust to damage a child's emotional well-being. Child abuse and neglect are most common among the youngest and most vulnerable children (Van Biema, 1994; Besharov & Laumann, 1996).

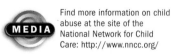 Find more information on child abuse at the site of the National Network for Child Care: http://www.nncc.org/

Although child abusers conform to no simple stereotype, they are more like to be women (60 percent) than men (40 percent). But almost all abusers share one trait: having been abused themselves as children. Research shows that violent behavior in close relationships is learned; in families, then, violence begets violence (Widom, 1996; Browning & Laumann, 1997; Levine, 2001; U.S. Department of Health and Human Services, 2003).

ALTERNATIVE FAMILY FORMS

Most families in the United States are still composed of a married couple who, at some point, raise children. But in recent decades, our society has displayed greater diversity in family life.

ONE-PARENT FAMILIES

Twenty-nine percent of U.S. families with children under eighteen have only one parent in the household, a proportion that more than doubled during the last generation. Put another way, 27 percent of U.S. children now live with only one parent, and about half will do so before reaching eighteen. One-parent families—80 percent of which are headed by a single mother—result from divorce, death, or an unmarried woman's decision to have a child.

Single parenthood increases a woman's risk of poverty because it limits her ability to work and to further her education. The converse is also true: Poverty raises the odds that a young woman will become a single mother (Trent, 1994). But single parenthood goes well beyond the poor, since at least one-third of women in the United States become pregnant as unmarried teenagers, and many decide to raise their children whether they marry or not. Looking back to Figure 18–2, note that 52 percent of African American families are headed by a single parent. Single parenting is less common among Hispanics (32 percent), Asian Americans (20 percent), and non-Hispanic whites (18 percent). In many single-parent families, mothers turn to their own mothers for support. In the United States, then, the rise in single parenting is tied to a declining role for fathers and the growing importance of grandparenting.

Research shows that growing up in a one-parent family usually disadvantages children. Some studies claim that because a father and a mother each make distinctive contributions to a child's social development, it

In recent years, the proportion of young people who cohabit—that is, live together without being married—has risen sharply. This trend contributes to the debate over what is and is not a family: Do you consider a cohabiting couple a family? Why or why not?

is unrealistic to expect one parent alone to do as good a job. But the most serious problem for one-parent families, especially if that parent is a woman, is poverty. On average, children growing up in a single-parent family start out poorer, get less schooling, and end up with lower incomes as adults. Such children are also more likely to be single parents themselves (Astone & McLanahan, 1991; Li & Wojtkiewicz, 1992; Biblarz & Raftery, 1993; Popenoe, 1993; Blankenhorn, 1995; Shapiro & Schrof, 1995; Webster, Orbuch, & House, 1995; Wu, 1996; Duncan et al., 1998; Kantrowitz & Wingert, 2001; McLanahan, 2002).

COHABITATION

Cohabitation is *the sharing of a household by an unmarried couple.* The number of cohabiting couples in the United States increased from about 500,000 in 1970

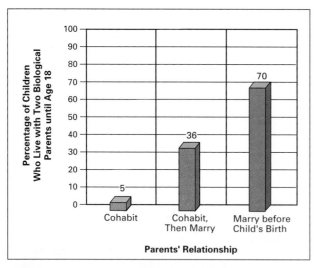

FIGURE 18-5 Parental Involvement in Children's Lives: Cohabiting and Married Parents

Source: Phillips (2001).

to about 5.5 million today (almost 5 million heterosexual couples and 0.6 million homosexual couples), or about 9 percent of all couples (Miller, 1997; U.S. Census Bureau, 2003).

In global perspective, cohabitation as a long-term form of family life, with or without children, is common in Sweden and other Scandinavian nations. But it is rare in more traditional (and Roman Catholic) nations such as Italy. Cohabitation is gaining in popularity in the United States, with almost half of people between ages twenty-five and forty-four having cohabited at some point.

Cohabiting tends to appeal to more independent-minded individuals as well as those who favor gender equality (Brines & Joyner, 1999). Most couples cohabit for no more than a few years, about half then deciding to marry and half ending the relationship. Mounting evidence suggests that living together may actually discourage marriage because partners (some research points especially to men) become used to low-commitment relationships. For this reason, cohabiting couples who have children—currently representing about one in eight births—may not always be long-term parents. Figure 18–5 shows that just 5 percent of

For research reports on cohabitation and other intimate relationships, visit the Web site of The National Marriage Project at Rutgers University: http://marriage.rutgers.edu

children born to cohabiting couples will live until age eighteen with both biological parents who remain unmarried. The share rises to 36 percent among children whose parents marry at some point, but even this is half of the 70 percent figure among children whose parents married before they were born. When cohabiting couples with children separate, the involvement of both parents, including financial support, is far from certain (Popenoe & Whitehead, 1999; Smock, 2000; Phillips, 2001; Zimmer, 2001; Scommegna, 2002).

GAY AND LESBIAN COUPLES

In 1989, Denmark became the first country to lift its legal ban on same-sex marriages. This change offered social legitimacy to gay and lesbian couples and equalized advantages in inheritance, taxation, and joint property ownership. Norway (in 1993), Sweden (1995), the Netherlands (2001), and Canada (2003) have followed suit. In 1996, however, the U.S. Congress passed a law banning gay marriage. Homosexual marriage is also illegal in all fifty states, although Vermont and Hawaii, as well as a number of major cities, including San Francisco and New York, confer limited marital benefits on gay and lesbian couples. Whereas about one-third of U.S. adults support gay marriage, half support civil unions providing the rights enjoyed by married couples (Gallup, 2002). Among U.S. college students, as Figure 18–6 shows, opposition to homosexual relationships fell from almost half in the 1970s to about one-fourth in 2001 (Astin et al., 2002).

Most gay couples with children in the United States are raising the offspring of previous heterosexual unions; some couples have adopted children. But many gay parents are quiet about their sexual orientation, not wishing to draw unwelcome attention to their children. Moreover, in several widely publicized cases, courts have removed children from homosexual couples, citing the best interests of the children.

Gay parenting challenges many traditional ideas. But it also shows that many gay people want to form families just as heterosexuals do (Gross, 1991; Pressley & Andrews, 1992; Henry, 1993).

SINGLEHOOD

Because nine out of ten people in the United States marry, we tend to see singlehood as a passing stage of life. In recent decades, however, more people are deliberately choosing to live alone. In 1950, just one household in ten contained a single person; by 2002, this share had risen to one in four: a total of 51 million single adults (U.S. Census Bureau, 2003).

Most striking is the rising number of single young women. In 1960, 28 percent of U.S. women aged twenty to twenty-four were single; by 2002, the proportion had soared to 74 percent. Underlying this trend is women's greater participation in the labor force. Women who are economically secure view a husband as a matter of choice rather than a financial necessity (Edwards, 2000).

By midlife, as described in the case of Diane Carp at the opening of this chapter, many unmarried women sense a lack of available men. Because we expect a woman to "marry up," the older a woman is, the more education she has, and the better her job, the more difficulty she has finding a suitable husband.

NEW REPRODUCTIVE TECHNOLOGY AND THE FAMILY

Recent medical advances involving *new reproductive technology* are changing families, too. A generation ago, England's Louise Brown became the world's first "test-tube baby"; since then, tens of thousands of children have been conceived this way. A decade from now, 2 or 3 percent of the children in high-income nations may be the result of new reproductive technologies.

Test-tube babies result from *in vitro fertilization*, in which doctors unite a woman's egg and a man's sperm "in glass" rather than in a woman's body. When the process is successful, the doctor implants the resulting embryo in the womb of the woman who is to bear the child or freezes it for use at a later time.

At present, new reproductive technologies help some couples who cannot conceive normally to have children. These techniques eventually may help to reduce the incidence of birth defects, as genetic screening of sperm and eggs allows medical specialists to increase the odds of having a healthy baby. But new reproductive technology also raises fascinating and troubling questions: When one woman carries an embryo made from the egg of another, who is the mother? When a couple divorces, which spouse is entitled to use the frozen embryos? Can one partner later have a child against the will of the other? Such questions remind us that technology changes faster than our ability to understand the consequences of its use (Thompson, 1994; Cohen, 1998; Nock, Wright, & Sanchez, 1999).

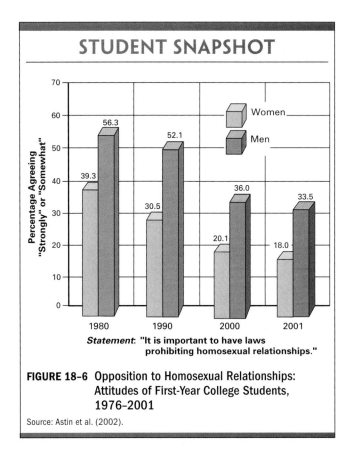

STUDENT SNAPSHOT

Statement: "It is important to have laws prohibiting homosexual relationships."

FIGURE 18-6 Opposition to Homosexual Relationships: Attitudes of First-Year College Students, 1976–2001

Source: Astin et al. (2002).

LOOKING AHEAD: THE FAMILY IN THE TWENTY-FIRST CENTURY

Family life in the United States will continue to change, and change, of course, causes controversy. In the case of the family, advocates of "traditional family values" line up against those who support greater personal choice; the final box on pages 482–83 sketches some of the issues. Sociologists cannot predict the outcome of this debate, but we can suggest five likely future trends.

First, divorce rates are likely to remain high, even in the face of evidence that marital breakups harm children. Bear in mind that today's marriages are no less durable than they were a century ago, when many were cut short by death (Kain, 1990). The difference is that more couples now *choose* to end marriages that fail to live up to their expectations. Thus, although the divorce rate declined slightly in the 1990s, it is unlikely to return to the low rates that marked the early decades of the twentieth century.

CONTROVERSY & DEBATE

Should We Save the Traditional Family?

What are "traditional families"? Are they vital to our way of life or a barrier to progress? To begin with, people use the term *traditional family* to mean a married couple who, over the life course, raise children. Statistically speaking, traditional families are less common than they used to be. In 1950, as the figure shows, 90 percent of U.S. households were families—two or more persons related by blood, marriage, or adoption. By 2001, just 68 percent of households were families, due to rising levels of divorce, cohabitation, and singlehood.

Of course, "traditional family" is more than just a term, it is also a moral statement. That is, belief in the traditional family implies giving high value to becoming and staying married, putting children ahead of careers, and favoring two-parent families over various "alternative lifestyles."

On one side of the debate, David Popenoe warns that there has been a serious erosion of the traditional family since 1960. Then, married couples with young children accounted for almost half of all households; today, the figure is 24 percent. Singlehood is up, from 10 to 24 percent of present households. The divorce rate has doubled since 1960, so that almost half of today's marriages end in permanent separation. Moreover, because of both divorce and having children out of wedlock, the share of youngsters who will live with a single parent before age eighteen has

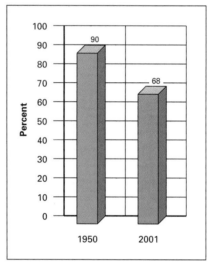

Share of U.S. Households That the Census Bureau Classifies as Families, 1950 and 2001

quadrupled since 1960, to 50 percent. In other words, just one in four of today's children will grow up with two parents and go on to maintain a stable marriage as an adult.

In light of such data, Popenoe concludes, it may not be an exaggeration to say that the family is falling apart. He sees a fundamental shift from a "culture of marriage" to a "culture of divorce." Traditional vows of marital commitment—"til death us do part"—now amount to little more than "as long as I am happy." Daniel Yankelovich (1994:20) sums it up this way:

> The quest for greater individual choice clashed directly with the obligations and social norms that held families and communities together in earlier years. People came to feel that questions of how to live and with whom to live were a matter of individual choice not to be governed by restrictive norms. As a nation, we came to experience the bonds of marriage, family, children, job, community, and country as constraints that were no longer necessary. Commitments have loosened.

Second, family life in the twenty-first century will be highly variable. Cohabiting couples, one-parent families, gay and lesbian families, and blended families are all on the increase. Most families are still based on marriage, and most married couples still have children. But the variety of family forms, taken together, reveals a trend toward more personal choice.

Third, men will play a limited role in child rearing. In the 1950s, a decade that many people view as the "golden age" of families, men began to withdraw from active parenting (Snell, 1990; Stacey, 1990). In recent years, a small countertrend—the stay-at-home

dad—is evident, with some older, highly educated fathers of young children staying at home, yet remaining active in their careers thanks to computer technology. But they represent no more than 15 percent of fathers with preschool children (Gardner, 1996). The bigger picture is that the high U.S. divorce rate and the increase in single motherhood are weakening children's ties to fathers. At the same time, the evidence is building that the absence of fathers is harmful to children, at the

Here is a resource Web site for stay-at-home fathers: http://www.slowlane.com

The negative consequences of the cultural trend toward weaker families, Popenoe continues, are obvious and can be found everywhere: As we pay less and less attention to children, the juvenile crime rate goes up, along with a host of other troublesome behaviors ranging from underage smoking and drinking to premarital sex to teen suicide.

As Popenoe sees it, then, we must work hard and act quickly to reverse current trends. Government cannot be the solution and may even be part of the problem: Since 1960, as families have weakened, government spending on social programs has soared fivefold. To save the traditional family, says Popenoe, we need a cultural turnaround. We must replace our "me-first" attitudes with commitment to our spouse and children and publicly endorse the two-parent family as best for the well-being of children.

But Judith Stacey says "good riddance" to the traditional family and provides a counterpoint. To her, the traditional family is more problem than solution. Striking to the heart of the matter, Stacey writes (1990:269):

The family is not here to stay. Nor should we wish it were. On the contrary, I believe that all

democratic people, whatever their kinship preferences, should work to hasten its demise.

The main reason for rejecting the traditional family, Stacey explains, is that it supports social inequality. Families play a key role in maintaining the class hierarchy, by transferring wealth as well as "cultural capital" from one generation to another. Moreover, feminists criticize the traditional family's patriarchal form, which subjects women to their husbands' authority and saddles them with most of the responsibility for housework and child care. From a gay rights perspective, she adds, a society that values traditional families also denies homosexual men and women equal participation in social life.

Stacey thus applauds the breakdown of the family as social progress. She considers the family not a necessary social institution but a political construct that places one category of people—rich white males—above others, including women, homosexuals, and poor people.

Stacey also claims that the concept of "traditional family" is increasingly irrelevant in a diverse society where both men and women work for income. What our society needs, Stacey concludes, is not a return to some golden

age of the family but political and economic change, including income parity for women, universal health care and child care, programs that reduce unemployment, and expanded sex education in the schools. Only with such programs can we support our children and ensure that people in diverse family forms receive the respect and dignity everyone deserves.

Continue the debate . . .

1. *To strengthen families, David Popenoe suggests that parents put children ahead of their own careers by limiting their joint workweek to sixty hours. Do you agree? Why or why not?*

2. *Judith Stacey thinks that marriage is weaker today because women are rejecting patriarchal relationships. What do you think about this argument?*

3. *Do we need to change family patterns for the well-being of our children? As you see it, what specific changes are called for?*

Sources: Stacey (1990, 1993), Popenoe (1993a), Council on Families in America (1995), Sawhill (2002), and U.S. Census Bureau (2002, 2003).

very least because such families are at high risk of being poor.

Fourth, we will continue to feel the effects of economic changes in our families (Hochschild & Machung, 1989). In most homes, both household partners work, rendering marriage the interaction of weary men and women who try to squeeze in a little "quality time" for themselves and their children (Dizard & Gadlin, 1990). Two-career couples may advance the goal of gender equality, but the long-term effects on families as we have known them are likely to be mixed.

Fifth and finally, the importance of new reproductive technology will increase. Ethical concerns about whether what *can* be done *should* be done will surely slow these developments, but new forms of reproduction will continue to alter the traditional experience of parenthood.

Despite the changes and controversies that have buffeted the family in the United States in recent decades, most people still report being happy as partners and parents. Marriage and family life are likely to remain a foundation of our society for many years to come.

SUMMARY

1. All societies are built on kinship, although family forms vary across cultures and over time.

2. In industrialized societies such as the United States, marriage is monogamous. Many preindustrial societies, however, permit polygamy, of which there are two types: polygyny and polyandry.

3. In global perspective, patrilocality is most common, whereas industrial societies favor neolocality and a few societies have matrilocal residence. Industrial societies use bilateral descent, while preindustrial societies are either patrilineal or matrilineal.

4. Structural-functional analysis identifies major family functions: socialization of the young, regulation of sexual activity, social placement, and provision of material and emotional support.

5. Social-conflict theories explore how the family perpetuates social inequality by transmitting divisions based on class, ethnicity, race, and gender.

6. Micro-level analysis highlights the variety of family life as experienced by various family members.

7. Courtship leads to the formation of new families. Romantic love is central to mate selection in the United States, but not in much of the rest of the world. Even in this country, moreover, romantic love usually joins people with similar social backgrounds.

8. The vast majority of married couples have children, although family size has decreased over time. The main reason for this decline is industrialization, which transforms children into economic liabilities, encourages women to gain an education and join the labor force, and reduces infant mortality.

9. Married life changes as children leave home to form families of their own. Many middle-aged couples, however, care for aging parents, and many older couples are active grandparents. The final transition in marriage begins with the death of one's spouse, usually the husband.

10. Families differ according to class position, race, and ethnicity. Hispanic families, for example, are more likely than others to maintain extended kinship ties. African American families are more likely than others to be headed by single women. Among all categories of people, well-to-do families enjoy the most options and the greatest financial security.

11. Gender affects family dynamics since husbands dominate in most marriages. Research suggests that marriage provides more benefits for men than for women.

12. The divorce rate today is ten times what it was a century ago; at least four in ten current marriages will end in divorce. Most people who divorce—especially men—remarry, often forming blended families that include children from previous marriages.

13. Family violence, which victimizes mostly women and children, is far more common than official records indicate. Most adults who abuse family members were themselves abused as children.

14. Our society's family life is becoming more varied. One-parent families, cohabitation, gay and lesbian couples, and singlehood have proliferated in recent years. While the law does not recognize homosexual marriages, many gay men and lesbians form long-lasting relationships and, increasingly, are becoming parents.

15. Although ethically controversial, new reproductive technology is changing conventional ideas of parenthood.

KEY CONCEPTS

family (p. 461) a social institution found in all societies that unites people in cooperative groups to oversee the bearing and raising of children

kinship (p. 461) a social bond based on blood, marriage, or adoption

family unit (p. 462) a social group of two or more people, related by blood, marriage, or adoption, who usually live together

marriage (p. 462) a legally sanctioned relationship, usually involving economic cooperation as well as sexual activity and childbearing, that people expect to be enduring

extended family (consanguine family) (p. 462) a family unit that includes parents and children as well as other kin

nuclear family (conjugal family) (p. 462) a family unit composed of one or two parents and their children

endogamy (p. 464) marriage between people of the same social category

exogamy (p. 464) marriage between people of different social categories

monogamy (p. 464) marriage that unites two partners

polygamy (p. 464) marriage that unites three or more people

polygyny (p. 464) marriage that unites one man and two or more women

polyandry (p. 464) marriage that unites one woman and two or more men

patrilocality (p. 464) a residential pattern in which a married couple lives with or near the husband's family

matrilocality (p. 464) a residential pattern in which a married couple lives with or near the wife's family

neolocality (p. 464) a residential pattern in which a married couple lives apart from both sets of parents

descent (p. 464) the system by which members of a society trace kinship over generations

patrilineal descent (p. 464) a system tracing kinship through men

matrilineal descent (p. 464) a system tracing kinship through women

bilateral descent (p. 464) a system tracing kinship through both men and women

incest taboo (p. 466) a norm forbidding sexual relations or marriage between certain relatives

homogamy (p. 470) marriage between people with the same social characteristics

infidelity (p. 470) sexual activity outside marriage

family violence (p. 478) emotional, physical, or sexual abuse of one family member by another

cohabitation (p. 479) the sharing of a household by an unmarried couple

CRITICAL-THINKING QUESTIONS

1. Identify important changes in U.S. families since 1960. What factors are responsible for these changes?

2. A rising number of companies are extending benefits such as health insurance to unmarried gay partners. Do you approve of this trend? Why or why not? Should companies also extend benefits to cohabiting heterosexual partners?

3. Child psychiatrist Stanley Greenspan (2001) suggests that parents limit their workweek to four-thirds time— that is, each working two-thirds time, or one working full-time and the other one-third time—so that they may devote two-thirds of the working day to their children. What do you see as the benefits and challenges of such a plan?

4. On balance, are families in the United States becoming weaker or simply different? What evidence can you cite?

APPLICATIONS AND EXERCISES

1. Parents and grandparents can be a wonderful source of information about changes in marriage and the family. Spend an hour or two with married people of two different generations and ask at what ages they married, what their married lives have been like, and what changes in family life today stand out for them.

2. Relationships with various family members differ. With which family member—mother, father, brother, sister—do you most readily and least readily share confidences? Why? Which family member would you turn to first in a crisis? Why?

3. A recent survey found that just one-third of families agreed that members often eat dinner together (Myers, 2000:179). Does your family do this? What other regular family rituals do you participate in? Do members of your family feel that they spend enough time together?

4. Packaged in the back of this new textbook is an interactive CD-ROM that offers a variety of video and interactive review materials intended to help you better understand the material covered in this chapter. For this chapter, the CD-ROM contains a relevant clip from *ABC News*, an author's tip video, interactive map animations, an interactive time line, and flashcards with audio pronunciations of the more difficult words.

 **SITES TO SEE**

http://www.prenhall.com/macionis

Visit the interactive Companion Website™ that accompanies this text. Begin by clicking on the cover of your book. You will find a chapter-by-chapter study guide, practice tests, suggested Web links, and links to other relevant material.

http://www.urban.org

Visit the site of the Urban Institute and look for research reports on the economic effects of family type on children, especially those living in or near poverty.

http://www.frc.org

This is the Web address for the Family Research Council, a conservative organization supporting what it calls "traditional family values." What does the council consider a "traditional family"? What values does it defend? Why? Are there family problems that it ignores?

http://www.contemporaryfamilies.org

The Council on Contemporary Families conducts research on today's family patterns.

http://www.genhomepage.com

Interested in tracing your ancestors? Learn more about genealogy at this resource site.

www.redthreadmag.com

This site provides information about cross-cultural adoptions—specifically, the experiences of people in the United States adopting young girls from China, as described in the opening of this chapter.

http://childstats.gov

This is the site for the Federal Interagency Forum on Child and Family Statistics, which compiles information from eighteen government agencies.

http://www.savethechildren.org

This organization provides information on how families and, especially, children around the world are affected by war, poverty, and AIDS and explains how you can help.

http://www.polyamorysociety.org

Survey the increasing diversity of family life at the Web site for the Polyamory Society. What do you make of the society's views of family life?

http://www.singlemothers.org

The National Organization of Single Mothers offers advice and assistance to women who are single mothers by choice or chance.

 **INVESTIGATE WITH RESEARCH NAVIGATOR™**

Follow the instructions on page 24 of this text to access the features of **Research Navigator™**. Once at the Web site, enter your Login Name and Password. Then, to use the **Content Select™** database, enter keywords such as "family," "cohabitation," and "divorce," and the search engine will supply relevant and recent scholarly and popular press publications. Use the *New York Times* **Search-by-Subject Archive** to find recent news articles related to sociology and the **Link Library** feature to find relevant Web links organized by the key terms associated with this chapter.

March 24, 2002

With the Blessing of Society, Europeans Opt Not to Marry

By SARAH LYALL

OSLO, Norway—Bjorn Lindahl and Nina Kjolaas do not feel inclined to declare their love in front of some anonymous official in a municipal building, or in a church. So they have never married—not when they moved in together, not when they bought their first house, not when they had their son, now 16. . . .

In a profound shift that has changed the notion of what constitutes a family in many countries, more and more European children are being born out of wedlock into a new social order in which, it seems, few of the old stigmas apply. The trend is far more pronounced in the Nordic countries, in France and in Britain, and less so in southern countries like Italy and Switzerland, but the figures as a whole are startling, particularly because they tend to hold up across all social classes. . . .

Marriage in Europe is by no means obsolete; most Europeans still marry at some point in their lives, and after a precipitous drop in marriage rates throughout the 1990s, some countries have actually experienced incremental increases of late. But with changing attitudes toward religion and toward the role of the individual and the state, the questions of when and whether to marry are increasingly seen as deeply personal choices free from the traditional moral judgments of community, family or church. . . .

The attitude in Europe is substantially different from that in the United States, where the government recently announced that it was actively committed to promoting marriage. The British government has all but abandoned that position, acknowledging in a recent position paper that there were many alternatives to the classic family structure. . . .

Policies enacted in the last two decades by many European governments include legislation ensuring that children born out of wedlock have the same inheritance rights as other children; financial grants to the children of single parents; and the removal, in Britain, of a special tax break for married couples and an increase in cash allowances for families with children. . . .

In deeply religious countries like Italy, few children are born to unwed parents, just 9 percent in 1998. But even in Italy, the old rules are breaking down. Most couples live together before marriage, and in a country where children, and fecundity, are adored, it is no longer unusual or embarrassing to see a heavily pregnant bride strolling down the aisle. . . .

Eric Larrayadieu, a photographer in France, has not married his girlfriend, Olivia, after more than three years of living together and the birth of Marius, their 6-month-old son. . . .

But the two are now considering marrying, purely for practical reasons—they want to ensure legal and financial protection for the family if one of them dies or falls ill. In France, as in most countries, a surviving live-in partner has no automatic inheritance rights.

Many of the couples decide to split up, of course, and the result has been a significant rise in single parents, most of them mothers.

. . . Buoyed in part by policies that allow them substantial financial grants even when they return to work, single mothers in many European countries are considerably better off than in the United States, where some 45 percent to 50 percent of single mothers live beneath the poverty line.

"As a single mother, you don't have to be ashamed anymore," said Kathrine Lorenz, 35, a child psychologist in Oslo, who is rearing her 3-year-old daughter alone. . . .

Ms. Lorenz was reared by a single mother, too, after her parents divorced when she was 5. Her mother, she said, was ashamed and could not work; Ms. Lorenz was taunted at school. "But our children don't hear this. It's much more normal now."

What do you think?

1. Do you think the trend away from marriage described in this article is good or bad for society? Why?
2. Should the government use tax advantages or other incentives to encourage marriage, to discourage it, or should government remain neutral about marriage? Explain your view.

CHAPTER

19

RELIGION

LOUIS DELAPORTE (FRENCH)
Festival in a Pagoda at Ngong Kair, Laos

From *Atlas du Voyage d'Exploration de Indos-Chine effectué pendant les Années 1866, 1867, & 1868 par une Commission Francaise* by Francis Garnier, engraved by Ange Luis Janet (1815–72) and Bachelier, published 1873 (color litho). Private Collection/The Stapleton Collection/The Bridgeman Art Library.

ITH ITS MANY churches, synagogues, temples, and mosques (a recent study put the figure at one for every 865 people), one nation stands out as among the most religious on Earth. For its entire history, its leaders have proclaimed that God is responsible for its prosperity and liberty; today, four out of five of this nation's people say they have "experienced God's presence or a spiritual force." Together, they give more than $55 billion each year to religious organizations—more than the total economic output of most low-income countries. In schools, their children stand before the national flag and pledge their allegiance to "one nation under God" (Sheler, 2002).

You have already guessed that the country described is the United States. But while the United States is a

religious nation, it is also a country of immigrants, and as a result, its people imagine God in many different ways. In countless places of worship—from soaring Gothic cathedrals in New York City to small storefront tabernacles in Los Angeles—one can find Christians, Muslims, Jews, Buddhists, Hindus, Sikhs, Jains, Zoroastrians, and followers of dozens of other religions (Ebaugh & Chafetz, 2000; Yang & Ebaugh, 2001; Sheler, 2002). One scholar of religion recently described the United States as the world's most religiously diverse nation, a country in which Hindu and Jewish children go to school together and Muslims, Buddhists, and Sikhs work in the same factories and offices as Protestants and Catholics (Eck, 2001). Furthermore, as we shall see, many more people in the United States today are spiritual without being part of an organized religion.

This chapter begins by explaining, from a sociological point of view, what religion is. We then explore the changing face of religious belief throughout history and around the world and examine the vital—yet sometimes controversial—place of religion in today's culture.

RELIGION: BASIC CONCEPTS

French sociologist Emile Durkheim stated that religion involves "things that surpass the limits of our knowledge" (1965:62; orig. 1915). Human beings define most objects, events, or experiences as **profane** (from the Latin, meaning "outside the temple"), *that which people define as an ordinary element of everyday life.* But we also view some things as **sacred,** *that which people set apart as extraordinary, inspiring awe and reverence.* Distinguishing the sacred from the profane is the essence of all religious belief. **Religion,** then, is *a social institution involving beliefs and practices based on a conception of the sacred.*

Religion is founded on the concept of the sacred: that which is set apart as extraordinary and which demands our submission. Bowing, kneeling, or prostrating oneself are all ways of symbolically surrendering to a higher power. This monk is performing an act of prostration circumambulation, a complicated way of saying that he falls flat on the ground every few steps as he moves around a holy shrine. In this way, he expresses his complete surrender to his faith.

When we consider the religious diversity of the United States—and that of the entire world—we realize that nothing is sacred to everyone. Although people regard most books as profane, Jews believe the Torah (the first five books of the Hebrew Bible or Old Testament) is sacred, in the same way that Christians revere the Old and New Testaments of the Bible and Muslims exalt the Qur'an (Koran).

But no matter how a community of believers draws religious lines, Durkheim (1965:62) explained, people understand profane things in terms of their everyday usefulness: We log onto the Internet with our computer or turn a key to start our car. What is sacred we reverently set apart from everyday life, giving it a "forbidden" aura. Marking the boundary between the sacred and the profane, for example, Muslims remove their shoes before entering a mosque, to avoid defiling a sacred place with soles that have touched the profane ground outside.

The sacred is embodied in **ritual**, or *formal, ceremonial behavior*. Holy communion is the central ritual of Christianity; to the Christian faithful, the wafer and wine consumed during communion are never treated in a profane way as food but as the sacred symbols of the body and blood of Jesus Christ.

RELIGION AND SOCIOLOGY

Because religion deals with ideas and truth that transcend everyday experience, neither common sense nor sociology can verify or disprove religious doctrine.

Religion is a matter of **faith**, *belief anchored in conviction rather than scientific evidence*. The New Testament of the Bible, for instance, describes faith as "the conviction of things not seen" (Heb. 11:1) and exhorts Christians to "walk by faith, not by sight" (2 Cor. 5:7).

Some people with strong faith may be disturbed by the thought of sociologists investigating what they hold sacred. In truth, however, a sociological study of religion poses no threat to anyone's faith. Sociologists study religion just as they study the family, to understand what religious experiences are around the world and how religion is tied to other social institutions. They make no judgments that a specific religion is right or wrong. Rather, scientific sociology takes a more worldly approach, asking why religions take particular forms in one society or another and how religious activity affects society as a whole.

THEORETICAL ANALYSIS OF RELIGION

Sociologists have applied various theoretical paradigms to the study of religion. Each provides distinctive insights into the way religion shapes social life.

FUNCTIONS OF RELIGION: STRUCTURAL-FUNCTIONAL ANALYSIS

According to Durkheim (1965; orig. 1915), society has an existence and power of its own beyond the life of any individual. In other words, society itself is "god-like," surviving the death of its members, whose lives it shapes. Thus, in religion, people celebrate the awesome power of their society.

No wonder, then, that people around the world transform certain everyday objects into sacred symbols of their collective life. Members of technologically simple societies do this with a **totem,** *an object in the natural world collectively defined as sacred.* The totem—perhaps an animal or an elaborate work of art—becomes the centerpiece of ritual, symbolizing people's collective life. In U.S. society, the flag is a sacred totem that is to be treated with respect, not used in a profane manner (say, as clothing) or allowed to touch the ground.

Similarly, putting the words "In God We Trust" on all currency (a practice begun in the 1860s at the time of the Civil War) or adding the words "under God" to the Pledge of Allegiance (in 1954) implies that our society is bound together with common beliefs. Across the United States local communities also gain a sense of unity through totemic symbolism attached to sports teams: from the New England Patriots, to the Iowa State University Cyclones, to the San Francisco 49ers.

Why is the religious dimension of social life so important? Durkheim pointed out three major functions of religion for the operation of society:

1. **Social cohesion.** Religion unites people through shared symbolism, values, and norms. Religious thought and ritual establish rules of fair play, making social life orderly.

2. **Social control.** Every society uses religious ideas to promote conformity. Societies give many cultural norms—especially mores that deal with marriage and reproduction—religious justification. Religion even legitimizes the political system. Although few of today's political leaders claim to rule by divine right (as they did centuries ago), many publicly ask for God's blessing, implying to audiences that their efforts are right and just.

3. **Providing meaning and purpose.** Religious belief offers the comforting sense that our brief lives serve some greater purpose. Strengthened by such beliefs, people are less likely to despair when one of life's calamities strikes. For this reason, we mark major life course transitions—including birth, marriage, and death—with religious observances.

Critical evaluation. In Durkheim's structural-functional analysis, religion represents the collective life of society. The major weakness of this approach is that it downplays religion's dysfunctions, especially the fact that strongly held beliefs can generate social conflict. Recently, terrorists have claimed that God supports their actions, and many nations march to war under the banner of their God. Few would deny that religious beliefs have provoked more violence in human history than differences of social class have.

CONSTRUCTING THE SACRED: SYMBOLIC-INTERACTION ANALYSIS

From a symbolic-interaction point of view, religion (like all of society) is socially constructed (although perhaps with divine inspiration). Through various rituals—from daily prayers to annual religious observances like Easter, Passover, and Ramadan—individuals sharpen the distinction between the sacred and the profane. Furthermore, says Peter Berger (1967:35–36), placing our fallible, brief lives within some "cosmic frame of reference" gives us "the semblance of ultimate security and permanence."

Marriage is a good example. If two people look on marriage as merely a contract, they can walk away whenever they want to. But defined as holy matrimony, their bond makes far stronger claims on them. This is why the divorce rate is lower among people who are religious. More generally, whenever we confront uncertainty or life-threatening situations—such as illness, natural disaster, terrorist attack, or war—we turn to our sacred symbols.

Critical evaluation. Using the symbolic-interaction approach, religion puts everyday life under a "sacred canopy" of meaning (Berger, 1967). Of course, Berger adds, the sacred's ability to give meaning and to stabilize society depends on people's ignoring its constructed character. After all, how much strength could we derive from beliefs we saw as mere strategies for coping with tragedy? Also, this micro-level analysis ignores religion's link to social inequality, to which we now turn.

INEQUALITY AND RELIGION: SOCIAL-CONFLICT ANALYSIS

The social-conflict paradigm highlights religion's support of the social hierarchy. Karl Marx claimed religion serves ruling elites by legitimizing the status quo and diverting people's attention from social inequities.

Even today, for example, the British monarch is the formal head of the Church of England, illustrating

DIVERSITY: RACE, CLASS, AND GENDER

Religion and Patriarchy: Does God Favor Males?

Why do two-thirds of U.S. adults envision God as "father" rather than "mother" (NORC, 2003:146)? Probably because we link godly attributes such as wisdom and power to men. Thus, it is hardly surprising that organized religions tend to favor males, a fact evident in passages from the sacred writings of major world religions.

The Qur'an (Koran), the sacred text of Islam, declares that men are to dominate women:

> Men are in charge of women.... Hence good women are obedient.... As for those whose rebelliousness you fear, admonish them, banish them from your bed, and scourge them. (quoted in Kaufman, 1976:163)

Christianity, the major religion of the Western world, also supports patriarchy. While many Christians revere Mary, the mother of Jesus, the New Testament also includes the following passages:

> A man . . . is the image and glory of God; but woman is the glory of

man. For man was not made from woman, but woman from man. Neither was man created for woman, but woman for man. (1 Cor. 11:7–9)

> As in all the churches of the saints, the women should keep silence in the churches. For they are not permitted to speak, but should be subordinate, as even the law says. If there is anything they desire to know, let them ask their husbands at home. For it is shameful for a woman to speak in church. (1 Cor. 14:33–35)

> Wives, be subject to your husbands, as to the Lord. For the husband is the head of the wife as Christ is the head of the church. . . . As the church is

---

the close alliance between religious and political elites. In practical terms, working for political change may mean opposing the church and, by implication, God. Religion also encourages people to endure without complaint social problems of this world as they look hopefully to a "better world to come." In a well-known statement, Marx dismissed religion as "the sigh of the oppressed creature, the sentiment of a heartless world, and the soul of soulless conditions. It is the opium of the people" (1964:27; orig. 1848).

Religion and social inequality are also linked through gender. Virtually all the world's major religions are patriarchal, as the box explains.

For centuries, the Christian nations of Western Europe justified the conquest of Africa, the Americas, and Asia by claiming that they were "converting heathens." In the United States, churches in the South viewed enslaving African Americans as consistent with

God's will. Moreover, many churches across the country remain segregated to this day. In the words of the African American writer Maya Angelou, "Sunday at 11:30 A.M., America is more segregated than at any time of the week."

Critical evaluation. Social-conflict analysis reveals the power of religion to legitimize social inequality. Yet religion also promotes change toward equality. Nineteenth-century religious groups in the United States, for example, were at the forefront of the movement to abolish slavery. During the 1950s and 1960s, religious organizations led by the Reverend Martin Luther King, Jr., and others were the core of the civil rights movement. In the 1960s and 1970s, many clergy actively opposed the Vietnam War just as, in 2003, Pope John Paul II and Archbishop Desmond Tutu spoke out against the War in Iraq.

subject to Christ, so let wives also be subject in everything to their husbands. (Eph. 5:22–24)

Let a woman learn in silence with all submissiveness. I permit no woman to teach or to have authority over men; she is to keep silent. For Adam was formed first, then Eve; and Adam was not deceived, but the woman was deceived and became a transgressor. Yet woman will be saved through bearing children, if she continues in faith and love and holiness, with modesty. (1 Tm. 2:11–15)

Judaism, too, traditionally supports patriarchy. Male Orthodox Jews say the following words in daily prayer:

Blessed art thou, O Lord our God, King of the Universe, that I was not born a gentile.
Blessed art thou, O Lord our God, King of the Universe, that I was not born a slave.

Blessed art thou, O Lord our God, King of the Universe, that I was not born a woman.

Major religions have also remained patriarchal by excluding women from the clergy. Even today, Islam and the Roman Catholic church ban women from the priesthood, as do about half of Protestant denominations. But a growing number of Protestant religious organizations, including the Church of England, ordain women, who now represent 15 percent of U.S. clergy. Orthodox Judaism upholds the traditional prohibition against women serving as rabbis, but Reform and Conservative Judaism look to both men and women as spiritual leaders. Across the United States, the proportion of women in seminaries has never been higher (now roughly one-third), further evidence that change is ongoing (Chaves, 1996; 1997; Nesbitt, 1997).

Challenges to the patriarchal structure of organized religion—from ordaining women to gender-neutral language

in hymnals and prayers—have sparked heated controversy between progressives and traditionalists. Propelling these developments is a lively feminism in many religious communities. According to feminist Christians, for example, patriarchy in the church stands in stark contrast to the largely feminine image of Jesus Christ in the Scriptures as "nonaggressive, noncompetitive, meek and humble of heart, a nurturer of the weak and a friend of the outcast" (Sandra Schneiders, quoted in Woodward, 1989:61).

Feminists argue that, unless traditional notions of gender are removed from our understanding of God, women will never be equal to men in the church. The theologian Mary Daly puts the matter bluntly: "If God is male, then male is God" (quoted in Woodward, 1989:58).

RELIGION AND SOCIAL CHANGE

Religion is not just the conservative force portrayed by Karl Marx. At some points in history, as Max Weber (1958; orig. 1904–5) explained, religion has promoted dramatic social transformation.

MAX WEBER: PROTESTANTISM AND CAPITALISM

Max Weber claimed that new ideas can be an engine of change. It was the religious doctrine of Calvinism, for example, that sparked the Industrial Revolution in Western Europe.

As Chapter 4 ("Society") explains in detail, John Calvin (1509–1564), a leader in the Protestant Reformation, preached the doctrine of predestination. According to Calvin, an all-powerful and all-knowing God predestined some people for salvation and condemned most to

eternal damnation. Each individual's fate, sealed even before birth and known only to God, was either eternal glory or endless hellfire.

Driven by anxiety over their fate, Calvinists understandably looked for evidence of God's favor in *this* world and came to regard prosperity as a sign of divine blessing. Religious conviction and a rigid devotion to duty led Calvinists to work all the time, and many amassed great wealth. But money was not for self-indulgent spending or for sharing with the poor, whose plight Calvinists saw as a mark of God's rejection. As agents of God's work on Earth, Calvinists believed that they best fulfilled their "calling" by reinvesting profits, reaping ever-greater success in the process.

All the while, Calvinists lived thrifty lives and were quick to adopt technological advances, thereby laying the groundwork for the rise of industrial capitalism. In time, the religious fervor that motivated early Calvinists weakened, leaving a profane "Protestant work ethic." To Max Weber, industrial capitalism itself was a "disenchanted" religion, further showing the power of religion to alter the shape of society.

LIBERATION THEOLOGY

While Weber explained how one type of Christianity had helped capitalism develop, other variations of Christianity offer harsh criticism of this economic system. A case in point is **liberation theology,** *a fusion of Christian principles with political activism, often Marxist in character.*

Historically, Christianity has reached out to suffering and oppressed people, urging all to a stronger faith in a better life to come. In the late 1960s, numerous clergy in Latin America's Roman Catholic church sought to use their position and their teachings to help liberate the poor from abysmal poverty. The message of liberation theology is simple: Social oppression runs counter to Christian morality, so as a matter of faith and justice, Christians must promote greater social equality.

Pope John Paul II condemns liberation theology, despite its Roman Catholic beginnings, for distorting traditional church doctrine with left-wing politics. But over the pontiff's objections, the liberation theology movement remains powerful in Latin America, where many people find their Christian faith drives them to improve conditions for the world's poor (Neuhouser, 1989; Williams, 2002).

TYPES OF RELIGIOUS ORGANIZATION

Sociologists categorize the hundreds of different religious organizations found in the United States along a continuum, with *churches* at one end and *sects* at the other. We can describe any actual religious organization, then, in relation to these two ideal types by locating it on the church-sect continuum.

CHURCH

Drawing on the ideas of his teacher Max Weber, Ernst Troeltsch (1931) defined a **church** as *a type of religious organization that is well integrated into the larger society.* Churchlike organizations usually persist for centuries and include generations of the same families. Churches have well-established rules and regulations and expect leaders to be formally trained and ordained.

While concerned with the sacred, a church accepts the ways of the profane world, which gives it broad appeal. Church members conceive of God in highly intellectualized terms (say, as a force for good) and favor abstract moral standards ("Do unto others as you would have them do unto you") over specific rules for day-to-day living. By teaching morality in safely abstract terms, church leaders avoid social controversy. For example, many congregations that celebrate the unity of all peoples have an all-white membership. Such duality minimizes conflict between a church and political life (Troeltsch, 1931).

December 11, Casablanca, Morocco. The waves of the Atlantic crash along the walls of Casablanca's magnificent coastline mosque, reputedly the largest in the world. From the top of the towering structure, a green laser cuts through the night sky, pointing eastward to Mecca, the holy city of Islam, toward which the faithful bow in prayer. To pay for this monumental house of worship, King Hassam II, Morocco's head of state and religious leader, levied a tax on every citizen in his realm, all of whom are officially Muslim. This example of "government religion" contrasts sharply with our ideas about the separation of church and state.

A church may operate with or apart from the state. A **state church** is *a church formally allied with the state*, as illustrated by Islam in Morocco. State churches have existed throughout human history; for centuries Roman Catholicism was the official religion of the Roman Empire, as Confucianism was the official religion of China until early in the twentieth century. Today, the Anglican church is the official church of England, as Islam is the official religion of Pakistan and Iran. State churches count everyone in the society as a member, a practice that discourages religious tolerance.

A **denomination,** by contrast, is *a church, independent of the state, that recognizes religious pluralism.* Denominations exist in nations that formally separate church and state, such as the United States, which has dozens of Christian denominations—including Catholics, Baptists, Episcopalians, and Lutherans—as well as various categories of Judaism, Islam, and other traditions. Although members of any denomination hold to their own beliefs, they recognize the right of others to disagree.

SECT

The second general religious form is the **sect,** *a type of religious organization that stands apart from the larger society.* Sect members have rigid religious convictions and deny the beliefs of others. Whereas the term "catholic" also means "universal," a sect deliberately does not try to appeal to everyone but instead forms an exclusive group. Generally, to members of a sect, religion is not just one aspect of life but a firm plan for how to live. In extreme cases, members of a sect may withdraw completely from society in order to practice their religion without interference. The Amish are one example of a North American sect that isolates itself. Since our culture holds up religious tolerance as a virtue, members of sects are sometimes accused of being narrow-minded in insisting that they alone follow the true religion (Kraybill, 1994; Williams, 2002).

In organizational terms, sects are less formal than churches. Thus, sect members are often highly spontaneous and emotional in worship, while members of churches tend to listen passively to their leader. Sects also reject the intellectualized religion of churches, stressing instead the personal experience of divine power. Rodney Stark (1985:314) contrasts a church's vision of a distant God ("Our Father, who art in Heaven") with a sect's more immediate God ("Lord, bless this poor sinner kneeling before you now").

A further distinction between church and sect turns on patterns of leadership. The more churchlike an organization, the more likely it is that its leaders will be formally trained and ordained. Sectlike organizations, which celebrate the personal presence of God, expect their leaders to exhibit divine inspiration in the form of **charisma** (from the Greek, meaning "divine favor"), *extraordinary personal qualities that can infuse people with emotion and turn them into followers.*

Sects generally form as breakaway groups from established religious organizations (Stark & Bainbridge, 1979). Their psychic intensity and informal structure render them less stable than churches, and many sects blossom only to disappear soon after. The sects that do endure typically become more like churches, losing fervor as they become more bureaucratic and established.

To sustain their membership, many sects actively recruit, or *proselytize,* new members. Sects highly value the experience of *conversion,* a personal transformation or religious rebirth. For example, members of Jehovah's Witnesses visit door to door to share their faith with others in hopes of attracting new members.

Finally, churches and sects differ in their social composition. Because they are more closely tied to the

In global perspective, the range of religious activity is truly astonishing. Members of this Southeast Asian cult show their devotion to God by suspending themselves in the air using ropes and sharp hooks that pierce their skin.

world, well-established churches tend to include people of high social standing. Sects, by contrast, attract more disadvantaged people. A sect's openness to new members and its promise of salvation and personal fulfillment appeal to people who may perceive themselves as social outsiders.

CULT

A **cult** is *a religious organization that is largely outside a society's cultural traditions.* Whereas most sects spin off from a conventional religious organization, a cult typically forms around a highly charismatic leader who

Typically, societies with simple technology are animistic, meaning they recognize divine power in the elements of the natural world, such as the animals they hunt for food. This painting, located in the Lascaux caves in France, was created some 17,000 years ago.

offers a compelling message about a new and very different way of life. As many as 5,000 cults now exist in the United States (Marquand & Wood, 1997).

Because some cult principles or practices are unconventional, the popular view is that they are deviant or even evil. The deaths of more than eighty cult members in Waco, Texas, in 1993 and the suicides of thirty-nine members of California's Heaven's Gate cult in 1997—people who claimed that dying was a doorway to a higher existence, perhaps in the company of aliens from outer space—confirmed the negative image the public holds of most cults. In short, say some scholars, calling any religious community a "cult" amounts to dismissing its members as crazy (Richardson, 1990; Shupe, 1995; Gleick, 1997).

This charge is unfortunate because there is nothing intrinsically wrong with this kind of religious organization. Many longstanding religions—Christianity, Islam, and Judaism included—began as cults. Of course, few cults exist for very long. One reason is that they are even more at odds with the larger society than sects. Many cults demand that members not only accept their doctrine but embrace a radically new lifestyle. Such lifestyle changes have prompted people to accuse cults of brainwashing their members, although research suggests that most people who join cults experience no psychological harm. Fear of cults reached a peak during the late 1970s and has declined since (Barker, 1981; Kilbourne, 1983; Williams, 2002).

RELIGION IN HISTORY

Like other social institutions, religion shows considerable variation both historically and cross-culturally. We now note several ways religion has changed over the course of history.

RELIGION IN PREINDUSTRIAL SOCIETIES

Early hunters and gatherers embraced **animism** (from the Latin, meaning "the breath of life"), *the belief that elements of the natural world are conscious life forms that affect humanity*. Animistic people view forests, oceans, mountains, and even the wind as spiritual forces. Many Native American societies are animistic; thus their historical reverence for the natural environment.

Belief in a single divine power responsible for creating the world arose with pastoral and horticultural societies, which first appeared 10,000 to 12,000 years ago. Our conception of God as a "shepherd" should be no surprise, because Christianity, Judaism, and Islam had their beginnings among pastoral peoples.

In agrarian societies, religion becomes more important, with a specialized priesthood in charge of religious organizations. The centrality of religion is evident in the huge cathedrals that dominated the towns of medieval Europe.

RELIGION IN INDUSTRIAL SOCIETIES

The Industrial Revolution ushered in a growing emphasis on science. More and more, people looked to physicians and scientists for the knowledge and comfort they had sought from priests. Even so, religion persists because science is powerless to address issues of ultimate meaning in human life. In other words, learning *how* the world works is a matter for scientists, but *why* we and the rest of the universe exist at all is a question for religion to answer.

WORLD RELIGIONS

The diversity of religious expression in the world is almost as wide-ranging as the diversity of culture itself. Many of the thousands of different religions are highly

 For more information on world religions, go to http://www.adherents.com

localized with few followers. *World religions*, by contrast, are widely known and have millions of adherents. We shall briefly describe six world religions, which together claim 4 billion believers—representing fully three-fourths of humanity.

CHRISTIANITY

Christianity is the most widespread religion, with 2 billion followers, roughly one-third of the world's people. Most Christians live in Europe or the Americas; more than 85 percent of the people in the United States and Canada identify with Christianity. Moreover, as shown in Global Map 19–1 on page 498, people who are at least nominally Christian represent a large share of the population in many other world regions, with the notable exceptions of northern Africa and Asia. European colonization spread Christianity throughout much of the world over the last 500 years. Its dominance in the West is shown by the fact that our calendar numbers years beginning with the birth of Christ.

Christianity originated as a cult, incorporating elements of its much older predecessor, Judaism. Like many cults, Christianity was propelled by the personal charisma of a leader, Jesus of Nazareth, who preached a message of personal salvation. Jesus did not directly challenge the political powers of his day, admonishing his followers to "render therefore to Caesar things that are Caesar's" (Matt. 22:21). But his message was revolutionary, nonetheless, promising that faith and love would triumph over sin and death.

Christianity is one example of **monotheism,** *belief in a single divine power,* and it thus broke with the Roman Empire's traditional **polytheism,** *belief in many gods.* Yet Christianity has a unique vision of the Supreme Being as a sacred Trinity: God the Creator; Jesus Christ, Son of God and Redeemer; and the Holy Spirit, a Christian's personal experience of God's presence.

The claim that Jesus was divine rests on accounts of his final days on Earth. Tried and sentenced to death in Jerusalem on charges that he was a threat to established political leaders, Jesus was executed by crucifixion. Therefore, the cross became a sacred Christian symbol. Three days later, according to Christian belief, Jesus arose from the dead, showing that he was the Son of God.

Jesus' followers, especially the twelve apostles, spread Christianity throughout the Mediterranean region. At first, the Roman Empire persecuted Christians; by the fourth century, however, Christianity had become a state church—the official religion of what later became known as the Holy Roman Empire. What had begun as a cult four centuries before was now an established church.

Christianity took various forms, including the Roman Catholic church and the Orthodox church, based in Constantinople (now Istanbul, Turkey). Toward the end of the Middle Ages, the Protestant Reformation in Europe created hundreds of new denominations. Dozens of these denominations—the Baptists and Methodists are the two largest—now command sizable followings in the United States (Smart, 1969; Kaufman, 1976; Jacquet & Jones, 1991).

ISLAM

Islam has some 1.2 billion followers (about 20 percent of humanity); followers of Islam are called Muslims. A majority of people in the Middle East are Muslims, so

 Here is a new report on Muslims in the United States from the Council on American-Islamic Relations: http://www.cair-net.org/mosquereport/

we tend to associate Islam with Arabs in that region of the world. But most Muslims live else-

where: Global Map 19–2 on page 498 shows that most people in northern Africa and Indonesia are also Muslims. Moreover, significant concentrations of Muslims are found in western Asia in Pakistan, India, Bangladesh, and the southern republics of the former Soviet Union. There are roughly 7 million Muslims in the United States alone, making Islam a significant

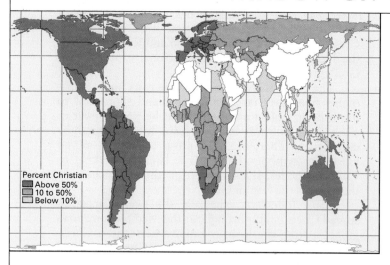

GLOBAL MAP 19–1
Christianity in Global Perspective
Source: *Peters Atlas of the World* (1990).

Percent Christian
- Above 50%
- 10 to 50%
- Below 10%

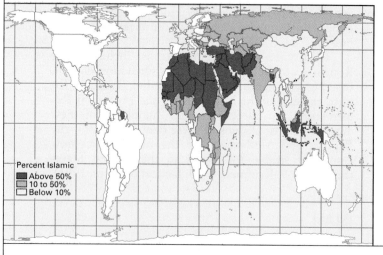

GLOBAL MAP 19–2
Islam in Global Perspective
Source: *Peters Atlas of the World* (1990).

Percent Islamic
- Above 50%
- 10 to 50%
- Below 10%

part of this country's religious life. Because Muslims have a higher birth rate than followers of any other major religion, some analysts predict Islam could become the world's dominant religion by 2050 (Weeks, 1988; University of Akron Research Center, 1993; Blank, 1998; Eck, 2001).

Islam is the word of God as revealed to Muhammad, who was born in the city of Mecca (now in Saudi Arabia) about the year 570. To Muslims, Muhammad is a prophet, not a divine being as Jesus is to Christians. The text of the Qur'an (Koran), sacred to Muslims, is

the word of Allah (Arabic for God) as transmitted through Muhammad, Allah's messenger. In Arabic, the word "Islam" means both "submission" and "peace," and the Qur'an urges submission to Allah as the path to inner peace. Muslims express this personal devotion in a ritual of prayers five times a day.

Islam spread rapidly after the death of Muhammad, although divisions arose, as they did within Christianity. All Muslims, however, accept the Five Pillars of Islam: (1) recognizing Allah as the one, true God and Muhammad as God's messenger; (2) ritual prayer; (3) giving alms to the poor; (4) fasting during the month of Ramadan; and (5) making a pilgrimage at least once in one's lifetime to the Sacred House of Allah in Mecca (Weeks, 1988; El-Attar, 1991). Like Christianity, Islam holds people accountable to God for their deeds on Earth. Those who live obediently will be rewarded in heaven, and evil-doers will suffer unending punishment.

Muslims are also obligated to defend their faith, which has led to calls for holy wars against unbelievers (in roughly the same way that medieval Christians fought in the Crusades). Recent decades have witnessed a rise in militancy and anti-Western feeling in much of the Muslim world, where many people see the United States as both militarily threatening and supportive of a way of life that they judge to be materialistic and immoral. Many Westerners—who typically know little about Islam and often stereotype all Muslims in terms of the terrorist actions of a few—respond with confusion and sometimes hostility (Eck, 2001; Ryan, 2001).

From a Western perspective, however, there has long been agreement that Muslim women are among the most socially oppressed people on Earth. Of course, there are differences among Muslim nations in this regard: Tunisia, for example, allows women far more opportunities than, say, Saudi Arabia (Ganley, 1998). In general, however, Muslim women do lack many of the personal freedoms enjoyed by Muslim men, yet many—and perhaps most—accept the mandates of their religion and find security in a system that guides the behavior of both women and men (S. Peterson, 1996). Muslims also point out that patriarchy was well established in the Middle East long before the birth of Muhammad. Some defenders argue that Islam actually improved the social position of women by requiring that husbands deal justly with their wives. Further, although Islam permits a man to have up to four wives, it admonishes men to have only one wife if having more would cause him to treat any woman unjustly (Qur'an, "The Women," v. 3).

JUDAISM

Simply in terms of numbers, Judaism's 15 million followers worldwide make it something less than a world religion. Moreover, only in Israel do Jews represent a national majority. But Judaism has special significance to the United States because the largest concentration of Jews (6 million people) is found in North America.

Jews look to the past as a source of guidance in the present and for the future. Judaism has deep historical

Many religions promote literacy because they demand followers study sacred texts. As part of their upbringing, most Islamic parents teach their children lessons from the Qur'an (Koran); later, the children will do the same to a new generation of believers.

roots that extend some 4,000 years before the birth of Christ to the ancient cultures of Mesopotamia. At this time, Jews were animistic, but this belief changed after Jacob—grandson of Abraham, the earliest great ancestor—led his people to Egypt.

Jews endured centuries of slavery in Egypt. In the thirteenth century B.C.E., Moses, the adopted son of an Egyptian princess, was called by God to lead the Jews from bondage. This exodus (this word's Latin and Greek roots mean "a marching out") from Egypt is commemorated by Jews today in the annual ritual of Passover. Once liberated, the Jews became monotheistic, recognizing a single, all-powerful God.

A distinctive concept of Judaism is the *covenant*, a special relationship with God by which the Jews became the "chosen people." The covenant implies a duty to observe God's law, especially the Ten Commandments as revealed to Moses on Mount Sinai. Jews regard the Old Testament of the Bible as both a record of their history and a statement of the obligations of Jewish life. Of special importance are the Bible's first five books (Genesis, Exodus, Leviticus, Numbers, and Deuteronomy), designated the *Torah* (a word roughly meaning "teaching" and "law"). In contrast to Christianity's central concern with personal salvation, therefore, Judaism emphasizes moral behavior in this world.

Judaism has three main denominations. Orthodox Jews (including more than 1 million people in the United States) strictly observe traditional beliefs and practices, wear traditional dress, segregate men and women at religious services, and eat only kosher foods. Such traditional practices set off Orthodox Jews in the United States as the most sectlike. In the mid-nineteenth century, many Jews sought greater acceptance by the larger society, and this led to the formation of more churchlike Reform Judaism (now including more than 1.3 million people in this country). A third segment—Conservative Judaism (with about 2 million U.S. adherents)—has since established a middle ground between the other two denominations.

Whatever their denomination, Jews share a cultural history of prejudice and discrimination. A collective memory of centuries of slavery in Egypt, conquest by Rome, and persecution in Europe has shaped Jewish identity. It was Jews in Italy who first lived in an urban ghetto (derived from the Italian word *borghetto*, meaning "settlement outside of the city walls"), and this residential segregation soon spread to other parts of Europe.

Jewish immigration to the United States began in the mid-1600s. Many early immigrants prospered, and many were also assimilated into largely Christian communities. But as larger numbers entered the country toward the end of the nineteenth century, prejudice and discrimination against them—commonly termed *anti-Semitism*—increased. During World War II, anti-Semitism reached a vicious peak as the Nazi regime in Germany systematically annihilated 6 million Jews.

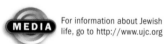
For information about Jewish life, go to http://www.ujc.org

On average, Jews have well-above-average social standing. Still, many Jews are concerned about the future of their religion because, in recent years, more than half of the Jews in the United States have married non-Jews. In only a few cases are non-Jewish spouses converting to Judaism. Just as significantly, only about half the children raised in Jewish households are learning Jewish culture and ritual. For the present, such patterns symbolize Jewish success in gaining acceptance into society. In the minds of some, however, they cast doubt on the future of Judaism in the United States (B. Wilson, 1982; Eisen, 1983; Dershowitz, 1997; Van Biema, 1997; Keister, 2003).

HINDUISM

Hinduism is the oldest of all the world religions, originating in the Indus River valley about 4,500 years ago. Hindus number some 800 million (14 percent of humanity). Global Map 19–3 shows that Hinduism remains an Eastern religion, mostly practiced in India and Pakistan, but with a significant presence in southern Africa and Indonesia.

Over the centuries, Hinduism and the culture of India have become intertwined, so that now one is not easily described apart from the other (although India also has a sizable Muslim population). This connection also explains why Hinduism, unlike Christianity, Islam, and Judaism, has not diffused widely to other nations. Nevertheless, with 1.5 million followers in the United States, Hinduism is a significant part of this country's cultural diversity.

Hinduism differs from most other religions by not being linked to the life of any single person. Hinduism also has no sacred writings comparable to the Bible or the Qur'an. Nor does Hinduism envision God as a specific entity. For this reason, Hinduism—like other Eastern religions, as we shall see—is sometimes described as an "ethical religion." Hindu beliefs and practices vary widely, but all Hindus recognize a moral force in the universe that presents everyone with responsibilities, termed *dharma*. Dharma, for example, calls people to observe the traditional caste system, described in Chapter 10 ("Social Stratification").

Another Hindu principle, *karma*, embodies a belief in the spiritual progress of the human soul. To a Hindu, all actions have spiritual consequences, and proper living contributes to moral development. Karma works through *reincarnation*, a cycle of death and rebirth, by which the individual is reborn into a spiritual state corresponding to the moral quality of a previous life. Unlike Christianity and Islam, Hinduism proclaims no ultimate judgment at the hands of a supreme god, although in the cycle of rebirth, people reap exactly what they have sown. *Moksha* is the sublime state of spiritual perfection: Only when a soul reaches this level is it no longer reborn.

Hinduism stands as evidence that not all religions can be neatly labeled monotheistic or polytheistic. Hinduism is monotheistic insofar as it envisions the universe as a single moral system; yet Hindus see this

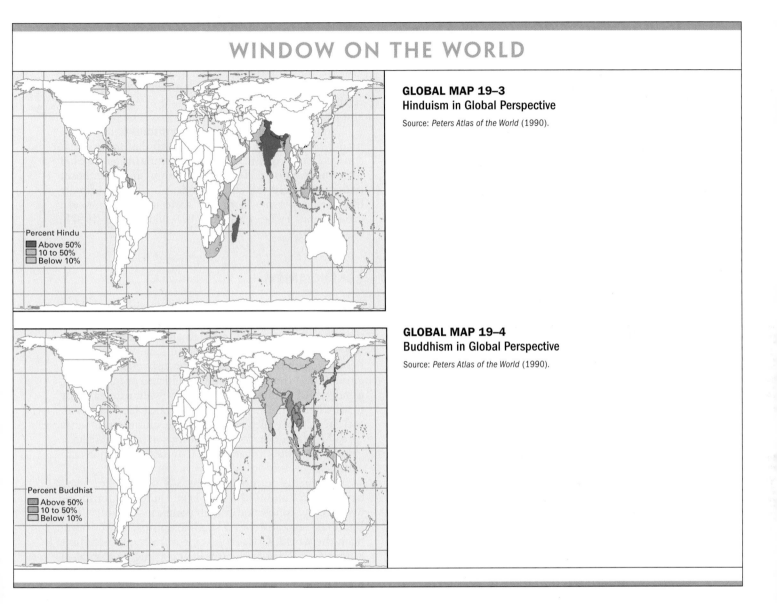

GLOBAL MAP 19–3
Hinduism in Global Perspective
Source: *Peters Atlas of the World* (1990).

Percent Hindu
■ Above 50%
▨ 10 to 50%
□ Below 10%

GLOBAL MAP 19–4
Buddhism in Global Perspective
Source: *Peters Atlas of the World* (1990).

Percent Buddhist
■ Above 50%
▨ 10 to 50%
□ Below 10%

moral order at work in every element of nature. More-over, many Hindus participate in public rituals, such as the *Kumbh Mela*, which every twelve years brings some 20 million pilgrims to the sacred Ganges River to bathe in its purifying waters. At the same time, Hindus practice private devotions, which vary from village to village across the vast nation of India.

While elements of Hindu thought have character-ized some cults in the United States over the years, Hinduism is still unfamiliar to most Westerners. But, with 1.7 million people claiming Asian Indian ancestry and the number of immigrants from India on the rise, Hinduism is becoming more and more a part of the U.S. religious landscape (Kaufman, 1976; Schmidt, 1980; Larson, 2000; Eck, 2001).

BUDDHISM

Twenty-five hundred years ago, the rich culture of India also gave rise to Buddhism. Today some 350 million people (6 percent of humanity) are Buddhists, almost all of them Asians. As shown in Global Map 19–4,

The Dalai Lama is the spiritual leader of the Tibetan people. His followers believe he is the most recent incarnation in a line of leaders beginning with Buddha. He has written many books that are gaining popularity in the United States.

Buddhists make up more than half the populations of Myanmar (Burma), Thailand, Cambodia, and Japan; Buddhism is also widespread in India and the People's Republic of China. Of the world religions considered so far, Buddhism most resembles Hinduism in doctrine, but like Christianity, its inspiration stems from the life of one individual.

Siddhartha Gautama was born to a high-caste family in Nepal about 563 B.C.E. As a young man, he was preoccupied with spiritual matters. At the age of twenty-nine, he underwent a radical personal transformation, and set off for years of travel and meditation. His journey ended when he achieved what Buddhists describe as *bodhi*, or enlightenment. Understanding the essence of life, Gautama became a Buddha.

Energized by his personal charisma, followers spread Buddha's teachings—the *dhamma*—across India. In the third century B.C.E., the ruler of India became a Buddhist and sent missionaries throughout Asia, making Buddhism a world religion.

Buddhists believe that much of life involves suffering. This idea is rooted in the Buddha's own travels in a society rife with poverty. But, Buddha claimed, the solution to suffering is not wealth. On the contrary,

materialism actually holds backs spiritual development. Instead, Buddha taught that we must transcend our selfish concerns and desires through meditation. Only by quieting the mind can people hope to connect with the power of the larger universe—the goal described as obtaining *nirvana*, a state of enlightenment and peace.

Buddhism closely parallels Hinduism in recognizing no god of judgment; yet each daily action has spiritual consequences. Another similarity is a belief in reincarnation. Here again, only enlightenment ends the cycle of death and rebirth and finally liberates a person from the suffering of the world (Schumann, 1974; Thomas, 1975; Van Biema, 1997b; Eckel, 2001).

CONFUCIANISM

From about 200 B.C.E. until the beginning of the twentieth century, Confucianism was a state church—the official religion of China. But after the 1949 Revolution, the communist government of the new People's Republic of China vigorously repressed religion. Today, though officials provide no precise count, hundreds of millions of Chinese are still influenced by Confucianism. Almost all followers of Confucianism live in China, although Chinese immigration has spread this religion to other nations in Southeast Asia. Perhaps 100,000 followers of Confucius live in North America.

Confucius or, more properly, K'ung-Fu-tzu, lived between 551 and 479 B.C.E. Like Buddha, Confucius was deeply concerned about people's suffering. The Buddha's response was a sectlike spiritual withdrawal from the world; Confucius, by contrast, instructed his followers to engage the world according to a code of moral conduct. Thus it was that Confucianism became fused with the traditional culture of China. Here we see a second example of what might be called a national religion: As Hinduism has remained largely synonymous with Indian culture, Confucianism is enshrined in the Chinese way of life.

A central concept of Confucianism is *jen*, meaning "humaneness." In practice, this means that we must always subordinate our self-interest to moral principle. People should look to tradition for guidance in how to live. In the family, the individual must be loyal and considerate. Families must remain mindful of their duties toward the larger community. In this way, layer upon layer of moral obligation ties together society as a whole.

Most of all, Confucianism stands out as lacking a clear sense of the sacred. Recalling Durkheim's analysis, we might view Confucianism as the celebration of the sacred character of society itself. Or we might argue that Confucianism is less a religion than a model of disciplined living. Certainly the historical dominance of Confucianism helps explain why Chinese culture is skeptical of the supernatural. But even as a disciplined way of life, Confucianism shares with religion a body of beliefs and practices that have as their goal goodness, concern for others, and social harmony (Kaufman, 1976; Schmidt, 1980; McGuire, 1997; Ellwood, 2001).

RELIGION: EAST AND WEST

This overview of world religions points up two general differences between the belief systems of Eastern and Western societies. First, religions that arose in the West (Christianity, Islam, Judaism) are typically deity-based, with a clear focus on God. Eastern religions (Hinduism, Buddhism, Confucianism), however, tend to be ethical codes; therefore, they make a less clear-cut distinction between the sacred and the secular.

Second, believers in Western religions form congregations. That is, people join an organization and worship formally in groups at a specific time and place. Eastern religious thinking, by contrast, is fused with culture itself. For this reason, for example, a visitor finds a Japanese temple filled with tourists and worshipers alike, who come and go as they please and pay little attention to those around them.

But these two distinctions do not overshadow the common element of all religions: a call to look beyond selfish, everyday concerns for a higher moral force or purpose. Although they take different paths towards this goal, all religions encourage a spiritual sense that there is more to life than what we see around us.

RELIGION IN THE UNITED STATES

As we noted in the opening to this chapter, the United States is a relatively religious nation. As Figure 19–1 shows, eight in ten members of our society say they gain "comfort and strength from religion," a substantially higher share than in most other countries.

That said, scholars debate exactly how religious this nation is. While some claim that religion remains central to our way of life, others conclude that a decline of the traditional family and the growing importance of science and technology are weakening religious

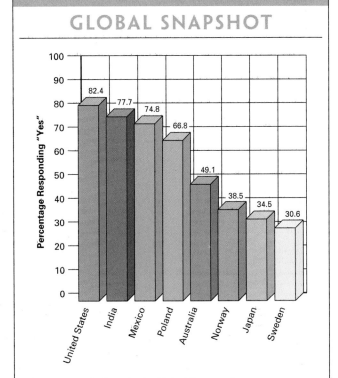

GLOBAL SNAPSHOT

FIGURE 19-1 Religiosity in Global Perspective

Survey Question: "Do you gain comfort and strength from religion?"

Source: Inglehart et al. (2000).

commitment and faith (Greeley, 1989; Woodward, 1992a; Hadaway, Marler, & Chaves, 1993).

RELIGIOUS AFFILIATION

National surveys show that about 85 percent of U.S. adults claim a religious preference (NORC, 2003:131). Table 19–1 on page 504 shows that more than 52 percent of U.S. adults consider themselves Protestants, 24 percent are Catholics, and nearly 2 percent claim they are Jews. Significant numbers of people also adhere to dozens of other religions—from animism to Zen Buddhism—making our society as religiously diverse as any on Earth (Eck, 2001).

About 60 percent of U.S. adults say they are a member of some religious organization, and 90 percent say they had at least some formal religious instruction when growing up (NORC, 2003:355). National

TABLE 19-1	Religious Identification in the United States, 2002

Religion	Percentage Indicating Preference
Protestant denominations	52.8%
Baptist	17.4
Methodist	7.5
Lutheran	5.4
Presbyterian	2.9
Episcopalian	2.1
All others or no denomination	17.5
Catholic	24.3
Jewish	1.7
Other or no answer	7.4
No religious preference	13.7

Source: *General Social Surveys, 1972-2002: Cumulative Codebook* (Chicago: National Opinion Research Center, 2003), pp. 131-32.

Map 19–1 shows the share of people who claim to belong to any church across the United States.

National Map 19–2 takes us one more step, showing that the religion most people identify with varies by region. New England and the Southwest are predominantly Catholic, the South is overwhelmingly Baptist, and in the northern Plains states, Lutherans predominate. In and around Utah, there is a heavy concentration of members of the Church of Jesus Christ of Latter Day Saints (Mormons).

RELIGIOSITY

Religiosity is *the importance of religion in a person's life.* Identifying with a religion is only one measure of religiosity, of course, and a superficial one at that. How religious people turn out to be, therefore, depends on how we operationalize this concept. For example, when asked directly, 86 percent of U.S. adults claim to believe in a divine power of some kind, although just 60 percent claim that they "know that God exists and have no doubts about it" (NORC, 2003:357). Just 56 percent claim to pray at least once a day, and about 30 percent attend religious services on a weekly or almost-weekly basis (Caplow, 1998; Hout & Greeley, 1998; Woodberry, 1998; NORC, 2003:140, 133).

Clearly, the question "How religious are we?" yields no easy answers, and it is likely that many people in the United States claim to be more religious than they really are (Hadaway, Marler, & Chaves, 1993).

Overall, although most people in the United States claim to be at least somewhat religious, probably no more than about one-third actually are. Moreover, religiosity varies among denominations. Members of sects

 Find online resources for the study of religion at http:// www.princeton.edu/~csrelig/ links/links.html

are the most religious of all, followed by Catholics and then "mainstream" Protestants. In general, older people are more religious than younger people, and women are more religious than men (Hadaway, Marler, & Chaves, 1993; Sherkat & Ellison, 1999; Miller & Stark, 2002).

What are the consequences of greater religiosity? Researchers have linked a number of social patterns to strong religious beliefs, including low rates of delin-

quency among young people and low rates of divorce among adults. According to one recent study, religiosity helps bind children, parents, and local communities in ways that benefit young people, enhancing their educational achievement (Muller & Ellison, 2001).

RELIGION: CLASS, ETHNICITY, AND RACE

Religious affiliation is related to several other factors. We shall consider three: social class, race, and ethnicity.

Social Class

A study of *Who's Who in America*, which profiles U.S. high achievers, showed that 33 percent of the people who gave a religious affiliation were Episcopalians, Presbyterians, and United Church of Christ members, denominations that together account for less than 10 percent of the population. Jews, too, enjoy high social position, with this 2 percent of the population accounting for 12 percent of the listings in *Who's Who*.

Research shows that other denominations—including Congregationalists, Methodists, and Catholics—have a moderate social position. Lower social standing is typical of Baptists, Lutherans, and members of sects. Within all denominations, of course, there is considerable variation (Davidson, Pyle, & Reyes, 1995; Waters, Heath, & Watson, 1995; Pyle & Koch, 2001).

Ethnicity and Race

Throughout the world, religion is tied to ethnicity. Many religions predominate in a single nation or

SEEING OURSELVES

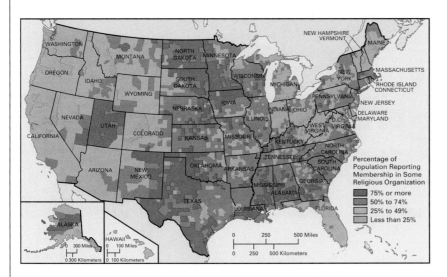

NATIONAL MAP 19–1
Religious Membership across the United States

In general, people in the United States are more religious than people in other high-income nations. Yet membership in a religious organization is more common in some parts of the country than in others. What pattern do you see in the map? Can you explain the pattern?

Source: From Rodger Doyle, *Atlas of Contemporary America.* Copyright © 1994 by Facts on File, Inc. Reprinted with the permission of Facts on File, Inc.

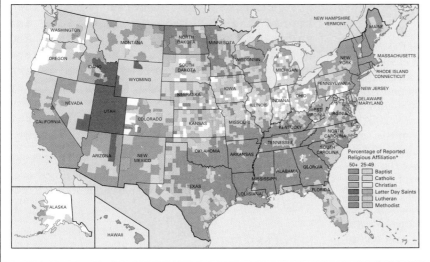

NATIONAL MAP 19–2
Religious Diversity across the United States

In most counties, at least 25 percent of people who report having an affiliation are members of the same religious organization. Thus, although the United States is religiously diverse at the national level, most people live in communities where one denomination predominates. What historical facts might account for this pattern?

*When two or more churches have 25 to 49 percent of the membership in a county, the largest is shown. When no church has 25 percent of the membership that county is left blank.

Source: The Glenmary Research Center (2002).

geographic region. Islam predominates in the Arab societies of the Middle East; Hinduism is fused with the culture of India; Confucianism runs deep in Chinese society. Christianity and Judaism do not follow this pattern; although these religions are mostly Western, Christians and Jews are found all over the world.

Religion and national identity come together in the United States as well. We have, for example, Anglo-Saxon Protestants, Irish Catholics, Russian Jews, and people who are Greek Orthodox. This linking of nation and creed results from the influx of immigrants from nations with a single major religion. Still, nearly every ethnic category displays some religious diversity. For example, people of English ancestry may be Protestants, Roman Catholics, Jews, Hindus, Muslims, or followers of other religions.

The church continues to play a central part in African American communities throughout the United States. In 2003, when California governor Gray Davis tried to mobilize African Americans to vote against the recall vote that turned him out of office, he and supporter Bill Clinton delivered their message in a Los Angeles church.

Scholars claim that the church is both the oldest and the most important social institution within the African American community. Transported to the Western Hemisphere in slave ships, most Africans became Christians—the dominant religion in the Americas—but they blended Christian belief with elements of African religions. Guided by this religious mix, African American Christians, therefore, have developed rituals that are, by European standards, quite spontaneous and emotional (Frazier, 1965; Roberts, 1980; Paris, 2001).

When African Americans migrated from the rural South to the industrial cities of the North around 1940, the church played a major role in addressing the problems of dislocation, poverty, and prejudice (cf. Pattillo-McCoy, 1998). Further, black churches have provided an important avenue of achievement for talented men and women. The Reverends Ralph Abernathy, Martin Luther King, Jr., and Jesse Jackson have all won recognition as national, and even world, leaders.

Recent years have witnessed an increasing number of non-Christian African Americans, especially in large U.S. cities. The most common non-Christian religion is Islam, with an estimated 1 million African American followers (Paris, 2001).

RELIGION IN A CHANGING SOCIETY

June 4, Ticonderoga, New York. Our summer church is small—maybe forty people attend on a Sunday in summer.

These days, Ed Keller says, it's tough for churches to survive with kids' sports teams scheduling practices and games on Sunday morning, Wal-Mart and all the other stores open for shopping, and many dog-tired people taking advantage of the opportunity to sleep a little later. The people here seem very committed to the church, but there are just not very many of them.

All social institutions evolve over time. Just as the economy, politics, and the family have changed over the course of the past century, so has our society's religious life.

SECULARIZATION

Secularization refers to *the historical decline in the importance of the supernatural and the sacred.* For society as a whole, secularization involves a declining influence of religion in everyday life. For religious organizations, becoming more secular means less focus on otherworldly issues (such as life after death) and more on worldly affairs (such as sheltering the homeless and feeding the hungry). Secularization also means that functions once performed by the church (such as charity) are now primarily the responsibility of other organizations, such as the United Way and government.

With Latin roots meaning "the present age," sec-ularization is associated with modern, technologically advanced societies, in which science is the dominant mode of understanding. Today, for example, people are more likely to experience the transitions of birth, illness, and death in the presence of physicians (with scientific knowledge) than of religious leaders (whose knowledge is based on faith). This shift alone suggests that religion's relevance to our everyday lives has de-clined. Harvey Cox elaborates:

> The world looks less and less to religious rules and rituals for its morality or its meanings. For some, religion provides a hobby, for others a mark of national or ethnic identification, for still others an aesthetic delight. For fewer and fewer does it provide an inclusive and commanding system of personal and cosmic values and explanations. (1971:3; orig. 1965)

If Cox is right, should we expect religion to disap-pear someday? The consensus among sociologists is "no." The vast majority of people in the United States still profess a belief in God, and as many people claim to pray each day as vote in national elections. In fact, religious affiliation today is actually proportionately higher than it was in 1850. Secularization, then, does not signal the death of religion. For one thing, some dimensions of religiosity (such as belief in life after death) have declined while others (such as religious af-filiation) have increased. Further, while affiliation with some religious organizations is declining, the numbers joining others are increasing. Finally, as Figure 19–2 shows, the share of new college students who say they have no religious preference almost doubled between 1970 and 2001. Even now, however, this share remains a clear minority. Overall, then, there is good reason to look upon the secularization thesis critically (Gorski, 2000; Stark & Finke, 2000; Astin et al., 2002; Hout & Greeley, 2002).

Secularization does not, then, signal the death of religion. More correctly, some dimensions of religion (such as belief in life after death) have declined, while others (such as religious affiliation) have increased. Moreover, people are of two minds about whether secularization is good or bad. Conservatives see any weakening of religion as a mark of moral decline. Progressives view secularization as liberation from the all-encompassing beliefs of the past, so peo-ple can choose what to believe. Secularization has also helped bring some practices of many religious organi-zations (such as ordaining only men) into line with

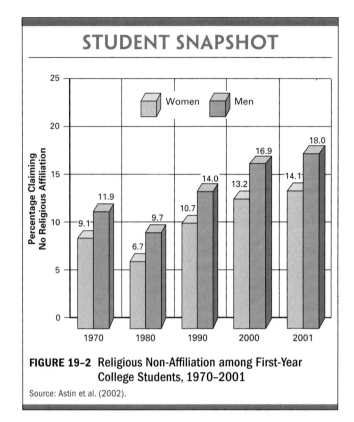

STUDENT SNAPSHOT

FIGURE 19-2 Religious Non-Affiliation among First-Year College Students, 1970–2001

Source: Astin et al. (2002).

widespread social attitudes (such as support for gen-der equality, by opening ordination to women as well as men).

In 1963, the U.S. Supreme Court banned prayer in public schools on the grounds that it is a violation of the constitutional separation of church and state. In recent years, however, religion has returned to many public schools—the box on page 508 takes a closer look.

CIVIL RELIGION

One dimension of secularization is what sociologist Robert Bellah (1975) calls **civil religion,** *a quasi-religious loyalty binding individuals in a basically secular society.* In other words, even in a largely secular society such as the United States, citizenship has taken on re-ligious qualities.

Most people in the United States consider our way of life a force for moral good in the world. Many people also find religious qualities in political move-ments, whether liberal or conservative (Williams &

CRITICAL THINKING

Should Students Pray in School?

It is late afternoon on a cloudy spring day in Minneapolis, and two dozen teenagers have come together to pray. They share warm smiles as they enter the room. As soon as everyone is seated, the prayers begin, with one voice following another. One girl prays for her brother; a boy prays for the success of an upcoming food drive; another asks God to comfort a favorite teacher who is having a hard time. Then they join their voices to pray for all the teachers at their school who are not Christians. Following the prayers, the young people sing Christian songs, discuss a Scripture lesson, and bring their meeting to a close with a group hug.

What is so unusual about this prayer meeting is that it is taking place in Room 133 of Patrick Henry High School, a *public* institution. Indeed, in public schools from coast to coast, something of a religious revival is taking place as more and more students hold meetings like this one.

You would have to be fifty or older to remember when it was routine for public school students to begin the day with Bible reading and prayer. In 1963, the Supreme Court ruled that doing so violated the separation of church and state mandated by the U.S. Constitution. Most school

officials took this decision as banning any religious activity anywhere in public schools. But right from the outset, critics charged that, by supporting a wide range of other activities and clubs while banning any religious activity, schools were really being *anti*religious. In 1990, the Supreme Court handed down a new ruling, stating that religious groups can meet on school property if group membership is voluntary, meetings are held outside regular class hours, and students rather than adults run them.

Today, student religious groups have formed in perhaps one-fourth of all public schools. Evangelical Christian organizations such as First Priority and National Network of Youth are using the Internet as well as word of mouth in

an effort to expand the place of religion in every public school across the country. Others, however, worry that religious zeal may lead some students to pressure others to join these groups. Given this tension, the controversy over prayer in public schools is sure to continue.

What do you think?

1. *Do you think that religious clubs should have the same freedom to operate on school grounds as other organizations? Why or why not?*

2. *The writers of our Constitution stated in the First Amendment that Congress should not establish any official religion and should also pass no law that would interfere with the free practice of religion. How do you think this amendment applies to the issue of prayer in school?*

3. *In 1995, President Bill Clinton said, "Nothing in the First Amendment converts our public schools into religion-free zones." Do you think schools should support spiritual education and development, be neutral to religious activity, or oppose such activity? Why?*

Source: Based on Van Biema (1998, 1999).

Demerath, 1991). Civil religion also involves a range of rituals, from singing the national anthem at sporting events to waving the flag at public parades. At all such events, the U.S. flag serves as a sacred symbol of our national identity, and we expect people to treat it with respect.

"NEW AGE" SEEKERS: SPIRITUALITY WITHOUT FORMAL RELIGION

In recent decades, an increasing number of people are seeking spiritual development outside of established religious organizations. This trend toward spirituality

New Age "seekers" are people in pursuit of spiritual growth, often using the age-old technique of meditation. The goal of this activity is to quiet the mind so that, by moving away from everyday concerns, one can hear an inner, divine voice. Countless people attest to the spiritual value of meditation; it has also been linked to improved physical health.

but away from established religious organizations has led some analysts to conclude that the United States is becoming a *post-denomination society*. In simple terms, more people seem to be "spiritual seekers," sometimes called New Age spiritualists, who believe that there is a vital spiritual dimension to human existence, which they pursue at least partly separate from any formal denomination. Exactly what is the difference between a focus on spirituality and a concern with religion? As one recent account puts it (Cimino & Lattin, 1999:62):

> [Spirituality] is the search for . . . a religion of the heart, not the head. It's a religious expression that downplays doctrine and dogma, and revels in direct experience of the divine—whether it's called the "holy spirit" or "divine consciousness" or "true self." It's practical and personal, more about stress reduction than salvation, more therapeutic than theological. It's about feeling good rather than being good. It's as much about the body as the soul.

Millions of people in the United States take part in New Age spirituality. Anthropologist and New Age spiritual teacher Hank Wesselman (2001:39–42) identifies the core values that define this approach:

1. **Seekers believe in a higher power.** There exists a higher power, a vital force that is found within all things and all people. Humans, then, are partly divine.

2. **Seekers believe we're all connected.** Everything and everyone is part of a universal divine pattern and thus interconnected.

3. **Seekers believe in a spirit world.** The physical world is not all there is; an alternative reality (or "spirit world") also exists.

4. **Seekers strive to experience the spirit world.** As people become more spiritually aware, they gain the ability to experience this spirit world. They also come to understand that helpers and teachers who dwell in the spirit world can and do touch their lives.

5. **Seekers pursue transcendence.** Various techniques (such as yoga, meditation, and prayer) give people the increasing ability to transcend the immediate physical world (the experience of "transcendence"), which is the larger purpose of life.

From a traditional point of view, this concern with spirituality may seem more like psychology than religion (Tucker, 2002). Yet, as in civil religion, we see religious interest in the modern world taking new forms.

RELIGIOUS REVIVAL: "GOOD OL'-TIME RELIGION"

At the same time as New Age spirituality is flourishing, there has also been a revival of "good ol'-time religion." In the United States, membership in liberal mainstream churches like the Episcopalian and Presbyterian denominations has plummeted by almost

CONTROVERSY & DEBATE

Does Science Threaten Religion?

Some 400 years ago, the Italian physicist and astronomer Galileo (1564–1642) helped start the scientific revolution with a series of startling discoveries. Dropping objects from the Leaning Tower of Pisa, he discovered some of the laws of gravity; fashioning his own telescope, he surveyed the heavens and found that the Earth orbited the sun, not the other way around.

For his trouble, Galileo was denounced by the Roman Catholic church, which had preached for centuries that the Earth stood motionless at the center of the universe. In response, Galileo only made matters worse by declaring that religious leaders and biblical doctrine had little to say about matters of science. Before long, he found his work banned and himself under house arrest.

From its beginnings, science has had an uneasy relationship with religion. In the twentieth century, clashes arose mainly over the issue of creation. Charles Darwin's masterwork, *On the Origin of Species*, theorizes that humanity evolved from lower forms of life over the course of a billion years. Yet the theory of evolution seems to fly in the face of the biblical account of creation found in Genesis, which states that "God created the heavens and the earth," introducing life on the third day and, on the fifth and sixth days, animal life, including human beings fashioned in God's own image.

Galileo would certainly have been an eager observer of the famous "Scopes monkey trial." In 1925, the state of Tennessee put a small-town science teacher named John Thomas Scopes on trial for teaching evolution in the local high school. State law forbade teaching "any theory that denies the story of the Divine Creation of man as taught in the Bible" and especially the idea that "man descended from a lower order of animals." Scopes was found guilty and fined $100. His conviction was reversed on appeal, so the case never reached the U.S. Supreme Court. The Tennessee law stayed on the books until 1967. A year later, the U.S. Supreme Court (*Epperson v. Arkansas*) struck down all such laws as an unconstitutional case of government-supported religion.

Today—almost four centuries after Galileo was silenced—many people still ponder the apparently conflicting claims of science and religion. A third of U.S. adults believe that the Bible is the literal word of God, and many of them reject any scientific findings that run counter to it (NORC, 2003:157).

But a middle ground is emerging: Half of U.S. adults (and also many church leaders) say the Bible is a book of truths inspired by God without being correct in a literal, scientific sense. That

50 percent since 1960. During the same period, affiliation with conservative religious organizations (including the Mormons, the Seventh-Day Adventists, and especially Christian sects) has risen just as fast.

These opposing trends suggest a limitation of secularization: As many churchlike organizations become more worldly, many people abandon them in favor of more sectlike communities offering a more intense religious experience (Stark & Bainbridge, 1981; Roof & McKinney, 1987; Jacquet & Jones, 1991; Warner, 1993; Iannaccone, 1994; Hout, Greeley, & Wilde, 2001).

Religious Fundamentalism

Fundamentalism is *a conservative religious doctrine that opposes intellectualism and worldly accommodation in favor of restoring traditional, otherworldly religion.* In response to what they see as the growing influence of science and the weakening of the conventional family, religious fundamentalists defend what they call "traditional values." As they see it, liberal churches are simply too open to compromise and change. Religious fundamentalism is distinctive in five ways (Hunter, 1983, 1985, 1987):

1. **Fundamentalists interpret sacred texts literally.**
   Fundamentalists insist on a literal interpretation of the Bible and other sacred texts in order to counter what they see as excessive intellectualism among more liberal religious organizations. Fundamentalist Christians, for example, believe that God created the world precisely as described in Genesis.

is, science and religion represent two levels of understanding that respond to different questions. Both Galileo and Darwin devoted their lives to investigating *how* the natural world operates. Yet only religion can address *why* humans and the natural world exist in the first place.

This basic difference between science and religion helps explain why our nation is both the most actively scientific and the most devoutly religious in the world. Moreover, as one scientist recently noted, the mathematical odds that a cosmic Big Bang 12 billion years ago created the universe and led to the formation of life as we know it are utterly infinitesimal—smaller than the chance of winning a state lottery twenty weeks in a row. Doesn't such a scientific fact suggest an intelligent and purposeful power in our creation? Can't a person be a religious believer and at the same time a scientific investigator?

In 1992, a Vatican commission created by Pope John Paul II concluded that the church's silencing of Galileo was wrong. Today, most scientific and religious leaders agree that science and religion represent important, but different, truths. Many also believe that, in today's rush to scientific discovery, our world has never been more in need of the moral guidance afforded by religion.

Clarence Darrow was the lawyer who defended John Scopes in the 1925 Tennessee trial that sought to determine whether or not evolution should be taught in the public schools.

Continue the debate . . .

1. Why do you think some scientific people reject religious accounts of human creation? Why do some religious people reject scientific accounts?

2. Do you think the sociological study of religion challenges anyone's faith? Why or why not?

3. Does it surprise you that about half of U.S. adults think science is changing our way of life too fast? Do you agree? Why or why not?

Sources: Based on Gould (1981), Huchingson (1994), and Applebome (1996).

2. **Fundamentalists reject religious pluralism.** Fundamentalists believe that tolerance and relativism water down personal faith. They maintain, therefore, that their religious beliefs are true and other beliefs are not.

3. **Fundamentalists pursue the personal experience of God's presence.** In contrast to the worldliness and intellectualism of other religious organizations, fundamentalism seeks a return to "good ol'-time religion" and spiritual revival. To fundamentalist Christians, being "born again" and having a personal relationship with Jesus Christ should be evident in a person's everyday life.

4. **Fundamentalism opposes "secular humanism."** Fundamentalists think accommodation to the changing world undermines religious conviction.

Secular humanism is a general term that refers to our society's tendency to look to scientific experts rather than God for guidance about how to live. There is nothing new in this tension between science and religion; it has existed for several centuries, as the box explains.

5. **Many fundamentalists endorse conservative political goals.** Although fundamentalism tends to back away from worldly concerns, some fundamentalist leaders (including Ralph Reed, Pat Robertson, and Gary Bauer) have entered politics to oppose the "liberal agenda" that includes feminism and gay rights. Fundamentalists oppose abortion and gay marriages; they support the traditional two-parent family, seek a return of prayer in schools, and claim that the mass media color the news

with liberal sentiments (Hunter, 1983; Ellison & Sherkat, 1993; Green, 1993; Manza & Brooks, 1997; Thomma, 1997; Rozell, Wilcox, & Green, 1998).

Opponents regard fundamentalism as rigid and self-righteous. But many find in fundamentalism—with its greater religious certainty and emphasis on the emotional experience of God's presence—an appealing alternative to the more intellectual, tolerant, and worldly "mainstream" denominations (Marquand, 1997).

Which religions are "fundamentalist"? In recent years, the world has become familiar with an extreme form of fundamentalist Islam that is intolerant of other beliefs and even supports violence against Western culture. In the United States, the term is most correctly applied to conservative Christian organizations in the evangelical tradition, including Pentecostals, Southern Baptists, Seventh-Day Adventists, and Assemblies of God. But fundamentalism has also taken root among both Jews and Muslims. In national surveys, 30 percent of U.S. adults describe their religious upbringing as "fundamentalist"; 40 percent claim a "moderate" religious background; and 24 percent, a "liberal" background (NORC, 2003:150).

The Electronic Church

In contrast to the small village congregations of years past, some religious organizations, especially those that are fundamentalist, have become electronic churches featuring "prime time preachers" (Hadden & Swain, 1981). Electronic religion is found only in the

 These sites provide different views of the fundamentalist doctrine of creationism: http://www.creationists.org and http://www.enconnect.net/rjtolle/index.htm

United States. It has propelled people such as Billy Graham, Oral Roberts, Pat Robertson, and Robert Schuller to prominence greater than that of all but a few clergy of the past. About 5 percent of the national television audience (some 10 million people) regularly view religious television, and 20 percent (about 40 million) watch or listen to some religious program every week (NORC, 2003).

LOOKING AHEAD: RELIGION IN THE TWENTY-FIRST CENTURY

The popularity of media ministries, the growth of fundamentalism, the flourishing of spiritual movements, and the connection of millions more people to mainstream churches show that religion will remain a major part of U.S. society. Moreover, high levels of immigration from many religious countries (in Latin America and elsewhere) will continue to diversify the religious character of U.S. society in this new century (Yang & Ebaugh, 2001).

The world is becoming more complex, and rapid change seems to outstrip our ability to make sense of it all. But rather than undermining religion, this process fires the religious imagination. Tensions between the spiritual realm of religion and the secular world of science and technology will surely continue to fire the religious imagination. No doubt, this is why religion—in new as well as traditional forms—remains a powerful force in U.S. society.

Science is simply unable to provide answers to the most basic human questions about the purpose of our lives. Moreover, new technology that can alter, extend, and even create life confronts us with vexing moral dilemmas as never before. Against this backdrop of uncertainty, it is little wonder that many people look to their faith for assurance and hope.

SUMMARY

1. Religion is a major social institution based on setting the sacred apart from the profane. Religion is grounded in faith (not scientific evidence), which people express through various rituals.

2. Sociologists study how religion is linked to other social patterns but make no claims about the truth of any religious belief.

3. Through religion, said Durkheim, people celebrate the power of their society. His structural-functional analysis suggests that religion promotes social cohesion and conformity and confers meaning and purpose on life.

4. Using the symbolic-interaction paradigm, Peter Berger explains that people construct religious beliefs as a response to life's uncertainties and disruptions.

5. Social-conflict analyst Karl Marx claimed that religion supports inequality. On the other hand, Max Weber's analysis of Calvinism's contribution to the rise of industrial capitalism shows how religion can trigger social change.

6. Churches, which are religious organizations well integrated into their society, fall into two categories: state churches and denominations.

7. Sects, the result of religious division, are marked by charismatic leadership and suspicion of the larger society.

8. Cults are religious organizations based on new and unconventional beliefs and practices.

9. Technologically simple human societies were generally animistic, with religion incorporated into family life; in more complex societies, religion emerges as a distinct social institution.

10. Followers of six world religions—Christianity, Islam, Judaism, Hinduism, Buddhism, and Confucianism—represent three-fourths of all humanity. While Western religions (the first three) share a focus on God and have well-defined congregations, Eastern religions (the second three) tend to be ethical codes widely diffused through the broader culture.

11. A slight majority of U.S. adults say they are Protestants. Overall, the United States is the most religiously diverse nation on Earth.

12. How religious a society is depends on exactly what one measures. In the United States, 85 percent of adults claim a religious preference; 60 percent profess a firm belief in God, but just 30 percent say they attend religious services weekly.

13. Secularization is the diminishing importance of the supernatural and the sacred. In the United States, while some indicators of religiosity (like membership in mainstream churches) have declined, others (such as membership in sects) have risen. Thus, it is doubtful that secularization will bring an end to religion.

14. Civil religion is the quasi-religious patriotism that ties people to their society.

15. Spiritual seekers are part of the growing "New Age" movement that pursues spiritual development outside conventional religious organizations. Seekers believe in a higher power that links everything; they pursue transcendence of the physical world and the experience of connection with a higher power.

16. Also on the rise is fundamentalism, which opposes religious accommodation to the world, favoring an otherworldly focus. Fundamentalists interpret religious texts literally and reject religious diversity as they pursue the personal experience of God's presence.

17. Some of the continuing appeal of religion lies in the inability of science (and also sociology) to address timeless questions about the ultimate meaning of human existence.

KEY CONCEPTS

profane (p. 489) that which people define as an ordinary element of everyday life

sacred (p. 489) that which people set apart as extraordinary, inspiring awe and reverence

religion (p. 489) a social institution involving beliefs and practices based on a conception of the sacred

ritual (p. 490) formal, ceremonial behavior

faith (p. 490) belief anchored in conviction rather than scientific evidence

totem (p. 491) an object in the natural world collectively defined as sacred

liberation theology (p. 494) a fusion of Christian principles with political activism, often Marxist in character

church (p. 494) a type of religious organization that is well integrated into the larger society

state church (p. 494) a church formally allied with the state

denomination (p. 494) a church, independent of the state, that recognizes religious pluralism

sect (p. 495) a type of religious organization that stands apart from the larger society

charisma (p. 495) extraordinary personal qualities that can infuse people with emotion and turn them into followers

cult (p. 495) a religious organization that is largely outside a society's cultural traditions

animism (p. 496) the belief that elements of the natural world are conscious life forms that affect humanity

monotheism (p. 497) belief in a single divine power

polytheism (p. 497) belief in many gods

religiosity (p. 504) the importance of religion in a person's life

secularization (p. 506) the historical decline in the importance of the supernatural and the sacred

civil religion (p. 507) a quasi-religious loyalty binding individuals in a basically secular society

fundamentalism (p. 510) a conservative religious doctrine that opposes intellectualism and worldly accommodation in favor of restoring traditional, otherworldly religion

CRITICAL-THINKING QUESTIONS

1. What is the basic distinction between the sacred and the profane that underlies all religious belief?

2. How did Karl Marx view religion's effect on society's ability to change? How did Max Weber's analysis of Calvinism lead to a different conclusion?

3. In what ways do churches, sects, and cults differ?

4. What evidence suggests that religion is declining in importance in the United States? In what ways does religion seem to be getting stronger?

APPLICATIONS AND EXERCISES

1. Some colleges are decidedly religious; others are passionately secular. Investigate the place of religion on your campus. Is your school affiliated with a religious organization? Was it ever? Is there a chaplain or other religious official? See if you can learn from campus sources what share of students regularly attend any religious service.

2. How religious people seem to be depends on exactly what questions one asks them. Develop five questions measuring religiosity that might be used on a questionnaire or in an interview. Present them to several people: How well do they seem to work?

3. Is religion getting weaker? To test the secularization thesis, go to the library or local newspaper office; obtain an issue of your local newspaper published 50 years ago and, if possible, 100 years ago. Compare the amount of attention to religious issues then and now.

4. Packaged in the back of this new textbook is an interactive CD-ROM that offers a variety of video and interactive review materials intended to help you better understand the material covered in this chapter. For this chapter, the CD-ROM contains a relevant clip from *ABC News*, an author's tip video, interactive map animations, an interactive time line, and flashcards with audio pronunciations of the more difficult words.

 ## SITES TO SEE

http://www.prenhall.com/macionis

Visit the interactive Companion Website™ that accompanies this text. Begin by clicking on the cover of your book. You will find a chapter-by-chapter study guide, practice tests, suggested Web links, and links to other relevant material.

http://www.parishioners.org/

Here is a site offering information on a variety of religious issues, including cults and toleration of religious differences.

http://www.trinityumc.net/youth/cool.htm

This is a Web site just for fun: Check it out!

http://www.bwanet.org
http://www.churchworldservice.org
http://www.catholicrelief.org
http://www.jdc.org

A number of religious organizations are involved in addressing hunger and other social problems. These are the Web sites that describe the activities of Baptist World Aid, Church World Service, Catholic Relief Services, and the American Jewish Joint Distribution Committee.

 ## INVESTIGATE WITH RESEARCH NAVIGATOR™

Follow the instructions on page 24 of this text to access the features of **Research Navigator™**. Once at the Web site, enter your Login Name and Password. Then, to use the **Content Select™** database, enter keywords such as "religion," "cults," and "Islam," and the search engine will supply relevant and recent scholarly and popular press publications. Use the *New York Times* **Search-by-Subject Archive** to find recent news articles related to sociology and the **Link Library** feature to find relevant Web links organized by the key terms associated with this chapter.

September 7, 2003

Putting the American in 'American Muslim'

By MUQTEDAR KHAN

WASHINGTON—Muslims in America. American Muslims. The difference between these two labels may seem a matter of semantics, but making the transition from the first to the second represents a profound, if somewhat silent, revolution that many of us in the Muslim community have been undergoing in the two years since Sept. 11.

On its face, this shift would seem to threaten the very core of Muslim identity and empowerment. After all, in the decade before the events of Sept. 11, Islam was one of the fastest-growing religions in North America. Mosques and Islamic schools were going up in every major city. Groups like the Council on American-Islamic Relations and the American Muslim Alliance established chapters in nearly every area with a Muslim population. . . .

At the time, the word that best summed up the Muslim sense of self was "fateh," a conqueror. Many religious and community leaders were convinced that Islam would not only manifest itself in its truest form in this country, but would also make America, already a great power, into a great society. Some even proclaimed that one day America would be an Islamic state.

On Sept. 11, of course, that dream evaporated. Today, the civil rights environment has declined drastically with the passage of the USA Patriot Act and other antiterrorism measures. Both sources of Islam's growth—immigration and conversion—are now in jeopardy, and we continue to face hostility and prejudice in many corners of society. There is no more talk of making America an Islamic state. Any reminder of this pre-9/11 vision generates sheepish giggles and snorts from Muslim audiences. . . .

Today, many Muslims realize that it is not their Islamic identity but their American citizenship that is fragile. Before Sept. 11, Muslims in America focused primarily on changing United States policy toward Palestine, Kashmir and Iraq. Since Sept. 11, the attempt to reconstitute our identity as American Muslims is making domestic relations and civil rights and interfaith relations more important.

Much of this is playing out at the local level. In Miami, for example, efforts are underway by a group of progressive Muslims to endow chairs in Islamic studies at American universities. In the Muslim community in Duluth, Minn., fund-raising has begun to support social services, including housing and health care initiatives for the poor. In Indianapolis, Muslim residents are opening soup kitchens. And think of the familiar advertising campaign by the Council on American-Islamic Relations in which Muslims announce, "We are American and we are Muslims." It is not without design that "American" is stated first.

Even more vital, many Muslims in this country have come to acutely understand the vulnerabilities of minorities and the importance of democracy and civil rights. Because we took our American citizenship for granted, we did not acknowledge its value and virtues. But now that it is imperiled, the overwhelming desire of many Muslims is that America remain true to its democratic and secular values. . . .

There is still much progress to be made. We need to continue to demonstrate that Muslims in this country constitute an ethical and philanthropic community that cares about humanitarian causes, about America and Americans and stands for justice and rights as embodied in the Constitution. Just like other ethnic groups before us, we have to pay our dues to this nation before we demand that they change themselves and the world for us.

But Americans, too, must play a role. They cannot allow events overseas to foster anti-Muslim sentiments and Islamophobia at home. They must recognize the insecurities and fears of their Muslim neighbors and extend a hand of friendship and support. The choices we face are tough, but Muslims must realize that the interests of our sons and daughters, who are American, must come before the interests of our brothers and sisters, whether they are Palestinian, Kashmiri or Iraqi. Only then will Muslims in America become American Muslims. . . .

What do you think?

1. What are the reasons for a rise in anti-Muslim attitudes in the United States since the September 11 terrorist attacks? Is this a clear case of unfair prejudice or is some of this bias justified? Explain your position.
2. Considering that there are some 7 million Muslims in the United States—more than the membership of many Protestant denominations—should Islam play a greater role in this country's national life? Explain your position.

EDUCATION

ALPHONSE ETIENNE DINET (1861–1929, FRENCH)
Writing Lessons in a Koranic School in an Algerian Village

1918 (color lithograph). Private Collection/Archives Charmet/The Bridgeman Art Library.

THE EXECUTIVES AT J. C. Penney had not planned to get involved in the controversy over schooling in the United States when they included on their clothing racks a novelty T-shirt that pictured a trailer home with the words "HOME SKOOLED." Many customers, however, were not amused. One week later, the store pulled the shirt from all its branches after angry letters poured in from across the country from parents who had a much more positive view of home schooling.

If Penney's had done a bit of sociological research, it probably would never have tried to sell the offending T-shirt. For one thing, home schooling is rapidly gaining in popularity: Estimates place the number of children being schooled at home at close to 1.5 million. This number represents about 3 percent of the K–12 population, or roughly the same as all the school-aged children living in Michigan. Moreover, these children are commonly from families that are middle-class or higher in terms of social standing, and most home-schooled children have parents who are well educated and place a high value on learning. But most important, home-schooled children turn out to be pretty good spellers: On average, they academically outperform children who attend public schools (Cloud & Morse, 2001).

The fact that so many parents undertake schooling their own children is one indication of the controversy that surrounds public schooling in the United States. While most people support public schooling, there is considerable evidence that public schools are not meeting the needs of many of this country's young people.

This chapter investigates this and many other issues related to **education,** *the social institution through which society provides its members with important knowledge, including basic facts, job skills, and cultural norms and values.* In high-income nations such as the United States, education is largely a matter of **schooling,** *formal instruction under the direction of specially trained teachers.*

EDUCATION: A GLOBAL SURVEY

From Maine to Hawaii, from Alaska to Texas, people expect children to spend much of their first eighteen years of life in school. This was not the case a century ago, when just a small elite in the United States had the privilege of attending school. In poor countries, even today, most young people receive only a few years of formal schooling.

SCHOOLING AND ECONOMIC DEVELOPMENT

The extent of schooling in any society is closely tied to its level of economic development. Chapter 4 ("Society") explained that our hunting and gathering ancestors lived a simple life in families without governments, churches, or schools. For these people, "schooling" amounted to the knowledge and skills parents transmitted directly to their children (Nolan & Lenski, 1999).

In low- and middle-income nations, where most of the world's people live, boys and girls spend several years in school learning the practical knowledge they need to farm or perform other production tasks. The

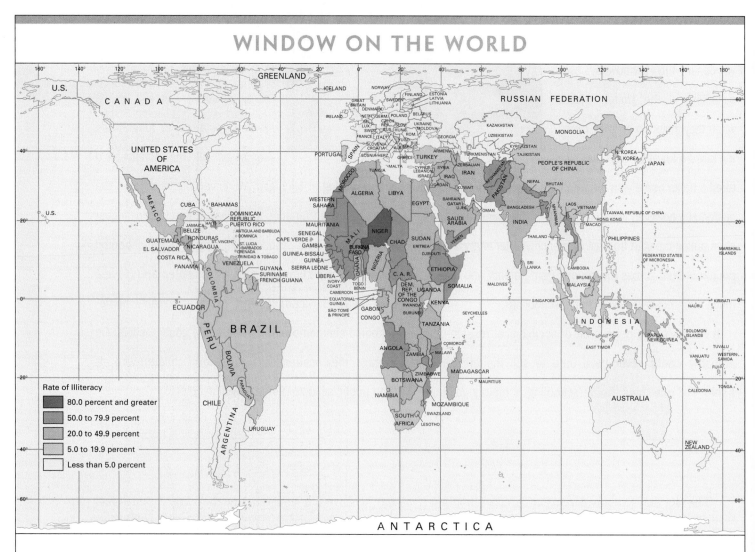

GLOBAL MAP 20–1 Illiteracy in Global Perspective

Reading and writing skills are widespread in high-income countries, where illiteracy rates generally are below 5 percent. In much of Latin America, however, illiteracy is more common, one consequence of limited economic development. In twenty-seven nations—twenty of them in Africa—illiteracy is the rule rather than the exception; there, people rely on the oral tradition of face-to-face communication rather than the written word.

Sources: United Nations Development Programme (2003) and The World Bank (2003); map projection from *Peters Atlas of the World* (1990).

opportunity to study literature, art, history, and science is generally available only to the lucky few who are wealthy and do not need to work. After all, the Greek root of the word "school" means "leisure." In ancient Greece, the students of renowned teachers such as Socrates, Plato, and Aristotle were almost all aristocratic young men. The same was true in ancient China, where the famous philosopher K'ung Fu-tzu (Confucius) shared his wisdom with just a select few. During the Middle Ages in Europe, the first

In many low-income nations, girls are as likely to work as to attend school. In Afghanistan under the strict rule of the Taliban, girls were all but absent from school. By the beginning of 2002, however, the picture was changing. Here we see girls at the Manu Chera school for girls in central Kabul completing a classroom assignment.

colleges and universities founded by the Roman Catholic church admitted only males from privileged families.

Today, schooling in low-income nations reflects local culture. In Iran, for example, schooling is closely tied to Islam. Similarly, schooling in Bangladesh (Asia), Zimbabwe (Africa), and Nicaragua (Latin America) has been molded by distinctive cultural traditions. But all low-income countries have one trait in common when it comes to schooling: There is not very much of it. In the world's poorest nations (including several in Central Africa), only half of all children ever get to school at all; in the world as a whole, just half of all children reach the secondary grades (Najafizadeh & Mennerick, 1992). As a result, 15 percent of Latin Americans, 30 percent of Asians, and 40 percent of Africans cannot read or write. Global Map 20–1 shows the extent of illiteracy around the world.

High-income nations endorse the idea that everyone should go to school. For one thing, workers who use machinery or computers need at least basic reading, writing, and arithmetic skills. In high-income nations, literacy is also necessary to carry on political democracy.

The following national comparisons illustrate the link between schooling and economic development. Notice, too, that various high-income nations differ in their approach to educating their populations.

SCHOOLING IN INDIA

India is a middle-income country where people earn less than 10 percent of the income standard in the United States, and poor families often depend on the earnings of children. Thus, even though India has outlawed child labor, many Indian children work in factories—weaving rugs or making handicrafts—up to sixty hours per week, so their chances for schooling are greatly limited.

Today, most children in India receive some primary education, typically in crowded schoolrooms where one teacher faces perhaps sixty children (twice as many as in typical U.S. public school classrooms). Less than half continue to secondary school, and very few enter college. The result is that only slightly more than half of the people in this vast country are literate.

Patriarchy also shapes Indian education. Indian parents are joyful at the birth of a boy, since he and his future wife will contribute income to the family. By contrast, girls are a financial liability because parents must provide a dowry at the time of marriage, and a daughter's work then benefits her husband's family. Thus, many Indians see less reason to invest in the schooling of girls, so only 30 percent of girls (compared to 45 percent of boys) reach the secondary grades. The flip side of this pattern is that a large majority of the children working in Indian factories are girls—a family's way of benefiting from their

TABLE 20-1	Educational Achievement in the United States, 1910–2002*		
Year	High School Graduates	College Graduates	Median Years of Schooling
1910	13.5%	2.7%	8.1
1920	16.4	3.3	8.2
1930	19.1	3.9	8.4
1940	24.1	4.6	8.6
1950	33.4	6.0	9.3
1960	41.1	7.7	10.5
1970	55.2	11.0	12.2
1980	68.7	17.0	12.5
1990	77.6	21.3	12.4
2000	84.1	25.6	12.7
2002	84.1	26.7	12.7

*For people twenty-five years of age and over. Percentage of high school graduates includes those who go on to college. Percentage of high school dropouts can be calculated by subtracting percentage of high school graduates from 100 percent.

Source: U.S. Census Bureau (2003).

daughters while they can (United Nations Development Programme, 1995).

SCHOOLING IN JAPAN

`September 30, Kobe, Japan. Compared to people in the United States, the Japanese are, above all, orderly. Young boys and girls on their way to school stand out in their uniforms, their arms filled with books and a look of seriousness and purpose on their faces.`

Schooling has not always been part of the Japanese way of life. Before industrialization brought mandatory education in 1872, only a privileged few attended school. Today, Japan's educational system is widely praised for producing some of the world's highest achievers.

The early grades concentrate on transmitting Japanese traditions, especially a sense of obligation to family. Starting in their early teens, students take a series of rigorous and highly competitive examinations. These written tests, which resemble the Scholastic Assessment Tests (SATs) used for college admissions in the United States, decide a Japanese student's future.

More men and women graduate from high school in Japan (96 percent) than in the United States (84 percent). But competitive examinations allow just 45 percent of high school graduates—compared to 62 percent in the United States—to enter college. Understandably, then, Japanese students take entrance examinations very seriously, and about half attend "cram schools" to prepare for them.

Japanese schooling produces impressive results. In a number of fields, notably mathematics and science, Japanese students outperform students in every other high-income nation, including the United States (Hayneman & Loxley, 1983; Rohlen, 1983; Brinton, 1988; Simons, 1989).

SCHOOLING IN GREAT BRITAIN

During the Middle Ages, schooling was a privilege of the British nobility, who studied classical subjects, because they had little need for practical skills to earn a living. But as the Industrial Revolution created a need for an educated labor force, and as working-class people demanded access to schools, a rising share of the population entered the classroom. British law now requires every British child to attend school until age sixteen.

Traditional social distinctions, however, persist in British education. Most wealthy families send their children to what the British call *public schools*, the equivalent of U.S. private boarding schools. These elite schools, which enroll about 7 percent of British students, not only teach academic subjects but also convey to children from wealthy (especially newly rich) families the distinctive patterns of speech, mannerisms, and social graces of the British upper class. These academies are far too expensive for most students, however, who attend state-supported day schools (Ambler & Neathery, 1999).

Since 1960, the British have lessened the influence of social background on schooling by expanding their university system and using competitive entrance examinations. For those who score the highest, the government pays most of the college costs. But these exams are less important than those in Japan, since many well-to-do children who do not score well still manage to attend Oxford or Cambridge, the most prestigious British universities, on a par with Yale, Harvard, and Princeton in the United States. "Oxbridge" graduates go on to take their place at the center of the British power elite: More than two-thirds of the top members of the British government, for example, have "Oxbridge" degrees (Sampson, 1982; Gamble, Ludlam, & Baker, 1993).

These brief sketches of schooling in India, Japan, and Great Britain show the crucial importance of economic development. In poor countries, many children—especially girls—work rather than go to school. Rich nations adopt mandatory education laws to prepare an industrial work force as well as to satisfy demands for greater equality. But rich nations vary, as we see in the intense competition of Japanese schools, the traditional social stratification that shapes schools in Great Britain, and the practical emphasis found in the schools of the United States.

SCHOOLING IN THE UNITED STATES

The United States was among the first countries to set a goal of mass education. By 1850, about half the young people between the ages of five and nineteen were enrolled in school. By 1918, all states had passed a *mandatory education law* requiring children to attend school until the age of sixteen or the completion of the eighth grade. Table 20–1 shows that a milestone was reached in the mid-1960s, when, for the first time, a majority of U.S. adults had high school diplomas. Today, more than four out of five have a high school education, and more than one in four has a four-year college degree.

The U.S. educational system is shaped by both affluence and our democratic principles. Thomas Jefferson thought the new nation could become democratic only if people "read and understand what is going on in the world" (quoted in Honeywell, 1931:13). As Figure 20–1 shows, the United States has an outstanding record of higher education for its people: No other country has as large a share of adults with a university degree (U.S. Census Bureau, 2002).

Schooling in the United States also tries to promote *equal opportunity*. National surveys show that

 Find a Census Bureau report on schooling and income at http://www.census.gov/population/www/socdemo/fld-of-trn.html

most people think schooling is crucial to personal success, and a majority also believe that everyone

has the chance to get an education consistent with personal ability and talent (NORC, 2003). In truth, this opinion expresses our aspirations better than our achievement. Earlier in this century, for example,

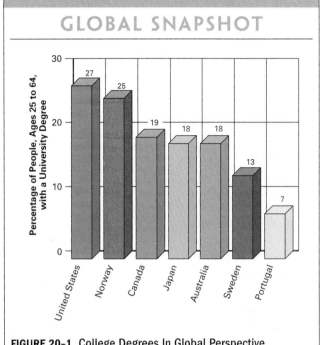

GLOBAL SNAPSHOT

FIGURE 20-1 College Degrees In Global Perspective
Source: U.S. Census Bureau (2002).

women were all but excluded from higher education, and even today, most people who attend college come from families with above-average incomes.

In the United States, the educational system stresses the value of *practical* learning, that is, knowledge that prepares people for their future jobs. This emphasis is in line with what educational philosopher John Dewey (1859–1952) called *progressive education*, by which schools in the United States generally try to make learning relevant to people's lives. Similarly, students seek out subjects of study that they find relevant to their lives and to their prospects for future jobs. As concerns about international terrorism have risen in recent years, for example, so have the numbers of students choosing to study geography, international conflict, and Middle Eastern history and culture (Lord, 2001).

THE FUNCTIONS OF SCHOOLING

Structural-functional analysis looks at how formal education contributes to the operation of society. As the following analysis suggests, schooling does this in many ways.

SOCIALIZATION

Technologically simple societies transmit their ways of life informally from parents to children. As societies develop complex technology, though, they turn to trained teachers to convey the specialized knowledge that adults will need for jobs and maintaining a household.

In primary school, children learn language and basic mathematical skills. Secondary school builds on this foundation, and for many, college allows further specialization. In addition, all schooling transmits cultural values and norms. Civics classes, for example, instruct students in our political way of life, and rituals such as saluting the flag foster patriotism. Likewise, activities such as spelling bees develop competitive individualism and a sense of fair play.

CULTURAL INNOVATION

Schools create and transmit culture. Especially at centers of higher education, scholars conduct research that leads to discovery and changes in our way of life. For example, medical research at major universities has helped increase life expectancy, just as research by sociologists and psychologists helps us take advantage of our longevity.

SOCIAL INTEGRATION

Schooling molds a diverse population into a unified society. This integrative function is especially important in nations with pronounced social diversity, such as the United States, with its history of immigration. This is one reason states enacted mandatory education laws a century ago as immigration increased. With minority students now a majority in many urban areas, schooling continues to serve this purpose today.

SOCIAL PLACEMENT

Schools identify and develop talent in students. Thus, schools enhance meritocracy by rewarding ability and effort regardless of social background. This helps explain the fact that, in the United States, schooling has long opened the door to upward social mobility.

LATENT FUNCTIONS OF SCHOOLING

Schooling also serves less widely recognized functions. It provides child care for the growing number of one-parent and two-career families. In addition, schooling

occupies thousands of young people in their late teens and twenties who would otherwise be competing for limited opportunities in the job market. High schools, colleges, and universities also bring together people of marriageable age. Finally, schools establish networks that are a valuable career resource throughout life.

Critical evaluation. Structural-functional analysis stresses the ways in which formal education supports the operation of a modern society. However, this approach overlooks the problems inherent in our educational system and ignores how schooling helps reproduce the class structure in each generation. Social-conflict analysis turns our attention to precisely these issues.

SCHOOLING AND SOCIAL INEQUALITY

Social-conflict analysis counters the functionalist idea that schooling develops everybody's talents and abilities. Rather, this approach argues that schools cause and perpetuate social inequality in several ways.

SOCIAL CONTROL

Social-conflict analysis suggests that schooling acts as a means of social control, reinforcing acceptance of the status quo. Samuel Bowles and Herbert Gintis (1976) point out that the clamor for public education in the late nineteenth century arose at precisely the time that factory owners were seeking a literate, docile, and disciplined work force. Mandatory education laws ensured that schools would teach immigrants not only English but also cultural values that supported capitalism, such as compliance, punctuality, and discipline. These traits were—and still are—part of what conflict theorists call the **hidden curriculum,** *subtle presentations of political or cultural ideas in the classroom.*

STANDARDIZED TESTING

Here is a question of the kind historically used to measure the academic ability of school-age children in the United States:

Painter is to painting as _____ is to sonnet.

Answer: (a) driver   (c) priest
            (b) poet   (d) carpenter

The correct answer is (b) *poet*: A painter creates a painting just as a poet creates a sonnet. This question supposedly measures logical reasoning, but demonstrating this skill depends on knowing what each term

Sociological research has documented the fact that young people living in low-income communities suffer in school due to large class sizes, poor quality teaching, and insufficient budgets for technology and other instructional materials. In a nation where people believe that schools should give everyone a chance to develop talents and abilities, should such inequalities exist?

means. Unless students are familiar with sonnets as a Western European form of written verse, they are not likely to answer the question correctly.

Educational specialists claim that bias of this kind has been all but eliminated from standardized tests, since testing organizations carefully study response patterns and drop any question that favors one racial or ethnic category over another. Critics, however, maintain that some bias based on class, race, or ethnicity cannot be avoided in formal testing, because questions inevitably reflect our society's dominant culture, thereby placing minority students at a disadvantage (Owen, 1985; Crouse & Trusheim, 1988; Putka, 1990).

SCHOOL TRACKING

Despite continuing controversy over standardized tests, most schools in the United States use them as the basis for **tracking,** *assigning students to different types of educational programs*, such as gifted programs, college preparatory classes, general education, and vocational and technical training.

Tracking supposedly helps schools provide appropriate instruction for students with different interests and aptitudes. However, educational critic Jonathan Kozol (1992) considers tracking one of the "savage inequalities" in our school system. Most students from privileged families tend to do well on standardized tests and get assigned to higher tracks, where they receive the best the school can offer. Students from disadvantaged backgrounds typically do less well on these tests and end up in lower tracks, where teachers stress memorization and classroom drill.

In light of these criticisms, schools across the United States are more cautious about making tracking assignments and give students more chances to move between tracks. Some schools have even dropped tracking entirely. While some tracking seems to be necessary to match instruction with student abilities, rigid tracking has a powerful impact on students' learning and self-concept. Young people who spend years in higher tracks tend to see themselves as bright and able, whereas students in lower tracks have less ambition and low self-esteem (Bowles & Gintis, 1976; Oakes, 1982, 1985; Hallinan & Williams, 1989; Kilgore, 1991; Gamoran, 1992; Kozol, 1992).

INEQUALITY AMONG SCHOOLS

Just as students are treated differently within schools, schools themselves differ in basic ways. The biggest difference is between public and private schools.

Public and Private Schools

Across the United States, 89 percent of the 54 million primary and secondary schoolchildren attend state-funded public schools. The rest go to private schools.

DIVERSITY: RACE, CLASS, AND GENDER
Schooling in the United States: Savage Inequality

"Public School 261? Head down Jerome Avenue and look for the mortician's office." On his way to doing fieldwork for his study of New York City schools, Jonathan Kozol parks his car and walks toward PS 261. Finding PS 261 is not easy because the school has no sign. In fact, the building is a former roller rink and doesn't look much like a school at all.

The principal explains that PS 261 is in a minority area of the North Bronx, so the school population is 90 percent African American and Hispanic. Officially, the school should serve 900 students, but it actually enrolls 1,300. The rules say class size should not exceed 32, but later Kozol notes that it sometimes approaches 40. Because of the small cafeteria, the children must eat in three shifts. After lunch, since there is no place to play, students just squirm in their seats until told to return to their classrooms. Only one classroom in the entire school has a window to the world outside.

Toward the end of the day, Kozol asks a teacher about the overcrowding and the poor condition of the building. She sums up her thoughts: "I had an awful room last year. In the winter, it was 56 degrees. In the summer, it was up to 90." "Do the children ever comment on the building?" Kozol asks. "They don't say," she responds, "but they know. All these kids see TV. They know what suburban schools are like. Then they look around them at their school. They don't comment on it, but you see it in their eyes. They understand."

Several months later, Kozol visits PS 24, in the affluent Riverdale section of New York City. This school is set back from the road, beyond a lawn planted with magnolia and dogwood trees, which are now in full bloom. On one side of the building is a playground for the youngest children; behind the school are playing fields for the older kids. Many people buy expensive homes in Riverdale because the local schools have an excellent reputation. There are 825 children here;

most are white and a few are Asian, Hispanic, or black. The building is in good repair and has a large library and even a planetarium. All the classrooms have windows with bright curtains.

Entering one of the many classes for gifted students, Kozol asks the children what they are doing today. A young girl answers confidently, "My name is Laurie, and we're doing problem solving." A tall, good-natured boy continues, "I'm David. One thing that we do is logical thinking. Some problems, we find, have more than one good answer." Kozol asks if such reasoning is innate or if it is something a child learns. Susan, whose smile reveals her braces, responds, "You know some things to start with when you enter school. But we learn some things that other children don't. We learn certain things that other children don't know because we're *taught* them."

Source: Adapted from Kozol (1992:85–88, 92–96).

Most private school students attend one of the 8,000 *parochial schools* (from the Latin, meaning "of the parish") operated by the Roman Catholic church. The Catholic school system grew rapidly a century ago as cities swelled with immigrants. These schools helped the new arrivals maintain their religious heritage in the midst of a predominantly Protestant society. Today, after decades of flight from the city by white people, many parochial schools enroll non-Catholics, including a growing number of African Americans whose families want an alternative to the neighborhood public school.

Protestants also have private schools, or Christian academies. These schools are favored by parents who want religious instruction for their children or who seek higher academic and disciplinary standards (James, 1989; Dent, 1996).

Some 6,000 nonreligious private schools also enroll young people, mostly from well-to-do families. Many of these are prestigious and expensive preparatory schools, modeled on British boarding schools, that not only provide strong academic programs but teach the mannerisms, attitudes, and social graces of the upper class. Many "preppies" maintain lifelong school-based networks that provide numerous social advantages.

Are private schools better than public schools? Research shows that, given similar backgrounds, students in private schools do outperform their public school counterparts. Private schools seem to generate greater interest in learning, probably because of smaller class size, more student-teacher contact, higher academic standards, and greater discipline (Coleman, Hoffer, & Kilgore, 1981; Coleman & Hoffer, 1987).

SEEING OURSELVES

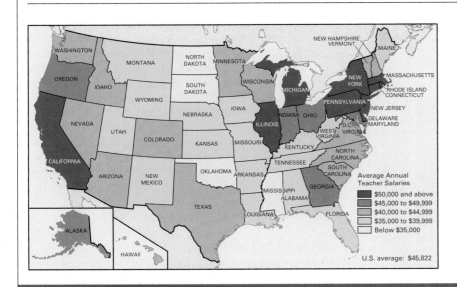

NATIONAL MAP 20–1
Teachers' Salaries
across the United States

In 2002, the average public school teacher in the United States earned $45,822. The map shows the average teacher salary for all the states; they range from a low of $32,416 in South Dakota to a high of $56,283 in California. Looking at the map, what pattern do you see? What do high-salary (and low-salary) states have in common?

Source: National Education Association, *Rankings and Estimates: Rankings of the States and Estimates of School Statistics 2003*. Washington, D.C.: NEA, 2003, p. 65.

Average Annual Teacher Salaries

- $50,000 and above
- $45,000 to $49,999
- $40,000 to $44,999
- $35,000 to $39,999
- Below $35,000

U.S. average: $45,822

Inequality in Public Schooling

But even the public schools are not all the same. For example, Winnetka, Illinois, one of the richest suburbs in the United States, spends more than $8,000 annually per student, compared to less than $3,000 in a poor area like Socorro, Texas (Carroll, 1990; Edwards, 1998). The box takes a closer look at differences in school quality within New York City.

Funding is important because schools in affluent areas can offer a better education than less well-funded schools in poor communities. National Map 20–1 shows the differences in average teacher salaries from state to state. Funding disparities also benefit whites over minorities. For this reason, some districts have started a policy of *busing*, transporting students to achieve racial balance and more equal opportunity in all schools. Although only 5 percent of U.S. schoolchildren are bused to schools outside their neighborhoods, this policy is controversial. Advocates claim that the only way government will adequately fund schools in poor, minority neighborhoods is if white children from richer areas attend them. Critics respond that busing is expensive and undermines the concept of neighborhood schools. But almost everyone agrees on one thing: Given the racial imbalance of most urban areas, an effective busing scheme would have to join inner cities and suburbs, a plan that has never been politically feasible.

But schooling is not only about money. A classic report by a research team headed by James Coleman (1966) confirmed that predominantly minority schools suffer more problems, ranging from larger class size to insufficient libraries and fewer science labs. But the Coleman report cautioned that making more money available would not magically increase learning. Even more important are the cooperative efforts and enthusiasm of teachers, parents, and the students themselves. In other words, even if school funding were exactly the same everywhere, students who benefit from more *social capital*—that is, those whose parents value schooling, read to their children, and encourage the development of imagination—would still perform better (Schneider et al., 1998; Israel, Beaulieu, & Hartless, 2001).

ACCESS TO HIGHER EDUCATION

Schooling is the main path to good jobs. But only 62 percent of U.S. high school graduates enroll in college the following fall (U.S. National Center for Education Statistics, 2003). Moreover, among young people eighteen to twenty-four years old, about 36 percent are enrolled in college.

Here is a report from the National Center for Educational Statistics that profiles U.S. college faculty: http://nces.ed.gov/pubsearch/pubsinfo.asp?pubid=2001201

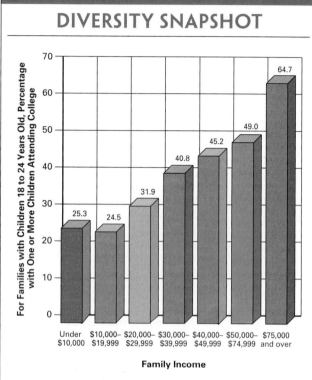

DIVERSITY SNAPSHOT

FIGURE 20–2 College Attendance and Family Income, 2001

Source: U.S. Census Bureau (2003).

The most crucial factor affecting access to U.S. higher education is family income. College is expensive: Even at state-supported institutions, annual tuition averages at least $3,000, and admission to the most exclusive private colleges and universities is almost $40,000 a year. As shown in Figure 20–2, families with incomes above $75,000 annually (roughly the richest 20 percent, who fall within the upper and upper-middle classes) can afford to send two-thirds of their children to college, whereas only one-fourth of young people from families earning less than $20,000 each year reach college (U.S. Census Bureau, 2003).

The cost of higher education prevents many minorities, typically with below-average incomes, from attending college. As Figure 20–3 shows, non-Hispanic whites are more likely than African Americans and Hispanics to complete high school, and this disparity remains with each step up in the educational system. For some, schooling is a path to social mobility, but it has not overcome entrenched racial inequality in the United States (Epps, 1995).

Completing college carries numerous rewards, including intellectual and personal growth, as well as higher income. Over an individual's working lifetime, a college degree adds almost $500,000 to income (Speer, 1994). Table 20–2 shows why. In 2001, women with an eighth-grade education typically earned $16,170; high school graduates averaged $24,217, and college graduates, $39,818. The ratios in parentheses show that a woman with a bachelor's degree earns two-and-one-half times as much as a woman with eight or fewer years of schooling. Across the board, men earn about 40 percent more than women; moreover, more schooling boosts income faster for men than for women. Finally, for both men and women, some of the greater earnings that come with more schooling have to do with social background, since the people with the most schooling are likely to come from relatively rich families to begin with.

GREATER OPPORTUNITY: EXPANDING HIGHER EDUCATION

With some 15.3 million people enrolled in colleges and universities, the United States is the world leader in providing a college education to its people. This country also enrolls more students from abroad than any other.

One reason for this achievement is that there are more than 4,000 colleges and universities in the United States. This number includes 2,364 four-year institutions (which award bachelor's degrees) as well as 1,833 two-year colleges (which award associate's degrees). While some two-year colleges are private, most are publicly funded community colleges that serve a local area (usually a county) and charge a low tuition (U.S. National Center for Education Statistics, 2003).

Historically, higher education has been a key path to better jobs and higher income. To offset the high cost of college, public funds have been used to allow many more people to enroll. After World War II, the GI Bill provided college funds to veterans, so that tens of thousands of men and women became the first generation in their family to attend college.

Community Colleges

Since the 1960s, the expansion of state-funded community colleges has further increased access to higher education. According to the U.S. National Center for Education Statistics (2003), the 1,833 two-year colleges across the United States now enroll 39 percent of all college undergraduates.

Community colleges provide a number of specific benefits. First, their low tuition cost places college courses and degrees within the reach of millions of families that could not otherwise afford them. Today, it is at community colleges that we find many students who are the first generation of their families to pursue a postsecondary degree. Compared to students who attend four-year colleges, a larger share of community college students are also paying their own way. The low cost of community colleges is especially important during periods of economic recession, such as the slowdown beginning in 2001. Typically, when the economy slumps (and people lose their jobs), college enrollments—especially at community colleges—soar.

Second, community colleges have special importance to minorities. Currently, one-half of all African American and Hispanic undergraduates in the United States attend community colleges.

Third, although it is true that community colleges serve local populations, many two-year colleges also attract students from around the world. Many community colleges recruit students from abroad, and more than one-third of all foreign students enrolled on a U.S. campus are studying at community colleges (Briggs, 2002; Golden, 2002).

Finally, while the highest priority of faculty who work at large universities typically is research, the most important job for community college faculty is teaching. Thus, although teaching loads are high (typically four or five classes each semester), community colleges appeal to faculty who find their greatest pleasure in the classroom. Community college students often get more attention from faculty than their counterparts at large universities (Jacobson, 2003).

CREDENTIALISM

Sociologist Randall Collins (1979) has dubbed the United States a *credential society* because people regard diplomas and degrees so highly. In modern, technologically advanced societies, credentials say "who you are" as much as family background.

Credentialism, then, is *evaluating a person on the basis of educational degrees.* On the one hand, credentialism is simply the way our modern society goes about filling jobs with well-trained people. On the other hand, Collins explains that credentials often bear little relation to the responsibilities of a specific job. In reality, advanced degrees often are an easy way to sort out the people with the manners, attitudes, and even skin

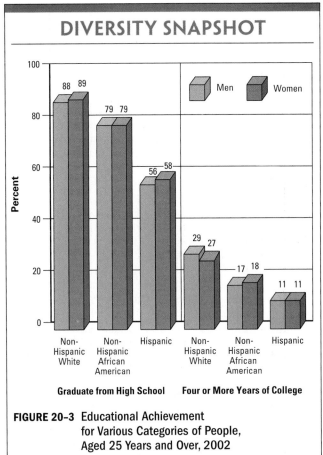

FIGURE 20–3 Educational Achievement for Various Categories of People, Aged 25 Years and Over, 2002

Source: U.S. Census Bureau (2003).

TABLE 20-2 Median Income by Sex and Educational Attainment[*]

Education	Men	Women
Professional degree	$100,000 (4.7)	$60,093 (3.7)
Doctorate	81,077 (3.8)	60,425 (3.7)
Master's	66,934 (3.2)	48,276 (3.0)
Bachelor's	53,108 (2.5)	39,818 (2.5)
1–3 years of college	40,159 (1.9)	28,839 (1.8)
4 years of high school	33,037 (1.6)	24,217 (1.5)
9–11 years of school	25,857 (1.2)	17,937 (1.1)
0–8 years of school	21,139 (1.0)	16,170 (1.0)

[*]Persons aged twenty-five years and over working full time, 2001. The earnings ratio, in parentheses, indicates how many times the lowest income level a person with additional schooling earns.

Source: U.S. Census Bureau (2002).

color favored by many employers. Credentialism is thus a gate-keeping strategy that restricts important occupations to a limited segment of the population.

PRIVILEGE AND PERSONAL MERIT

If attending college is a rite of passage for affluent men and women, as social-conflict analysis suggests, then *schooling transforms social privilege into personal merit*. But given our cultural emphasis on individualism, we tend to see credentials as "badges of ability" rather than as symbols of family affluence (Sennett & Cobb, 1973).

When we congratulate the new graduate, we rarely recognize the resources—both financial and cultural—that made this achievement possible. Yet the fact is that young people from families with incomes exceeding $100,000 a year average about 260 points higher on the SAT college entrance examination than young people from families with less than $10,000 in annual income. Furthermore, although effort is important for any and all students, research supports the conclusion that the higher the social background, the more educational benefit comes from a student's effort. Obviously, then, social background spills into what we commonly view as personal achievement (Deluca & Rosenbaum, 2001).

Critical evaluation. Social-conflict analysis links formal education and social inequality, to show how schooling transforms privilege into personal worthiness, and social disadvantage into personal deficiency. However, critics say that social-conflict analysis ignores the common pattern by which schooling provides upward social mobility for talented men and women from all backgrounds. Further, despite the claims that schooling supports the status quo, today's college curricula challenge social inequality on many fronts.

PROBLEMS IN THE SCHOOLS

An intense debate revolves around schooling in the United States today. Perhaps because we expect our schools to do so much—equalize opportunity, instill dis-

 For details on this national poll, go to htttp://www.pdkintl.org

cipline, fire the imagination—people are divided on whether public schools are doing their job. Although half of adults give schools in their local community a grade of A or B, just as many give a grade of C or below (Phi Delta Kappa International, 2003).

DISCIPLINE AND VIOLENCE

When many of today's older teachers think back to their own student days, school "problems" consisted of talking out of turn, chewing gum, breaking the dress code, or cutting class. But today, schools are grappling with serious issues such as drug and alcohol abuse, teenage pregnancy, and outright violence. It is little wonder that, while almost everyone agrees that schools should teach personal discipline, many think the job is no longer being done.

In recent years, violence has claimed the lives of students and teachers alike in high schools across the United States. Moreover, in national surveys, about 25 percent of students and 11 percent of teachers report being victims of violence each year in and around schools in hundreds of thousands of cases that do not capture national headlines (Arnette & Walsleben, 1998).

Schools do not create violence; in most cases, violence spills into the schools from the surrounding society. In the wake of a number of school shootings during the 1990s, many school districts have adopted zero-tolerance policies that mandate suspension or expulsion for serious misbehavior (Toby, 1998). But such policies have become controversial in the wake of data that show that schools are far more likely to suspend African American students than white students. The box takes a closer look.

STUDENT PASSIVITY

If some schools are plagued by violence, many more are filled with passive, bored students. Some of the blame for passivity can be placed on television (which now consumes more of young people's time than school), on parents (who are not involved enough with their children), and on the students themselves. But schools, too, play a part, since our educational system itself generates student passivity (Coleman, Hoffer, & Kilgore, 1981).

Bureaucracy

The small, personal schools that served countless local communities a century ago have evolved into huge educational factories. In a study of high schools across the United States, Theodore Sizer (1984: 207–9) identified five ways in which large, bureaucratic schools undermine education:

1. **Rigid uniformity.** Bureaucratic schools run by outside specialists (such as state education officials) generally ignore the cultural character

DIVERSITY: RACE, CLASS, AND GENDER

School Discipline: A Case of Racial Profiling?

Ken Russell was known as a troublemaker in his Modesto, California, high school. He doesn't deny it. But he also thinks he has been punished for more than his behavior. Ken, who is African American, recently got into a scuffle with another boy, who is white. It started with name calling, and then Ken threw a punch, and a fistfight ensued. Ken took some lumps, but the white boy required five stitches to close a wound over his left eye.

The school responded with suspensions: The white boy was sent home for three days, and Ken was suspended for more than a month. The administration justified the difference by pointing to the greater harm Ken caused to the white student. But after hearing school officials describe the fight as "mutual," Ken's father thought his son's longer suspension was unfair. He filed a civil rights complaint, claiming that his son was being punished more severely because he was black.

Records in the Modesto school district indicate a clear pattern: African American students are two-and-one-half times more likely than white students to be kicked out of school for misbehaving. Research confirms that this pattern holds nationwide; African Americans are more likely than whites to be suspended, expelled, or arrested at school.

The question, however, is why? One Modesto school official claims the answer is simply that African American youngsters are more likely to misbehave. While he concedes that African Americans are punished more often, he points out that the school district also suspends far more males than females. "Does that mean," he asks, "that we discriminate against men?"

But others charge that racial bias is real. One recent study of school discipline in a large school district in Indiana concluded that African American students were more likely than white

students to be disciplined for the same behaviors, especially relatively minor issues such as making too much noise or acting disrespectfully. "You can choose not to use the word racism," the researcher concluded, "but districts need to look seriously at what is going on."

Perhaps both theories contain some truth. The National Association of Secondary School Principals confirms that African Americans are more likely than whites to misbehave, but it claims the cause is not race but differences in social background. In other words, African American children have more disciplinary problems in school because they are more likely to come from poor families, where they are subject to disadvantages ranging from less parenting to exposure to lead-based paint. But if this is so, we are still left with the question: "Whose fault is that?"

Source: Morse (2002a).

---

of local communities and the personal needs of their children.

2. **Numerical ratings.** School officials define success in terms of numerical attendance records, dropout rates, and achievement test scores. Therefore, they overlook dimensions of schooling that are difficult to quantify, such as creativity and enthusiasm.

3. **Rigid expectations.** Officials expect fifteen-year-olds to be in the tenth grade and eleventh-graders to score at a certain level on a standardized verbal achievement test. Rarely are exceptionally bright and motivated students permitted to graduate early. Likewise, the system pushes poor performers on from grade to grade.

4. **Specialization.** High school students learn Spanish from one teacher, receive guidance from another,

and are coached in sports by still others. Although specialized teachers may know more about their subjects, no school employee comes to know and appreciate the complete student. Students experience this division of labor as a continual shuffling from one fifty-minute period to another throughout the school day.

5. **Little individual responsibility.** Highly bureaucratic schools do not empower students to learn on their own. Similarly, teachers have little latitude in what and how they teach their classes; they dare not accelerate learning for fear of disrupting the system.

Of course, with 54 million schoolchildren in the United States, schools have to be bureaucratic to get the job done. But, Sizer maintains, we can "humanize"

The degree to which students are active or passive depends largely on how the classroom is structured. Big lecture classes are designed to convey information to large numbers of students who passively take notes. What classroom arrangements encourage a more active discussion?

schools by reducing rigid scheduling, cutting class size, and training teachers more broadly so that they become more involved in the lives of their students. Overall, as James Coleman (1993) suggested, schools need to be less "administratively driven" and more "output-driven." Perhaps this transformation could begin by ensuring that graduation from high school depends on what students have learned rather than simply on the number of years spent in the building.

College: The Silent Classroom

Passivity is also common among college and university students. Martha E. Gimenez (1989) describes college as the "silent classroom" because the only voice heard is usually the teacher's. Sociologists rarely study the college classroom—a curious fact considering how much time they spend there. One exception was a study at a coeducational university where David Karp and William Yoels (1976) found that—even in small classes—only a few students spoke up. They concluded that passivity is a classroom norm, noting that students even become irritated if one of their number is especially talkative.

According to Karp and Yoels, most students think classroom passivity is their own fault. Yet, as anyone who observes young people *outside* class knows, they are usually active and vocal; it is schools that teach students to be passive and to view instructors as experts who serve up "truth." Thus, Karp and Yoels conclude, students find little value in classroom discussion and

perceive their proper role as listening quietly and taking notes. As a result, they estimate, just 10 percent of college class time is used for discussion.

Faculty can bring students to life in their classrooms by actively involving them in learning. One study of classroom dynamics, for example, linked greater student participation to four teaching strategies: (1) calling on students by name when they volunteer; (2) positively reinforcing students' willingness to contribute; (3) asking analytical rather than factual questions and giving students time to answer; and (4) directly soliciting student opinions even when no one volunteers a response (Auster & MacRone, 1994).

DROPPING OUT

If many students are passive in class, others are not there at all. The problem of *dropping out*—quitting school before earning a high school diploma—leaves young people (many of whom are disadvantaged to begin with) ill equipped for the world of work and at high risk of poverty.

The dropout rate has eased slightly in recent decades; currently 10.9 percent of people between the ages of sixteen and twenty-four have dropped out of school, a total of some 3.8 million young women and men. Dropping out is least pronounced among non-Hispanic whites (6.9 percent), higher among non-Hispanic African Americans (13.1 percent), and highest of all among Hispanics (27.8 percent) (U.S. National

SEEING OURSELVES

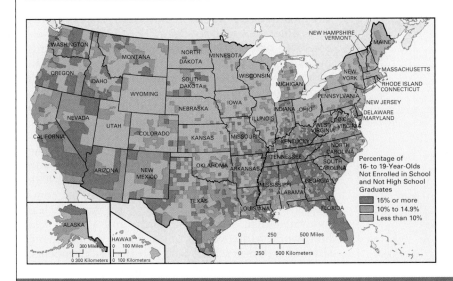

NATIONAL MAP 20–2
High School Dropouts across the United States

Across the United States, the highest dropout rate is found in Holmes County, Ohio, where more than half of young people are not enrolled in school or are not high school graduates. This county has a largely Amish population, and young people leave school to work on farms. Regionally, dropout rates are high across the South—from West Virginia down to Florida and from the Carolinas to Louisiana and east Texas. Rates are also high in the Southwest. What factors do you think account for this pattern?

Percentage of 16- to 19-Year-Olds Not Enrolled in School and Not High School Graduates
- 15% or more
- 10% to 14.9%
- Less than 10%

Source: From *Atlas of Contemporary America* by Rodger Doyle. Map copyright © 1994 by Facts on File, Inc. Reprinted with permission of Facts on File, Inc.

Center for Education Statistics, 2002). National Map 20–2 shows the dropout rate across the United States.

Some students drop out because of problems with the English language or because of pregnancy; others, whose families are poor, must go to work. The dropout rate (10.0 percent) among children growing up in the bottom 20 percent of households by income is more than six times as high as that (1.6 percent) for youngsters whose households fall in the top 20 percent (U.S. National Center for Education Statistics, 2002). The dropout rate is also higher in both rural and inner-city areas, where young people lack cultural and financial resources. These data point to the fact that many dropouts are young people whose parents also have little schooling, revealing a multigenerational cycle of disadvantage (Pirog & Magee, 1997; Roscigno & Crowley, 2001).

ACADEMIC STANDARDS

Perhaps the most serious educational issue confronting our society is the quality of schooling. *A Nation at Risk*, a comprehensive report on the quality of U.S. schools published in 1983 by the National Commission on Excellence in Education, begins with this alarming statement:

If an unfriendly foreign power had attempted to impose on America the mediocre educational performance that exists today, we might well have viewed it as an act of war. As it stands, we have allowed this to happen to ourselves. (1983:5)

Supporting this conclusion, the report notes that "nearly 40 percent of seventeen-year-olds cannot draw inferences from written material; only one-fifth can write a persuasive essay; and only one-third can solve mathematical problems requiring several steps" (1983:9). Furthermore, scores on the Scholastic Assessment Test (SAT) show little improvement over time. In 1967, median scores for students were 516 on the mathematical test and 543 on the verbal test; by 2003, the average in mathematics had risen slightly to 519, and the verbal average had slipped to just 507. Nationwide, one-third of high school students—and more than half in urban schools—fail to master even the basics in reading, math, and science on the National Assessment of Education Progress examination (Sanchez, 1998; Marklein, 2000; Barnes, 2002).

For many, even basic literacy is at issue. **Functional illiteracy,** *a lack of the reading and writing skills needed for everyday living,* is a problem for one in eight children who leave secondary school in the United States. For older people, the problem is even worse, so that, overall,

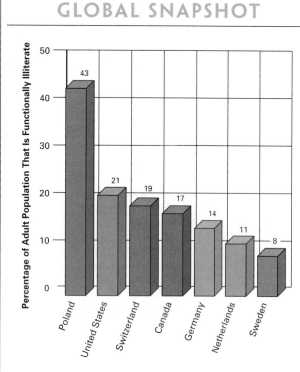

GLOBAL SNAPSHOT

FIGURE 20–4 Functional Illiteracy in Global Perspective

Source: Adapted with permission from *The Christian Science Monitor*. © 1997 The Christian Science Publishing Society. All rights reserved.

some 40 million U.S. adults (about 20 percent of the total) read and write at an eighth-grade level or below. As Figure 20–4 shows, the extent of functional illiteracy in the United States is below that of middle-income nations (such as Poland), but higher than in other high-income countries (such as Canada and Sweden).

A Nation at Risk recommended drastic reform. First, all schools should require students to complete several years of English, mathematics, social studies, general science, and computer science courses. Second, schools should not promote students until they meet achievement standards. Third, teacher training must improve, and teachers' salaries should rise to draw talent into the profession. *A Nation at Risk* concluded that schools must meet public expectations and that citizens must be prepared to pay for a job well done.

What has happened in the years since this report was issued? In some respects, schools have improved. A report by the Center on Education Policy (2000) noted a decline in the dropout rate, a trend toward schools' offering more challenging courses, and a larger share of high school graduates going on to college. Despite several tragic cases of shootings, school violence overall was down during the 1990s. At the same time, the evidence suggests that a majority of elementary school students are falling below standards in reading; in many cases, they can't read at all. In short, although some improvement is evident, much remains to be done.

In global perspective, this nation spends more on schooling its children than almost anywhere else. Even so, U.S. eighth-graders lag behind their counterparts in other countries, placing seventeenth in the world in science achievement and twenty-eighth in mathematics (Bennett, 1997; Finn & Walberg, 1998). Cultural values play a big part in international comparisons. For example, U.S. students are generally less motivated than students in Japan and also do less homework. Moreover, Japanese young people spend sixty more days in school each year than U.S. students. Perhaps one approach to improving schools is simply to have students spend more time there.

GRADE INFLATION

Academic standards depend on using grades that have clear meaning and are awarded for work of appropriate quality. Yet, in recent decades, there has been a substantial amount of *grade inflation*, by which teachers give higher and higher grades for average work. While not necessarily found in every school, grade inflation is evident in both high schools and colleges.

One recent study of high school grades shows how dramatic the change has been. In 1969, as Figure 20–5 shows, the high school records of students who had just entered college included more grades of C+ and below than grades of A-, A, and A+. By 2001, however, these A grades outnumbered grades of C+ and below by seven to one.

According to these researchers, there is no evidence that grade inflation will slow down any time soon. As a result, they suggest, the C grade (which used to mean "average") may virtually disappear, so just about every student will be "above average."

What accounts for grade inflation? In part, teachers are clearly not as "tough" as they used to be. At the same time, however, the ever more competitive process of getting into college (and also graduate schools) puts pressure on schools to give high grades to make their graduates more successful (Astin et al., 2002).

RECENT ISSUES IN U.S. EDUCATION

Our society's schools continuously confront new challenges. This final section explores several recent and important educational issues.

SCHOOL CHOICE

Some analysts claim that the reason our schools do not teach very well is that they have no competition. Thus, giving parents options for schooling their children might force all schools to do a better job. This is the essence of a policy called *school choice*.

Proponents of school choice want to provide more than one schooling option, so that parents and students can shop for the best value. According to the most sweeping proposal, the government would give vouchers to families with school-aged children and allow them to spend that money at public, private, or parochial schools. In recent years, major cities, including Indianapolis, Minneapolis, Milwaukee, Cleveland, Chicago, and Washington, D.C., as well as the states of Florida and Illinois, have experimented with choice plans aimed at making public schools perform better to win the confidence of families. In addition, the Children's Scholarship Fund, a privately funded charity, has supported 40,000 children who wish to attend nonpublic schools and has more than 1 million children on its waiting list (Lord, 2002).

Supporters claim that giving parents a choice about where to enroll their children is the only sure way to improve all schools. In 2002, moreover, the U.S. Supreme Court advanced the idea of school choice by upholding a Cleveland, Ohio, voucher program. But critics (including teachers' unions) continue to oppose a policy that they see as weakening this nation's commitment to public education, especially in the central cities, where the need is greatest (Godwin et al., 1998; Cohen, 1999; Forstmann, 1999; Morse, 2002b).

In 2002, President George W. Bush signed a new education bill that downplayed vouchers in favor of another approach to greater choice. Starting in the 2005–2006 school year, all public schools must test every child in reading, mathematics, and science in grades 3 through 8. Although the federal government may provide more aid to schools where students do not perform well, if those schools do not show improvements in test scores over time, their students will have the choice of either special tutoring or transportation to another school (Lindlaw, 2002).

Another type of school choice involves *magnet schools*, 1,700 of which now exist across the country.

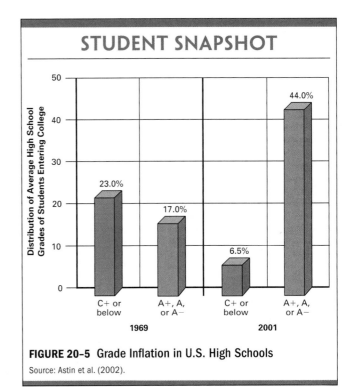

STUDENT SNAPSHOT

FIGURE 20-5 Grade Inflation in U.S. High Schools

Source: Astin et al. (2002).

Magnet schools offer special facilities and programs that promote educational excellence in a particular area, such as computer science, foreign languages, science and mathematics, or the arts. In school districts with magnet schools, parents can choose the school best suited to their child's particular talents and interests.

Another school choice strategy involves *charter schools*, which are public schools that are given more freedom to try out new policies and programs. There are about 2,400 such schools in thirty-eight states, Washington, D.C., and Puerto Rico; they enroll about 700,000 students (about 1.2 percent of student enrollment nationwide). In many of these schools, students have demonstrated high academic achievement—a condition that is necessary in order for the charter to be continued. Compared to traditional public schools, in which 40 percent of students are minorities, charter schools have a minority majority, with 51 percent minority enrollment (Dervarics, 2001; U.S. Department of Education, 2001). Not all charter schools have strong records, however. Critics point out that students attending underfunded charter schools—like those in any underfunded schools—do less well (Rimer, 2003).

A final development in the school choice movement is *schooling for profit*. Advocates of this plan say school systems can be operated by private profit-making companies more efficiently than by local governments. Private schooling is nothing new, of course; more than 25,000 U.S. schools are currently run by private organizations and religious groups. What is new, however, is the idea that hundreds of public schools enrolling hundreds of thousands of students are run by private businesses for profit.

Research confirms that many public school systems suffer from bureaucratic bloat, spending too much and teaching too little. And our society has long looked to competition and private initiative to improve quality and cut costs. Evidence suggests that for-profit schools have greatly reduced administrative costs, but the educational results appear mixed. Several companies claim to have improved student learning, yet some cities have cut back on business-run schools. In recent years, school boards in Baltimore, Maryland; Miami, Florida; Hartford, Connecticut; and, most recently, in Boston, Massachusetts, have canceled the contracts of for-profit schooling corporations. But other cities are deciding to give for-profit schooling a try. For example, after Philadelphia's public school system failed to graduate one-third of its students, the state of Pennsylvania took over that city's schools and has recently turned over most of them to for-profit companies. Emotions—both for and against privately run public schools—run high, and each side claims it speaks for the well-being of those caught in the middle: the schoolchildren (Greenwald, 2000; Caruso, 2002; McGurn, 2002; Winters, 2002).

HOME SCHOOLING

Home schooling is gaining popularity across the United States. As noted in the opening of this chapter, about 1.5 million children (about 3 percent of all school-aged children) have their formal schooling at home, and the number is increasing rapidly. Thus, home schooling involves more school-aged children than magnet schools, charter schools, and for-profit schools combined.

Why do parents undertake the enormous challenge of schooling their own children? Some twenty years ago, the parents who pioneered home schooling (which is now legal in every state) did so mainly because they wanted to give their children a strongly religious upbringing. Today, however, many are mothers and fathers who simply do not believe that public schools are doing a good job, and who think they can

do better. To benefit their children, they are willing to alter work schedules as well as to relearn algebra or other skills as necessary. Many belong to groups in which parents pool their efforts, each specializing in what he or she knows best.

Advocates of home schooling point out that, given the poor performance of many public schools, no one should be surprised that a growing number of parents are willing to step in to teach their own children. Moreover, this system works—on average, students who learn at home outperform those who learn in school. Critics counter that home schooling reduces the amount of funding going to local public schools, and the reduced funding ends up hurting the majority of students. Moreover, as one critic points out, home schooling "takes some of the most affluent and articulate parents out of the system. These are the parents who know how to get things done with administrators" (Lubienski, cited in Cloud & Morse, 2001:48).

SCHOOLING PEOPLE WITH DISABILITIES

Many of the 6 million children with disabilities in the United States face special challenges getting to and from school; once there, many with crutches or wheelchairs cannot negotiate stairs and other obstacles inside school buildings. Children with developmental disabilities like mental retardation require extensive personal attention from specially trained teachers. As a result, many children with mental and physical disabilities have received a public education only because of persistent efforts by parents and other concerned citizens (Horn & Tynan, 2001).

About one-half of children with disabilities are schooled in special facilities; the rest attend public schools, many participating in regular classes. Thus, most schools avoid expensive "special education" in favor of **mainstreaming,** *integrating special students into the overall educational program.* Mainstreaming is a form of *inclusive education* that works best for physically impaired students who have no difficulty keeping up with the rest of the class. Moreover, putting children with and without disabilities in the same classroom allows everyone to learn to interact with people who differ from themselves.

ADULT EDUCATION

In 2000, more than 88 million U.S. adults were enrolled in some type of schooling. These older students range in age from the middle twenties to the seventies and beyond. From another angle, 21 percent of students in degree-granting programs are now older students. Adults in school are more likely to be women than men, and most have above-average incomes.

Why do adults return to the classroom? The most obvious reasons given are to advance a career or train for a new job (66 percent), but many (43 percent) also point to the simple goal of personal enrichment (U.S. Census Bureau, 2002).

THE TEACHER SHORTAGE

A final challenge for U.S. schools is hiring enough teachers to fill the classrooms. A number of factors—including low salaries, frustration, and retirement, as well as rising enrollment and a reduction in class size—have combined to create more than 200,000 teaching vacancies in the United States each year.

How will these slots be filled? About the same number of people graduate with education degrees annually, but except for their education courses, most lack a degree in a specific field (such as mathematics, biology, or English), and many have trouble passing state certification tests in the area they wish to teach.

As a result, schools have adopted new recruitment strategies. Some analysts suggest that community colleges could play a larger role in teacher education. Others support using incentives such as higher salaries and signing bonuses to draw into teaching people who have already established successful careers. In addition, states could make it easier to gain teaching certification. Finally, many school districts are going global—actively recruiting in countries such as Spain, India, and the Philippines to bring talented women and men to U.S. classrooms (Dervarics, 1999; Lord, 2001; Philadelphia, 2001; Evelyn, 2002).

Of course, the debates about education in the United States extend beyond the issues noted here. The final box on page 536 takes a look at the recent trend by which men represent a declining share of students on college campuses.

LOOKING AHEAD: SCHOOLING IN THE TWENTY-FIRST CENTURY

Even though the United States leads the world in sending people to college, the public school system continues to struggle with serious problems, many of which have their roots in the larger society. Thus, we cannot expect schools *by themselves* to provide high-quality education. Schools will improve only to the extent that students, teachers, parents, and local

Educators have long debated the proper manner in which to school children with disabilities. On one hand, such children may benefit from distinctive facilities and specially trained teachers. On the other hand, they are less likely to be stigmatized as "different" if included in regular classroom settings. What do you consider to be the ramifications of the "special education" versus "inclusive education" debate for the classroom experience of all children, not only those who have disabilities?

communities commit themselves to educational excellence. In short, educational dilemmas are *social* problems, and there is no quick fix.

For much of the twentieth century, there were just two models for education in the United States: public schools run by the government and private schools operated by nongovernmental organizations. In the last decade, however, many new ideas about schooling have come on the scene, including schooling for profit and a wide range of "choice" programs (Finn & Gau, 1998). In the decades ahead, we are likely to see some significant changes in mass education, guided in part by social science research pointing out the consequences of different strategies.

Whatever decisions are made about who controls education, another factor that will continue to reshape schools is new information technology. Today, 97 percent of conventional primary and secondary schools use computers for instruction. Computers prompt students to be more active and allow them to progress at their own pace. For students with disabilities who cannot write using a pencil, computers permit easier self-expression.

Even so, computers have their limitations. Computers will never bring to the educational process the

CONTROVERSY & DEBATE

The Twenty-First-Century Campus: Where Are the Men?

A century ago, the campuses of colleges and universities across the United States might as well have hung out a sign that read "Men Only!" The fact is that almost all of the students and faculty were male. While there were a number of women's colleges, many more schools, including some of the best known U.S. universities (such as Yale, Harvard, and Princeton), barred women outright.

As the twentieth century proceeded, however, women won greater and greater social equality. Therefore, few people were surprised when, in 1980, the number of women enrolled at U.S. colleges finally matched the number of men.

What is surprising is what has happened since then: The share of women on the campus has continued to increase.

 MEDIA For a National Center for Education Statistics (NCES) report titled "Trends in Educational Equity of Girls & Women," go to http://nces.ed.gov/pubs2000/2000030.pdf

As a result, in 2000, men accounted for only 44 percent of all U.S. undergraduates. Meg DeLong noticed the gender imbalance right away when she moved into her dorm at the University of Georgia at Athens; she soon learned that just 39 percent of her first-year students were men. In classes, DeLong found, there were few men, and women dominated discussions. Out of class, she and many other women soon complained that having so few men on campus hurt their social life (not surprisingly, most of the men felt otherwise about their own social life).

Why the shifting gender balance on U.S. campuses? No one knows for sure, but several theories have been put forward. Some suggest that young men are drawn away from college by the lure of jobs, especially in high technology. This pattern is sometimes termed the "Bill Gates syndrome," after the Microsoft founder, who dropped out of college and soon became the world's richest person. In addition, analysts point to an anti-intellectual male culture. That is, while young women are drawn to learning and seek to do well in school, young men are more likely to see studying negatively and to dismiss schoolwork as "something for girls." Rightly or wrongly, in short, more men seem to think they can get a good job without investing years of their lives and a considerable amount of money in getting a college degree.

The gender gap is evident in all racial and ethnic categories. In fact, only 37 percent of African American college students are men. It is also found at all class levels. Indeed, the lower the income level, the greater the gender gap in college attendance.

Many college officials are concerned about this trend. In an effort to attract more balanced enrollments, some colleges are adopting what amounts to affirmative action programs that favor males. In several states, however, the courts have ruled that such policies are illegal. Many colleges, therefore, are turning to more vigorous recruitment, having admission officers pay special attention to male applicants, and stressing a college's strength in mathematics and science—areas that traditionally have attracted men. While colleges across the country are striving to increase their number of minority students, the hope is that they can also succeed in attracting men as well as women.

Continue the debate . . .

1. *Do you think that, among high school students, men are less concerned than women about academic achievement? Why or why not?*

2. *Is there a lack of males on your campus? Does it create problems? What problems? For whom?*

3. *What programs or policies do you think might increase the number of men going to college?*

Source: Based on Fonda (2000).

---

personal insight or imagination of a motivated human teacher. Nor can computers tap what one teacher calls the "springs of human identity and creativity" that we discover by exploring literature and language rather than simply manipulating mathematical codes. Indeed, despite the growing number of computers in the classroom, these machines have yet to change teaching and learning in any fundamental sense or even to replace the traditional blackboard (Skinner, 1997). Nor will technology ever solve the problems—including violence and rigid bureaucracy—that plague our schools. What we need is a broad plan for social change that refires this country's early ambition to provide high-quality universal schooling, a goal that has so far eluded us.

SUMMARY

1. Education is the major social institution for transmitting knowledge and skills, as well as teaching cultural norms and values. In preindustrial societies, education occurs informally within the family; industrial societies develop formal systems of schooling.

2. The United States was among the first countries to institute compulsory mass education, reflecting both democratic political ideals and the needs of the industrial-capitalist economy.

3. Structural-functional analysis highlights major functions of schooling, including socialization, cultural innovation, social integration, and the placement of people in the social hierarchy. Latent functions of schooling include providing child care and building social networks.

4. Social-conflict analysis links schooling to the hierarchy involving class, race, and gender. Formal education also serves as a means of generating conformity to produce compliant adult workers.

5. The use of standardized achievement tests is controversial. Some see them as a reasonable measure of academic aptitude and learning, while others say they are culturally biased tools that may lead to labeling less privileged students as personally deficient.

6. Tracking is another controversial issue. Some see tracking as the way schools provide appropriate instruction for students with different interests and aptitudes; others say tracking gives privileged youngsters a richer education.

7. The great majority of young people in the United States attend state-funded public schools. Most private schools offer a religious education. A small proportion of students—usually well-to-do—attend elite private preparatory schools.

8. Nearly 27 percent of U.S. adults over the age of twenty-five are now college graduates, marking the emergence of a "credential society." People with college degrees enjoy much higher lifetime earnings.

9. Most adults in the United States are critical of public schools. Violence permeates many schools, especially those in poor neighborhoods. The bureaucratic character of schools also fosters high dropout rates and student passivity.

10. Declining academic standards are reflected in today's lower average scores on achievement tests, the functional illiteracy of a significant proportion of high school graduates, and grade inflation.

11. The school choice movement seeks to make schools more responsive to the public. Innovative options include magnet schools, schooling for profit, and charter schools, all of which are topics of continuing policy debate. In addition, an increasing number of parents now choose to school their children at home.

12. Children with mental or physical disabilities historically have been schooled in special classes or not at all. Mainstreaming affords them broader opportunities.

13. Adults represent a growing proportion of students in the United States. Most older learners are women who are engaged in job-related study.

14. The Information Revolution is changing schooling through increasing use of computers. Although computers permit interactive, self-paced learning, they are not suitable for teaching every subject.

KEY CONCEPTS

education (p. 517) the social institution through which society provides its members with important knowledge, including basic facts, job skills, and cultural norms and values

schooling (p. 517) formal instruction under the direction of specially trained teachers

hidden curriculum (p. 522) subtle presentations of political or cultural ideas in the classroom

tracking (p. 523) assigning students to different types of educational programs

credentialism (p. 527) evaluating a person on the basis of educational degrees

functional illiteracy (p. 531) a lack of the reading and writing skills needed for everyday living

mainstreaming (p. 534) integrating special students into the overall educational program

CRITICAL-THINKING QUESTIONS

1. Why does industrialization lead societies to expand their systems of schooling?

2. In what ways is schooling in the United States shaped by our economic, political, and cultural systems?

3. From a structural-functional perspective, why is schooling important to the operation of society? From a social-conflict point of view, how does formal education reproduce social inequality in each generation?

4. Do you agree with the research findings presented in this chapter that, by and large, college students are passive in class? If so, what do you think colleges can do to make everyone a more active participant in learning?

APPLICATIONS AND EXERCISES

1. Arrange to visit a secondary school near your college or home. Does it have a tracking policy? If so, find out how it works. How much importance does a student's social background have in making a track assignment?

2. Most people agree that teaching our children is a vital task. Yet teachers earn relatively low salaries. Check the prestige ranking for teachers in Table 11–2. See what you can learn about the average salaries of teachers compared to those of other workers. Can you explain this pattern?

3. Since the passage of the Americans with Disabilities Act of 1990, schools have sought to "accommodate" students with a broader range of physical and mental disabilities. Do some research or contact officials on your campus to learn how laws of this kind are changing education.

4. Packaged in the back of this new textbook is an interactive CD-ROM that offers a variety of video and interactive review materials intended to help you better understand the material covered in this chapter. For this chapter, the CD-ROM contains a relevant clip from *ABC News*, an author's tip video, interactive map animations, an interactive time line, and flashcards with audio pronunciations of the more difficult words.

 SITES TO SEE

http://www.prenhall.com/macionis

Visit the interactive Companion Website™ that accompanies this text. Begin by clicking on the cover of your book. You will find a chapter-by-chapter study guide, practice tests, suggested Web links, and links to other relevant material.

http://www.publicagenda.org

Visit Public Agenda Online, a site that investigates a number of educational issues.

http://nces.ed.gov/

The National Center for Education Statistics provides data about U.S. education, including a profile of those who have earned various degrees, by gender and race.

http://www.acpe.asu.edu/VirtualU/

To explore how new information technology is reshaping education, read about the founding of Western Virtual University, this country's first "cyber-college." Think about the advantages and disadvantages of this type of schooling.

http://www2.kenyon.edu/projects/famfarm/

Visit the Family Farm Web site at Kenyon College. This site was created by students to share what they have learned about farming and rural life in a rural county in central Ohio.

http://nces.ed.gov/pubs2002/crime2001/

Read the U.S. government's new report on crime and safety in the schools at this Web site.

 INVESTIGATE WITH RESEARCH NAVIGATOR™

Follow the instructions on page 24 of this text to access the features of **Research Navigator**™. Once at the Web site, enter your Login Name and Password. Then, to use the **Content Select**™ database, enter keywords such as "tracking," "functional illiteracy," and "school choice," and the search engine will supply relevant and recent scholarly and popular press publications. Use the *New York Times* **Search-by-Subject Archive** to find recent news articles related to sociology and the **Link Library** feature to find relevant Web links organized by the key terms associated with this chapter.

November 14, 2003

Students' Scores Rise in Math, Not in Reading

By **DIANA JEAN SCHEMO**

WASHINGTON—Elementary and middle school children have continued a decade of progress on a nationally administered math test, with all groups showing gains in every state. But reading scores remained essentially flat in most of the country. . . .

The math results showed achievement rising among blacks and Latinos as well as white and Asian students, with greater gains among fourth graders than among eighth graders. North Carolina showed the largest gain among students since 1992, with the share of students ranked proficient in math soaring to 41 percent from 13 percent in fourth grade and to 32 percent from 12 percent in eighth grade.

The test, officially called the National Assessment of Educational Progress, is widely referred to as the nation's report card. It ranks students on a numerical scale as having either advanced, proficient, basic, or below-basic skills in math, reading and a variety of other subjects. . . .

Secretary of Education Rod Paige, who has often used the release of the national test scores to lament the quality of public education, hailed the math results as "stellar" and said, "I think our nation's teachers, administrators and students have a lot to be proud of " . . . .

Still, the Education Trust, which represents urban schools, expressed concern because the math scores of white students in eighth grade rose more than those of Latinos and black students, meaning a widening achievement gap.

In 1990, only 1 percent of black fourth graders and 2 percent of black eighth graders were proficient at math. The new results showed 10 percent of black fourth graders, and 7 percent of black eighth graders, have reached proficiency. "Clearly there's more work that needs to be done," said Johnny W. Lott, president of the National Council of Teachers of Mathematics. . . .

The results . . . came from a test given in February to a national sample of 686,000 students at 13,600 schools in all 50 states. Under the No Child Left Behind law, states must administer the national tests every two years. . . .

The rising math scores were seen as a vindication for curriculum guidelines developed by the National Council of Teachers of Math in 1989 and now used in nearly all states. They recommended that teachers spend less time on computational drills and more on data analysis, probability and reasoning.

In reading, the results were far less encouraging than in math.

Unlike the math results, where scores along each level of achievement rose, reading scores have remained fairly stagnant since 1992.

The share of students considered proficient in reading rose to 32 percent, from 29 percent, among both fourth and eighth graders, and the increases in the share of children with basic skills rose only modestly. . . .

Nor was there any real narrowing of the gap in reading ability between whites, blacks and Latinos at either the fourth or the eighth grades.

Among whites, 41 percent were proficient in reading in both grades, up from 35 percent in 1992. Among black students, only 13 percent in both grades were proficient readers, up from 8 percent of fourth graders, and 9 percent of eighth graders, in 1992. About 15 percent of Latino fourth and eighth graders were proficient in reading, up from 12 and 13 percent in 1992 respectively. . . .

Dr. Paige called the math results the early fruit of No Child Left Behind, saying, "These numbers represent a turning point for our nation."

But Dr. Lott of the math teachers' council said he saw little connection between the act and a trend that has held steady since the 1990's. "These standards have been out for 14 years now, and it takes 10 to 15 years to see changes take effect in education," Dr. Lott said. "It's certainly a strong indicator that what's been recommended now is working."

What do you think?

1. Students in the United States trail their counterparts in many other high-income countries in academic performance. What do you think accounts for this lower performance?
2. In your opinion, what can be done to close the performance gap between white students and minority students?

HEALTH AND MEDICINE

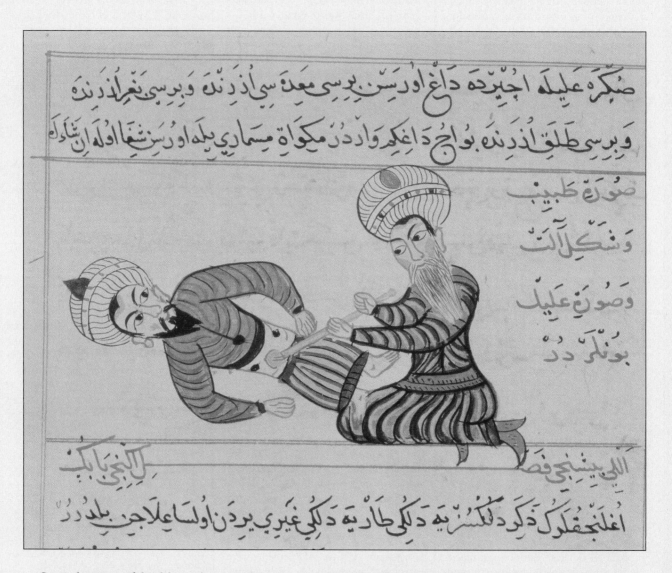

Surgical puncture of the abdominal cavity and the aspiration of peritoneal fluid with a canula on a patient suffering from dropsy

From an Ottoman translation of a surgical work by Sharaf ad-Din (vellum) by Turkish School (15th Century)
Bibliothéque Nationale, Paris, France/Bridgeman Art Library/Archives Charmet.

BRIAN, AARON, AND McLean, three middle school students in a central Ohio town, step up to the counter to order their lunch— three "value meals," one Number 4, one Number 5, and one Number 7. "Would you like to supersize that?" the young woman behind the counter asks before totaling the cost. "Sure," the boys nod together. Three sandwiches are then served with extra-large orders of French fries and extra-large soft drinks.

In a society where fast food has become something of a national dish and the term "supersize" is now used as a verb, maybe no one should be surprised that people are getting fat. Not some people. Most people. According to the experts, more than 60 percent of U.S. adults are overweight (generally defined as ten to thirty pounds over a healthy weight), including about 25 percent who are clinically obese (thirty pounds or more overweight). One recent study found that even most military personnel are overweight.

Being overweight is not just a matter of how one looks. It is a health issue, linked to higher rates of serious illness, including diabetes, heart disease, and stroke. Each year in the United States, about 300,000 people die early from diseases related to high body weight.

It is easy to dismiss being overweight as a personal flaw, as if to say that people get fat just because they eat too much. The choices we make do matter, but we are up against some powerful cultural forces. Consider the fact that the U.S. population is confronted with unhealthy fast food at every turn. Our national consumption of salty snacks (such as potato chips), soft drinks, pizza, and candy bars rises every year. And meals are simply getting bigger: The Department of Agriculture recently reported that, in 2000, the typical U.S. adult consumed 140 pounds more of food than ten years earlier. New editions of cookbooks contain recipes that used to say they would feed six but now say they will feed four (Blumenthal, 2002; Hellmich, 2002; Nash, 2002; Bellandi, 2003; Cullen, 2003).

WHAT IS HEALTH?

The World Health Organization defines **health** as *a state of complete physical, mental, and social well-being* (1946:3). This definition underscores the major

MEDIA For the Web site of the World Health Organization, go to http://www.who.org

theme of this chapter: *Health is not just a matter of personal choice, nor it is only a biological issue; patterns of well-being and illness are rooted in the organization of society.*

The profession of surgery has existed only for several centuries. Before that, barbers offered their services to the very sick, often cutting the skin to "bleed" a patient. Of course, this "treatment" was rarely effective, but it did produce plenty of bloody bandages, which practitioners hung out to dry. This practice identifies the origin of the red and white barber poles we see today.

Jan Sanders von Hemessen (c. 1504–1566), The Surgeon, oil on panel. Prado, Madrid, Spain/Giraudon/Bridgeman Art Library.

HEALTH AND SOCIETY

Society shapes people's health in four major ways:

1. **Cultural patterns define health.** Standards of health vary from place to place. A century ago, yaws, a contagious skin disease, was so common in sub-Saharan Africa that people there considered it normal (Dubos, 1980). Similarly, the U.S. Centers for Disease Control and Prevention (2000) says that, because of the rich diet common in the United States, more than 60 percent of U.S. adults are overweight. "Health," it turns out, is sometimes a matter of having the same disease as one's neighbors (Pinhey, Rubinstein, & Colfax, 1997).

   What people see as healthful also reflects what they think is morally good. Members of our society (especially men) think a competitive way of life is "healthy" because it fits our cultural mores, but it is a fact that stress contributes to heart disease and many other illnesses. On the other hand, people who object to homosexuality on moral grounds call this sexual orientation "sick," even though it is natural from a biological point of view. Thus, ideas about health serve to encourage conformity to cultural norms.

2. **Cultural standards of health change over time.** In the early twentieth century, some doctors warned that going to college might strain the female brain. Today, the majority of college students are women, and their brains are thriving. Fifty years ago, few physicians understood the dangers of cigarette smoking or too much sun exposure, practices that we now recognize as serious health risks. Even patterns of basic hygiene change over time: Whereas 75 percent of U.S. adults report bathing every day, back in 1950 only 30 percent did so (Gallup, 2000).

3. **A society's technology affects people's health.** A century ago in the United States, the three leading causes of death were all contagious diseases, as shown in Table 21–1. Today, improved living standards and advancements in medical technology have sharply reduced the number of deaths from these diseases.

   Likewise, the poor sanitation and inadequate medical resources in poor societies today explains why infectious diseases are rampant in these countries. As industrialization raises living standards, health improves. But industrial technology also creates new threats to health. As Chapter 22 ("Population, Urbanization, and Environment") explains, high-income countries threaten human health by overtaxing the world's resources and creating pollution.

4. **Social inequality affects people's health.** All societies distribute resources unequally. Overall, the rich have far better physical and mental health than the poor.

HEALTH: A GLOBAL SURVEY

Because health is closely linked to social life, we find that human well-being has improved over the long course of history as societies have developed economically. For the same reason, we see striking differences in the health of rich and poor societies today.

HEALTH IN HISTORY

With only simple technology, our ancestors could do little to improve health. Hunters and gatherers faced frequent food shortages, which sometimes forced mothers to abandon their children. Those lucky enough to survive infancy were still vulnerable to injury and illness, so half died by the age of twenty and few lived to the age of forty (Nolan & Lenski, 1999; Scupin, 2000).

As societies developed agriculture, food became more plentiful. Yet social inequality also increased, so that the elites enjoyed better health than the peasants and slaves, who lived in crowded, unsanitary shelters and often went hungry. In the growing cities of medieval Europe, human waste and other refuse piled up in the streets, spreading infectious diseases and plagues that periodically wiped out entire towns (Mumford, 1961).

HEALTH IN LOW-INCOME COUNTRIES

November 1, central India. Poverty is not just a matter of what you have; it shapes what you are. Probably most of the people we see in the villages here have never had the benefit of a doctor or a dentist. The result is easy to see: People look old before their time.

Severe poverty in much of the world cuts life expectancy far below the seventy or more years typical of rich societies. A look back at Global Map 15–2, on page 389, shows that people in most parts of Africa have a life expectancy of barely fifty, and in the poorest countries of the world, most people die before reaching their teens.

The World Health Organization reports that 1 billion people around the world—one in six—suffer from serious illness due to poverty. Bad health results not just from eating only one kind of food but, more

TABLE 21–1	The Leading Causes of Death in the United States, 1900 and 2001	
	1900	**2001**
	1. Influenza and pneumonia	1. Heart disease
	2. Tuberculosis	2. Cancer
	3. Stomach and intestinal disease	3. Stroke
	4. Heart disease	4. Lung disease (noncancerous)
	5. Cerebral hemorrhage	5. Accidents
	6. Kidney disease	6. Diabetes
	7. Accidents	7. Pneumonia and influenza
	8. Cancer	8. Alzheimer's disease
	9. Disease in early infancy	9. Kidney disease
	10. Diphtheria	10. Blood disease

Sources: Information for 1900 is from William C. Cockerham, *Medical Sociology*, 2d ed. (Englewood Cliffs, N.J.: Prentice Hall, 1986), p. 24; information for 2001 is from U.S. National Center for Health Statistics, *National Vital Statistics Report* (Hyattsville, Md.: The Center, 2003), vol. 52, no. 9 (November 7, 2003).

commonly, from simply having too little to eat. Poor sanitation and malnutrition kill people of all ages, especially children.

In impoverished countries, safe drinking water is as hard to come by as a balanced diet, and bad water carries a number of infectious diseases, including influenza, pneumonia, and tuberculosis, which are widespread killers in poor societies today. To make matters worse, medical personnel are few and far between, so that the world's poorest people—many of whom live in Central Africa—never see a physician. Global Map 21–1 on page 544 shows the availability of doctors throughout the world.

In poor nations with minimal medical care, it is no wonder that 10 percent of children die within a year of their birth. In some countries, half the children never reach adulthood—a pattern that parallels the death rates in Europe two centuries ago (George, 1977; Harrison, 1984).

In much of the world, illness and poverty form a vicious circle: Poverty breeds disease, which, in turn, undermines people's ability to work. Moreover, when medical technology does control infectious disease, the populations of poor nations rise. Without resources to ensure the well-being of the people they have now, poor societies can ill afford population increases. Thus, programs that lower death rates in poor countries will succeed only if they are coupled with programs that reduce birth rates as well.

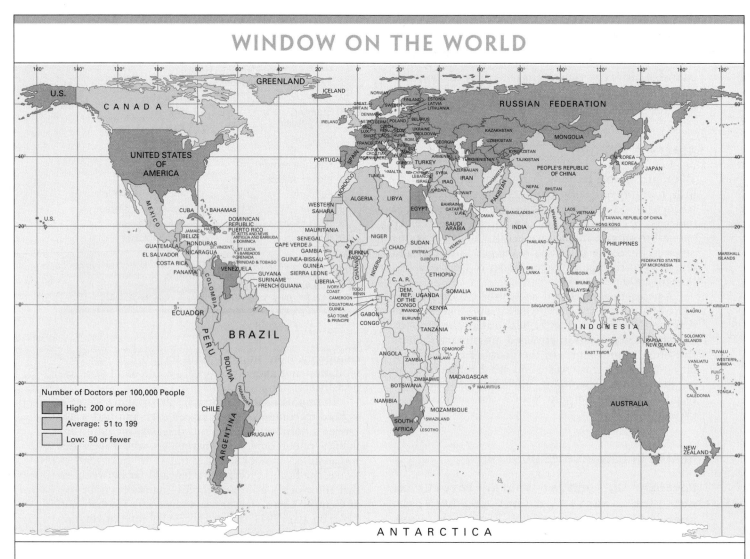

GLOBAL MAP 21–1 The Availability of Physicians in Global Perspective

Medical doctors, widely available to people in rich nations, are perilously scarce in poor societies. Although traditional forms of healing do improve health, antibiotics and vaccines—vital for controlling infectious diseases—often are in short supply. In poor countries, therefore, death rates are high, especially among infants.

Sources: United Nations Development Programme (2003) and The World Bank (2003); map projection from *Peters Atlas of the World* (1990).

HEALTH IN HIGH-INCOME COUNTRIES

Industrialization dramatically changed patterns of human health in Europe, although at first not for the better. By 1800, as the Industrial Revolution took hold, factory jobs drew people from all over the countryside. Cities quickly became overcrowded, a condition creating serious sanitation problems. Moreover, factories fouled the air with smoke, which few saw as a threat to health until well into the

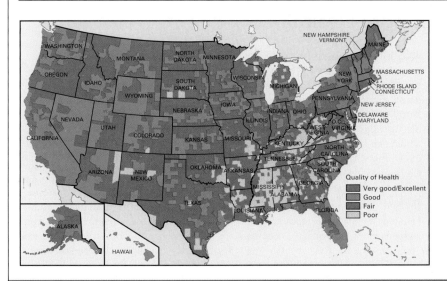

NATIONAL MAP 21–1
Health across the United States

Average health varies from place to place throughout the United States. This map shows the results of a survey that asked people across the country about their personal health, including their smoking habits, nutritional diet, and frequency of illness. Looking at the map, what pattern do you see? Can you explain it?

Source: *American Demographics* magazine, October 2000, p. 50. Reprinted with permission from *American Demographics*. © 2000 by Intertec Publishing, a Primedia Company.

Quality of Health
- Very good/Excellent
- Good
- Fair
- Poor

twentieth century. Accidents in the workplace were common.

But industrialization gradually improved health in Western Europe and North America by providing better nutrition and safer housing for most people.

For information on nutrition and health, go to http:// www.nal.usda.gov/fnic/etext/ 000056.html

After 1850, medical advances began to control infectious diseases. In 1854, for example, John Snow mapped the street addresses of London's cholera victims and found they all had drunk contaminated water from the same well (Rockett, 1994). Not long afterward, scientists linked cholera to a specific bacterium and developed a vaccine against the deadly disease. Armed with scientific knowledge, early environmentalists campaigned against age-old practices such as discharging raw sewage into the rivers used for drinking water. By the early twentieth century, death rates from infectious diseases had fallen sharply.

A glance back at Table 21–1 shows that the leading killers in 1900—influenza and pneumonia—account for just a small percentage of deaths today in the United States; it is now chronic illnesses, such as heart disease, stroke, and cancer, that cause most deaths. Nothing alters the reality of death, but industrial societies manage to delay death until old age (Edmondson, 1997a).

HEALTH IN THE UNITED STATES

Because the United States is a rich nation, health is generally good by world standards. Still, some categories of people are better off than others.

WHO IS HEALTHY? AGE, GENDER, CLASS, AND RACE

Social epidemiology is *the study of how health and disease are distributed throughout a society's population.* Just as early social epidemiologists traced the spread of epidemic diseases, researchers today examine the connection between health and our physical and social environments. National Map 21–1 surveys the health of the population of the United States, where there is a twenty-year difference in average life expectancy between the richest and poorest communities. This difference can be viewed in terms of age and sex, social class, and race.

Age and Gender

Death is now rare among young people. Still, young people do fall victim to accidents and, more recently, to acquired immune deficiency syndrome (AIDS).

Across the life course, women fare better in health than men. They have a slight biological advantage that

DIVERSITY: RACE, CLASS, AND GENDER

Masculinity: A Threat to Health?

Doctors call it "coronary-prone behavior." Psychologists call it the "Type A personality." Most everyone recognizes it as our culture's concept of masculinity. This pattern of attitudes and behavior—common among men in our society—includes (1) chronic impatience ("C'mon! Get outta my way!"); (2) uncontrolled ambition ("I've gotta have it . . . I *need* that!"); and (3) free-floating hostility ("Why are so many people *such idiots!?*").

This pattern, although normal from a cultural point of view, is one major reason that men who are driven to succeed are at high risk of heart disease. By acting out the Type A personality, we may get the job done, but we set in motion complex biochemical processes that are very hard on the human heart.

Here are a few questions to help you assess your own degree of risk (or that of someone important to you):

1. *Do you believe that a person has to be aggressive to succeed?* For

you, do "nice guys finish last"? For your heart's sake, try to remove hostility from your life. One starting point: How about eliminating profanity from your speech? Try replacing aggression with compassion, which can be surprisingly effective in dealing with other people. Medically speaking, compassion and humor—rather than irritation and aggravation—will enhance your life.

2. *How well do you handle uncertainty and opposition?* Do you have moments

when you fume "Why won't the waiter take my order?" or "Terrorists are plain nuts!" We all like to know what's going on and we like others to agree with us. But the world often doesn't work this way. Accepting uncertainty and opposition makes us more mature and certainly healthier.

3. *Are you uneasy showing positive emotion?* Many men think giving and accepting love—from women, from children, and from other men—is a sign of weakness. But the medical truth is that love supports health and anger damages it.

As human beings, we have a great deal of choice about how to live. Think about the choices you make, and reflect on how our society's idea of masculinity often makes us hard on others (including those we love) and—just as important—hard on ourselves.

Sources: Based on Friedman & Rosenman (1974) and Levine (1990).

renders them less likely than men to die before or immediately after birth. Then, as socialization begins, men become more aggressive and individualistic, which contributes to their higher rates of accidents, violence, and suicide. As the box explains, the combination of chronic impatience, uncontrolled ambition, and frequent outbursts of hostility that doctors call "coronary-prone behavior" is a fairly close match with our culture's definition of masculinity.

Social Class and Race

Infant mortality—the death rate among children under one year of age—is twice as high for disadvantaged

children as for children born to privilege. While the health of the richest children in our nation is the best in the world, our poorest children are as vulnerable as those in low-income countries such as Lebanon and Vietnam. Further, research shows that the negative effects of childhood poverty on well-being continue into adult life (Reynolds & Ross, 1998).

Researchers tell us that 78 percent of adults in families with incomes over $35,000 think their health is very good or excellent, but only 53 percent of adults in families earning less than $20,000 say the same. Conversely, only about 5 percent of higher-income people describe their health as fair or poor, compared with 19 percent of low-income people (U.S. National

Center for Health Statistics, 2003). Higher income boosts people's health in a number of obvious ways, including having better food and better health care, and living in more healthful surroundings (Robert, 1999).

Poverty among African Americans—at three times the rate among whites—helps explain why black people are more likely to die in infancy and, as adults, are more likely to suffer the effects of violence, drug abuse, and poor health (Hayward et al., 2000). Figure 21–1 shows that life expectancy of white children born in 2001 is five years greater than that of African Americans (77.7 years compared to 72.2). Gender is an even stronger predictor of health than race, since African American females outlive males of either race. From another angle, 79 percent of white men—but just 64 percent of African American men—will live to age sixty-five. The comparable figures for women are 87 percent for whites and 78 percent for African Americans.

With a higher risk of poverty, African Americans are four times as likely as whites to die of tuberculosis. Poor people of all races also suffer nutritional deficiencies. About 20 percent of the U.S. population—more than 50 million people—cannot afford a healthful diet or adequate medical care. As a result, while wealthy people can expect to die in old age of chronic illnesses such as heart disease and cancer, poor people are likely to die younger from infectious diseases such as pneumonia.

CIGARETTE SMOKING

Cigarette smoking tops the list of preventable hazards to health. Cigarettes became popular in the United States after World War I, and their popularity peaked in 1960, when almost 45 percent of U.S. adults smoked. By 2001, only 23 percent were still lighting up (U.S. Centers for Disease Control and Prevention, 2003). Quitting is difficult because cigarette smoke contains nicotine, a physically addictive drug. But people also smoke to cope with stress: Divorced and separated people are likely to smoke, as are the unemployed and people serving in the armed forces.

Generally speaking, the less schooling people have, the greater their chances of smoking. A slightly larger share of men (26 percent) than women (22 percent) smoke. But cigarettes—the only form of tobacco popular with women—have taken a toll on women's health. By 1990, lung cancer surpassed breast cancer as a cause of death among U.S. women, who now account for about 40 percent of all smoking-related deaths (Neergaard, 2001).

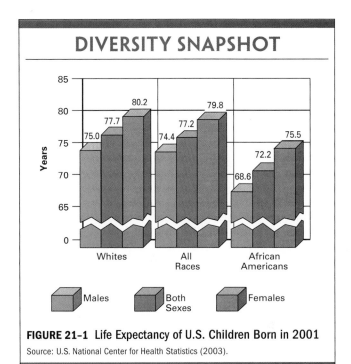

DIVERSITY SNAPSHOT

FIGURE 21-1 Life Expectancy of U.S. Children Born in 2001

Source: U.S. National Center for Health Statistics (2003).

Some 440,000 men and women in the United States die prematurely each year as a direct result of cigarette smoking, a figure that exceeds the death toll from obesity and also the death toll from alcohol, cocaine, heroin, homicide, suicide, automobile accidents, and AIDS combined (Mosley & Cowley, 1991; U.S. Centers for Disease Control and Prevention, 2003). Smokers also suffer more frequent minor illnesses such as the flu, and pregnant women who smoke increase the likelihood of spontaneous abortion and low-birthweight babies. Even nonsmokers exposed to cigarette smoke have a higher risk of smoking-related diseases.

Tobacco is a $45-billion industry in the United States. In 1997, the tobacco industry conceded that cigarette smoking is harmful to health and agreed to end marketing strategies that targeted young people. But despite the antismoking trend in the United States, smoking among college students has been creeping up, to 29 percent in 2001 (U.S. Centers for Disease Control and Precention, 2002). In addition, the use of chewing tobacco—also a threat to health—is increasing among the young.

Today, the tobacco industry is selling more products abroad, especially in low-income societies where there is less regulation of tobacco marketing and sales

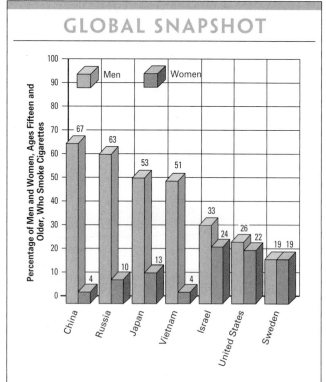

FIGURE 21-2 Cigarette Smoking in Selected Countries

Sources: U.S. Centers for Disease Control and Prevention (2003) and the World Bank (2003).

(Scherer, 1996; Pollack, 1997). Figure 21–2 shows that in many countries (especially in Asia) a large majority of men smoke. Worldwide, more than 1 billion adults (about 30 percent of the total) smoke, consuming some 6 trillion cigarettes annually, and the number is increasing. The good news is that about ten years after quitting, an ex-smoker's health is as good as that of someone who never smoked at all.

EATING DISORDERS

Being overweight is not the only way eating can harm our health. An **eating disorder** is *an intense form of dieting or other unhealthy method of weight control driven by the desire to be very thin.* One eating disorder, anorexia nervosa, is characterized by dieting to the point of starvation; another is bulimia, which involves binge eating followed by induced vomiting to prevent weight gain.

One clue that eating disorders have a cultural component is that 95 percent of people who suffer from anorexia nervosa or bulimia are women, mostly from white affluent families. For women, U.S. culture equates slenderness with being successful and attractive to men. Conversely, we tend to stereotype overweight women (and, to a lesser extent, men) as "lazy," "sloppy," and even "stupid" (Levine, 1987).

Research shows that most college-age women believe that (1) "guys like thin girls," (2) being thin is critical to physical attractiveness, and (3) they are not as thin as men would like. In fact, most college women want to be even thinner than most college men say women should be. For their part, men display much less dissatisfaction with their body shape (Fallon & Rozin, 1985).

Since few women approach our culture's unrealistic standards of beauty, many women develop a low self-image. Moreover, our idealized image of beauty leads many young women to diet to the point of risking their health. The box explains how the introduction of U.S. culture to the island of Fiji soon resulted in a notable increase in eating disorders among women.

SEXUALLY TRANSMITTED DISEASES

Sexual activity, though both pleasurable and vital to the continuation of our species, can transmit more than fifty kinds of infection called *sexually transmitted diseases* (STDs). Since our culture associates sex with sin, some people regard these diseases not only as illnesses but also as marks of immorality.

STDs grabbed national attention during the "sexual revolution" of the 1960s, when infection rates rose as people began sexual activity earlier and had a greater number of partners. As a result, STDs are an exception to the general decline of infectious diseases during the twentieth century. By the late 1980s, however, the rising dangers of STDs—especially AIDS—generated a sexual counterrevolution against casual sex (Kain, 1987; Kain & Hart, 1987; Laumann et al., 1994). The following sections briefly describe several common STDs.

Gonorrhea and Syphilis

Gonorrhea and syphilis are caused by microscopic organisms that are almost always transmitted by sexual contact. Untreated, gonorrhea causes sterility; syphilis damages major organs and can result in blindness, mental disorders, and death.

GLOBAL SOCIOLOGY

Gender and Eating Disorders: A Report from Fiji

In 1995, television came to Fiji, a small island in the South Seas of the Pacific Ocean. A single cable channel carried programming from the United States, Great Britain, and Australia. Anne Becker, a Harvard researcher specializing in eating disorders, read the news with great interest, wondering what effect the new culture being poured in via television would have on young women in Fiji.

Traditionally, Fijian culture emphasizes good nutrition and looking strong and healthy. The idea of dieting to look very thin was almost unknown. So, it is not surprising that, in 1995, Becker found just 3 percent of teenage girls reported ever vomiting to control their weight. By 1998, however, a striking change was evident in that 15 percent of teenage girls—a fivefold increase—reported this practice. Moreover, Becker found that 62 percent of girls claimed they had dieted during the previous month, and 74 percent reported feeling "too big" or "fat."

The rapid rise in eating disorders in Fiji, which Becker linked to the introduction of television, shows the power of culture to shape patterns of health.

Eating disorders, including anorexia nervosa and bulimia, are even more common in the United States, where about half of college women report engaging in such behavior. This is so even though most of these women, medically speaking, are not overweight. Indeed, Fijian women are now learning what many women in the United States already believe: "You are never too thin to feel fat."

Source: Becker (1999).

In 2001, some 362,000 cases of gonorrhea and 32,000 cases of syphilis were recorded in the United States, although the actual numbers may be several times higher. Most cases are contracted by non-Hispanic African Americans (75 percent), with lower numbers among non-Hispanic whites (16 percent), Latinos (7 percent), and Asian Americans and Native Americans (almost 2 percent) (U.S. Centers for Disease Control and Prevention, 2003).

Both gonorrhea and syphilis are easily cured by antibiotics such as penicillin. Thus, neither disease is currently a major health problem in the United States.

Genital Herpes

Genital herpes is a virus that infects as many as 50 million (one in five) people in the United States (U.S. Centers for Disease Control and Prevention, 2002). Though far less dangerous than gonorrhea and syphilis, herpes is incurable. People with genital herpes may exhibit no symptoms, or they may experience periodic, painful blisters on the genitals accompanied by fever and headache. Although not fatal to adults, women with active genital herpes can transmit the disease during vaginal delivery, and it can be deadly to a newborn. Therefore, such women typically give birth by Cesarean section (Sobel, 2001).

AIDS

The most serious of all sexually transmitted diseases is acquired immune deficiency syndrome, or AIDS. Identified in 1981, it is incurable and almost always fatal, although a few people have lived with the disease for more than twenty years. AIDS is caused by the human immunodeficiency virus (HIV), which attacks white blood cells, weakening the immune system. AIDS thus renders a person vulnerable to a wide range of other diseases that eventually cause death.

AIDS deaths dropped to 15,603 in 2001. But officials recorded 43,000 new cases in the United States that year, raising the total number of cases on record to more than 816,000. Of these, about 468,000 have died (U.S. Centers for Disease Control and Prevention, 2002).

Globally, HIV infects some 60 million people—half of them under age twenty-five—and the number is expected to continue to rise through 2010. The global AIDS death toll is 3 million each year, the total since 1981 exceeding 25 million. This means that, around the world each day, 8,000 people die of AIDS and 14,000 more are infected; about 2 percent of all deaths are in the United States. As Global Map 21–2 on page 550 shows, Africa (more specifically, countries south of the Sahara Desert) has the highest HIV infection rate

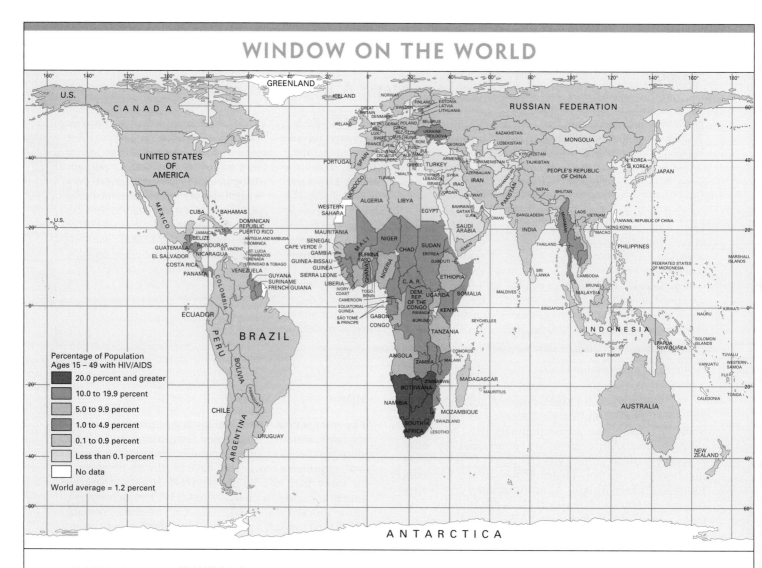

Percentage of Population Ages 15 – 49 with HIV/AIDS

- 20.0 percent and greater
- 10.0 to 19.9 percent
- 5.0 to 9.9 percent
- 1.0 to 4.9 percent
- 0.1 to 0.9 percent
- Less than 0.1 percent
- No data

World average = 1.2 percent

GLOBAL MAP 21–2 HIV/AIDS Infection of Adults in Global Perspective

Almost 70 percent of all global HIV infections are in sub-Saharan Africa. In countries such as Botswana, Swaziland, and Zimbabwe, more than one-third of people between the ages of fifteen and forty-nine are infected with HIV/AIDS. This very high infection rate reflects the prevalence of other sexually transmitted diseases and infrequent use of condoms, two factors that promote heterosexual transmission of HIV. All of Southeast Asia accounts for about 20 percent of global HIV infections. In countries such as Cambodia and Myanmar, 2 to 3 percent of people aged fifteen to forty-nine are now infected. All of North and South America taken together account for 8 percent of global HIV infections. In the United States, 0.6 percent of people aged fifteen to forty-nine are infected. The incidence of infection in Muslim nations is extremely low by world standards.

Source: Population Reference Bureau (2003); map projection from *Peters Atlas of the World* (1990).

The Nyumbani Children Center in Nairobi, Kenya, cares for young children infected with HIV. According to the World Health Organization, Kenya has about 120,000 children with HIV. Many mothers, assuming their children will die, abandon them, creating a crisis of needed care. This center is home to sixty-five children between the ages of six months and seventeen years.

and accounts for about 70 percent of global AIDS. A recent United Nations study found that, across much of sub-Saharan Africa, fifteen-year-olds face a fifty-fifty chance of becoming infected with HIV. The risk is especially high for girls, not only because HIV is transmitted more easily from men to women than vice versa but also because many African cultures encourage women to be submissive to men. According to some analysts, the AIDS crisis now threatens the political and economic security of Africa and, indeed, the entire world (Ashford, 2002; Reaney, 2002; Lamptey et al., 2002; United Nations, 2002).

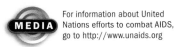 For information about United Nations efforts to combat AIDS, go to http://www.unaids.org

Upon infection, people with HIV display no symptoms at all, so most are unaware of their condition. Not for a year or longer do symptoms of HIV infection appear. Within five years, one-third of infected people in the United States develop full-blown AIDS; half develop AIDS within ten years, and most become sick within twenty years. In low-income countries, however, the progression of this illness is much more rapid, with many people dying within a few years.

HIV is infectious but not contagious. In other words, HIV is transmitted from person to person through blood, semen, vaginal secretions, and breast milk, but not through casual contact such as shaking hands, hugging, sharing towels or dishes, or swimming together, or even by coughing and sneezing. The risk of transmitting the virus through saliva (as in kissing) is extremely low. Moreover, the chance of passing HIV through sexual activity is greatly reduced by the use of latex condoms. But in the age of AIDS, abstinence or an exclusive relationship with an uninfected person is the only sure way to avoid infection through sexual contact.

Specific behaviors put people at high risk of HIV infection. The first is *anal sex*, which can cause rectal bleeding, allowing easy transmission of HIV from one person to another. The fact that many homosexual and bisexual men practice anal sex is a reason that these categories of people account for 46 percent of AIDS cases in the United States.

Sharing needles used to inject drugs is a second high-risk behavior. At present, intravenous drug users account for 25 percent of persons with AIDS. Sex with an intravenous drug user is also very risky. Because intravenous drug use is more common among poor people in the United States, AIDS is now becoming a disease of the socially disadvantaged. Minorities make up the majority of people with AIDS: African Americans (12 percent of the population) represent 38 percent of people with AIDS, and Latinos (13 percent of the population) represent 18 percent of AIDS cases. Moreover, about two-thirds of all women and children with the disease are African American or Latino. By contrast, Asian Americans and Native Americans

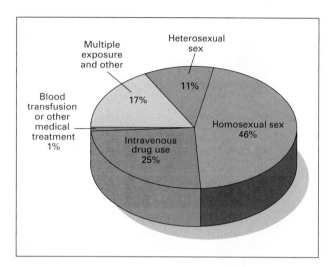

FIGURE 21–3 Types of Transmission for Reported U.S. AIDS Cases as of 2001

Source: U.S. Centers for Disease Control and Prevention (2001).

together account for only about 1 percent of people with AIDS (U.S. Centers for Disease Control and Prevention, 2002).

Using any drug, including alcohol, also increases the risk of HIV infection to the extent that it impairs one's judgment. In other words, even people who understand what places them at risk of infection may act less responsibly if they are under the influence of alcohol, marijuana, or some other drug.

As Figure 21–3 shows, only 11 percent of people with AIDS in the United States became infected through heterosexual contact (although heterosexuals, infected in various ways, account for more than 30 percent of AIDS cases). But heterosexual activity does transmit HIV, and the danger rises with the number of sexual partners, especially if they fall into high-risk categories. Worldwide, heterosexual relations are the primary means of HIV transmission, accounting for two-thirds of all infections.

In the United States, treating just one person with AIDS costs hundreds of thousands of dollars, and this figure may rise as new therapies appear. Government health programs, private insurance, and personal savings rarely cover more than a fraction of the cost of treatment. In addition, there is the mounting cost of caring for at least 75,000 U.S. children (globally, more than 13 million) orphaned by AIDS. Overall, there is little doubt that AIDS represents both a medical and a social problem of monumental proportions.

The U.S. government responded slowly to the AIDS crisis, largely because gays and intravenous drug users are widely viewed as deviant. But funds allocated for AIDS research and education have increased rapidly (now totaling some $11 billion annually), and researchers have identified some drugs, including protease inhibitors, that suppress the symptoms of the disease. But educational programs remain the most effective weapon against AIDS, since prevention is the only way to stop a disease that so far has no cure.

ETHICAL ISSUES SURROUNDING DEATH

Another social dimension of health and illness involves ethics. Now that technological advances give human beings the power to draw the line separating life and death, we must decide how and when to do so.

When Does Death Occur?

Common sense suggests that life ceases when breathing and heartbeat stop. But the ability to replace a heart and artificially sustain respiration makes such a definition of death obsolete. Medical and legal experts in the United States now define death as an *irreversible* state involving no response to stimulation, no movement or breathing, no reflexes, and no indication of brain activity (Ladd, 1979; Wall, 1980; Jones, 1998).

Do People Have a Right to Die?

Today, medical personnel, family members, and patients themselves face the agonizing burden of deciding when a terminally ill person should die. Among the most difficult cases are the roughly 10,000 people in the United States in a permanent vegetative state who cannot express their desires about life and death. Generally speaking, the first duty of physicians and hospitals is to protect a patient's life. Even so, a mentally competent person in the process of dying may refuse medical treatment and even nutrition (either at the time or, in advance, through a document called a "living will").

What about Mercy Killing?

Mercy killing is the common term for **euthanasia,** *assistance in the death of a person suffering from an incurable disease.* Euthanasia (from the Greek, meaning "a good death") poses an ethical dilemma, being at once an act of kindness and a form of killing.

Whether there is a "right to die" is one of today's most difficult issues. All people with incurable diseases have a right to forgo treatment that might prolong their lives. But whether a doctor should be allowed to help bring about death is the heart of the debate. In 1994, three states—Washington, California, and Oregon—placed before voters propositions that stated that physicians should be able to help people who wanted to die. Only Oregon's proposition passed, and the law was quickly challenged and remained tied up in state court until 1997, when Oregon voters again endorsed it. Since then, Oregon doctors have legally assisted in the death of terminally ill patients. In 1997, however, the U.S. Supreme Court decided that, under the U.S. Constitution, there is no "right to die," so the spread of such laws has been slowed. Moreover, in 1999, Congress began debating a law that would prohibit states from adopting laws similar to the one in Oregon, and in 2002, the Bush administration made unsuccessful efforts to block physician-assisted suicide in Oregon.

Supporters of *active* euthanasia—allowing a dying person to enlist the services of a physician to bring on a quick death—argue that there are circumstances (such as when a dying person suffers great pain) that make death preferable to life. Critics, however, counter that permitting active euthanasia invites abuse (see Chapter 15, "Aging and the Elderly"). They fear that patients will feel pressure to end their lives in order to spare family members the high costs of hospitalization and the burden of caring for them. Further, research in the Netherlands, where physician-assisted suicide is legal, indicates that about one-fifth of all such deaths have occurred without a patient's explicitly requesting to die (Gillon, 1999).

In the United States, a majority of adults express support for giving dying people the right to choose to die with a doctor's help (Rosenbaum, 1997; NORC, 2003). Therefore, the right-to-die debate is sure to continue.

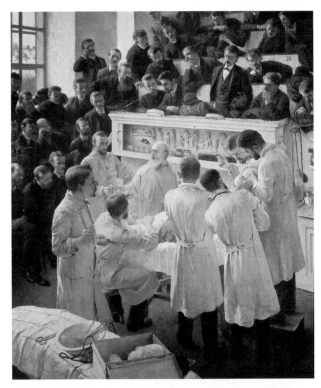

The rise of scientific medicine during the nineteenth century resulted in new skills and technology for treating many common ailments that had afflicted humanity for centuries. At the same time, however, scientific medicine pushed forms of health care involving women to the margins and placed medicine under the control of men living in cities. We see this pattern in the A. F. Seligmann painting General Hospital, *showing an obviously all-male medical school class in Vienna in 1880.*

THE MEDICAL ESTABLISHMENT

Medicine is *the social institution that focuses on combating disease and improving health.* Through most of human history, health care was entirely the responsibility of individuals and their families. Medicine emerges as a social institution only as societies become more productive and people take on specialized work.

In agrarian societies, health practitioners, including herbalists and acupuncturists, play a central part in improving health. In industrial societies, health care falls to specially trained and licensed healers, from anesthesiologists to x-ray technicians. Today's medical establishment in the United States has taken form over the last 150 years.

THE RISE OF SCIENTIFIC MEDICINE

In colonial times, doctors, herbalists, druggists, midwives, and ministers practiced the healing arts. But not all were effective: Unsanitary instruments, lack of anesthesia, and simple ignorance made surgery a terrible ordeal, and doctors probably killed as many patients as they saved.

But by studying human anatomy and physiology, doctors gradually established themselves as self-regulating professionals with medical degrees. The American Medical Association (AMA) was founded in 1847 and symbolized the growing acceptance of a scientific model of medicine.

Still, traditional approaches to health care had their defenders. The AMA opposed them by seeking control of the certification process. In the early 1900s, state licensing boards agreed to certify only physicians trained in scientific programs approved by the AMA. With control of the certification process, the AMA began closing down schools teaching other healing skills and thus limited the practice of medicine to those holding an M.D. degree. In the process, both the prestige and the income of physicians rose dramatically; today, men and women with M.D. degrees earn, on average, $200,000 annually.

Practitioners of other approaches, such as osteopathic physicians, concluded that they had no choice but to fall in line with AMA standards. Most osteopaths (with D.O. degrees), who originally manipulated the skeleton and muscles, today treat illness with drugs in much the same way as medical doctors (with M.D. degrees). Other practitioners—such as chiropractors, herbal healers, and midwives—have held to traditional roles but have been relegated to the fringe of the medical profession.

Scientific medicine, taught in expensive, urban medical schools, also changed the social profile of doctors. After the AMA standards were adopted, most physicians came from privileged backgrounds and practiced in cities. Furthermore, women, who had figured in many fields of healing, were scorned by the AMA. Some early medical schools did train women and African Americans, but faced with declining financial resources, most of these schools eventually closed. Only in recent decades has the social diversity of medical doctors increased, with women and African Americans representing 31 percent and 5 percent, respectively, of all physicians (Gordon, 1980; Starr, 1982; Huet-Cox, 1984; U.S. Department of Labor, 2003).

HOLISTIC MEDICINE

Recently in the United States, the scientific model of medicine has been tempered by the more traditional model of **holistic medicine,** *an approach to health care that emphasizes the prevention of illness and takes into account a person's entire physical and social environment.* Holistic practitioners agree on the need for drugs, surgery, artificial organs, and high technology, but they don't want technological advances to turn medicine into narrow specialties concerned with symptoms rather than people and with disease instead of health. Here are three foundations of holistic health care (Duhl, 1980; Gordon, 1980; Patterson, 1998):

1. **Patients are people.** Holistic practitioners concern themselves not only with symptoms but with how people's environment and lifestyle affect their physical, emotional, and even spiritual health. Holistic practitioners extend the bounds of conventional medicine, taking an active role in combating poverty, environmental pollution, and other dangers to public health.

2. **Responsibility, not dependency.** In the scientific model, patients are dependent on physicians. Holistic medicine tries to shift some responsibility for health from physicians to people themselves by encouraging health-promoting behavior. Holistic medicine thus favors an *active* approach to *health*, rather than a *reactive* approach to *illness*.

3. **Personal treatment.** Conventional medicine locates medical care in impersonal offices and hospitals, which are disease-centered settings. By contrast, holistic practitioners favor, as much as possible, a personal and relaxed environment such as the home.

In sum, holistic care does not oppose scientific medicine but shifts the emphasis from treating disease toward achieving the greatest well-being for everyone. Since the AMA currently recognizes more than fifty medical specialties, there is a need for practitioners who are concerned with the whole patient.

PAYING FOR MEDICAL CARE: A GLOBAL SURVEY

As medicine has come to rely on high technology, the costs of health care have skyrocketed. To meet these costs, countries have adopted various strategies.

Medicine in Socialist Societies

In societies with mostly socialist economies, government provides medical care directly to the people. These nations hold that all citizens have the right to basic medical care. In practice, then, people do not pay physicians and hospitals directly; instead, the government uses public funds to pay medical costs. The state owns and operates medical facilities and pays salaries to practitioners, who are government employees.

The People's Republic of China. The People's Republic of China faces the daunting task of providing for the health of more than 1 billion people. China has experimented with private medicine, but the government controls most health care.

China's famed "barefoot doctors," roughly comparable to U.S. paramedics, bring some modern methods of medical care to millions of peasants in rural villages. Otherwise, traditional healing arts, including acupuncture and the use of medicinal herbs, are still widely practiced in China. In addition, the Chinese approach to health is based on a holistic concern for the interplay of mind and body (Sidel & Sidel, 1982b; Kaptchuk, 1985).

The Russian Federation. The Russian Federation is transforming a state-dominated economy into more of a market system. For this reason, medical care is in transition. Nonetheless, the idea that everyone has a right to basic medical care remains widespread.

As in China, people do not choose a physician but report to a local government-operated health facility. Physicians in the Russian Federation have lower income than their counterparts in the United States, earning about the same salary as skilled industrial workers (compared to roughly a five-to-one ratio in this country). Worth noting, too, is that about 70 percent of Russian physicians are women, compared to 31 percent in the United States. As in our society, occupations dominated by women yield fewer financial rewards.

In recent years, the Russian Federation has suffered setbacks in health care, partly because of a falling standard of living, as the box on page 556 explains. Moreover, a rising demand for medical care has strained a bureaucratic system that, at best, provides highly standardized and impersonal care. The optimistic view is that, as market reforms proceed, both living standards and the quality of medical services will improve. In any case, what does seem certain is that disparities in the medical care among various segments of the Russian population will increase (Specter, 1995; Landsberg, 1998).

Medicine in Capitalist Societies

People living in nations with mostly capitalist economies usually pay for their own health care.

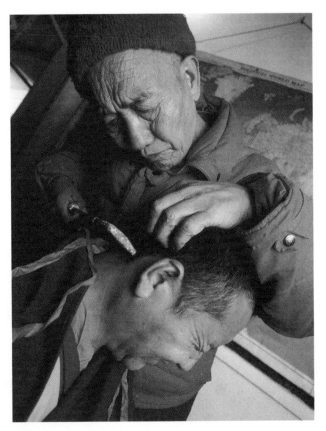

Traditional healers work to improve people's health throughout the world, especially in low-income nations. Here, a Chinese practitioner treats a patient by burning rolled herbs into his scalp.

However, because high cost puts medical care beyond the reach of many people, government programs underwrite a considerable share of the expense.

Sweden. In 1891, Sweden instituted a compulsory, comprehensive system of government medical care. Citizens pay for this program with their taxes, which are among the highest in the world. Typically, physicians are government employees, and most hospitals are government-managed. Because this medical system resembles that found in socialist societies, Sweden's system is called **socialized medicine**, *a medical care system in which the government owns and operates most medical facilities and employs most physicians.*

Great Britain. In 1948, Great Britain, too, established socialized medicine. The British did not do away with

When Health Fails: A Report from Russia

Night is falling in Pitkyaranta, a small town on the western edge of Russia, near the Finnish border. Andrei, a thirty-year-old man with a round face and a long ponytail, weaves his way through the deepening shadows along a busy street. He has spent much of the afternoon in a bar with friends watching music videos, smoking cigarettes, and drinking vodka. Andrei is a railroad worker, but several months ago he was laid off. "Now," he explains bitterly, "I have nothing to do but drink and smoke." Andrei shrugs off a question about his health. "The only thing I care about is finding a job. I am a grown man. I don't want to be supported by my mother and father." Andrei still thinks of himself as young, yet, according to current health patterns in Russia, for a man of thirty life is half over.

After the collapse of the Soviet Union in 1991, living conditions worsened every year. One result, say doctors, is massive stress—especially on men who earn too little to support their families or are out of work entirely. Few

people eat well anymore, and Russian men now drink and smoke heavily. The World Health Organization reports that alcohol abuse is Russia's number one killer, with cigarette smoking not far behind.

In towns like Pitkyaranta, signs of poor health are everywhere: Women no longer breast-feed their babies, adults suffer higher rates of accidents and illness, and people look old before their time. Doctors work to stop the health slide, but with poorly equipped hospitals, they are simply overwhelmed. Statistically, while life expectancy has dropped several years for women, it has gone into free fall for men and now stands at just fifty-nine years, about where it was half a century ago. Just 100 miles to the west in Finland—where economic trends are far better—the comparable figure is seventy-five years. In a global context, the life expectancy for Russian women has fallen below that in rich countries to the west; for Russian men, life expectancy is now the same as in some of the world's lowest-income nations.

Among young Russian men like Andrei, a joke is making the rounds. Their health may be failing, they say, but this cloud has a silver lining: At least they no longer have to worry about retirement.

Source: Adapted from Landsberg (1998).

---

private care, however; instead, they created a "dual system" of medical service. All British citizens are entitled to medical care provided by the National Health Service, but those who can afford to may purchase more extensive care from doctors and hospitals that operate privately.

Canada. Since 1972, Canada has had a "single-payer" model of health care that provides care to all Canadians. Like a vast insurance company, the Canadian government pays doctors and hospitals according to a set schedule of fees. But Canada also has a two-tiered system similar to Great Britain's, with some physicians

working outside the government-funded system and setting fees, although these are regulated by the government.

Canada boasts of providing care for everyone at a lower cost than the (nonuniversal) medical system in the United States. However, the Canadian system uses less state-of-the-art technology and responds slowly to people's needs, so that people may wait months to receive major surgery. At the same time, Canadians point out that lower-income people are not denied medical care as is often the case in the United States (Grant, 1984; Vayda & Deber, 1984; Rosenthal, 1991; Macionis & Gerber, 2002).

July 31, Montreal, Canada. I am visiting the home of an oral surgeon who
appears (judging by the large home)
to be doing pretty well. Yet he com-
plains that the Canadian government,
in an effort to hold down medical
costs, caps doctors' salaries at
about $125,000 (U.S.). Therefore,
he explains, many specialists have
left for the United States, where
they can earn much more; other doctors and dentists simply limit their
practice.

Japan. Physicians in Japan have private practices, but a combination of government programs and private insurance pays medical costs. As shown in Figure 21–4, the Japanese approach health care much as the Europeans do, with most medical expenses paid through government.

PAYING FOR MEDICAL CARE: THE UNITED STATES

With our primarily private system of medical care, the United States stands alone among industrialized nations in not having a government-sponsored medical system that provides care for every citizen. Called a **direct-fee system,** ours is *a medical care system in which patients pay directly for the services of physicians and hospitals.* Thus, while Europeans look to government to fund about 80 percent of their medical costs (paid for through taxation), the U.S. government pays less than 50 percent of this country's medical costs (Lohr, 1988; U.S. Census Bureau, 2002).

The government report Healthy People 2010 is found at http://www.cdc.gov/nchs/hphome.htm

In the United States, rich people can purchase the best medical care in the world. Yet the poor fare worse than their counterparts in Europe. This disparity explains the relatively high death rates among both infants and adults in the United States compared to those in many European countries (United Nations Development Programme, 2003).

Why does the United States have no national health care program? First, our society historically has limited government in the interest of greater personal liberty. Second, political support for a national medical program has not been strong, even among labor unions, which have concentrated on winning health

care benefits from employers. Third, the AMA and the health insurance industry have strongly and consistently opposed national health care proposals (Starr, 1982).

Expenditures for medical care in the United States increased dramatically from $12 billion in 1950 to more than $1 trillion in 2002. This sum amounts to more than $4,000 per person, which is more than any other nation in the world spends for medical care. Who pays the medical bills?

Private insurance programs. In 2002, 175 million people (61 percent) received some medical care benefits from a family member's employer or labor union. Another 27 million people (9 percent) purchased private coverage on their own. Of our population, then, 70 percent have private insurance, although few such programs pay all medical costs (U.S. Census Bureau, 2003).

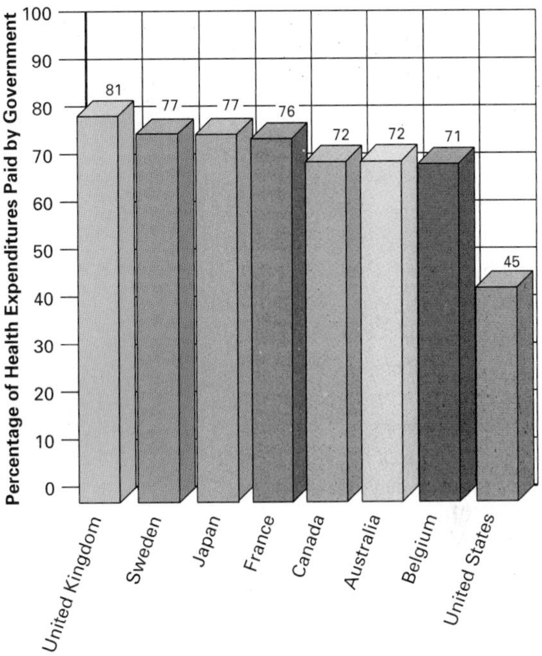

FIGURE 21-4 Extent of Socialized Medicine in Selected Countries

Sources: U.S. Census Bureau (2002) and The World Bank (2003).

Percentage of Health Expenditures Paid by Government

United Kingdom 81
Sweden 77
Japan 77
France 76
Canada 72
Australia 72
Belgium 71
United States 45

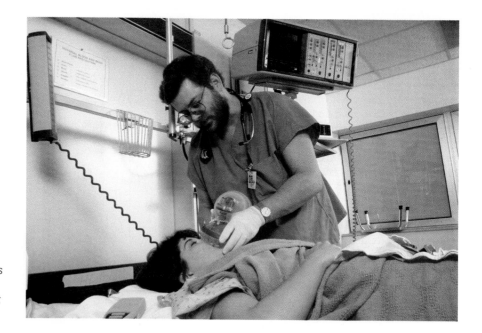

Throughout the United States, there is a serious shortage of nurses. One strategy for filling the need is for nursing programs to recruit more men into this profession; currently, men account for only 6 percent of nurses with R.N. degrees.

Public insurance programs. In 1965, Congress created Medicare and Medicaid. Medicare pays a portion of the medical costs of men and women over sixty-five; in 2002, it covered 38 million women and men, 13 percent of the population. During the same year, Medicaid, a medical insurance program for the poor, provided benefits to 33 million people, about 12 percent of the population. An additional 10 million veterans (4 percent of the population) can obtain free care in government-operated hospitals. In all, 26 percent of people in the United States enjoy some medical care benefits from the government, but most also have private insurance.

Health maintenance organizations. About 80 million people (28 percent) in the United States belong to a **health maintenance organization (HMO),** *an organization that provides comprehensive medical care to subscribers for a fixed fee.* HMOs vary in their costs and benefits, and none provides full coverage. Fixed fees make these organizations profitable to the extent that their subscribers stay healthy; therefore, many take a preventive approach to health. At the same time, HMOs have come under fire for refusing to pay for medical procedures that they consider unnecessary. Therefore, Congress is currently debating the extent to which patients can sue HMOs in order to obtain better care.

In all, 85 percent of the U.S. population has some medical care coverage, either private or public. Yet most plans do not provide full coverage, so serious illness threatens even middle-class people with financial hardship. Most programs also exclude certain medical services, such as dental care and treatment for mental health and substance abuse problems. Worse, more than 43 million people (about 15 percent of the population) have no medical insurance at all, even though 80 percent of these people are working. Almost as many lose their medical coverage temporarily each year due to layoffs or job changes. Some of these people choose to forgo medical coverage (especially young people who take good health for granted), but most are part-time or full-time workers who receive no health care benefits. As a result, many low- and moderate-income people cannot afford to become ill and cannot afford to pay for the preventive medical care they need to remain healthy (Hersch & White-Means, 1993; Smith, 1993; Brink, 2002; U.S. Census Bureau, 2003).

THE NURSING SHORTAGE

Another issue in medical care is the shortage of nurses across the United States. In 2002, there were some 1.9 million nurses (people with the degree of R.N., registered nurse), but about 11 percent of the available jobs (roughly 200,000 positions) are currently unfilled.

The immediate cause of the shortage is that fewer people are entering the nursing profession. During the last decade, enrollments in nursing programs have dropped by one-third, even as the need for nurses (driven by the aging of the U.S. population) goes up. Why this decline? One factor is that today's young women have a wide range of occupational choices, and fewer are drawn to the traditionally female occupation of nursing. This fact is evident in the rising median age of working nurses, which is now forty-three. Another is that many  of today's nurses are unhappy with their working conditions, citing heavy patient loads, too much required overtime, a stressful working environment, and a lack of recognition and respect from supervisors, physicians, and hospital managers. In fact, one recent survey found that a majority of working nurses say they would not recommend the field to others, and more R.N.s are leaving the field for other jobs.

A hopeful sign is that the nursing shortage is bringing change to this profession. Salaries, which range from about $45,000 for general-duty nurses to $100,000 for certified nurse anesthetists, are rising, although slowly. Some hospitals and physicians are also offering signing bonuses in efforts to attract new nurses. In addition, nursing programs are trying harder to recruit a more diverse population, seeking more minorities (which are currently underrepresented) and, especially, more men (who now make up only 6 percent of R.N.s) (DeFrancis, 2002a, 2002b; Dworkin, 2002; Yin, 2002).

THEORETICAL ANALYSIS OF HEALTH AND MEDICINE

Each of the major theoretical paradigms in sociology helps us organize and interpret facts and issues concerning human health.

STRUCTURAL-FUNCTIONAL ANALYSIS

Talcott Parsons (1964; orig. 1951) viewed medicine as society's strategy to keep its members healthy. In this scheme, illness is dysfunctional because it undermines people's abilities to perform their roles.

The Sick Role

Society responds to sickness not only by providing medical care, but also by affording people a **sick role,** *patterns of behavior defined as appropriate for people who are ill.* According to Parsons, the sick role has three characteristics:

1. **Illness exempts people from routine responsibilities.** Serious illness relaxes or suspends normal obligations such as going to work or attending school. To prevent abuse of this privilege, however, people cannot simply say they are ill; they must enlist the support of others—especially a recognized medical expert—before assuming the sick role.

2. **A sick person must want to be well.** We assume that no one wants to be sick, and we withdraw the benefits of the sick role when someone pretends to be sick to avoid responsibility or to get attention.

3. **A sick person must seek competent help.** People who are ill must seek out and cooperate with health care practitioners. By failing to get medical help or to follow doctor's orders, a person risks losing the benefits of the sick role.

The Physician's Role

Physicians evaluate people's claims of sickness and try to restore the sick to normal routines. To do this, physicians use their specialized knowledge. Physicians expect patients to cooperate with them, providing necessary information and following the doctor's orders to complete the treatment.

Critical evaluation. Parsons's analysis links illness and medicine to the broader organization of society. Others have usefully extended the concept of the sick role to some nonillness situations such as pregnancy (Myers & Grasmick, 1989).

One limitation of the sick-role concept is that it applies to acute conditions (like the flu or a broken leg) better than to chronic illnesses (like heart disease), which may not be reversible. In addition, a sick person's ability to take time off from work to regain health depends on the available resources; many working poor, for example, cannot afford to assume a sick role (Ehrenreich, 2001). Then, too, illness can have some positive consequences: Many people who experience serious illness report reevaluating their lives and gaining a better sense of what is truly important (Myers, 2001).

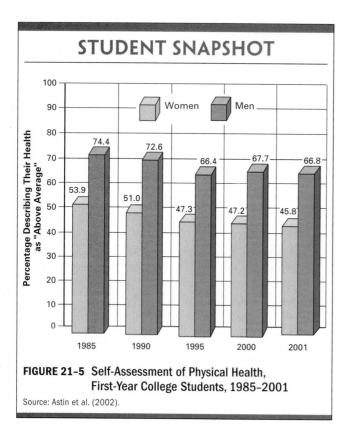

STUDENT SNAPSHOT

FIGURE 21-5 Self-Assessment of Physical Health, First-Year College Students, 1985–2001

Source: Astin et al. (2002).

How we respond to illness, too, is based on social definitions that may or may not square with medical facts. For instance, people with AIDS contend with fear and sometimes outright bigotry that has no medical basis. Likewise, students may pay no attention to signs of illness on the eve of a vacation but may dutifully report to the infirmary hours before a midterm examination. Health, in short, is less an objective commodity than a negotiated outcome.

Indeed, how people define a medical situation may actually affect how they feel. Medical experts marvel at *psychosomatic* disorders (a fusion of Greek words for "mind" and "body"), when state of mind guides physical sensations (Hamrick, Anspaugh, & Ezell, 1986). Applying sociologist W. I. Thomas's theorem (1931), we can say that when health or illness is defined as real, it becomes real in its consequences.

The Social Construction of Treatment

In Chapter 6 ("Social Interaction in Everyday Life"), we used Erving Goffman's dramaturgical approach to explain how physicians tailor their physical surroundings ("the office") and their behavior ("the presentation of self") so that others see them as competent and in charge.

Sociologist Joan Emerson (1970) further illustrates this process of constructing reality in her analysis of the gynecological examination carried out by a male doctor. This situation is vulnerable to serious misinterpretation, since a man's touching of a woman's genitals is conventionally viewed as a sexual act and possibly an assault.

To ensure that people define the situation as impersonal and professional, the medical staff wear uniforms and furnish the examination room with nothing but medical equipment. The doctor's manner and overall performance are designed to make the patient feel that, to him, examining the genital area is no different from treating any other part of the body. A female nurse is usually present during the examination, not only to assist the physician but to dispel any impression that a man and a woman are "alone together."

Managing situational definitions in this way is only rarely taught in medical schools. The oversight is unfortunate because, as Emerson's analysis shows, understanding how people construct reality in the examination room is as important as mastering the medical skills required for treatment.

Critical evaluation. A strength of the symbolic-interaction paradigm lies in revealing that what people

Finally, critics point out that Parsons's analysis gives doctors—rather than people themselves—the primary responsibility for health. A more prevention-oriented approach makes physicians and patients equal partners in the pursuit of health.

SYMBOLIC-INTERACTION ANALYSIS

According to the symbolic-interaction paradigm, society is less a grand system than a series of complex and changing realities. Therefore, health and medical care are socially constructed by people in everyday interaction.

The Social Construction of Illness

If we socially construct our ideas of health and illness, it follows that members of a very poor society may view hunger and malnutrition as normal. Similarly, people in rich nations, such as our own, may give little thought to the harmful effects of a rich diet.

Despite the efforts of exemplary physicians such as Dr. Joe Greer, homeless people throughout the United States have a great need for medical support but receive little health care. In your opinion, what changes are needed to meet the needs of society's most vulnerable members?

view as healthful or harmful depends on numerous factors, many of which are not, strictly speaking, medical. This approach also shows that in any medical procedure, both patient and medical staff engage in a subtle process of reality construction.

Critics fault this approach, however, for implying that there are no objective standards of well-being. Certain physical conditions do indeed cause definite changes in people, regardless of how we view those conditions. People who lack sufficient nutrition and safe water, for example, suffer from their unhealthy environment, whether they define their surroundings as normal or not.

Figure 21–5 shows that, since 1985, the share of first-year college students in the United States who characterize their physical health as "above average" has been dropping. Do you think this trend reflects just changing perceptions or a real decline in health (due, say, to eating more unhealthy food)? Why do you think more men than women see their health as above average?

SOCIAL-CONFLICT ANALYSIS

Social-conflict analysis draws a connection between health and social inequality and, taking a cue from Karl Marx, ties medicine to the operation of capitalism. Researchers have focused on three main issues:

access to medical care, the effects of the profit motive, and the politics of medicine.

Access to Care

Health is important to everyone. Yet, by making health a commodity, capitalist societies allow health to follow wealth. The access problem is more serious in the United States than in other industrialized nations because our country has no universal medical care system.

Conflict theorists concede that capitalism provides excellent health care for the rich, but not for much of the population. At greatest risk are the 43 million people who lack health care coverage and cannot afford the cost of treating a serious illness.

The Profit Motive

Some conflict analysts go further, arguing that the real problem is not access to medical care but the character of capitalist medicine itself. The profit motive turns physicians, hospitals, and the pharmaceutical industry into multibillion-dollar corporations. The quest for higher profits encourages unnecessary tests and surgery as well as an overreliance on drugs (Ehrenreich, 1978; Kaplan et al., 1985).

Of some 24 million surgical operations performed in the United States each year, three-fourths

CONTROVERSY & DEBATE

The Genetic Crystal Ball: Do We Really Want to Look?

The liquid in the laboratory test tube seems ordinary enough, rather like a syrupy form of water. But this liquid is one of the greatest medical breakthroughs of all time; it may even hold the key to life itself. The liquid is deoxyribonucleic acid, or DNA, the spiraling molecule found in cells of the human body that contains the blueprint for making each one of us human as well as different from every other person.

The human body is composed of some 100 trillion cells, most of which contain a nucleus of twenty-three pairs of chromosomes (one of each pair comes from each parent). Each chromosome is packed with DNA, in segments called genes. Genes guide the production of protein, the building block of the human body.

If genetics sounds complicated (and it is), the social implications of genetic knowledge are even more complex. Scientists discovered the structure of the DNA molecule in 1952, and in recent years they have made great gains in "mapping" our genetic landscape. Doing this may lead to understanding how each bit of DNA shapes our being. But do we really want to unlock the secrets of life itself?

In the Human Genome Project, many scientists see a chance to stop illness before it begins. Research already has identified genetic abnormalities that cause sickle cell anemia, muscular dystrophy, Huntington's disease, cystic fibrosis, some forms of cancer, and other crippling and deadly afflictions. During this century, genetic screening—a scientific "crystal ball"—could let people know their medical destiny and allow doctors to manipulate segments of DNA to prevent diseases before they appear.

But many people urge caution in such research, warning that genetic information could easily be abused. At its worst, genetic mapping opens the door to Nazi-like efforts to breed a "superrace." Indeed, in 1994, the People's Republic of China began to regulate marriage and childbirth to prevent "new births of inferior quality."

It seems inevitable that some parents will want to use genetic testing to

are "elective"; that is, they promote long-term health but are not prompted by a medical emergency. In addition, of course, any medical procedure or use of drugs is risky and results in harm to between 5 and 10 percent of patients. Worse still, at least 50,000 patients die each year from poor treatment within the current medical system. Therefore, social-conflict theorists contend that surgery is too closely tied to the financial interests of surgeons and hospitals and too often ignores the medical needs of patients (Illich, 1976; Sidel & Sidel, 1982a; Cowley, 1995; Nuland, 1999).

Finally, say social-conflict analysts, our society is all too tolerant of physicians having a direct financial interest in the tests and procedures they order for their patients (Pear & Eckholm, 1991). Health care should be motivated by a concern for people, not profits.

Medicine as Politics

Although science declares itself politically neutral, scientific medicine frequently takes sides on significant social issues. For example, the medical establishment opposes government regulation of fees and services and has always campaigned against proposals for government health care programs. Moreover, the history of medicine itself shows how racial and sexual discrimination has been supported by "scientific" opinions (Leavitt, 1984). Consider the diagnosis of "hysteria," a term that has its origins in the Greek word *hyster,* meaning "uterus." In choosing this word to describe a wild, emotional state, the medical profession suggested that being a woman is somehow the same as being irrational.

Even today, according to conflict theory, scientific medicine explains illness exclusively in terms of bacteria and viruses and ignores the ways in which poverty threatens people's health. In effect, scientific medicine depoliticizes health by reducing social issues to simple biology.

Critical evaluation. Social-conflict analysis provides still another view of the relationships among health, medicine, and society. According to this paradigm,

evaluate the health (or even the eye and hair color) of their future child. What if they want to abort a fetus because it falls short of their standards? Or as genetic manipulations become ever more possible, should parents be permitted to create "designer children"?

Then there is the issue of "genetic privacy": Can a prospective spouse request a genetic evaluation of her fiancé before agreeing to marry? Can life insurance companies demand genetic testing before issuing policies? Can an employer screen job applicants to weed out those whose future illnesses might drain health care funds? Clearly, what is scientifically possible is not always morally desirable. Society is already grappling with questions about the proper use of

our expanding knowledge about human genetics. Such ethical dilemmas will

Scientists are learning more and more about the genetic factors that prompt the eventual development of serious diseases. If offered the opportunity, would you want to undergo a genetic screening that would predict the long-term future of your own health?

only mount as genetic research moves forward in the years to come.

Continue the debate . . .

1. Traditional wedding vows join couples "in sickness and in health." Do you think individuals have a right to know the future health of their potential partner before tying the knot?

2. What about the desire of some parents to genetically design their children?

3. Is it right that private companies doing genetic research are able to patent their work so that they can control (and profit from) the results?

Sources: Nash (1995), D. Thompson (1999), and Golden & Lemonick (2000).

social inequality is the reason some people have better health than others.

The most common objection to the conflict approach is that it minimizes the gains in U.S. health brought about by scientific medicine and higher living standards. Though there is plenty of room for improvement, health indicators for our population as a whole rose steadily over the course of the twentieth century and compare well with those of other industrial nations.

In sum, sociology's three major theoretical paradigms convincingly argue that health and medicine are social issues. Indeed, as the final box explains, advancing technology is making it more and more true as time goes on. The renowned French scientist Louis Pasteur (1822–1895), who spent much of his life studying how bacteria cause disease, said just before he died that health depends less on bacteria than on the social environment in which the bacteria are found (Gordon, 1980:7). Explaining Pasteur's insight is sociology's contribution to human health.

LOOKING AHEAD: HEALTH AND MEDICINE IN THE TWENTY-FIRST CENTURY

At the beginning of the twentieth century, deaths from infectious diseases like diphtheria and measles were widespread, and scientists had yet to develop penicillin and other antibiotics. Even a simple infection from a minor wound was sometimes life-threatening. Today, a century later, most members of U.S. society take good health and long life for granted. It seems reasonable to expect the improvements in U.S. health to continue throughout the twenty-first century.

Another encouraging trend is that more people are taking responsibility for their own health (Caplow et al., 1991). Every one of us can live better and longer if we avoid tobacco, eat healthful meals in moderation, and exercise regularly.

Yet health problems will continue to plague U.S. society in the decades to come. The biggest problem, discussed throughout this chapter, is this nation's double standard in health: more well-being for the rich and higher rates of disease for the poor. International comparisons reveal that the United States lags in many measures of human health because we neglect those at the margins of our society. An important question for this new century, then, is how a rich society can afford to let millions of people live without the security of medical care.

 For a World Health Organization report on the health habits of young people in twenty-eight countries, including the United States, go to http://www.ruhbc.ed.ac.uk/hbsc/download/hbsc.pdf

Finally, we find that health problems are far greater in low-income nations than they are in the United States. The good news is that life expectancy for the world as a whole has been on the rise—from forty-eight years in 1950 to sixty-seven years today—and the biggest gains have been made in poor countries (Population Reference Bureau, 2003). But in much of Latin America, Asia, and especially Africa, hundreds of millions of adults and children lack not only medical attention but also adequate food and safe drinking water. Improving the health of the world's poorest people is a critical challenge in the twenty-first century.

SUMMARY

1. Health is a social issue because personal well-being depends on a society's technology as well as its distribution of resources. Culture shapes definitions of health and patterns of health care.

2. Historically, human health was poor by today's standards. Health improved dramatically in Western Europe and North America in the nineteenth century, first because of industrialization and later because of medical advances.

3. Poor nations suffer from inadequate sanitation, hunger, and other problems linked to poverty. Life expectancy is about twenty years less than in the United States; in the poorest nations, half the children do not survive to adulthood.

4. Infectious diseases were leading killers a century ago. Today, most people in the United States die in old age of chronic illnesses such as heart disease, cancer, or stroke.

5. More than three-fourths of U.S. children born today will live to at least age sixty-five. Throughout the life course, women have better health than men, and people of high social position enjoy better health than the poor.

6. Cigarette smoking is the greatest preventable cause of death in the United States.

7. The incidence of sexually transmitted diseases has risen since 1960, an exception to the general decline in infectious disease.

8. Advancing medical technology presents ethical dilemmas concerning how and when death should occur.

9. Historically a family concern, health care is now the responsibility of trained specialists. The model of scientific medicine underlies the U.S. medical establishment.

10. The holistic approach seeks to give people greater responsibility for their own health.

11. Socialist societies define medical care as a right that governments offer equally to everyone. Capitalist societies view medical care as a commodity to be purchased, although most capitalist governments support medical care through socialized medicine or national health insurance.

12. The United States, with a direct-fee system, is the only high-income nation with no comprehensive medical care program. Most people have private or government health insurance. About 43 million people in the United States do not have medical insurance.

13. A major part of the structural-functional analysis of health is the sick role, which excuses the ill person from routine social responsibilities.

14. The symbolic-interaction paradigm investigates how health and medical treatments are largely matters of socially constructed definitions.

15. Social-conflict analysis focuses on the unequal distribution of health and medical care. It criticizes the U.S. medical establishment for its overreliance on drugs and surgery, its giving free rein to the profit motive in medicine, and its overemphasis on the biological rather than the social causes of illness.

KEY CONCEPTS

health (p. 541) a state of complete physical, mental, and social well-being

social epidemiology (p. 545) the study of how health and disease are distributed throughout a society's population

eating disorder (p. 548) an intense form of dieting or other unhealthy method of weight control driven by the desire to be very thin

euthanasia (mercy killing) (p. 552) assistance in the death of a person suffering from an incurable disease

medicine (p. 553) the social institution that focuses on combating disease and improving health

holistic medicine (p. 554) an approach to health care that emphasizes the prevention of illness and takes into account a person's entire physical and social environment

socialized medicine (p. 555) a medical care system in which the government owns and operates most medical facilities and employs most physicians

direct-fee system (p. 557) a medical care system in which patients pay directly for the services of physicians and hospitals

health maintenance organization (HMO) (p. 558) an organization that provides comprehensive medical care to subscribers for a fixed fee

sick role (p. 559) patterns of behavior defined as appropriate for people who are ill

CRITICAL-THINKING QUESTIONS

1. Why is health as much a social as a biological issue?

2. Which diseases are widespread killers in low-income nations? Which diseases are the leading killers in high-income countries such as the United States?

3. In what ways can people take responsibility for their own health? In what ways can a society improve the health of the population?

4. Should the United States follow the lead of other high-income countries and enact a government program of health care for everyone? Why or why not?

APPLICATIONS AND EXERCISES

1. In most communities, a trip to the local courthouse or city hall is all it takes to find public records showing people's cause of death. Compare such records for people a century ago with those in recent years. What patterns emerge in life expectancy? How do causes of death differ?

2. Is there a medical school on or near your campus? If so, obtain a course catalogue and see how much (if any) of the medical curriculum highlights the social dimensions of health care.

3. Arrange to speak with midwives (many list their services in the Yellow Pages) about their work helping women bear their babies. How do midwives differ from medical obstetricians in their approach?

4. Packaged in the back of this new textbook is an interactive CD-ROM that offers a variety of video and interactive review materials intended to help you better understand the material covered in this chapter. For this chapter, the CD-ROM contains a relevant clip from *ABC News*, an author's tip video, interactive map animations, an interactive time line, and flashcards with audio pronunciations of the more difficult words.

SITES TO SEE

http://www.prenhall.com/macionis

Visit the interactive Companion Website™ that accompanies this text. Begin by clicking on the cover of your book. You will find a chapter-by-chapter study guide, practice tests, suggested Web links, and links to other relevant material.

http://www.cdc.gov

Visit the Web site for the Centers for Disease Control and Prevention. Here you will find information about this organization, health news, statistical data, and even travelers' health advisories. This site offers considerable evidence of the social dimensions of health.

http://www3.who.int/whosis/menu.cfm

Visit the World Health Organization's Statistical Information System to find basic health indicators for many of the world's nations, as well as data profiling the health of the U.S. population.

http://www.aegis.org/
http://www.nlm.nih.gov/

These sites provide a enormous database of articles and information concerning HIV and AIDS.

http://www.doctorsoftheworld.org
http://www.imc-la.org
http://www.dwb.org

Here are Web sites for several organizations of physicians involved in improving health around the world. The first is operated by Doctors of the World; the second presents the International Medical Corps; and the third profiles Doctors without Borders.

INVESTIGATE WITH RESEARCH NAVIGATOR™

Follow the instructions on page 24 of this text to access the features of **Research Navigator™**. Once at the Web site, enter your Login Name and Password. Then, to use the **Content Select™** database, enter keywords such as "holistic medicine," "AIDS," "cigarette smoking," and "euthanasia," and the search engine will supply relevant and recent scholarly and popular press publications. Use the *New York Times* **Search-by-Subject Archive** to find recent news articles related to sociology and the **Link Library** feature to find relevant Web links organized by the key terms associated with this chapter.

The New York Times
In the Times

October 22, 2002

Good and Bad Marriage, Boon and Bane to Health

By SHARON LERNER

In the early 1970's, demographers began to notice a strange pattern in life span data: married people tended to live longer than their single, divorced and widowed counterparts.

The so-called marriage benefit persists today, with married people generally less likely to have surgery and to die from all causes, including stroke, pneumonia and accidents. At its widest, the gap is striking, with middle-aged men in most developed countries about twice as likely to die if they are unmarried.

Many have argued that the difference in life expectancy is . . . because healthier people are more likely to marry. But an emerging group of marriage advocates has put a spotlight on the medical potential of the institution. . . .

But even as marriage is being packaged as a boon to health, there is a new caveat. While people in good, stable partnerships do, on average, have less disease and later death, mounting evidence suggests that those in strained and unhappy relationships tend to fare worse medically. . . .

Men and women who reported low-quality marriages had more gum disease and cavities than happily married people. Two studies found marital strain to be linked to ulcers in the stomach and intestine. And people's satisfaction with their relationships appears to alter how they experience pain.

Some of these physical effects seem to be direct results of behavior. . . . [A]ccording to Dr. James Coyne, a professor of psychiatry at the University of Pennsylvania, who has studied the effects of marital quality on recovery from congestive heart failure, a good marriage can give a person a reason to stay alive. . . .

In contrast, he said, a bad marriage can be worse than none at all. . . . [A]ccording to Dr. Coyne's study, published last year in *The American Journal of Cardiology* . . . the quality of patients' marriages predicted their recoveries as well as the pumping ability of their hearts.

According to Dr. Janice Kiecolt-Glaser, a professor of psychiatry at Ohio State University, and her husband, Dr. Ronald Glaser, an immunologist, marital arguments cause changes in the endocrine and immune systems.

During and after stressful conversations, levels of the hormones epinephrine and cortisol rise and can stay elevated for more than 22 hours afterward. Blood pressure and heart rate also tend to go up with relationship stress. . . .

. . . [I]n what may be the oddest study in the field, Dr. Kiecolt-Glaser and Dr. Glaser are now researching how the quality of a marriage affects the body's ability to repair itself.

In the continuing study, the scientists admit subjects to a hospital, inflict minor wounds on their arms, and then chart their interactions with their spouses and their progress in healing.

As with the overall "marriage benefit," which for women is smaller than for men and possibly even nonexistent, according to some researchers, women are more vulnerable to relationship-related health problems.

. . . [A] 15-year study of members of a large health maintenance organization in Oregon found that having unequal decision making power in marriage was associated with a higher risk of death for women, though not for men.

In Dr. Coyne's study of congestive heart failure, there was a stronger association between marital discord and death among women. Seven of the eight women with the poorest marital quality died within two years of the first assessment. . . .

For Dr. Alex Zautra, a professor of psychology at Arizona State University in Tempe, who has shown an association between criticism from intimate partners and joint pain in women with rheumatoid arthritis, the lesson from this growing literature is not to think of interpersonal ties as either all positive or negative.

"In truth, all relationships have both good and bad aspects to them," Dr. Zautra said. The point, he said, is that, in all their complexity, they matter. "At the heart of this is how people's emotions affect their health. People need to start thinking about that."

What do you think?

1. Recalling Durkheim's study of suicide described in Chapter 1 ("The Sociological Perspective"), how might he respond to this article?
2. Would you expect the "marriage benefit" to extend to members of same-sex couples? Why or why not?

POPULATION, URBANIZATION, AND ENVIRONMENT

FRIDA KAHLO
My Dress Hangs Here

THERE'S NOT MUCH choice when people decide to eat out in Bisbee, North Dakota: The Chocolate Shop is the only place in town. Sylvia Schmidt, who has lived in Bisbee all her life, owns

the small eatery. Shaking her head, she explains that by keeping her doors open to serve the dwindling number of locals and the occasional visitor who passes through town, she loses money every day. But she has enough saved to get by and so, although she's past what most folks call retirement age, she keeps the business going if only because she can't bear the thought of her town folding up. Thinking back, she smiles wistfully, "You can't imagine what it used to be like."

Bisbee is, indeed, in decline. The town now has just 227 people, down from about 300 ten years ago, making the population lower than when Bisbee was a frontier town in the mid-1800s. Pettsinger's movie house closed long ago, Brannon's Drug Store is gone, and Dick's Red Owl no longer sells groceries. The local church cannot afford the salary of a priest. The local high school has just sixty-nine students; the elementary school, thirty-one. Houses in Bisbee sell for as little as $2,000, yet no one is moving in.

Bob Weltin also grew up in Bisbee and, at forty-three, is now the town mayor. But as he sips a cup of Sylvia's coffee at The Chocolate Shop, he says that he has finally decided to call it quits; after he steps down as mayor, he's planning to move on to a larger community (Johnson, 2001).

There are hundreds of towns like Bisbee on the Great Plains that are hanging on by a thread. This chapter investigates population patterns, explaining why people move from place to place, why some cities get so large, and why small towns sometimes die. We shall also look at how population change and our entire way of life affect the physical environment.

DEMOGRAPHY: THE STUDY OF POPULATION

When humans first began to cultivate plants some 12,000 years ago, life for our ancestors was brutal and usually short: People fell victim to countless diseases, frequent injuries, and periodic natural disasters. Some scholars put the average lifespan 12,000 years ago at

only ten years. The population of the entire planet was only about 5 million, or about the population of Alaska today. Very slow growth pushed the global total in 1 B.C.E. to perhaps 300 million or a bit more than the population of today's United States (Haub, 2002a).

About 1750, world population began to spike upward, and it has continued to increase ever since. We now add 73 million people to the planet each year, for a total of 6.4 billion in 2004.

The causes and consequences of this drama are the basis of **demography,** *the study of human population.* Demography (from the Greek, meaning "writing about people") is a specialty within sociology that analyzes the size and composition of a population and studies how people move from place to place. Demographers not

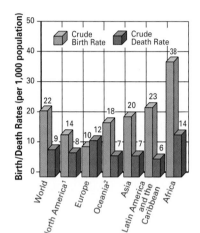 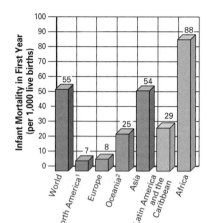 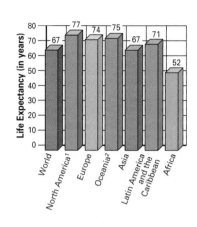

FIGURE 22-1 (a) Crude Birth Rates and Crude Death Rates, (b) Infant Mortality Rates, and (c) Life Expectancy, 2002

[1] United States and Canada.

[2] Australia, New Zealand, and South Pacific Islands.

Source: Population Reference Bureau (2003).

only collect statistics but also pose important questions about the effects of population growth and how it might be controlled. The following sections present basic demographic concepts.

FERTILITY

The study of human population begins with how many people are born. **Fertility** is *the incidence of childbearing in a country's population.* During her childbearing years, from the onset of menstruation (typically in the early teens) to menopause (usually in the late forties), a woman is capable of bearing more than twenty children. But *fecundity,* or maximum possible childbearing, is sharply reduced by cultural norms, finances, and personal choice.

Demographers gauge fertility using the **crude birth rate,** *the number of live births in a given year for every thousand people in a population.* To calculate a crude birth rate, divide the number of live births in a year by the society's total population and multiply the result by 1,000. In the United States in 2001, there were 4.1 million live births in a population of 284 million (U.S. National Center for Health Statistics, 2002), so the crude birth rate was 14.5.

January 18, Coshocton County, Ohio. Having just finished the mountains of meat and potatoes that make up a typical Amish meal, we have gathered in the livingroom of Jacob Raber, a member of this rural Amish community. Mrs. Raber, a mother of four, is telling us about Amish life. "Most of the women I know have five or six children," she says with a smile, "but certainly not everybody—some have eleven or twelve!"

A country's birth rate is described as "crude" because it is based on the entire population, not just women in their childbearing years. Furthermore, a crude birth rate also ignores differences between various categories of the population: Fertility among the Amish, for example, is high, whereas fertility among Asian Americans is low. But this measure is easy to calculate and allows rough comparisons of the fertility of one country or region in relation to others. Figure 22–1 shows that, in global perspective, the crude birth rate of North Americans is low.

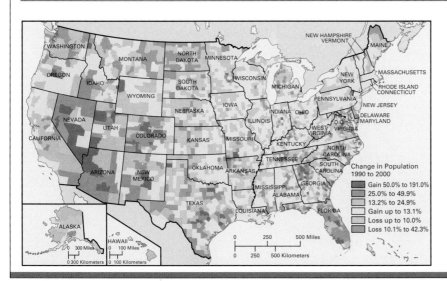

NATIONAL MAP 22–1
Population Change across the United States

This map, based on results of the 2000 Census, shows that population is moving from the heartland of the United States toward the coasts. What do you think is causing this internal migration? Can you offer a demographic profile of the people who remain in counties that are losing population?

Source: U.S. Census Bureau (2001).

Change in Population 1990 to 2000

- Gain 50.0% to 191.0%
- 25.0% to 49.9%
- 13.2% to 24.9%
- Gain up to 13.1%
- Loss up to 10.0%
- Loss 10.1% to 42.3%

MORTALITY

Population size also reflects **mortality,** *the incidence of death in a country's population.* To measure mortality, demographers use a **crude death rate,** *the number of deaths in a given year for every thousand people in a population.* This time, we take the number of deaths in a year, divide by the total population, and multiply the result by 1,000. In 2001, there were 2.4 million deaths in the U.S. population of 284 million, yielding a crude death rate of 8.5. Figure 22–1 shows that, in a global context, this rate is about average.

A third useful demographic measure is the **infant mortality rate,** *the number of deaths among infants under one year of age for each thousand live births in a given year.* To compute infant mortality, divide the number of deaths of children under one year of age by the number of live births during the same year and multiply the result by 1,000. In 2001, there were 28,000 infant deaths and 4.1 million live births in the United States. Dividing the first number by the second and multiplying the result by 1,000 yields an infant mortality rate of 6.8. The second part of Figure 22–1 indicates that, by world standards, North American infant mortality is low.

But remember the differences among various categories of people. For example, African Americans, with nearly three times the burden of poverty as

whites, have an infant mortality rate of 13.8—more than twice the white rate of 5.8.

Low infant mortality greatly raises **life expectancy,** *the average life span of a country's population.* U.S. males born in 2001 can expect to live 74.4 years, and females can look toward 79.8 years. As the third part of Figure 22–1 shows, life expectancy in North America is twenty-five years greater than in low-income countries of Africa.

MIGRATION

Population size is also affected by **migration,** *the movement of people into and out of a specified territory.* Movement into a territory—or *immigration*—is measured as an *in-migration rate,* calculated as the number of people entering an area for every thousand people in the population. Movement out of a territory—or *emigration*—is measured in terms of an *out-migration rate,* the number leaving for every thousand people. Both types of migration usually occur at once; the difference is the *net-migration rate.*

All nations also experience internal migration, that is, movement within their borders from one region to another. National Map 22–1 shows where the U.S. population is moving, and the places left behind (as suggested by the chapter opening, notice the heavy

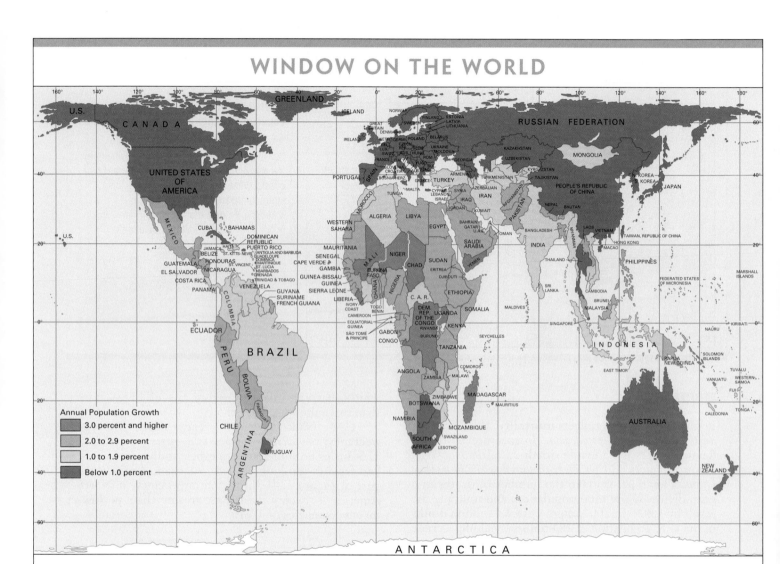

GLOBAL MAP 22–1 Population Growth in Global Perspective

The richest countries of the world—including the United States, Canada, and the nations of Europe—have growth rates below 1 percent. The nations of Latin America and Asia typically have growth rates around 1.6 percent, which double a population in forty-four years. Africa has an overall growth rate of 2.4 percent (despite only small increases in countries with a high rate of AIDS), which cuts the doubling time to twenty-nine years. In global perspective, we see that a society's standard of living is closely related to its rate of population growth: Population is rising fastest in the world regions that can least afford to support more people.

Source: Population Reference Bureau (2003); map projection from *Peters Atlas of the World* (1990).

losses in North Dakota). Migration is sometimes voluntary, as when people leave a dying town and move to a larger city. In such cases, "push-pull" factors are typically at work, as lack of jobs "pushes" people to move and more opportunity elsewhere "pulls" them to a larger city. Migration can also be involuntary, such as the forcible transport of 10 million Africans to the Western Hemisphere as slaves (Reed, 1999).

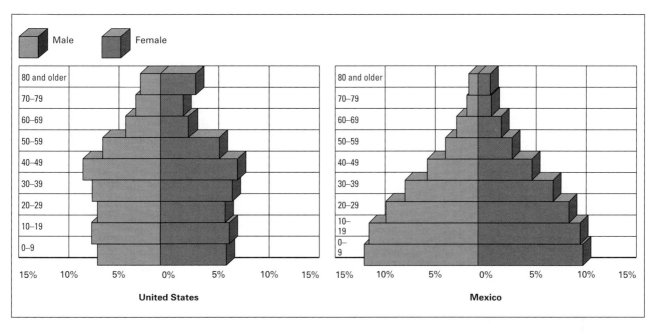

FIGURE 22–2 Age-Sex Population Pyramids for the United States and Mexico, 2002

Source: U.S. Census Bureau (2003).

POPULATION GROWTH

Fertility, mortality, and migration all affect the size of a society's population. In general, rich nations (like the United States) grow as much from immigration as from natural increase; poor nations (such as India) grow almost entirely from natural increase.

To calculate a population's natural growth rate, demographers subtract the crude death rate from the crude birth rate. The natural growth rate of the U.S. population in 2001 was 6.0 per thousand (the crude birth rate of 14.5 minus the crude death rate of 8.5), or about 0.60 percent annual growth.

Global Map 22–1 shows that population growth in the United States and other high-income nations is well below the world average of 1.3 percent. The Earth's low-growth continents are Europe (currently posting a slight decline, expressed as −0.2 percent annual growth), North America (0.5 percent), and Oceania (1.1 percent). Close to the global average are Asia (1.3 percent) and Latin America (1.7 percent). The highest growth region in the world is Africa (2.4 percent).

A handy rule of thumb for estimating population growth is to divide a society's population growth rate into the number 70 to calculate the *doubling time* in

years. Thus, an annual growth of 2 percent (found in parts of Latin America) doubles a population in thirty-five years, and a 3 percent growth rate (found in some of Africa) drops the doubling time to just twenty-four years. The rapid population growth of the poorest countries is deeply troubling because these countries can barely support the populations they have now.

POPULATION COMPOSITION

Demographers also study the makeup of a society's population at a given point in time. One variable is the **sex ratio,** *the number of males for every hundred females in a nation's population.* In 2000, the sex ratio in the United States was 96, or 96 males for every 100 females. Sex ratios are usually below 100 because, on average, women outlive men. In India, however, the sex ratio is 107, because parents value sons more than daughters and may either abort a female fetus or, after birth, give more care to a male infant, so that more male than female infants survive to adulthood.

A more complex measure is the **age-sex pyramid,** *a graphic representation of the age and sex of a population.* Figure 22–2 presents the age-sex pyramids for the

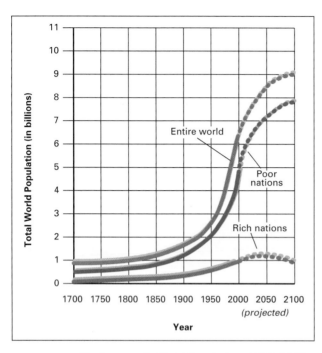

FIGURE 22–3 The Increase in World Population, 1700–2100

populations of the United States and Mexico. Higher mortality with advancing age gives these figures a rough pyramid shape. In the U.S. pyramid, the bulge corresponding to ages thirty through age fifty reflects high birth rates during the *baby boom* from the mid-1940s to 1970. The contraction just below—that is, people under thirty—reflects the subsequent *baby bust* as the birth rate dipped from 25.3 in 1957 to 14.5 in 2001.

Comparison of the U.S. and Mexican age-sex pyramids shows different demographic trends. The age-sex pyramid for Mexico, like that of other lower-income nations, is wide at the bottom (reflecting higher birth rates) and narrows quickly by what we would term middle age (due to higher mortality). Mexico, in short, is a much younger society with a median age of twenty compared to thirty-five in the United States. With a larger share of females still in their childbearing years, therefore, Mexico's crude birth rate (23) is nearly twice our own (14.5), and its annual rate of population growth (1.4 percent) is almost three times the U.S. rate (0.60 percent).

To find out more about U.S. demography, go to http://www.census.gov

HISTORY AND THEORY OF POPULATION GROWTH

In the past, people favored large families because human labor was the key to productivity. Moreover, until rubber condoms appeared 150 years ago, the prevention of pregnancy was an uncertain proposition at best. But high death rates from widespread infectious diseases put a constant brake on population growth.

A major demographic shift, shown in Figure 22–3, began about 1750 as the world's population turned upward, reaching the 1 billion mark by 1800. This milestone (which took all of human history up to this point) was repeated by 1930, barely a century later, when a second billion people were added to the planet. In other words, not only was population increasing but the *rate* of growth was accelerating. Global population reached 3 billion by 1962 (just thirty-two years later) and 4 billion by 1974 (a scant twelve years later). The rate of world population increase has slowed in recent years, but our planet passed the 5 billion mark in 1987 and the 6 billion mark in 1999. In no previous century did the world's population even double. In the twentieth century, it quadrupled.

Currently, the world is adding about 73 million people each year; 96 percent of this increase is in poor countries. Experts predict that the Earth's population will reach between 8 billion and 9 billion by 2050 (O'Neill & Balk, 2001). Given the world's troubles in feeding the present population, such an increase is a matter of urgent concern.

MALTHUSIAN THEORY

It was the sudden population growth two centuries ago that sparked the development of demography. Thomas Robert Malthus (1766–1834), an English economist and clergyman, warned that population increase would soon lead to social chaos. Malthus (1926; orig. 1798) calculated that population would increase by what mathematicians call a *geometric progression*, illustrated by the series of numbers 2, 4, 8, 16, 32, and so on. At such a rate, Malthus concluded, world population would soon soar out of control.

Food production would also increase, Malthus explained, but only in *arithmetic progression* (as in the series 2, 3, 4, 5, 6) because, even with new agricultural technology, farmland is limited. Thus, Malthus presented a distressing vision of the future: people reproducing

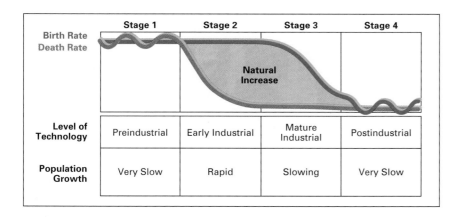

	Stage 1	Stage 2	Stage 3	Stage 4
Birth Rate Death Rate		Natural Increase		
Level of Technology	Preindustrial	Early Industrial	Mature Industrial	Postindustrial
Population Growth	Very Slow	Rapid	Slowing	Very Slow

FIGURE 22–4
Demographic Transition Theory

beyond what the planet could feed, leading ultimately to widespread starvation.

Malthus recognized that artificial birth control or abstinence might change the equation. But he found one morally wrong and the other quite unlikely. Thus, famine and war stalked humanity in Malthus's scheme, and he was justly known as "the dismal parson."

Critical evaluation. Fortunately, Malthus's prediction was flawed. First, by 1850, the European birth rate began to drop, partly because children were becoming an economic liability rather than an asset, and partly because people began using artificial birth control. Second, Malthus underestimated human ingenuity: Modern irrigation techniques, fertilizers, and pesticides have increased farm production far more than he could have imagined.

Some criticized Malthus for ignoring the role of social inequality in world abundance and famine. Karl Marx (1967; orig. 1867), for one, objected to viewing suffering as a "law of nature" rather than the curse of capitalism. More recently, "critical demographers" have claimed that saying high birth rates in low-income countries are responsible for poverty amounts to blaming the victims. On the contrary, they see global inequality as the real issue (Kuumba, 1999; Horton, 1999).

Still, Malthus offers an important lesson. Habitable land, clean water, and fresh air are limited resources, and, as we explain presently, greater economic productivity has taken a heavy toll on the natural environment. In addition, medical advances have lowered death rates, pushing up world population. Common sense tells us that no level of population growth can go on forever. Thus, people everywhere must become aware of the dangers of population increase.

DEMOGRAPHIC TRANSITION THEORY

A more complex analysis of population change is **demographic transition theory,** *the thesis that population patterns reflect a society's level of technological development.* Figure 22–4 shows the demographic consequences at four levels of technological development. Preindustrial, agrarian societies—those at Stage 1—have high birth rates because of the economic value of children and the absence of birth control. Death rates are also high because of low living standards and limited medical technology. Outbreaks of disease neutralize births, so population rises and falls with only a modest overall increase. This was the case for thousands of years in Europe before the Industrial Revolution.

Stage 2—the onset of industrialization—brings a demographic transition as death rates fall due to greater food supplies and scientific medicine. But birth rates remain high, resulting in rapid population growth. It was during Europe's Stage 2 that Malthus formulated his ideas, which explains his pessimistic view of the future. The world's poorest countries today are in this high-growth stage.

In Stage 3—a mature industrial economy—the birth rate drops, curbing population growth once again. Fertility falls, first, because most children survive to adulthood and, second, because high living standards make raising children expensive. Affluence, in short, transforms children from economic assets into economic liabilities. Smaller families, made possible by effective birth control, are also favored by women working outside the home. As birth rates follow death rates downward, population growth slows further.

In Stage 4—a postindustrial economy—the demographic transition is complete. The birth rate keeps falling, partly because dual-income couples gradually become the norm and partly because the cost of raising

Fertility in the United States has fallen during the past century and is now quite low. But some categories of the U.S. population have much higher fertility rates. One example is the Amish, a religious society living in rural areas of Ohio, Pennsylvania, and other states. It is common for Amish couples to have five, six, or more children. Why do you think the Amish favor large families?

children continues to rise. This trend, coupled with steady death rates, means that, at best, population grows only very slowly or even decreases. This is the case today in Japan, Europe, and the United States.

Critical evaluation. Demographic transition theory suggests that the key to population control lies in technology. Instead of the runaway population increase feared by Malthus, this theory sees technology reining in growth and spreading material plenty.

Demographic transition theory dovetails with modernization theory, one approach to global development discussed in Chapter 12 ("Global Stratification"). Modernization theorists are optimistic that poor countries will solve their population problems as they industrialize. But critics—notably, dependency theorists—strongly disagree. Unless there is a redistribution of global resources, they maintain, our planet will become increasingly divided into industrialized "haves," enjoying low population growth, and nonindustrialized "have-nots," struggling in vain to feed more and more people.

GLOBAL POPULATION TODAY: A BRIEF SURVEY

What can we say about population in today's world? Drawing on the discussion so far, we can identify important patterns and reach several conclusions.

The Low-Growth North

When the Industrial Revolution began in the Northern Hemisphere, the population increase in Western Europe and North America was a high 3 percent annually.

But in the centuries since, the growth rate has steadily declined and, in 1970, fell below 1 percent. As our

To find out more about population growth, go to http://www.populationconnection.org

postindustrial society enters Stage 4, the U.S. birth rate is less than the replacement level of 2.1 children per woman, a point demographers term **zero population growth**—*the level of reproduction that maintains population in a steady state.* More than sixty nations, almost all of them rich, are at or below the point of zero population growth.

Factors holding down population in these postindustrial societies include a high proportion of men and women in the labor force, rising costs of raising children, trends toward later marriage and singlehood, and widespread use of contraceptives and abortion.

In industrial nations, therefore, population increase is not the pressing problem that it is in poor countries. Indeed, some analysts point to a future problem of *underpopulation* in countries such as Russia, Japan, and Italy, where the swelling ranks of the elderly have fewer and fewer young people to look to for support in old age. Such decline is unlikely in the United States, where a younger population as well as higher immigration is causing slow but steady population increase (Chesnais, 1997; Wattenberg, 1997; McDonald, 2001; Kent & Mather, 2002).

The High-Growth South

Population is a critical problem in poor nations of the Southern Hemisphere. No nation of the world lacks industrial technology entirely; demographic transition

DIVERSITY: RACE, CLASS, AND GENDER

Empowering Women: The Key to Controlling Population Growth

Sohad Ahmad lives with her husband in a farming village fifty miles south of Cairo, Egypt's capital. Ahmad is poor, like hundreds of millions of other women in the world. Yet her situation differs in an important respect: She has had only two children and will have no more.

Why do Ahmad and her husband reject the conventional wisdom that children are an economic asset? One part of the answer is that Egypt's growing population has already created such a demand for land that Ahmad's family could not afford more even if they had the children to farm it. But the main reason is that she does not want her life defined only by childbearing.

Like Sohad Ahmad, more women in Egypt are taking control of their fertility and seeking more opportunities. Indeed, this country has made great progress in reducing its annual population growth from 3.0 percent just ten years ago to 2.1 percent today.

With its focus on raising the standing of women, the 1994 Cairo conference broke new ground. Past population control programs have simply tried to make birth control technology available to women. This effort is vital, since only half the world's married women use effective birth control. But even with birth

A simple truth: Women who have more opportunity for schooling and paid work have fewer children. As more women attend school in traditional societies, the fertility rate in these countries is falling.

control available, the population continues to expand in societies that define women's primary responsibility as raising children.

Dr. Nafis Sadik, an Egyptian woman who heads the United Nations efforts at population control, sums up the new approach to lowering birth rates this way: *Give women more life choices and they will have fewer children.* In other words, women who have access to schooling and jobs, who can decide when and whether to marry, and who bear children as a matter of choice will limit their own fertility. Schooling must be available to older women, too, Sadik adds, because elders exercise great influence in local communities.

Evidence from countries around the world is that controlling population and raising the social standing of women are one and the same.

Sources: Ashford (1995), Axinn & Barber (2001), and Population Reference Bureau (2003).

---

theory's Stage 1, therefore, applies to remote rural areas of low-income nations. But much of Latin America, Africa, and Asia is at Stage 2, with a mix of agrarian and industrial economies. Advanced medical technology, supplied by rich societies, has sharply reduced death rates, but birth rates remain high. Thus poor societies now account for two-thirds of the Earth's people and 96 percent of global population increase.

In poor countries throughout the world, birth rates have fallen from an average of about six children per woman in 1950 to about four today. But fertility this high will only intensify global poverty. At a 1994 global population conference in Cairo, delegates from

180 nations agreed that a key element in controlling world population growth was improving the status of women. The box takes a closer look.

In the last decade, the world has made significant progress in lowering fertility. Mortality also has come down. Although few would oppose medical programs that save lives—mostly children's—lower death rates mean rising population. In fact, population growth in most low-income regions of the world results *mostly* from falling death rates. Around 1920, Europe and North America began taking steps to spread scientific medicine and better nutrition around the world. Since then, inoculations against infectious diseases and the use of antibiotics and insecticides have pushed down death rates with stunning effectiveness. For example, in Sri Lanka, malaria caused half of all deaths in the 1930s; a decade later, use of insecticides to kill malaria-carrying mosquitoes cut the death toll from this disease in half. Although this is a great medical achievement, Sri Lanka's population began to soar. Similarly, India's infant mortality rate slid from 130 in 1975 to 66 in 2002, boosting that nation's population over the 1 billion mark.

 Read about efforts to control population increase in South Asia at http://www. asia-initiative.org/

In short, in much of the world, mortality is falling, especially among children. Now we must control birth in poor countries as successfully as we are fending off death.

URBANIZATION: THE GROWTH OF CITIES

October 8, Hong Kong. The cable train grinds to the top of Victoria Peak, where we behold one of the world's most spectacular vistas: the city of Hong Kong at night! A million bright, colorful lights ring the harbor as ships, ferries, and traditional Chinese "junks" churn by. Few places match Hong Kong for sheer energy. This small city is as economically productive as the state of Wisconsin or the nation of Finland. One could sit here for hours entranced by the spectacle of Hong Kong.

For most of human history, the sights and sounds of great cities such as Hong Kong, New York, and Los Angeles were simply unimaginable. Our distant ancestors lived in small, nomadic groups, moving as they depleted vegetation or hunted migratory game. The tiny settlements that marked the emergence of civilization in the Middle East some 12,000 years ago held only a small fraction of the Earth's people. Today the largest three or four cities of the world hold as many people as the entire planet did back then.

Urbanization is *the concentration of humanity into cities.* Urbanization redistributes population within a society and transforms many patterns of social life. We will trace these changes in terms of three urban revolutions: the emergence of cities 10,000 years ago, the development of industrial cities after 1750, and the explosive growth of cities in poor countries today.

THE EVOLUTION OF CITIES

Cities are a relatively new development in human history. Only about 12,000 years ago did our ancestors begin founding permanent settlements, launching the *first urban revolution.*

The First Cities

As explained in Chapter 4 ("Society"), hunting and gathering forced people to move all the time; raising food, however, required people to stay in one place (Nolan & Lenski, 1999). Raising their own food also created a material surplus, which freed some people from food production and allowed them to build shelters, make tools, weave cloth, and take part in religious rituals. The emergence of cities, then, led to specialization and higher living standards.

The first city—Jericho, which lies to the north of the Dead Sea and dates back some 10,000 years—was home to only around 600 people. But as the centuries passed, cities grew to tens of thousands of people and became the centers of vast empires. By 3000 B.C.E., Egyptian cities flourished, as did cities in China about 2000 B.C.E. and in Central and South America about 1500 B.C.E. In North America, however, only a few Native American societies formed settlements, so that widespread urbanization had to await the arrival of European settlers in the seventeenth century (Lamberg-Karlovsky & Lamberg-Karlovsky, 1973; Change, 1977; Coe & Diehl, 1980; Macionis & Parrillo, 2004).

Preindustrial European Cities

European cities date back some 5,000 years to the Greeks and, later, the Romans, both of whom created great empires and founded cities across Europe, including Vienna, Paris, and London. With the fall of the Roman Empire, the so-called Dark Ages began, as people withdrew within defensive walled settlements and warlords battled for territory. Only in the eleventh century did trade flourish once again, allowing cities to grow.

Medieval cities were quite different from those familiar to us today. Beneath towering cathedrals, the narrow and winding streets of London, Brussels, and Florence teemed with merchants, artisans, priests, peddlers, jugglers, nobles, and servants. Occupational groups such as bakers, carpenters, and metalworkers clustered together in distinct sections or "quarters." Ethnicity also defined communities, as residents sought to keep out people who differed from themselves. The term "ghetto" (from the Italian *borghetto,*

The oldest New York neighborhoods, near the southern tip of Manhattan, were settled between 1625 and 1650, before the industrial era shaped streets in a rigid grid pattern. The streets of New York's Chinatown show the irregular pattern characteristic of these early settlements. Also evident is the loss of vibrant street life usually found in such neighborhoods, a result of the terrorist attacks of September 11, 2001.

meaning "outside the city walls") first described the segregation of Jews in Venice.

Industrial European Cities

As the Middle Ages came to a close, steadily increasing commerce enriched a new urban middle class, or *bourgeoisie* (French, meaning "of the town"). With more and more money, the bourgeoisie soon rivaled the hereditary nobility.

By about 1750, the Industrial Revolution triggered a *second urban revolution*, first in Europe and then in North America. Factories unleashed tremendous productive power, causing cities to grow to unprecedented size. London, the largest European city, reached 550,000 people by 1700 and exploded to 6.5 million by 1900 (A. Weber, 1963, orig. 1899; Chandler & Fox, 1974).

Cities not only grew but changed shape as well. Older winding streets gave way to broad, straight boulevards that held the flow of commercial traffic and, eventually, motor vehicles. Steam and electric trolleys, too, crisscrossed the expanding cities. Since land was now a commodity to be bought and sold, developers divided cities into regular-sized lots (Mumford, 1961). The center of the city was no longer the cathedral but a bustling central business district, filled with banks, retail stores, and tall office buildings.

With a new focus on business, cities became more crowded and impersonal. Crime rates rose. Especially at the outset, a few industrialists lived in grand style, but most men, women, and children worked in factories for bare subsistence.

Organized efforts by workers to improve their lives eventually brought changes to the workplace, better housing, and the right to vote. Public services such as water, sewerage, and electricity further improved urban living. Today, some urbanites still live in poverty, but a rising standard of living has partly fulfilled the city's historical promise of a better life.

THE GROWTH OF U.S. CITIES

Most of the Native Americans who inhabited North America for thousands of years before the arrival of Europeans were migratory people who formed few permanent settlements. The spread of villages and towns, then, came after European colonization.

Colonial Settlement: 1565–1800

In 1565, the Spanish built a settlement at St. Augustine, Florida, and in 1607, the English founded Jamestown, Virginia. The first lasting settlement, however, came in 1624, when the Dutch established New Amsterdam, later called New York City.

New York and Boston (founded by the English in 1630) started out as tiny villages in a vast wilderness. They resembled medieval towns in Europe, with narrow, winding streets, some of which still curve through lower Manhattan and downtown Boston. When the first census was completed in 1790, as

TABLE 22-1 The Urban Population of the United States, 1790–2000		
Year	Population (in millions)	Percentage Urban
1790	3.9	5.1%
1800	5.3	6.1
1820	9.6	7.3
1840	17.1	10.5
1860	31.4	19.7
1880	50.2	28.1
1900	76.0	39.7
1920	105.7	51.3
1940	131.7	56.5
1960	179.3	69.9
1980	226.5	73.7
1990	253.0	75.2
2000	281.4	80.3

Source: U.S. Census Bureau (2001).

Table 22–1 shows, just 5 percent of the nation's people lived in cities. But economic growth would soon make cities not only far larger but also give them a new form, with wide streets typically laid out in a grid pattern.

Urban Expansion: 1800–1860

Early in the eighteenth century, as cities along the East Coast became bigger, towns sprang up along the transportation routes that opened the American West. By 1860, Buffalo, Cleveland, Detroit, and Chicago were changing the face of the Midwest, and about one-fifth of the entire U.S. population lived in cities.

Urban expansion was greatest in the northern states; New York City, for example, had ten times the population of Charleston, South Carolina. The division of the United States into the industrial-urban North and the agrarian-rural South was one major cause of the Civil War (Schlesinger, 1969).

The Metropolitan Era: 1860–1950

The Civil War (1861–65) gave an enormous boost to urbanization, as factories strained to produce weapons. Waves of people deserted the countryside for cities in hopes of obtaining better jobs. Joining them were tens of millions of immigrants, mostly from Europe, forming a culturally diverse urban mix.

In 1900, New York's population soared passed the 4 million mark, and Chicago—a city of only 100,000

people in 1860—was close to 2 million. Such growth marked the era of the **metropolis** (from Greek words, meaning "mother city"), *a large city that socially and economically dominates an urban area.* Metropolises became the economic centers of the United States. By 1920, cities were home to a majority of the U.S. population.

Industrial technology pushed the urban skyline ever higher. In the 1880s, steel girders and mechanical elevators raised structures more than ten stories high. In 1930, New York's Empire State Building became an urban wonder, an early skyscraper stretching 102 stories into the clouds.

Urban Decentralization: 1950–Present

The industrial metropolis reached its peak about 1950. Since then, something of a turnaround—termed *urban decentralization*—has occurred as people have deserted downtown areas for outlying **suburbs,** *urban areas beyond the political boundaries of a city.* Thus, the old industrial cities of the Northeast and Midwest stopped growing, and some lost considerable population in the decades after 1950. The urban landscape of densely packed central cities evolved into sprawling suburban regions.

SUBURBS AND URBAN DECLINE

Imitating European nobility, some of the rich always kept townhouses as well as country homes beyond the city limits (Baltzell, 1979a). It was not until after World War II that ordinary people found a suburban home within their reach. With more and more cars, new four-lane highways, government-backed mortgages, and inexpensive tract homes, the suburbs grew rapidly. By 1999, most of the U.S. population lived in the suburbs, and they frequented nearby shopping malls rather than the older downtown shopping districts in the cities (Rosenthal, 1974; Tobin, 1976; Geist, 1985; Peterson, 1999).

As many older cities of the Snowbelt—the Northeast and Midwest—lost affluent taxpayers to the suburbs, they struggled to fund expensive social programs for the poor who stayed behind. Many cities fell into financial crisis, and inner-city decay became severe. Especially to white people, the inner cities became synonymous with slums, crime, drugs, unemployment, the poor, and minorities (Sternlieb & Hughes, 1983; Logan & Schneider, 1984; Stahura, 1986; Galster, 1991).

Urban critic Paul Goldberger (2002) points out that the decline of central cities also has led to a decline in the importance of public space. Historically, the heart of city life was played out on public streets. The French word for a sophisticated person is "boulevardier," which literally means "street person." In the United States today, however, this term has a decidedly negative meaning. On the contrary, the active life that once took place on public streets and in public squares now takes place in shopping malls, cineplex lobbies, and gated communities—all privately owned spaces. Further reducing the vitality of today's urban places is the spread of television, the Internet, and other media that people use within their homes.

POSTINDUSTRIAL SUNBELT CITIES

As older Snowbelt cities fell into decline, Sunbelt cities in the South and the West began growing. The rapid growth of cities such as Los Angeles and Houston reflects a population shift to the Sunbelt, where 60 percent of U.S. people now live. In addition, most of today's immigrants enter the country in the Sunbelt region. The result: Back in 1950, nine of the ten biggest U.S. cities were in the Snowbelt; in 2000, six of the top ten were in the Sunbelt (U.S. Census Bureau, 2001).

Unlike their colder counterparts, Sunbelt cities came of age *after* urban decentralization began. So while cities like Chicago have long been enclosed by a ring of politically independent suburbs, cities like Houston have pushed their boundaries outward, along with the population flow. Thus, Chicago covers 227 square miles, while Houston covers more than 550 square miles (and the greater Houston urban area covers 8,778 square miles, which is bigger than the state of New Jersey).

The great sprawl of Sunbelt cities has drawbacks, however. Many people in cities like Atlanta, Dallas, Phoenix, and Los Angeles see unplanned growth as producing only clogged roads leading to slapdash developments. Not surprisingly, voters in many communities across the United States have passed ballot initiatives seeking to limit sprawl (Lacayo, 1999; Romero & Liserio, 2002).

MEGALOPOLIS: REGIONAL CITIES

Another result of urban decentralization is urban regions. The U.S. Census Bureau (2001) recognizes 276 urban regions, which the bureau calls *metropolitan statistical areas (MSAs)*. Each MSA includes at least one city with 50,000 or more people plus densely populated surrounding counties. Almost all of the fifty fastest-growing MSAs are in the Sunbelt.

The biggest MSAs, containing more than 1 million people, are called *consolidated metropolitan statistical areas (CMSAs)*. In 2000, there were eighteen CMSAs. Heading the list is New York and adjacent urban areas in Long Island, western Connecticut, and northern New Jersey, with a total population of more than 21 million. Next in size is the CMSA in southern California that includes Los Angeles, Riverside, and Anaheim, with a population of more than 16 million.

As regional cities grow, they begin to overlap each other. For example, along the East Coast a 400-mile supercity stretches all the way from New England to Virginia. In the early 1960s, the French geographer Jean Gottmann (1961) coined the term **megalopolis** to designate *a vast urban region containing a number of cities and their surrounding suburbs*. Other supercities cover the eastern coast of Florida and stretch from Cleveland west to Chicago. More megalopolises will undoubtedly emerge, especially in the fast-growing Sunbelt.

EDGE CITIES

Urban decentralization has also created *edge cities*, business centers some distance from the old downtowns. Edge cities—a mix of corporate office buildings, shopping malls, hotels, and entertainment complexes—differ from suburbs, which contain mostly homes. Thus, while the population of suburbs peaks at night, the population of edge cities peaks during the workday.

As part of expanding urban regions, most edge cities have no clear physical boundaries. Some do have names, including Los Colinas (near the Dallas–Fort Worth airport), Tyson's Corner (in Virginia, near Washington, D.C.), and King of Prussia (northwest of Philadelphia). Other edge cities are known only by the major highways that flow through them, including Route 1 in Princeton, New Jersey, and Route 128 near Boston (Garreau, 1991; Macionis & Parrillo, 2004).

THE RURAL REBOUND

Over the course of U.S. history, as the data in Table 22–1 showed, the urban population of the nation has steadily increased. Immigration has played a part in this increase, because most newcomers settle in cities. At the same time, there has been considerable migration from rural areas to urban places, typically by people seeking more economic opportunity.

The rural rebound has been most pronounced in towns that offer spectacular natural beauty. There are times when people living in the scenic town of Park City, Utah, cannot even find a parking space.

Even so, since 1990, many rural areas have been gaining population—a trend analysts have dubbed the "rural rebound." During the 1990s, three-fourths of the rural counties across the United States gained population. Most of this gain resulted from the migration of people from urban areas. This trend has not affected all rural places: As the opening to this chapter explains, many small towns in rural areas (especially in the mid-section of the country from North Dakota down to Texas; look back to National Map 22–1) are struggling simply to stay alive. But, even there, losses slowed during the 1990s (Johnson, 1999, 2001).

The greatest gains have come to rural communities that offer scenic and recreational attractions, such as lakes, mountains, and ski areas. In addition, some people are drawn to rural areas by lifestyle considerations, preferring a slower pace, lower traffic, less crime, and cleaner air. A number of companies, too, have relocated to rural counties, which has increased economic opportunity for the rural population (Baldauf, 1996; Johnson, 1999; Johnson & Fuguitt, 2000).

URBANISM AS A WAY OF LIFE

Early sociologists in Europe and the United States focused their attention on the rise of cities and how urban life differed from rural life. We briefly present their accounts of urbanism as a way of life.

FERDINAND TÖNNIES: *GEMEINSCHAFT* AND *GESELLSCHAFT*

In the late nineteenth century, the German sociologist Ferdinand Tönnies (1855–1937) studied how life in the new industrial metropolis differed from life in rural villages. From this contrast, he developed two concepts that have become a lasting part of sociology's terminology.

Tönnies (1963; orig. 1887) used the German word *Gemeinschaft* (meaning roughly "community") to refer to *a type of social organization by which people are closely tied by kinship and tradition*. The *Gemeinschaft* of the rural village joins people in what amounts to a single primary group.

By and large, argued Tönnies, *Gemeinschaft* is absent in the modern city. On the contrary, urbanization fosters *Gesellschaft* (a German word meaning roughly "association"), *a type of social organization by which people come together only on the basis of individual self-interest*. In the *Gesellschaft* way of life, individuals are motivated by their own needs rather than a drive to enhance the well-being of everyone. City dwellers display little sense of community or common identity and look to others mostly as a means of advancing their individual goals. Thus, Tönnies saw in urbanization the erosion of close, enduring social relations in favor of the fleeting and impersonal ties typical of business.

Peasant Dance *(above, c. 1565)*, by Pieter Breughel the Elder, conveys the essential unity of rural life forged by generations of kinship and neighborhood. By contrast, Ernest Fiene's Nocturne *(left)* communicates the impersonality common to urban areas. Taken together, these paintings capture Tönnies's distinction between Gemeinschaft and Gesellschaft.

Pieter Breughel the Elder (c. 1525/30–1569), Peasant Dance, c. 1565, Kunsthistorisches Museum, Vienna/Superstock. Ernest Fiene (1894–1965), Nocturne. Photograph © Christie's Images.

EMILE DURKHEIM: MECHANICAL AND ORGANIC SOLIDARITY

The French sociologist Emile Durkheim (see Chapter 4, "Society") agreed with much of Tönnies's thinking about cities. But, Durkheim countered, urbanites do not lack social bonds; they simply organize social life differently than rural people.

Durkheim described traditional, rural life as *mechanical solidarity*, social bonds based on common sentiments and shared moral values. With its emphasis on tradition, Durkheim's concept of mechanical solidarity bears a striking similarity to Tönnies's *Gemeinschaft*. Urbanization erodes mechanical solidarity, Durkheim explained, but it also generates a new type of bonding, which he called *organic solidarity*, social bonds based on specialization and interdependence. This concept, which parallels Tönnies's *Gesellschaft*, reveals an important difference between the two thinkers. While they agreed that the growth of industrial cities undermined tradition, Durkheim optimistically pointed to a new kind of solidarity. Where societies had been built on *likeness*, Durkheim now saw social life based on *difference*.

For Durkheim, urban society offered more individual choice, moral tolerance, and personal privacy than people found in rural villages. In sum, something was lost in the process of urbanization, but much was gained.

GEORG SIMMEL: THE BLASÉ URBANITE

The German sociologist Georg Simmel (1858–1918) offered a microanalysis of cities, studying how urban life shapes individual experience. According to Simmel, individuals perceive the city as a crush of people, objects, and events. To prevent being overwhelmed by all this stimulation, urbanites develop a *blasé attitude*, tuning out much of what goes on around them. Such detachment does not mean that city dwellers lack compassion for others; they simply keep their distance as a survival strategy so they can focus their time and energy on those who really matter to them.

THE CHICAGO SCHOOL: ROBERT PARK AND LOUIS WIRTH

Sociologists in the United States soon joined the study of rapidly growing cities. Robert Park, a leader of the first U.S. sociology program at the University of Chicago, sought to add a street-level perspective by getting out and studying real cities. As he said of himself:

I suspect that I have actually covered more ground, tramping about in cities in different parts of the world, than any other living man. (1950:viii)

Walking the streets, Park found the city to be an organized mosaic of distinctive ethnic communities, commercial centers, and industrial districts. Over time, he observed, these "natural areas" develop and change in relation to each other. To Park, then, the city was a living organism—a human kaleidoscope.

Another major figure in the Chicago School of urban sociology was Louis Wirth (1897–1952). Wirth (1938) is best known for blending the ideas of Tönnies, Durkheim, Simmel, and Park into a comprehensive theory of urban life.

Wirth began by defining the city as a setting with a large, dense, and socially diverse population. These traits result in an impersonal, superficial, and transitory way of life. Living among millions of others, urbanites come into contact with many more people than rural residents. Thus, when city people notice others at all, they usually know them not in terms of *who they are* but *what they do*—as, for instance, the bus driver, florist, or grocery store clerk. Specialized urban relationships can be pleasant enough for all concerned. But we should remember that self-interest rather than friendship is usually the main reason for the interaction.

Finally, limited social involvement coupled with great social diversity makes city dwellers more tolerant than rural villagers. Rural communities often jealously enforce their narrow traditions, but the heterogeneous population of a city rarely shares any single code of moral conduct (Wilson, 1985; Wilson, 1995).

Critical evaluation. Both in Europe and in the United States, early sociologists presented a mixed view of urban living. On the one hand, rapid urbanization was troubling. Tönnies and Wirth saw personal ties and traditional morality lost in the anonymous rush of the city. On the other hand, Durkheim and Park emphasized urbanism's positive face, pointing to more personal autonomy and greater personal choice.

One problem is that early analysis of urbanism tended to overlook the extent to which close-knit communities persist in the city (Greeley, 2002). In addition, general descriptions of urbanism by Wirth and others overlook the powerful effects of class, race, and gender. There are many kinds of urbanites—rich and poor, young and old, black and white, Anglo and Latino, women and men—all leading distinctive lives (Gans, 1968). Indeed, as the box explains, the share of minorities in the largest U.S. cities has increased sharply in recent years. Further, cities intensify social differences. That is, because various categories of people can form "critical masses," we see the extent of social diversity most clearly in cities (Macionis & Parrillo, 2004).

URBAN ECOLOGY

Sociologists (especially those who were part of the Chicago School) also developed **urban ecology,** *the study of the link between the physical and social dimensions of cities.* They asked, first, why cities are located where they are. Concerned with defense, early urbanites built many cities on mountains (ancient Athens was perched on an outcropping of rock) or in areas surrounded by water (Paris and Mexico City were founded on islands). With the Industrial Revolution, economic considerations situated all the major U.S. cities near rivers and natural harbors that facilitated trade.

Urban ecologists also study the physical design of cities. In 1925, Ernest W. Burgess, a student and colleague of Robert Park, described land use in Chicago in terms of *concentric zones.* City centers, Burgess observed, are business districts bordered by a ring of factories, followed by residential rings with housing that becomes more expensive the farther it is from the noise and pollution of the city's center.

Homer Hoyt (1939) refined Burgess's observations, noting that distinctive districts sometimes form *wedge-shaped sectors.* For example, one fashionable area may develop next to another, or an industrial district may extend outward from a city's center along a train or trolley line.

Chauncy Harris and Edward Ullman (1945) added yet another insight: As cities decentralize, they lose their single-center form in favor of a *multicentered model.* As cities grow, residential areas, industrial parks, and shopping districts typically push away from one another. Few people wish to live close to industrial areas, for example, so the city becomes a mosaic of distinct districts.

Social area analysis investigates what people in particular neighborhoods have in common. Three factors seem to explain most of the variation: family patterns, social class, and race and ethnicity (Shevky & Bell, 1955; Johnston, 1976; Fetto, 2002). Single people and couples without children predominate in areas with many apartment buildings; families with children gravitate to areas with single-family homes and good schools. The rich seek high-prestige neighborhoods, often in the central city near cultural attractions.

DIVERSITY: RACE, CLASS, AND GENDER

Census 2000: The Minority-Majority in the Largest U.S. Cities

According to the results of the 2000 U.S. Census, minorities—Hispanics, African Americans, and Asians—are now a majority of the population in 48 of the 100 largest U.S. cities, up from 30 in 1990. Why the change? One reason is that large cities have been losing their non-Hispanic white population. Santa Ana, California, for example, lost 38 percent of its 1990 white population; the drop was 40 percent in Birmingham, Alabama; and it was a whopping 53 percent in Detroit, Michigan. For all 100 of the largest cities taken as a whole, minorities are now a majority, with 56 percent of the total population, up from 48 percent in 1990.

But perhaps the biggest reason for the minority-majority trend is the increase in immigration. Immigration, coupled with higher birth rates among new immigrants, resulted in a 43 percent gain in the Hispanic population (almost 4 million people) of the largest 100 cities between 1990 and 2000. The Asian population also surged by 40 percent (more than 1.1 million people). The African American population was about steady over the course of the last decade.

Political officials and other policy makers are taking a close look at these figures. Clearly, the future vitality of the largest U.S. cities depends on meeting the needs and taking advantage of the contributions of the swelling minority population.

Sources: Based on Schmitt (2001) and U.S. Census Bureau (2001).

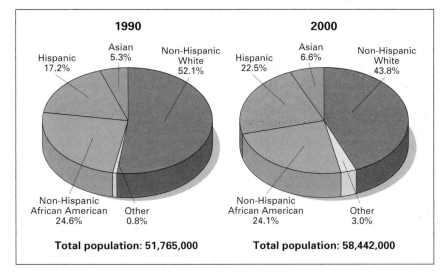

Minority Population Change in the 100 Largest U.S. Cities

People with a common social heritage cluster in distinctive communities.

Finally, Brian Berry and Philip Rees (1969) tie together many of these insights. They explain that distinct family types tend to settle in the concentric zones described by Ernest Burgess. Specifically, households with few children tend to cluster toward the city's center, while those with more children live farther away. Social class differences are primarily responsible for the sector-shaped districts described by Homer Hoyt as, for instance, the rich occupy one "side of the tracks" and the poor, the other. And racial and ethnic neighborhoods are found at various points throughout the city, consistent with Harris and Ullman's multi-centered model.

URBAN POLITICAL ECONOMY

In the late 1960s, many large U.S. cities were rocked by rioting. In the wake of such rioting, some analysts turned away from the ecological approach to a social-conflict understanding of city life. The *urban political economy* model applies Karl Marx's analysis of conflict in the workplace to conflict in the city (Lindstrom, 1995).

The ecological approach sees the city as a natural organism, with particular districts and neighborhoods developing according to an internal logic. Political economists disagree. They claim that city life is defined by people with power: corporate leaders and political

officials. Capitalism, which transforms the city into real estate traded for profit and concentrates wealth in the hands of a few, is the key to understanding city life. From this point of view, for example, the decline in industrial Snowbelt cities after 1950 was the result of deliberate decisions by the corporate elite to move their production facilities to the Sunbelt (where labor is cheaper and less likely to be unionized) or to move them out of the country entirely to low-income nations (Harvey, 1976; Molotch, 1976; Castells, 1977, 1983; Feagin, 1983; Lefebvre, 1991; Jones & Wilson, 1999).

Critical evaluation. Compared to the older urban ecology approach, the political economy view seems better able to address the fact that many U.S. cities are in *crisis*, with widespread poverty, high crime, and barely functioning schools. But one criticism applies to both approaches: They focus on U.S. cities during a limited period of history. Much of what we know about industrial cities does not apply to preindustrial U.S. towns or to the rapidly growing cities in many poor nations today. Therefore, it is unlikely that any single model of cities can account for the full range of urban diversity that we find in the world today.

URBANIZATION IN POOR SOCIETIES

November 16, Cairo, Egypt. People call the vast Muslim cemetery in Old Cairo "The City of the Dead." In truth, it is very much alive: Tens of thousands of squatters have moved into the mausoleums, making this place an eerie mix of life and death. Children run across the stone floors, clotheslines stretch between the monuments, and an occasional television antenna protrudes from a tomb roof. With Cairo gaining 1,000 people a day, families live where they can.

Twice in human history the world has experienced a revolutionary expansion of cities. The first urban revolution began about 8000 B.C.E. with the first urban settlements and continued until permanent settlements were in place on several continents. Then, about 1750, the second urban revolution took off and lasted for two centuries as the Industrial Revolution led to the rapid growth of cities in Europe and North America.

A third urban revolution is now underway. Today, 75 percent of people in industrial societies are already city dwellers. But extraordinary urban growth is occurring in low-income nations. In 1950, about 25 percent of the people in poor countries lived in cities; by 2005, the figure will exceed 50 percent. Moreover, in 1950, only seven cities in the world had populations over 5 million, and only two of these were in low-income countries. By 2000, forty-eight cities had passed this mark, and thirty-two of them were in less developed nations (Brockerhoff, 2000; *Time Almanac 2001*, 2000).

This third urban revolution is taking place because many poor nations have entered the high-growth Stage 2 of demographic transition theory. Falling death rates have fueled population increases in Latin America, Asia, and, especially, Africa. For urban areas, the rate of increase is *twice* as high because, in addition to natural increase, millions of people leave the countryside each year in search of jobs, health care, education, and conveniences like running water and electricity.

Cities do offer more opportunities than rural areas, but they provide no quick fix for the massive problems of escalating population and grinding poverty. Many cities in less economically developed nations—including Mexico City, Egypt's Cairo, India's Calcutta, and Manila in the Philippines—are simply unable to meet the basic needs of much of their population. All these cities are surrounded by wretched shantytowns—settlements of makeshift homes built from discarded materials. As noted in Chapter 12 ("Global Stratification"), even city dumps are home to thousands of poor people, who pick through the waste hoping to find enough to survive for another day.

ENVIRONMENT AND SOCIETY

Our species has prospered, rapidly increasing the population of the planet. Moreover, within the next twenty-five years, most people will live in the cities, settlements that offer the promise of a better life than that found in rural villages.

But these advances have come at a high price. Never before in history have human beings placed such demands on the Earth. This disturbing development brings us to the final section of this chapter: the interplay between the natural environment and society. Like demography, **ecology** is another cousin of sociology; it is *the study of the interaction of living organisms and the natural environment*. Ecology rests on the research not only of social scientists but of natural scientists as well. Here, however, we focus on those aspects of ecology that involve now-familiar sociological concepts and issues.

The **natural environment** is *the Earth's surface and atmosphere, including living organisms, air, water, soil, and other resources necessary to sustain life.* Like every other species, humans depend on the natural environment to live. Yet, with our capacity for culture, humans stand apart from other species. We alone take deliberate action to remake the world according to our own interests and desires, for better *and* for worse.

Why is the environment of interest to sociologists? Simply because environmental problems—from pollution to acid rain to global warming—do not arise from the "natural world" operating on its own. Rather, as we shall explain, such issues result from the specific actions of human beings, so they are *social* problems (Marx, 1994).

THE GLOBAL DIMENSION

The study of the natural environment requires a global perspective. The reason is simple: Regardless of political divisions among nations, the planet is a single **ecosystem,** *a system composed of the interaction of all living organisms and their natural environment.*

The Greek meaning of *eco* is "house," reminding us that this planet is our home and that all living things and their natural environment are *interrelated.* In practice, change in any part of the natural environment ripples throughout the entire global ecosystem.

Consider, from an ecological point of view, our national love of eating hamburgers. People in North America (and, increasingly, around the world) have created a huge demand for beef, which has greatly expanded the ranching industry in Brazil, Costa Rica, and other Latin American nations. To produce the lean meat sought by fast-food corporations, cattle in Latin America feed on grass, which requires a great deal of land. Latin American ranchers get the land for grazing by clearing thousands of square miles of forests each year. These tropical forests are vital to maintaining the Earth's atmosphere. Deforestation ends up threatening everyone, including people in the United States who enjoy hamburgers without giving a thought to the environment (Myers, 1984a).

TECHNOLOGY AND THE ENVIRONMENTAL DEFICIT

Sociologists point to a simple formula: I = PAT, where environmental impact (I) reflects a society's population

The most important insight sociology offers about our physical world is that environmental problems do not simply "happen." Rather, the state of the natural environment reflects the ways in which social life is organized—how people live and what they think is important. Moreover, the greater the technological power of a society, the greater that society's ability to threaten the natural environment.

(P), its level of affluence (A), and its level of technology (T). Members of societies with simple technology—the hunters and gatherers described in Chapter 4 ("Society")—have scarcely any ability to affect the environment because they are small in number and poor and have only simple technology. On the contrary, nature affects their lives as they follow the migration of game, watch the rhythm of the seasons, and suffer from natural catastrophes such as fires, floods, droughts, and storms.

Societies at intermediate stages of technological development have a somewhat greater capacity to affect the environment. Such societies are both larger and richer. But the environmental impact of horticulture (small-scale farming), pastoralism (the herding of animals), and even agriculture (the use of animal-drawn plows) is limited because people still rely on muscle power to produce food and other goods.

Human ability to control the natural environment grew dramatically with the Industrial Revolution.

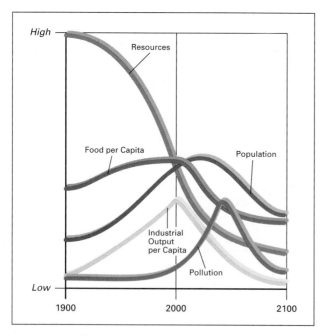

FIGURE 22-5 The Limits to Growth: Projections

Source: Based on Meadows et al. (1972).

Populations rose, along with living standards. Muscle power gave way to engines that burned fossil fuels: coal at first and then oil. With such machinery, people consume more natural resources and release more pollutants into the atmosphere. Even more important, humans armed with industrial technology are able to bend nature to their will, tunneling through mountains, damming rivers, irrigating deserts, and drilling for oil on the ocean floor. Thus, people in rich nations, who represent just 18 percent of humanity, now use 80 percent of the world's energy (Connett, 1991; Miller, 1992; York, Rosa, & Deitz, 2002).

The environmental impact of industrial technology goes beyond energy consumption. Just as important is the fact that members of industrial societies produce 100 times more goods than people in agrarian societies. Higher living standards, in turn, increase the problem of solid waste (since people ultimately throw away most of what they produce) and pollution (since industrial production generates smoke and other toxic substances).

From the start, people recognized the material benefits of industrial technology. But only a century later did they begin to see the long-term effects on the natural environment. Indeed, one trait of the recent postindustrial era is a growing concern about environmental quality (Abrahamson, 1997; Kidd & Lee, 1997). Today, we realize that the technological power to make our lives better can also put the lives of future generations in jeopardy (Voight, cited in Bormann & Kellert, 1991:ix–x).

Evidence is mounting that we are running up an **environmental deficit,** *profound and long-term harm to the natural environment caused by humanity's focus on short-term material affluence* (Bormann, 1990). The concept of environmental deficit is important for three reasons. First, it reminds us that the state of the environment is a *social issue,* reflecting choices people make about how to live. Second, it suggests that much environmental damage—to the air, land, and water—is *unintended.* By focusing on the short-term benefits of, say, cutting down forests, strip mining, or using throwaway packaging, we fail to see their long-term environmental effects. Third, in some respects, the environmental deficit is *reversible.* Inasmuch as societies have created environmental problems, in other words, societies can undo many of them.

CULTURE: GROWTH AND LIMITS

Whether we recognize environmental dangers and decide to do something about them is a cultural matter. Thus, along with technology, culture has powerful environmental consequences.

The Logic of Growth

When this country sets aside specific areas as parks and game preserves, we seem to be saying that, except for these special areas, people can use and abuse natural resources for their own purposes (Myers, 1991). This aggressive approach to the natural environment has long been central to our way of life.

Chapter 3 ("Culture") described the core values that underlie social life in the United States. One of these is *material comfort,* the belief that money and the things it buys enrich our lives. We also believe in the idea of *progress,* thinking that the future will be better than the present. Moreover, we look to *science* to make our lives easier and more rewarding. Taken together, such cultural values form *the logic of growth.*

The logic of growth is an optimistic view of the world. It holds that more powerful technology has improved our lives and new discoveries will make the future better still. In simple terms, the logic of growth asserts that "People are clever," "Having things is good," and "Life gets better." A powerful force throughout the history of the United States and other

Western industrial societies, the logic of growth is the driving force behind settling the wilderness, building towns and roads, and pursuing material affluence.

Even so, "progress" can lead to unexpected problems, including harming the environment. The logic of growth responds by arguing that people (especially scientists and other technology experts) will find a way out of any problem that growth places in our path. If, say, the world runs short of oil, we will come up with solar, hydrogen, or nuclear engines (or some other, yet unknown, technology) to meet the world's energy needs.

But environmentalists counter that the logic of growth is flawed in assuming that natural resources such as oil, clean air, fresh water, and topsoil will always be plentiful. On the contrary, they claim, these are *finite* resources that we can and will exhaust if we continue to pursue growth at any cost. Echoing Malthus, environmentalists warn that if we call on the Earth to support increasing numbers of people, we will surely deplete finite resources, destroying the environment—and ourselves—in the process (Livernash & Rodenburg, 1998; Smail, 2003).

The Limits to Growth

If we cannot invent our way out of the problems created by the logic of growth, perhaps we need another way of thinking about the world. Environmentalists, therefore, counter that growth must have limits. Stated simply, the *limits to growth thesis* is that humanity must implement policies to control the growth of population, production, and use of resources in order to avoid environmental collapse.

In *The Limits to Growth*, a controversial book that was influential in launching the environmental movement, Donella Meadows and her colleagues (1972) used a computer model to calculate the planet's available resources, rates of population growth, amount of land available for cultivation, levels of industrial and food production, and amount of pollutants released into the atmosphere. The model reflects changes that have occurred since 1900 and projects forward to the end of the twenty-first century. The authors concede that such long-range predictions are speculative, and some critics think they are plain wrong (Simon, 1981). But right or wrong, the conclusions of the study, shown in Figure 22–5, call for serious consideration.

According to the limits to growth thesis, we are quickly consuming the Earth's finite resources. Supplies of oil, natural gas, and other energy sources are already falling sharply and will continue to drop, a

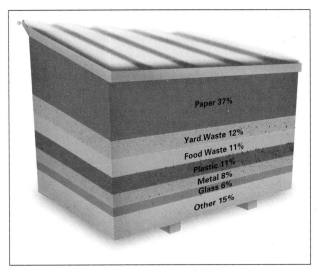

FIGURE 22-6 Composition of Community Trash
Source: U.S. Environmental Protection Agency (2002).

little faster or slower depending on the conservation policies of rich nations and the speed with which other nations industrialize. While food production per person will continue to rise during this century, world hunger will persist because existing food supplies are so unequally distributed. By 2050, the model predicts, hunger will reach a crisis level, first stabilizing population and then sending it back downward. Eventually, depleted resources will cripple industrial output as well. Only then will pollution rates fall.

Limits to growth theorists are also known as neo-Malthusians because they share Malthus's pessimism about the future. They doubt that current patterns of life are sustainable for even another century. If so, we face a fundamental choice: Either we make deliberate changes in how we live, or widespread calamity will force change upon us.

SOLID WASTE: THE DISPOSABLE SOCIETY

As an interesting exercise, carry a trash bag around for a single day and collect everything you throw away. Most people are surprised to find that the average person in the United States discards close to five pounds of paper, metal, plastic, and other materials daily (over a lifetime, that's about 50 tons). For the country as a whole, this amounts to about 1 billion pounds of solid waste *each and every day*. Figure 22–6 shows the average composition of a community's solid waste.

APPLYING SOCIOLOGY

Why Grandmother Had No Trash

Grandma Macionis, we always used to say, never threw away anything. She was born and raised in Lithuania—the "old country"—where life in a poor village shaped her in ways that never changed, even after she emigrated to the United States as a young woman and settled in Philadelphia.

After opening a birthday present, she would carefully save the box, wrapping paper, and ribbon, which meant as much to her as the gift they contained. Grandma never wore new clothes; her kitchen knives were worn narrow from decades of sharpening; and all her garbage was "recycled" as compost for her vegetable garden.

As strange as Grandma sometimes seemed to her grandchildren, she was a product of her culture. A century ago, in fact, there was little "trash." If a pair of socks wore thin, Grandma mended them, probably more than once. When they were beyond repair, she used them as rags for cleaning or sewed them (with other old clothing) into a quilt. For her, everything had value—if not in one way, then in another.

During the twentieth century, as women joined men in working outside the home, income went up and families began buying more and more "time-saving" products. Before long, few people cared about the home recycling that Grandma practiced. Soon, cities sent crews from block to block to pick up truckloads of discarded material. The era of "trash" had begun.

As a rich nation of people who value convenience, the United States has become a *disposable society*. We consume more products than virtually any other nation, and many of these products have throwaway packaging. The most familiar case is fast food, served with cardboard, plastic, and Styrofoam containers that we discard within minutes. And countless other products—from film to fishhooks—are elaborately packaged to make the product more attractive to the customer and to discourage tampering and theft.

Consider, too, that manufacturers market soft drinks, beer, and fruit juices in aluminum cans, glass jars, and plastic containers, which not only consume finite resources but also generate mountains of solid waste. Then there are countless items intentionally designed to be disposable: pens, razors, flashlights, batteries, even cameras. Other products—from light bulbs to automobiles—are designed to have a limited useful life and then become unwanted junk. As Paul Connett (1991) points out, even the words we use to describe what we throw away—*waste, litter, trash, refuse, garbage, rubbish*—show how little we value what we cannot immediately use. But this was not always the case, as the box explains.

Living in a rich society, the average person in the United States consumes 50 times more steel, 170 times more newspaper, 250 times more gasoline, and 300 times more plastic each year than the typical person in India (Miller, 1992). This high level of consumption means not only that we in the United States use a disproportionate share of the planet's natural resources but also that we generate most of the world's refuse.

We like to say that we "throw things away." But 80 percent of our solid waste is not burned or recycled and never "goes away." Rather, it ends up in landfills, which are, literally, filling up. And what goes into landfills all too often stays there, sometimes for centuries. Tens of millions of tires, diapers, and other items that we bury in landfills each year do not decompose and will be an unwelcome legacy for future generations. Often too, material in landfills can pollute groundwater. Although, in most places, laws now regulate what can be discarded in a landfill, the Environmental Protection Agency has identified 30,000 dump sites across the United States containing hazardous materials that are polluting water both above and below the ground.

Environmentalists argue that we should address the problem of solid waste by doing what many of our grandparents did: Turn waste into a resource. One way to do this is through *recycling*, reusing resources we would otherwise discard. Recycling is an accepted practice in Japan and many other nations, and it is becoming more common in the United States, where we now reuse about 30 percent of waste materials. The share is increasing as laws require reuse of certain materials such as glass bottles and aluminum cans. In addition, because our nation has a market-based economy, recycling is bound to increase as it becomes more profitable.

WATER AND AIR

Oceans, lakes, and streams are the lifeblood of the global ecosystem. Humans depend on water for drinking, bathing, cooling, and cooking, for recreation, and for a host of other activities.

According to what scientists call the *hydrologic cycle*, the Earth naturally recycles water and refreshes the land. The process begins as heat from the sun causes the Earth's water, 97 percent of which is in the oceans, to evaporate and form clouds. Because water evaporates at lower temperatures than most pollutants, the water vapor that rises from the seas is relatively pure, leaving various contaminants behind. Water then falls to the Earth as rain, which drains into streams and rivers and, finally, returns to the sea. Two major concerns about water, then, are supply and pollution.

Water Supply

For thousands of years, since the time of the ancient civilizations of China, Egypt, and Rome, water rights have figured prominently in codes of law. Today, as Global Map 22–2 on page 592 shows, some regions of the world, especially the tropics, enjoy a plentiful supply of water. But high demand, coupled with modest reserves, makes the water supply a matter of concern in much of North America and Asia, where people look to rivers rather than rainfall for their water. In China, deep aquifers are dropping rapidly. In the Middle East, water supply is reaching a critical level. Iran is rationing water in its capital city. In Egypt, the Nile River provides just one-sixth as much water per person as it did in 1900. Across northern Africa and the Middle East, as many as 1 billion people may lack the water they need within thirty years (Myers, 1984c; Postel, 1993; *Popline*, 2001).

In the United States, most of us take safe water for granted. But people, and especially children, in poor countries around the world are at high risk from infectious diseases that are spread by unclean water used for bathing, cooking, and drinking.

Rising population and the development of more complex technology have greatly increased the world's appetite for water. The global consumption of water (now more than 6 billion cubic feet per year) has tripled since 1950 and is expanding even faster than the world's population. As a result, even in those parts of the world that receive plenty of rainfall, people are using groundwater faster than it can be replenished naturally. In the Tamil Nadu region of southern India, for example, so much groundwater is being used that the water table has fallen 100 feet over the last several decades. Mexico City—which has sprawled to some 1,400 square miles—has pumped so much water from its underground aquifer that the city has sunk thirty feet during the last century and is dropping about two more inches per year. Farther north, in the United States, the Ogallala aquifer, which lies below seven states from South Dakota to Texas, is now being pumped so rapidly that some experts fear it could run dry within several decades.

WINDOW ON THE WORLD

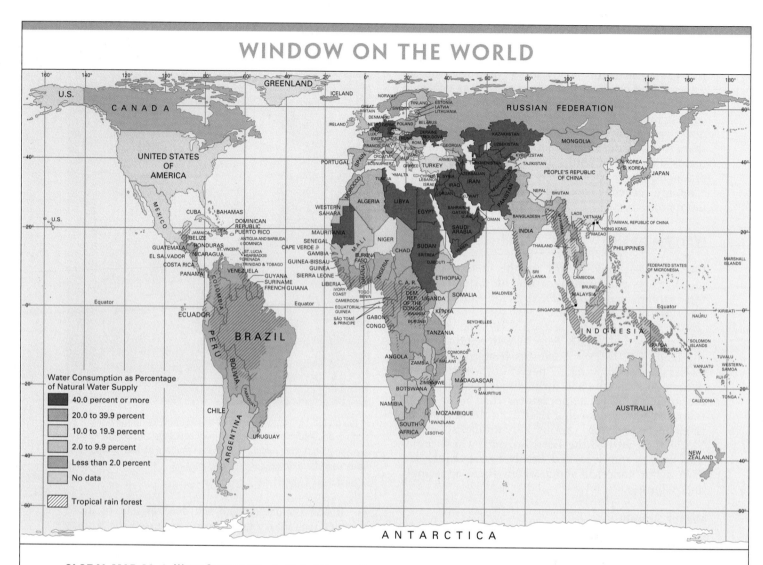

GLOBAL MAP 22–2 Water Consumption in Global Perspective

This map shows water consumption as a percentage of each country's renewable water resources. Nations near the equator consume only a tiny share of their available resources; indeed, much of this region is covered with rain forest. Northern Africa and the Middle East are a different story, however, with dense populations drawing on very limited water resources. As a result, in countries such as Libya, Egypt, and Saudi Arabia, people (especially the poor) do not have as much water as they would like or, often, as they need.

Source: United Nations Development Programme (2000).

In light of such developments, we must face the reality that water is a valuable, finite resource. Greater conservation of water by individuals (the average person consumes 10 million gallons in a lifetime) is part of the answer. However, households around the world account for just 10 percent of water use. It is even more crucial that we curb water consumption by industry, which uses 25 percent of the global total, and farming, which consumes two-thirds of the total for irrigation.

592 CHAPTER 22 Population, Urbanization, and Environment

New irrigation technology may reduce the demand for water in the future. But here again, we see how population increase, as well as economic growth, strains our ecosystem (Myers, 1984a; Goldfarb, 1991; Falkenmark & Widstrand, 1992; Postel, 1993; Population Action International, 2000).

Water Pollution

In large cities—from Mexico City to Cairo to Shanghai—many people have no choice but to drink contaminated water. Infectious diseases like typhoid, cholera, and dysentery, all caused by waterborne microorganisms, spread rapidly through these populations (Clarke, 1984b; Falkenmark & Widstrand, 1992). Besides ensuring ample *supplies* of water, then, we must protect the *quality* of water.

Water quality in the United States is generally good by global standards. However, even here the problem of water pollution is steadily growing. According to the Sierra Club, an environmental activist organization, rivers and streams across the United States absorb some 500 million pounds of toxic waste each year. This pollution results not just from intentional dumping but also from the runoff of agricultural fertilizers and lawn chemicals.

A special problem is *acid rain*—rain made acidic by air pollution—that destroys plant and animal life. Acid rain (or snow) begins with power plants burning fossil fuels (oil and coal) to generate electricity; this burning releases sulfuric and nitrous oxides into the air. As the wind sweeps these gases into the atmosphere, they react with the air to form sulfuric and nitric acids, which turns atmospheric moisture acidic.

This is a clear case of one type of pollution causing another: Air pollution (from smokestacks) ends up contaminating water (in lakes and streams that collect acid rain). Moreover, acid rain is truly a global phenomenon because the regions that suffer the harmful effects may be thousands of miles from the original pollution. For instance, British power plants have caused acid rain that has devastated forests and fish in Norway and Sweden, up to a thousand miles to the northeast. In the United States, we see a similar pattern as midwestern smokestacks have harmed the natural environment of upstate New York and New England (Clarke, 1984a).

Air Pollution

Because we are surrounded by air, most people in the United States are more aware of air pollution than contaminated water. One of the unexpected consequences of industrial technology, especially the factory and the motor vehicle, has been a decline in air quality. In London in the mid-twentieth century, factory smokestacks, automobiles, and coal fires used to heat households all added to what was probably the worst urban air quality of the last century. What some British jokingly called "pea soup" was, in reality, a deadly mix of pollution. For five days in 1952, an especially thick haze that hung over London killed 4,000 people (Clarke, 1984a).

Air quality improved in the final decades of the twentieth century. Rich nations passed laws that banned high-pollution heating, including the coal fires that choked London fifty years ago. In addition, scientists devised ways to greatly make factories as well as automobiles and trucks operate more cleanly.

If high-income countries can breathe a bit more easily than they once did, the problem of air pollution in poor societies is becoming more serious. One reason is that people in low-income countries still rely on wood, coal, peat, and other "dirty" fuels for cooking fires and to heat their homes. Moreover, nations eager to encourage short-term industrial development may pay little heed to the longer-term dangers of air pollution. As a result, many cities in Latin America, Eastern Europe, and Asia are plagued by air pollution as bad as London's fifty years ago.

THE RAIN FORESTS

Rain forests are *regions of dense forestation, most of which circle the globe close to the equator.* A glance back at Global Map 22–2 shows that the largest tropical rain forests are in South America (notably Brazil), west-central Africa, and Southeast Asia. In all, the world's rain forests cover some 2 billion acres, or 7 percent of the Earth's total land surface.

Like other global resources, rain forests are falling victim to the needs and appetites of the surging world population. As noted earlier, to meet the demand for beef, ranchers in Latin America burn forested areas to increase their supply of grazing land. We are also losing rain forests to the hardwood trade. People in rich nations pay high prices for mahogany and other woods because, as environmentalist Norman Myers (1984b:88) puts it, they have "a penchant for parquet floors, fine furniture, fancy paneling, weekend yachts, and high-grade coffins." Under such economic pressure, the world's rain

 **MEDIA** For more information, visit http://www.rainforestweb.org

Members of small, simple societies, such as the Tan't Batu, who thrive in the Philippines, live in harmony with nature; such people do not have the technological means to greatly affect the natural world. Although we in complex societies like to think of ourselves as superior to such people, the truth is that there is much we can—and must—learn from them.

Experts estimate that the atmospheric concentration of carbon dioxide is now 20 to 30 percent higher than it was 150 years ago (Revkin, 2002).

High above the Earth, carbon dioxide acts like the glass roof of a greenhouse, letting heat from the sun pass through to the Earth while preventing much of it from radiating away from the planet. The result of this *greenhouse effect*, say ecologists, is **global warming,** *a rise in the Earth's average temperature due to an increasing concentration of carbon dioxide in the atmosphere.* Over the last century, the global temperature has risen about 1.0° Fahrenheit (to an average of 58° F). And scientists warn that it could rise by 5° F to 10° F during this century, which would melt vast areas of the polar ice caps and raise the sea level to cover low-lying land around the world. Were this to happen, water would cover

 A government study claims that one in four houses within 500 feet of a shoreline is in danger over the next sixty years: http://www.heinzcenter.org

all of Bangladesh, for example, and much of the coastal United States, including Washington, D.C., right up to the steps of the White House. On the other hand, the U.S. Midwest, currently one of the most productive agricultural regions in the world, would very likely become arid.

Not all scientists share this vision of future global warming. Some point out that global temperature changes have been taking place throughout history, apparently with little or nothing to do with rain forests. Moreover, higher concentrations of carbon dioxide in the atmosphere might speed up plant growth (since plants thrive on this gas), and this increase would correct the imbalance and nudge the earth's temperature downward once again. A few scientists think global warming might even have benefits, including longer growing seasons and lower food prices (Silverberg, 1991; Moore, 1995; Begley, 1997; McDonald, 1999).

forests are now just half their original size, and they continue to shrink by about 1 percent (65,000 square miles) annually. Unless we stop this loss, the rain forests will vanish before the end of this century, and with them will go protection for the Earth's biodiversity and climate.

Global Warming

Why are rain forests so important? One reason is that they cleanse the atmosphere of carbon dioxide (CO_2). Since the beginning of the Industrial Revolution, pollutants from factories, automobiles, and other sources have risen dramatically. Much of this carbon dioxide is absorbed by the oceans. But plants take in carbon dioxide and expel oxygen. This is why rain forests are vital to maintaining the chemical balance of the atmosphere.

The problem, then, is that production of carbon dioxide is rising while the amount of plant life on the Earth is shrinking. To make matters worse, rain forests are being destroyed mostly by burning, which releases even more carbon dioxide into the atmosphere.

Declining Biodiversity

Clearing rain forests also reduces the Earth's *biodiversity* because rain forests are home to almost half this planet's living species.

On Earth, there are as many as 30 million species of animals, plants, and microorganisms. Several dozen unique species of plants and animals cease to exist every day. But given the vast number of living species, why should we be concerned? Environmentalists give three reasons. First, our planet's biodiversity provides a varied source of human food. Using agricultural high technology, scientists can "splice" familiar crops with more exotic plant life, making food more bountiful as well as more resistant to insects and disease. Thus, biodiversity is needed to feed our planet's rapidly increasing population.

Second, the Earth's biodiversity is a vital genetic resource. Medical and pharmaceutical research rely on it to provide hundreds of new compounds each year that cure disease and improve our lives. For example, children in the United States now have a good chance of surviving leukemia, a disease that was almost a sure killer two generations ago, because of a compound derived from a tropical flower called the rosy periwinkle. The oral birth control pill, used by tens of millions of women in this country, is another product of plant research, this time involving the Mexican forest yam.

Third, with the loss of any species of life—whether it is the magnificent California condor, the famed Chinese panda, the spotted owl, or even one variety of ant—the beauty and complexity of our natural environment are diminished. And there are clear warning signs of such loss: Three-fourths of the world's 9,000 species of birds are declining in number.

Finally, note that, unlike pollution, the extinction of any species is irreversible and final. An important ethical question, then, is whether we who live today have the right to impoverish the world for those who live tomorrow (Myers, 1984b, 1991; E. Wilson, 1991; Brown et al., 1993).

ENVIRONMENTAL RACISM

Conflict theory has given rise to the concept of **environmental racism,** *the pattern by which environmental hazards are greatest for poor people, especially minorities.* Historically, factories that spew pollution stand near neighborhoods of the poor and people of color. Why? In part, because the poor themselves were drawn to factories in search of work; also their low incomes often meant they could afford housing only in undesirable neighborhoods. Sometimes the only housing that fit their budgets stood in the very shadow of the plants and mills where they worked.

Nobody wants a factory or dump nearby, but the poor have little power to resist. Through the years, then, the most serious environmental hazards have been located near Newark, New Jersey (not in upscale Bergen County), in southside Chicago (not wealthy Lake Forest), or on Native American reservations in the West (not in affluent suburbs of Denver or Phoenix) (Commission for Racial Justice, United Church of Christ, 1994; Szasz, 1994; Pollock & Vittas, 1995; Bohon & Humphrey, 2000).

LOOKING AHEAD: TOWARD A SUSTAINABLE WORLD

The demographic analysis presented in this chapter points to some disturbing trends. We see, first, that Earth's population has reached record levels because birth rates remain high in poor nations and death rates have fallen just about everywhere. Reducing fertility will remain a pressing problem throughout this century. Even with some recent decline in population increase, the nightmare Thomas Malthus described is still a real possibility, as the final box on page 596 explains.

Further, population growth remains greatest in the poorest countries of the world, those without the means to support their present populations, much less their future ones. Supporting 73 million additional people on our planet each year—almost all of whom are born in low-income societies—will require a global commitment to provide not only food but housing, schools, and employment. The well-being of the entire world may ultimately depend on resolving the economic and social problems of poor, overly populated countries and bridging the widening gulf between "have" and "have-not" nations.

Urbanization, too, is continuing, especially in poor countries. Throughout human history, people have sought out cities with the hope of finding a better life. But the sheer numbers of people who live in the emerging global supercities—Mexico City, São Paulo (Brazil), Kinshasa (Democratic Republic of the Congo), Bombay (India), Manila (the Philippines)—have created urban problems on a massive scale.

Throughout the entire world, humanity is facing a serious environmental challenge. Part of this problem is population increase, which is greatest in poor societies. But part of the problem is also high levels of consumption, which mark rich nations such as our own. By increasing the planet's environmental deficit, our present way of life is borrowing against the well-being of our children and their children. Globally, members of rich societies, who currently consume so much of the Earth's resources, are mortgaging the future security of the poor countries of the world.

The answer, in principle, is to form an **ecologically sustainable culture,** *a way of life that meets the needs of the present generation without threatening the environmental legacy of future generations.* Sustainable living depends on three strategies.

First, the world needs to bring population growth under control. The current population of more than 6 billion is already straining the natural environment. Clearly, the higher the world's population climbs, the

CONTROVERSY & DEBATE

Apocalypse: Will People Overwhelm the Earth?

In the few minutes it takes to read this box, more than 1,000 people will be added to our planet. By this time tomorrow, global population will rise by 200,000. Currently, as the table below shows, there are four births for every two deaths on the planet, pushing the world's population upward by 73 million annually. Put another way, global population growth amounts to adding the population of Gambia each week, Paraguay each month, or Egypt to the world each year.

Maybe Thomas Robert Malthus—who predicted that overpopulation would push the world into war and suffering—was right after all. Lester Brown

and other neo-Malthusians predict an apocalypse if we do not change our ways. Brown maintains that the Earth's rising population is rapidly outstripping its finite resources. In many poor countries, people can find little firewood; in rich countries, people are depleting the oil reserves; everyone is draining our supply of clean water and poisoning the planet with waste. Some analysts argue that we have already passed the Earth's "carrying capacity" for population and we need to reduce global population to perhaps half of what it is today (Smail, 2004).

But other analysts, the anti-Malthusians, sharply disagree. Julian Simon points out that two centuries after Malthus

predicted catastrophe, the Earth supports almost six times as many people who, on average, live longer, healthier lives than ever before. With more advanced technology, people have devised ways to increase productivity and control population growth. As Simon sees it, this is cause for celebration. Human ingenuity has consistently proven the doomsayers wrong, and Simon is betting it will continue to do so.

Continue the debate . . .

1. *Where do you place your bet? Is Brown or Simon more correct? Why?*

2. *Ninety-six percent of current population growth is in poor countries. What does this mean for the future of rich nations? For the future of poor ones?*

3. *What should people in rich countries do to ensure the future of children everywhere?*

Global Population Increase

	Births	Deaths	Net Increase
Per Year	128,758,963	55,508,568	73,250,395
Per Month	10,729,914	4,625,714	6,104,200
Per Day	352,764	152,078	200,686
Per Hour	14,699	6,337	8,362
Per Minute	245	106	139
Per Second	4.1	1.8	2.3

Sources: Based, in part, on Brown (1995), Simon (1995), Scanlon (2001), Haub (2002b), and Smail (2004).

more difficult environmental problems will become. Even if the recent slowing of population growth continues, the world will have 8 billion people by 2050. Few analysts think that the Earth can support this many people; most argue that we must hold the line at about 7 billion, and some argue that we must *decrease* population in the coming decades (Smail, 2004).

A second strategy is *conservation of finite resources.* This means meeting our needs with a responsible eye toward the future by using resources efficiently, seeking alternative sources of energy, and, in some cases, learning to live with less.

A third strategy is *reducing waste.* Whenever possible, simply using less is the best solution. But recycling programs, too, are part of the answer.

In the end, making all these strategies work depends on a more basic change in the way we think about ourselves and our world. Our *egocentric* outlook sets our own interests as standards for how to live, but a sustainable environment demands an *ecocentric* outlook that helps us see how the present is tied to the future and why everyone must work together. Most nations in the southern half of the world are *underdeveloped,* unable to meet the basic needs of their people. At the same time, most countries in the northern half of the world are *overdeveloped,* using more resources than the Earth can sustain over time. The changes needed to create a sustainable ecosystem will not come easily, and they will be costly. But the price of not responding to the growing environmental deficit will certainly be greater (Burke, 1984; Kellert & Bormann, 1991; Brown et al., 1993; Population Action International, 2000).

Finally, consider that the great dinosaurs dominated this planet for some 160 million years and then perished forever. Humanity is far younger, having existed for a mere 250,000 years. Compared to the rather dim-witted dinosaurs, our species has the gift

 Explore connections between population increase, global inequality, and the natural environment at http://www.peopleandplanet.net/

of great intelligence. But how will we use this ability? What are the chances that our species will continue to flourish 160 million years—or even 1,000 years—from now? The answer depends on the choices that will be made by one of the 30 million species living on Earth: human beings.

SUMMARY

Population

1. Fertility and mortality, measured as crude birth rates and crude death rates, are major factors affecting population size. In global terms, U.S. population growth is low.

2. Migration, another key demographic concept, has special importance to the historical growth of the United States and to cities everywhere.

3. Demographers use age-sex pyramids to show graphically the composition of a population and to project population trends. *Sex ratio* refers to a society's balance of females and males.

4. Historically, world population grew slowly because high birth rates were largely offset by high death rates. About 1750, a demographic transition began as world population rose sharply, mostly due to falling death rates.

5. Thomas Robert Malthus warned that population growth would outpace food production and the result would be social calamity. Demographic transition theory, however, contends that technological advances gradually slow population increase.

6. World population is expected to reach between 8 billion and 9 billion by 2050. Such an increase is likely to overwhelm many poor societies, where most of the increase will take place.

Urbanization

1. The first urban revolution began with the appearance of cities about 8000 B.C.E. By the start of the common era, cities had emerged in most regions of the world except for North America.

2. Preindustrial cities have low-rise buildings; narrow, winding streets; and personal social ties.

3. A second urban revolution began about 1750, as the Industrial Revolution propelled rapid urban growth in Europe. The physical form of cities changed, as planners created wide, regular streets to facilitate trade. The

emphasis on commerce, as well as the increasing size of cities, made urban life more anonymous.

4. Urbanism came to North America with Europeans, who settled in a string of colonial towns along the Atlantic coastline. By 1850, hundreds of new cities had been founded from coast to coast.

5. By 1920, a majority of the U.S. population lived in urban areas, and the largest metropolises were home to millions of people.

6. About 1950, cities began to decentralize with the growth of suburbs and edge cities. Nationally, Sunbelt cities—but not the older Snowbelt cities—are increasing in size and population.

7. Rapid urbanization in Europe during the nineteenth century led early sociologists to contrast rural and urban life. Ferdinand Tönnies built his analysis on the concepts of *Gemeinschaft* and *Gesellschaft*, and Emile Durkheim proposed parallel concepts of mechanical solidarity and organic solidarity. Georg Simmel claimed that the overstimulation of city life produced a blasé attitude in urbanites.

8. At the University of Chicago, Robert Park believed cities permit greater social freedom. Louis Wirth saw large, dense, heterogeneous populations creating an impersonal and self-interested, though tolerant, way of life. Other researchers have explored urban ecology and urban political economy.

9. A third urban revolution is now occurring in poor countries, where most of the world's largest cities will soon be found.

Environment

1. A key factor affecting the natural environment is how human beings organize social life. Thus, ecologists study how living organisms interact with their environment.

2. Societies increase the environmental deficit by focusing on short-term benefits and ignoring the long-term consequences brought on by their way of life.

3. Our ability to alter the natural world lies in our capacity for culture. Humanity's effect on the environment has increased along with the development of complex technology.

4. The "logic of growth" thesis supports economic development, claiming that people can solve environmental problems as they arise. The opposing "limits to growth" thesis states that societies must curb development to prevent eventual environmental collapse.

5. Environmental issues include disposing of solid waste and protecting the quality of air and water. The supply of clean water is already low in some parts of the world.

6. Rain forests help remove carbon dioxide from the atmosphere and are home to a large share of this planet's living species. Under pressure from commercial interests, the world's rain forests are now half their original size and are shrinking by about 1 percent annually.

7. *Environmental racism* refers to the pattern by which the poor, especially minorities, suffer most from environmental hazards.

8. To achieve a sustainable environment that does not threaten the well-being of future generations, we must control world population, conserve finite resources, and reduce waste and pollution.

KEY CONCEPTS

Population

demography (p. 569) the study of human population

fertility (p. 570) the incidence of childbearing in a country's population

crude birth rate (p. 570) the number of live births in a given year for every thousand people in a population

mortality (p. 571) the incidence of death in a country's population

crude death rate (p. 571) the number of deaths in a given year for every thousand people in a population

infant mortality rate (p. 571) the number of deaths among infants under one year of age for each thousand live births in a given year

life expectancy (p. 571) the average life span of a country's population

migration (p. 571) the movement of people into and out of a specified territory

sex ratio (p. 573) the number of males for every hundred females in a nation's population

age-sex pyramid (p. 573) a graphic representation of the age and sex of a population

demographic transition theory (p. 575) the thesis that population patterns reflect a society's level of technological development

zero population growth (p. 576) the level of reproduction that maintains population in a steady state

Urbanization

urbanization (p. 578) the concentration of humanity into cities

metropolis (p. 580) a large city that socially and economically dominates an urban area

suburbs (p. 580) urban areas beyond the political boundaries of a city

megalopolis (p. 581) a vast urban region containing a number of cities and their surrounding suburbs

Gemeinschaft (p. 582) a type of social organization by which people are closely tied by kinship and tradition

Gesellschaft (p. 582) a type of social organization by which people come together only on the basis of individual self-interest

urban ecology (p. 584) the study of the link between the physical and social dimensions of cities

Environment

ecology (p. 586) the study of the interaction of living organisms and the natural environment

natural environment (p. 587) the Earth's surface and atmosphere, including living organisms, air, water, soil, and other resources necessary to sustain life

ecosystem (p. 587) a system composed of the interaction of all living organisms and their natural environment

environmental deficit (p. 588) profound and long-term harm to the natural environment caused by humanity's focus on short-term material affluence

rain forests (p. 593) regions of dense forestation, most of which circle the globe close to the equator

global warming (p. 594) a rise in the Earth's average temperature due to an increasing concentration of carbon dioxide in the atmosphere

environmental racism (p. 595) the pattern by which environmental hazards are greatest for poor people, especially minorities

ecologically sustainable culture (p. 595) a way of life that meets the needs of the present generation without threatening the environmental legacy of future generations

CRITICAL-THINKING QUESTIONS

1. What are fertility and mortality rates? Which one has been more important in increasing global population?

2. Evaluate the environmental prediction of Thomas Robert Malthus. On balance, do you think he was more wrong or more right? Why?

3. According to demographic transition theory, how does economic development affect population patterns?

4. According to Ferdinand Tönnies, Emile Durkheim, Georg Simmel, and Louis Wirth, what characterizes urbanism as a way of life? Note several differences in the ideas of these thinkers.

APPLICATIONS AND EXERCISES

1. Here is an illustration of the problem of runaway growth (Milbrath, 1989:10): *A pond has a single water lily growing on it. The lily doubles in size each day. In thirty days, it covers the entire pond. On which day does it cover half the pond?* When you realize the answer, discuss the implications of this example for population increase.

2. Draw a mental map of a city familiar to you with as much detail of specific places, districts, roads, and transportation facilities as you can. Compare your map to a real one or, better yet, a map drawn by someone else. Try to account for the differences.

3. In the Bible, read the first chapter of Genesis, especially verses 28–31. According to this account of creation, are humans empowered to do what we wish to the Earth? Or are we charged to care for the Earth? For more on this idea, see Wolkomir et al. (1997).

4. Packaged in the back of this new textbook is an interactive CD-ROM that offers a variety of video and interactive review materials intended to help you better understand the material covered in this chapter. For this chapter, the CD-ROM contains a relevant clip from *ABC News*, an author's tip video, interactive map animations, an interactive time line, and flashcards with audio pronunciations of the more difficult words.

SITES TO SEE

http://www.urban.nyu.edu/
New York University's Taub Urban Research Center Web site provides recent research on urban issues.

http://www.wri.org/
The World Resources Institute provides information on the state of the planet's environment.

http://www.hud.gov
This is the Web site for the U.S. government's Department of Housing and Urban Development.

http://www.sierraclub.org
http://www.greenpeace.org
These two environmental sites are maintained by the Sierra Club and Greenpeace. Visit the sites and see how these two organizations are similar to one another and how they differ.

http://www.eclac.org
This site, created by the Economic Commission for Latin America and the Caribbean (part of the United Nations), provides statistics on population patterns for this region of the world. Most of the site is available in English and Spanish.

INVESTIGATE WITH RESEARCH NAVIGATOR™

Follow the instructions on page 24 of this text to access the features of **Research Navigator™**. Once at the Web site, enter your Login Name and Password. Then, to use the **Content Select™** database, enter keywords such as "demography," "urbanism," and "rain forest," and the search engine will supply relevant and recent scholarly and popular press publications. Use the *New York Times* **Search-by-Subject Archive** to find recent news articles related to sociology and the **Link Library** feature to find relevant Web links organized by the key terms associated with this chapter.

COLLECTIVE BEHAVIOR AND SOCIAL MOVEMENTS

EDWARD BURRA (1905–1976, ENGLISH)
The Riot

1948, watercolor on paper, 79 × 110 cm. Private Collection/The Lefevre Gallery, London/The Bridgeman Art Library.

A CCORDING TO THE Internet message making the rounds in 2003, the Shell Oil Company had just issued an urgent warning: Cellular phones can cause fires at gas stations. What prompted the warning was an accident involving a motorist fueling her car who placed a cellular phone on the trunk lid; the phone suddenly rang, causing a spark that ignited gasoline fumes and caused a fire that destroyed both her car and the gas pump.

The Internet alert reported that this was only one of many similar incidents. The message ended with stern instructions from an oil company official to motorists using gas stations: Never use a cellular telephone at a gas station, and while refueling, turn cell phones off and leave them in the car.

This message went to tens of thousands of computers across the United States, generally spread by well-meaning people wanting to warn their friends and co-workers of the danger posed by cellular phones. The only problem with the message, as you may have guessed, is that it is not true. No such incident ever happened. But in a society in which millions of people have cellular phones (which few people really understand), it is easy to see how a rumor of this kind can spread.

The false rumor involving cellular phones causing gasoline explosions is just one example of **collective behavior,** *activity involving a large number of people, often spontaneous, and sometimes controversial.* This chapter investigates various forms of collective behavior—ranging from crowds, mobs and riots, rumor and gossip, public opinion, panic and mass hysteria, and fashions and fads to social movements aimed at changing the course of people's lives around the world.

For much of the twentieth century, sociologists focused on established social patterns like the family and social stratification. They paid less attention to

To read more about the cell phone rumor and other bogus stories on the Internet, go to http://www.truthorfiction.com/rumors/cellgas.htm

cases of collective behavior, considering most of it trivial, unusual, or even deviant. But numerous social movements characterized the tumultuous 1960s, and many are still changing society today.

Therefore, in recent decades, sociological interest in all types of collective behavior has increased (Weller & Quarantelli, 1973; G. Marx & Wood, 1975; Aguirre & Quarantelli, 1983; McAdam, McCarthy, & Zald, 1988; Turner & Killian, 1993).

STUDYING COLLECTIVE BEHAVIOR

Despite its importance, collective behavior is difficult for sociologists to study for three main reasons:

1. **Collective behavior is wide-ranging.** Collective behavior involves a bewildering array of human action. The traits common to fads, rumors, and mob behavior, for example, are far from obvious.

2. **Collective behavior is hard to explain.** Occasionally a rumor, like the one described in the opening of this chapter, is spread widely across the United States. But others quickly die out. Why does one

Looking down at the people in this park, are we observing a collectivity or a social group? What characteristics distinguish the two types of gatherings?

States; sociologists interested in how disasters affect behavior need to be prepared to begin research on short notice (Miller, 1985). A number of researchers are at work studying how the terrorist attacks of September 11, 2001, have affected U.S. society.

Sociologists now know a great deal about collective behavior, but they still have much to learn. The most serious shortcoming, according to Benigno Aguirre and E. L. Quarantelli (1983), is that sociologists have yet to devise a theory that ties together all the different actions termed "collective behavior."

At the least, all collective behavior involves the action of some **collectivity,** *a large number of people whose minimal interaction occurs in the absence of well-defined and conventional norms.* Collectivities are of two kinds. A *localized collectivity* refers to people in physical proximity to one another; this first type is illustrated by crowds and riots. A *dispersed collectivity* or *mass behavior* involves people who influence one another even though they are separated by great distances; examples here include rumors, public opinion, and fashion (Turner & Killian, 1993).

It is important to distinguish collectivities from the already familiar concept of social groups (see Chapter 7, "Groups and Organizations"). Here are three key differences:

1. **Collectivities are based on limited social interaction.** Group members interact frequently and directly. People in mobs or other localized collectivities interact very little. Most people taking part in dispersed collectivities, such as a fad, do not interact at all.

2. **Collectivities have no clear social boundaries.** Group members share a sense of identity that is usually missing among people engaged in collective behavior. Localized crowds may have a common object of attention (such as someone on a ledge threatening to jump), but they show little sense of unity. Individuals involved in dispersed collectivities, such as the "public" that is alarmed by the epidemic SARS (severe acute respiratory syndrome), have almost no awareness of shared membership. Of course, some issues divide the public into well-defined factions, but often, it is difficult to say who falls within the ranks of, say, the environmentalist or feminist movement.

3. **Collectivities generate weak and unconventional norms.** Conventional cultural norms usually regulate the behavior of group members. Some collectivities, such as people traveling on an airplane, observe conventional norms, but their interaction is

such rumor catch on, while another does not? More important, why, over the course of this nation's history, did millions of African Americans patiently endure second-class standing for so long before beginning the modern civil rights movement in the mid-1950s?

3. **Much collective behavior is transitory.** Sociologists can readily study the family because it is a continuing element of social life. Rumors, fashions, and riots, however, come and go quickly, so they are difficult to study.

Some researchers point out that these problems apply not just to collective behavior but to *most* forms of human behavior (Aguirre & Quarantelli, 1983). Moreover, collective behavior is not always so surprising; anyone can predict that crowds will form at sports events and music festivals, and sociologists can study these gatherings firsthand or record them on videotape to study later. Researchers can even anticipate natural disasters and study the human responses they provoke. Each year, for example, about sixty major tornadoes occur in particular regions of the United

usually limited to polite small talk, respectful of the privacy of people sitting nearby. Other collectivities—such as excited soccer fans who destroy property as they leave a stadium—spontaneously develop very unconventional norms (Weller & Quarantelli, 1973; Turner & Killian, 1993).

LOCALIZED COLLECTIVITIES: CROWDS

One major form of collective behavior is the **crowd,** *a temporary gathering of people who share a common focus of attention and who influence one another*. Historian Peter Laslett (1984) points out that very large crowds are a modern development; in medieval Europe, about the only time large numbers of people gathered in one place was when armies faced off on the battlefield. Today, however, crowds of 25,000 or more are common at sporting events, rock concerts, and even the registration halls of large universities.

But all crowds are not alike. Herbert Blumer (1969) identified four categories of crowds:

A *casual crowd* is a loose collection of people who interact little, if at all. People at the beach or at the scene of an automobile accident have only a passing awareness of one another.

A *conventional crowd* results from deliberate planning, as illustrated by a country auction, a college lecture, or a celebrity's funeral. In each case, interaction conforms to norms appropriate to the situation.

An *expressive crowd* forms around an event with emotional appeal, such as a religious revival, a World Wrestling Federation match, or the New Year's Eve celebration in New York City's Times Square. Excitement is the main reason people join expressive crowds, which makes this experience spontaneous and exhilarating for those involved.

An *acting crowd* is a collectivity motivated by an intense, single-minded purpose, such as an audience rushing the doors of a concert hall or fleeing from a burning theater. Acting crowds are ignited by very powerful emotions, which can reach a feverish intensity and sometimes erupt into mob violence.

Any crowd can change from one type to another. In 2001, for example, a conventional crowd of more than 10,000 fans filed into a soccer stadium in Johannesburg, South Africa, to watch a match between two rival teams. After a goal was scored, the crowd erupted and people began to push toward the field. Within seconds, a stampede was under way, which crushed forty-seven people to death. By the time order was restored, the dead lay in the stands and across the playing field as if a battle rather than a sporting event had taken place (Nessman, 2001).

Deliberate action by a crowd is not simply the product of rising emotions. Participants in *protest crowds*—a fifth category we can add to Blumer's list—may stage strikes, boycotts, sit-ins, and marches for political purposes (McPhail & Wohlstein, 1983). Examples of protest crowds are the antiwar demonstrations that took place on many campuses and in many large cities in the months prior to the War in Iraq. In such crowds, most participants display the low-level energy characteristic of a conventional crowd, while some are emotional enough to be in an acting crowd. Sometimes, too, a protest begins peacefully, but people may become aggressive when faced with resistance by police or counterdemonstrators or when they are intent on disrupting "business as usual."

MOBS AND RIOTS

When an acting crowd turns violent, we may witness the birth of a **mob,** *a highly emotional crowd that pursues a violent or destructive goal*. Despite, or perhaps because of, their intense emotion, mobs tend to dissipate quickly. How long a mob exists often depends on its precise goals and whether its leadership tries to inflame or stabilize the crowd.

Lynching is the most notorious example of mob behavior in the United States. The term is derived from Charles Lynch, a Virginia colonist who sought to maintain law and order in his own way before formal courts were established. The word soon became synonymous with violence and murder outside the law.

Lynching has always been colored by race. After the Civil War, lynch mobs became a terrorist form of social control over emancipated African Americans. African Americans who challenged white superiority risked being hanged or burned alive by hateful whites.

Lynch mobs—typically composed of poor whites threatened by competition from freed slaves—reached their peak between 1880 and 1930. Police recorded some 5,000 lynchings in that period, though, no doubt, many more occurred. Often, lynchings were popular events, attracting hundreds of spectators; sometimes victims were quickly killed, and sometimes they were tortured before being put to death. Most of these terrorist killings were committed in the Deep South, where a farming economy depended on a cheap and docile labor force. On the western frontier, lynch mobs targeted people of Mexican and Asian descent. In about 25 percent of known cases, whites lynched other whites. Lynching women, however, was rare; only about a hundred such instances are known, almost all involving women of color (White, 1969, orig. 1929; Grant, 1975; Lacayo, 2000).

A frenzied crowd without any particular purpose is a **riot**, *a social eruption that is highly emotional, violent, and undirected.* Unlike the action of a mob, a riot usually has no clear goal, except perhaps to express dissatisfaction. Underlying most riots is longstanding anger that is ignited by some minor incident so that participants become violent, destroying property or harming other persons (Smelser, 1962; M. Rosenfeld, 1997). Whereas a mob action usually ends when a specific violent goal has been achieved (or decisively blocked), a riot tends to disperse only as the participants run out of steam or police and community leaders gradually bring them under control.

Throughout our nation's history, riots have erupted as a reaction to social injustice. Industrial workers, for example, have rioted to vent rage over their working conditions. In 1886, a bitter struggle by Chicago factory workers for an eight-hour workday led to the explosive Haymarket Riot, which left eleven dead and scores injured. Rioting born of anger and despair also takes place frequently in prisons.

In addition, race riots have occurred in this country with striking regularity. Early in this century, crowds of whites attacked African Americans in Chicago, Detroit, and other cities. In the 1960s, violent riots rocked numerous inner-city ghettos when seemingly trivial events sparked rage at continuing prejudice and discrimination. In Los Angeles in 1992, the acquittal of police officers involved in the beating of motorist Rodney King set off an explosive riot. Violence and fires killed more than fifty people, injured thousands, and destroyed property worth hundreds of millions of dollars.

Riots are not always fired by hate. They can also begin with very positive feelings. In 2000, for example, young men attending New York City's National Puerto Rican Day Parade began spraying water on young women in their midst. Within the next few hours, dozens of women reported being groped, stripped, and assaulted—apparently resulting, as one report put it, from a mixture of "marijuana, alcohol, hot weather, testosterone idiocy, and lapses in police [protection]" (Barstow & Chivers, 2000:1). Similarly, a win by the Los Angeles Lakers basketball team a few days later was all that was needed to set hundreds of young people in Los Angeles on a jubilant rampage in which they turned over cars, broke windows, started fires, and injured several dozen people. As one analyst put it, in an "anything goes" culture, some people think they can do whatever they feel like doing (Pitts, Jr., 2000).

CROWDS, MOBS, AND SOCIAL CHANGE

April 13, Cincinnati, Ohio. The city has been under siege all week by African American demonstrators enraged by the police shooting of an unarmed black man. In the mayhem, however, dozens of innocent people—both black and white—have been seriously hurt by flying bricks and swinging baseball bats. Does such violence help bring attention to a just cause, or does it obscure it?

What does a riot accomplish? Ordinary people can gain power by acting collectively. The Cincinnati demonstrators succeeded in calling national attention to charges of racial bias on the part of police and causing that police department to carefully review officer conduct. The power of the crowd to disrupt the routine social order and force some social change is the reason crowds are controversial. Throughout history, defenders of the status quo have feared "the mob" as a threat. By contrast, those seeking change have viewed mobs sympathetically.

Moreover, crowds share no single political cast. Demonstrators and counterdemonstrators shout slogans for and against abortion, for example, displaying objectives that reflect all positions along the political spectrum (Rudé, 1964; Canetti, 1978; Tarrow, 1994).

EXPLAINING CROWD BEHAVIOR

What accounts for the behavior of crowds? Social scientists have developed several different explanations.

Contagion Theory

An early explanation of collective behavior was formulated by French sociologist Gustave Le Bon (1841–1931). According to Le Bon's *contagion theory* (1960; orig. 1895), crowds exert a hypnotic influence over their members. Shielded by the anonymity afforded by large numbers, people abandon personal responsibility and surrender to the contagious emotions of the crowd. A crowd thus assumes a life of its own, stirring up emotions and driving people toward irrational, even violent, action.

In 2003, a new type of collective behavior emerged—the "smart mob" or "flash mob." In this case, a large number of people—connected by cell phones or instant messaging—come together in a designated place for a few minutes to perform some specific action and then disperse. Here, hundreds of young people in Paris converged on the Louvre museum with the instructions "fall on the floor and don't move." Minutes later, they were gone.

Critical evaluation. Le Bon's idea that crowds foster anonymity and sometimes generate strong emotions is surely true. Yet, as Clark McPhail (1991) points out, a considerable body of research shows that "the madding crowd" does not take on a life of its own; its actions result from the policies and decisions made by specific individuals. In the case of the 2003 nightclub fire in Rhode Island that killed ninety-seven people, the high death toll did not result simply from the crowd "going wild" and thereby becoming trapped inside the flaming building. Later investigation showed that the band had used dangerous fireworks onstage, causing flames that ignited flammable soundproofing material on the ceiling, in a room that had no sprinkler system. As a result, fire engulfed the entire building in minutes, before many of the people realized what was happening (Apuzo, 2003; Forliti, 2003).

Furthermore, although collective behavior may involve strong emotions, such feelings are not necessarily irrational as contagion theory suggests. On the contrary, emotions—as well as action—can reflect real fear (as in the nightclub fire) or result from a sense of injustice (as in the Cincinnati racial protests) (Jasper, 1998).

Convergence Theory

Convergence theory holds that crowd behavior is not a product of the crowd itself but is carried into the crowd by particular individuals. That is, the crowd is a convergence of like-minded individuals. While contagion theory states that crowds cause people to act in a certain way, convergence theory says the opposite: People who wish to act in a certain way come together to form crowds.

In 2003, the crowds that formed at demonstrations opposing the War in Iraq, for example, did not cause people to speak out against this policy. On the contrary, participants came together because of their political attitudes.

Critical evaluation. By linking crowds to broader social forces, convergence theory claims that crowd behavior is not irrational, as Le Bon maintained. Rather, people in crowds express existing beliefs and values (Berk, 1974). But in fairness to Le Bon, people sometimes do things in a crowd that they would not have the courage to do alone, because crowds can diffuse responsibility. In addition, crowds can intensify a sentiment simply by creating a critical mass of like-minded people.

Emergent-Norm Theory

Ralph Turner and Lewis Killian (1993) developed the *emergent-norm theory* of crowd dynamics. These researchers concede that social behavior is never entirely predictable, but if similar interests draw people together, distinctive patterns of behavior may emerge in the crowd.

According to Turner and Killian, crowds begin as collectivities containing people with mixed interests

CRITICAL THINKING

The Rumor Mill: Paul Is Dead!

Everyone knows the Beatles. The music of Paul McCartney, John Lennon, George Harrison, and Ringo Starr caused a cultural revolution in the 1960s. Not everyone today, however, knows the rumor that circulated about Paul McCartney at the height of the group's popularity.

On October 12, 1969, a young man telephoned a Detroit disk jockey to say that he had discovered "evidence" that Paul McCartney was dead:

1. At the end of the song "Strawberry Fields Forever" on the *Magical Mystery Tour* album, filtering out background noise allows the listener to hear a voice saying, "I buried Paul!"

2. The phrase "Number 9, Number 9, Number 9" from the song "Revolution 9" on the *White Album*, when played backward, seems to intone, "Turn me on, dead man!"

Two days later, the University of Michigan student newspaper ran a story entitled "McCartney Is Dead: Further Clues Found." It sent millions of Beatles fans scurrying for their albums.

3. A picture inside the *Magical Mystery Tour* album shows John, George, and Ringo wearing red carnations, while Paul is wearing a black flower.

4. The cover of the *Sergeant Pepper's Lonely Hearts Club Band* album

shows a grave with yellow flowers arranged in the shape of Paul's bass guitar.

5. On the inside of that album, McCartney wears an armpatch with the letters "OPD." Is this the insignia of some police department or confirmation that Paul had been "Officially Pronounced Dead"?

6. On the back cover of the same album, three Beatles are facing forward while McCartney has his back to the camera.

7. On the album cover of *Abbey Road*, John Lennon is clothed as a clergyman, Ringo Starr wears an undertaker's black tie, and George Harrison

and motives. Especially in the case of less stable crowds—expressive, acting, and protest crowds—norms may be vague and changing. Consider how many Iraqi citizens began looting government buildings after U.S. troops toppled Saddam Hussein; over time, while some continued to steal anything they could carry, others tried to stop the lawlessness. In short, people in crowds make their own rules as they go along.

Critical evaluation. Emergent-norm theory represents a symbolic-interaction approach to crowd dynamics. Turner and Killian (1972:10) explain that crowd behavior is neither as irrational as contagion theory suggests nor as deliberate as convergence theory implies. Certainly, crowd behavior reflects the desires of participants, but it is also guided by norms that emerge as the situation unfolds.

Decision making, then, plays a major role in crowd behavior, although casual observers of the crowd may not realize it. For example, frightened people clogging the exits of a burning nightclub may appear to be victims of irrational panic, but from their point of view, fleeing a rapidly spreading fire makes a lot of sense.

Further, emergent-norm theory points out that people in a crowd take on different roles. Some step forward as leaders, others become lieutenants, rank-and-file followers, inactive bystanders, or even opponents (Weller & Quarantelli, 1973; Zurcher & Snow, 1981).

DISPERSED COLLECTIVITIES: MASS BEHAVIOR

It is not just people clustered together in crowds who participate in collective behavior. **Mass behavior** refers to *collective behavior among people dispersed over a wide geographic area.*

RUMOR AND GOSSIP

A common type of mass behavior is **rumor,** *unsubstantiated information people spread informally, often by word of mouth.* People pass along rumors through face-to-face communication, of course, but today's modern technology—including telephones, the mass

is clad in workman's attire as if ready to dig a grave. For his part, McCartney is barefoot, which is how Tibetan ritual prepares a corpse for burial. Behind Paul is parked John Lennon's Volkswagen displaying the license plate "28 IF," apparently stating that McCartney would be *28 if* he were alive.

The rumor explained that McCartney had died of head injuries suffered in an automobile accident in November 1966. After the accident, record company executives had secretly replaced Paul with a double.

Of course, Sir Paul McCartney is very much alive and still jokes about the episode. Few doubt that Paul himself dreamed up some of the details of his "death" with a little help from his friends to encourage the interest of their

fans. But the incident has a serious side, showing how quickly rumors can arise and persist in a climate of distrust. In the late 1960s, many disaffected young people were quite ready to believe that the media and other powerful interests were concealing McCartney's death.

In 1969, McCartney himself denied the rumor in a *Life* magazine story. But thousands of suspicious readers noticed that on the other side of the page with McCartney's picture was an ad for an automobile: Holding this page up to the light, the car lay across McCartney's chest and blocked his head. Another clue!

What do you think?

1. *What can we say about the kind of issues that give rise to rumors?*
2. *Have there been rumors this year on your campus? About what?*
3. *On balance, do you think rumors are helpful or harmful? Why?*

Sources: Based on Rosnow & Fine (1976) and Kapferer (1992).

media, and now the Internet—spreads rumors faster and farther than ever before.

Rumor has three essential characteristics:

1. **Rumor thrives in a climate of ambiguity.** Rumors arise when people lack definitive information about an important issue. The fact that many people now carry cellular phones that use a technology few understand helps explain why many would believe these phones might cause fires, as described in the opening to this chapter.

2. **Rumor is unstable.** People change a rumor as they pass it along, usually giving it a "spin" that serves their own interests. Before long, many competing versions exist.

3. **Rumor is difficult to stop.** The number of people aware of a rumor increases exponentially as each person spreads information to several others.

 Another site that tracks the truth about recent Internet rumors is http://www.nonprofit.net/hoax/

Rumors dissipate with time, but in general, the only way to control rumors is for a believable source to issue a clear and convincing statement of the facts.

Rumor can trigger the formation of crowds or other collective behavior. For this reason, officials establish rumor-control centers during a crisis in order to manage information. Yet some rumors persist for years, perhaps just because people enjoy them; the box gives one notable example.

Gossip is *rumor about people's personal affairs.* Charles Horton Cooley (1962; orig. 1909) explained that rumor involves an issue of concern to a large audience, but gossip interests only a small circle of people who know a particular person. Rumors, therefore, spread widely, while gossip tends to be more localized.

Communities use gossip as a means of social control, praising or scorning someone to encourage conformity to local norms. Moreover, people gossip about others to raise their own standing as social "insiders" just as more powerful people use gossip to keep those who are socially marginal "in their place" (Baumgartner, 1998; Nicholson, 2001). Yet no community wants gossip to get out of control so that no one knows what to believe, which may be the reason people who gossip *too* much are criticized as "busybodies."

SEEING OURSELVES

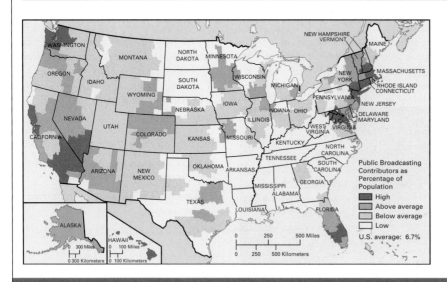

NATIONAL MAP 23–1
Support for Public Broadcasting across the United States

About 7 percent of people in the United States pledge money to support the Public Broadcasting System (PBS). As the map shows, PBS supporters are concentrated in particular regions of the country. What do you think accounts for this pattern?

Source: *Time* (January 16, 1995). Copyright © 1995 Time, Inc. Reprinted by permission.

Public Broadcasting Contributors as Percentage of Population

■ High
■ Above average
□ Below average
□ Low

U.S. average: 6.7%

0 250 500 Miles
0 250 500 Kilometers

PUBLIC OPINION AND PROPAGANDA

Another form of dispersed collective behavior is **public opinion,** *widespread attitudes about controversial issues.* Exactly who is, or is not, included in any "public" depends on the issue involved. Over the years in the United States, "publics" have formed over numerous controversial issues, from water fluoridation, air pollution, and the social standing of women, to handguns and health care (Lang & Lang, 1961; Turner, Killian, & Snow, 2001). More recently, the public has debated affirmative action, welfare reform, and government funding of public radio and television. National Map 23–1 shows where supporters of public broadcasting reside.

On any given issue, a small share of people offer no opinion at all because of ignorance or indifference. Even on some important issues, many people don't know enough to have clear opinions. In 2003, for example, researchers discovered that 60 percent of U.S. adults claimed they did not understand the U.S. income tax system well enough to know if they supported it or not (Rosenbaum, 2003).

Over time, as well, public interest in issues rises and falls. For example, interest in the social position of women in the United States ran high a century ago during the women's suffrage movement but declined

after 1920 when women gained the right to vote. Since the 1960s, a second wave of feminism has again created a public with strong opinions on gender-related issues.

Also, keep in mind that on any issue, not everyone's opinion carries the same weight. Some categories of people have more clout because they are better educated, wealthier, or better connected. Small, well-organized groups also can have a big effect on public policy. Physicians, for example, represent a very small share of the U.S. public, but they have a lot to say about health care in the United States, just as members of the National Education Association have a great deal to say about public education in the United States.

Special-interest groups and political leaders all try to shape public tastes and attitudes by using **propaganda,** *information presented with the intention of shaping public opinion.* Although the term has negative connotations, propaganda is not necessarily false. A thin line separates information from propaganda; the difference depends mostly on the presenter's intention. We offer *information* to enlighten others; we use *propaganda* to sway an audience toward some viewpoint. Political speeches, commercial advertising, and even some college lectures may disseminate propaganda in an effort to steer people toward thinking or acting in some specific way.

PANIC AND MASS HYSTERIA

A **panic** is *a form of localized collective behavior by which people react to a threat or other stimulus with irrational, frantic, and often self-destructive behavior.* The classic illustration of a panic is people streaming toward exits of a crowded theater after someone yells, "Fire!" As they flee, they trample one another, blocking exits so that few actually escape.

 To hear the 1938 radio broadcast that started a national panic, go to http:// www.waroftheworlds.org

Closely related to panic is **mass hysteria** or **moral panic,** *a form of dispersed collective behavior by which people react to a real or imagined event with irrational and even frantic fear.* Whether the cause of the hysteria is real or not, a large number of people certainly take it very seriously.

Some causes of mass hysteria or moral panic emerge within popular culture. In recent years, moral panics have centered on flag burning (Welch, 2000), fear of AIDS (or of people with AIDS), and, more recently, fear of SARS (severe acute respiratory syndrome). Sometimes the fears prove to be overblown, as in the case of flag burning, which outraged many people but did not threaten the country in any major way, and sometimes the fears prove to be justified, as in concern about the deadly AIDS crisis, which has killed more than 25 million people worldwide.

What makes moral panics common, especially in light of the fact that the danger may be overstated? Erich Goode (2000:549) explains that "the mass media *thrives* on scares; contributing to moral panics is the media's stock in trade." Thus, many people become more fearful than they should be because of what they learn from the mass media (Glassner, 1999).

Mass hysteria can also be triggered by an event, which, at the extreme, sends people into chaotic flight. Of course, people who see others overcome by fear may become more afraid themselves, so that hysteria feeds on itself. So it was on the morning of September 11, 2001, in the wake of the terrorist attacks. While there were countless acts of heroism, panic was also widespread, especially in Washington, D.C, after a plane crashed into the Pentagon, causing tens of thousands of people to flee the city and producing a citywide gridlock. People thought they were in danger, they found that they were unable to escape, and fear built upon itself (Gibbs, 2001).

At the same time, it is important to note that *most* disasters do not result in panics. Research has shown that most people, faced with fire, flood, tornado, or earthquake, act in an orderly and disciplined way, taking care of themselves and typically helping others (Clarke, 2002).

FASHIONS AND FADS

Two more kinds of collective behavior—fashions and fads—involve people spread over a large area. A **fashion** is *a social pattern favored by a large number of people.* Some fashions last for years, while others change after just a few months. The arts (including painting, music, drama, and literature), the shape of buildings, automobiles, and clothes, our use of language, and public opinion all change as ideas go in and out of fashion.

In preindustrial societies, clothing and personal appearance reflect traditional *style,* which changes very little. Women and men, the rich and the poor, lawyers and carpenters wear distinctive clothes and hairstyles that indicate their occupations and social standing (Lofland, 1973; Crane, 2000).

In industrial societies, however, established style gives way to changing fashion. For one thing, modern people care less about tradition and often eagerly embrace new ways of living. Then, too, high social mobility means that people use their "looks" to make a statement about themselves. German sociologist Georg Simmel (1971; orig. 1904) explained that affluent people are usually the trendsetters, since people look to them and they have the money to spend on luxuries. Or as U.S. sociologist Thorstein Veblen (1953; orig. 1899) put it, fashion involves *conspicuous consumption,* as people buy expensive products (from bottled water to Hummers) simply to show off their wealth.

Ordinary people who want to appear wealthy often snap up less expensive copies of what the rich make fashionable. In this way, a fashion trickles downward through the class structure. But before long, the fashion loses its prestige when too many average people now share "the look," so the rich have moved on to something new. In short, fashions are born along the Fifth Avenues and Rodeo Drives of the rich and rise to mass popularity in discount stores across the country.

A reversal of this pattern has been more common since the 1960s, by which better-off people mimic fashions found among people of lower social position. This pattern began when blue jeans, or dungarees (from a Hindi word for a coarse fabric), rose to the height of fashion among affluent college students. For decades, manual laborers had worn blue jeans, but in the era of civil rights and antiwar movements, jeans became the uniform of liberal political activists and were soon worn by just about everyone on college

Because change in high-income societies is so rapid, we see differences in personal appearance—one important element of fashion—over relatively short periods of time. These six photographs (beginning at the top, left) show hair styles commonly worn by women in the 1950s, 1960s, 1970s, 1980s, 1990s, and since 2000.

campuses across the country. Cargo pants and other emblems of the hip-hop culture do much the same today—allowing even the most affluent entertainers and celebrities to mimic the styles of those with much less.

A **fad** is *an unconventional social pattern that people embrace briefly but enthusiastically*. Fads, sometimes called *crazes*, are commonplace in high-income societies, where many people have the money to spend on amusing, if often frivolous, products. During the 1950s, two young entrepreneurs in California produced a brightly colored plastic version of a popular Australian toy, a three-foot-diameter hoop that one could swing around the waist by gyrating the hips. In no time, the "hula hoop" was a national craze. But in less than a year, hula hoops vanished from the scene. The recent rise and fall in popularity of Pokemon cards is another example of this process (Aguirre, Quarantelli, & Mendoza, 1988).

How do fads differ from fashions? Fads are passing fancies that capture the mass imagination but quickly burn out. Fashions, by contrast, reflect basic cultural values like individuality and sexual attractiveness and tend to evolve over time. Therefore, a fashion—but rarely a fad—is incorporated into a society's

culture. The fad of streaking, for instance, came out of nowhere and soon vanished; the fashion of wearing blue jeans, on the other hand, originated in the rough mining camps of Gold Rush California more than a century ago and still influences clothing designs today. This "staying power" explains why we are happy to be called "fashionable" but are put off by being called "faddish" (Blumer, 1968; Turner & Killian, 1993).

SOCIAL MOVEMENTS

A **social movement** is *an organized activity that encourages or discourages social change*. Social movements are perhaps the most important type of collective behavior because they are deliberately organized and often have lasting effects on the shape of our society.

Social movements occur more frequently in today's world than in the past. Preindustrial societies are tightly bound by tradition, making social movements extremely rare. Industrial and postindustrial societies, however, foster diverse subcultures and countercultures so that social movements develop around a wide range of public issues. In recent decades, for example, the gay rights movement has won legal changes in numerous cities and several states, forbidding discrimination based on sexual orientation and allowing formal domestic partnership. Like any social movement that seeks change, the gay rights movement has prompted a countermovement made up of traditionalists who want to limit the social acceptance of homosexuality. In today's society, almost every important public issue gives rise to a social movement favoring change and an opposing countermovement resisting it (Lo, 1982; Meyer & Staggenborg, 1996).

As Figure 23–1 shows, many—but not most—students consider influencing society to be an important goal during their college years, with the exact share rising and falling over time. Even so, this priority remains somewhat stronger among college women than among college men.

TYPES OF SOCIAL MOVEMENTS

Sociologists classify social movements according to several variables (Aberle, 1966; Cameron, 1966; Blumer, 1969). One variable asks *who is changed?* Some movements target selected people, while others try to change everyone. A second variable asks *how much change?* Some movements seek only limited change in our lives, while others are radical. Combining these variables results in four types of social movements, shown in Figure 23–2 on page 612.

Alterative social movements are least threatening to the status quo because they seek limited change in only a part of the population. Promise Keepers, one example of an alterative social movement, encourages men to be more spiritual and supportive of their families.

 Visit the Promise Keepers Web site at http://www.promisekeepers.org

Redemptive social movements also have a selective focus, but they seek radical change in those they engage. For example, Alcoholics Anonymous is an organization that helps alcoholics achieve a sober life.

Reformative social movements aim for only limited social change but target everyone. Multiculturalism, described in Chapter 3 ("Culture"), is an educational and political movement that advocates working toward social equality for people of all races and ethnicities. Reformative social movements generally work inside the existing political system. Some are *progressive* (promoting a new social pattern), while others are *reactionary* (countermovements trying to preserve the status quo or to revive past social patterns). Thus, just as multiculturalists push for greater racial

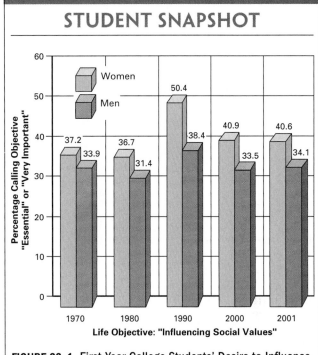

STUDENT SNAPSHOT

FIGURE 23–1 First-Year College Students' Desire to Influence Social Values, 1970–2001

Source: Astin et al. (2002).

equality, so white supremacist organizations try to maintain the historical dominance of white people.

Revolutionary social movements are the most extreme of all, striving for the basic transformation of an entire society. Sometimes pursuing specific goals, sometimes spinning utopian dreams, these social movements reject existing social institutions as flawed while promoting radically new alternatives. Both the left-wing Communist party (pushing for government control of the economy) and the right-wing militia groups (advocating the destruction of "big government") seek to radically change our way of life (Van Dyke & Soule, 2002).

EXPLAINING SOCIAL MOVEMENTS

Because social movements are intentional and long-lasting, sociologists find this type of collective behavior easier to explain than fleeting incidents of mob behavior or mass hysteria. Several theories have come to the fore.

 SOCIOLOGY @ WORK

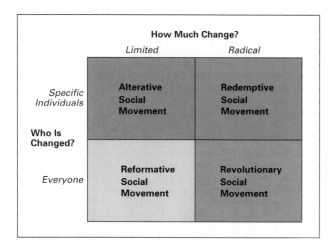

How Much Change?

	Limited	Radical
Specific Individuals	Alterative Social Movement	Redemptive Social Movement
Everyone	Reformative Social Movement	Revolutionary Social Movement

Who Is Changed?

FIGURE 23–2 Four Types of Social Movements

Source: Based on Aberle (1966).

Deprivation Theory

Deprivation theory holds that social movements arise among people who feel deprived. People who feel they lack enough income, safe working conditions, basic political rights, or plain human dignity may organize a social movement to bring about a more just state of affairs (Morrison, 1978; Rose, 1982).

The rise of the Ku Klux Klan and the passage of Jim Crow laws by whites intent on enforcing segregation in the South after the Civil War illustrate deprivation theory. With the end of slavery, white landowners lost a source of free labor and poorer whites lost the claim that they were socially superior to African Americans. Many reacted to their sense of deprivation by trying to keep all people of color "in their place" (Dollard et al., 1939). African Americans' deprivation was much greater, of course, but as slaves they had little opportunity to organize. During the twentieth century, however, African Americans organized successfully in pursuit of racial equality.

 For information on the Ku Klux Klan and other hate groups, visit http://www.splcenter.org/intelligenceproject/ip-index.html

As Chapter 7 ("Groups and Organizations") explained, deprivation is a relative concept. Regardless of anyone's absolute amount of money and power, people feel either better or worse off than some category of others. **Relative deprivation,** then, is *a perceived disadvantage arising from some specific comparison* (Stouffer et al., 1949; Merton, 1968).

A century and a half ago, Alexis de Tocqueville (1955; orig. 1856) studied the French Revolution.

Why, he asked, did rebellion occur in progressive France rather than in more traditional Germany, where peasants were, by any objective measure, worse off? Tocqueville's answer was that, as bad as their condition was, German peasants had known nothing but feudal servitude and thus had no basis for feeling deprived. French peasants, on the other hand, had seen improvements in their lives that whetted their appetites for more. Thus, the French—not the Germans—felt a keen sense of relative deprivation. The irony, as Tocqueville saw it, was that increasing freedom and prosperity did not satisfy people as much as stimulate their desire for an even better life (1955:175; orig. 1856).

Closer to home, Tocqueville's insight helps explain patterns of rioting during the 1960s. Then, protest riots involving African Americans took place not in the South, where many black people lived in miserable poverty and most were not even registered to vote, but in Detroit, where the auto industry was booming, black unemployment was low, and black home ownership was highest in the country (Thernstrom & Thernstrom, 1998).

James C. Davies (1962) agrees that, as life gets better, people take their rising fortunes for granted and expect even more. But what happens if the standard of living suddenly stops improving or, worse, begins to drop? As Figure 23–3 illustrates, relative deprivation is the result, generating unrest and social movements aimed at change.

Critical evaluation. Deprivation theory challenges our commonsense assumption that the worst-off people are the most likely to organize for change. People do not organize simply because they suffer in an absolute sense; rather, they form social movements because of *relative* deprivation. Indeed, both Tocqueville and Marx—as different as they were in many ways—agreed on the importance of relative deprivation in the formation of social movements.

But most people experience some discontent all the time, so deprivation theory leaves us wondering why social movements arise among some categories of people and not others. A second problem is that deprivation theory suffers from circular reasoning: We assume that deprivation causes social movements, but often the only evidence of deprivation is the social movement itself (Jenkins & Perrow, 1977). A third limitation of this approach is that it focuses exclusively on the cause of a social movement and tells us little about movements themselves (McAdam, McCarthy, & Zald, 1988).

Mass-Society Theory

William Kornhauser's mass-society theory (1959) argues that social movements attract socially isolated people who feel personally insignificant. From this point of view, social movements occur in large *mass* societies. Social movements are *personal* as well as *political* in that they offer a sense of belonging and purpose to people otherwise adrift in society (Melucci, 1989).

It follows, says Kornhauser, that categories of people with weak social ties are those who most readily join a social movement. People who are well integrated socially, by contrast, are unlikely to seek membership in a social movement.

Like Gustave Le Bon, discussed earlier, Kornhauser offers a conservative view of social movements. Activists tend to be psychologically vulnerable people who eagerly join groups and are often manipulated by group leaders. Social movements, in Kornhauser's view, are unlikely to be very democratic.

Critical evaluation. To Kornhauser's credit, his theory focuses on both the kind of society that produces social movements and the kinds of people who join them. But one criticism is that, if we try to test the idea that mass societies foster social movements, we run up against the problem of having no clear standard for measuring the extent to which we live in a "mass society."

A second criticism is that explaining social movements in terms of people hungry to belong ignores the social justice issues that movements address. Put otherwise, mass society theory suggests that flawed people—rather than a flawed society—are responsible for social movements.

What does research show about mass-society theory? The record is mixed. On the down side, some studies conclude that the Nazi movement in Germany did not draw heavily from socially isolated people (Lipset, 1963; Oberschall, 1973). Similarly, many of the people who took part in urban riots during the 1960s had strong ties to their communities (Sears & McConahay, 1973). Evidence also suggests that most young people who join religious movements have fairly normal family ties (Wright & Piper, 1986). Finally, researchers who have examined the biographies of 1960s political activists find evidence of deep and continuing commitment to political goals rather than isolation from society (McAdam, 1988, 1989; Whalen & Flacks, 1989).

On the up side, research by Frances Piven and Richard Cloward (1977) supports this approach. Piven and Cloward found that a breakdown of routine social

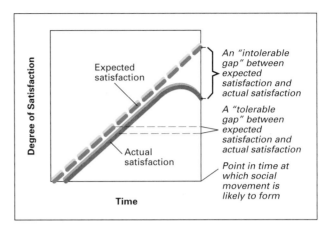

FIGURE 23-3 Relative Deprivation and Social Movements

In this diagram, the solid line represents a rising standard of living over time. The dotted line indicates the expected standard of living, which is typically somewhat higher. James C. Davies describes the difference between the two as "a tolerable gap between what people want and what they get." If the standard of living suddenly drops in the midst of rising expectations, however, the gap becomes intolerable. At this point, we can expect social movements to form.

Source: Davies (1962).

patterns has encouraged poor people to form social movements. Also, a study of the New Mexico State Penitentiary found that, when prison programs that promoted social ties among inmates were suspended, inmates were more likely to protest their conditions (Useem, 1997).

Structural-Strain Theory

One of the most influential theories about social movements was developed by Neil Smelser (1962). *Structural-strain theory* identifies six factors that encourage the development of social movements. Smelser's theory also suggests which kinds of situations lead to unorganized mobs or riots and which to highly organized social movements. We will use the prodemocracy movement that transformed Eastern Europe during the late 1980s to illustrate Smelser's theory.

1. **Structural conduciveness.** Social movements arise as people come to think their society has some serious problems. In Eastern Europe, these problems included low living standards and political repression by national governments.

A curious fact is that rioting by African Americans in U.S. cities during the 1960s was more common in the North (here, in Detroit) where good factory jobs were available and living standards were higher rather than in the South where a larger share of people lived in rural areas with lower incomes. Relative deprivation theory explains this contradiction by pointing out that it was in the North—where life had improved—that people came to expect equality. Relative to that goal, the reality of second-class citizenship became intolerable.

2. **Structural strain.** People begin to experience relative deprivation when their society fails to meet their expectations. Eastern Europeans joined the prodemocracy movement because they knew their living standards were far lower than living standards in Western Europe and much below what years of propaganda about prosperous socialism had led them to expect.

3. **Growth and spread of an explanation.** Forming a well-organized social movement requires a clear statement of a problem, its causes, and its solutions. If people are confused about their suffering, they are likely to express their dissatisfaction in an unorganized way such as rioting. In the case of Eastern Europe, intellectuals played a key role in the prodemocracy movement by pointing out economic and political flaws in the system and proposing strategies to increase democracy.

4. **Precipitating factors.** Discontent frequently festers for a long time only to be transformed into collective action by a specific event. In Eastern Europe, such an event occurred in 1985 when Mikhail Gorbachev came to power in the Soviet Union and began his program of *perestroika* (restructuring). As Moscow relaxed its rigid control over Eastern Europe, people there saw a historic opportunity to reorganize political and economic life and claim greater freedom.

5. **Mobilization for action.** Once people share a concern about some public issue, they are ready to take action—to distribute leaflets, stage protest rallies, and build alliances with sympathetic organizations. The initial success of the Solidarity movement in Poland—quietly aided by the Reagan administration in the United States and by Pope John Paul II in the Vatican—mobilized people throughout Eastern Europe to press for change. The rate of change accelerated as reform movements gained strength: What had taken a decade in Poland required only months in Hungary and only weeks in other Eastern European nations.

6. **Lack of social control.** The success of any social movement depends, in large part, on how political officials, police, and the military respond. Sometimes the state moves swiftly to crush a social movement, as happened in the case of prodemocracy forces in the People's Republic of China. But Gorbachev adopted a policy of nonintervention in Eastern Europe, thereby opening the door for change. Ironically, the movements that began in Eastern Europe soon spread to the Soviet Union itself, ending the historic domination of the Communist party and producing a new political confederation in 1992.

Critical evaluation. Smelser's analysis recognizes the complexity of social movements and suggests how various factors encourage or inhibit their development. Structural-strain theory also explains why people may respond to their problems either by forming organized social movements or through spontaneous mob action.

Yet Smelser's theory contains some of the same circularity of argument found in Kornhauser's analysis. A social movement is caused by strain, says Smelser, but the only evidence of underlying strain appears to be the social movement itself. Finally, structural-strain theory is incomplete, overlooking the important role that resources like the mass media or international alliances play in the success or failure of a social movement (Oberschall, 1973; Jenkins & Perrow, 1977; McCarthy & Zald, 1977; Olzak & West, 1991).

Resource-Mobilization Theory

Resource-mobilization theory points out that no social movement is likely to succeed—or even get off the ground—without substantial resources, including money, human labor, office and communications facilities, access to the mass media, and a positive public image. In short, any social movement rises or falls on its ability to attract resources, mobilize people, and forge alliances.

Outsiders can be just as important as insiders in affecting the outcome of a social movement. Because socially disadvantaged people, by definition, lack the money, contacts, leadership skills, and organizational know-how that a successful movement requires, sympathetic outsiders fill the resource gap. In U.S. history, well-to-do white people, including college students, performed a vital service to the black civil rights movement in the 1960s, and affluent men have joined women as leaders of the women's movement.

Resources connecting people are also vital. The 1989 prodemocracy movement in China was fueled by students whose location on campuses clustered together in Beijing allowed them to build networks and recruit new members (Zhao, 1998). More recently, the Internet has been a vital resource enabling organizations to link hundreds of thousands of people across the country. Prior to the War in Iraq, for example, two individuals using their computers were able to get 120,000 people in 190 countries to sign a petition opposing the war. In addition, the use of computers and cellular phones has now created "smart crowds," by which people across the country and around the world can coordinate their efforts to maximum effect.

The availability of organizing ideas online has helped many social movements to grow over time. For example, "Take Back the Night" is an annual occasion for rallies where people speak out in opposition to violence against women,

For more about Take Back the Night, go to http://www.campusoutreachservices.com/tbtn2.htm

children, and families. Using resources available online, even a small number of people can plan and carry out an effective political event (Killian, 1984; Snow, Rochford, Jr., Worden, & Benford, 1986; Baron, Mittman, & Newman, 1991; Burstein, 1991; Meyer & Whittier, 1994; Valocchi, 1996; Passy & Giugni, 2001; Packer, 2003).

Critical evaluation. Resource-mobilization theory recognizes that resources as well as discontent are necessary to the success of a social movement. Research confirms that forging alliances to gain resources is especially important and notes that movements with few resources may, in desperation, turn to violence to call attention to their cause (Grant & Wallace, 1991).

Critics of this theory counter that "outside" people and resources are not always needed to ensure a movement's success. They argue that even relatively powerless segments of a population can promote change if they are able to organize effectively and have strongly committed members (Donnelly & Majka, 1998). Aldon Morris (1981) adds that the success of the civil rights movement of the 1950s and 1960s was due to people of color who drew mostly on their own skills and resources. A second problem with this theory is that it overstates the extent to which powerful people are willing to challenge the status quo. Some rich white people did provide valuable resources to the black civil rights movement, but probably more often, elites were indifferent or opposed to significant change (McAdam, 1982, 1983; Pichardo, 1995). Third, keep in mind that movements and countermovements compete for the same resources and may show different patterns of success. For example, the gay rights movement has advanced by gaining support from government officials; the movement opposing gay rights has gained ground using ballot initiatives (Werum & Winders, 2001).

Culture Theory

In recent years, sociologists have recognized that social movements depend not only on material resources and the structure of political power, but also on cultural symbols. That is, people in any particular situation are likely to mobilize to form a social movement only to the extent that they develop "shared understandings of the world that legitimate and motivate collective action" (McAdam, McCarthy, & Zald, 1996:6; Williams, 2002).

In part, mobilization depends on a sense of injustice, as suggested by deprivation theory. In addition, people must come to believe that they are not able to

A symbol is a powerful way to rally support to a social movement. The peace symbol, which originated in 1958 as part of the movement against nuclear weapons, has been an important part of the peace movement ever since.

respond to their situation effectively acting as individuals. Finally, social movements gain strength as they develop symbols and a sense of community that both generate strong feelings and direct this emotional energy into organized action. Media images of the burning World Trade Center after the September 11, 2001, terrorist attacks helped mobilize people to support the "war against terrorism." Likewise, photos of children harmed by bombing helped fuel the antiwar movement during the War in Iraq just as they had during the Vietnam War (Morris & Mueller, 1992; Giugni, 1998; Staggenborg, 1998; Gibbs, 2001).

Critical evaluation. A strength of this approach is reminding us that not just material resources but also cultural symbols form the foundation of social movements. At the same time, powerful symbols (such as the flag and ideas about patriotism and respecting our leaders) help support the status quo. How and when symbols come to turn people from supporting the system toward protest are questions in need of further research.

Political-Economy Theory

The Marxist-based political-economy approach also has something to say about the rise of social movements. From this point of view, social movements arise within capitalist societies because the capitalist economic system fails to meet the needs of the majority of people. Despite great economic productivity, in other words, U.S. society is in crisis, with millions of people unable to find good jobs, living below the poverty line, and living without health insurance.

Social movements arise as a response to such conditions. Workers organize in order to demand higher wages, citizens rally for a health policy that will protect everyone, and people march in opposition to spending billions to fund wars at the expense of social welfare programs (Buechler, 2000).

Critical evaluation. A strength of political-economy theory is its macro-level approach. While other theories explain the rise of social movements in terms of traits of individuals (such as weak social ties or a sense of relative deprivation) or traits of movements (such as their available resources), this approach focuses on the institutional structures (the economy and political system) of society itself.

This approach explains social movements concerned with economic issues, although, as Chapter 16 ("The Economy and Work") points out, scholars disagree as to whether capitalism is incapable of meeting people's needs. In addition, the approach offers little insight into the recent rise of social movements concerned with the environment, animal rights, or other noneconomic issues.

New Social Movements Theory

A final theoretical approach addresses the changing character of what are often called "new social movements." *New social movements theory* emphasizes the distinctive features of recent social movements in the postindustrial societies of North America and Western

TABLE 23-1	Theories of Social Movements: A Summary
Deprivation Theory	People experiencing relative deprivation begin social movements. The social movement is a means of seeking change that brings participants greater benefits. Social movements are especially likely when rising expectations are frustrated.
Mass-Society Theory	People who lack established social ties are mobilized into social movements. Periods of social breakdown are likely to spawn social movements. The social movement gives members a sense of belonging and social participation.
Structural-Strain Theory	People come together because of their shared concern about the inability of society to operate as they believe it should. The growth of a social movement reflects many factors, including a belief in its legitimacy and some precipitating event that provokes action.
Resource-Mobilization Theory	People may join for all the reasons noted above and also because of social ties to existing members. But the success or failure of a social movement depends largely on the resources available to it. Also important is the extent of opposition within the larger society.
Culture Theory	People are drawn to a social movement by cultural symbols that define some cause as just. The movement itself usually becomes a symbol of power and justice.
Political-Economy Theory	People unite to address the societal ills caused by capitalism, including unemployment, poverty, and lack of health care. Social movements are necessary because a capitalist economy inevitably fails to meet people's basic needs.
New Social Movements Theory	People who join social movements are motivated by quality-of-life issues, not necessarily economic concerns. Mobilization is national or international in scope. New social movements arise in response to the expansion of the mass media and new information technology.

Europe (Melucci, 1980; McAdam, McCarthy, & Zald, 1988; Kriesi, 1989; Pakulski, 1993; Wallace, 1996).

First, while traditional social movements such as labor organizations are concerned mostly with economic issues, new social movements tend to focus on cultural change and improving our social and physical surroundings. The international environmental movement, for example, opposes practices that aggravate global warming and other environmental dangers.

Second, most of today's social movements are international, focusing on the global ecology, the social standing of women and gay people, animal rights, and opposition to war. As the process of globalization connects the world's nations in more and more ways, in other words, social movements, too, are becoming global.

For information on laws involving animal rights, see http://www.animal-law.org

Third, whereas most social movements of the past drew strong support from working-class people, new social movements, with their noneconomic agendas, usually draw support from the middle and upper-middle classes. The reason is, as discussed in Chapter 17 ("Politics and Government"), that more affluent people tend to be more conservative on economic issues (because they have wealth to protect) but more liberal on

social issues (partly as a result of extensive education). Furthermore, in the United States and other rich nations, the number of highly educated professionals—the people who most support "new social movements"—is increasing, a fact suggesting that these movements will grow (Jenkins & Wallace, 1996; Rose, 1997).

Critical evaluation. One clear strength of this theory is its recognition that social movements have increased in scale in response to the development of a global economy and international political connections. This theory also highlights the power of the mass media and new information technology to unite people around the world in pursuit of political goals.

Critics, however, claim that this approach exaggerates the differences between past and present social movements. The women's movement, for example, focuses on many of the same issues—workplace conditions and pay—that have concerned labor organizations for decades. Similarly, many of those protesting the use of U.S. military power consider economic equality around the world their primary goal.

Each of the seven theories we have presented offers some explanation of the emergence of social movements; no single theory can stand alone (Kowalewski & Porter, 1992). Table 23–1 summarizes the theories.

GENDER AND SOCIAL MOVEMENTS

Gender figures prominently in the operation of social movements. In keeping with traditional ideas about gender in the United States, men more than women tend to take part in public life—including spearheading social movements.

Investigating "Freedom Summer," a 1964 voter registration project in Mississippi, Doug McAdam (1992) found that most people viewed the job of registering African American voters in the midst of considerable hostility from whites dangerous, and therefore "men's work" unsuitable for women. He also discovered that project leaders were likely to assign women volunteers to clerical and teaching assignments, leaving the actual field activities to men. This was so even though women who participated in Freedom Summer were more qualified than their male counterparts in terms of years of activism. McAdam concluded that only the most committed women were able to overcome the movement's gender barriers. In short, while women have played leading roles in many social movements (including the abolitionist and feminist movements in the United States), male dominance has been the norm even in social movements that otherwise oppose the status quo (Herda-Rapp, 1998).

STAGES IN SOCIAL MOVEMENTS

Despite the many differences that set one social movement off from another, all unfold in roughly the same way, as shown in Figure 23–4. Researchers have identified four stages in the life of the typical social movement (Blumer, 1969; Mauss, 1975; Tilly, 1978):

Stage 1: Emergence. Social movements are driven by the perception that all is not well. Some, such as the civil rights and women's movements, are born of widespread dissatisfaction. Others emerge only as a small vanguard group increases public awareness of some issue. Gay activists, for example, initially raised public concern about the threat posed by AIDS.

Stage 2: Coalescence. After emerging, a social movement must define itself and develop a strategy for "going public." Leaders must determine policies, decide on tactics, build morale, and recruit new members. At this stage, the movement may engage in collective action like rallies or demonstrations to attract media attention and thereby public notice. The movement may also form alliances with other organizations to acquire necessary resources.

Stage 3: Bureaucratization. To become a political force, a social movement must take on bureaucratic traits, described in Chapter 7 ("Groups and Organizations"). Thus, as it becomes established, the social movement depends less on the charisma and talents of a few leaders and relies more on a capable staff. When social movements do not become established in this way, they risk dissolving. For example, many activist organizations on college campuses during the late 1960s were energized by a single charismatic leader and, consequently, did not last long. On the other hand, the National Organization for Women (NOW), despite its changing leadership, is well established and can be counted on to speak for feminists.

Even so, bureaucratization can sometimes hinder a social movement. In reviewing social movements in U.S. history, Frances Piven and Richard Cloward (1977) found that leaders can become so engrossed in building an organization that they neglect the need to keep people "fired up" for change. In such cases, the radical edge of protest is lost.

Stage 4: Decline. Eventually, most social movements begin to decline. Frederick Miller (1983) suggests four reasons that this can occur.

First, if members have met their goals, decline may simply signal success. For example, the women's suffrage movement disbanded after it won women in the United States the right to vote. Such clear-cut successes are rare, however, since few social movements have a single goal. More commonly, winning one victory leads to new campaigns. Because issues related to gender extend far beyond voting, the women's movement has recast itself time and time again.

Second, a social movement may fold because of organizational factors, such as poor leadership, loss of interest among members, insufficient funds, or repression by authorities. Some people lose interest when the excitement of early efforts is replaced by day-to-day routine. Fragmentation due to internal conflicts over goals and strategies is another common problem. Students for a Democratic Society (SDS), a student movement promoting participatory democracy and opposing the war in Vietnam, splintered into several small factions by the end of the 1960s, as members disagreed over strategies for social change.

Third, a social movement can fall apart if the established power structure, through offers of money, prestige, and other rewards, diverts leaders from their goals. "Selling out" is one facet of the iron law of

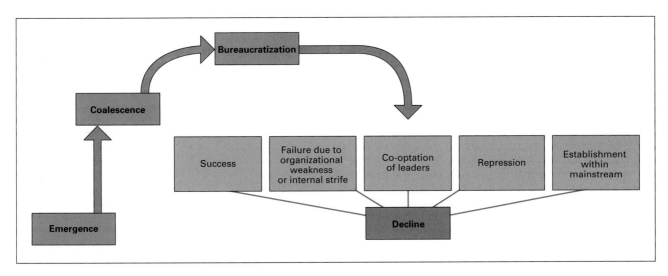

FIGURE 23-4 Stages in the Lives of Social Movements

oligarchy, discussed in Chapter 7 ("Groups and Organizations"). That is, organizational leaders use their position to enrich themselves. For example, Vernon Jordan, once head of the activist National Urban League, became a close adviser to President Clinton and a rich and powerful Washington "insider." But this process can also work the other way: Some people leave lucrative, high-prestige occupations to become activists. Cat Stevens, a rock star of the 1970s, became a Muslim, changed his name to Yusuf Islam, and since then has devoted his life to the spread of his religion.

Fourth and finally, a social movement can collapse because of repression. Officials may crush a social movement by frightening away participants, discouraging new recruits, and even imprisoning leaders. In general, the more revolutionary the social movement, the more officials try to repress it. Until 1990, the government of South Africa, for example, banned the African National Congress (ANC), a political organization seeking to overthrow the state-supported system of apartheid. Even suspected members of the ANC were subject to arrest. Only after 1990, when the government lifted the decades-old ban and released from prison ANC leader Nelson Mandela (who was elected the country's president in 1994) did South Africa begin the journey away from apartheid.

Beyond the reasons noted by Miller, a fifth cause of decline is that a social movement may "go mainstream."

Some movements become an accepted part of the system—typically after realizing some of their goals—so that while they continue to flourish, they no longer challenge the status quo. The U.S. labor movement, for example, is now well established; its leaders control vast sums of money and, according to some critics, now have more in common with the business tycoons they opposed in the past than with rank-and-file workers.

SOCIAL MOVEMENTS AND SOCIAL CHANGE

Social movements exist to encourage—or to resist—social change. Whatever the intention, their success varies from case to case. The civil rights movement has certainly pushed this country toward racial equality, despite opposition from a handful of white supremacist countermovements like the Aryan Nation and what's left of the Ku Klux Klan.

Sometimes we overlook the success of past social movements and take for granted the changes that other people struggled so hard to win. Beginning a century ago, workers' movements in the United States fought to end child labor in factories, limit working hours, make the workplace safer, and establish the right to bargain collectively with employers. Laws protecting the environment are another product of successful social movements during this century. In addition, women today have greater legal rights and

Are you satisfied with our society as it is? Surely, everyone would change some things about our way of life. Indeed, surveys show that, if they could, a lot of people would change plenty! There is considerable pessimism about the state of U.S. society: Two-thirds of U.S. adults think that the average person's situation "is getting worse, not better," and three-fourths of respondents stated that most government officials are "not interested" in the average person's problems (NORC, 2003:208).

But in light of such concerns, few people are willing to stand up and try to bring about change. Within the past five years, only 13 percent of U.S. adults have attended a public meeting organized to protest against the government; just 9 percent say they have

taken part in a protest march or demonstration (NORC, 2003:974–75).

Many college students probably suspect age has something to do with such apathy. That is, young people have the interest and idealism to challenge the status quo, while older adults worry only about their families and their jobs. Indeed, one of the popular sayings of the activist 1960s was "You can't trust people over thirty!" But the facts are otherwise: Students entering college in 2002 expressed less interest in political issues than their parents.

Asked to select important goals in life from a list, 33 percent of first-year students included "keeping up with political affairs" and just 22 percent checked off "participating in community action programs." As the figure shows, the same share of students (22 percent) say

they voted in a student election during the past year. An even smaller share (19 percent) claimed to discuss politics frequently in the past year.

Certainly, people cite some good reasons to avoid political controversy. Any time we challenge the system—whether on campus or in the national political arena—we risk making enemies, losing a job, or perhaps even sustaining physical injury.

But the most important reason that people in the United States avoid joining in social movements may have to do with cultural norms about how change should occur. In our individualistic culture, people favor taking personal responsibility over collective action as a means of addressing social problems. For example, when asked about the best way for women or African Americans to

economic opportunities won by earlier generations of women.

Seen one way, major social transformations such as the Industrial Revolution and capitalism give rise to social movements, including those involving workers and women. On the other hand, the efforts of workers, women, racial and ethnic minorities, and gay people have sent ripples of change throughout our society. In short, social change is both the cause and the consequence of social movements.

LOOKING AHEAD: SOCIAL MOVEMENTS IN THE TWENTY-FIRST CENTURY

Especially since the turbulent 1960s—a decade marked by widespread social protests—U.S. society has been pushed and pulled by many social movements and countermovements calling attention to issues from abortion to financing political campaigns to health care

to war. Of course, different people define the problems in different ways, just as they are likely to settle on different policies as solutions. In short, social movements and the problems they address are always *political* (Macionis, 2005).

Just as social movements have always been part of U.S. society, there is little doubt that they will continue to shape our way of life throughout the twenty-first century. Indeed, for three reasons, the scope of social movements is likely to increase. First, protest should increase as women, African Americans, and other historically marginalized categories of people gain a greater political voice. Second, at a global level, the technology of the Information Revolution means that anyone with a cable or satellite television or a personal computer can stay abreast of political events, often as they happen. Third, new technology and the emerging global economy mean that social movements are now uniting people throughout the entire world. Moreover, since many problems are global in scope, only international cooperation can solve them.

improve their social position, most U.S. adults say that individuals should rely on their own efforts, while only a few point to women's groups or civil rights activism as the best way to bring about change (NORC, 2003:221, 343, 345). This individualistic orientation explains why adults in this country are half as likely as their European counterparts to join in lawful demonstrations (Inglehart et al., 2000).

Sociology, of course, poses a counterpoint to our cultural individualism. As C. Wright Mills (1959) explained decades ago, many of the problems we encounter as individuals are caused by the structure of society. Thus, said Mills, solutions to many of life's problems depend on collective effort—that is, people willing to take a stand for what they believe.

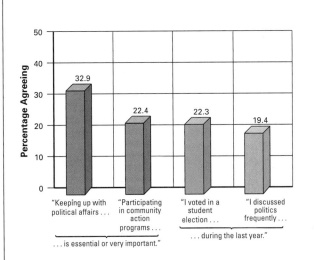

STUDENT SNAPSHOT

Political Involvement of Students Entering College in 2002: A Survey

Source: Sax et al. (2002).

Continue the debate . . .

1. *Do you think the reluctance of people in the United States to address problems through collective action shows that they are basically satisfied with their lives? Do they think individuals acting together can't make a difference?*

2. *Have you ever participated in a political demonstration? What were its goals? What did it accomplish?*

3. *Does it surprise you that two-thirds of eighteen- to twenty-four-year-olds in the United States do not even bother to vote? How would you explain such political apathy?*

SUMMARY

1. Collective behavior differs from group behavior because it involves limited social interaction within vague social boundaries, and also weak and often unconventional norms.

2. Crowds, an important type of collective behavior, take various forms: casual crowds, conventional crowds, expressive crowds, acting crowds, and protest crowds.

3. Crowds that become emotionally intense spawn violence in the form of mobs and riots. Mobs pursue a specific goal; rioting involves undirected destructiveness.

4. Crowds have figured heavily in social change throughout history, although the value of their action depends on one's political outlook.

5. Contagion theory views crowds as anonymous, suggestible, and subject to rising emotions. Convergence theory links crowd behavior to the traits of participants. Emergent-norm theory suggests that crowds develop their own behavioral norms.

6. One form of mass behavior is rumor, which thrives in a climate of ambiguity. While rumor involves public issues, gossip deals with personal issues.

7. Public opinion consists of people's positions on important, controversial issues. Public attitudes change over time; at any time on any given issue, some share of people hold no opinion at all.

8. A panic (in a local area) or mass hysteria (across an entire society) are types of collective behavior by which people respond to a significant event, real or imagined, with irrational, frantic, and often self-destructive behavior.

9. In industrial societies, people use fashion as a source of social prestige. A fad is more unconventional than a fashion and is also of shorter duration, although people embrace fads with greater enthusiasm.

10. Social movements exist to promote or discourage change. Sociologists classify social movements according

to the range of people they seek to involve and the extent of the change they seek.

11. According to deprivation theory, social movements arise as people feel deprived in relation to some standard of well-being.

12. Mass-society theory holds that people join social movements to gain a sense of belonging and moral direction.

13. Structural-strain theory explains the development of a social movement as a cumulative effect of six factors. Well-formulated grievances and goals encourage the formation of social movements; undirected anger, by contrast, promotes rioting.

14. Resource-mobilization theory ties the success or failure of a social movement to the availability of resources such as money, human labor, and alliances with other organizations.

15. Culture theory notes the importance of symbols as well as material resources to the success of a social movement.

16. The political-economy approach claims that social movements arise within capitalist societies that fail to meet the needs of a majority of people.

17. New social movements theory focuses on quality-of-life issues that are usually international in scope.

18. A typical social movement proceeds through consecutive stages: emergence (defining the public issue), coalescence (entering the public arena), bureaucratization (becoming formally organized), and decline (due to failure or, sometimes, success).

19. Past social movements have shaped society in ways that people now take for granted. Just as movements produce change, change itself causes social movements.

KEY CONCEPTS

collective behavior (p. 601) activity involving a large number of people, often spontaneous, and sometimes controversial

collectivity (p. 602) a large number of people whose minimal interaction occurs in the absence of well-defined and conventional norms

crowd (p. 603) a temporary gathering of people who share a common focus of attention and who influence one another

mob (p. 603) a highly emotional crowd that pursues a violent or destructive goal

riot (p. 604) a social eruption that is highly emotional, violent, and undirected

mass behavior (p. 606) collective behavior among people dispersed over a wide geographic area

rumor (p. 606) unsubstantiated information people spread informally, often by word of mouth

gossip (p. 607) rumor about people's personal affairs

public opinion (p. 608) widespread attitudes about controversial issues

propaganda (p. 608) information presented with the intention of shaping public opinion

panic (p. 609) a form of localized collective behavior by which people react to a threat or other stimulus with irrational, frantic, and often self-destructive behavior

mass hysteria or **moral panic** (p. 609) a form of dispersed collective behavior by which people react to a real or imagined event with irrational and even frantic fear

fashion (p. 609) a social pattern favored by a large number of people

fad (p. 610) an unconventional social pattern that people embrace briefly but enthusiastically

social movement (p. 610) an organized activity that encourages or discourages social change

relative deprivation (p. 612) a perceived disadvantage arising from some specific comparison

CRITICAL-THINKING QUESTIONS

1. The concept of collective behavior encompasses a broad range of social patterns. List some of these patterns. What traits do they all have in common?

2. Imagine the aftermath of a football game in which the revelry turns into a destructive rampage. How might contagion theory, convergence theory, and emergent-norm theory explain such behavior?

3. The 1960s were a decade of both great affluence and widespread social protest. What sociological insights help explain this apparent paradox?

4. In what respects do some recent social movements (those concerned with the environment, animal rights, and gun control) differ from older crusades (focusing on, say, the right of workers to form unions or the right of women to vote)?

APPLICATIONS AND EXERCISES

1. With ten friends, try this experiment: One person writes down a detailed "rumor" about someone important and then whispers it to the second person, who whispers it to a third, and so on. The last person to hear the rumor writes it down again. Compare the two versions of the rumor.

2. With other members of the class, identify recent fad products. What makes people want them? Why do they drop from favor so quickly?

3. What social movements are represented by organizations on your campus? Your class might invite several leaders to describe their groups' goals and strategies.

4. Packaged in the back of this new textbook is an interactive CD-ROM that offers a variety of video and interactive review materials intended to help you better understand the material covered in this chapter. For this chapter, the CD-ROM contains a relevant clip from *ABC News*, an author's tip video, interactive map animations, an interactive time line, and flashcards with audio pronunciations of the more difficult words.

 ## SITES TO SEE

http://www.prenhall.com/macionis

Visit the interactive Companion Website™ that accompanies this text. Begin by clicking on the cover of your book. You will find a chapter-by-chapter study guide, practice tests, suggested Web links, and links to other relevant material.

http://www.gallup.com

Tracking trends in public opinion is the job of various "pollsters," including the Gallup Organization. Visit this Gallup site to see what they do and read about some of their recent surveys.

http://organizenow.net/cco/

Organizing in support of various social movements has long been a characteristic of college campuses across the United States. This site describes the Center for Campus Organizing, which provides information on campus-based social movements.

http://www.natlnorml.org

Visit the Web site for the National Organization for the Reform of Marijuana Laws. What are the goals of this organization? How is it trying to expand the social movement in favor of legalizing marijuana use?

 ## INVESTIGATE WITH RESEARCH NAVIGATOR™

Follow the instructions on page 24 of this text to access the features of **Research Navigator™**. Once at the Web site, enter your Login Name and Password. Then, to use the **Content Select™** database, enter keywords such as "social movements," "riots," and "animal rights," and the search engine will supply relevant and recent scholarly and popular press publications. Use the *New York Times* **Search-by-Subject Archive** to find recent news articles related to sociology and the **Link Library** feature to find relevant Web links organized by the key terms associated with this chapter.

SOCIAL CHANGE: TRADITIONAL, MODERN, AND POSTMODERN SOCIETIES

THE FIVE-STORY, RED BRICK APARTMENT building at 253 East Tenth Street in New York City has been standing for more than a century. In 1900, one of the twenty small apartments in the building was occupied by thirty-nine-year-old Julius Streicher and his thirty-three-year-old wife, Christine—both of whom had immigrated from Germany—and their four young children.

The Streichers probably considered themselves successful. Julius operated a small clothing shop a few blocks from his apartment; Christine stayed at home, raised the children, and did housework. Like the vast majority of people in the country at that time, neither Julius nor Christine had graduated from high school, and they worked for ten to twelve hours, six days a week. Their income—average in the United States for that time—was about $35 a month

or about $425 a year. (In today's dollars, that would be slightly more than $8,000, which would put the family well below today's poverty line.) They spent almost half of their income for food; most of the rest went for rent.

Today, Dorothy Sabo resides at 253 East Tenth Street, living alone in the same apartment where the Streichers spent much of their lives. Now eighty-seven, she is retired from a career teaching art at a nearby museum. In many respects, Sabo's life has been far easier than the life the Streichers knew. For one thing, when the Streichers lived there, the building had no electricity (people used kerosene lamps and candles) and no running water (Christine Streicher spent most of every Monday doing laundry, using water she carried from a public fountain at the end of the block). There were no telephones, no television, and, of course, no computers. Today, Dorothy Sabo takes such conveniences for granted. Although Dorothy Sabo is hardly rich, her pension and Social Security are several times as much as the Streichers earned.

Sabo has her own worries. She is concerned about the environment and often speaks out about global warming. Here again, a look back in time is instructive. A century ago, the Streichers and their neighbors also complained about "the environment," but they meant the smell coming up from the street. At a time when motor vehicles were just beginning to appear in New York City, carriages, trucks, and trolleys were all pulled by horses—thousands of them. These animals dumped 60,000 gallons of urine and 2.5 million pounds of manure on the streets each and every day (based on Simon & Cannon, 2001).

It is scarcely possible for most people today to imagine how different life was a century ago. Not only was life much harder back then, but it was also much shorter. Statistical records show that life expectancy was just forty-six years for men and forty-eight years for women, compared to seventy-four and seventy-nine years today.

Certainly, over the course of the last century, much has changed for the better. Yet, as this chapter explains, social change is not all positive. On the contrary, change has negative consequences, too, creating unexpected new problems. Indeed, as we shall see, early sociologists were mixed in their assessment of

 Examine the lives of men and women, black and white, living in New York City between 1900 and 1920: http://www.albany. edu/mumford/1920/groups.html

modernity, changes brought about by the Industrial Revolution. Likewise, today's sociologists point to both good and bad aspects of *postmodernity*, the recent transformations of society caused by the Information Revolution and the postindustrial economy. The one thing that is clear is that—for better and worse—the rate of change has never been faster than it is now.

WHAT IS SOCIAL CHANGE?

In earlier chapters, we examined relatively *static* social patterns, including status and role, social stratification, and social institutions. We also looked at the *dynamic* forces that have shaped our way of life, ranging from innovations in technology to the growth of bureaucracy and the expansion of cities. These are all dimensions of **social change**, *the transformation of culture and social institutions over time*. The process of social change has four major characteristics:

1. **Social change happens all the time.** "Nothing is constant except death and taxes" goes the old saying. Yet even our thoughts about death have changed dramatically as life expectancy in the United States has doubled over the course of a century. Back in 1900, the Streichers and almost all other people in the United States paid little or no tax on their earnings; taxes increased dramatically over the course of the twentieth century, along with the size and scope of government. In short, virtually everything is subject to the twists and turns of change.

   Still, some societies change faster than others. As Chapter 4 ("Society") explained,

hunting and gathering societies change quite slowly; members of today's high-income societies, on the other hand, experience significant change within a single lifetime.

Moreover, in any society, some cultural elements change faster than others. William Ogburn's (1964) theory of *cultural lag* (see Chapter 3, "Culture") states that material culture (that is, things) usually changes faster than nonmaterial culture (ideas and attitudes). For example, the

 For an introduction to the recent controversy over stem cell research, visit http:// stemcells.nih.gov/index.asp

genetic technology that allows scientists to alter and

perhaps even to create life has developed more rapidly than ethical standards for deciding when and how to use it.

2. **Social change is sometimes intentional but often unplanned.** Industrial societies actively encourage many kinds of change. For example, scientists seek more efficient forms of energy, and advertisers try to convince us that life is incomplete without this or that new gadget. Yet rarely can anyone envision all the consequences of the changes that are set in motion.

   Back in 1900, when the country still relied on horses for transportation, many people looked ahead to motor vehicles that would carry them in a single day distances that had taken weeks or months in the past. But no one could see how profoundly the mobility provided by automobiles would alter life in the United States, scattering family members, threatening the environment, and reshaping cities and suburbs. Nor could automotive pioneers have predicted the more than 40,000 deaths that occur in car accidents each year in the United States alone.

3. **Social change is controversial.** The history of the automobile shows that social change brings both good and bad consequences. Capitalists welcomed the Industrial Revolution because new technology increased productivity and swelled profits. However, workers feared that machines would make their skills obsolete and resisted the push toward "progress."

   Today, as in the past, changing patterns of social interaction between black people and white people, women and men, and gays and heterosexuals give rise to both celebration and opposition as people disagree about how we ought to live.

4. **Some changes matter more than others.** Some changes (such as clothing fads) have only passing significance, whereas others (like computers) last a long time and may change the entire world. As we look ahead, will the Information Revolution turn out to be as pivotal as the Industrial Revolution? Like the automobile and television, the computer has both positive and negative effects, providing new kinds of jobs while eliminating old ones, isolating people in offices while linking people in global electronic networks, offering vast amounts of information while threatening personal privacy.

CAUSES OF SOCIAL CHANGE

Social change has many causes. Then, too, in a world linked by sophisticated communication and transportation technology, change in one place often begets change elsewhere.

CULTURE AND CHANGE

Chapter 3 ("Culture") identified three important sources of cultural change. First, *invention* produces new objects, ideas, and social patterns. Rocket propulsion research, which began in the 1940s, has produced spacecraft that reach toward the stars. Today we take such technology for granted; during the twenty-first century a significant number of people may well travel in space.

Second, *discovery* occurs when people take note of existing elements of the world. Medical advances, for example, offer a growing understanding of the human body. Beyond the direct effects on human health, medical discoveries have stretched life expectancy, setting in motion the "graying" of U.S. society (see Chapter 15, "Aging and the Elderly").

Third, *diffusion* creates change as products, people, and information spread from one culture to another. Ralph Linton (1937a) recognized that many familiar elements of our culture came from other lands. Cloth (developed in Asia), clocks (invented in Europe), and coins (devised in Turkey) are all part of our way of life. In general, material objects diffuse more readily than cultural ideas. That is, new breakthroughs (such as the science of cloning) occur faster than our understanding of when—and even whether–they are desirable.

Today, as throughout our entire history as a nation, immigrants bring change to the United States. In

Today, most of the people with access to computers live in rich countries such as the United States. But the number of people in low-income nations going "online" is on the rise. How do you think the introduction of new information technology will change more traditional societies? Are all the changes likely to be for the good?

recent decades, people from Latin America and Asia have introduced new cultural patterns, clearly evident in the sights, smells, and sounds of cities across the country. Conversely, the global power of the United States ensures that much of our culture—from cheeseburgers to hip-hop to M.B.A. degrees—is being diffused to other societies.

CONFLICT AND CHANGE

Tension and conflict in a society also produce change. Karl Marx saw class conflict as the engine that drives societies from one historical era to another (see Chapter 4, "Society," and Chapter 10, "Social Stratification"). In industrial-capitalist societies, he maintained, the struggle between capitalists and workers propels society toward a socialist system of production.

In the more than a century since Marx's death, this model has proven simplistic. Yet Marx correctly foresaw that social conflict arising from inequality (involving not just class but also race and gender) would force changes in every society, including our own.

SEEING OURSELVES

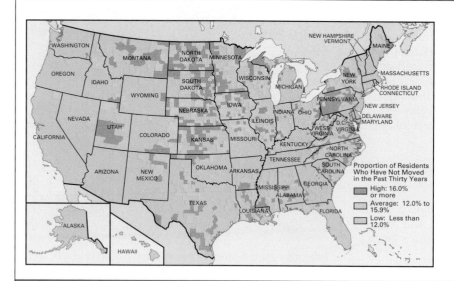

NATIONAL MAP 24–1

Who Stays Put? Residential Stability across the United States

Overall, only about 9 percent of U.S. residents have not moved during the last thirty years. Counties with a higher proportion of "long-termers" typically have experienced less change over recent decades: Many neighborhoods have been in place since before World War II, and many of the same families live in them. As you look at the map, what can you say about these stable areas? Why are most of these counties rural and some distance from the coasts?

Source: U.S. Census Bureau (1996).

IDEAS AND CHANGE

Max Weber also contributed to our understanding of social change. Weber acknowledged that conflict could bring about change, but he traced the roots of most social change to ideas. For example, people with charisma can carry a message that sometimes changes the world.

Weber also highlighted the importance of ideas by showing how the religious beliefs of early Protestants set the stage for the spread of industrial capitalism (see Chapter 4, "Society"). The fact that industrial capitalism developed primarily in areas of Western Europe where the Protestant work ethic was strong proved to Weber the power of ideas to bring about change (1958; orig. 1904–5).

Ideas also direct social movements. Chapter 23 ("Collective Behavior and Social Movements") explained how change comes when people join together to, say, clean up the environment or try to improve the lives of oppressed people.

DEMOGRAPHIC CHANGE

Population patterns also play a part in social change. A century ago, as the chapter opening suggested, the typical household (4.8 people) was far larger than it is today (2.6 people). Women are having fewer children, for one thing, and more people are living alone. In addition, change is taking place as our population, collectively speaking, grows older. As Chapter 15 ("Aging and the Elderly") explained, 12 percent of the U.S. population was over age sixty-five in 2000, three times the proportion in 1900. By the year 2030, seniors will account for 20 percent of the total (U.S. Census Bureau, 2001). Medical research and health care services already focus extensively on the elderly, and life will change in countless additional ways as homes and household products are redesigned to meet the needs of older consumers.

Migration within and among societies is another demographic factor that promotes change. Between 1870 and 1930, tens of millions of immigrants entered the industrial cities in the United States. Millions more from rural areas joined the rush. As a result, farm communities declined, cities expanded, and, for the first time, the United States became a predominantly urban nation. Similarly, changes are taking place today as people move from the Snowbelt to the Sunbelt and mix with new immigrants from Latin America and Asia.

Where in the United States have demographic changes been greatest, and which areas have been least

TABLE 24-1 The United States: A Century of Change

	1900	2000
National population	76,000,000	281,000,000
Percentage urban	40%	80%
Life expectancy	46 years (men), 48 years (women)	74 years (men), 79 years (women)
Median age	22.9 years	35.3 years
Average household income	$8,000 (in 2000 dollars)	$40,000 (in 2000 dollars)
Share of income spent on food	43%	15%
Share of homes with flush toilets	10%	98%
Average number of cars	1 car for every 2,000 households	1.3 cars for every household
Divorce rate	About 1 in 20 marriages ends in divorce	About 8 in 20 marriages end in divorce
Average gallons of petroleum products consumed per person per year	34	1,100

affected? National Map 24–1 provides one answer, showing counties where the largest share of people have lived in their present homes for thirty years or more.

MODERNITY

A central concept in the study of social change is **modernity**, *social patterns resulting from industrialization.* In everyday usage, modernity (its Latin root means "lately") designates the present in relation to the past. Sociologists include in this catchall concept the social patterns set in motion by the Industrial Revolution beginning in Western Europe in the mideighteenth century. **Modernization,** then, is *the process of social change begun by industrialization.* The time line inside the front cover of the text highlights important events that mark the emergence of modernity. Table 24–1 provides a snapshot of change over the course of the twentieth century.

FOUR DIMENSIONS OF MODERNIZATION

Peter Berger (1977), in his influential study of social change, identified four major characteristics of modernization:

1. **The decline of small, traditional communities.** Modernity involves "the progressive weakening, if not destruction, of the . . . relatively cohesive communities in which human beings have found solidarity and meaning throughout most of history" (Berger 1977:72). For thousands of years, in the camps of hunters and gatherers and

in the rural villages of Europe and North America, people lived in small communities where social life revolved around family and neighborhood. Such traditional worlds gave each person a well-defined place that, while limiting range of choice, offered a strong sense of identity, belonging, and purpose.

Small, isolated communities still exist in remote corners of the United States, of course, but they are home to only a small percentage of our nation's people. And their isolation is little more than geographic. Cars, telephones, television, and, increasingly, computers give rural families the pulse of the larger society and connect them to the entire world.

2. **The expansion of personal choice.** Members of traditional, preindustrial societies view their lives as shaped by forces beyond human control—gods, spirits, or simply fate. But as the power of tradition erodes, people come to see their lives as an unending series of options, a process Berger calls *individualization*. Many people in the United States, for example, choose a "lifestyle" (sometimes adopting one after another), showing an openness to change. Indeed, a common belief is that people *should* take control of their lives.

3. **Increasing social diversity.** In preindustrial societies, strong family ties and powerful religious beliefs enforce conformity and discourage diversity and change. Modernization promotes a more rational, scientific worldview as tradition loses its hold and people gain more and more individual choice. The growth of cities, the expansion of

In response to the accelerating pace of change in the nineteenth century, Paul Gauguin left his native France for the South Seas where he was captivated by a simpler and seemingly timeless way of life. He romanticized this environment in his painting, Nave Nave Moe (Sacred Spring).

Paul Gauguin, French (1848–1903), Nave Nave Moe
(Sacred Spring), 1894. Hermitage, St. Petersburg, Russia. Oil on
canvas, 73 × 98 cm. © The Bridgeman Art Library International Ltd.

impersonal bureaucracy, and the social mix of people from various backgrounds combine to foster diverse beliefs and behavior.

4. **Future orientation and growing awareness of time.** While premodern people focus on the past, people in modern societies think more about the future. Modern people are not only forward-looking but optimistic that new inventions and discoveries will improve their lives.

Modern people also organize their daily routines down to the very minute. With the introduction of clocks in the late Middle Ages, Europeans began to think not in terms of sunlight and seasons but in terms of days, hours, and minutes. Preoccupied with personal gain, modern people demand precise measurement of time and are likely to agree that "Time is money." Berger points out that one good indicator of a society's degree of modernization is the proportion of people wearing wristwatches.

Finally, recall that modernization touched off the development of sociology itself. As Chapter 1 ("The Sociological Perspective") explained, the discipline originated in the wake of the Industrial Revolution in Western Europe, where social change was proceeding most rapidly. Early European and U.S. sociologists tried to analyze the rise of modern society and its consequences, both good and bad, for human beings.

FERDINAND TÖNNIES: THE LOSS OF COMMUNITY

The German sociologist Ferdinand Tönnies (1855–1937) produced a lasting account of modernization in his theory of *Gemeinschaft* and *Gesellschaft* (see Chapter 22, "Population, Urbanization, and Environment"). Like Peter Berger, whose work he influenced, Tönnies (1963; orig. 1887) viewed modernization as the progressive loss of *Gemeinschaft*, or human community. As Tönnies saw it, the Industrial Revolution weakened the social fabric of family and tradition by introducing a businesslike emphasis on facts, efficiency, and money. European and North American societies gradually became rootless and impersonal as people came to associate mostly on the basis of self-interest—the state Tönnies called *Gesellschaft*.

Early in the twentieth century, at least some areas of the United States approximated Tönnies's concept of *Gemeinschaft*. Families that had lived for generations in small villages and towns were bound together in a hard-working, slow-moving way of life. Telephones (invented in 1876) were rare; it wasn't until 1915 that someone placed the first coast-to-coast call (see the time line inside the front cover of this book). Living without television (introduced in 1939, and not widespread until after 1950), families entertained themselves, often gathering with friends in the evening to share stories, sorrows, or song. Without rapid transportation (Henry Ford's assembly line began in 1908, but cars became commonplace only

George Tooker's 1950 painting The Subway *depicts a common problem of modern life: Weakening social ties and eroding traditions create a generic humanity in which everyone is alike yet each person is an anxious stranger in the midst of others.*

George Tooker, The Subway, 1950, egg tempera on gesso panel, 18⅛ × 36⅛", Whitney Museum of American Art, New York. Purchased with funds from the Juliana Force Purchase Award, 50.23. Photograph © 2000 Whitney Museum of American Art.

after World War II), many people's own town was their entire social world.

Inevitable tensions and conflicts divided these communities of the past. But according to Tönnies, because of the traditional spirit of *Gemeinschaft*, people were "essentially united in spite of all separating factors" (1963:65; orig. 1887).

Modernity turns societies inside out so that, as Tönnies put it, people are "essentially separated in spite of uniting factors" (1963:65; orig. 1887). This is the world of *Gesellschaft*, where, especially in large cities, most people live among strangers and ignore others they pass on the street. Trust is hard to come by in a mobile and anonymous society where people tend to put their personal needs ahead of group loyalty, and a majority of adults believe "you can't be too careful" in dealing with people (NORC, 2003:181). No wonder researchers conclude that, even as we become more affluent, the social health of modern societies has declined (Myers, 2000).

For a short biography of Ferdinand Tönnies, visit the Gallery of Sociologists at http://www.TheSociologyPage.com

Critical evaluation. Tönnies's theory of *Gemeinschaft* and *Gesellschaft* is the most widely cited model of modernization. The theory's strength lies in combining various dimensions of change: growing population, the rise of cities, and increasing impersonality in social interaction. But modern life, though often impersonal, is not completely devoid of *Gemeinschaft*. Even in a world of strangers, modern friendships can be strong and lasting. Some analysts also think that Tönnies favored— perhaps even romanticized—traditional societies while overlooking bonds of family, neighborhood, and friendship in modern societies.

EMILE DURKHEIM: THE DIVISION OF LABOR

The French sociologist Emile Durkheim, whose work is discussed in Chapter 4 ("Society"), shared Tönnies's interest in the profound social changes wrought by the Industrial Revolution. For Durkheim, modernization is defined by an increasing *division of labor*, or specialized economic activity (1964a; orig. 1893). Whereas every member of a traditional society performs more or less the same daily round of activities, modern societies function by having people perform highly specific roles.

Durkheim explained that preindustrial societies are held together by *mechanical solidarity*, or shared moral sentiments. In other words, members of preindustrial societies view everyone as basically alike, doing the same kind of work and belonging together. Durkheim's concept of mechanical solidarity is virtually the same as Tönnies's *Gemeinschaft*.

With modernization, the division of labor becomes more and more pronounced. To Durkheim, this change means *less* mechanical solidarity but *more* of another kind of tie: *organic solidarity*, or the mutual dependency of people engaged in specialized work. Put simply, modern societies are held together not by likeness but by difference: All of us must depend on others to meet most of our needs. Organic solidarity corresponds to Tönnies's concept of *Gesellschaft*.

Despite obvious similarities in their thinking, Durkheim and Tönnies viewed modernity somewhat differently. To Tönnies, modern *Gesellschaft* amounts to the loss of social solidarity, because modern people lose the "natural" and "organic" bonds of the rural village, leaving only the "artificial" and "mechanical" ties of the big, industrial city. Durkheim had a different take on modernity, even reversing Tönnies's language to bring home the point. Durkheim labeled modern society "organic," arguing that modern society is no less natural than any other, and he described traditional societies as "mechanical" because they are so regimented. Thus, Durkheim viewed modernization not as the loss of community but as a change from community based on bonds of likeness (kinship and neighborhood) to community based on economic interdependence (the division of labor). Durkheim's view of modernity is thus both more complex and more positive than Tönnies's view.

Critical evaluation. Compared to Tönnies, Durkheim was more optimistic about modern society. Still, he feared that modern societies might become so diverse that they would collapse into a state of *anomie*, a condition in which norms and values are so weak and inconsistent that society provides little moral guidance to individuals. Living with weak moral norms, modern people can become egocentric, placing their own needs above those of others and finding little purpose in life.

The suicide rate—which Durkheim considered a good index of anomie—did, in fact, increase in the United States over the course of the twentieth century. Moreover, the vast majority of U.S. adults report that they see moral questions not in clear terms of right and wrong but in confusing "shades of gray" (NORC, 2003:359).

Yet, shared norms and values still seem strong enough to give most individuals some sense of meaning and purpose. Moreover, whatever the hazards of anomie, most people seem to value the personal freedom modern society affords.

MAX WEBER: RATIONALIZATION

In Max Weber's work (also discussed in Chapter 4, "Society"), modernity means replacing a traditional worldview with a rational way of thinking. In preindustrial societies, tradition acts as a constant brake on change. To traditional people, "truth" is roughly the same as "what has always been" (1978:36; orig. 1921). To modern people, however, "truth" is the result of rational calculation. Because they value efficiency and have little reverence for the past, modern people adopt whatever social patterns allow them to achieve their goals.

Echoing Tönnies and Durkheim, who held that industrialization weakens tradition, Weber declared modern society to be "disenchanted." The unquestioned truths of an earlier time had been challenged by rational thinking. In short, modern society turns away from the gods. Throughout his life, Weber studied various modern "types"—the capitalist, the scientist, the bureaucrat—all of whom share the detached worldview that Weber believed was coming to dominate humanity.

Critical evaluation. Compared with Tönnies and especially Durkheim, Weber was critical of modern society. He knew that science could produce technological and organizational wonders but worried that science was turning us away from more basic questions about the meaning and purpose of human existence. Weber feared that rationalization, especially in bureaucracies, would erode the human spirit with endless rules and regulations.

Finally, some of Weber's critics think that the alienation he attributed to bureaucracy actually stemmed from social inequality. That criticism leads us to the ideas of Karl Marx.

KARL MARX: CAPITALISM

For Karl Marx, modern society was synonymous with capitalism; he saw the Industrial Revolution as primarily a *capitalist revolution*. Marx traced the emergence of the bourgeoisie in medieval Europe to the expansion of commerce. The bourgeoisie gradually displaced the feudal aristocracy as the Industrial Revolution placed a powerful new system of production under their control.

Marx agreed that modernity weakened small communities (as described by Tönnies), sharpened the division of labor (as noted by Durkheim), and fostered a rational worldview (as Weber claimed). But he saw all these simply as conditions necessary for capitalism to flourish. Capitalism, according to Marx, draws population from farms and small towns into an ever-expanding market system cen-

 For more on Durkheim, Weber, and Marx, visit the Gallery of Sociologists at http://www.TheSociologyPage.com

tered in cities; specialization is needed for efficient factories; and rationality is exemplified by the capitalists' endless pursuit of profit.

Earlier chapters have painted Marx as a spirited critic of capitalist society, but his vision of modernity also has a good bit of optimism. Unlike Weber, who viewed modern society as an "iron cage" of bureaucracy, Marx believed that social conflict in capitalist societies

Max Weber maintained that the distinctive character of modern society was its rational worldview. Virtually all of Weber's work on modernity centered on types of people he considered typical of their age: the scientist, the capitalist, and the bureaucrat. Each is rational to the core: The scientist is committed to the orderly discovery of truth, the capitalist to the orderly pursuit of profit, and the bureaucrat to orderly conformity to a system of rules.

would sow seeds of revolutionary change, leading to an egalitarian socialism. Such a society, as he saw it, would harness the wonders of industrial technology to enrich people's lives and also rid the world of social classes, the source of social conflict and dehumanization. Although Marx was an outspoken critic of modern society, he nevertheless imagined a future of human freedom, creativity, and community.

Critical evaluation. Marx's theory of modernization is a complex theory of capitalism. But he underestimated the dominance of bureaucracy in modern societies. In socialist societies, in particular, the stifling effects of bureaucracy turned out to be as bad as, or even worse than, the dehumanizing aspects of capitalism. The upheavals in Eastern Europe and the former Soviet Union in the early 1990s reveal the depth of popular opposition to oppressive state bureaucracies.

THEORETICAL ANALYSIS OF MODERNITY

The rise of modernity is a complex process involving many dimensions of change, as described in previous chapters and summarized in Table 24–2 on page 634. How can we make sense of so many changes going on all at once? Sociologists have developed two broad explanations of modern society, one guided by the structural-functional paradigm and one based on social-conflict theory.

STRUCTURAL-FUNCTIONAL THEORY: MODERNITY AS MASS SOCIETY

`November 11, on the Interstate 275 outerbelt.` From the car, we see a BP and a Sunoco station, K-Mart and Wal-Mart, AmeriSuites hotel, a Bob Evans, and a McDonald's. This road happens to circle Cincinnati. But it could be almost anywhere in the United States.

One broad approach—drawing on the ideas of Ferdinand Tönnies, Emile Durkheim, and Max Weber—understands modernization as the emergence of *mass society* (Dahrendorf, 1959; Kornhauser, 1959; Nisbet, 1966, 1969; Stein, 1972; Berger, Berger, & Kellner, 1974; Pearson, 1993). A **mass society** is *a society in which prosperity and bureaucracy have eroded traditional social ties.* A mass society is highly productive; on average, people have more income than ever. At the same time, it is marked by weak kinship and impersonal neighborhoods, so individuals often feel socially isolated. Although many people have material plenty, in short, they are spiritually weak and often experience moral uncertainty about how to live.

The Mass Scale of Modern Life

Mass-society theory argues, first, that the scale of modern life has greatly increased. Before the Industrial

TABLE 24–2 Traditional and Modern Societies: The Big Picture

Elements of Society	Traditional Societies	Modern Societies
Cultural Patterns		
Values	Homogeneous; sacred character; few subcultures and countercultures	Heterogeneous; secular character; many subcultures and countercultures
Norms	High moral significance; little tolerance of diversity	Variable moral significance; high tolerance of diversity
Time orientation	Present linked to past	Present linked to future
Technology	Preindustrial; human and animal energy	Industrial; advanced energy sources
Social Structure		
Status and role	Few statuses, most ascribed; few specialized roles	Many statuses, some ascribed and some achieved; many specialized roles
Relationships	Typically primary; little anonymity or privacy	Typically secondary; much anonymity and privacy
Communication	Face to face	Face-to-face communication supplemented by mass media
Social control	Informal gossip	Formal police and legal system
Social stratification	Rigid patterns of social inequality; little mobility	Fluid patterns of social inequality; high mobility
Gender patterns	Pronounced patriarchy; women's lives centered on the home	Declining patriarchy; increasing number of women in the paid labor force
Settlement patterns	Small-scale; population typically small and widely dispersed in rural villages and small towns	Large-scale; population typically large and concentrated in cities
Social Institutions		
Economy	Based on agriculture; much manufacturing in the home; little white-collar work	Based on industrial mass production; factories become centers of production; increasing white-collar work
State	Small-scale government; little state intervention in society	Large-scale government; much state intervention in society
Family	Extended family as the primary means of socialization and economic production	Nuclear family retains some socialization functions but is more a unit of consumption than of production
Religion	Religion guides worldview; little religious pluralism	Religion weakens with the rise of science; extensive religious pluralism
Education	Formal schooling limited to elites	Basic schooling becomes universal, with growing proportion receiving advanced education
Health	High birth and death rates; short life expectancy because of low standard of living and simple medical technology	Low birth and death rates; longer life expectancy because of higher standard of living and sophisticated medical technology
Social Change	Slow; change evident over many generations	Rapid; change evident within a single generation

Revolution, Europe and North America formed a mosaic of countless rural villages and small towns. In these small communities, which inspired Tönnies's concept of *Gemeinschaft*, people lived out their lives surrounded by kin and guided by a shared heritage. Gossip was an informal yet highly effective way to ensure conformity to community standards. These small communities, with their strong moral values and their low tolerance of social diversity, exemplified the state of mechanical solidarity described by Durkheim.

For example, before 1690, English law demanded that everyone regularly participate in the Christian ritual of Holy Communion (Laslett, 1984). In the New England colonies, only Rhode Island tolerated religious dissent. Because social differences were repressed, subcultures and countercultures rarely arose, and change proceeded slowly.

Increasing population, the growth of cities, and specialized economic activity driven by the Industrial Revolution gradually altered this pattern. People came to know one another by their jobs (for example, as "the doctor" or "the bank clerk") rather than by their kinship group or hometown. People looked on most others simply as strangers. The face-to-face communication of the village was eventually replaced by the mass media: newspapers, radio, television, and, more recently, computer networks—furthering the process of social atomization. Large organizations steadily assumed more and more responsibility for seeing to the daily tasks that had once been carried out by family, friends, and neighbors; public education drew more and more people to schools; police, lawyers, and courts supervised a formal criminal justice system. Even charity became the work of faceless bureaucrats working for various social welfare agencies.

Geographic mobility and exposure to diverse ways of life all erode traditional values. People become more tolerant of social diversity, defending individual rights and freedom of choice. Treating people differently—because of their race, sex, or religion—comes to be defined as backward and unjust. In the process, minorities at the margin of society acquire greater power and broader participation in public life.

The mass media give rise to a national culture that washes over traditional differences that set off one region from another. As one analyst put it, "Even in Baton Rouge, La., the local kids don't say 'y'all' anymore; they say 'you guys' just like on TV" (Gibbs, 2000:42). In this way, mass-society theorists fear, transforming people of various backgrounds into a generic mass may end up dehumanizing everyone.

The Ever-Expanding State

In the small-scale, preindustrial societies of Europe, government amounted to little more than a local noble. A royal family formally reigned over an entire nation, but without efficient transportation or communication, the power of even absolute monarchs fell far short of the power wielded by today's political leaders.

As technological innovation allowed government to expand, the centralized state grew in size and importance. At the time the United States gained independence from Great Britain, the federal government was a tiny organization whose main job was national defense. Since then, government has entered more and more areas of social life: schooling the population, regulating wages and working conditions, establishing standards for products of all sorts, and offering financial assistance to the ill and the unemployed. To pay for such programs, taxes have soared: Today's average worker labors more than four months each year to pay for the broad array of services that government provides.

In a mass society, power resides in large bureaucracies, leaving people in local communities little control over their lives. For example, state officials mandate that local schools must have a standardized educational program, local products must be government-certified, and every citizen must maintain extensive tax records. While such regulations may protect people and advance social equality, they also force us to deal more and more with nameless officials in distant and often unresponsive bureaucracies, and they undermine the autonomy of families and local communities.

Critical evaluation. The growing scale of modern life certainly has positive aspects, but only at the price of losing some of our cultural heritage. Modern societies increase individual rights, tolerate greater social differences, and raise standards of living (Inglehart & Baker, 2000). But they are prone to what Weber feared most—excessive bureaucracy—as well as Tönnies's self-centeredness and Durkheim's anomie. Their size, complexity, and tolerance of diversity all but doom traditional values and family patterns, leaving individuals isolated, powerless, and materialistic. As Chapter 17 ("Politics and Government") noted, voter apathy is a serious problem in the United States. But should we be surprised that individuals in vast, impersonal societies think no one person can make a difference?

Critics contend that mass-society theory romanticizes the past. They remind us that many people in small towns were actually eager to set out for a higher standard of living in cities. Moreover, mass-society theory ignores problems of social inequality. Critics say this theory attracts conservatives who defend conventional morality while being indifferent to the historical plight of women and other minorities.

SOCIAL-CONFLICT THEORY: MODERNITY AS CLASS SOCIETY

The second interpretation of modernity derives largely from the ideas of Karl Marx. From a social-conflict perspective, modernity takes the form of a **class society,** *a capitalist society with pronounced social stratification.* That is, while agreeing that modern societies have expanded to a mass scale, this approach views the heart of modernization as an expanding capitalist economy, rife with inequality (Miliband, 1969; Habermas, 1970; Polenberg, 1980; Blumberg, 1981; Harrington, 1984; Buechler, 2000).

Capitalism

Class-society theory follows Marx in claiming that the increasing scale of social life in modern society results from the insatiable appetite of capitalism. Because a capitalist economy pursues ever-greater profits, both production and consumption steadily increase.

According to Marx, capitalism rests on "naked self-interest" (Marx & Engels, 1972:337; orig. 1848).

Many people marveled at the industrial technology that was changing the world a century ago. But some critics pointed out that the social consequences of the Industrial Revolution were not all positive. Children worked long hours in mind-numbing jobs, as portrayed in this 1870 engraving of twinemakers in New York City.

This self-centeredness erodes the social ties that once cemented small communities. Capitalism also treats people as commodities: a source of labor and a market for capitalist products.

Capitalism supports science, not just as the key to greater productivity but as an ideology that justifies the status quo. That is, modern societies encourage people to view human well-being as a technical puzzle to be solved by engineers and other experts rather than as a moral issue to be realized through the pursuit of social justice (Habermas, 1970). A capitalist culture, for example, seeks to improve health through scientific medicine rather than by eliminating poverty, which is a core cause of poor health.

Business also raises the banner of scientific logic, trying to increase profits through greater efficiency. As Chapter 16 ("The Economy and Work") explains, today's capitalist corporations have reached enormous size and control unimaginable wealth as a result of "going global" and becoming multinationals. From the class-society point of view, then, the expanding scale of life is less a function of *Gesellschaft* than the inevitable and destructive consequence of capitalism.

Persistent Inequality

Modernity has gradually worn away the rigid categories that set nobles apart from commoners in preindustrial societies. But class-society theory maintains that elites persist—albeit now as capitalist millionaires rather than nobles born to wealth and power. In the United States, we may have no hereditary monarchy, but the richest 5 percent of the population nevertheless controls about 60 percent of all privately held property.

What of the state? Mass-society theorists contend that the state works to increase equality and combat social problems. Marx was skeptical that the state could accomplish more than minor reforms because, as he saw it, the real power lies in the hands of capitalists, who control the economy. Other class-society theorists add that, to the extent that working people and minorities do enjoy greater political rights and a higher standard of living today, these changes are the fruits of political struggle, not expressions of government goodwill. In short, they conclude, despite our pretensions of democracy, most people are powerless in the face of wealthy elites.

Critical evaluation. Class-society theory also dismisses Durkheim's argument that people in modern societies suffer from anomie, claiming instead that they suffer from alienation and powerlessness. Not surprisingly, then, the class-society interpretation of modernity enjoys widespread support among liberals (and radicals) who favor greater equality and call for extensive regulation (or abolition) of the capitalist marketplace.

A basic criticism of class-society theory is that it overlooks the increasing prosperity of modern societies and the fact that discrimination based on race, ethnicity, and gender is now illegal and is widely regarded as a social problem. Furthermore, most people in the

United States do not want a society in which everyone is equal; they prefer a system of unequal rewards that reflects personal differences in talent and effort.

Moreover, few observers think a centralized economy would cure the ills of modernity in light of socialism's failure to generate a high overall standard of living. Many other problems in the United States—from unemployment, homelessness, and industrial pollution to unresponsive government—are also found in socialist nations such as the former Soviet Union.

Table 24–3 summarizes the two interpretations of modernity. Whereas mass-society theory focuses on the increasing scale of life and the growth of government, class-society theory stresses the expansion of capitalism and the persistence of inequality.

MODERNITY AND THE INDIVIDUAL

Both mass- and class-society theories look at the broad societal changes that have taken place since the Industrial Revolution. But from these macro-level approaches we can also draw micro-level insights into how modernity shapes individual lives.

Mass Society: Problems of Identity

Modernity liberated individuals from the small, tightly knit communities of the past. Most people in modern societies, therefore, have the privacy and freedom to express their individuality. Mass-society theory suggests, however, that so much social diversity, widespread isolation, and rapid social change make it difficult for many people to establish any coherent identity at all (Wheelis, 1958; Riesman, 1970; Berger, Berger, & Kellner, 1974).

Chapter 5 ("Socialization") explained that people's personalities are largely a product of their social experiences. The small, homogeneous, and slowly changing societies of the past provided a firm, if narrow, foundation for building a personal identity. Even today, the Amish communities that flourish in the United States and Canada teach young men and women "correct" ways to think and behave. Not everyone born into an Amish community can tolerate strict demands for conformity, but most members establish a well-integrated and satisfying personal identity (cf. Hostetler, 1980; Kraybill & Olshan, 1994).

Mass societies are quite another story. Socially diverse and rapidly changing, they offer only shifting sands on which to build a personal identity. Left to make many life decisions on their own, many people—especially those with greater affluence and thus more

TABLE 24-3 Two Interpretations of Modernity: A Summary

	Mass Society	Class Society
Process of Modernization	Industrialization; growth of bureaucracy	Rise of capitalism
Effects of Modernization	Increasing scale of life; rise of the state and other formal organizations	Expansion of the capitalist economy; persistence of social inequality

freedom—face a bewildering range of options. Choice has little value without standards to guide our selections, and in a tolerant mass society, people may find one path no more compelling than the next. Not surprisingly, many people shuttle from one identity to another, changing their lifestyle, relationships, and even religion in search of an elusive "true self." Beset by the widespread "relativism" of modern societies, people without a moral compass lack the security and certainty once provided by tradition.

To David Riesman (1970; orig. 1950), modernization brings changes in **social character,** *personality patterns common to members of a particular society.* Preindustrial societies foster what Riesman calls **tradition-directedness,** *rigid conformity to time-honored ways of living.* Members of traditional societies model their lives on those of their ancestors, so that "living a good life" amounts to "doing what our people have always done."

Tradition-directedness corresponds to Tönnies's *Gemeinschaft* and Durkheim's mechanical solidarity. Culturally conservative, tradition-directed people think and act alike. Unlike the conformity sometimes found in modern societies, the uniformity of tradition-directedness is not an effort to mimic one another. Instead, people are alike because they all draw on the same solid cultural foundation. Amish women and men exemplify tradition-directedness; in Amish culture, tradition ties everyone to ancestors and descendants in an unbroken chain of righteous living.

Members of diverse and rapidly changing societies consider a tradition-directed personality deviant because it seems so rigid. Modern people, by and large, prize personal flexibility and sensitivity to others, what Riesman describes as **other-directedness,** *a receptiveness to the latest trends and fashions, often expressed by imitating others.* Because their socialization occurs in societies that are constantly in flux, other-directed

Mass-society theory attributes feelings of anxiety, isolation, and lack of meaning in the modern world to rapid social change that washes away tradition. Edvard Munch captured this vision of modern emptiness in his painting The Scream (left). Class-society theory, by contrast, ties such feelings to social inequality, by which some categories of people are made into second-class citizens (or not made citizens at all). Paul Marcus portrays modern injustice in the painting Crossing the Rio Grande (right).

Edvard Munch, The Scream, Oslo, National Gallery, Scala/Art Resource, N.Y. © 2004 Artists Rights Society (ARS), NY/ADAGP, Paris (left);
© Paul Marcus, Crossing the Rio Grande, 1999, oil painting on canvas, 63 × 72 in. Studio SPM Inc. (right).

people develop fluid identities marked by superficiality, inconsistency, and change. They try on different "selves," almost like so many pieces of new clothing, seek out role models, and engage in varied "performances" as they move from setting to setting (Goffman, 1959). In a traditional society, such "shiftiness" makes a person untrustworthy, but in a changing, modern society, the chameleonlike ability to fit in virtually anywhere is very useful.

In societies that value the up-to-date rather than the traditional, people anxiously solicit the approval of others, looking to members of their own generation rather than to elders as significant role models. Peer pressure can be irresistible to people with no enduring standards to guide them. Our society urges individuals to be true to themselves. But when social surroundings change so rapidly, how can people develop the self to which they should be true? This problem lies at the root of the identity crisis so widespread in industrial societies today. "Who am I?" is a nagging question that many of us struggle to answer. In truth, this problem is not so much us as the society in which we live, that is, the inherent instability of modern mass society.

Class Society: Problems of Powerlessness

Class-society theory paints a different picture of modernity's effects on individuals. This approach maintains that persistent social inequality undermines modern society's promise of individual freedom. For some, modernity serves up great privilege, but for many, everyday life means coping with economic uncertainty and a gnawing sense of powerlessness (Newman, 1993; Ehrenreich, 2000).

For racial and ethnic minorities, the problem of relative disadvantage looms even larger. Similarly, although women enjoy increasing participation in modern societies, they continue to run up against traditional barriers of sexism. In short, this approach rejects mass-society theory's claim that people suffer from too much freedom. Instead, class-society theory holds that our society still denies a majority of people full participation in social life.

On a global scale, as Chapter 12 ("Global Stratification") explained, the expanding scope of world capitalism has placed more of the Earth's population under the influence of multinational corporations. As a result, about two-thirds of the world's income is concentrated in the high-income nations where only 18 percent of its people live. Is it any wonder, class-society theorists ask, that people in poor nations seek greater power to shape their own lives?

The problem of widespread powerlessness led Herbert Marcuse (1964) to challenge Max Weber's statement that modern society is rational. Marcuse condemned modern society as irrational for failing to meet the needs of so many people. While modern capitalist societies produce unparalleled wealth, poverty remains the daily plight of more than a billion people. Moreover, Marcuse argues, technological advances further reduce people's control over their own lives. High technology confers great power on a core of specialists—not the majority of people—who now control events and dominate the public agenda, whether the issue is computing, energy production, or health care. Countering the common view that technology *solves* the world's problems, Marcuse believed that science *causes* them. In sum, class-society theory asserts that people suffer because modern, scientific societies concentrate both wealth and power in the hands of a privileged few.

MODERNITY AND PROGRESS

In modern societies, most people expect, and applaud, social change. We link modernity to the idea of *progress* (from Latin, meaning "moving forward"), a state of continual improvement. By contrast, we see stability as stagnation.

Given our bias in favor of change, our society tends to look upon traditional cultures as backward. But change, particularly toward material affluence, is a mixed blessing. As the box on page 640 shows, social change is too complex simply to equate with progress.

Even getting rich has its disadvantages, as the case of the Kaiapo shows. Historically, among people in the United States, a rising standard of living has made lives longer and, in a material sense, more comfortable. At the same time, many people wonder if today's routines are too stressful, with families often having little time for relaxation or simply spending time together.

Science, too, has its pluses and minuses. A recent survey (Inglehart et al., 2000) showed that people in the United States are confident—more than those in most other industrial nations—that science improves our lives. But surveys also show that many adults in the United States feel that science "makes our way of life change too fast" (NORC, 2003:346).

New technology has always sparked controversy. A century ago, the introduction of automobiles and telephones allowed more rapid transportation and more efficient communication. But at the same time, such technology weakened traditional attachments to hometowns and even to families. Today, people might well wonder if computer technology will do the same thing, giving us access to people around the world, but shielding us from the community right outside our doors; providing more information than ever before but, in the process, threatening personal privacy. In short, we all realize that social change comes faster all the time, but we may disagree about whether a particular change is progress or a step backward.

MODERNITY: GLOBAL VARIATION

October 1, Kobe, Japan. Riding the computer-controlled monorail high above the streets of Kobe or the 200-mile-per-hour bullet train to Tokyo, we see Japan as the society of the future, in love with high technology. Yet the Japanese remain strikingly traditional in other respects: Few corporate executives and almost no senior politicians are women; young people still accord their elders considerable respect; and public orderliness contrasts with the sometime chaos of U.S. cities.

Japan is a nation at once traditional and modern. This contradiction reminds us that, while it is useful to contrast traditional and modern societies, the old and the new often coexist in unexpected ways. In the People's Republic of China, ancient Confucian principles are mixed with contemporary socialist thinking. Similarly, in Saudi Arabia and Qatar, the embrace of modern technology is mixed with respect for the ancient principles of Islam. Likewise, in Mexico and much of Latin America, people observe centuries-old Christian rituals even as they struggle to move ahead economically. In short, combinations of traditional and modern are far from unusual—indeed, they are found throughout the world.

POSTMODERNITY

If modernity was the product of the Industrial Revolution, is the Information Revolution creating a postmodern era? A number of scholars think so and use the term **postmodernity** to refer to *social patterns characteristic of postindustrial societies.*

GLOBAL SOCIOLOGY

Does "Modern" Mean "Progress"?
Brazil's Kaiapo and Georgia's Gullah Community

The firelight flickers in the gathering darkness. Chief Kanhonk sits, as he has done at the end of the day for many years, ready to begin an evening of animated talk and storytelling (Simons, 2004). This is the hour when the Kaiapo, a small society in Brazil's lush Amazon region, celebrate their heritage. Because the Kaiapo are a traditional people with no written language, the elders rely on evenings by the fire to pass along their culture to their children and grandchildren. In the past, evenings like this have been filled with tales of brave Kaiapo warriors fighting off Portuguese traders who were in pursuit of slaves and gold.

But as the minutes pass, only a few older villagers assemble for the evening ritual. "It is the Big Ghost," one man grumbles, explaining the poor turnout. The "Big Ghost" has indeed descended upon them; its bluish glow spills from windows throughout the village. The Kaiapo children—and many adults as well—are watching television. The installation of a satellite dish in the village several years ago has had consequences far greater than anyone imagined. In the end, what their enemies failed to do with guns, the Kaiapo may well do to themselves with primetime programming.

The Kaiapo are among Brazil's 230,000 native peoples. They stand out because of their striking body paint and ornate ceremonial dress. In the 1980s, they became rich from gold mining and harvesting mahogany trees. Now they must decide whether their newfound fortune is a blessing or a curse.

To some, affluence means the opportunity to learn about the outside world through travel and television. Others, like Chief Kanhonk, are not so

sure. Sitting by the fire, he thinks aloud, ". . . people must buy useful things like knives and fishing hooks. Television does not fill the stomach. It only shows our children and grandchildren white people's things." Bebtopup, the oldest priest, nods in agreement: "The night is the time the old people teach the young people. Television has stolen the night" (Simons, 2004:494).

To see images of Brazil's Kaiapo, go to http://www. ddbstock.com/largeimage/ amindns.html

Far to the north, in the United States, half an hour by ferry from the coast of Georgia, lies the swampy island community of Hog Hammock. The seventy African American residents of the island today trace their ancestry back to the first slaves who settled there in 1802.

Walking past the colorful houses nestled among pine trees draped with Spanish moss, visitors feel transported back in time. The local people, known as Gullahs (or, in some places, Geechees) speak a mixture of English and West African languages. They fish, living much as they have for hundreds of years.

But the future of this way of life is now in doubt. Few young people who are raised in Hog Hammock can find work beyond fishing and making traditional crafts. "We have been here nine generations and we are still here," says one local. Then, referring to the island's nineteen children, she adds, "It's not that they don't want to be here, it's that there's nothing here for them—they need to have jobs" (Curry, 2001:41).

Just as important, with people on the mainland looking for waterside homes

for vacations or year-round living, the island is now becoming prime real estate. Not long ago, one of the larger houses went up for sale and the community was shocked to learn that its asking price was more than $1 million. The locals know only too well that higher property values will mean high taxes that few can afford to pay. In short, Hog Hammock is likely to become another Hilton Head, once a Gullah community on the South Carolina coast that is now home to well-to-do people from the mainland.

Before long, the odds are that the people of Hog Hammock will be selling out and moving inland. But few people are happy thinking about the economic windfall they will gain by selling their homes. On the contrary, moving away will mean the end of their cultural heritage.

The stories of both the Kaiapo and the people of Hog Hammock show us that change is not a simple path toward "progress." These people may be moving toward modernity, but this process will have both positive and negative consequences. In the end, both groups of people may enjoy a higher standard of living with better shelter, more clothing, and new technology. On the other hand, their new affluence will come at the price of their traditions. The drama of these people is now being played out around the world as more and more traditional cultures are being lured away from their heritage by the affluence and materialism of rich societies.

To learn more about Gullah culture, go to http://www. knowitall.org/gullahnet

Source: Based on Curry (2001) and Simons (2004).

Many people see modernity as a mix of promise and danger. The mural Read between the Lines by Mexican American artist David Botello (1975), found in East Los Angeles, contains the words, "Cuisense Amigos" ("Be careful, friends"). Looking at the mural, what about the modern U.S. way of life is Botello worried about? (In what ways is the heritage of Mexican Americans threatened in the United States?)

David Botello, Read between the Lines, 1975, mural on Ford and Olympic Boulevards, East Los Angeles, acrylic on stucco, 10 × 20 ft.

Precisely what postmodernism is remains a matter of debate. The term has been used for decades in literary, philosophical, and even architectural circles. It moved into sociology on a wave of social criticism that has been building since the spread of left-leaning politics in the 1960s. Although there are many variants of postmodern thinking, all share the following five themes (Bernstein, 1992; Borgmann, 1992; Crook, Pakulski, & Waters, 1992; Hall & Neitz, 1993; Inglehart, 1997; Rudel & Gerson, 1999):

1. **In important respects, modernity has failed.** The promise of modernity was a life free from want. As postmodernist critics see it, however, the twentieth century was unsuccessful in solving social problems like poverty, since many people still lack financial security.

2. **The bright light of "progress" is fading.** Modern people look to the future, expecting that their lives will improve in significant ways. Members (even leaders) of postmodern societies, however, are less confident about what the future holds. Furthermore, the buoyant optimism that carried society into the modern era more than a century ago has given way to stark pessimism; most U.S. adults believe that life is getting worse (NORC, 2003:208).

3. **Science no longer holds the answers.** The defining trait of the modern era was a scientific outlook and a confident belief that technology would make life better. But postmodern critics contend that science has not solved many old problems (like poor health) and has even created new problems (such as degrading the environment).

More generally, postmodernist thinkers discredit science, claiming that it implies a singular truth. On the contrary, they maintain, objective reality and truth do not exist at all. Reality amounts to social construction, they say; moreover, we can deconstruct science to see how it has been widely used for political purposes, especially by powerful segments of society.

4. **Cultural debates are intensifying.** Modernity was to be an era of enhanced individuality and expanding tolerance. But it has fallen short here as well. Feminism points out that patriarchy continues to limit the lives of women, and multiculturalism seeks to empower minorities who remain at the margins of social life.

Moreover, now that more people have all the material things they really need, ideas are taking on more importance. Thus, postmodernity is also a postmaterialist era, in which issues like social justice, as well as the environment and gay rights, command more and more public attention.

5. **Social institutions are changing.** Just as industrialization brought a sweeping transformation to social institutions, the rise of a postindustrial society is remaking society all over again. For example, just as the Industrial Revolution placed *material things* at the center of productive

CRITICAL THINKING

Tracking Change: Is Life in the United States Getting Better or Worse?

We began this chapter with a look at what life was like in a large U.S. city in 1900, more than a century ago. It is easy to see that, in many ways, life is far better for us than it was for our grandparents and great-grandparents. In recent decades, however, not all indicators have been good. Here is a look at some trends shaping the United States since 1970.

First, the good news: By some measures, shown in the first set of figures, life in this country is clearly improving. Infant mortality has fallen steadily; that is, fewer and fewer children die soon after birth. Moreover, more people are reaching old age, and after reaching sixty-five, they are living longer than ever. More good news: The poverty rate among the elderly is well below what it was in 1970. Schooling is another area of improvement: The share of people dropping out of high school is down, while the share completing college is up compared to a generation ago.

Second, some "no-news" results: A number of indicators show that life is

The good news . . .

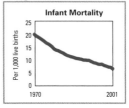

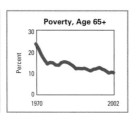
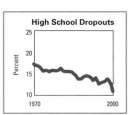
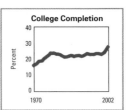

No news . . .

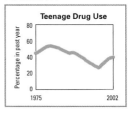
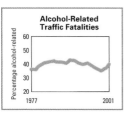
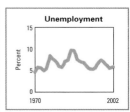
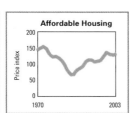

life, now the Information Revolution emphasizes *ideas*. Similarly, the postmodern family no longer conforms to any single pattern; on the contrary, individuals are choosing among many new family forms.

Critical evaluation. Analysts who claim that the United States and other high-income societies are entering a postmodern era criticize modernity for failing to meet human needs. Yet few think that modernity has failed completely; after all, we have seen marked increases in longevity and living standards over the course of the last century. Moreover, even if we accept postmodernist views that science is bankrupt and progress is a sham, what are the alternatives?

Finally, many voices offer very different understandings of recent social trends. The box provides one case in point.

LOOKING AHEAD: MODERNIZATION AND OUR GLOBAL FUTURE

Back in Chapter 1, we imagined the entire world reduced to a village of 1,000 people. About 175 residents of this "global village" come from high-income

The bad news . . .

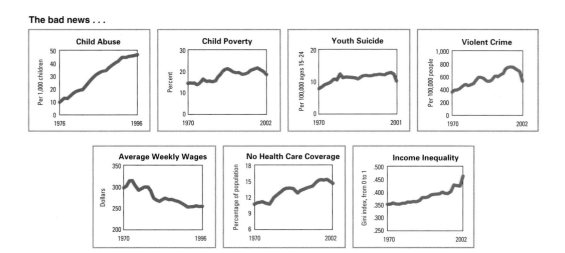

about the same as it was in the 1970s. Teenage drug use, for example, changed little over the last generation. Likewise, alcohol-related traffic deaths show only a slight decline. Unemployment has had its ups and downs, but the overall level has stayed about the same. Finally, there was about the same amount of affordable housing in the United States in 2003 as there was in 1970.

Third, the bad news: By some measures, several having to do with children, the quality of life in the United States has actually fallen. The official rate of child abuse is up, as is the level of child poverty and the rate of suicide among teenagers. Although the level of violent crime fell through the 1990s, it is still above the 1970 level. Average hourly wages—one measure of economic security—show a downward trend, so that families have had to rely on two or more earners to maintain family income. The number of people without health insurance is also on the rise. Finally, economic inequality in this country has been increasing.

Overall, then, the evidence does not support any simple ideas about "progress over time." Social change has been—and probably will continue to be—a complex process that reflects the kinds of priorities we set for this nation as well as our will to achieve them.

What do you think?

1. *Some analysts claim that U.S. society embodies a paradox: Over decades, we see increasing economic health but declining social health. Based on the data here, do you agree? Why or why not?*

2. *Which of the trends do you find most important? Why?*

3. *On balance, do you think the quality of life in the United States is improving or not? Why?*

Source: Miringoff & Miringoff (1999) and Myers (2001).

countries. At the same time, 200 people are so poor that their lives are at risk.

The tragic plight of the world's poor shows that some desperately needed change has not yet occurred. Chapter 12 ("Global Stratification") presented two competing views of why 1 billion people around the world are poor. *Modernization theory* claims that in the past the entire world was poor and that technological change, especially the Industrial Revolution, enhanced human productivity and raised living standards in many nations. From this point of view, the solution to global poverty is to promote technological development around the world.

For reasons suggested earlier, however, global modernization may be difficult. Recall that David Riesman portrayed preindustrial people as *tradition-directed* and likely to resist change. So modernization theorists advocate that the world's rich societies help poor countries grow economically. Industrial nations can speed development by exporting technology to poor regions, welcoming students from these countries, and providing foreign aid to stimulate economic growth.

The review of modernization theory in Chapter 12 points to some success with policies in Latin America, and to greater success in the small Asian countries of Taiwan, South Korea, Singapore, and Hong Kong.

CONTROVERSY & DEBATE

Personal Freedom and Social Responsibility: Can We Have It Both Ways?

Shortly after midnight on a crisp March evening in 1964, a car pulled to a stop in the parking lot of a New York apartment complex. Kitty Genovese turned off the headlights, locked the doors of her vehicle, and headed across the blacktop toward the entrance to her building. Seconds later, a man wielding a knife lunged at her, and as she shrieked in terror, he stabbed her repeatedly. Windows opened above, as curious neighbors looked down for the cause of the commotion. But the attack continued—for more than thirty minutes—until Genovese lay dead in the doorway. The police never identified her assailant, but they did discover a stunning fact: *Not one of dozens of neighbors who witnessed the attack on Kitty Genovese went to her aid or even called the police.*

Decades after this tragic event, we still confront the question of what we owe others. As members of modern societies, we prize our individual rights and personal privacy, but we sometimes withdraw from public responsibility

and turn a cold shoulder to people in need. When a cry for help is met with indifference, have we pushed our modern idea of personal autonomy too far? In a cultural climate of expanding individual rights, can we keep a sense of human community?

These questions point up the tension between traditional and modern social systems, which we can see in the writings of all the sociologists discussed in this chapter. Tönnies, Durkheim, and others concluded that, in some respects, traditional community and modern individualism don't go together. That is, society can unite its members in a moral community, but only to the extent that it limits their range of personal choices about how to live. In short, while we value both community and autonomy, we can't have it both ways.

Sociologist Amitai Etzioni (1993, 1996, 2003) has tried to strike a middle ground. The *communitarian movement* rests on the simple premise that "strong rights presume strong responsibilities."

Or, put another way, an individual's pursuit of self-interest must be balanced by a commitment to the larger community.

Etzioni claims modern people have become too concerned about individual rights. That is, people expect the system to work for them, but they are reluctant to support the system. For example, while we believe in the principle of trial by a jury of one's peers, fewer and fewer people today are willing to perform jury duty; similarly, the public is quick to accept government services but reluctant to pay for these services with taxes.

Specifically, the communitarians advance four proposals to balance individual rights and public responsibilities. First, our society should halt the expanding "culture of rights" by which people put their own interests ahead of social responsibility (after all, nothing in the Constitution allows us to do whatever we want to). Second, communitarians remind us, all rights involve responsibilities (we cannot simply take

---

But jump-starting development in the poorest countries of the world poses greater challenges. And even where dramatic change has occurred, modernization entails a trade-off. Traditional people, such as Brazil's Kaiapo, may acquire wealth through economic development, but they lose their cultural identity and values as they are drawn into global "McCulture," which is based on Western materialism, pop music, trendy clothes, and fast food. One Brazilian anthropologist expressed hope about the future of the Kaiapo: "At least they quickly understood the consequences of watching television. . . . Now [they] can make a choice" (Simons, 2004:495).

But not everyone thinks that modernization is really an option. According to a second approach to global stratification, *dependency theory*, today's poor societies have little ability to modernize, even if they want to. From this point of view, the major barrier to economic development is not traditionalism but the global domination of rich capitalist societies. Initially, domination took the form of colonialism when European societies seized much of Latin America, Africa, and Asia. Trading relationships soon enriched England, Spain, and other colonial powers, and their colonies became poorer and poorer. Almost all societies that were colonized are now politically independent, but colonial-style ties continue

from society without giving something back). Third, there are certain responsibilities that no one is free to ignore (such as upholding the law and protecting the natural environment). And fourth, defending some community interests may require limiting individual rights (protecting public safety, for example, might mean subjecting workers to drug tests).

The communitarian movement appeals to many people who, along with Etzioni, seek to balance personal freedom with social responsibility. But critics have attacked this initiative from both sides of the political spectrum. To those on the left, problems such as voter apathy and street crime cannot be solved with some vague notion of "social reintegration." Instead, we need expanded government programs to ensure equality in U.S. society. Specifically, these critics say, we must curb the political influence of the rich and actively combat racism and sexism.

Conservatives, on the political right, also find fault with Etzioni's proposals, but for different reasons (cf. Pearson, 1995). To these critics, the communitarian movement amounts to little more than a rerun of the 1960s leftist agenda. That is, the communitarian vision of a good society favors liberal goals (such as protecting the environment) but ignores conservative goals (such as allowing prayer in school or restoring the strength of traditional families). Moreover, conservatives ask whether a free society should permit the kind of social engineering that Etzioni advocates to build social responsibility (such as institutionalizing antiprejudice programs in schools and requiring people to perform a year of national service).

Perhaps, as Etzioni himself has suggested, the fact that both the left and the right find fault with his views shows that he has found a moderate, sensible answer to a serious problem. But it may also be that, in a society as diverse as the United States, people will not readily agree on what they owe to themselves and to each other.

In today's world, people can find new ways to express age-old virtues such as concern for their neighbors and extending a hand to those in need. Habitat for Humanity, an organization with chapters in cities and towns across the United States, is made up of people who want to help local families realize their dream of owning a home.

Continue the debate. . .

1. *Have you ever failed to come to the aid of someone in need or danger? Why?*

2. *President Kennedy admonished us, "Ask not what your country can do for you—ask what you can do for your country." Do you think people today support this idea? What makes you think so?*

3. *Do you agree or disagree that our society needs to balance rights with more responsibility? Explain your position.*

in the form of multinational corporations operating throughout the world.

In effect, dependency theory asserts that rich nations achieved their modernization at the expense of poor ones, plundering poor nations' natural resources and exploiting their human labor. Even today, the world's poorest countries remain locked in a disadvantageous economic relationship with rich nations, dependent on wealthy countries to buy their raw materials and in return provide them with whatever manufactured products they can afford. Overall, dependency theorists conclude, ties with rich societies only perpetuate current patterns of global inequality.

Whichever approach one finds more convincing, we can no longer isolate change in the United States from change in the rest of the world. At the beginning of the twentieth century, most people in today's high-income countries lived in relatively small settlements with limited awareness of the larger world. Today, a century later, the entire world has become one huge village because the lives of all people are increasingly linked.

The last century witnessed unprecedented human achievement. Yet solutions to many problems of human existence—including finding meaning in life, resolving conflicts between nations, and eradicating poverty—have eluded us. The final box examines one dilemma: balancing individual freedom and personal responsibility. To this list of pressing matters new concerns have been added, such as the dangers posed by the spread of nuclear weapons and terrorism, the need to control population growth, and the goal of establishing an environmentally sustainable society. In the next hundred years, we must be prepared to tackle such problems with imagination, compassion, and determination. Our unprecedented understanding of human society gives us reason to look to the task ahead with optimism.

SUMMARY

1. Every society changes continuously, although at varying speeds. Social change often generates controversy.

2. Social change results from invention, discovery, and diffusion, as well as social conflict.

3. *Modernity* refers to the social consequences of industrialization, which, according to Peter Berger, include the erosion of traditional communities, expanding personal choice, increasingly diverse beliefs, and a keen awareness of the future.

4. Ferdinand Tönnies described modernization as the transition from *Gemeinschaft* to *Gesellschaft*, which signifies the progressive loss of community amid growing individualism.

5. Emile Durkheim saw modernization as a function of a society's expanding division of labor. Mechanical solidarity, based on shared activities and beliefs, gradually gives way to organic solidarity, in which specialization makes people interdependent.

6. According to Max Weber, modernity replaces tradition with rationality. Weber feared the dehumanizing effects of rational organization.

7. Karl Marx saw modernity as the triumph of capitalism over feudalism. Viewing capitalist societies as fraught with social conflict, Marx advocated revolutionary change to achieve a more egalitarian socialist society.

8. According to mass-society theory, modernity increases the scale of life, enlarging the role of government and other formal organizations in carrying out tasks previously performed by family members and neighbors. Cultural diversity and rapid social change make it difficult for people in modern societies to develop stable identities and to find meaning in their lives.

9. Class-society theory states that capitalism is central to Western modernization. This approach charges that, by concentrating wealth in the hands of a few, capitalism generates widespread feelings of powerlessness.

10. Social change is too complex and controversial simply to be equated with social progress.

11. *Postmodernity* refers to the cultural traits of postindustrial societies. Postmodern criticism of society centers on the failure of modernity, and specifically science, to fulfill its promise of prosperity and well-being.

12. In a global context, modernization theory links global poverty to the power of tradition. Therefore, some modernization theorists advocate that rich societies intervene to stimulate economic development in poor nations.

13. Dependency theory explains global poverty as the product of the world economic system. The operation of multinational corporations ensures that poor nations will remain economically dependent on rich nations.

KEY CONCEPTS

social change (p. 626) the transformation of culture and social institutions over time

modernity (p. 629) social patterns resulting from industrialization

modernization (p. 629) the process of social change begun by industrialization

mass society (p. 633) a society in which prosperity and bureaucracy have eroded traditional social ties

class society (p. 635) a capitalist society with pronounced social stratification

social character (p. 637) personality patterns common to members of a particular society

tradition-directedness (p. 637) rigid conformity to time-honored ways of living

other-directedness (p. 637) a receptiveness to the latest trends and fashions, often expressed by imitating others

postmodernity (p. 639) social patterns characteristic of postindustrial societies

CRITICAL-THINKING QUESTIONS

1. How well do you think Tönnies, Durkheim, Weber, and Marx predicted the character of modern society? How are their visions of modernity the same? How do they differ?

2. What traits lead some to call the United States a "mass society"? Why do other analysts describe the United States as a "class society"?

3. What is the difference between *anomie* (a trait of mass society) and *alienation* (a characteristic of class society)? Among which categories of the U.S. population would you expect each to be more evident?

4. Why do some analysts believe that the United States has become a postmodern society? Do you agree? Why or why not?

APPLICATIONS AND EXERCISES

1. Do you have an elderly relative or friend? Most older people will be happy to tell you about the social changes they have seen in their lifetimes.

2. Ask people in your class or friendship group to make five predictions about U.S. society in the year 2050, when today's twenty-year-olds will be senior citizens. Compare notes. On what issues is there agreement?

3. Has the rate of social change been increasing? Do some research about inventions over time and see for yourself. Consider, for example, modes of travel, including walking, riding animals, trains, cars, airplanes, and

rockets in space. The first two characterized society for tens of thousands of years; the last four emerged in barely two centuries.

4. Packaged in the back of this new textbook is an interactive CD-ROM that offers a variety of video and interactive review materials intended to help you better understand the material covered in this chapter. For this chapter, the CD-ROM contains a relevant clip from *ABC News*, an author's tip video, interactive map animations, an interactive time line, and flashcards with audio pronunciations of the more difficult words.

 ## SITES TO SEE

http://www.prenhall.com/macionis

Visit the interactive Companion Website™ that accompanies this text. Begin by clicking on the cover of your book. You will find a chapter-by-chapter study guide, practice tests, suggested Web links, and links to other relevant material.

http://www.gwu.edu/~ccps/

This Web site describes the Communitarian Network, including its goals and how it proposes to achieve them.

http://www.utoronto.ca/utopia/

Deliberate change is sometimes inspired by visions of utopia—ideal societies that exist nowhere. Read about the Society for Utopian Studies at this Web site.

http://www.TheSociologyPage.com or
http://www.macionis.com

Finally, on a personal note, I hope this book has helped you and will be a useful resource for courses later on. Please visit my Web page, and send an e-mail message (macionis@kenyon.edu) with your thoughts and suggestions. And yes, I *will* write back!

John J. Macionis

 ## INVESTIGATE WITH RESEARCH NAVIGATOR™

Follow the instructions on page 24 of this text to access the features of **Research Navigator™**. Once at the Web site, enter your Login Name and Password. Then, to use the **Content Select™** database, enter keywords such as "social change," "modernization," and "postmodernity," and the

search engine will supply relevant and recent scholarly and popular press publications. Use the *New York Times* **Search-by-Subject Archive** to find recent news articles related to sociology and the **Link Library** feature to find relevant Web links organized by the key terms associated with this chapter.

NOVEMBER 15, 2003

No Wiggle Room in a Window War

By LISA W. FODERARO

CHAUTAUQUA, N.Y.—In the unyielding world of the Old Order Amish, very little changes, not the horse and buggy they ride in, not the capes and bonnets they wear.

The Amish home, too, remains a bulwark of simplicity and modesty. Religious tradition in this community in western New York, conservative even by Amish standards, dictates everything from the plumbing (gravity fed, cold water only) to the oil lamps used in place of electricity (kerosene) to the size of window openings (five square feet).

It is those windows that have suddenly thrust the 50 Amish families here into an uncomfortable spotlight, placing them and town officials at loggerheads with the state. The problem is a new state code that requires a minimum opening for bedroom windows, meant to ease both the escape of residents during a fire and access by rescuers.

Under the code, which went into effect in January, bedroom windows in newly built houses must measure at least 5.7 square feet. The double-hung, rectangular Amish window, which met the previous code requirement of four square feet, falls short of the new standard, town officials say.

This summer, John H. Rasmussen, Chautauqua's code enforcement officer, went to the home of Amos Byler, one of the three Amish residents seeking permits to build new houses, and measured an existing window. Mr. Rasmussen said that he did not record the exact dimensions but that he remembered that the window was roughly five square feet and just shy of what the state now requires by an inch and a half on each side. "I said, 'Amos, you can't do that,'" he recalled. He denied the permits for all three houses.

To the outsider, the solution is obvious: enlarge the windows by a smidgen. "It sounds easy to someone who isn't Amish, but if you're Old Order Amish it's not easy," said Mose Byler, the bishop of one of the two Amish districts in Chautauqua, clad in the traditional male uniform of a navy denim jacket fastened by hooks and eyes. "If you break a tradition, where's the tradition? You're not a faithful member."

The Amish are heartened that the town board is backing them. The board voted unanimously this summer to issue permits for the three houses, illegal windows and all, overruling Mr. Rasmussen. The town supervisor, James R. Willcockson, signed the permits himself in August and September, and the houses are now up and occupied.

Mr. Willcockson said he had spoken with local firefighters who said the difference in size, a fraction of a square foot, would not hinder rescue efforts. Given the rural location of the Amish houses and the lack of phones with which to dial 911, "there is not going to be much left standing" anyway, Mr. Willcockson added.

"It gets to the point where sometimes you have to do what you think is morally right," Mr. Willcockson explained. "We had a lot of support from people in the community. The Amish are a real benefit. They pay their taxes for everything although they don't use a lot of the services. They don't complain. They're just a great bunch of people to have around."

The state sees things differently. In a sternly worded letter to Mr. Willcockson dated Aug. 25, the codes division of the Department of State said the town was "in violation of the state laws and regulations that were enacted for the purpose of protecting the public" from fire and inadequate construction. While highlighting the improper window opening, the state also took issue with the building plans, noting that they lacked the signature of an architect or an engineer.

The letter, which came before construction began, said the town should stop the work on the houses immediately and threatened to begin an audit of the town's code enforcement. The letter noted that the state was working on a change in the new code that would permit houses to be built without plumbing and electricity, subject to local approval, a change that would "favor the Amish tradition." (The old code allowed such exemptions, but the new code does not.)

But there appears to be little wiggle room on window size. The letter concluded by saying that there was "no plan to change such life-safety features as the size of emergency egress and rescue openings," adding that the issue had been studied and adopted internationally.

The Amish could still apply for a variance for a smaller window opening to a regional state review board in

Buffalo, as the letter advised. But Mr. Willcockson said that his talks with a midlevel state official this summer left him with the impression that the state would not be inclined to give such a variance.

Town officials did not respond to the state's letter, and the state recently sent another warning letter reiterating the first, according to Peter Constantakes, a spokesman for the Department of State.

Nationwide, the degree to which the Amish embrace modern ways varies from congregation to congregation. According to Donald B. Kraybill, a senior fellow at the Young Center for Anabaptist and Pietist Studies at Elizabethtown College in Pennsylvania, there are 1,400 local Amish congregations, or districts, in 28 states and Ontario, Canada.

"People think of the Amish as though they are monolithic," said Dr. Kraybill, editor of "The Amish and the State" (Johns Hopkins University Press, 2003). "Each local congregation has autonomy so there are really 1,400 different ways of being Amish."

Some Amish communities use cell-phones, in-line skates and automatic milking machines despite adherence to such bedrock traditions as transportation by horse and buggy, schooling only through the eighth grade and the speaking of a Pennsylvania German dialect.

Over in Cattaraugus County, for instance, there are a number of Amish districts willing to tweak their window sizes to conform to the new code, Mr. Rasmussen said.

But ultraconservative communities like the Chautauqua Amish, which exist in only a half-dozen states, have "frozen history around 1915," Dr. Kraybill said. For these more traditional communities, customs like the architecture and decor of houses are considered an integral part of their religious faith and practice. The Amish tradition, which emerged after the Protestant Reformation in Europe, forcefully advocates the separation of church and state, with the corresponding principle that the state should not dictate religious practice.

"It's a cultural clash," Dr. Kraybill said of the dispute between the Chautauqua Amish and the state. "Probably the state bureaucrats who are enforcing this are just doing their job, but they don't understand how it infringes on the religious tradition of this community."

Standing by the roadside in the deepening twilight, Mr. Byler, a father of nine, said he hoped the window conflict could be resolved. He cited the fact that the community's children were allowed to stop their formal education after the eighth grade, a practice that was upheld in 1972 by the United States Supreme Court in *Wisconsin v. Yoder*.

But Mr. Byler held out the possibility that the Amish families would move elsewhere if the state forced them to install larger windows. "I don't know what we're going to do," he said. "I really don't."

Some local residents hope it does not come to that. While the Amish families make up a small part of the town's population of 4,500, many non-Amish seem to be rallying to their defense. "Sometimes there's too much government interference," said Danielle Morgan, a sales clerk at the Chautauqua Bookstore, referring to the new state code. "I think the town was right. The Amish contribute a lot to the community. They are nice people."

What do you think?

1. Would the Amish way of life illustrate David Riesman's concept of "tradition direction?" Explain.
2. Why would the Amish object to enlarging their windows a little bit in order to meet local building codes? As they see it, what larger issues are involved?
3. If it were your decision to make, would you allow the Amish to remain true to their own standards or force them to comply with state building codes? Why?
4. Do you think culture conflicts such as this one will become more or less common in the future? Why?
5. Can you think of other cases in which the local traditions of a subculture clash with government regulations that set standards within a mass society?

GLOSSARY

abortion the deliberate termination of a pregnancy

absolute poverty a deprivation of resources that is life-threatening

achieved status a social position a person assumes voluntarily that reflects personal ability and effort

activity theory the idea that a high level of activity enhances personal satisfaction in old age

Afrocentrism the dominance of African cultural patterns

ageism prejudice and discrimination against older people

age-sex pyramid a graphic representation of the age and sex of a population

age stratification the unequal distribution of wealth, power, and privilege among people at different stages of the life course

agriculture large-scale cultivation using plows harnessed to animals or more powerful energy sources

alienation the experience of isolation and misery resulting from powerlessness

animism the belief that elements of the natural world are conscious life forms that affect humanity

anomie Durkheim's designation of a condition in which society provides little moral guidance to individuals

anticipatory socialization learning that helps a person achieve a desired position

ascribed status a social position a person receives at birth or assumes involuntarily later in life

asexuality no sexual attraction to people of either sex

assimilation the process by which minorities gradually adopt patterns of the dominant culture

authoritarianism a political system that denies popular participation in government

authority power that people perceive as legitimate rather than coercive

beliefs specific statements that people hold to be true

bilateral descent a system tracing kinship through both men and women

bisexuality sexual attraction to people of both sexes

blue-collar occupations lower-prestige work that involves mostly manual labor

bureaucracy an organizational model rationally designed to perform tasks efficiently

bureaucratic inertia the tendency of bureaucratic organizations to perpetuate themselves

bureaucratic ritualism a preoccupation with rules and regulations to the point of thwarting an organization's goals

capitalism an economic system in which natural resources and the means of producing goods and services are privately owned

capitalists people who own and operate factories and other businesses in pursuit of profits

caregiving informal and unpaid care provided to a dependent person by family members, other relatives, or friends

caste system social stratification based on ascription, or birth

cause and effect a relationship in which change in one variable (the independent variable) causes change in another (the dependent variable)

charisma extraordinary personal qualities that can infuse people with emotion and turn them into followers

charismatic authority power legitimized through extraordinary personal abilities that inspire devotion and obedience

church a type of religious organization that is well integrated into the larger society

civil religion a quasi-religious loyalty binding individuals in a basically secular society

class conflict conflict between entire classes over the distribution of a society's wealth and power

class consciousness Marx's term for workers' recognition of themselves as a class unified in opposition to capitalists and, ultimately, to capitalism itself

class society a capitalist society with pronounced social stratification

class system social stratification based on both birth and individual achievement

cohabitation the sharing of a household by an unmarried couple

cohort a category of people with a common characteristic, usually their age

collective behavior activity involving a large number of people, often spontaneous, and sometimes controversial

collectivity a large number of people whose minimal interaction occurs in the absence of well-defined and conventional norms

colonialism the process by which some nations enrich themselves through political and economic control of other nations

communism a hypothetical economic and political system in which all members of a society are socially equal

community-based corrections correctional programs located within society at large rather than behind prison walls

concept a mental construct that represents some part of the world in a simplified form

concrete operational stage Piaget's term for the level of human development at which individuals first perceive causal connections in their surroundings

conglomerate a giant corporation composed of many smaller corporations

control holding constant all variables except one in order to see clearly the effect of that variable

corporate crime the illegal actions of a corporation or people acting on its behalf

corporation an organization with a legal existence, including rights and liabilities, apart from that of its members

correlation a relationship in which two (or more) variables change together

counterculture cultural patterns that strongly oppose those widely accepted within a society

credentialism evaluating a person on the basis of educational degrees

crime the violation of a society's formally enacted criminal law

crimes against the person (violent crimes) crimes that direct violence or the threat of violence against others

crimes against property (property crimes) crimes that involve theft of property belonging to others

criminal justice system a formal response by police, courts, and prison officials to alleged violations of the law

criminal recidivism subsequent offenses by people previously convicted of crimes

critical sociology the study of society that focuses on the need for social change

crowd a temporary gathering of people who share a common focus of attention and who influence one another

crude birth rate the number of live births in a given year for every thousand people in a population

crude death rate the number of deaths in a given year for every thousand people in a population

cult a religious organization that is largely outside a society's cultural traditions

cultural integration the close relationships among various elements of a cultural system

cultural lag the fact that some cultural elements change more quickly than others, disrupting a cultural system

cultural relativism the practice of evaluating a culture by its own standards

cultural transmission the process by which one generation passes culture to the next

cultural universals traits that are part of every known culture

culture the values, beliefs, behavior, and material objects that together form a people's way of life

culture shock personal disorientation when experiencing an unfamiliar way of life

Davis-Moore thesis the assertion that social stratification is a universal pattern because it has beneficial consequences for the operation of a society

deductive logical thought reasoning that transforms general theory into specific hypotheses suitable for testing

democracy a type of political system that gives power to the people as a whole

demographic transition theory the thesis that population patterns reflect a society's level of technological development

demography the study of human population

denomination a church, independent of the state, that recognizes religious pluralism

dependency theory a model of economic and social development that explains global inequality in terms of the historical exploitation of poor nations by rich ones

dependent variable a variable that is changed by another (independent) variable

descent the system by which members of a society trace kinship over generations

deterrence the attempt to discourage criminality through punishment

deviance the recognized violation of cultural norms

direct-fee system a medical care system in which patients pay directly for the services of physicians and hospitals

discrimination treating various categories of people unequally

disengagement theory the idea that society enhances its orderly operation by disengaging people from positions of responsibility as they reach old age

division of labor specialized economic activity

dramaturgical analysis Erving Goffman's term for the study of social interaction in terms of theatrical performance

dyad a social group with two members

dysfunction (*see* social dysfunction)

eating disorder an intense form of dieting or other unhealthy method of weight control driven by the desire to be very thin

ecologically sustainable culture a way of life that meets the needs of the present generation without threatening the environmental legacy of future generations

ecology the study of the interaction of living organisms and the natural environment

economy the social institution that organizes a society's production, distribution, and consumption of goods and services

ecosystem a system composed of the interaction of all living organisms and their natural environment

education the social institution through which society provides its members with important knowledge, including basic facts, job skills, and cultural norms and values

ego Freud's term for a person's conscious efforts to balance innate pleasure-seeking drives with the demands of society

empirical evidence information we can verify with our senses

endogamy marriage between people of the same social category

environmental deficit profound and long-term harm to the natural environment caused by humanity's focus on short-term material affluence

environmental racism the pattern by which environmental hazards are greatest for poor people, especially minorities

ethnicity a shared cultural heritage

ethnocentrism the practice of judging another culture by the standards of one's own culture

ethnomethodology Harold Garfinkel's term for the study of the way people make sense of their everyday surroundings

Eurocentrism the dominance of European (especially English) cultural patterns

euthanasia (mercy killing) assisting in the death of a person suffering from an incurable disease

exogamy marriage between people of different social categories

experiment a research method for investigating cause and effect under highly controlled conditions

expressive leadership group leadership that focuses on collective well-being

extended family (consanguine family) a family unit that includes parents and children as well as other kin

fad an unconventional social pattern that people embrace briefly but enthusiastically

faith belief anchored in conviction rather than scientific evidence

false consciousness Marx's term for explanations of social problems as the shortcomings of individuals rather than as the flaws of society

family a social institution found in all societies that unites people in cooperative groups to oversee the bearing and raising of children

family unit a social group of two or more people, related by blood, marriage, or adoption, who usually live together

family violence emotional, physical, or sexual abuse of one family member by another

fashion a social pattern favored by a large number of people

feminism the advocacy of social equality for men and women, in opposition to patriarchy and sexism

feminization of poverty the trend by which women represent an increasing proportion of the poor

fertility the incidence of childbearing in a country's population

folkways norms for routine or casual interaction

formal operational stage Piaget's term for the level of human development at which individuals think abstractly and critically

formal organization a large secondary group organized to achieve its goals efficiently

functional illiteracy a lack of the reading and writing skills needed for everyday living

fundamentalism a conservative religious doctrine that opposes intellectualism and worldly accommodation in favor of restoring traditional, otherworldly religion

Gemeinschaft a type of social organization by which people are closely tied by kinship and tradition

gender the personal traits and social positions that members of a society attach to being female or male

gender roles (sex roles) attitudes and activities that a society links to each sex

gender stratification the unequal distribution of wealth, power, and privilege between men and women

generalized other George Herbert Mead's term for widespread cultural norms and values we use as a reference in evaluating ourselves

genocide the systematic killing of one category of people by another

gerontocracy a form of social organization in which the elderly have the most wealth, power, and prestige

gerontology the study of aging and the elderly

Gesellschaft a type of social organization by which people come together only on the basis of individual self-interest

global economy expanding economic activity with little regard for national borders

global perspective the study of the larger world and our society's place in it

global warming a rise in the Earth's average temperature due to an increasing concentration of carbon dioxide in the atmosphere

gossip rumor about people's personal affairs

government a formal organization that directs the political life of a society

groupthink the tendency of group members to conform, resulting in a narrow view of some issue

hate crime a criminal act against a person or a person's property by an offender motivated by racial or other bias

Hawthorne effect a change in a subject's behavior caused simply by the awareness of being studied

health a state of complete physical, mental, and social well-being

health maintenance organization (HMO) an organization that provides comprehensive medical care to subscribers for a fixed fee

heterosexism a view stigmatizing anyone who is not heterosexual as "queer"

heterosexuality sexual attraction to someone of the other sex

hidden curriculum subtle presentations of political or cultural ideas in the classroom

high culture cultural patterns that distinguish a society's elite

high-income countries nations with very productive economic systems in which most people have relatively high incomes

holistic medicine an approach to health care that emphasizes the prevention of illness and takes into account a person's entire physical and social environment

homogamy marriage between people with the same social characteristics

homophobia the dread of close personal interaction with people thought to be gay, lesbian, or bisexual

homosexuality sexual attraction to someone of the same sex

horticulture the use of hand tools to raise crops

hunting and gathering the use of simple tools to hunt animals and gather vegetation

hypothesis an unverified statement of a relationship between variables

id Freud's term for the human being's basic drives

ideal type an abstract statement of the essential characteristics of any social phenomenon

ideology cultural beliefs that justify particular social arrangements, including patterns of inequality

incest taboo a norm forbidding sexual relations or marriage between certain relatives

income wages or salary from work and earnings from investments

independent variable a variable that causes change in another (dependent) variable

inductive logical thought reasoning that transforms specific observations into general theory

industrialism the production of goods using advanced sources of energy to drive large machinery

infant mortality rate the number of deaths among infants under one year of age for each thousand live births in a given year

infidelity sexual activity outside marriage

in-group a social group commanding a member's esteem and loyalty

institutional prejudice and discrimination bias inherent in the operation of society's institutions

instrumental leadership group leadership that emphasizes the completion of tasks

intergenerational social mobility upward or downward social mobility of children in relation to their parents

interpretive sociology the study of society that focuses on the meanings people attach to their social world

intersection theory the investigation of the interplay of race, class, and gender, often resulting in multiple dimensions of disadvantage

intersexual people (hermaphrodites) people whose anatomy (including genitals) includes both female and male characteristics

interview a series of questions a researcher administers in person to respondents

intragenerational social mobility a change in social position occurring during a person's lifetime

kinship a social bond based on blood, marriage, or adoption

labeling theory the assertion that deviance and conformity result not so much from what people do as from how others respond to those actions

labor unions organizations of workers that seek to improve wages and working conditions through various strategies, including negotiations and strikes

language a system of symbols that allows people to communicate with one another

latent functions the unrecognized and unintended consequences of any social pattern

liberation theology a fusion of Christian principles with political activism, often Marxist in character

life expectancy the average life span of a country's population

looking-glass self Cooley's term for a self-image based on how we think others see us

low-income countries nations with less productive economic systems in which most people are poor

macro-level orientation a broad focus on social structures that shape society as a whole

mainstreaming integrating special students into the overall educational program

manifest functions the recognized and intended consequences of any social pattern

marriage a legally sanctioned relationship, usually involving economic cooperation as well as sexual activity and childbearing, that people expect to be enduring

Marxist political-economy model an analysis that explains politics in terms of the operation of a society's economic system

mass behavior collective behavior among people dispersed over a wide geographic area

mass hysteria (moral panic) a form of dispersed collective behavior by which people react to a real or imagined event with irrational and even frantic fear

mass media impersonal communications aimed at a vast audience

mass society a society in which prosperity and bureaucracy have eroded traditional social ties

master status a status that a society defines as having special importance for social identity, often shaping a person's entire life

material culture the tangible things created by members of a society

matriarchy a form of social organization in which females dominate males

matrilineal descent a system tracing kinship through women

matrilocality a residential pattern in which a married couple lives with or near the wife's family

measurement a procedure for determining the value of a variable in a specific case

mechanical solidarity Durkheim's term for social bonds, based on common sentiments and shared moral values, that are strong among members of preindustrial societies

medicalization of deviance the transformation of moral and legal deviance into a medical condition

medicine the social institution that focuses on combating disease and improving health

megalopolis a vast urban region containing a number of cities and their surrounding suburbs

meritocracy social stratification based on personal merit

metropolis a large city that socially and economically dominates an urban area

micro-level orientation a close-up focus on social interaction in specific situations

middle-income countries nations with moderately productive economic systems in which people's incomes are about the global average

migration the movement of people into and out of a specified territory

military-industrial complex the close association of the federal government, the military, and defense industries

minority any category of people distinguished by physical or cultural difference that a society sets apart and subordinates

miscegenation biological reproduction by partners of different racial categories

mob a highly emotional crowd that pursues a violent or destructive goal

modernity social patterns resulting from industrialization

modernization the process of social change begun by industrialization

modernization theory a model of economic and social development that explains global inequality in terms of technological and cultural differences between nations

monarchy a type of political system in which a single family rules from generation to generation

monogamy marriage that unites two partners

monopoly the domination of a market by a single producer

monotheism belief in a single divine power

mores norms that are widely observed and have great moral significance

mortality the incidence of death in a country's population

multiculturalism an educational program recognizing the cultural diversity of the United States and promoting the equality of all cultural traditions

multinational corporation a large business that operates in many countries

natural environment the Earth's surface and atmosphere, including living organisms, air, water, soil, and other resources necessary to sustain life

neocolonialism a new form of global power relationships that involves not direct political control but economic exploitation by multinational corporations

neolocality a residential pattern in which a married couple lives apart from both sets of parents

network a web of weak social ties

nonmaterial culture the intangible world of ideas created by members of a society

nonverbal communication communication using body movements, gestures, and facial expressions rather than speech

norms rules and expectations by which a society guides the behavior of its members

nuclear family (conjugal family) a family unit composed of one or two parents and their children

nuclear proliferation the acquisition of nuclear weapons technology by more and more nations

objectivity personal neutrality in conducting research

oligarchy the rule of the many by the few

oligopoly the domination of a market by a few producers

operationalize a variable specifying exactly what one is to measure before assigning a value to a variable

organic solidarity Durkheim's term for social bonds, based on specialization and interdependence, that are strong among members of industrial societies

organizational environment factors outside an organization that affect its operation

organized crime a business supplying illegal goods or services

other-directedness a receptiveness to the latest trends and fashions, often expressed by imitating others

out-group a social group toward which one feels competition or opposition

panic a form of localized collective behavior by which people react to a threat or other stimulus with irrational, frantic, and often self-destructive behavior

paradigm (*see* theoretical paradigm)

participant observation a research method in which investigators systematically observe people while joining them in their routine activities

pastoralism the domestication of animals

patriarchy a form of social organization in which males dominate females

patrilineal descent a system tracing kinship through men

patrilocality a residential pattern in which a married couple lives with or near the husband's family

peer group a social group whose members have interests, social position, and age in common

personality a person's fairly consistent patterns of acting, thinking, and feeling

personal space the surrounding area over which a person makes some claim to privacy

plea bargaining a legal negotiation in which a prosecutor reduces a charge in exchange for a defendant's guilty plea

pluralism a state in which people of all races and ethnicities are distinct but have social parity

pluralist model an analysis of politics that sees power as dispersed among many competing interest groups

political action committee (PAC) an organization formed by a special-interest group, independent of political parties, to raise and spend money in support of political aims

political revolution the overthrow of one political system in order to establish another

politics the social institution that distributes power, sets a society's agenda, and makes decisions

polyandry marriage that unites one woman and two or more men

polygamy marriage that unites three or more people

polygyny marriage that unites one man and two or more women

polytheism belief in many gods

popular culture cultural patterns that are widespread among a society's population

population the people who are the focus of research

pornography sexually explicit material that causes sexual arousal

positivism a way of understanding based on science

postindustrial economy a productive system based on service work and high technology

postindustrialism technology that supports an information-based economy

postmodernity social patterns characteristic of postindustrial societies

power the ability to achieve desired ends despite resistance from others

power-elite model an analysis of politics that sees power as concentrated among the rich

prejudice a rigid and unfair generalization about an entire category of people

preoperational stage Piaget's term for the level of human development at which individuals first use language and other symbols

presentation of self Erving Goffman's term for a person's efforts to create specific impressions in the minds of others

primary group a small social group whose members share personal and enduring relationships

primary labor market jobs that provide extensive benefits to workers

primary sector the part of the economy that draws raw materials from the natural environment

primary sex characteristics the genitals, organs used for reproduction

profane that which people define as an ordinary element of everyday life

profession a prestigious white-collar occupation that requires extensive formal education

proletarians people who sell their productive labor for wages

propaganda information presented with the intention of shaping public opinion

prostitution the selling of sexual services

public opinion widespread attitudes about controversial issues

queer theory a growing body of research findings that challenges the heterosexual bias in U.S. society

questionnaire a series of written questions a researcher presents to subjects

race a socially constructed category composed of people who share biologically transmitted traits that members of a society consider important

racism the belief that one racial category is innately superior or inferior to another

rain forests regions of dense forestation, most of which circle the globe close to the equator

rationality a way of thinking that emphasizes deliberate, matter-of-fact calculation of the most efficient means to accomplish a particular task

rationalization of society Weber's term for the historical change from tradition to rationality as the dominant mode of human thought

rational-legal authority (also **bureaucratic authority**) power legitimized by legally enacted rules and regulations

reference group a social group that serves as a point of reference in making evaluations and decisions

rehabilitation a program for reforming the offender to prevent subsequent offenses

relative deprivation a perceived disadvantage arising from some specific comparison

relative poverty the deprivation of some people in relation to those who have more

reliability consistency in measurement

religion a social institution involving beliefs and practices based on a conception of the sacred

religiosity the importance of religion in a person's life

replication repetition of research by other investigators

research method a systematic plan for conducting research

resocialization radically changing an inmate's personality by carefully controlling the environment

retribution an act of moral vengeance by which society inflicts on the offender suffering comparable to that caused by the offense

riot a social eruption that is highly emotional, violent, and undirected

ritual formal, ceremonial behavior

role behavior expected of someone who holds a particular status

role conflict conflict among the roles corresponding to two or more statuses

role set a number of roles attached to a single status

role strain tension among the roles connected to a single status

routinization of charisma the transformation of charismatic authority into some combination of traditional and bureaucratic authority

rumor unsubstantiated information people spread informally, often by word of mouth

sacred that which people set apart as extraordinary, inspiring awe and reverence

sample a part of a population that represents the whole

Sapir-Whorf thesis the thesis that people perceive the world through the cultural lens of language

scapegoat a person or category of people, typically with little power, whom people unfairly blame for their own troubles

schooling formal instruction under the direction of specially trained teachers

science a logical system that bases knowledge on direct, systematic observation

scientific management Frederick Taylor's term for the application of scientific principles to the operation of a business or other large organization

scientific sociology the study of society based on systematic observation of social behavior

secondary analysis a research method in which a researcher uses data collected by others

secondary group a large and impersonal social group whose members pursue a specific goal or activity

secondary labor market jobs that provide minimal benefits to workers

secondary sector the part of the economy that transforms raw materials into manufactured goods

secondary sex characteristics bodily development, apart from the genitals, that distinguishes biologically mature females and males

sect a type of religious organization that stands apart from the larger society

secularization the historical decline in the importance of the supernatural and the sacred

segregation the physical and social separation of categories of people

self George Herbert Mead's term for that part of an individual's personality composed of self-awareness and self-image

sensorimotor stage Piaget's term for the level of human development at which individuals experience the world only through their senses

sex the biological distinction between females and males

sexism the belief that one sex is innately superior to the other

sex ratio the number of males for every hundred females in a nation's population

sexual harassment comments, gestures, or physical contact of a sexual nature that are deliberate, repeated, and unwelcome

sexual orientation a person's romantic and emotional attraction to another person

sick role patterns of behavior defined as appropriate for people who are ill

social change the transformation of culture and social institutions over time

social character personality patterns common to members of a particular society

social conflict the struggle between segments of society over valued resources

social-conflict paradigm a framework for building theory that sees society as an arena of inequality that generates conflict and change

social construction of reality the process by which people creatively shape reality through social interaction

social control attempts by society to regulate people's thought and behavior

social dysfunction any social pattern that may disrupt the operation of society

social epidemiology the study of how health and disease are distributed throughout a society's population

social functions the consequences of any social pattern for the operation of society as a whole

social group two or more people who identify and interact with one another

social institutions major spheres of social life, or societal subsystems, organized to meet human needs

social interaction the process by which people act and react in relation to others

socialism an economic system in which natural resources and the means of producing goods and services are collectively owned

socialization the lifelong social experience by which individuals develop their human potential and learn culture

socialized medicine a medical care system in which the government owns and operates most medical facilities and employs most physicians

social mobility a change in one's position in the social hierarchy

social movement an organized activity that encourages or discourages social change

social stratification a system by which a society ranks categories of people in a hierarchy

social structure any relatively stable pattern of social behavior

societal protection a means by which society renders an offender incapable of further offenses temporarily through incarceration or permanently by execution

society people who interact in a defined territory and share a culture

sociobiology a theoretical paradigm that explores ways in which human biology affects how we create culture

sociocultural evolution Lenski's term for the changes that occur as a society acquires new technology

socioeconomic status (SES) a composite ranking based on various dimensions of social inequality

sociology the systematic study of human society

special-interest group a political alliance of people interested in some economic or social issue

spurious correlation an apparent, although false, relationship between two (or more) variables caused by some other variable

state capitalism an economic and political system in which companies are privately owned but cooperate closely with the government

state church a church formally allied with the state

status a social position that a person occupies

status consistency the degree of consistency in a person's social standing across various dimensions of social inequality

status set all the statuses a person holds at a given time

stereotype an exaggerated description applied to every person in some category

stigma a powerfully negative label that greatly changes a person's self-concept and social identity

structural-functional paradigm a framework for building theory that sees society as a complex system whose parts work together to promote solidarity and stability

structural social mobility a shift in the social position of large numbers of people due more to changes in society itself than to individual efforts

subculture cultural patterns that set apart some segment of a society's population

suburbs urban areas beyond the political boundaries of a city

superego Freud's term for the cultural values and norms internalized by an individual

survey a research method in which subjects respond to a series of statements or questions in a questionnaire or an interview

symbolic-interaction paradigm a framework for building theory that sees society as the product of the everyday interactions of individuals

symbols anything that carries a particular meaning recognized by people who share a culture

technology knowledge that people use to make a way of life in their surroundings

terrorism acts of violence or the threat of such violence used as a political strategy by an individual or group

tertiary sector the part of the economy that involves services rather than goods

theoretical paradigm a basic image of society that guides thinking and research

theory a statement of how and why specific facts are related

Thomas theorem W. I. Thomas's assertion that situations that are defined as real are real in their consequences

total institution a setting in which people are isolated from the rest of society and manipulated by an administrative staff

totalitarianism a highly centralized political system that extensively regulates people's lives

totem an object in the natural world collectively defined as sacred

tracking assigning students to different types of educational programs

tradition sentiments and beliefs passed from generation to generation

traditional authority power legitimized through respect for long-established cultural patterns

tradition-directedness rigid conformity to time-honored ways of living

transsexuals people who feel they are one sex even though biologically they are the other

triad a social group with three members

underground economy economic activity involving income unreported to the government as required by law

urban ecology the study of the link between the physical and social dimensions of cities

urbanization the concentration of humanity into cities

validity actually measuring exactly what one intends to measure

values culturally defined standards by which people assess desirability, goodness, and beauty and that serve as broad guidelines for social living

variable a concept whose value changes from case to case

victimless crimes violations of law in which there are no readily apparent victims

war organized, armed conflict among the people of various nations, directed by their governments

wealth the total value of money and other assets, minus outstanding debts

welfare capitalism an economic and political system that combines a mostly market-based economy with extensive social welfare programs

welfare state a range of government agencies and programs that provides benefits to the population

white-collar crime crime committed by people of high social position in the course of their occupations

white-collar occupations higher-prestige work that involves mostly mental activity

zero population growth the level of reproduction that maintains population in a steady state

REFERENCES

ABBOTT, ANDREW. *The System of Professions: An Essay on the Division of Expert Labor*. Chicago: University of Chicago Press, 1988.

ABERLE, DAVID F. *The Peyote Religion among the Navaho*. Chicago: Aldine, 1966.

ABRAHAMSON, PAUL R. "Postmaterialism and Environmentalism: A Comment on an Analysis and a Reappraisal." *Social Science Quarterly*. Vol. 78, No. 1 (March 1997):21–23.

ADELSON, JOSEPH. "Splitting Up." *Commentary* (September 1996).

ADLER, JERRY. "When Harry Called Sally . . ." *Newsweek* (October 1, 1990):74.

ADORNO, T. W., et al. *The Authoritarian Personality*. New York: Harper & Brothers, 1950.

AGUIRRE, BENIGNO E., and E. L. QUARANTELLI. "Methodological, Ideological, and Conceptual-Theoretical Criticisms of Collective Behavior: A Critical Evaluation and Implications for Future Study." *Sociological Focus*. Vol. 16, No. 3 (August 1983):195–216.

AGUIRRE, BENIGNO E., E. L. QUARANTELLI, and JORGE L. MENDOZA. "The Collective Behavior of Fads: Characteristics, Effects, and Career of Streaking." *American Sociological Review*. Vol. 53, No. 4 (August 1988):569–84.

AIZCORBE, ANA M., ARTHUR B. KENNICKELL, and KEVIN B. MOORE. "Recent Changes in U.S. Family Finances: Evidence from the 1998 and 2001 Survey of Consumer Finances." *Federal Reserve Bulletin*. Vol. 89, No. 1 (January 2003):1–32. [Online] Available September 25, 2003, at http://www.federalreserve.gov/pubs/bulletin/2003/0103lead.pdf

AKERS, RONALD L., MARVIN D. KROHN, LONN LANZA-KADUCE, and MARCIA RADOSEVICH. "Social Learning and Deviant Behavior." *American Sociological Review*. Vol. 44, No. 4 (August 1979):636–55.

THE ALAN GUTTMACHER INSTITUTE. "Can More Progress Be Made? Teenage Sexual and Reproductive Behavior in Developed Countries." 2001. [Online] Available August 14, 2002, at http://www.agiusa.org/pubs/euroteens_summ.pdf

———. "Teen Pregnancy: Trends and Lessons Learned." *Issues in Brief*. 2002 Series, No. 1. 2002. [Online] Available August 14, 2002, at http://www.agi-usa.org/pubs/ib_1-02.pdf

———. *U.S. Teenage Pregnancy Statistics with Comparative Statistics for Women Aged 20–24*. [Online] Available September 30, 2003, at http://www.agi-usa.org/pubs/teen_stats.pdf

ALBA, RICHARD D. *Ethnic Identity: The Transformation of White America*. Chicago: University of Chicago Press, 1990.

ALBON, JOAN. "Retention of Cultural Values and Differential Urban Adaptation: Samoans and American Indians in a West Coast City." *Social Forces*. Vol. 49, No. 3 (March 1971):385–93.

ALFORD, RICHARD. "The Structure of Human Experience: Expectancy and Affect; The Case of Humor." Unpublished paper, Department of Sociology, University of Wyoming, 1979.

ALLAN, EMILIE ANDERSEN, and DARRELL J. STEFFENSMEIER. "Youth, Underemployment, and Property Crime: Differential Effects of Job Availability and Job Quality on Juvenile and Young Adult Arrest Rates." *American Sociological Review*. Vol. 54, No. 1 (February 1989):107–23.

ALLEN, MICHAEL PATRICK, and PHILIP BROYLES. "Campaign Finance Reforms and the Presidential Campaign Contributions of Wealthy Capitalist Families." *Social Science Quarterly*. Vol. 72, No. 4 (December 1991):738–50.

ALLEN, THOMAS B., and CHARLES O. HYMAN. *We Americans: Celebrating a Nation, Its People, and Its Past*. Washington, D.C.: National Geographic, 1999.

ALLEN, WALTER R. "African American Family Life in Social Context: Crisis and Hope." *Sociological Forum*. Vol. 10, No. 4 (December 1995):569–92.

ALTER, JONATHAN. "The Death Penalty on Trial." *Newsweek* (June 12, 2000):24–34.

AMATO, PAUL R. "What Children Learn from Divorce." *Population Today*. Vol. 29, No. 1 (January 2001):1, 4.

AMATO, PAUL R., and JULIANA M. SOBOLEWSKI. "The Effects of Divorce and Marital Discord on Adult Children's Psychological Well-Being." *American Sociological Review*. Vol. 66, No. 6 (December 2001):900–21.

American Demographics. Zandi Group survey. Vol. 20 (March 3, 1998):38.

———. (April 2002):6.

AMERICAN SOCIOLOGICAL ASSOCIATION. "Code of Ethics." Washington, D.C.: 1997.

AMNESTY INTERNATIONAL. Website against the Death Penalty. [Online] Available August 27, 2003, at http://web.amnesty.org/pages/deathpenalty-countries-eng

ANDERSON, ELIJAH. "The Code of the Streets." *Atlantic Monthly*. Vol. 273 (May 1994):81–94.

———. "The Ideologically Driven Critique." *American Journal of Sociology*. Vol. 197, No. 6 (May 2002):1533–50.

ANDERSON, JOHN WARD. "Early to Wed: The Child Brides of India." *Washington Post* (May 24, 1995):A27, A30.

ANGIER, NATALIE. "Scientists, Finding Second Idiosyncrasy in Homosexuals' Brains, Suggest Orientation Is Physiological." *New York Times* (August 1, 1992):A7.

ANNAN, KOFI. "Astonishing Facts." *New York Times* (September 27, 1998):16.

APA. *Violence and Youth: Psychology's Response*. Washington, D.C.: American Psychological Association, 1993.

APPLEBOME, PETER. "70 Years after Scopes Trial, Creation Debate Lives." *New York Times* (March 10, 1996):1, 10.

ARENDT, HANNAH. *Between Past and Future: Six Exercises in Political Thought*. Cleveland, Ohio: Meridian Books, 1963.

ARIÈS, PHILIPPE. *Centuries of Childhood: A Social History of Family Life*. New York: Vintage Books, 1965.

———. *Western Attitudes toward Death: From the Middle Ages to the Present*. Baltimore: Johns Hopkins University Press, 1974.

ARMSTRONG, ELISABETH. *The Retreat from Organization: U.S. Feminism Reconceptualized*. Albany: State University of New York Press, 2002.

ARNETTE, JUNE L., and MARJORIE C. WALSLEBEN. "Combating Fear and Restoring Safety in Schools." *Juvenile Justice Bulletin* (April 1998). Washington, D.C.: U.S. Department of Justice.

ARRIGHI, BARBARA A., ed. *Understanding Inequality: The Intersection of Race/Ethnicity, Class, and Gender*. New York: Roman & Littlefield, 2001.

ARROW, KENNETH, SAMUEL BOWLES, and STEVEN DURLAUF. *Meritocracy and Economic Inequality*. Princeton, N.J.: Princeton University Press, 2000.

ASANTE, MOLEFI KETE. *Afrocentricity*. Trenton, N.J.: Africa World Press, 1988.

ASCH, SOLOMON. *Social Psychology*. Englewood Cliffs, N.J.: Prentice Hall, 1952.

ASHFORD, LORI S. "New Perspectives on Population: Lessons from Cairo." *Population Bulletin*. Vol. 50, No. 1 (March 1995).

ASTIN, ALEXANDER W., LETICIA OSEGUERA, LINDA J. SAX, and WILLIAM S. KORN. *The American Freshman: Thirty-Five Year Trends*. Los Angeles: UCLA Higher Education Research Institute, 2002.

ASTONE, NAN MARIE, and SARA S. McLANAHAN. "Family Structure, Parental Practices and High School Completion." *American Sociological Review*. Vol. 56, No. 3 (June 1991):309–20.

ATCHLEY, ROBERT C. "Retirement as a Social Institution." *Annual Review of Sociology*. Vol. 8. Palo Alto, Calif.: Annual Reviews, 1982:263–87.

AXINN, WILLIAM G., and JENNIFER S. BARBER. "Mass Education and Fertility Transition." *American Sociological Review*. Vol. 66, No. 4 (August 2001):481–505.

BABWIN, DOHN. "Illinois Governor to Commute Death-Row Sentences." Yahoo! News. [Online] Available January 11, 2003, at http://dailynews.yahoo.com

BACHRACH, PETER, and MORTON S. BARATZ. *Power and Poverty*. New York: Oxford University Press, 1970.

BACKMAN, CARL B., and MURRAY C. ADAMS. "Self-Perceived Physical Attractiveness, Self-Esteem, Race, and Gender." *Sociological Focus*. Vol. 24, No. 4 (October 1991):283–90.

BAKER, MARY ANNE, CATHERINE WHITE BERHEIDE, FAY ROSS GRECKEL, LINDA CARSTARPHEN GUGIN, MARCIA J. LIPETZ, and MARCIA TEXLER SEGAL. *Women Today: A Multidisciplinary Approach to Women's Studies*. Monterey, Calif.: Brooks/Cole, 1980.

BAKER, PATRICIA S., WILLIAM C. YOELS, JEFFREY M. CLAIR, and RICHARD M. ALLMAN. "Laughter in the Triadic Geriatric Encounters: A Transcript-Based Analysis." In Rebecca J. Erikson and Beverly Cuthbertson-Johnson, eds., *Social Perspectives on Emotion*. Vol. 4. Greenwich, Conn.: JAI Press, 1997:179–207.

BALDAUF, SCOTT. "More Americans Move Off the Beaten Path." *Christian Science Monitor* (August 7, 1996):1, 4.

BALTES, PAUL B., and K. WARNER SCHAIE. "The Myth of the Twilight Years." *Psychology Today*. Vol. 7, No. 10 (March 1974):35–39.

BALTZELL, E. DIGBY. *The Protestant Establishment: Aristocracy and Caste in America*. New York: Vintage Books, 1964.

———. *Philadelphia Gentlemen: The Making of a National Upper Class*. Philadelphia: University of Pennsylvania Press, 1979a; orig. 1958.

———. *Puritan Boston and Quaker Philadelphia*. New York: Free Press, 1979b.

———. *Sporting Gentlemen: From the Age of Honor to the Cult of the Superstar*. New York: Free Press, 1995.

BANFIELD, EDWARD C. *The Unheavenly City Revisited*. Boston: Little, Brown, 1974.

BARASH, DAVID. *The Whispering Within*. New York: Penguin Books, 1981.

BARKER, EILEEN. "Who'd Be a Moonie? A Comparative Study of Those Who Join the Unification Church in Britain." In Bryan Wilson, ed., *The Social Impact of New Religious Movements*. New York: Rose of Sharon Press, 1981:59–96.

BARON, JAMES N., MICHAEL T. HANNAN, and M. DIANE BURTON. "Building the Iron Cage: Determinants of Managerial Intensity in the Early Years of Organizations." *American Sociological Review*. Vol. 64, No. 4 (August 1999):527–47.

BARON, JAMES N., BRIAN S. MITTMAN, and ANDREW E. NEWMAN. "Targets of Opportunity: Organizational and Environmental Determinants of Gender Integration within the California Civil Service, 1979–1985." *American Journal of Sociology*. Vol. 96, No. 6 (May 1991):1362–401.

BARONE, MICHAEL. "Lessons of History." *U.S. News & World Report*. Vol. 132, No. 17 (May 20, 2002):24.

BARONE, MICHAEL, and GRANT UJIFUSA. *The Almanac of American Politics*. Washington, D.C.: Barone and Co., 1981.

BAROVICK, HARRIET. "Tongues That Go Out of Style." *Time*. Vol. 159, No. 22 (June 10, 2002):22.

BARRY, KATHLEEN. "Feminist Theory: The Meaning of Women's Liberation." In Barbara Haber, ed., *The Women's Annual 1982–1983*. Boston: G. K. Hall, 1983:35–78.

BARTLETT, DONALD L., and JAMES B. STEELE. "Corporate Welfare." *Time*. Vol. 152, No. 19 (November 9, 1998):36–54.

———. "How the Little Guy Gets Crunched." *Time*. Vol. 155, No. 5 (February 7, 2000):38–41.

———. "Wheel of Misfortune." *Time*. Vol. 160, No. 25 (December 16, 2002):44–58.

BASSUK, ELLEN J. "The Homelessness Problem." *Scientific American*. Vol. 251, No. 1 (July 1984):40–45.

BAUER, P. T. *Equality, the Third World, and Economic Delusion*. Cambridge, Mass.: Harvard University Press, 1981.

BAUMGARTNER, M. P. "Introduction: The Moral Voice of the Community." *Sociological Focus*. Vol. 31, No. 2 (May 1998):105–17.

BAYDAR, NAZLI, and JEANNE BROOKS-GUNN. "Effect of Maternal Employment and Child-Care Arrangements on Preschoolers' Cognitive and Behavioral Outcomes: Evidence from Children from the National Longitudinal Survey of Youth." *Developmental Psychology*. Vol. 27 (1991):932–35.

BAYLEY, DAVID H. "Policing in America." *Society*. Vol. 36, No. 1 (November–December 1998):16–19.

BEARAK, BARRY. "Lives Held Cheap in Bangladesh Sweatshops." *New York Times* (April 15, 2001):A1, A12.

BEARMAN, PETER S., and HANNAH BRÜCKNER. "Opposite-Sex Twins and Adolescent Same-Sex Attraction." *American Journal of Sociology*. Vol. 107, No. 5 (March 2002):1179–1205.

BECKER, ANNE. Paper presented at the annual meeting of the American Psychiatric Association, Washington, D.C., May 19, 1999. Reported in "Eating Disorders Jump When Fiji Gets Television." *Toledo Blade* (May 20, 1999):12.

BECKER, HOWARD S. *Outside: Studies in the Sociology of Deviance*. New York: Free Press, 1966.

BEDARD, PAUL. "Washington Whispers." *U.S. News & World Report*. Vol. 132, No. 9 (March 25, 2002):2.

BEEGHLEY, LEONARD. *The Structure of Social Stratification in the United States*. Needham Heights, Mass.: Allyn & Bacon, 1989.

BEGLEY, SHARON. "Gray Matters." *Newsweek* (March 7, 1995):48–54.

———. "How to Beat the Heat." *Newsweek* (December 8, 1997):34–38.

BEINS, BARNEY, cited in "Examples of Spuriousness." *Teaching Methods*. No. 2 (Fall 1993):3.

BELL, DANIEL. *The Coming of Post-Industrial Society: A Venture in Social Forecasting*. New York: Basic Books, 1973.

BELLAH, ROBERT N. *The Broken Covenant*. New York: Seabury Press, 1975.

BELLAH, ROBERT N., RICHARD MADSEN, WILLIAM M. SULLIVAN, ANN SWIDLER, and STEVEN M. TIPTON. *Habits of the Heart: Individualism and Commitment in American Life*. New York: Harper & Row, 1985.

BELLANDI, DEANNA. "Study Finds Meal Portion Sizes Growing." Yahoo! News. [Online] Available January 3, 2003, at http://www.yahoo.com.

BELLAS, MARCIA L. "Comparable Worth in Academia: The Effects on Faculty Salaries of the Sex Composition and Labor-Market Conditions of Academic Disciplines." *American Sociological Review*. Vol. 59, No. 6 (December 1994):807–21.

BELLAS, MARCIA L., and BARBARA THOMAS COVENTRY. "Salesmen, Saleswomen, or Sales Workers? Determinants of the Sex Composition of Sales Occupations." *Sociological Forum*. Vol. 16, No. 1 (March 2001):73–98.

BEM, SANDRA LIPSITZ. *The Lenses of Gender: Transforming the Debate on Sexual Inequality*. New Haven, Conn.: Yale University Press, 1993.

BENEDICT, RUTH. "Continuities and Discontinuities in Cultural Conditioning." *Psychiatry*. Vol. 1 (May 1938):161–67.

BENET, SULA. "Why They Live to Be 100, or Even Older, in Abkhasia." *New York Times Magazine* (December 26, 1971):3, 28–29, 31–34.

BENJAMIN, LOIS. *The Black Elite: Facing the Color Line in the Twilight of the Twentieth Century*. Chicago: Nelson-Hall, 1991.

BENJAMIN, MATTHEW. "Suite Deals." *U.S. News & World Report*. Vol. 132, No. 14 (April 29, 2002):32–4.

BENNETT, WILLIAM J. "School Reform: What Remains to Be Done." *Wall Street Journal* (September 2, 1997):A18.

BENOKRAITIS, NIJOLE, and JOE FEAGIN. *Modern Sexism: Blatant, Subtle, and Overt Discrimination*. 2d ed. Englewood Cliffs, N.J.: Prentice Hall, 1995.

BERGAMO, MONICA, and GERSON CAMAROTTI. "Brazil's Landless Millions." *World Press Review*. Vol. 43, No. 7 (July 1996):46–47.

BERGEN, RAQUEL KENNEDY. "Interviewing Survivors of Marital Rape: Doing Feminist Research on Sensitive Topics." In Claire M. Renzetti and Raymond M. Lee, eds., *Researching Sensitive Topics*. Thousand Oaks, Calif.: Sage, 1993.

BERGER, PETER L. *Invitation to Sociology*. New York: Anchor Books, 1963.

———. *The Sacred Canopy: Elements of a Sociological Theory of Religion*. Garden City, N.Y.: Doubleday, 1967.

———. *Facing Up to Modernity: Excursions in Society, Politics, and Religion*. New York: Basic Books, 1977.

———. *The Capitalist Revolution: Fifty Propositions about Prosperity, Equality, and Liberty*. New York: Basic Books, 1986.

BERGER, PETER, BRIGITTE BERGER, and HANSFRIED KELLNER. *The Homeless Mind: Modernization and Consciousness*. New York: Vintage Books, 1974.

BERGER, PETER L., and HANSFRIED KELLNER. *Sociology Reinterpreted: An Essay on Method and Vocation*. Garden City, N.Y.: Anchor Books, 1981.

BERGER, PETER L., and THOMAS LUCKMANN. *The Social Construction of Reality*. Garden City, N.J.: Doubleday, 1966.

BERGESEN, ALBERT, ed. *Crises in the World-System*. Beverly Hills, Calif.: Sage, 1983.

BERK, RICHARD A. *Collective Behavior*. Dubuque, Iowa: Wm. C. Brown, 1974.

BERNARD, JESSIE. *The Female World*. New York: Free Press, 1981.

BERNSTEIN, NINA. "On Frontier of Cyberspace, Data Is Money, and a Threat." *New York Times* (June 12, 1997):A1, B14–15.

BERNSTEIN, RICHARD J. *The New Constellation: The Ethical-Political Horizons of Modernity/Postmodernity*. Cambridge, Mass.: MIT Press, 1992.

BERRILL, KEVIN T. "Anti-Gay Violence and Victimization in the United States: An Overview." In Gregory M. Herek and Kevin T. Berrill, *Hate Crimes: Confronting Violence against Lesbians and Gay Men*. Newbury Park, Calif.: Sage, 1992:19–45.

BERRY, BRIAN L., and PHILIP H. REES. "The Factorial Ecology of Calcutta." *American Journal of Sociology*. Vol. 74, No. 5 (March 1969):445–91.

BERSCHEID, ELLEN, and ELAINE HATFIELD. *Interpersonal Attraction*. 2d ed. Reading, Mass.: Addison-Wesley, 1983.

BESHAROV, DOUGLAS J., and LISA A. LAUMANN. "Child Abuse Reporting." *Society*. Vol. 34, No. 4 (May/June 1996):40–46.

BESHAROV, DOUGLAS J. and PETER GERMANIS. "Welfare Reform: Four Years Later." *The Public Interest*. Vol. 140 (Summer 2000):17–35.

BEST, JOEL. "Victimization and the Victim Industry." *Society*. Vol. 34, No. 2 (May/June 1997):9–17.

BEST, RAPHAELA. *We've All Got Scars: What Boys and Girls Learn in Elementary School*. Bloomington: Indiana University Press, 1983.

BIAN, YANJIE. "Chinese Social Stratification and Social Mobility." *Annual Review of Sociology*. Vol. 28 (2002):91–116.

BIANCHI, SUZANNE M., and DAPHNE SPAIN. "Women, Work, and Family in America." *Population Bulletin*. Vol. 51, No. 3 (December 1996).

BIBLARZ, TIMOTHY J., and ADRIAN E. RAFTERY. "The Effects of Family Disruption on Social Mobility." *American Sociological Review*. Vol. 58, No. 1 (February 1993):97–109.

BILLINGS, DWIGHT B., and KATHLEEN M. BLEE. *The Road to Poverty: The Making of Wealth and Hardship in Appalachia*. Cambridge, U.K.: Cambridge University Press, 2000.

BLACKWOOD, EVELYN, and SASKIA WIERINGA, eds. *Female Desires: Same-Sex Relations and Transgender Practices across Cultures*. New York: Columbia University Press, 1999.

BLANK, JONAH. "The Muslim Mainstream." *U.S. News & World Report*. Vol. 125, No. 3 (July 20, 1998):22–25.

BLANKENHORN, DAVID. *Fatherless America: Confronting Our Most Urgent Social Problem*. New York: HarperCollins, 1995.

BLAU, JUDITH R., and PETER M. BLAU. "The Cost of Inequality: Metropolitan Structure and Violent Crime." *American Sociological Review*. Vol. 47, No. 1 (February 1982):114–29.

BLAU, PETER M. *Exchange and Power in Social Life*. New York: Wiley, 1964.

———. *Inequality and Heterogeneity: A Primitive Theory of Social Structure*. New York: Free Press, 1977.

BLAU, PETER M., TERRY C. BLUM, and JOSEPH E. SCHWARTZ. "Heterogeneity and Intermarriage." *American Sociological Review*. Vol. 47, No. 1 (February 1982):45–62.

BLAU, PETER M., and OTIS DUDLEY DUNCAN. *The American Occupational Structure*. New York: Wiley, 1967.

BLAUSTEIN, ALBERT P., and ROBERT L. ZANGRANDO. *Civil Rights and the Black American*. New York: Washington Square Press, 1968.

BLOOM, LEONARD. "Familial Adjustments of Japanese-Americans to Relocation: First Phase." In Thomas F. Pettigrew, ed., *The Sociology of Race Relations*. New York: Free Press, 1980:163–67.

BLUM, LINDA M. *Between Feminism and Labor: The Significance of the Comparable Worth Movement*. Berkeley: University of California Press, 1991.

BLUMBERG, PAUL. *Inequality in an Age of Decline*. New York: Oxford University Press, 1981.

BLUMENTHAL, SUSAN J. "Prescriptions for a New Year." *U.S. News & World Report*. Vol. 132, No. 1 (January 14, 2002):52.

BLUMER, HERBERT G. "Fashion." In David L. Sills, ed., *International Encyclopedia of the Social Sciences*. Vol. 5. New York: Macmillan and Free Press, 1968:341–45.

———. "Collective Behavior." In Alfred McClung Lee, ed., *Principles of Sociology*. 3d ed. New York: Barnes & Noble Books, 1969:65–121.

BLUMSTEIN, ALFRED, and RICHARD ROSENFELD. "Assessing the Recent Ups and Downs in U.S. Homicide Rates." *National Institute of Justice Journal*. Vol. 237 (October 1998):9–11.

BLUMSTEIN, PHILIP, and PEPPER SCHWARTZ. *American Couples*. New York: William Morrow, 1983.

BOBO, LAWRENCE, and VINCENT L. HUTCHINGS. "Perceptions of Racial Group Competition: Extending Blumer's Theory of Group Position to a Multiracial Social Context." *American Sociological Review*. Vol. 61, No. 6 (December 1996):951–72.

BOGGESS, SCOTT, and JOHN BOUND. "Did Criminal Activity Increase during the 1980s? Comparisons across Data Sources." *Social Science Quarterly*. Vol. 78, No. 3 (September 1997):725–39.

BOHANNAN, CECIL. "The Economic Correlates of Homelessness in Sixty Cities." *Social Science Quarterly*. Vol. 72, No. 4 (December 1991):817–25.

BOHLEN, CELESTINE. "Facing Oblivion, Rust-Belt Giants Top Russian List of Vexing Crises." *New York Times* (November 8, 1998):1, 6.

BOHON, STEPHANIE A., and CRAIG R. HUMPHREY. "Courting LULUs: Characteristic of Suitor and Objector Communities." *Rural Sociology*. Vol. 65, No. 3 (September 2000):376–95.

BOLI, JOHN, and GEORGE M. THOMAS. "World Culture in the World Polity: A Century of International Non-Governmental Organization." *American Sociological Review*. Vol. 62, No. 2 (April 1997):171–90.

BONILLA-SANTIAGO, GLORIA. "A Portrait of Hispanic Women in the United States." In Sara E. Rix, ed., *The American Woman 1990–91: A Status Report*. New York: Norton, 1990:249–57.

BONNER, JANE. Research presented in *The Two Brains*. Public Broadcasting System telecast, 1984.

BOOTH, WILLIAM. "By the Sweat of Their Brows: A New Economy." *Washington Post* (July 13, 1998):A1, A10–A11.

BORGMANN, ALBERT. *Crossing the Postmodern Divide*. Chicago: University of Chicago Press, 1992.

BORMANN, F. HERBERT. "The Global Environmental Deficit." *BioScience*. Vol. 40 (1990):74.

BORMANN, F. HERBERT, and STEPHEN R. KELLERT. "The Global Environmental Deficit." In Herbert F. Bormann and Stephen R. Kellert, eds., *Ecology, Economics, and Ethics: The Broken Circle*. New Haven, Conn.: Yale University Press, 1991:ix–xviii.

BOSWELL, TERRY E. "A Split Labor Market Analysis of Discrimination against Chinese Immigrants, 1850–1882." *American Sociological Review*. Vol. 51, No. 3 (June 1986):352–71.

BOSWELL, TERRY E., and WILLIAM J. DIXON. "Marx's Theory of Rebellion: A Cross-National Analysis of Class Exploitation, Economic Development, and Violent Revolt." *American Sociological Review*. Vol. 58, No. 5 (October 1993):681–702.

BOTT, ELIZABETH. *Family and Social Network*. New York: Free Press, 1971; orig. 1957.

BOULDING, ELISE. *The Underside of History*. Boulder, Colo.: Westview Press, 1976.

BOWEN, WILLIAM G., and DEREK K. BOK. *The Shape of the River: Long-Term Consequences of Considering Race in College and University Admissions*. Princeton, N.J.: Princeton University Press, 1999.

BOWLES, SAMUEL, and HERBERT GINTIS. *Schooling in Capitalist America: Educational Reform and the Contradictions of Economic Life*. New York: Basic Books, 1976.

BOYER, DEBRA. "Male Prostitution and Homosexual Identity." *Journal of Homosexuality*. Vol. 17, Nos. 1–2 (1989):151–84.

BOYLE, ELIZABETH HEGER, FORTUNATA SONGORA, and GAIL FOSS. "International Discourse and Local Politics: Anti-Female-Genital-Cutting Laws in Egypt, Tanzania, and the United States." *Social Problems*. Vol. 48, No. 4 (November 2001):524–44.

BOZA, TANYA GOLASH. *Proposed* American Sociological Association Statement on "Race." [Online] Available October 24, 2002, at http://www.unc.edu/~tatiana/

BRAITHWAITE, JOHN. "The Myth of Social Class and Criminality Reconsidered." *American Sociological Review*. Vol. 46, No. 1 (February 1981):36–57.

BRANEGAN, JAY. "Is Singapore a Model for the West?" *Time*. Vol. 141, No. 3 (January 18, 1993):36–37.

BRIANS, CRAIG LEONARD, and BERNARD GROFMAN. "Election Day Registration's Effect on U.S. Voter Turnout." *Social Science Quarterly*. Vol. 82, No. 1 (March 2001):170–83.

BRINES, JULIE, and KARA JOYNER. "The Ties That Bind: Principles of Cohesion in Cohabitation and Marriage." *American Sociological Review*. Vol. 64, No. 3 (June 1999):333–55.

BRINK, SUSAN. "Living On the Edge." *U.S. News & World Report*. Vol. 133, No. 14 (October 14, 2002):58–64.

BRINTON, CRANE. *The Anatomy of Revolution*. New York: Vintage Books, 1965.

BRINTON, MARY C. "The Social-Institutional Bases of Gender Stratification: Japan as an Illustrative Case." *American Journal of Sociology*. Vol. 94, No. 2 (September 1988):300–34.

BROCKERHOFF, MARTIN P. "An Urbanizing World." *Population Bulletin*. Vol. 55, No. 3 (September 2000).

BRODER, DAVID S. "Stock Options belong in the Line of Fire." *Columbus Dispatch* (April 21, 2002):G3.

BRODKIN, KAREN. "How Jews Became White Folks." In Paula S. Rothenberg, ed., *White Privilege*. New York: Worth, 2001.

BROOKS, DAVID. *Bobos in Paradise: The New Upper Class and How They Got There*. New York: Simon & Schuster, 2000.

BROUGHTON, PHILIP DELVES. "Mississippi Vote to Keep Confederate Flag Symbol." *Electronic Telegraph*. Issue 2155 (April 19, 2001).

BROWN, LESTER R. "Reassessing the Earth's Population." *Society*. Vol. 32, No. 4 (May–June 1995):7–10.

BROWN, LESTER R., et al., eds. *State of the World 1993: A Worldwatch Institute Report on Progress toward a Sustainable Society*. New York: Norton, 1993.

BROWN, MARY ELLEN, ed. *Television and Women's Culture: The Politics of the Popular*. Newbury Park, Calif.: Sage, 1990.

BROWNING, CHRISTOPHER R., and EDWARD O. LAUMANN. "Sexual Contact between Children and Adults: A Life Course Perspective." *American Sociological Review*. Vol. 62, No. 5 (August 1997):540–60.

BUCKLEY, STEPHEN. "A Spare and Separate Way of Life." *Washington Post* (December 18, 1996):A1, A32–3

Bulletin of the Atomic Scientists. Current time of the doomsday clock. [Online] Available December 28, 2003, at http://www.thebulletin.org/media/current.html

BUECHLER, STEVEN M. *Social Movements in Advanced Capitalism: The Political Economy and Cultural Construction of Social Activism*. New York: Oxford University Press, 2000.

Bulletin of the Atomic Scientists. Current time of the doomsday clock. [Online] Available December 28, 2003, at http://www.thebulletin.org/media/current.html

BURAWAY, MICHAEL. "Review Essay: The Soviet Descent into Capitalism." *American Journal of Sociology*. Vol. 102, No. 5 (March 1997):1430–44.

BURCH, ROBERT. Testimony to House of Representatives Hearing in "Review: The World Hunger Problem." October 25, 1983, Serial 98–38.

BUREAU OF ALCOHOL, TOBACCO, AND FIREARMS. *Firearms Commerce in the United States 2001/2002*. Washington, D.C.: The Bureau, 2002.

BURKE, TOM. "The Future." In Sir Edmund Hillary, ed., *Ecology 2000: The Changing Face of the Earth*. New York: Beaufort Books, 1984:227–41.

BURKETT, ELINOR. "God Created Me to Be a Slave." *New York Times* Sunday Magazine (October 12, 1997):56–60.

BURNS, PETER F., PETER L. FRANCIA, and PAUL S. HERRNSON. "Labor at Work: Union Campaign Activities and Legislative Payoffs in the U.S. House of Representatives." *Social Science Quarterly*. Vol. 81, No. 2 (June 2000):507–22.

BURSTEIN, PAUL. "Legal Mobilization as a Social Movement Tactic: The Struggle for Equal Employment Opportunity." *American Journal of Sociology*. Vol. 96, No. 5 (March 1991):1201–25.

BUTLER, ROBERT N. *Why Survive? Being Old in America*. New York: Harper & Row, 1975.

CAIN, BRAD. "Ashcroft Overturns Assisted Suicide." Yahoo! News. [Online] Available November 7, 2001, at http://dailynews.yahoo.com

CALLAHAN, DANIEL. *Setting Limits: Medical Goals in an Aging Society*. New York: Simon & Schuster, 1987.

CAMARA, EVANDRO. Personal communication, 2000.

CAMERON, WILLIAM BRUCE. *Modern Social Movements: A Sociological Outline*. New York: Random House, 1966.

CAMPBELL, KIM. "On the Road . . . Again." *Christian Science Monitor* (September 6, 2002): Arts and Leisure, pp. 15, 18.

CAMPO-FLORES, ARIAN. "'Macho' or 'Sweetness'?" *Newsweek* (July 1, 2002)

CAMPOLO, ANTHONY. *Partly Right: Learning from the Critics of Christianity*. Dallas: Word Publishing, 1985.

CANETTI, ELIAS. *Crowds and Power*. New York: Seabury Press, 1978.

CAPIZANO, JEFFREY, KATHRYN TOUT, and GINA ADAMS. *Child Care Patterns of School-Age Children with Employed Mothers. Report of the Urban Institute*. [Online] Available February 14, 2001, at http://www.newfederalism.urban.org/html/op41/occa41.html#childcare

CAPLOW, THEODORE. "The Case of the Phantom Episcopalians." *American Sociological Review*. Vol. 63, No. 1 (February 1998):112–13.

CAPLOW, THEODORE, et al. *Middletown Families*. Minneapolis: University of Minnesota Press, 1982.

CAPLOW, THEODORE, HOWARD M. BAHR, JOHN MODELL, and BRUCE A. CHADWICK. *Recent Social Trends in the United States, 1960–1990*. Montreal: McGill-Queen's University Press, 1991.

CARLEY, KATHLEEN. "A Theory of Group Stability." *American Sociological Review*. Vol. 56, No. 3 (June 1991):331–54.

CARLSON, NORMAN A. "Corrections in the United States Today: A Balance Has Been Struck." *American Criminal Law Review*. Vol. 13, No. 4 (Spring 1976):615–47.

CARMICHAEL, STOKELY, and CHARLES V. HAMILTON. *Black Power: The Politics of Liberation in America*. New York: Vintage Books, 1967.

CARROLL, GINNY. "Who Foots the Bill?" *Newsweek*. Special Issue (Fall–Winter 1990):81–85.

CARROLL, JAMES R. "Congress Is Told of Coal-Dust Fraud UMW; Senator from Minnesota Rebukes Industry." *Louisville Courier Journal* (Thursday, May 27, 1999):1A.

CARUSO, DAVID B. "42 Philadelphia Schools Privatized." Yahoo! News. [Online] Available April 18, 2002, at http://www.yahoo.com

CASTELLS, MANUEL. *The Urban Question*. Cambridge, Mass.: MIT Press, 1977.

———. *The City and the Grass Roots*. Berkeley: University of California Press, 1983.

CATALYST. *2000 Catalyst Census of Women Corporate Officers and Top Earners*. [Online] Available November 1, 2002, at http://www.catalystwomen.org/research/censuses.htm#2000cote

———. *2001 Catalyst Census of Women Board of Directors of the Fortune 1000*. [Online] Available November 1, 2003, at http://www.catalystwomen.org/research/censuses.htm

————. *Women Corporate Officers and Top Earners.* [Online] Available December 26, 2003, at http://www.catalystwomen.org/press_room/factsheets/factcote98.htm

CBS. News report on female achievement in U.S. schools, November 1, 2002.

CENTER FOR AMERICAN WOMEN AND POLITICS. Women in Statewide Elective Executive Office 2003. Eagleton Institute of Politics, Rutgers University. [Online] Available February 11, 2003, at http://www.cawp.rutgers.edu/facts/stwide-03.html

CENTER FOR RESPONSIVE POLITICS. *Election Overview, 2000 Cycle: Fundraising at a Glance.* [Online] Available November 1, 2002, at http://www.opensecrets.org/overview/index.asp

————. The Big Picture: 2002 Cycle: Totals by Sector. [Online] Available December 28, 2003, at http://www.opensecrets.org/bigpicture/sectors.asp?cycle=2002

————. The Big Picture: 2002 Cycle: Where the Money Came From. [Online] Available December 28, 2003, at http://www.opensecrets.org/bigpicture/sherefrom.asp?cycle=2002

CENTER ON EDUCATION POLICY. "The Good News about American Education." Reported in Brigette Greenberg, "Report Finds America's Public Schools Showing Improvement." *Naples Daily News* (January 8, 2000):4a.

CHAGNON, NAPOLEON A. *Yanomamö: The Fierce People.* 4th ed. New York: Holt, Rinehart & Winston, 1992.

CHANDLER, TERTIUS, and GERALD FOX. *3000 Years of Urban History.* New York: Academic Press, 1974.

CHANGE, KWANG-CHIH. *The Archaeology of Ancient China.* New Haven, Conn.: Yale University Press, 1977.

CHAUNCEY, GEORGE. *Gay New York: Gender, Urban Culture, and the Making of the Gay Male World 1890–1940.* New York: Basic Books, 1994.

CHAVES, MARK. "Ordaining Women: The Diffusion of an Organizational Innovation." *American Journal of Sociology.* Vol. 101, No. 4 (January 1996):840–73.

————. *Ordaining Women: Culture and Conflict in Religious Organizations.* Cambridge, Mass.: Harvard University Press, 1997.

CHAVEZ, LINDA. "Promoting Racial Harmony." In George E. Curry, ed., *The Affirmative Action Debate.* Reading, Mass.: Addison-Wesley, 1996.

CHERLIN, ANDREW J., P. LINDSAY CHASE-LANSDALE, and CHRISTINE MCRAE. "Effects of Parental Divorce on Mental Health throughout the Life Course." *American Sociological Review.* Vol. 63, No. 2 (April 1998):239–49.

CHESNAIS, JEAN-CLAUDE. "The Demographic Sunset of the West?" *Population Today.* Vol. 25, No. 1 (January 1997):4–5.

CHIRICOS, TED, RANEE MCENTIRE, and MARC GERTZ. "Perceived Racial and Ethnic Composition of Neighborhood and Perceived Risk of Crime." *Social Problems.* Vol. 48, No. 3 (August 2001):322–40. *Chronicle of Higher Education. Almanac 2002–3.* [Online] Available October 23, 2002, at http://chronicle.com/weekly/almanac/2002/nation/0103201.htm

CHOLDIN, HARVEY M. "How Sampling Will Help Defeat the Undercount." *Society.* Vol. 34, No. 3 (March/April 1997):27–30.

Chronicle of Higher Education. Almanac 2002–3. [Online] Available October 23, 2002, at http://chronicle.com/weekly/almanac/2002/nation/0103201.htm

CHUA-EOAN, HOWARD. "Profiles in Outrage." *Time.* Vol. 156, No. 13 (September 25, 2000):38–39.

CHURCH, GEORGE J. "Unions Arise—with New Tricks." *Time.* Vol. 143, No. 24 (June 13, 1994):56–58.

————. "Ripping Up Welfare." *Time.* Vol. 148, No. 8 (August 12, 1996):18–22.

CIMINO, RICHARD, and DON LATTIN. "Choosing My Religion." *American Demographics.* Vol. 21, No. 4 (April 1999):60–65.

CLARK, CURTIS B. "Geriatric Abuse: Out of the Closet." In *The Tragedy of Elder Abuse: The Problem and the Response.* Hearings before the Select Committee on Aging, House of Representatives (July 1, 1986):49–50.

CLARK, KIM. "Bad CEO? Go to Your Room." *U.S. News and World Report.* Vol. 132, No. 16 (May 13, 2002a):39.

————. "Bankrupt Lives." *U.S. News & World Report.* Vol. 133, No. 10 (September 16, 2002b):52–4.

CLARK, MARGARET S., ed. *Prosocial Behavior.* Newbury Park, Calif.: Sage, 1991.

CLARKE, LEE. "Panic: Myth or Reality?" *Social Contexts.* Vol. 1, No. 3 (Fall 2002):21–6.

CLARKE, ROBIN. "Atmospheric Pollution." In Sir Edmund Hillary, ed., *Ecology 2000: The Changing Face of the Earth.* New York: Beaufort Books, 1984a:130–48.

————. "What's Happening to Our Water?" In Sir Edmund Hillary, ed., *Ecology 2000: The Changing Face of the Earth.* New York: Beaufort Books, 1984b:108–29.

CLAWSON, DAN, and MARY ANN CLAWSON. "What Has Happened to the U.S. Labor Movement? Union Decline and Renewal." *Annual Review of Sociology.* Vol. 25 (1999):95–119.

CLEMETSON, LYNETTE. "Grandma Knows Best." *Newsweek* (June 12, 2000):60–61.

CLINARD, MARSHALL, and DANIEL ABBOTT. *Crime in Developing Countries.* New York: Wiley, 1973.

CLOUD, JOHN, and JODIE MORSE. "Home Sweet School." *Time.* Vol. 158, No. 8 (August 27, 2001):46–54.

CLOWARD, RICHARD A., and LLOYD E. OHLIN. *Delinquency and Opportunity: A Theory of Delinquent Gangs.* New York: Free Press, 1966.

COE, MICHAEL D., and RICHARD A. DIEHL. *In the Land of the Olmec.* Austin: University of Texas Press, 1980.

COHEN, ADAM. "Test-Tube Tug-of-War." *Time.* Vol. 151, No. 13 (April 6, 1998):65.

————. "A First Report Card on Vouchers." *Time.* Vol. 153, No. 16 (April 26, 1999):36–38.

COHEN, ALBERT K. *Delinquent Boys: The Culture of the Gang.* New York: Free Press, 1971; orig. 1955.

COHEN, ELIAS. "The Complex Nature of Ageism: What Is It? Who Does It? Who Perceives It?" *The Gerontologist.* Vol. 41, No. 5 (October 2001):576–8.

COHEN, LLOYD R. "Sexual Harassment and the Law." *Society.* Vol. 28, No. 4 (May–June 1991):8–13.

COHN, RICHARD M. "Economic Development and Status Change of the Aged." *American Journal of Sociology.* Vol. 87, No. 2 (March 1982):1150–61.

COLE, GEORGE F., and CHRISTOPHER E. SMITH. *Criminal Justice in America.* 3d ed. Belmont, Calif.: Wadsworth, 2002.

COLEMAN, JAMES S. "Rational Organization." *Rationality and Society.* Vol. 2, (1990):94–105.

COLEMAN, JAMES S., and THOMAS HOFFER. *Public and Private High Schools: The Impact of Communities.* New York: Basic Books, 1987.

COLEMAN, JAMES, THOMAS HOFFER, and SALLY KILGORE. *Public and Private Schools: An Analysis of Public Schools and Beyond.* Washington, D.C.: National Center for Education Statistics, 1981.

COLEMAN, RICHARD P., and BERNICE L. NEUGARTEN. *Social Status in the City.* San Francisco: Jossey-Bass, 1971.

COLEMAN, RICHARD P., and LEE RAINWATER. *Social Standing in America.* New York: Basic Books, 1978.

COLLINS, RANDALL. "A Conflict Theory of Sexual Stratification." *Social Problems.* Vol. 19, No. 1 (Summer 1971):3–21.

COLLOWAY, N. O., and PAULA L. DOLLEVOET. "Selected Tabular Material on Aging." In Caleb Finch and Leonard Hayflick, eds., *Handbook of the Biology of Aging.* New York: Van Nostrand Reinhold, 1977:666–708.

COLLYMORE, YVETTE. "Migrant Street Children on the Rise in Central America." *Population Today.* Vol. 30, No. 2 (February/March 2002):1, 4.

COLTON, HELEN. *The Gift of Touch: How Physical Contact Improves Communication, Pleasure, and Health.* New York: Seaview/Putnam, 1983.

COMMISSION FOR RACIAL JUSTICE, UNITED CHURCH OF CHRIST. *CRJ Reporter.* New York: Commission for Racial Justice, the United Church of Christ, 1994.

CONNETT, PAUL H. "The Disposable Society." In F. Herbert Bormann and Stephen R. Kellert, eds., *Ecology, Economics, and Ethics: The Broken Circle.* New Haven, Conn.: Yale University Press, 1991:99–122.

COOK, RHODES. "House Republicans Scored a Quiet Victory in '92." *Congressional Quarterly Weekly Report.* Vol. 51, No. 16 (April 17, 1993):965–68.

COOLEY, CHARLES HORTON. *Social Organization.* New York: Schocken Books, 1962; orig. 1909.

————. *Human Nature and the Social Order.* New York: Schocken Books, 1964; orig. 1902.

COONEY, MARK. "From Warfare to Tyranny: Lethal Conflict and the State." *American Sociological Review.* Vol. 62, No. 2 (April 1997):316–38.

CORCORAN, MARY, SANDRA K. DANZIGER, ARIEL KALIL, and KRISTIN S. SEEFELDT. "How Welfare Reform Is Affecting Women's Work." *Annual Review of Sociology.* Vol. 26 (2000):241–69.

CORLEY, ROBERT N., O. LEE REED, PETER J. SHEDD, and JERE W. MOREHEAD. *The Legal and Regulatory Environment of Business.* 9th ed. New York: McGraw-Hill, 1993.

CORNELL, BARBARA. "Pulling the Plug on TV." *Time.* Vol. 152, No. 16 (October 16, 2000):F16.

CORRELL, SHELLEY J. "Gender and the Career Choice Process: The Role of Biased Self-Assessment." *American Journal of Sociology.* Vol. 106, No. 6 (May 2001):1691–1730.

COSE, ELLIS. "Census and the Complex Issue of Race." *Society.* Vol. 34, No. 6 (September/October, 1997):9–13.

COSER, LEWIS. *Masters of Sociological Thought: Ideas in Historical and Social Context.* New York: Harcourt Brace Jovanovich, 1971.

COUNCIL ON FAMILIES IN AMERICA. *Marriage in America: A Report to the Nation.* New York: Institute for American Values, 1995.

COURTNEY, ALICE E., and THOMAS W. WHIPPLE. *Sex Stereotyping in Advertising.* Lexington, Mass.: D.C. Heath, 1983.

COURTWRIGHT, DAVID T. *Violent Land: Single Men and Social Disorder from the Frontier to the Inner City.* Cambridge, Mass.: Harvard University Press, 1996.

COVINGTON, JEANETTE. "Racial Classification in Criminology: The Reproduction of Racialized Crime." *Sociological Forum.* Vol. 10, No. 4 (December 1995):547–68.

COWLEY, GEOFFREY. "The Prescription That Kills." *Newsweek* (July 17, 1995):54.

COX, HARVEY. "Church and Believers: Always Strangers?" In Thomas Robbins and Dick Anthony, *In Gods We Trust: New Patterns of Religious Pluralism in America.* 2d ed. New Brunswick, N.J.: Transaction, 1990:449–62.

COYOTE (Call Off Your Old Tired Ethics). [Online] Available April 2, 2000, at http://www.freedomusa.org/coyotela/what–is.html

CQ Weekly. "Women and Minorities in the 108th Congress." Vol. 61, No. 4 (January 25, 2003):192.

CRANE, DIANA. *Fashion and Its Social Agenda: Class, Gender, and Identity in Clothing.* Chicago: University of Chicago Press, 2000.

CRISPELL, DIANE. "Grandparents Galore." *American Demographics.* Vol. 15, No. 10 (October 1993):63.

CROOK, STEPHAN, JAN PAKULSKI, and MALCOLM WATERS. *Postmodernity: Change in Advanced Society.* Newbury Park, Calif.: Sage, 1992.

CROSSETTE, BARBARA. "Female Genital Mutilation by Immigrants Is Becoming Cause for Concern in the U.S." *New York Times International* (December 10, 1995):11.

CROUSE, JAMES, and DALE TRUSHEIM. *The Case against the SAT.* Chicago: University of Chicago Press, 1988.

CUFF, E. C., and G. C. F. PAYNE, eds. *Perspectives in Sociology.* London: Allen & Unwin, 1979.

CULLEN, LISA TAKEUCHI. "Will Manage for Food." *Time.* Vol. 160, No. 16 (October 14, 2002):52–6.

CUMMING, ELAINE, and WILLIAM E. HENRY. *Growing Old: The Process of Disengagement.* New York: Basic Books, 1961.

CURRIE, ELLIOTT. *Confronting Crime: An American Challenge.* New York: Pantheon Books, 1985.

CURRY, ANDREW. "The Gullahs' Last Stand?" *U.S. News & World Report.* Vol. 130, No. 24 (June 18, 2001):40–1.

CURTIS, JAMES E., EDWARD G. GRABB, and DOUGLAS BAER. "Voluntary Association Membership in Fifteen Countries: A Comparative Analysis." *American Sociological Review.* Vol. 57, No. 2 (April 1992):139–52.

CURTISS, SUSAN. *Genie: A Psycholinguistic Study of a Modern-Day "Wild Child."* New York: Academic Press, 1977.

CUTCLIFFE, JOHN R. "Hope, Counseling and Complicated Bereavement Reactions." *Journal of Advanced Nursing.* Vol. 28, No. 4 (October 1998):754–62.

CUTRIGHT, PHILLIP. "Occupational Inheritance: A Cross-National Analysis." *American Journal of Sociology.* Vol. 73, No. 4 (January 1968):400–16.

DAHL, ROBERT A. *Who Governs?* New Haven, Conn.: Yale University Press, 1961.

———. *Dilemmas of Pluralist Democracy: Autonomy vs. Control.* New Haven, Conn.: Yale University Press, 1982.

DAHRENDORF, RALF. *Class and Class Conflict in Industrial Society.* Stanford, Calif.: Stanford University Press, 1959.

DALY, MARTIN, and MARGO WILSON. *Homicide.* New York: Aldine, 1988.

DANFORTH, MARION M., and J. CONRAD GLASS, JR. "Listen to My Words, Give Meaning to My Sorrow: A Study in Cognitive Constructs in Middle-Aged Bereaved Widows." *Death Studies.* Vol. 25, No. 6 (September 2001):413–30.

DARROCH, JACQUELINE E., JENNIFER J. FROST, SUSHEELA SINGH, and THE STUDY TEAM. "Teenage Sexual and Reproductive Behavior in Developed Countries: Can More Progress Be Made?" New York: The Alan Guttmacher Institute (November 2001). [Online] Available August 14, 2002, at http://www.agi-usa.

DAVIDSON, JAMES D., RALPH E. PYLE, and DAVID V. REYES. "Persistence and Change in the Protestant Establishment, 1930–1992." *Social Forces.* Vol. 74, No. 1 (September 1995):157–75.

DAVIES, CHRISTIE. *Ethnic Humor around the World: A Comparative Analysis.* Bloomington: Indiana University Press, 1990.

DAVIES, JAMES C. "Toward a Theory of Revolution." *American Sociological Review.* Vol. 27, No. 1 (February 1962):5–19.

DAVIES, MARK, and DENISE B. KANDEL. "Parental and Peer Influences on Adolescents' Educational Plans: Some Further Evidence." *American Journal of Sociology.* Vol. 87, No. 2 (September 1981):363–87.

DAVIS, BYRON BRADLEY. "Sports World." *Christian Science Monitor* (September 9, 1997):11.

DAVIS, DONALD M., cited in "T.V. Is a Blonde, Blonde World." *American Demographics,* special issue: *Women Change Places.* Ithaca, N.Y.: 1993.

DAVIS, KAREN A. "Ex-Grocery Clerk Wins California Lottery." Yahoo! News. [Online] Available June 29, 2001, at http://www.dailynews.yahoo.com

DAVIS, KINGSLEY. "Extreme Social Isolation of a Child." *American Journal of Sociology.* Vol. 45, No. 4 (January 1940):554–65.

———. "Final Note on a Case of Extreme Isolation." *American Journal of Sociology.* Vol. 52, No. 5 (March 1947):432–37.

———. "Sexual Behavior." In Robert K. Merton and Robert Nisbet, eds., *Contemporary Social Problems.* 3d ed. New York: Harcourt Brace Jovanovich, 1971:313–60.

DAVIS, KINGSLEY, and WILBERT MOORE. "Some Principles of Stratification." *American Sociological Review.* Vol. 10, No. 2 (April 1945):242–49.

DEDRICK, DENNIS K., and RICHARD E. YINGER. "MAD, SDI, and the Nuclear Arms Race." Manuscript in development. Georgetown, Ky.: Georgetown College, 1990.

DeFINA, ROBERT H., and THOMAS M. ARVANITES. "The Weak Effect of Imprisonment on Crime: 1971–1998." *Social Science Quarterly.* Vol. 83, No. 3 (September 2002):635–53.

DeFRANCIS, MARC. "U.S. Elder Care Is in a Fragile State." *Population Today.* Vol. 30, No. 1 (January 2002a):1–3.

———. "A Spiraling Shortage of Nurses." *Population Today.* Vol. 30, No. 2 (February/March 2002b):8–9.

DeJONG, GORDON F., and ANNA B. MADAMBA. "A Double Disadvantage? Minority Group, Immigrant Status, and Underemployment in the United States." *Social Science Quarterly.* Vol. 82, No. 1 (March 2001):117–30.

DELACROIX, JACQUES, and CHARLES C. RAGIN. "Structural Blockage: A Crossnational Study of Economic Dependency, State Efficacy, and Underdevelopment." *American Journal of Sociology.* Vol. 86, No. 6 (May 1981):1311–47.

DELLA CAVA, MARCO R. "For Dutch, It's as Easy as Asking a Doctor." *USA Today* (January 7, 1997):4A.

DeLUCA, TOM. "Joe the Bookie and the Class Voting Gap." *American Demographics.* Vol. 20, No. 11 (November 1998):26–29.

DE MENTE, BOYE. *Japanese Etiquette and Ethics in Business.* 5th ed. Lincolnwood, Ill.: NTC Business Books, 1987.

DEMERATH, N. J., III. "Who Now Debates Functionalism? From *System, Change, and Conflict* to 'Culture, Choice, and Praxis.'" *Sociological Forum.* Vol. 11, No. 2 (June 1996):333–45.

DENT, DAVID J. "African-Americans Turning to Christian Academies." *New York Times,* Education Life supplement (August 4, 1996):26–29.

DERSHOWITZ, ALAN. *The Vanishing American Jew.* Boston: Little, Brown, 1997.

DERVARICS, CHARLES. "The Coming Age of Older Women." *Population Today.* Vol. 27, No. 2 (February 1999):2–3.

DEVINE, JOEL A. "State and State Expenditure: Determinants of Social Investment and Social Consumption Spending in the Postwar United States." *American Sociological Review.* Vol. 50, No. 2 (April 1985):150–65.

DICKINSON, AMY. "When Dating Is Dangerous." *Time.* Vol. 158, No. 8 (August 27, 2001):76.

DIXON, WILLIAM J., and TERRY BOSWELL. "Dependency, Disarticulation, and Denominator Effects: Another Look at Foreign Capital Penetration." *American Journal of Sociology.* Vol. 102, No. 2 (September 1996):543–62.

DIZARD, JAN E., and HOWARD GADLIN. *The Minimal Family.* Amherst: The University of Massachusetts Press, 1990.

DOBSON, RICHARD B. "Mobility and Stratification in the Soviet Union." *Annual Review of Sociology.* Vol. 3. Palo Alto, Calif.: Annual Reviews, 1977:297–329.

DOBYNS, HENRY F. "An Appraisal of Techniques with a New Hemispheric Estimate." *Current Anthropology.* Vol. 7, No. 4 (October 1966):395–446.

DOLLARD, JOHN, et al. *Frustration and Aggression.* New Haven, Conn.: Yale University Press, 1939.

DOMHOFF, G. WILLIAM. *Who Rules America Now? A View of the '80s.* Englewood Cliffs, N.J.: Prentice Hall, 1983.

DONAHUE, JOHN J., III, and STEVEN D. LEAVITT. Research cited in "New Study Claims Abortion Is Behind Decrease in Crime." *Population Today.* Vol. 28, No. 1 (January 2000):1, 4.

DONNELLY, PATRICK G., and THEO J. MAJKA. "Residents' Efforts at Neighborhood Stabilization: Facing the Challenges of Inner-City Neighborhoods." *Sociological Forum.* Vol. 13, No. 2 (June 1998):189–213.

DOYLE, JAMES A. *The Male Experience.* Dubuque, Iowa: Wm. C. Brown, 1983.

D'SOUZA, DINESH. "The Billionaire Next Door." *Forbes.* Vol. 164, No. 9 (October 11, 1999):50–62.

DU BOIS, W. E. B. *The Philadelphia Negro: A Social Study.* New York: Schocken Books, 1967; orig. 1899.

DUBOS, RENÉ. *Man Adapting.* New Haven, Conn.: Yale University Press, 1980; orig. 1965.

DUDLEY, KATHRYN MARIE. *Debt and Dispossession: Farm Loss in America's Heartland.* Chicago: University of Chicago Press, 2000.

DUHL, LEONARD J. "The Social Context of Health." In Arthur C. Hastings et al., eds., *Health for the Whole Person: The Complete Guide to Holistic Medicine.* Boulder, Colo.: Westview Press, 1980:39–48.

DUNBAR, LESLIE. *The Common Interest: How Our Social Welfare Policies Don't Work and What We Can Do about Them.* New York: Pantheon, 1988.

DUNCAN, CYNTHIA M. *Worlds Apart: Why Poverty Persists in Rural America.* New Haven, CT: Yale University Press, 1999.

DUNCAN, GREG J., W. JEAN YEUNG, JEANNE BROOKS-GUNN, and JUDITH R. SMITH. "How Much Does Childhood Poverty Affect the Life Chances of Children?" *American Sociological Review.* Vol. 63, No. 3 (June 1998):406–23.

DUREX GLOBAL SEX SURVEY. Reported in *Time* (October 30, 2000):31.

DURKHEIM, EMILE. *The Division of Labor in Society.* New York: Free Press, 1964a; orig. 1893.

———. *The Rules of Sociological Method.* New York: Free Press, 1964b; orig. 1895.

———. *The Elementary Forms of Religious Life.* New York: Free Press, 1965; orig. 1915.

———. *Suicide.* New York: Free Press, 1966; orig. 1897.

———. *Sociology and Philosophy.* New York: Free Press, 1974; orig. 1924.

DWORKIN, ANDREA. *Intercourse.* New York: Free Press, 1987.

DWORKIN, RONALD W. "Where Have All the Nurses Gone?" *Public Interest.* Vol. 148 (Summer 2002):23–36.

EBAUGH, HELEN ROSE, and JANET SALTZMAN CHAFETZ. *Religion and the New Immigrants: Continuities and Adaptations in Immigrant Congregations.* Walnut Creek, Calif.: AltiMira Press, 2000.

EBAUGH, HELEN ROSE FUCHS. *Becoming an EX: The Process of Role Exit.* Chicago: University of Chicago Press, 1988.

EBOH, CAMILLUS. "Nigerian Woman Loses Appeal against Stoning Death." Yahoo! News. [Online] Available August 19, 2002, at http://dailynews.yahoo.com

ECK, DIANA L. *A New Religious America: How a "Christian Country" Has Become the World's Most Religiously Diverse Nation.* New York: HarperSanFrancisco, 2001.

EDIN, KATHRYN, and LAURA LEIN. "Work, Welfare, and Single Mothers' Economic Survival Strategies." *American Sociological Review.* Vol. 62, No. 2 (April 1996):253–66.

EDMONDSON, BRAD. "Fountains of Youth." *American Demographics.* Vol. 18, No. 7 (July 1996):60.

———. "The Facts of Death." *American Demographics*. Vol. 49, No. 4 (April 1997):47–53.

EDWARDS, DAVID V. *The American Political Experience*. 3d ed. Englewood Cliffs, N.J.: Prentice Hall, 1985.

EDWARDS, TAMALA M. "Revolt of the Gentry." *Time*. Vol. 151, No. 23 (June 15, 1998):34–35.

———. "Flying Solo." *Time*. Vol. 156, No. 9 (August 28, 2000):47–55.

EHRENREICH, BARBARA. *The Hearts of Men: American Dreams and the Flight from Commitment*. Garden City, N.Y.: Anchor Books, 1983.

———. "The Real Truth about the Female Body." *Time*. Vol. 153, No. 9 (March 15, 1999):56–65.

———. *Nickel and Dimed: On (Not) Getting By in America*. New York: Henry Holt, 2001.

EHRENREICH, JOHN. "Introduction." In John Ehrenreich, ed., *The Cultural Crisis of Modern Medicine*. New York: Monthly Review Press, 1978:1–35.

EICHLER, MARGRIT. *Nonsexist Research Methods: A Practical Guide*. Winchester, Mass.: Unwin Hyman, 1988.

EISEN, ARNOLD M. *The Chosen People in America: A Study of Jewish Religious Ideology*. Bloomington: Indiana University Press, 1983.

EISENBERG, DANIEL. "Paying to Keep Your Job." *Time*. Vol. 158, No. 17 (October 15, 2001):80–3.

EISLER, BENITA. *The Lowell Offering: Writings by New England Mill Women 1840–1845*. Philadelphia: J.B. Lippincott, 1977.

EKMAN, PAUL. "Biological and Cultural Contributions to Body and Facial Movements in the Expression of Emotions." In A. Rorty, ed., *Explaining Emotions*. Berkeley: University of California Press, 1980a:73–101.

———. *Face of Man: Universal Expression in a New Guinea Village*. New York: Garland Press, 1980b.

———. *Telling Lies: Clues to Deceit in the Marketplace, Politics, and Marriage*. New York: Norton, 1985.

EL-ATTAR, MOHAMED. Personal communication, 1991.

ELIAS, ROBERT. *The Politics of Victimization: Victims, Victimology and Human Rights*. New York: Oxford University Press, 1986.

ELLIOT, DELBERT S., and SUZANNE S. AGETON. "Reconciling Race and Class Differences in Self-Reported and Official Estimates of Delinquency." *American Sociological Review*. Vol. 45, No. 1 (February 1980):95–110.

ELLISON, CHRISTOPHER G., JOHN P. BARTKOWSKI, and MICHELLE L. SEGAL. "Do Conservative Protestant Parents Spank More Often? Further Evidence from the National Survey of Families and Households." *Social Science Quarterly*. Vol. 77, No. 3 (September 1996):663–73.

ELLISON, CHRISTOPHER G., and DARREN E. SHERKAT. "Conservative Protestantism and Support for Corporal Punishment." *American Sociological Review*. Vol. 58, No. 1 (February 1993):131–44.

ELMER-DEWITT, PHILIP. "The Revolution That Fizzled." *Time*. Vol. 137, No. 20 (May 20, 1991):48–49.

———. "Battle for the Internet." *Time*. Vol. 144, No. 4 (July 25, 1994):50–56.

———. "Now for the Truth about Americans and Sex." *Time*. Vol. 144, No. 16 (October 17, 1994c):62–70.

EMBER, MELVIN, and CAROL R. EMBER. "The Conditions Favoring Matrilocal versus Patrilocal Residence." *American Anthropologist*. Vol. 73, No. 3 (June 1971):571–94.

———. *Anthropology*. 6th ed. Englewood Cliffs, N.J.: Prentice Hall, 1991.

EMBREE, AINSLIE T. *The Hindu Tradition*. New York: Vintage Books, 1972.

EMERSON, JOAN P. "Behavior in Private Places: Sustaining Definitions of Reality in Gynecological Examinations." In H. P. Dreitzel, ed., *Recent Sociology*. Vol. 2. New York: Collier, 1970:74–97.

EMERSON, MICHAEL O., GEORGE YANCEY, and KAREN J. CHAI. "Does Race Matter in Residential Segregation? Exploring the Preferences of White Americans." *American Sociological Review*. Vol. 66, No. 6 (December 2001):922–35.

ENDICOTT, KAREN. "Fathering in an Egalitarian Society." In Barry S. Hewlett, ed., *Father-Child Relations: Cultural and Bio-Social Contexts*. New York: Aldine, 1992:281–96.

ENGELS, FRIEDRICH. *The Origin of the Family*. Chicago: Charles H. Kerr & Company, 1902; orig. 1884.

ENGLAND, PAULA. *Comparable Worth: Theories and Evidence*. Hawthorne, N.Y.: Aldine, 1992.

———. "Three Reviews on Marriage." *Contemporary Sociology*. Vol. 30, No. 6 (November 2001):564–5.

ENGLAND, PAULA, JOAN M. HERMSEN, and DAVID A. COTTER. "The Devaluation of Women's Work: A Comment on Tam." *American Journal of Sociology*. Vol. 105, No. 6 (May 2000):1741–60.

EPPS, EDGAR G. "Race, Class, and Educational Opportunity: Trends in the Sociology of Education." *Sociological Forum*. Vol. 10, No. 4 (December 1995):593–608.

ERBER, ERNEST. "Virtues and Vices of the Market: Balanced Correctives to a Current Craze." *Dissent*. Vol. 37 (Summer 1990):353–60.

ERIKSON, ERIK H. *Childhood and Society*. New York: Norton, 1963; orig. 1950.

———. *Identity and the Life Cycle*. New York: Norton, 1980.

ERIKSON, KAI T. *Wayward Puritans: A Study in the Sociology of Deviance*. New York: Wiley, 1966.

ERIKSON, ROBERT S., NORMAN R. LUTTBEG, and KENT L. TEDIN. *American Public Opinion: Its Origins, Content, and Impact*. 2d ed. New York: Wiley, 1980.

ESTES, RICHARD J. "The Commercial Sexual Exploitation of Children in the U.S., Canada, and Mexico." Reported in "Study Explores Sexual Exploitation." Yahoo! News. [Online] Available September 10, 2001, at http://dailynews.yahoo.com

ETZIONI, AMITAI. *A Comparative Analysis of Complex Organization: On Power, Involvement, and Their Correlates*. Rev. and enlarged ed. New York: Free Press, 1975.

———. "Too Many Rights, Too Few Responsibilities." *Society*. Vol. 28, No. 2 (January–February 1991):41–48.

———. "How to Make Marriage Matter." *Time*. Vol. 142, No. 10 (September 6, 1993):76.

———. "The Responsive Community: A Communitarian Perspective." *American Sociological Review*. Vol. 61, No. 1 (February 1996):1–11.

———. *My Brother's Keeper: A Memoir and a Message*. Rowman & Littlefield Publishers, 2003.

ETZIONI-HALEVY, EVA. *Bureaucracy and Democracy: A Political Dilemma*. Rev. ed. Boston: Routledge & Kegan Paul, 1985.

EVELYN, JAMILAH. "Community Colleges Play Too Small a Role in Teacher Education, Report Concludes." *Chronicle of Higher Education Online*. [Online] Available October 24, 2002, at http://chronicle.com/daily/2002/10/2002102403n.htm

FAGAN, JEFFREY, FRANKLIN E. ZIMRING, and JUNE KIM. "Declining Homicide in New York City: A Tale of Two Trends." *National Institute of Justice Journal*. Vol. 237 (October 1998):12–13.

FALK, GERHARD. Personal communication, 1987.

FALKENMARK, MALIN, and CARL WIDSTRAND. "Population and Water Resources: A Delicate Balance." *Population Bulletin*. Vol. 47, No. 3 (November 1992). Washington, D.C.: Population Reference Bureau.

FALLON, A. E., and P. ROZIN. "Sex Differences in Perception of Desirable Body Shape." *Journal of Abnormal Psychology*. Vol. 94, No. 1 (1985):100–5.

FALLOWS, JAMES. "Immigration: How It's Affecting Us." *Atlantic Monthly*. Vol. 252 (November 1983):45–52, 55–62, 66–68, 85–90, 94, 96, 99–106.

FARLEY, CHRISTOPHER JOHN. "Winning the Right to Fly." *Time*. Vol. 146, No. 9 (August 28, 1995):62–64.

FARRELL, MICHAEL P., and STANLEY D. ROSENBERG. *Men at Midlife*. Boston: Auburn House, 1981.

FATTAH, HASSAN. "A More Diverse Community." *American Demographics*. Vol. 24, No. 7 (July/August 2002):39–43.

FEAGIN, JOE. *The Urban Real Estate Game*. Englewood Cliffs, N.J.: Prentice Hall, 1983.

———. "Death By Discrimination?" *Newsletter, Society for the Study of Social Problems*. Vol. 28, No. 1 (Winter 1997):15–16.

FEAGIN, JOE R., and VERA HERNÁN. *Liberation Sociology*. Boulder, Colo.: Westview, 2001.

FEATHERMAN, DAVID L., and ROBERT M. HAUSER. *Opportunity and Change*. New York: Academic Press, 1978.

FEATHERSTONE, MIKE, ed. *Global Culture: Nationalism, Globalization, and Modernity*. London: Sage, 1990.

FEDARKO, KEVIN. "Land Mines: Cheap, Deadly, and Cruel." *Time*. Vol. 147, No. 20 (May 13, 1996):54–55.

FELLMAN, BRUCE. "Taking the Measure of Children's T.V." *Yale Alumni Magazine* (April 1995):46–51.

FENYVESI, CHARLES. "Walled Streets." *U.S. News & World Report*. Vol. 132, No. 9 (March 25, 2002):57.

FERNANDEZ, ROBERTO M., and NANCY WEINBERG. "Sifting and Sorting: Personal Contacts and Hiring in a Retail Bank." *American Sociological Review*. Vol. 62, No. 6 (December 1997):883–902.

FERREE, MYRA MARX, and ELAINE J. HALL. "Rethinking Stratification from a Feminist Perspective: Gender, Race, and Class in Mainstream Textbooks." *American Sociological Review*. Vol. 61, No. 6 (December 1996):929–50.

FERREE, MYRA MARX, and BETH B. HESS. *Controversy and Coalition: The New Feminist Movement across Four Decades of Change*. 3d ed. New York: Routledge, 1995.

FETTO, JOHN. "Down for the Count." *American Demographics*. Vol. 21, No. 11 (November 1999):46–47.

———. "Lean on Me." *American Demographics*. Vol. 22, No. 12 (December 2000):16–17.

———. "Gay Friendly?" *American Demographics*. Vol. 24, No. 5 (May 2002):16.

———. "A View from the Top?" *American Demographics*. Vol. 24, No. 7 (July-August 2002):14.

———. "Me Gusta TV." *American Demographics*. Vol. 24, No. 11 (January 2003):14–5.

———. "Drug Money." *American Demographics*. Vol. 25, No. 2 (March 2003):48.

FINEMAN, HOWARD, and TAMARA LIPPER. "Spinning Race." *Newsweek* (January 27, 2003):26–9.

FINKELSTEIN, NEAL W., and RON HASKINS. "Kindergarten Children Prefer Same-Color Peers." *Child Development*. Vol. 54, No. 2 (April 1983):502–8.

FINN, CHESTER E., JR., and HERBERT J. WALBERG. "The World's Least Efficient Schools." *Wall Street Journal* (June 22, 1998):A22.

FIREBAUGH, GLENN. "Growth Effects of Foreign and Domestic Investment." *American Journal of Sociology*. Vol. 98, No. 1 (July 1992):105–30.

———. "Does Foreign Capital Harm Poor Nations? New Estimates Based on Dixon and Boswell's Measures of Capital Penetration." *American Journal of Sociology*. Vol. 102, No. 2 (September 1996):563–75.

———. "Empirics of World Income Inequality." *American Journal of Sociology*. Vol. 104, No. 6 (May 1999):1597–1630.

———. "The Trend in Between-Nation Income Inequality." *Annual Review of Sociology*. Vol. 26 (2000):323–39.

FIREBAUGH, GLENN, and FRANK D. BECK. "Does Economic Growth Benefit the Masses? Growth, Dependence, and Welfare in the Third World." *American Sociological Review*. Vol. 59, No. 5 (October 1994):631–53.

FIREBAUGH, GLENN, and KENNETH E. DAVIS. "Trends in Antiblack Prejudice, 1972–1984: Region and Cohort Effects." *American Journal of Sociology*. Vol. 94, No. 2 (September 1988):251–72.

FIREBAUGH, GLENN, and DUMITRU SANDU. "Who Supports Marketization and Democratization in Post-Communist Romania?" *Sociological Forum*. Vol. 13, No. 3 (September 1998):521–41.

FISCHER, CLAUDE W. *The Urban Experience*. 2d ed. New York: Harcourt Brace Jovanovich, 1984.

FISHER, ELIZABETH. *Woman's Creation: Sexual Evolution and the Shaping of Society*. Garden City, N.Y.: Anchor/Doubleday, 1979.

FISHER, ROGER, and WILLIAM URY. "Getting to YES." In William M. Evan and Stephen Hilgartner, eds., *The Arms Race and Nuclear War*. Englewood Cliffs, N.J.: Prentice Hall, 1988:261–68.

FISKE, ALAN PAIGE. "The Cultural Relativity of Selfish Individualism: Anthropological Evidence that Humans Are Inherently Sociable." In Margaret S. Clark, ed., *Prosocial Behavior*. Newbury Park, Calif.: Sage, 1991:176–214.

FITZPATRICK, MARY ANNE. *Between Husbands and Wives: Communication in Marriage*. Newbury Park, Calif.: Sage, 1988.

FLAHERTY, MICHAEL G. "A Formal Approach to the Study of Amusement in Social Interaction." *Studies in Symbolic Interaction*. Vol. 5. New York: JAI Press, 1984:71–82.

———. "Two Conceptions of the Social Situation: Some Implications of Humor." *Sociological Quarterly*. Vol. 31, No. 1 (Spring 1990).

FLYNN, PATRICIA. "The Disciplinary Emergence of Bioethics and Bioethics Committees: Moral Ordering and Its Legitimation." *Sociological Focus*. Vol. 24, No. 2 (May 1991):145–56.

FOBES, RICHARD. "Creative Problem Solving." *The Futurist*. Vol. 30, No. 1 (January–February 1996):19–22.

FOLIART, DONNE E., and MARGARET CLAUSEN. "Bereavement Practices among California Hospices: Results of a Statewide Survey." *Death Studies*. Vol. 25, No. 5 (July 2001):461–8.

FONDA, DAREN. "The Male Minority." *Time*. Vol. 156, No. 24 (December 11, 2000):58–60.

———. "Selling in Tongues." *Time*. Vol. 153, No. 23 (Global Business edition, November 2001):B12–B16.

Forbes 400. Special Issue: *The Richest People in America*. Vol. 170, No. 6 (September 30, 2002).

FORD, CLELLAN S., and FRANK A. BEACH. *Patterns of Sexual Behavior*. New York: Harper & Row, 1951.

FORLITI, AMY. "R.I. Nightclub Fire Kills at Least 39." Yahoo! News. [Online] Available February 21, 2003, at http://www.yahoo.com

FORSTMANN, THEODORE J. "A Competitive Vision for American Education." *Imprimis*. Vol. 28, No. 9 (September 1999):1–4.

FOST, DAN. "American Indians in the 1990s." *American Demographics*. Vol. 13, No. 12 (December 1991):26–34.

FOUCAULT, MICHEL. *The History of Sexuality: An Introduction*. Vol. 1, trans. Robert Hurley. New York: Vintage, 1990; orig. 1978.

FRANK, ANDRÉ GUNDER. *On Capitalist Underdevelopment*. Bombay: Oxford University Press, 1975.

———. *Crisis: In the World Economy*. New York: Holmes & Meier, 1980.

———. *Reflections on the World Economic Crisis*. New York: Monthly Review Press, 1981.

FRANKLIN, JOHN HOPE. *From Slavery to Freedom: A History of Negro Americans*. 3d ed. New York: Vintage Books, 1967.

FRANKLIN ASSOCIATES. *Characterization of Municipal Solid Waste in the United States, 1960–2000*. Prairie Village, Kans.: Franklin Associates, 1986.

FRAZIER, E. FRANKLIN. *Black Bourgeoisie: The Rise of a New Middle Class*. New York: Free Press, 1965.

FREDRICKSON, GEORGE M. *White Supremacy: A Comparative Study in American and South African History*. New York: Oxford University Press, 1981.

FREE, MARVIN D. "Religious Affiliation, Religiosity, and Impulsive and Intentional Deviance." *Sociological Focus*. Vol. 25, No. 1 (February 1992):77–91.

FREEDMAN, ESTELLE B. *No Turning Back: The History of Feminism and the Future of Women*. New York: Ballantine Books, 2002.

FREEDOM HOUSE. *Freedom in the World 1998–1999*. New York: Freedom House, 1999.

———. *Freedom in the World 2001–2002*. New York: Freedom House, 2002.

———. *Freedom in the World 2002–2003*. New York: Freedom House, 2003.

FRENCH, HOWARD W. "Teaching Japan's Salarymen to Be Their Own Men." *New York Times* (November 27, 2002):A4.

FRENCH, MARILYN. *Beyond Power: On Women, Men, and Morals*. New York: Summit Books, 1985.

FRIEDAN, BETTY. *The Fountain of Age*. New York: Simon & Schuster, 1993.

FRIEDMAN, MEYER, and RAY H. ROSENMAN. *Type A Behavior and Your Heart*. New York: Fawcett Crest, 1974.

FRIEDMAN, MILTON, and ROSE FRIEDMAN. *Free to Choose: A Personal Statement*. New York: Harcourt Brace Jovanovich, 1980.

FUGITA, STEPHEN S., and DAVID J. O'BRIEN. "Structural Assimilation, Ethnic Group Membership, and Political Participation among Japanese Americans: A Research Note." *Social Forces*. Vol. 63, No. 4 (June 1985):986–95.

FUJIMOTO, ISAO. "The Failure of Democracy in a Time of Crisis." In Amy Tachiki et al., eds., *Roots: An Asian American Reader*. Los Angeles: UCLA Asian American Studies Center, 1971:207–14.

FULLER, REX, and RICHARD SCHOENBERGER. "The Gender Salary Gap: Do Academic Achievement, Intern Experience, and College Major Make a Difference?" *Social Science Quarterly*. Vol. 72, No. 4 (December 1991):715–26.

FULLERTON, HOWARD, JR., and MITRA TOOSSI. "Labor Force Projections to 2010: Steady Growth and Changing Composition." *Monthly Labor Review* (November 2001):32–33. [Online] Available September 10, 2002, at http://www.bls.gov/opub/mlr/2001/11/art2full.pdf

FUREDI, FRANK. "New Britain: A Nation of Victims." *Society*. Vol. 35, No. 3 (April 1998):80–84.

FURSTENBERG, FRANK F., JR., and ANDREW CHERLIN. *Divided Families: What Happens to Children When Parents Part*. Cambridge, Mass.: Harvard University Press, 1991.

GAGNÉ, PATRICIA, and RICHARD TEWKSBURY. "Conformity Pressures and Gender Resistance among Transgendered Individuals." *Social Problems*. Vol. 45, No. 1 (February 1998):81–101.

GAGNÉ, PATRICIA, RICHARD TEWKSBURY, and DEANNA MCGAUGHEY. "Coming Out and Crossing Over: Identity Formation and Proclamation in a Transgender Community." *Gender and Society*. Vol. 11, No. 4 (August 1997):478–508.

GALLAGHER, MAGGIE. "Does Bradley Know What Poverty Is?" *New York Post* (October 28, 1999):37.

GALLUP. Gallup poll data reported in "Americans and Homosexual Civil Unions." *Society*. Vol. 40, No. 1 (December 2002):2.

GALSTER, GEORGE. "Black Suburbanization: Has It Changed the Relative Location of Races?" *Urban Affairs Quarterly*. Vol. 26, No. 4 (June 1991):621–28.

GAMORAN, ADAM. "The Variable Effects of High-School Tracking." *American Sociological Review*. Vol. 57, No. 6 (December 1992):812–28.

GAMSON, WILLIAM A. "Beyond the Science-versus-Advocacy Distinction." *Contemporary Sociology*. Vol. 28, No. 1 (January 1999):23–26.

GANLEY, ELAINE. "Among Islamic Countries, Women's Roles Vary Greatly." *Washington Times* (April 15, 1998):A13.

GANS, HERBERT J. *People and Plans: Essays on Urban Problems and Solutions*. New York: Basic Books, 1968.

GARDNER, MARILYN. "At-Home Dads Give Their New Career High Marks." *Christian Science Monitor* (May 30, 1996):1, 12.

GARDYN, REBECCA. "Retirement Redefined." *American Demographics*. Vol. 22, No. 11 (November 2000):52–57.

———. "The Mating Game." *American Demographics*. Vol. 24, No. 7 (July/August 2002):33–7.

GARFINKEL, HAROLD. "Conditions of Successful Degradation Ceremonies." *American Journal of Sociology*. Vol. 61, No. 2 (March 1956):420–24.

GARREAU, JOEL. *Edge City*. New York: Doubleday, 1991.

GEIST, WILLIAM. *Toward a Safe and Sane Halloween and Other Tales of Suburbia*. New York: Times Books, 1985.

GELLES, RICHARD J., and CLAIRE PEDRICK CORNELL. *Intimate Violence in Families*. 2d ed. Newbury Park, Calif.: Sage, 1990.

GELMAN, DAVID. "Born or Bred?" *Newsweek* (February 24, 1992):46–53.

GENDELL, MURRAY. "Boomers' Retirement Wave Likely to Begin in Just Six Years." *Population Today*. Vol. 30, No. 3 (April 2002):1–2.

GERBER, THEODORE P. "Structural Change and Post-Socialist Stratification: Labor Market Transitions in Contemporary Russia." *American Sociological Review*. Vol. 67, No. 5 (October 2002):629–59.

GERBER, THEODORE P., and MICHAEL HOUT. "More Shock Than Therapy: Market Transition, Employment, and Income in Russia, 1991–1995." *American Journal of Sociology*. Vol. 104, No. 1 (July 1998):1–50.

GERGEN, DAVID. "King of the World." *U.S. News & World Report*. Vol. 132, No. 6 (February 25–March 4, 2002):84.

GERLACH, MICHAEL L. *The Social Organization of Japanese Business*. Berkeley: University of California Press, 1992.

GERSTEL, NAOMI. "Divorce and Stigma." *Social Problems*. Vol. 43, No. 2 (April 1987):172–86.

GERTH, H. H., and C. WRIGHT MILLS, eds. *From Max Weber: Essays in Sociology*. New York: Oxford University Press, 1946.

GESCHWENDER, JAMES A. *Racial Stratification in America*. Dubuque, Iowa: Wm. C. Brown, 1978.

GEST, TED. "Law Schools' New Female Face." *U.S. News & World Report*. Vol. 130, No. 14 (April 9, 2001):76–77.

GEWERTZ, DEBORAH. "A Historical Reconsideration of Female Dominance among the Chambri of Papua New Guinea." *American Ethnologist*. Vol. 8, No. 1 (1981):94–106.

GIBBONS, DON C., and MARVIN D. KROHN. *Delinquent Behavior*. 4th ed. Englewood Cliffs, N.J.: Prentice Hall, 1986.

GIBBS, NANCY. "When Is It Rape?" *Time*. Vol. 137, No. 22 (June 3, 1991):48–54.

———. "The Pulse of America Along the River." *Time*. Vol. 156, No. 2 (July 10, 2000):42–46.

———. "What Kids (Really) Need." *Time*. Vol. 157, No. 17 (April 30, 2001a):48–49.

———. "If You Want to Humble an Empire." *Time.* September 11, 2001b. Special issue.

GIDDENS, ANTHONY. *The Transformation of Intimacy.* Cambridge, UK: Polity Press, 1992.

GIELE, JANET Z. "Gender and Sex Roles." In Neil J. Smelser, ed., *Handbook of Sociology.* Newbury Park, Calif.: Sage, 1988:291–323.

GIGLIOTTI, RICHARD J., and HEATHER K. HUFF. "Role Related Conflicts, Strains, and Stresses of Older-Adult College Students." *Sociological Focus.* Vol. 28, No. 3 (August 1995):329–42.

GILBERTSON, GRETA A., and DOUGLAS T. GURAK. "Broadening the Enclave Debate: The Dual Labor Market Experiences of Dominican and Colombian Men in New York City." *Sociological Forum.* Vol. 8, No. 2 (June 1993):205–20.

GILLIGAN, CAROL. *In a Different Voice: Psychological Theory and Women's Development.* Cambridge, Mass.: Harvard University Press, 1982.

———. *Making Connections: The Relational Worlds of Adolescent Girls at Emma Willard School.* Cambridge, Mass.: Harvard University Press, 1990.

GILLON, RAANAN. "Euthanasia in the Netherlands: Down the Slippery Slope?" *Journal of Medical Ethics.* Vol. 25, No. 1 (February 1999):3–4.

GINSBURG, FAYE, and ANNA LOWENHAUPT TSING, eds. *Uncertain Terms: Negotiating Gender in American Culture.* Boston: Beacon Press, 1990.

GIOVANNINI, MAUREEN. "Female Anthropologist and Male Informant: Gender Conflict in a Sicilian Town." In John J. Macionis and Nijole V. Benokraitis, eds., *Seeing Ourselves: Classic, Contemporary, and Cross-Cultural Readings in Sociology.* 2d ed. Englewood Cliffs, N.J.: Prentice Hall, 1992:27–32.

GIROUX, GREGORY L. "GOP Maintains Thin Edge." *CQ Weekly.* Vol. 58, No. 44 (November 11, 2000):2652.

GIUGNI, MARCO G. "Structure and Culture in Social Movements Theory." *Sociological Forum.* Vol. 13, No. 2 (June 1998):365–75.

GLADUE, BRIAN A., RICHARD GREEN, and RONALD E. HELLMAN. "Neuroendocrine Response to Estrogen and Sexual Orientation." *Science.* Vol. 225, No. 4669 (September 28, 1984):1496–99.

GLASSNER, BARRY. *The Culture of Fear: Why Americans Are Afraid of the Wrong Things.* New York: Basic Books, 1999.

GLEICK, ELIZABETH. "The Marker We've Been Waiting For." *Time.* Vol. 149, No. 14 (April 7, 1997):28–42.

GLENMARY RESEARCH CENTER. Major Religious Families by Counties of the United States: 2000 (map). Nashville, Tenn., 2002.

GLENN, NORVAL D., and BETH ANN SHELTON. "Regional Differences in Divorce in the United States." *Journal of Marriage and the Family.* Vol. 47, No. 3 (August 1985):641–52.

GLUECK, SHELDON, and ELEANOR GLUECK. *Unraveling Juvenile Delinquency.* New York: Commonwealth Fund, 1950.

GODWIN, KENNETH, FRANK KEMERER, VALERIE MARTINEZ, and RICHARD RUDERMAN. "Liberal Equity in Education: A Comparison of Choice Options." *Social Science Quarterly.* Vol. 79, No. 3 (September 1998):502–22.

GOESLING, BRIAN. "Changing Income Inequalities within and between Nations: New Evidence." *American Sociological Review.* Vol. 66, No. 5 (October 2001):745–61.

GOETTING, ANN. *Getting Out: Life Stories of Women Who Left Abusive Men.* New York: Columbia University Press, 1999.

GOFFMAN, ERVING. *The Presentation of Self in Everyday Life.* Garden City, N.Y.: Anchor Books, 1959.

———. *Asylums: Essays on the Social Situation of Mental Patients and Other Inmates.* Garden City, N.Y.: Anchor Books, 1961.

———. *Interactional Ritual: Essays on Face to Face Behavior.* Garden City, N.Y.: Anchor Books, 1967.

———. *Gender Advertisements.* New York: Harper Colophon, 1979.

GOLDBERG, BERNARD. *Bias: A CBS Insider Exposes How the Media Distort the News.* Washington, D.C.: Regnery, 2002.

GOLDBERG, STEVEN. *The Inevitability of Patriarchy.* New York: William Morrow, 1974.

———. Personal communication, 1987.

GOLDBERGER, PAUL. Lecture delivered at Kenyon College, Gambier, Ohio, September 22, 2002.

GOLDEN, FREDERIC. "Good Eggs, Bad Eggs." *Time.* Vol. 153, No. 1 (January 11, 1999a):56–59.

———. "Lying Faces Unmasked." *Time.* Vol. 153, No. 13 (April 5, 1999b):52.

GOLDFARB, WILLIAM. "Groundwater: The Buried Life." In F. Herbert Bormann and Stephen R. Kellert, eds., *Ecology, Economics, and Ethics: The Broken Circle.* New Haven, Conn.: Yale University Press, 1991:123–35.

GOLDFIELD, MICHAEL. "Rebounding Unions Target Service Sector." *Population Today.* Vol. 28, No. 7 (October 2000):3, 10.

GOLDSMITH, H. H. "Genetic Influences on Personality from Infancy." *Child Development.* Vol. 54, No. 2 (April 1983):331–35.

GOLDSTEIN, JOSHUA R., and CATHERINE T. KENNEY. "Marriage Delayed or Marriage Foregone? New Cohort Forecasts of First Marriage for U.S. Women." *American Sociological Review.* Vol. 66, No. 4 (August 2001):506–19.

GOODE, ERICH. "No Need to Panic? A Bumper Crop of Books on Moral Panics." *Sociological Forum.* Vol. 15, No. 3 (September 2000):543–52.

GOODE, WILLIAM J. "The Theoretical Importance of Love." *American Sociological Review.* Vol. 24, No. 1 (February 1959):38–47.

———. "Encroachment, Charlatanism, and the Emerging Profession: Psychology, Sociology and Medicine." *American Sociological Review.* Vol. 25, No. 6 (December 1960):902–14.

GORDON, JAMES S. "The Paradigm of Holistic Medicine." In Arthur C. Hastings et al., eds., *Health for the Whole Person: The Complete Guide to Holistic Medicine.* Boulder, Colo.: Westview Press, 1980:3–27.

GORING, CHARLES BUCKMAN. *The English Convict: A Statistical Study.* Montclair, N.J.: Patterson Smith, 1972; orig. 1913.

GORMAN, CHRISTINE. "Stressed Out Kids." *Time.* Vol. 156, No. 26 (December 25, 2000/January 1, 2001):168.

GORSKI, PHILIP S. "Historicizing the Secularization Debate: Church, State, and Society in Late Medieval and Early Modern Europe, ca. 1300 to 1700." *American Sociological Review.* Vol. 65, No. 1 (February 2000):138–67.

GOTHAM, KEVIN FOX. "Race, Mortgage Lending, and Loan Rejections in a U.S. City." *Sociological Focus.* Vol. 31, No. 4 (October 1998):391–405.

GOTTFREDSON, MICHAEL R., and TRAVIS HIRSCHI. "National Crime Control Policies." *Society.* Vol. 32, No. 2 (January–February 1995):30–36.

GOTTMANN, JEAN. *Megalopolis.* New York: Twentieth Century Fund, 1961.

GOULD, STEPHEN J. "Evolution as Fact and Theory." *Discover* (May 1981):35–37.

GOULDNER, ALVIN. *The Coming Crisis of Western Sociology.* New York: Avon Books, 1970.

GRANT, DON SHERMAN, II, and MICHAEL WALLACE. "Why Do Strikes Turn Violent?" *American Journal of Sociology.* Vol. 96, No. 5 (March 1991):1117–50.

GRANT, DONALD L. *The Anti-Lynching Movement.* San Francisco: R & E Research Associates, 1975.

GRANT, KAREN R. "The Inverse Care Law in the Context of Universal Free Health Insurance in Canada: Toward Meeting Health Needs through Public Policy." *Sociological Focus.* Vol. 17, No. 2 (April 1984):137–55.

GRATTET, RYKEN. "Hate Crimes: Better Data or Increasing Frequency?" *Population Today.* Vol. 28, No. 5 (July 2000):1, 4.

GREELEY, ANDREW M. *Religious Change in America.* Cambridge, Mass.: Harvard University Press, 1989.

GREEN, GARY PAUL, LEANN M. TIGGES, and DANIEL DIAZ. "Racial and Ethnic Differences in Job-Search Strategies in Atlanta, Boston, and Los Angeles." *Social Science Quarterly.* Vol. 80, No. 2 (June 1999):263–90.

GREEN, JOHN C. "Pat Robertson and the Latest Crusade: Resources and the 1988 Presidential Campaign." *Social Sciences Quarterly.* Vol. 74, No. 1 (March 1993):156–68.

GREENBERG, DAVID F. *The Construction of Homosexuality.* Chicago: University of Chicago Press, 1988.

GREENFIELD, LAWRENCE A. *Child Victimizers: Violent Offenders and Their Victims.* Washington, D.C.: U.S. Bureau of Justice Statistics, 1996.

GREENHOUSE, LINDA. "Justices Uphold Stiffer Sentences for Hate Crimes." *New York Times* (June 12, 1993):1, 8.

GREENSPAN, STANLEY I. *The Four-Thirds Solution: Solving the Child-Care Crisis in America.* Cambridge, Mass.: Perseus, 2001.

GREENWALD, JOHN. "The New Service Class." *Time.* Vol. 144, No. 20 (November 14, 1994):72–74.

———. "School for Profit." *Time.* Vol. 155, No. 11 (March 20, 2000):56–57.

GREGORY, PAUL R., and ROBERT C. STUART. *Comparative Economic Systems.* 2d ed. Boston: Houghton Mifflin, 1985.

GROSS, JANE. "New Challenge of Youth: Growing Up in a Gay Home." *New York Times* (February 11, 1991):A1, B7.

GROTH, NICHOLAS A., and H. JEAN BIRNBAUM. *Men Who Rape: The Psychology of the Offender.* New York: Plenum, 1979.

GURAK, DOUGLAS T., and JOSEPH P. FITZPATRICK. "Intermarriage among Hispanic Ethnic Groups in New York City." *American Journal of Sociology.* Vol. 87, No. 4 (January 1982):921–34.

GURNETT, KATE. "On the Forefront of Feminism." *Albany Times Union* (July 5, 1998):G-1, G-6.

GWYNNE, S. C., and JOHN F. DICKERSON. "Lost in the E-Mail." *Time.* Vol. 149, No. 15 (April 21, 1997):88–90.

HABERMAS, JÜRGEN. *Toward a Rational Society: Student Protest, Science, and Politics.* Jeremy J. Shapiro, trans. Boston: Beacon Press, 1970.

HACKER, HELEN MAYER. "Women as a Minority Group." *Social Forces.* Vol. 30 (October 1951):60–69.

———. "Women as a Minority Group: 20 Years Later." In Florence Denmark, ed., *Who Discriminates against Women?* Beverly Hills, Calif.: Sage, 1974:124–34.

HADAWAY, C. KIRK, PENNY LONG MARLER, and MARK CHAVES. "What the Polls Don't Show: A Closer Look at U.S. Church Attendance." *American Sociological Review.* Vol. 58, No. 6 (December 1993):741–52.

HADDEN, JEFFREY K., and CHARLES E. SWAIN. *Prime Time Preachers: The Rising Power of Televangelism.* Reading, Mass.: Addison-Wesley, 1981.

HAFNER, KATIE. "Making Sense of the Internet." *Newsweek* (October 24, 1994):46–48.

HAGAN, JACQUELINE MARIA. "Social Networks, Gender, and Immigrant Incorporation: Resources and Restraints." *American Sociological Review.* Vol. 63, No. 1 (February 1998):55–67.

HAGAN, JOHN, and PATRICIA PARKER. "White-Collar Crime and Punishment: The Class Structure and Legal Sanctioning of Securities Violations." *American Sociological Review.* Vol. 50, No. 3 (June 1985):302–16.

HALBERSTAM, DAVID. *The Reckoning.* New York: Avon Books, 1986.

HALEDJIAN, DEAN. "How to Tell a Businessman from a Businesswoman." Annandale, Va.: Northern Virginia Community College, 1997.

HALL, JOHN R., and MARY JO NEITZ. *Culture: Sociological Perspectives.* Englewood Cliffs, N.J.: Prentice Hall, 1993.

HALL, KELLEY J., and BETSY LUCAL. "Tapping in Parallel Universes: Using Superhero Comic Books in Sociology Courses." *Teaching Sociology.* Vol. 27, No. 1 (January 1999):60–66.

HALLINAN, MAUREEN T., and RICHARD A. WILLIAMS. "Interracial Friendship Choices in Secondary Schools." *American Sociological Review.* Vol. 54, No. 1 (February 1989):67–78.

HAMEL, RUTH. "Raging against Aging." *American Demographics.* Vol. 12, No. 3 (March 1990):42–45.

HAMER, DEAN, and PETER COPELAND. *The Science of Desire: The Search for the Gay Gene and the Biology of Behavior.* New York: Simon & Schuster, 1994.

HAMILTON, ANITA. "Speeders, Say Cheese." *Time.* Vol. 158, No. 11 (September 17, 2001):32.

HAMILTON, RICHARD F. "*The Communist Manifesto* at 150." *Society.* Vol. 38, No. 2 (January/February 2001):75–80.

HAMRICK, MICHAEL H., DAVID J. ANSPAUGH, and GENE EZELL. *Health.* Columbus, Ohio: Merrill, 1986.

HANDLIN, OSCAR. *Boston's Immigrants 1790–1865: A Study in Acculturation.* Cambridge, Mass.: Harvard University Press, 1941.

HANEY, CRAIG, CURTIS BANKS, and PHILIP ZIMBARDO. "Interpersonal Dynamics in a Simulated Prison." *International Journal of Criminology and Penology.* Vol. 1 (1973):69–97.

HANEY, LYNNE. "After the Fall: East European Women since the Collapse of State Socialism." *Contexts.* Vol. 1, No. 3 (Fall 2002):27–36.

HARBERT, ANITA A., and LEON H. GINSBERG. *Human Services for Older Adults.* Columbia: University of South Carolina Press, 1991.

HARLOW, HARRY F., and MARGARET KUENNE HARLOW. "Social Deprivation in Monkeys." *Scientific American.* Vol. 207 (November 1962):137–46.

HARPSTER, PAULA, and ELIZABETH MONK-TURNER. "Why Men Do Housework: A Test of Gender Production and the Relative Resources Model." *Sociological Focus.* Vol. 31, No. 1 (February 1998):45–59.

HARRIES, KEITH D. *Serious Violence: Patterns of Homicide and Assault in America.* Springfield, Ill.: Charles C. Thomas, 1990.

HARRINGTON, MICHAEL. *The New American Poverty.* New York: Penguin Books, 1984.

HARRIS, CHAUNCY D., and EDWARD L. ULLMAN. "The Nature of Cities." *The Annals.* Vol. 242 (November 1945):7–17.

HARRIS, DAVID R., and JEREMIAH JOSEPH SIM. "Who Is Multiracial? Assessing the Complexity of Lived Race." Vol. 67, No. 4 (August 2002):614–27.

HARRIS, MARVIN. *Cultural Anthropology.* 1st ed., 1983; 2d ed. New York: Harper & Row, 1987.

HARVEY, DAVID. "Labor, Capital, and Class Struggle around the Built Environment." *Politics and Society.* Vol. 6 (1976):265–95.

HAUB, CARL. "Has Global Growth Reached Its Peak?" *Population Today.* Vol. 30, No. 6 (August–September 2002a):6.

———. "How Many People Have Ever Lived on Earth?" *Population Today.* Vol. 30, No. 8 (November–December 2002b):3–4.

HAWTHORNE, PETER. "South Africa's Makeover." *Time.* Vol. 154, No. 2 (July 12, 1999).

HAYWARD, MARK D., EILEEN M. CRIMMINS, TONI P. MILES, and YU YANG. "The Significance of Socioeconomic Status in Explaining the Racial Gap in Chronic Health Conditions." *American Sociological Review.* Vol. 65, No. 6 (December 2000):910–30.

HEATH, JULIA A., and W. DAVID BOURNE. "Husbands and Housework: Parity or Parody?" *Social Science Quarterly.* Vol. 76, No. 1 (March 1995):195–202.

HELGESEN, SALLY. *The Female Advantage: Women's Ways of Leadership.* New York: Doubleday, 1990.

HELIN, DAVID W. "When Slogans Go Wrong." *American Demographics.* Vol. 14, No. 2 (February 1992):14.

HENLEY, NANCY, MYKOL HAMILTON, and BARRIE THORNE. "Womanspeak and Manspeak: Sex Differences in Communication, Verbal and Nonverbal." In John J. Macionis and Nijole V. Benokraitis, eds., *Seeing Ourselves: Classic, Contemporary, and Cross-Cultural Readings in Sociology.* 2d ed. Englewood Cliffs, N.J.: Prentice Hall, 1992:10–15.

HENRY, WILLIAM A., III. "Gay Parents: Under Fire and on the Rise." *Time.* Vol. 142, No. 12 (September 20, 1993):66–71.

HENSHAW, STANLEY K. "U.S. Teenage Pregnancy Statistics." New York: Alan Guttmacher Institute (March 5, 2001). [Online] Available August 14, 2002, at http://www.agi-usa.org/pubs/teen_preg.pdf

HERDT, GILBERT H. "Semen Transactions in Sambian Culture." In David N. Suggs and Andrew H. Miracle, eds., *Culture and Human Sexuality.* Pacific Grove, Calif.: Brooks Cole, 1993:298–327.

HEREK, GREGORY M. "Myths about Sexual Orientation: A Lawyer's Guide to Social Science Research." *Law and Sexuality.* No. 1 (1991):133–72.

HERMAN, DIANNE. "The Rape Culture." In John J. Macionis and Nijole V. Benokraitis, eds., *Seeing Ourselves: Classic, Contemporary, and Cross-Cultural Readings in Sociology.* 5th ed. Upper Saddle River, N.J.: Prentice Hall, 2001.

HERPERTZ, SABINE C. Study reported in Alan Mozes, "Psychopathic Criminals Lack Fear Factor, Emotion." Yahoo! News. [Online] Available October 12, 2001, at http://dailynews.yahoo.com

HERRNSTEIN, RICHARD J., and CHARLES MURRAY. *The Bell Curve: Intelligence and Class Structure in American Life.* New York: Free Press, 1994.

HERRSTROM, STAFFAN. "Sweden: Pro-Choice on Child Care." *New Perspectives Quarterly.* Vol. 7, No. 1 (Winter 1990):27–28.

HERSCH, JONI, and SHELLY WHITE-MEANS. "Employer-Sponsored Health and Pension Benefits and the Gender/Race Wage Gap." *Social Science Quarterly.* Vol. 74, No. 4 (December 1993):850–66.

HESS, BETH B. "Breaking and Entering the Establishment: Committing Social Change and Confronting the Backlash." *Social Problems.* Vol. 46, No. 1 (February 1999):1–12.

HEWLETT, BARRY S. "Husband-Wife Reciprocity and the Father-Infant Relationship among Aka Pygmies." In Barry S. Hewlett, ed., *Father-Child Relations: Cultural and Bio-Social Contexts.* New York: Aldine, 1992:153–76.

HEYMANN, PHILIP B. "Civil Liberties and Human Rights in the Aftermath of September 11." *Harvard Journal of Law and Public Policy.* Vol. 25, No. 2 (Spring 2002):441–77.

HILL, MARK E. "Race of the Interviewer and Perception of Skin Color: Evidence from the Multi-City Study of Urban Inequality." *American Sociological Review.* Vol. 67, No. 1 (February 2002):99–108.

HIMES, CHRISTINE L. "Elderly Americans." *Population Bulletin.* Vol. 56, No. 4 (December 2001). Washington, D.C.: Population Reference Bureau.

HIROSHI, MANNARI. *The Japanese Business Leaders.* Tokyo: University of Tokyo Press, 1974.

HIRSCHI, TRAVIS. *Causes of Delinquency.* Berkeley: University of California Press, 1969.

HOBSON, KATHERINE. "Kissing Cousins." *U.S. News & World Report* (April 15, 2002):77.

HOCHSCHILD, ARLIE. "Emotion Work, Feeling Rules, and Social Structure." *American Journal of Sociology.* Vol. 85, No. 3 (November 1979):551–75.

———. *The Managed Heart.* Berkeley and Los Angeles: University of California Press, 1983.

HOCHSCHILD, ARLIE, and ANNE MACHUNG. *The Second Shift: Working Parents and the Revolution at Home.* New York: Viking Books, 1989.

HOFFERTH, SANDRA. "Did Welfare Reform Work? Implications for 2002 and Beyond." *Contexts.* Vol. 1, No. 1 (Spring 2002):45–51.

HOLLANDER, PAUL. "We Are All (Sniffle, Sniffle) Victims Now." *Wall Street Journal* (January 18, 1995):A14.

HOLMES, STEVEN A. "U.S. Reports Drop in Rate of Births to Unwed Women." *New York Times* (October 5, 1996a):1, 9.

———. "For Hispanic Poor, No Silver Lining." *New York Times* (October 13, 1996b): section 4, p. 5.

HOLMES, THOMAS H., and RICHARD H. RAHE. "The Social Readjustment Rating Scale." *Journal of Psychosomatic Research.* Vol. 11 (1967):213–18.

HOLMSTROM, DAVID. "Abuse of Elderly, Even by Adult Children, Gets More Attention and Official Concern." *Christian Science Monitor* (July 28, 1994):1.

HONEYWELL, ROY J. *The Educational Work of Thomas Jefferson.* Cambridge, Mass.: Harvard University Press, 1931.

HORATIO ALGER ASSOCIATION and PETER D. HART RESEARCH ASSOCIATES. *2001 State of Our Nation's Youth* (Update). Alexandria, Va.: Horatio Alger Association, 2001. [Online] Available June 26, 2003, at http://www.horatioalger.org

HORN, WADE F., and DOUGLAS TYNAN. "Revamping Special Education." *Public Interest.* Vol. 144 (Summer 2001):36–53.

HOROWITZ, IRVING LOUIS. *The Decomposition of Sociology.* New York: Oxford University Press, 1993.

HORTON, HAYWARD DERRICK. "Critical Demography: The Paradigm of the Future?" *Sociological Forum.* Vol. 14, No. 3 (September 1999):363–67.

HORTON, HAYWARD DERRICK, BEVERLY LUNDY ALLEN, CEDRIC HERRING, and MELVIN E. THOMAS. "Lost in the Storm: The Sociology of the Black Working Class, 1850 to 1990." *American Sociological Review.* Vol. 65, No. 1 (February 2000):128–37.

HOSTETLER, JOHN A. *Amish Society.* 3d ed. Baltimore: Johns Hopkins University Press, 1980.

HOUT, MICHAEL. "More Universalism, Less Structural Mobility: The American Occupational Structure in the 1980s." *American Journal of Sociology.* Vol. 95, No. 6 (May 1998):1358–400.

HOUT, MICHAEL, and ANDREW M. GREELEY. "What Church Officials' Reports Don't Show: Another Look at Church Attendance Data." *American Sociological Review.* Vol. 63, No. 1 (February 1998):113–19.

HOUT, MICHAEL, ANDREW GREELEY, and MELISSA J. WILDE. "The Demographic Imperative in Religious Change in the United States." *American Journal of Sociology.* Vol. 107, No. 2 (September 2001):468–500.

HOUT, MIKE, CLEM BROOKS, and JEFF MANZA. "The Persistence of Classes in Post-Industrial Societies." *International Sociology.* Vol. 8, No. 3 (September 1993):259–77.

HOYT, HOMER. *The Structure and Growth of Residential Neighborhoods in American Cities.* Washington, D.C.: Federal Housing Administration, 1939.

HSU, FRANCIS L. K. *The Challenge of the American Dream: The Chinese in the United States.* Belmont, Calif.: Wadsworth, 1971.

HUD. "The Forgotten Americans: Homelessness—Programs and the People They Serve." December 1999. [Online] Available October 21, 2002, at http://www.huduser.org/publications/homeless/homelessness/contents.html

HUET-COX, ROCIO. "Medical Education: New Wine in Old Wine Skins." In Victor W. Sidel and Ruth Sidel, eds., *Reforming Medicine: Lessons of the Last Quarter Century.* New York: Pantheon Books, 1984:129–49.

HUFFMAN, KAREN. *Psychology in Action.* New York: Wiley, 2000.

HUFFMAN, MATT L., STEVEN C. VELASCO, and WILLIAM T. BIELBY. "Where Sex Composition Matters Most: Comparing the Effects of Job versus Occupational Sex Composition of Earnings." *Sociological Focus*. Vol. 29, No. 3 (August 1996):189–207.

HULS, GLENNA. Personal communication, 1987.

HUMAN RIGHTS WATCH. "Children's Rights: Child Labor" (2003). [Online] Available December 30, 2003, at http://www.hrw.org/children/labor.htm

HUMPHREY, DEREK. *Final Exit: The Practicalities of Self-Deliverance and Assisted Suicide for the Dying*. Eugene, Ore.: The Hemlock Society, 1991.

HUNNICUT, BENJAMIN K. "Are We All Working Too Hard? No Time for God or Family." *Wall Street Journal* (January 4, 1990).

HUNTER, JAMES DAVISON. *American Evangelicalism: Conservative Religion and the Quandary of Modernity*. New Brunswick, N.J.: Rutgers University Press, 1983.

———. "Conservative Protestantism." In Philip E. Hammond, ed., *The Sacred in a Secular Age*. Berkeley: University of California Press, 1985:50–66.

———. *Evangelicalism: The Coming Generation*. Chicago: University of Chicago Press, 1987.

HYMOWITZ, CAROL. "World's Poorest Women Advance by Entrepreneurship." *Wall Street Journal* (September 9, 1995):B1.

HYMOWITZ, KAY S. "Kids Today Are Growing Up Way Too Fast." *Wall Street Journal* (October 28, 1998):A22.

IANNACCONE, LAURENCE R. "Why Strict Churches Are Strong." *American Journal of Sociology*. Vol. 99, No. 5 (March 1994):1180–211.

ICELAND, JOHN, and JOSH KIM. "Poverty among Working Families: New Insights from an Improved Poverty Measure." *Social Science Quarterly*. Vol. 82, No. 2 (June 2001):253–67.

IDE, THOMAS R., and ARTHUR J. CORDELL. "Automating Work." *Society*. Vol. 31, No. 6 (September–October 1994):65–71.

ILLICH, IVAN. *Medical Nemesis: The Expropriation of Health*. New York: Pantheon Books, 1976.

INCIARDI, JAMES A. *Elements of Criminal Justice*. 2d ed. New York: Oxford University Press, 2000.

INCIARDI, JAMES A., HILARY L. SURRATT, and PAULO R. TELLES, *Sex, Drugs, and HIV/AIDS in Brazil*. Boulder, Colo.: Westview Press, 2000.

INGLEHART, RONALD. *Modernization and Postmodernization: Cultural, Economic, and Political Change in 43 Societies*. Princeton, N.J.: Princeton University Press, 1997.

INGLEHART, RONALD, et al. *World Values Surveys and European Values Surveys, 1981–1984, 1990–1993, and 1995–1997*. [Computer file] ICPSR version. Ann Arbor, Mich.: Interuniversity Consortium for Political and Social Research, 2000.

INGLEHART, RONALD, and WAYNE E. BAKER. "Modernization, Cultural Change, and the Persistence of Traditional Values." *American Sociological Review*. Vol. 65, No. 1 (February 2000):19–51.

INTERNATIONAL MONETARY FUND. *World Economic Outlook* (April 2000). [Online] Available http://www.imf.org/external/pubs/ft/weo/2000/01/index.htm

INTERNATIONAL TELECOMMUNICATION UNION. *World Telecommunication Development Report 2001*. Data cited in The World Bank, *World Development Indicators 2002*. Washington, D.C.: The World Bank, 2002.

INTER-PARLIAMENTARY UNION. "Women in National Parliaments." [Online] Available June 30, 2003, at http://www.ipu.org/wmn-e/classif.htm and http://www.ipu.org/wmn-e/world.htm

ISAY, RICHARD A. *Being Homosexual: Gay Men and Their Development*. New York: Farrar, Straus, & Giroux, 1989.

ISRAELY, JEFF. "Something in the Air." *Time*. Vol. 160, No. 24 (December 9, 2002):16.

JACOBS, DAVID, and JASON T. CARMICHAEL. "The Political Sociology of the Death Penalty: A Pooled Time-Series Analysis." *American Sociological Review*. Vol. 67, No. 1 (February 2002):109–31.

JACOBS, DAVID, and RONALD E. HELMS. "Toward a Political Model of Incarceration: A Time-Series Examination of Multiple Explanations for Prison Admission Rates." *American Journal of Sociology*. Vol. 102, No. 2 (September 1996):323–57.

JACOBS, JAMES B. "Should Hate Be a Crime?" *Public Interest*. No. 113 (Fall 1993):3–14.

JACOBY, RUSSELL, and NAOMI GLAUBERMAN, eds. *The Bell Curve Debate*. New York: Random House, 1995.

JACQUET, CONSTANT H., and ALICE M. JONES. *Yearbook of American and Canadian Churches 1991*. Nashville, Tenn.: Abingdon Press, 1991.

JAGAROWSKY, PAUL A., and MARY JO BANE. *Neighborhood Poverty: Basic Questions*. Discussion paper series H-90-3. John F. Kennedy School of Government. Cambridge, Mass.: Harvard University Press, 1990.

JAGGER, ALISON. "Political Philosophies of Women's Liberation." In Laurel Richardson and Verta Taylor, eds., *Feminist Frontiers: Rethinking Sex, Gender, and Society*. Reading, Mass.: Addison-Wesley, 1983.

JAMES, DAVID R. "City Limits on Racial Equality: The Effects of City-Suburb Boundaries on Public-School Desegregation, 1968–1976." *American Sociological Review*. Vol. 54, No. 6 (December 1989):963–85.

JANIS, IRVING. *Victims of Groupthink*. Boston: Houghton Mifflin, 1972.

———. *Crucial Decisions: Leadership in Policymaking and Crisis Management*. New York: Free Press, 1989.

JANUS, CHRISTOPHER G. "Slavery Abolished? Only Officially." *Christian Science Monitor* (May 17, 1996):18.

JARRETT, ROBIN L. "Living Poor: Family Life among Single Parent, African-American Women." *Social Problems*. Vol. 41, No. 1 (February 1994):30–49.

JASPER, JAMES M. "The Emotions of Protest: Affective and Reactive Emotions in and around Social Movements." *Sociological Forum*. Vol. 13, No. 3 (September 1998):397–424.

JEFFERSON, THOMAS. Letter to James Madison, October 28, 1785. In Julian P. Boyd, ed., *The Papers of Thomas Jefferson*. Princeton, N.J.: Princeton University Press, 1953:681–83; orig. 1785.

JENCKS, CHRISTOPHER. "Genes and Crime." *New York Review* (February 12, 1987):33–41.

JENKINS, J. CRAIG, and CHARLES PERROW. "Insurgency of the Powerless: Farm Worker Movements (1946–1972)." *American Sociological Review*. Vol. 42, No. 2 (April 1977):249–68.

JENKINS, J. CRAIG, and MICHAEL WALLACE. "The Generalized Action Potential of Protest Movements: The New Class, Social Trends, and Political Exclusion Explanations." *Sociological Forum*. Vol. 11, No. 2 (June 1996):183–207.

JENNESS, VALERIE, and RYKEN GRATTET. *Making a Hate Crime: From Movement to Law Enforcement*. New York: Russell Sage Foundation, 2001.

JOHNSON, CATHRYN. "Gender, Legitimate Authority, and Leader-Subordinate Conversations." *American Sociological Review*. Vol. 59, No. 1 (February 1994):122–35.

JOHNSON, DIRK. "Census Finds Many Claiming New Identity: Indian." *New York Times* (March 5, 1991):A1, A16.

JOHNSON, KENNETH M., and GLENN V. FUGUITT. "Continuity and Change in Rural Migration Patterns, 1950–1995." *Rural Sociology*. Vol.65, No. 1 (March 2000):27–49.

JOHNSON, PAUL. "The Seven Deadly Sins of Terrorism." In Benjamin Netanyahu, ed., *International Terrorism*. New Brunswick, N.J.: Transaction Books, 1981:12–22.

JOHNSON, ROLAND. [Online] Available in 1996 at http://www.personalwebs.myriad.net/Roland

JOHNSTON, DAVID CAY. "Voting, America's Not Keen On. Coffee Is Another Matter." *New York Times* (November 10, 1996): section 4, p. 2.

JOHNSTON, R. J. "Residential Area Characteristics." In D. T. Herbert and R. J. Johnston, eds., *Social Areas in Cities. Vol. 1: Spatial Processes and Form*. New York: Wiley, 1976:193–235.

JONES, ANDREW E. G., and DAVID WILSON. *The Urban Growth Machine: Critical Perspectives*. Albany: State University of New York Press, 1999.

JONES, D. GARETH. "Brain Death." *Journal of Medical Ethics*. Vol. 24, No. 4 (August 1998):237–43.

JONES, JUDY. "More Miners Will Be Offered Free X-Rays; Federal Agency Wants to Monitor Black-Lung Cases." *Louisville Courier Journal* (Thursday, May 13, 1999b):1A.

JONES, KATHARINE W. *Accent on Privilege: English Identities and Anglophilia in the U.S.* Philadelphia: Temple University Press, 2001.

JORDAN, ELLEN, and ANGELA COWAN. "Warrior Narratives in the Kindergarten Classroom: Renegotiating the Social Contract?" *Gender and Society*. Vol. 9, No. 6 (December 1995):727–43.

JOSEPHY, ALVIN M., JR. *Now That the Buffalo's Gone: A Study of Today's American Indians*. New York: Alfred A. Knopf, 1982.

JOYNSON, ROBERT B. "Fallible Judgments." *Society*. Vol. 31, No. 3 (March–April 1994):45–52.

KADLEC, DANIEL. "Everyone, Back in the (Labor) Pool." *Time*. Vol. 160, No. 5 (July 29, 2002):22–31.

KADUSHIN, CHARLES. "Friendship among the French Financial Elite." *American Sociological Review*. Vol. 60, No. 2 (April 1995):202–21.

KAIN, EDWARD L. "A Note on the Integration of AIDS into the Sociology of Human Sexuality." *Teaching Sociology*. Vol. 15, No. 4 (July 1987):320–23.

———. *The Myth of Family Decline: Understanding Families in a World of Rapid Social Change*. Lexington, Mass.: Lexington Books, 1990.

KAIN, EDWARD L., and SHANNON HART. "AIDS and the Family: A Content Analysis of Media Coverage." Presented to National Council on Family Relations, Atlanta, 1987.

KALLEBERG, ARNE, BARBARA F. RESKIN, and KEN HUDSON. "Bad Jobs in America: Standard and Nonstandard Employment Relations and Job Quality in the United States." *American Sociological Review*. Vol. 65, No 2 (April 2000):256–78.

KALLEBERG, ARNE L., and MARK E. VAN BUREN. "Is Bigger Better? Explaining the Relationship between Organization Size and Job Rewards." *American Sociological Review*. Vol. 61, No. 1 (February 1996):47–66.

KAMINER, WENDY. "Volunteers: Who Knows What's in It for Them." *Ms.* (December 1984):93–94, 96, 126–28.

———. "Demasculinizing the Army." *New York Times Review of Books* (June 15, 1997):7.

KANAZAWA, SATOSHI. "Comment: Why We Love Our Children." *American Journal of Sociology*. Vol. 106, No. 6 (May 2001):771–6.

KANE, EMILY W. "Racial and Ethnic Variations in Gender-Related Attitudes." *Annual Review of Sociology*. Vol. 26 (2000):419–39.

KANTER, ROSABETH MOSS. *Men and Women of the Corporation*. New York: Basic Books, 1977.

KANTER, ROSABETH MOSS, and BARRY A. STEIN. "The Gender Pioneers: Women in an Industrial Sales Force." In R. M. Kanter and B. A. Stein, eds., *Life in Organizations*. New York: Basic Books, 1979:134–60.

KANTROWITZ, BARBARA, and PAT WINGERT. "Unmarried with Children." *Newsweek* (May 28, 2001):46–52.

——. "What's at Stake." *Newsweek* (January 27, 2003):30–7.

KAO, GRACE. "Group Images and Possible Selves among Adolescents: Linking Stereotypes to Expectations by Race and Ethnicity." *Sociological Forum*. Vol. 15, No. 3 (September 2000):407–30.

KAPFERER, JEAN-NOEL. "How Rumors Are Born." *Society*. Vol. 29, No. 5 (July–August 1992):53–60.

KAPLAN, DAVID E., and MICHAEL SCHAFFER. "Losing the Psywar." *U.S. News & World Report* (October 8, 2001):46.

KAPLAN, ERIC B., et al. "The Usefulness of Preoperative Laboratory Screening." *Journal of the American Medical Association*. Vol. 253, No. 24 (June 28, 1985):3576–81.

KAPTCHUK, TED. "The Holistic Logic of Chinese Medicine." In Shepard Bliss et al., eds., *The New Holistic Health Handbook*. Lexington, Mass.: The Steven Greene Press/Penguin Books, 1985:41.

KARATNYCKY, ADRIAN. "The 2001–2002 Freedom House Survey of Freedom: The Democracy Gap." In *Freedom in the World: The Annual Survey of Political Rights and Civil Liberties, 2001–2002*. New York: Freedom House, 2002:7–18.

KASINITZ, PHILIP, and JAN ROSENBERG. "Missing the Connection: Social Isolation and Employment on the Brooklyn Waterfront." *Social Problems*. Vol. 43, No. 2 (May 1996):180–96.

KAUFMAN, MARC. "Becoming 'Old Old.'" *Philadelphia Inquirer* (October 28, 1990):1-A, 10-A.

KAUFMAN, MICHAEL T. "Face It: Your Looks Are Revealing." *New York Times*. 2002.

KAUFMAN, ROBERT L. "Assessing Alternative Perspectives on Race and Sex Employment Segregation." *American Sociological Review*. Vol. 67, No. 4 (August 2002):547–72.

KAUFMAN, ROBERT L., and SEYMOUR SPILERMAN. "The Age Structures of Occupations and Jobs." *American Journal of Sociology*. Vol. 87, No. 4 (January 1982):827–51.

KAUFMAN, WALTER. *Religions in Four Dimensions: Existential, Aesthetic, Historical and Comparative*. New York: Reader's Digest Press, 1976.

KAY, PAUL, and WILLETT KEMPTON. "What Is the Sapir-Whorf Hypothesis?" *American Anthropologist*. Vol. 86, No. 1 (March 1984):65–79.

KEISTER, LISA. *Wealth in America: Trends in Wealth Inequality*. Cambridge, UK: Cambridge University Press, 2000.

——. "Religion and Wealth: The Role of Religious Affiliation and Participation in Early Adult Asset Accumulation." *Social Forces* (September 2003).

KEISTER, LISA A., and STEPHANIE MOLLER. "Wealth Inequality in the United States." *Annual Review of Sociology*. Vol. 26 (2000):63–81.

KEITH, PAT M., and ROBERT B. SCHAFER. "They Hate to Cook: Patterns of Distress in an Ordinary Role." *Sociological Focus*. Vol. 27, No. 4 (October 1994):289–301.

KELLER, HELEN. *The Story of My Life*. New York: Doubleday, Page, 1903.

KELLERT, STEPHEN R., and F. HERBERT BORMANN. "Closing the Circle: Weaving Strands among Ecology, Economics, and Ethics." In F. Herbert Bormann and Stephen R. Kellert, eds., *Ecology, Economics, and Ethics: The Broken Circle*. New Haven, Conn.: Yale University Press, 1991:205–10.

KELLEY, JONATHAN, and M. D. R. EVANS. "Class and Class Conflict in Six Western Nations." *American Sociological Review*. Vol. 60, No. 2 (April 1995):157–78.

KENNICKELL, ARTHUR B., MARTHA STARR-MCCLUER, and BRIAN J. SURETTE. "Recent Changes in U.S. Family Finances: Results from the 1998 Survey of Consumer Finances." [Online] Available April 7, 2000, at http://www.federalreserve.gov/pubs/bulletin/2000/0100lead.pdf

KENT, MARY M., and MARK MATHER. "What Drives U.S. Population Growth?" *Population Bulletin*. Vol. 57, No. 4 (December 2002):3–40.

KENTOR, JEFFREY. "The Long-Term Effects of Foreign Investment Dependence on Economic Growth, 1940–1990." *American Journal of Sociology*. Vol. 103, No. 4 (January 1998):1024–46.

——. "The Long-Term Effects of Globalization on Income Inequality, Population Growth, and Economic Development." *Social Problems*. Vol. 48, No. 4 (November 2001):435–55.

KERCKHOFF, ALAN C., RICHARD T. CAMPBELL, and IDEE WINFIELD-LAIRD. "Social Mobility in Great Britain and the United States." *American Journal of Sociology*. Vol. 91, No. 2 (September 1985):281–308.

KEYS, JENNIFER. "Feeling Rules That Script the Abortion Experience." Paper presented at the annual meeting of the American Sociological Association, Chicago, August 2002.

KIDD, QUENTIN, and AIE-RIE LEE. "Postmaterialist Values and the Environment: A Critique and Reappraisal." *Social Science Quarterly*. Vol. 78, No. 1 (March 1997):1–15.

KIDRON, MICHAEL, and RONALD SEGAL. *The New State of the World Atlas*. New York: Simon & Schuster, 1991.

KILBOURNE, BROCK K. "The Conway and Siegelman Claims against Religious Cults: An Assessment of Their Data." *Journal for the Scientific Study of Religion*. Vol. 22, No. 4 (December 1983):380–85.

KILGORE, SALLY B. "The Organizational Context of Tracking in Schools." *American Sociological Review*. Vol. 56, No. 2 (April 1991):189–203.

KILLIAN, LEWIS M. "Organization, Rationality and Spontaneity in the Civil Rights Movement." *American Sociological Review*. Vol. 49, No. 6 (December 1984):770–83.

KING, KATHLEEN PIKER, and DENNIS E. CLAYSON. "The Differential Perceptions of Male and Female Deviants." *Sociological Focus*. Vol. 21, No. 2 (April 1988):153–64.

KINKEAD, GWEN. *Chinatown: A Portrait of a Closed Society*. New York: HarperCollins, 1992.

KINSEY, ALFRED, et al. *Sexual Behavior in the Human Male*. Philadelphia: Saunders, 1948.

——. *Sexual Behavior in the Human Female*. Philadelphia: Saunders, 1953.

KISER, EDGAR, and JOACHIM SCHNEIDER. "Bureaucracy and Efficiency: An Analysis of Taxation in Early Modern Prussia." *American Sociological Review*. Vol. 59, No. 2 (April 1994):187–204.

KITTRIE, NICHOLAS N. *The Right to Be Different: Deviance and Enforced Therapy*. Baltimore: Johns Hopkins University Press, 1971.

KLEINER, CAROLYN. "What's So Funny?" *U.S. News & World Report*. Vol. 132, No. 9 (March 25, 2002):38–39.

KLEINFELD, JUDITH. "Student Performance: Males versus Females." *Public Interest*. No. 134 (Winter 1999):3–20.

——. Research reported in Ben Wildavsky, "Small World, Isn't It?" *U.S. News & World Report*. Vol. 132, No. 10 (April 1, 2002):68.

KLUCKHOHN, CLYDE. "As an Anthropologist Views It." In Albert Deuth, ed., *Sex Habits of American Men*. New York: Prentice Hall, 1948.

KOELLN, KENNETH, ROSE M. RUBIN, and MARION SMITH PICARD. "Vulnerable Elderly Households: Expenditures on Necessities by Older Americans." *Social Science Quarterly*. Vol. 76, No. 3 (September 1995):619–33.

KOHLBERG, LAWRENCE. *The Psychology of Moral Development: The Nature and Validity of Moral Stages*. New York: Harper & Row, 1981.

KOHLBERG, LAWRENCE, and CAROL GILLIGAN. "The Adolescent as Philosopher: The Discovery of Self in a Postconventional World." *Daedalus*. Vol. 100 (Fall 1971):1051–86.

KOHN, MELVIN L. *Class and Conformity: A Study in Values*. 2d ed. Homewood, Ill.: Dorsey Press, 1977.

——. "The 'Bell Curve' from the Perspective of Research on Social Structure and Personality." *Sociological Forum*. Vol. 11, No. 2 (1996):395.

KONO, CLIFFORD, DONALD PALMER, ROGER FRIEDLAND, and MATTHEW ZAFONTE. "Lost in Space: The Geography of Corporate Interlocking Directorates." *American Journal of Sociology*. Vol. 103, No. 4 (January 1998):863–911.

KOONTZ, STEPHANIE. *The Way We Never Were: American Families and the Nostalgia Trap*. New York: Basic Books, 1992.

KORNHAUSER, WILLIAM. *The Politics of Mass Society*. New York: Free Press, 1959.

KORPI, WALTER, and JOAKIM PALME. "The Paradox of Redistribution and Strategies of Equality: Welfare State Institutions, Inequality, and Poverty in the Western Countries." *American Sociological Review*. Vol. 65, No. 5 (October 1998):661–87.

KORZENIEWICZ, ROBERTO P., and KIMBERLY AWBREY. "Democratic Transitions and the Semiperiphery of the World Economy." *Sociological Forum*. Vol. 7, No. 4 (December 1992):609–40.

KOSTERS, MARVIN. "Looking for Jobs in All the Wrong Places." *The Public Interest*. Vol. 125 (Fall 1996):125–31.

KOWALEWSKI, DAVID, and KAREN L. PORTER. "Ecoprotest: Alienation, Deprivation, or Resources?" *Social Sciences Quarterly*. Vol. 73, No. 3 (September 1992):523–34.

KOZOL, JONATHAN. *Rachel and Her Children: Homeless Families in America*. New York: Crown Publishers, 1988.

——. *Savage Inequalities: Children in America's Schools*. New York: Harper Perennial, 1992.

KRAFFT, SUSAN. "¿Quién es Numero Uno?" *American Demographics*. Vol. 15, No. 7 (July 1993):16–17.

KRANTZ, MICHAEL. "Say It with a :-)." *Time*. Vol. 149, No. 15 (1997):29.

KRAYBILL, DONALD B. *The Riddle of Amish Culture*. Baltimore: Johns Hopkins University Press, 1989.

——. "The Amish Encounter with Modernity." In Donald B. Kraybill and Marc A. Olshan, eds., *The Amish Struggle with Modernity*. Hanover, N.H.: University Press of New England, 1994:21–33.

KRAYBILL, DONALD B., and MARC A. OLSHAN, eds. *The Amish Struggle with Modernity*. Hanover, N.H.: University Press of New England, 1994.

KRIESI, HANSPETER. "New Social Movements and the New Class in the Netherlands." *American Journal of Sociology*. Vol. 94, No. 5 (March 1989):1078–116.

KRIVO, LAUREN J., RUTH D. PETERSON, HELEN RIZZO, and JOHN R. REYNOLDS. "Race, Segregation, and the Concentration of Disadvantage: 1980–1990." *Social Problems*. Vol. 45, No. 1 (February 1998):61–80.

KRUGMAN, PAUL. "For Richer: How the Permissive Capitalism of the Boom Destroyed American Equality." *New York Times Magazine* (September 20, 2002):62–7, 76–7, 141–2.

KRUKS, GABRIEL N. "Gay and Lesbian Homeless/Street Youth: Special Issues and Concerns." *Journal of Adolescent Health*. Special Issue. No. 12 (1991):515–18.

KRYSAN, MARIA. "Community Undesirability in Black and White: Examining Racial Residential Preferences through Community Perceptions." *Social Problems*. Vol. 49, No. 4 (November 2002):521–43.

KÜBLER-ROSS, ELISABETH. *On Death and Dying*. New York: Macmillan, 1969.

KUUMBA, M. BAHATI. "A Cross-Cultural Race/Class/Gender Critique of Contemporary Population Policy: The Impact of Globalization." *Sociological Forum*. Vol. 14, No. 3 (March 1999):447–63.

KUZNETS, SIMON. "Economic Growth and Income Inequality." *American Economic Review*. Vol. 14, No. 1 (March 1955):1–28.

———. *Modern Economic Growth: Rate, Structure, and Spread*. New Haven, Conn.: Yale University Press, 1966.

LACAYO, RICHARD. "The Brawl over Sprawl." *Time*. Vol. 153, No. 11 (March 22, 1999):44–48.

———. "Blood at the Root." *Time*. Vol. 155, No. 14 (April 10, 2000):122–3.

LACH, JENNIFER. "The Color of Money." *American Demographics*. Vol. 21, No. 2 (February 1999):59–60.

LADD, JOHN. "The Definition of Death and the Right to Die." In John Ladd, ed., *Ethical Issues Relating to Life and Death*. New York: Oxford University Press, 1979:118–45.

LAI, H. M. "Chinese." In *Harvard Encyclopedia of American Ethnic Groups*. Cambridge, Mass.: Harvard University Press, 1980:217–33.

LAMBERG-KARLOVSKY, C. C., and MARTHA LAMBERG-KARLOVSKY. "An Early City in Iran." In *Cities: Their Origin, Growth, and Human Impact*. San Francisco: Freeman, 1973:28–37.

LANDSBERG, MITCHELL. "Health Disaster Brings Early Death in Russia." *Washington Times* (March 15, 1998):A8.

LANE, DAVID. "Social Stratification and Class." In Erik P. Hoffman and Robbin F. Laird, eds., *The Soviet Polity in the Modern Era*. New York: Aldine, 1984:563–605.

LANG, KURT, and GLADYS ENGEL LANG. *Collective Dynamics*. New York: Thomas Y. Crowell, 1961.

LANGBEIN, LAURA I. "Politics, Rules, and Death Row: Why States Eschew or Execute Executions." *Social Science Quarterly*. Vol. 80, No. 4 (December 1999):629–47.

LANGBEIN, LAURA, and ROSEANA BESS. "Sports in School: Source of Amity or Antipathy?" *Social Science Quarterly*. Vol. 83, No. 2 (June 2002):436–54.

LAPPÉ, FRANCES MOORE, JOSEPH COLLINS, and DAVID KINLEY. *Aid as Obstacle: Twenty Questions about Our Foreign Policy and the Hungry*. San Francisco: Institute for Food and Development Policy, 1981.

LAPPÉ, FRANCES MOORE, JOSEPH COLLINS, and PETER ROSSET. *World Hunger: Twelve Myths*. New York: Grove Press, 1998.

LAREAU, ANNETTE. "Invisible Inequality: Social Class and Childrearing in Black Families and White Families." *American Sociological Review*. Vol. 67, No. 5 (October 2002):747–76.

LaROSSA, RALPH, and DONALD C. REITZES. "Two? Two and One-Half? Thirty Months? Chronometrical Childhood in Early Twentieth-Century America." *Sociological Forum*. Vol. 166, No. 3 (September 2001):385–407.

LARSON, GERALD JAMES. "Hinduism in India and in America." In Jacob Neusner, ed., *World Religions in America: An Introduction*. Louisville, Ky.: Westminster John Knox Press, 2000:124–41.

LASLETT, BARBARA. "Family Membership, Past and Present." *Social Problems*. Vol. 25, No. 5 (June 1978):476–90.

LASLETT, PETER. *The World We Have Lost: England before the Industrial Age*. 3d ed. New York: Charles Scribner's Sons, 1984.

LASSWELL, MARK. "A Tribe at War: Not the Yanomami: The Anthropologists." *Wall Street Journal* (November 17, 2000):A17.

LAUMANN, EDWARD O., JOHN H. GAGNON, ROBERT T. MICHAEL, and STUART MICHAELS. *The Social Organization of Sexuality: Sexual Practices in the United States*. Chicago: University of Chicago Press, 1994.

LAVELLA, MARIANNA. "Payback Time." *U.S. News & World Report*. Vol. 132, No. 7 (March 11, 2002):36–40.

LAVELLE, MARIANNE. "Rogue of the Year." *U.S. News & World Report*. Vol. 133, No. 25 (December 30, 2002–January 6, 2003):32–45.

LAVIN, DANIELLE, and DOUGLAS W. MAYNARD. "Standardization vs. Rapport: Respondent Laughter and Interviewer Reaction during Telephone Surveys." *American Sociological Review*. Vol. 66, No. 3 (June 2001):453–79.

LEACH, COLIN WAYNE. "Democracy's Dilemma: Explaining Racial Inequality in Egalitarian Societies." *Sociological Forum*. Vol. 17, No. 4 (December 2002):681–96.

LEACOCK, ELEANOR. "Women's Status in Egalitarian Societies: Implications for Social Evolution." *Current Anthropology*. Vol. 19, No. 2 (June 1978):247–75.

LEAVITT, JUDITH WALZER. "Women and Health in America: An Overview." In Judith Walzer Leavitt, ed., *Women and Health in America*. Madison: University of Wisconsin Press, 1984:3–7.

LEE, FELICIA R. "Long Buried, Death Goes Public Again." *New York Times*. [Online] Available November 2, 2002, at www.researchnavigator.com

LEE, SHARON M. "Poverty and the U.S. Asian Population." *Social Science Quarterly*. Vol. 75, No. 3 (September 1994):541–59.

LEFEBVRE, HENRI. *The Production of Space*. Oxford, U.K.: Blackwell, 1991.

LELAND, JOHN. "Bisexuality." *Newsweek* (July 17, 1995):44–49.

LEMERT, EDWIN M. *Social Pathology*. New York: McGraw-Hill, 1951.

———. *Human Deviance, Social Problems, and Social Control*. 2d ed. Englewood Cliffs, N.J.: Prentice Hall, 1972.

LENGERMANN, PATRICIA MADOO, and RUTH A. WALLACE. *Gender in America: Social Control and Social Change*. Englewood Cliffs, N.J.: Prentice Hall, 1985.

LENNON, MARY CLARE, and SARAH ROSENFELD. "Relative Fairness and the Doctrine of Housework: The Importance of Options." *American Journal of Sociology*. Vol. 100, No. 2 (September 1994):506–31.

LENSKI, GERHARD E. *Power and Privilege: A Theory of Social Stratification*. New York: McGraw-Hill, 1966.

LENSKI, GERHARD, PATRICK NOLAN, and JEAN LENSKI. *Human Societies: An Introduction to Macrosociology*. 7th ed. New York: McGraw-Hill, 1995.

LEONARD, EILEEN B. *Women, Crime, and Society: A Critique of Theoretical Criminology*. New York: Longman, 1982.

LESLIE, GERALD R., and SHEILA K. KORMAN. *The Family in Social Context*. 7th ed. New York: Oxford University Press, 1989.

LeVAY, SIMON. *The Sexual Brain*. Cambridge, Mass.: MIT Press, 1993.

LEVER, JANET. "Sex Differences in the Complexity of Children's Play and Games." *American Sociological Review*. Vol. 43, No. 4 (August 1978):471–83.

LEVINE, MICHAEL. "Reducing Hostility Can Prevent Heart Disease." *Mount Vernon News* (August 7, 1990):4A.

LEVINE, MICHAEL P. *Student Eating Disorders: Anorexia Nervosa and Bulimia*. Washington, D.C.: National Educational Association, 1987.

LEVINE, ROBERT V. "Is Love a Luxury?" *American Demographics*. Vol. 15, No. 2 (February 1993):27–28.

LEVINE, SAMANTHA. "The Price of Child Abuse." *U.S. News & World Report*. Vol. 130, No. 14 (April 9, 2001):58.

———. "Playing God in Illinois." *U.S. News & World Report*. Vol. 134, No. 1 (January 13, 2003):13.

LEVINSON, DANIEL J., CHARLOTTE N. DARROW, EDWARD B. KLEIN, MARIA H. LEVINSON, and BRAXTON McKEE. *The Seasons of a Man's Life*. New York: Alfred A. Knopf, 1978.

LEWIS, FLORA. "The Roots of Revolution." *New York Times Magazine* (November 11, 1984):70–71, 74, 77–78, 82, 84, 86.

LEWIS, OSCAR. *The Children of Sanchez*. New York: Random House, 1961.

LEWIS, PEIRCE, CASEY McCRACKEN, and ROGER HUNT. "Politics: Who Cares?" *American Demographics*. Vol. 16, No. 10 (October 1994):20–26.

LI, JIANG HONG, and ROGER A. WOJTKIEWICZ. "A New Look at the Effects of Family Structure on Status Attainment." *Social Science Quarterly*. Vol. 73, No. 3 (September 1992):581–95.

LIAZOS, ALEXANDER. "The Poverty of the Sociology of Deviance: Nuts, Sluts and Preverts." *Social Problems*. Vol. 20, No. 1 (Summer 1972):103–20.

———. *People First: An Introduction to Social Problems*. Boston: Allyn and Bacon, 1982.

LICHTER, DANIEL T., and MARTHA L. CROWLEY. "Poverty in America: Beyond Welfare Reform." *Population Bulletin*. Vol. 57, No. 2 (June 2002):3–34.

LICHTER, S. ROBERT, and DANIEL R. AMUNDSON. "Distorted Reality: Hispanic Characters in TV Entertainment." In Clara E. Rodriguez, ed., *Latin Looks: Images of Latinas and Latinos in the U.S. Media*. Boulder, Colo.: Westview Press, 1997:57–79.

LICHTER, S. ROBERT, STANLEY ROTHMAN, and LINDA S. LICHTER. *The Media Elite: America's New Powerbrokers*. New York: Hastings House, 1990.

LIGHT, PAUL C. "Big Government Is Bigger Than You Think." *Wall Street Journal* (January 13, 1999):A22.

LIN, GE, and PETER ROGERSON. Research reported in Diane Crispell, "Sons and Daughters Who Keep in Touch." *American Demographics*. Vol. 16, No. 8 (August 1994):15–16.

LIN, NAN, and WEN XIE. "Occupational Prestige in Urban China." *American Journal of Sociology*. Vol. 93, No. 4 (January 1988):793–832.

LINDAUER, DAVID L., and AKILA WEERAPANA. "Relief for Poor Nations." *Society*. Vol. 39, No. 3 (March–April 2002):54–8.

LINDEN, EUGENE. "Can Animals Think?" *Time*. Vol. 141, No. 12 (March 22, 1993):54–61.

LINDSTROM, BONNIE. "Chicago's Post-Industrial Suburbs." *Sociological Focus*. Vol. 28, No. 4 (October 1995):399–412.

LING, PYAU. "Causes of Chinese Emigration." In Amy Tachiki et al., eds., *Roots: An Asian American Reader*. Los Angeles: UCLA Asian American Studies Center, 1971:134–38.

LINN, MICHAEL. Noted in *Cornell Alumni News*. Vol. 99, No. 2 (September 1996):25.

LINO, MARK. *Expenditures on Children by Families, 2002*. U.S. Department of Agriculture, Center for Nutrition Policy and Promotion. Miscellaneous Publication No. 1528–2002. Washington, D.C.: U.S. Government Printing Office, 2003.

LINTON, RALPH. "One Hundred Percent American." *American Mercury*. Vol. 40, No. 160 (April 1937a):427–29.

———. *The Study of Man*. New York: D. Appleton-Century, 1937b.

LIPS, HILARY. *Sex and Gender: An Introduction*. 2d ed. Mountain View, Calif.: Mayfield Publishing Co., 1993.

LIPSET, SEYMOUR MARTIN. *Political Man: The Social Bases of Politics*. Garden City, N.Y.: Anchor/Doubleday, 1963.

———. "Canada and the United States." Charles F. Donan and John H. Sigler, eds. Englewood Cliffs, N.J.: Prentice Hall, 1985.

LIPSET, SEYMOUR MARTIN, and REINHARD BENDIX. *Social Mobility in Industrial Society*. Berkeley: University of California Press, 1967.

LISKA, ALLEN E. *Perspectives on Deviance*. 3d ed. Englewood Cliffs, N.J.: Prentice Hall, 1991.

LISKA, ALLEN E., and BARBARA D. WARNER. "Functions of Crime: A Paradoxical Process." *American Journal of Sociology*. Vol. 96, No. 6 (May 1991):1441–63.

LITTLE, CRAIG, and ANDREA RANKIN. "Why Do They Start It? Explaining Reported Early-Teen Sexual Activity." *Sociological Forum*. Vol. 16, No. 4 (December 2001):703–29.

LITTMAN, DAVID L. "2001: A Farm Odyssey." *Wall Street Journal* (September 14, 1992):A10.

LIVERNASH, ROBERT, and ERIC RODENBURG. "Population Change, Resources, and the Environment." *Population Bulletin*. Vol. 53, No. 1 (March 1998).

LIVINGSTON, GRETCHEN, and JOAN R. KAHN. "An American Dream Unfulfilled: The Limited Mobility of Mexican Americans." *Social Science Quarterly*. Vol. 83, No. 4 (December 2002):1003–12.

LIVINGSTON, KEN. "Politics and Mental Illness." *Public Interest*. Vol. 143 (Winter, 1999):105–9.

LO, CLARENCE Y. H. "Countermovements and Conservative Movements in the Contemporary U.S." *Annual Review of Sociology*. Vol. 8. Palo Alto, Calif.: Annual Reviews, 1982:107–34.

LOBO, SUSAN. "Census-Taking and the Invisibility of Urban American Indians." *Population Today*. Vol. 30, No. 4 (May–June 2002):3–4.

LOFLAND, LYN. *A World of Strangers*. New York: Basic Books, 1973.

LOFTUS, JENI. "America's Liberalization in Attitudes toward Homosexuality, 1973 to 1998." *American Sociological Review*. Vol. 66, No. 5 (October 2001):762–82.

LOGAN, JOHN R., RICHARD D. ALBA, and WENQUAN ZHANG. "Immigrant Enclaves and Ethnic Communities in New York and Los Angeles." *American Sociological Review*. Vol. 67, No. 2 (April 2002):299–322.

LOGAN, JOHN R., and MARK SCHNEIDER. "Racial Segregation and Racial Change in American Suburbs, 1970–1980." *American Journal of Sociology*. Vol. 89, No. 4 (January 1984):874–88.

LOHR, STEVE. "British Health Service Faces a Crisis in Funds and Delays." *New York Times* (August 7, 1988):1, 12.

LONGINO, JR., CHARLES F. "Myths of An Aging America." *American Demographics*. Vol. 16, No. 8 (August 1994):36–42.

LORD, MARY. "Good Teachers, the Newest Imports." *U.S. News & World Report*. Vol. 130, No. 13 (April 9, 2001):54.

———. "A Battle for Children's Futures." *U.S. News & World Report*. Vol. 132, No. 6 (March 4, 2002):35–6.

LORD, WALTER. *A Night to Remember*. Rev. ed. New York: Holt, Rinehart & Winston, 1976.

LORENZ, FREDERICK O., and BRENT T. BRUTON. "Experiments in Surveys: Linking Mass Class Questionnaires to Introductory Research Methods." *Teaching Sociology*. Vol. 24, No. 3 (July 1996):264–71.

LOVEMAN, MARA. "Is 'Race' Essential?" *American Sociological Review*. Vol. 64, No. 6 (December 1999):890–98.

LOVGREN, STEFEN. "Will All the Blue Men End Up in Timbuktu?" *U.S. News & World Report* (December 7, 1998):40.

LUND, DALE A. "Conclusions about Bereavement in Later Life and Implications for Interventions and Future Research." In Dale A. Lund, ed., *Older Bereaved Spouses: Research with Practical Applications*. London: Taylor-Francis-Hemisphere, 1989:217–31.

———. "Caregiving." *Encyclopedia of Adult Development*. Phoenix, Ariz.: Oryx Press, 1993:57–63.

LUND, DALE A., MICHAEL S. CASERTA, and MARGARET F. DIMOND. "Gender Differences through Two Years of Bereavement among the Elderly." *The Gerontologist*. Vol. 26, No. 3 (1986):314–20.

LUNDMAN, RICHARD L. Correspondence to author, 1999.

LUO, JAR-DER. "The Significance of Networks in the Initiation of Small Businesses in Taiwan." *Sociological Focus*. Vol. 12, No. 2 (June 1997):297–317.

LUTZ, CATHERINE A. *Unnatural Emotions: Everyday Sentiments on a Micronesia Atoll and Their Challenge to Western Theory*. Chicago: University of Chicago Press, 1988.

LUTZ, CATHERINE A., and GEOFFREY M. WHITE. "The Anthropology of Emotions." In Bernard J. Siegel, Alan R. Beals, and Stephen A. Tyler, eds., *Annual Review of Anthropology*. Palo Alto, Calif.: Annual Reviews, Vol. 15 (1986):405–36.

LYNCH, MICHAEL, and DAVID BOGEN. "Sociology's Asociological 'Core': An Examination of Textbook Sociology in Light of the Sociology of Scientific Knowledge." *American Sociological Review*. Vol. 62, No. 3 (June 1997):481–93.

LYND, ROBERT S. *Knowledge for What? The Place of Social Science in American Culture*. Princeton, N.J.: Princeton University Press, 1967.

LYND, ROBERT S., and HELEN MERRELL LYND. *Middletown in Transition*. New York: Harcourt, Brace & World, 1937.

LYNOTT, PATRICIA PASSUTH, and BARBARA J. LOGUE. "The 'Hurried Child': The Myth of Lost Childhood on Contemporary American Society." *Sociological Forum*. Vol. 8, No. 3 (September 1993):471–91.

MA, LI-CHEN. Personal communication, 1987.

MABRY, MARCUS, and TOM MASLAND. "The Man after Mandela." *Newsweek* (June 7, 1999):54–55.

MCADAM, DOUG. *Freedom Summer*. New York: Oxford University Press, 1988.

———. "The Biographical Consequences of Activism." *American Sociological Review*. Vol. 54, No. 5 (October 1989):744–60.

———. "Gender as a Mediator of the Activist Experience: The Case of Freedom Summer." *American Journal of Sociology*. Vol. 97, No. 5 (March 1992):1211–40.

MCADAM, DOUG, JOHN D. MCCARTHY, and MAYER N. ZALD. "Social Movements." In Neil J. Smelser, ed., *Handbook of Sociology*. Newbury Park, Calif.: Sage, 1988:695–737.

MCBROOM, WILLIAM H., and FRED W. REED. "Recent Trends in Conservatism: Evidence of Non-Unitary Patterns." *Sociological Focus*. Vol. 23, No. 4 (October 1990):355–65.

MCCAFFREY, DAWN, and JENNIFER KEYS. "Competitive Framing Processes in the Abortion Debate: Polarization-Vilification, Frame Saving, and Frame Debunking." *Sociological Quarterly*. Vol. 41, No. 1 (Winter 2000):41–61.

MCCALL, LESLIE. *Complex Inequality: Gender, Class, and Race in the New Economy*. New York: Routledge, 2001a.

———. "Sources of Racial Wage Inequality in Metropolitan Labor Markets: Racial, Ethnic, and Gender Differences." *American Sociological Review*. Vol. 66, No. 4 (August 2001b):520–41.

MCCALL, WILLIAM. "Oregon Suicides More than Double." Yahoo! News. [Online] Available March 4, 2003, at http://dailynews.yahoo.com

MCCARTHY, JOHN D., and MAYER N. ZALD. "Resource Mobilization and Social Movements: A Partial Theory." *American Journal of Sociology*. Vol. 82, No. 6 (May 1977):1212–41.

MACCOBY, ELEANOR EMMONS, and CAROL NAGY JACKLIN. *The Psychology of Sex Differences*. Palo Alto, Calif.: Stanford University Press, 1974.

MCCOLM, R. BRUCE, JAMES FINN, DOUGLAS W. PAYNE, JOSEPH E. RYAN, LEONARD R. SUSSMAN, and GEORGE ZARYCKY. *Freedom in the World: Political Rights & Civil Liberties, 1990–1991*. New York: Freedom House, 1991.

MCDONALD, KIM A. "Debate over How to Gauge Global Warming Heats Up Meeting of Climatologists." *Chronicle of Higher Education*. Vol. 45, No. 22 (February 5, 1999):A17.

MCDONALD, PETER. "Low Fertility Not Politically Sustainable." *Population Today*. Vol. 29, No. 6 (August/September 2001):3, 8.

MCGEARY, JOHANNA. "Nukes . . . They're Back." *Time*. Vol. 151, No. 20 (May 25, 1998):34–42.

MCGURN, WILLIAM. "Philadelphia Dims Edison's Light." *Wall Street Journal* (March 20, 2002):A22.

MACIONIS, JOHN J. "Intimacy: Structure and Process in Interpersonal Relationships." *Alternative Lifestyles*. Vol. 1, No. 1 (February 1978):113–30.

———. "A Sociological Analysis of Humor." Presentation to the Texas Junior College Teachers Association, Houston, 1987.

MACIONIS, JOHN J., and LINDA GERBER. *Sociology: Third Canadian Edition*. Scarborough, Ontario: Prentice Hall Allyn & Bacon Canada, 2001.

———. *Sociology: Fourth Canadian Edition*. Scarborough, Ontario: Prentice Hall Allyn & Bacon Canada, 2002.

MACIONIS, JOHN J., and VINCENT R. PARRILLO. *Cities and Urban Life*. 3d ed. Upper Saddle River, N.J.: Prentice Hall, 2004.

MACKAY, JUDITH. *The Penguin Atlas of Human Sexual Behavior*. New York: Penguin Group, 2000.

MCKEE, VICTORIA. "Blue Blood and the Color of Money." *New York Times* (June 9, 1996):49–50.

MCLANAHAN, SARA. "Life without Father: What Happens to the Children?" *Contexts*. Vol. 1, No. 1 (Spring 2002):35–44.

MCLEOD, JANE D., and MICHAEL J. SHANAHAN. "Poverty, Parenting, and Children's Mental Health." *American Sociological Review*. Vol. 58, No. 3 (June 1993):351–66.

MCLEOD, JAY. *Ain't No Makin' It: Aspirations and Attainment in a Low-Income Neighborhood*. Boulder, Colo.: Westview Press, 1995.

MCLUHAN, MARSHALL. *The Gutenberg Galaxy*. New York: New American Library, 1969.

MCNEIL, DONALD G., JR. "Should Women Be Sent into Combat?" *New York Times* (July 21, 1991):E3.

MCNULTY, PAUL J. "Who's in Jail and Why They Belong There." *Wall Street Journal* (November 9, 1994):A23.

MCPHAIL, CLARK. *The Myth of the Maddening Crowd*. New York: Aldine, 1991.

MCPHAIL, CLARK, and RONALD T. WOHLSTEIN. "Individual and Collective Behaviors within Gatherings, Demonstrations, and Riots." *Annual Review of Sociology*. Vol. 9. Palo Alto, Calif.: Annual Reviews, 1983:579–600.

MACPHERSON, KAREN. "Children Have a Full-Time Media Habit, Study Says." *Toledo Blade* (November 18, 1999):3.

MADDOX, SETMA. "Organizational Culture and Leadership Style: Factors Affecting Self-Managed Work Team Performance." Paper presented at the annual meeting of the Southwest Social Science Association, Dallas, February 1994.

MADSEN, AXEL. *Private Power: Multinational Corporations for the Survival of Our Planet*. New York: William Morrow, 1980.

MAINES, DAVID R. "Charting Futures for Sociology: Culture and Meaning." *Contemporary Sociology*. Vol. 29, No. 4 (July 2000):577–84.

MALTHUS, THOMAS ROBERT. *First Essay on Population 1798*. London: Macmillan, 1926; orig. 1798.

MANZA, JEFF, and CLEM BROOKS. "The Religious Factor in U.S. Presidential Elections, 1960–1992." *American Journal of Sociology*. Vol. 103, No. 1 (July 1997):38–81.

MARCUSE, HERBERT. *One-Dimensional Man*. Boston: Beacon Press, 1964.

MARE, ROBERT D. "Five Decades of Educational Assortative Mating." *American Sociological Review*. Vol. 56, No. 1 (February 1991):15–32.

MARGOLIS, LYNNE. "Still the Stones' Age." *Christian Science Monitor* (September 6, 2002): Arts and Leisure, pp. 15, 18, 19.

MARÍN, GERARDO, and BARBARA VANOSS MARÍN. *Research with Hispanic Populations*. Newbury Park, Calif.: Sage, 1991.

MARKLEIN, MARY BETH. "Optimism Rises as SAT Math Scores Hit 30-Year High." *USA Today* (August 30, 2000):1A.

MARKOFF, JOHN. "Remember Big Brother? Now He's a Company Man." *New York Times* (March 31, 1991):7.

MARKOVSKY, BARRY, JOHN SKVORETZ, DAVID WILLER, MICHAEL J. LOVAGLIA, and JEFFREY ERGER. "The Seeds of Weak Power: An Extension of Network Exchange Theory." *American Sociological Review*. Vol. 58, No. 2 (April 1993):197–209.

MARKS, ALEXANDRA. "U.S. Shelters Swell—With Families." *Christian Science Monitor*. [Online] Available December 4, 2001, at http://www.csmonitor.com

MARKSON, ELIZABETH W. "Moral Dilemmas." *Society*. Vol. 29, No. 5 (July–August 1992):4–6.

MARQUAND, ROBERT. "Worship Shift: Americans Seek Feeling of 'Awe.'" *Christian Science Monitor* (May 28, 1997):1, 8.

MARQUAND, ROBERT, and DANIEL B. WOOD. "Rise in Cults as Millennium Approaches." *Christian Science Monitor* (March 28, 1997):1, 18.

MARQUARDT, ELIZABETH, and NORVAL GLENN. *Hooking Up, Hanging Out, and Hoping for Mr. Right*. New York: Institute for American Values, 2001.

MARSHALL, SUSAN E. "Ladies against Women: Mobilization Dilemmas of Antifeminist Movements." *Social Problems*. Vol. 32, No. 4 (April 1985):348–62.

MARTIN, CAROL LYNN, and RICHARD A. FABES. Research cited in Marianne Szegedy-Maszak, "The Power of Gender." *U.S. News & World Report*. Vol. 130, No. 22 (June 4, 2001):52.

MARTIN, JOHN R., and ANNE T. ROMANO. *Multinational Crime: Terrorism, Espionage, Drug and Arms Trafficking*. Newbury Park, Calif.: Sage, 1992.

MARTINEZ, RAMIRO, JR. "Latinos and Lethal Violence: The Impact of Poverty and Inequality." *Social Problems*. Vol. 43, No. 2 (May 1996):131–46.

MARULLO, SAM. "The Functions and Dysfunctions of Preparations for Fighting Nuclear War." *Sociological Focus*. Vol. 20, No. 2 (April 1987):135–53.

MARX, GARY T., and JAMES L. WOOD. "Strands of Theory and Research in Collective Behavior." In Alex Inkeles et al., eds., *Annual Review of Sociology*. Vol. 1. Palo Alto, Calif.: Annual Reviews, 1975:363–428.

MARX, KARL. Excerpt from "A Contribution to the Critique of Political Economy." In Karl Marx and Friedrich Engels, *Marx and Engels: Basic Writings on Politics and Philosophy*, Lewis S. Feurer, ed. Garden City, N.Y.: Anchor Books, 1959:42–46.

———. *Karl Marx: Early Writings*. T. B. Bottomore, ed. New York: McGraw-Hill, 1964.

———. *Capital*. Friedrich Engels, ed. New York: International Publishers, 1967; orig. 1867.

MARX, KARL, and FRIEDRICH ENGELS. "Manifesto of the Communist Party." In Robert C. Tucker, ed., *The Marx-Engels Reader*. New York: Norton, 1972:331–62; orig. 1848.

———. *The Marx-Engels Reader*. 2d ed. Robert C. Tucker, ed. New York: Norton, 1978.

MARX, LEO. "The Environment and the 'Two Cultures' Divide." In James Rodger Fleming and Henry A. Gemery, eds., *Science, Technology, and the Environment: Multidisciplinary Perspectives*. Akron, Ohio: University of Akron Press, 1994:3–21.

MASSEY, DOUGLAS. "Housing Discrimination 101." *Population Today*. Vol. 28, No. 6 (August/September 2000):1, 4.

MASSEY, DOUGLAS S. "A Brief History of Human Society: The Origin and Role of Emotion in Social Life." *American Sociological Review*. Vol. 67, No. 1 (February 2002):1–29.

MASSEY, DOUGLAS S., and NANCY A. DENTON. "Hypersegregation in U.S. Metropolitan Areas: Black and Hispanic Segregation along Five Dimensions." *Demography*. Vol. 26, No. 3 (August 1989):373–91.

MATLOFF, JUDITH. "Nomadic 'Blue Men' of the Desert Try to Go Roam Again." *Christian Science Monitor* (September 9, 1997):7.

MATTHIESSEN, PETER. *Indian Country*. New York: Viking Press, 1984.

MAUER, MARC. "Americans behind Bars: U.S. and International Use of Incarceration 1995." [Online] Available April 1, 2000, at http://www.sentencingproject.org/pubs/tsppubs/9030data.html

MAURO, TONY. "Ruling Likely Will Add Fuel to Already Divisive Debate." *USA Today* (January 7, 1997):1A, 2A.

MAUSS, ARMAND L. *Social Problems of Social Movements*. Philadelphia: Lippincott, 1975.

MAY, ELAINE TYLER. "Women in the Wild Blue Yonder." *New York Times* (August 7, 1991):21.

MAYO, KATHERINE. *Mother India*. New York: Harcourt, Brace, 1927.

MEAD, GEORGE HERBERT. *Mind, Self, and Society*. Charles W. Morris, ed. Chicago: University of Chicago Press, 1962; orig. 1934.

MEAD, MARGARET. *Sex and Temperament in Three Primitive Societies*. New York: William Morrow, 1963; orig. 1935.

MEADOWS, DONELLA H., DENNIS L. MEADOWS, JORGAN RANDERS, and WILLIAM W. BEHRENS III. *The Limits to Growth: A Report on the Club of Rome's Project on the Predicament of Mankind*. New York: Universe, 1972.

MELTZER, BERNARD N. "Mead's Social Psychology." In Jerome G. Manis and Bernard N. Meltzer, eds., *Symbolic Interaction: A Reader in Social Psychology*. 3d ed. Needham Heights, Mass.: Allyn & Bacon, 1978.

MELUCCI, ALBERTO. "The New Social Movements: A Theoretical Approach." *Social Science Information*. Vol. 19, No. 2 (May 1980):199–226.

———. *Nomads of the Present: Social Movements and Individual Needs in Contemporary Society*. Philadelphia: Temple University Press, 1989.

MENCKEN, F. CARSON, and IDEE WINFIELD. "Employer Recruiting and the Gender Composition of Jobs." *Sociological Focus*. Vol. 32, No. 2 (May 1999):210–20.

MENJIVAR, CECILIA. "Immigrant Kinship Networks and the Impact of the Receiving Context: Salvadorans in San Francisco in the Early 1990s." *Social Problems*. Vol. 44, No. 1 (February 1997):104–23.

MERGENHAGEN, PAULA. "Sun City Gets Boomerized." *American Demographics*. Vol. 18, No. 8 (August 1996a):16–20.

———. "Her Own Boss." *American Demographics*. Vol. 18, No. 12 (December 1996b):37–41.

MERTON, ROBERT K. "Social Structure and Anomie." *American Sociological Review*. Vol. 3, No. 6 (October 1938):672–82.

———. *Social Theory and Social Structure*. New York: Free Press, 1968.

METZ, MICHAEL E., and MICHAEL H. MINER. "Psychosexual and Psychosocial Aspects of Male Aging and Sexual Health." *Canadian Journal of Human Sexuality*. Vol. 7, No. 3 (Summer 1998):245–60.

METZGER, KURT. Data presented in "Cities and Race." *Society*. Vol. 39, No. 1 (December 2001):2.

MEYER, DAVID S., and SUZANNE STAGGENBORG. "Movements, Countermovements, and the Structure of Political Opportunity." *American Journal of Sociology*. Vol. 101, No. 6 (May 1996):1628–60.

MEYER, DAVIS S., and NANCY WHITTIER. "Social Movement Spillover." *Social Problems*. Vol. 41, No. 2 (May 1994):277–98.

MICHELS, ROBERT. *Political Parties*. Glencoe, Ill.: Free Press, 1949; orig. 1911.

MILGRAM, STANLEY. "Behavioral Study of Obedience." *Journal of Abnormal and Social Psychology*. Vol. 67, No. 4 (1963):371–78.

———. "Group Pressure and Action against a Person." *Journal of Abnormal and Social Psychology*. Vol. 69, No. 2 (August 1964):137–43.

———. "Some Conditions of Obedience and Disobedience to Authority." *Human Relations*. Vol. 18 (February 1965):57–76.

———. "The Small World Problem." *Psychology Today*. Vol. 2 (1967):60–67.

MILIBAND, RALPH. *The State in Capitalist Society*. London: Weidenfield & Nicolson, 1969.

MILLER, ALAN S., and RODNEY STARK. "Gender and Religiousness: Can Socialization Explanations Be Saved?" *American Journal of Sociology*. Vol. 107, No. 6 (May 2002):1399–1423.

MILLER, ARTHUR G. *The Obedience Experiments: A Case of Controversy in Social Science*. New York: Praeger, 1986.

MILLER, DAVID L. *Introduction to Collective Behavior*. Belmont, Calif.: Wadsworth, 1985.

MILLER, FREDERICK D. "The End of SDS and the Emergence of Weatherman: Demise through Success." In Jo Freeman, ed., *Social Movements of the Sixties and Seventies*. New York: Longman, 1983:279–97.

MILLER, G. TYLER, JR. *Living in the Environment: An Introduction to Environmental Science*. Belmont, Calif.: Wadsworth, 1992.

MILLER, WALTER B. "Lower Class Culture as a Generating Milieu of Gang Delinquency." In Marvin E. Wolfgang, Leonard Savitz, and Norman Johnston, eds., *The Sociology of Crime and Delinquency*. 2d ed. New York: Wiley, 1970:351–63; orig. 1958.

MILLER, WILLIAM J., and RICK A. MATTHEWS. "Youth Employment, Differential Association, and Juvenile Delinquency." *Sociological Focus*. Vol. 34, No. 3 (August 2001):251–68.

MILLS, C. WRIGHT. *The Power Elite*. New York: Oxford University Press, 1956.

———. *The Sociological Imagination*. New York: Oxford University Press, 1959.

MIRACLE, TINA S., ANDREW W. MIRACLE, and ROY F. BAUMEISTER. *Human Sexuality: Meeting Your Basic Needs*. Upper Saddle River, N.J.: Prentice Hall, 2003.

MIRINGOFF, MARC, and MARQUE-LUISA MIRINGOFF. "The Social Health of the Nation." *The Economist*. Vol. 352, No. 8128 (July 17, 1999):suppl. 6–7.

MIROWSKY, JOHN, and CATHERINE ROSS. "Working Wives and Mental Health." Presentation to the American Association for the Advancement of Science, New York, 1984.

MITCHELL, ALISON. "Give Me a Home Where the Buffalo Roam Less." *New York Times* (January 20, 2002):section 4, p. 5.

MOEN, PHYLLIS, DONNA DEMPSTER-McCLAIN, and ROBIN M. WILLIAMS. "Successful Aging: A Life-Course Perspective on Women's Multiple Roles and Health." *American Journal of Sociology*. Vol. 97 (May 1992):1612–38.

MOGELONSKY, MARCIA. "Reconfiguring the American Dream (House)." *American Demographics*. Vol. 19, No. 1 (January 1997):31–35.

MOLOTCH, HARVEY. "The City as a Growth Machine." *American Journal of Sociology*. Vol. 82, No. 2 (September 1976):309–33.

MONTAGU, ASHLEY. *The Nature of Human Aggression*. New York: Oxford University Press, 1976.

MONTAIGNE, FEN. "Russia Rising." *National Geographic*. Vol. 200, No. 5 (September 2001):2–31.

MOORE, GWEN. "Gender and Informal Networks in State Government." *Social Science Quarterly*. Vol. 73, No. 1 (March 1992):46–61.

MOORE, GWEN, SARAH SOBIERAJ, J. ALLEN WHITT, OLGA MAYOROVA, and DANIEL BEAULIEU. "Elite Interlocks in Three U.S. Sectors: Nonprofit, Corporate, and Government." *Social Science Quarterly*. Vol. 83, No. 3 (September 2002):726–44.

MOORE, WILBERT E. "Modernization as Rationalization: Processes and Restraints." In Manning Nash, ed., *Essays on Economic Development and Cultural Change in Honor of Bert F. Hoselitz*. Chicago: University of Chicago Press, 1977:29–42.

———. *World Modernization: The Limits of Convergence*. New York: Elsevier, 1979.

MORRIS, ALDON. "Black Southern Sit-In Movement: An Analysis of Internal Organization." *American Sociological Review*. Vol. 46, No. 6 (December 1981):744–67.

MORRISON, DENTON E. "Some Notes toward Theory on Relative Deprivation, Social Movements, and Social Change." In Louis E. Genevie, ed., *Collective Behavior and Social Movements*. Itasca, Ill.: Peacock, 1978:202–9.

MOSLEY, W. HENRY, and PETER COWLEY. "The Challenge of World Health." *Population Bulletin.* Vol. 46, No. 4 (December 1991). Washington, D.C.: Population Reference Bureau.

MOUW, TED. "Job Relocation and the Racial Gap in Unemployment in Detroit and Chicago, 1980 to 1990." *American Sociological Review.* Vol. 65, No. 5 (October 2000):730–53.

MULLER, CHANDRA, and CHRISTOPHER G. ELLISON. "Religious Involvement, Social Capital, and Adolescents' Academic Progress: Evidence from the National Education Longitudinal Study of 1988." *Sociological Focus.* Vol. 34, No. 2 (May 2001):155–83.

MULRINE, ANNA. "Risky Business." *U.S. News & World Report.* Vol. 132, No. 18 (May 27, 2002):42–49.

MUMFORD, LEWIS. *The City in History: Its Origins, Its Transformations, and Its Prospects.* New York: Harcourt, Brace & World, 1961.

MURDOCK, GEORGE PETER. "Comparative Data on the Division of Labor by Sex." *Social Forces.* Vol. 15, No. 4 (May 1937):551–53.

———. "The Common Denominator of Cultures." In Ralph Linton, ed., *The Science of Man in World Crisis.* New York: Columbia University Press, 1945:123–42.

———. *Social Structure.* New York: Free Press, 1965; orig. 1949.

MURRAY, STEPHEN O., and WILL ROSCOE, eds. *Studies of African Homosexualities.* New York: St. Martin's Press, 1998.

MYERS, DAVID G. *The American Paradox: Spiritual Hunger in an Age of Plenty.* New Haven and London: Yale University Press, 2000.

MYERS, NORMAN. "Humanity's Growth." In Sir Edmund Hillary, ed., *Ecology 2000: The Changing Face of the Earth.* New York: Beaufort Books, 1984a:16–35.

———. "The Mega-Extinction of Animals and Plants." In Sir Edmund Hillary, ed., *Ecology 2000: The Changing Face of the Earth.* New York: Beaufort Books, 1984b:82–107.

———. "Disappearing Cultures." In Sir Edmund Hillary, ed., *Ecology 2000: The Changing Face of the Earth.* New York: Beaufort Books, 1984c:162–69.

———. "Biological Diversity and Global Security." In F. Herbert Bormann and Stephen R. Kellert, eds., *Ecology, Economics, and Ethics: The Broken Circle.* New Haven, Conn.: Yale University Press, 1991:11–25.

MYERS, SHEILA, and HAROLD G. GRASMICK. "The Social Rights and Responsibilities of Pregnant Women: An Application of Parsons' Sick Role Model." Paper presented to the Southwestern Sociological Association, Little Rock, Arkansas, March 1989.

MYRDAL, GUNNAR. *An American Dilemma: The Negro Problem and Modern Democracy.* New York: Harper & Brothers, 1944.

NAGEL, JOANE. *American Indian Ethnic Renewal: Red Power and the Resurgence of Identity and Culture.* New York: Oxford University Press, 1996.

NAJAFIZADEH, MEHRANGIZ, and LEWIS A. MENNERICK. "Sociology of Education or Sociology of Ethnocentrism: The Portrayal of Education in Introductory Sociology Textbooks." *Teaching Sociology.* Vol. 20, No. 3 (July 1992):215–21.

NASH, J. MADELEINE. "To Know Your Own Fate." *Time.* Vol. 145, No. 14 (April 3, 1995):62.

———. "Cracking the Fat Riddle." *Time.* Vol. 160, No. 10 (September 2, 2002):50–5.

NAVARRO, MIREYA. "Puerto Rican Presence Wanes in New York." *The New York Times* (February 28, 2000):A1, A20.

NEERGAARD, LAURAN. "Tobacco Devastating Women's Health." Yahoo! News. [Online] Available March 28, 2001, at http://www.yahoo.com

NELSON, AMY L. "The Effect of Economic Restructuring on Family Poverty in the Industrial Heartland, 1970–1990." *Sociological Focus.* Vol. 31, No. 2 (May 1998):201–16.

NELSON, JOEL I. "Work and Benefits: The Multiple Problems of Service Sector Employment." *Social Problems.* Vol. 42, No. 2 (May 1994):240–55.

NESBITT, PAULA D. *Feminization of the Clergy in America: Occupational and Organizational Perspectives.* New York: Oxford University Press, 1997.

NESSMAN, RAVI. "Stampede at Soccer Match Kills 47." Associated Press news report, April 11, 2001. [Online]. Accessed at http://www.dailynews.yahoo.com

NEUGARTEN, BERNICE L. "Grow Old with Me. The Best Is Yet to Be." *Psychology Today.* Vol. 5 (December 1971):45–48, 79, 81.

———. "Personality and the Aging Process." *The Gerontologist.* Vol. 12, No. 1 (Spring 1972):9–15.

———. "Personality and Aging." In James E. Birren and K. Warner Schaie, eds., *Handbook of the Psychology of Aging.* New York: Van Nostrand Reinhold, 1977:626–49.

NEUHOUSER, KEVIN. "The Radicalization of the Brazilian Catholic Church in Comparative Perspective." *American Sociological Review.* Vol. 54, No. 2 (April 1989):233–44.

NEUMAN, W. LAURENCE. *Social Research Methods: Qualitative and Quantitative Approaches.* 3d ed. Boston: Allyn & Bacon, 1997.

NEWMAN, KATHERINE S. *Declining Fortunes: The Withering of the American Dream.* New York: Basic Books, 1993.

NEWMAN, WILLIAM M. *American Pluralism: A Study of Minority Groups and Social Theory.* New York: Harper & Row, 1973.

NIELSEN, A. C. Survey data cited in *Information Please Almanac 1997.* Boston: Houghton Mifflin, 1997.

NIELSEN, FRANCOIS, and ARTHUR S. ALDERSON. "The Kuznets Curve: The Great U-Turn: Income Inequality in U.S. Counties, 1970 to 1990." *American Sociological Review.* Vol. 62, No. 1 (February 1997):12–33.

NIELSEN, JOYCE MCCARL, ed. *Feminist Research Methods: Exemplary Readings in the Social Sciences.* Boulder, Colo.: Westview Press, 1990.

1991 Green Book. U.S. House of Representatives. Washington, D.C.: U.S. Government Printing Office, 1991.

NISBET, ROBERT A. *The Sociological Tradition.* New York: Basic Books, 1966.

———. *The Quest for Community.* New York: Oxford University Press, 1969.

NOCK, STEVEN L., JAMES D. WRIGHT, and LAURA SANCHEZ. "America's Divorce Problem." *Society.* Vol. 36, No. 4 (May/June 1999):43–52.

NOLAN, PATRICK, and GERHARD LENSKI. *Human Societies: An Introduction to Macrosociology.* 8th ed. New York: McGraw-Hill, 1999.

NORBECK, EDWARD. "Class Structure." In *Kodansha Encyclopedia of Japan.* Tokyo: Kodansha, 1983:322–25.

NORC. *General Social Surveys, 1972–1991: Cumulative Codebook.* Chicago: National Opinion Research Center, 1991.

———. *General Social Surveys, 1972–2002: Cumulative Codebook.* Chicago: National Opinion Research Center, 2002.

NORD, MARK. "Does It Cost Less to Live in Rural Areas? Evidence from New Data on Food Scarcity and Hunger." *Rural Sociology.* Vol. 65, No. 1 (March 2000):104–25.

NOVAK, VIVECA. "The Cost of Poor Advice." *Time.* Vol. 154, No. 1 (July 5, 1999):38.

NULAND, SHERWIN B. "The Hazards of Hospitalization." *Wall Street Journal* (December 2, 1999):A22.

OAKES, JEANNIE. "Classroom Social Relationships: Exploring the Bowles and Gintis Hypothesis." *Sociology of Education.* Vol. 55, No. 4 (October 1982):197–212.

———. *Keeping Track: How High Schools Structure Inequality.* New Haven, Conn.: Yale University Press, 1985.

OBERSCHALL, ANTHONY. *Social Conflict and Social Movements.* Englewood Cliffs, N.J.: Prentice Hall, 1973.

O'BRIEN, DAVID J., EDWARD W. HASSINGER, and LARRY DERSHEM. "Size of Place, Residential Stability, and Personal Social Networks." *Sociological Focus.* Vol. 29, No. 1 (February 1996):61–72.

O'CONNOR, RORY J. "Internet Declared Protected Speech." *Post-Star* (Glens Fall, N.Y.: June 27, 1997):A1–A2.

OGAWA, NAOHIRO, and ROBERT D. RETHERFORD. "Shifting Costs of Caring for the Elderly Back to Families in Japan: Will It Work?" *Population and Development Review.* Vol. 23, No. 1 (March 1997):59–95.

OGBURN, WILLIAM F. *On Culture and Social Change.* Chicago: University of Chicago Press, 1964.

OGDEN, RUSSEL D. "Nonphysician-Assisted Suicide: The Technological Imperative of the *Deathing* Counterculture." *Death Studies.* Vol. 25, No. 5 (July 2001):387–402.

O'HARE, WILLIAM P. "The Rise of Hispanic Affluence." *American Demographics.* Vol. 12, No. 8 (August 1990):40–43.

———. "Managing Multiple-Race Data." *American Demographics.* Vol. 20, No. 4 (April 1998):42–44.

———. "Tracking the Trends in Low-Income Working Families." *Population Today.* Vol. 30, No. 6 (August/September 2002):1–3.

O'HARE, WILLIAM P., WILLIAM H. FREY, and DAN FOST. "Asians in the Suburbs." *American Demographics.* Vol. 16, No. 9 (May 1994):32–38.

OKRENT, DANIEL. "Raising Kids Online: What Can Parents Do?" *Time.* Vol. 154, No. 18 (May 10, 1999):38–43.

OLSEN, GREGG M. "Re-Modeling Sweden: The Rise and Demise of the Compromise in a Global Economy." *Social Problems.* Vol. 43, No. 1 (February 1996):1–20.

OLZAK, SUSAN. "Labor Unrest, Immigration, and Ethnic Conflict in Urban America, 1880–1914." *American Journal of Sociology.* Vol. 94, No. 6 (May 1989):1303–33.

OLZAK, SUSAN, and ELIZABETH WEST. "Ethnic Conflict and the Rise and Fall of Ethnic Newspapers." *American Sociological Review.* Vol. 56, No. 4 (August 1991):458–74.

OMESTAD, THOMAS. "A Balance of Terror." *U.S. News & World Report.* Vol. 134, No. 3 (February 3, 2003):33–5.

O'NEILL, BRIAN, and DEBORAH BALK. "World Population Futures." *Population Bulletin.* Vol. 56, No. 3 (September 2001):3–40.

ORECKLIN, MICHELLE. "Earnings Report: J.K. and Judy." *Time.* Vol. 161, No. 2 (January 13, 2003):72.

ORLANSKY, MICHAEL D., and WILLIAM L. HEWARD. *Voices: Interviews with Handicapped People.* Columbus, Ohio: Merrill, 1981:85, 92, 133–34, 172.

ORWIN, CLIFFORD. "All Quiet on the Western Front?" *Public Interest.* Vol. 123 (Spring 1996): 3–9.

OSGOOD, D. WAYNE, JANET K. WILSON, PATRICK M. O'MALLEY, JERALD G. BACHMAN, and LLOYD D. JOHNSTON. "Routine Activities and Individual Deviant Behavior." *American Sociological Review.* Vol. 61, No. 4 (August 1996):635–55.

OSTRANDER, SUSAN A. "Upper Class Women: The Feminine Side of Privilege." *Qualitative Sociology.* Vol. 3, No. 1 (Spring 1980):23–44.

———. *Women of the Upper Class.* Philadelphia: Temple University Press, 1984.

OUCHI, WILLIAM. *Theory Z: How American Business Can Meet the Japanese Challenge.* Reading, Mass.: Addison-Wesley, 1981.

"Our Cheating Hearts." Editorial in *U.S. News & World Report* (May 6, 2002):4.

OVADIA, SETH. "Race, Class, and Gender Differences in High School Seniors' Values: Applying Intersection Theory in Empirical Analysis." *Social Science Quarterly.* Vol. 82, No. 2 (June 2001):341–56.

OWEN, CAROLYN A., HOWARD C. ELSNER, and THOMAS R. McFAUL. "A Half-Century of Social Distance Research: National Replication of the Bogardus Studies." *Sociology and Social Research*. Vol. 66 (1977):80–98.

OWEN, DAVID. *None of the Above: Behind the Myth of Scholastic Aptitude*. Boston: Houghton Mifflin, 1985.

PACKARD, MARK. Personal communication (2002).

PACKER, GEORGE. "Smart-Mobbing the War." *New York Times Magazine* (March 9, 2003):46–9.

PADAWER, RUTH. "Striking Transformations for Nation's Families, Seniors." *Bergen Record* (May 15, 2001):A1, A13.

PAGE, SUSAN. "New Tactics Pushed in Terror War." *USA Today* (January 7, 2000):1A.

PAKULSKI, JAN. "Mass Social Movements and Social Class." *International Sociology*. Vol. 8, No. 2 (June 1993):131–58.

PALLONE, NATHANIEL J., and JAMES J. HENNESSY. "Brain Dysfunction and Criminal Violence." *Society*. Vol. 35, No. 6 (September–October 1998):20–27.

PALMORE, ERDMAN. "Predictors of Successful Aging." *The Gerontologist*. Vol. 19, No. 5 (October 1979):427–31.

PARINI, JAY. "The Meaning of Emeritus." *Dartmouth Alumni Magazine* (July/August 2001):40–43.

PARK, ROBERT E. *Race and Culture*. Glencoe, Ill.: Free Press, 1950.

PARRILLO, VINCENT N. "Diversity in America: A Sociohistorical Analysis." *Sociological Forum*. Vol. 9, No. 4 (December 1994):42–45.

———. "Updating the Bogardus Social Distance Studies: A New National Survey." Revised version of a paper presented at the annual meeting of the American Sociological Association (August 17, 2002). Provided by the author, 2003.

———. *Strangers to These Shores*. 7th ed. Boston: Allyn & Bacon, 2003.

PARSONS, TALCOTT. "Age and Sex in the Social Structure of the United States." *American Sociological Review*. Vol. 7, No. 4 (August 1942):604–16.

———. *Essays in Sociological Theory*. New York: Free Press, 1954.

———. *The Social System*. New York: Free Press, 1964; orig. 1951.

———. *Societies: Evolutionary and Comparative Perspectives*. Englewood Cliffs, N.J.: Prentice Hall, 1966.

PARSONS, TALCOTT, and ROBERT F. BALES, eds. *Family, Socialization and Interaction Process*. New York: Free Press, 1955.

PASSY, FLORENCE, and MARCO GIUGNI. "Social Networks and Individual Perceptions: Explaining Differential Participation in Social Movements." *Sociological Forum*. Vol. 16, No. 1 (March 2001):123–53.

PATTERSON, ELISSA F. "The Philosophy and Physical of Holistic Health Care: Spiritual Healing as a Workable Interpretation." *Journal of Advanced Nursing*. Vol. 27, No. 2 (February 1998):287–94.

PATTILLO-McCOY, MARY. "Church Culture as a Strategy of Action in the Black Community." *American Sociological Review*. Vol. 63, No. 6 (December 1998):767–84.

PAUL, ELLEN FRANKEL. "Bared Buttocks and Federal Cases." *Society*. Vol. 28, No. 4 (May–June, 1991):4–7.

PAUL, PAMELA. "News, Noticias, Nouvelles." *American Demographics*. Vol. 23, No. 11 (November, 2001):26–31.

———. "Corporate Responsibility." *American Demographics*. Vol. 24, No. 5 (May 2002):24.

PEAR, ROBERT. "Women Reduce Lag in Earnings, but Disparities with Men Remain." *New York Times* (September 4, 1987):1, 7.

PEAR, ROBERT, and ERIK ECKHOLM. "When Healers Are Entrepreneurs: A Debate over Costs and Ethics." *New York Times* (June 2, 1991):1, 17.

PEARSON, DAVID E. "Post-Mass Culture." *Society*. Vol. 30, No. 5 (July–August 1993):17–22.

———. "Community and Sociology." *Society*. Vol. 32, No. 5 (July–August 1995):44–50.

PEASE, JOHN, and LEE MARTIN. "Want Ads and Jobs for the Poor: A Glaring Mismatch." *Sociological Forum*. Vol. 12. No. 4 (December 1997):545–64.

PERLMUTTER, PHILIP. "Minority Group Prejudice." *Society*. Vol. 39, No. 3 (March–April 2002):59–65.

PERRUCCI, ROBERT. "Inventing Social Justice: SSSP and the Twenty-First Century." *Social Problems*. Vol. 48, No. 2 (May 2001):159–67.

PESSEN, EDWARD. *Riches, Class, and Power: America before the Civil War*. New Brunswick, N.J.: Transaction Books, 1990.

Peters Atlas of the World. New York: Harper & Row, 1990.

PETERSEN, TROND, ISHAK SAPORTA, and MARC-DAVID L. SEIDEL. "Offering a Job: Meritocracy and Social Networks." *American Journal of Sociology*. Vol. 106, No. 3 (November 2000):763–816.

PETERSILIA, JOAN. "Probation in the United States: Practices and Challenges." *National Institute of Justice Journal*. No. 233 (September 1997):4.

PETERSON, SCOTT. "Women Live on Own Terms behind the Veil." *Christian Science Monitor* (July 31, 1996):1, 10.

PHI DELTA KAPPA INTERNATIONAL. Phi Delta Kappa International/Gallup Poll. [Online] Available December 16, 2002, at http://www.pdkintl.org/kappan/k0209pol.htm#1a

PHILADELPHIA, DESA. "Rookie Teacher, Age 50." *Time*. Vol. 157, No. 14 (April 9, 2001):66–68.

———. "Tastier, Plusher—and Fast." *Time*. Vol. 160, No. 14 (September 30, 2002):57.

PHILIPSON, ILENE J., and KAREN V. HANSEN. "Women, Class, and the Feminist Imagination." In Karen V. Hansen and Ilene J. Philipson, eds., *Women, Class, and the Feminist Imagination: A Socialist-Feminist Reader*. Philadelphia: Temple University Press, 1992:3–40.

PHILLIPS, MELANIE. "What about the Overclass?" *Public Interest*. No. 145 (Fall 2001):38–43.

PHILLIPSON, CHRIS. *Capitalism and the Construction of Old Age*. London: Macmillan, 1982.

PIERCE, EMILY. "Momentum Swing." *CQ Weekly*. Vol. 58, No. 44 (Nov. 11, 2000):2646.

PILLEMER, KARL. "Maltreatment of the Elderly at Home and in Institutions: Extent, Risk Factors, and Policy Recommendations." In U.S. Congress. House, Select Committee on Aging and Senate, Special Committee on Aging. *Legislative Agenda for an Aging Society: 1988 and Beyond*. Washington, D.C.: U.S. Government Printing Office, 1988.

PINCHOT, GIFFORD, and ELIZABETH PINCHOT. *The End of Bureaucracy and the Rise of the Intelligent Organization*. San Francisco: Berrett-Koehler, 1993.

PINES, MAYA. "The Civilization of Genie." *Psychology Today*. Vol. 15 (September 1981):28–34.

PINHEY, THOMAS K., DONALD H. RUBINSTEIN, and RICHARD S. COLFAX. "Overweight and Happiness: The Reflected Self-Appraisal Hypothesis Reconsidered." *Social Science Quarterly*. Vol. 78, No. 3 (September 1997):747–55.

PINKER, STEVEN. *The Language Instinct*. New York: W. W. Morrow, 1994.

PIQUERO, ALEX R., JOHN M. MacDONALD, and KAREN F. PARKER. "Race, Local Life Circumstances, and Criminal Activity." *Social Science Quarterly*. Vol. 83, No. 3 (September 2002): 654–70.

PITTS, LEONARD, JR. "When a Win Sparks a Riot." *Philadelphia Inquirer* (June 26, 2000):A11.

PIVEN, FRANCES FOX, and RICHARD A. CLOWARD. *Poor People's Movements: Why They Succeed, How They Fail*. New York: Pantheon Books, 1977.

PLOMIN, ROBERT, and TERRYL T. FOCH. "A Twin Study of Objectively Assessed Personality in Childhood." *Journal of Personality and Social Psychology*. Vol. 39, No. 4 (October 1980):680–88.

PODOLNY, JOEL M., and JAMES N. BARON. "Resources and Relationships: Social Networks and Mobility in the Workplace." *American Sociological Review*. Vol. 62, No. 5 (October 1997):673–93.

POHL, RUDIGER. "The Transition from Communism to Capitalism in East Germany." *Society*. Vol. 33, No. 4 (June 1996):62–65.

POLENBERG, RICHARD. *One Nation Divisible: Class, Race, and Ethnicity in the United States since 1938*. New York: Pelican Books, 1980.

POLLACK, ANDREW. "Happy in the East (^-^) or Smiling :-) in the West." *New York Times* (August 12, 1996).

———. "Overseas, Smoking Is One of Life's Small Pleasures." *New York Times* (August 17, 1997):E5.

POLLOCK, PHILIP H., III, and M. ELLIOT VITTAS. "Who Bears the Burdens of Environmental Pollution: Race, Ethnicity, and Environmental Equity in Florida." *Social Science Quarterly*. Vol. 76, No. 2 (June 1995):294–310.

POLSBY, NELSON W. "Three Problems in the Analysis of Community Power." *American Sociological Review*. Vol. 24, No. 6 (December 1959):796–803.

POMER, MARSHALL I. "Labor Market Structure, Intragenerational Mobility, and Discrimination: Black Male Advancement out of Low-Paying Occupations, 1962–1973." *American Sociological Review*. Vol. 51, No. 5 (October 1986):650–59.

POPENOE, DAVID. "Family Decline in the Swedish Welfare State." *Public Interest*. No. 102 (Winter 1991):65–77.

———. "American Family Decline, 1960–1990: A Review and Appraisal." *Journal of Marriage and the Family*. Vol. 55, No. 3 (August 1993a):527–55.

———. "Parental Androgyny." *Society*. Vol. 30, No. 6 (September–October 1993b):5–11.

———. "Scandinavian Welfare." *Society*. Vol. 31, No. 6 (September–October, 1994):78–81.

———. "Can the Nuclear Family Be Revived?" *Society*. Vol. 36, No. 5 (July/August 1999):28–30.

POPENOE, DAVID, and BARBARA DAFOE WHITEHEAD. *Should We Live Together? What Young Adults Need to Know about Cohabitation before Marriage*. New Brunswick, N.J.: The National Marriage Project, 1999.

POPKIN, SUSAN J. "Welfare: Views from the Bottom." *Social Problems*. Vol. 17, No. 1 (February 1990):64–79.

Popline. "Terrorist Attacks Spur Unseen Human Toll." Vol. 23 (December 2001):1–2.

POPULATION ACTION INTERNATIONAL. *People in the Balance: Population and Resources at the Turn of the Millennium*. Washington, D.C.: PAI, 2000.

POPULATION REFERENCE BUREAU. *2002 World Population Data Sheet*. Washington, D.C.: Population Reference Bureau, 2002.

———. *2003 World Population Data Sheet*. Washington, D.C.: Population Reference Bureau, 2003.

Population Today. "Majority of Children in Poverty Live with Parents Who Work." Vol. 23, No. 4 (April 1995):6.

PORTER, EDUARDO. "Even 126 Sizes Do Not Fit All." *Wall Street Journal* (March 2, 2001):B1.

PORTES, ALEJANDRO, and LEIF JENSEN. "The Enclave and the Entrants: Patterns of Ethnic Enterprise in Miami before and after Mariel." *American Sociological Review*. Vol. 54, No. 6 (December 1989):929–49.

POSTEL, SANDRA. "Facing Water Scarcity." In Lester R. Brown et al., eds., *State of the World 1993: A Worldwatch Institute Report on Progress toward a Sustainable Society*. New York: Norton, 1993:22–41.

POWELL, CHRIS, and GEORGE E. C. PATON, eds. *Humour in Society: Resistance and Control*. New York: St. Martin's Press, 1988.

PRESSER, HARRIET B. "The Housework Gender Gap." *Population Today*. Vol. 21, No. 7/8 (July–August 1993):5.

PRESSLEY, SUE ANNE, and NANCY ANDREWS. "For Gay Couples, the Nursery Becomes the New Frontier." *Washington Post* (December 20, 1992):A1, A22–23.

PRIMEGGIA, SALVATORE, and JOSEPH A. VARACALLI. "Southern Italian Comedy: Old to New World." In Joseph V. Scelsa, Salvatore J. LaGumina, and Lydio Tomasi, eds., *Italian Americans in Transition*. New York: The American Italian Historical Association, 1990:241–52.

PRINDLE, DAVID F. *Risky Business: The Political Economy of Hollywood*. Boulder, Colo.: Westview Press, 1993.

PRINDLE, DAVID F., and JAMES W. ENDERSBY. "Hollywood Liberalism." *Social Science Quarterly*. Vol. 74, No. 1 (March 1993):136–49.

PUTERBAUGH, GEOFF, ed. *Twins and Homosexuality: A Casebook*. New York: Garland, 1990.

PUTKA, GARY. "SAT to Become a Better Gauge." *Wall Street Journal* (November 1, 1990):B1.

PYLE, RALPH E., and JEROME R. KOCH. "The Religious Affiliation of American Elites, 1930s to 1990s: A Note on the Pace of Disestablishment." *Sociological Focus*. Vol. 34, No. 2 (May 2001):125–37.

QUEENAN, JOE. "The Many Paths to Riches." *Forbes*. Vol. 144, No. 9 (October 23, 1989):149.

QUILLIAN, LINCOLN, and DEVAH PAGER. "Black Neighbors, Higher Crime? The Role of Racial Stereotypes in Evaluations of Neighborhood Crime." *American Journal of Sociology*. Vol. 107, No. 3 (November 2001):717–67.

QUINNEY, RICHARD. *Class, State and Crime: On the Theory and Practice of Criminal Justice*. New York: David McKay, 1977.

RABKIN, JEREMY. "The Supreme Court in the Culture Wars." *Public Interest*. Vol. 125 (Fall 1996):3–26.

RAGAVAN, CHITRA. "Coming to America." *U.S. News & World Report*. Vol. 132, No. 5 (February 18, 2002):16–24.

RANK, MARK R., and THOMAS A. HIRSCHL. "Rags or Riches? Estimating the Probabilities of Poverty and Affluence across the Adult American Life Span." *Social Science Quarterly*. Vol. 82, No. 4 (December 2001):651–69.

RAPHAEL, RAY. *The Men from the Boys: Rites of Passage in Male America*. Lincoln: University of Nebraska Press, 1988.

RATNESAR, ROMESH. "Not Gone, but Forgotten?" *Time*. Vol. 153, No. 15 (February 8, 1999):30–31.

RAY, PAUL H. "The Emerging Culture." *American Demographics*. Vol. 19, No. 2 (February 1997):29–34, 56.

RAYMOND, JOAN. "The Multicultural Report." *American Demographics*. Vol. 23, No. 11 (November 2001):S1–S6.

RECKLESS, WALTER C., and SIMON DINITZ. "Pioneering with Self-Concept as a Vulnerability Factor in Delinquency." *Journal of Criminal Law, Criminology, and Police Science*. Vol. 58, No. 4 (December 1967):515–23.

RECTOR, ROBERT. "America Has the World's Richest Poor People." *Wall Street Journal* (September 24, 1998):A18.

REED, HOLLY E. "Kosovo and the Demography of Forced Migration." *Population Today*. Vol. 27, No. 6 (June 1999):4.

REICH, ROBERT B. *The Work of Nations: Preparing Ourselves for 21st-Century Capitalism*. New York: Alfred A. Knopf, 1991.

REIMAN, JEFFREY. *The Rich Get Richer and the Poor Get Prison: Ideology, Class, and Criminal Justice*. Boston: Allyn & Bacon, 1998.

REMOFF, HEATHER TREXLER. *Sexual Choice: A Woman's Decision*. New York: Dutton/Lewis, 1984.

RESKIN, BARBARA F., and DEBRA BRANCH MCBRIER. "Why Not Ascription? Organizations' Employment of Male and Female Managers." *American Sociological Review*. Vol. 65, No. 2 (April 2000):210–33.

REVKIN, ANDREW C. "Can Global Warming Be Studied Too Much?" *New York Times* (December 3, 2002):D1, D4.

REYNOLDS, JOHN R., and CATHERINE E. ROSS. "Social Stratification and Health: Education's Benefit beyond Economic Status and Social Origins." *Social Problems*. Vol. 45, No. 2 (May 1998):221–45.

RICHARDSON, JAMES T. "Definitions of Cult: From Sociological-Technical to Popular Negative." Paper presented to the American Psychological Association, Boston, August 1990.

RICHE, MARTHA FARNSWORTH. "America's Diversity and Growth: Signposts for the 21st Century." *Population Bulletin*. Vol. 55, No. 2 (June 2000).

RIDDLE, JOHN M., J. WORTH ESTES, and JOSIAH C. RUSSELL. "Ever since Eve: Birth Control in the Ancient World." *Archaeology*. Vol. 47, No. 2 (March/April 1994):29–35.

RIDGEWAY, CECILIA L. *The Dynamics of Small Groups*. New York: St. Martin's Press, 1983.

RIDGEWAY, CECILIA L., and KRISTAN GLASGOW ERICKSON. "Creating and Spreading Status Beliefs." *American Journal of Sociology*. Vol. 106, No. 3 (November 2000):579–615.

RIESMAN, DAVID. *The Lonely Crowd: A Study of the Changing American Character*. New Haven, Conn.: Yale University Press, 1970; orig. 1950.

RILEY, MATILDA WHITE, ANNE FONER, and JOAN WARING. "Sociology of Age." In Neil J. Smelser, ed., *Handbook of Sociology*. Newbury Park, Calif.: Sage, 1988:243–90.

RILEY, NANCY E. "Gender, Power, and Population Change." *Population Bulletin*. Vol. 52, No. 1 (May 1997).

RIMER, SARA. "Blacks Carry Load of Care for Their Elderly." *New York Times* (March 15, 1998):1, 22.

RITZER, GEORGE. *The McDonaldization of Society: An Investigation into the Changing Character of Contemporary Social Life*. Thousand Oaks, Calif.: Pine Forge Press, 1993.

———. *The McDonaldization of Society*. Revised ed. Thousand Oaks, Calif.: Sage, 1996.

———. *The McDonaldization Thesis: Explorations and Extensions*. Thousand Oaks, Calif.: Sage, 1998.

———. "The Globalization of McDonaldization." *The Spark* (February 2000):8–9.

RITZER, GEORGE, and DAVID WALCZAK. *Working: Conflict and Change*. 4th ed. Englewood Cliffs, N.J.: Prentice Hall, 1990.

RIVERA-BATIZ, FRANCISCO L., and CARLOS SANTIAGO, cited in Sam Roberts, "Puerto Ricans on Mainland Making Gains, Study Finds." *New York Times* (October 19, 1994):A20.

ROBERT, STEPHANIE A. "Socioeconomic Position and Health: The Independent Contribution of Community Socioeconomic Context." *Annual Review of Sociology*. Vol. 25 (1999):489–516.

ROBERTS, J. DEOTIS. *Roots of a Black Future: Family and Church*. Philadelphia: Westminster Press, 1980.

ROBINSON, JOHN P., PERLA WERNER, and GEOFFREY GODBEY. "Freeing Up the Golden Years." *American Demographics*. Vol. 19, No. 10 (October 1997):20–24.

ROBINSON, LINDA. "A Timeworn Terrorism List." *U.S. News & World Report*. Vol. 132, No. 17 (May 20, 2002):18, 21.

ROBINSON, THOMAS N., MARTA L. WILDE, LISA C. NAVRACRUZ, K. FARISH HAYDEL, and ANN VARADY. "Effects of Reducing Children's Television and Video Game Use on Aggressive Behavior." *Archives of Pediatrics and Adolescent Medicine*. Vol. 155 (January 2001):17–23.

ROCHE, TIMOTHY. "A Psychotic Killer Sues His Psychiatrist." *Time*. Vol. 153, No. 15 (April 19, 1999):8.

ROESCH, ROBERTA. "Violent Families." *Parents*. Vol. 59, No. 9 (September 1984):74–76, 150–52.

ROETHLISBERGER, F. J., and WILLIAM J. DICKSON. *Management and the Worker*. Cambridge, Mass.: Harvard University Press, 1939.

ROGERS-DILLON, ROBIN H. "What Do We Really Know about Welfare Reform?" *Society*. Vol. 38, No. 2 (January/February 2001):7–15.

ROMAINE, SUZANNE. *Communicating Gender*. Mahwah, NJ: Erlbaum, 1999.

ROMERO, FRANCINE SANDERS, and ADRIAN LISERIO. "Saving Open Spaces: Determinants of 1998 and 1999 'Antisprawl' Ballot Measures." *Social Science Quarterly*. Vol. 83, No. 1 (March 2002):341–52.

ROOF, WADE CLARK, and WILLIAM MCKINNEY. *American Mainline Religion: Its Changing Shape and Future*. New Brunswick, N.J.: Rutgers University Press, 1987.

ROSE, FRED. "Toward a Class-Cultural Theory of Social Movements: Reinterpreting New Social Movements." *Sociological Forum*. Vol. 12, No. 3 (September 1997):461–94.

ROSE, JERRY D. *Outbreaks*. New York: Free Press, 1982.

ROSEN, ELLEN ISRAEL. *Bitter Choices: Blue-Collar Women In and Out of Work*. Chicago: University of Chicago Press, 1987.

ROSENBAUM, DAVID E. "Americans Want a Right to Die. Or So They Think." *New York Times* (June 8, 1997):E3.

ROSENBAUM, MARC. "Americans' Views on Taxes." Report of an NPR/Kaiser Family Foundation/Kennedy School of Government poll. Lecture delivered at Kenyon College, Gambier, Ohio, April 23, 2003.

ROSENDAHL, MONA. *Inside the Revolution: Everyday Life in Socialist Cuba*. Ithaca, N.Y.: Cornell University Press, 1997.

ROSENFELD, MEGAN. "Little Boys Blue: Reexamining the Plight of Young Males." *Washington Post* (March 26, 1998):A1, A17–A18.

ROSENFELD, MICHAEL J. "Celebration, Politics, and Selective Looting and Riots: A Micro-Level Study of the Bulls Riot of 1992 in Chicago." *Social Problems*. Vol. 44, No. 4 (November 1997):483–502.

ROSENFELD, RICHARD. "Crime Decline in Context." *Contexts: Understanding People in Their Social Worlds*. Vol. 1, No. 1 (Spring 2002):20–34.

ROSENTHAL, ELIZABETH. "Canada's National Health Plan Gives Care to All, with Limits." *New York Times* (April 30, 1991):A1, A16.

ROSENTHAL, JACK. "The Rapid Growth of Suburban Employment." In Lois H. Masotti and Jeffrey K. Hadden, eds., *Suburbia in Transition*. New York: New York Times Books, 1974:95–100.

ROSNOW, RALPH L., and GARY ALAN FINE. *Rumor and Gossip: The Social Psychology of Hearsay*. New York: Elsevier, 1976.

ROSS, CATHERINE E. "Neighborhoods and Guns in America." *Sociological Focus*. Vol. 34, No. 3 (August 2001):287–98.

ROSS, CATHERINE E., JOHN MIROWSKY, and JOAN HUBER. "Dividing Work, Sharing Work, and In-Between: Marriage Patterns and Depression." *American Sociological Review*. Vol. 48, No. 6 (December 1983):809–23.

ROSS, JOHN. "To Die in the Street: Mexico City's Homeless Population Boom as Economic Crisis Shakes Social Protections." *SSSP Newsletter*. Vol. 27, No. 2 (Summer 1996):14–15.

ROSSI, ALICE S. "Gender and Parenthood." In Alice S. Rossi, ed., *Gender and the Life Course*. New York: Aldine, 1985:161–91.

ROSSI, PETER H. Review of Christopher Jencks, *The Homeless* (Cambridge, Mass.: Harvard University Press). *Society*. Vol. 32, No. 4 (May–June 1995):80–81.

ROSTOW, WALT W. *The Stages of Economic Growth: A Non-Communist Manifesto*. Cambridge, U.K.: Cambridge University Press, 1960.

———. *The World Economy: History and Prospect.* Austin: University of Texas Press, 1978.

ROTHMAN, BARBARA KATZ. "Of Maps and Imaginations: Sociology Confronts the Genome." *Social Problems.* Vol. 42, No. 1 (February 1995):1–10.

ROTHMAN, STANLEY, and AMY E. BLACK. "Who Rules Now? American Elites in the 1990s." *Society.* Vol. 35, No. 6 (September–October 1998):17–20.

ROTHMAN, STANLEY, STEPHEN POWERS, and DAVID ROTHMAN. "Feminism in Films." *Society.* Vol. 30, No. 3 (March–April 1993):66–72.

ROUSSEAU, CARYN. "Unions Rally at Wal-Mart Stores." Yahoo! News. [Online] Available November 22, 2002, at http://dailynews.yahoo.com

ROZELL, MARK J., CLYDE WILCOX, and JOHN C. GREEN. "Religious Constituencies and Support for the Christian Right in the 1990s." *Social Science Quarterly.* Vol. 79, No. 4 (December 1998):815–27.

RUBENSTEIN, ELI A. "The Not So Golden Years." *Newsweek* (October 7, 1991):13.

RUBIN, LILLIAN BRESLOW. *Worlds of Pain: Life in the Working-Class Family.* New York: Basic Books, 1976.

RUDÉ, GEORGE. *The Crowd in History: A Study of Popular Disturbances in France and England, 1730–1848.* New York: Wiley, 1964.

RUDEL, THOMAS K., and JUDITH M. GERSON. "Postmodernism, Institutional Change, and Academic Workers: A Sociology of Knowledge." *Social Science Quarterly.* Vol. 80, No. 2 (June 1999):213–28.

RUDOLPH, ELLEN. "Women's Talk: Japanese Women." *New York Times Magazine* (September 1, 1991).

RULE, JAMES, and PETER BRANTLEY. "Computerized Surveillance in the Workplace: Forms and Delusions." *Sociological Forum.* Vol. 7, No. 3 (September 1992):405–23.

RUSSELL, CHERYL. "True Crime." *American Demographics.* Vol. 17, No. 8 (August 1995):22–31.

RUSSELL, CHERYL, and MARCIA MOGELONSKY. "Riding High on the Market." *American Demographics.* Vol. 22, No. 4 (April 2000):44–54.

RUTHERFORD, MEGAN. "Women Run the World." *Time.* Vol. 153, No. 25 (June 28, 1999):72.

———. "Simply Grand." *Time.* Vol. 154, No. 15 (October 11, 1999). Special section.

RYAN, PATRICK J. "The Roots of Muslim Anger." *America.* Vol. 185, No. 17 (November 26, 2001):8–16.

RYAN, WILLIAM. *Blaming the Victim.* Rev. ed. New York: Vintage Books, 1976.

RYMER, RUSS. *Genie.* New York: HarperPerennial, 1994.

ST. JEAN, YANICK, and JOE R. FEAGIN. *Double Burden: Black Women and Everyday Racism.* Armonk, N.Y.: M. E. Sharpe, 1998.

SACHS, JEFFREY. "The Real Causes of Famine." *Time.* Vol. 152, No. 17 (October 26, 1998):69.

SALE, KIRKPATRICK. *The Conquest of Paradise: Christopher Columbus and the Columbian Legacy.* New York: Alfred A. Knopf, 1990.

SAMPSON, ROBERT J., and JOHN H. LAUB. "Crime and Deviance over the Life Course: The Salience of Adult Social Bonds." *American Sociological Review.* Vol. 55, No. 5 (October 1990):609–27.

SAMUELSON, ROBERT J. "The Rich and Everyone Else." *Newsweek* (January 27, 2003):57.

SANCHEZ, RENE. "Urban Students Not Making the Mark." *Washington Post* (January 8, 1998):A18.

SAPIR, EDWARD. "The Status of Linguistics as a Science." *Language.* Vol. 5 (1929):207–14.

———. *Selected Writings of Edward Sapir in Language, Culture, and Personality.* David G. Mandelbaum, ed. Berkeley: University of California Press, 1949.

SAPORITO, BILL. "Can Wal-Mart Get Any Bigger?" *Time.* Vol. 161, No. 2 (January 13, 2003):38–43.

SAVISHINSKY, JOEL S. *Breaking the Watch: The Meanings of Retirement in America.* Ithaca, N.Y.: Cornell University Press, 2000.

SAWHILL, ISABEL V. "The Perils of Early Motherhood." *Public Interest.* Vol. 146 (Winter 2002):74–84.

SCANLON, JAMES P. "The Curious Case of Affirmative Action for Women." *Society.* Vol. 29, No. 2 (January–February 1992):36–42.

SCANLON, STEPHAN J. "Food Availability and Access in Lesser-Industrialized Societies: A Test and Interpretation of Neo-Malthusian and Technoecological Theories." *Sociological Forum.* Vol. 16, No. 2 (June 2001):231–62.

SCHAFFER, MICHAEL. "American Dreamers." *U.S. News & World Report.* Vol. 133, No. 8 (August 26–September 2, 2002):12–16.

SCHAIE, K. WARNER. "Intelligence and Problem Solving." In James E. Birren and R. Bruce Sloane, eds., *Handbook of Mental Health and Aging.* Englewood Cliffs, N.J.: Prentice Hall, 1980:262–84.

SCHEFF, THOMAS J. *Being Mentally Ill: A Sociological Theory.* 2d ed. New York: Aldine, 1984.

SCHERER, RON. "Worldwide Trend: Tobacco Use Grows." *Christian Science Monitor* (July 17, 1996):4, 8.

SCHILLER, BRADLEY. "Who Are the Working Poor?" *Public Interest.* Vol. 155 (Spring 1994):61–71.

SCHLESINGER, ARTHUR. "The City in American Civilization." In A. B. Callow, Jr., ed., *American Urban History.* New York: Oxford University Press, 1969:25–41.

SCHLESINGER, ARTHUR, JR. "The Cult of Ethnicity: Good and Bad." *Time.* Vol. 137, No. 27 (July 8, 1991):21.

SCHLESINGER, JACOB M. "Finally, U.S. Median Income Approaches Old Heights." *Wall Street Journal* (September 25, 1998):B1.

SCHMIDT, ROGER. *Exploring Religion.* Belmont, Calif.: Wadsworth, 1980.

SCHMITT, ERIC. "Whites in Minority in Largest Cities, the Census Shows." *New York Times* (April 30, 2001):A1, A12.

SCHOFER, EVAN, and MARION FOURCADE-GOURINCHAS. "The Structural Contexts of Civil Engagement: Voluntary Association Membership in Comparative Perspective." *American Sociological Review.* Vol. 66, No. 6 (December 2001):806–28.

SCHULTZ, T. PAUL. "Inequality in the Distribution of Personal Income in the World: How It Is Changing and Why." *Journal of Population Economics.* Vol. 11, No. 2 (1998):307–44.

SCHUMAN, HOWARD, and MARIA KRYSAN. "A Historical Note on Whites' Beliefs about Racial Inequality." *American Sociological Review.* Vol. 64, No. 6 (December 1999):847–55.

SCHUMANN, HANS WOLFGANG. *Buddhism: An Outline of Its Teachings and Schools.* Wheaton, Ill.: The Theosophical Publishing House/Quest Books, 1974.

SCHUR, LISA A., and DOUGLAS L. KRUSE. "What Determines Voter Turnout? Lessons from Citizens with Disabilities." *Social Science Quarterly.* Vol. 81, No. 2 (June 2000): 571–87.

SCHUTT, RUSSELL K. "Objectivity versus Outrage." *Society.* Vol. 26, No. 4 (May–June 1989):14–16.

SCHWARTZ, BARRY. "Memory as a Cultural System: Abraham Lincoln in World War II." *American Sociological Review.* Vol. 61, No. 5 (October 1996):908–27.

SCHWARTZ, FELICE N. "Management, Women, and the New Facts of Life." *Harvard Business Review.* Vol. 89, No. 1 (January–February 1989):65–76.

SCHWARTZ, MARTIN D. "Gender and Injury in Spousal Assault." *Sociological Focus.* Vol. 20, No. 1 (January 1987):61–75.

SCHWARZ, JOHN E., and THOMAS J. VOLGY. *The Forgotten Americans: Thirty Million Working Poor in the Land of Opportunity.* New York: Norton, 1992.

SCOMMEGNA, PAOLA. "Increased Cohabitation Changing Children's Family Settings." *Population Today.* Vol. 30, No. 7 (July 2002):3, 6.

SCOTT, JOHN, and CATHERINE GRIFF. *Directors of Industry: The British Corporate Network, 1904–1976.* New York: Blackwell, 1985.

SCOTT, JOSEPH E., and J. CUVELIER. "Violence in *Playboy* Magazine: A Longitudinal Analysis." *Archives of Sexual Behavior.* Vol. 16 (1987):279–88.

SCOTT, W. RICHARD. *Organizations: Rational, Natural, and Open Systems.* Englewood Cliffs, N.J.: Prentice Hall, 1981.

SEAGER, JONI. *The State of Women in the World Atlas.* New revised 2d ed. New York: Penguin Group, 1997.

SEARS, DAVID O., and JOHN B. McCONAHAY. *The Politics of Violence: The New Urban Blacks and the Watts Riot.* Boston: Houghton Mifflin, 1973.

SEGAL, MADY WECHSLER, and AMANDA FAITH HANSEN. "Value Rationales in Policy Debates on Women in the Military: A Content Analysis of Congressional Testimony, 1941–1985." *Social Science Quarterly.* Vol. 73, No. 2 (June 1992):296–309.

SEIDMAN, STEVEN. *Queer Theory/Sociology.* Oxford, U.K.: Blackwell, 1996.

SEKULIC, DUSKO, GARTH MASSEY, and RANDY HODSON. "Who Were the Yugoslavs? Failed Sources of Common Identity in the Former Yugoslavia." *American Sociological Review.* Vol. 59, No. 1 (February 1994):83–97.

SENNETT, RICHARD. *The Corrosion of Character: The Personal Consequences of Work in the New Capitalism.* New York: Norton, 1998.

SENNETT, RICHARD, and JONATHAN COBB. *The Hidden Injuries of Class.* New York: Vintage Books, 1973.

THE SENTENCING PROJECT. "New Prison Population Figures Show Slowing of Growth but Uncertain Trends." [Online] Available August 14, 2002, at http://www.sentencingproject.org/brief/pub1044.pdf

SEPLOW, STEPHEN, and JONATHAN STORM. "How TV Defined Our Lives." *Philadelphia Inquirer* (November 30, 1997):A1, A16–17.

SHAPIRO, JOSEPH P. "Back to Work, on Mission." *U.S. News & World Report.* Vol. 130, No. 22 (June 4, 2001).

SHAPIRO, JOSEPH P., and JOANNIE M. SCHROF. "Honor Thy Children." *U.S. News & World Report.* Vol. 118, No. 8 (February 27, 1995):39–49.

SHARPE, ANITA. "The Rich Aren't So Different After All." *Wall Street Journal* (November 12, 1996):B1, B10.

SHAWCROSS, WILLIAM. *Sideshow: Kissinger, Nixon and the Destruction of Cambodia.* New York: Pocket Books, 1979.

SHEA, RACHEL HARTIGAN. "The New Insecurity." *U.S. News & World Report.* Vol. 132, No. 9 (March 25, 2002):40.

SHEEHAN, TOM. "Senior Esteem as a Factor in Socioeconomic Complexity." *The Gerontologist.* Vol. 16, No. 5 (October 1976):433–40.

SHELDON, WILLIAM H., EMIL M. HARTL, and EUGENE McDERMOTT. *Varieties of Delinquent Youth.* New York: Harper, 1949.

SHELER, JEFFREY L. "Faith in America." *U.S. News & World Report.* Vol. 132, No. 15 (May 6, 2002):40–4.

SHELEY, JAMES F., JOSHUA ZHANG, CHARLES J. BRODY, and JAMES D. WRIGHT. "Gang Organization, Gang Criminal Activity, and Individual Gang Members' Criminal Behavior." *Social Science Quarterly.* Vol. 76, No. 1 (March 1995):53–68.

SHERKAT, DARREN E., and CHRISTOPHER G. ELLISON. "Recent Developments and Current Controversies in the Sociology of Religion." *Annual Review of Sociology.* Vol. 25 (1999):363–94.

SHERMAN, LAWRENCE W., and DOUGLAS A. SMITH. "Crime, Punishment, and Stake in Conformity: Legal and Informal Control of Domestic Violence." *American Sociological Review.* Vol. 57, No. 5 (October 1992):680–90.

SHEVKY, ESHREF, and WENDELL BELL. *Social Area Analysis*. Stanford, Calif.: Stanford University Press, 1955.

SHIPLER, DAVID K. *Russia: Broken Idols, Solemn Dreams*. New York: Penguin Books, 1984.

SHIPLEY, JOSEPH T. *Dictionary of Word Origins*. Totowa, N.J.: Roman & Allanheld, 1985.

SHIVELY, JOELLEN. "Cowboys and Indians: Perceptions of Western Films among American Indians and Anglos." *American Sociological Review*. Vol. 57, No. 6 (December 1992):725–34.

SHUPE, ANSON. *In the Name of All That's Holy: A Theory of Clergy Malfeasance*. Westport, Conn.: Praeger, 1995.

SHUPE, ANSON, WILLIAM A. STACEY, and LONNIE R. HAZLEWOOD. *Violent Men, Violent Couples: The Dynamics of Domestic Violence*. Lexington, Mass.: Lexington Books, 1987.

SIDEL, RUTH, and VICTOR W. SIDEL. *A Healthy State: An International Perspective on the Crisis in United States Medical Care*. Rev. ed. New York: Pantheon Books, 1982a.

———. *The Health Care of China*. Boston: Beacon Press, 1982b.

SILVERBERG, ROBERT. "The Greenhouse Effect: Apocalypse Now or Chicken Little?" *Omni* (July 1991):50–54.

SIMMEL, GEORG. *The Sociology of Georg Simmel*. Kurt Wolff, ed. New York: Free Press, 1950:118–69; orig. 1902.

———. "Fashion." In Donald N. Levine, ed., *Georg Simmel: On Individuality and Social Forms*. Chicago: University of Chicago Press, 1971; orig. 1904.

SIMON, JULIAN. *The Ultimate Resource*. Princeton, N.J.: Princeton University Press, 1981.

———. "More People, Greater Wealth, More Resources, Healthier Environment." In Theodore D. Goldfarb, ed., *Taking Sides: Clashing Views on Controversial Environmental Issues*. 6th ed. Guilford, Conn.: The Dushkin Publishing Group, 1995.

SIMON, ROGER, and ANGIE CANNON. "An Amazing Journey." *U.S. News & World Report*. Vol. 131, No. 5 (August 6, 2001):10–19.

SIMONS, MARLISE. "The Price of Modernization: The Case of Brazil's Kaiapo Indians." In John J. Macionis and Nijole V. Benokraitis, eds., *Seeing Ourselves: Classic, Contemporary, and Cross-Cultural Readings in Sociology*. 5th ed. Upper Saddle River, N.J.: Prentice Hall, 2001:496–502.

SIMPSON, GEORGE EATON, and J. MILTON YINGER. *Racial and Cultural Minorities: An Analysis of Prejudice and Discrimination*. 4th ed. New York: Harper & Row, 1972.

SIVARD, RUTH LEGER. *World Military and Social Expenditures, 1987–88*. 12th ed. Washington, D.C.: World Priorities, 1988.

———. *World Military and Social Expenditures, 1992–93*. 17th ed. Washington, D.C.: World Priorities, 1993.

SIZER, THEODORE R. *Horace's Compromise: The Dilemma of the American High School*. Boston: Houghton Mifflin, 1984.

SKOCPOL, THEDA. *States and Social Revolutions: A Comparative Analysis of France, Russia, and China*. Cambridge, U.K.: Cambridge University Press, 1979.

SLOAN, ALLAN. "Bad Boys Club." *Newsweek*. (July 1, 2002):44–6.

SMAIL, J. KENNETH. "Let's *Reduce* Global Population!" In John J. Macionis and Nijole V. Benokraitis, eds., *Seeing Ourselves: Classic, Contemporary, and Cross-Cultural Readings in Sociology*. 6th ed. Upper Saddle River, N.J.: Prentice Hall, 2004:422–6.

SMART, NINIAN. *The Religious Experience of Mankind*. New York: Charles Scribner's Sons, 1969.

SMART, TIM. "Not Acting Their Age." *U.S. News & World Report*. Vol. 130, No. 22 (June 4, 2001):54–60.

———. ". . . and Those Who Came When Called." *U.S. News & World Report*. Vol. 133, No. 25 (December 30, 2002-January 6, 2003):48.

SMELSER, NEIL J. *Theory of Collective Behavior*. New York: Free Press, 1962.

SMITH, ADAM. *An Inquiry into the Nature and Causes of the Wealth of Nations*. New York: The Modern Library, 1937; orig. 1776.

SMITH, CRAIG S. "Authorities Took Victim's Organs, His Brother Says." *Columbus Dispatch* (March 11, 2001):A3.

SMITH, DOUGLAS A. "Police Response to Interpersonal Violence: Defining the Parameters of Legal Control." *Social Forces*. Vol. 65, No. 3 (March 1987):767–82.

SMITH, DOUGLAS A., and PATRICK R. GARTIN. "Specifying Specific Deterrence: The Influence of Arrest on Future Criminal Activity." *American Sociological Review*. Vol. 54, No. 1 (February 1989):94–105.

SMITH, DOUGLAS A., and CHRISTY A. VISHER. "Street-Level Justice: Situational Determinants of Police Arrest Decisions." *Social Problems*. Vol. 29, No. 2 (December 1981):167–77.

SMITH, ROBERT B. "Health Care Reform Now." *Society*. Vol. 30, No. 3 (March–April 1993):56–65.

SMITH, RYAN A. "Race, Gender, and Authority in the Workplace: Theory and Research." *Annual Review of Sociology*. Vol. 28 (2002):509–42.

SMITH-LOVIN, LYNN, and CHARLES BRODY. "Interruptions in Group Discussions: The Effects of Gender and Group Composition." *American Journal of Sociology*. Vol. 54, No. 3 (June 1989):424–35.

SMOCK, PAMELA J. "Cohabitation in the United States: An Appraisal of Research Themes, Findings, and Implications." *Annual Review of Sociology*. Vol. 26 (2000):1–20.

SMOLOWE, JILL. "When Violence Hits Home." *Time*. Vol. 144, No. 1 (July 4, 1994):18–25.

SNELL, MARILYN BERLIN. "The Purge of Nurture." *New Perspectives Quarterly*. Vol. 7, No. 1 (Winter 1990):1–2.

SNOW, DAVID A., E. BURKE ROCHFORD, JR., STEVEN K. WORDEN, and ROBERT D. BENFORD. "Frame Alignment Processes, Micromobilization, and Movement Participation." *American Sociological Review*. Vol. 51, No. 4 (August 1986):464–81.

Society. "Female Opinion and Defense since September 11th." Vol. 39, No. 3 (March/April 2002):2.

SONENSTEIN, FREYA L., GARY J. GATES, STEFANIE SCHMIDT, and NATALYA BOLSHUN. *Primary Child Care Arrangements of Employed Parents: Findings from the 1999 National Survey of America's Families*. Washington, D.C.: The Urban Institute, 2002. [Online] Available September 12, 2002, at http://www.urban.org

SOUTH, SCOTT J., and STEVEN F. MESSNER. "Structural Determinants of Intergroup Association: Interracial Marriage and Crime." *American Journal of Sociology*. Vol. 91, No. 6 (May 1986):1409–30.

SOWELL, THOMAS. *Ethnic America*. New York: Basic Books, 1981.

SOYINKA, WOLE. "Africa's Culture Producers." *Society*. Vol. 28, No. 2 (January–February 1991):32–40.

SPECTER, MICHAEL. "Plunging Life Expectancy Puzzles Russia." *New York Times* (August 2, 1995):A1, A2.

———. "Deep in the Russian Soul, a Lethal Darkness." *New York Times* (June 8, 1997a): section 4, pp. 1, 5.

———. "Moscow on the Make." *New York Times Magazine* (June 1, 1997b):48–55, 72, 75, 80, 84.

———. "Yogurt? Caucasus Centenarians 'Never Eat It.'" *New York Times* (March 14, 1998):A1, A4.

SPEER, TIBBETT L. "Are College Costs Cutting Enrollment?" *American Demographics*. Vol. 16, No. 11 (November 1994):9–10.

———. "Digging Into the Underground Economy." *American Demographics*. Vol. 17, No. 2 (February 1995):15–16.

SPEIER, HANS. "Wit and Politics: An Essay on Laughter and Power." Ed. and trans. by Robert Jackall. *American Journal of Sociology*. Vol. 103, No. 5 (March 1998):1352–1401.

SPITZER, STEVEN. "Toward a Marxian Theory of Deviance." In Delos H. Kelly, ed., *Criminal Behavior: Readings in Criminology*. New York: St. Martin's Press, 1980:175–91.

SPLAIN, CHERYL S. "Homeless Problem Not Just in Big Cities." *Mount Vernon News* (March 6, 2000):1A, 3A.

STACEY, JUDITH. *Patriarchy and Socialist Revolution in China*. Berkeley: University of California Press, 1983.

———. *Brave New Families: Stories of Domestic Upheaval in Late Twentieth-Century America*. New York: Basic Books, 1990.

———. "Good Riddance to 'The Family': A Response to David Popenoe." *Journal of Marriage and the Family*. Vol. 55, No. 3 (August 1993):545–47.

STAGGENBORG, SUZANNE. "Social Movement Communities and Cycles of Protest: The Emergence and Maintenance of a Local Women's Movement." *Social Problems*. Vol. 45, No. 2 (May 1998):180–204.

STAHURA, JOHN M. "Suburban Development, Black Suburbanization and the Black Civil Rights Movement since World War II." *American Sociological Review*. Vol. 51, No. 1 (February 1986):131–44.

STAPINSKI, HELENE. "Let's Talk Dirty." *American Demographics*. Vol. 20, No. 11 (November 1998):50–56.

STARK, RODNEY. *Sociology*. Belmont, Calif.: Wadsworth, 1985.

STARK, RODNEY, and WILLIAM SIMS BAINBRIDGE. "Of Churches, Sects, and Cults: Preliminary Concepts for a Theory of Religious Movements." *Journal for the Scientific Study of Religion*. Vol. 18, No. 2 (June 1979):117–31.

———. "Secularization and Cult Formation in the Jazz Age." *Journal for the Scientific Study of Religion*. Vol. 20, No. 4 (December 1981):360–73.

STARR, PAUL. *The Social Transformation of American Medicine*. New York: Basic Books, 1982.

STAVRIANOS, L. S. *A Global History: The Human Heritage*. 3d ed. Englewood Cliffs, N.J.: Prentice Hall, 1983.

STEELE, RANDY. "Awful but Lawful." *Boating* (June 2000):36.

STEELE, SHELBY. *The Content of Our Character: A New Vision of Race in America*. New York: St. Martin's Press, 1990.

STEIN, MAURICE R. *The Eclipse of Community: An Interpretation of American Studies*. Princeton, N.J.: Princeton University Press, 1972.

STEPHENS, JOHN D. *The Transition from Capitalism to Socialism*. Urbana: University of Illinois Press, 1986.

STERNLIEB, GEORGE, and JAMES W. HUGHES. "The Uncertain Future of the Central City." *Urban Affairs Quarterly*. Vol. 18, No. 4 (June 1983):455–72.

STEVENS, GILLIAN, and GRAY SWICEGOOD. "The Linguistic Context of Ethnic Endogamy." *American Sociological Review*. Vol. 52, No. 1 (February 1987):73–82.

STIER, HAYA. "Continuity and Change in Women's Occupations following First Childbirth." *Social Science Quarterly*. Vol. 77, No. 1 (March 1996):60–75.

STODGHILL, RON, and AMANDA BOWER. "Where Everyone's a Minority." *Time*. Vol. 160, No. 10 (September 2, 2002):25–30.

STONE, LAWRENCE. *The Family, Sex and Marriage in England 1500–1800*. New York: Harper & Row, 1977.

STONE, ROBYN, GAIL LEE CAFFERATA, and JUDITH SANGL. *Caregivers of the Frail Elderly: A National Profile*. Washington, D.C.: U.S. Department of Health and Human Services, 1987.

STORMS, MICHAEL D. "Theories of Sexual Orientation." *Journal of Personality and Social Psychology*. Vol. 38, No. 5 (May 1980):783–92.

STOUFFER, SAMUEL A., et al. *The American Soldier: Adjustment during Army Life.* Princeton, N.J.: Princeton University Press, 1949.

STRATTON, LESLIE S. "Why Does More Housework Lower Women's Wages? Testing Hypotheses Involving Job Effort and Hours Flexibility." *Social Sciences Quarterly.* Vol. 82, No. 1 (March 2001):67–76.

STRAUS, MURRAY A., and RICHARD J. GELLES. "Societal Change and Change in Family Violence from 1975 to 1985 as Revealed by Two National Surveys." *Journal of Marriage and the Family.* Vol. 48, No. 4 (August 1986):465–79.

STROSS, RANDALL E. "The McPeace Dividend." *U.S. News & World Report.* Vol. 132, No. 10 (April 1, 2002):36.

SUDNOW, DAVID N. *Passing On: The Social Organization of Dying.* Englewood Cliffs, N.J.: Prentice Hall, 1967.

SULLIVAN, BARBARA. "McDonald's Sees India as Golden Opportunity." *Chicago Tribune.* Business section (April 5, 1995):1.

SUMNER, WILLIAM GRAHAM. *Folkways.* New York: Dover, 1959; orig. 1906.

SUN, LENA H. "WWII's Forgotten Internees Await Apology." *Washington Post* (March 9, 1998):A1, A5, A6.

SUNG, BETTY LEE. *Mountains of Gold: The Story of the Chinese in America.* New York: Macmillan, 1967.

SUTHERLAND, EDWIN H. "White Collar Criminality." *American Sociological Review.* Vol. 5, No. 1 (February 1940):1–12.

SUTTON, JOHN R. "Imprisonment and Social Classification in Five Common-Law Democracies: 1955–1985." *American Journal of Sociology.* Vol. 106, No. 2 (September 2000):350–86.

SWARTZ, STEVE. "Why Michael Milken Stands to Qualify for Guinness Book." *Wall Street Journal.* Vol. 70, No. 117 (March 31, 1989):1, 4.

SZASZ, THOMAS S. *The Manufacturer of Madness: A Comparative Study of the Inquisition and the Mental Health Movement.* New York: Dell, 1961.

———. *The Myth of Mental Illness: Foundations of a Theory of Personal Conduct.* New York: Harper & Row, 1970; orig. 1961.

———. "Mental Illness Is Still a Myth." *Society.* Vol. 31, No. 4 (May–June 1994):34–39.

———. "Idleness and Lawlessness in the Therapeutic State." *Society.* Vol. 32, No. 4 (May–June 1995):30–35.

TAJFEL, HENRI. "Social Psychology of Intergroup Relations." *Annual Review of Psychology.* Palo Alto, Calif.: Annual Reviews, 1982:1–39.

TAKAKI, RONALD. *Strangers from a Different Shore.* Boston: Back Bay Books, 1998.

TANBER, GEORGE J. "Freed from Death Row." *Toledo Blade* (November 22, 1998):B1, B2.

TANNAHILL, REAY. *Sex in History.* Scarborough House Publishers, 1992.

TANNEN, DEBORAH. *You Just Don't Understand: Women and Men in Conversation.* New York: Wm. Morrow, 1990.

———. *Talking from 9 to 5: How Women's and Men's Conversational Styles Affect Who Gets Heard, Who Gets Credit, and What Gets Done at Work.* New York: Wm. Morrow, 1994.

TANNENBAUM, FRANK. *Slave and Citizen: The Negro in the Americas.* New York: Vintage Books, 1946.

TARMANN, ALLISON. "Out of the Closet and onto the Census Long Form." *Population Today.* Vol. 30, No. 4 (May/June 2002):1, 6.

TARROW, SIDNEY. *Social Movements, Collective Action and Politics.* New York: Cambridge University Press, 1994.

TAVRIS, CAROL, and CAROL WADE. *Psychology in Perspective.* 3d ed. Upper Saddle River, N.J.: Prentice Hall, 2001.

TAX FOUNDATION. [Online] Available June 15, 2000, at http://www.taxfoundation.org

———. [Online] Available November 15, 2003, at http://www.taxfoundation.org

TAYLOR, JOHN. "Don't Blame Me: The New Culture of Victimization." *New York Magazine* (June 3, 1991):26–34.

TERRY, DON. "In Crackdown on Bias, A New Tool." *New York Times* (June 12, 1993):8.

TEWKSBURY, RICHARD, and PATRICIA GAGNÉ. "Transgenderists: Products of Non-normative Intersections of Sex, Gender, and Sexuality." *Journal of Men's Studies.* Vol. 5, No. 2 (November 1996):105–29.

THERNSTROM, ABIGAIL, and STEPHAN THERNSTROM. "American Apartheid? Don't Believe It." *Wall Street Journal* (March 2, 1998):A18.

THOMAS, EDWARD J. *The Life of Buddha as Legend and History.* London: Routledge & Kegan Paul, 1975.

THOMAS, EVAN, JOHN BARRY, and MELINDA LIU. "Ground Zero." *Newsweek* (May 25, 1998):28–32A.

THOMAS, PIRI. *Down These Mean Streets.* New York: Signet, 1967.

THOMAS, W. I. "The Relation of Research to the Social Process." In Morris Janowitz, ed., *W. I. Thomas on Social Organization and Social Personality.* Chicago: University of Chicago Press, 1966:289–305; orig. 1931.

THOMMA, STEVEN. "Christian Coalition Demands Action from GOP." *Philadelphia Inquirer* (September 14, 1997):A2.

THOMPSON, DICK. "Gene Maverick." *Time.* Vol. 153, No. 1 (January 11, 1999):54–55.

THOMPSON, LARRY. "Fertility with Less Fuss." *Time.* Vol. 144, No. 20 (November 14, 1994):79.

THOMPSON, MARK. "Fatal Neglect." *Time.* Vol. 150, No. 17 (October 27, 1997):34–38.

———. "Shining a Light on Abuse." *Time.* Vol. 152, No. 5 (August 3, 1998):42–43.

THOMPSON, MARK, and DOUGLAS WALLER. "Shield of Dreams." *Time.* Vol. 155, No. 19 (May 8, 2001):45–47.

THORNBERRY, TERRANCE, and MARGARET FARNSWORTH. "Social Correlates of Criminal Involvement: Further Evidence on the Relationship between Social Status and Criminal Behavior." *American Sociological Review.* Vol. 47, No. 4 (August 1982):505–18.

THORNE, BARRIE, CHERIS KRAMARAE, and NANCY HENLEY, eds. *Language, Gender and Society.* Rowley, Mass.: Newbury House, 1983.

THUROW, LESTER C. "A Surge in Inequality." *Scientific American.* Vol. 256, No. 5 (May 1987):30–37.

TILLY, CHARLES. *From Mobilization to Revolution.* Reading, Mass.: Addison-Wesley, 1978.

———. "Does Modernization Breed Revolution?" In Jack A. Goldstone, ed., *Revolutions: Theoretical, Comparative, and Historical Studies.* New York: Harcourt Brace Jovanovich, 1986:47–57.

Time Almanac 2001. Boston: Information Please, 2000.

TIRYAKIAN, EDWARD A. "Revisiting Sociology's First Classic: The Division of Labor in Society and Its Actuality." *Sociological Forum.* Vol. 9, No. 1 (March 1994):3–16.

TITTLE, CHARLES R., and WAYNE J. VILLEMEZ. "Social Class and Criminality." *Social Forces.* Vol. 56, No. 22 (December 1977):474–502.

TITTLE, CHARLES R., WAYNE J. VILLEMEZ, and DOUGLAS A. SMITH. "The Myth of Social Class and Criminality: An Empirical Assessment of the Empirical Evidence." *American Sociological Review.* Vol. 43, No. 5 (October 1978):643–56.

TOBIN, GARY. "Suburbanization and the Development of Motor Transportation: Transportation Technology and the Suburbanization Process." In Barry Schwartz, ed., *The Changing Face of the Suburbs.* Chicago: University of Chicago Press, 1976.

TOBY, JACKSON. "Getting Serious about School Discipline." *Public Interest.* Vol. 133 (Fall 1998):68–83.

TOCQUEVILLE, ALEXIS DE. *The Old Regime and the French Revolution.* Stuart Gilbert, trans. Garden City, N.Y.: Anchor/Doubleday Books, 1955; orig. 1856.

TOLNAY, STEWART E. "The Great Migration Gets Underway: A Comparison of Black Southern Migrants and Nonmigrants in the North, 1920." *Social Science Quarterly.* Vol. 82, No. 2 (June 2001):235–51.

TOLSON, JAY. "The Trouble with Elites." *Wilson Quarterly.* Vol. 19, No. 1 (Winter 1995):6–8.

TÖNNIES, FERDINAND. *Community and Society (Gemeinschaft und Gesellschaft).* New York: Harper & Row, 1963; orig. 1887.

TORRES, LISA, and MATT L. HUFFMAN. "Social Networks and Job Search Outcomes among Male and Female Professional, Technical, and Managerial Workers." *Sociological Focus.* Vol. 35, No. 1 (February 2002):25–42.

TREAS, JUDITH. "Older Americans in the 1990s and Beyond." *Population Bulletin.* Vol. 50, No. 2 (May 1995). Washington, D.C.: Population Reference Bureau.

TREIMAN, DONALD J. "Industrialization and Social Stratification." In Edward O. Laumann, ed., *Social Stratification: Research and Theory for the 1970s.* Indianapolis: Bobbs-Merrill, 1970.

TRENT, KATHERINE. "Family Context and Adolescents' Expectations about Marriage, Fertility, and Nonmarital Childbearing." *Social Science Quarterly.* Vol. 75, No. 2 (June 1994):319–39.

TROELTSCH, ERNST. *The Social Teaching of the Christian Churches.* New York: Macmillan, 1931.

TROIDEN, RICHARD R. *Gay and Lesbian Identity: A Sociological Analysis.* Dix Hills, N.Y.: General Hall, 1988.

TUCKER, JAMES. "New Age Religion and the Cult of the Self." *Society.* Vol. 39, No. 2 (February 2002):46–51.

TUMIN, MELVIN M. "Some Principles of Stratification: A Critical Analysis." *American Sociological Review.* Vol. 18, No. 4 (August 1953):387–94.

———. *Social Stratification: The Forms and Functions of Inequality.* 2d ed. Englewood Cliffs, N.J.: Prentice Hall, 1985.

TURNER, JONATHAN. *On the Origins of Human Emotions: A Sociological Inquiry into the Evolution of Human Emotions.* Stanford: Stanford University Press, 2000.

TURNER, RALPH H., and LEWIS M. KILLIAN. *Collective Behavior.* 2d ed. Englewood Cliffs, N.J.: Prentice Hall, 1972; 3d ed., 1987; 4th ed., 1993.

TYLER, S. LYMAN. *A History of Indian Policy.* Washington, D.C.: United States Department of the Interior, Bureau of Indian Affairs, 1973.

TYREE, ANDREA, MOSHE SEMYONOV, and ROBERT W. HODGE. "Gaps and Glissandos: Inequality, Economic Development, and Social Mobility in 24 Countries." *American Sociological Review.* Vol. 44, No. 3 (June 1979):410–24.

UDRY, J. RICHARD. "Biological Limitations of Gender Construction." *American Sociological Review.* Vol. 65, No. 3 (June 2000):443–57.

———. "Feminist Critics Uncover Determinism, Positivism, and Antiquated Theory." *American Sociological Review.* Vol. 66, No. 4 (August 2001):611–18.

UGGEN, CHRISTOPHER. "Ex-Offenders and the Conformist Alternative: A Job-Quality Model of Work and Crime." *Social Problems.* Vol. 46, No. 1 (February 1999):127–51.

UGGEN, CHRISTOPHER, and JEFF MANZA. "Democratic Contraction? Political Consequences of Felon Disenfranchisement in the United States." *American Sociological Review.* Vol. 67, No. 6 (December 2002):777–803.

UNESCO. Data reported in "Tower of Babel is Tumbling Down—Slowly." *U.S. News & World Report.* Vol. 131, No. 1 (July 2, 2001):9.

UNITED NATIONS DEVELOPMENT PROGRAMME. *Human Development Report 1990.* New York: Oxford University Press, 1990.

———. *Human Development Report 1994.* New York: Oxford University Press, 1994.

———. *Human Development Report 1995.* New York: Oxford University Press, 1995.

———. *Human Development Report 1996.* New York: Oxford University Press, 1996.

———. *Human Development Report 1997.* New York: Oxford University Press, 1997.

———. *Human Development Report 1998.* New York: Oxford University Press, 1998.

———. *Human Development Report 1999.* New York: Oxford University Press, 1999.

———. *Human Development Report 2000.* New York: Oxford University Press, 2000.

———. *Human Development Report 2001.* New York: Oxford University Press, 2001.

———. *Human Development Report 2002.* New York: Oxford University Press, 2002.

———. *Human Development Report 2003.* New York: Oxford University Press, 2003.

UNIVERSITY OF AKRON RESEARCH CENTER. *National Survey of Religion and Politics 1992.* Akron, Ohio: University of Akron Research Center, 1993.

UNRUH, JOHN D., JR. *The Plains Across.* Urbana: University of Illinois Press, 1979.

U.S. BUREAU OF ECONOMIC ANALYSIS. Foreign Direct Investment in the United States: Country Detail for Selected Items. [Online] Available December 26, 2003, at http://www.bea.doc.gov/bea/di/fdilongcty.htm

U.S. BUREAU OF JUSTICE STATISTICS. *Intimate Partner Violence and Age of Victim, 1993–99.* Washington, D.C.: The Bureau, 2001. [Online] Available December 4, 2001, at http://www.ojp.usdoj.gov/bjs/pub/pdf/ipva99.pdf

———. *Compendium of Federal Justice Statistics, 2000.* NCJ 194067. Washington, D.C.: U.S. Department of Justice, 2002. [Online] Available October 9, 2002, at http://www.albany.edu/sourcebook/

———. *Sourcebook of Criminal Justice Statistics Online.* [Online] Available November 22, 2002, at http://www.albany.edu/sourcebook/1995/pdf

———. *Capital Punishment 2001.* Washington, D.C.: The Bureau, 2002. [Online] Available December 30, 2003, at http://www.ojp.usdoj.gov/bjs/pub/pdf/cp01.pdf

———. *Criminal Victimization 2001: Changes 2000–01 with Trends 1993–2001.* Washington, D.C.: The Bureau, 2002.

———. *Criminal Victimization, 2002.* Washington, D.C.: U.S. Government Printing Office, 2003.

———. *Prison and Jail Inmates at Midyear 2002.* Washington, D.C.: The Bureau, 2003.

U.S. CENSUS BUREAU. "Census Bureau Counts 170,000 at Homeless Shelters." News release, October 31, 2000.

———. *Educational Attainment in the United States: March 2000* (Update). Current Population Reports, P20–536. Washington, D.C.: U.S. Government Printing Office, 2000.

———. *Age: 2000.* Census 2000 Brief, C2KBR/01-12. Washington, D.C.: U.S. Government Printing Office, 2001. [Online] Available September 2001 at http://www.census.gov/population/www/cen2000/briefs.html

———. *America's Families and Living Arrangements: 2000.* Current Population Reports, P20-537. Washington, D.C.: U.S. Government Printing Office, 2001. [Online] Available November 6, 2002, at http://www.census.gov/prod/2001pubs/p20-537.pdf

———. *The Black Population: 2000.* Census 2000 Brief, C2KBR/01-5. Washington, D.C.: U.S. Government Printing Office, 2001. [Online] Available October 24, 2002, at http://www.census.gov/population/www/cen2000/briefs.html

———. *Census 2000 PHC-T-5. Ranking Tables for Incorporated Places of 100,000 or More: 1990 and 2000.* [Online] Available October 24, 2001, at http://www.census.gov/population/cen2000/phc-t5/tab02.pdf

———. *Census 2000 PHC-T-15. General Demographic Characteristics by Race for the United States: 2000.* [Online] Available October 10, 2001, at http://www.census.gov/population/www/cen2000/phc-t15.html

———. *Census 2000 Supplementary Survey Summary Tables.* Tables QT-01, QT-02, and QT-03. [Online] Available September 12, 2001, at http://factfinder.census.gov/

———. *CPS Annual Demographic Survey, March Supplement.* [Online] Available March 2001 at http://ferret.bls.census.gov/macro/032001/perinc/new06-000.htm

———. *Gender: 2000.* Census 2000 Brief, C2KBR/01-9. Washington, D.C.: U.S. Government Printing Office, 2001. [Online] Available September 2001 at http://www.census.gov/population/www/cen2000/briefs.html

———. *The Hispanic Population: 2000.* Census 2000 Brief, C2KBR/01-3. Washington, D.C.: U.S. Government Printing Office, 2001. [Online] Available October 24, 2002, at http://www.census.gov/population/www/cen2000/briefs.html

———. *Home Computers and Internet Use in the United States.* August 2000. Current Population Reports (P23-201). Washington, D.C.: U.S. Government Printing Office, 2001.

———. *Households and Families: 2000.* Census 2000 Brief, C2KBR/01-8. Washington, D.C.: U.S. Government Printing Office, 2001. [Online] Available September 2001 at http://www.census.gov/population/www/cen2000/brief.html

———. *Interracial Tables.* Table 2, "Race of Couples: 1990." [Online] Available December 4, 2001, at http://www.census.gov/population/socdemo/race/interractab2.txt

———. *Mapping Census 2000: The Geography of U.S. Diversity.* Census Special Reports, Series CENSR/01-1. Washington, D.C.: U.S. Government Printing Office, 2001.

———. *The Native Hawaiian and Other Pacific Islander Population: 2000.* Census 2000 Brief, C2KBR/01-14. Washington, D.C.: U.S. Government Printing Office, 2001. [Online] Available October 24, 2002, at http://www.census.gov/population/www/cen2000/briefs.html

———. *Overview of Race and Hispanic Origin: 2000.* Census 2000 Brief, C2KBR/01-1. Washington, D.C.: U.S. Government Printing Office, 2001. [Online] Available October 24, 2002, at http://www.census.gov/population/www/cen2000/briefs.html

———. *Population Change and Distribution: 1990 to 2000.* Census 2000 Brief, C2KBR/01-2. [Online] Available April 2001 at http://www.census.gov/population/www/cen2000/briefs.html

———. *Money Income in the United States: 2000.* Current Population Reports, P60-213. Washington, D.C.: U.S. Government Printing Office, 2001.

———. *Poverty in the United States: 2000.* Current Population Reports, P60-214. Washington, D.C.: U.S. Government Printing Office, 2001.

———. *Resident Population Estimates of the United States by Sex, Race, and Hispanic Origin: April 1, 1990 to July 1, 1999, with Short-Term Projection to November 1, 2000.* [Online] Available September 19, 2001, at http://www.census.gov/population/estimates/nation/intfile3-1.txt

———. *School Enrollment: Social and Economic Characteristics of Students: October 2000.* PPL-148. Washington, D.C.: The Bureau, 2001. [Online] Available October 17, 2001, at http://www.census.gov/population/socdemo/school/ppl-148/

———. *The 65 Years and Over Population: 2000.* Census 2000 Brief, C2KBR/01-10. Washington, D.C.: U.S. Government Printing Office, 2001. [Online] Available October 24, 2002, at http://www.census.gov/population/www/cen2000/briefs.html

———. *The Two or More Races Population: 2000.* Census 2000 Brief, C2KBR/01-6. Washington, D.C.: U.S. Government Printing Office, 2001. [Online] Available October 24, 2002, at http://www.census.gov/population/www/cen2000/briefs.html

———. *The White Population: 2000.* Census 2000 Brief, C2KBR/01-4. Washington, D.C.: U.S. Government Printing Office, 2001. [Online] Available October 24, 2002, at http://www.census.gov/population/www/cen2000/briefs.html

———. *The American Indian and Alaska Native Population: 2000.* Census 2000 Brief, C2KBR/01-15. Washington, D.C.: U.S. Government Printing Office, 2002. [Online] Available October 24, 2002, at http://www.census.gov/population/www/cen2000/briefs.html

———. *The Asian Population: 2000.* Census 2000 Brief, C2KBR/01-16. Washington, D.C.: U.S. Government Printing Office, 2002. [Online] Available October 24, 2002, at http://www.census.gov/population/www/cen2000/briefs.html

———. Current Population Survey. Detailed Income Tabulations—Families. Table FINC-01. [Online] Available August 9, 2003, at http://ferret.bls.census.gov/macro/032002/faminc/new01_003.htm

———. Current Population Survey. Detailed Income Tabulations—People. Tables PINC-01, PINC-03, PINC-05, PINC-06, PINC-11. [Online] Available August 9, 2003, at http://ferret.bls.census.gov/macro/032002/perinc/new11_002.htm

———. Current Population Survey. Detailed Poverty Tables: 2001. Tables 1, 10, 16a, 20. [Online] Available October 22, 2002, at http://ferret.bls.census.gov/macro/032002/pov/toc.htm

———. *Custodial Mothers and Fathers and Their Child Support.* Current Population Reports (P60-217). Washington, D.C.: U.S. Government Printing Office, 2002. [Online] Available November 5, 2002, at http://www.census.gov/prod/2002pubs/p60-217.pdf

———. *Health Insurance Coverage: 2001. Current Population Reports* (P60-220). Washington, D.C.: U.S. Government Printing Office, 2002.

———. Historical Income Tables—Families. Tables F-1, F-2, F-3, F-7, F-7C. [Online] Available October 18, 2002, at http://www.census.gov/hhes/income/histinc/histinctb.html

———. Historical Income Tables—Households. Table H-17. [Online] Available October 21, 2002, at http://www.census.gov/hhes/income/histinc/histinctb.html

———. Historical Income Tables—People. Tables P-10, P-36. [Online] Available September 26, 2002, at http://www.census.gov/hhes/income/histinc/histinctb.html

———. *Housing Vacancies and Home Ownership Annual Statistics: 2001.* Table 20. [Online] Available October 22, 2002, at http://www.census.gov/hhes/www/housing/hvs/annual01/an01t20.html

———. *Money Income in the United States: 2001.* Current Population Reports (P60-218). Washington, D.C.: U.S. Government Printing Office, 2002. [Online] Available September 24, 2002, at http://www.census.gov/prod/2002pubs/p60-218.pdf

——. *Poverty in the United States: 2001.* Current Population Reports (P60-219). Washington, D.C.: U.S. Government Printing Office, 2002. [Online] Available September 24, 2002, at http://www.census.gov/prod/2002pubs/p60-219.pdf

——. Sex by Age. Summary File 1 tables. [Online] Available September 26, 2002, at http://www.census.gov/

——. *Statistical Abstract of the United States: 2002.* Washington, D.C.: U.S. Government Printing Office, 2002.

——. *Voting and Registration in the Election of November 2000.* Current Population Reports, P20-542. Washington, D.C.: U.S. Government Printing Office, 2002. [Online] Available September 10, 2002, at http://www.census.gov/population/socdemo/voting/p20-542/tab08.pdf

——. Historical Income Tables—Families. Table F-7C. Revised September 30, 2002. [Online] Available December 24, 2003, at http://www.census.gov/hhes/income/histinc/f07c.html

——. *The Asian and Pacific Islander Population in the United States: March 2002.* Current Population Reports (P20-540). Washington, D.C.: U.S. Government Printing Office, 2003.

——. *The Black Population in the United States: March 2002.* Current Population Reports (P20-541). Washington, D.C.: U.S. Government Printing Office, 2003.

——. Current Population Survey, March 2002. Tables 7, 14. [Online] Available May 28, 2003, at http://www.census.gov/population/socdemo/race/api/ppl-163/tab07.pdf

——. *Educational Attainment in the United States: March 2002.* Detailed tables (PPL-169) (2003). [Online] Available August 9, 2003, at http://www.census.gov/population/socdemo/education/ppl-169/tab01.pdf

——. *The Hispanic Population in the United States: March 2002.* Current Population Reports (P20-545). Washington, D.C.: U.S. Government Printing Office, 2003.

——. Income 2001. Table 4. Median Income of Families by Selected Characteristics, Race and Hispanic Origin of Householder: 2001, 2000, and 1999. [Online] Available August 9, 2003, at http://www.census.gov/hhes/income/income01/inctab4.html

——. International Data Base. [Online] Available October 16, 2003, at http://www.census.gov/cgi-bin/ipc/idbagg

——. *Married-Couple and Unmarried-Partner Households: 2000.* Washington, D.C.: The Bureau, 2003.

——. Table F1. Family Households, by Type, Age of Own Children, Age of Family Members, and Age, Race and Hispanic Origin of Householder: March 2002: Total Family Households: Black. [Online] Available June 12, 2003, at http://www.census.gov/population/socdemo/hh-fam/cps2002/tabF1-black.pdf

——. Table 4. Language Spoken at Home and Ability to Speak English for the Population 5 Years and Over by State: 2000. [Online] Available February 25, 2003, at http://www.census.gov/population/cen2000/phc-t20/tab04.pdf

——. Table 4. Poverty Status of Families, by Type of Family, Presence of Related Children, Race, and Hispanic Origin: 1959 to 2002. [Online] Available October 6, 2003, at http://www.census.gov/hhes/poverty/histpov/hstpov4.html

——. Table MS-3. Interracial Married Couples: 1980 to Present. [Online] Available June 30, 2003, at http://www.census.gov/population/socdemo/hh-fam/tabMS-3.pdf

——. Table QT-P13. Ancestry: 2000. [Online] Available November 5, 2003, at http://factfinder.census.gov

U.S. CENSUS OFFICE. *Census of the United States (1900).* Vol. II: Population. Washington, D.C.: The Office, 1902.

U.S. CENTERS FOR DISEASE CONTROL AND PREVENTION. "National and State-Specific Pregnancy Rates among Adolescents–United States, 1995–1997." *Morbidity and Mortality Weekly Report.* Vol. 49, No. 27 (July 14, 2000):605–11.

——. *HIV/AIDS Surveillance Report.* Vol. 13, No. 1 (Midyear 2001 edition). Atlanta, Ga.: The Centers, 2001.

——. *HIV/AIDS Surveillance Report.* Vol. 13, No. 2 (Year-end 2001 edition). Atlanta, Ga.: The Centers, 2001.

——. *2000 Sexually Transmitted Disease Surveillance Report.* Atlanta, Ga.: The Centers, 2001.

——. "Cigarette Smoking among Adults—United States, 2000." *Morbidity and Mortality Weekly Report.* Vol. 51, No. 29 (July 26, 2002):642–45.

——. "Trends in Cigarette Smoking among High School Students—United States, 1991–2001." *Morbidity and Mortality Weekly Report.* Vol. 51, No. 19 (May 17, 2002):409–12.

U.S. CITIZENSHIP AND IMMIGRATION SERVICES. *2002 Yearbook of Immigration Statistics.* [Online] Available December 24, 2003, at http://uscis.gov/graphics/shared/aboutus/statistics/IMM02yrbk/IMM2002list.htm

U.S. DEPARTMENT OF COMMERCE. *Statistical Abstract of the United States: 1930.* Washington, D.C.: U.S. Government Printing Office, 1930.

U.S. DEPARTMENT OF HEALTH AND HUMAN SERVICES. *Administration for Children and Families. Temporary Assistance for Needy Families (TANF) Program; Third Annual Report to Congress,* August 2000. Washington, D.C.: The Administration, 2000.U.S. DEPARTMENT OF JUSTICE. "Nearly Three Percent of College Women Experienced a Completed Rape or Attempted Rape During the College Year, According to a New Justice Department Report." [Online]. Accessed February 15, 2001, at http://www.ojp.usdoj.gov/bjs/pub/press/svcw.pr

U.S. DEPARTMENT OF LABOR. Bureau of Labor Statistics. Tables from *Employment and Earnings.* [Online] Available August 30, 2003, at http://www.bls.gov/cps/#annual

——. Bureau of Labor Statistics. *International Comparisons of Hourly Compensation Costs for Production Workers in Manufacturing, 2002.* [Online] Available September 30, 2003, at http://www.bls.gov/fls

U.S. DEPARTMENT OF STATE. *World Military Expenditures and Arms Transfers 1999–2000.* [Online] Available December 28, 2003, at http://www.state.gov/documents/organization/18738.pdf

USEEM, BERT. "Disorganization and the New Mexico Prison Riot of 1980." *American Sociological Review.* Vol. 50, No. 5 (October 1985):677–88.

U.S. EQUAL EMPLOYMENT OPPORTUNITY COMMISSION. Occupational Employment in Private Industry by Race/Ethnic Group/Sex, and by Industry, United States, 2001. [Online] Available June 5, 2003, at http://www.eeoc.gov/stats/jobpat/2001/national.html

U.S. FEDERAL BUREAU OF INVESTIGATION. *Crime in the United States 2000.* Washington, D.C.: The Bureau, 2001. [Online] Available November 11, 2001, at http://www.fbi.gov/ucr/cius-00/

——. *Crime in the United States 2001.* Washington, D.C.: The Bureau, 2002.

U.S. FEDERAL ELECTION COMMISSION. "FEC Issues Semi-Annual Federal PAC Count." News release (August 29, 2003).

U.S. HOUSE OF REPRESENTATIVES. "Street Children: A Global Disgrace." Hearing on November 7, 1991. Washington, D.C.: U.S. Government Printing Office, 1992.

U.S. IMMIGRATION AND NATURALIZATION SERVICE. *Legal Immigration, Fiscal Year 2000.* Washington, D.C.: The Service, 2002. [Online] Available August 13, 2002, at http://www.ins.usdoj.gov/graphics/aboutins/statistics/IMM2000AR.pdf

U.S. INTERNAL REVENUE SERVICE. "Personal Wealth, 1998." *Statistics of Income Bulletin* (April 2003):88.

U.S. NATIONAL CENTER FOR EDUCATION STATISTICS. *Dropout Rates in the United States: 2000.* Washington, D.C.: U.S. Government Printing Office, 2001. [Online] Available November 6, 2002, at http://nces.ed.gov/pubs2002/droppub_2001/

——. *Digest of Education Statistics, 2002.* Washington, D.C.: U.S. Government Printing Office, 2003.

U.S. NATIONAL CENTER FOR HEALTH STATISTICS. *National Vital Statistics Report.* Vol. 48, No. 11 (July 24, 2000).

——. *National Vital Statistics Report.* Vol. 49, No. 8 (September 21, 2001).

——. *National Vital Statistics Report.* Vol. 49, No. 12 (October 9, 2001).

——. *National Vital Statistics Report.* Vol. 50, No. 5 (February 12, 2002).

——. *National Vital Statistics Report.* Vol. 50, No. 6 (March 21, 2002).

——. *National Vital Statistics Report.* Vol. 50, No. 12 (August 28, 2002).

——. *National Vital Statistics Report.* Vol. 50, No. 14 (September 11, 2002).

——. *National Vital Statistics Report.* Vol. 50, No. 15 (September 16, 2002).

——. "Births: Final Data for 2001." *National Vital Statistics Report.* Vol. 51, No. 2 (December 18, 2002):44.

——. *National Vital Statistics Report.* Vol. 51, No. 3 (December 19, 2002).

——. "Deaths: Preliminary Data for 2001." *National Vital Statistics Report.* Vol. 51, No. 5 (March 14, 2003):7.

——. *National Vital Statistics Report.* Vol. 52, No. 3 (September 18, 2003).

——. *Summary Health Statistics for the U.S. Population: National Health Interview Survey, 2000. Vital and Health Statistics.* Series 10, No. 214. Hyattsville, Md.: The Center, 2003.

U.S. SMALL BUSINESS ADMINISTRATION. *Minorities in Business, 2001.* 2001. [Online] Available October 26, 2002, at http://www.sba.gov/advo/stats/min01.pdf

——. *Women in Business, 2001.* October 2001. [Online] Available October 23, 2002, at http://www.sba.gov/advo/stats/wib01.pdf

U.S. STATE DEPARTMENT. *Patterns of Global Terrorism: 2002.* [Online] Available December 26, 2003, at http://www.usis.usemb.se/terror/rpt2002/index.html

VALDEZ, A. "In the Hood: Street Gangs Discover White-Collar Crime." *Police.* Vol. 21, No. 5 (May 1997):49–50, 56.

VALLAS, STEPHEN P., and JOHN P. BECK. "The Transformation of Work Revisited: The Limits of Flexibility in American Manufacturing." *Social Problems.* Vol. 43, No. 3 (August 1996):339–61.

VALOCCHI, STEVE. "The Emergence of the Integrationist Ideology in the Civil Rights Movement." *Social Problems.* Vol. 43, No. 1 (February 1996):116–30.

VAN BIEMA, DAVID. "Parents Who Kill." *Time.* Vol. 144, No. 20 (November 14, 1994):50–51.

——. "Buddhism in America." *Time.* Vol. 150, No. 15 (October 13, 1997):71–81.

——. "Spiriting Prayer into School." *Time.* Vol. 152, No. 20 (April 27, 1998):38–41.

——. "A Surge of Teen Spirit." *Time.* Vol. 153, No. 20 (May 31, 1999):58–59.

VAN DER LIPPE, TANJA, and LISET VAN DIJK. "Comparative Research on Women's Employment." *Annual Review of Sociology.* Vol. 28 (2002):221–41.

VAN DYKE, NELLA, and SARAH A. SOULE. "Structural Social Change and the Mobilizing Effect of Threat: Explaining Levels of Patriot and Militia Organizing in the United States." *Social Problems.* Vol. 49, No. 4 (November 2002):497–520.

VAUGHAN, MARY KAY. "Multinational Corporations: The World as a Company Town." In Ahamed Idris-Soven et al., eds., *The World as a Company Town: Multinational Corporations and Social Change.* The Hague: Mouton Publishers, 1978:15–35.

VAYDA, EUGENE, and RAISA B. DEBER. "The Canadian Health Care System: An Overview." *Social Science and Medicine.* Vol. 18, No. 3 (1984):191–97.

VEBLEN, THORSTEIN. *The Theory of the Leisure Class.* New York: The New American Library, 1953; orig. 1899.

VEDDER, RICHARD, and LOWELL GALLAWAY. "Declining Black Employment." *Society.* Vol. 30, No. 5 (July–August 1993):56–63.

VINOVSKIS, MARIS A. "Have Social Historians Lost the Civil War? Some Preliminary Demographic Speculations." *Journal of American History.* Vol. 76, No. 1 (June 1989):34–58.

VOGEL, EZRA F. *The Four Little Dragons: The Spread of Industrialization in East Asia.* Cambridge, Mass.: Harvard University Press, 1991.

VOGEL, LISE. *Marxism and the Oppression of Women: Toward a Unitary Theory.* New Brunswick, N.J.: Rutgers University Press, 1983.

VOLD, GEORGE B., and THOMAS J. BERNARD. *Theoretical Criminology.* 3d ed. New York: Oxford University Press, 1986.

VON HIRSH, ANDREW. *Past or Future Crimes: Deservedness and Dangerousness in the Sentencing of Criminals.* New Brunswick, N.J.: Rutgers University Press, 1986.

VONNEGUT, KURT, JR. "Harrison Bergeron." In *Welcome to the Monkey House.* New York: Delacorte Press/Seymour Lawrence, 1968:7–13; orig. 1961.

WAITE, LINDA J., and MAGGIE GALLAGHER. *The Case for Marriage: Why Married People Are Happier, Healthier, and Better Off Financially.* New York: Doubleday, 2000.

WALDER, ANDREW G. "Career Mobility and the Communist Political Order." *American Sociological Review.* Vol. 60, No. 3 (June 1995):309–28.

WALDFOGEL, JANE. "The Effect of Children on Women's Wages." *American Sociological Review.* Vol. 62, No. 2 (April 1997):209–17.

WALKER, KAREN. "'Always There For Me': Friendship Patterns and Expectations among Middle- and Working-Class Men and Women." *Sociological Forum.* Vol. 10, No. 2 (June 1995):273–96.

WALL, THOMAS F. *Medical Ethics: Basic Moral Issues.* Washington, D.C.: University Press of America, 1980.

WALLER, DOUGLAS. "Onward Cyber Soldiers." *Time.* Vol. 146, No. 8 (August 21, 1995):38–44.

WALLERSTEIN, IMMANUEL. *The Modern World-System: Capitalist Agriculture and the Origins of the European World-Economy in the Sixteenth Century.* New York: Academic Press, 1974.

———. *The Capitalist World-Economy.* New York: Cambridge University Press, 1979.

———. "Crises: The World Economy, the Movements, and the Ideologies." In Albert Bergesen, ed., *Crises in the World-System.* Beverly Hills, Calif.: Sage, 1983:21–36.

———. *The Politics of the World Economy: The States, the Movements, and the Civilizations.* Cambridge, U.K.: Cambridge University Press, 1984.

WALLERSTEIN, JUDITH S., and SANDRA BLAKESLEE. *Second Chances: Men, Women, and Children a Decade after Divorce.* New York: Ticknor & Fields, 1989.

WALSH, KENNETH H. "On the Job." *U.S. News & World Report.* Vol. 132, No. 6 (Feb. 25-March 4, 2002):70–2.

WALSH, MARY WILLIAMS. "No Time to Put Your Feet Up as Retirement Comes in Stages." *New York Times* (April 15, 2001):1, 18.

WALTON, JOHN, and CHARLES RAGIN. "Global and National Sources of Political Protest: Third World Responses to the Debt Crisis." *American Sociological Review.* Vol. 55, No. 6 (December 1990):876–90.

WARNER, R. STEPHEN. "Work in Progress toward a New Paradigm for the Sociological Study of Religion in the United States." *American Journal of Sociology.* Vol. 98, No. 5 (March 1993):1044–93.

WARNER, W. LLOYD, and PAUL S. LUNT. *The Social Life of a Modern Community.* New Haven, Conn.: Yale University Press, 1941.

WARR, MARK, and CHRISTOPHER G. ELLISON. "Rethinking Social Reactions to Crime: Personal and Altruistic Fear in Family Households." *American Journal of Sociology.* Vol. 106, No. 3 (November 2000):551–78.

WATERS, MELISSA S., WILL CARRINGTON HEATH, and JOHN KEITH WATSON. "A Positive Model of the Determination of Religious Affiliation." *Social Science Quarterly.* Vol. 76, No. 1 (March 1995):105–23.

WATTENBERG, BEN J. "The Population Explosion Is Over." *New York Times Magazine* (November 23, 1997):60–63.

WATTS, DUNCAN J. "Networks, Dynamics, and the Small-World Phenomenon." *American Journal of Sociology.* Vol. 105, No. 2 (September 1999):493–527.

WEBER, ADNA FERRIN. *The Growth of Cities.* New York: Columbia University Press, 1963; orig. 1899.

WEBER, MAX. *The Protestant Ethic and the Spirit of Capitalism.* New York: Charles Scribner's Sons, 1958; orig. 1904–5.

———. *Economy and Society.* G. Roth and C. Wittich, eds. Berkeley: University of California Press, 1978; orig. 1921.

WEBSTER, ANDREW. *Introduction to the Sociology of Development.* London: Macmillan, 1984.

WEBSTER, MURRAY, JR., and STUART J. HYSOM. "Creating Status Characteristics." *American Sociological Review.* Vol. 63, No. 3 (June 1998):351–78.

WEBSTER, PAMELA S., TERRI ORBUCH, and JAMES S. HOUSE. "Effects of Childhood Family Background on Adult Marital Quality and Perceived Stability." *American Journal of Sociology.* Vol. 101, No. 2 (September 1995):404–32.

WEEKS, JOHN R. "The Demography of Islamic Nations." *Population Bulletin.* Vol. 43, No. 4 (December 1988). Washington, D.C.: Population Reference Bureau.

WEICHER, JOHN C. "Getting Richer (at Different Rates)." *Wall Street Journal* (June 14, 1995):A18.

WEIDENBAUM, MURRAY. "The Evolving Corporate Board." *Society.* Vol. 32, No. 3 (March/April 1995):9–20.

WEINBERG, GEORGE. *Society and the Healthy Homosexual.* Garden City, N.Y.: Anchor Books, 1973.

WEINER, TIM. "Head of C.I.A. Plans Center to Protect U.S. Cyberspace." *New York Times* (June 26, 1996):B7.

WEINRICH, JAMES D. *Sexual Landscapes: Why We Are What We Are, Why We Love Whom We Love.* New York: Charles Scribner's Sons, 1987.

WEISBERG, D. KELLY. *Children of the Night: A Study of Adolescent Prostitution.* Lexington, Mass.: D.C. Heath, 1985.

WEITZMAN, LENORE J. *The Divorce Revolution: The Unexpected Social and Economic Consequences for Women and Children in America.* New York: Free Press, 1985.

———. "The Economic Consequences of Divorce Are Still Unequal: Comment on Peterson." *American Sociological Review.* Vol. 61, No. 3 (June 1996):537–38.

WELCH, MICHAEL. *Flag Burning: Moral Panic and the Criminalization of Protest.* New York: Aldine de Gruyter, 2000.

WELLER, JACK M., and E. L. QUARANTELLI. "Neglected Characteristics of Collective Behavior." *American Journal of Sociology.* Vol. 79, No. 3 (November 1973):665–85.

WELLFORD, CHARLES. "Labeling Theory and Criminology: An Assessment." In Delos H. Kelly, ed., *Criminal Behavior: Readings in Criminology.* New York: St. Martin's Press, 1980:234–47.

WELLNER, ALISON STEIN. "Discovering Native America." *American Demographics.* Vol. 23, No. 8 (August 2001):21.

———. "The Census Report." *American Demographics.* Vol. 24, No. 1 (January 2002a):S3–S6.

———. "The Power of the Purse." *American Demographics.* Vol. 24, No. 7 (January/February 2002b):S3–S10.

WERTHEIMER, BARBARA MAYER. "The Factory Bell." In Linda K. Kerber and Jane De Hart Mathews, eds., *Women's America: Refocusing the Past.* New York: Oxford University Press, 1982:130–40.

WERUM, REGINE, and BILL WINDERS. "Who's 'In' and Who's 'Out': State Fragmentation and the Struggle over Gay Rights." *Social Problems.* Vol. 48, No. 3 (August 2001):386–410.

WESSELMAN, HANK. *Visionseeker: Shared Wisdom from the Place of Refuge.* Carlsbad, Calif.: Hay House, 2001.

WESTERN, BRUCE. "Postwar Unionization in Eighteen Advanced Capitalist Countries." *American Sociological Review.* Vol. 58, No. 2 (April 1993):266–82.

———. "A Comparative Study of Working-Class Disorganization: Union Decline in Eighteen Advanced Capitalist Countries." *American Sociological Review.* Vol. 60, No. 2 (April 1995):179–201.

———. "The Impact of Incarceration on Wage Mobility and Inequality." *American Sociological Review.* Vol. 67, No. 4 (August 2002):526–46.

WHALEN, JACK, and RICHARD FLACKS. *Beyond the Barricades: The Sixties Generation Grows Up.* Philadelphia: Temple University Press, 1989.

WHEELIS, ALLEN. *The Quest for Identity.* New York: Norton, 1958.

WHELAN, DAVID. "The Asian American Blind Spot." *American Demographics.* Vol. 23, No. 7 (July 2001):16–17.

WHITAKER, MARK. "Ten Ways to Fight Terrorism." *Newsweek* (July 1, 1985):26–29.

WHITE, RALPH, and RONALD LIPPITT. "Leader Behavior and Member Reaction in Three 'Social Climates.'" In Dorwin Cartwright and Alvin Zander, eds., *Group Dynamics.* Evanston, Ill.: Row, Peterson, 1953:586–611.

WHITE, WALTER. *Rope and Faggot.* New York: Arno Press and New York Times, 1969; orig. 1929.

WHITMAN, DAVID. "Shattering Myths about the Homeless." *U.S. News & World Report* (March 20, 1989):26, 28.

WHORF, BENJAMIN LEE. "The Relation of Habitual Thought and Behavior to Language." In *Language, Thought, and Reality.* Cambridge, Mass.: The Technology Press of MIT/New York: Wiley, 1956:134–59; orig. 1941.

WHYTE, WILLIAM FOOTE. *Street Corner Society.* 3d ed. Chicago: University of Chicago Press, 1981; orig. 1943.

WHYTE, WILLIAM H., JR. *The Organization Man.* Garden City, N.Y.: Anchor Books, 1957.

WIARDA, HOWARD J. "Ethnocentrism and Third World Development." *Society.* Vol. 24, No. 6 (September–October 1987):55–64.

WICKHAM, DEWAYNE. "Homeless Receive Little Attention from Candidates." Accessed October 24, 2000, at http://www.usatoday.com/usatonline

WIDOM, CATHY SPATZ. "Childhood Sexual Abuse and Its Criminal Consequences." *Society.* Vol. 33, No. 4 (May/June 1996):47–53.

WILCOX, CLYDE. "Race, Gender, and Support for Women in the Military." *Social Science Quarterly.* Vol. 73, No. 2 (June 1992):310–23.

WILES, P. J. D. *Economic Institutions Compared.* New York: Halsted Press, 1977.

WILLIAMS, RHYS H., and N. J. DEMERATH III. "Religion and Political Process in an American City." *American Sociological Review.* Vol. 56, No. 4 (August 1991):417–31.

WILLIAMS, ROBIN M., JR. *American Society: A Sociological Interpretation.* 3d ed. New York: Alfred A. Knopf, 1970.

WILLIAMS, TIMOTHY. "Bloomberg Spent $69 Million in Mayor's Race." Yahoo! News. [Online] Available December 4, 2001, at http://dailynews.yahoo.com

WILLIAMSON, JEFFREY G., and PETER H. LINDERT. *American Inequality: A Macroeconomic History*. New York: Academic Press, 1980.

WILSON, BARBARA. "National Television Violence Study." Reported by Julia Duin, "Study Finds Cartoon Heroes Initiate Too Much Violence." *Washington Times* (April 17, 1998):A4.

WILSON, BRYAN. *Religion in Sociological Perspective*. New York: Oxford University Press, 1982.

WILSON, EDWARD O. "Biodiversity, Prosperity, and Value." In F. Herbert Bormann and Stephen R. Kellert, eds., *Ecology, Economics, and Ethics: The Broken Circle*. New Haven, Conn.: Yale University Press, 1991:3–10.

WILSON, JAMES Q. *Bureaucracy: What Government Agencies Do and Why They Do It*. New York: Basic Books, 1991.

———. "Crime, Race, and Values." *Society*. Vol. 30, No. 1 (November–December 1992):90–93.

WILSON, JAMES Q., and RICHARD J. HERRNSTEIN. *Crime and Human Nature*. New York: Simon & Schuster, 1985.

WILSON, LOGAN. *American Academics Then and Now*. New York: Oxford University Press, 1979.

WILSON, THOMAS C. "Urbanism and Unconventionality: The Case of Sexual Behavior." *Social Science Quarterly*. Vol. 76, No. 2 (June 1995):346–63.

WILSON, WILLIAM JULIUS. "Work." *New York Times Magazine* (August 18, 1996):26–31, 40, 48, 52, 54.

WINNICK, LOUIS. "America's 'Model Minority.'" *Commentary*. Vol. 90, No. 2 (August 1990):22–29.

WINSHIP, CHRISTOPHER, and JENNY BERRIEN. "Boston Cops and Black Churches." *The Public Interest*. Vol. 136 (Summer 1999):52–68.

WINTERS, REBECCA. "Who Needs an M.B.A.?" *Time Select: Business*. Vol. 153, No. 19 (May 17, 1999).

———. "Trouble for School Inc." *Time*. Vol. 159, No. 21 (May 27, 2002):53.

WIRTH, LOUIS. "Urbanism as a Way of Life." *American Journal of Sociology*. Vol. 44, No. 1 (July 1938):1–24.

WITKIN, GORDON. "The Crime Bust." *U.S. News & World Report*. Vol. 124, No. 20 (May 25, 1998):28–40.

WITKIN-LANOIL, GEORGIA. *The Female Stress Syndrome: How to Recognize and Live with It*. New York: Newmarket Press, 1984.

WITT, G. EVANS. "Say What You Mean." *American Demographics*. Vol. 21, No. 2 (February 1999):23.

WOLF, DIANE L., ed. *Feminist Dilemma of Fieldwork*. Boulder, Colo.: Westview Press, 1996.

WOLF, NAOMI. *The Beauty Myth: How Images of Beauty Are Used against Women*. New York: William Morrow, 1990.

WOLFE, DAVID B. "Targeting the Mature Mind." *American Demographics*. Vol. 16, No. 3 (March 1994):32–36.

WOLFGANG, MARVIN E., ROBERT M. FIGLIO, and THORSTEN SELLIN. *Delinquency in a Birth Cohort*. Chicago: University of Chicago Press, 1972.

WOLFGANG, MARVIN E., TERRENCE P. THORNBERRY, and ROBERT M. FIGLIO. *From Boy to Man, From Delinquency to Crime*. Chicago: University of Chicago Press, 1987.

WOLFSON, ADAM. "Killing Off the Dying?" *Public Interest*. No. 131 (Spring 1998):50–70.

WONG, BUCK. "Need for Awareness: An Essay on Chinatown, San Francisco." In Amy Tachiki et al., eds., *Roots: An Asian American Reader*. Los Angeles: UCLA Asian American Studies Center, 1971:265–73.

WOODBERRY, ROBERT D. "When Surveys Lie and People Tell the Truth: Church Attenders." *American Sociological Review*. Vol. 63, No. 1 (February 1998):119–22.

WOODWARD, KENNETH L. "Feminism and the Churches." *Newsweek*. Vol. 13, No. 7 (February 13, 1989):58–61.

———. "Talking to God." *Newsweek*. Vol. 119, No. 1 (January 6, 1992a):38–44.

———. "The Elite, and How to Avoid It." *Newsweek* (July 20, 1992b):55.

THE WORLD BANK. *World Development Report 1993*. New York: Oxford University Press, 1993.

———. *World Development Report 1995: Workers in an Integrating World*. New York: Oxford University Press, 1995.

———. *World Development Report 1997: The State in a Changing World*. New York: Oxford University Press, 1997.

———. *World Development Report: Knowledge for Development*. New York: Oxford University Press, 1999.

———. *Entering the 21st Century: World Development Report 1999/2000*. New York: Oxford University Press, 2000.

———. *World Development Report 2000/2001*. Washington, D.C.: The World Bank, 2001.

———. *2003 World Development Indicators*. Washington, D.C.: The World Bank, 2003.

WORLD HEALTH ORGANIZATION. *Constitution of the World Health Organization*. New York: World Health Organization Interim Commission, 1946.

WORSLEY, PETER. "Models of the World System." In Mike Featherstone, ed., *Global Culture: Nationalism, Globalization, and Modernity*. Newbury Park, Calif.: Sage, 1990:83–95.

WREN, CHRISTOPHER S. "In Soweto-by-the-Sea, Misery Lives on as Apartheid Fades." *New York Times* (June 9, 1991):1, 7.

WRIGHT, ERIC R. "Personal Networks and Anomie: Exploring the Sources and Significance of Gender Composition." *Sociological Focus*. Vol. 28, No. 3 (August 1995):261–82.

WRIGHT, ERIK OLIN, and BILL MARTIN. "The Transformation of the American Class Structure, 1960–1980." *American Journal of Sociology*. Vol. 93, No. 1 (July 1987):1–29.

WRIGHT, JAMES D. "Address Unknown: Homelessness in Contemporary America." *Society*. Vol. 26, No. 6 (September–October 1989):45–53.

WRIGHT, JAMES D. "Ten Essential Observations on Guns in America." *Society*. Vol. 32, No. 3 (March–April 1995):63–68.

WRIGHT, RICHARD A. *In Defense of Prisons*. Westport, Conn.: Greenwood Press, 1994.

WRIGHT, ROBERT. "Sin in the Global Village." *Time*. Vol. 152, No. 16 (October 19, 1998):130.

WRIGHT, STUART A., and ELIZABETH S. PIPER. "Families and Cults: Familial Factors Related to Youth Leaving or Remaining in Deviant Religious Groups." *Journal of Marriage and the Family*. Vol. 48, No. 1 (February 1986):15–25.

WU, LAWRENCE L. "Effects of Family Instability, Income, and Income Instability on the Risk of a Premarital Birth." *American Sociological Review*. Vol. 61, No. 3 (June 1996):386–406.

YAMAGATA, HISASHI, KUANG S. YEH, SHELBY STEWMAN, and HIROKO DODGE. "Sex Segregation and Glass Ceilings: A Comparative Static Model of Women's Career Opportunities in the Federal Government over a Quarter Century." *American Journal of Sociology*. Vol. 103, No. 3 (November 1997):566–632.

YANG, FENGGANG, and HELEN ROSE EBAUGH. "Transformations in New Immigrant Religions and Their Global Implications." *American Sociological Review*. Vol. 66, No. 2 (April 2001):269–88.

YANKELOVICH, DANIEL. "How Changes in the Economy Are Reshaping American Values." In Henry J. Aaron, Thomas E. Mann, and Timothy Taylor, eds., *Values and Public Policy*. Washington, D.C.: The Brookings Institution, 1994:20.

YATES, RONALD E. "Growing Old in Japan; They Ask Gods for a Way Out." *Philadelphia Inquirer* (August 14, 1986):3A.

YEATTS, DALE E. "Self-Managed Work Teams: Innovation in Progress." *Business and Economic Quarterly* (Fall–Winter 1991):2–6.

———. "Creating the High Performance Self-Managed Work Team: A Review of Theoretical Perspectives." Paper presented at the annual meeting of the Southwest Social Science Association, Dallas, February 1994.

YIN, SANDRA. "Wanted: One Million Nurses." *American Demographics*. Vol. 24, No. 8 (September 2002):63–65.

YOELS, WILLIAM C., and JEFFREY MICHAEL CLAIR. "Laughter in the Clinic: Humor in Social Organization." *Symbolic Interaction*. Vol. 18, No. 1 (1995):39–58.

YORK, RICHARD, EUGENE A. ROSA, and THOMAS DEITZ. "Bridging Environmental Science with Environmental Policy: Plasticity of Population, Affluence, and Technology." *Social Science Quarterly*. Vol. 83, No. 1 (March 2002):18–34.

YUDELMAN, MONTAGUE, and LAURA J. M. KEALY. "The Graying of Farmers." *Population Today*. Vol. 28, No. 4 (May/June, 2000):6.

YUNKER, JAMES A. "A New Statistical Analysis of Capital Punishment Incorporating U.S. Postmoratorium Data." *Social Science Quarterly*. Vol. 82, No. 2 (June 2001):297–311.

ZAKARIA, FAREED. "How to Wage the Peace." *Newsweek* (April 21, 2003):38, 48.

ZEITLIN, IRVING M. *The Social Condition of Humanity*. New York: Oxford University Press, 1981.

ZHAO, DINGXIN. "Ecologies of Social Movements: Student Mobilization during the 1989 Prodemocracy Movement in Beijing." *American Journal of Sociology*. Vol. 103, No. 6 (May 1998):1493–1529.

ZHOU, MIN, and JOHN R. LOGAN. "Returns of Human Capital in Ethnic Enclaves: New York City's Chinatown." *American Sociological Review*. Vol. 54, No. 5 (October 1989):809–20.

ZHOU, XUEGUANG, and LIREN HOU. "Children of the Cultural Revolution: The State and the Life Course in the People's Republic of China." *American Sociological Review*. Vol. 64, No. 1 (February 1999):12–36.

ZICKLIN, G. "Re-Biologizing Sexual Orientation: A Critique." Paper presented at the Annual Meeting of the Society for the Study of Social Problems, Pittsburgh, Penn., 1992.

ZIMBARDO, PHILIP G. "Pathology of Imprisonment." *Society*. Vol. 9 (April 1972):4–8.

ZIMMER, MICHAEL. "Explaining Marital Dissolution: Explaining the Role of Spouses' Traits." *Social Science Quarterly*. Vol. 82, No. 3 (September 2001):464–77.

ZOGBY INTERNATIONAL. Poll, reported in Sandra Yin, "Race and Politics." *American Demographics*. Volume 23, No. 8 (August 2001):11–13.

ZUBERI, TUKUFU, *Thicker than Blood: How Racial Statistics Lie*. Minneapolis: University of Minnesota Press, 2001.

ZUBOFF, SHOSHANA. "New Worlds of Computer-Mediated Work." *Harvard Business Review*. Vol. 60, No. 5 (September–October 1982):142–52.

ZURCHER, LOUIS A., and DAVID A. SNOW. "Collective Behavior and Social Movements." In Morris Rosenberg and Ralph Turner, eds., *Social Psychology: Sociological Perspectives*. New York: Basic Books, 1981:447–82.

PHOTO CREDITS

Paul W. Liebhardt, *dedication page;* Courtesy of George Breithaupt, *xxxi.*

CHAPTER 1: The Bridgeman Art Library International Ltd., *xxxii;* EyeWire Collection/Getty Images-EyeWire, Inc., *1;* Caroline Penn/Corbis, *2 (top left);* Minh-Thu Duong Pham, *2 (top center);* Takahara, Takeshi/Photo Researchers, Inc., *2 (top right);* Paul Liebhardt, *2 (bottom left, bottom center, bottom right);* Lineair/Peter Arnold, Inc., *7;* English School (19th Century) *The Spitalfields Soup Kitchen,* 1867, engraving. *The Illustrated London News* Picture Library, London, UK/The Bridgeman Art Library, *11;* North Wind Picture Archives, *12;* Corbis Bettman, *13 (left);* Brown Brothers, *13 (right);* Janet Marquesee Fine Arts Ltd., *15;* Brown Brothers, *16;* Paul Marcus/Studio SPM, Inc., *17;* Lisa Harris Gallery, *18.*

CHAPTER 2: The Bridgeman Art Library International Ltd., *26;* Photo by Ruben Burrell, Courtesy of Hampton University, *27;* 35464/13 *Creation of North Sacred Mountain* by Harrison Begay, Navajo. In the Collections of the Museum of Indian Arts and Culture/Laboratory of Anthropology, Museum of New Mexico. Photograph by Blair Clark, *29;* Brian Smith/ Gamma Press USA, Inc., *30;* Bob Daemmrich/Stock Boston, *32;* © Doranne Jacobson/International Images, *34;* Steve McCurry/ Magnum Photos, Inc., *35 (left);* Argas/ Getty Images, Inc.-Liaison, *35 (right);* Tony Freeman/ PhotoEdit, *39;* Philip G. Zimbardo, Inc., Department of Psychology, Stanford University, *40;* Spencer Grant/ Stock Boston, *42;* David Bradnum/ Robert Estall Photo Agency, *46 (left);* Carol Beckwith & Angela Fisher/Robert Estall Photo Agency, *46 (right);* Cheryl Gerber/ AP/Wide World Photos, *48.*

CHAPTER 3: The Bridgeman Art Library International Ltd., *56;* Charles Schwab & Company, Inc., *57;* Paul W. Liebhardt, *34 (top left, middle left);* Carlos Humberto/TDC/Contact/Corbis/Stock Market, *34 (top center);* © Doranne Jacobson/International Images, *34 (top right, bottom left);* David Austen/Stock Boston, *34 (middle center);* Hubertus Kanus/Photo Researchers, Inc., *34 (middle right);* Art Wolfe/Getty Images, Inc./Stone, *34 (bottom right);* Dimitri Lovetsky/ AP/Wide World Photos, *59;* G. Humer/ Getty Images, Inc.-Liaison, *60;* Pearson Education/PH College, *61;* AP/Wide World Photos, *62;* Mrs. *Warhol Is of Two Minds about What to Cook for Dinner,* from *Great Housewives of Art* by Sally Swain. © 1988, 1989 by Sally Swain. Used by permission of Viking Penguin, a division of Penguin Putnam Inc., *66;* Peter Menzel Photography, *67;* David Young Wolff/ PhotoEdit, *69;* Margaret Courtney-Clarke/ Tom Keller and Associates LLC, *70;* Barbara Salz, *71;* AP/Wide World Photos, *74;* Catherine Karnow/ Corbis Bettman, *76;* Shehzad Nooran/Still Pictures/ Peter Arnold, Inc., *78;* Jesse Levine, Laguna Sales, Palo Alto, *79;* Joseph Sohm/ChromoSohm Inc./ Corbis Bettman, *81;* © 1952, 1980 Ruth Orkin, *82.*

CHAPTER 4: Art Resource, N.Y., *88;* © 1996, *The Washington Post.* Photo by Carol Guzy. Reprinted with permission, *89;* Patrick Bordes/ Photo Researchers, Inc., *90;* Victor Englebert/ Photo Researchers, Inc., *91;* Robert Frerck/ Woodfin Camp & Associates, *92;* Getty Images Inc.-Hulton Archive Photos, *95 (left);* Corbis/Sygma, *95 (right);* Picture Desk, Inc./Kobal Collection, *99;* Corbis Bettmann, *100;* Fatih Saribas/Getty Images Inc.-Hulton Archive Photos, *102;* The Museum of Modern Art/Film Stills Archive, *103;* DC Moore Gallery, *106;* Elliot Landy/Magnum Photos, Inc., *107 (left; center; left; center right);* Robert Sorbo/AP/Wide World Photos, *107 (right);* Paul W. Liebhardt, *108.*

CHAPTER 5: Wayne Healy, *114;* Jose Luis Pelaez/ Corbis Bettmann, *115;* Ted Horowitz/Corbis/Stock Market, *116 (left);* Henley & Savage/Corbis/Stock Market, *116 (center);* Tom Pollack, *116 (right);* Ken Heyman/ Woodfin Camp & Associates, *117;* Isaacs Gallery Toronto, *119;* Elizabeth Crews/ Elizabeth Crews Photography, *120;* Rimma Gerlovina and Valeriy Gerlovin, *Manyness,* 1990. © the artists, New City, NY, *123;* Henry Ossawa Tanner, *The Banjo Lesson,* 1893. Oil on canvas. 49 × 35 1/2". Hampton University Museum, Hampton, Virginia, *125;* The Bridgeman Art Library International Ltd., *130;* CBS/CBS 2003 CBS Worldwide Inc. All Rights Reserved/Landov, *134.*

CHAPTER 6: The Bridgeman Art Library International Ltd., *138;* John Macionis, *139;* Jim Anderson/ Woodfin Camp & Associates, *140;* AP/Wide World Photos, *141;* Richard Lord Enterprises, Inc., *142;* DiMaggio/Kalish/ Corbis/Stock Market, *144;* Staton R. Winter/*The New York Times,* *147;* The Cartoon Bank, *148;* Paul W. Liebhardt, *149 (3 photos);* Paul Ekman, Ph.D. Professor of Psychology, University of California, San Francisco, *150 (2 photos);* David Cooper/Getty Images, Inc., *152 (top left);* Alan Weiner/Getty Images, Inc., *152 (top, second from left);* Joel Gordon Photography, *152 (top, second from right;* © Guido Alberto Rossi/TIPS Images, *152 (top right);* Chris Carroll/Corbis, *152 (bottom left);* Costa Manos/Magnum Photos, Inc., *152 (bottom right);* Najlah Feanny/Stock Boston, *153;* Angela Maynard/Getty Images, Inc.-Photodisc, *155;* Michael Newman/PhotoEdit, *156;* AP/Wide World Photos, *159.*

CHAPTER 7: The Bridgeman Art Library International Ltd., *162;* Spencer Grant/PhotoEdit, *163;* Alon Reininger/Woodfin Camp & Associates, *164;* Jonathan Green Studios, Inc., *169;* Spencer Grant/PhotoEdit, *170;* Cliche Bibliotheque nationale de France, Paris. From *The Horizon History of China* by the editors of *Horizon* Magazine, The Horizon Publishing Co., Inc., 551 5th Avenue, New York, N.Y. 10017. © 1969 Bibliotheque nationale de France, *174;* The Metropolitan Museum of Art, *176;* Paul W. Liebhardt, *177;* © Hulton Getty/Archive Photos, *178;* Courtesy: Google, *182 (left);* Michael Newman/ PhotoEdit, *182 (right).*

CHAPTER 8: Adam Hernandez, *188;* Tony Freeman/PhotoEdit, *189;* SIPA Press, *191;* Rick Reinhard, *193;* Robert Yager/Getty Images Inc.-Stone Allstock, *195;* Edward Gargan/*New York Times* Pictures, *197;* Jahi Chikwendiu/AFP/Corbis, *198;* Andrew Lichtenstein/The Image Works, *199;* AP/Wide World Photos, *201;* Jeremy Hogan/Gamma Press USA, Inc., *203;* Rich Pedroncelli/AP/Wide World Photos, *207;* The Cartoon Bank, *208;* A. Ramey/Woodfin Camp & Associates, *211;* Bob Daemmrich/The Image Works, *212;* A. Ramey/PhotoEdit, *216.*

CHAPTER 9: AP/Wide World Photos, *220;* Paul Solomon/Woodfin Camp & Associates, *221;* Andre Gallant/ Getty Images Inc.-Image Bank., *222 (top left);* Pete Turner/ Getty Images Inc.-Image Bank, *222 (top, center);* Brun/Photo Researchers, Inc., *222 (top right);* Bruno Hadijh/ Getty Images, Inc.-Liaison, *222 (bottom, left);* Elliot Erwitt/Magnum Photos, Inc., *222 (bottom center);* George Holton/Photo Researchers, Inc., *222 (bottom right);* Corbis, *225;* Bill Aron/ PhotoEdit, *237;* AKG London Ltd., *239.*

CHAPTER 10: Picture Desk, Inc./Kobal Collection, *246;* Wilton, Chris Alan/ Getty Images Inc.-Image Bank, *247;* Sebastiao Salgado/ Contact Press Images Inc., *248;* Lindsay Hebberd/Corbis, *249;* Abbas/ Magnum Photos, Inc., *250;* AP/Wide World Photos, *252;* Francisco Conde, *254;* SuperStock, Inc., *256;* Kevork Djansezian/ AP/Wide World Photos, *259;* The Granger Collection, *260;* © Doranne Jacobson/International Images, *262;* Joel Stettenheim/ Corbis, *265.*

CHAPTER 11: © Paul Marcus, *Upstairs-Downstairs,* Studio SPM Inc., *270;* AP/Wide World Photos, *271;* Bachmann/Stock Boston, *277;* Grapes/Michaud/ Photo Researchers, Inc., *278 (left);* Burt Glinn/ Magnum Photos, Inc., *278 (right);* Ed Bock/Corbis/Stock Market, *279;* Russell Lee/Corbis, *281;* The Cartoon Bank, *282;* North Wind Picture Archives, *287;* William Julius Wilson, *290;* Richard Pasley/ Stock Boston, *291;* Argus Fotoarchiv/ Peter Arnold, Inc., *294.*

CHAPTER 12: The Art Archive/Dagli Orti/ Picture Desk, Inc./Kobal Collection, *298;* Agence France-Presse AFP, *299;* Reuters NewMedia Inc./Corbis, *301 (left);* Chip Hires/ Gamma Press USA, Inc., *301 (right);* Martin Benjamin/The Image Works, *302 (top, left);* Peter Turnley/Corbis, *302 (top, right);* Pablo Bartholomew/Getty Images, Inc.-Liaison, *302 (bottom);* Yuri Cortez/AFP Photo/Corbis, *307;* Malcolm Linton/ Getty Images, Inc.-Liaison, *309;* Steve Maines/ Stock Boston, *311;* Joe McDonald/Corbis, *313 (left);* Robert van der Hilst/Corbis, *313 (center);* Wolfgang Kaehler/Corbis, *313 (right);* The Art Archive/Biblioteca National do Rio de Janiero Brazil/Dagli Orti/Picture Desk, *315;* Mark Edwards/Still Pictures/ Peter Arnold, Inc., *317.*

CHAPTER 13: The Bridgeman Art Library International Ltd., *324;* Getty Images Inc.-Hulton Archive Photos, *325;* Andy Cox/ Getty Images Inc.-Stone Allstock, *326;* Angela Fisher/Carol Beckwith/ Robert Estall Photo Agency, *328;* Carol Beckwith/Angela Fisher/ Robert Estall Photo Agency, *330;* Tony Freeman/ PhotoEdit, *332;* AP/Wide World Photos, *336;* Sonda Dawes/ The Image Works, *339;* R. W. Jones/Corbis, *342;* Willinger/ Getty Images, Inc.-Taxi, *343;* Bettmann/Corbis, *346 (left);* APA/Getty Images Inc.-Hulton Archive Photos, *346 (center);* Hulton-Deutsch Collection/Corbis, *346 (right);* Richard B. Levine, *349.*

CHAPTER 14: The Bridgeman Art Library International Ltd., *352;* Myrleen Ferguson Cate/PhotoEdit, *353;* Joel Gordon/Joel Gordon Photography, *354 (top left);* Leong Ka Tai, *354 (top center);* Owen Franken/Corbis, *354 (top right);* Charles O'Rear/Corbis, *354 (bottom left);* Paul W. Liebhardt, *354 (bottom center);* Lisi Dennis/Getty Images, Inc./Image Bank, *354 (bottom right);* Joel Gordon Photography, *355;* Rob Crandall, Photographer, *358;* Sean Sprague/Stock Boston, *362;* Western History Collections, University of Oklahoma Libraries, *364;* AP/Wide World Photos, *365;* Corbis, *369 (far left);* Culver Pictures, Inc., *369 (left center);* Photographs and Prints Division, Schomburg Center for Research in Black Culture/The New York Public Library/ Astor, Lenox and Tilden Foundations, *369 (center right);* UPI/Corbis, *369 (far right);* UPI/Corbis, *372;* Carmen Lomas Garza, *376;* Gary Conner/ PhotoEdit, *378.*

CHAPTER 15: The Bridgeman Art Library International Ltd., *382;* Photo by Steve Azzara/Corbis Sygma, *383;* Elliott Erwitt/ Magnum Photos, Inc., *388 (left);* AP/Wide World Photos *388 (right);* Philip Gould/Corbis, *391;* Alese and Mort Pechter/ Corbis/Stock Market, *393;* Laima Druskis/ Pearson Education/PH College, *397;* Chris Rainier/Corbis, *399;* Spencer Grant/ Stock Boston, *401;* Alan Oddie/ PhotoEdit, *402.*

CHAPTER 16: The Bridgeman Art Library International Ltd., *406;* Jose Carillo/ PhotoEdit, *407;* Catherine Karnow/ Woodfin Camp & Associates, *408;* Underwood & Underwood/ Library of Congress, *409;* Sven-Olof Lindblad/ Photo Researchers, Inc., *411;* Courtesy of the Library of Congress, *413;* Gamma Press USA, Inc., *414;* Bellavia/REA/ Corbis/SABA Press Photos, Inc., *415 (left);* John Bryson/ Corbis/Sygma, *415 (right);* FSA/National Archives/ Franklin D. Roosevelt Library, *420;* Chris Brown, *423;* AP/Wide World Photos, *424.*

CHAPTER 17: The Bridgeman Art Library International Ltd., *432;* Getty Images, Inc., *433;* Durand/ SIPA Press. *435;* David Ball/ Index Stock Imagery, Inc., *439;* Timothy Fadek/ Gamma Press USA, Inc., *442 (left);* Joel Gordon Photography, *442 (right);* Paul Fusco/ Magnum Photos, Inc., *448;* David Hoffman Photo Library, *449;* Joe McNally, Life Magazine © TimePix, *452.*

CHAPTER 18: Gordon Woodside/John Braseth Gallery, *460;* Beth Balbierz/ The Record, *461;* David Botello, *462;* Bo Zaunders/ Corbis/Stock Market, *463;* The Bridgeman Art Library International Ltd., *466;* © Susan Pyzow, *Bridal Bouquet,* watercolor on paper, 10 × 13.5 in. Studio SPM Inc., *467;* The Bridgeman Art Library International Ltd., *468;* The Cartoon Bank, *471;* Mark J. Barrett/ Creative Eye/MIRA.com, *476;* Bill Bachmann/ The Image Works, *479.*

CHAPTER 19: The Bridgeman Art Library International Ltd., *488;* Getty Images, Inc., *489;* Michael Freeman/Corbis, *490;* Mathieu Polak/ Corbis/Sygma, *492;* (C)Doranne Jacobson/International

Images, *495;* Topham/ The Image Works, *496;* Annie Griffiths Belt/NGS Image Collection, *499;* Allison Wright/ Stock Boston, *502;* Ric Francis/AFP/ Getty Images, Inc.-Liaison, *506;* James L. Amos/Corbis, *508;* Philip North-Coombes/ Getty Images Inc.-Stone Allstock, *509;* Library of Congress, *511.*

CHAPTER 20: The Bridgeman Art Library International Ltd., *516;* Getty Images, Inc., *517;* AP/Wide World Photos, *519;* Mary Kate Denny/ PhotoEdit, *523 (left);* Getty Images, Inc., *523 (right);* Patrick Ward/Corbis, *530;* Mugshots/ Corbis/Stock Market, *535.*

CHAPTER 21: The Bridgeman Art Library International Ltd., *540;* Martin Parr/ Magnum Photos, Inc., *541;* The Bridgeman Art Library International Ltd., *542;* Steve Prezant/ Corbis/Stock Market, *546;* Sayyid Azim/ AP/Wide World Photos, *551;* Adalbert Franz Seligmann, *Allgemeines Krankenhaus (General Hospital),* 19th Century Painting, canvas, *Professor Theodor Billroth lectures at the General Hospital, Vienna,* 1880, Erich Lessing/Art Resource, N.Y., *553;* Galen Rowell/ Mountain Light Photography, Inc., *555;* John Cancalosi/ Stock Boston, *556;* Billy E. Barnes/ PhotoEdit, *558;* Al Diaz, *561;* Steve Murez/ Black Star, *563.*

CHAPTER 22: Christie's Images Inc., *568;* Joyce Benson/ North Central Grain Coop, *569;* David and Peter Turnley/Corbis, *576;* Lauren Goodsmith/ The Image Works, *577;* Getty Images, Inc., *579;* Steve C. Wilson/Online USA, Inc./ Getty Images Inc.-Hulton Archive Photos, *582;* Christie's Images Inc., *583 (left);* Pieter Breughel the Elder (c. 1525/30–1569), *Peasant Dance,* c. 1565, Kunsthistorisches Museum, Vienna/Superstock, Inc., *583 (right);* James King-Holmes/Science Photo Library/ Photo Researchers, Inc., *587;* Culver Pictures, Inc., *590;* Paul W. Liebhardt, *591;* Eric Pasquier/ Corbis/Sygma, *594.*

CHAPTER 23: The Bridgeman Art Library International Ltd., *600;* Romeo Gacad/ Agence France-Presse AFP, *601;* Dion Ogust/ The Image Works, *602;* Olivier Coret/In Visu/Corbis, *605;* Sabina Dowell, *607;* Tom Kelley, *610 (top left);* Inge Morath/Magnum Photos, Inc., *610 (top center);* Kimberly Maier, *610 (top right);* Willie L. Hill, Jr./Stock Boston, *610 (bottom left);* Michael Grecco/Stock Boston, *610 (bottom center);* © Mike Blake/Reuters NewMedia Inc./Corbis, *610 (bottom right);* AP/Wide World Photos, *614;* Agenzia Giornalistica Italia, *616.*

CHAPTER 24: © Christie's Images Inc. 1918, *624;* Culver Pictures, Inc., *625 (left);* PhotoEdit, *625 (right);* Robert Essel/Corbis, *627;* The Bridgeman Art Library International Ltd., *630;* Whitney Museum of American Art, *631;* Pearson Education/PH College, *633;* North Wind Picture Archives, *636;* Art Resource, N.Y., *638 (left);* Paul Marcus/Studio SPM, Inc., *638 (right);* David Botello, *645.*

TIMELINE: *1807:* Courtesy of The New-York Historical Society, New York City; *1829:* Dorling Kindersley/Science Museum; *1848:* North Carolina Museum of History; *1876:* Property of AT&T Archives, reprinted with permission of AT&T; *1886:* Irene Springer/Pearson Education/PH College; *1886:* "Coca-Cola" is a registered trademark of The Coca-Cola Company and is reproduced with kind permission from The Coca-Cola Company; *1893:* Library of Congress; *1903:* Courtesy of the Library of Congress; *1912:* Chris Alan Wilton/Getty Images, Inc.-Image Bank; *1910:* Tim Ridley/Dorling Kindersley Media Library; *1927:* Bettmann/Corbis; *1931:* Texas State Library and Archives Commission; *1945:* U.S. Air Force; *1946:* Unisys Corporation; *1947:* Dorling Kindersley Media Library; *1950:* Dorling Kindersley Media Library; *1952:* Dorling Kindersley Media Library; *1955:* AP/Wide World Photos; *1964:* Dorling Kindersley Media Library; *1969:* NASA/Johnson Space Center; *1969:* AP/ Wide World Photos; *1970:* Jason Laure/Woodfin Camp & Associates; *1980:* Laima Druskis/Pearson Education/PH College; *1981:* Artwork provided courtesy of MTV: Music Television. MTV: Music Television and all related titles, characters, and logos are trademarks owned by MTV Networks, a division of Viacom International, Inc. All rights reserved; *1987:* John Serafin; *1990s:* Gerald Lopez/ Dorling Kindersley Media Library; *2000:* Brady/Pearson Education/PH College.

NAME INDEX

Cloward, Richard A., 194–195, 613, 618
Cobain, Kurt, 107–108
Cobb, Jonathan, 293, 528
Cockerham, William C., 543
Coe, Michael D., 578
Cohen, Adam, 481, 533
Cohen, Albert K., 194–195
Cohen, Elias, 396
Cohen, Lloyd R., 342
Cohn, Richard M., 390
Cole, George F., 217
Coleman, James S., 177, 524–525, 528, 530
Coleman, Richard P., 276–277
Cole, Stephen, 217
Colfax, Richard S., 542
Collins, Joseph, 316–317
Collins, Randall, 344, 527
Collymore, Yvette, 308
Colton, Helen, 224
Comte, Auguste, 11–14, 30
Connett, Paul H., 588, 590
Cook, Rhodes, 171, 444
Cooley, Charles Horton, 123, 164, 607
Copeland, Peter, 231
Copernicus, Nicolaus, 12
Cordell, Arthur J., 183
Corley, Robert N., 589
Cornell, Barbara, 127
Cornell, Claire Pedrick, 341
Correll, Shelley J., 331
Cose, Ellis, 31
Cotter, David A., 336
Courtney, Alice E., 331
Courtwright, David T., 208
Coventry, Barbara Thomas, 333
Covington, Jeanette, 208
Cowan, Angela, 126
Cowan, Carolyn Pope, 126
Cowley, Geoffrey, 562
Cowley, Peter, 547
Cox, Harvey, 507
Crane, Diana, 609
Cressey, Donald R., 201
Crimmins, Eileen M., 547
Crispell, Diane, 472
Crockett, Davy, 71
Crook, P. J., 382
Crook, Stephen, 641
Crossette, Barbara, 239, 341
Crouse, James, 523
Crowley, Martha L., 293
Cuff, E. C., 98, 102
Cullen, Francis T., 202, 420
Cullen, Lisa Takeuchi, 541
Cumming, Elaine, 396
Cummings, Scott, 358
Curie, Marie, 77
Currie, Elliott, 209
Curry, Andrew, 640
Curtis, James E., 173
Curtiss, Susan, 118
Cutcliffe, John R., 401
Cutright, Phillip, 251

Dahl, Robert A., 446–447
Dahrendorf, Ralf, 260, 633
Daly, Martin, 190–191
Danforth, Marion M., 402
Darroch, Jacqueline E., 232
Darrow, Charlotte N., 130
Darwin, Charles, 82, 116, 257, 510–511
David, Antonio, 130
Davidson, James D., 276, 504
Davies, Christie, 159
Davies, James C., 448, 612–613
Davies, Mark, 127
Davis, Donald M., 331
Davis, Karen A., 271
Davis, Kenneth E., 370
Davis, Kingsley, 115, 117–118, 238, 257–258
De Beauvoir, Simone, 346
Deber, Raisa, 556

Dedrick, Dennis K., 454
Defina, Robert H., 214
DeFrancis, Marc, 559
Deitz, Thomas, 588
DeJong, Gordon F., 369
Delacroix, Jacques, 316, 426
Delaporte, Louis, 488
della Cava, Marco R., 400
DeLuca, Tom, 445, 528
Demerath, N. J., III, 34, 508
Dempster-McClain, Donna, 398
Dent, David J., 524
Denton, Nancy A., 364
Dershem, Larry, 171
Dershowitz, Alan, 203, 500
Dervarics, Charles, 533, 535
Despont, Thierry, 285
Deutscher, Irwin, 10
Devine, Joel A., 441
Dewey, John, 521
Diana, Princess of Wales, 254
Diaz, Daniel, 171
Dickens, Charles, 124
Dickerson, John F., 176–177
Dickinson, Amy, 237
Dickson, William J., 40
Diehl, Richard A., 578
Dimond, Margaret F., 401
Dinitz, Simon, 191
Disraeli, Benjamin, 52
Dixon, William J., 261, 316, 426
Dizard, Jan E., 483
Dobson, Richard B., 255
Dobyns, Henry F., 365
Dodge, Hiroko, 336
Dollard, John, 360, 612
Domhoff, G. William, 261
Donahue, John J., III, 216
Donnelly, Patrick G., 615
Donovan, Virginia K., 119
Doyle, James A., 347
Doyle, Rodger, 368, 505
D'Souza, Dinesh, 284
Du Bois, W. E. B., 13, 15–16, 27, 370
Dubos, René, 542
Dudley, Kathryn Marie, 418
Duhl, Leonard J., 554
Duncan, Cynthia M., 289
Duncan, Greg J., 133, 282, 472, 479
Duncan, Otis Dudley, 282
Durkheim, Emile, 3, 13–14, 30, 48, 89, 106–111, 192–193, 196, 202, 214, 489–491, 503, 583–584, 631–635, 644
Durlauf, Steven, 267
Duvalier, François, 318
Dworkin, Andrea, 240, 345–346, 559

Ebaugh, Helen Rose Fuchs, 143, 489, 512
Eboh, Camillus, 204
Eck, Diana L., 489, 498–499, 501, 503
Eckholm, Erik, 562
Edin, Kathryn, 289
Edmonson, Brad, 386, 545
Edwards, David V., 436
Edwards, Tamala M., 20, 481, 525
Ehrenreich, Barbara, 326, 329, 559, 561
Eichler, Margrit, 37
Einstein, Albert, 452
Eisen, Arnold M., 500
Eisenberg, Daniel, 421
Eisler, Benita, 409
Ekman, Paul, 150, 153
El-Attar, Mohamed, 499
Elias, Robert, 207
Elizabeth, Queen II, 252
Elliot, Delbert S., 2–7
Ellison, Christopher G., 125, 195, 504, 512
Ellison, Lawrence, 259
Elmer-DeWitt, Philip, 171
Elsner, Howard C., 359
Ember, Carol R., 464

Ember, Melvin, 464
Emerson, Joan P., 364, 560
Emerson, Michael O., 364
Emerson, Ralph Waldo, 440
Endersby, James W., 129
Endicott, Karen, 90
Engels, Friedrich, 81, 99–100, 102, 260, 344, 346, 467–468, 635
England, Paula, 336, 467
Epps, Edgar G., 526
Erber, Ernst, 427
Erger, Jeffrey, 171
Erickson, Kristan Glasgow, 144
Erikson, Erik H., 124–125, 392
Erikson, Kai, 193
Erikson, Robert S., 442
Eshref, Shevky, 584
Estes, Richard J., 234
Etzioni, Amitai, 68, 172, 476, 644–645
Etzioni-Halevy, Eva, 436
Evans, M.D.R., 272
Evelyn, Jamilah, 535
Ezell, Gene, 560

Fabes, Richard A., 331
Fagan, Jeffrey, 216
Falkenmark, Malin, 593
Falk, Gerhard, 65
Fallon, A. E., 548
Fallows, James, 376
Farnsworth, Margaret, 207
Farrell, Michael P., 132
Fastow, Andrew S., 201
Fattah, Hassan, 57
Feagin, Joe, 36, 159, 336, 339, 387, 467, 586
Featherman, David L., 80, 282–283
Fellman, Bruce, 128
Fernandez, Roberto M., 171
Ferree, Myra Marx, 325, 344–345, 347
Fetto, John, 129, 379, 395, 445, 584
Fiene, Ernest, 583
Figlio, Robert M., 207, 215
Finch, Donna, 142
Fine, Gary Alan, 607
Fineman, Howard, 379
Finkelstein, Neal W., 126
Finn, Chester E., Jr., 532
Finn, James, 414
Firebaugh, Glenn, 311, 314–315, 317, 319, 370, 426, 428
Fischer, Claude W., 33
Fisher, Angela, 46
Fisher, Elizabeth, 91, 93
Fisher, Roger, 454
Fiske, Alan Paige, 260
Fitzpatrick, Mary Anne, 472
Flacks, Richard, 613
Flaherty, Michael G., 159
Fletcher, Kay, 158
Flynn, Patricia, 401
Foch, Terryl T., 117
Foliart, Donne E., 401
Fonda, Daren, 78, 536
Foner, Anne, 133
Ford, Clellan S., 229
Ford, Henry, 178, 630
Forliti, Amy, 605
Forstmann, Theodore J., 533
Foss, Gail, 341
Fost, Dan, 366, 370
Foucault, Michel, 229
Fourcade-Gourinchas, Marion, 173
Fox, Gerald, 579
Francia, Peter L., 436
Frank, André Gunder, 315–316
Franklin, Benjamin, 105
Franklin, John Hope, 367–368
Frazier, E. Franklin, 506
Fredrickson, George M., 250
Freedman, Estelle B., 328, 343–345
Free, Marvin D., 199
French, Marilyn, 253, 328, 345
Freud, Sigmund, 118–120, 122–123, 191

Frey, William H., 370
Friedan, Betty, 396
Friedland, Roger, 425
Friedman, Meyer, 546
Friedman, Milton, 427
Friedman, Rose, 427
Frost, Jennifer J., 232
Fugita, Stephen S., 372
Fuguitt, Glenn V., 582
Fujimoto, Isao, 372
Fuller, Rex, 336
Fullerton, Howard, Jr., 422
Furedi, Frank, 66
Furstenberg, Frank F., Jr., 476, 478

Gadlin, Howard, 483
Gagné, Patricia, 223
Gagnon, John H., 69, 226, 228–229, 231, 237, 239, 470, 548
Galileo, 12, 510–511
Gallagher, Maggie, 288, 467
Gallup, George, 480
Galster, George, 580
Gamble, Andrew, 521
Gamoran, Adam, 523
Gamson, William A., 37
Gandhi, Mahatma, 435
Ganley, Elaine, 499
Gans, Herbert J., 584
Gardner, Marilyn, 482
Gardyn, Rebecca, 1, 74, 393
Garfinkel, Harold, 145, 197
Garreau, Joel, 581
Gartin, Patrick R., 200
Gates, Bill, 176
Gates, Gary J., 473
Gauguin, Paul, 624
Gau, Rebecca L., 535
Gautama, Siddhartha, 502
Geertz, Clifford, 223
Geist, William, 580
Gelles, Richard J., 341, 478
Gelman, David, 231
Gendell, Murray, 383, 393
Geoffrey, Jan Jules, 99
George, Susan, 543
Gerber, Linda, 83, 556
Gerber, Theodore P., 255
Gergen, David, 411, 451
Gerlach, Michael L., 415
Gerlovina, Rimma, 123
Gerlovin, Valeriy, 123
Gerson, Judith M., 641
Gerstel, Naomi, 476
Gerth, H. H., 103
Gertz, Marc, 208
Geschwender, James A., 362
Gest, Ted, 337
Gewertz, Deborah, 327
Gibbons, Don C., 191
Gibbs, Nancy, 125, 237, 347, 609, 616, 635
Giddens, Anthony, 238
Giele, Janet Z., 344
Gigliotti, Richard J., 143
Gilbertson, Greta A., 371
Gilligan, Carol, 121–122, 330
Gillon, Raanan, 401, 553
Gimenez, Martha E., 530
Ginsberg, Leon H., 385
Ginsburg, Faye, 339
Gintis, Herbert, 16, 522–523
Giovannini, Maureen, 37–38
Giroux, Gregory L., 178
Giugni, Marco G., 615–616
Gladue, Brian A., 231
Glass, J. Conrad, Jr., 402
Glassner, Barry, 609
Glauberman, Naomi, 267
Gleick, Elizabeth, 496
Glenn, Norval D., 236, 477
Glueck, Eleanor, 190
Glueck, Sheldon, 190
Gnida, John J., 20
Godbey, Geoffrey, 397

Spain, Daphne, 333, 461
Specter, Michael, 255, 391, 417, 555
Speer, Tibbett L., 421, 526
Speier, Hans, 159
Spencer, Earl, 254
Spencer, Herbert, 14, 257
Spilerman, Seymour, 390
Spitzer, Steven, 200–201, 398
Splain, Cheryl S., 294
Stacey, Judith, 345, 482–483
Stacey, William A., 341, 478
Staggenborg, Suzanne, 611, 616
Stahura, John M., 580
Stalin, Josef, 364
Stanton, Elizabeth Cady, 325, 344
Stapinski, Helene, 335, 467
Stark, Rodney, 495, 504, 507, 510
Starr, Paul, 554, 557
Stavrianos, L. S., 93
Steele, James B., 367, 424, 441, 446
Steele, Randy, 192
Steele, Shelby, 20, 362
Steffensmeier, Darrell J., 195
Stein, Barry A., 179
Stein, Maurice R., 633
Stephens, John D., 261
Sternlieb, George, 580
Stevens, Gillian, 375
Stewart, Martha, 282
Stewman, Shelby, 336
Stier, Haya, 336
St. Jean, Yanick, 339
Stodghill, Ron, II, 234, 353
Stofferahn, Curtis W., 420
Stone, Lawrence, 469
Stone, Robyn, 392
Storm, Jonathan, 127
Stouffer, Samuel A., 168, 612
Stratton, Leslie S., 335
Straus, Murray A., 478
Streib, Gordon, 396
Stross, Randall E., 163
Stuart, Robert C., 416
Sudnow, David N., 399
Sullivan, Anne Mansfield, 62
Sullivan, Barbara, 183
Sullivan, William M., 67
Sumner, William Graham, 68
Sung, Betty Lee, 370
Sun, Lena H., 372
Surratt, Hilary L., 354
Sussman, Leonard R., 414
Sutherland, Edwin H., 199–201
Sutton, John R., 214
Sutton, Willy, 157
Swain, Charles E., 512
Swain, Sally, 66
Swartz, Steve, 201
Swicegood, Gray, 375
Swidler, Ann, 67
Szasz, Thomas S., 197–198, 595

Tajfel, Henri, 168
Takaki, Ronald, 370–371, 373
Tallichet, Suzanne E., 335
Tanber, George J., 214
Tannahill, Reay, 241
Tannenbaum, Frank, 367
Tannen, Deborah, 139, 156, 179
Tanner, Henry Ossawa, 125
Tarmann, Allison, 231
Tarrow, Sidney, 604
Taubman, Alfred, 202
Tavris, Carol, 326, 331
Taylor, Frederick Winslow, 178, 180–181, 185
Taylor, John, 69
Tedin, Kent L., 442
Telles, Paulo R., 354
Terkel, Studs, 101
Terry, Don, 203
Tewksbury, Richard, 223
Thernstrom, Abigail, 612
Thernstrom, Stephan, 612
Thomas, Edward J., 502

Thomas, Evan, 452
Thomas, George M., 440
Thomas, Melvin E., 369
Thomas, W. I., 145, 196, 363, 560
Thomma, Steven, 512
Thompson, D., 563
Thompson, Larry, 481
Thompson, Mark, 395, 453
Thorlindsson, Thorolfur, 3
Thornberry, Terrance, 207
Thorne, Barrie, 149–151, 155
Thurow, Lester C., 275
Tigges, Leann M., 171
Tilly, Charles, 448, 618
Tipton, Steven M., 67
Tittle, Charles R., 207
Tobin, Gary, 580
Toby, Jackson, 528
Tocqueville, Alexis de, 11, 448, 612
Tolnay, Stewart E., 369
Tolson, Jay, 178
Tönnies, Ferdinand 582–584, 630–633, 635, 644
Tooker, George, 106, 176
Toossi, Mitra, 422
Torres, Lisa, 171
Treas, Judith, 386–387
Treiman, Donald J., 251
Trent, Katherine, 479
Troeltsch, Ernst, 494
Troiden, Richard R., 231
Trusheim, Dale, 523
Truth, Sojourner, 369
Tsing, Anna Lowenhaupt, 339
Tubman, Harriet, 71, 369
Tucker, James, 509
Tumin, Melvin M., 248, 258
Turner, Ralph H., 153, 601–603, 605–606, 608, 611
Turner, Tina, 383
Tutu, Desmond, 492
Tyler, S. Lehman, 365–366
Tynan, Douglas, 534
Tyree, Andrea, 251

Udry, J. Richard, 330
Uggen, Christopher, 195, 445
Ujifusa, Grant, 441
Ullman, Edward L., 584–585
Ulmer, Adrienne, 133–134
Unruh, John D., 365
Upthegrove, Tayna R., 19
Ury, William, 454
Useem, Bert, 613
Utagawa Kunisada, 56

Valdez, A., 202
Vallas, Stephen P., 423
Valocchi, Steve, 615
Van Biema, David, 478, 500, 502, 508
van der Lippe, Tanja, 333
van Dijk, Liset, 333
Van Dyke, Nella, 611
Van Hemessen, Jan Sanders, 298
Varacalli, Joseph A., 159
Vayda, Eugene, 556
Veblen, Thorstein, 609
Velasco, Steven C., 336
Villemez, Wayne J., 207
Vinovskis, Maris A., 450
Visher, Christy A., 212
Vittas, M. Elliot, 595
Vogel, Ezra F., 317, 344–345
Vold, George B., 200–201
Volgy, Thomas J., 289
von Hirsh, Andrew, 198
Vonnegut, Kurt, Jr., 265
Voss, Jacqueline, 234

Wade, Carol, 326, 331
Waite, Linda J., 467
Walberg, Herbert J., 532
Walczak, David, 419
Waldfogel, Jane, 336

Walker, Karen, 281
Walker-Taylor, Yvonne, 44
Wallace, Michael, 615, 617
Wallace, Ruth A., 326, 339, 343–344
Waller, Douglas, 453
Wallerstein, Immanuel, 315–316, 426
Wallerstein, Judith S., 477
Wall, Thomas F., 399, 471, 552
Walsh, Mary Williams, 166, 397
Walsleben, Marjorie C., 528
Walton, John, 316, 426
Walton, Sam, 407
Waring, Foner, 133
Warner, Barbara D., 195
Warner, R. Stephen, 510
Warner, W. Lloyd, 276
Warr, Mark, 195
Waters, Malcolm, 641
Waters, Melissa S., 504
Watson, John B., 116, 121–122
Watson, John Keith, 504
Wattenberg, Ben J., 576
Watt, James, 408
Watts, Duncan J., 170
Weber, A., 579
Weber, Max, 18, 34, 36, 49, 89, 102–103, 105–106, 108–111, 174, 176–179, 183–184, 258, 261–262, 276, 312, 417, 433–436, 493–494, 628, 632, 635, 639
Webster, Murray, Jr., 141
Webster, Pamela S., 479
Weeks, John R., 498–499
Weerapana, Akila, 320
Weicher, John C., 277
Weidenbaum, Murray, 425
Weinberg, George, 232
Weinberg, Nancy, 171
Weiner, Tim, 453
Weinrich, James D., 231
Weisberg, D. Kelly, 234
Weitzman, Lenore J., 10, 132, 283, 476
Welch, Michael, 609
Weller, Jack M., 601, 603, 606
Wellford, Charles, 200
Wellner, Alison Stein, 366, 375
Wells-Barnett, Ida, 369
Werner, Perla, 397
Wertheimer, Barbara Mayer, 409
Werum, Regine, 615
Wesselman, Hank, 509
West, Elizabeth, 615
Western, Bruce, 419
Whalen, Jack, 613
Wheelis, Allen, 637
Whelan, Christine B., 373
Whipple, Thomas W., 331
Whitaker, Mark, 450
White, Geoffrey M., 153
Whitehead, Barbara Dafoe, 480
White-Means, Shelly, 558
White, Ralph, 166
White, Walter, 604
Whitman, David, 292
Whittier, Nancy, 615
Whitt, J. Allen, 446
Whorf, Benjamin Lee, 65
Whyte, William Foote, 46–47, 177
Wiarda, Frank D., 314
Wickham, DeWayne, 291
Widom, Cathy Spatz, 479
Widstrand, Carl, 593
Wiedner, Peter A. B., 285
Wieringa, Saskia, 230
Wilcox, Clyde, 339, 512
Wilde, Marta L., 129, 510
Wilde, Oscar, 157, 388
Wiles, P. J. D., 416
Willer, David, 171
Williamson, Jeffrey G., 263
Williams, Rhys H., 507
Williams, Richard A., 523
Williams, Robin, 66–67
Williams, Robin M., Jr., 80, 398
Williams, Serena, 18

Williams, Timothy, 436
Wilson, Barbara, 129
Wilson, Bryan, 383, 500
Wilson, David, 586
Wilson, Edward O., 595
Wilson, James Q., 185, 190, 370
Wilson, Janet K., 199
Wilson, L., 34
Wilson, Margo, 191
Wilson, William Julius, 27, 289–290
Winders, Bill, 615
Winfield, Idee, 171
Winfield-Laird, Idee, 253
Winfrey, Oprah, 258
Wingert, Pat, 379, 479
Winkler, Karen, 122
Winship, Christopher, 216
Winters, Rebecca, 335, 534
Winter, Staton R., 147
Wirth, Louis, 584
Witkin, Gordon, 216
Witkin-Lanoil, Georgia, 116
Witt, G. Evans, 43
Wohlstein, Ronald T., 603
Wojtkiewicz, Roger A., 479
Wolf, Diane L., 36
Wolfe, David B., 388
Wolfgang, Marvin E., 207, 215
Wolf, Naomi, 132, 332
Wolfson, Adam, 401
Wong, Buck, 371
Woodberry, Robert D., 504
Wood, Daniel B., 496
Woodhull, Victoria, 337
Wood, James L., 601
Woodward, Charlotte, 325
Woodward, Kenneth L., 129, 493, 503
Worden, Steven K., 615
Worsley, Peter, 317
Wright, Eric R., 171
Wright, J., 209
Wright, James D., 194, 477, 481
Wright, Quincy, 450
Wright, Richard A., 215
Wright, Robert, 185
Wright, Stuart A., 613
Wu, Lawrence L., 479

Xie, Wen, 275
Xie, Xie, 275

Yamagata, Hisashi, 336
Yancey, George, 364
Yang, Fenggang, 489, 512
Yang, Yu, 547
Yankelovich, Daniel, 482
Yates, Ronald E., 391
Yeatts, Dale E., 181
Yeh, Kuang S., 336
Yeung, W. Jean, 133, 282, 472, 479
Yinger, J. Milton, 454
Yin, Sandra, 559
Yoels, William C., 159, 530
York, Richard, 588
Yudelman, Montague, 390
Yunker, James A., 214

Zafonte, Matthew, 425
Zald, Mayer N., 601, 612, 615, 617
Zangrando, Robert L., 368
Zarycky, George, 414
Zeitlin, Irving M., 99
Zhang, Joshua, 194, 363
Zhang, Wenquan, 362
Zhao, Dingxin, 615
Zhou, Min, 371
Zimbardo, Philip, 40–41, 51
Zimmer, Michael, 480
Zimring, Franklin E., 216
Zuberi, Tukufu, 355
Zuboff, Shoshana, 423
Zurcher, Louis A., 606

SUBJECT INDEX

Aborigines (Australia), hunting and gathering, 90
Abortion
  defined, 242
  and emotion management, 154
  fundamentalist view, 511
  as political issue, 442
  proponents and opponents, 240–41
  as reproductive right, 345
Absolute monarchy, 436, 438
Absolute poverty
  decline and industrialism, 312, 313
  defined, 286
  global, 307
Academic standards, 531–32
Achieved status, 141
Achievement (see also Educational achievement)
  racial and ethnic minorities' conceptions of, 133
  as U.S. value, 66
Acid rain, 593
Acquaintance rape (see Date rape)
Acquired immune deficiency syndrome (AIDS), 549–52
  HIV infection, global map, 550
  and prostitutes, 235
  and sexual counterrevolution, 227–28
  types of transmission as of 2001, 552
Acting crowds, 603
Action, as U.S. value, 66
Active euthanasia, 553
Activity theory of aging, 397–98
Addictions, and blame, 68
Adolescents
  adolescence, stage of, 130
  identity development, 124, 130, 133
  September 11 attacks, effects on, 133–34
  sexuality, 130
  teen pregnancy, 232–33
Adoption
  by gay couples, 480
  by single parents, 461
Adult education, 534–35
Adultery (see Extramarital sex)
Adulthood, stages of, 130–32
Advertising
  fashion, sexually provocative, 245
  gender role representation, 331–32
Affection, toward leaders, 165
Affirmative action
  gender discrimination, 349
  proponents/critics of, 378–79
Affluence (see Income; Wealth)
Afghanistan
  land mines, 452
  Taliban, 318, 453, 454
  terrorists of, 450
  U.S. troops in, 451
  women's status, 328
Africa (see also specific countries)
  and AIDS, 549–50
  colonization of, 314, 315
  female genital mutilation, 341
  illiteracy in, 518, 519
  immigrants to U.S., 73
  income inequality, 264

low-income countries of, 6, 305, 307
middle-income countries of, 305
poverty, extent of, 307, 319
slavery (modern) in, 309
African Americans, 367–70
  affirmative action, 378–79
  affluent, 44, 49, 277
  Afrocentrism, 75
  in cities, 364, 368, 369, 370, 585
  as crime victims, 208
  and criminality, 207–8
  and development of sociology, 13, 16
  and discrimination (see Civil rights movement; Racial discrimination; Racism)
  educational achievement, 369, 378–79, 524, 526, 527
  elderly, 394
  family life, 208, 474–75
  geographic distribution, national map, 374
  Gullah community, 640
  health status, 547, 551
  income of, 275, 276, 277, 283, 369, 474
  infant mortality, 547
  intelligence debate, 361
  interracial marriage, 475
  in labor force (2002), 416
  life expectancy, 547
  in managerial positions, 179
  mass media portrayals, 128–29
  in medical profession, 554
  and multicultural movement, 75–76
  personal achievement and racism, 43–45
  political affiliation, 443
  in politics, 370
  population, national map, 357
  poverty of, 208, 287, 394, 474
  in professional sports, 19–21
  religious affiliation, 506
  slavery, 315, 367–68
  social standing of (2001), 370
  social stratification, 276
  stereotyping of, 21, 129, 208
  and suicide, 3–4
  unemployment, 290, 369, 420–21
  voter participation, 444
  women (see African American women)
African American women
  accomplished, 369
  earnings of, 340
  female-headed households, 208, 479
  and feminism, 347
  grandmothers, status of, 472
  intersection theory, 339
  lynching, 604
African National Congress (ANC), 619
Afrocentrism, 75
Age
  and criminal behavior, 206, 216
  life course stages, 129–34
  poverty, rates by age, 395
  and voter participation, 444
Ageism, defined, 396
Age-sex pyramid, 573–74
Aggression, and men, 329, 330, 546

Aging, 383–402 (see also Elderly; Life expectancy)
  activity theory of, 397–98
  age stratification, 389–91
  biological changes, 387
  death and dying, 398–402
  disengagement theory, 397
  and family life, 472
  future view, 402–3
  and health decline, 387
  life expectancy, rise in, 384–86
  old age, stage of, 132
  personality and coping, 392
  psychological changes, 387–88
  social-conflict view, 398
  structural-functional view, 396–97
  symbolic-interaction view, 397–98
  of U.S. population, 383–86
Agrarian societies
  and caste system, 249–50
  characteristics of, 92–93, 96–97
  economic development, 408
  elderly in, 390
  leadership of, 435
  Marxist revolution in, 263
  religion in, 496
  social inequality in, 93, 263, 310
  women's status in, 93, 327
Agriculture
  agribusiness, 418
  agricultural revolution, 408
  development of, 92
  Green Revolution, 313, 316, 321
  without technology, 310
  work, decline of, 417–18
  work force, global map, 412
Aid for Dependent Children (AFDC), 292–93
AIDS (see Acquired Immune Deficiency Syndrome [AIDS])
Air pollution, 593
Aka people (Africa), hunting and gathering, 90
Alaska, purchase, 315
Albania
  as middle-income country, 302
  religious displays, ban on, 192
Alcoholics Anonymous, 611
Alcohol use, medicalization of, 198
Algeria, as middle-income country, 305
Alienation
  and voter apathy, 444–45
  Weber's view, 106
  of workers (see Worker alienation)
Al Jezeera, 452
Alterative social movements, 611
America dilemma, 368
American colonies, cities of, 579–80
American Dream
  and las colonias, 303
  status of, 283–84
American Medical Association (AMA), 554
American Revolution, 448
American Sociological Association (ASA), research ethics, 38
Amish
  cultural clash, example of, 648
  culture of, 80, 103
  fertility of, 570
  material culture, rejection of, 70
  personal identity, 637
  as sect, 495

technology, opposition to, 312
Amnesty International, 439
Anal sex, 551
Ancestry, and social standing, 275
Androcentricity, meaning of, 37
Anger, and death, 132
Animals
  diversity, decline of, 594–95
  domestication of, 91–92
  and language learning, 65
Animism, 496
Anomie
  defined, 632
  Durkheim's concept, 108
Anorexia nervosa, 548
Anticipatory socialization, 127
  and conformity, 167
Anti-Semitism, 500
Apartheid, 250, 257
Apathy, voter, 444–45
Applied sociology
  applications and exercises, 23, 55, 86, 113, 137, 161, 187, 219, 244, 269, 296, 323, 351, 381, 405, 430, 457–58, 485, 514, 538, 565, 599, 623, 647
  corporate welfare, 424
  day-care centers, 473
  drop in crime rate, 216
  home recycling and modernization, 590
  language and reality, 145
  lying, detection of, 149–50
  sociological imagination, 9
  sociological perspective, 8–10
  statistical measures, 31
  tables, reading of, 45
  technology, sociological viewpoints on, 109
  worker alienation, 101
Approval ratings, and wording of survey, 43
Arab Americans, post-September 11
  detention/civil liberties issue, 459
  Muslim community, activism of, 515
  social acceptance, 360
Arabs (see Islam; Islamic countries; Muslim women)
Arapesh people (New Guinea), Mead's gender studies, 327
Argentina
  as high-income country, 301
  income inequality in, 273
  nuclear disarmament, 452
Arithmetic progression, 574
Arms dealing, 209
Arms reduction, 452, 454
Artifacts of culture, 69
Aryan Nation, 619
Ascribed status, 140–41
Asexuality, 229
Asia (see also specific countries)
  high-income countries of, 305
  immigrants to U.S., 73
  low-income countries of, 305
  middle-income countries of, 305, 312
Asian Americans, 370–73
  and achievement, 208
  affluent, 49
  in cities, 585
  and criminality, 208
  diversity initiatives, 57

educational achievement, 208, 370, 371
  ethnicities of, 356, 370–73
  family life, 208, 475
  geographic distribution, national map, 374
  income of, 275, 276, 370, 371, 373
  increase in U.S. population, 75
  interracial marriage, 372, 475
  IQ scores, 361
  population, national map, 357
  population growth, 370
  poverty of, 370, 371
  social standing of (2000), 371
  stereotyping of, 129, 358
  in U.S. population, 370
Asian Indian Americans, 370
Assemblies of God, 512
Assimilation, 363–64
  defined, 363
  miscegenation, 364
Athletics (see Sports)
Australia
  Aborigine hunting and gathering, 90
  government, size of (2001), 440
  as high-income country, 6, 305
  income inequality in, 273
  manufacturing, hourly wages, 425
  poverty, public opinion of, 293
  socialized medicine, 557
Austria, television ownership, 127
Authoritarianism
  authoritarian leadership, 165–66, 176
  as political system, 438
Authoritarian personality theory, of prejudice, 360
Authority, 433–35
  charismatic, 434–35, 495
  defined, 434
  family patterns, 465–66
  rational-legal, 434
  traditional, 434
  Weber's concept, 434
Automation, and McDonaldization, 183
Automobile ownership, as U.S. ideal, 69
Autonomy versus shame and doubt, 124
Average middle-class, 279

Baby boom
  aging population, 383, 472
  and sexual revolution, 226
  time span of, 574
Baby bust, time span of, 574
Bahrain, divine right in, 438
Bangladesh
  garment workers of, 299–300, 301, 308
  as low-income country, 302, 303, 304, 305, 312
  schooling in, 519
Baptists, 497, 504
  social standing, 276
Barter, agrarian societies, 93
Batek people (Malaysia), hunting and gathering, 90
Bay of Pigs, and groupthink, 167
B.C.E. (before the common era), use of term, 11*n*
Beauty (see also Physical attractiveness)
  beauty myth, 332
Behaviorism
  focus of, 116, 121–22
  social behaviorism, 121–22
Belarus, nuclear disarmament, 452
Belgium
  African colonies, 314
  socialized medicine, 557

Beliefs
  defined, 65
  and values, 65–66
Bell Curve, The (Herrnstein and Murray), 266–67, 361
Bereavement, 401–2
Bias
  research, 34–35, 40
  standardized tests, 522–23
  and women (see Gender bias)
Bible, 490
  creationism issue, 510–11
Bilateral descent, 464
Bill Gates syndrome, 536
Bill of Rights, 211, 440
Biodiversity, decline of, 594–95
Biology
  and aging, 387
  and deviance, 190–91
  gender differences, 326, 330
  and human behavior, 116–17
  and racial variation, 353–54
  and sex determination, 222–23
  and sexual orientation, 230–31
Biracial (see Interracial marriages; Multiracial)
Birth control
  birth control pill, 226–27
  global use of, 227, 345, 577
  lack of, low-income countries, 308
  as reproductive freedom, 345, 346, 347
Birth rate
  births per woman, global view, 4
  decline and industrialization, 384, 575
  decline in U.S., 384
  demographic concept, 570
  and poverty, 308
Bisexuality, defined, 229
Black Americans (see African Americans)
Black church, 506
Black power movement, 369
Blame the victim, and poverty, 288–89, 314
Blasé urban attitude, 583
Blau, Peter, and symbolic-interaction paradigm, 18
Blended families, 477–78
Blue-collar occupations
  decline of, 418
  defined, 261
  types of, 274
Blue jeans, 609
Bodhi (enlightenment), 502
Body language (see Nonverbal communication)
Bonding, human, 117–18
Boot camp, shock probation, 217
Bosnia
  genocide of Bosnians, 365
  regional conflict, 451
  U.S. troops in, 451
Botswana
  gross domestic product (GDP), 305–6
  as middle-income country, 303, 305
Bourgeoisie, Marxist view, 99, 258, 579, 632
Brady bill, 209
Branch Davidians, 496
Brazil
  crime rates, 209
  economic inequality, 255
  income inequality, 264
  as middle-income country, 303, 305
  nuclear disarmament, 452
  racial categories in, 354
  street children, 308
Brown v. the Board of Education of Topeka (1954), 362, 364

Brunei, divine right in, 436
Buddhism
  global map, 501, 502
  history and beliefs of, 501–2
Bulgaria, 416, 417
Bulimia, 548
Burakumin (outcasts), 253
Bureaucracy, 174–78
  characteristics of, 174–75
  defined, 174
  informality of, 175–76
  oligarchy, 177–78
  organizational environment, 175
  origins of, 174
  privacy issue, 184–85
  problems of, 176–77
  of schools, 528–30
  and social movements, 618
  U.S. government, 436
  Weber's view, 106, 109
Bureaucratic authority, 434
Bushmen (Africa), hunting and gathering, 90
Busing, 525

Cable television, 127
Call girls, 234
Calvinism, and capitalism, 103–5, 493–94
Cambodia, genocide in, 365
Campaign financing, political action committees (PACs), 443–44
Canada
  and crime rate, 209
  culture, compared to United States, 83
  government, size of (2001), 440
  gross domestic product (GDP), 305
  health care in, 556–57
  as high-income country, 6, 305
  immigrants to U.S., 73
  income inequality in, 273
  television ownership, 127
Cannibalism, 92
Capitalism
  and bureaucracy, 106
  and Calvinism, 103–5, 493–94
  and class conflict, 99–100
  defined, 413
  and democracy, 436, 438
  and deviance, 200–202
  and elderly, 398
  endurance, reasons for, 260–61
  features of, 413–14
  and gender stratification, 343, 345, 346
  and global economy, 315–18
  government regulation, 414
  and health care, 555–57
  Marx on, 97–98, 256, 259–60, 632–33, 635–37
  and materialism, 81
  and medical care, 561–63
  and modernity, 632–33, 635–37
  relative advantages of, 415–16
  compared to socialism, 415–16, 436, 438
  state capitalism, 415
  and urbanization, 585–86
  welfare capitalism, 415
  and worker alienation, 100–101
Capitalists, defined, 97
Capitalist world economy, 315–16
Capital punishment
  global map, 210
  and Middle Eastern countries, 209
  as political issue, 442
  and retribution, 213
  in U.S., national map, 214
Caregiving, 392, 395

Care and responsibility perspective, moral development, 121–22
Case studies, 45
Caste system, 248–51
  feudal Japan, 253
  India, 249
Casual crowds, 603
Category, social groups, 163
Catholic Church
  institutionalization of, 435
  liberation theology, 494
  materialism, view of, 105
  origin of, 497
  as patriarchy, 493–94
  and Protestant Reformation, 312
  region of U.S., 504
  schools of, 519, 524
Catholics
  ethnicity of, 355
  religiosity, 504
  and suicide, 3
Caucasoid racial type, 354–55
Cause and effect, and variables, 32
C.E. (common era), use of term, 11*n*
Cellular telephones, 410, 440, 601, 607
Chad
  as low-income country, 303
  population growth, 310
  women's status, 328
Change, and culture, 318
Charisma, defined, 495
Charismatic authority, 434–35, 495
Charter schools, 533
Chastity belt, 239
Chattel slavery, 309
Cheating, increase in, 196
Chechnya, regional conflict, 451
Chicago School, on urbanism, 584–85
Child abuse
  abusers, traits of, 479
  and foster children, 191
  isolated/neglected children, 115, 117–18
  statistics on, 478
Child custody
  and blended family, 478
  mother-custody, 349, 477
Childhood, stage of, 129–30
Child labor
  factory workers, 409
  global map, 131
  India, 519
  in low-income countries, 78, 309, 313, 519
Child rearing
  discipline and culture, 87
  and family characteristics, 471–72
  future view, 482
  and maternal employment, 332–33, 335
Children
  child weddings, India, 469
  day-care centers, 473
  death, global view, 306, 307
  development of (see Human development; Socialization)
  divorce, effects of, 477
  family context (see Family)
  hurried child syndrome, 130
  life expectancy, U.S. (2001), 547
  poverty, global view, 307–8
  poverty, U.S., 287
  in single-parent family, 479
  as slaves, 309
  street children, 307–8
Child support
  deadbeat dads, 349, 477
  payment, statistics on, 478
Chile
  as middle-income country, 300, 302, 303
  totalitarian regime, 438

China (see People's Republic of China)
Chinatowns, 363, 370–71
Chinese Americans
  parental discipline, 87
  profile of, 370–71
Chinese language, global map, 64
Christianity
  global map, 498
  history and beliefs of, 497
  as patriarchy, 492
  view of God, 92, 497
  women, status of, 492–93
Chromosomes
  gay gene, 231
  and sex differentiation, 222
Chukchee people, transgendered persons, 230
Church
  electronic, 512
  as organization, 494
Church of Jesus Christ of the Latter Day Saints (Mormons), 504, 505, 510
Cigarette smoking, 547–48
  decline, 402
Circumcision, male and female, 239
Cities (see also Urbanization)
  African Americans in, 364, 368, 369, 370, 585
  decline, post World War II, 580–81
  edge cities, 581
  ethnic villages, 363, 370–71, 376, 378
  evolution of, 10, 578–80
  homeless in, 294
  industrialization and growth, 313, 579
  inner city, problems of, 290
  poverty in, 288
  and presidential election (2000), 443, 444–45
  racial segregation in, 364
  shantytowns of, 311, 586
  urban ecology, 584–85
  urbanism, theories of, 582–86
  U.S. growth of, 579–82
  white flight, 364, 370
City-states, 435
Civil law, defined, 201
Civil liberties, 461
Civil religion, 507–8
Civil Rights Act of 1964, 379
Civil rights movement
  Brown decision, 362, 364
  impact of, 369
  Montgomery bus boycott, 141
  against racism, 360
  religious roots of, 492
  as social movement, 612, 618
Civil War, 580, 612
Class conflict (see also Marxism; Social conflict; Social-conflict paradigm)
  and capitalism, 99–100
  defined, 100
Class consciousness, Marxist view, 99–100
Class society, defined, 635
Class-society theory, 635–37
Class system, 251–56 (see also Social class)
  China, 256
  estate system (United Kingdom), 251–53
  feudal system (Japan), 253
  meritocracy, 251
  Soviet Union, 254
  and status consistency, 251
Closed-end questionnaire format, 42
Coercive organizations, 173
Cognitive development, 119–21
Cohabitation, 462, 479–80

Europe, new attitude towards, 487
Cohort, defined, 133
Collective behavior, 601–21 (see also Social movements)
  crowds, 164, 603–6
  defined, 601
  fashions and fads, 609–10
  panic and mass hysteria, 609
  rumor and gossip, 601, 606–7
  study, difficulties of, 601–2
  theories of, 604–6
Collective conscience, 108
Collectivism
  Japanese organizations, 180
  and socialism, 414
Collectivities, compared to social groups, 602–3
College
  access to, 525–26
  community colleges, 526–27
  cost of, 526, 528
College attendance
  affirmative action, 349, 378
  African Americans, 369, 378–79
  Asian Americans, 371
  and future earnings, 526, 527
  and income level, 3, 526
  and intelligence level, 266
  as personal merit, 528
College students
  activism of, 618
  careers chosen by, 419
  date rape, 237, 340
  death penalty, view of, 215
  feminism, opposition to, 347
  gender and areas of study, 337
  on homosexual relationships, 481
  hooking up, 236
  life objectives, 77
  on marriage and romantic love, 470
  passivity of, 530
  political affiliation, 443
  political involvement, 620–21
  and revolution, 448
  and social distance, 359–60
  social diversity of, 170
  women, increase in enrollment, 536
Colombia, drug trade, 209
Colonialism
  Africa, map of, 314
  defined, 310
  and dependency theory, 315–16
  and genocide, 364
  neocolonialism, 310
  and slavery, 367–68
Command economy, 414
Common sense
  versus scientific evidence, 29–30
  truth of, 8–9
Communication
  gender differences in, 156
  nonverbal, 148–49
Communications (see also Information Revolution)
  advances and society, 103
  and bureaucracy, 175, 176
  global, 80
  high-tech methods, 410, 440, 453
  industrial era inventions, 94
  organizational, 176
  satellite, 54, 80, 440
Communism
  China, 255–56
  defined, 98, 414
  and socialism, 414–15
  Soviet Union, 254
Communitarian movement, 644–45
Community
  las colonias, 303
  modern, decline of, 629, 630–31, 634–35

Community-based corrections, 215–17
Community colleges, 526–27
Community policing, 216
Comparable worth policy, 336
Competition
  and capitalism, 413
  and corporations, 425
  as male trait, 329
Competitive work teams, 181
Complementarity, gender roles, 343–44
Computers (see also Information Revolution)
  global map, 104
  and social movements, 615
  and workplace changes, 423
Concentric zone urban model, 584
Concept
  defined, 30
  in sociological research, 30–31
Concrete operational stage, Piaget's theory, 120
Conflict (see also Social conflict)
  and humor, 159
  role conflict, 143
  between values, 67
Conflict subculture, 194
Conflict theory (see Marxism; Social-conflict paradigm)
Conformity, 166–67
  versus deviance, 193–94
  group study of, 166
  groupthink, 167
  obedience to authority study, 167–68
Confucianism, 11, 78, 174, 518
  history and beliefs of, 502–3
Conglomerates, 424–25
Congo, Democratic Republic of the
  authoritarian regime, 438
  as low-income country, 303, 305, 306
Conjugal family, 462
Consanguine family, 462
Conscience
  and delinquency, 191
  superego, 119, 191
Conservatism
  affiliation with, 442–43
  family values agenda, 228, 442, 471
  and fundamentalism, 511–12
  and mass media, 129
Consolidated metropolitan statistical areas (CMSAs), 581
Conspicuous consumption, 278, 281
Constitutional monarchy, 436
Consumption, and economic development, 278, 281, 313
Contagion theory, crowd behavior, 604–5
Containment theory, 191
Contraception (see Birth control)
Control, in scientific investigation, 33
Control group, 39–40
Control theory, 199, 200
Controversy, and humor, 158
Conventional crowds, 603
Conventional level, moral development, 121
Convergence theory, crowd behavior, 605
Conversion, religious, 495
Corporations, 423–26
  agribusiness, 418
  CEOs, compensation of, 285
  and competition, 425
  conglomerates, 424–25
  corporate crime, 201–2
  corporate welfare, 424
  diversity in, 57, 422
  downsizing, 286, 290, 420

and global economy, 425–26
  government regulation of, 425
  multinational (see Multinational corporations)
  scandals, 176, 189, 202, 282
  sizes of, 424
  white-collar crime, 201
Corrections system, 212–17
  community-based corrections, 215–17
  probation, 215, 217
  punishment, reasons for, 213–15
  and resocialization, 134
Correlation of variables, 32–33
  spurious correlation, 33
Cottage industry, 409
Countercultures, 77
  and industrialization, 94
Coup d'état, 448
Courtship, 469–70
  social-exchange view, 468
Court system, criminal processing, 212
Craze, 610
Creationism, 510–11
Creative autonomy, of workers, 181
Credentialism, 527–28
Credit agencies, and personal privacy, 185
Credit cards, average per adult, 185
Crime, 205–9 (see also Corrections system; Criminal justice system; Violence)
  components of, 205
  defined, 191
  Durkheim on, 107
  as form of deviance, 194–95
  gender and criminality, 207, 348
  global perspective, 209
  hate crimes, 203–4
  men as victims, 348
  and modern society, 110
  multinational crimes, 209
  against persons, 205
  property crimes, 205
  prostitution, 233–35
  and racial and ethnic minorities, 207–8
  rates in U.S., 206
  recidivism, 214
  and social class, 207
  statistics, compilation of, 205–6
  street crime, 193
  victimless, 205
  white-collar, 201
  women as victims, 205
Criminal justice system, 209–17
  corrections system, 212–17
  courts, 212
  defined, 190
  due process, 211
  police, role of, 211–12
Criminal law, defined, 201
Criminal subculture, 194
Critical sociology, elements of, 36–37
Cross-dressing, 223
Crowds, 603–6
  behavior, theories of, 604–6
  in evolution of group, 164
  mobs and riots, 603–4
  types of, 603
Crude birth rate, global view, 570
Crude death rate, global view, 570
Crusades, 499
Cuba
  foreigners in, 192
  as Marxist society, 263, 415, 437
  U.S. access to, 315
Cuban Americans, profile of, 376
Cults, 495–96
Cultural capital, and social class, 281

Cultural change (*see also* Industrialization; Modernity; Social change)
  causes of, 77
  cultural lag, 77
Cultural conventions, and gender inequality, 326
Cultural diversity, 70–72 (*see also* Ethnicity; Race; Racial and ethnic minorities; Social diversity)
  and conflict of values, 67
  counterculture, 76
  cultural relativism, 78–79
  ethnocentrism, 78
  high culture, 72
  multiculturalism, 74–76
  popular culture, 72
  and role and status, 141–42
  subculture, 72–74
  United States, 70–74
Cultural elite, and television industry, 129
Cultural integration, defined, 76
Cultural lag
  defined, 626
  elements of, 76–77
Cultural relativism, 78–79
Cultural transmission, of language, 63, 65
Cultural universals, 80–81
Culture, 59–84
  aging, views of, 388–91
  as constraint, 84
  cultural change, 76–77
  defined, 59
  development of (*see* Sociocultural evolution)
  and deviance, 193
  and diversity (*see* Cultural diversity)
  facial expressions and emotions, 152
  as freedom, 84
  and gender roles, 326–28
  global diversity, 58
  and global inequality, 310–14
  and health status, 542
  high culture, 93
  and human intelligence, 60–61
  and humor, 158–59
  ideal and real, 69
  and language, 62–65
  material culture, 69
  and modernization, 312
  norms, 67–68
  and parental discipline, 87
  sexuality, regulation of, 238
  sexual orientation, views of, 229
  and sexual practices, 223–24
  and social change, 627
  social-conflict view, 81
  sociobiological view, 81–83
  structural-functional view, 80–81
  subculture, 72–74
  symbols, 61–62
  and technology, 69–70
  values and beliefs, 39, 65–67
  of victimization, 68–69
  virtual, 72
Culture of poverty, 289
Culture shock, 59–60
  defined, 59
  as two-way process, 62
Culture theory
  of prejudice, 360–61
  of social movements, 615–16
Cyber (*see also* Information Revolution; Internet)
  global network, 171–72
  symbols, 63
Czech Republic, 416, 417

Darwinism, social, 257, 288–89
Date rape, 237, 340
Davis-Moore thesis, 257–58, 265, 266
Day-care programs, 473
Death, 398–402
  bereavement, 401–2
  dying, stages of, 132
  historical patterns of, 398–99
  leading causes, U.S. (1900 and 2000), 543
  median age, global map, 306
  medical and legal definition, 399, 552
  poverty as cause of, 305, 306
  right-to-die debate, 399–401, 552–53
  of spouse, 392, 474
  stages of dying, 401
Death instinct, 118
Death penalty (*see* Capital punishment)
Death rate
  demographic concept, 571
  and industrialization, 575
Debt bondage, 309
Decision making, collective, 180
Declaration of Independence
  on equality and freedom, 368
  individual rights, 11
Deductive logical thought, 50–51
De facto segregation, 364
Defense mechanisms, 119
Degradation ceremony, 197
Deindustrialization (*see also* Postindustrial economy)
  and global economy, 286
  and job loss, 292
De jure segregation, 364
Delinquency, as subculture, 194
Democracy, 436–38
  defined, 436
  gap and Islamic countries, 454–55
  political freedom, global map, 437
  as U.S. value, 66
Democratic leadership, 166, 176
Democratic Party
  on economic issues, 441–42
  on social issues, 442
  voters for, 443
Demographic transition theory, 575–76
Demography, 569–74 (*see also* Population)
  defined, 569
  fertility, 570
  migration, 571–72
  mortality, 571
  population composition, 573–74
  population growth, 573
  and social change, 628–29
Denial, of death, 132, 401
Denmark, government, size of (2001), 440
Denomination, religious, 494
Dependency theory of development, 311–18
  colonialism, 315–16
  evaluation of, 317–18
  high-income countries, role of, 315–16
  historical view, 315, 318
  on modernization, 644–45
Dependent variable, 30, 36–37
Deprivation theory, social movements, 612, 617
Descent, kinship patterns, 464
Deterrence, and criminals, 213–14
Development, human, 118–29
  cognitive development, 119–21
  Erikson's stages, 124–25
  Freudian theory of personality, 118–19
  life course, 129–34

moral development, 121–22
  nature versus nurture, 116–17
  self, development of, 121–24
Deviance, 190–217
  and biology, 190–91
  and capitalism, 200–202
  control theory, 199, 200
  and criminality (*see* Crime)
  and culture, 192
  defined, 190
  differential association theory, 199
  Durkheim on, 192
  functions of, 192, 195
  and gender, 204–5
  labeling theory, 195–98
  medicalization of, 198
  and personality traits, 191
  and power, 200
  primary and secondary, 196–97
  social-conflict view, 200–202
  and social diversity, 203–4
  social foundations, 191–92
  strain theory of, 193–94, 204
  structural-functional view, 192–95, 202
  subcultures, 194–95
  symbolic-interaction view, 195–200, 202
Dhamma (Buddha's teachings), 502
Dharma (responsibility), 311, 500
Differential association theory, 199, 200
Diffusion of culture, 77, 627
Diplomacy, 454
Direct-fee system, health care, 557
Disabled people
  disability as master status, 142
  education of, 534
  as outsiders, 8
Disarmament, 452, 454
Discrimination (*see also* Gender discrimination; Racial discrimination)
  ageism, 396
  defined, 362
  institutional, 362
  relationship to prejudice, 363
  reverse discrimination, 378
Disease (*see* Infectious disease)
Disengagement theory of aging, 397
Dispersed collectivities, 602
Diversity (*see also* Cultural diversity; Social diversity)
  diversity initiatives, 57
  global diversity, 58
  physical, 353–54
  and sociological perspective, 9
Divine right, 10, 436, 438
Division of labor
  Durkheim's view, 108–9, 631–32
  and sociocultural evolution, 343
Divorce, 476–77
  child custody, 349, 477
  effects on children, 477
  increasing rate, reasons for, 470, 476–77
  and modern society, 110
  and women's financial decline, 283
Djibouti, women's status, 328
DNA (deoxyribonucleic acid), 562
Domestication of animals, 91–92
Domestic violence (*see* Family violence)
Double standard
  gender and crime victimization, 348
  and sexuality, 226
  sociobiological view, 82
  and sociological research, 37
Doubling time, 573
Downsizing
  and global competition, 185
  and job loss, 290, 420
Downward social mobility, 282

Dramaturgical analysis, 18, 147–52
  embarrassment/tact, 151–52
  idealization, 151–52
  nonverbal communication, 148–49
  performances, 147–51
Dred Scott case (1847), 368
Dropping out, 530–31
  rates, national map, 531
Drug trade
  decline of, 216
  global view, 210
Drug use, medicalization of, 198
Due process, elements of, 211
Dyads, 169

Early adulthood, 131
Eastern Europe (*see also* specific countries)
  dependency theory, 318, 319
  economic transition, 416–17
  industrialization of, 94
  middle-income countries of, 302, 305
  pro-democracy social movements, 613–14
Eastern Orthodox Church, ethnicities of members, 355
Eating disorders, 548–49
Ecologically sustainable culture, 595–96
Ecology (*see also* Natural environment)
  defined, 586
  urban ecology, 584–85
Economic development (*see* Global stratification; Industrialization)
Economic inequality (*see* Income inequality; Poverty; Wealth)
Economic systems
  capitalism, 413–14
  Eastern Europe transition, 416–17
  market, and invisible hand, 413, 427
  socialism, 414–15
  state capitalism, 415
  welfare capitalism, 415
Economy, 407–13 (*see also* Work)
  corporations, 423–26
  and crime rate, 216
  defined, 407
  economic issues and politics, 443–44
  future view, 426
  global (*see* Global economy)
  government regulation, 414, 425, 441
  historical overview, 407–11
  and organizations, 175
  and politics, 10–11, 441–42
  postindustrial, 410, 417–21
  sectors of, 410–11
  and sexual attitudes, 226
  underground, 421
Ecosystem, defined, 587
Ecuador
  as middle-income country, 302
  physical attractiveness, 222
Edge cities, 581
Education, 517–37 (*see also* Schooling; Schools)
  academic standards, 531–32
  adult education, 534–35
  defined, 517
  of disabled, 534
  dropping out, 530–31
  and gender stratification, 337
  and multiculturalism, 75–76
  sex education, 234
  and stratification, 525–27
  teacher shortage, 535

Gay people (*see also* Homosexuality; Lesbians)
and AIDS, 551
gay prostitutes, 234
gay rights movement, 231–32
and hate crimes, 204, 205
homophobia, 232
marriage and children, 1, 480
as outsiders, 8
in U.S. population, 230, 231
GDP (*see* Gross domestic product [GDP])
Gemeinschaft, 582–83, 630–31, 634
Gender (*see also* Men; Women)
and behavior (*see* Gender differences; Gender roles; Gender socialization)
definition of, 223, 325
inequality. (*see* Gender bias; Gender discrimination; Gender inequality; Gender stratification)
newborn preference, 466
and reproduction, 83–84
compared to sex, 223, 326
sex ratio, 573
and social standing (*see* Gender stratification)
Gender bias
double standard, 37, 82, 226
in English language, 155–56
in formal organization, 179
and labeling, 204–5
and research, 37–38, 122
sexism, 328–30
Gender blindness, meaning of, 37
Gender differences
athletic performance, 327
communication style, 156
criminality, 207, 348
deviance, 204–5
eye contact/staring, 151
health status, 545–46
leadership role, 165
life expectancy, 326, 384, 386–87, 472
mathematical ability, 236
moral development, 121–22, 331
network preferences, 171
personal performances, 149–51
personal space, intrusions, 151
physical differences, 326, 330
smiling, 151
social mobility, 283
social stratification, 275–76
suicide, 3–4, 329, 348
touching, meaning of, 151
and traits (*see* Feminine traits; Masculine traits)
verbal skills, 326
violent behavior, 329, 339–40, 348
workplace demeanor, 150–51
Gender discrimination (*see also* Gender inequality)
and affirmative action, 349
against men, 349
professional sports, 19
in research studies, 37–38
women as outsiders, 8
Gender equality
athletic performance, 326, 327
and bilateral descent, 464
Chinese claim, 235
and cohabitation, 480
feminist views, 345–48
future view, 347–48
global view, 328, 329
income, progress in, 283
and industrialization, 328, 348
in intelligence, 326
opposition to, 347
and population control, 577
and reproductive rights, 345, 346, 347

Gender inequality (*see also* Gender stratification)
income inequality, 283, 335–36, 339, 526
Japan, 253
in low-income countries, 308–10
and minority women, 339
occupational, 275, 283, 333–34
and sexism, 328–30
and sexuality, 238–39
social inequality, 275–76
voting rights, 337
women as minority, 339
women as slaves (modern era), 309–10
and workplace (*see* Women and workplace)
Gender reassignment surgery, 223
Gender roles
in agrarian societies, 93, 327
and complementarity, 343–44
and culture, 326–28
defined, 330
global comparisons, 326–28
and housework, 335, 476
in hunting and gathering societies, 90–91, 327
and marriage experience, 475–76
in mass media, 331–32
Mead's research (preindustrial societies), 327
role conflict, 143
and social class, 281
and socialization (*see* Gender socialization)
Gender socialization
complementarity theory, 343–44
and family, 330–31
and mass media, 331–32
and peers, 331
and schooling, 331
Gender stratification, 325–49 (*see also* Gender inequality)
defined, 325
and education, 337
feminist views, 344–46
minority women, 339
and patriarchy, 328–30
in politics, 337–38
social-conflict view, 344
and socialization, 330–32
structural-functional view, 343–44
and violence against women, 339–43
workplace inequality, 332–37
General deterrence, 213, 214
Generalized other, Mead's concept, 123
General Motors, 425
Generation gap, 126
Genetics
and criminality, 190
genetic screening, 562–63
and sexual orientation, 230–31
Genital herpes, 549
Genital mutilation (*see* Female genital mutilation)
Genocide, 364–65
defined, 364
historical examples, 364–65
Geometric progression, 574
German Americans, 376
as undesirables, 367
Germany
income inequality in, 273
manufacturing, hourly wages, 425
market system, 416
poverty, public opinion of, 293
television ownership, 127
Geronticide, 398
Gerontocracy, 390
Gerontology, defined, 387
Gesellschaft, 582–83, 630–31, 636

Gestures, and communication, 65, 149
Ghana, as low-income country, 7, 314
GI Bill, 378, 526
Glass ceiling, 336, 422
Global Crossing, 202
Global culture (*see also* Culture)
diversity of, 58
links in, 80
official languages, global maps, 64
Global economy, 5–8
and corporations, 425–26
defined, 411
development, global map, 6
global culture, growth of, 80
high-income countries, 5
impact of, 411
low-income countries, 7
middle-income countries, 5, 7
and neocolonialism, 310
and postindustrialism, 95
and stratification (*see* Global stratification)
and U.S. class structure, 286
Global political system, 440
Global population, 576–78
growth, global views, 572, 574
low-income countries, 308, 310, 321, 576–78
Northern Hemisphere, 576
Southern Hemisphere, 577–78
Global poverty, 304–11 (*see also* Low-income countries)
absolute poverty, 304–5
as cause of death, 305
and children, 305–7
correlates of, 310, 318
death, median age, global map, 306
dependency theory, 317–18
existing with wealth, example of, 304
extent of, 307
India, example of, 311
low-income countries, 302–3
and malnutrition, 307, 319, 321
versus modernization, 312
relative poverty, 304–5
severity of, 305–7
and slavery, 308–10
and women, 308
Global stratification, 299–321
dependency theory, 311–18
high-income countries, 301–2
income distribution statistics, 300, 304
low-income countries, 303–4
middle-income countries, 302–3
modernization theory, 311–14
and poverty (*see* Global poverty)
trends related to, 318–20
Global village
example of, 5
and technological advance, 96
Global warming, 594
GNP (*see* Gross national product [GNP])
Goal orientation, instrumental leaders, 165
God, common view of, 92, 496
Golf, popularity, national map, 146
Gonorrhea, 548–49
Goods, defined, 407
Gossip, 607, 634
Government (*see also* Government, United States; Political systems; Politics)
defined, 433
governments, size of (2001), 440
Government, United States (*see also* Politics, United States)
as bureaucracy, 436
democracy, 436–38

economic regulation, 414, 425, 441
size of, 440, 442–43, 635
and welfare state, 440–41
Grade inflation, 532, 533
Grandparenting, 472, 479
Graphs, manipulation of data, 52–53
Great Britain
air pollution, 593
colonization by, 314, 315, 316
economic inequality, 255
estate system, 251–53
health care in, 555–56, 557
high-income countries, 305
income inequality in, 273
Industrial Revolution, 312–13
manufacturing, hourly wages, 425
monarchy in, 435–36
nuclear capability, 452
religion in, 491–92
schooling in, 520–21, 524
social mobility, 253
teenage pregnancy, 232
Great Depression, 8, 420, 441
job creation, 290
sexual attitudes, 226
Great Wall of China, 93
Greece, ancient, 11, 12*n*
cities, 578
education in, 518
justice, Plato's view, 256
Greek Americans, 376
Greenhouse effect, 594
Greenpeace, 439
Green Revolution
benefits of, 321
dependency theory, 316
methods of, 313
modernization theory, 313
Gross domestic product (GDP)
capitalism versus socialism, 418
defined, 305*n*
economic development, global map, 6
global view, 305–6, 311
Gross national product (GNP), defined, 305*n*
Groups (*see* Social groups)
Group superiority, as U.S. value, 67
Groupthink, 167
Guam, U.S. control, 315
Guilt, and social control, 70
Guinea, as low-income country, 305
Gullah community, 640
Gun ownership, and murder, 209
Gynocentricity, meaning of, 37

Haiti
as low-income country, 305, 314
militaristic regime, 318
U.S. troops in, 451
Hand gestures, as communication, 149
Handgun Control, Inc., 443
Hate crimes, 203–4, 205
Hawaiian Islands
brother-sister marriage, 466
U.S. control, 315
Hawthorne effect, 40
Haymarket Riot, 604
Health, 541–64
defined, 541
influencing factors (*see* Health status)
Health care (*see* Medical care; Medicine)
Health maintenance organizations (HMOs), 558
Health problems
cigarette smoking, 547–48
eating disorders, 548–49
infectious disease, 384–85, 542, 543, 545, 563, 578, 602

Lithuania
    gross domestic product (GDP), 305–6
    as middle-income country, 305
Living wills, 400, 552
Lobbyists, 443–44
Localized collectivities, 602
Logical thought, inductive and deductive, 50–51
Looking-glass self, 122–23
Love, romantic, 470
Lowell factory system, 409
Lower-class, 279
    British, 252–53
Lower-upper class, 278
Low-income countries (see also Global poverty; specific countries)
    air pollution, 593
    childbearing, global map, 4
    child labor, 78, 309, 313, 519
    death, median age, global map, 306
    defined, 300
    and dependency theory, 316–17
    economic development in, 6, 7, 303–4
    family size, 471
    foreign debt, 316
    gross domestic product in, 6, 304
    health status, 543
    and modernization theory, 311
    per capita annual income of, 301n
    population growth, 308, 310, 321, 576–78
    schooling in, 517–19
    urbanization in, 586, 595
Low-income earners, 284
Lutherans, 504
Lying, detection of, 149–50
Lynching
    of African Americans, 368
    mob behavior, 603–4

McCulture, 644
McDonaldization, 182–83
    history of, 163
Machismo, 474
Macro-level orientation
    defined, 17
    and social-conflict paradigm, 19
    and structural-functional paradigm, 19
Mafia, 202
Magnet schools, 533
Mainstreaming in schools, 534
Malaysia
    exports of, 316
    as middle-income country, 302, 305
Mali, freedom in, 454
Malnutrition
    and caloric intake, 307
    and childhood death, 307
    future view, 321
    in low-income countries, 307, 319, 321
    and political manipulation, 318
    in U.S., 547
Malthusian theory, 574–75
    proponents and opponents of, 596
Management
    race/sex/ethnicity in (2001), 179
    scientific management, 178, 180–81
Mandatory education, 521, 522
Manifest functions, 14
Manufacturing
    decline of, 286, 292
    and industrialization, 408–9
    Industrial Revolution, 10
Maoris (New Zealand), displays of affection, 223

Marginality, social, 8
Marital forms
    and authority, 465–66
    descent patterns, 464
    endogamous and exogamous, 464
    monogamy, 464
    polyandry, 464
    polygamy, 464
    polygyny, 464
    residence patterns, 464
    worldwide, global map, 465
Marital rape, 478
Marriage (see also Family)
    arranged, 469
    average age of, 284
    and courtship, 469–70
    defined, 462
    divorce, 477
    extramarital sex, 69, 228–29, 470–71
    first-cousin, national map, 224
    forms of (see Marital forms)
    and health status, 567
    and homogamy, 470
    idealized view, 470
    interracial, 249, 364, 475
    marital sex, 470
    and mental health status, 475–76, 567
    mental health of wives, 475–76
    as religious bond, 491
    remarriage, 477–78
    same-sex, 1, 480
    servile forms of, 309
    and social mobility, 282
    and social structure, 1
    and sociocultural evolution, 92
Marxism, 96–102
    on capitalism, 97–98, 256, 260–61, 632–33, 635–37
    on class conflict, 99–100
    communist society, view of, 417
    on culture and society, 81
    economic system, 414–15
    formation of theory of, 96–97
    on gender inequality, 344
    Marxist societies, current, 415
    on modernity, 632–33, 635–37
    political-economy model, 446–47
    on religion, 491–92
    on social change, 98–99, 627
    on social class, 256, 259–60
    on social conflict, 89, 97
    socialism, conception of, 102
    socialist feminism, 346
    on worker alienation, 100–101
Marxist revolution
    in agrarian societies, 263
    Russian Revolution as, 254
Masculine traits (see also Gender roles; Men)
    and culture, 326–28
    health effects, 328–29, 546
    instrumental traits, 343
    risk-taking, 328–29, 348
    Type A personality, 329, 546
    types of, 331
    violent behavior, 329, 339–40
Massage parlors, 234
Mass behavior, defined, 606 (see also Collective behavior)
Mass consumption, and industrialization, 313
Mass hysteria, 609
Mass media (see also Television)
    advertising, 332–33
    electronic religion, 512
    gender role portrayals, 331–32
    minorities, portrayal of, 128–29
    national map, 128
    and sexuality, 129, 130
    and socialization, 127–29
    violence in, 129
    and warfare, 452

Mass production
    and industrialization, 408–9
    modernization theory, 312–13
Mass society, defined, 633
Mass-society theory
    identity issues, 637–38
    and modernity, 633–35
    social movements, 613, 617
Master status
    defined, 141
    race as, 357
    stigma as, 197
Material culture
    and cultural values, 69
    meaning of, 59
Materialism
    and capitalism, 81
    Marxist view, 98
    as U.S. value, 66
Mathematical ability
    gender differences, 236
    math scores, rise in, 539
Matriarchy, defined, 328
Matrilineal descent, 464
Matrilocality, 464
Mauritania, female slavery in, 309
"Me", Mead's concept, 123
Mean, 29
Measurement, scientific, 28
Mecca, 499
Mechanical solidarity, 108, 583, 631
Media (see Mass media)
Median, 29
Medicaid, 558
Medical care
    in capitalist societies, 555–57, 561–63
    nursing shortage, 559
    physician availability, global, 544
    social-conflict view, 561–63
    in socialist societies, 438, 554–55
    structural-functional view, 559–60
    symbolic-interaction view, 560–61
    U.S., medical care programs, 557–58
Medicalization of deviance, 198
Medical technology
    birth control, 226
    in genetics, 562–63
    and health status, 542
    and life expectancy, 384–85
    and plant biodiversity, 595
    reproductive, 481
Medicare, 441, 558
Medicine, 553–62 (see also Medical care)
    holistic, 554
    political involvement, 562
    scientific medicine, 553–54, 562–63
Megalopolis, 581
Melanesians (New Guinea), child sexuality, 239
Melting pot, 74, 363–64
Men
    as crime victims, 348
    educational achievement, 337
    extramarital sex, 228–29
    in labor force, 333
    male-female differences (see Gender differences; Gender roles; Masculine traits)
    male rape, 348
    marriage, average age of, 284
    at midlife, 131–32, 472
    networks of, 171
    occupations of, 333
    patriarchy, 328–30, 469
    patrilineal descent, 464
    patrilocal residence, 464
    political affiliation, 443
    and premarital sex, 228
    sex determination, 222–23
    and social mobility, 283

Men's rights movement, 348–49
Mental illness, labeling of, 198–99
Mercy killing, 400–401, 552–53
Meritocracy, defined, 250
Metaphysical stage of history, 12
Methodists, 497, 504
Metropolis, 580
Metropolitan statistical areas (MSAs), 580–81
Mexican Americans, profile of, 375
Mexico
    age-sex population pyramid, 573–74
    immigrants to U.S., 72
    manufacturing, hourly wages, 425
    as middle-income country, 6, 305, 316
    poverty, public opinion of, 293
    street children, 308
    technological maturity, 313
Micro-level orientation
    defined, 17
    and symbolic-interaction paradigm, 19
Middle adulthood, 132–33
Middle Ages (see also Agrarian societies)
    cities, 10–11, 578–79
    estate system, 251–52
    higher education, 518–19
    time, awareness of, 630
    view of crime, 213
Middle class, 278–79
    British, 252
    friendship pattern, 281–82
    gender roles, 281
Middle East (see also Islamic countries; individual countries)
    middle-income countries of, 305
    oil wealth, 455
    water scarcity, 591
Middle-income countries (see also individual countries)
    death, median age, global map, 306
    defined, 300
    economic development in, 5, 7, 302–3, 304, 316
    gross domestic product in, 6, 304
    per capita annual income of, 301n, 302
Middletown study, 447
Migration
    demographic concept, 571–72
    and global culture, 80
    and household membership, 473
    internal, U.S., national map, 571
    and racial variation, 353–54
    and social change, 628
Militarism, costs and causes of, 451–52
Military
    fighting force, demographics of, 25
    language of, 145
    women in, 338–39
Military-industrial complex, 451–52
Minimum wage
    amount of, 289
    immigrant workers, 358
Minorities (see also Racial and ethnic minorities)
    defined, 339, 356
    elderly as, 396
    features of, 356–57
    minority-majority population, national map, 357
    minority-majority population trends, 585
    stereotyping of, 357–58
    women as, 339
Minority-majority interactions, 363–65
    assimilation, 363–64

genocide, 364–65
pluralism, 363
segregation, 364
Miscegenation, of racial traits, 364
Mixed marriage (see Interracial marriage)
Mobs, 603–4
Mode, 29
Modernity, 629–39
and capitalism, 632–33, 635–37
community, loss of, 629, 630–31, 634–35
defined, 626, 629
division of labor, 631–32
global view, 639–40
Marxist view, 632–33, 635–37
mass-society theory, 633–35
postmodernity, 626, 639–42
progress, attitudes toward, 639
and social change, 629–30
social-conflict view, 635–37
structural-functional view, 633–35
traditional versus modern societies, 634
Modernization
defined, 629
dimensions of, 629–30
stages of, 312–13
Modernization theory of development, 311–14, 426
culture in, 312
evaluation of, 314
high-income countries, role of, 313–14
historical view, 312, 318
Rostow's stages, 312–13
Modesty, and culture, 224
Moksha (spiritual perfection), 500
Monarchy, 435–36
Money
earnings (see Income)
and sociocultural evolution, 93
Mongoloid racial type, 354–55
Monoculture, Japan, 71
Monogamy, 464
Monopoly, 425
Monotheism, 497
Moral development
Gilligan's theory, 121–22, 331
Kohlberg's theory, 121
Moral panic, 609
Mores, as norm, 68
Mormons, 504, 510
Morocco
descriptions of, 5, 77, 209–10
as middle-income country, 302
physical attractiveness, 222
state religion, 494
Moro reflex, 116
Mortality (see also Death rate)
decline, low-income countries, 577–78
defined, 571
infant, 571
Multiculturalism, 74–76
defined, 61, 74
language diversity, national map, 75
and marketing, 57
proponents and critics of, 75–76
as social movement, 611
Multinational corporations
defined, 310
and global economy, 310, 316
impact on poor countries, 425–26
political power of, 440
Multiracial
as Census Bureau category, 355
Native Americans, 366
people, national map, 475
Mundugumor people (New Guinea), Mead's gender studies, 327

Muslims (see Arab Americans, post-September 11; Islam; Islamic countries; Muslim women)
Muslim women
and prostitution, 235
Qur'an on women, 492
repression of, 147, 192, 454, 499
as slaves, 309
veiling, 204, 224
as workers, 308, 334
Mutually assured destruction (MAD), 453
Myanmar, physical attractiveness, 222

Namibia, as middle-income country, 303
Nation, defined, 61
National Assessment of Educational Progress, math scores, rise in, 539
National Organization for Women (NOW), 618
National political surveys, 43
National Rifle Association (NRA), 444
National Urban League, 619
Nation-states, 435
Native Americans, 365–67
and animism, 496
citizenship of, 366
cultural revival, 356, 366
family life, 473
reservations, national map, 366
settlements, 578
social standing of (2000), 366, 367
Nativist movements, 377
Natural environment
conservation strategies, 595–96
deficit in, 588
defined, 587
disasters, and global poverty, 317
ecologically sustainable culture, 595–96
global study of, 587
industrialization effects, 96, 587–88, 591–95
limits to growth theory, 589
logic of growth theory, 588–89
Natural environment issues
air pollution, 593
biodiversity, decline of, 594–95
deforestation, 593–94
environmental racism, 595
global warming, 594
population growth, 595–96
solid waste disposal, 589–91
water pollution, 593
water scarcity, 591–93
Natural selection, 83
Nature versus nurture, 116–17
Navajo Indians
code talkers, 365
incest taboo, 224, 466
intersexual persons, 223
Nazi Germany
fascism, 438
Holocaust, 364, 500
and social movements, 613
Negroid racial type, 354–55
Neocolonialism, and global economy, 310
Neolocality, 464
Neo-Malthusians, 589
Netherlands, euthanasia, 400–401, 553
Networks, 170–72
corporate, 425
defined, 170
information (see Internet)
Milgram study, 170
New Age spirituality, 509
New Deal, 427, 441

New Guinea
child sexuality, 239
Mead's gender studies, 327
Sambia, homosexual behavior, 230
New information technology (see Information Revolution)
New social movements theory, 616–17
Newspapers, reading, national map, 128
New Zealand, as high-income country, 301
Nicaragua
as low-income country, 314
Marxist revolution, 263
schooling in, 519
Niger
as low-income country, 312
women's status, 328
Nigeria
exports of, 316
female genital mutilation, 341
physical attractiveness, 222
Nineteenth Amendment, 337, 444
Nirvana (enlightenment), 502
Nisei, 371–72
Nomads
pastoralists, 91–92
Tuareg, 89, 103
Nonconformity, as deviance, 190
Nongovernmental organizations (NGOs), 440
Nonmaterial culture, meaning of, 59
Nonverbal communication, 148–49
and deception/lying, 149–50
facial expressions, 148–49
Normative organizations, 173
Norms, 67–68
defined, 67
deviance and rule-breaking, 190
folkways, 68
mores, 68
prescriptive and proscriptive, 67
regional, 192
and social control, 68
North Korea
communist regime, 438
as Marxist society, 415
nuclear capability, 452
Norway
as high-income country, 305, 307
quality of life, 307
socialized medicine, 557
women in parliament, 338
women's status, 328
Nuclear family, 462
Nuclear weapons
arms race, 450
disarmament, 452, 454
nuclear proliferation, 96, 425
Nurses, shortage of, 558–59
Nurture versus nature, 116–17
Nutritional deficiencies (see Malnutrition)

Obedience to authority experiment, 166–67
Obesity, 541
Objectivity
defined, 34
and research, 34–35
Occupational prestige
gender differences, 275, 283, 333–34, 337
professions, 419–20
scale of, in U.S., 274
and social inequality, 275
and social worth, 257–58
Occupational specialization
and bureaucracy, 174
division of labor, 108–9
and industrialization, 94, 313, 409
of rational society, 105

Occupations (see also Occupational specialization; Work)
blue-collar, 261, 274
and childhood cultural capital, 281
and gender stratification, 333–35
job projections (to 2010), national map, 426
and social standing (see Occupational prestige)
white-collar, 261, 274
Odessa, Ukraine, economic problems, 255
Old age (see Aging)
Old-age dependency ratio, 386
Old-boy networks, 171
Oligarchy, 177–78
Oligopoly, 425
Open-ended questionnaire format, 42
Operationalizing a variable, 30–31
Operation Iraqi Freedom, 433, 451, 452, 603, 606, 614, 616
Opportunity, as U.S. value, 66
Optimism, about modern society, 110
Oral cultural tradition, 63
Organic solidarity, 108, 583, 631
Organizational environment, bureaucracy, 175
Organizations (see also Formal organizations)
bureaucracy, 174–78
corporate scandals, 176, 189, 202
female advantage, 179
formal organizations, 173–74
in postindustrial economy, 180–82
of rational society, 105
Organized crime
and human trafficking, 310
nature of, 202
as subculture, 194
Other-directedness, 637–38
Out-groups, 168
Overgeneralization, in sociological research, 37
Overweight, rise in U.S., 541

Pacific Islanders, population, national map, 357
Pakistan, nuclear capability, 452
Panama, militaristic regime, 318
Panic, 609
Paradigms, sociological, 14–18 (see also individual topics)
social-conflict paradigm, 15–17, 19
structural-functional paradigm, 14–15, 19
symbolic-interaction paradigm, 17–18, 19
Paraprofessionals, 420
Parochial schools, 524
Parole, 217
Participant observation, 45–48, 50
Street Corner Society study, 46–48
Pastoral societies
characteristics of, 91–92, 96–97
elderly in, 390
religion in, 496
and social stratification, 263
Patriarchy
defined, 328, 434
and education, 519
in families, 467
and female genital mutilation, 341
feminist view, 641
and Islamic societies, 235
and religious organizations, 492–93, 499
and sexism, 328–30
Patrilineal descent, 464
Patrilocality, 464
Peace, approaches to, 452–54

Pearl Harbor attack, 167, 371, 449
Peer group
  and gender socialization, 331
  and socialization, 126–27
Pentagon attack (*see* September 11
  attacks)
Pentecostals, 512
People's Republic of China
  capital punishment, 209
  cigarette smoking, 550
  class system, modern, 256
  displays of affection, 223
  gender equality claim, 235
  gross domestic product (GDP),
    304
  health care in, 555
  industrialization of, 94
  as middle-income country, 305
  nuclear capability, 452
  premarital sex, 224
  religion in, 502
  socialist economy, 414, 415
Perestroika (restructuring), 254, 614
Performances
  dramaturgical analysis, 147–48
  embarrassment and tact, 151–52
  and gender, 149–51
  and idealization, 151
Persian Gulf War, women in, 338
Personality
  aging and changes, 387–88
  aging and coping, 392
  authoritarian, 360
  charismatic, 495
  and culture, 59
  defined, 115
  and deviance, 191
  Freudian model of, 118–19
  and social regulation, 108
  Type A, 329, 546
Personality disorders, Freudian view,
  119
Personal orientation, of primary
  groups, 164–65
Personal space
  and culture, 39, 78
  defined, 151
  and gender, 151
Peru, brother-sister marriage, 224,
  466
Pessimism
  about modern society, 110
Philippines
  crime rate, 209
  exports of, 316
  militaristic regime, 318
  poverty and wealth in, 304
  U.S. control, 315
Physical appearance, and criminality,
  190
Physical attraction, and courtship,
  466
Physical attractiveness
  beauty myth, 332
  and culture, 58, 328
  and eating disorders, 548–49
  fashions and fads, 609–10
Physicians (*see also* Medical care;
  Medicine)
  availability, global map, 544
  presentation and performance of,
    148
  role of, 559–60
Piaget's theory
  cognitive development, 119–21
  moral reasoning, 121
Pink-collar occupations, 333
Placebo, 40
Plants, biodiversity, decline of,
  594–95
Play
  and learning, 123
  play stage, Mead's concept, 123
Plea bargaining, 212

Pluralism, defined, 363
Pluralist model of power, 446
Pokot people (Africa), intersexual
  persons, 223
Poland
  as middle-income country, 302,
    305, 417
  Solidarity, 614
Police
  community police, 216
  role of, 211–12
Political action committees (PACs),
  443–44
Political affiliation
  college students (1970–2001), 443
  conservatives, 442–43
  Democratic Party, 443
  and income level, 281, 442–43
  liberals, 442–43
  political spectrum survey (2002),
    441
  of racial and ethnic minorities, 443
  Republican Party, 443
  and social class, 281, 442–43
  weakness in, 443
Political change, and economic
  development, 10–11
Political correctness, and mass
  media, 129
Political economy
  defined, 436
  and social movements, 616, 617
  urban, 585–86
Political party identification (*see*
  Political affiliation)
Political spectrum, national survey
  (2002), 441
Political state, 435
Political surveys, 43
Political systems
  authoritarianism, 438
  democracy, 436–38
  monarchy, 435–36
  totalitarianism, 438
Politics, 433–55
  and authority, 433–35
  and critical sociology, 36
  defined, 433
  global system issue, 440
  and Information Revolution, 440
  and medical establishment, 562
  political freedom, global map, 437
  revolution, 448–49
  terrorism, 449–50
  theoretical analysis of, 447–48
  war and peace, 450–54
Politics, United States
  African Americans in, 370
  and economy, 10–11, 441–42
  effects on organizations, 175
  Marxist political-economy model,
    446–47
  participation and social class, 281
  and political parties (*see* Political
    affiliation)
  power-elite model, 446
  social issues, 442
  special-interest groups, 443–44
  voter apathy, 444–45
  women in, 337–38
Polls, survey wording, effects of, 43
Pollution
  air, 593
  water, 593
Polyandry, 464
Polygamy, 464
Polygyny, 464
Polytheism, 497
Popular culture, 72
  national map, 73
Population (*see also* Demography)
  aging of (*see* Aging; Elderly)
  changes, effects on organizations,
    175

in survey research, 41
Population composition,
  demographic measures, 573–74
Population control (*see also* Birth
  control)
  and economic development, 312
  and gender equality, 577
Population growth
  demographic aspects, 573
  demographic transition theory,
    575–76
  doubling time, 573
  as environmental problem, 595–96
  global (*see* Global population)
  global views, 572, 574
  Malthusian theory, 574–75, 596
  and sociocultural evolution, 93
  zero population growth, 576
Pornography, 342–43
  as power issue, 240, 342
  and sexual violence, 342–43
  and violence against women, 233,
    342–43
Portugal, African colonies, 314
Positivism, focus of, 12, 30
Postconventional level, moral
  development, 121
Postindustrial economy, 417–21
  features of, 410
  organizations in, 180–82
  work and workers in, 417–20
Postindustrialism, defined, 95
Postindustrial societies,
  characteristics of, 94–97
Postmodernity, 639–42
  defined, 626, 639
  themes of, 641–42
Poverty, 286–94
  absolute poverty, 286
  of African Americans, 208, 287,
    394, 474
  and age, 287
  of Asian Americans, 370, 371
  blame the poor position, 288–89,
    314
  blame society position, 289
  and children, 287
  culture of, 289
  of elderly, 393–95
  and environmental racism, 595
  and female-headed households,
    276, 283, 479
  feminization of, 287–88
  global (*see* Global poverty)
  and health status, 280, 543,
    546–47
  of Hispanic Americans (Latinos),
    287, 394
  homelessness, 291–94
  public opinion on, 288–89, 293
  and racial and ethnic minorities,
    394
  rates by age, in U.S., 395
  rate in U.S. (1960–2001), 286
  relative poverty, 286
  and street code, 193–94
  in urban areas, 288
  and welfare reform, 297
  and women, 287–88, 308, 310
  working poor, 289, 291
Power (*see also* Politics)
  authority, 433–35
  control functions of language, 155
  defined, 433
  and deviance, 200
  gender inequality, 326–30
  and global relationships, 310
  and in-group relations, 168
  over women, and pornography,
    240
  and personal space, 151
  political models, U.S., 446–47
  and sexual violence, 341
  and social inequality, 274, 275

and wealth, 274
  women's, global map, 329
Power-elite model, 446
Practicality, as U.S. value, 66
Practical learning, 521
Preconventional level, 121
Predestination, 104, 493
Pregnancy
  and abortion, 240–41
  teen pregnancy, 232–33
Preindustrial societies (*see* Agrarian
  societies; Horticultural societies;
  Hunting and gathering societies;
  Pastoral societies)
Prejudice, 357–61
  authoritarian personality theory,
    360
  conflict theory, 362
  culture of, 360, 362
  defined, 357
  ethnocentrism, 78
  institutional, 362
  measurement of, 358–59
  positive and negative, 357
  relationship to discrimination, 363
  scapegoat theory, 360
Premarital sex, attitude survey, 228
Preoperational stage, 120
Prescriptive norms, 67
Presentation of self (*see also*
  Dramaturgical analysis)
  defined, 147
Presidential election (2000)
  popular vote by county, national
    map, 445
  rural versus urban votes, 444–45
Prestige, and work (*see* Occupational
  prestige)
Pretesting, 42
Primary deviance, 196
Primary economic sector, 410
Primary groups, 164–65
Primary labor market, 418
Primary sex characteristics, 223
Primates, 59–60
  Harlow social isolation study, 117
  and human evolution, 60
  and language learning, 65
Primogeniture, 252
Prisons
  incarceration rates in U.S., 214
  justification for use, 213–14
  population, rise in U.S., 216
  prohibition from voting, 445
  and resocialization, 134
  violence in, 40–41, 51
  women versus men in population,
    348
Privacy
  genetic, 563
  and information technology,
    184–85
Privacy Act (1974), 185
Private schools, versus public
  schools, 523–24
Probation
  parole, 217
  requirements of, 215
  shock probation, 217
Pro-choice, 240–41
Profane, defined, 489
Professions, 419–20
Profit, and capitalism, 413
Progress
  modern attitude toward, 639
  as U.S. value, 66
Progressive education, 521
Progressive social movements, 611
Prohibition era, 202
Projective labeling, 197
Proletarians, 259
  defined, 98
Pro-life, 240–41
Promise Keepers, 611

Propaganda, 608
Property crimes, 205
Property ownership
 and capitalism, 413
 collective, 414
 inheritance, 467
Proposition 187, 377
Proscriptive norms, 67
Proselytize, 495
Prostitution, 233–35
 functions of, 236–37
 global map, 235
 latent functions of, 238
 sexual slavery, 309–10
 and social inequality, 239–40
Protestantism
 and capitalism, 103–5, 493–94
 denominations, 497
 and social status, 504
 and suicide, 3, 13
 women, ordination of, 493
 work ethic, 367, 493–94
Protestant Reformation, 104
 cultural changes from, 312
Protest crowds, 603
Psychological changes, and aging, 387–88
Psychosomatic disorders, 560
Public broadcasting, support for, national map, 608
Public opinion, 608
Public policy, and sociology, 10
Public schools
 inequality in, 524–25
 versus private schools, 523–24
Puerto Rican Day Parade riot (2000), 604
Puerto Ricans
 family structure, 474
 profile of, 375
Puerto Rico
 technological maturity, 313
 U.S. control, 315
Punishment for crime (see Corrections system)
Purchasing power parities, 305
Puritans
 sexual attitudes of, 225
 sociological investigation of, 48–50
 witchcraft trials, 193
Pygmies (Africa), hunting and gathering, 90
Pyramids of Giza, 92, 93

Qatar, wealth in, 455
Quakerism, sociological investigation of, 48–50
Qualitative data, 36
Qualitative research, 46
Quality circles, 180
Quality of life index, global view, 305–6
Quantitative data, 36
Quantitative research, 46
Queer theory, 241–42
Questionnaires, 41–42
Quid pro quo sexual harassment, 342
Qur'an (Koran), 490, 492, 498

Race (see also Racial and ethnic minorities)
 classification by, 354–55
 defined, 353
 and intelligence issue, 361
 and professional sports, 19–20
 as social construction, 354–55
 and social stratification, 276
 typologies, 355–56
 U.S. Census Bureau definition, 31
Race consciousness, 362

Race riots, 604
Racial discrimination
 civil rights movement, 141, 369, 492, 612, 618
 Du Bois on, 16, 370
 in formal organizations, 179
 and hate crimes, 203
 institutional, 362
 Jim Crow, 369, 378, 612
 lynching, 368, 603–4
 personal achievement and racism, 43–45
 personal effects of, 27
 and prejudice, 360–62
 and professional sports, 19–20
 and racism, 360
 school discipline, racial profiling, 529
 segregation (see Racial segregation)
 and stereotyping, 21, 129
 voting rights, 444
Racial and ethnic minorities, 353–79
 (see also specific minority and ethnic groups)
 achievement, conceptions of, 133
 African Americans, 367–70
 Asian Americans, 370–73
 characteristics of, 356–57
 family, 472–75
 future view, 377–78
 health status, 546–47, 551–52
 Hispanic Americans (Latinos), 373–77
 income inequality, 276–77, 283, 369, 375
 in labor force (2002), 416, 422
 in managerial positions, 179
 minority-majority interactions, 363–65
 minority-majority population, national map, 357
 Native Americans, 365–67
 negative views of (see Discrimination; Prejudice; Racial discrimination; Racism)
 political affiliation, 443
 poverty of, 287
 and social inequality, 276
 social mobility, 283
 white Anglo-Saxon Protestants (WASPs), 367
 white ethnics, 376–77
Racial segregation
 caste, 248–51
 de jure and de facto, 364
 Japanese American internment, 371–72
 and multiculturalism, 75–76
 school desegregation, 362, 364, 525
Racism
 and African Americans, 27, 41–43
 anti-Semitism, 500
 defined, 360
 environmental, 595
 and hate crimes, 203
 personal effects of, 27
 as U.S. value, 67
Radical feminism, 347
Rain forests, deforestation, 593–94
Random sampling, 42
Rape, 235–37
 culture of, 341
 date rape, 237, 340
 defined, 237
 male rape, 237
 marital, 478
 pornography connection, 233
Rationality
 defined, 102
 Weber's concept, 103
Rationality and society, 102–6
 and alienation, 106
 and bureaucracy, 106, 174, 183

and capitalism, 103–5
 meaning of, 103
 and modernity, 632
 social organization, 105–6
 and tradition, 103
Rational-legal authority, 434
Reactionary social movements, 611
Reading (see also Illiteracy)
 literacy and service workers, 410
 scores, stagnation of, 539
Real culture, 69
Reality, social construction of, 143–47
Rebellion, as form of deviance, 194
Recidivism, criminal, 214
Recycling, 590, 591, 596
Redemptive social movements, 611
Red tape, and bureaucracy, 177
Reference groups, 167–68
Reflexes, infant, 116
Reformative social movements, 611
Reformatories, 213
Rehabilitation, criminals, 213
Reincarnation, 500
Relationships, and social class, 281–82, 473
Relative deprivation, 612
Relative opportunity structure, 194
Relative poverty
 defined, 286
 global, 307
Relativism, cultural, 78–79
Reliability
 defined, 31
 in sociological research, 31–32
Religion, 489–512
 civil religion, 507–8
 defined, 489
 electronic church, 512
 functions of, 491
 future view, 512
 importance to individuals (see Religiosity)
 membership and participation (see Religious affiliation)
 and patriarchy, 492–93, 499
 and science, 497, 510–11
 and secularization, 506–7
 and social change, 312, 492–94
 social-conflict view, 491–92
 and sociological investigation, 490
 versus spirituality, 508–9
 structural-functional view, 490–91
 symbolic-interaction view, 491
 world (see World religions)
Religiosity
 defined, 504
 fundamentalism, 510–12
 global view, 503
 measurement of, 31–32
 social impact of, 504
 variation among denominations, 504
Religious affiliation
 diversity in U.S., national map, 505
 and ethnicity, 355
 membership in U.S., national map, 505
 and race and ethnicity, 504–5
 and social class, 504
 and social inequality, 276
 in U.S., 503–4
Religious organizations
 church, 494
 cult, 495–96
 sect, 495
Remarriage, 477–78
Renaissance, 12
Replication of research, 35
Repression, 119
Reproduction
 incest taboo, 224, 238, 466
 low-income countries, 308

reproductive technology, 481
 sex determination, 222–23
 sociobiological view, 83
 women's right to choose, 345, 346, 347
Republican Party
 on economic issues, 441–42
 on social issues, 442
 voters for, 443
Research
 bias in, 34–35, 39
 and ethics, 38
 gender bias, 37–38, 122
 and human behavior, 35
 Internet sources, 48
 methods (see Sociological investigation)
 objectivity in, 34–35
 and politics, 34–35
 summary of methods, 50
 value-free, 34–35
Reservations, Native American
 gambling casinos, 367
 national map, 366
Residence patterns
 of affluent minorities, 49
 preindustrial societies, 464
 in U.S., national map, 628
Resocialization, of prison inmate, 134
Resource-mobilization theory, 615, 617
Respect, toward leaders, 165
Retirement, 392–93
 transition to, 132
Retreatism
 as form of deviance, 194
 retreatist subculture, 194
Retribution, and crime, 213
Retrospective labeling, 197
Reverse discrimination, 379
Revolution, 448–49
 Marxist view, 102
 revolutionary social movements, 611
Rights of individual, 11, 66, 436, 438
Right-to-die debate, 399–401, 552–53
Riots, 603–4
Risk-taking, and men, 328–29, 348
Ritual, defined, 490
Ritualism
 bureaucratic, 177
 as deviance, 194
RJR-Nabisco, 424
Roaring Twenties, sexual attitudes, 226
Robber barons, 259
Rock-and-roll
 tragic deaths in, 107, 108
 transition to mainstream, 192
Role, defined, 141
Role conflict, 142–43
 causes of, 143
 defined, 143
 minimizing, 143
Role models, teachers, 141
Roles, 141–43
 gender (see Gender roles)
 role exit, 143
 role set, 142
 role-taking, 123
Role strain, causes of, 143, 336
Romania, 416, 417
Romantic love, 470
Rome, ancient, 11, 12n
 and Christianity, 497
 cities, 578
 population growth, 92–93
Routinization of charisma, 435
Royalty, divine right, 10
Rules and regulations
 and bureaucracy, 174
 of everyday interaction, 146

Rumor, 601, 606–7
Rural areas
  homelessness, 294
  population trend, 581–82
  poverty in, 288
  and presidential election (2000), 443, 444–45
Rural life (*see* Gemeinschaft; Mechanical solidarity)
Russia
  economic problems, 302, 417
  health care in, 555–56
  industrialization of, 94
  as middle-income country, 303, 305
  nuclear capability, 452
  social stratification, 254–55
Russian Revolution (1917), 254, 448
Rwanda
  genocide in, 365
  as low-income country, 314

Sacred, defined, 489
Salem witch trials, 193
Sambia people (New Guinea), homosexual behavior, 230
Same-sex marriage, 1, 480
Samoan Islanders, 372
Sampling
  focus of, 41
  snowball sampling, 44
Samurai (warrior caste), 253
Sanctions, and social control, 68
Sandwich generation, 395, 472
Sansei, 372
Sapir-Whorf thesis, 65
Sardinia, elderly in, 391
SARS (severe acute respiratory syndrome), 602
Satellite systems, 54, 80, 440
Saudi Arabia
  capital punishment, 209
  divine right in, 436, 438
  as high-income country, 301, 318, 455
  women, repression of, 204
Saving face, 152
Scandals, corporate, 176, 189, 202, 282
Scapegoat, defined, 360
Scapegoat theory, of prejudice, 360
Scholastic Aptitude Test (SAT), scores, 531
Schooling (*see also* Education)
  defined, 517
  functions of, 521–22
  future view, 535–36
  and gender socialization, 331
  in Great Britain, 520–21, 524
  home schooling, 517, 534
  in India, 518–19
  in Japan, 520
  latent functions of, 15, 522
  levels of completion in U.S. (2002), 275
  in low-income countries, 517–19
  social-conflict view, 522–25
  and social inequality, 275, 522–26
  and socialization, 126, 522
  structural-functional view, 521–22
  student performance, 539
  in U.S., 521
Schooling for profit movement, 534
Schools
  charter schools, 533
  desegregation of, 362
  discipline problems, 528–29
  grade inflation, 532, 533
  hidden curriculum, 126, 522
  magnet schools, 533
  parochial schools, 525
  public versus private schools, 523–24

racial desegregation, 362, 364
school choice, 533–34
school prayer issue, 508
standardized testing, 522–23
student passivity, 528–30
teacher salaries, national map, 525
tracking in, 15–16, 523
violence in, 528
Science
  versus common sense, 29–30
  defined, 26
  elements of, 30–33
  postmodern view, 641
  and religion, 497, 510–11
  and sociology, 11–12
  U.S. belief about, 66
Scientific management, 178, 180–81
Scientific medicine, 553–54, 562–63
Scientific sociology
  concepts in, 30–31
  focus of, 28
  limitations of, 35
  and objectivity, 34–35
  reliability and validity in, 31–32
  variables in, 32–33
Scientific stage of history, 12
Scopes monkey trial, 510
Search engines, 171
Secondary deviance, 196–97
Secondary economic sector, 410
Secondary groups, 164–65
Secondary labor market, 418
Secondary research (*see* Historical analysis)
Secondary sex characteristics, 223
Second estate, 252
Second World
  and former Soviet Union, 302
  meaning of, 300
Sects, 495
Secular humanism, 511
Secularization, 506–7
Segregation (*see* Racial segregation)
Self
  components of, 123
  definition of, 122
  development of, 121–24
  looking-glass self, 122–23
  presentation of (*see* Dramaturgical analysis)
Self-administered survey, 42
Self-discipline, of rational society, 105
Self-employment, 420
Self-esteem, and gender, 122
Self-managed work teams, 181
Semai people (Malaysia)
  hunting and gathering, 90, 312
  peace-loving, 450
  Westerner meeting with, 61
Seneca Falls conference, 325, 344
Seneca tribe, as matriarchy, 328
Sensorimotor stage, 120
September 11 attacks (*see also* Arab Americans, post-September 11)
  and bureaucratic ritualism, 177
  casualties of, 449
  and construction of reality, 147
  and counterculture groups, 76
  effect on young people, 133–34
  and group bonds, 164, 192
  national security measures, 185
Serbia, 196
Serbs, genocide of Bosnians, 365
Serial monogamy, 464
Service economy
  and earnings, 286, 418
  employment, global map, 412
  in postindustrial era, 417–21
  rise of, 418
Services, defined, 407
Servile marriage, 309
Settlement house, 13

Seventh-Day Adventists, 512
Sex
  defined, 222, 223
  compared to gender, 223, 326
  primary and secondary sex characteristics, 223
  sex determination, 222–23
Sex education, 234
Sexism (*see also* Gender bias; Gender inequality)
  and gender inequality, 328–30
  impact of, 328–29
  institutional, 328
  and patriarchy, 328–30
Sex ratio, 573
Sexual attitudes
  attitudes/behaviors, in U.S., 225–32
  and culture, 225
  double standard, 226
  on extramarital sex, 228–29
  freedom, feminist view, 345
  on homosexuality, 230, 231
  incest taboo, 224, 238, 466
  on premarital sex, 228
  sexual counterrevolution, 227–28
  sexual revolution, 225–26, 232
Sexual counterrevolution, 227–28
Sexual harassment
  blame on women, 205
  defined, 342
  forms of, 342
Sexual issues
  abortion, 240–41
  fashion, 245
  pornography, 232–33, 342–43
  prostitution, 233–35
  sexual violence, 236–37
  teenage pregnancy, 232–33
Sexuality, 221–41
  adolescent, 130, 232
  extramarital sex, 69, 228–29
  family and regulation of, 466
  Freudian view, 119
  and gender inequality, 238–39
  global comparison, 238
  Kinsey studies, 226, 231
  marital, 470
  in mass media, 129, 130
  practices and culture, 223–24
  premarital sex, 228
  sexual orientation, 229–30
  social-conflict view, 239–42
  social control of, 238
  structural-functional view, 235–37
  symbolic-interaction view, 238–39
  virginity, 238–39
Sexually transmitted diseases (STDs)
  and sexual counterrevolution, 227–28
  types of, 548–52
Sexual orientation, 229–30
  biological basis of, 230–31
  defined, 229
  social construction of, 229–30
  and socialization, 230
Sexual slavery, 308
Sexual violence, 236–37 (*see also* Rape; Violence against women)
  rape, 236–37
  and sexual language, 240–41
Shamans, hunting and gathering societies, 91
Shame, and social control, 68
Shantytowns, 311, 586
Sherman Antitrust Act (1890), 427
Shogun (military leader), 253
Sick role, 559
Sierra Club, 593
Sierra Leone
  as low-income country, 305, 307
  quality of life, 307
Significant others, 123

Singapore
  chewing gum ban, 192
  economic development, of, 313, 317, 439
  as high-income country, 301
  mass consumption, 313
  political system, 439
  state capitalism, 415
Singlehood, 480–81
Single-parent households (*see also* Female-headed households)
  characteristics of, 479
  children, effects on, 479
  and racial/ethnic minorities, 208, 375
  statistics on, 479
Slavery
  African Americans, 367–68
  child, 309
  and colonialism, 315
  forms of, 309–10
  Marxist view, 99
  modern, in poor societies, 308–10
  racial inferiority belief, 360
  and sociocultural evolution, 92, 93
  women as slaves (modern era), 309–10
Slovakia, as high-income country, 301, 417
"Smart crowds," 615
Smiling
  and gender, 151
  as nonverbal communication, 148–49
Snowball sampling, 44
Snowbelt, 581, 586
Social area analysis, 584–85
Social behaviorism, focus of, 121–22
Social capital
  networks as, 171
  and schooling, 525
Social change, 626–46 (*see also* Industrialization; Modernity; Sociocultural Evolution)
  and conflict, 627
  cultural change, factors in, 76–77
  and culture, 627
  defined, 626
  demographic change, 628–29
  deviance, transition to mainstream, 192
  modernity, 629–39
  and religion, 312, 492–94
  and social movements, 619–20
  and sociological thinking, 8
  and study of sociology, 10–11
Social character, 637
Social class, 276–81 (*see also* Class system; Social stratification)
  categories of, 276–80
  and conflict, 99–100
  and crime, 207
  and family life, 281–82, 472
  and gender roles, 281
  and health status, 281, 546–47
  and inequality (*see* Social inequality)
  and intelligence, 266–67
  lower class, 279, 281
  Marxist view, 259–60
  middle class, 278–79
  and political affiliation, 281
  and relationships, 281–82, 473
  and religious affiliation, 504
  and social inequality, 275
  and socialization, 125–26
  and social mobility, 276
  upper class, 276–78
  and values, 280, 280–81
  working class, 279
Social conflict
  defined, 97
  Marxist view, 89, 97–102, 258–60, 627

Social-conflict paradigm (*see also* Marxism; individual topics)
and critical approach, 37
elements of, 15–17, 19
Social construction of reality, 143–47 (*see also* Dramaturgical analysis; Symbolic-interaction paradigm)
defined, 144
ethnomethology, 145–46
social class/culture in, 146–47
street smarts, 144–45
Thomas theorem, 145
Social control
control theory, 199, 200
defined, 68, 190
and norms, 68
and religion, 490
and schooling, 522
Social crisis, and sociological thinking, 8
Social Darwinism, 257, 288–89
Social distance, and college students, 359–60
Social distance scale, prejudice measure, 358–59
Social diversity (*see also* Cultural diversity)
and deviance, 203–4, 203–5
and group dynamics, 169–70
and social change, 629–30
in the workplace, 422
Social dysfunctions, defined, 15
Social epidemiology, 545–47
Social-exchange analysis, focus of, 18
Social experience, and development of self, 122–23
Social facts, 107
Social function, defined, 14
Social groups, 163–73
conformity, 166–67
defined, 163
diversity of, 169–70
compared to formal organizations, 175
group leadership, 165–66
group size, 168–69
in-groups and out-groups, 168
leadership, 165–66
networks, 170–72
primary and secondary, 164–65
reference groups, 167–68
Social inequality (*see also* Social-conflict paradigm; Social stratification)
and elderly, 398
and gender, 275–76
and income level, 272–73
and occupation, 275
and power imbalance, 274
and race and ethnicity, 276
and religious affiliation, 276
and schooling, 275, 522–36
and social class, 275
and sociocultural evolution, 92, 93, 98–99
and wealth, 273–74
Social institutions, defined, 98
Social integration
and schooling, 522
and suicide, 3–4, 13
Social interaction, 139–59
defined, 139
dramaturgical analysis, 147–52
and emotions, 153–55
and humor, 156–59
and language, 155–56
majority-minority interaction, 363–65
social construction of reality, 143–47
and social structure, 139–41
and sporting events, 20–21

Socialism
compared to capitalism, 415–16, 436, 438
and communism, 414–15
defined, 414
Eastern Europe, end of, 416–17
features of, 414–15
Marxist concept, 102
and medical care, 554–55
relative advantages of, 415–16
Social isolation, 117–18
of abused children, 115, 117–18
of elderly, 392
primate studies, 117
Social issues, and politics, 444
Socialist feminism, 346
Socialization
agents of, 125–29
anticipatory, 127, 167
defined, 115
and education, 126
and family, 125–26, 466
and freedom, 135
and gender roles (*see* Gender socialization)
and life course, 129–34
and mass media, 127–29
and peer groups, 126–27
and schools, 522
and sexual orientation, 230
and social class, 125–26
versus social isolation, 115, 117–18
in total institutions, 134
in totalitarian regimes, 438
Socialized medicine, 555–57
Social marginality, sociological perspective, 8
Social mobility, 282–85
defined, 248
and gender, 283
by gender, 283–84
by income, 283
and income level, 283
and industrialization, 282
and marriage, 282
and race and ethnicity, 283
and schooling, 526
and social class, 276
in Soviet Union, 255
structural social mobility, 255
and United Kingdom, 253
Social movements, 610–20
classification of, 611
defined, 610
future view, 620
gender and participation, 618
and social change, 619–20
stages in, 618–19
theories of, 612–17
Social Register, 447
Social responsibility, and personal freedom, 644–45
Social Security, 441
Social self (*see* Self)
Social stratification, 247–66 (*see also* Income inequality; Marxism; Social class; Social inequality)
and aging, 389–91
and ancestry, 275
caste system, 248–51
class system, 251–57
Davis-Moore thesis, 257–58
defined, 248
global view, 262–65, 310
historical view, 262
ideology related to, 256–57
income disparity, global map, 264
Marxist view, 258–61
and racial and ethnic minorities, 276
and religious affiliation, 276, 504–6
social-conflict view, 258–61

structural-functional view, 261–62, 266
and technology, 262–65
variation in positions on, 265–66
Weber's view, 261–62
Social structure, 139–41
defined, 14
role, 141–43
status, 140–41
Social unity, and response to deviance, 192
Societal protection, and incarceration, 214–15
Society, 89–111
defined, 61, 89
Durkheim's view, 106–9
Marxist view, 96–102
and rationality, Weber's view, 102–6, 174
and technology, 90, 95–96
Sociobiology, 81–83
critics of, 83
mate selection, 222
Sociocultural evolution, 90–95
agrarian societies, 92–93
horticultural/pastoral societies, 91–92
hunting and gathering societies, 90–91
industrial societies, 93–94
Marxist view, 98–99
political systems, 435
postindustrial societies, 94–95
and religion, 496
and social stratification, 263
and sublimation, 119
summary of stages, 96–97
Socioeconomic status (SES)
defined, 261
dimensions of, 262, 272
and education, 15–16
and suicide, 3–4
Sociological imagination, application of, 9
Sociological investigation, 28–53
basic requirements of, 28–30
critical sociology, 36–37
ethical guidelines, 38
experiments, 38–41
gender, effects of, 37–38
historical analysis, 48–50
induction and deduction in, 50–51
interpretive sociology, 36
participant observation, 45–48
scientific sociology, 28–35
survey research, 41–45
ten steps in, 51–52
theory and method relationship, 50–51
Sociological paradigms (*see* Paradigms, sociological)
Sociological perspective, 1–10
application of, 8–10
benefits of use, 8–9
focus of, 1–4, 28
meaning of, 1
of social crisis, 8
of social marginality, 8
Sociologist, education and work of, 10
Sociology
critical sociology, 36–37
defined, 1
first use of term, 11–12
in global perspective, 5–8
and historical development stages, 12
interpretive sociology, 36
investigation and research (*see* Sociological investigation)
origins of, 10–13
and science, 11–12
scientific sociology, 28–35
and social change, 10–11

Soft authoritarianism, 439
Solidarity (*see* Mechanical solidarity; Organic solidarity)
Solidarity movement, 614
Solid waste issue, 589–91
Somalia
female genital mutilation, 341
as low-income country, 312
starvation in, 318
U.S. troops in, 451
South Africa
African National Congress (ANC), 619
apartheid, 250, 257
economic inequality, 255
as middle-income country, 302, 303, 316
nuclear disarmament, 452
physical attractiveness, 222
Southern Baptists, 512
South Korea
as high-income country, 301, 305
industrialization of, 94, 313, 314, 317
manufacturing, hourly wages, 425
state capitalism, 415
Soviet Union
breakup of, 254–55, 300, 416–17, 613–14 (*see also* Eastern Europe; Russia)
dependency theory, 318, 319
income inequality, 264
as Marxist society, 263, 415
socialist economy, 414–15
Stalin era, 102
Space (*see* Personal space)
Spain, African colonies, 314
Spanish language
global map, 64
Puerto Rican Americans, 375
speakers in U.S., 75
Special-interest groups, 443–44
Specialization
in schooling, 529
of work (*see* Occupational specialization)
Specific deterrence, 213
Spiritual beliefs (*see also* Religion)
preindustrial societies, 92–93
Spirituality, 508–9
Sports
gender and performance, 326, 327
golf popularity, national map, 146
sociological paradigm applied to, 18–21
Spurious correlation, 33
Sri Lanka
arranged marriage, 469
economic development, 317
population growth, 578
Stacking, in professional football, 20
Stalking laws, 478
Standardized testing
bias in, 522–23
and college admission, 266
Standard of living, global map, 320
Stanford County Prison experiment, 40–41
Staring, and dominance, 151
Starvation (*see* Malnutrition)
State capitalism, 415
State church, 494
State terrorism, 449
Statistical measures, mode/mean/median, 31
Statistics, manipulation of, 52–53
Statue of Liberty, inscription on, 365
Status
ascribed and achieved, 140–41
defined, 140
master, 141, 197, 357
socioeconomic, 261–62
status set, 140
Status consistency, 251

ABOUT THE AUTHOR

John J. Macionis (pronounced ma-SHOW-nis) was born and raised in Philadelphia, Pennsylvania. He earned a bachelor's degree from Cornell University and a doctorate in sociology from the University of Pennsylvania. His publications are wide-ranging, focusing on community life in the United States, interpersonal intimacy in families, effective teaching, humor, new information technology, and the importance of global education. He and Nijole V. Benokraitis have edited the anthology *Seeing Ourselves: Classic, Contemporary, and Cross-Cultural Readings in Sociology.* Macionis has also authored *Society: The Basics,* the leading brief text in the field, and he collaborates on international editions of the texts: *Sociology: Canadian Edition; Society: The Basics, Canadian Edition; Seeing Ourselves, Canadian Edition;* and *Sociology: A Global Introduction* (published by Prentice Hall Europe). *Sociology* is also available for high school students and in various foreign language editions. In addition, Macionis and Vincent Parrillo have written the urban studies text *Cities and Urban Life* (Prentice Hall). Macionis's most recent textbook is *Social Problems* (Prentice Hall). The latest on all the Macionis textbooks, as well as information and dozens of Internet links of interest to students and faculty in sociology, are found at the author's personal Web site: http://www. macionis.com or http://www. TheSociologyPage.com Additional information, instructor resources, and online student study guides for the texts are found at the Prentice Hall site, http://www.prenhall.com/ macionis

John Macionis is Professor and Distinguished Scholar of Sociology at Kenyon College in Gambier, Ohio. During his career at Kenyon, he has chaired the Sociology Department, directed the college's multidisciplinary program in humane studies, presided over the campus senate and also the college's faculty, and, most important, taught sociology to thousands of students.

S. Georgia Nugent, president of Kenyon College, congratulates John Macionis on his receiving the Philander Chase medal for twenty-five years of teaching at Kenyon.

In 2002, the American Sociological Association named Macionis recipient of the Award for Distinguished Contributions to Teaching, citing his innovative use of global material as well as introduction of new teaching technology in the development of his textbooks.

Professor Macionis has been active in academic programs in other countries, having traveled to some fifty nations. During his last study tour, he directed the global education course for the University of Pittsburgh's Semester at Sea program, teaching 400 students on a floating campus that visited twelve countries as it circled the globe.

Macionis writes, "I am an ambitious traveler, eager to learn and, through the texts, to share much of what I discover with students, many of whom know little about the rest of the world. For me, traveling and writing are all dimensions of teaching. First and foremost, I am a teacher—a passion for teaching animates everything I do." At Kenyon, Macionis offers a wide range of upper-level courses, but his favorite course is Introduction to Sociology, which he teaches every year. He enjoys extensive contact with students and each term invites members of his classes to enjoy a home-cooked meal.

The Macionis family— John, Amy, and children McLean and Whitney—live on a farm in rural Ohio. In his free time, John practices yoga and enjoys swimming and bicycling through the Ohio countryside. During the summer, he is a competitive sailor, and year-round, he enjoys performing oldies rock and roll and playing the Scottish bagpipes.

Professor Macionis welcomes (and responds to) comments and suggestions about this book from faculty and students. Write to the Sociology Department, Palme House, Kenyon College, Gambier, Ohio 43022, or direct e-mail to MACIONIS@KENYON. EDU

SINGLE PC LICENSE AGREEMENT AND LIMITED WARRANTY

READ THIS LICENSE CAREFULLY BEFORE OPENING THIS PACKAGE. BY OPENING THIS PACKAGE, YOU ARE AGREEING TO THE TERMS AND CONDITIONS OF THIS LICENSE. IF YOU DO NOT AGREE, DO NOT OPEN THE PACKAGE. PROMPTLY RETURN THE UNOPENED PACKAGE AND ALL ACCOMPANYING ITEMS TO THE PLACE YOU OBTAINED THEM [[FOR A FULL REFUND OF ANY SUMS YOU HAVE PAID FOR THE SOFT-WARE]]. *THESE TERMS APPLY TO ALL LICENSED SOFTWARE ON THE DISK EXCEPT THAT THE TERMS FOR USE OF ANY SHAREWARE OR FREEWARE ON THE DISKETTES ARE AS SET FORTH IN THE ELECTRONIC LICENSE LOCATED ON THE DISK:*

1. **GRANT OF LICENSE and OWNERSHIP:** The enclosed computer programs <<and data>> ("Software") are licensed, not sold, to you by Pearson Education, Inc. publishing as Prentice Hall ("We" or the "Company") and in consideration [[of your payment of the license fee, which is part of the price you paid]] [[of your purchase or adoption of the accompanying Company textbooks and/or other materials,]] and your agreement to these terms. We reserve any rights not granted to you. You own only the disk(s) but we and/or our licensors own the Software itself. This license allows you to use and display your copy of the Software on a single computer (i.e., with a single CPU) at a single location for <u>academic</u> use only, so long as you comply with the terms of this Agreement. You may make one copy for back up, or transfer your copy to another CPU, provided that the Software is usable on only one computer.

2. **RESTRICTIONS:** You may <u>not</u> transfer or distribute the Software or documentation to anyone else. Except for backup, you may <u>not</u> copy the documentation or the Software. You may <u>not</u> network the Software or otherwise use it on more than one computer or computer terminal at the same time. You may <u>not</u> reverse engineer, disassemble, decompile, modify, adapt, translate, or create derivative works based on the Software or the Documentation. You may be held legally responsible for any copying or copyright infringement that is caused by your failure to abide by the terms of these restrictions.

3. **TERMINATION:** This license is effective until terminated. This license will terminate automatically without notice from the Company if you fail to comply with any provisions or limitations of this license. Upon termination, you shall destroy the Documentation and all copies of the Software. All provisions of this Agreement as to limitation and disclaimer of warranties, limitation of liability, remedies or damages, and our ownership rights shall survive termination.

4. **LIMITED WARRANTY AND DISCLAIMER OF WARRANTY:** Company warrants that for a period of 60 days from the date you purchase this SOFTWARE (or purchase or adopt the accompanying textbook), the Software, when properly installed and used in accordance with the Documentation, will operate in substantial conformity with the description of the Software set forth in the Documentation, and that for a period of 30 days the disk(s) on which the Software is delivered shall be free from defects in materials and workmanship under normal use. The Company does <u>not</u> warrant that the Software will meet your requirements or that the operation of the Software will be uninterrupted or error-free. Your only remedy and the Company's only obligation under these limited warranties is, at the Company's option, return of the disk for a refund of any amounts paid for it by you or replacement of the disk. THIS LIMITED WARRANTY IS THE ONLY WARRANTY PROVIDED BY THE COMPANY AND ITS LICENSORS, AND THE COMPANY AND ITS LICENSORS DISCLAIM ALL OTHER WARRANTIES, EXPRESS OR IMPLIED, INCLUDING WITHOUT LIMITATION, THE IMPLIED WARRANTIES OF MERCHANTABILITY AND FITNESS FOR A PARTICULAR PURPOSE. THE COMPANY DOES NOT WARRANT, GUARANTEE OR MAKE ANY REPRESENTATION REGARDING THE ACCURACY, RELIABILITY, CURRENTNESS, USE, OR RESULTS OF USE, OF THE SOFTWARE.

5. **LIMITATION OF REMEDIES AND DAMAGES:** IN NO EVENT, SHALL THE COMPANY OR ITS EMPLOYEES, AGENTS, LICENSORS, OR CONTRACTORS BE LIABLE FOR ANY INCIDENTAL, INDIRECT, SPECIAL, OR CONSEQUENTIAL DAMAGES ARISING OUT OF OR IN CONNECTION WITH THIS LICENSE OR THE SOFTWARE, INCLUDING FOR LOSS OF USE, LOSS OF DATA, LOSS OF INCOME OR PROFIT, OR OTHER LOSSES, SUSTAINED AS A RESULT OF INJURY TO ANY PERSON, OR LOSS OF OR DAMAGE TO PROPERTY, OR CLAIMS OF THIRD PARTIES, EVEN IF THE COMPANY OR AN AUTHORIZED REPRESENTATIVE OF THE COMPANY HAS BEEN ADVISED OF THE POSSIBILITY OF SUCH DAMAGES. IN NO EVENT SHALL THE LIABILITY OF THE COMPANY FOR DAMAGES WITH RESPECT TO THE SOFTWARE EXCEED THE AMOUNTS ACTUALLY PAID BY YOU, IF ANY, FOR THE SOFT-WARE OR THE ACCOMPANYING TEXTBOOK. BECAUSE SOME JURISDICTIONS DO NOT ALLOW THE LIMITATION OF LIABILITY IN CERTAIN CIRCUMSTANCES, THE ABOVE LIMITATIONS MAY NOT ALWAYS APPLY TO YOU.

6. **GENERAL:** THIS AGREEMENT SHALL BE CONSTRUED IN ACCORDANCE WITH THE LAWS OF THE UNITED STATES OF AMERICA AND THE STATE OF NEW YORK, APPLICABLE TO CONTRACTS MADE IN NEW YORK, AND SHALL BENEFIT THE COMPANY, ITS AFFILIATES AND ASSIGNEES. HIS AGREEMENT IS THE COMPLETE AND EXCLUSIVE STATEMENT OF THE AGREEMENT BETWEEN YOU AND THE COMPANY AND SUPERSEDES ALL PROPOSALS OR PRIOR AGREEMENTS, ORAL, OR WRITTEN, AND ANY OTHER COMMUNICATIONS BETWEEN YOU AND THE COMPANY OR ANY REPRESENTATIVE OF THE COMPANY RELATING TO THE SUBJECT MATTER OF THIS AGREEMENT. If you are a U.S. Government user, this Software is licensed with "restricted rights" as set forth in subparagraphs (a)-(d) of the Commercial Computer-Restricted Rights clause at FAR 52.227-19 or in subparagraphs (c)(1)(ii) of the Rights in Technical Data and Computer Software clause at DFARS 252.227-7013, and similar clauses, as applicable.

Should you have any questions concerning this agreement or if you wish to contact the Company for any reason, please contact in writing: Social Sciences Media Editor, Prentice Hall, One Lake Street Upper Saddle River, NJ 07458.

Make the Most of Your Study Time!

SOCIOLOGY

TENTH EDITION

INTERACTIVE CD-ROM

Offering you an invitation to think sociologically about the world around you, this innovative CD-ROM is filled with great media resources and interactive study material for every chapter in *Sociology, Tenth Edition*. Organized by the concepts of **seeing, thinking,** and **doing,** the CD-ROM challenges you to think critically about the topics covered in each chapter and uses interesting videos and animations to guide you through the finer theoretical points.

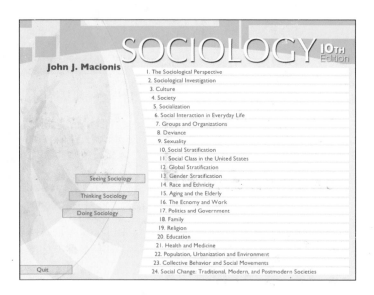

You will benefit from access to this great resource that comes FREE in the back of every new copy of *Sociology, Tenth Edition.* Its features include:

ABC News **Videos**   Imagine using the power and depth of the *ABC News* archives to bring to life sociological concepts. These high-quality actual news videos are tied to topics in the text and include study questions that underscore the relevance of sociological concepts to real life. They literally pull you from your seat to explore sociologically the world outside the classroom.

Author Tip Videos   The textbook author, John J. Macionis, offers a personal insight on each chapter's topic and encourages you to consider why the particular chapter is a part of this textbook. These clips will motivate you to reflect on key points from the chapter and strengthen your connection with the textbook. A very valuable tool!

Map Animations   Every map in the textbook becomes interactive on the CD-ROM. Roll-over graphics allow you to focus in on the sociological relevance of each of the more than sixty Window on the World global maps and Seeing Ourselves national maps.

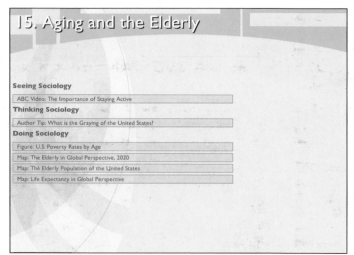

Flashcards   All key terms from the text are available for review in our innovative flashcard feature. Hear the more difficult terms pronounced, study their definitions, and discard terms as you master them.